Growing Without Schooling:
The Complete Collection
Vol. 3, 1982 to 1984

John C. Holt, editor and founder

Series Edited by Patrick Farenga and Carlo Ricci

Growing Without Schooling: The Complete Collection Vol. 3, 1982 to 1984

John C. Holt, editor (1977 to 1985) and founder
Series edited by Patrick Farenga and Carlo Ricci

Printed in the United States of America
HoltGWS LLC, 13 Hume Avenue, Medford, MA 02155

Cover design by Stephen Tedesco
Book layout and design by Patrick Farenga

Copyright © 2019 HoltGWS LLC
All rights reserved.

ISBN-13: 978-1-7321885-2-5

Acknowledgments

This collection—just like the original issues of GWS—would not be possible without the volunteer efforts of many people. The following people helped scan, retype, edit, and layout each of the 141 issues of GWS; we are very grateful for your help and diligence to see this massive project (over 6,000 pages!) to completion.

Hafidha Acuay	Harman Singh Goraya	Karugia Ndirangu
Tane Akamatsu	Elaine Greenwood	Katherine Norman
C. Tane Akamatsu	Sandra Gurton	Jean Nunnally
Qubsa Ali	Tracy Hall	Jessica Nurmsoo
Amy Andrews	Cindy Harasen	Deb O'Rourke
Ellen Behm	Brooke Haugh	Mercedes Oli
Christine Behnen	Renée Herbert	Dana Pelletier
Anne Bolger	Amanda Hewitt	Krista Tucker Petrick
Joey Breiannis	Adrian Hill	Hussam Qasem
Courtney Anne Brewer	Dagmar Hoffmeier	Stephanie Quigley
Jeff Brinson	Emma Howitt	Colleen Raja
Sarah Brooks	Viola Huang	Marian S. Remple
Shannon Butler	Greg Huneault	Rocco Ricci
Jeff Cappleman	Chris Hunt	Gina Riley, Ph.D
Amanda Carvalho	Laura Johnson	Babette Rossj
Jess Clausen	Kirsten Jork	Pabloi Sepulveda Rosso
Michelle Cloutier	Deborah Joyce	Aleksandra Serebrenik
Jason Corcoran	Janine Kam-Lal	Thérèse Shere
Oliver & Teresa Costes	Juliet Kemp	Francesca Silvester
Jesse Cull	Barbara Klapperich Senn	Melissa Silvestri
Malcolm Dow	Heidi Klein	Tatiana Yvette Smith
Angie Drake	Dr. Marianne Kuzujanakis	Robin Stevens
Emma Draper	Friedmund Labmann	Nina Sutcliffe
Nate Dvorak	Oleg Legusov	Kathryn Szrodecki
Amy Edwards	Rob Lennox	Dr. Gudrun Taresch
Meghan Edwards	Jane Levicki	Dagmar Tatomir
Sheila Etches	Karen MacKay	Jennifer G. Taus
Dawn Evans	Natasha Mansouri	Stephen Tedesco
Nada Fakhro	Gabrielle Martell	Karen Thiel
Michelle Feather	Tara McGoey	Tosh Tipler
Aaron Fewkes	Amy Milstein	Tracey Verney
Donna Garstin	Kristan Morrison	Chun Wah Chiu
Maddie Gillespie	Kristiina Myllymäki	Anna Maria Wesener
Emily Gonyer	Kathyann Natkie	

Introduction

By Patrick Farenga

When I first arrived at *Growing Without Schooling* (*GWS*) magazine in 1981 I thought it would be a steppingstone for me to another job in the magazine industry; instead, it became a focus of my life's work. Being around people who not only criticized school methods but actually took action to help their children learn and grow in ways that schools will not or cannot proved exciting to me. From kindergarten to college, every educational precept was challenged and alternatives presented and I eventually realized that John Holt was creating something new and different in the world of education that I wanted to be part of. Unlike most schools and corporations, John did not want or encourage slavish devotion to an institutional mission as the primary purpose of one's life. John encouraged everyone, including me, to focus on our interests and concerns that engaged us, no matter how big or small, rather than to always put our own development aside in favor of proving to school officials that we can focus on their interests and concerns.

In formatting and editing these issues for digital readers I realized what an incredible individual and group effort GWS was and still is. John Holt almost single-handedly wrote many of the first ten issues and much of his thinking generated some incredibly thoughtful and brave responses. I say "brave" because simply saying you were homeschooling in those days often led to severe personal and public criticism or a court appearance, as you can readily read in this volume. You can see a grassroots movement developing its reach, finding allies and resources, defending its right to exist in the face of bigger, more organized, and well-funded opposition, and celebrating the unique power to learn and grow that is in each of us.

A note about *GWS* issue dates and style: John Holt didn't want to date the issues of *GWS* because he felt they contained much timeless material about children and learning, so he decided that a simple number system—*GWS* 1, *GWS* 2, etc.—was more useful. When we reached a certain number of subscribers the postal service required us to print the date of publication in each issue, so starting with *GWS* 31 there are accurate publication dates. But we can only guess at the dates of some of the early issues based on the references we see and the fact that Holt only published when he had enough material, not because it was a certain date. It wasn't until associate editor Donna Richoux came on board (see *GWS* 11) that *GWS* maintained a steady bimonthly publishing schedule.

While we wanted to make this volume as easy to read as possible by using standard spelling conventions, the abbreviations and other shorthand John and readers used to write and comment in the issues is preserved. We feel it helps give you a sense of all the activity and new ideas Holt and others were sharing in those days. The *GWS* Directory, where people listed their contact info and the ages of their children, is not reproduced in these volumes, but you can see from the many references it receives in the issues that networking was an important function of *GWS*.

I had a lot of misgivings about doing this project at first. Accurately collecting, editing, and formatting the more than six thousand pages of the original, single-spaced *GWS* articles is an enormous undertaking that I long avoided due to the amount of time and effort it required not just by me, but by anyone who joined. I am grateful that Carlo is persistent and over the course of several conversations he showed me that volunteers, good will, and using some of the graduate students at the school where he teaches, Nipissing University in North Bay, Ontario, were good, low-tech ways to tame the thousands of pages printed during *GWS'* 24 years. The manual labor involved was enormous—every issue was essentially retyped—and I am grateful to every typist and proofreader who helped us create this collection.

This is the first of many volumes of *Growing Without Schooling*; I look forward to sharing them all and hearing back about what you think about parents and children directing their own learning without conventional schooling. Homeschooling has grown tremendously since Holt published *GWS* 1 in August 1977; Holt estimated there might have been perhaps 25,000 children being homeschooled in the late 1970s; there are now nearly 2 million children being taught outside of school and in their local communities by their parents. How did this wild growth happen? The answer is right in your hands.

—Patrick Farenga

By Carlo Ricci

First, I need to thank all of the volunteers, which includes technical experts who created solutions for us, since they all helped make this enormous project possible. Although, republishing all of the issues of *Growing Without Schooling* seems simple enough, the task required thousands and thousands of human hours and some ingenious technical mastery. I will spare you the details, but suffice it to say that a lot of the work was tedious, time consuming, and took a whole team of us (including over 100 volunteers) over 5 years, so far, to get to where we are today.

For many of us *GWS* remains one of the most inspirational and important windows into unschooling, self-determination, and willed learning. The insights gleaned by reading *GWS* are seminal. Years after it was last published, the legend of *GWS* remains ubiquitous. I believe that *GWS* is still the turning point for many. For this reason, I hoped that reprinting the issues in volumes to make it accessible would be a great service. So in 2011, I emailed Pat Farenga to ask if he is interested in republishing *GWS*. Of course, he was. However, he warned me that they tried to do this before, and after putting out one volume containing 12 of the 141 issues, they realized that the task was enormous and required too many people hours to complete.

With the good fortune and hope in newer technology to assist us, we decided to move forward. Initially, Pat, Stephen Tedesco (without his technical expertise, I am not sure if we could have pulled this off. Early into the project Stephen had to leave and we were sad to see him go), and I thought we would tackle this project. It quickly became clear that if it was left to the three of us, this project could not be completed. The hours required to do what needed to be done were far too many for three people, no matter how committed, to complete. In short, the first step required that we either retype every single issue, or that we follow Stephen's technical solution which converted a hard copy of the document into a digital document so that we could manipulate the text. We decided to follow Stephen's solution. Regardless, because of the format of the original issues, converting the issues into a digital document was still very time-consuming, and required heavy proofreading and editing, since the conversion resulted in an error-filled document.

It became clear very quickly that if we were going to do this we required help, and lots of it. In life, I believe that meeting and having great people in your life that you know personally is a great fortune. Another great fortune is to be a part of a larger community of people that you might not know personally, but that are nonetheless a part of your world. And if you are really lucky, you will have both personal friends and belong to a strong community. Fortunately, I am really, really lucky. So when I suggested to Pat and Stephen that we try and tap into our networks to see if we can get a few volunteers to help, we were hopeful that we might get a few people.

In fact, seconds after we put out the call asking for volunteers, offers came flooding in, for which we remain thankful and humbled. I like to think that they agreed to volunteer because, of course they are special people, and also because they believe in the value of sharing *GWS* with the world as much as we do. I also believe that Holt remains such a beacon of hope and inspiration that people want to be a part of what his legend and work continues to offer. Holt still brings people and communities together, as this project attests.

GWS is interesting as a historical document, but much more than that. It is as relevant for people today as it was when it was first published. I believe Holt felt the same. When people would subscribe to *GWS* they would start with receiving issue 1 regardless of when they subscribed. This indicates to me that it was not written for a particular time, but it was meant to be a record for future readers where all of the information in all of the issues is timeless. In fact in issue 5, Holt writes, "Some people, now or in the future, who read

GWS." This quote makes clear to me that *GWS* was meant to be timeless. It was written with present and future readers in mind.

GWS, in part, is about how we learn best. It offers clear examples and narratives from people who are learning through unschooling. There are lots and lots of examples of how people successfully learn naturally. *GWS* shares tips about what people are doing to learn and how and what they are learning. It also offers powerful insights into how to get credentialed by going to school less.

GWS is the best way to learn about "learning." It's great because it's not just theory, but it is what people are actually doing. Again, the tips and insights are just as helpful and relevant today, maybe even more so.

In part, *GWS* connects people with each other; informs people about friendly post-secondary options, which is helpful for both unschoolers and mainstream schoolers, and it connects and informs people about alternative possibilities and even friendly schools.

GWS is useful for everyone to read since all of us learn. There are also narratives of people in mainstream schools who see understanding "learning" as a high priority, who report in *GWS* that what is written in *GWS* is helpful to them as mainstream schoolers. They report finding it worthwhile, and clearly provocative.

It is clear that *GWS* helped and continues to help many. It contributed to normalizing homeschooling and to bringing and organizing the homeschooling community. *GWS* connected people with each other, gave people the information they needed to navigate and challenge the laws, and gave people the confidence and ideas about what it means to learn as an unschooler. Of course, it continues to do this for everyone who takes the time to read the issues of this seminal magazine.

In *GWS* 19 Tom Wesley writes: "When I first wrote *GWS* I was too insecure to use my name. Now I feel safe enough after four years of tolerant, helpful teachers and school board members to come out of the unschooling closet." The security felt by Tom Wesley was made possible, in part, by the pages of *GWS*. Like Tom, many more of us can now feel safe and confident.

I am extremely proud and happy to have such a great social circle and to be a part of such a wonderful project and community, and I sincerely hope that *GWS* will live on and be a source of peace, love, and inspiration well into the future.

—Carlo Ricci

Editorial Note

We want to preserve the original tone and context of the original issues as much as possible in this collection, but we have discovered that some conventions from the printed issues do not carry over well to the digital realm, particularly *Growing Without Schooling's* use of ellipses.

John Holt and Donna Richoux, the editors for these issues, made meticulous deletions to the original letters in order to squeeze the text into a few printed pages. In editing these volumes, we have edited out many of the ellipses in readers' letters and found doing so does not change the meaning of the letter and removes a lot of visual clutter from the page, making it easier to read. We have not removed ellipses from quoted materials or where they are needed for comprehension.

A note about *GWS* issue dates and style: John Holt didn't want to date the issues of *GWS* because he felt they contained much timeless material about children and learning, so he decided that a simple number system—*GWS* 1, *GWS* 2, etc.—was more useful. When we reached a certain number of subscribers the postal service required us to print the date of publication in each issue, so starting with *GWS* 31 there are accurate publication dates. But we can only guess at the dates of some of the early issues based on the references we see and the fact that Holt only published when he had enough material, not because it was a certain date. It wasn't until editor Donna Richoux joined *GWS* (see *GWS* 11) that it maintained a steady bimonthly publishing schedule.

Starting with *GWS* 27, one can see the expansion of the *GWS* Resource Lists to include the following categories that were updated in all future issues: Certified Teachers (willing to help homeschoolers); Homeschooling Groups (by state);

other organizations that support self-reliance, child-raising, and educational issues as homeschooling allies or help; Friendly Lawyers, Professors and others allies willing to help homeschooler develop curriculum, evaluate progress, or in other ways; Correspondence Schools and Books; Helpful Private Schools that enrol or help home study students; Friendly School Districts; the Directory of Families willing to network with others and be contacted by people interested in learning more about homeschooling. From this issue forward, the Resource Lists took up the last pages of each issue of *GWS*. We chose not to reproduce those lists as this information is quite dated, but they were a vital tool used by many homeschoolers, whether subscribers and nonsubscribers, until the advent of the internet.

While we wanted to make this as easy to read as possible by using standard spelling conventions, the abbreviations and other shorthand John used to write and comment in the issues is preserved. We feel it helps give you a sense of all the excitement about the ideas Holt and others were sharing in those days.

Table of Contents

Introduction……………………………………...…………………...4

Growing Without Schooling 31…………………………………..9

Growing Without Schooling 32………………………………….61

Growing Without Schooling 33………………………………….121

Growing Without Schooling 34………………………………….183

Growing Without Schooling 35………………………………….234

Growing Without Schooling 36………………………………….283

Growing Without Schooling 37………………………………….332

Growing Without Schooling 38………………………………….399

Growing Without Schooling 39………………………………….457

Growing Without Schooling 40………………………………….514

About John Holt………………………………..…….……..572

Growing Without Schooling 31

December 1982

We had our first open house at the *GWS* office—a great success. I had thought that perhaps, because of the rather short notice, very few people would come, but there were twelve or so families there, probably forty or more people in all. Everyone had a wonderful time, above all the children. It was lovely, as is usual at homeschool gatherings, to see children of many ages playing happily together, the big ones looking out for the little ones—a thing that too rarely happens with children who go to school. Were looking forward to the next ones (second Thursday every month, 6–8 p.m.).

Wherever there are a number of homeschooling families and a convenient place for them to meet, it might be fun to have regular gatherings like this, as often as seems desirable and convenient. The advantage of having them at a regular time and place is, of course, that it saves the trouble and expense of sending out notices, and also lets people plan to attend well ahead of time. If any groups decide to do this, please let us know—and tell us how it works out.

Only one other word—try to avoid making these "business meetings," complete with agenda, etc. Just have them a nice occasion for people to get to know each other and have a good time together.—John Holt

Important Michigan Ruling

Time *magazine, 1/10/83:*

> In a strong, unambiguous decision, a Michigan judge reaffirmed the First Amendment guarantee of separation of church and state by exempting private Christian schools from state supervision of their curriculum and teachers. Ministers, teachers and parents of the Bridgeport Baptist Academy and the Sheridan Road Christian School, both near Saginaw, had charged that attempts by the state's board of education to supervise curriculum and teacher qualifications violated their religious freedom. Judge Ray Hotchkiss agreed, ruling that the board, by imposing its secular standards of education on religious schooling, "interfered with plaintiffs' constitutional right to freely exercise their religion." Said Hotchkiss: "This court fails to see a compelling state interest in requiring nonpublic schools to be of the 'same standard' as public schools in the same district. Such a scheme does not ensure even a minimum degree of quality of education." Hotchkiss, however, did uphold the state's right to impose on the Christian schools health and safety requirements, to which they had never objected.

The fundamentalists were jubilant at their victory. Said Sheridan Road Principal Bill Swain: "We knew our position was strongly supported by the Bible. We thought we had the Constitution on our side. But I didn't expect to get a favorable decision." William Bentley Ball, a leading constitutional lawyer who argued for the two schools, called the judgment "very strong on religious liberty, clarifying the right to teach and the right to learn."

While the decision applies only to Michigan, it may influence other states. As independent Christian schools have proliferated over the past decade—with an estimated enrollment of 600,000 students nationwide—so have conflicts with state authorities. In Nebraska, the Rev. Everett Sileven of Louisville was jailed four times in 1982 for defying a court decision requiring him to hire state-approved teachers for his Faith Baptist School. In Massachusetts, Assistant Attorney General Maria Lopez has asked a civil court to impose a $100-a-day fine on two ministers who operate the Grace Bible Church Christian School in Dracut until they agree to report the names, ages and residences of their 30 students. In Maine, a major case will be tried in

February. The issue: whether the teachers at the Bangor Baptist Church School and some 20 other Christian schools need to have state approval and whether the schools must maintain and report educational records. In the Michigan trial, the issue of teacher certification turned out to be more of an embarrassment to state officials than to the Christian schools. Education experts could not agree on which standards the Christian teachers needed to follow, nor could they prove any link between certified teachers and good education. Noted Judge Hotchkiss, a former public school teacher: "The overwhelming evidence shows that teacher certification does not ensure teacher competency and may even inhibit it." Since each student who leaves a Michigan public school to attend a Christian academy deprives the local school district of about $2,000 in state aid, the judge also observed that state officials were hardly disinterested guardians of education. He called state regulation of private schools "an incredible conflict of interest."

Michigan officials intend to appeal Judge Hotchkiss's verdict. Says Assistant Attorney General Richard Gartner: "The state now has no process to approve nonpublic schools." Part of Michigan's compulsory education law says that parents must send children to state-approved schools. According to Gartner, there is now a legal doubt as to whether the compulsory attendance requirement is legal.

John's Coming Schedule

Feb. 21, 1983: Guest of Honor, Harvard Dinner Series, Cambridge, MA.

Apr. 9 (tent.): Homeschooling meetings and lectures, Chico CA area. Contact: Richard Roth, 703 Salem St, Chico CA 95926; 916-345-9682.

Apr. 30: 6th Mass. Area La Leche League Conf., Walsh Middle School, Framingham MA. Contact: Roberta Jalbert, 8 Brown St, Ipswich MA 01938; 617-356-7345.

May 3: International Reading Assoc. meeting, Anaheim CA. Contacts: Carole Vinograd-Bausell, 807 Beaverbank Cir., Towson MD 21204, or Jack Cassidy, PO Box 55, Kemblesville PA 19347; 215-255-4058.

June 28–30: 7th Annual Kephart Memorial Child Study Center Symposium, Univ. of Northern Colorado, Aspen/Snowmass, CO. Contact: Dr. Robert Reinert, KMCSC, UNC, Greeley co 80639; 303-351-2691.

Aug. 1–2: Child Development Symposium, Assoc. for Research & Enlightenment, Virginia Beach, VA. Contact: Robert Witt, PO Box 595, Va. Bch. 23451; 804-428-3588.

Anyone who wants to coordinate other meetings or lectures around these times and locations should contact me directly.—Peg Durkee

Success In Michigan

Cheryl Wustman (MI) wrote:

Jacob went through kindergarten last year, but this year we're teaching him at home. It was so much easier than I thought it would be.

We wrote a letter to the Superintendent of the Kent County intermediate school district.... We were told that *if* we wanted to we could enroll Jacob as a homebound student. This would mean he could receive all the material that the first graders are covering free. To receive this we would meet the first grade teacher every other Tuesday after school let out. It was that simple. So we've been doing this for the last month and a half. It has worked out perfect because the school is happy and we're happy.

Family Meets Legislator

From John Boston (CA):

When you spoke, John, in Anaheim, in 1981, you mentioned it would be helpful if our legislators knew about homeschooling. You suggested we visit them. Well—that's just what we did.

I first contacted our state senator's office trying to find out if he could help clarify why some school districts were contacting some home schools on their legal status and others were not. His office said they would get back to me. A few days later, I got a call from one of his staff informing me as to the man who I could talk to about private schools in the State Dept. of Education. More importantly she asked if I would like an appointment to talk to the senator. I said yes, my son would like to meet him to learn about state government as a real-person experience. She gave us an appointment.

My wife and I, with our son (age 13), went to his office about 20 miles away. His secretary showed us into his office and introduced us. The senator was dressed leisurely, as were we, and he asked us to relax by sitting in some comfortable lounge chairs in one area of his office. We told him of our son's unusual schooling arrangement, home learning, and of our private school. He wanted to hear from our son about what he did at home. Our son told him about his bicycles and model airplanes he built. He told him about his Boy Scout group, his religion classes, and his Humane Society volunteer work. We talked, informally, for close to 50 minutes. We found out the senator knows people we do so we had some things in common.

He invited our son (and us) to come up to Sacramento after the new legislative session starts and he would personally tour the Capitol with us. He was very interested in our son learning about government and gave him a booklet on our state's constitution and how a bill becomes law. All in all a very pleasurable experience, both for our son and us.

I'm sure if anything about homeschooling comes up in Sacramento our senator will feel more knowledgeable and positive about it. We would encourage other homeschoolers to do this. Our legislators are the people who make the laws the school officials must follow! Get them on our side! Let them know we are families concerned about our children!

Notes From Donna

We had a nice visit from Rosalyn Frank of the Mass. Department of Education. She's in charge of the "Gifted and Talented Special Programs" throughout the state, and is very sympathetic to the notion of homeschooling. She would like to know how many homeschoolers there are in Massachusetts, and would be willing to help someone do a survey of the various school districts. Would someone like to take on this research project?

Yet another homeschooler has sold an article to the "Mother's Children" section of *Mother Earth News*; that's three at least. In the Jan. issue, Joshua Wood wrote about the same business selling sprout jars that his mother told us about in *GWS* 21. Pat Stone of *TMEN* (105 Stoney Mountain Rd, Hendersonville NC 28791) is always looking for how-to articles by young people. And if by chance he's not interested in your story, we at *GWS* probably would be.

A 12-year-old reader suggests we put in a pen pal section for kids. We're willing to do this if it doesn't take up too much space. So, any children wanting pen pals, send in your name, age, address, and, if you want, *1–3 words* about your hobbies, interests, favorite authors, etc.

We were distressed to hear that reader Rena Caudle's son Jeremy has a massive brain tumor and is not expected to live beyond another year or so. Rena says, "If there are any readers that would like to boost up a little boy, cards would be welcomed. He's collecting his cards and he's collecting stickers, too." Jeremy's address is 1417 First, Everett WA 98201.

Another reader asks if we could print more about divorced homeschooling parents, especially if the other parent disapproves of the homeschooling. Has it ever been an issue in a custody case? Any of you who think your experiences would be useful to others, please write us.

Someone asked if we have any videotapes of TV programs with John Holt. We don't; none of us here have any video equipment. Do any of our readers have such videotapes, and if so, are they willing to loan them out, or can they make copies?

Rachael Solem has just finished the 24-page index to *GWS* 1–30, which is available here for $2.50. She's done a thorough job with the help of a computer. Entries are in the following categories: Alternative Schools, Art, At Home, Authors, Books Quoted, Books Reviewed, Children Working,

Colleges, Communities, Contributors, Correspondence Schools, Court Cases, Curriculum, Friendly Lawyers, Games, General, In School, Language, Learning, Local Schools & Legal Issues, Mathematics, Money, Music, Newsletters, Organizations, Poetry, Politics, Printing, Publications, Reading, Religion, Reports, Resources, Social Issues, Tapes, Teaching, Tests, Teens Working, Travel, Work, Writing, and Young Graduates. Rachael welcomes suggestions for future editions of the index.

At John's suggestion, Mary and Mark Van Doren brought in a little table and chair for our office toddler, Anna. Our extra typewriter sits on it, and sometimes Anna will busy herself for a long time with the machine. Mary has a neat trick of taping two sheets of paper together into a loop, so that no matter how much Anna presses the "Return" key, she never runs out of paper.—Donna Richoux

News Of Court Cases

We have recently gotten word of two homeschooling court cases lost, and a number of others pending. Of the losses, the bigger was the Virginia State Supreme Court ruling (12/3/82) against Robert and Vicky Grigg of Chesapeake. The court, using reasoning similar to California and Florida cases, said that since the Virginia compulsory education law has a specific exemption for "home instruction by a qualified tutor," the Griggs could not claim exemption by a different route, namely, that their home was a private school. How this will affect other homeschoolers in Virginia remains to be seen.

The other loss was in Stephens County Superior Court, Georgia, involving Terry and Vickie Roemhild. We do not yet have any details on this decision.

Other families who are being prosecuted are: Wayne and Margaret Burrow, Little Rock, Arkansas; Mary and Garfield Morgan of Lebanon, Connecticut; Bob & Jean Smith, Albert Lea, Minnesota; the Warren Parker family, Alexandria, Minnesota; Pat Baker of the Southside School District, San Antonio, Texas; and Tahca Ska, Poplar, Wisconsin.—DR

Georgia Regulations

[JH:] In two states, Georgia and Maryland, the State Boards of Education have proposed regulations that will make homeschooling difficult or impossible for most families. First, the Georgia situation. As *The Atlanta Constitution* of 1/13/83, in a story by Jane Hansen, reported it:

Rules Pushed To End Homeschooling In GA

The state school superintendent has recommended standards to eliminate homeschooling in Georgia in response to the growing number of parents who are teaching their children themselves. . . . The new policy would further define private schools by requiring them to meet these criteria: 1) A minimum of 15 students must be enrolled in the program at least 4½ hours daily and 180 days annually. 2) The building must be used primarily for instruction and must meet fire inspection codes. 3) At least one teacher must have a college degree from an accredited institution.

[JH:] Homeschool families and parents and teachers involved in small church-based schools are banding together to try to block these regulations. The board is expected to vote on the policy on Feb. 10, so by the time you read this they will have decided either to pass these regulations or an amended version of them, or, if public pressure is strong enough, as we hope will be the case, to let the whole matter drop. We will tell you what happened in *GWS* 32.

Meanwhile, because education officials in other states, thrown into needless panic by stories about growing numbers of homeschooling families, may try to make similar regulations, we might look at these a bit more closely. About them, three things can be said: 1) There is not the slightest educational justification for them. 2) They will probably be struck down in most or all courts in which they are put to the test. 3) Even if they were upheld by the courts, they would not automatically or necessarily make homeschooling impossible.

We should understand ourselves, and help the public to understand, that the first two of these proposed board regulations have nothing whatever to do with education or learning or even the quality of private schools. In defending the need for these regulations, the board has apparently said that it wants only to "clarify" the status of homeschooling under law, so that it will know where and how to enforce the state's compulsory school laws. This word "clarify" has been used in similar circumstances by education authorities in other states. In using the word, the board in Georgia is, to put it very politely, not being candid; as the newspaper story itself makes clear, they do not want to "clarify," but to prohibit. More specifically, they want to make private schooling so expensive that only a few rich can afford it.

The public schools have for a long time had a kind of silent bargain with the richest five percent of the parents of this country. They have said, in effect, "We will let you teach your children any way you want, *if you will give us a monopoly over the other 95%.*" Until recently, this is what has happened. Private schools, meaning schools in buildings not used for other purposes and staffed by paid teachers, have been so expensive that with few exceptions only affluent parents could afford them. Almost all the private schools started by moderate or low income parents in the past twenty years have failed for lack of money, and those that have survived for any length of time have almost all been rich ones, with high tuitions and often large endowments. With very few exceptions, state and local public education authorities have never interfered with these rich schools. They could hire any teachers they wanted, not just those with education degrees and teacher's credentials. They could teach any kind of curriculum they wanted, or none at all. State laws might mandate courses in state history, or health, or (as in NY) the dangers of alcoholism; rich private schools ignored such laws. In the fourteen years I taught in private schools we were never once visited or inspected by *public* education authorities. Rich private schools do have their own private accrediting agencies, but these are to allay the anxieties of rich parents of prospective students, not to satisfy any requirements of the state. The state's position has always been and is now, whatever rich people want in the way of schooling for their kids, they can have—*if the state can have complete control of all the rest.*

What now scares the public education authorities is that the second part of this bargain is breaking down. More and more people who twenty or even ten years would never have considered sending their children to private schools are now doing so. Despite hard times and inflation, the median income of parents of private school children has been dropping every year now for a number of years. One reason is that more and more parents are becoming so critical of public schools that they are willing to make ever larger money sacrifices to get their children out of them. But an even more important reason is that people are beginning to invent ways, among them homeschooling, to make private schooling cost so much less that more and more people can afford it. This growth of *low-cost* private schooling is what the public school authorities are trying to stop, since it threatens their effective monopoly over the education of the great majority of American children. They say that it is the low quality of homeschooling that worries them, but what really worries them is its low price tag.

Perhaps the best evidence that there is no educational need whatever for these regulations, let alone any compelling need, comes from Georgia itself. One of the books on our list is the *Peterson's Guide To Independent Study Through Correspondence Instruction*, which lists over 12,000 courses offered for academic credit not just at the high school but also the undergraduate and even the graduate level, by sixty-nine leading private and state colleges and universities. By happy chance one of these universities is the University of Georgia. Pages 52 and 53 of the Guide list 68 lower level college and 96 upper level college courses which the university offers, for credit, by correspondence. Lest any suspect these are some kind of Mickey Mouse courses, not really academic, here are the fields of study offering upper level courses: Agriculture, Archaeology, Anthropology, Ecology, Latin, American Literature, History (American, English, European, etc.), Philosophy, Government, Psychology, Sociology, Economics, Business Law and Management, Education, Forestry, Nutrition, and Journalism.

None of these many major departments or divisions at the leading university of the state seem to feel that in order for someone to learn the material in their courses they must be in a room with at least fourteen other people in a building not used for any other purposes, etc., etc. The University, like all the other universities listed in the guide, says, in effect, "We don't care where, or how, or when, or in whose company, or with whose assistance (if any) you learn this material. If you can show that you have learned it, we will give you full academic credit for it." This should be enough to dispose of any idea that effective learning can only take place in certain special places where nothing else takes place, and in the company of some minimum number of people, and in the presence of a college graduate.

Beyond this we have as evidence the experience over many years and even decades of such correspondence schools as Calvert Institute, Home Study Institute, and a host of others we have listed in *GWS*. Calvert alone has estimated that over the years over 300,000 have used their home study course; the total figure for all the home correspondence courses put together must be close to half a million, and might well be more than that. Beyond that, there are right now many thousands of families in Alaska, in the northern parts of Canada, and in the "outback," the great interior desert of Australia, where children are being educated, with the support and approval of state school systems, if only for the very good reason that they are many miles away from the nearest school. No one has ever produced a shred of evidence that all this homeschooling has not produced satisfactory results. So, as I say, there is not the slightest educational justification for the regulations which the Georgia State Board of Education is proposing, or for similar regulations which we may see put forward in other states.

But let me say again, as at the start of this piece, that even if through some strange piece of twisted judicial reasoning a Georgia court were to uphold these regulations, they would still not necessarily or automatically close down all homeschooling in the state. The regulations say there must be at least fifteen children in a school, but it should be easy for more than fifteen Georgia homeschooling families to register their children in one or more schools, perhaps the Horizons School which already exists and in which many of them are already registered. Beyond that, there is no reason why homeschooling families could not register their children with each others' schools, so that family A would have in its school the children of families B, C, D, etc., while family B would have in its school the children of family A, C, D, etc., and so on. Indeed, this would be a good thing for homeschooling families to do in any state where homeschooling may come under attack.

The regulations also say that the school must be in a building primarily used for instruction. But who could say, far less prove, that any home in which children were growing up, certainly any home school, was not being used primarily for instruction? What else happens in the home that is more important, or that occupies more of the time, thought, and energy of the parents? No reasonable person would claim that a home was used primarily for cooking, or eating, or sleeping. The regulations also talk about 4 ½ hours a day of instruction, 180 days a year. But as countless parents have pointed out, in a homeschool learning goes on twelve or more hours a day, 365 days a year. Again, who could reasonably claim, let alone prove, otherwise?

With such arguments as these, I think homeschoolers may be able to persuade most state boards of education or comparable bodies, or the state legislatures themselves, that there is no good reason to try to pass regulations or laws such as those proposed in Georgia, which can serve no useful or legitimate purpose and will only produce a great deal of litigation for our already terribly overcrowded courts—so overcrowded, it may be worth pointing out publicly, that all over the country they are unable to bring to a speedy trial criminals, often with long records, who have been arrested for violent crimes, but instead must let them back on the streets or, as is common, let them off with a greatly reduced sentence. We cannot say too often that our courts have far more important and indeed urgent things to do than pursue conscientious parents who are doing a capable job of teaching their own children.

Action By GA Homeschoolers

Connie Shaw, editor of the Georgia homeschooling newsletter, A Different Drummer, *sent us a copy of the information packet, including a list of recommended actions, that she sent to Georgia homeschoolers in order to fight the proposed regulations. It seems like such a thorough job, especially for being done on short notice, that we thought it would be useful to reprint in case other GWS readers faced a similar battle:*

Here is a checklist of things each of you can do to help in the days ahead:

1) Call your local legislators in the Georgia Assembly. Let them know what has happened and ask them to call their state board representative for their district (provide them with a phone number) and tell them to vote *no* on the proposed policy. This is where the real power is going to come from. If you know someone or have a friend that knows someone in the Capitol or on the Board of Education, let us know.

2) Call *all* 10 members of the Board of Education and let them know why you are opposed to the proposed ruling. Be careful not to attack openly the public schools. Calling is going to have more of an impact because they can easily overlook letters which they delegate to their secretaries to take care of. If you cannot call, then do write everyone a letter.

3) Sit down and compose a sincere letter for your local newspaper. Try to be tactful and project a good image of homeschooling. If you are willing to be interviewed, contact local radio and TV stations and let them know what is happening and why you oppose it. We need favorable publicity.

4) Get signatures on the petition that is enclosed. Make copies if you need more. Return all petitions to Phillis Bostar before Feb. 5, so they can be presented to the school board at their meeting.

5) Duplicate this material as many times as you are able, and pass it along to other groups or individuals that you may know that are interested in the family and basic rights of citizens.

6) We need money. Whatever you can donate, please send. Money is needed to cover all the printing costs of this mailing, postage, envelopes, long distance calls, and other items.

7) Attend the meeting of homeschoolers and interested citizens on Sat., Jan. 22.... Bring copies of any letters you have written. Please share them with us so we can benefit from your ideas.

8) Attend the State School Board of Education meetings on Wed., Feb. 9 and Thur., Feb.

9) If you are seeking permission to speak out at the school board meetings, please bring a copy of your prepared speech to the meeting on the 22nd, to share with us

10) Our numbers will carry a lot of weight at these meetings.... Bring as many others as you can—parents, grandparents, friends, and other interested parties.

If everyone will actively participate, we will be able to win and maintain our rights to continue teaching at home.

Do not let individual philosophies, religious beliefs, opposing lifestyles, or other differences divide us. We must stand solidly together on this one issue.

There is not much time. We need to move as quickly and deliberately as possible.

Maryland Regulations

At the same time, the Maryland State Board of Education is proposing even more stringent regulations. Manfred Smith of the Maryland Home Education Association *tells us that homeschoolers will be at the public hearing Jan. 26 to testify against them.* The Baltimore Sun *of 1/16/83, in a story by Gail Campbell, sub headlined "State move would virtually eliminate parent as teacher," summarized the regulations and added some interesting comment. We quote, in part:*

> Parents' freedom to teach children at home instead of sending them to school will virtually end if the State Board of Education adopts a proposed revision of its bylaws.
>
> A draft bylaw would allow only parents with college degrees or certification in the subjects they teach their children to do home teaching.
>
> The draft also would require children to receive at home a minimum of 180 days, or 1,080 hours, of instruction in courses such as English, language arts, mathematics, science and social studies.
>
> These home courses would have to be described to school officials in a written curriculum *citing specific objectives* and submitted to the local school superintendent for approval.
>
> Parents teaching at home would also have to provide books and materials comparable to those found in public school systems [JH: the regulations actually say they shall be "of good quality . . . and in sufficient variety and quantity . . ."], and the local superintendent would determine how often children should be tested to measure their progress.
>
> Last January, a Harford county couple were refused permission to teach their 7-year-old daughter at home. The county school board voted with one abstention to uphold Superintendent Alfonso A. Roberty's decision and ordered Miguel and Ellen Andriola to enroll their daughter Zoe in school immediately.
>
> Mrs. Andriola is not a college graduate and therefore would not qualify as a home teacher under the proposed bylaw, but she said she felt she did a good job teaching her daughter at home in spite of that.
>
> "*My daughter tested three grade levels above her own*," Mrs. Andriola said. School officials tested Zoe after she had been taught for a year and a half at home.
>
> Dr. Roberty said he totally supported the proposed bylaw. "The qualifications are stringent, there's no doubt about it, but it needs to be stringent. Otherwise, we'll have everybody teaching everywhere with no specific curriculum," Dr. Roberty said.
>
> "Some people don't like uniformity, but when you're running a school system, that's what you need," he added.
>
> Rabbi Kenneth B. Block, vice president of the Harford county school board, said he was equally opposed to the bylaw. . . . "I think it's too restrictive and unnecessary. They're trying to legislate home instruction out of existence," Rabbi Block said. . . . He said . . . he believes families should have the option of teaching at home if they wish. W. Eugene Graybeal, president of the Harford county school board, saying he spoke as an individual citizen . . . said he too believes parents should have the choice of teaching at home.
>
> "But this bylaw the state board has in the works is to strengthen its control over home teaching. The trend should be to loosen its hold," Mr. Graybeal said.

[JH:] Some comment on this particular story. It seems very likely that a reasonable court would rule that the Harford county school board erred in not allowing Mrs. Andriola to continue teaching her own daughter, since she was obviously working more than twice as effectively as the schools. And, though a court would not say this, most reasonable citizens would further conclude 1) that Dr. Roberty was not competent to judge the qualifications of a home teacher, since he so obviously judged wrongly in this case, and/or 2) Dr. Roberty and the Harford county school board were clearly not acting in good faith, that is, in the best interests of the child, in acting as they did.

Beyond that, we can only wonder, since two members of the Harford county board said in these hearings that they thought people should be able to teach their own children, how did it happen that this same county board voted *3–0* against Mrs. Andriola?

In quoting the news story, I underlined the words "citing specific objectives." They refer to a certain kind of meaningless school jargon—every teacher's lesson plan is supposed to list "Objectives." In many places, teachers are required to list both "Outcomes" *and* "Objectives," and have to do verbal handsprings to make them sound different, since there is in fact no real difference. But the schools could use this clause as a way of penalizing parents for not using the approved private jargon. Of course, top rated private schools and colleges do not use this kind of jargon at all.

More Local News

For addresses of the organizations mentioned, see the Directory in GWS 30, or our "Home Schooling Resource List" ($1). If you have a local newsletter, we'd really appreciate being on your mailing list; that way we can let the rest of our readers know what you're doing.

California: We list the San Juan Ridge Union School District in California as a "Friendly School District." It's Independent Study Director, Marilyn DeVore, has just told us that although its *mailing* address is in Nevada City, the district is *actually* in North San Juan, 16 miles away. She writes, "Our Nevada City mailing address has presented some problems. A family reading your publication moved to Nevada City, only to find that the school district there does not offer Independent Study...."

Connie Warthan in San Jose writes, "In the Bay Area we have been meeting for almost a year now.... It is an informal picnic and anybody interested in unschooling is welcome. Date is second Saturday of the month." For location, call Connie at 408-266-1494 or the Blomquists, 408-243-7870.

Connecticut: From Jeanine Lupinek: "As a result of a picnic held at the home of Madalene and Tom Murphy last summer, many families have gotten together and the Murphys are putting out a newsletter, *Hearth Notes*. Laura Pritchard and I have put together an information packet on homeschooling in Connecticut, which contains the guidelines on home education from the state department, our letter to the supt., an extensive list of resources, and names of homeschoolers. We have to ask $2 for the packet to cover printing and mailing expenses...."

Florida: Ann Mordes writes in the *FLASH* newsletter, 1/83: "I have received many telephone calls and letters from all over the state since October, from people who are complaining of harassment by truant officers. *FLASH* was happy to supply these many people with copies of our letters from the Governor's office, and the Health and Rehabilitative Services letter which 'let my husband and me off the hook' here in Jackson County [*GWS* 28]. Indeed these letters have helped every homeschooler who needed and used them."

Illinois: The Demmins sent us a report submitted to the State Board of Education, dated 6/24/82, called "Informational Report and Preliminary Recommendations Regarding the State's Relationship to Illinois Nonpublic Schools." It recommended that the state "add to the current list of assurances required for registration (i.e., immunization/health examination; health and fire safety; an academic term of 176 days or 880 clock hours; and non-discriminatory policies) the following: that children are taught the branches of education also taught to children of corresponding ages and grades in the public schools. . . ." Anyone knowing of the fate of these recommendations, please let us know.

Kentucky: According to some newspaper articles sent by Ruth McCutchen, the state Superintendent of Public Instruction told the local districts that they were responsible for bringing legal action against parents whose children attended unapproved schools, and officials in at least two districts have started truancy proceedings against families in Christian schools. However, the Rev. B.C. Gillespie has filed suit against the state board in U.S. District Court.

Massachusetts: Deborah Armer, 36 Shorecrest Dr, E Falmouth MA 02536, writes, "Some of us here in the Falmouth area are now calling ourselves the *Cape Cod Homeschooling Cooperative*. At last we have a name for ourselves (and some discounts when we go places as a group). We consist of eight families at the moment; six actually have their children out of school, the others are not yet of school age. We are beginning to get lots of phone calls from others in surrounding towns, as well. . . . We have finished putting out our second monthly newsletter."

Michigan: Dr. Raymond Moore, author of *School Can Wait, Home-Grown Kids*, etc, has started a newsletter, *Family Report,* for members of his *Hewitt Research Foundation* (553 Tudor Rd, Berrien Springs, MI 49103). Membership is $15/year.

Oklahoma: Toni O' Leary (405-332-9284) told us that the *Oklahoma Homeschoolers Association* was to have its first meeting on Feb. 12.

Pennsylvania: A story in the Fall '82 *Pa. Unschoolers Network* began with this quote by Wendell Phillips: "What is defeat? Nothing but education, nothing but the first step to something better," and then went on to say, "This was borne out in the experiences of the Rattenni family in Canonsburg. Jean and Richard had applied to their local superintendent about homeschooling their two daughters. The reply was negative because of their lack of teaching certificate. Drawing deep gulps of faith, they set about collecting recommendations from local elementary faculty, regional overseer of their church, etc. Based on these, the superintendent *reversed his decision*."

Texas: The *Texas Home Education Coalition* (1112 Millsprings, Richardson TX 75080) is planning seminars on how to defend your own case in court, and is considering submitting a pro-homeschooling bill in the state legislature.

Vermont: Jerry Mintz of the Shaker Mountain School has started a newsletter for the *Vermont Alternative Education Network* (PO Box 74, Hinesburg VT 05461). He says, "The woman who typed up the mailing list is about to start homeschooling her granddaughter when she takes her on a three-month trip down south."

Australian Newsletter

The Dec. 82 issue of *Other Ways*, ($10 Aus. per yr. from *Alternative Education Resources Group*, c/o Heather Keck, 22 Rix St. Glen Iris 3146, Victoria, Australia) has much exciting news of alternative school and homeschool developments in that country. Not only is homeschooling continuing to grow in the state of Victoria (where the city of Melbourne is located), but it is spreading to and growing in other states: New South Wales, Southern Australia, Queensland, Western Australia—which covers most of the country. Lorraine and Adrian Doesburg, with whom I had a very interesting long distance phone conversation a few months ago, are the resource people for Western Australia—write them at P.O. Roleystene, W.A. 6111. In Queensland the contact person is Lyn Cargill, 148 Henson Rd., Salisbury 4107.

Other Ways, which at first concerned itself mainly with doings in the state of Victoria, seems to have become the Australian national newsletter of alternative and homeschooling—at least, I don't know of any other. Any who are interested in the growth of homeschooling in Australia, and certainly any who think they might be visiting or moving there in the near future, should subscribe. Also, it may be a good way for children to make some Australian pen pals.—JH

Legal Insurance Working

[DR:] In January 1981, Ed Nagel and the National Association For The Legal Support Of Alternative Schools *(PO Box 2823, Santa Fe NM 87501) started an insurance program for homeschooling families concerned about facing legal action. We asked how it was going, and Lu Vorys wrote on Ed's behalf:*

Ed feels the Legal Insurance For Education (LIFE) program is working very well as a protection for home study families from intimidation and/or prosecution. Of the 52 families who have taken out policies, only two have made claims. In most cases, strong letters from Ed to threatening school officials have averted legal action.

The rates are the same as originally explained in *Tidbits* #8: $80 a year for up to $20,000 coverage, $40 a year for up to $10,000 coverage, and $20 a year up to $5,000.

More News From Carver

From Pat Montgomery (MI):

I thought you might like to know that Norman Bossio, superintendent of Carver Schools in Carver, Massachusetts, is very supportive of homeschooling. In the last two years he has gone before his board four times and recommended that families in his district do homeschooling, and, specifically, Clonlara's Home Based Education Program. He called the other day regarding one of the families and was lavish in his praise of our program.

He was also seriously concerned about another family in his district who were not following any program and were apparently feeding him misinformation about their homeschooling. He seemed genuinely disturbed by this in view of the fact that he is known to support homeschooling.

You will probably recall [GWS 21] that Carver is the place where, two or three years ago, a judge ordered a family of a frequently absent from school teenager to enroll in Clonlara's program and he also ordered the school district to pay the bill.

Commission For Ads

As you can see, our campaign to get display and classified advertising in *GWS* is off to a good start. Many thanks to all of you who bought these ads. In order to make *GWS* as close as possible to self-supporting, and less dependent than it is on the very uncertain and declining lecture business, we want to increase this advertising as fast as we can; our target, which we hope to reach in a year or two, is four pages of ads in each issue, which by that time would be 28 and more probably 32 pages.

We plan to solicit ads actively from this office; Pat Farenga will be our Director of Advertising. But because we are small and already very busy, we will only be able to do a limited amount of this. What we would like is to have as many readers as possible solicit ads for us, from any businesses they may know of or read about that they think might like to advertise in *GWS.* To encourage you, we make this offer: for every display ad that you recruit for us (from someone else, of course—an ad for yourself wouldn't count), and send in together with the check in payment, we will pay you a commission of 10% of the cost of the ad.

The only other thing I would like to say about our advertising is that it would be very helpful if, whenever you buy anything advertised here, you mention to the company that you saw their ad in *GWS*—perhaps writing them a letter, perhaps just making a little note on the order blank.

For any help you can give us in either of these ways, thanks very much.—JH

Young Farmers' Earnings

Betty Anderson (FL) wrote:

In April of '81 my daughter and son opened bank accounts for their own business practice. The bank loaned them each $800 to purchase a steer and feed for the year. In February of '82 their steers were sold at auction (this was their 4-H project). In our county bids on these 4-H animals go beyond the average market price for beef animals. The profits have paid for many college degrees and set up independent businesses for young people. My children were fortunate to add approximately $4500 to their bank accounts through the sale of their steers (profit).

According to the bank, the money belongs solely to me. How ridiculous. They were the ones who were up at 6 a.m. daily to feed, water, and groom the animals. They were the ones who missed out or were late arriving at social functions because they were tending the steers in the afternoons. They were the ones to balance bank statements, write checks for feed bills and keep daily records of the project. They did all the work—but the bank does not recognize an 11-year-old girl and a 9-year-old boy as established customers of their bank.

You should have seen the look on the piano salesman's face when my 11-year-old walked into his showroom and began to make a deal on the purchase of a piano. At first he wanted to speak with me, but I made it clear that he and Tammy would be conversing. He was astonished. Tammy was indignant that he didn't treat her as a valid customer. The purchase was made and I heard him say to Tammy, "Your mom can make the check out for $X." Tammy looked up at him sweetly and said, "No sir, my mother doesn't have enough money to buy this piano, so I'll write you a check from my account." Without hesitation she opened her check book and began to write out a check for the full amount of a brand new Kimball. The man began to chuckle at his own ignorance of her ability. When the piano tuner came, he said "Is Tammy Anderson here?"

Children do need more rights and more respect. Scott (9) would like the right to vote. This past election I feel he made wise choices. I believed it enough that when I went into the booth I voted on the candidates he had chosen. I did that because I wanted to prove to him his political choices were as sound as mine. . . . Actually, he made an effort to become well informed about each candidate—I didn't and I'm 31 years old. I would have voted a straight ticket because I was less informed.

They Learned At Home

From Rosalie Schultz, 3755 N Kedzie Av, Chicago IL 60618:

My parents and I collaborated to keep me out of school as much as possible. We did it with creatively written excuse notes. It's a lot like the more common art of creative menu writing. You've seen how hamburgers get dramatized into "delicately diced boeuf au jus naturel" on a menu. Well, my watery eye would be written up in the absence note as a true epic of "lachrymatory excess limiting the ocular field." Described that way, it was worth a good week to ten days at home.

My absences allowed me to grow up with large open spaces in my life. It was like being a pioneer into frontier territory.

I read myself into the rhythms of other worlds. For three voyaging months the language of *Moby Dick* rolled me on the ocean. At other times I walked briskly to the clipped affectation of Lord Peter Wimsey.

Then too, there were the comforting rhythms of our adjoining family printing business. I'd been collating printed sheets into booklets since I was two years old. Now I added typing, addressing, filing and metering to my repertoire. Much of the work was what most adults might shun as routine, but I enjoyed the almost mystical monotony very much. The work left the mind uncluttered and receptive.

My parents never filled my free time with any formal instruction. They were there, and we were part of a way of life together. That was enough.

Now I'm well into adulthood and am in charge of the family business.

From Eileen Perkins (VT):

My senior year I had a concussion and was physically out of school for over a month. (Mentally it took me a couple years to recover.) My assignments were sent home. That semester I received my first straight A's and in my English class not only did I get top score in the class, but top score in the four English sections that teacher taught. I assure you, I spent much less time on schoolwork than the six hours a day I would have spent at school. My parents had predicted that my grades would drop because I spent hours working on plays.

From the last experience I changed my study habits when I got to college. I relaxed, enjoyed my classes, didn't worry about grades, and I think I learned more than if I were trying to please the teacher or outguess him.

Self-Taught Scientist

A Christian Science Monitor *article, reprinted in the* L.A. Times, *12/22/82:*

> Rotterdam, NY—Vincent J. Schaefer, "the father of rainmakers" and one of the world's leading atmospheric scientists, did not take the conventional academic route to eminence.
>
> Until 1961, when he founded the Atmospheric Sciences Research Center at the State University of New York at Albany, which he directed as its leading professor for 15 years, he had never set foot inside a college or university—except as a distinguished lecturer or to receive some honorary degree.
>
> Schaefer never aspired to become a self-instructed scientist. He had hoped to go to college to become a forester.
>
> "But we had a large family," he said in an interview at his home in rural Rotterdam. "Being the eldest of the family, with our parents in poor health, it was necessary for me to go to work to bring in enough money to keep us in food." After only two years in high school, he left to become an apprentice at General Electric in nearby Schenectady.
>
> Four years later, he had mastered the machinist trade and was making experimental models for scientists at GE's Research Laboratory.
>
> Schaefer refers to his experience at General Electric as "Langmuir University." Under the tutelage of the late Irving Langmuir, for whom he was building test models, Schaefer's natural talents came to flower. In a short time he was conducting his own experiments in the General Electric lab.
>
> That unorthodox beginning launched him on a career as a highly inventive natural scientist. In 1946, Schaefer discovered the first feasible method of seeding clouds.
>
> What is his secret of success?
>
> —Work on your own.
>
> —Learn by doing.
>
> —Seek out worthwhile people and make them your friends.
>
> —Read books.
>
> —Take advantage of every good opportunity to learn something.
>
> —Remember that mature people enjoy helping young people who are trying to find themselves and realize their potential.
>
> Schaefer insists that anyone with the desire could do what he has done. "You have to have a sense of wonder," he says, "and be aware of everything that goes on. You have to develop what I call 'intelligent eyes'—be intrigued with the world and everything in it."
>
> "A book is a distillation of a person's ideas," said Schaefer, a voracious reader. "If you have a book, you have an open door to the area of knowledge the author is interested in. It is a tremendous resource to take advantage of."
>
> A boyhood interest in collecting rocks and arrowheads in this geologically and historically rich region introduced him to the first of his long list of "worthwhile people."
>
> Two farmers, both self-educated men, stirred in young Vince an admiration for their knowledge of local history, where Indian lore mingles with tales of early Dutch settlers.
>
> In retrospect, he gives much credit to the Lone Scouts of America, an organization

for farm boys who were too isolated to be active in Boy Scout troops. They took all their tests by correspondence. "It gave you a sense of independence because you were on your own honor," Schaefer said.

Eventually, with three other boys, he formed the Lone Scout Mohawk Tribe. The boys published a little magazine on archeology, which attracted the attention of the New York State Department of Archeology. Through the head of the research laboratory, Schaefer eventually met the state archaeologist, Arthur Parker, who invited the 17-year-old to join him on a month-long archeological field trip.

Homeschooler Helps School

From Jacque Williamson (WV):

I direct and teach an early school for children ages 2–5 which is similar to a parent co-op school in that most parents rotate helping me in the classroom. This is the second year I've had a homeschooler helping me (she was 10 last year, 11 this). It's been great for us both. As we only meet two mornings a week, it isn't too demanding of her time and gives her a chance to use her skills with others. I'm constantly amazed at how she can breeze into situations with children who won't try a new activity and have them rapidly enjoying the very thing they've avoided. I think she has a "kid-sense" we have lost. I'm quite open with parents who ask about her presence and now we have several more families interested in homeschooling since they see it in action. One of these days I hope Chris will write you about her experience helping in the school.

High Schoolers At Work

Theodore Sizer, chairman of "A Study of High School" sent us an interesting paper by Eleanor Farrar. Some excerpts:

> Our field studies in fifteen high schools around the country are in the final phase. . . . One widespread phenomenon which has taken many of the staff by surprise is the amount of time and energy that so many public high school students commit to working. We've noticed that, regardless of family circumstances or plans for life after high school, most students are holding jobs, many virtually as full-time employees. The recently published report from the NORC High School and Beyond Study, "Youth Employment During High School," captures in quantitative form the impressions we have formed in the field: the NORC study reports that 50% of all students surveyed in spring, 1980 (a national sample of nearly 60,000 sophomores and seniors), had worked the previous week; and in the senior year, 63% had worked. Furthermore, over half the seniors worked more than fifteen hours per week, 10% worked full-time, and the average weekly hours of work was 19. These figures include private schools. If privates were excluded, the number would be even higher. Why are they working? . . . First and foremost, students say that they work for the paycheck. Some are saving for college, or a car, or a trip. Others work to support cars, or their closets, or their weekend fun. Many students work because they have to; but a surprising number of students say that though their parents willingly provide an allowance, they feel uncomfortable taking it. As one girl puts it, "My mom got a job when my sister went to college. They'd give me an allowance if I asked, but I'd feel funny taking it." Like so many young people, she relishes the freedom and independence that her own money brings, but she also feels obligated to lighten the burden at home. In this sense, students work not because they "have to" for financial reasons, but because their sense of self-esteem and of family membership requires it.

> Work also seems to provide a larger arena, beyond the school, in which young people can take a measure of themselves. While school provides a test of academic achievement or, for some, athletic or journalistic skill, it seems to

fall short as a yardstick of such qualities as responsibility, initiative, and ability to get on in the world. The opportunities schools provide in these domains seem to "top off" at a point which is too low for many students. They want bigger challenges—"responsibility" is a word that comes up over and over again—and they want the recognition that comes with success, such as a raise, or a promotion, or a more difficult assignment. As Ted Sizer recently noted, "A student may work forty hours a week as assistant manager at a fast food place, but at school he still needs a pass to go to the bathroom: it's crazy!" Whether or not they see craziness in the situation, many students are voting with their free hours after school for a chance to be treated like the adults they believe they are.

Kids In The News

A UPI article from Sandy, UT:

Karisa Rothey, 6, thinks her neighbors in suburban Sandy should take a lesson from Mormon history to get rid of a plague of hungry grasshoppers, so she has gone into the rent-a chicken business.

Before the days of insecticides, flocks of seagulls helped save the Mormon settlers from swarms of grasshoppers that were devouring their crops in 1847.

Karisa has once again found that birds are a terrific answer to the insect plague. Only she uses a flock of Leghorn chickens, which she rents to neighbors a week at a time.

The voracious chickens, along with domestic ducks, seem to be succeeding in partially curbing a nasty grasshopper infestation that has resisted insecticides and brush fires set by the fire department.

Sandy city officials have asked Governor Scott Matheson to provide state assistance and even call out the Utah National Guard to deal with the hungry chompers that have been stripping gardens and even fruit trees throughout the suburb south of Salt Lake City.

But Karisa said, "All people need are some chickens. They love to eat bugs. The grasshoppers used to eat all of the plants in our garden. We had to plant the corn twice. But the chickens just gobble up the grasshoppers."

Karisa said her father, Kenneth Rothey, a lawyer, bought her some baby chicks for Easter and she raised them specifically to attack the bugs that invade her yard yearly from nearby fields.

After the chickens cleaned the insects out of her yard, Karisa began renting them to her neighbors for 25 cents per chicken per week. She also collects and sells the eggs.

"We're now getting some beautiful eggs from all that protein," said her father. "Karisa is selling them for 50 cents a dozen, and she has $140 in her savings account."

Neighbors up and down the block have been renting the birds.

The Oregon Journal, *5/4/82:*

Eugene—There are kids in this town who tell some pretty tall tales—and when they do, others listen. In fact, they listen so well that sometimes they forget where they are.

And that's the best compliment you can give these young people—Roosevelt's Troupe of Storytellers, in its 13th year and still the only troupe of its kind in the nation.

They may spin their yarns in the classroom, but they transport their audience to far-off fairy tale lands with monsters and princesses, or scary places with haunted houses, or magical kingdoms where anything can happen.

These "spellbinder apprentices," as they

have been called, are in reality a group of junior high students who have performed for more than 26,000 elementary school students throughout the state, have given demonstrations at libraries and for college education classes, have had their work recorded for radio and television and are occasionally called on to exhibit their skills at teacher workshops.

During the summer months many of the tellers perform for children's festivals, summer camp or park programs, and at hospitals. One girl spent a summer as a guest storyteller in Hilo, Hawaii, and others turn their well-practiced talents to high school dramatic presentations.

Wherever they perform, it is as professionals.

"I will not save them if they are up in front of a class," says Robert E. Rubinstein, creator and director of the troupe. It is the kind of discipline they expect from this man.

A professional storyteller himself, Rubinstein learned the craft while working as a children's librarian in Boston and continues to work at it in addition to fulltime teaching duties at Roosevelt Junior High School.

"It's a hard life," says Rubinstein, of those who attempt to make a career of storytelling. "A few of the very best can make a living at it, but they just about have to be single and willing to travel all over the country."

Each of the students in the travelling troupe must develop a repertoire of four stories and be ready to perform any or all of them on call, which, of course, is one of the true storyteller's greatest assets.

Some have written original stories to tell. Most, however, choose tales with good characters and exciting dialogue, which make their job easier in the long run. They learn fast.

"I like short stories because they are easier to tell and you can make up more," says Jean Tobin, 13.

"It is a challenge to be able to tell something to take the place of the pictures," adds Dawn Germain, 13.

"It's fun. It makes other people happy and I like that," says Claire Ferres, 12.

"What's really hard is when you are scared and begin to fidget when you stand up," confides another member of the troupe.

But when it comes time to pull on the red troupe T-shirts and climb into the van heading for the next school, they soon lose the jitters by wisecracking and singing songs. . . .

"The most important thing to keep in mind when selecting a story," Rubinstein tells his students, "is that the teller must genuinely like the story, want to tell it and want to share it with his audience."

14-Year-Old On TV

From Doris Newman (NY):

My 14-year-old daughter, Joy Newman, just taped a television pilot called *The Kid's Connection*. She was one of five professional children chosen to participate in a talk show for teenagers, with an adult interviewer and a live audience of adolescents. The five children included two tap dancers (sister and brother), a model, a singer, and an actress.

Although Joy was hired as the actress, as soon as the producers found out that she does not attend school, they focused on her homeschooling for most of the questions. In rehearsal, the other kids were asked neutral questions like "How did you get your first job?" and "How old were you when you first got started?" Joy was asked, "Don't you feel isolated?" and "Aren't you lonely?"

When I spoke to the women who were running the show (teachers), they assured me that everyone was just interested, not challenging or threatening. Joy felt that she was put in the position of defending herself and her education.

Because she was so uncomfortable about the tone of the inquiries, we spent some time at home thinking of hostile questions, although it's hard for my husband and myself to assume a frame of mind where the most important things are tests, report cards, schedules and graded homework. At our private rehearsal, Joy's answers were better than the ones we would have given. We wanted to bring your book *Teach Your Own* and other materials to show, but they rejected the idea.

Yesterday, when they taped the show, Joy was smiling and confident, giving thoughtful answers. When she mentioned learning French from *Parlez-moi*, a public television program, she was asked how she could learn without a book. Joy's response was to explain how we sent away for the book of scripts, which is written in French, and how we read aloud with our own spontaneous translations. (She didn't have time to tell about going to a French restaurant, or seeing French films, or saving labels from products made in France or Quebec.)

Someone from the studio audience asked, "Someday, won't you be sorry you didn't get a well-rounded education?" The irony is this: All five kids (who were Long Islanders hired in New York City after auditioning for the show) had to travel a couple of hours to Tarrytown in Westchester County, where the TV studio was located. All of the others, whose education was not considered questionable, went home as soon as the show was over. Our family stayed overnight, then drove a few miles to visit Philipsburg Manor, which was built in 1720. At the mill on the estate, Joy studied the gears attached to the water wheel for grinding corn and wheat, she drew sketches of the ewes and rams near the barn, walked on the oyster shell paths, asked questions of the well-informed tour guides, and saw a short film on the history and restoration of the manor. We compared artifacts in the manor house to the ones used on stage for *The Crucible* at SUNY Stony Brook last summer. (Joy had played a role in the Arthur Miller play about the Salem witch trials of 1692.)

Joy's "schooling" didn't stop because it was Saturday, but the other students and their families apparently thought that since it wasn't in a school building, and it was a weekend, there was no need for any more education for the week. They were about three miles from this beautiful place when they left the TV studio and headed home. So much for the well-rounded education!

The education of all five children who were interviewed is actually much broader than that of the average child, because of special skills and work experiences. It was interesting to me that the model, the singer, and the two dancers kept assuring everyone that they were just "ordinary, regular, average kids." Joy acknowledged that her life is different. On the program her answers were unique because of her frankness about conflicts in her life, contrasted with the idealistic picture presented by the others. Joy was articulate, informative, and sometimes amusing. (Her answers were singularly lacking the "like, you know, like" speech pattern of our local adolescents.)

After the show, some of the boys went over to the model, while most of the kids in the studio audience flocked around Joy. Isn't it funny that the girl who is supposed to be missing socialization made the most new friends!

From The Mahers

From Mary Maher (MA):

I still have my dream of buying a piano, but the problem is—where to put it? . . . Mandy (6) has a real interest in the piano. She's been taking music classes (with note reading and some piano) from a very accomplished Russian pianist who lives up the street. She loves going there and is now after me to get her something to play on. In the meantime I'm going to buy her a recorder. A friend has offered to teach her to play. I'm going to learn to play also.

Mandy is doing so well as a homeschooler. I really see the benefits of never having let her attend school at all. Learning to read and do math is fun for her. She has no anxieties at all about whatever she wants to learn. It's so wonderful—and such a contrast from Scott!

Scott (12) is free and happy now, but some aspects of school work still cause him unhappiness.

Too many bad memories, I guess. One good thing, though—he is enrolled in the 7th grade science program at the junior high school—*his* choice. He's very excited about his class—lots of experiments and opportunities to ask questions. His grades are all A's. I don't care what his grades are, but he is proud to feel that he can succeed in school. In the past he always saw himself as a failure, and now he has a chance to see that he is smart. The science teacher told us that Scott is a child any teacher would love to have in his class—bright, eager, questioning. It makes me so happy to see Scott appreciated after all the years of criticism from elementary school teachers.

I remember telling you once how Scott couldn't write—he would just freeze up. Well, you should see him now! He writes page after page without any anxiety. Not forcing him to write at all in the beginning, and being oh so patient, has really paid off.

So many good things have come from homeschooling. The best is that my children hardly ever fight anymore. They are close friends and care about each other deeply. I did nothing to bring this about, it just happened. It makes me see more and more how terribly destructive school can be to a child's well-being and sense of self-worth.

You asked us to let you know how we are doing with our Sinclair Computer. We have bought several books on how to program it, and also bought a 16K memory RAM. There is an awful lot to learn and it's a rather slow process. Mandy and Scott have both put programs into it. Tom will write you all about it when he finally understands it!

Scott also wrote us a letter:

When I left school two years ago in fifth grade, I felt that I would not want to go back. I am now in seventh grade and I am very interested in science. My friends told me that the science class down at the junior high school was very exciting and they were doing a lot of experiments. When I heard this I decided to try it out.

In October my parents and I went for a meeting down at the school. The teachers were glad to hear that I wanted to go down there for a class and gave me the best teacher.

The first day of class I felt awkward because I didn't know most of the kids, but now I feel I fit in with the class. None of the other kids think I'm different because I'm a homeschooler. The homework is very easy and I do it in about 5 to 10 minutes. My teacher says I am one of his best students.

Some of the things we study are: matter and energy, atoms and molecules, and now machines.

Manhattan Homeschool

Articles from The Gorsetman—Landowne Homeschool of Manhattan Newsletter, *September, 1982:*

> "The History of our School" by Rose Landowne
>
> For the past ten years, Chaya (Gorsetman) and I have been dreaming about the type of Jewish education (including general education) that we want our daughters to have. Chaya had started a nursery school and kindergarten, and we wanted to find an elementary program which continued with the same philosophy of living Judaism, respect for individuals, and unpressured growth. We visited close to fifty schools, but did not find anything that was completely satisfying.
>
> At first the idea of keeping the children out of school was not much more than a fantasy, but then our consultant, Dr. Clara Loomanitz, pointed out that we really should do it. As our frustrations with institutions of any sort mounted, the idea began to seem better and better. When we read *Teach Your Own* by John Holt, we realized that, although we did not know any other people who were homeschooling their children, it was a growing trend, and made a lot of sense.
>
> Last spring we made our decision and began gathering textbooks and discussing what sort of curricular materials to use. We decided to use a curriculum which we had written for our

alternate program. The basis of this curriculum is the Jewish calendar, and it branches out into science, social studies, and Jewish textual material. We originally wrote it for the first two elementary grades, but found that we can go through fifth grade with it by studying the textual material in depth.

Chaya's sister got married and sublet her apartment to us, so we have a workspace. It's easier to get started when you have to leave the house in the morning. During the summer we cleaned the apartment, set up furniture and arranged our library. On Tuesday, September 7, the day after Labor Day, the Jewish Family School (un)officially opened its doors to our four students, Atara Gorsetman (grade 5), Dena Landowne (grade 5), Talya Gorsetman (grade 3), and Lea Landowne (grade 1).

"How We Work" by Atara Gorsetman

In our school we have a very different schedule than any other school. Our hours are from 9 a.m. to 3 p.m.. We start with Tefila (prayer). Then we have some sort of math scheduled until lunch. However, when or if someone finishes math before lunch time, then she can work on some project. This month we worked on two projects. One was our Rosh Hashanah cards and the other was hooked rugs, which we designed and began making. Hooked rugs are made with special tools.

After lunch we do our jobs. Then Chaya, Rose, Dena, and I work on a workbook called *You are the Editor*. It is supposed to help us write better. It is hard to tell right now, but I think it will help. Every day we work on Hebrew but in a different way each day. For instance, one day we might work in a workbook called *Sefatenu*. It has exercises with different words and questions to answer about a story. Sometimes we study texts. For example, before Yom Kippur we learned the book of Jonah and before Succoth we learned the holiday's sources in the book of Leviticus. After Hebrew we go upstairs to my house to practice piano. Then the day is almost over. Sometimes we plan trips to places like the apple orchard...

From "September Review" by Chaya R. Gorsetman:

We are studying animals, classifying them according to cold blooded and warm blooded, vertebrates: mammals, and reptiles, etc. All this came about because of the snake that we are buying.

Talya developed a math game that is appropriate for almost all ages. All four girls are taking piano lessons and are attending the Hebrew Arts School for art, choir and Israeli Dance. Dena and Atara are taking a jewelry class at the Walden School. Talya is taking a gymnastics class at a local gymnastic studio.

Success Stories

From Judith Wenz (NE):

This is our second year of homeschooling. We have four children, 8, 7, 5, and 2. We have our school set up as a private school since I am a certified teacher in this state. This seemed like the path of least resistance. We have our library with a card catalog, books with their Dewey decimal numbers on them and all the other little things we had to do to be approved. Even though these things can be a bother we are aware that we are the first homeschoolers in our area and want to make a good impression. What we seemed to be judged on is how cooperative we are willing to be rather than how well we are educating our children. And the issues they want us to cooperate on are so minor that we are willing to go along with them at this point.

Last year for school I tried to center our activities around the children's interests. This year my approach has been to let each child set his own goals. They have turned out to be very short term—

usually something that can be accomplished in an hour—but at least I don't feel a need to keep things going myself all day. When the kids bog down or get bored, then I get out a game or project that I've wanted to experiment with, and that gets us over the hump.

I have met people just as able as I am to teach, who say they couldn't possibly do it, simply because they had never finished college. Those who have finished college but have not specialized in teaching usually feel they could teach their children in their area of expertise, but not in other areas. *Those of us who have specialized in education know that our courses have helped us very little, and just dive in.*

From David Byram in Connecticut:

We have been successfully teaching our own at home for about two and a half months now.

We are using the Calvert system for Christi (6) and Jeremy (9). My wife Linda mainly does the teaching with my assistance on areas that may be unfamiliar to her.

The first meeting with the superintendent and his assistant ended up with what seemed to be a loss. They tried so much to discourage us, something of course that was expected. Before we even contacted them we did much research on Connecticut laws and had the aid of an attorney, Mr. Frank B. Cochran [see "Friendly Lawyers"], to whom we owe much thanks. Whenever the local board thought they could get us on some technicality, Mr. Cochran pointed us to what the law really says.

After the very first meeting with the superintendent, it seemed that we gained their cooperation, which was a great help. The monitoring requirements were not burdensome. We go to the local school every eight weeks to show the children's progress . . . The principal is very nice and cooperative and, since he knows Jeremy and Christi from their earlier school records, told the school board they are both excellent students and that he sees no problems. The only formal testing will be a standard achievement test given in April.

My wife does notice the lack of time she has now, but we both find it rewarding, especially as we see the children grow rapidly.

Carole Miller (MA) writes:

We are unschooling here in Saugus this year—at last—with the approval of the School Committee and Superintendent's Office. We began this venture in Florida, but I gave in to the prevailing pressures to put Adam in school when we moved to Massachusetts after my divorce from Adam's father. At that time I guess I wasn't up to another battle! Two years in the first grade for Adam gave me the courage to renew my commitment to homeschooling. Adam's adjustment has been beautiful (as I knew it would) and his progress has exceeded even my expectations.

I agreed to twenty hours per week of home instruction—fifteen of which are based on my summary of the town's language arts and mathematics curricula for Grade 2. We're pretty much on our own for science, social studies, music, art and physical education.

For materials, I am using my choice of town-supplied texts and workbooks as the core of Adam's program in language arts and math, although I am liberally supplementing these with other materials of my own choosing. Materials for science, social studies, etc., have been left to my own discretion. In all areas, the public library has proved to be an invaluable resource as our finances are *extremely* limited.

I have agreed to standardized testing at the end of the school years, although whether or not this testing will actually be required remains to be seen. Otherwise, we're on our own.

From a reader in Australia:

I have my 12-year-old stepdaughter out of school as we were told that she needed to be put away in a psychiatric institution for her "mad" behaviour at the local State school! How dangerously wrong they were!

Her real problems were caused by missing out on learning until age eight due to undiagnosed deafness. (I married her father when she was 7 and

I detected the deafness which is now quite cured.) She has comprehension problems with reading and her math level was three grades behind. After three weeks with me "teaching" her, she has made remarkable progress. She has already succeeded in completing eighteen months of math and is doing daily comprehension exercises at a great rate from an American series of books called *Increasing Comprehension Skills.* Her self-esteem is rising daily, and fortunately the memories of teacher and peer humiliations are fading.... As I only asked for permission to keep her out of school for one term (our system has the school year ending just before Christmas), I only needed a medical certificate stating that she was emotionally unfit for school.

Recovering From "Special Ed"

From Kristine Maihado in southern California:

We have three children, ages 11, 9, and 6. We took our two older children out of public school one and a half years ago, after much struggling and dissatisfaction on our part and unhappiness on theirs.

Our oldest boy, Jamie, had been labeled hyperactive.... They advised us to put him on medication and into a special class. Well, we did the special class but not the drugs.... Each year he and his brother Andy would fall farther and farther behind in reading....This was creating a very negative situation for them.

In the meantime, my youngest child, Emily, had started at a marvelous little school near our home that's based on your philosophy and that of Joseph Chilton Pearce and A. S. Neill of *Summerhill.* She was doing fine and was wonderfully happy.

Her two older brothers were developing a real curiosity about what was going on at this interesting school.... So with much enthusiasm, they started going there after school two days a week. It became a safe place for them to vent a lot of angry feelings. Creative things happened as well and many nice humane relationships were formed.

Then one day while browsing in the local library, I happened on the book *And The Children Played* by Patricia Joudry. I immediately fell in love with the author, her philosophy, and whole way of life. I wanted that for us.

I remember the turning point. I was sitting on our front porch one warm November Sunday afternoon reading this book, laughing, crying, and intermittently reading parts to my husband, Jim. When the three children all trooped out and announced that they wanted to cook, I looked at Jim, he looked at me, and we said sure. Amidst flour, butter and honey on the floor, I made dinner that night with a feeling of warmth and new freedom in my heart.

After Christmas, with lots of reservations and excitement, we took them out of public school. We decided they would attend the private school for two or three days a week, and the rest of the time they would be home. They loved it and very quickly fell into the routine.

Jamie has spent hours repairing bikes, had a job at a bike shop for a while. This year he built a beautiful bike for himself from scratch. He likes reading classified ads in the newspaper, bike magazines, and *Mad* magazine, though sometimes I suspect he mostly looks at pictures.

Both boys like building things and have made duck and fish ponds, forts, lofts, animal cages. Andy spent a lot of last year cooking, and cooks many things, from cookies to pizza, even a whole dinner for us at times. He also likes stained glass, music, aerobics, and several times last year spent days working in a math workbook. They are interested and enthusiastic about many things and are always busy.

Jamie reads and writes very little. Andy reads not at all—he sometimes recognizes words and other times can't remember the sounds of letters. I often get very scared that they lack so much self-confidence in that area and that they have so many negative feelings they may just grow up never learning to read or write.

It's hard to face our friends and family when they hear about our homeschooling and say, "But look at your children, they don't even read yet." They even sometimes ask our children if they can read. The children look down with long faces and reply, "No, I can't." It really hurts me when I see them feel ashamed of themselves.

I love homeschooling and can't count all the good things that have come of it. I see no other way; this is the best. Our little school here (all the other pupils are homeschoolers too) is great for breaking the isolation of homeschooling and getting together and sharing with other people, though it is, like you say, John, a lot of extra work. Every day I count my blessings that I can give my children this kind of freedom, and I'm feeling better and stronger and more relaxed about everything.

How should I handle this? If I just completely leave them alone, which is what I want to do, with their negative feelings, will they eventually teach themselves to read on their own?

My newest idea was to make a journal for them to keep and require that they write something in it once a week with pictures, stories, poems, mainly for the purpose of allowing the feelings to come up and working through them, not necessarily that they actually write.

Another idea was to have my husband and me play school with them in the evening sometimes, Jim and me being the pupils and the children being the teachers. I can imagine now all kinds of orders and reprimands going on. I truly believe that once these feelings are out they will feel so much freer and better about themselves and will reclaim that natural curiosity and true desire for learning that was theirs before they went to school.

I must say that my six-year-old Emily is thoroughly in love with life. She is constantly busy, plays great imaginary, detailed games with her friends. She begged to go to kindergarten this year. Well, freedom is freedom, so we let her go. After one month she still won't miss a day. She really likes doing homework, etc.

I will keep close tabs on what is happening there and will let her leave as soon as she even hints about it. I'm so afraid this natural enthusiasm of hers could be ruined all too easily.

John wrote in reply:

Thanks so much for your good letter.... I'm so glad the boys are recovering from their experience of schooling and "special education." Considering how big a dose they got, they seem to be doing very well.

About their reading, you say, ". . . they may just grow up never learning to read or write." There is about as much chance of that happening as that they will grow up to be crocodiles. If you must worry, worry about something else.

You say "Jamie reads and writes very little . . ." You later say that when people ask the boys if they can read, they look down with long faces and say that they can't. Why do they say that? It's not true. Don't let them say it anymore! Maybe they can't read very much, maybe they don't read very often, but if they can read *something*, even only a few words, then they can read. So don't let them say they can't. Don't even let them think it. As for your friends and family, ask them or tell them please to stop asking that question, which only makes things worse. More to the point, tell them that the boys' reading is none of their business.

Above all, don't let the boys feel ashamed of themselves. Even if it were true, and it isn't, that they couldn't read a single word, it would be nothing to be ashamed of. Reading is a useful skill as well as a source of much information and pleasure, and not being able to do it can be a nuisance. But it is not a crime. Reading has nothing to do with intelligence or competence, and I have heard of quite a few highly successful and even wealthy people in this country who could not read at all. There is no reason for shame. Make sure the boys understand that.

As I say, not being able to read is an inconvenience and a nuisance, like having a broken leg or being sick. But also, once people get over the idea that reading is terribly difficult or that they are too stupid to do it, neither of which is true, and once they decide that for their own reasons they really want to read, they can do it in a very short time, often only a few months or less—I myself personally saw adult illiterates in their 40s and 50s learning the essential skills of reading in only a few weeks. You can say to the boys, "You don't have to read unless and until you want to, and anytime you really want to, you can do it easily." You can add, "The only reason you think that perhaps you can't learn to read is because all those people in school told you so. But they have been proved wrong thousands of times."

One way of showing Andy how many words he does in fact know how to read might be to offer him a small payment, say 25¢, for every word he can read to you. Keep an alphabetical card file of these words. You and he will soon find that he can read many more words than your or he thought.

You say, "If I just completely leave them alone, with their negative feelings, will they eventually teach themselves to read on their own?" You don't leave them *completely* alone in anything else, so why should you in this? It's their negative feelings that you have to try to deal with. Once they stop feeling ashamed, or thinking that even if they did try to read they wouldn't be able to, their natural intelligence and curiosity will do the rest. As far as help goes, it will be enough to say, "Any time you want me to tell you what a word *says*, ask me and I'll tell you, and anytime you want me to write a word for you, ask me and I'll do that." That will almost certainly do the trick. Though if you can afford it, it would probably help if you bought them some kind of a typewriter—they will almost certainly like it and will want to learn to use it.

Please let me know what you think and feel about this letter, and if you discuss it with the boys, what they say about it. And after a few months, please write again and let us know how things are coming along. And please try to worry less. Good luck to you all.

Trying Out School

From Jacque Williamson (WV):

Our experiment of having Nathan (5) attend public kindergarten two mornings a week has about run its course. We had agreed to try it for three months. Nathan loved it the first month and I was feeling a mixture of relief and anxiety. I was glad he fit in and yet worried about what would happen if he really liked it and insisted on going to first grade which is against all our wishes—plus I was puzzled about why he liked such a structure which he's never liked before. I was beginning to question all our theories and plans for his schooling, thinking maybe I'd misjudged what he needed.

However, after eight mornings (one month), he started to ask to not go. A little talking about sticking it out until November, as we had agreed, was all it took to keep him going a few more times. However, near the end, he downright pleaded to not go so he skipped several days. Finally, I spent a morning with him to get a feel for the whole flow— I'd visited frequently for several years in this class but only brief visits. After our visit I told his teacher he wasn't happy and we agreed to teach him at home for the winter and see what he wants to do come spring. He's happy.

Why was he happy at first and later dissatisfied? At first the novelty was what he liked—new place, new toys, new activities, new friends. That soon wore off when every day was the same thing. In three months they finger painted once, the only time there was any free-form art (as opposed to what I call "preplanned parent pleasers"—those things that all look the same for each child and which parents can recognize as being a turkey, etc.). His frequent question during this time was "Mommy, how come in public school they don't let you make any decisions?" The lock-step of the system became apparent when they studied numbers 1–5 in November, even though his teacher admitted all but two children knew 1–5 before entering kindergarten, and those two she didn't expect to learn 1–5 all year. So Nathan was bored.

Now he's home doing his own projects, mostly non-academic. However, at times he gets interested in reading or math or science and in short order zooms ahead. He's on par with the first graders here in math and close in reading and I dare say he's spent less than two full school days' worth of time getting those skills.

Jesse Murphree (FL) wrote in the FLASH *newsletter, 1/83:*

I have been an unschooler all my life. But August 30, 1982, I stepped into a public middle school. It was the first public school I'd ever attended in my life. The reason I was going to school was I wanted to get out and meet some girls my own age. I was pretty scared since I'd never been to a real school before.

The thing I was most worried about was school work. Until I wanted to start school I'd never done any kind of work (and I'm no genius). For eleven years I'd done practically whatever I pleased and now I was in sixth grade.

I made friends but it was sort of hard because I'm kind of shy and some girls were not too friendly. But as time went by I learned which girls to avoid and which ones were nice.

After the first six week period the names of the people who made the honor roll were called over the intercom. I was one of them. The next day I got a blue card with my name and a little red ribbon on it.

I went to school two more weeks before I decided to quit. It wasn't that I didn't like school, it was just school wasn't all peaches and cream. Most of the work was pretty boring and it took up a lot of my time. I wanted more time to write stories and do other things.

I think school was a good experience. I made friends and had some good times. Most of all I learned that I could go to school and make the honor roll even though I'd never been to school before. That gave me a lot of confidence.

She Chose To Go

From Bonnie Kolodzy in Ontario:

Though my oldest is in kindergarten, it is by her choice. She knows that anytime she wishes to, she may switch to homeschooling.

I once had someone ask me in regard to my allowing her to choose to go to school, "If she wanted to eat a whole bag of sugar, would you let her?" Though I was dumbstruck, when reflected on it, I thought, "No, but I wouldn't deny her a taste." I feel that she needs to experience school in order to make an informed choice, hence my decision to allow her to go. I must admit, though, my husband and I were both a bit disappointed when she chose to go. We were all set to allow her to learn by curiosity as she has always done at home.

We still encourage her learning on her own, through all the ways mentioned in *GWS* over and over again....

Both Beth (5) and Joe (3) have been assisting me in so many areas! Last week, for instance, I was busy when my apple pie was done in the oven. Beth shut off the buzzer and the oven and, using potholders, removed the pie from the oven to cool—all without any prompting. This week, Joe made muffins for a friend who was ill. I measured the ingredients out, he put them in the bowl, beat it up and spooned the batter into muffin tins. He even delivered them to the door!

This is how we encourage self-sufficiency. Helping only when needed and allowing the children to grow into independence.

At Home In New Orleans

Marilyn Bohren (LA) writes:

When will I quit worrying? I have three children—boys 5 and 3, and a newborn girl. The 5-year-old has been picking up reading as it interests him—he's unafraid to tackle words phonetically and writes his own stuff (usually on the typewriter because it's faster), phonetically also. Since I've done crossword puzzles and shorthand, I have no problem deciphering the stories.

His math astounds all of us. "Can I have some hard-cooked egg?" he asked while we prepared dinner for company. I said to figure it out. He added our family to the visitors, counted the eggs and divided by 4 as I quartered them, and then subtracted to find he could have three pieces.

But Django's drawing was nonexistent. I didn't want him afraid of art but he wasn't interested because he couldn't do it. Then he saw something on TV at a friend's which explained something similar to a *GWS* article [#25] where everything is just broken down into basic shapes. Now we can hardly keep him and his brother Andre supplied with enough paper. At 3, Andre is drawing a circle head with circle eyes and line mouth. Often he'll watch Django tackle something—for as long as 10 minutes—and then maybe he'll do it himself or maybe he'll digest it for a couple of days.

Most days the boys will spend a couple of hours spontaneously at their desk: drawing, cutting, punching, pasting. A lot of it seems to be just practicing their skills. The concentration level amazes me. In the afternoons we read more—both are fanatic about books. And while Andre naps, Django generally has a quiet time where I rest from questions and he uses special materials Andre can't handle carefully enough yet. Both boys help me cook and Django has several special recipes he can make for their snacks.

I can see the advantage for the younger siblings as Django explains letters to Andre and even 2-month-old Corinna. Andre is learning his alphabet in a very different way from Django. Django learned the song and eventually asked about letters. Andre declares a new letter about once a week—I assume he gets it from Django.

My husband and I are around to answer questions a lot. As one gets worn out, the other usually takes over with rapid-fire conversation. Spencer, my husband, is a musician and out of town too much, so we're working on getting a bus to be a family on the road. We're all thrilled at the prospect of learning life first-hand. Why not learn about the formation of the earth at Yellowstone or where clothes come from in the Mississippi Delta where cotton is being farmed? I've been subscribing to and saving *Cobblestone* magazines as each month they have topics like a New England community or the Erie Canal or the Beaver trade of the 1800s with lots of listing to supplement the magazine, like museums and literature. I was explaining locks to Django when the Erie Canal issue came out, but he interrupted me since he knew about it from a local tour boat ride he'd taken several months ago.

Django took a real interest in maps for a while. We spent two weeks vacationing and used the map a lot as we were doing it pretty free form. When we got home, Django drew a map of a walk we were to take to a ferry that would get us downtown. It was perfect. So I drew a map of our errands downtown and he followed it.

Spencer bought a ukulele for the boys. It needed fixing so Django got into that aspect—he loves machines and knowing how they fit together (he loves going into factories to see the conveyor belts and such). As soon as the uke was together, he lost interest and Andre took over, strumming and writing songs and singing at the top of his lungs. When Spencer would sit down to play, Andre would get the uke and mimic his movements. Once Andre even got up on stage with Spencer at a loose outdoor gig and just stood next to him and got the feel of the audience. He didn't bother anyone—just soaked it all up. Both boys help Spencer change strings and voluntarily move the lighter equipment. They're so eager to be in the bus, too.

I feel so lucky to have time with my children. The last three years I've been a licensed midwife, delivering enough babies at home to keep me pretty busy. But as the boys get older and now that we have another baby, I find my priorities changing. I want to be available to answer all those questions and to teach them as they're ready. We also need to be on the road, so I'm letting midwifery slide for now. . . . It's amazing how my concentration level has changed now that I'm not keeping three or four women-who-could-deliver-any-second on my mind all the time. Much as I love mothers and babies, I love my family more. And I figure why go to the bother of a special birth if you're not going to follow through—which in our case means homeschooling.

My kids have a weekly exchange with other kids they love and who are not yet in school. And we visit other homeschoolers as we can. But whenever they're with schooled children, they inevitably complain later about how those kids are too rough or no fun. One exception was a little Spanish boy who was an outsider at school because of the language barrier. He and Django had great fun gently playing together.

I find both boys are nearly impossible to get out of the house some days as they're so busy. . . . It's encouraging to me that they find their security at home and I hope they'll transfer this to the bus.

I know none of this is so very spectacular, as I read this sort of thing in *GWS* and hear it from other homeschooling mothers all the time. But still—here's more fuel for your fire.

Time For Everyone

Joyce Kinmont (UT) wrote in her newsletter The Tender Tutor:

> From an Oregon mother of five, the oldest a second grader and the youngest not yet born, who is considering home school: "I've noticed that even when the young children are happily occupied, as soon as I sit down with an older child, both young ones are on my lap. Short of only having individual attention for the older children while the younger ones take naps (I enjoy resting also), I wonder if you have found something that works well for you? ... Have you found it possible to pursue your own individual projects while having all your children home all of the time?"
>
> In reading this letter, it suddenly hit me what a wonderful compliment it is to a person to be able to say that the minute she sits down her children run to sit on her lap. How privileged we are to be mothers. No other occupation in the world brings that kind of reward.
>
> When I work with my children individually we go into another room where I have a desk set up and where we can close the door for privacy. The other children accept this with no trouble because they all know they will get their own turn. (Our 2½-year-old is amusing in her insistence that nobody enter the room when it's her turn.)
>
> There is an old principle we have all heard that when a mother is busy in the kitchen and a child tugs on her apron strings, if she will stop and spend a minute answering his need he will go away satisfied and she will be free to finish her work. If she tries to put him off, he will continue to bother her until they are both frustrated.
>
> I find that the same principle works in homeschooling. If I spend my mornings with my children, they are usually happy to pursue their own projects in the afternoon, and I am left with plenty of free time

Making Life Easier

Susan Blount wrote in the Maine Home Education *newsletter, Fall-82:*

> I have developed a job list for the girls and every time a job is completed satisfactorily they can put a star on a chart. They receive a quarter allowance for every ten stars. There are a few rules to be followed: 1) They must cooperate on a job. No fighting or they will have to finish the job but not get a star; 2) They must do three things with their money: save some, give some, spend some. They have opened their own savings accounts.
>
> We have implemented this plan for over a year. I can't see us ever outgrowing it. . . . You wouldn't believe the work that gets done now. They will say, "No, Mom, I'll do that." I love it. And it's been so good for them, too. They don't take for granted the many hours it takes to run a household. Plus they've learned about job sharing, organizing and many other things.

From Therese Maria Pol (IL):

> I have heard and read how difficult it is to change and dress toddlers. Well, we were having our own frustrating, squirming sessions for a while. Then it dawned on me (certainly not a brainstorm, but a personal revelation nonetheless) to include Jessica (1½) *actively*. Now she holds her diaper pins for me while I'm putting on the diaper. I ask her for each pin, and as she decides to, she hands them to me. We laugh and play peek-a-boo and talk. Granted, Jessica may hold those pins for quite a while sometimes, but she is in control as much as I am. I know that she likes it that way.

From Helen Cave (BC):

> This morning the girls (9, 7, and 4) decided that

I was to have breakfast-in-bed as "it's been a long time since you've *had* to have breakfast in bed because you were sick." While preparing breakfast they decided to move our dishes (plates, bowls, cups from an upper, hard-to reach cupboard to a more accessible below-counter cupboard. I was so used to years of dishes kept in high cupboards that I was dubious at first of the new arrangement. But it's much more practical—easier to get at—not only for them, but also for me!

Nicole's Book

From Juanita Haddad (BC):

Since Nicole began to talk she's been saying things that sounded as good to me as A. A. Milne or Robert Frost so I began writing things down. Now I'm writing down for Tacy, too. One only has to glance at the book to know something of two very different little girls: of Tacy as she dances and whirls through life and of Nicole as she stops to study and inspect each phenomenon. (The hardback, a 175001 Record Book with a single line by Dominion Blueline Inc, is an excellent well-bound book.)

To begin with, none of what I wrote down was said for writing down. I got better at keeping notebooks in the truck, upstairs and downstairs, and in the garden, an inspiring place for Nicole, as it is for me. I'm terrible at remembering word for word what she's said so I put it down immediately or have to let it go. I'd never fill in the blanks for her. After Nicole understood I wouldn't be sending her book, just copies from it, she said I could send some to you. She remembers each entry, word for word. After all, they're her words and each is greater than itself, surrounded by the memories and meaning of the real context it was spoken in. We read that book more often than any other in the house. She hardly lets us catch our breath. She says, "Read!" It looks now like it may be the first thing she'll choose to read as I often see her with it, finding the words she knows.

I've always been a little uncomfortable about being the person who ultimately "chooses" what goes in her book. I've wanted it to be as much hers as possible until she can do it all herself. Yet, I realize I'm capturing thoughts, etc., that are unencumbered with the effort of writing. Things are changing fast though, of course. At first I subtly wrote what I heard, then Nicole began adding dictations that she "wanted in her book" and now she's begun with the copying.

I'll choose from all Nicole's entries up to the present:

> There was an owl in the summer when you had your summer clothes on. (4/81)

> Come back wind, come back wind and bring the sun. (5/81)

> It's funny when your bathrobe gets stretched out like a butterfly. (6/81)

> I'm drinking water buttons off the pea plants. (6/81)

> Mamma, I just saw a fixture. He sitting on the ramp. He was just a little one. Then he flew up in the tree and he was saying, "Fixture, fixture, fixture" (9/81—at the time we were putting in plumbing.)

> Oh! It's raining! See the windows all sparkly! Up came a rainbow drop! Look at the crowds of leaves! (10/81)

> When I see your old toys around I know you were a kid and Papa was a boy. That's how I know you were little tiny people. (2/82)

> When I cry and I get done crying I kind of laugh a nice kind of laugh. (1/82)

> The song gets louder and the drum gets louder; just the drum gets louder, and you sing softly to a loud drum. (3/82)

> Tip your cereal dish, Mama. The milk makes a piece of moon or a cradle or a leaf curling. (12/82)

On Reading & Math

From Susan Haverfield (WA):

When Ben was 3, we tried Doman's *Teach*

Your Baby To Read. I don't think people are monsters to try it, but I think it's possible to resent the child if he loses interest (the preparation is very time consuming). Ben learned, then lost interest, then forgot. I now feel confident that he will learn to read when he wants to and I probably wouldn't recommend the method. It was often fun, but not as much fun as when he figures out things for himself.

Dorothy Werner wrote in the 7/82 House Door:

> Using the Monthly Record the Home Based Education Program (MI) provides has shown all of us that we actually spend a lot more time on academics than we thought. We really hadn't noticed, since much of that time is not structured-at-desk-and-write kind.
>
> My 11-year-old was sure he was behind in math. Just for fun, we went through the Math outline to see. He discovered he is above grade-level in every area of math. That discovery let him relax about math, and now he spends more time with it.
>
> Joshua had done very little formal math work in the alternative school he had attended since the first grade. He was sure he was behind. And he found out it simply wasn't so.

From Miriam Mangione (NV):

Since Shanda has been home we have learned more about her. Since the second grade she has employed her own method of subtracting two digit numbers. For example, 15−8. First she adds the 1 and 5 of 15 and gets 6, then she counts back on her fingers 6, 7, *8;* there are seven fingers left, which is the answer. She uses this only for two digit numbers up to 19. Her teachers have always told her it couldn't be done that way but she persisted in using this method as it was the one she figured out for herself that she understood.

3 Rs At Home

Denise Hodges (IL) writes:

We haven't really changed our daily routine very much (or lack of one), since we began. Basically the kids have most of the day to follow their own interests. When the weather was nice we went to parks almost daily and they played, walked, or observed nature.

One change I have made is that Lucas (7) now does some academic type work every day. It usually takes him 30 to 45 minutes. I got a bit upset because for six solid months (starting when we took him out of school), he didn't write a word. He had previously flooded us with notes and letters. When, at my suggestion, he tried to write a letter requesting some free stuff from Ranger Rick, he got terribly frustrated and gave up.

For a long time I did nothing, but I finally decided that this was not a case where I should just leave him alone. He had set up a real mental block somewhere along the way. I read about D'Nealian handwriting in *GWS* 23, and ordered their work texts. I told him he was to do two pages a day, starting with the first-grade level book. He grumbled a little at first but in about four weeks he was writing easily and beautifully. He finished that book in about six weeks, and is now halfway through the Level 2 book and is learning cursive, and best of all is writing letters again! I got him his own address book and stationery and he writes to distant friends and relatives and can even address the envelopes himself.

As far as his reading ability goes, for some unexplained reason that's one thing I don't worry about. Don occasionally asks him to read one of his books out loud, and Lucas always does fine. He spends some time every day reading library books he picks out. I also read aloud every day. We just finished Madeline L'Engle's *A Wrinkle In Time,* which we both loved. That reminds me, Why isn't *The Education Of Little Tree* on your booklist anymore? [DR: Sad to say, it's out of print again.] We got it at the library, and that is now my all-time favorite book about Indian life. Lucas also loved it. Although I have read in many other books about the "trail of tears," when I read *Little Tree's* version I was crying so hard I couldn't see the words! And the explanation of spiritual life, and of what it means to love (to understand) is so beautiful and so simple that to my mind it's a classic. I read that book months ago and Lucas still quotes from it.

One area of Lucas's education I do worry about is his math ability (or lack of it). After playing dominoes with him and having him keep score I was shocked to find out that he had forgotten how to do even simple sums. I have tried to interest Lucas in several of *GWS*'s math type games (the grids, etc.) but he is just not interested. So here again I am in a quandary. Should I give him another "push" or should I leave him alone? Of course I am scared that one of his relatives (who are all worried about his education) will ask him a math question, or that sooner or later our school will be tested in some way and found lacking.

As of the last two weeks, I have tacked on a short math type assignment to his daily writing. We do a problem with Cuisenaire rods, or from the *I Hate Math* book, or something else I dream up concerning something we are doing (like cooking). I am not at all sure I am doing the right thing, but I am going to stick with it for a while and hope that light will go on again as it did with his writing. By the way, Lucas doesn't complain about doing this stuff. On the other hand he rarely does it without my reminder.

Another worry I have concerns Maia's (3½) insistence that she is going to kindergarten. True— it's 1½ years away, but she talks about it daily! She is doing beautifully on her writing, totally on her own initiative, and learning to recognize some words. She will literally spend hours sitting at the kitchen table writing in a practice book I made for her at her request. I hate to see that pure love of learning destroyed by a formal school experience. On the other hand, I'm afraid if I don't let her go to kindergarten she will resent me and feel that she is missing out on something terrific. But if I do let her go, I subject her to all the negative things in public schools that I am now so against. . . .

She is a very social creature. We joined a playgroup to fulfill that need for now. By the way, the playgroup was originally intended for 3-4 year-olds. Lucas was not going to be involved. But I quickly found out that he loved playing with the little ones, especially the two 10-month-old infants who come with their mothers!

Drama & Writing

Karen Holguin (CA) writes:

The University of Southern California has a summer campus, open to adults and kids, for the pursuit of the arts: drama, music, photography, ceramics, weaving, etc. Marti attended the Children's Theater last summer for two weeks, a very good group with a dynamic instructor. Marti was also able to secure a part in an adult cast last winter. His interest in drama grew out of an interest in special effects and now he is becoming quite serious about it. He plans to get a summer job on campus in exchange for classes. At present he spends 1 to 2 hours each day studying pantomime. This involves a lot of "Hey, look, Mom!" but I am enjoying it! I believe this is one of the big advantages of homeschooling.

The child is free to explore subjects in depth for prolonged times and as a result is better able to pursue subjects of interest as an adult.

For instance, Marti is writing a short paper on the history of pantomime. . . . As part of the paper, he is taking notes from what he reads. . . . I did not learn this skill until I was well out of school. . . . Marti's notes reflect what the book says as well as what he thinks about that. In the same vein, he has begun keeping a journal. This is his private place, though he shares occasionally. All this from the boy who four years ago was having hysterics and wheeze attacks over book reports! [See Karen's letter in "'Free Writing' At Home," *GWS* 21.]

Reading Via Computer

Our friend Bob Lawler sent us an excellent article he wrote for The Boston Review, *6/82. The Lawlers are now living in Paris, and Bob says, "My two older kids are in a French school (after three years of Calvert homeschooling) and doing well. Because it is a private school, they can take time off to travel with me, so their position is not oppressive. They began the year in English and will convert to French, course by course, during the year."*

From the article:

I have worked in the computer industry for over fifteen years, and when my children were born I became interested in the potential impact of early computer experience on children's learning. Several years ago, in collaboration with the Logo project at MIT [see "Mindstorms," *GWS* 24], began an intensive study of how daily access to a computer influenced the way my two older children—then aged eight and six—learned the basics of arithmetic. By the time their younger sister Peggy turned three, a microcomputer had become standard equipment in our household, and I began to develop several programs to give Peggy access to the machine. Playing with the programs in her own way and on her own initiative, Peggy has begun to do something that looks very much like the beginnings of reading and writing. Peggy, at the age of three, even living in a bookish family, did not know how to read in any substantial sense before her computer experience. Her knowledge of letters at three years and three months of age was quite specific and limited. She recognized only a few letters as distinct symbols with any meaning. For example, she knew that "P" was the first letter of her name. She also recognized "G" as the "mommy letter" because her mother's name is Gretchen.

What was Peggy's understanding of spelling? One incident gave me some inkling. My oldest daughter was learning a bit of French; one day Peggy claimed that she knew how to "spell French" and continued, "un, deux, trois, quatre, cinq." At another time her spelling of "French" was "woof boogle jig." (Some of you may recognize this as the Klopstockian love song from a W.C. Fields movie.) Peggy seemed to have the general idea of spelling as decomposing a meaningful whole into a string of essentially meaningless symbols, but she had not yet learned any of the culture standard assignments of letters to words.

After receiving a book as a gift from her older sister (who then wrote PEGGY LAWLER on the flyleaf), Peggy interpreted all small clusters of alphabetic symbols as "Peggy Lawler." Later, as a consequence of being read to, she became able to recognize the word "by," which appeared on the title page of every book we read to her. There is no reason to believe she had any idea of what "by" might mean in that context. She did recognize that same word "by" in quite a different context, spontaneously pointing out the word in the line "These Romans are crazy, by Jupiter" from an *Asterix* cartoon book. Her knowledge of reading as a process for interpreting graphic material is best seen in her observation that when we read a book together, she reads pictures and I read words. From her remark, we can infer she would "read" by inventing a story based on her best speculation about the pictures' meaning. She assumed that I was doing the same with the words. Not a bad assumption, but completely empty of any information about how written words signify as they do.

Contrast the foregoing sketch of Peggy's knowledge at three years and three months with what she now knows seven months later. Her knowledge of letters is essentially complete, in that she discriminates the 26 letters of the alphabet and can name them. Her knowledge of words, in the sense of interpreting them one at a time, is significantly greater. She reads more than 20 words, most with complete dependability. But unlike children who have learned to read and write by conventional means, she sees the spelling of words as step-by-step directions for typing a name into the computer. Although her general idea of what book reading is may not have changed, she has a different and powerful idea of what reading single words means that derives directly from her experience with computer programs I wrote. (I call the computer environments created by the programs I have written, "microworlds.")

Her desire to control the machine led her into typing on the computer her first "written" word. Having helped load programs by pushing buttons on a cassette tape recorder, one day on her own Peggy typed "LO" on the keyboard of the computer terminal and then came seeking direction as to what letter came next. A few days later, she typed the "LOAD" command while the rest of the family was at lunch in a different room.

The initial microworlds were one for moving colored blocks around on the computer's video display screen and another (made for her older sister but taken over by Peggy) which created designs by moving a colored cursor about on the screen. Her older sister used this drawing program to make designs, but Peggy's first design was a large box—which she immediately converted into a letter "P" by adding the stem. Letters intrigued Peggy. They were a source of power she didn't understand.

A few days later, Peggy keyed the letter "A" and explained to me that "A is for apple." Her comment suggested a way we could—on the computer—make a new kind of prereaders' ABC book.

In the ABC microworld we invented, the letter is the "key" for accessing the picture. That is, typing the key for the letter "D" on the computer's keyboard produces a picture of a dog on the computer screen. Peggy was able to try any letter on the keyboard, first, to see what it got her, and later, if the picture interested her, to inquire what was the letter's name. She was in control of her own learning. She could learn what she wanted, when she wanted to, and could ask for advice or information when she decided she wanted it. . . . The shapes were selected and created on the computer by Peggy's older sister and brother, aged ten and twelve.

More complex and interesting than the ABC microworld, the BEACH microworld provides a backdrop for action that can be controlled by the child. Waves and a beach in the foreground, with grass above, rise to a road, more grass, and clouds at the top of the display. Against that backdrop, Peggy could create a small picture of an object by specifying a name, then manipulate the picture with commands typed on the computer keyboard. Peggy typically began constructing a scene by typing the word SUN. A yellow circle would appear in the waves. She would raise it to the sky by keying the word UP repeatedly, change its color or set it in motion with another word, and go on to other objects. She could, for example, make a CAR image appear by keying that word, change its location with commands UP, DOWN, MOVE, and specify its heading and velocity with TURN, SLOW, FAST, FASTER, and HALT.

These microworlds were created using Logo, an easily comprehensible computer language which permits the programmer to assign meaning to any string of letters by writing a simple procedure that is activated whenever that string of letters is typed. Logo's procedure definition was especially valuable in customizing the BEACH world. When Peggy first used BEACH, she was unhappy with the speed of the objects and asked, "How can I make them zoom, Daddy?" Nothing was easier than to create a new word, ZOOM, the procedure for which would set the velocity of the object with a single Logo primitive command. In another instance, Peggy's older sister made a horse-and-rider design and wrote a PONY procedure to create that object and set it in motion. After watching her sister edit that shape design, Peggy imitated the specific commands to create her own new shape. (She could not well control the design and ended with a collection of perpendicular lines. Asked what it was, she first replied, "A pony," then later, "Something important.")

As a direct consequence of playing with the BEACH world, Peggy learned to "read" approximately twenty words. Initially, she keyed names and commands, copying them letter by letter from a set of 4×6 cards that I made up for her. Soon, her favorite words were keyed from memory. Less familiar words she would locate by searching through the pile of cards. When her mood was exploratory, she would try unfamiliar words if she encountered them by chance. Now, when shown these words—on the original 4×6 cards or printed elsewhere—she recognizes the pattern of letters and associates it with the appropriate vocal expression. Further, the words are meaningful to her. She knows what they represent, either objects or actions in the BEACH microworld. In the past, children have always learned to read words as alphabetic symbols for ideas to be evoked in the mind. For Peggy, words are that, but they are something else as well—a set of directions for specifying how to key a computer command. What is strikingly different in this new word-concept is that the child and computer together decode a letter string from a printed word to a procedure which the computer executes and whose significance the child can appreciate. Because the computer can interpret specific words the child does not yet know, she can learn from the computer through her self-directed exploration and experiment.

The basic lesson I draw from this story is *not* merely about "motivation"—although Peggy did enjoy playing with these microworlds and learned from doing so. There is a more revolutionary aspect, one that is paradoxical as well. This new technology, although it may seem highly artificial, can make possible a more "natural" absorption of knowledge than learning to read from the printed page. The character of words experienced as executable procedure names brought Peggy into a new relationship with language, one different from what has been characteristic of learning to read in the past. Learning to read from print is necessarily a passive process for the child. Words on the page stand for other people's meanings. Until children start to write they can't use written words for their own purposes. Microcomputers put reading and writing together from the start. A word that Peggy can read is also one she can use to produce on the computer effects that interest her. For Peggy, learning the alphabetic language has become more like what every infant's learning of the vocal language is like. Speaking is powerful for the infant, even for one who commands but a few words, when a responsive person listens and reacts. Likewise, the production of alphabetic symbols—even one letter and one word at a time—can become powerful for the young child when computer microworlds provide a patient, responsive intelligence to interpret them.

The change wrought by microcomputers may not be profound for Peggy. She would have learned to read anyway at six or five instead of three; but for many other children in the world—those with less responsive families and teachers, for example—the chance to use language symbols in microcomputers may give them a new access to the power of written words which can truly be called revolutionary. The computer revolution is worthwhile only if it liberates people. It has the potential to do so if those who care about individual's freedom and development join in shaping this plastic medium more to the service of mankind than narrow technical or commercial interests might be inclined to do.

Young Computer Teacher

From a New York reader:

We sent our son (12) to computer camp last summer and he came home quite knowledgeable on computers. We decided to buy one for my husband's business and it would double as an educational tool for our children. We found our son so enthusiastic over the computer that we suggested he teach a small computer class to fellow classmates.

So he gathered his notes together and got in contact with a teacher down the road from us (who will be teaching a computer course to her elementary students soon) and asked her if she would help him make up some kind of lesson plans. She was willing, for he shared with her what he knew and helped her design her course and she helped him make up his course. They visited libraries and viewed films and swapped magazines. By the end of all of this, his knowledge was doubled and so was hers.

He has been holding classes for a month now—ages range from nine years to adult. He includes a few workshops as well and will be doing an advanced course for students later in the year. In payment for this lady's help, he offered her son the entire series free. He has accepted barter but prefers to get paid (saving for his own computer and future computer courses). This has kept him quite busy after school and on weekends.

Not only has his knowledge on computers been reinforced through teaching, but it has given him a desire to keep two steps ahead of his students as well. He is learning business management, dealing with all types of people and how to invest his money. We feel this has been a very worthwhile experience for us all and are very excited about the months ahead.

His only advertisement so far has been with direct mailing of the computer print-out he made up of his course. He hopes to advertise in supermarkets and the local newspaper. So far his best source of promotion is word of mouth by his mom.

I called around to find a typing course for him through adult education and the instructor told me she would not take one so young for his attention span would not have the tolerance for her course (little does she know!).

Kohl On Computers

[JH:] Herb Kohl, a very humane and intelligent man and, as readers of his books will know, one who understands and loves children, underscores Bob Lawler's remarks in an article he wrote for the Sept.–Oct. '82 issue of the *Harvard Bulletin*. In it he said, in part:

> I was reminded of the continual pleasure I got (as a child) from building an electric-train world recently when I visited a local computer store. A number of girls and boys between nine and fifteen were hanging around, watching the salespeople's demonstrations, playing games, and writing their own programs whenever a demonstration machine became available. I asked the person waiting on me if she knew the youngsters, and she told me that they were the local computer buffs. They had no machines at home or at school, and the store had become a social center for them. As long as they made no trouble and freed the machines for customers, they were welcome. In fact, they were very helpful to the salespeople, because some of them knew more about computers and computing than anyone who worked at the store.
>
> I talked to several of the youngsters and found that they were indeed knowledgeable, and that the sense of power they felt when controlling the machines was close to what I had felt with my electric trains. Over the past few years I've been observing a number of young people working and playing with computers, and have discovered that it is not only the buffs who love the power that comes with control, but that most children seem to enjoy the complexity and challenge represented by computers. And even more, they seem to enjoy the fact that one doesn't need an adult teacher in order to learn to program or use a computer.
>
> A computer that is simply pre-programmed to take game cartridges or one with practically no memory is, over

a period of time, a dull machine, one that minimizes the user's power. But an expandable system, one that can lead to increasingly complex uses and control of greater computer capability, offers challenges that you can return to for years. This is not an exaggeration. My neighbor's son, thoroughly bored with school, has built a small computer into a very powerful system that he has used to reproduce arcade games, to develop programs that analyze the statistics of his high school basketball team, and to set up books for his parents' small business.

Joseph is not exceptional, even within our small community in northern California. There is a microcomputer that has been floating around Point Arena for over five years. A high-school student bought it originally, and after a year found it too limited for his purposes. So he sold it to another student and bought a system with a greater memory and better graphics. The second student went through the same experience, and now that machine is passed from student to student with the knowledge that he or she will soon outgrow it. To date, it has been owned by six youngsters and used by several dozen more. The local high school has held classes in computer science only for the past two years. Most of the students who know something about computers don't take the course because, as one boy told me, "I know more than the teacher, and he'll get angry at me for telling him things to do that require more than he knows." This student is fifteen, but he said he knew of a dozen fifth and sixth graders who also knew more than the teacher.

So much for the high-school teacher. There's a one-room school about five miles north of here with two teachers and 35 students. The man who teaches kindergarten through third grade discovered computers last year, and now he is a buff, perhaps even an expert. He and many of the children in our community have come to some agreement about "time on the machine," but what impresses me most is the fact that they don't relate to each other in the usual teacher/student or adult/child mode. Instead they relate to this open-ended machine that they are exploring together. It is possible for young people and adults to learn computing together, to randomize old notions of dominance, and to feel inventive and powerful. I am learning with my children on the Atari we have, and am finding out how to approach problem solving and complex thinking in a systematic way with the continual feedback a home computer provides.

[JH:] How sad it is that the high school teacher was jealous and fearful of the children who knew more about computers than he did. Why not instead applaud and welcome their skill, and encourage them to use it to help others? Teachers complain, with good reason, about their class loads. This high-school teacher could easily and greatly reduce his teaching load by sharing it with children—if he could only bring himself to ask them to help him.

For all that I am in many ways very skeptical about computers and the grandiose claims that are made for them, I can see that right now they are an important part of our world, and am therefore interested in them, and even more in the ways that children use them. Do readers know of other friendly computer stores where children are encouraged to hang out, use the machines, and become experts in the natural and painless way Kohl describes? If you know stories like the ones he tells about children using computers, please tell us about them, too.

Herb told me on the phone a couple of months ago that he was planning to start a newsletter about children and computers, and the first issue should be out soon. If you want more info on this, write him c/o *GWS* at our office.

I agree with all that Seymour Papert, Bob Lawler, and Herb Kohl have said about the value of making available to children a world in which they can make things happen, and in the ways they want. But there is a danger, and we have signs already how great it may be, that some children (adults too) may so love their power over the mini-world of the computer that they will hide in that world from the larger world outside in which they control so little. May not autistic children be in essence people who, bewildered and terrified by the unpredictability and uncontrollability of the real world, have drawn back into a shrunken world of their own making in which they can predict and control everything?

Our age worships power and control far too much, and I doubt very much that a remedy for this cultural disease will be to put some form of total power and control at the disposal of everyone—or everyone who can afford a computer. Let's discuss this further. We'd like to hear your thoughts.

Buying A Computer

I have been trying to find the cheapest computer on which you can use Logo. The leading candidate seemed to be the Texas Instruments TI-99/4A, which lists at $300 but for which dealers are for the time being giving a $100 rebate. If you have color TV, you don't need a monitor; TI's own monitor, with very vivid color, costs about $300. The Logo software to go with this costs an additional $200 or so. Logo for $800, maybe $500—not so bad. Then I read an article on home computers in a recent issue of the Boston *Phoenix*, and found:

> If you purchased a TI 99/4A because of the unit's low price and TI's long involvement in computer aided education, did the dealer tell you that you'll have to spend another $1000 on an expansion interface and disk drive before you can use the highly praised TI Logo learning language ?

Is this correct? If so, TI Logo will cost about $1500–1800. Is there a cheaper way to use Logo? If you know, please tell us.

When I saw a demo of TI Logo, the software package included another game, whose name I forget, in which many objects and groups of objects of different sizes and colors could be moved in different ways about the screen. It looked quite interesting. But the TI 99/4A has a limited memory, which means that you are not going to be able to do with it many of the fascinating things that Seymour Papert and Bob Lawler talk about. As another reviewer put it, with it, you soon "run out of ink."

Perhaps Logo with an Apple computer has more possibilities, because of its greater memory. Do any readers have experience with this? What is the minimum cost of Apple Logo? Are there other possibilities?

Since I agree with Papert that many children might be much more interested in writing if they had a quick and easy way to edit and add to what they had already written, I have wondered what is the least expensive equipment with which they could do this? The new Commodore 64 computer costs $600, and I read in *Popular Science* that a New York company called Quick Brown Fox— what a nice name!—offers a word processing program for the 64 that costs only around $150, much less than most word processing software. (I've written for more info.) With this you would need a monitor, which for word processing could be an inexpensive black-and-white TV, and a printer, which you can now get for about $600, for a total of around $1500. Of course, you would have limited memory, but then children are not going to be writing 50,000 word novels (at least, I don't think so). Is there a cheaper way to do this? Do any readers know children who have worked with word processors? Which ones? How did they like it? Does it in fact, as Papert predicted, encourage their writing? Thanks for anything you can tell us.

Until recently the cheapest complete computer and word processor package seemed to be the Osborne, which at $1800 (without printer) had the further advantage that it was portable—if you call 24 pounds portable. Anyway, it all fits together into a case with a handle, so you can carry it if you have to. But the unit has a very small screen, only five or so inches wide, and the further disadvantage that only 50 or so spaces of the 80-space width line will fit on the screen at a time, so that you can never see all of your text at once. This more or less defeats the whole point of having the screen. Also, when I tried out the Osborne, I didn't like the feel of the keyboard.

Since then a similar machine, the Kaypro, has come out at the same price. It offers a larger and full width screen, and Tim Chapman, who has used it, says the keyboard is a delight. An ad in a recent *New York Times* offered the Kaypro, with the Smith Corona letter quality printer, for about $2250, which is probably as good a buy in a new machine as you can find these days. But Osborne is supposed to be coming out soon with a new portable machine that corrects all the faults of the first, and a number of other companies, including Apple, are supposed to be bringing out portables within a year or so. If you can, wait; if you are eager to buy now, the Kaypro is probably worth looking at.

We don't have time or money to test these machines in the office, so must rely on you, or people like Herb Kohl, to tell us what children like best. Thanks for any news you can send.—JH

Foreign Language Tapes

Ann Bodine (NJ) told us with enthusiasm about *The Learnables*, a foreign language tape course available from the *International Linguistics Corporation*, 401 W 89th St, Kansas City MO 64114. She says, "I have tried several foreign language courses and find that this one promotes the fastest learning. It's also the most enjoyable. Like Suzuki in music, *The Learnables* is based on ear training first."

Courses available are French, German, and Spanish. We sent $1 for the sample lesson in Mandarin Chinese (further lessons *not* available) to get an idea of the method. In the sample, you look at a series of pictures (an apple, a boy, a doctor, an airplane) while the tape repeats the appropriate name or a short sentence. You do *not* say anything, you just listen. John and I enjoyed this, and remembered some of the names for days. According to Ann, only after you've gone through the entire series of lessons that way do you start saying any of the words. It sounds logical—after all, babies listen to a language for a long time before they try to speak it.

The cost is $35 for 5 tapes and a book. There are four levels of 5 tapes for each language, and the book is the same for all the languages, which, as Ann points out, saves a bit of money if you want to learn more than one. If you try these, please tell us how you like them.—DR

Photography At 6

From California:

We have a one-man store—a photography store. Zane (6) already takes fantastic pictures and did his first aerial work a few weeks ago of Yosemite Valley using an old camera of mine. You'd believe his work, but not many people could accept so much from a six-year-old. So far we haven't had time to do anything but make a contact sheet. Soon Zane will go into the darkroom with us and make his first print—all by himself.

His composition must be intuitive; even I don't understand it. His first roll of slides was fantastic. And what joy he had giving his first slide show—setting up the projector, putting the slides in, etc. He's so quick and spontaneous taking his pictures that, as a grown-up, I find it hard to believe he can get such good results. My thinking says you have to work to do it. He plays, and does it. Of course, he prefers color to black and white—and that is too expensive for how quickly he can go through a roll of film. Now we are bulk-loading black and white, so it is quite inexpensive. 100 feet of film for $17 goes a long way, even the way I shoot.

Suzuki In N.J.

From Joanne Lynt in New Jersey:

My husband's supervisor at work told us about a Suzuki violin program in a nearby town. We are *so* pleased. The teacher is so tolerant of family needs. Everyone brings their babies and toddlers along to the older child's class. There is no pressure to find babysitters. No trauma. All the parents participate fully in the classes and at home with practice. I have found some wonderful friends, many of them homeschoolers. There is much trading of experiences through the newsletter and the *Talent Education Journal* (a Suzuki publication from American-based translators; 236 Spring Av, St. Louis MO 63119; $6/yr). Greta (3½) has grown a whole lot from spending time with these families. I was amazed that so many parents would be willing to spend so much time with their children. It is really like a large family.

And helping Greta learn the violin is good practice for us as a future (present?) homeschooling family, because I am learning the truth of so many accounts I have read about leaving the children to learn on their own but *be there* when they do need you. The first few weeks I was intent on urging Greta to practice every day. I was being so bossy about it. Having taught myself several instruments by ear (with no parental intervention), I should have realized the value of personal incentive. But I was determined to spare her the poor habits I had developed through lack of discipline. Anyway, when I forced myself to stop being so demanding, her interest did pick up on its own, spurred by the inspiration of seeing the other kids in her class play their violins.

The Suzuki experience is really a total environment in which parents learn to improve their attitudes toward their children through love and patience. I must say that the class schedules themselves are so busy that most of the enlightenment I have acquired has been through the lending library which the teacher provides, and then I relate the theory back to the reality.

Suzuki In N.Y.

When I visited the Wallaces (NY) in November, I went to two very interesting Suzuki events. First I heard a rehearsal of a string orchestra in which Vita Wallace (7) was playing violin. The young conductor had written a short piece in three parts for them, and it was interesting to watch him help them put it together. Later we went to a formal recital. First a number of students, ranging from five-year-old beginners to very skillful teen-agers, played solo pieces, or in one case a piece for three players. Then the small orchestra of which Vita was a member played, in unison, a number of standard Suzuki pieces.

Recitals of children can often be tense and unhappy affairs, but this one was pure pleasure. One thing helped make it so; I don't know whether this is standard practice at Suzuki recitals everywhere, or an invention of this particular group. They did not start the recital with the youngest children and slowly work their way up to the experts; instead, they mixed beginners and experts more or less randomly. There was no feeling of stars, or competition; it was simply a group of children making music together for their pleasure and the pleasure of their parents and any others who might hear them. The feeling was very much like one of our homeschooling family parties.

One thing, though, struck me as odd. None of the soloists, not even the very talented girl who played the entire middle movement of the Bruch G minor concerto, one of the great pieces of the Romantic repertory, were allowed to tune their own violins; all had to bring them up for one of the adult teachers to tune. I can understand this for the beginners; not only can they probably not hear accurate fifths (the strings of violins and cellos are tuned a fifth apart), but their hands are not strong enough to turn the pegs. But why should the advanced players not have tuned their own instruments? I have to assume they knew how.

Perhaps the Suzuki people felt that letting some children tune their own instruments while making others bring theirs up for adults to tune might result in drawing just the kind of line between "good" and "bad" players that they did not wish to draw. If this was their idea, then a good case can be made for it. In any case, it is most important for even young and inexperienced players to learn as soon as possible to learn to tune their instruments accurately; it is a "basic skill" of string players. If we need to invent devices to make it possible for little children to do this, then let's get busy and invent them.—JH

Instead Of Testing

Freda Lynn Davies (Ont.) wrote:

I was able to convince the school authorities that it was in Kevin's best interests that standardized testing not be used to evaluate his out-of-school learning. The meeting I was to have had with the provincial attendance counselor was reduced to a phone call through which arrangements were made for a meeting with local officials, in which we were asked to try again to solve the evaluation problem locally. The new superintendent for our area was the most understanding school official I have yet encountered (and I thought I was lucky before to have been able to deal with pretty reasonable school people in this area). He brought to the meeting a kind-eyed lady who is now a member of the "support staff" which I gather is a group whose members go from school to school helping to solve individual students' problems. The result is that she is now our "evaluator" and comes to visit us. She has come twice this fall and will come again in the spring. She did not test Kevin in the usual sense of the word, but engaged him in friendly conversation. She asked him to do a few 3 R's type things, but never pushed him when he seemed uncomfortable. Kevin and I would of course rather be left alone entirely, but this seems like a pretty good compromise, and it's probably good to keep the communication lines open with the many caring people still within the school system.

Writing A Curriculum

After seeing her "Successful Curriculum" *printed in* GWS *27, Lynn Kapplow (MA) wrote:*

If any of you are planning a curriculum, just go ahead and write down what you're already doing; you'll be pleasantly surprised. Many of us don't realize what amazing things are happening with our kids until we're forced to commit it to paper. Suddenly we're made aware of the varied and inventive ways in which learning occurs in our homes.

When I made the curriculum I realized I'd now have school people being overly curious about what we do, so I began keeping a very informal record of what we accomplish each day. It's similar to Anna Quinn-Smith's learning record (*GWS* 27) but much less detailed, since I feel I'm only doing this as a concession to the schools. I personally don't need to look at these records once they're written to know how my kids are doing. In the year that I've been keeping them, I've never looked back at a single day's record. Still, they've proved very important. Towards the end of receiving our approval, the superintendent's office told us that they were holding up our approval because they didn't have a way to monitor us. They frankly expected that we'd be sitting each day from 9–3 doing school work. I was appalled and informed them that we left school because of what is imposed on children and had no intention of playing school at home. I went on to explain (in a nice way) how the rhythms of children at home who are free to study whenever they want are completely different from those at school. I then suggested that his office have free access to my daily records as a way to know what the kids are doing. They found this very satisfactory.

What's turned out to be more important to the girls are their activity boxes. Each one has a carton filled with all the work they've done for the year. It's got their art work, cards, letters, stories, ads, mock newspapers, jokes, math, spelling bees, compositions, crafts, grammar pages, etc. They love it, and our youngest is always going through it, showing us her achievements. We save them from year to year, feeling they'll be fun to look back on when the girls are grown up.

My biggest problem with keeping records is that I find myself pressuring my kids to do some school work so I can enter it on the record. I don't like doing that, and feel I have to come to terms with this and devise some new thinking and new types of record keeping that typifies homeschooling and what *we* find important. If I solve it, I'll share it, since I know many parents are struggling with the same problem.

Letter To Supt.

From Deirdre Purdy (WV):

I wanted to send you our letter to the school board asking for homeschooling for our oldest, Jed. The point of the letter is to tell the absolute and complete truth about Jed's schooling while never promising to follow a curriculum, study anything any number of hours every day, use certain texts, or generally commit ourselves in writing to holding school. The crux of the letter is paragraph 3. After saying something like that, you go on to elaborate on your child's learning in as much detail as you can muster. Every letter would be very different and full of convincing personal details of what the children are doing (rather than what they're supposed to do or what you're going to make them do).

[The Purdy's letter, addressed to the county superintendent of schools:]

We would like to request a continuance of Jedediah Purdy's homeschooling. We would also like to enroll Hannah in kindergarten but continue to teach her at home also. Jed was seven on November 29, 1981. He was enrolled last year at Minnora School, but learned at home. When he was tested at the end of the year on the CTBS, he scored very well, getting 100% on five sections of language arts and scoring above grade level in every area.

Jed will be instructed by both of us. We are both college graduates. Walter has a BA in philosophy. Deirdre has a BA in English, BA in American studies, MA in English, MA in philosophy, and did further graduate work toward her PhD. Deirdre was also a teaching assistant at Penn State and at the University of Pittsburgh, and an instructor of philosophy at Carnegie-Mellon University. She also has a particular interest in education and is the editor of *Alternatives in Education* newsletter.

Jed will be enrolled in the third grade. We would like the appropriate books to ensure that he is aware of the material being covered in the third grade at school. However, we plan to continue Jed's education in the same manner as we have conducted it so far:

Jed likes to read and regularly reads four or more hours per day when he is at home without friends visiting. A few of his favorite books are *20,000 Leagues Under the Sea, Treasure Island, The Adventures of Tom Sawyer, Kidnapped, Just So Stories,* and *Swiss Family Robinson.* He has read the original versions of all of these books several times. He also read superhero comic books, adventure stories such as *Star Trek, Tom Swift,* or the Hardy Boys, and a number of books with which you may be less familiar such as *Flaming Arrows* and *Black Stone Knife.* He visits the Knawha County Library in Charleston where he has had a library card for several years and borrows 5 to 10 books each month. Jed has special interests in science and science fiction. Another favorite book is *The Time Machine.* He recently made a series of diagrams which were designs for an android. Jed was given a number of junior high school science texts by a friend who is a teacher, and read sections in all of them. Jed also reads portions of the daily Charleston newspaper and the magazines which we receive. He follows the cartoons of Dan O'Neill and R. Crumb of the *CoEvolution Quarterly*. Because of Jed's high level of reading ability and his matching skills at articulation we feel it is important to teach him at home where we can ensure he has material to read and discussion concomitant with his level of understanding.

Jed's interest in science began with his rock collection. He has collected rocks since he was three and has a large and varied collection, mostly gathered in West Virginia. Among them are half a dozen fossils and a collection of floating rocks. He has studied several books on geology and on rock identification. We have visited quarries, strip mines, and stream beds for rock collection. Jed also has a bone collection with specimens from wild and domestic animals. He and his friends often go on nature walks together, gathering whatever interesting items they may find, including turtles, lizards, fish, and lost hound dogs, all of which we have kept for a time and then returned or released. Jed also takes complete responsibility for his pet rabbit which he hopes to breed soon. Jed is interested in the cows, horses, and gardens which we raise. He experimented with soil mixtures and bean seeds this spring to determine which soil mix produced the best bean seedlings. Jed is interested in plant and animal identification, and can identify most of the trees and flowers, many birds, 18 snakes, insects, and large animals which live in our area. He has helped tap trees and make maple syrup, and watched trees cut, hauled out, milled, returned, and made into buildings, so he is getting an intensive education in the use of natural resources. Jed reads regularly about space exploration and astronomy. He has a chemistry set with which he performs simple experiments. As part of our everyday conversation we discuss such issues as nuclear power, acid rain, soil erosion, and the causes of diseases, tying his scientific interests in with current events and more general knowledge. He also receives and reads *Ranger Rick* nature magazine cover-to-cover each month. We plan to encourage Jed to continue to explore these interests while broadening his knowledge in all of these areas.

Jed is interested in several areas of history: the American Revolution and civil war, the life of the American Indians, and pioneering in the 19th century. He has read all eight of the Laura Ingalls Wilder books many times. He has read a number of books about these periods as well as biographies of such figures as Frederick Douglass, Abraham Lincoln, and George Washington. He has been learning about Peter the Great recently. He is also learning to read maps and globes at present. We use road maps for trips and when discussing current events. We have also examined local topographic maps. National Public Radio is on for *Morning Edition* and *All Things Considered*, two news programs, so the whole family listens to portions of these three hours of daily news programming. We discussed the Falklands war and its causes, followed the action on the globe, and read about it in the newspaper. It was on public radio that Jed first learned (or at least ingested the fact) that nuclear weapons existed that could destroy the world. He has been bringing that fact up for discussion in many contexts. Jed's interest in cartoons has led him to examine the daily editorial cartoon in the newspaper, and usually to understand it and its object. Jed reads in *National Geographic* each month, and we have large collection of old *Geographics* which he and his sister can examine. We visit the Department of Culture and History in Charleston several times a year to see the art, craft, and history displays.

We regularly take the children to see appropriate movies, such as *E.T., On Golden Pond, Superman I & II, Star Wars, Coal Miner's Daughter* and so on. After the movies we discuss with them what parts they liked or didn't like and why. We do the same with books they read and programs heard on the radio, feeling that this provides the foundations of personal judgment for aesthetic appreciation and understanding. We do not criticize the children's art, however. They both draw with great pleasure. Jed does extensive cartooning and has developed several superhero characters such as Fish Man, Antimatter Man, and Mental Man. These characters occur in comic strips which he draws and each has an appropriate origin, strength, flaw, costume, alter identity, and so on. We keep pens, paint, pencils, crayons, markers, paper, and other art materials well supplied. We also examine reproductions of fine drawings, paintings, and other arts and crafts of many eras from many parts of the world. We visit the Carnegie Museum in Pittsburgh at least once a year and visit natural history and art displays (though the children's preference is for natural history). The children see us build buildings, do architectural drawings and auto mechanics, make books, knit and sew. Contact with and participation in ongoing productive creativity is, we believe, the most important part of education in the arts.

We often play music on the radio, and on record and cassette players. We all listen to jazz, bluegrass, rock, and folk music. We also sing songs. Jed is least interested in music of all subjects, particularly in his boyish resistance to dancing. Hannah loves to sing and dance and plans to take dancing lessons starting this fall. We will continue to play music and sing with the children, take them to dances and to hear live music, and giving them the chance to enjoy music without any pressure to perform.

Jed studies arithmetic from several elementary arithmetic books which we own. He is competent and working above grade level as shown by the CTBS tests. He is quite able, for example, to be the banker at Monopoly, figuring percentages for mortgages, as well as making change for property purchases and overseeing bankruptcies. We will continue to oversee his studies, using the third grade arithmetic books, as well as those he is already working with.

Both of our children have an extensive social life. They have friends from 3 to 73. Their young friends often spend the night, or they go to spend the night with their friends, both boys and girls, about once a week and sometimes more often. Many of their best friends are also homeschoolers, so they have the opportunity to participate in lessons whenever they visit. Once or twice a week they visit with our neighbors who are in their seventies. Every few months, they watch Saturday morning TV cartoons and have dinner with these friends. They attend adult softball games where they can play with their friends while the adults play softball. They have learned many group games such as tag, Red Rover, Red Light Green Light, and dodge ball at the children's sports group which several parents have been running. They both like to play chess and checkers. Jed plans to begin karate lessons this fall which will bring him in contact with new children in an atmosphere of education and discipline. I am particularly impressed with the children's ability to carry on conversations with adults who loan them books, talk with them, and take an interest in their education. For instance, Jed will travel to Washington, DC, for 3 days next month with a man who is his friend. Each child has several friends around their own age, with whom they are particularly close. Jed, for example, is friends with Lucy Perineau with whom I have overheard him discuss the intelligence of dolphins, life after death, and reincarnation, as well as books they both have read or their plans for the afternoon. One of the main reasons we wish the children to study at home is so that they have time to maintain these social relations.

Both children are learning to play softball and to swim this summer. They are extremely active all day long, when they are not quietly working or reading. Another reason for teaching them at home is so they will be able to complete their necessary schoolwork in shorter time, given individual attention, and not be forced to remain inactive for long periods of time that are often required in the classroom.

We would like Jed and Hannah to continue to participate in school activities, such as the Halloween party, at the Minnora School as they did last year. We would be very happy to share any of our activities with any students or classes at school.

Thank you for consideration of our request.

Montessori Legal Memo

We received a "Memorandum of Law—Private Montessori Schools" from the International

Montessori Society, 912 Thayer Av, Silver Spring MD 20910. It makes some very important points that apply just as well to people with private schools in their homes. From the memo:

> State control and regulation over Montessori schools has been legally justified to limit the free exercise of liberty in private education through a general application of "state police power." From *State v. Williams* (253 NC 337, 117 SE 2d 444, 92 ALR2d 513 1960):
>
> "... the state has a limited right, under the police solicitors, provided (1) there is a manifest present need which affects the health, morals, or safety of the public generally, (2) the regulations are not arbitrary, discriminatory, oppressive, or otherwise unreasonable, and (3) adequate legislative standards are established."
>
> However, application of such police power is limited by countervailing rights of private schools protected by the U.S. Constitution... From *Binet-Montessori, Inc. v. San Francisco Unified School District*, (160 Cal R 38, 98 Cal App 3d 991 1979):
>
> "A necessary corollary to the parent's right to send a child to private school is the right of the private school to operate. The right to send one's children to private school would be a hollow right if the state could prevent the operation of such schools."
>
> In *Milwaukee Montessori School v. Percy* (473 F Supp 1358 1979), a private non-profit Montessori school in Wisconsin successfully challenged the constitutionality of the pertinent day care law as a denial of equal protection of the laws since this law established a classification exemption for "parochial" schools, excluding other private schools. The court held that:
>
> "... there is no rational basis for the distinction created (by the statute) between private parochial schools and other private schools and therefore the enforcement of that statute ... is in violation of the equal protection clause of the Fourteenth Amendment ..."
>
> In *Griswold v. Connecticut*, (381 US 479 1964), the US Supreme Court specifically noted certain rights in private education as under the protection of the First Amendment:
>
> "... the right to educate one's children as one chooses is made applicable to the states by the force of the First and Fourteenth Amendments.... In other words, the state may not, consistent with the spirit of the First Amendment, contract the spectrum of available knowledge."
>
> In *Roe v. Wade*, 410 US 113 (1973), the Supreme Court noted the high judicial scrutiny afforded to "fundamental" rights such as those included under the First Amendment:
>
> "Where certain 'fundamental rights' are involved, the Court has held that regulation limiting these rights may be justified only by a 'compelling state interest.' ... Legislative enactments must be narrowly drawn to express only the legitimate state interests at stake."
>
> In application, a "compelling state interest" normally requires the state to show some special emergency or exceptional need, above and beyond a rational purpose related to the general public interest, to justify the infringing of fundamental rights.... However, even if a "compelling state interest" can be asserted within the state's compulsory school age range (normally, 6–16), the state must still further show that such interest does not extend past certain "minimum standards" of control or regulation.
>
> In *State v. Whisner* (351 NE 2d 750 1975), the court noted the Ohio "minimum standards" for private schools as beyond the bounds of reasonable

regulation.

"... these standards are so pervasive and all-encompassing that total compliance with each and every standard by a nonpublic school would effectively eradicate the distinction between public and nonpublic education, and thereby deprive these appellants of their traditional interest as parents to direct the upbringing and education of the children."

Changing Residency

[DR:] *When John was in New York, the Helmke-Scharfs told him that they changed their legal residency in order to be in a district that was more co-operative with homeschoolers. Other homeschoolers may want to consider doing the same thing, although we caution anyone thinking of this to check the legal requirements for their state and district thoroughly first.*

Bill Scharf later wrote us how they did it:

1) We informed school district #1 that we would be "relocating" to district #2. (When asked if we were selling our farm, we of course explained that we would still be running the farm and spending as much time there as possible.)

2) We rented (for $10 per month) a mailing address from a friend's mother in district #2.... We wrote a brief but legal paper with her saying that we were sub renting part of her apartment for $10 per month and that she would accept our mail. She could terminate the agreement at any time and for any reason. For this agreement and payment she added our name to her mailbox. We notified the post office.

3) We informed district #2 that we were now in their district and went through the usual routine paperwork.

4) District #2 informed us that their legal counsel advised that a resident of the school district was a person who filed their Federal Income Tax Return from an address within the district. This was good news because by attending to those details, everyone (administrators in both districts as well as ourselves) were off the hook. We telephoned the IRS, transferred our voter registration, and became legal residents of our chosen school district.

Graduates Lack Skills

From a story headlined "Survey Finds Young People Lack Work Skills," by Kathleen Teltsch, in the New York Times, *1/16/83:*

Industry in the United States is being severely undercut because young people entering the work force lack basic skills in reading, writing, mathematics and science, according to a survey of corporations and school systems across the country.

As a consequence, companies are spending millions of dollars for remedial training to learn skills that should have been accomplished in the ninth and tenth grades, the researchers concluded. The study was conducted by the Center for Public Resources and financed mainly by [several large corporations].

The responses to the questionnaires sent out, the study said, suggest that a "significant gap" exists between business' and educators' perceptions as to the adequacy of the job skills of young people. It said many companies reported that deficiencies in basic skills were apparent in a majority of job categories. By contrast, school officials insisted that the majority of graduates entering the job market were adequately prepared for employment.

But the study said there was "surprising" recognition by both schools and business that companies would have to be more precise in defining job-preparation requirements, in assisting with the development of curriculum and even in participating in classroom instruction. While the need for improving basic skills has long been recognized by educators, the report maintained that it had only recently become a "priority issue" for American industry as it faced stiffer economic competition from other nations. Changing technology has also compelled business to seek job applicants capable of handling more comprehensive tasks.

Of the 184 companies responding, half said skilled and semi-skilled employees, including bookkeepers, could not complete mathematics problems involving decimals and fractions. 50% of those responding also said managers and supervisors could not write paragraphs that had no grammatical or spelling errors. 40% of the companies said secretaries had difficulty reading at the level required by their jobs.

In contrast, of the schools surveyed, 80% said their graduates read well enough for employment, 66% said the writing ability of their graduates was adequate and 79% said their graduates' knowledge of mathematics was adequate.

A copy of the report can be obtained from the Center for Public Resources, 680 Fifth Ave., New York NY 10019.

[JH:] Ordinarily we don't give much space in *GWS* to stories like this of the schools' many troubles and failures. We would rather help those people who wish to teach their own children to do that as well as possible. But in states like Georgia and Maryland, where state school officials and boards of education are now trying to pass regulations designed only to make homeschooling impossible, the information in the *Times* story may be able to help homeschoolers block these efforts. And in any places where homeschooling families are being prosecuted in court, this information may also be helpful.

This survey makes clear that not only are the schools not doing a good job of instruction, but also that they are doing an equally poor job of monitoring or measuring learning. They like to claim that they are the only people who can either produce learning or measure it; the facts are clearly that they are not good at doing either.

The survey also disposes of the schools' claim that they, and only they, can prepare children for entry into the "real world" of employment. On the contrary, the evidence is strong that about half of their graduates are very badly prepared for that world. Nobody has produced or is likely to produce any such evidence about homeschooled children. Stories like the one from the *Times* quoted above give homeschoolers the means to make a strong case that it is precisely *because* they want their children to be prepared for the real world that they want to teach them at home.

We must be sure to use information like this with tact and discretion; we are not trying to make war on the schools, only to persuade them to stop trying to make war on us. When we talk to school officials or legislators or the general public about the problems of the schools, we would probably do well to say, first of all, that we understand very well that some of the serious problems of the schools have their origin in the world outside, and that the schools cannot fairly be blamed for them. Beyond that, we can say, as I have just said in an article for *Phi Delta Kappan* (Feb '83), a leading educational magazine, that we believe that much of what we are learning in our experiences as homeschoolers could in fact be very useful to the schools and might help them go a long way toward solving some of their more serious problems, and therefore that the schools have much to gain by cooperating with us rather than trying to fight us.

As I have written before, when homeschoolers find themselves in court they must be careful not to appear to be inviting the judge to say officially that he agrees that the schools are doing a poor job. Whatever may be their private thoughts, few judges will say this officially and publicly, for this reason among others, that to make such judgments is not their proper business or within their competence. If they think that by ruling in favor of a family they will be widely understood as making such a statement, they will not so rule. We should make clear that we are not asking the court in any way to condemn the schools, only to say that their record in teaching and monitoring children is not so good as to entitle them to say that they are the only ones who should be allowed to do it. In golf terms, we are not asking courts to say that people who have never broken 90 in golf should not be allowed to play golf, but only that they should not be allowed to say that everyone who plays golf should be made to play it their way.

Records Available Here

Tapiola Children's Choir: Sounds Of Finland and *Christmas Music* ($9 each + post). Here are the first two commercial recordings we have added to our list, two beautiful collections of songs by this astonishing children's chorus, of which I wrote in *GWS* 30. What I said about their singing at the concert is just as true of their singing on these records; I have never heard any singing group, children or adults, anywhere in the world that sings with more beauty of tone, perfection of pitch, and musical feeling than these children from Finland.

The first of these two recordings, *Sounds of Finland*, was made in Helsinki in November, 1977, either just before the chorus left for a six-week trip to Japan or just after they had returned—the cover photo shows some of the children in costumes made for that trip. Since the chorus, whenever they visit another country, always includes on their programs some songs of that country (always astonishing their hearers by how well they pronounce the language), on this record they sing three lovely Japanese folk songs, so beautifully that it must have practically undone their audiences to hear them. The other songs are Finnish songs of the 19th and 20th centuries, beginning with Sibelius' "Finlandia" —how I envy the Finns that beautiful national anthem. Some of these songs are traditional, some quite modern and extremely difficult—it is amazing how they keep these complicated and shifting harmonies so perfectly in tune—and all are beautiful.

On two songs there are interludes played by a string orchestra, the Espoo (the city of which Tapiola is a part) Chamber Orchestra, conducted by the brother of the man who directs the chorus. The record jacket describes them as a group of young players. My guess is that they are another and perhaps slightly older group than the chorus—they play like adult professionals, and I'd be happy to have a recording of them alone.

The first half of the recording of *Christmas Music* is made up of traditional Christmas songs, four of them old Finnish songs, the others by Praetorius, Bach, Handel, and Sibelius. The only melody familiar to me is the Handel, which I have known as the "Dead March" from his opera *Saul* (the melody is a Suzuki violin piece). But all have a strong Christmas feeling about them, made even more beautiful by the clear and pure sound of the children's singing.

The entire other side of the record is a new piece, written in 1975 for this group by the Finnish composer Rautavaara, "The Mysterious Legend of Marjatta, Lowly Maiden." The text is taken from the *Kalavela*, the great collection of Finnish legends. This particular legend is the story of the birth of Jesus, but changed many centuries ago into a Finnish context. Marjatta, the lowly maiden, chaste and pure, is made pregnant by a magic berry which begs her to eat it, which she does. When the time comes for her to bear her child, she looks for a sauna in which to ease her labor, but the man who controls all the saunas will not let her use one. Instead he sends her to a horse stall in some burnt out woods. There the breath of the animals makes the stall like a sauna and lets her have her baby. At the end, as the chorus sings the soft and mysterious song with which the piece started, the narrator, an adult man with a very gentle and beautiful speaking voice, says, "This is how the old legend ends, which came from afar to Finland, bringing a new time, a new belief to forests and lakes, new hope for their inhabitants, new love among people, good will."

The piece, for narrator, vocal soloists, solo flute, solo violin, organ, percussion, and the chorus, is modern in feeling and technique, but very beautiful—the music fits the legend perfectly, and of course the children sing it perfectly. They pronounce their words so clearly that, especially with the shorter songs on the first side, it is easy to follow them in the text.

Indeed, from the record we can get a little lesson in pronouncing Finnish, which for all its strange grammar and spelling sounds much less foreign than any Slavic language or, for that matter, French or German. The words sound very much the way they look. After hearing "Marjatta" only one or two times, you should be able, by following the text and the translation, to know the meaning of what is being sung. Even without the meaning, the music is very beautiful, but the meaning makes it even more so.

One more astonishing thing about this chorus is that they sing their music from memory, which is rarely done. A friend of mine sings in the Tanglewood Festival Chorus, which is one of the outstanding choruses of the world. The other night they sang in a superb performance of *The Damnation of Faust*. The conductor, Seiji Ozawa, had them sing it from memory, instead of from the music, as is usual, and my friend said to me how much more difficult this was. But that is how this very talented Tapiola Children's Choir does it.

The recordings themselves are made by a small Swedish company called BIS (a musical word meaning "again" or "repeat"). The company itself is something of a phenomenon. The founder was Robert von Bahr, who has run it for a number of years with only a few assistants. Most companies lose money making classical records, and must be subsidized by their popular divisions or in other ways. Von Bahr and BIS, without subsidies, make money, at least enough to continue to make recordings, of which they have by now over 200. In quality of sound they are among the finest recordings being made. When the big companies make a classical recording, they tend to go in with a big crew of engineers and about a ton of equipment. Von Bahr carries in his own Revox tape recorder and two mikes, and every one of his BIS recordings I have heard has a far more natural sound quality than almost any of the recordings of the big companies.

I hope you love this music as much as I do.— JH

New Books Available Here

The Borrowers Afield and *The Borrowers Afloat*, by Mary Norton ($2.65 each + post). I loved *The Borrowers* (*GWS* 16), the first book in this series, so much that I can't think why it has taken me so long to add the others (I will add *The Borrowers Aloft*, the fourth in the series, as soon as we get it in.) I faintly recall someone telling me that they were not as good, and I may have put off reading them for fear of being disappointed. Well, whoever told me that (if anyone did) was mistaken; these are every bit as interesting, beautiful, and exciting as *The Borrowers* itself.

Those of you who have read the first book will remember that the Clock family, father Pod, mother Homily, and teenaged daughter Arietty, all tiny human-like creatures only a few inches high, were discovered by the full-sized humans in whose house they had been living for many years, and were driven out of their comfortable home under the kitchen floor and forced to flee into the fields, where they hoped to find shelter with some relatives who were said to be living in an abandoned badger den. In these two books we follow their further adventures as, very much indoor creatures, they find shelter and learn to live in the wild outdoors, though they never give up their hope of finding a human house and living secretly in it, as true borrowers should. In time they meet another borrower, Spiller, a boy not much older than Arietty, who unlike themselves is at home in the wild and loves it, only going into human houses when he must.

This is all I will tell about these fascinating stories. What makes them seem so true—truer than much supposedly realistic fiction—is first of all Mary Norton's accurate and loving eye for the significant details of life, both indoors and outdoors, and secondly the fact that having created in imagination these fantastic tiny people, she then takes them seriously enough to treat them as if they were real. Having asked us to take on faith that there *are* people six inches high, she does not ask us to take anything else on faith. Instead, as seriously as any scientist, she explores the question: "If there *were* such creatures as these, how would they live, what would the world look like to them, what problems and dangers might they meet, how might they solve and overcome or escape them?"

And the more we see these little people dealing with uncertainty, hardship, and danger—not just the danger of death, but the even worse danger of being captured, imprisoned, and exhibited for the greed of some humans and the pleasure of others—the more we admire and love them.

Coot Club, by Arthur Ransome ($3.35 + post). In this next book in the *Swallows* series, we meet again not the Walker and Blackett children of the first two books, but Dorothea and Dick, she the romancer and writer, he the naturalist and scientist, whom we first met in *Winter Holiday*. They are going to Norfolk in the east of England to visit their mother's former teacher Mrs. Barrable, who is going to spend a week or so of the Easter holiday on her brother's small boat. The two Ds, as they came to be called in the earlier book, are overjoyed, because they think they will have a chance to learn to sail, and so will be able to meet their sailing friends as equals on the lake when summer comes. They are crushed when they learn that Mrs. Barrable doesn't know how to sail either, and is only planning to spend her time on the boat at anchor. But things happen, as they always do in these books, and before long they are having the sailing adventure they longed for, and becoming the competent sailors they dreamed of being.

I began to read this as I started off on a bus trip to New Hampshire. As always, it was like opening a window and getting a delicious breath of fresh air. Beginning a Ransome book, we find ourselves in a world full of energetic, serious, capable people, young and old, doing meaningful work that they enjoy and believe in. Some of these are moderately rich, many are not rich at all, but all recognize and respect serious and skillful work wherever they see it. Ransome's world is a democracy such as we might dream of living in, in which people are respected and honored, not for wealth and power, but for competence and character. Among all the people we meet in *Coot Club*, there is only one group of bad guys, rich vacationers down from London, who don't know how to handle boats or how to behave on the water. But all the others know they are bad guys and silently conspire to outwit them. And at the end, when they bring well-earned trouble on themselves, and in spite of the fact that they don't seem to have learned any lesson from it, we even feel a little bit sorry for them. A fine end to a fine story.

We Didn't Mean To Go To Sea, by Arthur Ransome ($3.35 + post). This story starts very much like the others, with some children, our friends the Walkers, off for some pleasant sailing with a college-age friend. For a while everything is as interesting and happy as Ransome knows how to make it. But it takes only a couple of small mistakes by the young captain, a little bad luck, and another mistake by John Walker to put the children into a real adventure, in which they are not in some kind of ingenious made-up contest with the Blacketts but are fighting with every drop of strength for their very lives. Despite being ignorant and confused, sick and exhausted, and terrified almost but not quite out of their wits, they don't give up or panic, as many surely would have, and in the end all the courage, skill, and judgment which they learned from their play adventures, plus some good luck, earn them the mercy of the sea, and at the end, a very moving tribute from one of the sea's veterans.

It is a very exciting and indeed frightening story, with which Ransome reminds us that the sea must be not just loved and enjoyed but respected and feared, that tide and fog and wind and wave do not allow or forgive many mistakes. On the water, things must be done right, or it may cost you your life—thus the tragic death last summer of the very gifted young black conductor Calvin Simmons, who while canoeing in the middle of a calm lake overturned his canoe and drowned before any could reach him. Ransome has already shown us that the water, whether in river, lake, or ocean, is a great teacher. Here he shows us that it can be a very stern one.

New Dinosaurs, by Robert Long and Samuel Welles ($2.65 + post). Here's your chance to know more dinosaurs and dinosaur names than any kid (or adult) on the block! All children love dinosaurs, and almost all know, as well as they know the family dog or cat, the shapes and names of the old standbys—*tyrannosaurus rex, brontosaurus, triceratops, stegosaurus, pterodactyl*, perhaps *allosaurus* and *diplodocus*. But this is just scratching the surface. On the cover of this book you will meet *deinonychus*, "only" twelve feet long but pound for pound probably the most vicious and fearsome killer of them all. After that come *brachylophosaurus, podopteryx, chanaresuchus, gracriisuchus, tanystropheus, hupesuchus* . . . and so on, probably close to a hundred of them in all. Along with the many drawings of animals and plants, all in black and white, with space to color for any who want to do that, is a great deal of information about the latest work being done by paleontologists, the people who dig up and identify and classify these old bones.

On the last page of the book the authors put forward a theory of Dr. Russell in Canada that a supernova in space killed all the dinosaurs by bathing the earth in intense radiation. Since this book was written, an even newer theory has been proposed, with much evidence to support it, that a very large meteorite actually hit the earth, sending so much dust into the sky that it produced a change in the earth's climate which the dinosaurs could not survive.

No dinosaur fan should be without this book.

Totto-Chan, by Tetsuko Kuroyanagi ($8.65 + post). This is the true story of a young child's adventures in a most unusual school run by a most gifted, humane, and imaginative teacher. The child grew up to become the leading TV personality in Japan, host for eight years now of Japan's #1 TV talk show, and the author of this book. The school was Tomoe Gakuen, a small elementary school founded in Tokyo in 1937 and destroyed in the great fire raids eight years later. The teacher, founder of the school and its headmaster during its short life, was Sosaku Kobayashi, a man I wish (as will many others) I had known, who died in 1963 at the age of seventy.

The book has been a publishing sensation in Japan; in only sixteen months it has sold more than five million copies. This is probably more than all the school reform books put together have sold in this country in the last twenty years. Of course it helps that the author is one of the best known and most often seen and heard people in Japan. But this alone would not explain the book's success; biographies of our most famous TV personalities don't do nearly as well. Perhaps millions of Japanese want for their children, at least while they are young, a kind of schooling very different from what they have had. Perhaps the idea that young children can and should be trusted and respected, which has certainly not taken root anywhere else that I know of, is about to take root in Japan. Let us hope so. They are setting us an example in many other things; perhaps they will do so in this.

The book itself is altogether charming. Totto-chan (the author was called that as a child) was a delightful little girl, curious, imaginative, warm-hearted, friendly, energetic, and logical and impulsive as happy children so often are—if a thing seemed sensible and interesting for her to do, she did it, without worrying about whether others were doing it or what they might later say about it. Her kind parents loved this innocent courage and adventurousness, but it quite naturally got her in trouble elsewhere—while still only seven years old she was expelled from her first school (which her mother didn't tell her until she was twenty), as she would probably have been expelled from almost any conventional school that could expel her. One of her chief crimes was that when something interesting happened outside the window, and since the school was right on the street this happened all the time, she could not keep from rushing to the window to see what it was; hence the subtitle of the book, "The Girl At The Window." (Today she would be called "hyperactive.") In her new school the kindly headmaster, knowing how much of this kind of trouble with adults Totto-chan got into, would always say to her, "You *really* are a good girl, you know." It was what she needed; as she says in her preface, without him she might very easily have grown up thinking of herself as a bad and worthless person.

It is impossible in this short space to give more than the barest hint of the wonderful character of this school or the wonderful man who ran it. Two details may help: the classrooms were in a group of old railroad cars that Mr. Kobayashi found somewhere and managed to have moved to the school; every day he looked at the children's lunches to be sure that, as he had asked them and as they were always happy to show him, they had brought "something from the mountain and something from the sea."

Perhaps the most characteristic and touching incident of all, the one that made me think when I read it, "We have to have this book on our list," took place when Totto-Chan first went to be interviewed by the headmaster.

> The headmaster offered her a chair and turned to Mother. "You may go home now. I want to talk to Totto-Chan."
>
> [After Mother left] The headmaster drew over a chair and put it facing Totto-chan, and when they were both sitting down close together, he said, "Now then, tell me all about yourself. Tell me anything at all you want to talk about."
>
> "Anything I like?" Totto-chan had expected him to ask questions she would have to answer. When he said she could talk about anything she wanted, she was so happy she began straight away.
>
> [After a long time] she could think of nothing more to say no matter how hard she tried. It made her rather sad. But just then the headmaster got up, placed his large, warm hand on her head, and said, "Well, now you're a pupil of this school."
>
> Only sometime later did she realize that she had talked for four hours. "And all that time the headmaster hadn't yawned once or looked bored, but seemed just as interested in what she had to say as she was."

A lovely man, a lovely book.

Giving Up The Gun, by Noel Perrin ($4.50 + post). This is a beautiful, astonishing, and encouraging book. Though it has practically nothing to do with homeschooling, it has much to do with the world that we and our children are living and will live in. I am adding it to our list for a number of reasons: 1) It is a beautiful book, finely printed and illustrated with many beautiful reproductions of Japanese prints. 2) It tells us something that I suspect none of us knew and that many of us will be glad to hear. 3) It shows us that something we have all been told was impossible has in fact been done. In the forward, Mr. Perrin tells us:

> This book tells the story of an almost unknown incident in history. A civilized country, possessing high technology, voluntarily chose to give up an advanced military weapon and to return to a more primitive one. It chose to do this, and it succeeded. . . . Guns arrived in Japan in 1543, brought by the first Europeans. They were adopted at once, and were used widely for the next hundred years. Then they were gradually abandoned.

How and why this all happened makes a fascinating story. From it I learned many things I did not know and would never have guessed, one being that in those days (16th−18th centuries) Japanese technology was in most respects far ahead of Europe's. At the end, Mr. Perrin writes:

> None of this proves in the least, to be sure, that what the Japanese once did with guns the whole world could now do with, say, plutonium. Japan's circumstances in the seventeenth century were utterly different from those of any military power now.
>
> What the Japanese experience *does* prove is two things. First, that a no-growth economy is perfectly compatible with prosperous and civilized life. And second, that human beings are *less* the passive victims of their own knowledge and skill than most men in the West suppose. "You can't stop progress," people say. . . . This is to talk as if progress—however one defines that elusive concept—were something semi divine, an inexorable force outside

human control. And, of course, it isn't. It is something we can guide, and direct, and even stop. Men can choose to remember; they can also choose to forget. As men did on Tanegashima.

Rocannon's World, by Ursula Le Guin ($2.00 + post). This very early novel of Le Guin is an adventure story set on a distant world, a planet of the star Fomalhaut (by which I remember navigating in submarine days), in a far distant future, when three technically advanced civilizations, one of them our own on Earth, have joined to form the League of Worlds. Rocannon has been sent with a small group of assistants by the League to study the primitive races and cultures of this world. As the story begins his ship, and with it all his companions and the instant communicator which is his only contact with the League, have been destroyed by a sudden attack by a rebel planet which plans to make this remote world a base for war on the League, leaving Rocannon alone and seemingly helpless against these powerful and ruthless enemies.

Against this background Le Guin spins an absorbing tale of fantasy and swashbuckling adventure. What makes this story stand out from hundreds of others of its general kind, and why so much of it sticks in memory, is that Le Guin has such an original, fertile, and detailed imagination; that she writes so well that she can make us see in our mind's eye what she sees in hers; that she takes such trouble to make the many details of her story consistent with each other; and finally, that even in this tale of pure adventure (which in the right hands could make a wonderful film) she writes from a thoughtful and coherent point of view about people and civilizations and what makes some better or worse than others. This book is far less philosophical than her later books (see booklist), but it holds hints of important ideas she was later to develop in much more depth. A fine story.

Many Dimensions, by Charles Williams ($4.50 + post). This is the second of seven remarkable novels written during the 1930s by the British theologian, who died in 1945 at the age of fifty-nine. The book jacket says, "There is nothing in fiction quite like these novels." It is an understatement; I don't know anything in fiction even remotely like them. They are, in one way or another, stories of exploration and adventure, of the body and/or the mind and spirit. They are all involved, in an astonishing variety of ways, with the supernatural. They are all to some extent, and again in many ways, about conflicts between good and evil. Finally they are all, again in many different ways, about the nature of time, death, and existence after death.

Many Dimensions was my introduction to Williams' novels, and having now read all of them, all more than once, I think it is the best introduction. Like all the novels, it is set in Williams's "present," that is, England in the 1930s. The villain (a really hateful one), a rich and powerful man whose supposedly scientific curiosity is at bottom only a desire to wield unlimited power over people and things, manages to have stolen for him a very ancient, powerful, and holy religious relic, a stone from the crown of King Solomon. This stone has two properties: it can be divided into an infinite number of replicas of itself, and to anyone holding any one of these replicas it gives the power to move anywhere in time and space, and also, to know and to have some power over other people's thoughts. The rightful guardians of the stone come to England to report the theft to the Lord Chief Justice, a man of great judgment and probity, and he and his young secretary set out to regain it. What happens to the stone in England, how it affects the lives of the many people who come in contact with it, and how the stone is restored, is what the *plot* of this novel is about. Like all serious fiction, it is of course about much more than that. If you like it, please let us know; if enough do, I will add others of Williams's novels to the list, which I would very much like to be able to do.

Mathematics: A Human Endeavor, 2nd Ed. by Harold Jacobs ($16.50 + post). I wrote about this book in *GWS* 7, but since it was expensive, and since I thought it might soon come out in paperback, I didn't add it to our list. But it has been such a success that the publishers have kept it in hardcover, and indeed printed this second edition. Meanwhile, many people have written us about how much they liked it. So I've decided to add it to our list. Families who find it too expensive could perhaps find a way to share the cost of the book with other families, sharing time with it as they might share time on a computer.

In *GWS* 7, I wrote:

> [This] is about the best book on mathematics, for beginners, that I have ever seen. What Jacobs tries to do, and does very well, is give the beginner, or even the math-hater, an idea of what mathematical *thinking* is about, why human beings have found it so interesting, and how (to some extent) it has grown over the centuries. It is a delightful book, for people of almost any age. People who (like me) have done school math (and even got good grades) without ever having the slightest idea of what math is really all about, may find it interesting and exciting. People who have always feared and hated math may find there is no reason to fear and hate it. And I can't think of any book on math that would be more fun to read aloud to and work on with quite young children. I believe that it was written for high-school or even college students, but I would guess that quite young children would like it if they could work on it with an adult, perhaps to help them with some of the long words.
>
> The book is laid out somewhat like a conventional text, in chapters, with questions and problems. But, unlike most texts, it begins by looking at the path of billiard balls on a table, and the ways in which we might think about that. From there it goes on to many other fascinating and unfamiliar topics. The mathematical illustrations are clear and well chosen, and the book is sprinkled with pertinent and very funny cartoons from *Peanuts, B.C.*, and other sources. I can't recommend it too highly.

Stewart Piano Preschool Book and *Teacher Instruction Book* ($4.50 each + post). Many readers will be familiar with Books I and II of Mrs. Stewart's Piano Method, which I reviewed in *GWS* 21, saying in part, "From the very beginning, children—the books are designed for children to use or for adults to use with children—are encouraged to transpose, i.e., to play the same tune in all keys and are given a simple device . . . which makes it easy for them to do so. . . . Where the other books I had seen made learning music look mysterious, difficult, and dull, these books made it look sensible, exciting, and easy . . . in the sense that at every point I know what I am doing and why I am doing it." I remain just as enthusiastic.

The *Preschool Book* is a book of thirteen songs for young children of four (or less) to hear, sing, and play. It precedes Book I of the Stewart Piano Lessons. The *Teacher Instruction Book* tells the adult teacher (who need not know how to play the piano her/himself) how to use this book (and by implication the later books) with children. It is full of sensible and helpful suggestions drawn from actual experience. Indeed, I would recommend it even to people who were using the later books, whether to teach children or themselves. One particularly wise suggestion is, "Play All Over The Piano." Another: "Be sure to move onto the second, third, etc., scales *right away*. Do not wait for each to be perfect—keep adding on new scales as you practice the old one." A very good point—if children ever tried to say a new word until they could say all their old words perfectly, they never would learn to speak. Learning is more interesting and exciting, therefore more efficient, when we are exploring many related things at once.

This insight seems to have been lost or given up in Suzuki music instruction, which is full of talk about making sure that the child does each step perfectly before going on to the next step. This is surprising, since it was precisely from listening to children teach themselves to speak that Dr. Suzuki got his original ideas about how they might best learn music. At any rate, it's one of the many merits of the Stewart method that it doesn't make this mistake.—JH

The First Homeschool Catalogue by Donn Reed ($10 + post). Mr. Reed, a homeschooling parent, has put together this 200+ page collection of articles, reference lists, and catalog descriptions in an attempt to make a kind of *Whole Earth Catalog* for homeschoolers. The first section deals with the how-to's and legalities of homeschooling, including copies of the correspondence between the Reeds and the school officials; a summary of the homeschooling laws in each state and province (which the author admits is "only very basic" and not up-to-date); and lists of correspondence schools and textbook publishers.

Most interesting to us are the dozens of items described in the remainder of the book. Many of these, such as rubber stamps (six pages' worth!) and stencils are the kind of simple learning materials that John has suggested using in the past. There are science kits, maps, globes, and an "eyescope" that lets you see the inner workings of your own eye. There are many pages of "Talking Books" and "Old-Time Radio Shows" on cassette tapes. There are 14 pages of free materials to send for, and the address of a man in Massachusetts who has over a million back issues of magazines to sell. Want the front page of the *New York Times* for any day in the last 130 years? Or a badge made with any design you choose? *The First Homeschool Catalogue* will help you.

Many of these items are available through the Reed family's *Brook Farm Books* service, which is located in Canada. They also offer hundreds of books such as all the Modern Library and Portable Library titles; all the Danny Dunn, Tintin and Tarzan books; the Foxfire series, the Made Simple series, the Bellerophon coloring books, and more.

The catalog is printed by the Reeds themselves, who welcome readers' ideas and contributions for future editions. We see this catalog as potentially very useful and valuable to many homeschoolers, and we wish the Reeds well in this venture.—DR

Editors—John Holt & Donna Richoux
Managing Editor—Peg Durkee
Editorial Assistant—Pat Farenga
Subscriptions & Books—Tim Chapman
Office Assistant—Mary Van Doren

Growing Without Schooling 32

March 1983

An unusual amount of legal information in this issue. For a while it seemed as if every day brought news of another family in court or another legislature acting against homeschoolers. You'll find many of John Holt's thoughts on how to deal with these situations inside.

Our friend and co-worker, Tim Chapman, is leaving us after two years to work in a completely different field. John thought that Tim's experience is such a good example of learning from the world instead of through formal schooling that he asked him to write about it, and you'll find Tim's letter in this issue. We welcome to our staff Mark Pierce who is now learning to handle book orders and subscriptions.

Beginning in March, John had a series of radio interviews, arranged by Delacorte (publishers of *Teach Your Own* and the revised editions of *How Children Fail* and *How Children Learn*). John was on the air in Winston-Salem, Muncie, Nashville, St. Louis, Atlanta, Cincinnati, and Des Moines. He also went to Philadelphia for a live TV show, and to West Virginia for a speaking engagement at Glenville State College. Next week he leaves for a series of homeschooling meetings in northern California and a lecture in Chico.

In early February I went to Arizona to visit family and friends in the Phoenix area, so I suggested to Brian Evans of the *Arizona Home Education Association* that it would be nice to meet some of the homeschooling families there. The Association invited me to a meeting where I answered questions for an hour about homeschooling and the work of Holt Associates, and later in the week I had lunch and dinner with various *GWS* readers. A most pleasant visit.—Donna Richoux

John's Coming Schedule

Apr. 30, 1983: 6th Mass. Area La Leche League Conf., Walsh Middle School, Framingham MA. Contact: Roberta Jalbert, 8 Brown St, Ipswich MA 01938; 617-356-7345.

May 3: International Reading Assoc. meeting, Anaheim CA. Contacts: Carole Vinograd-Bausell, 807 Beaverbank Cir., Towson MD 21204, or Jack Cassidy, PO Box 55, Kemblesville PA 19347; 215-255-4058.

May 4: Sky Mountain Life School, Escondido CA. Contact Dean Donald F. Hanley, 1084 Nostalgia l, Vista CA 92083; 619-726-7016.

May 5: Sacramento area homeschooling meeting. Contact Jane Williams, 8241 E Hidden Lakes Dr, Roseville CA 95678.

May 14–15: N.J. Homeschoolers meeting. Contact Nancy Plent, 2 Smith St, Farmingdale NJ 07727; 201-938-2473.

June 24: Center for Innovation in Education, Saratoga CA. Contact: Susan Iwamoto, CIE, 19225 Vineyard Ln, Saratoga CA 95070.

June 28–30: 7th Annual Kephart Memorial Child Study Center Symposium, Univ. of Northern Colorado, Aspen/Snowmass, CO. Contact: Dr. Robert Reinert, KMCSC, UNC, Greeley CO 80639; 303-351-2691.

Aug. 1–2: Child Development Symposium, Assoc. for Research & Enlightenment, Virginia Beach, VA. Contact Robert Witt, PO Box 595, Va. Bch. 23451; 804-428-3588.

Anyone who wants to coordinate other meetings or lectures around these times and locations should contact me directly—Peg Durkee

Self-Taught Computer Designer

From Barb Parshley (NH):

I wanted to send this as I read in *GWS* 29 what the physicist said about people learning science and not through college ["Becoming Experts" by David Deutsch].

I am presently apprenticing in the most positive sense of the word, under someone who designs computers. I have a love for science but have never studied anything about computers. Jim began by showing me how to wire the boards inside and I later began learning to read and draw the schematic diagrams. All the time I'm learning about how these things are put together, all on-the-job training. I stood in awe of the knowledge this man has.

One day, as I expressed my regret to him for my not having gone to college for a degree in this field so I could work better for him, I asked him what his degree was in. He chuckled and said he didn't have one. Being sure he misunderstood my question, and also sure he must be progressing toward his doctorate, I restated my question. He said once again that he didn't have a degree, not even on a high school level. In fact, he never went past 8th grade! He is self-taught, and is designing computers for companies both here and abroad.

This man has been a great inspiration to me as I homeschool my children (I take all my work home) and realize that they could do quite well in a highly technical field, if they choose to, learning on their own, as Jim did.

Resolution In Virginia

Jim O'Toole writes, "Recently the Virginia Legislature passed the following resolution. It is designed to study the conditions, if any, under which parents may pursue schooling of their children at home. If you reside in Virginia and wish to become part of the committee's work, please contact me at Box 256, King George VA 22485; 703-775-4867."

The resolution reads:

> *Whereas*, parents are traditionally and rightfully the primary educators of their children and have a fundamental responsibility to prepare their children for the obligations of later life; and
>
> *Whereas*, it is the joint responsibility of parents and the state to provide children with educational opportunities; and
>
> *Whereas*, our Compulsory Attendance Law has served well the educational goals of the Commonwealth and an overwhelming majority of its families; and
>
> *Whereas*, there are children who are more receptive to the educational process in the environment of their own homes; and
>
> *Whereas*, it is appropriate and desirable that families who believe that home instruction is better for their children be allowed to educate them at home; and
>
> *Whereas*, the Commonwealth is responsible for the delicate task of ensuring educational opportunity for children and encouraging the healthy growth of the family unit; now, therefore, be it
>
> *Resolved* by the Senate, the House of Delegates concurring, that the Education and Health Committee of the Senate and the Education Committee of the House of Delegates are requested to create a joint subcommittee on home education. The joint subcommittee is requested to establish guidelines whereby parents may qualify to educate their own children in their own home.
>
> The joint subcommittee shall consist of five members: two members of the Education and Health Committee of the Senate to be appointed by the Committee on Privileges and Elections of the Senate, and three members of the Education Committee of the House of Delegates to be appointed by the Chairman thereof.
>
> The joint subcommittee shall submit its recommendations to the 1984 Session of the General Assembly.
>
> The cost of this study shall not exceed $4,000.

[JH:] This is something that homeschoolers in many states could probably fairly easily persuade their legislators to do. In any case, we hope readers will tell as many legislators as possible about this.

Single Mother's Arrangements

From Valerie Vaughan (MA), who wrote "Mom & Son Travel," GWS 25:

After sending my son Gabe (almost 5) to a preschool for the last year because I'm a single working mother, and having seen his spirit dampened, I was getting more and more concerned. I felt under a terrible emotional and financial struggle, and then your Issues #25−30 arrived and I stayed up to 3 a.m. reading and regaining hope and determination to "go for" what I really want for my son. With the help of another *GWS* homeschooler, Diane Landis, and a little extra driving every week, Gabe will be at others' homes while I work, and will only be one afternoon at preschool per week (which I'll change if I can find another arrangement!)

The difference in his mood and my relief from a destructive guilt is so uplifting. *GWS*, I want to thank you for saving this situation. It was really the inspiration and push I needed to get the two of us out of the pits. I think one of the worst forms of self-negation is to believe so totally in one thing and to feel (financially or otherwise) forced to do the opposite.

I send out this message for other single working mothers—don't give up—the convenience of a daily preschool or other school is a deceptive illusion, and the price is the wearing away of the living drive and spirit of not just your child, but your own self! Hold the image strong that there *is* another way, and the answer will appear. I had to want this *enough* so that it could happen.

Good News From Sessions

[JH:] On Jan, 31, Bob Sessions wrote us an encouraging letter about latest developments in his case in Iowa. For those new readers of *GWS* who may not have read *Teach Your Own* and for whom the name Sessions may not mean anything, let me sum up very briefly what this is all about. Five years or so ago Bob and Linda Sessions began to teach their son at home. The local Superintendent (who retired last Dec.) was adamantly opposed to this and took the Sessions to court. They lost, appealed to District Court, and won there in a ruling which we quote in *Teach Your Own*. Later on, when another Iowa family appealed a weak First Amendment case to the state Supreme Court and lost there, the Decorah school district saw their chance to go after the Sessions family again, and it is about this second case that Bob is writing.

What has happened is that the Sessions and their lawyer have prepared such a strong case that the state DPI (Department of Public Instruction) is reluctant to press the suit against them, for fear that the Sessions may win and so set a strong homeschooling precedent for the whole state. Also, some members of the local school board are themselves beginning to wonder whether this suit is worth going on with, particularly since the superintendent who felt so strongly about it is gone. So the family, the DPI, and the local board are trying to find a solution acceptable to all of them. The DPI is no longer opposed in principle to homeschooling or determined that it shall only be done by certified teachers, but they do want the state to retain some control over it; no more in Iowa than anywhere else are they willing to give an absolutely blank check to homeschoolers.

I wrote to Bob that there were parts of his second paragraph that I couldn't understand. In his reply he admitted that it was unclear. What the DPI is struggling to do is to find a definition of the words "equivalent instruction by a certificated teacher" (which come from the statutes) that will not enable the Sessions or any other homeschoolers to show in court that these same requirements are nowhere met by the state's own schools—an argument which, as I have said elsewhere in this issue, should be extremely effective in many or most courts, including the Federal courts.

In his letter Bob wrote, in part:

We had our DPI hearing last week. It was quite interesting! We won't know the official outcome for a month or two, but some things are clear now.

The DPI officials (same ones we met with five years ago) would like to side with us, they would like to rule us "equivalent," if for no other reason than to stop our move toward a clear court decision in our favor. They told us they continue to have no problem finding our program equivalent.... Furthermore, they made it clear they hoped that their vague "certified instruction equivalent to that in public schools" statement of five years ago would suffice as a general policy across the state. They're now clear that saying "equivalent means equivalent" doesn't really settle anything, and they spent much time in the hearing trying to figure out some grounds for saying home schools must have X hours per week of certified instruction. . . . And they're finally facing the whole issue of quality.

The hearing will help us a lot in court if we have to go back there. . . . And if the DPI is willing to admit, for the public record, that it is very difficult to find a decision procedure to determine equivalency, the judge will surely wonder how they can justify harassing us for five years.

It became apparent to the local principals that we might be up to something acceptable; i.e., for the first time, perhaps, some local officials are beginning to see that non-school education could be legitimate.

Our best hope is that the DPI will go for us in a way which will set reasonable standards for all homeschoolers in Iowa. Possibly they will send it back to the locals with instructions to be reasonable and talk to us. And if they do set some policy we can't live with (four or five hours per day with a certified teacher), we should have a good chance to win in court. We're not anxious to return to court, but we're certainly not terribly fearful, given what we experienced at our hearing.

We'll be presenters at a workshop in Iowa City for school superintendents this summer on the topic of homeschooling. Our lawyer and the DPI lawyer also will be featured. Clearly the educational folks in this state are moving in the direction you take in your *Kappan* article.

Families Win In Court

From the latest issue of Tidbits *(PO Box 2823, Santa Fe NM 87501):*

> In August, 1982, Don and Paula Edgington of Socorro, New Mexico, won the right to teach their children at home without enrolling them in a state-recognized school. The couple had been found guilty in February of the petty misdemeanor charge of not complying with state law by failing to send their two minor children to a state-recognized school or adhering to an approved home study course. On appeal, the district court *reversed* their conviction, declaring that portion of the state law which allegedly excludes parents from teaching their children at home "is unreasonable, arbitrary, and does not rest upon some ground of difference having a fair and substantial relation to the objects of the Public School Code."
>
> Paula, who has a degree in education, is teaching their children at home as a satellite school of the Christian Liberty Academy, based in Illinois. The defense attorney claimed two constitutional violations in the matter: denial of equal protection and denial of due process of law. In his defense he also presented testimony that freedom of religion was denied the Edgingtons, stating that under the statute the family was being denied their choice of educational format based, in part, upon their belief "that a child's religious instruction and secular instruction should be integrated one with the other." However, freedom of religion as an issue in this case was not considered in the court's decision.
>
> In finding for the parents, District Court Judge Edmund Kase focused primarily upon the wording of the statute involved, where it states in part:
>
> "a private school means a school offering programs of instruction not under the control, supervision or management of a local school board exclusive of home instruction by the parent, guardian, or one having custody of the student."
>
> The state education statute did not exclude *all* home instruction—only home instruction by a parent or guardian, which defense attorney Neil Mertz said "lacked any reasonable relationship to power within the state to regulate." The ruling judge agreed, saying that clause "doesn't make sense" by leaving it open for an aunt or grandparent—in short,

anyone other than the parent or guardian—to instruct children at home.

The district court's ruling has been appealed by the State. . . . If it is upheld (as is likely) by the appellate court, deputy district attorney Charles Noland has indicated the State will ask the New Mexico Supreme Court to review the matter. If the Supreme Court chooses not to review the case or upholds the district court's decision, he said, then the legislature will probably be asked to rewrite the statute (again).

From the Quincy, Mass. Patriot Ledger, *1/18/83:*

Craig Bialick of Cedarville can teach his 7-year-old son at home now without fear of being dragged off to jail or fined for making the boy a truant.

The school committee voted unanimously last night to accept Bialick's home education plan for his son, Isaiah, who was pulled out of school 2 months ago by his parents.

Bialick's brush with the school department came to a head two weeks ago when he was arrested at his 46 Sharps Drive home for failing to bring his son to school. The arrest came the night after Bialick and his wife, Mary Lou, asked the school committee for permission to teach their son at home.

Bialick appeared in Plymouth District Court last week on the misdemeanor charge of "failing to send a child to school." His case was continued to tomorrow to give him time to work out his differences with the school department.

Bialick's home education plan consists of the basic subjects required by state law—reading, writing and mathematics. . . . The Bialicks also have lined up help from an aunt who worked for 33 years as a public school teacher, and a family friend who has worked as an art teacher.

The Bialicks have agreed to provide school officials with a portfolio of their son's educational accomplishments, and have agreed to periodic testing.

"I don't mind the tests. I'd like to know how he's doing, anyway," said Mrs. Bialick. "Not to put him up against a bunch of other kids, but to find out what he knows and what he needs to know."

The Bialicks are former commune members who lived and worked on a vegetarian cooperative in Tennessee called, simply, The Farm. They also lived in Guatemala. Mr. Bialick taught the Mayan Indians and Mrs. Bialick assisted midwives at birth

---

Nancy Coomes (TN) sent us a series of articles from Tennessee newspapers about two homeschooling families in Murfreesboro who were taken to court. The final story reads:

Two local children can continue attending school at home while the county school board investigates the quality of education their parents are giving them.

A General Sessions Court case against the parents—Charles and Linda Law and Natale and Geraldine Failla—was continued indefinitely today after the school board was ordered to investigate the home instruction before prosecuting the parents.

"The board of education is responsible for making a factual determination in each case," said local District Attorney General Guy Dotson. "I don't think the school board has visited the homes and they haven't made a determination of the curriculum being taught."

Dotson said an opinion he requested from state Attorney General William Leech suggested that it is the school board's responsibility to determine whether the children are receiving a quality education.

County schools Superintendent Carl Buckner said he is not sure whether the school system will even pursue an investigation into the homeschooling.

Nancy added, "I talked with Gerri Failla today. She said that her attorney and the County District Attorney reached an agreement. They agreed to an indefinite postponement. The DA assured them that they would not be hassled by the superintendent or school board. It seems that the schooling both families were doing was never investigated or evaluated. The DA was a bit embarrassed about this, and the judge reprimanded the superintendent for it."

More Homeschoolers In Court

Another win: Dorothy and Charles Calf of Seligman, MO.

Filing suit against district: Dave & Pat Wallace, Winnemucca, Nev.

Facing court action: The Charles Bergmans of Newfield, NY; Mr. and Mrs. Don Hole of Willow Shade, KY; homeschoolers incorporated under Faith Academy in Wisconsin; Edwin & Cheryl Burwell, Richard & Karen Helleman, Robert & Sandra Trower, all of Angleton, Texas.

Appealing a loss: Lynne & Erwin Leffel of Thompson, OH; the Sawyers of Kansas City, Kansas; and Martha Zamber of San Antonio, TX (attorney, Dave Haigler).

Confusion In California

In February, a dozen or more California homeschoolers phoned, wrote, or sent clippings about new developments out there. It all began when Robert Ponce, Assistant Superintendent of the California Department of Education, sent a memo, dated Jan. 21, to "Selected District Superintendents of Schools" which read in part:

> It has come to our attention that there are one or more households within your district attendance boundaries in which parents are providing private home instruction. The purpose of this letter is to tell you that private home instruction by persons not fully credentialed in the state of California has been declared an illegal activity since 1952. The two landmark court cases which have considered this have unequivocally concluded that private home instruction is *not* exempt from the compulsory attendance laws.... (*People v. Turner, People v. Shinn*).
>
> The mere fact that a school has filed a 1982 "Private School Affidavit" with the Department of Education, pursuant to Education Code Section 33190 does *not* make home instruction a private school.... The affidavit is only for statistical reporting purposes.
>
> We suggest that you conduct an investigation into these apparent violations of the compulsory attendance laws.
>
> Enclosed is a list of addresses of parents within your school attendance boundaries who we feel may be conducting private home instruction without being fully credentialed to do so.

[DR:] Several homeschooling families told us of receiving letters from their local districts or unannounced visits from truant officers after this memo was issued. The San Francisco Examiner *ran an article on the situation Feb. 20, "State Gets Tough on One-Family Schools," which was picked up by the UPI wire service and reprinted around the state.*

One homeschooler was particularly indignant because it was Robert Ponce himself who had told her some time ago that she would satisfy the law by filing a private school affidavit!

Jane Williams, who has started the California Home Education Clearinghouse *(8241 E Hidden Lakes Dr, Roseville CA 95678) was in touch with the state Dept. of Ed. early in February and told us:*

> Ponce has stated that his letter was sent in error. ... It was never meant to go out as it did. I have

talked with Ponce myself and also Janet McCormick, who is considered the state department's official liaison to nonpublic schools. . . . McCormick states one of her immediate jobs is to determine the need for a letter in response to Ponce's.

Ms. McCormick stated the law is unclear as to what constitutes a private school. . . . The court cases, Shinn (1961) and Turner (1953) were adjudicated prior to the state law allowing for registration of private schools through means of the Private School Affidavit form. (Ms. McCormick was guessing the year that became law; she thought 1967). Because of this, Ms. McCormick, although not an attorney, says she does not feel the state department can fall back on the court cases of Turner or Shinn to disqualify parents' use of the Private School Affidavit.

[DR:] There was not always agreement among local school officials about what to do. From some articles in the local Tuolumne County papers sent by Pat Tennant (CA):

> Almost all the superintendents [in the county] agree with superintendent Larry Naegeli of the Soulsbyville Elementary School District. . . . "There are one million things that have to be done at once right now, and home schools are not at the top of my list."

> Jack Price, a part-time attendance consultant for Stanislaus and Tuolumne counties . . . strongly disagrees. "A superintendent's primary duties are to see that all of the children in his district, not just those in his school, are getting a legal education."

> Norm Wiley, superintendent of Belleview School echoed comments of several other school officials when he said the state has put an unfair burden on local schools by asking them to enforce vague private school requirements. "I think it's up to the state to define this better," he said. "I've got better things to do with my time."

[DR:] From an article by Diane Divoky, "Home-Teaching Supporters Mobilize" that appeared in the Sacramento Bee *Feb. 24:*

> When state superintendent Bill Honig learned of Ponce's memo after the fact, he canceled the directive and asked Janet McCormick, the department's liaison for private schools, to draft a new policy statement on homeschooling.

> That directive is expected to continue California's laissez-faire approach to homeschooling, leaving the matter up to local school boards.

> As a result of the flap, the homeschooling community is mobilizing to push for state legislation on the issue.

> Sacramento homeschoolers have begun meeting among themselves and with those from El Dorado, Placer, and Solano counties to establish a statewide support group, the California Homeschoolers Network.

> One of the concerns of districts is the loss of funds each homeschooled child represents. One California district that has solved this problem is the tiny San Juan Ridge Union District in Nevada City, where 36 students are now homeschooled at no loss to the district. In that program, which operates under 1977 legislation that allows for independent learning arrangements, homeschooling families work out individual learning plans with the district, which monitors and supports their work.

> Similar independent learning programs are operating in Placer County, according to county superintendent Ken Lonergan.

[DR:] In mid-March, Jane Williams and also Pamela Pacula of Home Centered Learning *(34 Katrina Lane, San Anselmo CA 94960) sent us a copy of the memo written by Janet McCormick,*

dated March 1 (sent out under the name James R. Smith, Deputy Superintendent for Programs):

> *Subject*: Memo from Robert Poncere Private Home Instruction.
>
> Last month you received the above referenced memorandum which included a listing of certain small private schools in your district. There have been numerous questions and concerns regarding the State Department of Education's intent in distributing this listing, as well as the legal effect of the accompanying memorandum.
>
> First, this listing identifies, according to our current records, all private schools in your district with an enrollment of four or fewer students. The listing was provided merely as a result of the frequent requests we have received from districts for this information.
>
> Next, the "legal effect" of the memo must be addressed. The memo is not a declaration from the department that these schools are operating in violation of the law. The department does not have the information or the authority to make that judgement. Some districts have regarded the memo as a "directive" or "mandate" from the Department of Education to take legal action against the persons listed. This is not the case. The legal responsibility is invested in local school districts and governing boards to take action at their discretion in these matters.
>
> We understand that this issue is a very complex and sensitive one, and apologize for any confusion caused by prior Department of Education communications. If you have further questions, please contact Janet McCormick, Liaison, Non-Public Schools at 916-323-0547.

[DR:] So that's where the matter stands at present. As we go to press we have not heard what the effect of this second memo has been on any school districts that started investigations or prosecutions following the first memo.

A final postscript: Pam Pacula received this letter from Gary K. Hart, Chairman of the Calif. Senate Committee on Education, dated March 2:

> Thank you for your thoughtful letter regarding homeschooling. . . . I agree that homeschooling ought to be an option in California. There are many talented parents, some of whom are credentialed teachers, who can provide a stimulating, creative, and challenging educational environment for their children. They should have that choice.
>
> However, I also feel that we must make sure that all children receive instruction in safe surroundings. State law with respect to nonpublic schooling requires that facilities meet fire safety, health and sanitation standards. The law also sets forth requirements with respect to pupil records and teacher qualifications. I believe that these provisions are necessary and desirable.
>
> If you and your colleagues sponsor legislation to clarify homeschooling as an option, I will give it my careful consideration. I am confident that we can maintain homeschooling as a viable alternative, and still make sure that all children are in safe, secure, and challenging educational settings.

Legislative News

Georgia: The State Board of Education's hearing on its proposed policy for private schools (requiring a minimum of 15 students a school building, and a teacher with a college degree), which was postponed once to March 17 (*GWS* 31), was postponed again, this time indefinitely, apparently under the governor's influence. Meanwhile, opponents of the regulations introduced several bills into the legislature. The House passed a bill that would require the Board of Education to fall under the Administrative Procedures Act (and so limit its ability to make such regulations), and the Senate passed a bill that would remove the regulation of private schools from the Board's authority. The legislative session ended before any compromise could be reached, so the matter awaits the 1984 session.

Indiana: Jean Lafferty sent us a cop of House Bill 1447, introduced by Rep. Wilson, which would specify "home instruction" as an alternative to public school attendance. The bill would require parents to "furnish the superintendent with an educational plan, including curriculum and the qualifications of the parent who is providing instruction," and it also says, "The burden shall be on the parent to show that the instruction is equivalent to that given in the public schools."

Louisiana: Kathy Reves writes, "Citizens for Home Education urges all *GWS* subscribers who are Louisiana residents to write to La. state legislators to request that they vote *against* a repeal of Act 828 of 1980, La.'s private school deregulation and home study law. Rep Woody Jenkins, author of the law, expects an even tougher fight this year.... The Board of Elementary and Secondary Education... decided to ask Attorney General William Guste to determine whether home study violated the intent of traditional laws requiring every school age child to attend school."

Maryland: A note from Manfred Smith: "Everything's quiet in Md. The state is re-writing bylaws and a new public hearing will follow (April–May?). We will resist them as forcefully as we did the old ones [*GWS* 31]."

Missouri: Rebecca Osterhage, who says there is now "a loosely associated group" of 39 homeschooling families in St. Charles County, sent us a copy of House Bill 645, which, like the Indiana bill, would put onto the parents the burden of proving that home instruction is "substantially equivalent" to public education. Later she learned that Rep. Whitehall of Ballwin added several amendments favorable to homeschoolers, such as allowing them to use school libraries and texts. The bill then died in committee.

Montana: From the *Montana Homeschoolers Assoc. Newsletter* (PO Box 1008, Belgrade MT 59714; $8/yr): "House Bill 49 came before the House Education Committee a couple of weeks ago in favor of homeschooling. Many homeschoolers were there to speak in support of the bill.... The bill is on hold for the moment, but it isn't dead yet."

The newsletter goes on to say, "... The Board of Public Education is currently putting together a proposal to be presented in bill form to the '83 legislature... to regulate all private institutions (nonpublic schools).... One of the alternatives that is being frontally attacked by this bill is the home school option.... Homeschooling was an option specifically allowed in the Montana School laws from 1903 until 1971 when specific reference to it was dropped.

Nevada: Marian Sorenson (702-752-3566) sent us regulations proposed by the State Board of Education that would require homeschooling parents to hold a teaching credential. The latest news, from Kathy Erickson in Las Vegas (702-363-1849) is that the Education Committee of the State Assembly is to hold a hearing on the question in Carson City March 29, and homeschoolers will be there.

New York: A reader saw the state's Commissioner of Education, Gordon Ambach, on TV urging the compulsory school age to be lowered to age 4. She hopes New York homeschoolers will "deluge him with letters voicing their opinions on this proposal."

South Dakota: According to an *Omaha World-Herald* article (11/21/82) reprinted in the *Home Educator's Newsletter*, "A bill calling for the repeal of a 1981 state law allowing education at home has been requested by State Sen. Don Peterson, R-Yankton." We are trying to find out more about the 1981 law, as well as Peterson's bill.

Tennessee: Yet another state trying to pass restrictive regulations for private schools. Senate Bill 1136 and House Bill 1033 would require private schools to have at least 20 students, be elsewhere than a home, and have teachers with college degrees. Wolf Nemeth of Dry Creek Community School (Dowellton TN 37059; 615-536-5287) is organizing opposition.

Washington: Debra Stewart of the *Unschoolers Project* writes, "We have up before the legislature this session no less than three homeschooling bills, none of which will pass, it seems, and several really bad bills in both the House and Senate.... When the hearings came up I made about 15 phone calls to all the reps in our organizational districts, and the communication committee chairman in the *Stillaguamish Learning Exchange*, and the word got out. Each group was urged to call five people and commit each of those five people to calling one other person, and on and on. Some of the groups contacted many more than that. Several of those contacted were churches with hundreds of members, licensed teachers, and many other unexpected supporters. Surprisingly enough, licensed teachers were against the HB 492 which would extend the school age from 8–15 to 6–18. They said they didn't want older kids in their classes who didn't want to be there because they would be largely disruptive. Well, the network really seemed to work. I got calls from people wanting to know the text and numbers of the bills, wanting to get a newsletter.... Many were shocked to learn how government works. But they got involved by calling the toll-free hotline and leaving messages for their legislators and the education committee."

Debra continued, "Now the word is that the truancy and extended age bills look like they won't pass.... I always tell people that they should not let themselves feel helpless, they are actually very powerful if they will just call in at the right time.... This week the homeschooling bills are coming up for a hearing. We are sending down a group to testify, like we did for the other hearings.... Even if they don't pass, the legislators know we are here now, and even though they hope we are a passing fad, we know that we are not!"—DR

Organizational News

National: Two address changes—Cathy Bergman and the *Home Educator's Newsletter* have moved to PO Box 2487, Ft. Lauderdale FL 33303, phone 305-525-6014; and Raymond and Dorothy Moore of the *Hewitt Research Center* are at PO Box 9, Washougal WA 98671.

The folks at *Horizons School* in Georgia have started a publication, *Alternative Schooling Newsletter*, 229 Ponce de Leon Av, Atlanta GA 30308; $5/yr (4 issues).

Canada: Wendy Priesnitz, now at 3859-76th St, Edmonton, Alberta T6K 2P9, writes, "I am still the national coordinator of the *Canadian Alliance of Homeschoolers*.... The Alliance sells an information package for $4 (recently updated) which provides legal and contact information for homeschooling in Canada. I receive many orders for these and they seem to be of great help to people. I still maintain a network of provincial contacts for people to write for specific regional information."

And from Terry Faubert (3033 Cedar Hill Rd., Victoria, British Columbia V8T 3J2): "We now have about a dozen interested families in the Victoria area, nine of whom attended our last support meeting. We decided to hold meetings about once every two months.... Our next meeting will deal with local resources of use to homeschoolers, with everyone coming prepared to share their knowledge, books, and favourite places to go."

Connecticut: There will be a homeschooling picnic May 7th; contact Laura Pritchard, 634-0714.

Florida: *Bread for Children* (PO Box 1017, Arcadia FL 33821; 813-494-6214) will hold its second Home School Seminar April 7–8.

Louisiana: Judy Maranto (PO Box 368, Rodessa LA 71069; 318-223-4341) has started a local newsletter.

Maryland: A support group has formed in the western part of the state; contact Linda Morgan, 350 Welsh Hill, Frostburg MD 21532; 689-8760.

Nebraska: Beth Zuehlke of the *Nebraska Home Schooling Exchange* (Box 96, Rockville NE 68871) has started a newsletter; $5/5 issues or $1.25 for a sample.

Ohio: Lynne Leffel and Beth Kirchhausen have taken charge of the group *OCEAN (Ohio Coalition for Educational Alternatives Now)*: new address is PO Box 094, Thompson OH 44086. And Elizabeth Burns and Linda Cox have started *Christian Homeschoolers of Ohio*, PO Box 302, Cuyahoga Falls OH 44221. Elizabeth says, "July 29–31, we are having a camp-out weekend at our farm in

Ashland. Families are welcome to bring campers, tents, or just come for a day."

Utah: Laurie Huffman of the *Utah Home Education Association* (PO Box 6338, Salt Lake City UT 84106) informed us of the excellent TV, radio, and newspaper coverage Utah homeschoolers are getting, and said, "Ken and I keep busy fighting fires as families all over the state come to grips with their district officials who attempt to impose tighter restrictions than the law allows. We feel, however, that Utah's administrators are generally good with genuine concern for the welfare of children. They are easy to converse with, for the most part, and even seem to welcome our explanations of the statutes. What an unusual position we have found ourselves in, but what fun we are having at the same time!"

Wyoming: Kasey Michaels (Pioneer Academy, 917 N Lincoln, Casper WY 82601) and Cynthia Neilson (Box 1386, Lyman WY 82937; 307-787-6728) are organizing a homeschooling group for the state—DR

Ideas from Local Groups

[DR:] Here are some good ideas from local and regional homeschooling groups that others may want to adapt in their own area. First, in the Fall '82 *Maine Home Education* newsletter, editor Don Wismer put a form with the heading, "Yes, please list us in the Directory Issue of *Maine Home Education*." This was followed by lines for parents' names, address, phone number, children's names, ages, and interests; and below that, these remarks: "Use the remaining space for mentioning anything about yourself that you'd like to see in the Maine directory, such as a wish for a local group, the fact that you need someone to come in and work with the family on a particular subject field, skills that you have that you are willing to share with other families, etc."

The eleven replies printed in the next issue made fascinating reading, giving a vivid picture of each family. A simple way for distant families to become acquainted and find out what they would like to do together.

A list on the front page of the *Western Pa. Homeschoolers* newsletter:

> *Western Pa. School Districts that have cooperated with homeschooling families: Fox Chapel, West Jefferson Hills, North Hills, South West Butler, Pittsburgh Public Schools, Titusville, Woodland Hills, Armstrong, Jefferson-Morgan, Shaler, Kiski.*

Next, some activities of the *New Jersey Family Schools Association* (Pres., Carol Skidmore, 201-647-3506):

At the March General Meeting, according to the newsletter, "David O'Hearn will speak on 'What Kids Can Do With a Computer.' David is 13 years old and has been working with computers since he was ten or eleven, so he is well qualified to speak on this topic. Last summer David founded his own small but growing company, Telecom Communication."

Some of the ten "Activity Days" scheduled for March and April included: hiking and feeding ducks at Loantaka Park; a tour of Edmund Scientific Store; Fieldcrest Farm Sheep Shearing, which would have wood and iron crafters, Scottish dancers and music, shearers, sinners, and weavers; and a lecture and tour of the 19th century Cooper Grist Mill.

Lastly, Nancy Plent (NJ) has been sending us the monthly "Library Bulletin" of the *Unschoolers Network*. As she says in one of them, "Our monthly open house started as a homeschooling support group. Getting together regularly made it possible to start thinking about our food co-op, which is now one year old. Recycling bottles and newspapers to pay the expenses of the open house is our latest project. We also have a small but growing library of books about alternatives and have a learning exchange. We try to approach all projects in the least complicated, least expensive, most stress-free way we can devise! We want our networking to be a pleasure, not a chore."

Last year when these open houses (called

Library Days) began, I asked Nancy to tell us more about them. She wrote:

> The Library day, believe it or not, is a well-thought-out plan to *simplify* part of my life. . . . Having committed myself to having a get-together on a regular basis, I automatically follow through on things that have to be ready by meeting dates. Before, I was just spinning my wheels.
>
> After the initial work of planning what the day was for and getting the books together and catalogued, the library day itself requires very little work. There are two of us who do most of the preparations and planning. We talked for four months before we decided what we wanted to do. We wanted regular contact with other like-minded people, but not in a meeting atmosphere. I'm dismayed at the business-meeting tone that so many groups take. . . . I suppose that if you are fighting the state, some of that is necessary, but just social contact and an opportunity to meet people and swap ideas on *anything* seemed like what was needed.
>
> We had one "introductory meeting" in August which I advertised to the public, for the benefit of people who might not know they didn't have to send their kids to school in September. Since then, we just get together, sit and talk or picnic in the backyard, see a film, bring things in to show others (one member brought in an Animal Town game and I was impressed with the quality of the pieces. Stuff like I remember in games when I was a kid). We usually have no more than 10 people who show up. There's a regular core, but there's also always somebody new who wants to know more about homeschooling. I guess "laid back" is the way you might describe the day.
>
> Several people have come and met others who lived not far from them, and a couple of new friendships have formed. There's a little more community feeling than there was in the past.
>
> The film part is no problem, after we found out what was available and how to get it. Kathy Shoshin is my partner in craziness. . . . She lives near a library that lends projectors, but has boring films. I live near a library with neat films but not projectors. It's a perfect partnership. . . . I order a couple of months ahead and just pick up the films. We've started dividing the year into "areas" to focus on. This quarter is food, nutrition, and health. So we ordered *Diet for a Small Planet* as our film, and are concentrating on putting up flyers to get new co-op members. Next quarter will be on pregnancy, birth and infant nurturing.
>
> The only problem with all of this (which is, after all, only one day a month, basically) is that we can think of more to do than we have time for and we shoot down more ideas than we follow through on. We've learned not to expect too much of ourselves or too much of a response from others. And things that we've wanted to get into for years are slowly happening. Kathy and I both make decisions on the food co-op and both are trying to build it up, but Kathy handles all the paperwork. It's her main project. A friend nearby has watched our meetings from the sidelines for months and finally decided she would offer a crafts workshop once or twice a month at the local community center. We've talked about that for years, too. I'm helping her find people and materials, but she's going to handle all of the details . . . . We're hoping that more people will offer to do things that we can incorporate into the network of activities without having to become one bulky organization or have anybody overloaded. Which is just simply *networking*, not organizing.
>
> Back to the food co-op for a minute. We think we have solved a lot of the problems that are a persistent part of most co-ops and I've been meaning to write out our guidelines to share with people. A lot of people won't *like* the premises we're based on, but they are working. We've accepted the fact that a small handful of people wind up doing the work in any group, so we don't try to involve anybody else in the planning . . . . Everybody seems happy with the service so far, though new members still go through a period where they think we should be having lots of membership meetings or *something*.

About Address Changes

We have always gotten letters like the following, but lately they seem to be coming more often:

"Dear *GWS*—I haven't received an issue since #27, and I know I subscribed for three years. Could you please send me the issues I am missing? Oh, by the way, I moved last year; my new address is . . . ."

As we have said a number of times, the post office does not forward Third and Fourth class mail (the rates we have been using), which is why we have asked you to send address changes promptly. The post office doesn't return the issues to us, either; it throws them away.

In the past, we replaced the missing issues for free, but we can no longer afford to do this. Our policy now is that if you are missing back issues because of a change in address, you will have to replace them at your own expense.

If we get your address change at least *three weeks before the next issue is mailed*, we'll be able to enter it into the computer in time. For example, *GWS* 33 will be mailed in late June, so changes received in mid-June or later will be too late.

Additionally, we have applied for a permit for Second-class mail, the rate for publications. Second-class mail is not forwarded either, with this exception: you may have noticed that the post office's change-of-address form asks if you are willing to pay to have periodicals forwarded. If you mark "Yes," Second-class mail (as we hope *GWS* will be) will reach you for a small charge. (If you do not mark "Yes," and our label still has your old address, the post office will throw away your *GWS*.)

So to avoid extra expense and unnecessary frustration, please, please send us your new address as soon as you know it. Thanks.—DR

From Revised "Learn"

The revised edition of How Children Learn *is now available here ($7.15 + post). As with the revised edition of* How Children Fail, *John has left the original text intact, interspersed with new material (indented and marked with a line running along the left margin). Here are some excerpts from the new sections:*

All I am saying in this book can be summed up in two words—Trust Children. Nothing could be more simple—or more difficult. Difficult, because to trust children we must trust ourselves—and most of us were taught as children that we could not be trusted.

It is even possible that some kinds of mental activity may be largely centered in some parts of the brain, and other kinds in others. But it would be simple-minded and silly to say that all the complicated varieties of thought, of mental experience, can be neatly separated into two kinds and that one of these can be exclusively assigned to the left side of the brain, the other to the right. When I say that I am sometimes surprised by what my mind tells me, I am talking about a very common experience. But where in my brain is the "my mind" who does the telling, where the "me" who is surprised?

What of the fact that often, while thinking of something else, I will find that "my mind" has suddenly presented "me" with a complete sentence, sometimes even two or three, which "I" like so much that I rush to write them down before I forget them? "I" have certainly not produced those sentences in the way I am now producing these sentences on the typewriter, thinking about what words to use or where to put them. On which side of my brain is the producer of these sentences, on which side the observer, critic, editor who judges them to be good?

It is hardly ever possible to separate what we think about something from how we feel about it. . . . This notion, now very popular in leading universities, that organisms, including human beings, are nothing but machines, is for me one of the most mistaken, foolish, harmful, and dangerous of all the many bad ideas at large in the world today. If an idea can be evil, this one surely is.

It is only in the presence of loving, respectful, trusting adults like Millicent

Shinn or Glenda Bissex that children will learn all they are capable of learning, or reveal to us what they are learning.... Of two ways of looking at children now growing in fashion—seeing them as monsters of evil who must be beaten into submission, or as little two-legged walking computers whom we can program into geniuses, it is hard to know which is worse, and will do more harm. I write this book to oppose them both.

How much people can learn at any moment depends on how they feel at that moment about the task and their ability to do the task. When we feel powerful and competent, we leap at difficult tasks. The difficulty does not discourage us; we think, "Sooner or later, I'm going to get this." At other times, we can only think, "I'll never get this, it's too hard for me, I'm never any good at this kind of thing, why do I have to do it," etc. Part of the art of teaching is being able to sense which of these moods learners are in.

The only good reason for playing games with babies is because we love them, and delight in playing these games with them and in sharing their delight in playing—not because we want someday to get them into college. It is our delight in the baby and the games that make the games fun, and worthwhile and useful for the baby. Take away the delight, and put in its place some cold-hearted calculation about future I.Q. and SAT scores, and we kill the game, for ourselves and the baby.

The point is that if it takes a long time to develop a good habit, it will take just as long to develop a bad one. The idea that we must work hundreds of hours to make a good habit, but can make a bad one in a few seconds, is nonsense. And the point of this to us as teachers is that we don't always have to be in such a big hurry to correct children's mistakes. We can afford to give them time to notice and correct them themselves. And the more they do this, the better they will become at doing it, and the less they will need and depend on us to do it for them.

In this chapter I will say something very simple, that may not often have been said before. Children use fantasy not to get out of, but to get into, the real world.

It is a serious mistake to say that, in order to learn, children must first be able to "delay gratification," i.e., must be willing to learn useless and meaningless things on the faint chance that later they may be able to make use of some of them. It is their desire and determination to do real things, not in the future but right now, that gives children the curiosity, energy, determination, and patience to learn all they learn.

I would now add perhaps even more important reasons why testing—at least, unasked-for testing done by others—destroys learning.

The first reason has to do with the matter of hunches. When we constantly ask children questions to find out whether or not they know something (or prove to ourselves that they don't), we almost always cut short the slow process by which, testing their hunches against experience, they turn them into secure knowledge.

Every unasked-for test is above all else a statement of no confidence in the learner. That I check up at all on what you have learned proves that I fear you have not really learned it. For young children, these repeated votes of no confidence can be devastating.

It may be true enough that in learning purely physical skills, such as sports ... we generally have to learn easy movements before we learn hard ones. That is how the body works. But it is not how the mind works.... What makes things easy or hard for our minds has very little to do with how little or how much information they may contain, and everything to do with how interesting they are and, to say it once again, how much sense they make, how connected they seem to reality.

This book did not change, as I hoped it might, the way schools deal with children. I said, trust them to learn. The schools would not trust them, and even if they had wanted to, the great majority of the public would not have let them. Their reasons boil down to these: (1) Children are no good; they won't learn unless we make them. (2) The world is no good; children must be broken to it. (3) I had to put up with it; why shouldn't they? To people who think this way, I don't know what to say. Telling them about the real learning of real children only makes them cling to their theories about the badness and stupidity of children more stubbornly and angrily than ever. Why do they do this? Because it gives them a license to act like tyrants and to feel like saints.

What is lovely about children is that they can make such a production, such a big deal, out of everything, or nothing.... All that energy and foolishness, all that curiosity, questions, talk, all those fierce passions, inconsolable sorrows, immoderate joys, seem to many a nuisance to be endured, if not a disease to be cured. To me they are a national asset, a treasure beyond price, more necessary to our health and our very survival than any oil or uranium or—name what you will.

J.P. At Four

From Kathy Mingl (IL):

J.P. is a "*big* boy," now—he'll be 5 in April. He's still fascinated by all kinds of machinery, but his scope has increased. His big drive has always been to be able to do anything a grownup can do, and I think he's come to a point where he can see that within his reach, and that's a great relief to him. (I don't know what you think of reincarnation, but I've always had this picture of a really big, capable, forceful, no-nonsense sort of person who suddenly finds himself in this tiny, helpless body, feeling totally degraded, frustrated, terrified, and ridiculous, all at the same time.) He really had a bad time of it there, for a while, poor guy, but he's calmed down a lot, now. He's usually willing to wait for directions, these days, rather than trying to control things by beating them down by main force—he *knows*, you see, that he *can* make the thing behave itself, even if he doesn't have the details of how he's going to do it worked out yet.

He wants to know about death, and where babies come from, and whether I still love him when I'm mad at him—and those are the *easy* questions! Some of the stuff he comes up with is really startling, like "If there was a hole under our house, why wouldn't it fall all the way to the other side of the world?" and "Why can't you make a car that runs on hydrogen?" (He *must* have heard somebody talking about that sometime, but the way it came up, we had been looking up what makes balloons rise, and he had asked what made cars go, a few days before.) Sometimes the questions he asks sound strange, because he's thinking about things he doesn't have the words for yet, like the other day: "How do cats know to be a cat, when they just eat and aren't there?" I *think* that means, "How is a specific body form created and maintained without an intelligence in residence, directing the process?" I had a craven impulse to just say, "God does it," but I told him I didn't know, instead—let him read about theology vs. evolution for himself.

Reading has at last clicked for J.P. It's hard to pinpoint just when it happened, but it was fairly sudden, as all these new steps seem to be. One day it was just an interesting oddity that he could figure out what stop-signs said, and so on, and the next day, the world was filled with messages for him. He's learned a lot about spelling just from having jokes explained to him—many jokes, especially the ones within his range of humor, depend on words that sound the same but are spelled differently, and there are some incorrigible punsters in this family.

A while back, when he was wanting to use my paints and solvents, I had promised him I'd let him have them when he could read and understand the warning labels on them. He'd been sounding out words lately, so I tried him out on the "Keep out of reach of children" panel, and with a little encouragement, he made out the whole thing!

(Then we cleared all the new words, just to make sure he knew what it *meant*). Since he'd kept his part of the bargain, I've given him a job staining rocking horses for me, $1 per horse, and is he ever excited!

I'd say that J.P.'s main interest, right now, is money—which I suppose is understandable, considering that's what he hears adults talking about the most around here. He collects it, hoards it, counts it, leaves it all over the house, finds it again (always a big deal—lost treasure and all that, you know), and bugs the life out of his poor daddy to drive him to the store to spend it. He's intrigued with the idea of making things and selling them, but he's still a bit confused about exactly how that works—yesterday he made a "coat rack" (well, that's what he *said* it was), to sell for $6,000.06. He even made a price tag for it. He discovered the dollar-sign key on the typewriter last night—boy, what an acquisition! He covered most of a sheet of paper with dollar signs, and wouldn't give me my typewriter back.

Another thing he's confused about is change—he thinks it's a way you *get* money. I'm afraid that might have been our fault, because several times he's gone to the dime store with a dollar, and come back with a $3 toy and some change. I've told Tony he's going to have to start being hard-hearted about that, or the kid's going to get some very strange ideas about arithmetic.

Last fall, we went out to some garage sales, and J.P. asked if we could go to one with toys, because he wanted to buy a spaceship. I had him look through the list in the paper with me, and mark the ones that said t-o-y-s. Then I showed him how to find the street name on the alphabetical map directory, and then find the area from the directory code. We followed the street sign sequences with the map, and told Daddy which way to turn. I had J.P. compare the street sign with the name in the paper when we came to it, and then we counted the house numbers until we found the one with "his" garage sale. Guess what he found when we got there? The very spaceship he wanted, for 10¢ (it was a neat one, too when you put batteries in it and turn it on, it blinks and bumbles all over the floor. It was missing a piece of the mechanism, but it happened to be the very part that we had saved from one of J.P.'s former toys, and Tony and J.P. fixed it up just fine). Tony hadn't really believed before that a kid could learn useful information, comparable to "purposefully studied" stuff, just from doing ordinary things, but that garage sale worked out so perfectly that he had to be impressed.

J.P. is very interested in gardening and living things. Did you know that if you take a few scale divisions off a lily bulb before you plant it, and put them in a plastic bag with a little semi-moist peat moss, they'll make tiny new lily bulbs, right in your kitchen? J.P. was fascinated with mine, so we made him a "nursery pot" of his own, with his very own "lily-babies" in it (once they were big enough to leave their "mommies"). I gave him all the ones that grew a leaf, and to make it more interesting, I cut some pictures out of an old catalog of the flowers they'll have and stapled them on plastic markers, to put next to each bulb. J.P. mixes up "secret formula" fertilizers for them out of mud, bone meal, egg-shells, rock phosphate, and whatever else he can scrounge in the greenhouse, and feeds it to them with a turkey baster (I just have to keep him from drowning them). The very first word that J.P. ever spelled on his own was "lily." He wrote it out on an extra seed catalog order form I'd given him. I wasn't paying much attention when he told me he was sending for some lily-babies, but there it was, clear as anything.

J.P. has had his heart set on having a Venus Fly Trap, ever since he saw one on TV eat a frog (yech). Park Seed Co. has a very attractive, informative catalog, and when I made out my order, I let J.P. send for a Venus Fly Trap bulb. I had him look it up in the alphabetical index, count the numbers to the right page, and read me the catalog number and the price so I could write it down.

There's something about a bulb that's really neat—they're nice just to have, you know? They're filled with secret surprises, all round and heavy and alive, not tiny and dead-looking, like seeds. I gave J.P. all my gladiolus bulbs to grow last summer, and they make babies in a very satisfying and prolific way, too—J.P. is very proud of his flower garden.

J.P. has picked up a lot of interests from my dad, including a broad perspective on languages, and an appreciation for music. Many years ago, my father made a recording from an old 78 of Basil Rathbone narrating *Peter and the Wolf*, and J.P. has always loved it, asking to hear it over and over again. He's been gradually learning to hum and whistle all of the musical themes of the story—I think he has Peter, the cat, the wolf, and the hunters, now.... You hear him off by himself, playing, or staring out of the car window, humming those tricky chromatic changes to himself, searching for the right, elusive half-tone. He's getting them down pretty darned well.

I had to stop here, and help J.P. sew a "pet." (I think it's supposed to be some kind of squirrel, or maybe a beaver. J.P. says his name is "Brownie Pink-Nose.") J.P. does quite well with sewing—he doesn't stab himself nearly as often as I do myself, and he catches on quickly to anything you show him (he always has had an affinity for sharp objects). I let him have the extra bits of fur from the rocking horses, and he has a big cookie-tin for his sewing supplies. I've found that heavy thread and large needles are easiest for him to handle (though he astonished me by being able to thread a *regular*-sized needle, when he was a lot littler than he is now), because button-and-carpet thread doesn't tangle quite as enthusiastically as ordinary thread.

[JH:] A wonderful picture of a four-year-old human being doing what all human beings of that age (and other ages) do—though no two of them do it the same way: exploring the world around him, *creating* knowledge out of his own questions, thoughts, and experiences. All children do this, as we see when we pay a little thoughtful attention to what they do.

Learning Compassion

From Catherine King (MI):

I had written earlier about the challenge of homeschooling with a joyful toddler grabbing the pencils and sitting on the paper. You asked if I would write back about any successful arrangements that I might have worked out. Well, I thought about it and couldn't come up with a one! Oh yes, we do the classics like take advantage of toddler naptime, but I think what is important is deciding that *compassion* is a valid and valuable aspect of education for the older siblings. So perhaps they will sacrifice the terrible efficiency of the system that lumps similar ages together and marches them right along at supposedly the most rapid learning rate, in exchange for an understanding that life and learning are not linear and involve dealing with baby brother's urgent desire to scribble on the paper we're practicing letters on—and to deal compassionately! So, sorry, no concrete tips here—but if I come up with some, I'll be sure to let you know!

Dinosaurs From Real Books

Susan Richman (PA) wrote in the Unschoolers Network *#14:*

> Recently I scrounged through books at a library book sale. My son Jesse is 4, and I thought that perhaps it would be good to have a few *texts* around. I found a copy of a first grade science text used locally. I thumbed through. The illustrations were pedestrian and uninspired. The text was minimal or non-existent, trying vainly to keep within standard word lists, I'm sure. When I got to the unit on dinosaurs, my decision was clenched . . . the book would stay on the table.

> You see, two pages were all that were given to the ancient reptiles. No names, no descriptions, no information. Just a half-dozen of the most common dinosaurs dotted about the page, no flora or fauna, no drama. A question at the bottom asked, "How do we know about the past?" (I could hear some publisher's fantasy of a teacher intoning this in perfect sing-song).

> I closed the book and thought of my Jesse and what resources he has available already for extending his knowledge of

dinosaurs. We own probably two dozen varied books about dinosaurs and prehistoric life. We've picked most up second hand or at museums.

It's been especially fascinating to see how the books *disagree* with each other, giving Jesse a real feel for the "guess-iness" of our scientific thinking about other times. He's already aware of the conflicting theories about hot-blooded or cold-blooded dinosaurs, realizes that ideas about the duckbills' crests have changed, notes how some books describe Dimetrodon's "sail" as a strange mistake, while others present it as the first solar heating and cooling unit.

Our set of toy dinosaurs is growing all the time (including some wooden ones designed by Jesse) and they are used to act out incredible reptile dramas. Jesse is aware of extinction, and really grappling with a sense of time and history. Early questions were, "Well, did the first Indians see the dinosaurs?" Now his internal time-line is stretching, and he's even aware of which dinosaurs were around first, next, and last.

Jesse revels in pretending to be a museum scientist, tries his hand at putting together turkey bones and sheep skeletons, arranges "exhibits" of his toy dinosaurs after "excavating" them and dragging them back with bulldozers and dump trucks. We've watched the scaffolding raised beside Brontosaurus so that his bones could be cleaned, we've touched Tyrannosaurus Rex's teeth. We've imagined, pondered, wondered, from "Do dinosaurs have birthdays? I bet the plant-eating dinosaurs just ate plants on *their* birthdays, and the meat-eaters just ate meat. . . . They didn't get to eat good food on their birthdays . . . ." to trying to figure out his own possibilities for why the great creatures disappeared.

No, we don't have any need for these official textbooks. . . . We'll take real books, real life, real thinking, thank you.

Low-Cost Resource

From Kathy Kearney (GWS 30):

I've just discovered the wonders of ERIC, the computer database for education. . . . ERIC is the "Educational Resources Information Center" of the National Institute of Education of the US Department of Education.

Basically, ERIC works like this: You go to a local library (most college libraries should have the catalogs, as well as state libraries and some larger local libraries), and begin looking at the catalogs. When you find a document that interests you, you write down the "ED" number and total number of pages of that particular document, on the order blank. You also have to decide at that point if you want to order it in microfiche or paper copy— microfiche is *much* cheaper if you have access to a microfiche reader, and you can always have paper copy printed from the fiche if you need it.

Then you figure out the cost from the number of pages, following directions on the order blank, and send in the order. Up to 450 pages, if ordered on microfiche as a single entry, is only 97¢ plus postage.

They are very slow. I have had an order out for a month now and it isn't here yet. However, I also just found out that the Vermont Dept. of Education has the entire ERIC collection in Montpelier, and Vermont teachers get up to 50 fiche per year free. After that, and for all other Vermonters, the cost is 15¢ per fiche or paper copy, so it's actually a bit cheaper than sending to the Virginia headquarters. I would assume some other Dept.'s of Ed. or state libraries elsewhere in the country would also have a similar service, and it would certainly be worthwhile to ask. I am also going to ask if I can go up to Montpelier to preview some of this stuff before I purchase the fiche copies.

Getting stuff *into* ERIC is also quite easy. You would complete the "reproduction release" form and send it in with the document (address, PO Box 190, Arlington VA 22210; 703-841-1212). The only thing to remember is that once it's in ERIC, it's available to people for almost no money, and evidently no money comes back to you for having entered it. So it wouldn't be a good idea to enter books into ERIC that you wanted to earn money from selling, for instance.

My head is just spinning from everything I just looked at. Everything imaginable is in there. The Defense Department includes all its foreign language materials, so it's possible to learn French, German, Persian, Albanian, and a host of other languages. There are textbooks, songbooks, storybooks, teacher's guides, and everything you can imagine, including a complete course on nuclear power technology! Best of all, it costs very, very little on fiche.

There are many, many sample curriculum and scope and sequence charts from all over the country which would be helpful for parents who had to put together a curriculum to satisfy school officials.

I hope all this proves helpful to the homeschoolers out there—it looks like a perfectly marvelous resource, though of course some materials will be better than others.

Phi Delta Kappan Article

[JH:] The Feb. '83 issue of *Phi Delta Kappan*, a national magazine for educators, published an article by me called "Schools and Homeschoolers: A Fruitful Partnership." We have reprints available here for 15¢ (SASE required for single copy). Some excerpts from the article:

> I contend that it would be in the best interests of schools everywhere, even in the most narrowly conceived terms—budgets, jobs, etc.—to follow the example of the Barnstable School District in cooperating fully with homeschooling families rather than trying to oppose them. First of all, it is simply not realistic for school departments and districts to perceive homeschooling, as many seem to, as some kind of short-run or even long-run threat. It is true that the number of homeschooling families has grown rapidly in recent years and, if the legal situation does not change for the worse, is likely to continue to grow. But the number of families who, having the option to send children to school, have chosen not to send them, is at the moment hardly more than ten or fifteen thousand. Even at present rates of growth, it seems most unlikely that by a generation from now more than five or perhaps ten percent of families in this country will be choosing to teach their own children. Most children will remain in schools, public or private, for as far into the future as any of us can or dare to look.
>
> Schools would be wise not merely to refrain from opposing homeschoolers but to cooperate with them as fully as possible. For one thing, such cooperation might well bring schools some good publicity, and that would be a welcome change.
>
> Schools are burdened by a set of assumptions: first, assumptions about children; second, about learning; and finally, about teaching and the relationship between teaching and learning. These assumptions shape everything schools do, and I believe them to be a root cause of the schools' frustrations and failures.
>
> Schools tend to assume that children are not much interested in learning, are not much good at it, and are unlikely to learn anything useful and important unless adults tell them what to learn, tell them when and how to learn it, check up on them to make sure they are learning it, and reward or penalize ("reinforce") them according to whether they seem to be learning or not. . . . These assumptions about children are not supported by research or experience, but are rooted in popular Calvinist assumptions about the inherent badness of children and in the deep need of many adults to credit themselves for anything good that children may do. No one with eyes and ears open and a mind in working order can long remain in the company of babies or young children without observing that they are in fact voracious, tireless, and skillful learners

and they *create* learning out of their experiences in much the same way that scientists create it out of theirs.

One serious consequence of the prevalence of these assumptions, grounded more in folklore than in experience or research, is that they can scarcely be tested with a large enough population and over a long enough period to produce meaningful results. Many small-scale experiences, in homes and in schools, have shown that, when children are allowed to decide when they will begin the exciting task of learning to read and are allowed to work out for themselves the problems of doing so (with no more help or checking than they ask for), the great majority of them learn to read much more quickly, enthusiastically, and efficiently than most children in conventional schools. But not in the foreseeable future can we expect a school district to duplicate this experience with more than a tiny fraction of its pupils—if any at all.

Similarly, many experiences in homes and schools (even in the penal institution for boys described by Daniel Fader in *Hooked on Books*) have shown that, when children who can read at least a little are given access to a large and varied selection of books, told to read what they like, and given plenty of time without interruption, checking, testing, or competitive grading, not only does their reading skill improve but they come to love reading. Yet even those schools that have tried such programs on a small scale and found them successful have rarely applied them more widely. A number of schools in various parts of the U.S. have begun to devote a short time each day to "sustained silent reading," but even these schools rarely allow more than 10 minutes a day for this work. To give even as much as a single hour per day to silent reading (thus taking time away from reading instruction) would strike most educators as a dangerously radical experiment.

Not in the foreseeable future can we imagine a school district saying to its students, "You can read anything you like, and as much as you like, and we aren't going to grade you on it." Or, "You can study whatever you want, and we don't care what grade you're in." Or, "If you're working on some project, take as much time as you need to finish it." If educational experiments such as these are ever to be undertaken on a large scale (as they should be), it is not likely to be in schools as we know them. Nor are we likely to see large-scale and long-term research conducted to find out whether other methods of evaluating learning might not be better than the standardized testing now almost universally used. We are equally unlikely to see any research that questions or examines any other standard assumptions and practices in education.

There is only one place where this kind of research is likely to be carried out on a large enough scale and for a long enough time to yield significant results. That place is in the homes of families who are teaching their own children. This is the main reason why the homeschooling movement is so important to schools. It is—in effect, though certainly not by design—a laboratory for the intensive and long-range study of children's learning and of the ways in which friendly and concerned adults can help them learn. It is a research project, done at no cost, of a kind for which neither the public schools nor the government could afford to pay.

Even if our public institutions could afford such research, it would not be as good as that now taking place in homes . . . because of the flexibility of curriculum and schedule, and above all the closeness, the intimacy, the emotional warmth, and the security of those homes in which parents elect to teach their own children.

The absence of "professional distance" makes those homes effective environments not only for children's learning but also for the training of the parent/teachers themselves. All teachers who learn to teach well learn to do so mostly from their students, who show by their responses when teaching has been helpful and when it has not. But even the most attentive, perceptive, and thoughtful classroom teachers could never elicit from their students the amount and intensity of feed-back that homeschooling parents typically get from their children, because parents know and understand their children so much better.

So far, the homeschooling movement may not have generated statistically impressive numbers of success stories, but, if it is not legally prevented from growing, it is sure to do so. Meanwhile, as it grows, it gives more and more encouragement and support to those people within the schools who are trying to make fundamental changes.

But the homeschooling movement provides more than just encouragement to those who seek change in schools; it also provides much useful information. There is a great deal of internal communication within the homeschooling movement. As people who teach their own children discover new ways to help their children learn (sometimes finding that the children don't need help at all), they tell this to others. When homeschoolers have problems, they ask other homeschoolers for help; when they solve their own problems, they share their solutions. If they live near enough to each other, they usually meet informally, sometimes as often as once a month. At these gatherings, homeschoolers and their children get acquainted, share ideas and experiences, and often plan and carry out group projects. Since the bond between them is a strong one, many homeschoolers become close friends; indeed, many people in the homeschooling movement liken it to being a member of a very large but close family.

Much of this communication between friends and colleagues is printed in the magazine *Growing Without Schooling*. Admittedly, some of this information is of interest mainly to parents, but much of it could be of immediate use to classroom teachers and others working in schools.

As far as I know, there is nothing in public education that is comparable to this network. Certainly a great number of educational magazines exist, but none that I have seen are open forums in which teachers can talk freely to one another, especially about their problems and failures. Nothing would do more to improve the morale of teachers and raise the quality of their teaching than the creation of many such forums. Everything I learned about teaching I learned from my students, from my own experiences as a learner, and from talking, without fear of censure, to other teachers who were as puzzled and frustrated as I was. It is ironic that hardly anyone in the still small homeschooling movement feels as isolated as do many of the teachers and others working in our giant system of public education. Whatever educators may think of the content of the homeschooling publications, they do offer a rough model of a kind of network of communication and mutual support that, once established, could prove very useful to the public system. One can easily imagine a school district newsletter in which administrators, teachers, students, parents, and the general public share their ideas about the schools.

———

[JH:] I think it might be useful for local homeschooling groups to send copies of this article, perhaps along with copies of our proposed legislation (*GWS* 30), to as many as possible school officials, state and national legislators, governors, other politically influential people, and the media. We must make it as clear as we can that we are trying to live in cooperation and harmony with the schools, and that if there is conflict it is of their making, not ours.

"What's Wrong With Teachers?"

[JH:] The cover story of *US News and World Report*, 3/14/83, is entitled "What's Wrong with Our Teachers?" Since now in some states and perhaps soon in many more, homeschoolers are combating attempts to make it difficult or impossible for them to teach their own children, we are going to have to make a point of collecting all we can find of stories like these, about the incompetence of schools and the very poor qualifications of many of their teachers. Here are some significant quotes from the four-page article (the numbers in parentheses refer to my comments later in this story):

> On the one hand, too many classrooms are burdened with teachers improperly prepared for their work. On the other, thousands of competent instructors are being lured from their jobs by more rewarding work elsewhere. (1)
>
> Increasingly, leading scholars insist that reform of the nation's schools—crucial to maintaining America's technological leadership—must start with teachers. In a major study of the American teacher to be released in mid-March by a panel of top educators, project director Emily Feistritzer concludes: "The real crisis in teaching today is in who is entering the profession." (2)
>
> Fewer than 5% of the freshmen entering college last fall said they planned to become teachers—down from nearly 22% in 1966. Their low numbers were matched only by their low academic performances. The 1982 SAT scores for students entering education were 80 points below the national average in math and verbal skills—a combined score of 813 out of a possible 1,600. Future teachers ranked 26th in 29 academic fields surveyed. (3)
>
> Educators say many of the problems are traceable to a surge in public-school enrollment in the early '60s that put pressure on colleges of education to train thousands of teachers quickly. The boom also caused many states to certify new instructors who were not adequately prepared.
>
> "They were just trying to get warm bodies into the classroom," recalls Samuel Sava, executive director of the National Association of Elementary School Principals.
>
> Many young women have decided that the teaching profession, for decades one of the best jobs available to them, did not have enough prestige and chose other careers.
>
> The result has been an alarming decline in the quality of teachers entering many classrooms. A study conducted for the National Institute of Education, which looked at college graduates who entered teaching in the late '70s, found that those with the highest academic ability were much more likely to leave their jobs than those who were lower achievers. Among high achieving students, only 26% intended to teach at age 30, as compared with approximately 60% of those with the lowest academic ability. (4)
>
> One third of the nearly 7,000 prospective teachers who took California's first minimum competency test failed to meet the most basic skill requirements. (5)
>
> Notes Dan Alexander, president of the Mobile County, Ala., school board: "If the current test-failure rate is, say, 20%, then you have to figure that 20% of the people who would have failed in the past are still teaching in the system." (6)
>
> One of the worst effects of the crisis is the lowering of teachers' morale. A 1981 survey ... found that 24% of the teachers polled "probably would not" choose teaching as a career again. ... What has happened over the past two

decades to make teaching so unpopular? (7)

Low pay is the top complaint. . . . (8)

29% of the teachers surveyed in Texas last year had outside jobs, up from 22% in 1980. The experience can be humiliating. A Salt Lake City teacher finds his job at a gas station makes him the target of student ridicule: "Students that I had bring in their cars and ask for a dollar's worth of gas. They enjoy taunting me as their teacher who now has to wait on them." (9)

Many areas . . . have had to use teachers certified in other subject areas to teach math and science. In Pacific Coast states, 84% of the new math and science teachers were trained in other fields. (10)

Other reasons for leaving [the teaching profession] include problems of discipline in overcrowded classrooms that are filled with handicapped youngsters, children who speak little English, and the products of broken homes.

Teachers in many urban school districts live with the fear of violence. . . . In Dade County, Fla., public schools reported 84 student assaults on school personnel during the first half of the past school year. (11)

By 1985, half of the 50 states will require new teachers to take a basic-skills test before they can operate in a classroom. The tests screen out incompetent teachers and help pinpoint weak teacher-preparation programs. (12)

Improvements also are underway in many of the 1,340 colleges offering teacher-education programs—only 534 of which are approved by the National Council for Accreditation of Teacher Education. Concern has generally focused on the teaching-methods courses that critics say are boring and are driving away many bright, ambitious students. (13)

Secretary of Education Terrel Bell favors creating a position called "master teacher," which would command a salary several thousand dollars higher than a regular teacher's pay. Tennessee Governor Lamar Alexander has proposed such a program that would pay master teachers an average salary of $26,873, which is 60% more than the salary of a regular teacher. (14)

While such a program would reward excellence, many administrators say any type of merit-pay system would be hard to administer and might prove divisive. . . . (15)

[JH:] Some observations about the above quotes:

(1) This condition has been true through all the thirty years I have been involved in education.

(2) One of the first books about modern education (whose title I forget) was written by Joseph Wood Krutch in the early 1950s. In it he quoted an extensive study showing that of all college students entering graduate schools, the only ones whose grades were lower than those going into education were those going into physical education. In the years since then I have read a number of articles, reports, news stories, etc., on this question, and I do not remember one that did not in effect say the same thing.

(3) ". . . 80 points below the national average . . ." But that average itself is the lowest we have had in many years. As a former secondary school teacher I can assure you that a student whose combined math and verbal scores are barely above 800 is a very poor student indeed. The chances are that of all the students taking the SAT tests, only a very small percentage had a total score of less than 813, and of these, almost all went to schools of education. In other words, the *average* score of future teachers was lower than the scores of almost *any* scores of people going into other fields. Important to note that the only fields ranked lower than Education were Home Economics, Ethnic Studies, and Trade and Vocational.

(4) What this tells us is that the average of the

SAT scores *of the people who stayed for a long time in the schools* was lower and probably considerably lower than the math + verbal figure of 813 quoted above. It would be interesting, and people with access to the figures should find it not too difficult, to find out how much lower it was. Indeed, if we are ever forced to take a case into the high Federal courts, we ought to make a point of getting that figure. Beyond that, I have known a number of very bright people who, thinking that they wanted to teach, went to schools of education, but soon changed to other fields because the material they had to study in ed school was so boring and stupid. It seems very likely that schools of education lose a number of their best students for this reason, which would, of course, lower still further the average scores of those remaining.

(5) We are certainly entitled to assume that the people who went into teaching in California before this test was established did no better—and it's worth noting further that the California schools have long had the reputation of being one of our best state systems. Homeschoolers in California who are fighting the requirement that they must be state certified in order to teach their own children should make use of this information.

(6) For the reason given in #4, that most of the best people quit early, we have to assume that *many more than 20% of those now in the schools* would have failed that test.

(7) See #1 and #2. Teaching was "unpopular" for a long time before that.

(8) This is a very common, and mostly mistaken argument. In the first place, it has been true for a long time and still is true that on the whole private schools, even in the inner city, achieve much better results than public schools in the same area, *in spite of the fact that they pay their teachers less*. Beyond that, I have by now heard, either face to face or by letter, from many hundreds of former teachers (many of whom now teach their own children at home), and very few have ever said that money was an important reason for their leaving, or a reason at all. Most left because they were denied any real control over their own work, and/or because they could not stand to work in places where so many of their colleagues so obviously and so strongly distrusted and disliked children. Worth noting, too, that in the Scandinavian schools, where pay is relatively higher and only the best students, instead of the worst, are admitted to teacher's colleges, the schools are also in serious crisis and getting worse, and teacher morale is also very low.

(9) This is a sad and indeed a disgusting story. But we have to ask ourselves, what kind of atmosphere did that teacher create in that class, what kind of values did he and his fellow teachers communicate to their students that would lead them to act in such a shameful way. Even more to the point, what can we say about the "social life" of a school that would turn out students with such values?

(10) This says a good deal about the supposed qualifications of certified teachers. Homeschooling families in both California and Washington should make full use of this information. Many or most courts would agree that for the schools to impose upon parents requirements which they themselves do not even come close to meeting is to deny them equal treatment before the law.

(11) These conditions, which have made classrooms intolerable for more and more teachers, make up the very same "social life" which educators say is so good and indeed essential for children. When I was being interviewed by a Florida radio station, and a mother called in to say that she had taken her young child out of school because he was beaten up almost daily by other children, a male teacher phoned in to say that this mother was teaching her child "to run away from problems." In reply, I asked him when the last time someone had punched *him* in the face was. If violence in school is bad for teachers, as we all agree it is, then it is ten, a hundred times worse for children, and parents have every moral right to protect and withdraw their children from it, if they can.

(12) Well, but what good will this do if there are not enough teachers who *can* pass the tests to fill up all the necessary classrooms? Furthermore, the same week, *Newsweek* reported, "Like several

other cities, Houston now requires public-school teachers to be tested to assess their competence. Last week more than 3,000 teachers took the test, and many of them openly cheated. Some freely exchanged answers. Some passed their test booklets around. Others sauntered in and out of the room with answer sheets.... It appears that the flagrant cribbing was at least in part a protest against the test. Many of them thought the basic-skills exam was beneath their professional dignity. Some were concerned about flunking, though school superintendent Billy Reagan assured everyone that the test would be used merely to gauge district 'needs,' not to fire teachers who did poorly.... No one has taken the names of the cheaters."

(13) But it is not going to be any easier to get rid of the many incompetent professors of education who teach these boring courses than it is to get rid of incompetent teachers. Most of these professors of education have tenure, and many of them are presidents, deans, and heads of departments in schools of education. How are we to get out from under them?

(14) This is not a new idea at all—many schools during the '60s had "master teachers," and most of these were in fact paid more. But this scheme did not improve the quality of teaching and did not get to the bottom of what was wrong with schools.

(15) There is no reason whatever to believe that it would reward excellence, since most of the people who would decide who was or was not "excellent" would be administrators who were themselves indifferent teachers if indeed they had ever been teachers at all. "Excellence" in most schools has mostly to do not with results but with keeping your students quiet and doing whatever the administration tells you. James Herndon's *The Way It Spozed To Be* is a good and all-too-typical story of what really happens to excellent teachers, teachers who get results, in the average school.

Surviving Ed. School

Sue Radosti (1526 3rd St, Charleston IL 61920) wrote to John:

I'm taking my second shot at college after a 3-year absence, struggling through the elementary ed. program here.... School has always been a breeze for me, but I've hated all the superficial teaching/learning games. It was a major disappointment to me to discover that college was only more of the same, which was why I quit after my first two years. But during my three years out, I decided I wanted to do something to make it possible for kids to learn without being stuffed into rigid schedules and lesson plans. As I read through your books, my goals shifted from working within the system, to getting involved in alternative schooling, to helping sustain the homeschooling/unschooling "movement."... I feel that I'll be a lot freer to be of service to unschoolers in a variety of ways if my certification base is covered.

Teacher Ed. programs are certainly everything you've claimed, if not worse. I spend a lot of time with my mouth hanging open in amazement over the issues raised in class. I'm learning to be a little bolder with my objections, but it's an overwhelming task sometimes when an entire lecture presentation is permeated with learning myths and child stereotypes.

I've discovered first-hand some of the problems involved in trying to change the thinking of the traditional educators, a major one being the nature of educational research. I'm in a general methods course this semester (primarily focused on—what else?—classroom management), and one of the course requirements is proficiency in the Zaner-Bloser manuscript handwriting system (undoubtedly the ugliest writing style I've ever seen!). We were given assignments to be written in the Z-B style which were corrected by a grad assistant and returned to us with the more imperfect letters designated for extra practice. It took many of us 3 or 4 weeks to become proficient—and yet no one ever mentioned in class the obvious irony that this system was too difficult even for adults who have been writing with ease for years! ...

Anyway, I spent a great deal of time in the library, poring over ERIC abstracts and searching *Education Digest* for some scrap of research to support my belief that a rigid system of handwriting isn't necessary for learning to write. What I found was that a lot of study has been devoted to comparing one system with another, but no attempt has been made to compare a system with a *lack* of a system. Silly me—why should I expect educators to undermine their own purpose by disproving the necessity for systematized instruction? To quote one article I came across: "For a school to model its instructional program after the kind of free learning pupils do on their own out of school is to abandon most of its special value as a school, most of its very reason for existence." Indeed.

I do have an ally or two on campus, the more outstanding one being my Ed Psych professor: a marvelously sensitive and courageous psychologist. . . . As much as is possible within university regulations, his classes are student-oriented, with no tests, contract grading (the closest they'll let him come to eliminating grades altogether), and individualized learning projects. . . . But he has found that the strongest resistance to his methods, at least in recent years, comes from *the students themselves*. Even after all his talk about the evils of testing and grading, around midterm every semester at least one student asks, "When are we going to have a test?" Many of my classmates were still puzzling over the vaguely structured assignments in the final weeks of the semester and asking me, "Do you understand what he wants from us? I don't know what we're supposed to do." And on the final "feedback card" most of them indicate that they themselves still plan to use heavy testing and the traditional grading scale in their future classrooms.

The other subversive professor I've met practices many of the same classroom methods, but he's carried them a step farther. He himself enrolls in courses on campus, and he tells the profs at the outset why he's there, what he wants to learn, and how he'll go about it, refusing to take any tests or to do any assignments he doesn't care about. So far, no one's objected, but I'm sure the fact that he's a tenured, 52-year-old PhD. has a lot to do with that.

Learning about this man's experiences has helped me face my biggest worry in my training: student teaching. I've felt like a conscientious objector facing combat just thinking about it, but I see now that I had been envisioning myself at the beck and call of a supervising teacher, locked into her peculiar classroom structure. But I'm the one who's paying tuition for this experience and I'm the one who knows what I want to learn from it. So I plan to follow my prof-friend's example and tell my supervisor that I don't plan to be a traditional classroom teacher and have no interest in planning lessons and writing measurable objectives and devising tests, but that I'll be glad to spend time with individual students or in small groups, wherever extra attention is most needed. I'm not banking on getting a cooperative teacher, but I know that my chances of enduring the experience will be much greater if I can begin with such a firm-but-friendly, clear-cut attitude. I've got about 10 months to get my confidence built up in preparation. The big question for me right now is, what happens after graduation? I have so many ideas about things I could do, but very little knowledge of how to go about it. I'm fascinated by the idea of a community learning center, where kids could come to find people who share their interests, where all kinds of people could offer their skills or seek out teachers, and where young unschoolers could be under supervision when their parents were at work or school. But how to begin? Where on earth would the money come from, and how could I simultaneously bring in a liveable personal income? . . . I can hardly imagine how a person goes about creating his own occupation, especially without a lot of financial backing! I'd appreciate any thoughts on this idea.

Improving Ed. Course

Sue also sent us a copy of a letter she wrote to her college faculty:

As a student and prospective teacher, I am very concerned about the inclusion of a manuscript handwriting proficiency test as a requirement of the course. This requirement and the way in which it is approached in the classroom contradict many of my beliefs about children and education in general (as well as many of those commonly espoused in our classrooms), and it presents me with the painful situation of participating in what I consider to be a destructive activity in order to pass the course.

Written communication is a marvelous tool of mankind; to be able to convey thoughts, ideas, and feelings by merely scratching out a series of symbols on paper is little short of magical. But to squeeze that magic into an arbitrary, rigid system of instruction transforms it quickly into drudgery. Rather than encouraging a child to feel that writing is a part of himself, an expressive extension of his own personality, such a system *dis*courages creativity and individuality, and by placing an undue stress on cumbersome rules and precision, distorts the very purpose of handwriting. The message it communicates is subordinated to the form of the letters. Such is the concern of a calligrapher, whose form is an art in its own right; but for the first grade child, such an emphasis imposes unnecessary stress upon the simple task of writing his name.

Perhaps a more serious consequence of a strict adherence to a manuscript system is the message it conveys: that there is a "correct" way to write, and any deviations are therefore "wrong." As I understand it from the orientation to the Zaner-Bloser system in this course, this notion of correctness is advanced in the interest of "consistency" so that the child will not be confused by any irregularity in letter shapes. But is it really consistent to contradict what the child can see for himself in the world around him—in his story books, on the TV screen, on traffic signs, on food packages—that the world of print is a veritable carnival of variation, and that communication is effectively achieved (indeed, often enhanced) even when the letter forms deviate wildly from the Zaner-Bloser norms?

I also take issue with the implied assumption that children cannot learn from or will be distressed by anything that isn't uniform or consistent. Our spoken language, with its regional and personal accents and idioms, is far from uniform, and yet the vast majority of children are able to master it without noticeable anxiety at an incredibly tender age, despite the lack of systematic or "consistent" instruction. It is only after children are taught a concept of regularity that they become confused or distressed by the variations they encounter in reality.

Another justification given for the manuscript instruction is the fact that so many public school districts make use of such a system. That is indeed a good reason for acquainting student teachers with the method; but it is a poor reason in itself for actually promoting the method and requiring its mastery for completion of the course. The university does not/should not exist for the purpose of perpetuating public school tradition but should serve as a source of innovation and creative challenge. By gearing its curriculum to the demands of the public schools, it forfeits its role as a leader in the search for more effective educational techniques and alternatives and becomes instead a mere vocational training school, committed to the mediocrity and rigidity which is causing so much concern over the country's educational system.

In light of these arguments, I would like to seriously challenge the department and the developers of the curriculum to reconsider the mandatory proficiency requirement in a prescribed manuscript handwriting style.

———

Sue added, "I gave this letter to the man who designed the methods course and to the instructor of my class. The latter more or less ignored it, but the former took it quite seriously, sharing it with the department chairman and other colleagues, and presenting my views at a meeting of the grad students who are in charge of that aspect of the course. I'm quite sure that the requirement won't be eliminated, but he did ask my opinion about some possible changes, such as emphasizing the fact that the Z-B system is only one of many, that communication value is the highest priority in handwriting, and giving students the choice between several systems in which to seek proficiency. Certainly an improvement, maybe as much as I could hope for from a college. I was glad to have made the effort anyway."

Tim On Word Processors

Tim Chapman (see p. 1) wrote:

Today is the last day I will be doing my paid work for Holt Associates/*GWS*. I am starting a new job in less than two weeks, as a sales representative for Brookline Office Equipment in Brookline MA. I will be selling electronic typewriters and extensions made by Olympia, a German-based company. In popular jargon, machines such as Olympia's electronic typewriter with its visual display system and disk drive are known as word-processors. In six months, I am told, I will also be selling Olympia's soon-to-be-announced computers. In the meantime, I'll be sticking to Olympia's word processors, copiers, calculators, and other office supplies. I can't wait to begin!

I'm writing because John asked me to tell how I came to be qualified for my new job. I also want to say farewell. I can't imagine working for two nicer people than John and Peggy, and I will always stay in touch with the whole atmosphere of *Growing Without Schooling*.

I was first introduced to electric typewriters in the 11th grade. I was in Journalism I, which meant I wrote for the paper but didn't have much to say about how it looked. Needing typists, the editors, three 12th grade girls from Journalism II, taught me to use an electric IBM typewriter. A year later, I was one of two editors, responsible for putting out a 6–8 page paper every other week. By that time I typed longer blocks of text than anyone else on the newspaper staff. (To make a long block, all lines had to end flush with an imaginary right hand margin line.) Without knowing it, I was hooked to the typed word.

During my four years at college and the following two years, I had ample opportunity to type, as an English major who had to write ten to fifteen stories 10–20 pages long every ten weeks and, later, as a community organizer who wrote 20- to 50-page fund-raising and grant proposals. But it wasn't until a little over two years ago, when I began volunteering at *GWS*, that I met my first word processor, the Olivetti TES 401. My early assignments on the word processor were very routine, printing out personalized form letters. I only had to type in the person's name; the rest of the letter printed onto paper with the touch of a single key. I was soon back to the IBM Selectric, typing letters that John had dictated onto cassettes.

A month or so after I graduated from volunteer to employee, I decided to see if there was more to the word processor than printing out form letters. There was! In just four hours with Olivetti's training manual, I discovered I didn't even have to print onto paper a single word I typed. Everything I typed stayed in the typewriter until I was ready to run it off on paper. I could type a letter, fill out some new *GWS* subscriptions, saunter back to the word processor, hit a couple of keys, and watch my letter emerge from the machine's memory. I was hooked again, this time to the wonderful world of word processing.

Over the next year and a half, I didn't progress beyond the 15 character viewing screen on the Olivetti. I had seen electronic typewriters with separate TV screens that let you see 24 lines of type, but I never used one. Six months ago, I was hired as a two-day-a-week secretary for a small law office. The four attorneys who worked there created a mountain of handwritten documents every day and it was my job to turn them into typed script. After one month on the job, I'd had enough. I felt like a robot on an assembly line. Something had to change, and since I needed the job to survive, I decided to change how I did the job. The law office was planning to move within five months and was taking out a loan to cover the cost. One of the attorneys had been thinking about getting a word processor for over a year and soon the office decided to use part of the loan to get one.

With the attorneys' blessings, I took charge of locating a machine they could use. I immediately lined up meetings with ten different word-processing companies. Sometimes I went to their offices to test their machines, and sometimes their salespeople brought their machines to us. After several weeks of research, I decided on the Olympia ES 105 electronic typewriter with its 24-lined screen and the ability to remember 35 typed pages and store them on remove-able diskettes.

Two companies were trying to sell us these machines so I played one against the other, drove a hard bargain, and brought the price down $1400.

In the following months I began designing a way to learn to use the Olympia word processor that put the new user in control of it in just one hour. To discuss this training method, I met with the Director of Sales and Services for Brookline Office Equipment, the company from whom our law firm bought the word processor. After he had shown me every electronic machine in the office, he handed me an application form for the position of sales representative. Two weeks later, I was formally offered the job, and took it. Farewell and best wishes to all.

Apprentices In Germany

From a column by William Raspberry in the Washington Post, *11/12/82:*

> Fully half of Germany's young people leave full-time school by age 16 to begin three-year apprenticeships in their chosen trades.... "Both government and unions favor this [voluntary] approach," say Limprecht and Hayes (authors of an article in the *Harvard Business Review*), "because it helps address the problem of youth unemployment by providing teen-agers with a marketable trade and good discipline.... Industry likes the system because it builds a work force that is highly skilled—especially in the high-technology industries that are crucial to the German economy—as well as motivated and responsible.

> "When young people are trained by industry, not by the state, and are given considerable work experience and responsibility at an early age, they become very attractive to future employers. These employers are willing to furnish whatever retraining is necessary because they have found, through long experience, that apprentices adapt well to different work environments."

The German system, in other words, is producing young workers with precisely the skills our experts say will be in increasingly short supply here in the coming years.

Child In Food Co-Op

From Jill Bastian (MI):

I have gotten braver, recently, and taken Heather (7) to the food co-op with me, while I work my 2-hour stint once a month. I shop while I'm there.... I wasn't sure what would happen. Often mothers bring small children and expect them to play contentedly for two hours in a small carpeted area with toys. But the little ones invariably start getting into everything else—namely the food packages on the shelves.

Heather played for a while, the first time, by herself. Then she asked if she could help me. I package herbs in 1–2 oz. amounts. It's messy and very exacting work. Although I'm not normally very patient, I decided to let her help a little. I have to count 16 baggies and ties for each herb, write and stick on a small label, and, of course, spoon and weigh the herbs from a big bag into the small baggies. The weights are in grams and must be put on one side of the scale with tweezers so as not to get oil from your hands on them. Heather counted baggies and ties, affixed labels, twisted ties, put on weights, and even was allowed to measure some of each herb into a bag (it really is very messy even for an adult and must be *very* exact to come out in 16 equal amounts). I was really proud of her and felt good about her helping.

This last month, she found a very young child to play with, and it was interesting to watch their interaction. Later when she asked to help me, I wasn't very patient, as I was tired and in a hurry to get the last batch done. She had played most of the time with the young child, even when the child frustrated her by messing up arrangements of blocks Heather had built. She is very at ease, though, at the co-op: washing her hands very thoroughly before helping me, going around asking other adults what they are doing without interfering, and even paying for a snack at the cashier in the front of the store.

Last time I asked if I could switch jobs. The manager had others available, so next month I will learn to package other things. If I'm ever able to inventory, I'm sure Heather would like to help. I've told several of the women about Heather's homeschooling, and have had several calls as a result of leaving a notice on the wall that persons interested in homeschooling could call me.

Another Vet Helper

From Ruth McCutchen (KY):

After reading *GWS* 30, Alison (13) was inspired to begin volunteer work at both the library and our veterinarian's office. She enjoys both but favors the vet. During her first week she saw a dog spayed and our two 10-month-old kittens neutered. She described it to us in *glorious* detail and we all found it fascinating. She wasn't fazed by any of it.

The vet's family seem to appreciate her calmness and efficiency. They have school-age children and are considering trying homeschooling.

Teens At Home

From Christopher DeRoos (CA):

I have been home-taught and two years ago when I was 14, my mother started taking me to sit in on college courses. I am at Holy Names College in Oakland, where a friend also attends. He started there when he was 15. His mom home-taught all four of her children. I am in computer sciences and economics. I'm going to be taking an auto engineering class. My favorite computers are Apple II and III and Hewlett Packard HP900. . . . I am serving on a Planning Commission—Sign Committee, reviewing the Alameda County sign ordinances. My motto is from Auntie Marne, "Life's a banquet and most of you poor suckers are starving to death." Being home taught has been the best!

The most-asked question was about my socialization. Having exchange students in our home helped—because the students from Europe agreed that American schools over stress the social rather than the academic. . . . I could never understand why all 5-year-olds, etc., were stuck together when we each progress at different rates. . . . Usually when you get out in the work force you're with all ages. Homeschooling helped prepare me for the *real* world.

From Vanessa Keith in NH:

I'm 14. I've never been to school (except one day with my cousin). I have been trading with neighbors for two years. I trade babysitting, washing dishes, and money for lessons. I have four lessons a week: sewing, weaving, botany, and piano. It works great if you have friendly neighbors.

I am away from home approximately four months of the year picking apples in the fall and pruning apple trees in the winter and visiting my father who lives in Philadelphia. I started picking apples of my own accord when I was five. I started really picking a lot when I was ten. I haven't lost my enthusiasm for it yet.

I earn money doing these things. I have to buy my own clothes. I have to pay for Christmas presents, food, rent, and transportation while picking apples and pruning. If I want to go to a movie, restaurant, concert, etc., I also have to pay myself.

A parent in Brooklyn wrote:

About five years ago, I took my daughter out of the sixth grade, keeping her out of the seventh and eighth grade too. . . . She's attending high school now, a small private school.

Regarding the years my daughter stayed at home: they were really hard. We were both very isolated and the only reason she didn't go back to school was that school was worse than staying home. She wouldn't let me tutor her and she wouldn't do all the educational things I had planned, like go to museums and stuff. She hung around in her bathrobe and drew pictures all day. For nearly three years. Summers, too.

Well, you should see her art work today. Fantastic!

Staying home was hard for my daughter but we both think it was necessary, if only to recuperate from the previous six years of schooling.

From Sarah O'Keefe in California:

I do Sylvia Hare's Abilities Research Associates schooling program (I love it).

I'm taking this program because I hate school—that doesn't mean I hate schoolwork, I like schoolwork. I do Sylvia's courses and expand them. . . . By expand, I mean independent work I thought up. . . . Right now I'm reading archaeology, Egyptology and about Jupiter's 12th moon—whatever.

The other thing I love about independent courses is I'll work on Saturday and then on Tuesday take off and go to an open rock concert or a beach. You can't do that in school!.

Tammy Mills (TX) wrote last fall:

I am a teenaged homeschooler. . . . This year would be my first year in high school, so I'm feeling sort of isolated. I've been a homeschooler for almost two years and hadn't minded until now. All my friends here talk about what a "blast" high school is, and that I'm really missing out on something.

But I feel that education is more than having the best football team or the prettiest cheerleaders. Education should be learning things worth learning in a good atmosphere, and should be made interesting. Home education is all of the above.

Education is not someone you don't know telling you where to be—and when—or else. Education is someone who loves you as a person, patiently helping you where you need help, encouraging you to learn for yourself. In those six hours a day, I can read, play the piano, help one of the younger ones with their math, or cook, or whatever else I may feel like doing at the time.

I have gotten in touch with several other people my age whose addresses I found in the GWS directory, becoming "pen pals" with each. It is very interesting to hear about different ways of life in different parts of the country. And yet most of these people have returned to the public school. But every one of them who has, has stated clearly that they were not going back for the education, that in fact, they had loved homeschooling, except for one fact—they missed their friends.

I feel very good towards homeschooling, because of my pen pals, who make me feel that although I may be isolated from the public school group, I have friends everywhere who care about me and the homeschooling movement. I would love to get letters from any other homeschoolers who feel this way, and will answer all letters.

On Correspondence Courses

[JH:] I happened to see in the *US Air* magazine a very interesting article by Kate Ennis about correspondence courses. It said in part:

> For Joyce Gerig, the idea of being an interior decorator was more than a career goal. It was an obsession. . . . The problem was she had neither the time nor money to continue her education. Then, while browsing through a magazine called *1001 Decorating Ideas*, she came across what seemed to be the answer: correspondence courses.
>
> Eight months later, after completing a comprehensive course through the mail, she started her own interior-design business, and today is ready to hire her own full-time secretary.
>
> Lynell Scaff . . . five years ago was working as a clerk at a small electronics firm in Pennsylvania. Unable to support herself and go to school at the same time, she invested in a three-year [International Correspondence Schools] program to earn a bachelor's degree in accounting. Today, at age 23, she's earning $25,000 a year as a regional accountant for the McDonald's Corporation.
>
> These days, more and more people like Gerig are finding success through the U.S. mails, and correspondence schools are earning the respect of educators and business people. [JH: More than can be said for many public schools—see "Graduates Lack Skills," *GWS* 31.]
>
> While college enrollments continue to

drop, correspondence-school admissions are increasing by approximately 25% every year. Why? For one thing, correspondence schools—sometimes known as "proprietary" schools—offer many courses that aren't available elsewhere, occasionally at exceptionally low prices. At last count, over 1500 subjects were being offered in such non-traditional home-study areas as wine appreciation, stock-market science, paralegal training, landscape design, gem appraisal, and even robot-building. At least six of the country's proprietary schools offer bachelor and associate degrees in such subjects as electronics engineering, business management, and Bible theology all through the mail.

One of home study's strongest points is its flexibility. Students can take several years to complete a course, putting in as little as two hours a week for study.

For a free copy of the National Home Study Council's Directory of Accredited Home Study Schools, write to National Home Study Council, 1601 18th St. N.W., Washington DC 20009.

[JH:] We print this article for two reasons. One is that some of our readers might want to use some of these correspondence courses. The other, and more important one, is that the very existence of these courses, and the fact that their credentials are honored by businesses and other institutions and that their graduates are demonstrably competent in their chosen fields, is conclusive proof that the contention that we can only learn important things by spending many hours in a place designated as a "school" and in the face-to-face presence of someone designated as a "certified teacher," is wholly untrue.

This is important to homeschoolers from a legal point of view because it gives us strong grounds for saying in court (if we are pushed there) that any requirement of schools and/or legislatures that only people with teachers' certificates shall be allowed to teach children is unreasonable and a denial of our Fourteenth Amendment right to equal treatment under the law. It is clearly absurd to say that I can get a bachelor's degree for myself without spending a single minute in school buildings or in the presence of a certified teacher, but that my child can't learn without a certified teacher. Furthermore, the good track record of correspondence schools conclusively refutes the schools' argument that the higher we go in the grades, the more necessary it is for certified teachers to teach us.

This argument can be very useful, not just because it could carry considerable weight right now in many state and federal courts, but even more because, since it does not depend on *Pierce* or *Tokushife*, it will still carry weight even if we lose these valuable precedents (see p. 17).

How Many Are We?

[JH:] I asked our friend and colleague, Dr. Raymond Moore, of the *Hewitt Research Center*, to write us a letter explaining or defending his estimate that there are 500,000 or more homeschoolers in the country. I said I would print in GWS what he had to say about this question, and that if he convinced me I would say so, and if he didn't I would say why not. Out of his busy schedule he took time to write, saying in part (I have numbered the excerpted paragraphs for reference):

1. John, I could not live with my conscience if I ignored the handicapped children and migrant youngsters as homeschoolers. When was with the U.S. Office of Education, some of the leading Spanish officials were former migrant children. Why should we exclude these precious children?

2. I first picked up my figures from the *Wall Street Journal* which has figures in excess of 300,000, and then went to the U.S. Census and Labor Department and determined that there were close to 5,000,000 children in areas of handicapped, migrant, and normal children who are at home or at least away from school. Then we did some brief factoring in a town or two and concluded that at least five to ten percent of these youngsters were getting some kind of instruction at home. This would give a net figure of at least a quarter to half a

million youngsters who are receiving some kind of home instruction. And bear in mind that this does not include the family schools in which parents have their children going to institutional schools and coming home to study and work with them part of the day. And there are many Amish, Mennonite and other families who are doing exactly that.

3. It may be that such writers as John Naisbitt are thinking in terms of the gross figure of all students who are studying at home, when they give the figure of 1,000,000 or so, and they may very well be right, although I do not normally quote them. In any event, Bill Gothard, who is the leading marriage and family counselor in the nation, with seminars up to 15,000 or 20,000 people, has repeatedly told me that there must be at least 100,000 new families per year now going into this movement. He has gathered his data from his seminars. And he is now making the family school the center of his entire family and marriage counseling ministry.

4. Almost every day we get a new letter that tells us how they felt they were the only homeschoolers around and shortly found that there were 30 in their local town, or others who called meetings, as recently in Sacramento, and found several times as many showed up as expected. This was our experience not long ago in Vancouver where we were told that we might have 30 or 40 people, and we had over 200.

5. I still stick by my figure of quarter to a half million at least, and the figures probably range higher than that now. This does not include those children who are going to school as well as studying at home.

6. All I know is that when I inquire of the University of Nebraska I find that they have more than 10,000 homeschool students of all kinds, Missouri more than 5,000, Home Study Institute more than 8,000, and so on and on and on until we got tired of writing and telephoning all these people to obtain information that way. Christian Liberty Academy has 6,000 students itself, according to the last statement that they gave to us a year or so ago. Such figures as these put the figure of 10,000 to 15,000 totally out of the picture, it seems to me.

7. The facts are that there are probably thousands of families who have started their own private schools in the northern California area. I would tend to believe that there are a very small number of those who actually have registered with the state compared with those that are actually doing teaching at home.

8. You say that you do not know of a state that has as many as 1,000 homeschool families by your definition. Of course your definition may be more limiting than my definition, but we have far more than 1,000 homeschool records on California in our files. Now maybe some of these have gone out of business or whatever, for we have not made checks, but I would suggest that there are probably many thousands of homeschoolers in California. I do not know what the figure is in Utah, but it is considerable.

9. And the other night when I was in the Minneapolis suburb of Minnetonka, on a very, very bad night weather-wise and I thought we would be fortunate if we had 40 or 50 people, there turned out 400.

10. In Louisiana, my information from Woody Jenkins is that things are growing, not declining. There is a growth of opposition from the NEA and other vested interests, of course, but when they came by the legislature to make some changes in Woody's law, 2,000 people showed up on the capitol steps to oppose them.

11. I don't think we should use high figures to make impressions on anyone, but if those figures are accurate I am not going to worry a bit if they alarm the opposition. . . .

―――――

[JH:] In reply, I wrote:
Dear Ray—Thanks very much for your good letter. I remain unconvinced by your figures, for reasons I will give, but I'm sure our discussion will clarify some important issues and will be very useful to all who read it.

First of all, our numbers disagree because we are using the words "homeschoolers" or "homeschooled children" to mean very different things. There's nothing wrong with this, as long as the people who hear these words know what *we* mean by them. When people ask me, as they always do, how many homeschooling families there are, I now say, more or less, "That depends, of course, on what you mean by those words. If we mean, how many families are there whose children do not go to school, perhaps because they are handicapped, perhaps because they are migrant workers, perhaps for other reasons, we get a very large number. If we mean, how many families are there in which some instruction is done in the home, we get another very large number. I use the words 'homeschoolers' to mean families who, *having a choice of sending their children to school, choose not to send them, or to send them only on a part time basis for courses or activities which the children have chosen for themselves.*" It is this latter definition, and this alone, that interests people. I then say that my best guess, the guess I am most comfortable with, the guess for which I can find at least some hard support, is somewhere between ten and fifteen thousand *families*, perhaps going as high as twenty thousand. The number of homeschooled *children* would of course be larger than this, depending on the average size of the families. My guess here would be that the average homeschooling family is somewhat larger than the national average of 2+ children. A guess of three children per homeschooled family would give us a total, by my definition, of somewhere between thirty and sixty thousand children.

By the way, I should say that in his latest letter to me Ed Nagel guesses that the number of homeschooling families, which I think he defines much as I do, is between thirty and fifty thousand. I will ask him, as I did you, to write me explaining or defending this figure—but this will have to wait for a later issue of *GWS*.

Let me now comment on the paragraphs of your letter as I have numbered them.

1. I don't want to ignore these children, either. I don't include them in my estimates of homeschoolers, first, because that is not the question that people want answered, and secondly, because the overwhelming majority of these people *would send their children to school if they could.* This is one reason the American Civil Liberties Union has not been much interested in helping us; they are far more interested in making it possible for those parents who want to send their children to school, to be able to send them, a position with which I agree. Of course this is an important issue; I only say it is an issue which ought not to be confused with ours.

2. This doesn't help me at all. Where did the *Wall Street Journal* get its figures? This is hardly an area in which they have expertise. In all probability, they are simply using someone else's wild guess. But a wild guess remains a wild guess, no matter how many times it is passed from hand to hand. As for the Census figures, I don't know what their definitions are or how those figures were obtained. If their definition of homeschooled children is the same as yours, then it's not clear to me why you don't use their figure. If the definitions are different, then what is the difference? Unless we know what the definitions are, the numbers, even if accurate (which is questionable), are meaningless.

3. I have the same problem with these people. What does Naisbitt (author of *Megatrends*) mean by homeschoolers, and where does he get his figures? Same question for Bill Gothard. And how does he "gather this data" from a seminar of 15,000 people? What questions does he ask them? If you have an address for him, perhaps I can ask him directly.

4. Well, we've gotten letters like that, too. But if I got a letter *every day for a year* from someone saying that she or he had turned up 30 homeschoolers, that would add up to a little over 10,000, not a million. As for attendance at meetings, that tells us only how many people are interested in the idea of homeschooling, not how many are doing it. At such meetings I almost always ask how many are doing it, how many are seriously thinking about doing it, and how many are interested in the idea as such. The number actually doing it is never more than a fairly small percentage of the meeting, at the outside 20%.

5 and 6. These figures are impressive, but again we come back to definitions. How many of the people using University of Nebraska, Missouri, etc. courses, are using them to *supplement* regular

school work, and how many of them are using them *instead of* regular school work? Almost certainly, the universities, Home Study Institute, etc., do not know, because this is not a question they have asked or have any reason to ask. Beyond that, how many of the people using these courses are beyond compulsory school age, which would remove them from my definition of homeschoolers? Probably a large percentage, maybe a large majority. How many of these students are outside the United States? Unless we know, the numbers tell us nothing about the number of homeschoolers within the U.S.

7. "The facts are that there are probably . . ." If it's a "fact," then it's not "probably." The fact is that this isn't a fact, but a surmise, a guess, maybe a reasonably guess, but a guess none the less. What I need to know is, on the basis of what evidence can we make such a guess. Why would only a very small number of homeschoolers have registered with the state, when to do so was easy, cost nothing, and, at least until recently, seemed a sure way of staying out of trouble? Do we know of a community in which the number of unregistered homeschoolers is much larger than the number of registered? I don't.

8. We are indeed back at the matter of definitions. You speak of "far more than 1,000 homeschool records on our files." Does this mean you have letters from far more than 1,000 California families saying that they are not sending their children to school but are teaching them at home? Or does it mean something else, perhaps that more than 1,000 families are using some kind of home teaching materials? California homeschoolers have not until recently been very much organized, but those few communities which have active organizations have not reported any such large numbers. The Utah people are exceptionally active and well organized, with very good internal communications, yet they do not claim much more than two hundred or so homeschooling families.

9. See my earlier remarks about homeschoolers and meetings. Also, it is surely as true for you as for me that when the word gets out that you are going to be speaking somewhere, people come from a long distance to hear.

10. I quite agree; my information is the same. But no one I know in Louisiana has claimed much over two hundred homeschooling families. If there are more, nobody knows about them, which puts us back into wild guesses. As for those 2,000, we don't know how many were actual homeschoolers; there were many education bills up before the legislature, all of them bad, and many of these people may have been there to oppose some of them that had nothing to do with homeschooling. Say even that they are potential homeschoolers; I wouldn't disagree with you for a minute that there may well be a million or more people in the country who are *seriously considering* homeschooling. But how many are doing it right now is another matter.

11. I entirely agree; if we have accurate figures, let us by all means use them. But if we are guessing, as we are, then it makes more sense to guess conservatively. TR rightly said, "Speak softly, and carry a big stick." What use for us to speak loudly if in a pinch it turns out that all we are carrying is a little twig. I would rather say to a legislator that we have 100 homeschoolers in a state, and have all 100 turn up at a hearing, than say we have 10,000 and have only 100 turn up. Meanwhile, I insist that it doesn't make good tactical or political sense to throw the schools into unnecessary panic.

Well, so much for all of that. My mind remains open (more or less) on this question. I would rather believe that there are many homeschoolers than that there are few, and will welcome any and all hard evidence to support that idea, so any time you get some new information about all of this, I'll be grateful if you'll send it along for us to share with our readers.

Meanwhile, thanks for all your good work, enjoy your new home in the state of Washington, and keep in touch.

Freedom In Florida

Melanie Darst (FL) writes:

Ann Mordes helped me when we got started. At that time there were some bad signs for homeschoolers in Florida. So she suggested that I register Russell (6) at Grassroots private school at a special rate for homeschoolers. I did and the cost was $90 for the whole year. The director is interested in and supports homeschooling. Once a month I turn in three sheets which record the amount of time we have spent in three subject areas. Grassroots does not interfere with our homeschooling in any way. [See "Helpful Schools," GWS 30.]

When I undertook this experiment I had one main objective—to take all the pressure of learning out. I wanted Russell to relax, enjoy himself, and feel that he had some power and responsibility in his own life. Therefore I could not institute another regime with graded sheets and him reading aloud, etc. I decided to go completely to a non-structured learning situation. In fact, the only activity which I planned to do daily was read, which I was doing anyway, but read more. I have always let Russell and Lightsey (4) pick out the books.

It was difficult at first to be passive—not to ask questions, test, and worry. The hardest task to not worry about is reading. I have asked Russell several times if he wants to practice aloud or if he wants me to teach him. Each time he has said he would rather do it himself and just ask me a word when necessary. So I do not know at this moment how well he reads, but I do see him studying books and he does ask about certain words.

I am self-employed as a botanical artist and am part-owner of a native plants nursery. I am able to work almost entirely at home and this is ideal, but we could not have our home school without the support of Paul's full-time job. However, I have very little time to "teach." I estimate that Russell and Lightsey get about 1½ hours of undivided attention and help per school day.

I love our freedom from carpooling, school hours, and organized school activities. We can do a project when we want to, for hours if necessary. Russell is more confident and is very self-motivated about what he finds interesting. He has studied history and geography mostly. We have read about topics that are never studied such as the Mongol invasions, Russian folklore, Indian folklore, the origin of Japan, Confucius, and other things. He has a portfolio of artwork about three inches thick so far.

All this is great but there is one problem. Russell says he is ready to go back to school next year. I think there are several reasons. First, he misses the children he got to know during his kindergarten year. Second, he liked the independence of being out on his own, however nerve-wracking. Third, I think he feels he is missing something which the other kids share. When asked about homeschooling, he says he likes it. Lightsey says she wants to go to kindergarten, too. I have already told them that if next summer they still want to go to school, they can. I have also said that if later (the following year) they wanted to go back to homeschooling, we would.

[From a later letter:] The kids are currently not leaning toward going to public school. I try not to poll them about it, but I think they are hearing more negative things about it from schoolchildren they play with. We'll see.

From Costa Rica To U.S.

From Walter Marschner (LA):

Our letter about adopting our two boys, ages 14 and 12, from Costa Rica was published in *GWS* 26, and we thought readers may like to know how our boys are doing since their arrival in May '82.

We are homeschooling the boys, as well as our 17-year-old daughter. Up to this time, I have not wanted to ask the boys how they like school here as compared to schools in Costa Rica (which are Hispanic versions of schools in the US—enough said). I felt it was too manipulative a question.

But in letters to their former houseparents in Costa Rica last week, Joseph, our 12-year-old, said, "Thank God we don't go to these schools. We go to school at home." I then felt free to ask him why he liked school at home. His response was, "Because I do so much better! I did much worse there," which is very true. In five years of schooling, Joe could not write cursive, knew absolutely no math (could not even add 2 + 1 in his head without counting on his fingers). Also, though he had a desire to communicate with others, he had great trouble expressing his thoughts, particularly on paper. He had been labeled "perhaps learning disabled."

After several months of homeschooling, Joe now knows all his tables through the 10s, can do complicated addition, subtraction, and multiplication, generally without counting on his fingers or using stick figures any more. He writes a beautiful cursive hand. Most encouraging of all, he now sits down and writes his own letters to friends without help—that is, he can now express the thoughts that are in his head in his own words on paper. Of course, he needs lots of help with spelling and punctuation, but it is almost as if a bright light has been turned on in his head.

He is also asking many good questions and developing listening habits, which he did not have before. He has asked, just over the past several days, "Who invented airplanes?" "Who invented kites?" "Who was Hitler?" And he asked the very good question one day, "Why is the U.S. such a rich country and Costa Rica so poor?" leading us into a historical and religious analysis. We combine our answers to the boys' questions with trips to the public library for picture books which help to *show* what we are talking about.

As for the older boy, Saul, 14, we can't keep up with him! Neither boy had ever (or very rarely) opened a book for pleasure in their lives before. Now, Saul has devoured the several dozen books we brought back with us from Costa Rica and we are searching for other Spanish language books for him. (While the boys are learning English, we don't want them to forget Spanish. . . .) Saul likes both fiction and biographies, and has been fascinated to learn about Benjamin Franklin, Marquis de Lafayette, and other figures in American history. One of his favorite books was a biography of Isaac Newton. The great part of this is—as you and readers of *GWS* know—that such omnivorous reading leads one into learning about so many things!

Saul was always a good athlete, but Joe had never done anything physical in his life before. Now he not only rides a bike, does karate and exercises and running, but is making goals for his soccer team! He had somehow been led to think, in the past, that he could never do anything.

We read in English together every day. The boys are learning, though they don't understand everything as yet. We also read in Spanish (I read to them) at night before they go to bed. Their (and my) great favorites are the C. S. Lewis *Narnia Chronicles* in Spanish.

More Success Stories

From a Georgia mother:

We homeschooled in Tennessee for a year, during which time we were summoned to court twice. The last court appearance resulted in all charges being dropped, but with a warning from the court that they would continue to harass us. So, we bought a farm in Georgia and moved to friendlier territory.

The boys and I are thriving on the farm. I know when I say "The world is our classroom" that it sounds hokey, but it is so true. In the last few months the boys and I have sold our house, our car, bought a farm, learned to drive a standard shift (I couldn't have done it without the kids' support: "Hey, Mom, you're still in second!"), learned to split wood and build a fire (our farmhouse is heated by woodstove and fireplace), mended fence, learned to use power tools, etc., etc. And in spite of all this learning we've had to do, we still found time to read *To Kill A Mockingbird*, and *Animal Farm*, and *Slapstick* by Kurt Vonnegut (the boys' favorite), learn long division the fun way (without pressure), visit the library once a week, write to pen pals, etc., etc. Sometimes we get so busy with "etc., etc." that we don't have time to watch TV!

From Gwen Witmer (PA):

We're two months into our second year of homeschooling: this year without any hassle, after agreeing to allow our fifth grader to be tested with the local school's CTBS achievement test. After a discussion of the abnormality of testing our son in the alien environment of their school, the superintendent marvelously agreed to allow *me* to test D.N. myself!

We had a wonderful workout with those tests and I hope that D.N.'s fears of achievement testing have been forever allayed. The test was sent out to be graded with local fifth grade tests and will be returned with a printout advising his strengths and weaknesses.

We are using materials from *Christian Light Publications*, PO Box 1126, Harrisonburg VA, an individualized-study curriculum.

Mornings at our house center around math, language arts, science, social studies, and Bible study. Any daily assignment not completed by noon is considered "homework." Afternoons are for the extra-curricular activities such as signing, German, creativity, music, work skills, home economics, composition, memory work, and practicing parts to be given at church on Sunday mornings.

We take the children on a field trip each month and also seek out the skills of other "teachers." Right now we are learning how to make stocking caps on a homemade circular loom made of plywood and 46 golf tees.

At Home Until 10

From Georgeanne Poe (ME):

We don't plan to send our 4-year-old Rosie to school for a while. I thought I'd share with you my personal experiences with my first child, Annalee, who is now 18. Because we moved to a very rural commune in northern Vermont when she was first-grade age, we had the ideal situation to keep her at home with *no* legal hassles. We really didn't follow any program, but, as I look at your booklist for young children, I see that we had literally *every* book on it, and Annie read all of them until their covers wilted.

As things turned out, by age 10, Annie thought she'd like to go to school. The school tested her and placed her—along with all the other 9- and 10-year-olds—in the 4th grade. She was slightly deficient in math, but off the charts in reading. School gave her a band and flute lessons, and a championship basketball team, two things I could never have provided. We had given her a very strong sense of family and support and a good idea of personal worth. By her junior year in high school, she was attending Northfield Mt. Hermon School and was, last autumn, accepted at Bowdoin with a very generous scholarship. She chose to wait a year to enter, and is presently crewing and cooking on charter boats in the Caribbean.

I think that having home education, as well as public and private school, has been a plus for Annie and I hope we can be as successful with Rosie.

Law Review Articles

Two of our "Friendly Lawyers" (see list in *GWS* 31) have sent us law review articles they've written about home education. The first is by James W. Tabak and Perry A. Zirkel, "Home Instruction: An Analysis of the Statutes and Case Law," appearing in the Fall 1982 *University of Dayton Law Review* (300 College Park, Dayton OH 4546 9-0001). The other is "The Constitutionality of Home Education: The Role of the Parent, the State and the Child," by Brendan Stocklin-Enright. It was published in the Fall '82 *Willamette Law Review* (Willamette University, Salem OR 97301). This article looks especially useful for homeschoolers, as it is written from the point of view of arguing a case before the US Supreme Court, and has useful comparisons among the requirements of the different states.—DR

Our Legal Situation

At present, homeschoolers stand on a piece of legal and constitutional ground which, though narrow, is firm enough to support our weight and almost always does so; for all our talk of court cases, and our natural worry over them, the fact is that for every family now threatened with court there are hundreds teaching their children at home without legal problems or worry. My own fairly conservative estimate of the number of families who have chosen to teach their children at home is somewhere in the range of ten to fifteen thousand, perhaps even twenty thousand (see article elsewhere in this issue on "How Many Are We?"), and of these far less than a hundred are now facing court action.

In the draft of model homeschooling legislation we printed in *GWS* 30, I outlined, in effect, the legal and constitutional basis for homeschooling. Let me sum it up again here. The Constitution itself is silent on the matter of education. Whether the framers of the Constitution said nothing about education because they meant to leave it up to the states or because they wanted to leave it up to individual parents, we have no way of knowing. When, a century or so later, the states began to enact compulsory school attendance laws, a number of people went into the courts claiming that these laws were unconstitutional. In every case the U.S. Supreme Court turned them down, saying over and over again that under the police powers reserved to the states by the Constitution, they had the right, by enacting compulsory schooling laws, to protect themselves against the possibility that without such schooling children might grow up so ignorant as to be a burden on and danger to the state. Many honest and sincere homeschoolers devoutly wish that this were not so and have taken their wish for a fact. But it is not a fact. Compulsory school attendance laws are not on the face of them unconstitutional; quite the reverse.

What the U.S. Supreme Court did say, first in *Pierce v. Society of Sisters*, was that the states could not establish what we might call an educational monopoly, more specifically, that they could not deny to private schools the right to exist, or require through laws that they be in effect identical to the public schools, since this would deny parents their constitutional right, expressed here explicitly for the first time, to get for their children an education generally in harmony with their own principles and beliefs. The court said, in effect, that parents should have a right of choice among schools; it did not specifically include among their choices that of teaching their children at home. Since then a growing number of state courts have later extended the meaning of *Pierce* to include this additional possibility, locating this right of parents in the First, Ninth, and Fourteenth Amendments, though, as I said before, it is not specifically written in any of these.

A few years later, in *Farrington v. Tokushige*, the court established further that the states could not impose by regulations "unreasonable restrictions" on private schools.

This, then, is our Constitutional ground. Yes, say the courts, the states may regulate the education of children, including the right of parents to teach their own. But, the courts then say, if the states or their schools say No to these parents, they must have strong reasons for saying so, they must say what those reasons are, and they must give the parents the right to challenge, examine, and answer these reasons in formal hearings, according them full rights of due process. I think it very likely that, through the kind of legislation we have talked about, through the home education plans that we persuade school districts to accept, and now and then, if pushed that far, through court cases at the local and state level, we can gradually reduce the requirements that school authorities can impose on homeschooling parents. Thus in a number of cases we have already overcome and removed the requirement that parents must have teacher's certificates, and I think in time we will be able to do away with other requirements concerning curriculum, standardized tests, etc.

But this is a slow process, and one that requires us to keep talking to school authorities about the education of our children. Many people are for one reason or another impatient with this process and unwilling to talk to school authorities at all. They feel sorely cramped by the smallness of the constitutional turf on which we stand, and want to push its boundaries out past the horizon. They want the courts to hand homeschoolers what is in effect a blank check, that is to say that if people want to teach their own children, above all if their reasons for wanting to do so are primarily religious, then it is none of the state's business and it must leave them alone. To these impatient homeschoolers I have said many times why I don't think there is a chance in a billion that the present U.S. Supreme Court will say any such thing. On the contrary, if we take such a brief that far, the court will almost certainly cut out from under our feet most of the constitutional ground on which we are now standing. Specifically, I fear that they will say that

Pierce was only about private schools, not about homeschooling; that whether or not people can teach their own children is not a constitutional question but something for the state legislatures to decide as they wish; and finally, that the states do not have to show any compelling need for whatever laws and regulations they may want to establish.

Let me take a few words to say why I feel so certain that the present Supreme Court will rule this way. In his short but very interesting and important book, *The Nature Of The Judicial Process,* former Supreme Court Justice Benjamin Cardozo, explaining to law students (to whom these lectures were originally given) how judges arrive at their decisions, said that there were essentially four ways in which judges could and did look at cases.

In the "Philosophical" approach, they examine them in terms of basic legal principles, found perhaps in the Constitution itself, perhaps in the Anglo-Saxon Common Law from which the Constitution arose, perhaps in even older and more fundamental principles of right and justice. Such judges ask themselves, in effect, what is the right, the fair, the just thing to do in this case. Most people not familiar with the law, and not long ago I was certainly one of them, would have assumed as I did that all judges thought this way all the time. But for many and often very good reasons, this is not always so.

Another way of looking at cases, called by Cardozo the "Historical" approach, is to ask what the law itself has said about similar cases over the years. Historically-minded judges want to preserve, as far as they can, the unity and internal consistency of the law, so that as far as possible people will be able to predict, from what the courts have said in the past, what they will be likely to say in the future. In making their rulings they cannot to some degree avoid making new law, but they want this new law to disturb the existing body of law as little as possible. If the law must change, as it cannot avoid changing, to take account of new problems and conditions, they prefer it to change by gradual steps, not by sudden announcements of new positions or sudden reversals of old ones. In this frame of mind judges are much influenced by precedents, which tend to make the law predictable.

Still another kind of judge—I forget Cardozo's name for these—is what has elsewhere been called "strict constructionists." When facing a dispute over the meaning or application of a particular law, such judges ask, what did the lawmakers, when they wrote this law, *intend* to have happen, how would they have written it if they have known about the case now before us. In *People v. Turner*, of which we wrote in *GWS* 29 and 30, the court was thinking primarily in this way.

Finally we have what Cardozo called the "Sociological" approach to the law. In this, judges facing a case ask themselves, what will be the social consequences of our ruling this way or that? How must we rule in order to make happen what we want to have happen, or to prevent from happening what we don't want to have happen? In this frame of mind judges act primarily as if they were legislators. The judges who have so far refused to award damages to parents whose children the schools had completely failed to educate thought in this way; they said, in effect, if we start awarding money damages against schools for failing to teach, our courtrooms will soon be bursting with complaining parents and the schools will soon be broke, neither of which we want. So, in spite of the rights of the parents and the seriousness of the injuries which may have been done to them and their children, these judges have not awarded damages, and in my judgement are not likely to do so.

The present Burger court is, from the point of view of homeschoolers, probably the worst kind we could have. Like the Warren court of the '50s, they are a very sociologically-minded and legislative court, but unlike the Warren court, they are a very anti-libertarian one. They feel that in general the state has lost far too much of its power and authority over its citizens, and are determined to restore them. In any conflict between the power of the state and the liberties, and in the case of atomic energy even the physical safety of its citizens, they almost always come down strongly on the side of the state. Beyond that, they tend to be constructionists, preferring to interfere as little as possible with whatever legislative bodies want to do. Finally, they are very worried (and rightly) about the increasing over crowdedness of our courts, so much so that if they had no other reasons for saying that homeschooling was the business of the legislatures rather than the courts, they would find this reason enough.

Some of the homeschoolers who want to take broad constitutional cases up through the Federal courts claim that in *Wisconsin v. Yoder* a majority of the justices presently on the Supreme Court said, in effect, "if your religious convictions forbid your sending your children to school, then they don't have to go." The fact is that the Court went to great trouble to make clear that this is *not* what they were saying. They stressed instead that the Amish were a long-established sect; that the prohibition against sending their children to school past eighth grade was itself long-established and was uniformly observed through their church; that they had shown over many years that their children, despite their abbreviated schooling, grew up to be productive and useful citizens, and no burden or danger to the state; and finally, that this exemption granted to the Amish was *not* to be considered as applying to any individual who might for whatever personal reasons want to avoid the requirements of compulsory schooling. Indeed, three of the justices, in a concurring opinion, said that if even the Amish, instead of claiming the right not to send their children to school after eighth grade, had claimed the right not to send them at all, they might well have ruled the other way—as they put it, the difference between eight years of school and ten is probably not very great, in this case not enough to justify trampling on the Amish's religious convictions. This very cautious and heavily circumscribed ruling is a long way from some of the optimistic interpretations of *Yoder* presently circulating in the homeschooling movement.

For all of these reasons I have been trying for some time now, in *GWS* and through personal conversations and correspondence, to dissuade people from bringing broad cases into the Federal courts. Whether I was right or wrong in this, I have to recognize that the effort is failing. Many people active and prominent in the movement are continuing publicly to urge aggressive action in the courts, and indeed at least four cases seem already to have started on their way, three of them damage suits against the schools, and one what we might call a Leave-Us-Alone suit. Before long these will probably be followed by many others. What will happen to them in the lower courts, and how long it will take them to work their way, if any do, into the Supreme Court, I don't know. But I have started to accept it as a fact of life, and urge others to accept it, that within a few years we will see a Supreme Court ruling saying, first, that there is no generalized constitutional right of parents to escape, for whatever reasons, the compulsory education laws of the several states; secondly, that education is the constitutional province of the states and that in this area they may make whatever regulations they wish; and finally, that no burden of proof will rest on the states to show that these regulations are reasonable and necessary, but only on those who claim they are not. Or, which amounts to the same thing, we will get such a ruling from a lower Federal court and the Supreme Court will refuse to hear an appeal from it. This may not happen for two or three years, but I think we should be prepared for it. If and when it happens, we don't want the phones here to start ringing day and night with people saying, "Help! Help! The Supreme Court has just ruled against homeschooling, what do we do now?"

One thing to do now is to realize that though such a ruling would be a very serious setback, it would not be the end of homeschooling. As we know, there are active and growing homeschooling movements in Canada and Great Britain, yet neither of these countries have constitutions like ours, under which the courts can simply strike down legislation written by Parliament. When homeschoolers go to court there, what they say is not that the law is unconstitutional but that they, in teaching their own children, are in fact obeying it, meeting its requirements and satisfying its true intent. There is no reason why homeschoolers in this country could not, if they had to, fight and win many such cases in state courts, and in this and later issues of *GWS* we will discuss how we might prepare such cases.

The case of the Edgingtons in New Mexico, described elsewhere in this issue, is an example of how the law works, changes, and grows. If two parties are in dispute under a particular law, they both try to get the courts to interpret the law in their favor; if the courts disappoint one of the parties—as they must—then that party goes back to the legislature to try to get a more favorable law. As long as the schools see homeschoolers as a serious threat, this game of court-to-legislature-to-court is going to continue. It's unrealistic for us to think that we can, so to speak, end the game while we are ahead. The only way to end the game is to end the conflict, which is what we here at *GWS* want to find ways to do.

Note that in this ruling Judge Kase was thinking like (in Cardozo's terms) a philosophical judge. In saying that the statute in question made no sense, he was calling on an old Roman maxim of law (I forget the Latin), "The law is not an ass." Such judges feel that a fundamental requirement of any law, one much older than the Constitution itself, is that it makes sense, and not be self-contradictory or absurd. We would probably do well, as we continue our struggles in the courts, to take note and keep track of such philosophical judges, since, if we prepare our cases well, we have a much better chance of winning in their courts.

Meanwhile, this case is important for just the reason given in the story, that in finding for the parents Judge Kase "focused primarily upon the wording of the statute involved," rather than on any First Amendment or other constitutional rights. He threw out the law (which a "strict constructionist" judge would never have done) not because it was unconstitutional but because it didn't make sense and hence was bad law. Since his argument does *not* rest primarily on the U.S. constitution, it will remain available as a useful defense for homeschoolers even if our constitutional defenses should be lost. (Copy of the ruling available from NALSAS, Box 2823, Santa Fe NM 87501, for $1 and a business-size self-addressed and stamped envelope.)

Please do not take me to be saying that there are *no* kinds of cases that we can win in Federal courts. On the contrary, I think that we may be able to win there, (after first going through the state courts) whenever we can show that a particular family has been either 1. denied the right of due process, in short, that in prosecuting the family the state failed to follow its own required legal procedures, or 2. denied equal treatment under the law, that is, has been forbidden to do what other citizens are free to do, and/or required to do what other citizens are free not to do; still more specifically, has been required to obey laws and regulations which the state's own schools widely ignore or disobey. I think we may also be able to win at least some cases in which we can show that the effect of the state's education laws on a particular family is less to hold the parents and children *up* to the minimum standards of the state schools than to hold them *down* to them. To philosophical judges we can say that this is unfair and unjust; to political judges—and we should know which kind we have to deal with—we can say that it is not in the best interests of society, which is on the contrary best served by allowing and encouraging all parents, not just rich ones, to get the best education for their children that they can, if need be, making it for themselves.

Since these are the kinds of arguments that we will have to make if, as seems likely, we lose our constitutional support, we should start making them right now, both in the educational proposals we make to schools and in the legal briefs we draw up if and when we are forced into court. The advantage of cases won by such arguments is that, unlike constitutionally based cases, these Due Process and/or Equal Treatment cases will still stand as helpful precedents no matter how bad a future Supreme Court ruling may be.

But the main point of this article is that we must now greatly increase our efforts, first, to get good homeschooling laws passed in the legislatures, and secondly, to achieve cooperative relationships with as many as possible of the local schools. In any states which pass legislation saying in one form or another something reasonably close to what we put into our model legislation (*GWS* 30), parents would not have to worry much about what the courts might or might not say. And the strongest position of all will be, as it is right now, to have a really friendly, understanding, and cooperative local school district. If the local district not just grudgingly but warmly approves the idea of your teaching your own children and wants to help as much as it can and in whatever ways suit you best, then you don't have to worry about either legislatures or courts; with that much school support, you will easily find a legal way to homeschool. So our most urgent task, now more so than ever, is to persuade our local school people, and beyond them the state authorities, that homeschooling is not a threat to their existence and that their best interests will be served by working with it instead of fighting it. To convince them of this is not an easy job and will not be accomplished in a year or two. All the more reason to get to work on it as soon as we can. One way to do this will be to establish more effective local organization and lines of communication. Another way may be to give the widest possible circulation to our legislative proposal and to my article from *Phi Delta Kappan* (see excerpts in this issue).—JH

Minnesota v. Tollefsrud

State Of Minnesota, County Of Houston County Court, Criminal Division

State of Minnesota, Plaintiff, v. Thomas Tollefsrud, Defendant

The above-entitled matter came on for hearing on the 19th day of January, 1983 before the Honorable Robert E. Lee, County Judge.

It Is Ordered:

1. That as applied to this defendant, MSA 120.10 and MSA 120.12 are unconstitutional intrusions on the First and Fourteenth Amendment rights of the defendant.

2. That the motion of the defendant is granted.

3. That the complaint is dismissed.

Dated: February 9, 1983.

Memorandum

This prosecution is concerned with the constitutionality of imposing criminal penalties upon the Tollefsruds for their religiously based refusal to compel their children to attend a public school. The State of Minnesota is seeking to brand these parents as criminals for following their religious beliefs. This Court does not recognize that the State of Minnesota can constitutionally do so.

The First Amendment to the United States Constitution states, "Congress shall make no law respecting an establishment of religion or prohibiting the free exercise thereof."

The "free exercise" clause was made applicable to the respective States through the concept of "liberty" as embodied and defined in the Fourteenth Amendment. . . . The analysis or test of the concept of "free exercise" has a broad application (*United States v. Ballard*, 322 US 78, 1944) and the Court has indicated that a proper inquiry is limited to whether or not the party charged with the offense was sincere in his (or her) beliefs.

The Court has noted that non-traditional beliefs, including secular humanism and atheism are all "religions" for the purpose of the "free exercise" analysis. (*Fowler v. Rhode Island*, 345 US 67, 1953.) The Court held that it was "no business of the Courts to say that what is a religious practice or activity for one group is not a religion that comes within the protection of the First Amendment."

The free exercise of one's religious beliefs prohibits the invasions or intrusions of civil authority, and it is incumbent for one in such a case to show the coercive effect of a legislative enactment as it operates against him in the practice of his religion. (*School Dist. of Abington v. Schemysp*, 314 US 203.)

The stated religious beliefs and convictions of the Tollefsruds are on a collision course with the avowed determination of the school authorities to prosecute them, convict them of criminal offenses, and seek the adjudication of the Courts to sentence them to jail, impose monetary fines, or both.

The leading case on the proposition confronting this Court is *Wisconsin v. Yoder* (406 US 205, 1972; 92 S CT 1526).

The sincerity of the religious beliefs and convictions of the Tollefsruds is not challenged. The prosecution has filed no affidavits disputing the contentions of the Tollefsruds that as stated in their joint affidavit "to send a child to a system of education which does not center around the Bible and which does not teach faith in Jesus Christ, is to endanger the eternal destiny of that child and to bring God's judgment upon one's self as well."

Nor is it contended by the prosecution that the parents (Tollefsruds) are attempting to replace state educational requirements with their own idiosyncratic views of what a child needs to know to be useful and productive in our society. (See *Wisconsin v. Yoder*).

The Tollefsruds affirm that they are regularly using materials supplied by the Christian Liberty Academy and that the children are tested annually using the Iowa Tests of Basic Skills. The prosecution has filed no affidavits challenging or disputing the effectiveness of these education resources.

It is contended by the prosecution in this case that the *Yoder* case is distinguished, since in *Yoder*, the Amish children were required to attend the public schools from grades one to eight. A careful reading of that case compels this Court to conclude that the issue of the age of the student was not decided by the U. S. Supreme Court.

As appears from the affidavit submitted by the Tollefsruds, they sincerely accept the fundamental conviction that their children are a special gift of God, and that they are accountable to God, as parents, for the life of that child, from its first day on earth.

A considerable portion of the *Yoder* case is devoted to a historical analysis of the Amish religion and the unique life-style fundamental to the Amish communities. The US Supreme Court was vitally concerned with the possible consequences to the Amish beliefs and traditions if their children were required to attend secondary schools. That feature is not necessarily involved with the Tollefsruds, but it is of critical importance that the Amish rejection of formal secondary education is rooted in a literal Biblical context. It is the decision of this Court that the Tollefsruds must be afforded the same guarantees, even though they are not involved in a community of believers, as are the Amish, and even though they also reject formal elementary education.

It is also suggested by the prosecution that the State's interest in the compulsory school attendance of the Tollefsrud children is paramount to that of the parents and that the children's interests must be recognized.

This argument was rejected in *Yoder*. The children are not parties to the litigation.

"It is the parents who are subject to prosecution for failing to cause their children to attend school and it is their right of free exercise of religion, not their childrens', that must determine the State's power to impose criminal penalties on the parent" (*Wisconsin v. Yoder*).

The prosecution makes no claim that the health or safety of the Tollefsrud children is at stake, or is in any way jeopardized by the refusal of the parents to send their children to the public school.

In conclusion, this Court is eminently satisfied that the Tollefsruds sincerely believe, profess, and live their religious convictions.

It is urged by defendants that MSA 120.10 is unconstitutionally vague. Since this Court has determined that the present action should be dismissed as against these defendants, the Court is not disposed to make any further determination as to that issue; since it is not critical to the issue of the First and Fourteenth Amendment rights of these defendants.

[JH:] News clippings tell us that the county attorney does not plan to appeal; that the superintendent of the district says that the result will affect 17 or 18 students being educated at home in the district, and may cost the district $23,000+ in state aid and possibly a teacher in the schools; and that a similar case in another county was decided against the parents.

Sometimes, as here, these cases win; sometimes they lose. News clips and letters sent from around the country have given me the (perhaps false) impression that they lose more than they win. In the last year or so I wrote the Christian Liberty Academy, asking roughly how many cases they were winning and how many losing, but received no reply. Ray Moore says that in the First Amendment cases with which he has been associated the parents have won most of the cases. I am trying to persuade him to send me, or publish in his own newsletter, a list of cases won and lost. It would be extremely valuable information to homeschoolers; the longer the list of successful cases that we can show school districts, the greater the chance that they will decide against prosecution. But, what with moving his home and office, and with all his other work, he has not yet had time to make such a list. We must keep after this. The same goes for all *GWS* readers—please let us know about any homeschool court cases you hear about, whether the parents win or lose. Send news clips if you can; if possible, send the date of the ruling, the name of the court, name of judge, etc. Meanwhile, lacking hard evidence to the contrary, I tend to continue to believe that this basic First Amendment argument is not strong enough and, though it may win when it meets a friendly judge like Judge Lee, it loses more often than it should.

In any event, this argument has to my knowledge lost twice in state Supreme Courts (Nebraska and Iowa) and has not yet won at that level. In the Nebraska case, as a result of which a Christian minister running a private school has been sent to jail, the court said in effect that people couldn't get out of obeying laws they didn't like just by saying that it went against their religious beliefs. If such a case reaches the U.S. Supreme Court, and one (from Kentucky) seems headed in that direction, that court will almost certainly say the same thing. Like many others, Judge Lee seems to have read into *Yoder* a meaning almost the exact opposite of what the Supreme Court intended. His quote of the remark about people replacing educational requirements with their own idiosyncratic views is particularly ironic. These words come from the concurring opinion of Justice White, who of all the Justices is perhaps the most hard-nosed and unyielding supporter of compulsory public schools for everyone, and the surest to vote against homeschoolers in any case that may come up.

I would like to know more about why the county decided not to appeal. It may have been a wise decision; it is not *always* a good idea, and indeed is often a bad idea, to appeal a lost case to a higher court, because you cannot add anything to your original argument. It may often be better to prepare a stronger case the next time. The news clips, and the ruling itself, give the impression that the schools thought they had an easy win in this case and did not work very hard preparing it. They may well be looking for a more favorable case, perhaps one in which the children are not testing very well on achievement tests. Or perhaps they are waiting until they can lobby through the legislature laws which will make it easier to prosecute homeschoolers.

Another question in my mind. According to one news story, the Tollefsruds offered to show the effectiveness of their home education by comparing their children's standardized test results with those of children in the district, but the school "belittled the test." Might it not have been possible for the Tollefsruds and their attorney to use what is called the "discovery" process to compel the district to reveal the test scores of students within its schools? In the discovery part of a trial, each party to the dispute can submit to the other a list of questions which the other must answer. Whether this process is available in all states, in what sorts of trials it can and cannot be used, and what kinds of questions can or cannot be asked, is something we need to know more about. We'll be very grateful for any information that any of our readers who may be lawyers can give us.

Losing State Aid Money

If we are interested, as we should be, in making a friendly and cooperative working relationship with the schools, instead of just trying to run them out of business, we have to take seriously the concern of Superintendent Lewis in the Tollefsrud case, and many others like him, that homeschooling might cost school districts so much in state aid that they might have to fire one or more teachers, or cut out some programs, and (the corollary argument) that this loss of teachers and programs in already crowded school systems might make the schools worse for many more children than whatever number was being helped by homeschooling.

We should meet and answer this argument, not just because it has merit on its own and in any case may carry much weight with many legislators and other people whose support we need, but most of all because we really do have an answer for the problem. In our legislative proposal (*GWS* 30), we suggested that the schools continue to register homeschooled pupils, list them (which nothing in the law forbids) as being part of a Special Independent Study Program, and continue to collect for them (which, again, nothing in the law forbids) whatever state and other aid they get for their "regular" pupils.

In fact, when families first begin to discuss homeschooling with their local schools, they would probably be wise to say: "We know that you are concerned that this may cost you badly needed state aid, but we feel certain that with your support we can work out together a way of doing home education that will *not* cost you any state aid," this being the procedure named above.

No doubt some superintendents will continue to oppose homeschooling for other reasons. In this case, as we have said before, we should begin immediately to talk, or better yet write, to the school board itself, saying as we did to the Superintendent that we do not want our homeschooling to worsen the already difficult financial position of the schools, and that we are convinced that with the schools' support there is a way to avoid this. If the idea of collecting aid for students not physically present in the building makes the school people nervous, we could consider such possible remedies as having the family actually fill out school attendance slips, or whatever else may seem to help deal with the problem. If we keep making this offer to the Superintendent and the School Board, though here and there some diehards will continue to oppose us no matter what, we should be able to win over a much larger number for whom, except for money, homeschooling does not seem to present a problem. And we can offer still another strong reason for schools to carry homeschooled children on their rolls—not only will they continue to collect state aid for them, but they can improve their schools' test scores by averaging in the (in most cases much higher) scores of the homeschooled students.—JH

Damage Suits Bad Idea

A number of homeschooling families have either filed or are getting ready to file damage suits in the Federal courts against their local school superintendents and other education and law enforcement officials. They are claiming that these officials have acted to deprive them of their constitutional rights by refusing to allow them to homeschool their children, and they are asking for monetary compensation. Furthermore, several people active and prominent in the homeschooling movement are urging homeschoolers all over the country to file such suits whenever school authorities take them to court for violating truancy laws.

I feel I now have to say publicly what I have for some time been saying to some of these people privately, namely, that I am strongly opposed to these suits and strongly advise families against filing them, no matter how much trouble the schools may be making for them, and that I will not support such suits in any way.

Simply stated, my reasons are these: I don't think the families can win such suits; even if they did win, I don't think it would bring the desired results; and win or lose, I think these suits will make it much harder to do what we must eventually do, and the sooner the better—persuade the schools to support and cooperate with homeschoolers.

More specifically, my arguments are these:

1) The families are not going to be able to make a convincing argument in court. The one family whose case has been much discussed in other publications certainly has not done so; unless the opposing school officials hire a fool for a lawyer, they will easily demolish the family's argument. Since most of these damage suit cases are likely to be modeled after this first one, the same thing is likely to be true for all of them.

2) Even if the families are lucky enough to find themselves opposed by incompetent lawyers, the courts are unlikely to award damages against the schools, for the reasons that they have already several times refused to do so: they fear it would cripple the schools, and would flood the courts with similar cases.

3) In the (to me) very unlikely event that a court did award damages against a school system, it seems unlikely that the damages would be enough to have the deterrent effect sought by the homeschoolers. The school business, as we can't too often remind ourselves, is a 100+ *billion* dollar a year operation. If, as some claim, the managers of this business are for malicious and unprincipled reasons determined to use the threat of prosecution to frighten people out of exercising their legal right to teach their own children, then they will not be deterred from this by the kinds of damages courts are likely to award, if indeed they award any. To put this a little differently, if the managers of this giant business really believe that the homeschooling movement is so great a threat to their very existence that they must in self-defence use the law as a weapon against it, they will cheerfully pay, as a kind of insurance, whatever occasional damages the courts may award against them, just as large industrial firms find it easier and cheaper to pay whatever fines they must pay for dumping their poisons into our rivers than to find some other way of disposing of them.

4) In the (to me) extremely unlikely event that a lower court did award damages really large enough to hurt and worry the schools, they would surely appeal this all the way to the Supreme Court, which for reasons discussed elsewhere in this issue, is virtually certain to rule in their favor.

5) In the enormously improbable event that the Supreme Court did let stand lower court rulings awarding heavy damages against school systems, the schools across the country would soon find effective countermeasures against this danger. Without spending much time on it, I have already thought of four.

This talk about damage suits has much of the same unreal quality as a lot of the talk we hear about the arms race—as if all we had to do was find some new legal super-weapon in order to bring the schools to their knees. In the early '70s one book said, and for a while I helped spread this idea, that all you had to do to get your children out of public school was to say that you were going to send them to private school—and then not send them. It didn't take the public schools long to find an answer for that. Then all we had to do was enroll our children in a distant school and call our homes a branch of that school; or in many states, simply declare our own home a school. After a while the public schools began to find their answer to that. Now people talk as if some legal equivalent of the MX missile or the Trident submarine or whatever would finally stop the schools in their tracks. It's a dream; as long as the schools feel they are in a fight for their lives, for every legal weapon we invent they are going to invent a counter weapon—and they have vastly greater resources to spend on this than we do. It makes no sense for us to continue escalating this battle.

Of course, it will not be easy to persuade the schools as a whole to work with homeschoolers, and of course, if in the meanwhile we are forced into court, we must make the strongest defense we can. But our principal task must be not to think of newer and better legal weapons but *to find ways to end the war*. In terms of this task these damage suits even if now and then they win—seem to me a big step backward.—JH

Adult Learns To Read

Nancy Plent (NJ) wrote in the Unschoolers Network #14:

I heard a touching story from a family that came to one of our meetings here. The father never learned to read. School was a traumatic experience for him, and he's determined that his 8-month-old son won't go. So he's started from scratch with his son's baby books. He reads to his son every day. His wife says he often has tears in his eyes when he finds that he doesn't know a word in one of these books. She reassures him that their son doesn't know the difference right now if he misses a word, and that he'll learn it all as he goes along.

Un-Taught Reading

From a long article by Jeannette DeWyze in the San Diego Reader, *10/7/82, about John Boston (CA) teaching his son Sean at home:*

> The two began by sitting down at the family's dining table first thing every morning to work on such subjects as spelling, mathematics, and reading.
>
> [John Boston] had thought the secret of enticing Sean into reading would be simple: he would give Sean books that weren't boring. From the bookstore he brought home piles of Hardy Boys and other adventure stories; at the library he searched for entertaining reading material pertaining to flying, one of Sean's interests. But he was soon forced to ask himself, "What if Sean dislikes the act of reading itself?" As the weeks rolled by, Boston watched his son more and more reluctantly sit down to the table, and then stare out the window, his attention wandering. When Boston tried to review material he had covered with Sean only days before, he found "it was as if he had never seen it in the first place." Gradually he and Sean began shortening or skipping the sessions altogether.
>
> Boston changed tactics. Even as a preschooler, Sean's obvious forte was mechanics. "He was interested in machinery and bulldozers and windshield wipers and anything you can name. Machines and I don't get along at all," says the father, "but with Sean it's different. He makes machines talk." Since school hadn't destroyed that interest, Boston decided to let Sean turn his full attention to machines and to anything else that interested the lad. If the father no longer was taking an active role teaching, he saw a new role for himself in constantly being alert for things and people with which Sean might want to be in contact in order to learn.
>
> When Sean acquired a small Honda motorcycle and began tinkering with it, his father asked if the boy would like a service manual for it, to which Sean eagerly assented.
>
> He has become a regular reader of a few aviation magazines such as *Model Aviation* and *Bicycling*, which are devoted to some of his hobbies. In fact, his father says this year he administered to Sean a "quick assessment" reading test Boston obtained from a San Diego reading specialist. Boston says it

indicated that Sean has improved to where he's now reading at roughly a seventh-grade level, about the same as other children his age.

"But does he ever simply read for pleasure?" I asked Boston the first time we talked.

"Not really. They really turned him off and I don't know how to turn him back on again," Boston replied sadly. But then he remembered something that had momentarily slipped his mind. A few weeks before, Sean had discovered an adventure story series in which the reader has a choice of reading a number of different endings for the various dramas. "That was the first time in two and a half years he ever asked me to buy him something to read," Boston amended himself. Later, when I asked Sean himself if he thought that he would ever return to reading, I didn't tell him what his father had told me about the book, and the boy answered my question with a note of pride. "I already do read." He went and pulled out the volume, *The Curse of the Sunken Treasure* by R. G. Austin, and explained how the stories work. "It's a series," he told me. "I'd like to get all of them."

Reading Together

Susan Richman wrote in the Winter '83 Western Pa. Homeschoolers:

I remember wondering, while pregnant with my second child, how I'd ever be able to read to my older Jesse with a new baby around. I figured the early few months *might* go all right, as I could read while nursing the baby, but I really worried about what would happen as our little one began grabbing books from us—would he eat or rip them, or generally make a muddle of our good sharing times? Would the children be too far apart in age to ever enjoy the same stories at the same time?

I've been delighted with what's actually happened. The early months *were* very easy for reading aloud to Jesse. We'd all snuggle in bed together with a book, lots of nursing, and we'd all feel relaxed. I think my "reading voice" was lulling to Jacob in the same way as a crooning singing voice! I was often amazed to find both boys would drift off to sleep at the same time after our readings.

As Jacob grew, he began to open his eyes a bit as I'd read, pupils dilating with delight while Jesse and I would laugh over some delicious passage. Jacob began laughing with us over favorite parts just to share in our fun, began peeking away from the breast to see the pictures, began patting pages. We weren't reading *to* him, or *for* him; we weren't trying to give our baby a "boost" in reading ability by exposing him to print at a properly early age. It's just that as a part of our family, Jacob was always *there*, and took part as best he could at every stage. He did at times make very loud noises while we read, he did sometimes throw our books on the floor, but generally that just meant the timing was wrong, not that Jacob was destroying our reading time.

By a year, he'd fallen in love with *Goodnight Moon*, laughing as we'd touch the "hot" fire, pointing ecstatically to the real moon outside. We somehow passed over most of the cardboard baby books—Jacob seemed to be catching on so quickly to gentle handling of books since they were always about *everywhere*, and obviously treasured. He also seemed to prefer real *stories* to mere "point it out" books. We found our reading choices move towards Jacob's new favorites—we must have read and pored over the *Angus* and *Ask Mr. Bear* books by Marjorie Flack a thousand times the month Jacob was 15 months old. It was our delight to rediscover Jesse's old treasures and share them anew with Jacob. Jesse seemed to enjoy these simplest tales immensely, too. . . . It wasn't a boring experience for him to hear *Three Billy Goats Gruff* a hundred times—he loved acting it out with his little brother, and also would see these timeless stories from his new older perspective.... I remember Jesse musing, "Well, I think they should have sent the *Big* Billy Goat Gruff over the bridge—*first*, then the littlest one wouldn't have had to be so scared by the troll, the big one could have gotten rid of that troll right away."

Jesse also began to learn Jacob's favorites by heart. I remember him at 4½ "reading" all of the *Little Fur Family* by Margaret Wise Brown to Jacob, with engaging inflection and proper pauses to ask Jacob little questions.

Jacob usually seems to grasp the main characters of our books, and so can follow and participate in Jesse's play-acting versions (*everything* seems to get acted out in our house!) Shared stories have become a cement to their friendship, a vehicle for them to enjoy play together, as they both know and love the common themes of the stories woven through their days.... The years ahead look exciting and rich, and now we're wondering how next summer's baby-to-be #3 will enjoy it all.

And Writing Together

And a letter from Suzanne Erion in the same issue:

My 3½-year-old son, Matthew, said to me one cold fall morning, "Mommy, I want to learn to write my name." I thought, "What an opportunity." I got my big lined chart paper and with Matthew on my lap, he watched me print his name. Knowing all his letters, he named the letters in his name one by one. I printed it again two more times. The next time he said, "I want to make the T's," and he did so well, I was surprised how legible and neat. Matthew attempted the "H" along with the two T's next time and finally he included the "W." We printed his name ten times, each time he made the T, H, and W. My 18-month-old son Philip watched eagerly behind my shoulder, tugging on Matthew's shirt indicating he wanted a turn. Matthew said, "OK, Philip, your turn." Philip sat on my lap and he watched me print each letter in his name as I said them. After printing it a couple of times, unexpectedly Philip turned his head, touched my cheek with his little hand and kissed me as if saying "Thanks for taking the time to print my name with me." I could have just melted.

Letters On Computers

From Christine Hilston (OH):

We recently purchased a Texas Instruments TI99/4A home computer and are teaching ourselves programming. We hope to come up with some rather unique programs that may bring in a little income. But for right now we are having fun learning. We bought a couple of educational software cartridges (and a game cartridge, too), and it's amazing how well our boys are doing. They not only are learning the material presented, but also how to operate the computer. And they don't look on it as "learning" they say, "We want to *play* 'Early Learning Fun,' or 'Number Magic'", etc.

It is interesting to observe how Erik (6) and Brent (3) react differently to their computerized learning. Erik seems to want us watching every problem on the screen and giving our approval before he types in the answer and gets the programmed approval. He doesn't want to make a mistake!... Brent, on the other hand, is happy using the computer by himself and gets very excited over a correct answer. Age may play a part too, since Brent is 3. But he doesn't always want or need to get the answer correct. He sometimes says, "I want to see what happens if I get it wrong...."

From Wendy Baruch in Cambridge

We have the Commodore VIC-20 computer which comes with 4K of memory. For an extra $100, we bought 16K extra memory. Commodore sells a program called "VIC Typewriter" (word processor) for $12. It's a powerful word processing system for the money. We bought the VIC 1515 printer for $350, so including the $75 for the cassette tape machine, our word processing system cost us $837 (VIC itself was $300). The price of the VIC has gone down a hundred dollars since we bought our model so this package could be bought for $737. [DR: Not including TV.]

Our son, Shane (8), is very capable of using this system. For a while he was actively corresponding with my younger sister (10) who lives in Florida. The point is it's an economical and practical system and I've never run out of memory since we bought the 16K expander. I use the system all the time as I am using it now. There are a number of good editing features and a small convenient handbook of instructions.

The VIC-20's 1515 printer is not as efficient as I would like. Occasionally it repeats a word (of its own choosing) and sometimes the print head sticks and needs a push manually. If I had to do it over again, I would have spent a hundred dollars more and bought a different brand, better-quality printer.

Also, if any homeschoolers have the VIC-20, I would highly recommend investing an extra $40 to buy the Turtle Graphics cartridge. This changes the computer language from Basic to Turtle. Turtle uses very simple commands that make the cursor (called the Turtle) crawl across the screen and leave various colored trails. This interesting form of computer art (you can program sound into your picture too) is an excellent introduction to programming.

From Sheryl Schuff (8156 Lieber Rd, Indianapolis IN 46260; 317-259-4778):

In *GWS* 31 you asked for information concerning the cheapest way to run Logo. I hope the following thoughts will be helpful.

First, the prices you quoted in your article are "manufacturer's suggested list prices." Substantial discounts are available from discount stores (Children's Palace and Service Merchandise are two) and from many mail-order firms. These firms advertise in *Byte* magazine and *The 99'er* (published by Texas Instruments computer users).

You said that you read that you needed a disk drive before you could run Logo. While this may be the preferred setup, it is not necessary. A portable cassette recorder can be used instead.

The "game" you mentioned in which different size and color objects can be moved about the screen is actually a hardware feature of the TI 99/4A called Sprites. As far as the "limited memory," there is a newer version of Logo called Logo II which has twice as much memory available to the user. It also has music capabilities of up to three simultaneous tones which can be played across a five-octave range.

For a good discussion of Logo and its implementation on various machines, see *Byte*, 8/82. Some of the information is out of date now.

Last October, we implemented Logo on the TI 99/4A with the following equipment:

TI 99/4A with RF modulators; after $100 rebate: $200
Logo: $90
Peripheral expansion box: $220
32K memory expansion card: $250
Cassette cable: $15

For a monitor, we used a color TV already in our home. For a cassette recorder, we purchased a Sears model on sale at $44 for a total cost of $819.

We could have used a cassette recorder we already owned (purchased for $25) with an adaptor available for $6 through mail-order.

Prices for the equipment have come down in the last several months, so the system should now be able to be put together for less: while the $100 rebate is still in effect, for $656.

Logo is used primarily by our 3-year-old daughter. My husband and I also write procedures which are available to her including printing her name, dialing a touch-tone telephone, and building with geometric shapes.

Between the two of us, we have 20 years experience in data processing and are available to consult with homeschoolers.

More Electronic Bargains

In "Bargains In Electronics" (*GWS* 31 p. 14), I said that a good place to shop for cameras and various kinds of electronic equipment was the Thursday *New York Times*. Since then I have found that an even better place is the second half of the main news section of the Sunday *Times*, where the same companies tend to run even larger ads.

Thus in a recent ad for *47th Street Photo* (36 E. 19 St., Kew York NY 10003) we find, among other things, the Olivetti Praxis 35 Electronic Typewriter, an office-sized, daisy wheel typewriter, originally priced at $750 and now sold for $350. The Aiwa HS-J02 walkman-sized radio and tape recorder I described in *GWS* 30 is offered for $130. (*S & W Electronics*, 187 Ross St., Brooklyn NY 11211, sells it for $120.) At such prices it is a remarkable bargain. 47th St. Photo offers the Timex-Sinclair computer, listed at $100, for $55; the VIC 20, listed at $200, for $140, and so on.

If you are buying a computer for the first time, and *if* there is a computer store near you where the salespeople are both well informed and helpful, not an easy thing to find according to the computer magazines, it may make sense to buy from them, even if it costs a little more, just so that you can get advice and help when you need it. But if there is no such store near you, or if you have other sources of help you can go to, or if you already know a lot about computers, the Sunday *Times*, and also the computer magazines themselves, are very good places to shop.—JH

Arts And Crafts

From Suzanne Alejandre (Ger.):

April '82: . . . I once wrote the suggestion [*GWS* 23] that people buying art supplies should only buy red, blue, yellow, white, and black paint and that they could then mix for all other colors. My old paint tubes were one thing I eliminated in packing when we moved to Germany. So, I took my own advice! Having just the primary colors has been great because in painting with them the boys are discovering what colors they can create. As with most of their discovery experiences I try to keep my mouth shut. They've made some great discoveries. Because Lee tends to mix everything I sometimes leave out black as one of their colors, but otherwise the idea was sound.

I wrote a while back [*GWS* 28] about Niko wanting to knit. Since that letter we've had three more sessions. Each time he resumed the work as if he'd never stopped. (I still hold the needles while he works the yarn). Each time we knit he gets progressively faster. Right now we can knit together as fast as I can knit alone!

The fact that Niko didn't forget reminded me of my piano learning experience. When I was teaching myself piano, the things I learned I didn't forget, even though I might have weeks in between playing. I remember thinking at the time how I had often been told as a child or student that I *must* do something and continue doing it or I would "forget." I feel we only "forget" what we didn't "learn" in the first place! Once you learn to ride a bike (or roller skate, etc.) you never forget.

Dec. '82: Niko is still knitting but the intervals are very long in between—a "knitting teacher" would be very frustrated by now, but because Niko only knits when he really has the urge, we both enjoy it. The other night, *Lee* (3) said he wanted to knit. I thought, oh, no, I'll never have knitting time to myself! But, as with Niko, it is quite boring for Lee but he enjoys it for the little time he devotes to it. . . . As with Niko, I worked the needles as he did the yarn. He continually went around wrong and had to try again. He ended up doing five rows before tiring. . . . It will be interesting to see Lee's retention when we have a second session.

Niko was looking through all my stuff (I have loads of scraps, patterns, fabric, etc., etc.) and he came across a cross-stitch kit which Rich's brother had given me as a gift. I let him open it and he was intrigued by all the things—thread, needle, grid-canvas. He wanted to try it but the grid was so tiny I told him we'd buy a larger one. . . . I spent over an hour transferring the drawing, color coding it as Niko looked on. . . . By the time I was finished he'd lost most of his interest. He did try about 3 stitches—had a terrible time and we put it away. About one month later, he found it and wanted to try again. That time he did a whole row and could do one cross-stitch alone. I hadn't realized that he had even caught on to the concept but he had.

Jan. '83: I wrote once about having a lot of leftover art supplies from college. In among them were two pen holders with a large assortment of tips. . . . Niko found a feather one day and started telling me that "old time pens" were made from feathers (who knows where he learned that). So I bought some ink, Rich trimmed the feather end, and Niko had a quill pen. He was so intrigued that I waited over a week before I got out the other pens. Actually it worked out well because Lee had been too rough on *his* feather—the pen suited him better. We've all had great fun—Lee and I each use a holder and share the tips while Niko uses his feather pen.

Music In The Family

An article by Marion Pears in the Australian homeschooling newsletter, Otherways:

> Music just happened in our family. Or, rather, it *grew*. I had no musical training myself, but once Arnold could walk we played rhythmic music for him on our cheap record player, and he loved to dance to it. Later, we gave that record player to the children, along with a collection of their own records to use when they liked. Classical music appealed to me, emotionally, and I used to listen to it on the ABC radio stations, as I worked. Arnold listened, too. It was just there, in the environment.
>
> When Arnold was about five I decided to try to teach myself to play the recorder. I'd always wanted to play an instrument, and the recorder seemed the most realistic and approachable instrument. So I bought one, and a "how to" book, and got started. Arnold wanted to learn to play, too. So I bought him a recorder, and together we made slow progress. At the same time I bought a collection of percussion instruments; we had Bryn as well, by this time, and we used to have wonderful times together just experimenting with sound, making "cat music," or "train music," or imitating birds.
>
> At this time we became interested in the Gilbert and Sullivan operettas, largely because there was a G & S Company formed in Melbourne, and it was producing several a year. We started going down for the productions, bought full length recordings, and librettos. At one stage Arnold knew most of the G & S operettas by heart from start to finish. He could sing you every aria, knew each piece of dialogue, memorized and sang the patter songs with great delight.
>
> The two families whom we were very close to when we lived in Bendigo were very musical. Both the fathers of these families were music teachers, and all their children played instruments. Arnold badly wanted to learn to play the violin. Nevertheless, this wasn't possible until a few years later, when we came to Melbourne, and were lucky enough to find a wonderful, gentle, understanding teacher. After one year of Arnold learning, Bryn wanted to learn the violin, too, and so he also started.
>
> By this time we were involved with Malvern Community School, which had an old piano. I loved to experiment around with it, so bought myself a beginner's book and started trying to teach myself a few things. Before long, Bryn, Omi and I were arriving at school early each morning so that we could do our "piano lessons" before school started. Bryn never became good at the piano, but still loves to pick out tunes. For Omi, it became her great love and the instruments she eventually learned to play the best. Both Bryn and Omi had learned the recorder from me, too. (I'd eventually become reasonably competent.) I got a proper teacher for Omi, and bought a piano.
>
> Bryn and Arnold were at this time playing in a small chamber group run by their music teacher. It started to become obvious that Bryn had a good ear. He would whistle the cello part from *Eine Kleine Natchmusick,* and could play lots of things by ear on violin and piano. He wanted to learn the trumpet. Wendy, the music teacher at ERA, agreed to help him, and so we bought a cheap trumpet.

Every instrument you learn makes each new instrument easier to play. He could already read music, so with the aid of some "how to" books, a tape, and a few lessons from Wendy, he largely taught himself to play.

Omi was starting to become interested in the guitar, at this time, too, and has had lessons off and on.

While all this was happening, our knowledge of music was broadening, our finances improving, our record collection growing. We became interested in opera, and bought season tickets for one season. It was wonderful, and well worthwhile. We still try to go to one opera each season. We bought a hi-fi, and good recordings of our favorite operas.

People started developing a special interest in a special piece of music. I think Arnold must have played *Eine Kleine Natchmusick* a thousand times, and Bryn must have played the New World Symphony the same. In self-defense we bought earphones.

Arnold became interested in medieval music, bought recordings, and we went to hear the Ars Nova group play a number of times. Finally, he built the Celtic harp, and is planning to make further instruments himself.

Meanwhile, we had discovered that we had all become good enough to play together. Wendy arranged several pieces for us of a classical nature, and we play together as a bush band with the boys on their violins, and Omi and I on our recorders. Omi and I can play duets on our recorders. We can all play simple duets on the piano; Arnold and Bryn can play violin duets; and we can play together as a quartet—two violins, piano and recorder.

Bryn is becoming interested in jazz trumpet.... Omi is playing *Pavarotti's Greatest Hits*.

Looking back, it all seems to have happened so simply and naturally, and this is true.

It's also true that music was passionately interesting to me, and was therefore available in the environment all the time. There was the example of our competent musical friends who could play beautifully, and of me, happily messing around teaching myself to play things.

There was the fact that what they were interested in, I encouraged. There was the fact that they believed they could teach themselves these things (which helps a lot). You don't always need "experts" to teach you, though they may be helpful.

And most of all, there was the fact that we have always had a lot of *fun* with music, and we explored it together.

Suzuki Books Available Here

Suzuki Piano School, Vol. I and *Suzuki Violin School, Vol. I* ($4.65 each + post). A number of our readers have children who are taking some kind of Suzuki music instruction, and many others are interested in music and ways to open the world of music to their children, so we have decided to add to our list the first volumes of the Suzuki Violin and Piano Methods. If readers seem interested, we will add other volumes of these series, and also branch out into the cello, flute, and viola series. (Suzuki tuba is not yet available.)

Before I say why I like these books, let me say a few words about how I came to know about Suzuki and what I now feel is good, or not so good, about Suzuki instruction programs as I understand them.

I first read about Dr. Suzuki's work in Japan from an article in the *New York Times* years ago. It said that one day it occurred to him that since all Japanese children accomplish the difficult task of learning to speak Japanese, if they had the intelligence and skill to do this, they could, if they wanted to, learn to play the violin (Suzuki's own instrument) in the same way. Since he believed that children's lives would be much enriched by music, as his own had been, he set out to devise a way of learning the violin as close as possible to the method children use to learn their own language. He realized that children had to hear a lot of other people's speech before they could make their own, and that they did a lot of speaking before they did any reading and writing. He also realized that children want very much to do what they see the adults around them do. From these sound insights he developed his method. If a Japanese family wanted their child to study violin by this method, when the child was still a baby they would begin to play at home, every day if possible, and many times each day, recordings played by expert players of some of the simple violin tunes that the child would later learn to play. Soon the child would come to know the tunes and think of them as his or hers. (Later experiments have shown that babies six-months-old or younger can learn tunes well enough to respond happily when they hear them played.)

When the child was about three or four one of the parents, usually the mother, would begin taking violin lessons with a Suzuki teacher, *bringing her child with her*. At the teacher's house, the teacher would give the parent a violin, show her how to hold it, etc. and then would play one of the tunes that the child already knew. Then the teacher would show the mother how to play the tune—since it was the first, it would be simple enough so that she could learn to play it quickly. After the lesson the teacher would tell Mother to practice that little tune at home until the next lesson. This would go on for a few lessons, the child always going with the mother to the lesson. Then in perhaps the third or fourth lesson, if the child was still really interested—for Suzuki insisted that he would not force children to play—the teacher would mysteriously produce from somewhere a tiny child-sized violin, asking the child, "Would you like to try it?" Yes, indeed! So the mother and child would go home together with their violins, and would practice at home together the little tune they both knew. After a while the mother, though she was still expected to listen to the child play and required to come with him to the lessons, could if she wished stop playing herself—by this time, the child could go on alone. As time went on, he would learn other tunes, and along with his individual lessons would play in groups with other children, discovering with delight that they, too, knew the same tunes.

In the original method, only after a child gained considerable fluency on the violin, and could play fairly complicated tunes, was he introduced to the written notes for the tunes that he already could play. Not for still some time, I'm not sure how long, would he start learning new tunes from written notes instead of by ear.

So much for the basic method, which seemed to me then as it does now in good accord with all I know about children's learning. The *Times* article went on to say that children were encouraged to experiment with their instruments, to make sounds both fast and slow, high and low—remember it said children were asked to make sounds "like an elephant" or "like a little mouse." It then said that all over Japan, hundreds of four-, five-, and six-year-old children taught by these methods gathered to play music by Vivaldi, Handel, and Bach.

A few years later, when a group of these children came to the New England Conservatory on a tour of the U.S., I was there to hear them, along with several hundred others, many of them music teachers. The children, perhaps twenty of them, came onstage, healthy, energetic, and happy. At the time I thought the average age of the children might be five to six; I now think they may have been perhaps a year or two older. Dr. Suzuki and a young assistant checked the tuning of the children's violins. We waited in great suspense. What would they play? Perhaps some of the slower and easier tunes of Vivaldi, Handel, or Bach. Dr. Suzuki gave the downbeat, and away they went—playing not some easy tune but the Bach Double Concerto, in perfect tune, tempo, and rhythm, and with great energy and musicality. It was breathtaking, hair-raising. I could not have been more astonished if the children had floated up to the ceiling. Rarely in my life have I seen and heard anything so far beyond the bounds of what I would have thought possible.

During the question period, Dr. Suzuki told us (through his young interpreter) that the Japanese children we had heard were unusual in only two respects: their families could afford to pay for this trip to the U.S., and their mothers could go with them. But there were apparently many hundreds or even thousands of children in Japan who could play as well.

I have to emphasize before saying any more about Suzuki in this country that all I know about Suzuki instruction in Japan came from the *Times* story and a couple of others, and from what I learned from this short meeting. It is possible that the picture of Suzuki instruction that I made in my mind out of these brief materials was far from accurate. What actually happened then, or happens now, in Suzuki classes in Japan, I don't know. What I can say with certainty is that from all I have seen, heard, and read of it, Suzuki instruction in the U.S. today is very far from my idea of what it was, the one I have just described to you, and even further from the method by which children learn to speak their own language. Suzuki instruction today is in fact very much like most school instruction. The material to be learned is broken down into many very small pieces; each one is supposed to be done perfectly before the next one is attempted; mistakes are corrected instantly, from the outside, by the teacher or the parent; there is considerable pressure put on children to "practice"; and children are given little room or encouragement, if any at all, to improvise and experiment with the instrument.

Some of the reasons for this probably have to do with differences between Japanese and American family life and culture. Japanese women are much more likely to be at home with their children, and Japanese parents, if told by an expert that they must play recordings of simple violin tunes for several hours a day for years on end, are perhaps more likely to do it. To some extent, Dr. Suzuki surely had to modify his method, whatever it was, to take into account differences in American family life, in American adults' ideas about how to treat children (we are generally much more severe with them than the Japanese), and in American music teachers' ideas about how music had to be taught.

It is also important to note that not all Suzuki teachers are alike, any more than are all Montessori teachers, or any kind of teachers. Some are more inventive and flexible than others; indeed, as happened with Montessori, some Suzuki teachers have already broken off from the rather rigid American organization and call themselves independent Suzuki teachers, to give themselves the freedom, if they wish, to modify the strict methods handed down from above. If I ever teach string playing to adults and/or children, as someday I hope to, I will certainly use Suzuki materials, but much of the time I will use them in my own way. The only way to find out what Suzuki instruction is like in your town is to see the people doing it. I have seen some astonishingly bad teaching done under the name of Suzuki, and also some very good teaching. See and decide for yourself.

On the whole, though, it is safe to say that Suzuki instruction in this country has become very rigid. And whether because of this or for other reasons, it certainly is not producing the kind of results that we were told it once produced in Japan. Some very fine string players are coming out of Suzuki training, no question about it. But there are very few 6- to 8-year-old American children who can play the Bach Double Concerto. If you hear large numbers of Suzuki children playing in this country, what you are more likely to hear are simple variations of "Twinkle, Twinkle, Little Star," which (for good enough musical reasons) has become a kind of Suzuki national anthem. The organization and the method are certainly doing some good things, but much less than they apparently once did in Japan, and what is more to the point, much less than they could do here if they really practiced what they preach—that is, helped children to learn music in the same way that they once learned language.

What then is so good about Suzuki materials and methods, and why are we adding them to our list and recommending them to parents?

1) Their musical selections are very good. They are playable—not too hard and not too easy. They are fun to play, and what is just as important for the

parents who will have to hear them over and over again, they are fun (or at the very worst, at least tolerable) to hear. The children are very soon playing pieces written by the great masters. Some have objected that what the children play are simplified versions of what these composers wrote, but I see no objection to that. A child I know well has already moved from a simplified version of a Bach piece to one much closer to the real thing. It doesn't cause her any problems and I don't see why it should. She just thinks that a piece she already liked has become even more interesting.

2) There are recordings (see the review following this one) available of good performances of the music that the children will be playing. I suspect that most parents don't play these as much as they might or should; still, with these recordings you *can* do Suzuki as it was supposed to be done, that is, you can make it possible for your children to really know these tunes *before* they start trying to play them, so that, as in learning to talk, they can correct their own mistakes rather than have to have parents or teachers do this for them. One of the things American Suzuki teachers do that seems to me a complete mistake is to put little pieces of tape on the violin (or viola or cello) fingerboard so that children (or their parents) can tell by looking at them where the fingers are supposed to go. This is musical nonsense; it is our *ears*, not our eyes, that are supposed to tell us where to put our fingers.

3) The children become members of a musical community. In a performing art, like music, the uniform curriculum for which the schools so mistakenly strive in other areas actually makes sense. Wherever a Suzuki child goes, she will find that other Suzuki children at about her level of skill know the same pieces she does, *so they can play them together*, which is fun for the children and beyond that is one of the chief joys of music. Learning a musical instrument, at least until you got good enough to play in a band or orchestra, used to be a rather lonely business for children. Now it doesn't have to be. Not only do the Suzuki teachers in a community have their pupils play together every week or so, but there are in addition even larger gatherings of children, often hundreds of them, at various Suzuki conferences. These can be enormously exciting to the children. The actual classes and workshops may or may not be interesting, but in between them the children can rush around and play with other children all the music they know. One mother of two very talented children, who has gone to several of these big get-togethers, says that the best things that happen there, as far as the children are concerned, are the things that are not planned—informal, spontaneous music-making with other children. For me this is a very important asset, and one which outweighs any objections I have to the program.

So I think that the Suzuki materials and organization can be a very useful resource—*one of many*—for children learning music, and their parents (perhaps also learning music). The trick is to make use of those materials, but not restrict yourself to them. Branch out: encourage the children to improvise freely, to make up tunes, to write down tunes, to write compositions for each other to play, to begin as soon as possible to play real chamber music, which so far does not play a very big part in formal Suzuki instruction—though this may be changing, as it should and as I hope it is.

In short, put back into learning music the exploration, the discovery, the adventure, and above all the joy and excitement that is properly a part of it, and that too formal and rigid instruction can only kill.—JH

Suzuki Records Here

Violin-Varieties and *Recital Favorites* ($11 each + postage: 75¢ for 1, $1 for 2). These two recordings include the music from the first *two* books of the Suzuki violin and piano instruction series. The same company makes several other recordings in each series, to go with the later Suzuki books; if there is enough interest, we will add the later recordings, along with the later books, to our list.

A similar set of recordings has been produced in Japan, and is distributed here by Summy-Birchard, who publish the written music. But all the Suzuki people I know feel that the recordings produced in this country are quite a bit better—as well as somewhat cheaper—so these are the ones we have chosen.

As far as I know, the company has not yet produced any recordings to go with the cello, viola, or flute written music, but perhaps these will be available soon. We will let you know if we find out.—JH

Other Books Available Here

Women of the West, by Cathy Luchetti ($23.50 + post). This is one of the most unusual, beautiful, informative, and thought provoking books about history that I have ever seen, a book about what I call True History, as opposed to the textbook history that I, and I suppose most children, studied and still study in school. A British historian once said, very aptly, "History is the propaganda of the victors." We could as well say that it is the study of What The Big Shots Did. Reading it, one would hardly think there had ever lived anyone except kings, generals, and an occasional religious leader or two. What ordinary people did, how they worked, how they lived their lives, above all how they felt about their lives, is something we almost never find out.

This is as true of the history of our own West as of the kingdoms and empires of Europe. The textbook history of our West is almost entirely the history of men engaged in romantic and dangerous occupations and exploits—explorers, soldiers, gold-seekers, gunfighters, sheriffs, cowboys, miners. This, though true enough, is only a small part of the truth. Most of the true history of the West is a history of work, cruelly hard work done in a bitter and hostile environment, and much of this work was done by women. In this book, after a very interesting general description of the lives of pioneer women, we meet eleven of those women, and through their diaries, journals, and letters, hear the story of their own lives—the story of the Little House books as they might have been if Laura Ingalls Wilder's mother, the gentle and shadowy Caroline, had written them.

Along with the text, in itself fascinating, are reproductions of about a hundred photographs taken at the time. With a few wonderful exceptions—two women galloping on horseback at top speed, two little girls whispering and giggling to each other at school—the photographs are mostly stiff and formal portraits of women or their families, usually in front of the tiny sod or dugout houses or log cabins they lived in. Somehow these photos, in their many shades of black and gray, and their absence of motion, convey more of the harshness of the landscape and hardness of the life than modern color photos could do.

Text and photos are beautifully laid out and printed in a book which, just as a book, is a work of the printer's art. I know it is a more expensive book than many individual families will feel they can buy. But families who get together very often, as more and more homeschoolers do, could join together to buy it for their joint use. I hope they will do so, and also will try to get their local public libraries to buy it. This beautiful book is one that should be widely known and read, and kept alive for future generations of children to read.

A Sand County Almanac, by Aldo Leopold ($2.50 + post). This book, first published in 1949, is one of the great classics of ecology—a word, by the way, invented more than a hundred years ago. It is among other things a book about a kind of biology, and a way of looking at biology, that has almost but not quite gone out of fashion, though we need it now even more desperately than when Leopold wrote.

Joseph Wood Krutch, himself a great naturalist and writer, once made a very interesting and important distinction in speaking about biology. He spoke of the difference between "inside" biology and "outside" biology. "Inside" biology, the kind now very much in fashion, consists in exploring, with electronic microscopes and other exotic tools, the innermost parts, the very cells and genes of living creatures, to find out how these parts work and how to make them work differently—presumably better. "Outside" biology consists of trying to observe living things as they appear in nature, disturbing them as little as possible, to find out how they relate to each other, and we to all of them. "Inside" biology seeks to understand nature so that we may change and control it; outside biology seeks to understand it so that we may live harmoniously within it.

I had feared that the inside biologists, whose doings are in the headlines every week or so, had won the battle, and that outside biology was no longer a respectable science or perhaps even an active one at all. So I was greatly encouraged to read in the *New York Review of Books* of 1/20/83 a book review by a Professor of Biology and Zoology at Harvard named R. C. Lewontin. Reviewing the books *Against Biological Determinism* and *Towards A Liberatory Biology*, (both of which I plan to read, if they are not too technical), he writes:

What is surely the most powerful and influential metaphor-become-real in Western civilization was provided in 1637 by Rene Descartes. . . . It is the organism as machine.

What has happened since 1637 is that, in the minds of natural scientists and a large fraction of social scientists as well, the world has ceased to be *like* a machine, but instead is seen as if it were a machine. Cartesian reductionism, which regards the entire world of things as, in fact, a very complicated electro-mechanical device, is not simply the dominant mode of thought in natural science, but the only mode to enter the consciousness of the vast majority of modern scientists. It is no exaggeration to say that most scientists simply do not know how to think about the world except as a machine.

The natural historical approach to understanding the world consists in attempting to reconstruct the causes of events from observing systems in their normal state of motion or stasis. The experimental approach, on the other hand, uses perturbation as its primary tool. The object under study is pushed, picked, and nicked, bits and pieces are removed, foreign agents added and the normal working of the system generally disturbed in the hope that its response to these alterations will reveal its inner workings. The Cartesian reductionist view confuses the nature of the perturbation itself with the "cause" of the system's normal functioning. A Russian story tells of the psychologist who proves that fleas hear with their legs by training them to jump on command, and then observing that they no longer respond when their legs are amputated.

As the term is defined in this elegant comparison, Aldo Leopold was a natural historian. He liked to observe living things—plants, trees, birds, fish, animals—in their natural state, disturbing them (except for some occasional fly fishing) as little as possible. As a result of a lifetime of this kind of gentle and respectful observation, he was able to see what the inside biologist, the experimenter, the perturber, the tinkerer, never sees, which is the enormous number of interconnections between living things, and the many ways in which a small and supposedly unimportant change in one place may later, perhaps much later, bring about an important change in another.

Because he could see that tinkering with nature was risky and could lead to unexpected, unwanted, and irreversible results, but even more because he loved the variety and beauty of all the living creatures he saw, Leopold at the end of his book called for "a land ethic," which, as he put it, "changes the role of *Homo sapiens* from conqueror of the land community to plain member and citizen of it. It also implies respect for his fellow members, and also respect for the community as such." Later he writes: "It is inconceivable to me that an ethical relation to land can exist without love, respect, and admiration for land, and a high regard for its value. By value I of course mean something far broader than mere economic value; I mean value in the philosophical sense." Almost forty years later we still do not have a land ethic, though we perhaps have more people who see the need for one. One of the important reasons we don't have it is that most people, without being scientists, have absorbed through the skin or learned in school the supposedly scientific notion that everything, including every living thing, is just some kind of a machine. How can one, and more important, *why should one*, love a machine? Machines are for us to use for our own benefit, aren't they? What else would they be for?

But I run the risk of giving the impression that the book is a collection of sermons about ecology. It is not, though there are sermons in it. Mostly, it is a book of descriptions. For a while we look through the keen, informed, and loving eyes of Leopold at many different parts of our country, including the "barren" Sand County in Wisconsin, which most of us would otherwise consider uninteresting and not worth looking at. Because Leopold sees so much, and enjoys so much what he sees, and learns so much from it, we who read him will in our future contacts with nature see and learn and enjoy more than we did before.

The book has many illustrations of plants and animals, mostly in pencil, some in ink, by Charles Schwartz. They are so accurate, detailed, and full of life that we can easily imagine that we are seeing these drawings in color. My goodness, if I could draw like that I would never be without a pencil in my hand.

Generally Speaking—How Children Learn Language, by Ronald Macaulay ($9.95 + post). This is a very short—the text is only 61 pages long— very perceptive, interesting, wise, and witty book. I had met Dr. Macaulay in Nov. '82 when I spoke at Pitzer College, in Claremont, Calif., of which he was then acting Dean. We enjoyed each other's company, he was interested in and sympathetic to what I had to say about homeschooling, and as I left he gave me a copy of his book. On page 2 I found this:

> As adults we do not have a set of ready-made utterances from which to choose when we wish to speak. Instead we have the ability to produce and understand utterances we have never heard before. For example, it is unlikely that anyone will have heard the following sentence previously: "Karl Marx was playing bridge with Abraham Lincoln, Winston Churchill, and Mary Queen of Scots when Tarzan walked in."

At this bit of dry Scottish wit I began to feel that I was going to have to have this book for our list.

This is also a very scholarly book by an expert in the field—Dr. Macaulay has long been a Professor of Linguistics, and in the back of his book he has listed almost six pages, in very fine print, of references to other experts like himself. Since he is saying, as I have for years, that children learn to speak not by some combination of rote learning and blind imitation, but by the most careful listening and creative thinking, his book can be very valuable to many parents who do not want their children subjected to the blind rote learning that is the norm in so many schools. When I say that children, in their explorations of the world of language, act like very capable scientists, most educators find it easy to dismiss the idea as the work of a non-expert and a "romantic"— if not an outright nut. It will not be so easy for them so to dismiss Dr. Macaulay.

The book can be useful to parents in a number of ways. To those who have not observed at first hand the process by which children master language, or who never gave much thought to the process going on under their noses, it will make clearer to them the meaning of what their child is doing, and so enable them to share in this great human adventure. To all of them it will show what many, but not all, know by instinct— how important it is to listen to what little children say, to make every effort to understand them, to answer their questions as far as we can. And to parents wanting to teach their own children, and preparing for the schools a statement of their educational ideas and plans, it will furnish many valuable quotes, such as this, from page 1: ". . . it is obvious that the child does not learn language like a parrot by memorizing whole utterances." Or this, from page 61: "[helping a child develop linguistic competence] means creating a situation in which the child can be his or her natural self: happy, curious, and talkative."—JH

Editors—John Holt & Donna Richoux
Managing Editor—Peg Durkee
Advertising Director—Pat Farenga
Subscriptions & Books—Mark Pierce
Office Assistant—Mary Van Doren

Growing Without Schooling 33

May 1983

Since *GWS* 32 went to press I have spoken to many meetings that (because they were arranged later) were not listed on my schedule. On my April trip to California, along with listed meetings at Chico, I spoke in Marin County (wonderfully green after all that rain), San Francisco, Nevada City, and Eureka. On my May trip, along with the listed meetings, I spoke in Carson City NV, and San Diego. On a very quick trip in late May, I spoke to a number of good meetings at Georgia Southern College in Statesboro GA.

Thanks to a tremendous amount of good work by Nancy Plent and Meg Johnson (and in part to perfect weather), the May meeting of New Jersey homeschoolers was a great success—over 200 people came, with many children of all ages. Eric Plent was our capable sound engineer, and Corinne and Melissa Johnson did good work at the registration desk.

On the way to California in April I appeared in Detroit on the popular local TV show *Kelly & Co.* On the day that the newspapers announced the report of the President's Commission on Education (of which there is more later in this issue), Susan Stanberg of *All Things Considered* from National Public Radio interviewed me about it. The following day CBS *Sunday Morning* and the *Donahue* show both asked me to appear the following week, but since I was going to be on the West Coast I was not able to.

I have also been on radio shows in Saskatoon, St. Paul, San Antonio, and Boston. I also did one interview for the magazine *Learning Today*, and another for the largest English language magazine in Japan. Not sure yet when these will appear.

While I was in Sacramento, Jane Williams (CA) and I had a very pleasant and interesting meeting with Janet McCormack, the Private Schools Liaison officer for the State Department of Education. She was very interested, well informed, and helpful—she really knows how California government works. From what she told us, it seems likely that, for the time being at least, we will probably not be able to get any significant homeschooling legislation through the California legislature. On the other hand, we may not need to; the homeschooling picture looks much better than a few months ago.

Around the country, the picture remains mixed; in some states, homeschooling has become easier, in others the state authorities still seem to be looking for ways to put a stop to it. It is still and probably will be for some time an important part of our job to convince the schools that homeschooling is not a threat to them. In this connection, we keep getting good responses to my article in the *Phi Delta Kappan* (see *GWS* 32), one even coming from as far away as Germany.

Near the end of March I spent a weekend visiting the Wallaces in Ithaca NY, and there saw the last three of nine public performances of Ishmael Wallace's musical play (his second), "I Love You More Than a Grapefruit Squirts." It was a delight, and a well-deserved success, interesting, dramatic, and very funny. I hope by the next issue of *GWS* to be able to offer tapes of the performance and a complete script.

More good news from the Wallace family— Nancy found a publisher for her book on homeschooling, the Swedish firm Larson, which is beginning to publish in the U.S. The book is called *Better Than School,* and will be published in November. Congratulations to Nancy and the family!

Here in Boston we have a big change in the office. Our old friend and colleague Peggy Durkee, whom many of you know in person or at least over the phone, was suddenly offered the job of Office Manager by the company she worked for before she came to work here, fourteen years ago, the same company that handles the mailing of *GWS*. It was an offer far too good to turn down, and one we could never hope to match here, much as we would like to. So she will have left by the time you read this.

Fortunately for us all, Pat Farenga, who will be getting married in August, was in a position to (and eager to) work full-time, so he will be taking over

Peggy's duties and responsibilities. For a while we will be even busier than ever here, but we are all sure that the transition will go smoothly.

Please note in the Directory that we have a new address for both the Canadian Alliance of Homeschoolers and Education Otherwise in Great Britain.

To those who found *GWS* 32 a bit hard to read, my apologies. I thought that green would be a nice color for spring, but the ink turned out to be paler in print than I had expected from the sample. For the time being we'll stay with the blue, which people seem to like, though we may try some other colors later.

You will see from the reviews that we are adding our first musical instruments to our mail-order list. Hope you like these; in time we may add others.—John Holt

John's Coming Schedule

June 24, 1983: Center for Innovation in Education, Saratoga CA. Contact: Susan Iwamoto, CIE, 19225 Vineyard Ln, Saratoga CA 95070.

June 28–30: 7th Annual Kephart Memorial Child Study Center Symposium, Univ. of Northern Colorado, Aspen/Snowmass, CO. Contact: Dr. Robert Reinert, KMCSC, UNC, Greeley CO 80639; 303-351-2691.

July 21–23: Homesteaders Good Life Get-Together. Contact Sherrie & Norm Lee, Homesteaders News, Naples NY 14512.

July 30–31: West Virginia homeschoolers. Contact Jan Evergreen, Rt 1 Box 352, Alderson WV 24910.

Aug. 1–2: Child Development Symposium, Assoc. for Research & Enlightenment, Virginia Beach, VA. Contact: Robert Witt, PO Box 595, Va. Bch. 23451; 804-428-3588.

Anyone who wants to coordinate other meetings or lectures around these times and locations should contact Pat Farenga.

Wisconsin Supreme Court Ruling

From the Wisconsin News-Tribune & Herald, *4/27/83:*

A Wisconsin Supreme Court ruling Tuesday that the state's private school attendance law is unconstitutional apparently will deter prosecution of at least four "home schools" in Douglas County.

The high court said the law is "impermissibly vague" and could not be used in prosecutions involving attendance or non-attendance at private schools.

The ruling could affect at least three children in the Superior School District who have been considered truant, according to Joseph Regina, director of student services for the district. He said the children are attending private schools set up by their parents last school year but not sanctioned by the state.

Douglas County District Attorney Keith Peterson said similar cases have been raised in three other districts around the county, though charges are pending in only one.

In Tuesday's decision, the court directed that the Iowa County Circuit Court dismiss two misdemeanor convictions against Laurence Popanz, who was convicted of failure to send two daughters to a public or private school.

Popanz, a member of the Agency for the Church of the Free Thinker, Inc., had two daughters enrolled in the Free Thinker School, a private school in Avoca.

The local school district administrator refused to recognize the school as a private school because it was not listed in the "Wisconsin Nonpublic School District Directory" issued by the state Department of Public Instruction.

There is no requirement in state law or administrative regulations requiring that private schools be so listed, the Supreme Court said in a decision written by Justice Shirley Abrahamson.

"The administrator testified that the listing requirement was a matter of his own 'professional' standards," she wrote.

"Due process," she said, "requires that the law set forth fair notice of the conduct prohibited or required and proper standards for enforcement of the law adjudication."

[JH:] This is the first case I know of in which a state supreme court has overturned such a law on grounds of vagueness, so it will probably be useful to continue to make this point and to cite this ruling in support.

New Montana Law

The state of Montana has just passed a law which specifically permits home education. From an article by Ginny Baker in the newsletter of the Montana Homeschoolers Association (the actual words of the bill are underlined; other remarks are Ginny's):

[The law] will go into effect July 1, 1983, and will have the following provisions. A child between the ages of 7 and 16 must attend a public school unless the child is "enrolled in a nonpublic or home school that complies with the provisions of Section 2" of this bill. "For the purposes of this subsection (f), a home school is the instruction by a parent of his child, stepchild, or ward in his residence, and a nonpublic school includes a parochial, church, religious, or private school." To qualify for exemption, Section 2 states "a nonpublic or home school shall:

1. "maintain records on pupil attendance and disease immunization and make such records available to the county superintendent or schools on request." The parent merely must keep these records, even if he does not immunize his children.

2. "provide at least 180 days of pupil instruction or the equivalent in accordance with 20-1-301 and 20-1-302." These sections define 180 days of instruction to include at least 2 hours for preschool and kindergarten, 4 hours for grades 1 through 3, and 6 hours for grades 4 through 12.

3. "be housed in a building that complies with applicable local health and safety regulations." It is the intent of the legislature that if your home is safe enough to live in, it is safe enough to hold your home school in. This subsection should have no effect on the home school except for local zoning laws for all homes.

4. "provide an organized course of study that includes instruction in the subjects required of public schools as a basic instructional program pursuant to 20-7-111." The homeschooler may provide his own course of study that includes these subject areas: *Elementary school* (grades K–6): language arts (reading, writing, speaking, listening, spelling, penmanship, English); arithmetic (oral and written); science and conservation; social sciences (geography, history of the US, state history, agriculture, economics); fine arts (music and art); physical education; safety (including fire prevention); health education. *Junior high school* (grades 7–9): language arts, social sciences, mathematics, science, health and physical education, fine arts, practical arts (2 years). *High school* (grades 9–12): language arts, social sciences, mathematics, science, health and physical education, fine arts, practical arts (home economics, industrial arts, business, or agriculture), electives.

5. "in the case of home schools, notify the county superintendent of schools of the student's attendance at the school." It appears the parent who operates a home school must take the initiative to notify the county superintendent of the student(s)' attendance at such school. Montana takes no census of school-age children. The legislature included this subsection because it felt it had to keep

track of our children.

Home educators in Montana do not have to submit their children to testing of any kind. Nonpublic teachers do not have to be "certified." The home school curriculum and textbooks need no approval by anyone as long as the parent affirms that they include the above mentioned subjects. Any parents who claim to teach their children at home yet do not are "non-schoolers," not homeschoolers, and would be liable for prosecution under the current truancy laws. I recommend that all home educators get a copy of Revised Law 20-5-102, MCA to keep on hand in case you are challenged by local authorities who are unaware of the change that legalizes home education in Montana.

Victory In Alberta

The Calgary Herald, *3/17/83:*

A Calgary courtroom echoed with cheering Wednesday as a provincial judge found Pastor Larry Jones is not guilty of contravening School Act regulations by keeping his children out of a board-controlled school.

Judge Douglas Fitch ruled it is "the right of every person" to give efficient educational instruction to his children.

He based his ruling on Section 143 of the act and Section 7 of the federal Charter of Rights.

Section 143 of the School Act "preserves" the right of parents to educate their children outside a certified school, he ruled.

The section says children can be excused from attending a certified public school if an application by parents is granted by a superintendent of schools, or a Department of Education inspector feels the children are being properly instructed at home or elsewhere.

But defense lawyer Phillip Carr argued there is nothing in the act which says parents have to apply for such an exemption. He also said Jones's books have always been open for inspection.

"School authorities declined to send in their inspectors but (sent) school attendance officers" to explain to Jones he was breaking the law, Fitch said in his judgment.

Fitch also said Jones's rights were infringed upon under Section 7 of the Charter of Rights which says "everyone has the right to life, liberty and security of the person and the right not to be deprived thereof except in accordance with the principles of fundamental justice."

Since the school officials who challenge Jones's right to educate his children are the same officials who decide, under Section 143 of the School Act if his school provides proper instruction, that contradicts the notion of "fundamental justice," referred to in the Charter of Rights, the judge said.

The judge also ruled that in broad terms, the School Act doesn't infringe on freedom of religion.

One of the designers of the Alpha Omega curriculum, a Christian-based correspondence-type program which Jones uses, testified Wednesday the same curriculum is used in more than 2,000 schools in 20 countries.

Harold Wengert, also president of the Texas company which distributes the curriculum, said students who have taken the program often score much higher on university entrance exams than students who follow regular school-based programs.

Linda Matsalla, who performs psychological and educational testing for Foothills Educational Services, testified that an assessment of Jones's three daughters who currently attend his school showed all three scored average or well above average on achievement tests set for their grade level.

In some areas the oldest daughter, Laura, and the youngest, Alison, were three grades ahead of the standards of students the same age in a public school.

"It was a good victory but it's not over yet. We'll still fight it," Jones said, referring to charges which may yet be laid against him by the Department of Education for running his school.

President's Commission Report

The President's Commission on Excellence In Education has recently issued a report, entitled "A Nation At Risk," on the state of our public schools. In report card terms, they gave them an F. Among other things, they said that if a foreign country had done to us what our public schools have done to us, we might well consider it an act of war. Strong words.

What did the Commission recommend? Same old stuff—a longer school year, tougher courses, fewer electives, higher standards (code for "flunk more kids"), better teachers, more money.

A number of people, beginning with Susan Stanberg of NPR's *All Things Considered*, have asked me what I thought about the report. Among other things, I said:

The report was no surprise. If you set up a commission to study U.S. transportation, and put on the commission only General Motors executives, naturally they will say that what we need is more cars, better roads, cheaper gas, etc. This commission, being made up of people in the school business, naturally said that the remedy for our problems was more school.

The report was nothing new. Every commission that has taken a broad look at the schools since the end of World War II has said exactly the same thing. We had national crises in the schools in the late '40s, in the '50s when Sputnik went up, in the early '60s, again in the late '60s, in the early '70s when we went "Back To Basics"—that movement is now about ten years old—and almost continuously since then. There probably never was a time since universal compulsory public schools were invented when any overall look at what they were doing would have given them a good report.

The report will probably not do much of anything, but if it does, will do mostly harm. After all, if the medicine is what is making you sick, more of the same medicine will only make you sicker. The medicine, as I have said for many years, is Coerced, Controlled, Competitive Learning, which destroys most of the desire and capacity for learning of almost all on whom it is inflicted, even those who are good at school.

But, I was asked, won't it do some good if we just spend more money on schools. No. If you start from Chicago to go to San Francisco, and assume that it is due south, the further and faster you go, the worse off you will be. The schools are operating on the basis of fundamentally wrong assumptions about children, learning, and teaching, and as long as they do, the harder they try, the worse they will do. They assume that children will not learn unless made to and cannot learn unless shown how, and that the way to make them learn is to give them a lot of disconnected little "facts" to memorize and punish them if they fail. This never worked and never will.

The correct assumptions, as our readers learn every day from their own experiences with their children, are that children love to learn, are very good at it, and, like scientists, do it by looking at the world around them, asking themselves questions about it, and making up or finding, and then testing, their answers to these questions. Efforts to coerce, control, and measure this process simply turn it off, for the vast majority of children. Until the schools learn this and act on it, they will remain where they have been for eighty or more years now—in serious trouble.

Aside from that, the effect of every one of these reports, and indeed all efforts to legislate improvement in education, is to take away from teachers the power to run their own classrooms as they see fit, and so to drive most of the best of them out of teaching, since they won't stand for other people, most of whom have never done any teaching, telling them what to do in their classrooms and constantly checking up on them to be sure they do it. Telling teachers how to teach does not make bad teachers good; it only makes good teachers furious, and as the record shows, they don't put up with it for long.

Will this report, and the Democrats' hastily thrown together answer to it, help or hurt homeschooling? Perhaps some of both. The report will certainly give us an answer to the schools' claim that only they are competent to teach our children. But it may also breed a swarm of new curriculum requirements which could seriously limit our right to teach our children as we think best. Time will tell.—JH

Encouragement From California

[JH:] I received a very encouraging letter just the other day from Dr. Lynn P. Hartzler, Program Manager, Alternative Education and Independent Study, California Dept of Education, 721 Capitol Mall, Sacramento CA 95814, saying in part:

This is to acknowledge and thank you for your letter to Bill Honig, Superintendent of Public Instruction. Mr. Honig has asked me to write to you because I have been assigned the responsibility for alternative programs including homeschooling. We concur with the observation that home and public schools may exist in a mutually cooperative and supportive relationship. . . . At present there is much that can be done legally under the Independent Study option provided the local school authority adopts the required policy and procedures. Our position has been to encourage school boards and administrators to try to accommodate parents who request homeschooling under the existing Independent Study legislation.

[JH:] Along with this, Dr. Hartzler sent me a copy of a letter he or she wrote to some parents who had written their Assemblyman, Don Sebastiani, about homeschooling. This letter (a copy was sent to Mr. Sebastiani) says in part:

We are pleased with your report of success in conducting a home school last year for the benefit of one child and the mother. There is no doubt that homeschooling can be a fine experience especially for young children when the conditions are favorable, as they seem to have been in your case. It is our operational policy to encourage school district officials to attempt to accommodate parents who are willing and able to conduct home schools to do so via the Independent Study process. This is a legal option for citizens in California which safeguards school interests while allowing homeschooling on a conditional basis. . . . This office will be pleased to supply parents and school officials information and assistance in taking advantage of this option.

[JH:] I think California families would be wise to explore and pursue this Independent Study option *before* considering registering their own homes as private schools, for reasons I discuss in the article "Private School Option," page 24.

South Dakota Amends Law

[DR:] *I wrote to the South Dakota legislature and to some* GWS *readers in that state, trying to find out more about the 1981 homeschooling law and the possible repeal that we mentioned in* GWS *32. Shirley Frederick (SD) wrote back:*

The S.D. law you refer to is better known as the Christian Schools bill. It was promoted by various religious groups that wanted to set up schools without meeting state requirements for accreditation. Homeschooling was included in the bill. The legislature agreed . . . as long as the children were to be tested annually and demonstrated academic progress.

The sponsor of the original 1981 bill came back to the legislature in '83 to amend the law— apparently the supporters of the original bill didn't keep their end of the bargain and some children received no instruction whatsoever. Other children received dogmatic training under harsh conditions. The '83 fight was bitter—harsh words, name-calling, recriminations, bizarre demonstrations, and shady tactics. Legislators supported by the S.D. Education Association tried to require teacher certification for the "Christian schools." The compromise bill passed on the last day.

[DR:] The staff attorney at the S.D. State Capitol sent a copy of the amendments as they were passed in the 1983 session:

Be it enacted by the legislature of the state of South Dakota:

Section l. That S. 13-27-7 be amended to read as follows:

13-27-7. All applications for excuse from school attendance shall be on a standard form acknowledged before a notary or two witnesses. The form shall be provided by the state superintendent of elementary and secondary education. If the application is granted, a certificate of excuse also provided by the superintendent of elementary and secondary education shall be issued by the president of the school board having jurisdiction over the district in which the child has school residence, stating the reason for the excuse and be for a period not to exceed one year. Upon a showing by the superintendent of elementary and secondary education that a child excused from school attendance pursuant to S. 13-27-3 is not being instructed in compliance with 13-27-3, the school compliance with 13-27-3, the school board may immediately revoke the child's certificate of excuse.

All tests scores required by S. 13-27-3 shall be kept on file in the public school of the district where the child has school residence. If subsequent achievement test results reveal less than satisfactory academic progress in the child's level of achievement, the school board may refuse to renew the child's certificate of excuse.

Section 2. That S. 13-27-3 be amended to read as follows:

13-27-3. A child shall be excused from school attendance, pursuant to 13-27-2, because the child is otherwise provided with competent alternative instruction for an equivalent period of time, as in the public schools, in the basic skills of language arts and mathematics. The parent or guardian of the child shall identify in the application the place where the child shall be instructed and the individual or individuals who will instruct the child. The individuals are not required to be certified but the state superintendent of elementary and secondary education may investigate and determine if the instruction is being provided by a competent person. The child shall annually take a nationally standardized achievement test of the basic skills. The test shall be the same test designated to be used in the public school district where the child is instructed and may be monitored by a designee from the local school district where the child is instructed. The test shall be provided by the school district where the child is instructed. The superintendent of elementary and secondary education or his designee may visit any alternative education program at reasonable times during the school year.

Section 3. That Chapter 13-27 be amended by adding thereto a new section to be read as follows:

If a child of compulsory school age [who] has been attending an unaccredited school in another state or country or [who] has been receiving alternative instruction pursuant to 13-27-3 enrolls in a public school in this state, the child shall be placed at the child's demonstrated level of proficiency as established by one or more standardized tests. However, a child's placement may not be in a grade level higher than warranted by the child's chronological age assuming entry into the first grade at age six. [A similar provision for secondary students follows.]

More Legislative News

California: According to Jane Williams of the *California Home Education Clearinghouse*, some homeschoolers discussed the possibility of homeschool legislation with a State Assemblyman, an assistant to a State Senator, Janet McCormick of the Department of Education, a couple of lobbyists, and the general counsel for the Seventh Day Adventists. The general advice was that any homeschooling bill would be unlikely to pass, partly because the California Teachers Association was very powerful. They also advised that homeschooling legislation might bring more problems to the homeschooling movement, in the form of controls and aggressive opposition.

Illinois: Deb Martin of *HOUSE* writes, "Yes, we are aware of the 'Informational Report and Preliminary Recommendations Regarding the State's Relationship to Illinois Nonpublic Schools' [*GWS* 31]. There have been hearings throughout the state. What disturbs us most about this is that they want to make it mandatory for all nonpublic and home schools to register with the state. It is voluntary now. We are suggesting that people write their senators and representatives. . . . There is another study, 'Phase I Mandates Studies Final Staff Recommendations Presented to the Illinois State Board of Education Planning and Policy Committee.' In this they are trying to redefine schooling. Some of our people have appeared at hearings on this. The definition of schooling is a *formal process* which has as its primary purpose the *systematic transmission* of knowledge and culture, whereby children learn in areas fundamental to their continuing development. 'Formal' and 'systematic' are the words we object to. Also in this report they want to lower the mandatory school age. . . ."

Kansas: Jeanne Kasten writes, "Several months ago I was told about a group of homeschoolers in Wichita, and I attended a meeting in February. About 30 adults came. . . . There was some discussion of a bill which was pending which would have put restrictions on private schools and would have been bad news for those who had established private schools of their own. . . . We all wrote letters the following week and the bill never even made it to committee."

Jeanne continued, "After the meeting . . . I threw out the idea of writing our own bill, based on the 'legislative proposal' in *GWS* 30. Several people jumped at the idea. . . . At the March meeting . . . we spent the time familiarizing ourselves with the proposal. . . . I have written about half a dozen letters since that March meeting—to the Eagle Forum, to the lawyer who handled a homeschooling case, and to others I think might be interested. So far I have no responses. Anyone who wants to contact me on this may write or call (316-263-0225).

Louisiana: Rep. Louis "Woody" Jenkins writes, "Regarding the Private Education Deregulation Act here in Louisiana, it is true that for a time I urged people to utilize the 'private school' option in the act, instead of the 'home study' option in the same law. This was because the State Board of Elementary and Secondary Education (BESE) was attempting to impose additional regulations on home study parents, *contrary to law*. . . . BESE *did* rescind its regulations and institute a simple, one-page home study application form. Now I urge parents to use either the private school or the home study option. BESE is approving *all* home study applications.

"With respect to the possibility of the attorney general or some judge ruling that one-child private schools at home are illegal, the Louisiana attorney general has already ruled that they *are* legal under the Private Education Deregulation Act. . . ."

Minnesota: From Issue #1 of the *Minnesota Home Schooling Association Newsletter* ($5/year): "A major topic at the last few meetings was the possibility of introducing a bill to the Minnesota legislature to provide for homeschooling. We took John Holt's model bill as a starting point. It was decided not to introduce a bill at this time for three reasons: first, it would be difficult for homeschoolers to agree what should be put in the bill since each of us has diverse philosophies of education; second, a friendly legislator did not recommend we do this because once the bill was introduced it could be amended into something we don't want; third, one of the MHSA members gave (out) a copy of Arizona's homeschooling law which makes many restrictions on homeschooling which limited the freedom we wish for ourselves...."

Nevada: Kathy Erickson [*GWS* 32] wrote in early may that the testimony on March 29 before the State Legislature Education Committee "was surprising—we had 150 to 200 more people that we expected. The bill, we hope, will be out of Education Committee and on the Assembly floor this week. Then we will have testimony in the Senate. But the Legislature will close at the end of the month so we are pressured for time...."

Notes From Donna

New Reprints: We have two new reprints available here. One is John's "Legislative Proposal" from *GWS* 30; the other is a summary of the Massachusetts homeschooling situation that Tim Chapman put together before he left. Each is available for 10¢ (SASE required if you are not buying other material from us).

Questions: A reader asks if anyone knows where to pursue a doctorate in alternative education (including independent study and homeschooling).

Another reader would like to hear about any homeschooled twins, especially about the question of whether they grow too dependent on each other.

Thanks: Rena Caudle writes, "We want to thank you all very much for printing the article [*GWS* 31] about Jeremy," who had a brain tumor. "The response has been wonderful. It has been great for the kids." Rena had the marvelous news that Jeremy had "spontaneous remission"—at present there are no signs of the tumor.

I sent some books and magazines to Dr. K. D. Chauhan ["Request from India," GWS 29] and he wrote that when the children opened the package, "They were dancing here, having each copy of books and magazines in their hands and singing with joy and pleasures a unique wonderful and beautiful song with music of their own country hand instruments and drums in a circle.... After half an hour they became quiet and absorbed in magazines and I was pointing and hinting to make them understand...." Dr. Dhauhan especially appreciated the *National Geographics* we sent and hopes he can get more. If you can, please send materials to him at the Jagdish Society, Post Unjha 384170, N. Guj., India.

Finally, thanks to all those who have made a contribution, large or small, to our "Gift Sub Fund." Because of you, a dozen families are receiving *GWS* who could not otherwise afford it. When you give us extra money and say, "Keep the change," that's where it goes, and we hope these gifts will continue to come in.—Donna Richoux

Organizational News

All addresses will be found in the "Home Schooling Groups" list at the end of this issue. *New groups* on the list include *LEARN*, which publishes the *Rainbow Review*, Bloomington IN ($5/yr); *Michigan Association of Home Educators; San Fernando Valley Homeschoolers Association.*

Arizona: According to the *Arizona Families for Home Education* newsletter ($4/yr), the group will have a convention July 16, at Centennial Hall, 201 N Center, Mesa.

Arkansas: From the *Christian Home Education Association*: "We have a fast-growing group across our state at the present time. Several families have been challenged in various cities at the municipal court level have appealed the unjust rulings to Circuit Court. None have reached Circuit Court trial yet.... We have also had to fight proposed legislation this spring which would have defined private and parochial schools and placed several state "standards" upon all education, effectively shutting down home education. House Bill 554 ended up being referred to an Interim Education Committee between now and the 1985 legislative session.... We have published two issues of a statewide newsletter ($10/yr)."

California: Last year John Boston (CA) began organizing a "telephone network" across the state which was useful in alerting homeschoolers about legal news and events. If you would like to take part, write hi or phone 619-749-1522.

Florida: We have received information from the *Advanced Mindpower Institute*, 12522 Holyoke Av, Tampa FL 33624, a nonprofit organization and church with home education as a major religious principle.

Illinois: Deborah Martin of *HOUSE* wrote,

"You recommended that if homeschooling groups form, they stay very informal. . . . Our HOUSE groups have varied. The Chicago and the Lake County groups have usually had very informal meetings without an agenda or meeting topics. However, I found our DuPage County group needed to take a more formal approach or people who had previously attended meetings, or people who were actually homeschooling, would not return. . . . I have found it helpful for myself to have an agenda of group things to discuss. However, this has taken an awful lot of energy on my part. . . . I am looking forward to this summer as being a time of more informal meetings, possibly an open house.

Iowa: Barb Tetzlaff writes, "Our group, O!KIDS (Organization to Keep Iowa Deschoolers Strong) is really growing. . . . At our first meeting we had 49 adults and their children in attendance. It was really beautiful to see all the children socializing so nicely! Our son, Josh, said that it was the best day of his life! . . . We're planning a picnic for Independence Day.

New York: Peter Ackerman, now in Connecticut (RFD 1 Box 306, Kent 06757; 203-354-7003) says he gathered a great deal of information about the New York City school bureaucracy, regulations, etc., that should be most useful to would-be homeschoolers there, and he hopes they will contact him.

Oregon: From *Homeschoolers of Lane County*: We have formed a homeschooler group here in Eugene, involving about 10 or so families. It is a very informal and loose-knit gathering which we hold once a month. . . . At these meetings we share our homeschooling experience and any information involving legal or public school issues and whatever else people want to discuss. We also form field trips. . . . Each family will share with other families, one or two days a month, their particular field of expertise or interest. So far we have families willing to share home computer courses, first aid, goat care, typing, chemistry, nutrition, Spanish, bread dough art, baking, sewing, building, and farming

Utah: The *Utah Home Education Association's* Third Annual Convention will take place June 23–24 with guest speakers Raymond and Dorothy Moore, and Richard and Linda Eyre (advisors on President Reagan's Committee for Financing Elementary Education).

Washington: A group of homeschoolers, with the assistance of attorney Michael Ferris, have started the *Home School Legal Defense Association* (PO Box 1219, Olympia WA 98507). According to its brochure, "In the event that any legal action (or threats of legal action) are brought against a member family, the association will furnish free legal representation through the attorneys on staff or retained by the association. . . . Basic cost is $65 per year. . . . "

Wisconsin: Sue Brooks writes, "Chris Mayou and I are going to publish the *Wisconsin Regional Coalition of Alternative Community Schools Newsletter* beginning sometime in July. . . . I only hope it works—organizing has been *difficult* here due, in part, I think, to great differences in philosophy which seem to keep folks at arms' length. . . . Folks can send legal info to Chris (W8229 Tower St, Onalaska WI 54650) and general info on meetings or short paragraphs describing their dealings with their school district (please *name* that district) to me. Subscription orders ($10) can also be sent to me (Rt 2 Box 230, New Auburn WI 54757). . . ."—DR

An Ally in Colorado

Was delighted to hear the other day from my old friend Edward Pino in Colorado. Ed was for many years the Superintendent of the Cherry Creek School District (suburb of Denver), known nationally as one of the most innovative and by any measures successful school districts in the entire country. He retired from that post ten years ago, but is still active, energetic, and very interested in homeschooling. I asked him to find out for us what he could about the legal and administrative situation in Colorado. He very quickly replied with the following useful and encouraging information:

1) The Colo. Dept. of Education "monitors" homeschooling families, currently estimated at about 114, but essentially the Board's function is simply to provide information.

2) "Colo. law leaves responsibility to local boards, both authority and responsibility. Colo. law is very flexible and open to home study. . . ." The State Dept. of Ed. has no authority either to permit or forbid homeschooling, though of course they can always try to influence local boards to move one way or the other.

3) "Six boards out of 181 districts in the state have chosen to disapprove of home study for various reasons . . . if you want more help on this, let me know."

Since Ed is very well-known and highly respected among Colorado educators, his advice and help are likely to prove very helpful. Perhaps together we may before long find ways to bring around those few presently hostile school districts. A useful first step might be to put into the hands of the superintendents and board members copies of the *Phi Delta Kappan* article and our legislative proposal.—JH

Supporting Public Schools

From Pamela Pacula (CA):

Not knowing that I would not be sending my 4-year-son to the local public school, a neighbor called and asked me to help a group of mothers in their fight to keep the school in our area open.

The public school facility near us is in a very beautiful, serene location, surrounded by rolling hills and trees. The buildings are fairly new, and the children can see the lovely surroundings from inside their classrooms. I thought it was a shame that the children in our community might not be able to spend the better part of their days at this particularly beautiful school site, and was more than happy to help the other mothers take a survey to present to the school board.

As I called people from the list, some asked me as many questions as I asked them. When they found out that my son would not be going to public school, they invariably asked: "But why are *you* helping with the survey? Why do you care if the school remains open or not?"

I told them that I cared very much! I reminded them that the children who go to public school are part of the same society my children live in. They will become the adults my children will encounter when they enter adulthood—so how can I not care about their education, their health, and their happiness?! The people I spoke with were very pleased that I was willing to help.

I want others to know that I'm not being "elitist" or saying "To heck with society" by choosing to homeschool my child. I'm merely exercising my right to choose how *my* child is educated and raised. While helping with this survey I made some 5 new friends in the non-homeschool community. They saw that I was eager to help their children and they were supportive of my right to homeschool my child.

Four and a half years ago . . . I decided that when my youngest went to school, I would volunteer to teach French in his class. . . . Although I have since become firmly convinced that homeschool is best for Brian, still intend to volunteer (with Brian) to teach French at a local elementary school. I love the French language, I enjoy teaching young children, and feel it would be as beneficial to Brian and me as to the children.

[JH:] Many thanks to Pam for this very important letter. We are of course very eager to hear from parents whose local schools are working with and helping them; but we are equally eager to hear from parents who have found ways to cooperate and work with their local schools. For Pam is right—for a long time, the schools are going to be there, and most children are going to be going to them, and what happens to them there is going to affect the lives of all children, including homeschooled ones. It would be very short-sighted for us to assume that the worse things get in the schools, the better it will be for homeschooling. Quite the reverse.

Buying Our Books Helps

A reader told us that she and others she knew thought they were doing us a favor by *not* buying books from us—they thought—we didn't make any money from the books we sell and so they were saving us time and trouble. Well, let's clear this up without further ado. We do indeed make a profit on sales of books, and even at present levels of sales this profit makes a useful contribution to our total income. If we could double, and then double again, our book business, it would go a long way toward making *GWS* self-supporting, instead of depending very heavily, as we do now, on the uncertainties of the lecture and publishing business. There is no reason why we should not do this, since the list is already good enough so that many people, if they knew about it, might order many books from it even though they had no particular interest in homeschooling. Many people have told us that even though the Boston area is a great educational center, we offer a more varied and interesting set of books for and about children than they can find in any local bookstore—and we have many more good books and materials that we plan to add to the list as soon as we can.

In short, one of the easiest and most useful things that people can do to help *GWS* is to put our book list into the hands of as many people as possible, or otherwise make it known to them. To save on printing costs, we are designing a special short version of our list that will include descriptions of our most popular books. These will be ready by the time you read this, and you could help us a great deal by ordering a quantity of these short booklists (20/$1) and giving or sending them to people you know or with whom you have contact.

One possible thing to try—put classified ads in small local papers or magazines, asking people to send you a self-addressed stamped envelope and perhaps a small sum, 25¢ or so, to help cover the cost of the ad. For anything you can do along these lines, thank you very much—and if you find some particularly effective ways to distribute these lists, please let us know.

Another reader wondered how long after we reviewed a book in *GWS* could she still buy it from us. We continue stocking all titles as long as we can get them from the publishers, and only a few have gone out of print. Of course, many of the current prices are higher than what you'll find in the back issues of *GWS*. You can always get a free copy of our latest booklist by sending us a self-addressed, stamped envelope.—JH & DR

Life At Home

Kathy Lorimor (IL) writes:

We are now homeschoolers, and each day I think of a new benefit to our chosen course. Since Lisa is only kindergarten age now, she will not be required to enter school for two more years, when she is 7. This past summer Lisa taught herself to read and do math problems. In the past month she got interested in sign language, so we found a book at the library, and she is teaching herself. She has learned how to look words up in the Table of Contents and then find the page that she wants. She spent most of her birthday money to purchase the book, since the library couldn't let us keep it indefinitely. Her main desire for her birthday was a world map puzzle, since the US puzzle she received at age 4 is too easy. She daily practices 1–1½ hours on her cello with me, and then does up to an hour of piano on her own. Heather and Heidi are now 3 and watch Lisa very carefully.

My husband and I have noticed that the girls have stopped asking, "What can I do?", but more often say "May I . . .?", "Will you help me . . . .", and "Where can I find . . .?" They have become self-motivated in the home environment.

From Connie Colten (CA; GWS 29):

A few months ago, Shawn (8) was riding his bike on a weekday when two policemen stopped him and asked why he wasn't in school. He replied that he goes to homeschool. The police wanted to know what that was. Shawn told them that his mom teaches him at home. When they wanted to know why, Shawn told them it was because homeschooling was better than public schooling. That concluded the conversation as they didn't ask him for his name and address. The whole thing didn't seem to bother Shawn at all, but I must admit that I was a little upset.

Now, as to what the boys have been doing. Chris (11) has been on a Nancy Drew reading kick.

He also has read all of the Little House books. He found out some relatives are making money on the stock market so he and his father read about stocks and have some pretend shares to check in the newspaper. He is still very interested in sports and spends time watching games, sorting his playing cards, reading books about sports figures and playing the various games outdoors.

Devin (4) seems most interested in numbers lately. Chris taught him to play War with cards, and he quickly learned the lower and higher values involved there. Next he watched Chris and a friend play Stratego and he became obsessed with the game, wanting to play three to four times a day for two months.... Now he watches the digital clock, calling out the numbers. He also bought a book that he can "read" aloud, so he trades his story for the ones he wants us to read to him.

Shawn has been spending his time and money fixing up his bike. He saves and shops to get the equipment he wants. Money has taken on a value to him now that it didn't have before.

We were interviewed by a freelance writer on homeschooling. Chris and Shawn were very pleased to be questioned about their opinions. So far the article hasn't been published. Before the interview was finished Chris was interviewing the writer about being a writer!

Our homeschooling group meets weekly. It has offered an opportunity for social interaction for the boys as we moved here fairly recently. We have done some field trips with the group: visiting a vet's office, touring a bakery, picking apples, and going to the beach.

An art project of making piñatas was a disaster. Each boy wanted to make his own. We ended up covering very big balloons, so we papier-mâchéd for days. They dried funny and finally after a little painting, I came out on the porch to find the boys had smashed them open to get the goodies! I was glad to see the end of the whole project.

The boys have also been involved in my prenatal care. They come to the check-ups at the midwife's. They listen to the baby's heartbeat, have been shown how to measure the heartbeat and how to measure my iron count. We borrowed some childbirth films from the library to view.

From Miriam Mangione (NV):

Shanda (11) is doing fine at home—migraines have disappeared! We use the "open book" method for Calvert and employ other short cut methods as it's all non-essential information. She didn't like "learning to type"; however, she did learn the finger placement and *does type* when she wants to type up a play she wrote, etc. She spends most of her time reading, reading, reading; writing poetry, plays, cartoons; doing all the work in the house, yard, car repairs, fix-it jobs and child care; and just about everything else we do, she does too. The only time any of us were ever bored was when we were in school. Creativity leads to further creativity, so at home one thing just leads to another and we're always busy—even if it's *just* thinking.

Other than exceptional programs we watch very little TV. And I especially hate the Saturday fare of cartoons—I never liked them as a child—so they are never on. Shanda used to watch them years ago but I found she could not break away from their mesmerization and her temperament would change. Now she spends Saturdays at dance class and dressing up her baby sisters in costumes at home and they imitate her dancing, among other activities. *Anything* but cartoons!

We film a lot of their activities on our video camera and they watch themselves more than anyone else on television. Only thing is that the two-year-old doesn't know why she isn't on other people's televisions when she visits. She has an excellent vocabulary for a two-year-old and I think much of it came from just watching herself and the adults around her repeating their words and actions. We don't use it for any "educational" purpose; for us it's the best entertainment on TV!.

From Pam Gingold (CA):

I have a 6½-year-old son, Jeremiah, who is unschooled. I helped him learn how to read a couple of months short of his fifth birthday (I taught him phonics and he readied himself by doing jigsaw puzzles for two months straight—*literally,* he only wanted to do 150-piece puzzles day and night, then he picked up a second grade book and started to read). Now he reads at sixth grade level and spends 2–3 hours a day at it. We have thousands of books and magazines at home and we also go to the library every two weeks so he is free to dig up whatever information he can find. Mostly he is interested in historical fiction, biographies, and science.

He also thinks long division is nothing but great puzzles to figure out, and as far as adding and subtracting goes, he "looks it up in his head." ... He learned to write making NO NUKES signs and sometimes helps in the Alliance for Survival office doing mailings. He's sure we can stop war, he hates racial discrimination, sexual discrimination, etc.

I feel great about homeschooling. ... Now I know that if I know something I can teach it (if someone wants to learn it). It doesn't matter that I got rotten grades in high school and I didn't go to UCLA. I taught my neighbor's 8-year-old son to multiply and divide in *15 minutes* yesterday and his wonderfully trained teacher couldn't get him to learn his times tables (he didn't know what he was learning them for). I like things to make sense so I always make sense out of things for children.

Madalene Murphy (CT) wrote:

We began the school year rather structured because that's what Emily (8) suggested, and, although we hate to admit it now, we were more comfortable with that. The structure began to decay after the third day, until by Thanksgiving it had metamorphosed into a bulletin board with index cards that could be rearranged into any order and most cards were open to substitution or negotiation. One of Emily's favorite cards was a research question—sometimes very simple ("Was FDR a Democrat or a Republican?"), sometimes more complex ("How do frogs croak?")—which would send her on a search through our encyclopedias and other available books, and would often result in her finishing the encyclopedia entry even after she found the answer, and then looking for more books in the library on the subject, or at least involving Tom or me in a lengthy discussion ("What is a Democrat, anyway?").

Christian (6) is beginning to read and it is a beautiful thing to watch. In one of my "What if the school board . . . ?" moods I'll think for a moment that we should do some phonics exercises but then I listen to him and I realize, as he tries a new word, that he has learned a lot of phonics just by reading. Besides, we tried a beginning workbook for a while last fall until he looked up one day and said, "These sentences are really boring." He is primarily interested in woodworking and made all the Christmas presents he gave last year, ranging from spool holders to a box for his sister's doll clothes.

Clare (3) is involved in all the activities (even in the typing of this letter, as evidenced by the dots above). She decided that one of her goals for the next year would be to learn to read.

One of our primary sources of educational materials has been tag sales. About a month ago I picked up a "chemistry set" for $1.30 at one—no chemicals, just lots of beakers, test tubes, racks, and such. The kids have spent a couple of days, all day, messing around with them, mixing oil, water, flour, and dish detergent, recording what they observed. They want to expand this throughout the year.

We parents have found homeschooling demanding, primarily because we have had to change our value system. The more we learn about learning, the less time we spend over teaching. Ultimately, however, we are impressed with how efficient homeschooling is; in Emily's case, the elimination of the emotional static caused by school releases an impressive supply of energy that can keep her going from morning till night, pretending, arguing, fooling around, and even helping.

After spending a rather lonely winter in the sense that we seemed to be the only homeschooling family in the immediate area, we were quite surprised last spring to start getting phone calls from people who were interested in taking or keeping their children out of school. Many of them have now joined our *GWS* subscription.

From a New Jersey reader:

Homeschooling has given my children (8 and 6) and me the freedom and opportunity to accompany my husband on his many business trips. This takes a lot of coordination and patience on all our parts, but what better way for the children to learn those attributes! My husband's business plans are never set in stone, so our time schedules are always in limbo. A three-day trip can turn into a week or may be canceled at the last minute altogether. We trail a pop-up camper behind our van and cut expenses by camping when possible. I've always wondered what went through bellmen's heads when they see us to our hotel room followed by all our camping equipment. Finding an appropriate place to open up a wet tent in the middle of Chicago, Richmond, and Washington D.C. has been quite an experience, too! We're solving that problem and other inconveniences by purchasing a small R.V.

No matter where we go we can find a museum or historical site of interest. The children have grown an appreciation for their country's growth from visiting such places as Plymouth, Williamsburg, Old Salem, Washington D.C., Philadelphia, many national parks, and presidential libraries. . . . Both keep journals of their trips, and it's interesting to note the natural improvement in penmanship, sentence construction, grammar, and especially in their desire to write in general. They now don't think twice about sitting down and writing plays, stories, or poems.

Our trips have also influenced the children's play habits. More times than not, they will pretend that they are inventors, presidents, or park rangers instead of always playing school or nurse in stereotypical roles. . . . This carries over when we go to the library. Without my suggesting it, they usually seek out books having to do with a trip we just took or are planning to take. This could be anything from a geology book to a biography.

Our new TRS-80 color computer has taken the place of trips for the winter months. In three weeks' time, our son has learned enough to start programming. He started learning by systematically completing a chapter a day. By Chapter 7, he decided that he knew enough for his present needs and now types to his heart's content, and uses the index to find what specific language he needs. Our daughter's interest comes in spurts. She often feels threatened because her older brother progresses rapidly and is a self-proclaimed expert at programming. So she sits back, watches intently, and learns by observing what we do.

Seymour Papert wrote a marvelous book in 1980 called *Mindstorms: Children, Computers, and Powerful Ideas* [DR: we sell it here for $6.25; see John's review in *GWS* 24]. I strongly recommend this book to all *GWS* readers even if you don't have or plan to buy a computer. . . . Papert presents some approaches for making computers have a more humanistic relationship with mathematics. He discusses not only what the computer can do, but also offers a perspective on the process of learning itself.

From Debbie Hart (MI):

We just took a 4-day trip to visit a homeschooling family 150 miles west of us. They have six children (2–11 years). With my three we had quite a houseful, but we all enjoyed ourselves very much.

The children are so creative and have such imaginations that I know soon they will outdo me in my artwork. They already can observe things that it has taken me years to learn, things like perspective and shadowing of their pictures. I'm finding that I am relearning my own art skills. I was always taught to copy and do exactly like the mimeographed sheet said. If I used my own imagination I was punished for not following instructions. Now I am trying to un-program myself from these "rules."

My husband, Steve, is working on a wind generator and so both boys are learning all the mechanics of that. They build their own models along with him and sometimes even give him ideas.

We have started building a passive solar greenhouse/house. It's earth-bermed and will be compost-heated. The kids are learning how to construct a house (us, too, actually). We do a little at a time since our funds are short, but we are learning a lot. This summer we are going to let the kids have a sort of vacation, sending them to others' houses for a couple of weeks or so. I want them to be exposed to different environments that we can't provide, like our friends who play piano and other instruments, just so they know not everyone is a crazy artist like me or an inventor like Steve (he likes making different energy-saving devices). Maybe they need to get away from us once in a while and find out that just about every household has some sort of chores to do. Or that you have to do a little preparation before a meal can be made. Sometimes they think they are the only children who have to pick up clothes and clean their rooms. They like helping once in a while, but if you push it, it's "Do I have to?" Usually they come around when they tell me they're hungry and ask me for something to eat; I just say, "Do I have to cook?" They get the idea after a while.

From North Carolina:

We are entering Year Three of home school. As a single parent, sole supporter of our family and this venture, I must say home education has been difficult and terribly frustrating on many occasions . . . but, in the long run, promises to be well worth it! Our approach has varied from Calvert with Advisory Testing (we lasted six months), to Clonlara with whom I was completely independent (even when I should have sought assistance!), to Horizons in Atlanta for this year. Horizons offers the same type of service as Clonlara, but is only 5 hours away.

I've had a tendency in the past to look to unschooling as a panacea for all child rearing difficulties—thus, I've often become disheartened when "life wasn't perfect" and have erroneously blamed normal disruptions on unschooling. It's taken me two years to get over this tendency, but I think it's perhaps my most crucial lesson—i.e., brothers will disagree, kids will have mood fluctuations, teenage years do cause more emotion, houses get very messy when occupied by active people all day, my energy does have a limit—we all need R&R, our own space, etc., at times!.

Young Workers

Sharon Hillestad (MN) writes:

Holly (14) visited California friends for three weeks. They took her to Mexico with them on a church trip. A group of people journeyed to Baja to work on an orphanage. Holly took care of small children, painted fences, stacked wood, and distributed clothing to some Indians. She saw some of the worst poverty on the continent. She also saw a lot of caring people trying to help. She is determined to do it again next year and has set money aside for it. She wants her 12-year-old brother to go along next time. I think it is good social studies and I wish everyone else could do this or something similar. She will never take our relative prosperity for granted again.

By the way, she had studied Spanish from the tapes you recommended in *GWS* 20 [*Living Languages*, available from Publishers Central Bureau, 1 Champion Av, Avenel NJ 07131). She was able to speak the language as well as the high school students who studied two or three years in school.

Jenni Williams wrote in the PA Unschoolers Network, *#6:*

> Working at the Public Library in Gettysburg was an educational experience which boosted my self-confidence. I enjoyed helping others and the easy work. Other librarians at the library were surprised to find someone who is my age (12) being a volunteer. They didn't know quite how to handle it. Since I had experience with the children's librarian during the summer student apprenticeship program, she agreed to have me as her volunteer. The things I had to learn were to catalog books, put them in correct alphabetical or numerical order, how to properly check out books, magazines, etc., for others. The work involved shelving books, checking out articles, typing overdue notices and book orders, and slipping books (putting correct card in pocket when book is returned.)
>
> I would recommend working at a library to anyone who is willing to use the time and energy.

From Elaine Mahoney (MA; GWS 23):

The girls (15 and 13) have a new interest and job opportunity. They have been working part-time in a consignment shop earning $4.00 an hour. They are also helping me to landscape our lawn. We have never, ever done anything like this before but have discovered that when there is a will, there is a way. We are digging up ¾ of the grass, planting ground cover, cutting *small* trees, and planting flowers. I suggested to the girls that they go into the landscaping business, but they just grinned and walked away.

Homeschooled Teenagers

Vera Smith (ID) writes:

It's been a year now since we decided to take our two teen-aged boys out of school, and so far, so good. They seem to be learning at their own pace and with a lot more interest than while they were in school. They do the things that we feel are important to their education and then they have more than enough time to pursue their own interests, gardening, model building, and such.

Believe me, it's not the easiest age to work with because their interests are so wide and I'm just not up on everything they want to know and study. If it weren't for Time-Life books, National Geographic books, and sundry others, I'd be in a fog. I'm wading through Carl Sagan and David Attenborough. I'm in a sea of English history. I've battled at Gallipoli, and I've gazed at Gandhi. I threw my tea bags into Boston Harbor and had a cup of coffee with Thomas Jefferson. If the boys don't learn anything from this experience, *I'll* at least be well-read and able to speak intelligently on a number of subjects including black holes, neutron stars, and thermonuclear fusion. Too bad such things don't crop up in our everyday conversations.

We have a family-owned business and each boy gets a turn at working in the office, answering phones, making out repair orders, and scheduling appointments. It's good experience for both and they get an idea of how to deal with the public.

From Carla Emery in Idaho:

It's too bad I went through 16 years of homeschooling myself without the guidance and support of your magazine. Over all those years I tried just about every variation on that theme you can imagine, including hiring a certified teacher to come to my home every day. Technically I was supposed to assistant-teach under her supervision, but, really, she taught under mine because after all I was providing her paycheck. It's been quite an adventure and my seven wonderful children thoroughly disprove the many bad prophecies they've been offered. The family is growing up fast now. Instead of alphabets, I have to worry about sex education and driver's ed!.

Asks About Teens

Several readers have asked to see more about teens in GWS. *In particular, one mother writes:*

We are having a good experience with homeschooling—have been doing it for about six years.

I have noticed a growing restlessness in our 13-year-old. He's not a person who has great social needs—needing to be with others much—but he is feeling lonely, isolated. He does city soccer, local theater, swim team, etc., etc., but still really has no friends his age. I don't think he'd need but one. . . . He's always hated school but this need is pushing him toward school. He knows the need might not be filled there and yet school is a focus of activity with kids his age.

Do homeschoolers with kids age 12 and up find the children do become more restless, more aware of their isolation? Do most homeschooled kids return to school about that age? Are we, as parents, missing opportunities to keep the momentum going for home study?

Is there anything we can do to help fill this gap? So far pen pals don't do it; activities like working with kids in a play for a month don't do it. We don't get together with other homeschoolers or have family friends with kids their age. That would help, I'd think.

I wonder if we're missing opportunities (or participation in real-life activities like part-time jobs that the kids like, etc. (not necessarily paid).

We are apprehensive about homeschooling high school. We would do it if we had a miserable high school student, of course, but I almost think the kids should at least try high school. We can't provide tennis team, chorus, band, chemistry lab.

It would be easy if you had a child who was sure that he wanted none of that stuff. Maybe we shall just let the kids go and find out, maybe that's it. Maybe they're beginning to long for school and need to go and have a basis for comparison.

I do think teens have different needs than the young homeschoolers and I wonder about ways of meeting them. . . . I want to know more about what other teens do, have done, etc. If they continue learning at home, do they content themselves with trade-offs ("I can't be on the tennis team but neither do I have to take tests")? . . . I'd like to hear more from homeschooled kids who decided to go to school—did it fulfill their needs?

Life After Homeschool

Eileen Trombly (CT) wrote about her homeschooled daughters Lori (now in college) and Amy:

Thought you'd enjoy reading an article written by Lori concerning her presence at the Eugene O'Neill Theater Center. For both Lori and Amy, "life after homeschooling" has been super-charged with their dreams becoming realities. Lori has already been offered a position at O'Neill for next summer and was given her *own studio* this summer. Even though we're 15 minutes from the theater she sleeps nights at the mansion provided for the convenience of the N.Y. critics, etc. She often works late hours and is completely immersed in what she does. She looks, feels, and sounds totally healthy.

Likewise with Amy. She has done so well [at the school of the Hartford Ballet, a top professional company] she's already been recommended to dance in the company class this fall.

Their self-esteem is sky high and, as parents,

Spencer and I feel great satisfaction in their happiness.

Working With Adults

A follow-up to "Tutor in the Tropics," GWS *17:*

To briefly refresh your memory, you received a letter over two years ago now from me, then a New Alchemist interested in, among other things, worms. My wife and I had just accepted a position as personal tutors of a twelve-year-old boy who resided on his parents' privately-owned atoll of tropical islands (complete with library, tennis court, windsurfs, swimming pool, airplane, cooks, maids, launderer, etc.). You very kindly responded with a multitude of thoughtful suggestions.

It was a time of tremendous personal growth for each of us, of meeting some of the most interesting people we've ever encountered, of deepening as well as heightening our sense of harmony with the natural world, and of cultivating one of the most moving relationships (with the boy) I can recall.

Prior to this mutually educational experience, I was ambivalent about homeschooling my own prospective children. I am now convinced that no other form of education could be more beneficial, not only for my children but for my wife and myself as parents as well.

The educational background of the boy we tutored has almost solely been personal tutors. From the boy's perspective, his situation is akin to homeschooling; he has never known a traditional classroom, peer pressure, nor any of the other associated phenomena. It was clearly to his advantage.

As the boy was eventually destined to attend a European international school (which he did beginning this year), we had certain academic standards to take into account. Although this had to be a major focus in our curriculum, my wife and I would also routinely invite him to take part in our own current "pet projects." A couple examples of these were surveying and documenting the (previously un-surveyed) marine corals and fishes inhabiting the reef encircling the main island that we lived on, and carrying out some experiments a New Alchemy colleague requested on the freshwater ecology of a pond there. I believe the boy's eagerness to participate in projects such as these stemmed mainly from his experiencing our dedication to and love for such work. I share your philosophy that a younger person will tend to "learn best and most if his/her learning grows out of being associated with someone in serious adult work, not just school stuff." How well and much that person learns seems to me to be in direct proportion to how passionate that "someone" feels about his or her work, whether it be baking bread, building boats, or responsibly raising children.

Homeschooling In Louisiana

From a very encouraging story in the New Orleans Times—Picayune, *3/28/83, sent to us by our friends Mary and Walter Marschner:*

> The Marschners and the Andersons are two of 17 local families [JH: the Marschners wrote above this, "Many more"] continuing an old-fashioned practice that is resurfacing as a trend of the '80s: homeschooling.
>
> The Louisiana legislative act allowing home education of children is now in its second year—and though some parents have tried the system briefly and declined to continue, others are sold on the living room-as-classroom concept.
>
> "One of the prime advantages is family closeness," says Mary Marschner. "We do so many things together as a family now."
>
> "It allows concentration," adds her husband, Walter Marschner. "With 40 kids, you get one kid with a problem and you'll have trouble meeting his needs. If one of our kids has a special need, we take all the time necessary to get it right.
>
> "And flexibility—Jemmy was invited to a wedding in Mexico in the middle of the 'school year'—but what a wonderful educational opportunity. She spent a month there."
>
> "It doesn't take as much time as you might think," adds Anderson, who says her six years as a teacher were not much of a preparation for her present situation. "Now I'm not boxed into a certain time of day for a certain subject. Everything becomes a learning experience, and I've always loved learning. And it's easier for parents to teach today because there are so many materials available."
>
> The home study movement has spawned a whole industry of support materials. Entire curriculums are available by mail. Parents can order individual texts, workbooks and tape cassettes on every subject imaginable. Guides to educational programs on TV are available, as well as accompanying workbooks. National newsletters offer the latest information on homeschooling legislation, civic action, and educational materials.
>
> Jemmy and Andreas [Anderson] both say they do not miss daily association with other teens. . . . They pursue a number of extracurricular activities that, they say, provide plenty of outside companionship.
>
> As of February of this year, Louisiana Department of Education figures record *500 students throughout the state enrolled in home study—up from 265 at the same time a year ago.* . . . Assistant Director of the Bureau of Elementary Education Diane Reynolds . . . estimates that the figure will rise to 600 by the end of this school semester.
>
> As the law currently stands, there is virtually no way to judge how well homeschooling is working. . . . The department cannot oversee curriculums, review exams, test students or monitor home study in any way. . . . "With no monitoring," [says Reynolds] "we can't say if it's working. Probably some parents are doing a fine job. But it certainly isn't helping every child—I can't say that all 500 children are getting

a quality education."

Yet it is unbelievably easy to qualify for the home study program. Applicants simply fill out a one-page form listing the names and addresses of parents and names and grades of children. The form contains a pledge signed by parents stating that they will provide their children with an education "equal to the public system" and a school year of no less than 180 days. Parents need not tell the board of education what curriculum they will follow or what materials they will use. The application is renewed yearly and, if correctly completed, is approved routinely by the department.

Some parents avoid even that minimum of regulation by setting themselves up as private schools. . . . Parents who wish to operate their own schools simply write to the state department of education at the beginning of the school year stating when the year will begin and the number of students enrolled.

Better assessment of the program may be possible in years to come, as children who are products of homeschooling enter colleges or return to public schools. In the meantime, say educators, the movement is here to stay.

Letter From Mississippi

Sandi Myers (MS) sent an article from a local paper about her family's homeschooling (GWS 28), and wrote:

I was surprised that we did not get any crank calls from the article. We found two other homeschooling families and have talked with them but not gotten together yet. I also got many calls congratulating us on what we are doing. Being in an area where the schools are recognized to be poor sure does promote understanding of our choice. The nicest thing by far about doing the article is feeling like we made two real friends in the reporter and the photographer. Both were young, single girls who felt that someday they might choose to allow their own children to learn at home.

Of the two families we talked to, one has eight children, ranging from about four to fourteen. The oldest children went to school a year or so, but they have been homeschooling since then. They seem to do much as we do with occasional emphasis on doing "studies" but for the most part just living and enjoying all the very natural learning that goes on.

The mother of this family and I laughed about how we encourage getting down to studying specific subjects at specific times out of pressure *we* feel from outside sources. My own children have gotten very good at recognizing this and they become very solicitous to me—giving me backrubs, helping with anything I am trying to do, asking if I would like to talk about it, and so on; but rarely getting down to doing whatever I had "suggested" they do in whatever timetable. And, of course, their response meets the actual need better than what I had suggested would.

We received a call from an encyclopedia salesman who was very complimentary but was just sure she had the very thing we needed! She came out to show us her wares, and we found her to be like so many educators in that she would ask questions, but they were designed to bring about the answer she was looking for, not asking for our real thoughts. At one point, she asked if we knew the bird that flies the highest. We all thought and guessed, and none guessed right, so she astounded us with the *right* answer—a goose had been spotted— at 26,000 feet, above the Himalayas. The kids and I immediately started to wonder about special adaptations birds in general must have to fly where people cannot breathe without supplemental oxygen, or perhaps just birds in that area, and of course she didn't have the answer. To her, the little piece of information she could present to dazzle us was the whole issue—to us, finding out how they do it, and what species do it, and so on is the issue. I hope my children never lose their curiosity, and I have them to thank for the reawakening of mine.

Retired Teacher Supportive

Debra Stewart (WA) sent this letter which appeared in a local paper a few days after an article about the Stewarts' homeschooling:

In regard to Sunday's article about the Stillaguamish Learning Center, I question why the state officials can't leave these people alone.

Speaking as a retired teacher with many years of experience, I was thrilled to read about parents with that much interest in their children's learning. One of the problems of the public schools is to find parents who have time or interest to give to their children's learning.

It seems ridiculous that the state officials would demand home inspections. If the homes are safe for the children to live in when not studying why wouldn't they be safe for the shorter time when they are studying? The rules Tom Anderson, deputy attorney general, is trying to enforce there were made for larger groups of children. It seems as though he is trying to harass these people.

Here is a group that is doing much more than average parents to see their children get the type of education best suited to the child. They are hiring a certified person to test the children to be sure they are accomplishing scholastically. The children seem to be ahead of their contemporaries in the public schools with no cost to the taxpayers. The parents aren't begging the state for money to help. They aren't complaining about having to pay taxes to help other children have schools. My respect goes out to them.

It is my opinion that as long as the children are achieving, in the way this article purports, Tom Anderson should use this time and energy toward trying to help the neglected children who can't seem to fit into the public system.— Evalyn Pflueger, Snohomish

---

[JH:] Letters like this could probably be published in many papers where homeschoolers are having troubles. In general, letters to the editor are very good ways to reach the public.

Friendly Administrator

Denise Hodges (IL) writes:

I wrote up our curriculum and sent it to the regional superintendent in August. Haven't heard a thing from him personally.... My husband Don teaches at a public school. Recently his superintendent approached him and said, "I hear we're fellow administrators!" Don didn't know what he was talking about until he remembered we jokingly listed him as our principal (because he's not here all day!), when we filled out the form to register as a private school. Anyway, the superintendent went on to say that the regional superintendent had told him about our school and he was "very impressed" with our curriculum! So it looks like we'll have no problems!

Single Parent Homeschooler

From Pat Tennant (CA):

We have a friend who is a single parent raising her 7-year-old son. She is a licensed day-care person because that allows her to have some income and also be home with her son. But this is a low-income job so she uses some government services such as Medi-Cal. Because of this she has to meet once a year to have her "life reviewed" by a welfare person. This year, because of her son's age, she had to bring proof that he was enrolled in a school. We had agreed a while back that if she needed coverage we would enroll Mark in our school—he is enrolled but is at home with his mother. So, for her meeting with the welfare person, we gave her a letter stating that Mark was enrolled in Lothlorien. When the welfare person saw this she remembered reading about the home schools in the paper so she called the county schools office and asked if this school was a legal school. She was told that it was. She asked if it was one of the schools that was allegedly illegal and was told that no action was being taken at this time and until such time when action was taken, these schools were considered legal and that it was fine for Mark to be in that school.

Discussions With Ex-Husband

From a mother in Kansas:

I am interested in hearing more about divorced parent situations in which one disapproves of homeschooling. I was pleased to see it mentioned in *GWS* 31. I am just going ahead with my own plans to keep my almost-6-year-old son out of school (he's legal until age 7) but am apprehensive about what big guns an otherwise friendly but in this case very traditional father might use.

My tactics have been as follows: I know I would not be polite while discussing something I feel so strongly about face to face with him, so I wrote a series of essays for him explaining my beliefs and hopes, and inviting his participation and support. It was in a series because many people will not read much at a time, especially about a subject they don't want to know about. These essays I doled out to him at intervals of a week or two. Then when all four of us met (my spouse is behind me on the issue), there was a known basis for discussion. In my case this was not the road to unanimity, but at least I initiated controlled and less emotional debate than might have been generated by misunderstanding.

I have now suggested that my ex-husband and I meet to begin negotiations toward some middle ground, but he is visibly terrified of confrontation and has not yet responded.

Maybe these ideas will help someone start the ball rolling. It has been extremely difficult to be cast as revolutionary by family and friends, so this step-by-step process gives the chaos a semblance of order.

Job vs. Homeschool

From Deb Martin (IL):

The price of keeping one parent home most of the time with a child can be high if the parent is giving up a job. I know there are certain advantages in giving up a job that probably outweigh the disadvantages, like not having to pay for child care, cheaper transportation, clothing, food, not to mention the emotional cost for the children.

In our case I had a 2½-year-old and a 5-year-old and a new baby. I felt overwhelmed trying to teach the 5-year-old and handle the rest. We seriously considered putting our 5-year-old into Montessori school. We ended up keeping him home, however, for a couple of reasons. First of all, I decided that what *I* wanted to do most was to teach my own children and it was worth the cost to make that possible. So instead of spending money to have someone else teach, we are spending money to have a junior high school girl come in for two hours each afternoon to help do housework and relieve me so I can focus some time on our 5-year-old. The second reason I felt OK about doing this was a phone conversation I had with a Montessori teacher and teacher-trainer, who was also teaching her children at home. She told me that if I read to my children each day and made materials and equipment readily available to them, I would be doing as well as if I had my children in a Montessori school.

New Home Through *GWS*

From Jane McClung in Texas:

While I was reading *GWS* 28, I found the letter from Susan Corcoran, "Found a Home," which referred to the letter in *GWS* 24 about the Greenwood Forest Association. Over Christmas we drove over 900 miles to Missouri to see the last remaining 10 acre parcel.

When we arrived at that dirt road, all I could say is "What have I gotten us into this time?" as we stopped every few hundred feet to assess the road situation. We learned later the road has been there since the Civil War. It was full of big rocks, holes, water, etc.—we drove for 45 minutes in those woods before we found a living soul. We were beginning to wonder if someone wouldn't find us until the spring! What an adventure! Finally we found some humans and they directed us to the Paxton family's cabin. What lovely and intelligent people we met as they took us around to meet the neighbors. They really lived in cabins, teepees, etc. While we were visiting, the sun went down and they lit their lanterns. I've never had someone say to me, "Come closer. Let me push the lantern closer to you so I can see your face while we talk." I always felt I was born in the wrong century. The experience was like being transported back in time to a simpler life and one that was compatible with our beliefs in home birth, homeschool, and a more home-centered philosophy.

We stayed three days, even spending one night on our 10 acres in 20 degree weather to be sure it was right for us. We loved it. Then we signed the papers and everyone hugged each other. We didn't just get land in the deal—we got wonderful neighbors and a unique lifestyle too. We are busy planning what kind of home we'll build. Michael, 4, has volunteered to paint it red. We hope to return to plant fruit trees in the spring.

Dealing With Thoughtlessness

One aspect of homeschooling that concerns us is the child's feeling of being different from others. We live in a residential area surrounded by a group of all-American elementary school kids, who already make rude remarks about our son being a baby because he is not in kindergarten (which is not compulsory). He loyally espouses homeschooling, but admits he does feel bad when they set him apart.—A Kansas parent.

I am eleven years old, and am in my fourth year of homeschooling. . . . One of the girls in my neighborhood thought I was having school at home because I was retarded! She had asked her dad about me having school at home, and that's what he said. It took a lot of talking to her to get that out of her head.—Lisa Holway (OH).

A friend of his age told Shawn that Shawn couldn't spell since he didn't take spelling tests!—Connie Colten (CA).

[DR:] Sad to say, learning to deal with ignorant and cruel remarks is something all children have to do as they grow up, whether they go to school or not. It's important for homeschooled children to realize that; if the issue wasn't homeschooling, it would be something else, sooner or later—appearance, clothes, vocabulary, diet, possessions, beliefs, etc. People have many different reactions to the pain inflicted by such thoughtlessness; many, of course, decide to conform, to be so much like everyone else that no one could possibly notice them. Being different takes courage.

In *GWS* 15, John wrote, "From the age of 11 I felt left out, and never more so than when I was in school. . . . I think I would have been better off if I had felt, and been, *somewhat* less left out than I was. But it gave me the independence and moral courage I needed to do things in my adult life that most people weren't doing, to follow work that seemed important."

I'm sure many parents have discussed this issue with their children, and I hope more readers will write us about how they've handled situations like these.

Blaming The Unconventional

Denise Hodges (IL) wrote:

I have found that when you go against the status quo, *that* area of your life becomes the scapegoat for anything that goes wrong. At La Leche League meetings we often discuss how when there is anything wrong with a breast-fed baby, people (especially the pediatrician) will suggest that there is something wrong with the milk (not enough, too much, not the right kind, etc.) when in fact it usually has nothing to do with that. Maia still nurses frequently and I often hear, "She cries because she's still nursing" or other such nonsense, as if weaned 3-year-olds never cry!

Now homeschooling falls into this category, too. I'm hearing things like, "Lucas is crabby because he knows he should be in school," or "He fights with the neighbor kids because they are jealous of his not being in school," or "Lucas doesn't know how to get along with kids because he's not in school," etc. So, homeschoolers beware! If your kid gets warts or hiccups, someone may tell you it's because he's not in school!.

[JH:] I used to say to teachers, when you do

something the old way, if (as usual) it doesn't work, everyone blames the children; if you do it a new way, and it doesn't work—or even if it does—they blame you.

Going Back To School

From Lisa Holway (OH), who was homeschooled for four years:

Next year I will be in seventh grade, and will be going to Hilliard Middle School.

The main reason I want to go to middle school is to meet other girls my age. I'm a little worried about how people might accept me at first, but hopefully after the first few weeks we can be good friends.

Homeschooling has been a great experience for me, and I don't think I would have missed it for anything. But I need to grow and change, and going to middle school is just one of my ways of doing that. Other people might rather stay at home, and that is fine. We're each doing our own thing, and enjoying it!

One great advantage of having school at home is the time you have to do the things you want to do like reading, writing stories, drawing, cooking, playing the guitar, etc. . . . What I like about homeschooling is having your mom around to talk to, ask help from, have fun with, and do things with. But whether you have school at home, or go to a public school, the important thing is to be happy wherever you are.

From Sharon Hillestad (MN):

Holly has signed up for the 9th grade at Hastings Junior High. She literally skipped 6th, 7th, and 8th grades. It took less than 15 minutes to get her back in school in Hastings. Last year she tried to enroll in junior high in Huntsville, Alabama. The school secretary told her she couldn't come to school without records. Holly told her that she hadn't been to school for two years but the woman kept insisting on records. So that was that.

[DR: Since this was the first time we had ever heard of a homeschooler having trouble trying to get back into school, I asked Sharon if they had tried going over the secretary's head to someone with more authority to bend the rules. She replied, "Holly did her own inquiring in Alabama and did not go past the secretary."]

Part-Time School

Janet Williams (PA) writes:

My children are all doing well. I am holding my own despite having two pre-adolescents. Why is there so much fuss about adolescence? The real killer for me has been 9–11.

Jenni has come out of that stage beautifully. She is very together and has managed a hybrid of school and home. She can hold her own when there are problems in school (she doesn't get hostile or teary or frustrated anymore). Last June she told the Middle School principal that she would be willing to return to school fulltime *if* he would approve her skipping 7th grade and moving into the 8th where most of her friends are this year. He said no. She said, "Then I will be home again."

Her schedule is as follows:
Monday: 1st period Computers, then home.
Tuesday: 1st Industrial Arts, 4th Recess, 5th Lunch, 6th Science, 7th Phys. Ed, 8th Art.
Wednesday: 1st Speed Reading, 4th Recess, 5th lunch, 8th Chorus.
Thursday: 1st Spanish, 4th Recess, 5th Lunch, 6th Science, 7th Phys. Ed, 8th Bi-weekly clubs.
Friday: home all day.
Periods when she is not in a class, she works independently in the library or computer room

The three days seem just about right for Jenni. She does most of her school homework while she is there. She is more responsible about it than she was last year. It is such a pleasure not to have to nag and pressure her. It did not do either of us any good.

On Guilt

To a parent who had many concerns about the issue of homeschooling, John wrote:

Your letter raises an issue of great importance, to which I have given much thought.

We have printed and will print stories from

people who want very much to teach their children at home but for one reason or another have not been able to find a way to do so. Sometimes we or other *GWS* readers have been able to suggest a way out of the dilemma, sometimes not, in which case we consider how to make school less harmful to the child until a solution can be found. Meanwhile we say, "Be patient, keep hoping and trying, between us we will sooner or later turn up something."

But I take it this is not quite what you want. You say, "My point is that an ideal viewpoint can become a source of guilt rather than a source of support to the very people who believe in it." True; *Mothering* magazine, to name only one, prints many letters from women who feel badly because they were not able to have a home or natural childbirth, or to nurse their children, or to spend as much time with them as they would like. *Mothering* and other magazines usually reply as we do above, by telling people to do the best they can and keep trying for something better. But some people seem to be telling us that we should not say so strongly that natural home birth, or breastfeeding, or homeschooling, or whatever, are good for children, because it makes all those people feel bad who for whatever reason didn't or don't do it. Well, I'm sorry they feel bad; I often feel bad about a lot of things I have done or haven't done. But our job is to say what we think is best for children and help people come as close to it as they can.

Later you say that your daughter is in first grade, by her own choice. I've said often that if children and their parents are happy with their schools, I'm delighted. It is only if they are unhappy that I urge them to think about homeschooling. But I gather this is not the case with you and your daughter. . . . As long as your daughter is thriving and happy in school, why should guilt arise? If, on the other hand, the day comes when her school stops being a good experience and starts becoming a bad one, then you *may have* to make a choice, for a while at least, between some things you want very much to do and the health, happiness, and growth of your child. Perhaps this conflict can be avoided, perhaps ways can be found, as indeed they often can, to make it possible for both of you to have what you most need. But if a choice has to be made, surely there is no question as to which must come first.

You write of " . . . the insinuated philosophy that happy families spend *lots* of time together." It's not insinuated, and it's not a philosophy, in the sense of a *theory*; what we print are reports by real people about how they actually live their lives. You write, "How about happy families that have lots of different interests, activities and outlets and come together at dinner or whenever—with many exciting things to share?" There have been many such letters; if most letters are about families together, it is because most homeschooled children are still quite young. If the parents who write to us stress as much as they do how much they enjoy their children's company, it is largely because so many of the people *they* meet say things to them like, "How can you stand to have your children around all the time?" etc.

A bit earlier in your letter you wrote, "I wish you would stress differences in maturation." We stress, all the time, that children do not grow according to timetables, and that the best time for children (or adults) to learn or do things is when they are most eager to learn or do them, not when someone else's theory says they should be done. You speak of " . . . a precocity syndrome." There's no "syndrome"; we print what people tell us about their children. If many of these sound precocious, it is only because all children, when not pressured or afraid, are in plain fact far more intelligent and capable than almost anyone thinks possible.

An old friend of mine and of *GWS* once criticized us for writing so much about "super-kids." In practically the next breath he told us (showing us many photos, which I wish we could have printed) about his 15-year-old son, who on his own, working from books, without any previous experience, and without any instruction, advice, or help, built a small but complete house. I said to him, "Now who's talking about 'super-kids?' How many fifteen-year-olds do you think build their own houses?" He laughed, and admitted the point, which is that even people who really like their children get so used to them, take them so much for granted, that they may fail to notice what remarkable things they do—and all children do remarkable things. We are not in the business of saying that some children are more remarkable than others. One of the reasons you never see any talk in *GWS* about "gifted children" is because we insist that all children are gifted. We don't encourage people to wonder or worry about whether their children are less or more gifted than others; quite the reverse. We say, enjoy them for what they are.

We like to print and will continue to print what people tell us about the remarkable things that their children do. After all, we confront everywhere, among school people and the general public, a widespread conviction that children are lazy, incurious, incapable, untrustworthy, and just plain bad, and that they will never learn or do anything good unless made to. Here at *GWS* we do our best to combat and change this attitude, by printing stories that prove that children are curious, capable, extremely good at learning, and eager to do things well and to make a useful contribution to the life around them. To stop printing such stories because some people might find in them reason to feel ashamed of their own children would be a serious and self-defeating mistake. Every good thing done by any child helps break down the popular myth about all children's badness and stupidity, and so works for the good of all children, especially homeschooled children. Reading such stories should make our readers, as they make us, feel not ashamed but reassured, glad, and proud.

In this issue we tell about an 18-year-old Canadian cellist who has already made a commercial recording and appeared with major orchestras. Should I, a struggling amateur cellist of almost sixty, resent her talent and feel shame because I can't play as well and probably never will? No; I say, "Three cheers for her!" and go back to my own cello and work a little harder. All we can do is do the best we can. If we do that, we have no cause to feel shame.

Well, in any case, we are not going to stop printing good stories about homeschooled children. And if and when we print stories about people having problems, as we do when people (rarely) send us such stories, it is to help them find ways to solve these problems, rather than to relieve other people of whatever burden of guilt they may have laid on themselves.

I hope this letter may somewhat lessen the problem of guilt for you and other readers. In any case, it should make our own position a little more clear.

Letters on Learning Disabilities

*Thomas Armstrong (*Latebloomers Educational Consulting Services*, PO Box 2647, Berkeley CA 94702), who is writing a book on learning disabilities, writes:*

I was excited to get so many wonderful replies to my letter in *GWS* 28 about late bloomers and the "learning disabilities" scam. Many parents wrote in sharing stories of their late blooming children who were spared the scars of special education (labeling, testing, and "cure") by homeschooling and through the patience, faith, and trust of these parents in the natural growth processes of their children. I thought I'd share some selections from these letters with you and your readers. I'm still eager to hear from parents about their late blooming kids and from any and all who are willing to speak out against the distortions of the whole "learning disability" movement.

―――――

From a letter that a Wisconsin parent sent to Mr. Armstrong:

I have a very interesting child who is definitely a "late bloomer." . . . Seth seemed slow to master physical and mechanical skills, but would often suddenly learn a whole group of skills in one to two days. At 9 months Seth did not sit up, crawl, scoot, or walk. In one week, shortly before he was 10 months old, he learned to do all of them. . . . As he neared 3 years of age, Seth occasionally spoke a single full sentence but did not use any other words or gestures on a regular basis. By this time his younger sister was beginning to speak well. Again I became concerned. Suddenly Seth began talking and talked constantly. . . . At 4 his physical skills were really lacking. He couldn't catch a ball, hop, or even run very well. Stupidly, I let friends persuade me to enroll him in a special preschool program for "slow learners." It was neither a good nor a bad experience. Toward the end of the year, Seth made another of his miraculous advances, was suddenly doing everything he should be and was tired of preschool. I stopped sending him, but attributed his gains to the program. Looking back I realize that it was not the program at all, but Seth's pattern of learning. . . . Seth was 7, he couldn't read at all, still wrote many words backwards; his sister, his only friend, decided she was tired of playing with boys, another dark time for Seth. His physical coordination fell way behind his sister's. She began to lose her teeth—he didn't. But by now we had faith in Seth. We basically left him alone. The result, Seth lost 6 teeth in one week, developed a fascination with reading and suddenly shot ahead of his sister who we were sure would read before he did, began to make friends, became an ace at badminton, and can never get enough math problems to work. But he was almost 9 years old before all this happened.

Pearlene Gavlik (NH) wrote:

In previous school years, Sherry had been core-evaluated, placed in Title I and Chapter 766 programs. None of them really helped to a large degree. In my heart, I never really believed she had a learning disability. . . . While attending school she had a very low tolerance frustration level, a very hostile and sarcastic disposition, no memory retention, and no desire to learn at all. She hated to read, would refuse to read assigned chapters for homework, and most of the time would go around with a retarded look on her face.

In my home-study program, I've tried to give her a lot of space, not pressure her to learn, and be patient with a non-judgmental attitude. After about nine months of this, remarkable changes started occurring. She was becoming more thoughtful with a pleasant disposition, did not need her friends any more to amuse and distract her, her mind started getting more creative and she demonstrated more patience in her projects. Now she loves to read.

Lately she's been reading a book a day. She's excited about learning all about dinosaurs, insects, herbs, gardening, astronomy, mineralogy, wildlife, trees and plants, birds and fish, canning foods, sewing, Egyptian kings and relics, ancient Rome and Greece.

From Freda Davies (Ont.):

My son, ex-husband, brother and father were all placed in one or another of the above categories ["learning disabled," "slow," "lazy"] by the school system and the scars show on all of them. I think I have managed to counteract some of the ill effects on my son by taking him out of school. He is now nearly 12 years old and has been "unschooling" since age 8. During Kevin's three years in school, he almost constantly begged me to let him stay home. The only part of school that he liked were recesses and a few other occasions when he was able to choose his own activities. He had (and still has) a strong aversion to any organized learning programs including such apparently innocuous ones as swimming or skiing lessons. . . . At about age 10, Kevin made a sudden leap in his reading ability [See Freda's letter in *GWS* 17]. From reading only a few words, he jumped to whole sentences, often containing fairly difficult words. He still reads mainly comic books, saying that "chapter" books are too boring. . . . Kevin has no trouble doing math calculations in his head or using a calculator to solve more complex problems. . . . He does very little writing except occasionally when he wants to write a business letter to the Lego Corporation. Building with Lego sets is his great hobby and he often has questions or complaints which bother him until he writes and gets an answer from the company. . . . Besides Lego, Kevin likes making taped "radio" programs either by himself or with friends.

And from an Alaska mother:

My lovely sweet Anette, now 10, was labeled SLD [Specific Learning Disability] in first grade. . . . We went with the option of placing her in the SLD program, halfway through first grade! I know it's like crying over spilt milk but I wish I'd never done it.... She spent a lot of "sick" days, especially when I went into the classroom to help once a week. I knew the teacher felt I was catering to her when I'd let her come home with me. You see, I was beginning to feel something was wrong!

We then moved to our present home in the woods, 7 miles from school.... We were able to qualify for Home Correspondence. That was terrible! I was constantly battling the teachers who felt, it seems, that all children learn the same!... As winter went along... things went from bad to worse! The work was intense, the pressure also. I no longer felt like a mother, but a witch!... Needless to say, Anette learned little and in the end refused to even work, blocking out all learning. We went totally on our own the following year. They (the correspondence advisors) sent us a requisite for having your own school from the state laws; but have never bothered to see if we carry it out. We're in our second year now. With Anette, I let her totally alone! Never did I give her an assignment or pressure.... She now *reads*, picks up a book, even a comic book. She loves the Cuisenaire rods, we follow the series as she asks me to do it. Enjoys math this way.... Better late than never!

On "Dyslexia"

Mary Maher (MA) wrote:

I must tell you that while reading *Teach Your Own*, I became very excited over what you had to say about dyslexia. I have a vivid first grade memory of trying to copy the number 5 off the blackboard onto my paper. I *saw* the 5 correctly, but was unable to make my *hand* write what I saw. I was only able to make it backwards. I was terribly frustrated because I could see my five was not the same as the five on the board.

[JH:] Just the other day I watched a child trying to make a 5. She got the horizontal line OK, then the vertical line, but when she started to do the curved part, she couldn't get it to go the right way. Then when she saw it was going wrong, she tried to reverse it, which made it look even worse. She was very frustrated. Fortunately no one was pushing her to "do it right"—she didn't even see me watching. She has plenty of time to wait before trying it again.

Late Blooming Reader

From Debbie Jones (ID):

It's hard to believe we've been homeschooling for four years now. This year we have seen many rewards that we've had to be patient for.... Our Cori who is almost twelve finally took off in reading. He has been frustrated and discouraged since his school experiences (second grade). He didn't enjoy reading and didn't read on his own. Well, I read to the family quite a bit. We go to the library frequently. We read ourselves a lot. And this last year he would occasionally read a story or book to the other children. I was amazed at his improved ability. "All those years of working with him finally paid off," they would say in school, but that isn't it at all; he didn't read at all for almost two years! Then a friend introduced him to the Choose Your Own Adventure series. *Balloon to the Sahara* and *Mystery of the Maya* were two of the first ones he got and read and read and read. Recently he read some articles in *Mother Earth News* on raising chickens. And he just finished *My Side of the Mountain*, a very good book that I'm sure is at about the sixth grade level, according to the grade level people. If he was tested any time over the last few years you know what the verdict would have been: "He's terribly behind. He's not being taught!" etc....

A Down's Syndrome Champ

From Elaine Bechtold (see Resource List for Down's Syndrome at the end of this issue):

Our daughter's 4-H project earned her the 1982 champion poultry trophy for Wright County and a state fair trip.

This girl who has Down's Syndrome can now read the newspaper. Her reading ability helped her function at the state fair. She spent seven years in public school (Trainable Mentally Retarded) class where reading would not be taught. The past 4–5 years she is in a Christian day school where she is challenged just like everyone else. Here she is learning and progressing every day.

Competent Kids

From Marilyn Hall (CA):

A note on 2-year-olds. At 27 months, with a 3-month-old sister, Michael: cracks eggs, chops vegetables for soups and steaming, stirs soups or vegetables on stove; puts butter on tortillas for quesadillas—has not burned or cut himself and I have done both in the same time he's been cooking with me. He can use a screwdriver and knows the Phillips from regular, and removed the handles from my cupboard doors and only reluctantly replaced them; took the phone apart. (I put *that* back together); took apart all toys with screws (these are *tiny* screws—½" long). He took the torn webbing off my lawn chair—worked diligently for 2+ hours, occasionally asking for help with a screw too tight for him to loosen. . . . He is delighted in being useful. He helps me make biscuits and bread and granola. He is respectful of *real* danger and mindless of parent *fear*. He touches the cold stove, but not the hot burner.

He only in the last three months has allowed us to read to him; before that he was only interested in the covers or flypapers and absolutely *refused*, closing book, leaving, etc. He then chose four books and would let us read only those four for two months, and then suddenly was interested in others—I read a new book through and he simply sits. On the fourth or fifth reading he points to a picture or anticipates a word in the text. On Reading #10 or so, we hardly finish the book because he points out everything. Then on to a new book. He picks out books he likes and only occasionally indulges adult preferences.

From Elizabeth Swift (VT):

It's great to have a publication supporting children's competence. I used to think we were the only ones who allowed our under-two-year-old to use a real hammer. He also uses (at 4) a real screwdriver. He can take the reflectors off the truck and put them back on all by himself and *nobody taught him*. We just discovered him doing it.

We've seen recently how important it is to encourage this independence. Grandma was here last week and was stifling the independence we are encouraging. We had a real series of blow-ups between her and Gabriel until I made it clear to her that, yes, he was allowed to pour his own juice, set the table, help peel potatoes, decide whether he needed boots on or not. I'm sure she believes we're letting him "rule the roost," but I see all of this as encouraging him to make his own decisions.[From a later note:] Grandma may be beginning to see things our way. She just gave Gabriel his own eggbeater (regulation size) so that he can make pies (using instant pudding and graham cracker crusts) all by himself. He loves making the pies and loves the compliments they produce.

A California reader wrote:

May I tell you some of the things that my son does day in and day out, everyday, which I notice that most mothers do not allow their children to do? I am not proud that he "does" something, but I feel a little sorry for other children who do not even have the basic freedom to move as human beings in their own homes (something must be wrong).

At two years, he:
- selects a cassette tape to play; puts into tape player;
- does gardening: plants seeds, waters, conditions soil;
- finds aluminum cans outside, collects them to be recycled (on his own, I don't point them out);
- watercolor painting, etc., (gets out own materials and puts away nicely);
- butters a peanut butter sandwich from jar (with knife);
- washes dishes, puts on rack to dry; sweeps; mops up spills; cleans table with sponge;
- does errands: gets/finds things; puts things away in shelves, drawers, etc.;

- plays drums, ukulele, flute, hand cymbals, sometimes organ— seriously, with rhythm, etc.;
- brushes own teeth; washes face, hands, dries them; hangs up towel; etc.;
- feeds himself and is allowed to be a little messy (aren't we all) but he cleans it up.

Oops! Also forgot that he plays outside all day long without supervision from me on playground equipment, in games with older children. But most children under five years are not allowed outside for any period of time by themselves. If they do manage to make it outside, it is with Mother shouting, "No, No," etc.

On a different subject, I have found that photo-essay adult books seem to be the best and most interesting for my son now (the library kiddie books were just too weird). These are the books that deal with flowers, wild animals, fish, dogs, etc. They are interesting to me, also (The "kiddie" books were not).

Skyler At 2

From Meryl Runion (FL):

Skyler (2) has changed a lot since my last letter [*GWS* 29]. He's a mixture of very dependent and boldly independent. He still has to help much of the time but he's gone for stretches, too, visiting the boy next door. He sings, sings, sings, and he's much more reasonable.

Now that he has a social life of his own, I actually have occasional moments to do things without him. It's a funny feeling.... We live at the end of a dead-end street so I can let him go out without supervision. I check on him from time to time but he doesn't seem to want to go farther than next door, anyway. He and the four-year-old run back and forth every half hour or so.... I think it's good for his self-esteem for him to be able to come and go without me on his tail.

I remember when we lived in Thailand, we were in a resort that had cottages. There were about 15 adults on staff and a girl about two years old running around. The whole six months we were there, I never figured out who her parents were (someone told me later). She was very charming and happy and also very able to look after herself. She was comfortable with all the adults. I was so impressed with what a nice thing it is for a small child to be able to wander freely without an adult watching (and usually judging) her every move. She never did fall into the ocean.

Skyler is still nursing, nursing, nursing. I never like to push Skyler into or out of things and it just hasn't seemed appropriate to cut back at any point. I still don't use sitters for the same reason. Even so, my neighbors are noticing that the clingy child who always wanted *up* is coming into his own and being very independent. But he keeps coming back for "*my milk!*"

I used to read a lot while he nursed but now I read to *him*. It's funny, I would just as soon he learned to read late, rather than early, but I find myself reading to him two hours a day while he nurses and he's got a lot of books almost memorized. I used to dislike Mother Goosey type books, saying they were too silly. But then I obtained an album of Mother Goose. He loved it and used to ask to hear it all day long. Now the Mother Goose books are his favorite. If I try to read a verse he knows there's a tune for, he'll insist I sing it, and I've had to make up tunes for many of those I don't know tunes for.

He sings a lot during the day—but so do I. We're not a musical family, I don't play an instrument and don't put the radio or stereo on much and yet music is a big part of our lives. So many things inspire me to song—the squeak of a swing, the sound of the washer, some situation that reminds me of a passage of a song. Skyler is the same way. He rides down the street on his trike singing "Twinkle Twinkle Little Star" so the whole neighborhood can hear. I think it's great because it's so joyful. What I want Skyler to gain most from his early education is a sense of joy and delight.

Skyler doesn't help as much since he has his own life now but he's still there much of the time. Sometimes I hold him up to reach the clothesline so he can hang the clothes. He still sits on the vacuum—it hasn't broken yet. Some things he gets very upset if anyone else does. But generally he's more reasonable now. He doesn't get upset when I won't let him do something impossible and dangerous (with a few exceptions—he's dying to drive the car). He's happy with only a small part of a job—when we scoop grains at the store, I can fill the scoop and aim it in the bag as long as I let him tilt it that last little bit. I tie his shoes up to the very end and then he pulls the loops through. I think even that small involvement prepares him to do the job.

The neighbors are less of a problem now that Skyler is more reasonable. My next door neighbor was warning me Skyler would be a juvenile delinquent because I didn't spank him when he bit her son, but now they play together pretty well. So far, at least, the "terrible twos" are a piece of cake compared to 1½. It doesn't take the same energy I used to expend constantly trying to redirect (distract) him. Now I can ask him to put something back and he does. And some habits have dropped off without too much effort—I was able to put the knobs back on the oven, I was able to put my books in the shelves (I can even take him to the library), the trash can is no longer suspended from the ceiling. Someday I'm sure the chairs will remain upright—now they are always knocked over, but we walk around them and put them up when we need them, assured that this too will pass. Oh yes, he doesn't even walk on the tables at restaurants anymore.

When my friend tells me her son (now 3½) shares because she worked with him on it, I smile a little inside but also feel sad her son doesn't get any of the credit. She's sure all of his virtues exist because she put them there. I'm convinced they're there because they're natural. So we try to set good examples (I never walk on the tables of restaurants *or* at home), tolerate what we can, gently ask him not to do some things and if we need to, we distract him.

Sometimes of course we need to physically prohibit some activity. That's when I'm so glad he's nursing. When he gets upset and mad at me (for example when I don't let him use the garden hose to water the rug in the living room), he takes his comforting from me, so we're brought back together immediately. Nursing is his source of comfort and it's hard to be mad at someone who's giving you milk. "I like *my milk*," he says.

2-Year-Olds' Language

From Lezlie Long (OR):

One of the things I've noticed about Richard (2) that's different from Robert and Rebecca is that *anything* he says has to be *perfectly* correct. If he wants his coat from the car, it's:

Rich: Me go to car and to get my coat?
Me: Yes.
Rich: Can me go to car and to get my coat?
Me: Yes.
Rich: Can me go to the car and get my coat?
Me: Yes.
Rich: OK.

Then he goes and gets his coat. This can be very frustrating when it takes five minutes to get his sentence correct and you know what he's saying but he just has to say it right. Once I got good and mad at him and picked him up and took him with me rather than stand there patiently and listen. Of course he was heartbroken and cried for 30 minutes which made me madder so I was snapping at everybody. Now even if I'm irritated, I take the time to listen to him. It's hard but it's worth it.

And from Chris Laning (CA; see GWS *27, "Unrelated, But Family"):*

Leah has grown two whole clothing sizes in the past six months and her language is growing by leaps and bounds. Other kids come to play with her and Larry three mornings a week, and she goes to a friend's house the other two. We really notice the difference on those days when she doesn't have playmates. She wears us out instead! We just can't keep up with her two-year-old energy. We have *finally* found some other people who think it is perfectly natural to nurse a child until she is three or even older, if she still wants it. Most of the comments otherwise have been, "Aren't you afraid she'll get too clingy and dependent?" (No signs of that yet!) She does almost always want to nurse when going to sleep or when she's just waked up. If she wakes up alone in the bed she almost always cries—seems to feel very lonely and abandoned.

We are astonished at the length and complexity of the sentences she's coming out with. She and I were curled up on the floor, pretending to be cats (a favorite game), when she said "Turn off light!" I said, "But cats can go to sleep with the light on, can't they?" and she replied firmly, "*People* turn light off when people go to sleep in *beds*."

It is delightful to hear her talking away, often just to herself, experimenting. Fortunately she seems to enjoy it when we laugh at what she said! The other night, after searching for her papa and finding him in the bathroom, she came out into the living room and announced, "Papa brushing her teeth." She thought that over for a minute and then said, "Papa brushing his teeth," which seems to have been more satisfactory.

We try to keep an ear open for times when she's tired of grownups always being the ones that know all the answers. She does get quizzed on things, and most of the time doesn't seem to mind it, but occasionally will say "I don't know" when what she seems to mean is "I don't want to answer." We do try to teach her that her body is her own and that she can always say no if she doesn't want someone to touch her (doctoring being the only exception)—we have to be sure we don't assume we can walk into her mind without her permission, either.

Learning Through Play

Janet Williams wrote in the PA Unschoolers Network #6:

> Katie (4) has spent the better part of the winter absorbing phonics and playing with letters. She developed a game of alliterative speech. First she began with reciting nursery rhymes—with modifications. One of her favorites was "Dary dad a dittle damb." (Oh, the delight of the forbidden fruits!) Then we started speaking to each other in the "language" of a given letter. On B day, I would ask, "Bate, bhat bould bou bike for breakfast?" On S day, she would ask, "Som, slease sive se sa srink." The whole family would get into the act. When Kate would ask questions in her letter-talk, the replies would come back in letter-talk.
>
> Over and over, I am struck by how easily we learn if we "play" with something instead of "working" at it. All five of our children learned to read by playing with letters and sounds as Katie has. All five have learned ease with the typewriter/computer keyboard by using and playing in their own "improper" manners. All five are comfortable with the computer logic because they played tricks on each other. (Did you know that we are now capable of electronic teasing?) All five learned about numbers by playing number games in their heads, in Uno, in Yahtzee, in the *endless* "How old will I be in x years?" Then, "Amy is 3 years older so she will be y (x + 3) then, right?" All five have absorbed Spanish and sign language from *Sesame Street*, and now French from Mom.
>
> *But* I still hesitate (what if I'm wrong?) over pronouncing Hawaiian or Russian names. I still grit my teeth every time I approach the typewriter. I still have only the vaguest ideas about the computer. I still think I am so poor at languages—even though Catherine, my French friend, tells me how good my accent is. It seems that learning the *right* way (be it phonics or math or typing or French) becomes more important than *doing* it. The pressure of judgment destroys the pleasure of joyous doing.
>
> So let your silly beginning reader slaughter the phonics in his reader. (We recently had the absurdly unprofessional experience of laughing ourselves to tears over the *intentional* mispronunciations and gibberish that were read from the pre-primer. I am sure that a reading expert would say it was wrong, but we had a *grand* time . . . and that child is reading more each day.) So let your six-year-old develop her hunt-and-peck

typing. So let your four-year-old say, "Aqua, s'il vous plaît." It will all sort itself out in time if we just *let them be*. Playing and doing are the beginnings of learning. Don't criticize the acorn for not being an oak yet.

Making Their Own Rules

More from Lezlie Long (OR):

When the family went to town after Christmas, we picked up a Super Master Mind that was on sale. I saw all those ads saying what a terrific game it was. Well, it is! It has lots of colored pins that one person takes five of and arranges in a covered area, and the second person guesses or "decodes" them. Robert (5) kept begging to play with it so I finally let him. He made designs with the colored pegs. After watching Ken and me play several times, he asked to play. Total frustration! The game is too advanced for him. He finally talked me into letting him play with Rebecca (3). So I set them all up in the living room and went into the kitchen to work. Pretty soon I heard "Yea! Becca, all right! You won!" Rebecca comes running in to tell me she won. She was so excited and proud! I went in to watch them, and what they did was pick *one* color for all five pegs and all they had to do was guess which color. It took each of them five or six tries to get the right color but then there were cheers of "You won! You won!" They never keep track of how many tries they take; to them, it's not important. Robert tricked Becca once and slipped in an extra color. It took forever for her to figure it out. When she did they both laughed but have not tried to do that again.

From Kath Raymond, 3700 NE Van Buren, Minneapolis MN 55421:

I saw one evening that Seth (then age 4) was really having no fun playing Candy Land and neither was I, of course—it's not that great a game. So we began to make our own rules. We played it backward, we traded places, we let Seth take as many turns as he felt would make him happy—we had a *good* time. That was my first experience of the fact that we were the controllers now. I don't know who made the rules on the cover of a boring box game—so why was I following them?

Since then we have questioned so much more. We're coming up with our own answers—all ours—and that feels great!.

Letting Go Of TV

Mary Lee wrote in the Winter '83 Western Pa. Homeschoolers:

> We cast our TV into the attic this past Saturday.... I would say *the* most influential part of the whole deciding process... was Justin.
>
> Justin had destroyed a dollhouse I had been working on for some time—pushing out windows and breaking furniture. This was quite out of character for him and he showed no remorse. He even seemed proud of his "accomplishment." I was quite disturbed and felt he should be punished, so Reese and I decided no TV for 24 hours. Justin has always been fond of TV and watched it often more than I liked him to watch. In those 24 hours, I saw a child who often threw temper tantrums after a TV session, turn into a sweet cooperative little boy, the boy we knew Justin to be. (We couldn't understand these recent changes in behavior.) He played happily outside that day, "read" his books, built magnificent block castles, *really* helped around the house, took a short nap only to arise refreshed (he used to wake up cranky and mean), ate better than usual and generally knocked old Mom off her feet.
>
> TV was brought back the next day, old behavior resumed, and I pointed it all out to Reese, who was beginning to notice too. We also talked about our own habit of turning on the TV when wanting to avoid a certain chore, or person, or when not wanting to make an effort to find something more creative or constructive to do. We also wondered what effects TV was having that we weren't

recognizing. I knew TV made me dissatisfied with my life even though I like my life—explain that one!

So Saturday, for one week, up to the attic went the old TV. You know we honestly, truly—I do not lie or exaggerate—have not missed it. Justin asked about it once a day for three days, and has not since.

And behavior is changing. We are reading more, talking more, going outside more, becoming more involved in outside activities, and generally becoming more human. We're more satisfied, seem less cranky, go to bed earlier, and thus feel better. So, sorry, TV lovers—I think the Lees' TV shall stay in the attic until we decide to sell it!

Instead Of Teaching

A letter from Nancy Edmondson to Susan Richman in the Winter '83 Western Pa. Homeschoolers:

I thought your idea about going ahead and working on the alphabet book *alone* without trying to draw their interest purposely was helpful. Thinking of that the other night, I got out a puzzle and started doing it on the kitchen table. I might have met with resistance had I suggested they might want to help me. So I said nothing, but before I even had all the pieces turned over, they were there eager to help.

Kids Watch Parents Learn

Suzanne Alejandre wrote:

In moving to Germany, Rich and I learned a valuable lesson in what it is like to be a two-year-old child. . . . We could not communicate, everything we did was a new experience. Just buying groceries was a hard task. All the products were packaged strangely. We couldn't recognize them by sight, we couldn't read the labels, and we couldn't ask anyone! Then when we had decided what to buy, we were not familiar with the money. We had to learn each task as we were doing it and we experienced all the frustration that goes along with the process of figuring things out. At the same time, we experienced the exhilaration of a simple, completed task. I can still remember the joy of going through the "correct" steps of buying a loaf of bread in a bakery. I came home and recounted the entire dialogue to Richard. I was so proud of myself!

Even more important for us as a family was that our (then) 2- and 4-year-old sons were often with us through these experiences. They learned as much as we did by watching how we handled situations. They've seen me throw fits just as they have! They've seen me angry, fearful, crying, ecstatic, everything!—all the range of emotions. . . . It is an invaluable experience for a child to watch their parents go through the stages of learning. Rarely will they disrupt—they honor what you are experiencing because they have recently been there. They understand and are watching intently to see what *you* will do to make things work out.

Sometimes they even help. Recently Rich went downtown with Niko because a pair of gloves he had bought already had a hole in them and they were still quite new. When they got to the register where Rich was to make his complaint, Niko whispered, "Daddy, the word for hole in German is 'loch.'" And, actually, that helped because Rich hadn't known the word!.

Learning From Travel

Christine Gajzago wrote in the Australian newsletter, Otherways, *3/83:*

> I'd like to talk more personally about the experiences Ami (6) and Pablo (2½) and I had while overseas. Our aim was to enjoy ourselves and see and do as much as possible. . . . I see no reason why learning should not continue in the same way at home as it did on our trip. With all that concentrated novelty of experience, away from the many distractions and routines of home life, I could see our learnings and discoveries more clearly than usual. Our trip served to magnify, perhaps, what normally goes on at home.
>
> Most people have said: "It's all right to

stop lessons while overseas because it's so 'educational' and such a rare event. But at home children need structured input because they wouldn't learn enough otherwise." I disagree with this view. Often I wonder if behind it lies a lifestyle that may be dull and circumscribed for children and/or does not involve children in the daily ebb and flow. I know this from personal experience. If I am rundown and too preoccupied with my own problems, Ami and Pablo usually let me know. Boredom and frustration set in once they have finished their independent activities and they need external recharging.

The grandest palaces in Europe were not an insurance against ennui if my children's momentary needs for playfulness, energy discharge, food and rest were not met. I noticed from the start of our trip that everything was enjoyed from the context of playfulness. Playfulness does not necessarily require another child but any playful, interesting, energetic, amusing, available person.

Ami and Pablo learnt much on our plane journey to Europe. For instance, the length of the trip reinforced the idea of the distance between Australia and Germany. Even when Ami missed her daddy during the next three months, she did not ask for him, realizing he was too far away. We spoke a lot about the geography of the world which was becoming real now, about how planes work, about many things. But all this was in response to questions and while we played or she chatted to passengers of different nationalities. Ami became very excited about a Philippino girl with whom she played up and down the aisles and the Philippines really became a place in her inner map of the world. Especially after our 5-hour delay in Manila! Since then Germany, Hungary and England have also become concrete reference points in her inner map.

From the start I discovered that there was little point expecting Ami to be enthused about everything I was or to realize that she was in a once-in-a-lifetime situation. She and Pablo lived, and still do, very much in the present. . . . It took time and some effort to respect Ami's pace and style of learning about the world. Once I did, we enjoyed ourselves more. . . . When I *tried* less, I experienced more and generated more excitement.

And Ami did become ecstatic and creative and active so much without any prodding at all. From the moment we landed and entered the German landscape Ami was agog with excitement. "Look! Look!" she would say over and over as we passed mountains and forests and pretty chalets with shuttered windows and geraniums in profusion, and castles that looked like fairy tales.

She asked questions over and over like— "What was this room for?," "Where did the princess sleep?," "Who painted that picture?," "What is that painting (usually one with strong emotive or religious imagery) about?" The very same situations that aroused excitement or deeply absorbed her in long reverent silences, did not excite her if *I* chose to point them out at the wrong time.

Of course since we spent most of our time with distant relatives in a Bavarian village, she needed no prompting to learn German and she learnt with great speed in the daily context of play with children who spoke only German. She picked up a strong English accent while we were in England in a matter of days too, even though by this stage, she also spoke German with me sometimes. In bed at night she did her "homework" and rehearsed new words and phrases with me. Sometimes she would ask me what certain words mean that she had heard and not understood that day. . . . I saw over and over how children regulate their own learning and learn best that way. Adults learn a second language best when they need and want to use it. Why do we expect children to learn *anything* well any other way?

Ami wanted to *be* a princess in a castle (and was)—she wanted to be dressed appropriately and when she became a princess, her face exuded radiance. She became part of her surrounds, part of the past—not just a passive, detached observer. She also needed to extend herself physically wherever she was—to run up and down spiral tower stairs, to hide in the turrets of a castle wall, to explore and climb over and through the beautiful scenery—not just gaze at it. And everywhere, a landscape or special place took on importance when it was associated with special people.

Gwendolyn West (TN) wrote in a report on her family's homeschooling:

Our trip to England and Wales was a marvelous experience for the whole family. The boys readily figured out English money, subways and which double-decker to catch to go where. They loved Dover Castle (we studied feudal times and read King Arthur before we left) and the Tower of London with its crown jewels and rooms of armor. When we were out in the countryside in Rye, Sussex, we stayed in an old smuggler's hideout, an inn remodeled (!) in 1420. Our room was in the peak, full of beams, the lovely and authentic Elizabethan architecture surrounding us. Jason was in awe of Stonehenge (we studied that previously, too), and both boys found the ancient Roman baths of Bath fascinating.

But perhaps best of all may have been staying in our Evans family homestead (my maiden name) that dates back to the 1200s when King Edward II is thought to have hidden prior to being murdered; an official stone marks the spot. Here we stayed one night under down comforters in the thick-walled farmhouse. The boys had "high tea" complete with cakes, biscuits, etc., that my Evans relatives lavished on us as if we were royalty. They also gave us traditional meals of lamb and porridge! The boys played with the rural Welsh children, who were intrigued with meeting Americans, and lots of questions were exchanged with answers on both sides. The Welsh accent is very strong, and we all worked at comprehending it. While I attempted painting my old family homestead, about ten Welsh children gathered. Friendly and warm, they had many questions. They invited Jason and Nathan into a "den" (fort) they had made, to walk down the rocky footpath to the river, to climb trees, etc. My boys learned the internationality of children everywhere. They had a wonderful time. They also played with the Evans' donkey, cats and dog. We explored the area. It is a blustery, green, hilly country of unspeakable beauty, and I know the boys felt this, too.

They loved the experience of London taxis, double-decker buses and of their dad driving our Hertz car on the left-hand side of the road. They became masters at helping us conquer roundabouts and all road signs and were amazingly quick to spot a castle. (Their father, I might add, drove, to my surprise, like a true Briton!)

Language Through Action

[DR:] A few years ago, some foreign language teachers began using a new method called "Total Physical Response," or TPR, and homeschoolers might like to adapt some of its basic principles for their own use. As a GWS *reader writes:*

The book *Learning Another Language Through Actions*, by James Asher, PhD. ($10 from Sky Oaks Productions, PO Box 1102, Los Gatos CA 95031), subtitled "The Complete Teacher's Guidebook," intrigues me. He says this method of teaching foreign languages was invented from closely observing how children and infants learn language, and he says adults can learn this way even faster than kids, because of having a larger vocabulary to start with. . . . Imperative statements are the key. Also it's important not to intimidate students by requiring them to repeat words; rather, as far as speech goes, the students remain passive as long as they want, and, of course, testing in the usual sense is not done either.

Standing together with the students where s/he can be seen by them, the instructor gives a verbal command and immediately carries out that command him/herself, encouraging (not forcing) the students to do likewise. Initially, these are simple imperative statements, like "Sit down!" "Stand up!" "Jump!" "Turn around." Gradually, more and more elaborate imperatives are issued (involving body parts and common objects in the vicinity) which can be directed to individual students, e.g., "Joe, go touch the door!" "Lee, hit your knee!" "Marie, run to my desk!" The next stage is to introduce compound sentences, questions, and humor, but keeping to the imperative form, e.g., "Run to the door and slam it shut!" "Will you bring me your book?" "Did she slam the door?" "Joe, lie down on the floor and go to sleep!"

When the instructor knows what words students know, s/he can ask them individually or in groups to pass on a "command" to the teacher or other individuals or groups. . . . The book gives rather detailed step-by-step instructions, which can, of course, be varied considerably, but I think many readers would find a wealth of good ideas in it.

[DR:] You can find a slightly longer description of TPR methods in an article by James Asher in *Psychology Today*, 8/81. Dr. Asher recommends that instructors not ask students to speak until the 12th hour of training, at the earliest, and when they do speak, that students not be interrupted with corrections as long as their speech is intelligible. He describes several experiments in which students who learned with the TPR method remembered more than those taught by conventional methods.

Rave Reviews

Jane Filstrup ["Bilingual Family," GWS 30] writes:

Thank you for sending the neat little tape of John's trip to Sweden [Travel Diary Vol. I; $6 + post] . . . . You know Emma and Burton (5) are bilingual, by an artificially constructed home program in French. Somewhat to their sensible father's chagrin—"This thing is going too far!"— they are learning Italian from a recorded course. That is why they commented when their father found them listening raptly to this unconventional tape diary, "Oh, this is the friend of those children. We put it on when we got bored of Italian." How how how did John know a travel diary would be so appealing to (at least non-TV watching) young people? It must be the verisimilitude that hugs them in. Hearing sounds of the environment is interesting—one waits for them. Imagine, that is a Swedish police car whistle; maybe the kind Sjowall's and Wahloo's police darted around in (me); what happened to the car? (Burton).

Asked point-blank what they take away from the tape, my son says, "Ça me fait penser que je suis sur l'avion" (It makes me feel as though I'm on the plane), while Emma says, "Maman, je fais semblant que je suis en avion" (I pretend I'm on the plane, too).

I'm not sure whether I want to wire us up to do a tape diary in Paris this summer, but my book will definitely recommend it to other parents travelling with children of all ages. And if anybody *makes* one, my children, for two, would love to hear it!

Susan Richman (PA) writes:

We *love* the *Stewart Piano Preschool Book (GWS 31)*! Jesse has really been enjoying playing piano since we've received the book—he plays "Hot Cross Buns" all over the piano, and has discovered major chords all over (without the 1–3–5 chart, just discovered on his own, he thought they sounded so pretty.) We've been writing out lots of simple songs in numbers, noticing similar patterns in different songs, such as that "Row, Row, Row Your Boat" and "Why Doesn't My Goose" (an old round) both end with 5–4–3–2–1.

It inspired us to get our old piano repaired and tuned, and both boys thoroughly enjoyed seeing the old piano tuner at work, seeing the inside working of the piano. Made me realize that the piano is just a sort of "magic" instrument with no rhyme or reason to it, until you get to see all the fascinating inside mechanisms. I know Jesse and Jacob never imagined all those felt hammers, strings, and connecting rods were inside our old upright!

So glad you found out about the Stewart books. . . . Very fun to do at home—certainly less expensive than *lessons*.

[JH:] About Jesse discovering major chords—that's how and why human beings invented our musical scale and intervals—because they sounded so pretty.

Young Virtuoso Cellist

[JH:] The Jan./Feb. '83 issue of *Music Magazine* has a story about the outstanding young cellist Ofra Harney, who at 17 was the youngest first-prize winner in the 31-year history of the New York Concert Artists Guild, and who has already made a commercial recording and will soon play with several major orchestras. In the article she says, "When I was very young I grew up with music every day. Either my parents were playing or there were records on all the time. They tell me that when I was two years old I would break out in tears when I heard sad music being played." When she was six her mother gave her a quarter-sized cello, and she immediately began playing under her violinist father's instruction. *"There was no one there to tell me that it was difficult, so I started playing in all the positions right away."*

This is what I tell all the people I know, young or old, who take up the cello, and what my experienced piano teacher friends Phyllis Jansma (of Stewart Piano) and Norman Hess tell all their pupils—play all over the instrument, and in all the keys. Don't get the idea in your head that some parts of the instrument are harder than others, for on the piano and the stringed instruments, at least, it is not true. (Of course, it is true for most wind and brass instruments, where the high notes are definitely harder to play.)

When beginners think of their instruments as things on which and with which they can *explore*, and have adventures and make discoveries, they enjoy their playing more and make much more progress. Music approached in this spirit does not have to be drudgery, even for rank beginners.

Later the article quotes Harnoy as saying, "I don't have a teacher now. When I occasionally go back to Orloff or Pleeth it is to exchange ideas and renew inspiration. Even though I will always be learning, I'm not being taught."

Endless Cassettes

When John and I met Barry Kahn (ME) at the Massachusetts Suzuki Conference in Boston recently, he told us about "endless cassettes," devices used in Suzuki training which he thought had exciting possibilities for use in other sorts of learning as well. The cassettes look ordinary but are designed in a special way so the tape loops around to where it began, and so will play the same thing over and over and over until you shut it off. In the Suzuki program, tunes are recorded on these loops, and played often so the children learn them by heart.

The cassettes come in 3, 6, and 12 minute lengths, and can be ordered from *Ability Development*, Box 887, Athens OH 45701. Besides music, Barry thinks they would be great for learning languages, or anything requiring memorization. Recently I had to learn some lines for an acting class I was in, so I taped the scene and played it back a number of times; if I had had an "endless cassette," this job would have been a little simpler. Please let us know if you try these gadgets and if you come up with any other uses for them. —DR

Teaching Adult To Read

Dean Schneider (PA) writes:

I've been working in a local literacy program since July. Bill, the man I tutor, is 48 and never learned to read. He grew up in South Carolina, and his father always put him to work instead of teaching him or sending him to school. The adult literacy program is simple in concept, similar to a learning exchange. The YMCA acts as the administrator and compiles a list of volunteers and matches each volunteer with a person who is registered and seeking help learning to read.

I've been happy with my tutoring with Bill. He's learning to read and I'm seeing my same old methods work as well for an adult as they have for children [See Dean's letter in *GWS* 15, "Advice on Reading"].

Bill and I simply sit down for an hour or so and read together. When we begin a new story, I read the story aloud first so he hears what it's about, then he reads whatever amount of the story he can before getting tired or frustrated. I sit next to him telling him words or giving him clues whenever he gets stuck. We read the story several times until he knows the story fairly well, then we go on to the next. And when he reads on his own at home, he'll read the current story and some of the prior ones for practice.

We started right out reading real books. At first we read simply children's books. I especially like the Monster series published by Bowmar/Noble (4563 Colorado Blvd, Los Angeles CA 90039) and the fairy tales published by Ladybird (Hutchinson Books Inc., Chestnut St, Lewiston ME 04240). After reading just a few of these together, I decided to move to the Junior Great Books program, series 2 (Great Books Foundation, 40 E Huron St, Chicago IL 60611)—a much more difficult set of stories, but very good and Bill seems to like to push himself to read harder books. He enjoys working on a story until he "gets it right," as he says. There's no need for reading to be one long line of steady progress: there are plateaus and leaps.

I have yet to see a better general statement of how people learn to read than James Herndon in *How to Survive in Your Native Land*. He says, "Reading is best taught by somebody who can already read and who knows and likes the kid . . . sitting down with the kid with a book and reading to the kid and listening to the kid read and pointing out things about sounds and words as they go along," and perhaps talking to him about the book and what is going on in it. This is basically what I do with Bill. It works as well with an adult beginner as it does with a child.

The "phonics" work I do is simple. It's partly tied in to the "clues" I give as shown in the list below, and occasionally we'll take a break from the story we're reading and spend five minutes or so on variations of words from the story. For example, *rat*, sat, fat, mat, brat, that; *came*, same, tame, shame, blame; *mean*, bean, lean. There's no particular reason for choosing a certain word for this exercise except that, in the beginning, it should be a common sound. I don't try to do everything all at once. I only list a few possible variations, and I don't try to "cover" every sound he's unfamiliar with. I allow him time to assimilate his growing vocabulary and skill. I simply pick a couple basic sounds to work on for a few minutes, then we get back to reading the story. I do, however, keep an informal chart of the little lists of variations so we can review from time to time. Later on, I'll pick a sound on the list to expand further. For example, I might do fear, feast, beast, beat, meat, peat, peace, please, etc. We've been reading together twice a week since July and we've only accumulated a couple of pages of these phonetic variations. Yet, Bill's recognition of words and ability to figure them out goes beyond such a limited range of sounds. He seems to have absorbed some general rules for figuring out words from the limited phonics work we have done; in other words, he uses phonics for what it is—a *clue* to what a word might be, and *one way* to look at a word (i.e., by the sound).

I'm not against teaching phonics, at least when done in this manner and by syllables or whole words, but I don't agree with teaching phonics right away to a beginner. It's like trying to teach outlining before a student knows how to write. Get the person reading a lot first so he begins to see patterns, to relate unknown words to known words, and has a stock of known words you can compile for little charts. How can phonics make sense until the learner gets a sense of the terrain, of what it's all about, a sense of patterns, a familiarity with lots of sounds and words through just reading. Sure, you can force phonics down students' throats, but that's just a measure of your willingness to be authoritarian, not a measure of what is truly useful for the learner. Phonics should come *after* the student is already reading quite a bit. This early reading is mostly through a "sight" vocabulary and an acquired *sense* of phonics. Bill learned from easy but good books which he read over and over, a few pages at a time until he had learned to read particular books. Each book he learned made it easier to read the next since he was acquiring an increasingly large sight vocabulary. Then, a bit of organized instruction in phonics can help a person consolidate what he knows so far and be a basis for further learning. But still, you don't need much phonics instruction (if any!). We still continue to read and re-read stories and accumulate new phonics lists.

In the following chart, I list some of the "clues" I give when Bill gets stuck as we read together. These are clues only; if Bill doesn't get the clue and is still stuck, I simply tell him the word he's having trouble with. I do not sneak lessons into our reading time together. The only "lessons" I do at all are the variations on sounds I described above.

Clues and Aids to help a reader get unstuck:

- Read the story for him first, so he hears it, knows what's coming, and hears your model of how it should be read fluently.
- If he looks confused after reading a section, even though he reads it correctly, reread it for him.
- Just tell him the word so he'll keep going.
- If the unknown word is the same as a word he's seen before, say, "It's the same as this word up here" and point to both words.
- Tell him a word that rhymes with the unknown word. Tell him "you know this part of it" (such as "out" in "outstretched" or "ten" in "tender"). Cover the unknown part to show the known part by itself; then, cover the known part and see if he can figure out the unknown.
- Just say "Skip it," or "Skip it and come back to it when you've finished the sentence." This helps him figure out words through the context of the sentence. You can also re-read the sentence for him, up to the unknown word.

"Take a guess." Sometimes beginners are afraid to make a mistake, so they don't risk taking guesses. I've found that guessing at unknown words loosens him up; besides, more often than not, his guesses are correct or at least close. If he learns to make guesses, he will do the same when he reads alone and will not get stuck as often when there is no one right there to read with him.

Her Own Reading Improves

Judy Thompson in Washington State wrote to John:

I had been unable to read, or told I couldn't, for so long I really must have subconsciously believed it. I am 42 years old and after reading what you said in one of your books—I don't remember which one but you said kids shouldn't be made to worry about what they didn't know when they read—I tried it out on my 7-year-old girl after she had been on Dick and Jane for two years and hadn't been progressing hardly at all. Well, I dropped reading altogether and two weeks later, she picked out a book several levels above what she had been reading and just started to read and didn't worry about what she didn't know. She read much better than before, probably because she wasn't worried about the unknown.

So this made me think of what I always did. I only read what I knew I could read. So, I got something I wanted to read and I was surprised how well it worked. I read very slowly and still do, but I understand and retain everything. I started to love to read when before I hated to. I never thought I would ever say I love to read but I do. And I thank you for letting me see that I could.

I have a father who with tears in his eyes said to me, "I guess I am just dumb." He works on cars, built a house when first married, most of it himself, drew out the plans himself. He welds, made a sawmill by using odds and ends and was self-employed for most of my life at home.... He was a logger and I used to help him on Sunday. He cleared 3 acres of land and built barns, a shop, chicken coop, greenhouse, had a small farm—cows, chickens, garden. Made a real high swing for us kids. Got wood for the house. And yet he felt dumb.

Buying Standardized Tests

From a parent in Massachusetts:

Last year I mailed away for the free standardized test catalog described in *GWS* 26 [Bureau of Educational Measurements, Emporia State U., 1200 Commercial, Emporia KS 66801]. I then ordered the Metropolitan Achievement Test for 6th grade, and the Iowa Tests of Basic Skills, Levels 9–14, which covers grades 1–6. Each set includes a teacher's guide and answer sheet. The cost for both sets was about $17.

It is helpful to know which tests your school uses, such as Iowa, Metropolitan, etc. . . . Each level has many different forms (JH, H, AB) so it is unlikely you would get the same test your child would be taking in school.

I ordered the tests on my husband's school letterhead paper, but nowhere is it stated in the catalog that only educators can purchase these tests.

I think they're useful if your child is required to take the tests each year. You can get a good idea of content, format, and scoring. . . . The answers are recorded on a separate answer sheet by coloring in a circle:

No. 5 1 2 3 4
     0 0 0 0

It is easy for a child to lose his or her place, and then all the subsequent answers would be wrong. This happened to my child at school, and he felt so pressured knowing he only had a certain amount of time to complete the section that he became unable to find his place, and just continued to fill in any circle so the teacher wouldn't be angry. After practicing at home this year, he felt more confident about taking the tests.

It was helpful for me to see the range of skills that are tested: Vocabulary, Reading, Spelling, Capitalization, Punctuation, Language Usage, Map Reading, Reading Graphs/Tables, Use of Reference Materials, Math Concepts, and Math Problems.

Of course, you're much better off never having to take these tests at all. But if you have to take them, as we do, then you might find buying them a worthwhile investment.[DR: Did anyone else buy their own tests? Please tell us about your experience with them.]

Getting Good Materials

From Leslie Westrum (WI):

Recently visited a local preschool and was tremendously impressed—mostly, I realized, by the equipment. Michael and I have allotted in our family budget about $300–400 per year for our "education fund" (so far we've never spent that much in one year, but it's there if we need it.) Our friends think we're *crazy* to spend so much on the kids—and yet they send their own kids to a preschool—costs them about $800 per year per child! (Some here would cost closer to $1,800 per year.) For that amount of money the kid gets to take his turn with a dozen or more kids at using the great school equipment, and the day there is *very* regimented—and the kids come home tired and bored and flop in front of the TV—no energy left.

Our plan—so far working out just beautifully—is to provide good, sturdy, attractive equipment (I hesitate to use the word "toys" for our school things) and more importantly to provide a peaceful non-competitive atmosphere and lots of cuddling and individual attention.

It has been my experience that children (like adults) learn more easily when given attractive tools to work with— so I'm critical, I admit, of the things I choose for "Rabbit Mountain." Madeline (now 2½) loves our set of 170 colored blocks—wooden ones with a lovely feel to them and nice bright colors. They're made by T.C. Timber and will probably last *forever*! James (1½) prefers Duplo Blocks (made by Lego) because he can snap them together and they don't fall down.

We took Madeline to an educational supply store and she chose an alphabet frieze for the wall—caps and lower-case letters from A to Z and animals from alligator to zebra. She loves pictures on the wall, but then so do the rest of us. So now we have all those letters and animals marching across our *living room* wall. I'm sure the instructor from my interior decorating class would weep.

Our new townhouse has a big back yard and a sandbox (very dilapidated). We had one week of warm weather here last month, and spent most of the week in the back yard. What a delight! ... Michael has drawn up plans to re-build the sandbox and also to build a climbing structure for the kids.

Funny—I used to think that only schools or very, very rich people would have all the educational things we're accumulating, but we're not really a school, and we're *certainly* not rich— it's just a matter of priorities and preferences. Some people buy cigarettes, some buy tempera paint. Some pay a preschool, some create one. I realize, for instance, that our kindergarten blocks cost a bit (around $50) and I could have made perfectly good blocks myself—but I'm not eager to cut, sand, and paint little blocks. On the other hand, I'm awfully eager for good weather so we can cut, sand, put together and paint our climbing structure which will cost about $100, and I wouldn't even consider spending the $600—800 to buy one of those! (And of course we'll have lots of small leftovers for a birdhouse, squirrel feeder, maybe some kid-sized benches).

Cooperative Libraries

Many homeschoolers have said to me, "There are so many books on your list that I would love to buy, but I just can't afford them." For this and other reasons it might be useful for homeschoolers in a given area, even if they live far enough apart so that they only see each other once in a while, to join forces to make a homeschool library. A number of families could decide what books and materials they wanted. If they already had some kind of common gathering place, they could pool their money, send in their order, and have all the books delivered to that place. But it could work just as well if each of, say, six families ordered one-sixth of the books, and then every month or two passed their books along to the next family in some regular rotation, so that by the end of the year everyone would have seen all the books.

Some such arrangement could make it possible for groups of families not only to order more books from us, but other good books which we do not carry (because we cannot get a retailer's discount on them), like the splendid books put out by the National Geographic Society or the Sierra Club. And under such an arrangement families could subscribe to many more good magazines than any one family could afford, like *National Geographic, National Geographic World, Natural History, Ranger Rick, Smithsonian Magazine, Science 83, Odyssey* (a child's magazine of astronomy), *Cobblestones, Homesteader's News, Mother Earth News*, and many others.

Of course it would save families money and perhaps trouble if they could persuade local public libraries to buy the books they wanted. But where libraries are not able or willing to do this, the families could, as just described, have their own library.

Elsewhere in this issue we talk about ways of cooperating with schools. I can imagine a situation in which some of the members of this book-buying-and-sharing group would be teachers in schools. In such a case, as part of their regular rotation, the books and magazines would spend part of their time in these teachers' classroom libraries. For that matter, there is no reason why some *non-*homeschooling families might not also be part of this cooperative library. It would among other things be a good way for them to meet some homeschooling families, and vice versa. One way of finding such families might be to write a letter to the local paper. On second thought, it may be wise not to let this library group get too large, or the task of coordinating it, keeping track of books, etc., which someone will have to do, may become too much of a burden.

If some of you try, or are already trying, this joint library plan, we'll be grateful if you will let us know how it works out.—JH

Italic Workbooks

Ann Bodine wrote in the N.J. Family Schools Newsletter:

There is finally an excellent Italic handwriting series designed especially for children and sufficiently self-instructional to be ideal for homeschoolers. There is a book for each grade level from K through 5, one for adults and older children (who already know how to write) who want to learn Italic, as well as a manual which gives a rationale for Italic handwriting, discusses the historical development of alphabets, left or right handedness, and techniques for increasing speed and developing a personal handwriting style. The children's workbooks are artistic and interesting. Each book costs $3.95 ($3.16 for schools) and there is a $1.50 per order handling charge. Order from Portland State University, Division of Continuing Education, Box 1394, Portland, OR 97207.

[DR: We were interested to learn that the Portland school system has adopted this handwriting method for its elementary schools.]

Writing Contests

From Sharon Hillestad (MN):

Holly decided to enter a writing contest conducted by Avon publishers. It is for teenagers to write about teenagers. She is writing a book ... So far she's written about 4,000 words. I do the typing. First prize is $5,000 plus 6% royalty. Even if she doesn't win she will learn a lot about sentence structure, punctuation, and writing dialogue. She is using Louisa May Alcott as her role model. She has a great start.

The rules for the contest, from the January issue of *Seventeen*:

1. Last date to accept completed manuscripts, Sept. 30, 1983.
2. Each manuscript should contain 30,000 to 50,000 words.
3. Manuscripts must be typed, double spaced, single side.
4. Enclose a letter giving short description of novel with manuscript along with name, address, telephone number and age.
5. Eligible ages, 13 to 18.

For more info: Flare Novel competition, Avon Books, Rm. 413, 959 8th Av, NY, NY 10019.

[DR:] I heard about another contest *GWS* readers might like to enter, the annual Young Playwright's Festival. The winning one-act plays are given a full-scale Broadway production at the Circle Repertory Theater (111 8th Av, NY, NY 10011). We've written to the theater asking about age requirements, rules, etc., and will pass along whatever we find out. If readers know of other such opportunities for children's writing, please let us know.

Computer Letter For Pen Pals

From James Pagnoni (MA), age 10:

I used our Apple to get pen pals from all over the USA. First I typed a general letter to make contact with kids my age who, like me, are taught at home. Here's a copy of it:

Dear XXXXX,

I picked your name out of *Growing Without Schooling*. I am ten years old and my brother is seven. We are homeschoolers. We like board games, sports, reading, piano, and electronic games. I am doing this letter on an Apple II Plus computer. Do you have a computer?

We used to go to school but now we don't. Do you go to school? What kind of school work do you do? Hope you write back.

Your friend,
James Pagnoni

Then I used the Apple Writer II to edit it and to input the different addresses and to make letter-perfect printouts. If a pen pal wrote back, I responded with a more personal reply. Now I have friends from as far away as Virginia, South Dakota, and California. And I am expanding my search for friends to other countries. (I'm waiting to hear from places like Japan and Australia).

My friend from California has an Atari 800, an Apple II Plus, a Commodore 64, a Vic-20, and is thinking about getting an Atari 1200. But most of my pen pals don't have a word processor but want one.

I enjoy computer pen pals because I "meet" new friends and learn about other places. My dad likes it because it also makes me practice my writing skills. And my little brother Joey (who uses the word processor too) says "the best thing is when you erase your mistakes the paper doesn't scrunch up and tear."

Writing, Reading, Spelling

Toni Lenhardt in Oregon writes:

After receiving a Valentine card signed, "To Brooke, Love, Dawn Star," in Dawn's handwriting, my daughter Brooke decided she wanted to write a letter. I thought to myself, sure, you don't know how to write the alphabet, let alone words. I recalled several months before I tried to teach Brooke how to write ABC's and she wasn't interested. But now she was ready; she had asked for help. She dictated the letter to me and I printed it out. Brooke copied my letter onto her own paper. The letter S was hard for her, but without asking me how to do it, she traced what I had written to get the feel of it and then wrote it on her paper.

She's written four letters now.... This was Brooke's letter to Jessica who was looking for a pen-pal (Jessica's request was in Debra Stewart's *Unschoolers Project*):

Dear Jessica, I love ballet. I am 4. I have a baby sister, Rachel Leigh. She was born at home. I cut the cord. I'd like to be a pen pal.
Love,
Brooke

Brooke has started to make her own books—from words on index cards and pictures. She staples the left side and has a book.... She put "Mr. Blossom I like you" on page 1; then "Blossom" (& picture). 3rd page was "Crocus" (& picture); 4th page, "Bluebell too"; 5th, "Happy Spring & Rainbows too" (picture of rainbow); and she made up a tune, singing and dancing and turning pages.

Penny Gillie (IN) wrote in the 5/83 Rainbow Review:

Sometimes the nicest times in our home school are unplanned and unexpected. I was washing lunch dishes while Meegan, age 5, played with magnetic letters on the refrigerator door. Since she was asking me what sounds various letters made, I devised a spur-of-the-moment exercise that we both thoroughly enjoyed. Using the letters *at* and a variety of consonants, I made-up a story about Mat and Pat, employing as many other words ending in *at* as I could. Every time I came to an *at* word, I would tell her the appropriate consonant. She would find the letter, place it in front of *at*, and sound out the ensuing word.

When we had exhausted our *at* story, we switched to *et*. We had such a good time with the *et* story that she suggested combining the two, so our third story was about Mat and Pat and their search for a pet. The possibilities go on and on.

A good suggestion from a reader who has trouble spelling:

I have found that a Thesaurus is much more useful to me than a dictionary because I often do not know the second or third letter of the word I want, but most times can recall a word that means the same and find it that way, or quickly scan a list in the index, if I have no idea.

The Power Of Letter-Writing

[DR:] *An article in the* Greenpeace *newsletter (2007 R St NW, Wash DC 20009) reminds me that one of the best ways homeschooled children can practice their writing skills is by writing real letters, not just to friends but to government officials, companies, newspapers, etc. The article reads:*

Another success story ... As of April 3, 1983, the Turkish dolphin kill has been prohibited. Your letters were the key to giving an endangered species of dolphins a chance at survival.

A British group that visited Turkey last year ... brought back the shocking news that fishermen there were killing an average of 60,000 dolphins per year. Conservationists leveled an international writing campaign at the Turkish government, which was subsidizing the hunt, to demand that it be abolished. After receiving thousands of letters, including one signed by 32 members of the U.S. Senate, Turkey gave in.

We can tell you time and time again how important your letters are, but nothing tells it better than a victory like this. We would like to thank ... the many Greenpeace supporters who made it possible.

[DR:] There's a long list of issues that young people might feel strongly enough about to write letters—the environment (pollution, endangered wildlife, land use), peace, world hunger, honesty in government, discrimination, product safety, individual freedom, saving old buildings, and so on. There are many organizations connected with each of these issues that will be more than happy to tell you where your letters will be most effective, and to give you background information.

For example, Amnesty International *(304 W 58th St, New York, NY 10019) depends on letter-writing as a tool in preserving human rights, and as it happens they have just begun focusing on the imprisonment, torture, and killing of children in political struggles around the world. Some excerpts from the organization's literature, describing how it works:*

> Amnesty International ... founded in 1961 ... has worked to bring about the release of tens of thousands of "prisoners of conscience"—people imprisoned and often tortured for holding the wrong political views, expressing the wrong opinions, believing in the wrong religions or belonging to the wrong ethnic groups.... Once we have learned the identity of a prisoner of conscience, our research department in London investigates the case and digs out as many facts as possible about the prisoner's background, details of his or her arrest, trial (if the prisoner was fortunate enough to get one), and imprisonment.
>
> If the prisoner is "adopted" by Amnesty, our members write to him when possible, to his family and friends, to the officials in charge of his prison or his case, to the news media in his and other countries—even to the heads of state and government leaders.
>
> Such measures—mild though they may seem—have aided in bringing about the release of thousands of prisoners of conscience in many countries.... In recognition of its efforts, Amnesty International received the Nobel Peace Prize in 1977.

[DR:] Organizations like Greenpeace and Amnesty International usually ask for contributions for their publications, but if you are truly interested in one of these issues yet cannot afford to pay, you should not let that stop you. I imagine that if you wrote to these groups anyway, saying that you would like to support their cause by writing letters, they would send you information if they possibly could.

Children who think their letters will not be taken seriously because they are children can always type their letters. No need for them to mention their age unless they want.

The organization, Bread for the World *(32 Union Sq. E, NY, NY 10003) has an excellent pamphlet on writing effective letters to Congress. Of course, readers will find this advice helpful in writing to their representatives about many issues, in particular about homeschooling. Some excerpts:*

> Only one out of every 10 US citizens ever writes a letter to his or her congressional representative, senator, or to the President. The other nine remain silent for reasons such as "Congresspersons don't read their mail" and "One letter won't make any difference anyway." The experience of Bread for the World has proved these notions incorrect.

Congresspersons are the first to acknowledge the increasingly important role played by letters from their constituents:

"My mailbag is my best 'hot line' to the people back home. On several occasions a single, thoughtful, factually persuasive letter did change my mind. . . ."—Morris Udall, Representative from Arizona.

"Someone who sits down and writes a letter about hunger . . . almost literally has to be saving a life. . . . "—Paul Simon, Representative from Illinois.

Bread for the World is a grass roots lobbying movement that uses letters as the primary tool in shaping legislation. For example, an estimated 250,000 letters were generated in support of the Right-To-Food bill. As a result, this resolution was voted out of the committee where it had been held up and was passed by both the Senate and the House.

Rules of thumb . . . Rarely should a letter exceed one full page. Write your own views in your own words. . . . Concentrate on one issue per letter. . . . Don't threaten or demand . . . Be constructive. If a bill addresses a legitimate problem but proposes the wrong solution, express this and then go on to give your view as to the correct approach. . . . On occasion, you will be writing on a subject about which you have greater knowledge or access to information than your representative. Share such information by sending background papers and newspaper articles.

[DR:] About this last point—John often does this, sending to the Massachusetts senators copies of magazine articles that he thinks they should know about.

Writing to business companies can also be useful. I read somewhere recently about a teacher who always had her class send letters of complaint, suggestion, etc., to companies during the first week of the school-year, because when the replies started coming in two or three weeks later, the children became excited and developed a new respect for the power of the written word. If you make clear your disappointment over a particular product or service, many companies will send you a refund or a discount on future purchases. You can always write to the president of a corporation if you're not sure who else to write to; if the address is not on the product, you can find usually find it in the reference section of a library.

We'd love to hear some stories about letters that readers (especially younger readers, but not only them) have written that have made a difference, that have produced some kind of rewarding or unlooked-for response.

An Electronic Typewriter

Since I travel so much, and like to type, l have long wished that someone would invent a truly portable electric typewriter. A Japanese company named Brother has done it, and their EP-20 is one of the most useful tools I own. It is less than two inches thick, weighs only a few pounds, and can run off regular house current or four D-sized batteries—which last a long time. It is so quiet that you can type without disturbing people close to you, or waking up people who are asleep. It uses a dot matrix printer, which means that you can't make carbon copies, the type has the typical dot matrix look (some publishers will not accept manuscripts done in it), and the print is not very bold (though it is perfectly readable).

Perhaps the most astonishing thing of all about this little machine is that it has a fifteen-space correcting feature. When you type in the CP ("correcting print") mode, each letter you type appears at the right hand edge of a 15-space liquid crystal display, like the ones on small calculators. Only when a letter moves off the left hand edge of the screen is it typed on the paper. Everything on the screen can be changed, either deleted or added to. Once it gets on the page, it can't be fixed, of course, but the 15 spaces allow you to catch mistakes and even to change your mind about a word or two. All other machines with this correcting feature cost at least twice as much as this one.

The machine has another feature I have not seen on any typewriter at any price. There is a second shift key (green) which when pressed gives you an entire keyboard's worth of extra characters. The smart Brother people, wanting to sell their machine in all countries, have used these extra keys for the accents and special letters used in such languages as French, Spanish, Swedish, etc., and also for symbols for different kinds of money. It would be very useful for people writing in some of these languages.

But the most interesting thing to me about this typewriter is that it is so fascinating to children. I have had it with me when I have visited several families with children, and they just can't get enough of it. Something about its small size, and the correcting screen, has great appeal for them. They all say, "I'm going to get one like that!" Because it is small, and quiet, and correctable, and has no keys to jam up, I think it might be an ideal child's typewriter.

Along with the disadvantages of the dot matrix printer, it has one other disadvantage. It uses a special ribbon cartridge, which for the amount of typing you get from it is fairly expensive. They cost $3 each, and I think will last for about eight or ten single spaced pages—I haven't measured exactly. I don't think it would be a sensible machine to use as a full-time home typewriter, if you do a lot of writing—one of the larger correcting machines would do better. But if you travel a lot, and like to write when you do, or if you have children, it seems to me almost ideal.

The list price of the typewriter is about $200, but in today's news section of the Sunday *New York Times* I see that 47 Street Camera—of whom we wrote in *GWS* 32 as being a very good source for cameras, tape recorders, computers, etc.—is selling it for $160, which seems a very good buy. Their mail order address is 36 E. 19th St., New York NY 10003, and you can call them toll-free at 800-221-7774. I would even be tempted to add this machine to our own mail order list, except that we could never buy in large enough quantities to meet the prices of these big discount stores.

Another company which sells this typewriter (along with many other interesting products) is JS&A, One JS&A Plaza, Northbrook IL 60062. They charge $10 more for the machine, but they give an unconditional 30-day money back guarantee, so if after trying it you feel it's not for you, you can send it back.

If I had to choose between getting a child one of these typewriters and one of the $100 computers, I would certainly pick this typewriter.—JH

Learning From Computer Games

Herb Kohl wrote in Changing Schools, *Winter '83:*

> I have had arguments with teachers over the use of computer games in the classroom. They resist the games (even the same teachers who will use frilly versions of drill programs) because the children seem to be having too much fun to be learning. Of course they're having fun! And despite what many teachers feel, they're learning too.
>
> I said this to a group of teachers recently and received a challenge which seemed to me more hostile than pedagogic. "If they're learning, then tell us exactly what they are learning by playing computer games. How can what's learned be tested? How does it fit in the curriculum?"
>
> Whenever someone throws a question like that at me, I step back and think about specific children and specific instances where it was clear that something was being learned. In the case of computer games, what came to mind was:
>
> The time I saw a very frightened, demoralized boy sit for two hours and conquer a complex game that required considerable dexterity and a bit of thought.
>
> Another time when a girl I know learned enough chess from a computer to beat

her father.

A time when a twelve-year-old I have worked with, and who the school calls "educationally handicapped" and "hyperactive," worked his way through a space game that required weighing the relative values of fuel supplies, weapons, and speed, while charting his position on a map with 16 different segments. This same boy could not sit still in school for more than ten minutes.

A time when four ten-year-olds challenged me to play several computer games with them, and then wiped me out.

In my experience, even the most avid game player eventually wants more from computers than just playing games. He or she eventually wants to *make* games, to list and change programs, and to achieve that additional power which comes from understanding a machine and its language well enough to push it to its limits.

I believe that through the programming of some simple games, just about all of the Basic or Pilot computer language that one needs for programming competency can easily be mastered. In fact, this year I hope to work with a group of seven-year-olds and teach them the rudiments of programming this way.

A good game to start with is a simple number guessing game, or a graphics game. The game you start with, of course, will depend upon the qualities of the computer you work with. These days I work principally with the Atari 800 because I like its graphics and sound capabilities. It is a very easy machine to use with children because they can quickly see some elegant results of their work.

The challenge of my simple number guessing game is to program the computer so it will select a number from 1 to 20, and have the player guess the number. After we get that simple game written, the goal is to dress it up with sound graphics, to change the program so that numbers from 1 to 100 are selected by the computer, and to give the player hints.

All of this leads up to what I hold to be the central notion of gaming and programming—that there is *no single way* to do things, nor even a single "best" way. Like playing poker or chess, programming is an *art*, even though there is a structure to it.

Letters Wanted On Computers

From Daniel Chandler (8 Burnet, Stantonbury 1, Milton Keynes, Bucks MK14 6AJ, England), who promises to share the results with GWS:

I am writing a book with the title *Young Learners And The Microcomputer* for the Open University Press in England. It is to be both for parents and teachers in England and the US, and will discuss issues and practices, using as springboards the perceptions of kids themselves (up to age 12).

If your kids would like to describe how they've been using computers, I'd be very interested to hear from them (as well as from parents). As a de-schooler myself I'd like to be able to use some good examples from alternative education. . . . Any extracts will be gratefully acknowledged in the text.

Concerns About Computers

From Lisa Boken (MA):

Just a few quick thoughts on home computers—I love them, I hate them, they scare me, and they lure me.

Like many of the "wonders of technology," how much was researched before the masses were sold on them? . . . What about the problems that don't surface for years? Decades?

There are those who see computers as the key to future success. . . . Why, one parent actually wept and pleaded with a teacher of computer science in a middle school because her son's future would be *ruined* if he didn't squeeze him into his class.

Our family has access to three computers. We have also attended local interest groups for computers in our area and what we see and hear and share thrills us and frightens us. . . . We need people like you, John, to say, "Think about . . . ."

So, what do we do—lock ourselves and our children up, away from technology—until the implications are manifest? No . . . but think about the possibilities, picture (to the best of your ability) down the road a piece.

I guess I feel strongly that our society is becoming less and less questioning and more and more accepting unconditionally. . . . Look at the sacred cow, school, and how many years you and others have worked just to get people to question, to think.

From Shannon Bush (TN):

I, too, am excited about the potential that computers have in making homeschooling and self-reliant living richer and even more exciting for us. But it is crucial that parents understand the biological hazards to themselves and their children that VDTs (Video Display Terminals) may present. While there have been few conclusive studies yet, several are in progress, and one should not gamble with one's health in the meantime. The information I am passing on here is from an article in the March '83 issue of *Whole Life Times*, by Barbara Bialick.

Of 125 models that the U.S. Bureau of Radiological Health tested, 8 VDTs emitted more X-rays than the legal limit. Some of these were recalled or taken off the market.

More worrisome . . . are the 8 clusters of birth defects and miscarriages that have been reported in North America since 1979. . . . Other factors in the workplace could be implicated, but one cluster seems to point the finger at VDTs. . . . The other suspected health effect of VDT's is cataracts. A Scarsdale, NY ophthalmologist, Dr. Milton Zaiet, is currently the only eye doctor in North America who will state openly that he believes that "VDT's as currently shielded and constructed pose a grave radiation danger."

It is tempting for people who like their home computers to dismiss these problems as irrelevant to their situation on the grounds that they and their children certainly don't spend eight hours a day at their computers. But might they not spend three or four occasionally? People who are really fascinated do. . . . An hour or two a day of X-rays is worse for a growing nine-year-old than a fifty-year-old, as I know from the research I did a few years ago when they were building a nuclear plant near my home.

And from Kathie DeWees (VT):

I happened upon the following "letter to the editor" in a local newspaper that I thought you might be interested in:

Recently, President Reagan endorsed the idea that video games were ultimately going to benefit our country's military forces. He suggested the maneuvering handles on the games were similar to those in military aircraft. And so because we have millions of kids zeroing in for the kill, preparing to kill, developing the hand/eye coordination necessary to operate defense/offense systems, our president is pleased and I am horrified.[Kathie resumed:] I, too, am horrified . . . if there must be all these computer things, though I don't see why there needs to be, why can't they be peace games, why must it always be for power and control and killing?

So many people are getting further and further away from our Mother Earth and the life and love that our planet stands for, and are so much into all this super technology that in the end stand for death and hate. I'm glad my family lives simply, without electricity, etc., and I'm glad to see our children building things from bark and stones and branches and playing in the stream and the snow. They are at peace with nature and I hope they can always be. They have yet to play a computer war game and I hope that can always be, though that will have to be their decision. I hope they can always love to watch the seedlings grow and the animals run free and feed the birds from their hands and not want to play war games that in the end lead to the destruction of all these wondrous things.

The Ideas Behind Computers

Truly successful inventions are likely to have ideas behind them; that is, they meet human needs which are not merely physical or economic, but psychological and emotional.

The automobile is a good example. It has profoundly changed the face of the world and the patterns of human life. From where did it get its magic power? Mostly from a dream, a wish, which human beings have cherished and pursued since ancient times, but found only in myths, like Pegasus the flying horse or magic carpets—the dream of going wherever they want, and many times faster than their feet or even a horse could ever carry them.

A middle-aged Danish woman, who had just bought the first car she had ever owned or driven, once expressed this dream as we drove through Copenhagen, still mostly untroubled by severe traffic jams. In a voice of true rapture she said, "I feel so *free*!"

That was ten years ago. Whether she still feels so free, I do not know. Living in Boston, where I can walk to most of the places I go and take public transport to most others, I feel more free because I have not owned a car in ten years or so and do not expect ever again to own one. In recent years I have said this to many people; almost without exception they have said to me, "Oh, you're lucky! I wish I didn't have to own a car." Recent figures claim that for most Americans the cost of owning a car is now over $4000 a year. Clearly an invention, a tool, which most people feel they have no choice but to own and which costs them many thousand dollars a year is not a liberating but an enslaving tool. It has added much more to our burdens and problems than to our pleasures. Most things that we really love to do, we could do without cars; the things we have to use them to do are mostly things we feel we can't get out of doing.

The computer is clearly another successful invention. Whether it will prove to be as enduring as the automobile, or be a liberating or an enslaving tool, it is too early to tell, but successful it certainly is. What are the ideas behind its success, what psychic needs does it fill? Two seem very clear.

The first is the Cartesian idea about which I wrote in my review of *A Sand County Almanac* in *GWS* 32, namely, that all of reality, everything that exists, is a machine, of which every part can be expressed as a number. The early educational psychologist Thorndike stated this flatly: "Everything that exists can be measured"—an idea which has corrupted and crippled education to this day. Or, as we might put it, anything we can't count, doesn't count. Computers powerfully reinforce the modern myth that anything and everything important can and can only be expressed in numbers. People have of course believed this for many years before anything like the modern computer was invented. But computers make it much easier to believe and much harder to oppose.

The other idea embodied in the computer is the idea that *information* can somehow be a substitute for judgment, wisdom, courage, faith, and luck—that if you just have enough pure facts at your disposal you can know exactly what will happen, and make happen what you want to happen. This need for absolute certainty and absolute control, while understandable enough in a rapidly changing and dangerous world, is a weakness and a sickness. Like the wish for unlimited mobility, it is also long enshrined in myth. The ability to know the future is one of the things which human beings have always craved and for which many have been willing to sell their souls to the devil. Since on the whole we do not believe the truths that come down to us in stories, but only what moves pointers on dials, we still persist in the folly of thinking that we can get the best of that bargain.

One reason I am more fearful than hopeful about the future of computers is that I find it hard to see how much good can come of an invention which so strongly depends on and reinforces two such bad ideas. The first idea, that everything that exists can be measured and that whatever we can't count doesn't count, is from a scientific point of view absurd; from any conceivable religious point of view, it can only be called blasphemous, and it is astonishing that so few religious thinkers point this out. The second idea, that information can replace judgment, that if we have enough facts we can't go wrong, is equally silly, and is contradicted by every day's news. Within the last quarter Pan American Airlines announced what the financial columns said was the largest quarterly loss ever reported by an American corporation. Yet we may be sure that Pan Am had as many and as good computers, and as much raw information, as its rivals. Where it failed was in not knowing which of its information was important, or in making wise use of it. This is something that in the nature of things computers cannot do.

Not believing in faith or judgment, we don't believe in souls, still less the Devil. But if the busy makers and sellers of computers could convince us, as they are doing their best to, that with their machines we can really know and control the future, we might be willing to make any changes in our laws, customs, morals, ideas of right and wrong, that computers might seem to demand, not least of them the right to privacy, to reveal no more of ourselves to the world than we wish to reveal.

Let me be a bit more specific about these dangers. I have said that an important freedom for me is the right *not* to own a car—or for that matter, a television set. So far the government has not tried to deny me these choices. But there are already strong signs that it may soon try to deny me the choice of *not* owning a computer or spending time learning how to run it. A very slippery, tricky, and sinister little phrase is beginning to make its way, I should say force its way, into our language—"computer literacy." It has appeared in practically every statement about education that I have seen in the past six months. A recent *Christian Science Monitor* story reports: "Both [California State Superintendent of Education) Honig's proposal and one put forward by Democratic State Sen. Gary Hart . . . would require . . . one year of computer training for a high school diploma." My friend Ed Pino from Colorado told me just yesterday that already sixteen colleges require their entering freshmen to buy a computer, and *120* make some kind of computer training a requirement for admission.

What is it that these educators want to compel students to know? Probably a modest amount of computer vocabulary—names of computer hardware, etc.—most of which I have learned from a little casual browsing in computer magazines—and the ability to do some simple programming in BASIC. But BASIC is even now hardly ever used for any serious business or scientific purposes, and within a decade it will probably be useless. For many years the ability to type well has been a very valuable skill—I count it one of the most useful things I have ever learned. Even now it is a great deal more useful for most life purposes than the ability to do simple programming. But no schools, though they might have been wise to do so, have ever made typing a graduation requirement, or colleges made it an entrance requirement, or demanded that all their students own a typewriter. No doubt the makers of typewriters are kicking themselves for not having ever thought of the phrase "typewriter literacy." But then, typewriters never pretended to be more than a handy tool to write things with, instead of some magical way of knowing and controlling the future.

Who is going to be allowed to decide what people shall be compelled to know about computers? Who will write the textbooks for all those "computer literacy" courses? In all probability, the same people who are making and selling the computers. Will the students be taught to be skeptical about computers and cautious about buying them? I doubt it very much. Will they learn, as in my casual browsing I have learned, that most computer hardware is incompatible with most other hardware, and that most of the people who sell this hardware either don't know that or won't tell you? Or that the first word processing program put out by IBM for use with their personal computer was so bad that they soon had to withdraw it? Or that nothing done in homes (as opposed to businesses) *economically* justifies buying a computer? Or that when you buy a new model computer you will probably have to wait two or three years for the necessary programs to go with it? Or that businesses should not spend more than about one percent of their annual gross income on a computer? Or that at all price levels computers have been and are plagued by serious problems of reliability, and that most of the people who sell them do not know how to or will not service them? All this seems extremely unlikely. What is much more likely is that the schools, which have long been teaching Science-Worship, will now begin to teach Computer-Worship.

There's an old Arab saying that if you let the camel's nose into your tent you will soon have the entire camel. We have allowed into our tent—our society, our laws, our schools—the nose of a very large, determined, clever, unscrupulous, and in the long run possibly dangerous camel. Unless we are very careful, we may soon find ourselves obliged by law to buy whatever the computer industry wants to sell us. I still think there is a chance that computers may become, in Ivan Illich's phrase, "convivial tools," which, like bicycles, typewriters, and cassette tape recorders (to name only three of many), serve and empower their users, instead of, like autos and TV, burden and diminish them. But it will have to be up to us, not the computer industry, to make sure this happens. We at *GWS* will have more to say, from time to time, about how we may do this.—JH

If You Start A School

Nancy Plent wrote in the New Jersey Unschoolers Network:

> My two years with an alternative school, 13 years ago, were exhausting, discouraging, and emotionally draining. . . . I've learned that homeschoolers often want to start schools. It was an upsetting discovery at first. I wanted to shake people by the shoulders and tell them how *good* they had it without that complication.
>
> But many parents feel a longing for "something more," some replacement for the special children's place that school represents. As Eric grows, I see that he will probably want "something more" at some point, too. I've started wrestling with the painful ghosts of that school experience to see if I could decide where things went wrong, and if it seems possible to have a parent-run school which would bring pleasure and excitement instead of stress.
>
> *Children and adults should maintain and run their "school."* Some time should be spent each day in adults and children working together on the physical maintenance of the school. No adults giving assignments and children doing the work, or hiring outside maintenance people. This idea comes from Dr. Raymond Moore, and is being practiced in private schools at all levels including college. Two boys at our alternative school refused to pick up after using things and were indifferent to any project we tried to get them involved in. They felt the adults should do the picking up. (Fair enough, actually, since the projects were all adult ideas.) When their family later moved to a commune, an old warehouse in need of lots of fixing, the boys were viewed as potential workers and welcomed on adult work crews. Their mother reported that their attitude was entirely different. They felt they belonged in this place, were needed, and had a voice in decisions.
>
> *A school should either share a building or run a business.* Money problems can tear a school apart. If you're in constant danger of having to close down, can't buy any materials, etc., the school becomes drudgery. If you make tuition high, parents often demand unreasonable things of the school ("because after all, I'm sacrificing a lot to send my child there"). A sense of parent sacrifice makes the children feel guilty about enjoying the school. One school I know got a grant to run a health food co-op and expanded it into a store. Every effort should be made to keep expenses low or income stable.
>
> *Someone has to be in charge.* This was an unpopular notion in the '60s. Our school was started by an energetic mother of five with hundreds of ideas and a hang-up about being an "authority figure." We spent hours in meetings,

hashing out small things which she could have simply decided. *We* didn't know what direction we were going in. We wanted her to set the course. The confused atmosphere that some alternative schools project comes from this kind of "Well, what do *you* think?" lack of leadership. If a school is a group effort rather than the brainchild of one energetic person, at least have people in charge of different areas. . . . A lot of energy is released when somebody has to go-ahead to act upon their ideas, right or wrong.

[JH:] I agree 100% that the children and adults involved in a school—or learning center, club, whatever you want to call it—should do all the physical work of maintaining it. At the Friskole in Copenhagen this has been the rule from the first day. The one thing all children are expected to do is do their share of cleaning up, repairing, and cooking, and the interesting thing is that no children, even the most disturbed, angry and rebellious newcomers, ever refuse to do it. It makes them members of the community they need so much to feel a part of.

Private School Option

Many, perhaps even a majority, of the people who are teaching their children at home, are doing so by calling their own home a private school. Since in many states private schools are virtually unregulated, this has seemed the easiest way to go, and indeed we here at *GWS* have long recommended it. But I am beginning to feel more and more strongly that in the long run and even in the short it may not be the best way to go, and that the best way to go, if we can do so without making unacceptable concessions, is to reach a friendly and cooperative agreement with the local schools, of the kind we have often described, in which the children are registered with the school and can use as much of its facilities as they want, and in which the school continues to receive whatever state and federal aid it gets for its regular pupils.

The trouble with the private school option is that though it looks easy on the face of it—just fill out the simple form, and there you are—in the long run it is unstable. The public schools, that 100+ billion industry, with great political power in Congress and the state legislatures, must and always will see as an intolerable threat to their existence any homeschool arrangements which deprive them of the state (and perhaps federal) aid which is an increasingly important part of their budgets, and deny them the right to exercise any kind of educational control over what goes on. They will never stop trying to fight such arrangements, and in the long run, and not just because of their money, they will probably be able to persuade most legislatures, and most federal courts, to take their side. Even those legislatures (LA, AZ) which have passed what look like strong pro-homeschooling laws could very easily be persuaded to repeal them if the schools could only manage to turn up one or two cases of gross neglect or abuse or educational incompetence by homeschooling families—and sooner or later, as our numbers increase, there are very likely to be a few such cases.

In most of what we might call the private-school states, we homeschoolers are in a kind of cold war relationship with the schools. On any given day there may not be active hostilities—they may not actually be taking any families to court—but they are likely always to be thinking about ways in which they might do it. This makes the situation of homeschoolers more precarious than it ought to be; we never can tell when some court (as in Virginia and Florida) or some state Attorney General, or some educational official, as recently in California and Washington, may not suddenly be able to pull the rug out from under our feet. We have to keep thinking, "What might they try next, and if they do, what are we going to do about it?" instead of thinking about something more interesting—how to help our children grow up into the world.

Here in Massachusetts we don't have the private school option (since private schools must be approved by the local public schools). What we have is much better—a situation in which a growing number of school districts are cooperating with homeschoolers and in the process getting to know and trust them. Every year the number of districts grows in which superintendents and school boards can say, "Yes, we have homeschool families, and they're doing a fine job, and we like to help them all we can." Families whose school districts feel this way about them don't have to worry about what this or that judge or state official may say. As far as anyone can be secure in this world, they are secure, at least in their homeschooling. And, of course, they are able to use, if they want, those expensive school facilities which they could never duplicate and which their taxes help pay for.—JH

On "Discovery Proceedings"

From Theodore Amshoff (see "Friendly Lawyers," this issue):

In reference to the inquiry you made on Page 20 of GWS 32 concerning the use of discovery techniques in home education trials to ascertain test scores, etc., several problems present themselves. Normally the process of submitting written questions which must be answered by the opposing side (called "interrogatories") is available only in a civil trial. Discovery proceedings in criminal trials are much more severely limited in most states.

Juvenile courts in many states conduct their proceedings under the *civil* rules of procedure instead of the criminal rules. Thus, interrogatories may be available in that situation.

Even in the criminal context, some discovery is usually available under the laws of every state. We have been quite successful in our representation of homeschoolers in securing Court Orders, even in criminal cases, compelling the prosecutor to furnish test data from the local public schools, as well as state test norms. In our experience, as a practical matter, judges have been much more willing to uphold the constitutional rights of homeschoolers where they have been given evidentiary assurance that the children are receiving an education comparable or superior to that of their public school peers.

Obtaining such information in a criminal proceeding usually involves pre-trial motions to the court in order to secure appropriate orders for such discovery. We have done this in several states.

Incidentally, as a general principle, I wholeheartedly concur with your advice and recommendation against the filing of civil damage suits in the federal courts against the local school superintendents and other education and law enforcement officials. . . . While it is possible that some set of facts someday might justify such action, I have not yet seen that case. Other remedies are certainly available which have far greater strategic prospects for success.

For example, the same statute (42 USC S.1983) also provides for the granting of injunctive relief, and may be coupled with an action for a declaration of rights. Relatively speaking, I believe this remedy to be far more appropriate to homeschool situations, and might be a recommended strategy in those areas where state court precedent is strongly against homeschoolers, thereby foredooming a family's prospects in a state court criminal prosecution.

Needless to say, each schooling case is unique, and merits careful consideration of the alternatives applicable in each situation with competent legal counsel.

Michigan School Case

[DR:] We got a copy of the court decision described in "Important Michigan Ruling," GWS 31, and quote some of the relevant portions below. In case you're interested in how to obtain such documents, what we did was write to the County Courthouse in Saginaw, the city closest to the towns mentioned; someone there forwarded our letter to the Court Clerk of Ingham County in Lansing, who asked us for $5 for photocopying.

> *Sheridan Road Baptist Church, First Baptist Church Bridgeport, et al, Plaintiffs; v. State of Michigan, Department of Education, and Phillip E. Runkel, Superintendent of Public Instruction, Defendants.*

Opinion and Order, Docket #80-26205-AZ

Held in the Circuit Courtrooms, City of Lansing, County of Ingham, State of Michigan, on the 29th day of December, 1982. Present: Honorable Ray C. Hotchkiss, Circuit Judge

In July of 1980, Defendant, Michigan Dept. of Education, filed a complaint with the Superintendent of Public Instruction seeking suspension of the operation of Sheridan Road Christian School and the Bridgeport Baptist Academy. The complaint alleged that the schools failed to comply with the requirements of 1921 P.A. 302, S. 5; MCLA 388.555; MSA 15. 1925.

On Dec. 6, 1980, plaintiffs filed the present action seeking declaratory and injunctive relief. Plaintiffs challenge the constitutionality of 1921 P.A. 302 (hereafter referred to as "the act") and allege that said act is contrary to the First and Fourteenth Amendments to the Constitution of the United States and Article 1, Section 4, and Article VII, Section 1, of the Constitution of the State of Michigan.

The purpose of 1921 P.A. 302 is clearly stated in the preamble to that act. It provides:

"*an act* to provide for the supervision of private, denominational and parochial schools; to provide the manner of securing funds in payment of the expense of such supervision; to provide the qualifications of the teachers in such schools; and to provide for the endorsement of the provisions hereof."

Under Section 1 of this act, the superintendent of public instruction is given supervision over all private, denominational, and parochial schools. This section further provides that the sanitary conditions and the courses of study in religious schools must be of the same standard as provided by the public schools. Under Section 3 of the act, all teachers employed by non public schools must be certificated and must submit to an examination to obtain a certificate.

Section 5 provides for investigation and examination of records of non public schools by the superintendent of public education to determine whether that school is in compliance with the act. This section also provides that refusal to allow an investigation or examination of records is sufficient cause to suspend the operation of the school.

This Court is of the opinion that the religious beliefs of the plaintiffs are sincere and that the education of their children in schools which conform to their religious beliefs is an integral part of the churches' religious mission. This Court is further of the opinion that the regulations imposed on the schools by 1921 P.A. 302 interfere with the practice of plaintiffs' legitimate religious beliefs.

Freedom of worship is among the fundamental rights which are protected by the Fourteenth Amendment of the Constitution from infringement by the state.... The basic purpose of the free exercise and establishment clause of the Fourteenth Amendment is to see that no religion is favored, sponsored, commanded, or inhibited.... Only the highest state interests, and those not otherwise served, may overbalance the legitimate claims to the free exercise of religion (*Sherbert v. Verner, Wisconsin v. Yoder*).

The State of Michigan's interest in universal education can only be classified as a state interest of the highest order. To implement the responsibility for education, it is necessary that the state have power to impose reasonable regulations. However, even the state's interest in education is not above the balancing process when it impinges on fundamental rights like the free exercise of religion.

Section 3 of the act requires that all teachers employed by non public schools must be certified by the State of Michigan. Under MCLA 380.1531, the State Board of Education is responsible for determining the requirement for teacher certification. One requirement is that a candidate must hold a degree from a college or university with an approved teacher training program. Another requirement is that a candidate must complete a certain number of hours as a student teacher under the guidance of an experienced teacher.

The purpose of teacher certification in Michigan is to insure a minimal level of qualification for teachers, and to provide some minimum standards to address things a teacher ought to know in order to avoid harm or detriment to children.

Defendants' expert witness, Dr. Judith E. Lanier, stated that without teacher certification, there would be no safeguard or mechanism to represent the State's interest in the education of children by qualified instructors. However, Dr. Lanier admitted that she was aware of no specific research linking teacher certification with better teachers. Dr. Lanier also stated that she did not believe Michigan's teacher certification program has resulted in overall success in performance by Michigan students.

Dr. Donald Erickson, an expert in the field of education, testified that there is a distinct lack of consensus on the method to be used to train teachers. Dr. Erickson further testified that the factors that make certain teachers more effective than others are unknown.

Dr. Erickson stated that schools that employ only certified teachers are generally less effective when effectiveness is measured by student achievement. He criticized Michigan's teacher education system which he felt imposed certain methods of teaching at the expense of others. Dr. Erickson further testified that he believed teacher certification to be one of the weakest steps to guaranteeing educational quality.

Another expert in the field of education, Dr. Russell D. Kirk, testified that the requirements for teacher certification in Michigan are excessive in number and that the requirements for teacher training institutions are too restrictive. Dr. Kirk was of the opinion that the certification requirement produces mediocrity in the teaching profession and does not improve the quality of teaching in this state.

Defendant contends that the need to insure minimum standards for teaching in private schools constitutes a compelling state interest and that teacher certification is a reasonable means of assuring that state interest. The overwhelming weight of evidence presented, however, shows that teacher certification does not insure teacher competency and may even inhibit teacher competency.

Defendants have failed to show that teacher certification is a reasonable or effective means to carry out a legitimate state purpose. Further, this court is of the opinion that teacher certification causes excessive government entanglement with religion.

This Court is of the opinion that 1921 PA 302, Section 3, MCLA, is violative of the First Amendment to the United States Constitution, and is, therefore, void and without effect.

Plaintiffs object to the requirement that the courses of study must be of the same standard as the public school. The "general school laws" of the state do not specify any particular courses, but allow the local school boards to determine the courses of study in their districts.

State official, Paul DeRose, testified that the Department of Education makes a judgment as to what is comparable in terms of curriculum offered by non public schools. Mr. DeRose further testified that non public schools must be comparable to public schools in the same district but may not be comparable to public schools located in a different school district. Mr. DeRose was unaware of any guidelines for local school district officials in evaluating non public schools.

Jack R. Newton, Superintendent of the Bridgeport-Spalding Community School District, testified that it was within his power to evaluate the curriculum of non public schools to ascertain if that curriculum was comparable to the public schools in that area. . . . Mr. Newton admitted concern with the loss of $2,000 in State Aid for every student who leaves the public school and enrolls in area non public schools.

This Court fails to see a compelling state interest in requiring non public schools to be "of the same standard" as public schools in the same school district. Such a scheme does not insure uniformity in the quality of education in the state because the school districts throughout the state are not required to be comparable. Further, such a scheme does not insure even a minimum degree of quality in education; it merely requires that non public schools be as good as, or as bad as, the public schools in the district.

This Court is of the opinion that Section 1 of 1921 PA 302 causes excessive government entanglement with religion and does not forward any compelling state interest. It is, therefore, the opinion of this court that Section 1 of 1921 PA 302 is unconstitutional.

Metronome Available Here

Seiko Electronic Metronome (Available from Holt Associates; $63.50, postage included). A metronome, as most readers probably know, is a clock-like device which beats time, by giving a click and/or flashing a light, at whatever speed you want, from 40 to 208 beats per minute. It is an indispensable tool for any serious student of music, and has been used by virtually all musicians since it was first invented by Maelzel. I have tried out a number of metronomes since I first began making music, and of all the ones I have seen this compact and versatile little machine is the best. In its case, it measures about 5½ × 2¾ × 1⅓ inches, and weighs less than half a pound. It will give you an A to tune with, at any pitch from 440 to 445 cycles (useful if you want to play with a recording, or a piano, that is not tuned exactly to A 440). It will beat time with a flashing light, or a sound, or both. The sound can be at low level or high level, and at high level is strong enough (not true of most small metronomes) to be heard over loud instruments.

One of the most important features of this metronome, one I have found in few others, is that it will not only beat time but, like a conductor, will give you the first beat in the measure. You can set it for measures of anywhere from two to six beats. When it is set for, say, a three beat measure, it will flash a red light and give a high-pitched sound for one beat, then a green light and a lower pitched sound for the next two beats, and so on for as long as it runs. I have found this very useful in trying to play music with (for me) complicated rhythms—if I skip a rest, or don't hold a rest or a note long enough, this machine will tell me, where a conventional metronome might not. It is, as I say, like having a little conductor on the music stand.

We will send the metronome to you with its 9 volt transistor radio battery installed. When the time comes to change the battery (easily found in drugstores, etc.), you will find the battery cover a little bit stiff to open. Push with your thumb, as the instruction manual says, and don't be afraid to push hard— you can't hurt anything by doing so. When you put the battery cover back on (the metronome will work OK with the cover off), push down and in on the little arrow and the word "Open." You don't have to worry about putting the battery the wrong way, because you can't—the clips are designed so that they will only go on the right way.

There's a foolish printer's mistake in the instruction booklet, which is not of any importance but may puzzle you. A photo of the back of the metronome points out the battery cover and the prop-up stand, but the labels are reversed.

This may seem quite a lot of money to pay for a little device that doesn't do much except say "click-click-click." But, as I said, it is an extremely important musical tool, which you will use in many ways. If you and/or your children are seriously studying any of the major instruments, you will spend a great deal more than this in only a few years, on lessons, strings, repairs, sheet music, recordings, and the like. Even the cheapest metronomes cost about half as much as this one, and its convenience and extra features make it well worth the extra money. I am very glad to have one for my own use, and strongly recommend it.—JH

Two Instruments Available Here

Aulos Soprano Recorder (Available from Holt Associates, $10.00 including postage). When I first thought of adding a recorder to our music list, I asked several of my recorder playing friends what companies made the best plastic recorders (the ones in wood are much more expensive). They all said, "Aulos." So we tracked down their catalog, found they make a whole line of recorders—soprano, alto, tenor, etc.—and, again on the advice of friends, picked this one to start with. I am not a recorder expert, but it seems easy to blow, accurate in pitch, even in sound, and pleasant in tone. It is one of the best beginning musical instruments for children or adults, and in fairly large and musically active cities like Boston you can often find groups of people to play with who specialize in recorder music. Also, it is a no-worry instrument; short of running over it with the car, it is pretty hard to hurt it. So it's OK to leave it lying around where anyone who feels like it can pick it up and tootle on it.

Pianica ($47 incl. postage). For some time I have been looking for a small and inexpensive keyboard instrument, for families to use who do not own or have access to a piano. Keyboard instruments are the best and certainly the easiest ways to learn something about music theory, music notation, harmony, etc. As an experienced piano teacher once put it, "A piano is a perfect teaching machine; what you see is what you get." Also, it is one of the easiest of all instruments for young children to make *some* kind of sound on. Action leads to results, which little children like and need. And by their own investigations they can learn a lot about how (musically) a keyboard instrument works.

Unfortunately, not everyone can find or afford a piano. One inexpensive electronic substitute I like very much is the Casio VL-10, a tiny synthesizer, great fun to play with and to compose tunes on. But it won't play chords, and the cheapest machines that will play them cost $150 and more—and usually don't sound very good. Also, the Casio probably wouldn't stand much rough treatment. (For older children, it may still be worth looking into.)

Then we found the Pianica (Piano + Harmonica). As with a harmonica, you blow into it, in this case, through a flexible pipe that fits in one end. The air makes notes by vibrating little metal reeds, and you pick the notes you want by pressing down a key or keys on a piano-type keyboard, two and a half octaves wide. The Pianica is cheaper than other instruments of this kind, and sounds better—the pitches are accurate, the tone pleasant, and the chords actually sound like chords, and not, as on many expensive electronic instruments, like discords. Erik Sessions, who is a good violinist and pianist, was in the office from Iowa the other day, and he had a good time with it. I think you and your children will too.—JH

New Books Available Here

The Doll Book, by Karin Neuschutz ($8 + post). This book is subtitled "Soft Dolls and Creative Free Play," and is about both of those—how, if you can sew, with or without a machine, you can make soft dolls for children, and the many kinds of things children can do with them (and other simple objects). The dolls themselves are inexpensive, not hard to make, and completely charming—I can well imagine how much children would love them. But the book itself would be well worth its price just for what the author says about play. She understands clearly and illustrates vividly what I say in *How Children Learn*—that children use play as a way of exploring the world and making as much sense as they can out of it.

Later, talking about fairy tales and what children can get out of them, Neuschutz says something I have long felt, without quite being able to put it into words:

To give children realistic everyday stories in books with the motivation that that's how many children today live—that Charlie lives in an apartment building, that his mother and father often fight, that this is what it's like to be in a hospital or at the dentist's or in a barn or in Antarctica—is actually to fool both ourselves and the child. No film or book can show a child how it is. Only the reality that we ourselves experience can show us the workings of the outside world.

At the very end of the book, Neuschutz talks about what to do when a favorite doll gets worn out. Ask the child if it's all right to take the doll to the hospital, and if so, tell the child that when it gets all well and comes back it won't look *exactly* the same. Then re-make as much of the doll as is worn out, keeping the old head and face or perhaps only the hair. The doll can be almost totally new, but to the child it will be the same old friend. It reminds me of the story of the old woodsman who, showing a friend his house, pointed to an axe behind the door, and said, "I've had that axe all my life; it's had three new heads and seven new handles." That's how children can feel about fixed-up old dolls, and why these simple soft dolls are so nice.

It occurs to me that, using the patterns in this book, some homeschoolers might make a small cottage industry out of making these dolls for others. They'd make lovely presents.

This book, by the way, is published by Larson, the company that will be publishing Nancy Wallace's book. The book is very well made, with a sewn binding (I can't remember the last book of mine to have one—publishers these days usually just glue the pages together at the spine of the book, which they call a "perfect" binding).

Concise Oxford Dictionary of Music, Ed. by Michael Kennedy ($10.45 + post). 724 pages of fascinating information about composers, both famous and obscure, together with lists of their works; also many compositions (listed by title), performers, musical instruments, musical terms (the ones, like *allegro, più mosso*, etc., that you would find in written music), music theory (harmony, ornaments, etc.), musical history, and just about anything that might interest anyone who likes "classical" music. (A few great jazz players are mentioned, but only a few.) An excellent reference work for serious students, and a delightful book just to browse in—every time I pick it up to look up something, I find myself reading about a lot of other things. Of the one volume dictionaries of music I have seen, much the most complete and readable.

Peter and the Wolf ($5.35 + post) and *The Nutcracker* ($5.35 + post). Two famous ballet stories, charmingly illustrated in color, with selections (written for piano) of some of the best known and most beautiful music of each, so that as adults or children read the story they can play some of the music along with it. Thus, from *Peter*, we have the songs of Peter, the bird, the duck, the cat, the grandfather, the wolf, and the hunters. From *Nutcracker* we have Harlequin and Columbine, the Waltz of the Snowflakes, the Mice, the Dance of the Flutes, the Chinese Dance, and the Waltz of the Flowers.

The Story of Ferdinand, by Munro Leaf ($3.15 + post). The classic story of the little Spanish bull who would rather sit quietly smelling the flowers than fight. The black and white pen and ink illustrations by Robert Lawson have great life and vitality, almost more color than if they were in color. A wonderful story. By the way, the same pair did another book called *Wee Gillis* which though equally good is unfortunately out of print. It is about a little Scottish boy who learns to play some bagpipes that no one else can play. If you ever see a copy in a second hand bookstore, snap it up—and if there are extras, please get some for us—we'll buy them from you at cost.

Destination Moon, $4.45; *Explorers of the Moon*, $3.55; *The Shooting Star*, $4.45. Three more in the great series of Tintin comic books (see *GWS* 29 and #25). Can't add much to what I've said before about these: ingenious and exciting plots, lots of slapstick humor of the kind that kids like, plenty of interesting dialogue, and accurate, detailed, and often quite beautiful drawings—kids may not think much about color and composition in their comic books, but they probably respond to them, and they certainly add to the pleasure of any adults who read these books aloud (or by themselves).

Hergé wrote these books when people were first talking about going to the moon, but before anyone had gone there, so much of the "science" he had to make up out of his imagination. Events may have outdated some of it, but not enough to bother most young readers.

May I repeat what we said in *GWS* 29; if any of you are interested in foreign language versions of the Tintin books, please tell us. We have had one or two requests for Tintin in the original French, but so far there has not been enough demand to warrant stocking even a French edition.

The Man Who Kept Cigars in His Cap, by Jim Heynen ($4.50 + post). Many books on our list are unusual and beautiful, but this book, suggested by homeschooling friends in Yucaipa CA, is one of the most unusual and beautiful of all. It is a group of forty-one very short stories, really just accounts of incidents, in the life of a small, un-named farm community. The central figures in the book are a group of boys, who appear in all the incidents. We are not told how many there are, or their ages or names—they are only called "the boys." Only rarely will the storyteller even single out one as littlest or biggest. In my mind's eye I see perhaps three or four boys, the oldest of them not much more than ten. But this is only my guess; the storyteller does not tell us, nor do the few pen and ink illustrations.

In fact, only three characters of the many in the book are named: Maggie, a little girl with an extra toe; Maley, the midget shoemaker; and the stallion Bayard. This lack of names, of people or places, gives these short tales an almost mythic quality—they might have happened anywhere, they could be happening anywhere, anywhere at least that human beings grow food and raise animals and live in small towns. Many of the tales are about the daily realities of farm life, animals being born, getting sick, dying. Others have to do with life and death, happiness and grief, in a much larger sense. To give a hint of their flavor, here are some quotes:

> When the boys went to one neighbor's farm to ask him if they might pick some of his apples, they could not find him anywhere.... Finally—in a very dark corner of the barn—they saw him. He was praying to his animals.
>
> On his knees with his hands crossed in his lap. Praying to a piglet, a dog, a cat, and a bull calf. He had fed each of them their own kind of food, so they were quiet as he prayed.
>
> He was saying, Little animals with four feet on the ground, teach the rocks to lie in their places, tell the oceans never to rise and the mountains never to fall. Little ones, give your gentle ways to me.
>
> The boys slipped away and went to wait in the yard. When the man came out of the barn, they asked him about apples. He brought a large basket and said they could fill it with the ripest and largest apples from his trees. Not only that. He said they could keep the basket to carry feed to their animals.
>
> One night the boys were getting ready for bed.
>
> I smell a girl, said the smallest boy.
>
> There aren't any girls here, silly, said the biggest boy.
>
> They started looking anyway. Under the beds and inside drawers. One of the

window curtains moved a little and the smallest boy said, See, there! That was a girl!

But there were no arms or feet, only the curtain moving a little. The boys went to bed without finding the girl. Still, they could not sleep because they smelled the girl. The smell got stronger.

After a while, in the dark, one of them said, it's not a girl, it's a lady. It smells like a grown lady. They turned on the lights and looked for the lady. But she was not there.

Back in bed, they lay listening and smelling the strange smell. It's not a girl or a lady, one of them said. It smells like an old, old woman.

Again, the boys turned on the lights. The curtain was still moving. This time they saw something. It was dust, blowing in through the window. So they closed the window and went back to bed.

After that, they fell asleep.

The last story in the book, called "Death Death Death," might be (and is probably meant to be) a kind of parable of modern life. On a hot summer day, playing in the yard, the boys suddenly become aware of the smell of many dead creatures.

Death, Death, Death, said one of the boys.

There were dead animals all over the farmyard—if they'd look for them. . . . And this was not unusual. Things die. It's just that the boys happened to be noticing it all at once.

Look. One of the boys pointed to the sky. They were not alone, noticing all the death. A chicken hawk was circling overhead. Circling over the whole farmyard.

This place stinks like dead everything, said one of the boys.

There's only one thing to do about all this death, said the smallest boy.

But I will let you find out from this wonderful book what that was.

Well, There's Your Problem, by Edward Koren ($3.65 + post). This is a book of cartoons, all originally published in *The New Yorker*, done by one of my favorite cartoonists. If you see *The New Yorker* often, you probably know his work—many of his drawings are of large, incredibly shaggy, rather solemn looking animals, and all of his drawings are in ink, in a great many slightly wiggly lines, as if his hand shook a little when he tried to draw. Just about every cartoon in the book makes me laugh aloud when I see it, and the cover and title drawing, which I first saw many years ago, has made me laugh ever since, not just when I see it but when I even think of it—I won't give away what it is about. All in all, a lovely mixture of the gently satirical and the absurd. I'll think you'll have a lot of fun with this, our first cartoon book but not, I hope, our last.

The Amateur Naturalist's Handbook, by Vinson Brown ($7.15 + post). This splendid book was first published in 1948 and went through fourteen printings before the author prepared this thoroughly revised edition. By way of describing the book and what it is for, I can't do better than quote the author himself:

This book is for all who like the out-of-doors and would like to know more about the many interesting things they see.

In this book you will be given suggestions about how to go about your work so that you will learn more and more as you go along, and you will be given information about a number of tools useful in studying nature, many of which you can make yourself. The study of each of the great sections of nature is so arranged that there are things to learn and do for the Beginning, Student, Advanced, and Explorer Naturalist.

The table of contents will give an idea of the wealth of facts and ideas to be found here.

Introduction: The Trail Of The Naturalist; What Nature Study Is; Ideals Of A Naturalist; Nature In The City (each of these chapters has sub-sections of its own). *The Beginning Naturalist*: Animals and Animal Collecting; Plants and Plant Collecting; Rocks and Minerals and Their Collecting; Climate; Beginning Ecology. Then additional sections, each with chapters and sub-chapters, on *The Student Naturalist*; *The Advanced Naturalist*; and *Becoming an Explorer-Naturalist*.

The first two sections of the book take up about 100 of its 400 or so pages, and would alone be well worth its price; even if we look at it only as a school science textbook, rather than the source of interest, pleasure, and knowledge that it is, we can find enough material in it to enable homeschoolers to satisfy almost any school's science requirements well up into the high school years. Any child who knows a good part of what is in here will know much more about science than almost any children of her or his age. But the book is too interesting and beautiful to be used as a textbook—so many pages this day, so many pages that. It is a friendly and helpful guide to seeing and understanding more of the world around us.

About a third of the pages of the book are illustrated; many of them, like those in Eric Sloane's books (*Diary of an Early American Boy*, etc.) have many illustrations. Almost all of these are done in pen and ink, and with the loving accuracy and attention to detail that we see in Sloane's drawings. The artist signs himself only "Don G K." Astonishingly, the book does not name him—about the only thing in it that I can find to criticize.

Seeing in the contents that the next-to-last chapter in the book, "The Naturalist as a Scientist," contained a sub-chapter, The Scientific Attitude, I looked to see what Brown had to say about that, and was relieved to find that he is not a science-worshipper or busy science promoter and grant-grabber, but a true scientist, in the old and very best sense of the word. He says:

The scientific attitude recognizes first that truth is what is being sought; second, that no ways should be missed that might help find the truth; and third, that what may seem to be the truth at one time may later, under the advance of new facts, prove to be something less than truth.

All in all, a fascinating book, for adults or children, a book to sharpen our eyes and fire our imaginations.—JH

Editors—John Holt & Donna Richoux
Managing Editor—Pat Farenga
Subscriptions & Books—Mark Pierce
Office Assistant—Mary Van Doren

Growing Without Schooling 34

August 1983

Had very pleasant and productive meetings with homeschoolers in Colorado and Maine. The Colorado group met on a rainy evening in a large church in Denver. The audience had been given slips of paper on which they could write questions—a good idea, since even among homeschoolers some may be a bit shy about asking questions out loud. While in Denver I had an interview with the *Rocky Mountain News*, a big Denver daily, and the *Boulder Camera*, which put the story on the front page.

The Maine meeting was held in the Rockcraft Lodge in East Sebago, right on the edge of Lake Sebago. Parents (mostly of children still under school age) were there from Maine, New Hampshire, and even Florida (in Maine for their vacation). The lodge, which is a big old rambling house mostly used by church groups, was a perfect place for a meeting, not very expensive, with plenty of space for children to play, and a nice place to swim in the delicious lake water. The Maine homeschoolers hope to make this a regular annual event.

One of the people attending the Maine meeting was Samuel Lanham (see "Friendly Lawyers," *GWS* 33). He has been working with William Ball on a very important case involving the rights of private schools to be free of excessive state regulation. If they win, it will greatly strengthen the position of small private schools all over the country, and so will help homeschoolers. For the time being, the homeschooling situation in Colorado and Maine is much the same—the state law allows it, but only with the OK of the local schools, most (but not all) of which have been friendly or at least tolerant.

Since *GWS* 33 went to press, I have had radio telephone interviews with stations in Urbana IL, Columbus MO, and Philadelphia, and a TV interview for a Springfield, MA station.—John Holt

Homeschoolers Get Grant

From Patt Morris in California:

Due to unemployment, we've been below the official poverty line for two years, so the thought of applying for some sort of grant repeatedly crossed my mind. Some research at the library (a wonderful free resource!) convinced me that foundations give grants only to non-profit, tax-exempt organizations and I gave up. But—I received a free sample of *Gifted Children's Newsletter* in February (it was their Jan. issue) and read with interest the announcement of their grants competition for subscribers and including a category for individuals with an innovative idea for parenting or teaching gifted children. I immediately scraped together the money for a subscription [$24/12 iss.; RD 1 Box 128A, Sewell NJ 08080] and returned to the library to learn how to write a proposal. To make a long story short, they liked the proposal and the idea (to provide math and science materials and classes for gifted children being taught at home by their mother and father) and we'll be receiving $500 from them!

John's Coming Schedule

Sept. 2, 1983: Whole Life Expo. 5:15–6:00. Gardner Room, Sheraton Hotel, 39 Dalton St, Boston.

Oct. 13: Fairleigh Dickinson U., Rutherford, New Jersey. 8 p.m. Contact Vicki Roussman, 201-460-5330.

Dec. 2: DePauw U., Greencastle IN. 9–11 a.m. Contact Myra Rosenhaus, 317-658-4864.

Dec. 3: meeting with Central Indiana Home Educators. Contact Sherry Hamstra, 5724 Diana Dr, Indianapolis IN 46278.

High Scores On G.E.D.

From the mother who wrote "Hiding From School," *GWS 24:*

Our big news is, Jenifer (*age 16*) this spring decided to take the GED (high school equivalency) test. She heard on the radio about a YMCA program called "Operation Bootstrap," which gives free tutoring to pass the tests. She took a placement test and was told she *didn't need* the tutoring! She took the tests and passed with high scores (got only one wrong, on one test). I'm proud, because (1) she decided this on her own, (2) if still in school she'd have one more year, and (3) she never attended high school.

Now our 19-year-old married son is interested in taking the tutoring and the tests. He's teaching himself fractions, something he never caught on to while in school.

Wildlife Volunteer At 9

From Karen Olin Johnston (CA):

We have been mostly homeschooling for the past three years. Fawn (9) is involved in my own work as a volunteer with a wildlife conservation organization, the Elsa Wild Animal Appeal. One of my responsibilities is answering the many letters the group receives from children around the country. The majority of these letters are requests for information on an animal that the child is studying in school. In our home we maintain an extensive file of fact sheets on animal species, from which we answer children's requests.

Fawn gets involved by: reading the letters to determine what info is needed (which exposes her to some interesting penmanship and spelling!); finding the fact sheet on that animal (involving alphabetizing and categorizing as well as choosing material suitable to the writer's age); stuffing, weighing and applying postage to the envelopes; addressing the envelopes (penmanship practice); getting the week's work to the post office; letting me know when supplies are getting low and copying is needed.

Indirectly she is learning a lot about wildlife and conservation, and also about US geography as we often get out the atlas to see where the kid she's responding to lives. And, she *knows* that she is performing a valuable service for the Elsa Appeal.

By the way, homeschoolers are welcome to take advantage of this service, if they wish to learn more about a particular species, or about endangered species in general. 25¢ per request to cover postage and copying is appreciated, and requests should be sent to the Elsa Clubs of America, PO Box 4572, N Hollywood CA 91607.

What They Wanted To Learn

From Susan Jaffer, RD 2 Box 206, Waymart PA 18472:

Last year, at the beginning of summer, I asked my daughters what I thought was a casual question: "What would you like to learn about this summer?" They began answering me right away, without so much as a pause, and this is what we ended up with: Suzanne, 8, wanted to learn about stories, poems, science, math, art, music, books, people, planting, animals, places, food, colors, rocks, babies, cars, eyes, and electricity. Gillian, 6, wanted to learn about seeds, bones, plants, books, evolution, dinosaurs, and experiments. I tend to think that the fact that I asked them in the summer freed them from the boundaries of school subjects. In any case, I was stunned by the fact that they had so many subjects in mind, and that their lists were right there waiting for me to ask the right question.

Tax Break For Parents

Time, 7/11/83:

> Last week the [US Supreme] court appeared to soften its traditional stance by upholding a Minnesota statute that ... authorizes deductions of $500 to $700 spent by parents on "tuition, textbooks, and transportation" for any child in grade or high school. By a 5-to-4 vote, the court found Minnesota's plan crucially different from other tax programs that had been ruled unconstitutional because the benefit is available to all parents, whether their children attend private or public schools.
>
> A day after the court's action, New Jersey legislators introduced a new tax-exemption proposal, and other states are expected to follow.

Notes From Donna

Free Educational Software: Ed Freedland, chairman of *Krell Software* and publisher of the *Logo and Educational Computing Journal* (1320 Stonybrook RD, Stonybrook, NY 11790) is very interested in *GWS* and called us out of the blue to offer us 5 free sets of Logo software. They are suitable for Apple II computers, and each set contains 4 disks, a manual, a poster with Logo commands, and an issue of the *Journal*. We'll hold a drawing to give away these five sets, so if you'd like to win one, send your name and address on a postcard to *Free Logo Drawing*, c/o *GWS*. We'll set the deadline as *Oct. 31, 1983*, so that those in group subscriptions will have a chance. All we ask is that the winners tell us about their experiences in using the programs (and it would nice if they'd reimburse us the shipping cost—about $2).

Travel Network Report: Ted and Martha Laux offered to run the "Network for Educational Travel" in *GWS* 27, and they have just published a guide that lists 25 families across the US who are willing to host visitors. They write, "To help travelers know what to expect, we ask members to provide us with basic information such as their name, address, phone number, their children's names, sex, and birthdates, their interests, preferences, accommodations, location, and area attractions. If they send us a self-addressed stamped envelope, we'll send them a form to fill out. For the complete guide, we ask for $1 to cover our printing and mailing costs. Of course, people can always call or write us to see if there is anyone in the area in which they'll be travelling.

"We hope that this guide (though small) will make this year's travels more affordable and enjoyable. The *GWS* families we've encountered all seem to be pretty terrific. We'll probably do an updated and, we hope, expanded version next spring. . . ."

Homeschooling Films: Interesting that we've recently heard about two possible films on homeschooling being worked on in California. Larry and Suzanne Bischof of North Hollywood intend to write a fictional story for a television movie, and Toni Shy of Sherman Oaks is trying to make a documentary. Good luck to both of these projects.

New Resources: Our friend Wendy Priesnitz of the *Canadian Alliance Of Homeschoolers* sent us Issue #1 of her new publication, *Child's Play*, a "Family Learning Resources Newsletter" (1003-129 Wellington St, Brantford, Ontario N3T 5Z9; $15/6 issues; $2.50 sample). Among the resources Wendy recommends are materials that have been suggested in *GWS*, such as the Abrams Planetarium Sky Calendar and the Key Curriculum math workbooks, and this fact leads me to believe our readers would enjoy many of her other ideas.

Pat Montgomery of Clonlara School sent us information on ED/NET, "an educational computer network that is designed to serve the homeschooling community nationwide." Run by homeschoolers Gary and Gillian Anderson, the system is designed to provide legal information, lists of materials, and reviews of educational software, electronic mail, an electronic encyclopedia, and more. For $175, they will supply you with a complete "start-up package," which includes a Timex-Sinclair computer and a telephone modem. For more info, contact the Andersons at PO Box 191, Timberville VA 22853; 703-896-3358.

Steve Molnar of the *National Coalition Of Alternative Community Schools* tells us that the 1983 edition of their alternative schools directory is now available ($5; 1289 Jewett St, Ann Arbor MI 48104), and writes, "Up until now the books have essentially been sold one by one to individuals and stores. This year I'm looking to hook into other networks and distributors to help get the information out. If you know any people who might be able to help, please pass their names on to me."

New Materials Here: On June 6, the *Christian Science Monitor* ran a good article called "Unschooling—a learn-as-you-go experiment," which was based on an interview with John. We have reprints available—10¢ if you order with other materials; SASE required if ordered alone.

Thanks to many hours of work by volunteer Reba Karban, we now have a "Pinchpenny Press" edition of John's book *Freedom And Beyond*, which had gone out of print. (Send $4.50 + 75¢ postage to Holt Associates.)

Travel Plans: As soon as this issue is put together, I'm off for a three-week vacation—a hiking trip in England. This will be the longest I've been away from Boston since I came four years ago! Then later in August, Pat Farenga will be away, too—he and Day Yelland are getting married on the 20th, and are honeymooning in Denmark for two weeks.—Donna Richoux

Maine Pays For Schooling

From Adam Tomash, RFD 1 Box 1590, N Anson ME 04958:

We have for sale part or all of a forty-acre homestead in a rural part of central Maine.... The unique part is its location in what is described in Maine as an "unorganized territory." ... We pay our taxes ($150/year) directly to the state and they in turn pay for services such as schools and roads directly on a contract basis. They pay a local school district $1200 per pupil per year for tuition *but they are willing to pay any non-religious school the same amount.* We have actually sent our children to an alternative school without cost. A small community built on this property with its own certifiable teacher could collect $1200 per student from the state to defray school costs. For more information please send SASE or call 207-643-2510.

Homeschoolers In Court

From the Arkansas Democrat, *6/30/83:*

> Wayne and Margaret Burrow, who educated their 8-year-old daughter at home, were found in violation of the state's compulsory school attendance law Wednesday and fined $1,000 by Pulaski County Circuit Judge Lowber Hendricks.
>
> "As much as I like you folks and admire you, I feel you're in violation of state law," Hendricks said. "I really do think this can be solved at the highest level (of court)."
>
> Hendricks also recommended that the Burrows apply for a state permit to operate as a private school if they wanted to continue to teach their daughter at home.
>
> The Burrows could have been fined $4,000 in accordance with the state's provision of a $10 per day fine, but Hendricks said he felt the fine was excessive.
>
> After Hendricks' decision, Wayne Burrow said he would take the case to the U.S. Supreme Court if necessary. He also said he would not apply for a permit to operate as a private school.
>
> Hendricks said, "It seems to me through the testimony I've heard today that Mr. and Mrs. Burrow should not have to work too hard getting approved as a private school."

[DR:] A reader tells us that in spite of what the judge said, Arkansas laws require a private school to have a certified teacher and a minimum of 15 students. She also sent the July issue of the Christian Home Education Association *newsletter, in which Margaret Burrow writes:*

> On first appearances, the ruling Judge Lowber Hendricks gave us may have seemed unfair ... However ... we are now in a position to help all home schools in the state.
>
> Circuit Court does not set a precedent; Judge Hendricks set the $1,000 fine to assure that we will appeal to the State Supreme Court.
>
> In reference to state approval, the statute to which reference was made is for occupational private schools, such as real estate and beauty schools. What this has done is to give us tremendous grounds for appeal at a higher level since this reference is in error.

Dr. Raymond Moore and Dr. William Randall did fine jobs [testifying]. We appreciate the financial support given by many of you toward getting Dr. Moore here to testify. We were very fortunate to get all testimony in *without even one objection*. ... The state did not present a single expert witness.

Lawrence Williams (CA) of Oak Meadow School *writes about the May court decision involving Pamela Hackett of Los Angeles:*

After hearing the evidence and testimonies, the judge made a distinction between two charges: the charges relating to the period *before* they enrolled in the Independent Study Program of the Palisades Learning Center (the name of the Los Angeles branch of Oak Meadow School), and the charges relating to the period *after* they enrolled. For the period *before* their enrollment in PLC, the judge declared them *guilty*. ... However, for the period *after* their enrollment in PLC, the Judge *dismissed* the charges against them stating that the prosecution had not presented sufficient evidence to prove that they were not enrolled in a legal private school as of that date. The fines for the guilty portion of the verdict were waived (at the request of the prosecution) and Pamela and Maurice Hackett were placed on summary probation and ordered to obey the compulsory education laws.

So, technically, as long as the Hacketts remain enrolled in the Palisades Learning Center they won't have any further trouble from the school district.

From the Jan. newsletter of the Texas Home Education Coalition, *reprinted in* Home Educator's Newsletter:

> Don and Evelyn Culley are a missionary couple who recently returned to the United States. They were schooling their two boys, aged 8 and 10, at home in Odessa, Texas, when they were taken to court by the local school district. They lost at the J.P. level and filed an appeal. They received considerable adverse publicity from the news media. Their home support church, after hearing of their court battle, cut them off without a penny.
>
> But ... the county prosecutor who prosecuted them in J.P. court ... came away with the opinion that home education is an acceptable alternative. Last November he was elected County District Attorney. When the Culley's appeal came up for consideration, he moved that the case against them be dismissed and his motion was granted! The Culleys are now free to continue the home education of their children.

More Court News

Victories: Joe & Wimbric Padgett, McRae, Georgia; George & Irene Anderson, Kauai, Hawaii (Robert Grinpas, attorney); The Kirshenmans, Moorhead, Minnesota; May Phillips, Trinity School District, Pennsylvania; Scott Page, St. Matthews, South Carolina

Facing Court Action: Jean & Bob Smith, Albert Lea, Minnesota

Appealing A Loss: Terry & Vickie Roemhild, Stephens County, Georgia; Charles & Marlee Bergman, West Danby, New York (appeal tentative)

W.V. Law—Private Schools

[DR:] The West Virginia legislature recently passed two education bills: Senate Bill No. 184, which allows for the certification of private schools with minimal regulations; and Senate Bill No. 365, which lowers the compulsory school attendance age from 7 to 6 and establishes kindergartens.

First, some pertinent quotes from the private school bill, passed 3/5/83:

> Each private, parochial, or church school or school of religious order shall observe a minimum instructional term of 180 days, with an average of five hours of instruction per day, and shall make and maintain annual attendance and disease immunization records for each pupil. Upon the request of the county

superintendent of schools, any school to which this applies . . . shall furnish to the county board of education a list of the names and addresses of all children enrolled in such school. Each such school shall be subject to reasonable fire, health and safety inspections by state, county and municipal authorities as required by law.

Each . . . nonpublic school electing to operate under this statute . . . shall administer on an annual basis during each school year to every child enrolled therein between the ages of 7 and 16 years either the Comprehensive Test of Basic Skills, the California Achievement Test or the Stanford Achievement Test, which test will be selected by the chief administrative officer of each school. . . . Upon request of a duly authorized representative of the West Virginia department of education, the school composite test results shall be furnished by the school.

Each school to which this article applies shall:

(A) Establish curriculum objectives, the attainment of which will enable students to develop the potential for becoming literate citizens.

(B) Provide an instructional program that will make possible the acquisition of competencies necessary to become a literate citizen.

If such school composite test results for any single year . . . fall below the fortieth percentile . . . the school . . . shall initiate a remedial program. . . . If after two consecutive calendar years, school composite test results are not above the fortieth percentile level, attendance at the school may no longer satisfy the compulsory school attendance requirement. Any [school to which this article applies] may, on a voluntary basis, participate in any state operated or state sponsored program otherwise made available to such schools by law.

Any new school to which this article relates shall send to the state superintendent of schools . . . a notice of intent to operate, name and address of the school, and name of the school's chief administrator.

No [school to which this article applies] which complies with the requirements of this article, shall be subject to any other provision of law relating to education except requirements of law respecting fire, safety, sanitation, and immunization.

About this law, Richard Dulee of the Homeschool Education Association *(RT 1 Box 352, Alderson WV 24910) writes:*

The new regulations are the result of lobbying by a proliferation of "Christian academies" which have existed outside of previous certification requirements. We see it as an opening for homeschoolers. We have already notified the state superintendent of the establishment of Harmony Hill Private School. . . . They were surprised to hear of our plans. They were also unable to refute our interpretation. We are seeking out sympathetic legal counsel just in case.

The *Homeschool Education Association* is offering W.V. homeschoolers all necessary documentation and testing for compliance with the new regulations. We have recruited state certified teachers and a psychologist and are looking to establish a network of duly registered private home schools to counter any attempts to exclude us from coverage under the new statute.

W.V. Law—School Age

[DR:] Next, a look at West Virginia Senate Bill No. 365, passed one week later than the previous bill, on 3/12/83. The reader who told us about it thought it lowered the compulsory age from 7 to 5, but although the law is confusing and almost contradictory, it does clearly change the minimum age to 6. To quote:

18-8-1a . . . Compulsory school

attendance shall begin with the school year in which the sixth birthday is reached prior to September one of such year and continue to the sixteenth birthday.

The bill also requires county boards of education to provide kindergarten for children who have turned 5 before the school year begins. The difference between "The public schools are required to provide kindergartens" and "Parents are required to send their children to kindergarten" is vital, but easily confused in the press and in people's minds. Anyone involved in similar legislative confrontations in other states should make a point of being clear about which kind of compulsion is involved. (Just think how much happier homeschoolers would be if *all* compulsory education laws had been written in the form, "The community shall provide schools for children," not "Parents shall send their children to school"!)

Further confusion enters in the W.V. law when it states:

Prior to entrance in the first grade . . . each child must have either (1) successfully completed such publicly or privately supported, state-approved kindergarten program or Montessori kindergarten program, or (2) successfully completed an entrance test of basic readiness skills approved by the county in which the school is located: *Provided*, that such test be administered in lieu of kindergarten attendance only under extraordinary circumstances to be determined by the board. What this will mean to a family that wants to keep a child out of kindergarten but send her/him to first grade, I don't know. The fact that the compulsory age is 6 says they have the right to do this, but I can imagine some boards of education being upset about whether those were "extraordinary circumstances." Clearly this bill was not written with homeschoolers in mind.

Although we've heard of attempts in various states to lower the compulsory school age, this is the first bill we know of that has actually passed. We urge all readers to be alert for such bills. It's beginning to be a very popular notion in educational circles (see, for example, the highly publicized report of the National Commission for Excellence in Education) that the quality of education in this country would improve if children only spent *more* time in schools. The Japanese start school at age four, they say, and look how successful *they* are. (When you start using this kind of false logic, there's no end to what you can justify.)

Teachers' lobbies love this kind of legislation, of course, because it guarantees more jobs. Plus, the many parents who are now paying for daycare for their young children would be delighted to get it free from the schools. So, such a bill could easily slip through the system, as there is no organized, powerful opposition—unless we help create it.

Local News

Arizona: Sherri Pitman (6166 W Highland, Phoenix AZ 85033) has raised the price of her book on the Arizona homeschooling law to $9. She informed us of some small changes in the homeschooling statute, including the interesting addition, "The Department of Education shall upon request provide any information which the department provides to teachers and parents of public school children relating to the nationally standardized achievement test" which homeschooled children must take. Sherri also sent a letter from State Attorney General Bob Corbin in which he gave the opinion that "the private school exemption, as contained in Paragraph 2 of ARS 15-802.B, does not encompass what is, in fact, a home teaching situation. . . ."

Australia: Heather Cousland-Keck of the newsletter *Other Ways* (*GWS* 31) tells us that the rates for subscriptions to America are $24 (U.S.) for airmail, $16 for sea. Money should be in Australian bank draft or Australian travelers checks.

British Columbia: Tunya Audain of *Education Advisory* (2267 Kings Av, W Vancouver BC, Canada V7V 2Cl; 926-9081) has a "Home Learning Pack" of information and reprints useful for would-be homeschoolers in B.C.

California: Pamela Pacula writes, "Mailing list for the *Home Centered Learning* newsletter [34 Katrina Ln, San Anselmo CA 94960; free] has grown from 96 to over 250 since February. Our last picnic in San Jose two weeks ago was the biggest yet! I contacted the Lifestyles Editor of the *Independent Journal*, Marin County's largest newspaper, and she said, yes, she would like to do a story on homeschooling in the near future."

From Linda Simmons (CA): "We organized an informal get-together for homeschoolers in our area. Advertisement in our local newspaper, radio, and word-of-mouth brought together 15 homeschooling families. . . . Some knew each other, some did not; some had filed a private school affidavit, some had not; all had varying reasons for making their decision. It was *GWS* in person! . . . ."

After John appeared at a homeschoolers' meeting arranged by Jane Williams of the *California Home Education Clearinghouse*, she wrote, "Financially, we took in enough money to cover the cost of the hall, your [additional] plane fare, hotel, printing costs, and postage to cover the flyers sent out announcing your visit." This is encouraging news for any of you thinking of arranging for John to come to a homeschooling meeting when he has a fee-paying engagement in your state. But help us get those university and conference dates first!

From Pam Gingold (CA): "Thank you for listing Nancy Reckinger's name under 'Professors Willing to Help Homeschoolers.' Together we are working to get Los Angeles City Schools to accept Independent Study students in the primary grades. She knows many people in the State Education Dept. and perhaps they will allow her to try a pilot program because she is well-respected. . . . Also, she is becoming a well-loved friend, which is as important."

Colorado: In what the *Denver Post* called a "major victory for fundamentalist religious schools," the governor signed a bill that requires only that private schools be in session 172 days, that they provide a "basic academic education," and that they keep attendance records.

A handout of the *Colorado Homeschooling Network* (SASE to 365 Hooker St, Denver 80219) says they have been holding monthly meetings, their newsletter is $8 per year, and their "Homeschooling in Colorado" legal packet costs $5.

Florida: Ann Mordes of *FLASH* announces, "Barbara Plunket has agreed to become the South Florida Director of *FLASH*. I feel very lucky to have her aboard. Anyone from Sarasota down through Miami, feel free to contact Barbara (2012 N Huntington Av, Sarasota FL 33582; 813-921-6009)."

Georgia: A good idea from Connie Shaw in *A Different Drummer*: "Each year we have noticed that homeschooling children are sometimes sad and even upset on the day their friends go back to school. . . . We are planning a special day for all homeschoolers on this first day of the school year. The children will be doing much of the organizing and preparing. . . ." Connie's group also offers an info packet for Georgia homeschoolers for $5 (4818 Joy Ln, Lilburn GA 30247).

Phillis Bostar is publishing another newsletter for Georgia homeschoolers, *The Creative Mind* (4953 Womack Av, Acworth GA 30101; $6/6 issues).

Michigan: Pat Montgomery's booklet, *Home Sweet School*, has much good legal information for Michigan families. Don't know the price—contact her at Clonlara School, 1289 Jewett St, Ann Arbor MI 48104; 313-769-4515.

Oregon: Jane Joyce has started *The Learning Connection* (3530 Galice Rd, Merlin OR 97532) and says "Please list me in 'Schools that will help homeschoolers,' for all of Oregon. We've been operating since Nov. '82 without any hassles from the authorities, and will expand out of this area in September. . . ."

New Hampshire: There are monthly statewide homeschooling meetings, according to the *N.H. Home schools Newsletter*; for a copy, send a SASE to Kathie Dupont, RFD 2 Box 255, Laconia NH 03246.

Oklahoma: The Oklahoma Homeschool Association held its first meeting on Feb. 12 at the Native American Association in Oklahoma City. Speakers included attorney John Eidsmoe. Around 100 adults and children attended. There are three chapters of the OHSA that hold regular meetings:

Tulsa (918-455-6390), Oklahoma City (405-946-4600), and Lawton (405-355-6954).

Tennessee: According to the new *Assist Newsletter* (PO Box 1851, Knoxville TN 37901; $5/yr.), there was so much negative reaction to House Bill #1033 and Senate Bill #1116, which would have placed many restrictions on private schools (see *GWS* 32), the sponsors deleted the entire content of the bill and substituted a provision that would place on the parents the "burden of proving that a child is being afforded an academic program and curriculum comparable to that offered in the local public school system." The bill will be considered by the Subcommittee on Secondary Education over the summer.—DR

Worried School

From Sandy Hurst of Upattinas School *(see our "Helpful Schools" list, GWS 33):*

We have had some bad news from Harrisburg. Some superintendents and other people in Pa. have let it be known that we "enroll" homeschoolers, and the Director of Non-Public Schools has let me know that we are not allowed to do this—at the risk of losing our license to operate our school. He seems willing to cooperate as long as we don't use the school's name. I can use my own name as educational consultant, but the school must not be mentioned.

We are working on a correspondence course offering, which we'll have to have licensed. If we get the license, we'll be able to work through that more easily. I'm hoping that the superintendents will feel more comfortable with allowing people to work with us that way.

I would welcome any comments. . . . I don't have the support of my whole school community to just go on the way we've been doing it. We are really concerned about our license being pulled.

If you get calls, tell people to call me for more personal treatment. . . . We'll still do all we can to protect them or help them write up proposals for their superintendents.

A Psychologist Helps

Andy Peterson (PA) wrote in the Western Pa. Homeschoolers *#5:*

For the past two years I have had a home education specialty as part of my private practice of psychology [see *GWS* 20 and our "Professor & Allies" list]. There are three main services. The first is offering an information packet on home education specifically geared to our Pennsylvania situation. I ask six dollars to cover postage and copying costs.

Second is home education consultation and evaluation. This is for parents having difficulty with superintendent-approval. My official credentials are Professional Psychology License and School Psychology Certification. I can do a professional psychoeducational report regarding the prognosis for a child benefitting from home education and the extent to which the parents are "properly qualified" as tutors. . . . The purpose of this report is to present a specific home education recommendation in professional jargon, to critique past evaluations, and to provide the superintendent with a back-up professional opinion for his decision. In some cases, this strategy can smooth the approval process.

Usually, I interview family, parents, and child. Some traditional psychometric tests and a parent questionnaire might be used. A rough draft of the report is reviewed by the parents and corrections made. The final draft, along with cover letter and enclosures, is sent to the superintendent. I am then available for a school conference, if needed. Consultation by phone is included.

A third counseling service is sort of a de-programming conversation about past experiences with educationists. Parents may be either homeschooling or not, but would like an outsider such as me to comment on and question their view of Johnny's academic-type skills and his over-all development. This would include a meeting with the child, maybe some tests, and a critique of past school programs and evaluations. A subsequent meeting with the parents or the family would provide opportunity for discussion.

Notifying Superintendent Early

Susan Richman wrote in the same Western Pa. Homeschoolers:

Having a child just approaching age 6 who's never been enrolled in any school, I've been wondering for a good while about the best time to begin working out a homeschooling arrangement with our school district. It seemed silly to contact the superintendent when Jesse had just turned five, and I toyed with thoughts of waiting until age eight, PA compulsory school age. Finally a number of factors (baby #3 arriving in late summer, among them) helped me to decide to request official approval this spring, just before what would be considered Jesse's first grade year.

Although each family must find what is best for them, I think there are a lot of possible advantages for families in beginning a dialogue with school people early. Approaching the superintendent now put *us* in a very favorable light—we were showing we were ready and willing to cooperate, even though it was not legally necessary. I knew that the state held no power in the situation, and that my district had no reason to worry that *they* were doing anything even vaguely illegal by cooperating with us. Although in our situation, I knew beforehand that the superintendent would be very friendly and supportive of our choice, I also knew that if for some reason I didn't like any of his recommendations or conditions, I could simply say, politely, "Thanks, see you instead when Jesse is 8," and be free of all dealings for a few more years. Those years could give time for a change in the climate of acceptance for homeschooling, or possibly even a change in superintendents. And meanwhile, nothing would be lost. . . . I felt these two years could give a superintendent time to really get to know a family's situation, to slowly grow to trust in the parents' handling of their own child's education. Once two years of very informal cooperation go by, it seems to me that it's quite a simple matter for a superintendent to continue giving approval when a child reaches compulsory school age. After all, this was a family the superintendent already knew well, not a strange family he knew absolutely nothing about and suddenly had to make a decision about.

I presented a Home Education Plan for Jesse at my initial meeting with the superintendent and his assistant. It included a short statement on our philosophy of education, and a conventional subject matter breakdown—language arts (listening, talking, reading, and writing), mathematics, social studies, science, art, music, and physical education and health, and also a section on evaluation procedures. I had already looked over the district's curriculum outlines for kindergarten and first grade and felt *very* confident that what we were doing normally at home easily met *all* grade level requirements, and in fact went much farther. Under each subject heading, I simply described, in normal language, not educational jargon, our basic approach in the area and listed specific interests and activities that Jesse had been involved with over the past year, indicating that we planned to continue in the same manner in the upcoming year.

When I wrote these lists, I began to be amazed at how thorough, how *good*, we looked on paper. Why it even looked like it might have been *planned*! (Reminded me again that our learning is *never* chaotic or without form, but just naturally creates its own form and order. . . .) This type of curriculum write-up was almost a delight to do, since I was simply sharing some of the experiences of a favorite little person, and I could avoid the drudgery of trying to come up with dry behavioral objectives, goals, future teaching strategies, etc. And no superintendent could say, as one in western PA did when shown a homeschooling plan, "Pshaw! Idealism! It will never work!", for our plan wasn't describing what we vaguely hoped *might* happen, but what actually had *already* happened. It was fact and couldn't be argued with.... It also makes me feel more confident now when people ask what we do all day or how I can manage to know what to do *next*. I can now say, perhaps even with an air of mystery, that of course I have our written educational *plan* if they'd like to see it.... Also, by showing up at the initial interview, detailed plan in hand, I also showed I was organized, serious, self-motivated and ready to dialogue. I was not waiting to be told a format for our plan, or waiting for them to specify what to include.

So everything is going well with setting up a cooperative relationship with our district. Communication lines are open, feelings are good on all sides, and school facilities will be available to Jesse as we feel we want to use them. Glad we didn't wait until age 8 to begin the process!

Success In N.H.

Jan Olmstead (NH) writes:

We have just finished our first year of homeschooling. I wrote to you about a year ago to say we had submitted our homeschooling proposal. Taking our kids out of school was easier than we had dreamed it would be. We had absolutely no trouble. In New Hampshire there are state guidelines for homeschooling and the people at the state level were very helpful. They suggested that we not try to prove "educational hardship" (i.e., the school's shortcomings) but that we focus on the educational benefit of home study.

The basis of our argument was the Congressional report on the education of the gifted and talented. We had our kids professionally (privately) evaluated and had a letter from the psychologist stating that they are academically gifted. Then we addressed our proposal to each paragraph of the state guidelines. When, on the week before school opened, we approached the superintendent, we had a copy of our proposal in hand. He didn't even have a copy of the guidelines!

The kids had to attend school for one week— until the first school board meeting. The board asked the superintendent if we had met the legal guidelines and that was it. We contracted with the school to: meet quarterly with the principal, guidance counselor, and special ed. (who else?) coordinator; to submit a monthly portfolio; and to have the kids take yearly achievement tests and the Gates-MacGinite reading test twice a year. We felt the reading tests and monthly portfolios excessive but decided to comply since it had gone so smoothly.

As it turned out, the school had more trouble with the contract than we did and we only had three meetings (one of which was the week after school got out) and the guidance counselor did not attend any of them. The kids took the reading test only once and that they let us do at home. The school was ecstatic with the test results ("With results like this who could argue with your home program!").

We had a great year. The kids learned about anything they wanted (ancient Egypt, photography, parapsychology, whales, etc.). They worked with a number of people in the community—an artist, a biologist, a woman who had lived in France (for French). Our 11-year-old audited a university biology lab. Both children were guests of honor at the artist's show opening. Since both children are serious about performing arts (violin and ballet), being home gave them the time to take lots of classes, to be in performances, and to practice.

Their interest in the arts became a vehicle to academic subjects instead of the arts being extracurricular. We never had much structure to our learning at home or wherever. We went to all the cultural events that interested us, visited lots of museums, read many books, spent much time in the library, talked a lot, travelled (an extended trip along the southern coast), and the results of the California achievement tests just happened.

Our request for continuation of homeschooling was granted without hesitation. Our younger child (7) will be at home next year but our daughter (now 12) will be attending a performing arts boarding school only because she cannot find adequate opportunity here. We are in the process of lining up mentors in photography and violin-making.

We would like to invite anyone, especially in New Hampshire, who would like to look at our proposal or ask any questions to please do so.

A Traveling Family

A letter from South Carolina:

Last summer we ran across *Teach Your Own* and decided to keep our children home this past school year. For several years we have wanted to travel, but we have had no funds to travel on. So last summer we decided to experiment and see how much of civilization we could do without and still be happy and fairly comfortable. From June to October we lived in two tents in the mountains of Tennessee. My husband drove 120 miles round trip to work every day. We were just going good on our experiment when it was time to start worrying about getting the kids back in school somewhere. Since we were rootless and enjoying the freedom of being able to pull up stakes and move whenever we wanted to, we were overjoyed to read your book.

Our original plan was to get correspondence courses but we just could not come up with $800 for two children, so we started school out under the trees on a lake with whatever appropriate books we could find at flea markets. . . . We required the children to write one composition a week. . . . We all loved to go to the libraries.

Of course, it hasn't been easy and all fun. We have no records for last year's schoolwork. Though I tried to maintain a schedule, the demand of younger children and another pregnancy, plus my own lags in discipline and lesson-planning made it a stop-and-start-again experience. There were times they just did not want to have school and my insistence discouraged us all.

All in all, we're very glad we kept them home this past year. They are more family oriented, and not as much inclined to be led around by the nose by their peer groups.

This past week Jon (13) began working in a paint and body shop with his father, earning $115 a week; he was thrilled to be able to earn some money to help pay for his own clothes and education.

Famous Unschooler

From a column in the Sacramento Bee, *5/23/83:*

> Ansel Adams' father let him drop out of school at the age of 13 to fiddle with a Brownie box camera. "My father told me that he'd wait until I found exactly what I wanted to do before he made me go back to school. I never went back."
>
> He learned to fiddle pretty good with the Brownie. Today he can get as much as $71,000 for one of his snaps.

Teens At Home

A Canadian reader writes:

I am 15 years old, and have been partially homeschooled since Grade II, and fully since Grade V. I just finished my Grade IX correspondence course. *GWS* has been a spiritual life-saver for my parents and me. By putting us in touch with other homeschoolers, it has dispatched the feeling that we're isolated "freaks," battling alone against the cold, sterile system.

Also, after reading many issues of your magazine, I have finally stopped having terrifying nightmares about school, and have even learned to trust people again, after feeling persecuted by everyone because of my choice of an alternative lifestyle.

In our area, there is still a great deal of anger and jealousy directed at homeschoolers. Yesterday, I had to turn down a request for an interview on a radio talk-show. I would have loved to do it, but the situation is just too fragile now. If the authorities would have found out, it could have been the end. It is very frustrating to be constantly suppressed, when you feel you are not doing anything wrong.

From a Texas parent:

I have been reminded by a homeschooler friend that I never reported on an accomplishment of last summer concerning my now 13-year-old son. . . . We have been homeschoolers (we also have a nine-year-old son) since my oldest was in preschool.

We let him go to camp last summer for two weeks. He won numerous skill awards, but most prized of the camp was a sterling silver pin given to "best camper, citizen, and most congenial." He collected it also! I must say *we* were not surprised, but I feel all at camp realized (to *their* surprise) it was because he is *not* in school rather than in school, learning to be "social"!

I find that most think that socialization *must* be what he is lacking in being homeschooled. They aren't worried about his math, only that he isn't meeting *girls* (he has plenty of girl *friends*).

From a mother in Oregon, who sent clippings about her daughter's modeling, ballet, and acting career:

When my daughter was in the sixth grade she bought your book *Teach Your Own* and gave it to me. She had been earning her own money since she was nine and working toward a career goal since she was seven. Even though she liked her fellow students and teachers, she repeatedly complained about wasting half of her day in school accomplishing nothing.

I taught her for the next year and a half at home. She completed three grades easily in that time and once again expressed a need to go on.

At the age of 12 she confidently agreed to take a full college entrance exam in order to take one biology class at the college. The counselor told her she could go home and study for a week. She replied that she would rather take it then and there. He raised his eyebrows and took her in for testing. She emerged at the scheduled time having passed the test in the top 13% of all high school graduates taking it.

After many frustrations and tribulations she entered college as a full-time student at the age of 13. She is almost 14 now.

She is quick-witted, sees a charm in all people and looks at every new and unusual situation as a learning experience.

Margo Bauer (CA) wrote:

I am homeschooling my 14-year-old daughter. . . . When I volunteered in her sixth-grade classroom and saw just how terrible the whole school scene was, I decided to teach her at home.

I have had her tested every September (Iowa Test of Basic Skills) and she is above grade average in every subject. Her problem had always been math. She attended a private school which I found out later taught no math at all. We enrolled in our junior college last year, and bought a very helpful programmed-learning math book, and she is doing beautifully. (She was not allowed to enroll herself but she was allowed to attend classes with me.) We took basic writing and math (for her), and advanced writing for me. She was allowed to sit in there also, and she enjoyed hearing the poems and stories others had done. It was a remarkably good class, I thought.

Next September we may attend the University of California at Davis's extension class in writing. Cost is $125 a semester. We will see. Perhaps I will attend, and she can also do the assignments (she can legally attend Extension).

I have read extensively about education since deciding to take her out of school, and feel I could write my own book. (In fact, I plan to.) . . . I finally narrowed her education down to one hour (approx.) each day for each of these subjects—reading, writing, and arithmetic. The reading is from books I consider the most helpful, interesting, etc. I wonder if this is being too dictatorial. Still, I am afraid that if we are not all pushed a little, we will miss some excellent books. I know I would never have read many books if I had not had to for classes in college. The same with writing papers. I believe in allowing her to choose her topics sometimes, but I do expect her to write. In her reading, she does one chapter a day, and writes a brief summary of it.

She is also expected to clip one article from the

paper, and write a *brief* summary of it, and be prepared to discuss it at dinner. She is to learn one new word a day, know its origin, and use in a sentence. She does one Proverb a day, paraphrasing it and illustrating it briefly. And she also writes a half-page in her journal daily. Oh, yes, I have a most excellent history book. It covers world history from the early Greeks through present day times.

I now live on a small almond ranch in foothills west of Sacramento. I love it here . . . I wish that I could have known what I know now with my other children, and had them here on a farm. I would never have let them set foot in a classroom!

My daughter is in the Bay Area presently, one hour away, and will be back this weekend. This is one of the joys of homeschooling. She has a thin copy of a math and English book to take with her plus her current reading book. She is free. She has earned money doing babysitting and housecleaning. She trained in a child-care center for two weeks, and in fact she and I are opening a center here. She can be my legal assistant at age 14. We go to Davis often, where my husband works in grounds. There is so much to do. Just going to the library there is an education.

Life At Home

A letter from Florida:

We incorporated as a private school in Dec. 1982. . . . The children stay inside until the public schools let out and we try to stay at or above "grade level" in our lessons. And we try to produce enough paperwork to be able to show anyone who questions us.

We acquired boxes and boxes of textbooks from the surplus of the county schools. They were free . . . Even if we don't go through the books page by page, they are handy for reference. Some sections are very good. There is a "Computer Corner" in one set of math books—my son (12) and daughter (10) went through all the books from grade 2–8 doing the computer programs. I think that without knowing, they were learning some laws of math by the way the computer had to be programmed to get certain results.

We signed up as a school to take a self-guided tour of the animal areas of Busch Gardens. We got a very low admission price and they sent us a nice packet of pre-visit and post-visit activities to help us get the most out of our tour. I am checking into other local attractions to see if they have programs like this.

I am slowly working towards getting a teaching certificate as insurance so we never have to send our children back to school. I just began a class in Humanities. I was looking forward to being with adults in an intellectual atmosphere, learning things from the class discussion. Instead, the teacher simply reads the book to us. The most stimulating question heard in class is, "Will that be on the test?"

From Lezlie Long (OR):

Kindergarten has started and the twin neighbor boys are going. Robert (5) and I have been going round and round about that. "But Adam and Aaron are going." So I explain for the twentieth time that he may not go to school until he's 8. More arguments. Finally he wailed, "But mother, *I have to learn!!!*" We decided to do "school work" while the twins are at school and it has worked beautifully.

We started with his name and Rob decided he did not want to do that: "Too hard." "Sorry, chum, if you were in school you would do it anyway." "OK." So now he can write his name with no help and loves to write letters to people but does not want *any* help *at all* with arithmetic.

Rebecca (3) and Richard (2) of course are always there with us and how much they're picking up is hard to tell. Rebecca mostly sings and tells me how to take care of the baby. Richard watches and watches and watches.

We use clay and color and paint and cut and tape and write and read and sometimes we go for walks. I took a storytelling class and now the kids insist on at least one "not-read" story each day. Actually it's closer to three or four, but Mother can sometimes beg her way out of it.

Dave Porterfield (PA) writes:

Yesterday Link, Chik, and I went to a wholesaler of tropical birds. We just went without telling them we were coming. Even though the sign on the door said an appointment is needed on Monday, we were able to have our "field trip," seeing thousands of birds.

Thursday I'll drive nursery school kids to Pittsburgh's aviary/conservatory. Link and Chik will go. We've been there at least a dozen times and never tire of it. At the back there's a torpedo tube from the USS Maine. We eat lunch at that spot, where my brothers and cousins and I used to play many years ago.

It's handy being a school bus driver and being able to take the boys on trips.

Today Link wants to ask if he can help elderly people at Passavant Health Center. I help with IRS's volunteer tax program, and he got the idea last Tuesday of doing something useful while I work on the program.

Jan Risley (CA) writes:

We've been homeschooling since 1979 with no real problems. Do wish the girls would show more interest in reading—it seems to be a lack of confidence in the 9-year-old, resulting from being pushed into reading in kindergarten, before she was ready. Tammy (7) hasn't yet mastered all the sounds and how to blend them together—they both want to know how to read but haven't decided to put the necessary effort into it. Ryan (5) has shown more curiosity about words than either of the girls did, and I printed some on cards for him. I'm hoping for a major breakthrough here, but have to let it happen by itself. They love to be read to and to look at books and magazines, so I try to be patient.

We go to swap meets and garage sales quite often and the girls have learned a lot about money this way, more than any workbook could ever teach them. I've been pleasantly surprised to hear them adding up various coins and coming up with the right answers.

We do a lot of art and craft type things. The girls took an art class last summer from a lady who does beautiful water colors. It was a very small class—often they were the only two there. It met in a small park adjacent to the lady's art gallery, so there was no feeling of confinement. She let them draw or paint whatever they wanted, offering advice when asked. In getting to know her better I learned that she has taught art here in California and thinks the idea of homeschooling is great—and offered to be available if ever we need a certified teacher.

My husband thinks the kids should be in school so I could have more free time (I don't complain). . . . He agrees that some things in school are bad but thinks kids should be there anyway. He is a commercial fisherman and recently built his own fishing boat—with the kids' help!.

From Kris Rose in Kansas (see "Friendly Lawyers," *GWS 33):*

I took my son out of kindergarten last March after meetings with the teacher. . . . He still resists any attempt to learn new words or to read although he loves to be read to.

To encourage my son to read, I write out recipes for simple dishes he can prepare—he loves to cook and is very proud when he can do it by himself. He made his own loaf of yeast bread this way—I assembled the tools and ingredients and turned on the oven. He did almost everything else.

We enjoy playing backgammon, and have started to learn chess and Yahtzee. We plan to send him to first grade in the fall. However, we all understand that going to school is a voluntary choice on our part—and that we are the consumers, so to speak, of a service offered by this institution. This approach gives me the courage to confront teachers and administrators. Although I am an attorney and trained to deal with confrontations, I am intimidated by grade school teachers—the strict authoritarian figures of my timid girlhood. . . . I do anguish over losing Alan from 8 to 3:15 daily and I may see if I can bring him home at 1 or 1:30.

Growing Happy In England

From Mary Gwizdata in England:

The talk John gave in London was what finally

convinced me to take my son, Janek, who's nearly four, out of school, and never to send him or his sister, Anastasja (18 months old) to school. . . . In the last few months, my husband and I have split up, which—although it makes for all the usual financial and accommodation problems—actually means that I can arrange my life the way *I* want it (instead of around him). In just the few weeks since he left here, Anastasja has begun to talk and try to play (instead of just being whiny and miserable and wanting to be with me all the time) and Janek has settled down quite a bit.

Janek had been gradually becoming calmer anyway, like he was before his term and a half at school. His power of concentration had been returning, and although he is definitely the untidiest child since the child I used to be, he no longer wrecks things as his main pastime (the only thing he seemed to learn at school). He is interested in everything again; if only *I* weren't always so tired! I seem to hear myself so often saying "I don't know," "later," "one day," "in a minute."(Anastasja can say, "In a minute"!)

However, I am becoming less tired, anxious, worried, more human. My days aren't being spent screaming at and hustling my children because I'm afraid of what might happen when their father comes in; I even laugh sometimes! I guess what I mean is that poor Janek has had a double dose of negation, or even worse than that: (l) parents who seemed to hate each other; (2) school, promised as a place full of fun but in fact boring and causing even worse feelings of insecurity; and possibly (3) his sister, who was ill and didn't sleep much for most of the first year or so of her life, thus getting far more attention than Janek, or so it must have seemed to him. I love my children, even at two in the morning when Janek arrives freezing cold and clammy to announce that he's wet his bed again (more washing, impossible in this climate where nothing dries, unbelievable the amount of time I spend on laundry) and I hear he's woken Anastasja en route and I have to get up to make her a drink, etc., etc. . . . But lately I'm learning to like and respect *myself*, not easy after 35 years of trying to submerge myself and thinking there's something "wrong" with me: and it's reflected in my children's feelings and wellbeing. I've always *known* the theory that happiness breeds happiness, and confidence breeds confidence: that if you don't set the example, the child won't follow it. But now, instead of acting happy and confident, I'm making a conscious effort to *be* it.

Lately, Janek has taught himself to read numbers, I'm not sure how. And to trace pictures. And to draw around the outlines of pictures he's "supposed" to color in. He's also very keen on tying things up, and will play for hours with little bits of string. I think he's learning to read: he spends uncountable hours poring over his books. I think that sometime soon he will just read.

Overcame Shyness

From the N.J. Family Schools Assoc. Newsletter, *6/83:*

> Peggy Kimszal is particularly pleased with her daughter's unending stream of ideas, plans and projects. She writes, "Both girls are very creative and love to put on plays and puppet shows. Recently Alison (8) took one of her albums, *Antshillvania* (the story of the prodigal son with ants as characters), and made stick puppets for each of the characters, made a stage and props, and put on a puppet show. On another night Suzanne (5) and Alison acted out all the parts themselves, including making up dances to go with the songs. They also rounded up the neighborhood kids and put together their own version of *Annie*."
>
> Friends cautioned Peggy that Alison needed to attend school to overcome her shyness. But after several years of homeschooling Alison has become a sought-after social leader among neighborhood children, even older children. Other children look to Alison for ideas of what to play. Alison's abundance of ideas, which Peggy attributes to the freedom and time to explore which homeschooling provides, seems to have led Alison out of shyness.

Learning On Her Own

[JH:] We keep hearing the objection that homeschooling is bad, elitist, impractical, etc., because people who work out of the home can't do it. I keep saying that this is not so, that there have been and are families in which the parent or parents go to work every day and the children stay home, doing the things that interest them, until the parents return from work and they resume their family life. But as far as we know there are not yet a great many of these families, so it is always nice to meet new ones. On a recent lecture tour I met one such family, who later wrote me a letter about their experience, saying in part:

It all goes back about eight years. Our eldest daughter was then in the first grade and very bored. It occurred to us that she was not learning anything at school that she could not learn at home, so we pulled her out. At first I was concerned that she would be wasting her time but I was too busy to be terribly bothered about it and I soon found myself leaving her alone the way my parents had left me alone in the summers. I was amazed to see that she thrived. The next year we tried second grade and pulled her out again. The following year our youngest daughter started kindergarten and the oldest went to third grade. The little one was reading the original version of *Winnie The Pooh* before she entered and when the teacher was still teaching her the alphabet in November, I pulled both girls out and neither ever went back.

These girls have not had any lessons of any kind since and they are positively as literate and educated, creative and skillful in many areas as the wonder kids in school. To be sure, our house has always been full of wonderful books and records and tools, but the point here is we did not make any kind of learning mandatory unless it really was! For example, I decided years ago that they should help me by doing the laundry and other chores, so I showed them how. It was necessary and certainly part of "real" life. In fact, as time passed, the whole idea of creating situations outside of real life for the purpose of teaching about real life became positively ludicrous.

Even now when people wonder if the girls shouldn't be doing this or that I always wonder what is so wrong with just letting them live their lives.... Our girls are not being deprived of necessary experiences and teaching. They both exhibit astonishing common sense, clarity of thinking, sensitivity to each other and all people and life, and an elegant poise which says they truly like themselves. I am always learning from them. They are so fortunate.

I fear this letter got a bit rambly but I get so worked up when I feel forced to pick at the details when the huge human picture is so clear and important. It was meant only to say that young humans are being left alone all day while the parents work and it is just fine.

Enthusiastic Stranger

From a Cincinnati parent:

While at an appointment, my children waited quietly in a large waiting room with another client who was playing and talking to them. When I was finished, the client approached me and inquired how old my children were and where did they attend school. I replied that they were not of school age yet and they have not set foot inside a school or day-care center, and that I had been working with them at home.

At that, the lady was overcome with joy! She said that she felt all children should be taught at home by their parents and that the atmosphere was not the stiff competitiveness of school. She went on to tell me of how children are labeled "hyperactive" and "problem children" because they are required to stay still and not move about after completing a task before their classmates, whereas at home, the child could move on to something else when finished. This woman talked to me about forty-five minutes more and begged me not to put my children in school. This woman was a school teacher!

Husband Changes Mind

Bettelou Roberts wrote to Susan Richman (PA):

I no longer have a reluctant husband! I just kept passing info along as I read it in your newsletter and in *GWS*, shared my ideas of what I'd like to do and assured him I wouldn't make a move without him till he had made up his mind. Soon I noticed him sharing a few opinions and asking a few questions. Then came the notice in the newspaper about kindergarten enrollment this month. He told his folks we weren't enrolling Erin in school and explained homeschooling. I'm sure they'll be supportive as my parents are also.

Liking School Is Not Enough

Nola Evans (WA) writes:

Several people have written in to *GWS* about letting their young children try school. To carry on the sugar analogy from "She Chose to Go" in *GWS* 31, I think a taste of school can be dangerous, unless parents are willing to enforce their limiting powers after that, because it is not good for you. The question is not whether your child likes school or not (or likes sugar or not), the question is what effects does it have.... Schools teach a whole host of negative opinions and attitudes: to distrust yourself, use others, degrade others, disregard your interests and become out of touch with them, disown yourself; to be a fun-seeker, a non-producer, a consumer, a non-learner, an apathetic bystander.... This happens without your being aware of it and happens just as quickly and effectively if you like school as if you dislike it.

If you send your child to school and she or he later decides to stay home, you have a lot more to undo than their negative opinion about school or even about themselves. I contend that if they go to school and like it, they are oblivious to the harm they are doing to themselves and others.

My experience comes partly from my daughter, who enjoyed the social life at school and who did well enough with the academics that she wasn't concerned with them. Academics were like trivia—interesting but not something you would go out of your way to discover, not something you work with and use. School was like a TV game show; it was fun for her because she got the right answers, won the prizes, and was a celebrity (in the social circles). There were lots of things we saw happening to her in four years of school—things that John or Herbert Kohl or James Herndon have written about other children in schools. But we never thought of taking her out of school until we heard of *Teach Your Own*. It wasn't too difficult for us to convince her to try unschooling because it happened at a time when changes were being made in the school, friends moving, etc. A year earlier, she would have wanted to stay in school and I'm not sure how I would have handled it.

I'm also writing from my experience as a preschool teacher (ex-teacher, now).... I tried desperately to make the school work for the kids, not just so they learned to read letters or words or whatever, but so they would use the school to work out things they were interested in. I wanted it to provide the intrigue and the resources to investigate. What I saw every year was what happens in any ordinary school. Even (and maybe *especially*) when kids liked school, *it was not out of a love for learning.* I couldn't figure out what I was doing wrong, until I read *Teach Your Own* and it hit me: it wasn't that *I* couldn't make it work, it was that it *doesn't* work. Schools don't help people develop into human beings. They can't help with the essence of learning—they can't offer what I wanted to offer—not, at least, when there are one or two teachers and 20 or more children in one room, all required to be together for a specified amount of time.

Anyway, in this experience, I realized how easily influenced the children are. They adapt quickly to whatever methods and structures are imposed on them. Attitudes and ideas that are unplanned but develop out of the methods are quickly adopted as "The Way It Spozed To Be." If we can put off school entrance to age 10 or more, we have more of a chance that our children will see school as it really is.

People I've talked to tell me, it is not difficult [to keep a young child out] if it is not left open to question. They do not ask, "Would you like to go to school or stay home?" They simply let their children know well beforehand that the children will not be going to school. . . . If parents feel strongly about it, children are unlikely to resist. (If you're a vegetarian, it's not likely your preschooler would insist on eating meat.) If that did happen, you have to decide whether they are old enough or wise enough to be allowed to make their own choice. Will they see the consequences? Will they see, not just the overt experiences, but the implications—the subtle, underlying teachings that will shape them? . . . I believe that parents should learn all they can about school's effects and then, armed with this awareness, assume the responsibility for making the decision to keep their children out of school until the children are older and equal to the task of making this weighty decision.

Spaceship School

Earlier this year I visited for a few days some old friends who are not homeschoolers and whose children have always gone to school. Spending some time with their schooled kids made me realize that the combination of school plus "peer group" (an odd way to describe a group of people who have nothing in common with you except being the same age) can do children a kind of harm that I had not previously thought of.

My objection to the social life of almost all schools, as *GWS* readers know, is that it is for the most part mean-spirited, competitive, ruthless, snobbish, conformist, consumerist (you are judged by what you can buy, or your parents buy for you), fickle, heartless, and often cruel. Most children come out of school with far less self-esteem, less sense of their own identity, dignity, and worth, than they had when they went in. I know this was true of me. Most children in school feel like losers and outsiders, and most will do almost anything that will, if only for a short time, give them the feeling of being insiders, truly "One Of The Gang." But I had generally felt and said that there might be a few children who were so good at all the things that schools and "peer groups" considered important, so completely winners at the school game, that socially, at least, the school experience might be more positive than negative for them.

My friends' oldest child, about to enter high school, seemed at first to be such a person. She was very good at schoolwork (though not in the least interested in it), and got A's in all her courses; was very athletic, outstanding in a number of sports; was good-natured, friendly, lively, funny, and very popular with both boys and girls; and was astonishingly pretty. She seemed genuinely happy, was fond of and nice to her parents, and was pleasant and friendly to me. Surely this one was one of those rare children who was getting good rather than harm from the social life of school. And yet, after living with her and her family for a few days, I began to feel that even to her the combination of school plus "peer group" was doing some real harm, perhaps harm of a rather subtle kind, perhaps harm that she may soon outgrow, but harm none the less.

What school plus "peer group" had done was to enclose her in a world that was so small and so cut off from every other kind of reality that she might as well have been living in a spaceship. In spite of being very bright, and having very bright parents, she was as nearly as I could tell almost totally ignorant of and uninterested in the world around her. By this I do not mean just that she was not up on the latest newspaper headlines—I tend to agree more and more with Thoreau that most of the "news," even if true, is not worth knowing. What I mean is that she was not interested in *anything* about the world she lived in except the handful of cute boys and girls who were her companions and perhaps friends, plus perhaps a few stars from the world of popular mass culture—singers, actors and actresses, etc. For her, these were the most real or perhaps the only real people. As I have said, she seemed to love her kind and intelligent parents, who very much loved her. But she was not interested in them or what they thought and did, except perhaps as it impinged on her own spaceship life. Most healthy children are at least some of the time very curious about the adult world, and particularly any strange adults who appear in their families. But this child, though she answered very nicely the few questions I asked her, asked none of me, and paid no more real attention to me than she did to her parents.

I have to make clear that, perhaps because she was such an outstanding winner in her little world, perhaps also because she was a happy and good-natured person (no small thing), she had never learned to think of adults as enemies, and so was not in the least afraid of them, or rude, hostile, or contemptuous toward them. But she never gave the slightest sign that she thought that any adults, including her very intelligent and remarkable parents, might be interesting, or might have anything to say worth hearing, or any knowledge of the world or experience of life worth learning. Adults, those shadowy figures, were obviously *there*, and since they had money and power they had to be coped with one way or another, something she was very good at doing. But there was nothing interesting or useful to be learned by watching or listening to them; they were in no way models for the adult life she herself would one day lead. Friendly and charming though she was, she seemed as truly *alienated* from adult life, the (to me) fascinating community she lived in, and indeed the whole *"Real World"* the schools talk about, as the most enraged delinquent punk rocker. And this seems to me a serious loss and deprivation for her, and one that will probably make her own adult life less interesting and more difficult, when one day, as she must, she alights on Earth from her little spaceship.—JH

Interruptions At Home

Leslie Westrum (WI) writes:

The home pre-schooling is going fine here—except that my friends think that since I'm "just at home" I'm not really doing anything. I get a lot of uninvited, unexpected drop-in visitors. We do have regular lessons and try to stick to a basic schedule of study, work, and playtime, but we're constantly interrupted by visits and phone calls from friends who were just in the neighborhood, or who just want to call and chat for a couple of hours while they do the ironing. I guess they think I should send my kids to watch TV, or send them to play with a neighbor so I can spend the day with my ear to the phone. That's not my idea of good parenting, or even of a worthwhile way to spend my own time.

My other pet peeve, fresh in my mind because it happened *twice today,* is that friends who do know that I'm trying to teach the kids, for some reason feel free to drop their kids off while they do errands. I guess they figure since I'm just home with the kids all day anyway I'd be delighted to have a couple extras around. There also seems to be a feeling that if we're having a lesson it will be great for their kids to just sit in and have class with us. And yet none of these parents would drop a toddler off at work for a few hours since dad is "just sitting around the office anyway." They would never say, "As long as you're changing your baby you can change mine too," or "As long as you're going to the store here's my grocery list for the week." . . . Has anyone else got a problem like this? Do I get strict and risk losing a few friends?

Toddler: Homeschool Challenge

In a letter last fall, Kate Gilday (MA) mentioned that her 2½-year-old was "another challenge" in the homeschooling of her older daughter. Donna wrote in her reply:

A mother told us not long ago about trying to make a plaster-of-paris model with her older daughter—the baby came along and wrecked it and the whole thing was a tearful disaster. I don't see any solution except *not* to do activities when the baby is around that she cannot participate in, in some ways at least, and saving more complicated things for naptime. If that mother's only child was the baby, the mother simply would not have been making a plaster-of-paris model, right? Certainly not where the baby could reach it.

I think at some point you have to decide, is it more important that the older child be exposed to particular things *right now* (like making plaster-of-paris models), or to have harmony in the family? I think it's an American educational tradition to think that kids should be exposed to lots of things early.

But what difference does it make if a kid first uses plaster-of-paris at 6 or 8 or 12 or 15? Seems to me there'll be plenty of time later, and when both of the children are older it will be so much easier. *Recently Kate wrote again:*

3-year-old Ananda continues to be the factor in Suzi's homeschooling that we need to be the most creative in dealing with. Those projects that Suzi needs me close by for get done when Ananda is either (1) in for a nap or (2) at a friend's. It is sometimes frustrating to plan around her, for Suzi tends to want to get right into something she's decided upon and often when we wait it just doesn't get done.

However, two things are becoming clear as the months roll on. One comes from the letter you wrote in the fall, Donna, concerning the fact that the *really* important thing is harmony in the family. When there is, so much good feeling and easy energy is around that all kinds of interesting things happen. We're learning to trust that more and more. Also, I am beginning to realize that Suzi is not the only one home-schooling. We *all* are—and now with Ananda's "Whys" and desire to try anything and everything, I'm seeing she deserves our support in her ventures, too.

This whole experience is putting us through *so* many changes—some uncomfortable—all in helping our awareness of life grow.[See also "Learning Compassion," *GWS* 32.]

Sisters Cope With Baby

From Kathryn Finn (MA):

Danette (6) tells everyone that she likes puzzle-books (workbooks) better than anything. . . . Bridget (3½) is on the verge of reading and knows every bit as much math as her older sister, and the baby (Socorro, 2) wants to join the fun so much. The big girls are very good to her and find ways she can be a part of their activities without destroying things. If her crayon wanders out of bounds on to their stuff they simply move her back to her own page and agree that she's too young to know. They make booklets about colors and shapes and numbers for her to read and keep telling her that she can learn to read when she's three. When she sits on their book they get upset, but not otherwise.

Kids' Role In Housework

Nancy Wallace (NY) wrote:

I want to respond to something in Donna's last letter to me, an issue that has a lot to do with the philosophy behind *GWS*. Donna was concerned that I don't ask the kids to do their fair share of the housework and hence, while they are doing all kinds of wonderful things, I am stuck with all the mundane work that family life necessitates. As Donna writes, "I guess my concerns are twofold—one, that the kids, Ishmael in particular, are learning to be self-sufficient, and two, that *you* are respecting and valuing yourself as much as you value them." I think these are really legitimate concerns, particularly when you believe that children should in no way be treated with condescension because of their size and when you believe that they are capable of a lot more than most adults think they are. Many people I know, and many people who write in to *GWS*, take their children seriously enough to include them in their adult working lives, and, among other things, this means that they expect their children to share equally in their household chores. The attitude of these parents should in no way be confused with that of others, though, who believe that their children should be grateful to them for bringing them into the world and therefore have an *obligation* to help out with chores . . . (I think that perhaps parents who are really incapable of getting along without their children's help should have thought twice before they had children).

I don't know if you can teach self-sufficiency, or expect kids to learn it before they are ready. . . . I think they have to be ready, in much the same way they have to be ready to learn to read or whatever. Vita was ready practically from the day she was born. She's always been interested in dressing herself, vacuuming, cooking, sewing, and so on. Ishmael has been less interested. In fact, he was about 8 before he could zip a zipper or tie his shoes. We never even really suggested that he learn those things, but one day he just did, albeit 4 or so years later than most other children.

The other thing, I think, is that we tend to overemphasize the difficulty of performing household tasks and to assume that they have to be learned early to be learned well. But take me, for example. My mother not only cleaned the house all by herself, but she *wouldn't let* me make my bed or go near the kitchen. When I was 15 I was so unhappy in school that I made up my mind to go to a small private school (Pacific High School) instead, even if I had to earn the tuition myself, which is what I ended up doing. So that summer I got a job as a live-in maid and babysitter and I was responsible for making beds, doing all the cleaning, cooking, and serving all the meals, and looking after the kids. Somehow I managed, without any previous training. Knowing that, and knowing how relatively easy it was, I feel sure that even if Ishmael didn't do *any* housework, he'd be fine when he found himself on his own.

Now the truth is that the kids *do* help a lot, but I don't take it for granted, I always thank them for it. And it's also true that I *don't* ask Ishmael to help when he's busy composing. But could you? Besides, writing and music are what Bob and I do, and so I think of Vita and Ishmael as "working" when they "tinker" on the piano—work of more importance than doing the laundry or whatever.

It's true that I don't get enough time for myself, but can any homeschooling parent say that he or she does? And yet all of us would probably agree that having kids and watching them grow is worth any frustration we may feel about the lack of time we have to do our own work. Besides, our children *are* a large part of our work. . . . In some ways I, and most parents, live through my kids, and perhaps because of that, it looks as if I'm not fulfilled. I don't think living through your children is bad—I think it's natural. . . . I find that I delight in their accomplishments more than my own, and so often, although it seems as if I've been denying myself, I've been doing so happily. When we went to Philadelphia, for example, the kids got in two hours of music before we left, while Bob and I got ready for the trip. Self-denial? Yes, in a way. But I wanted it that way. Both kids are very aware of the work I do and both would have happily gotten us ready for the trip while I played the piano if I'd asked them to. I didn't, though, because I was happier listening to them play.

Perhaps the best thing we can do as parents is to show our kids examples of parents working together in households. Bob does the laundry and mending too, and he does the dishes and makes beds. Hopefully, unlike me, Vita will grow up assuming that housework isn't just women's work, and Ishmael will grow up thinking that housework is one of his responsibilities.

Having Fun With Housework

Susan Richman wrote in Western Pa. Homeschoolers #5 *(see her article* "Little Kids & Housework," *GWS 30):*

> Amazingly enough, housework is seeming like less of a problem to me these days. Partly this is due to changes in my attitudes after reading *Side-Tracked Home Executives*. Partly it's due to our growing repertoire of "clean-up games." It's becoming easier and easier to think these up on the spur of the moment, and certainly makes daily pick-up chores pleasanter.
>
> In one new game, Jesse works in one room, and I work in another. We must both pick up and put away *something*, then we must guess what it is that other person has put away. Involves a lot of going back and forth between rooms, but is good fun *and* gets two rooms neatened.
>
> I sometimes ask Jesse to pick up, say, the spilled contents of the Lincoln Log can, adding that I'll time him to see how long it takes. A stop-watch is great for this. This approach usually gets much more cooperation than a stern command, and even helps Jesse gain a firm sense of the meaning of seconds and minutes. If a friend is over, they can work cooperatively to do the task. Always good to see kids scurrying about to *help*

each other rather than to beat each other. Also it's surprising to all of us how *little* time these "put-away" jobs take.

The game Jacob, our almost-3-year-old, finds most delightful might be called the "Silly Mommy Nonsense Direction Game." I'll ask him to please put away the masking tape, *in the refrigerator*. He'll laugh at his silly mother, who must not know any better. I'll look confused, then maybe say, "Hmmm, in the *washing machine*?" More indulgent laughs, and finally Jacob himself says "Tape goes on the *tape hook*!" and runs to put it there. (We have *lots* of low-down hooks in our house—saves routing about in messy drawers.) Jacob's other favorite is when I pretend something very light-weight is very heavy—"Oh, Jacob, I couldn't let *you* put away this green marker, it's *much* too heavy, I can barely lift it!" More belly laughs and Jacob races away with the marker, usually now even putting it in the right place.

I'm also realizing that for many things the kids really don't need me sitting right by them "helping." Today when Jesse and Jacob built wonderful houses and people out of our "wild clay" from our stream, I got the dishes washed, the refrigerator and freezer tops cleaned off, scrubbed the stove and the oven door, and even did my 3-minute bathroom cleanup. I was right near, as they were working at the kitchen table, and we were all talking together happily the whole time. They didn't feel left out or ignored because I hadn't dropped everything just to sit and watch them work. I could always easily see what they were making, could comment as I felt like it, and none of these little jobs of mine were the type that couldn't bear an interruption of a minute or two. Perhaps some homeschooling parents worry that there are only two types of time in a day—time spent directly with a child, when *you* do nothing else, or time spent directly with household tasks when the child must be out of the way. Perhaps blending these times is a more realistic, fruitful approach. It seems to work best for us, anyway.

A children's book by Phyllis Krasilovsky. *The Man Who Didn't Wash His Dishes*, has also helped us greatly. I remember reading in John Holt's *Escape From Childhood* that probably most young children simply don't have our adult perspective to see the consequences of not doing various jobs. He writes [page 134]:

'When we take the garbage out, we know the reason: if we don't take it out, the kitchen will eventually be full of garbage. In our mind's eye we can see it there, we can almost smell it. In this sense we could be said to have a *more* active fantasy life than the children. The child has no such fantasy. We may ask him, 'What do you think would happen if we didn't take out the garbage?' He has no idea. He thinks, I suppose, the sack of garbage would just sit there where it is, what's so bad about that?'

The Krasilovsky book tells what happens to a man who decides, each night, that he's just *too* tired to do his dishes, and so keeps putting off the task day after day. Finally he can barely get in the front door, because of the dirty dishes stacked everywhere, and he's even eaten out of all his ashtrays, soap dishes, flower pots, and vases. The book ends with a rainstorm washing all the dishes clean in the back of the old man's pickup truck, and the man resolving that from then on he would always wash his dishes immediately after eating. Both of my boys think the story is very funny, and now whenever they nag me to stop washing dishes to help them with something, I'll say, "Oh, no! You want me to be the little old *woman* who never washed *her* dishes." That's usually enough to get them laughing and let me finish my job. We've transferred the idea to other tasks—we imagine what the house would be like if I *never* folded the laundry—the heaping piles on top of the dryer, the empty clothes drawers, the clean clothes falling to the floor and getting stepped on and made dirty again, the entire house stuffed to bursting with unfolded clothes. . . . And all this delicious imagining *while* we're folding and carrying the clothes!

One more children's book that's helped us cooperate better around the house is *Pelle's New Suit*, a charming Swedish picture book by Elsa Beskow, about a little boy who asks all of his relatives and the town tailor to help him out in making a new suit of clothes from his own little lamb's wool. Each person always answers Pelle's requests for help by very politely saying, "Oh! That I will gladly do, if while I'm doing ____ for you, you will do ____ for me. Pelle hauls wood, weeds carrots, tends cows, watches his baby sister, and ends up with a completed suit ready to show to his lamb. Now when Jesse asks me to do something for him, and it really is something he can't do for himself, I'll answer in "Pelle language"—"Oh, I will gladly mend your blue jeans for you, if while I am doing it you will kindly clear off the breakfast dishes for me." Jesse always catches the "literary reference" and is ready to do his part as I help him.

A "Continuum" Baby

From Jane Gaffney, 347 Lawrence Hargrave Dr, Clifton NSW 2510, Australia:

My little girl, Liesl, will be age one in a few days' time. Watching her explore the world is a real delight. . . . Just lately she's learned to turn our cassette deck off while it's playing and to adjust the volume, and she just *loves* to be able to have such an obvious and immediate effect on something. She's also learning to clean up—she puts her blocks back into their container. She knows what I mean if I say, "Where is your ball?" or "Get your shoes," and sets about finding these things and bringing them to me.

Liesl is a home-birth, *Continuum Concept* baby. By this I mean she was carried around nearly all the time until she could sit at 4 months, most of the time until she could crawl at 7 months, then quite a bit of the time (but much less) until she could walk at 10 months, and now she still likes lots of cuddles, a few ½–1 hour sessions in the backpack each day, and lots of hip rides. I am her base to which she comes when she's sick of playing, tired, or hungry.

For Liesl and me, the body contact part has and still does seem very right and I think that is the most important point Jean Liedloff makes. I'm afraid when it comes to trusting the baby's own instincts for self-preservation, I'm not so confident. We have wired in our 10-foot-high balcony and I don't let Liesl play near the 150-foot cliff in our backyard. However, I do make an effort not to panic over things that don't *really* matter, like her playing with not-very-sharp knives and forks, or sucking on stones and twigs and leaves, all of which she loves. I've seen so many mothers panicking, smacking and *no-no'ing* about little things. It surely must have an effect on that wonderful drive to learn and explore that all babies are born with.

I have read quite a few accounts in *GWS* of babies who want to be in on everything. Liesl is the same. Between the ages of about 3 and 7 months, before she could crawl, she would spend most of her waking hours in a pouch on my front facing out. She absolutely loved this as she was right in the center of everything and could "help" with whatever I was doing. Sometimes she was content to watch all the interesting things going on. Other times she would grab a spoon I was using to stir something, or pull on the clothes I was hanging out. Nowadays she gets absorbed in her own little games but if I'm doing something interesting like playing the piano, or cleaning my teeth or working in the vegetable garden (unfortunately she doesn't know the difference between a weed and a vegetable) or sewing or vacuuming or making the bed or folding clothes, she's right in there helping me. She's here right now on my lap trying to grab my pen. It can be rather frustrating but usually there's a solution if you just think about it, even if it means waiting until she goes to sleep to do some things.

False Idea About Learning

From a letter John wrote to Mothering *magazine, published Spring '83:*

> When I (now 60) was little, *nobody ever thought that children had to be TAUGHT colors and shapes*. Nobody ever taught me colors and shapes. I figured them out, just as I figured out thousands of other things, by seeing what people did around me and hearing what they said about what they did, and maybe asking a question if I wanted to confirm one of my hunches.
>
> Every year we get more and more deeply mired in the fundamentally false idea that learning is, must be, and can only be the result of teaching, in short, that ideas never get into children's heads unless adults put them there. No more harmful and mistaken idea was ever invented. The fact, as all parents of young children can easily observe, is that children *create* learning out of experience and they do it in almost exactly the same way that the people we call "scientists" do it—by observing, wondering, theorizing, and experimenting (which may include asking questions) to test their theories.
>
> The idea that, unless taught, a child *might* actually grow up not knowing squares from triangles or red from blue is so absurd that I hardly know what to say about it. But it is an astonishingly widespread idea.
>
> I suppose I'm doomed to spend the rest of my life battling it. The worst thing about it is that after a while kids come to believe it themselves.

Susan Richman (PA) wrote us:

> So glad to see your letter to *Mothering* magazine, John. . . .The bizarreness of teaching colors, etc., has struck me hundreds of times since becoming a parent—it's as if these people think colors don't exist all around the child *every*where until Mom or nursery school teacher holds up the proper construction paper circle (and anyone should know that construction paper has the most pallid, dead colors). How much more exciting to go to a huge carpet store and soak in all the hues and shades and textures, or look over paint sample cards, or look around any room, or any load of laundry.

Making Up Test Questions

From Anne Miles, 860 E 13th Av, Vancouver BC V5T 2L5:

> Recently my 4-year-old has been making up her own "Which one does not belong?" questions. She has a subscription to a kid's magazine which has many of these questions—ridiculously simple ones. Laura will make up questions like this: Which one does not belong—a cough, a sneeze, a burp, and a hankie? Answer—a hankie! She is also equal to any "Which one does not belong" questions I throw at her.

Simple Reading Ideas

Another good article by Susan Richman in the Western Pa. Homeschoolers #5:

> As Jesse has always found great delight in spinning off reels of rhyming words, we began making simple rhyming flip books. You'll need some small blank cards—index card size, printer's scraps, whatever. Cut most of the cards in half, and staple these on top of one full-size card, so you have a little booklet. Then start filling in words, putting the first letter or blend on the small cards, and having the rhyming ending on the one long card, as shown.

> C | AT

> As you flip through the book, a different rhyming word pops up—it seems almost magical to a beginning reader that one letter makes the change. Jesse helps in thinking up words for these books; he especially enjoys inventing silly-sounding nonsense words. Jacob (2½) has even had good fun with the

idea—not in reading the words, of course, but in thinking up his own rhyming combinations. He thinks it's a great joke to ask for "cinnamon-jinnamon-binnamon" for his breakfast oatmeal, loving to twirl the funny words on his tongue, laughing. Jesse notices rhymes everywhere, often saying, "Hey, that would make a good flip book."

Another game that evolved is the "Message Game," played with our refrigerator magnetic letters. Jesse is now in charge of alphabetizing the letters every Monday, and scrounging up lost ones from *under* the refrigerator. This usually takes him about the same time as my breakfast clean-up, and so gives us both some work to do in the kitchen (always good to have company during jobs!). When the letters are organized we start the game. First I write out a simple message with the letters—our usual favorite starting one that Jesse *always* can read is "*give mommy a hug.*" Then the message is changed to perhaps "Give Mommy a *rug*" or "*bug*" or "*jug*." Jesse must run to get me these things from about the house. Soon it's Jesse's turn to write *me* a message. (I'm never allowed to look while he's writing his, so I can often do another bit of needed neatening during this time.) He usually likes to use his favorite books to help him with spelling out words he needs, coming up with "*give Jesse a dinosaur*," etc, and then I must find those items for *him*. He's reluctant to just try putting words together as they sound to him, but he does know that he has resources to turn to other than just me. The game goes on until Jesse wants to stop, often a half-hour or more (or other times five minutes!). It is full of lots of laughs, hugs, and sitting on laps and leaping about—no quiet desk work for us!

Another idea that has been a help to us is making Jesse his own small word-book dictionary. We stapled together 26 long skinny pages, and wrote one letter at the top of each page. Any time Jesse needs to spell a word, for a letter to Grandma, the message game, a sign he's making, a note to Daddy, etc., I'll write it in his book, on the proper page. It's surprising how much learning comes from this simple device. First, of course, it saves all the innumerable scraps of paper we used to have lying about when Jesse wanted words written out for him—helps cut down on clutter! Jesse always wants me to read over all his old words on a page whenever a new one is added, absorbing again the initial sounds of the words. Often a word he needs is already in his book and Jesse can somehow figure out which one it is. He's getting more familiar with alphabetical order, and is now able to find the letter for the word he needs without looking through the entire book randomly. He can also guess what letter his word will start with, and is always pleased when he comes up with a word for a letter page that hasn't had any words up to then.

Using Neighborhood Library

From Marilyn Bohren (LA):

Jan. 27: . On our last move, we found the neighborhood library was across the street from our house. Django worked diligently at crossing the street safely and writing his name small enough to sign a library card. His father took him over finally after lots of practice, but the library made Spencer sign the card instead of Django. We were all really disappointed.

Nevertheless, at 5½, Django made his first library solo trip, returning a couple of books and checking out his five. And why not? He's been watching us for years. The only problem is the doors are heavy for him to open. But someone usually helps there. The librarian is chatty and kind—actually it seems noisy for adults to study, but kids seem to enjoy it.

One day Django ran across the row of Hardy Boys books and asked his father about them. Now there's always one around. Sometimes one is being read by Spencer and one is being read by me. They seem to be having several influences on Django: (l) the privacy and intimacy of sharing a story with someone; (2) his vocabulary is increasing as he asks for definitions at least once a page (sleuth, eavesdrop, villain, suspicious, etc.); (3) the Hardy Boys are not adults and yet are given credit for accomplishing what are normally considered adult tasks, i.e., cracking mysteries, recovering money, working with police; (4) there's a sound relationship between the Hardy Boys and their parents; (5) Django now wants to be a detective when he gets older, although his play shows that he's one now.

June 9: Django is quite the reader now. He's joining the library's summer reading program. At first he thought *we* could read Hardy Boys books to him. Once the librarian straightened him out on that, he found a book he could read and came home and read it to me. It was so smooth and fearless I couldn't believe it, as it's been several weeks since he's read aloud. I asked if he'd read it before and he said he had—to himself in the library. I know all our reading aloud helps as he asks questions on words and seems to follow along often. Django now knows about paragraphs and quotation marks from just watching us read. Most of all, I think these hours of reading provide him with the personal attention he still needs but can't get in too many other ways.

I'm getting better organized now that Corinna is 8 months. So I got a simple chemistry book out of the library and we did experiments. The kids loved hydrogen peroxide with bleach, which released oxygen to ignite a smoldering broomstraw. Django knows about molecules and atoms and compounds in a very in-a-matter-fact-way—same as the birthing process. He's also learning how to yodel from a record!

Andre (3½) writes some letters. Is it by accident the first three were A, N, D of his name? . . . He's also decided to play guitar like Spencer and imitates his posture and strumming technique perfectly. Now that Django goes up the street to play with the neighborhood kids, Andre will sometimes stay with me alone and we'll have a nice time together.

The library across the street from us is an exceptional place. . . . They suggest I bring a blanket to let the baby crawl around on while I look for books . . . Refreshing.

"Preschool" At Home

More from Leslie Westrum (WI):

Madeline (3) has some workbooks now written for preschool kids—things about reading readiness, numbers, the alphabet. We work in our books most days. She calls it "going to school" and I must admit I have thought of encouraging that notion. I like the idea that she thinks of schooling as something we do, not somewhere we go. Oh, I got the workbooks at a school supply store, but for some reason the local discount stores are starting to carry them. K-Mart carries a line of Golden Book Workbooks that are as good as what the local preschools and kindergartens are using. School Zone has some that are good, but not as colorful, so small ones probably won't like them as well. I realize you don't really need these things to do a perfectly good job of teaching, but they're a lot of fun, and at our house we believe in fun!

I must confess our workbooks would not get stars or stickers in a regular school, because we don't always do what the instructions say. In matching, for instance, Madeline circled the paintbrush and the spoon as being things a teacher would use because her father taught her to paint and I have been teaching her to mix cookies. I think that's very logical, so I gave her an extra kiss. Hugs and kisses are rewards around here. You get it right, you get a hug or a kiss. Get it wrong and you get a hug and kiss for encouragement. Don't tell me real schools operate that way!

Madeline and Daddy are fixing dinner. He just sent her downstairs for a can of green beans. They're "generic," so there's no picture on the can, and he told her to bring the can with a word that starts with a G and one that starts with a B. She did it! I hadn't realized that knowing her alphabet would be useful so soon—I'm very impressed with my kid!.

Her Own Books, Newspaper

From the N.J. Family Schools Assoc. *newsletter, 6/83:*

> Naomi Mather writes from Paris, "We've seen a big improvement in Mara's writing and it's all because of the flea market. There's an old man who sells books there. One day we bought a big old Larousse dictionary from him for about $5. He mentioned that he had rebound it himself. So I told Mara I would bind her stories. She immediately started writing and we had her books bound very cheaply. When we get back to the U.S. in September I will look for another cheap book binder." Naomi also writes that the best help to Mara in learning to read French has been French Walt Disney comic books.
>
> Mara Mather writes a newspaper from Paris. She cuts large letters out of newspaper and pastes them on paper to make her headings. Then she handwrites the articles under the very newspaper-looking headings and Xeroxes the whole sheet. A very nice effect.

Personalized Pencils

From the First Homeschool Catalog *(available here, $10 + post):*

> Our kids enjoy using pencils with their own names imprinted on them, and we all like having pencils with "Brook Farm School" imprinted.... We've found a company that charges about the same amount for imprinted pencils in small quantities as one usually has to pay for plain pencils.
>
> Set of 3 pencils, same name imprinted, 45¢ plus 5¢ postage.
>
> Wooden ruler, metric and U.S., name imprinted, 43¢ plus 5¢.
>
> 36 pencils, all same imprint, $4.95 plus $1.40 postage.
>
> 144 pencils, all same imprint, $11.95 plus $1.70 postage.
>
> *Minimum Order* $5.00. Add $1.00 handling charge per order. Print personalizing instructions clearly; send payment with your order to: *Amsterdam Company,* Wallins Corners Road, Amsterdam NY 12010.

"MotherScribe"

Yet another piece by Susan Richman (PA) in her newsletter:

> *At last ... the perfect word processor for children.* So many folks seem especially interested in hearing about home-computer use with kids that I thought I'd let you all in on a good discovery I made just last week. I've found the perfect, *very* low cost word-processor/printer package for children, especially useful for kids with little or no reading ability. Available everywhere, the unit is named the *Mother-Scribe*. It has quite an excellent memory bank, and perhaps most significantly it is able to take oral dictation, as well as processing even misspelled typing or hand lettering. The package comes complete with the ability to orally ask pertinent questions in nonthreatening language (clarifying who "he" refers to, or asking, "Oh! And what happened then?") Children can easily have the program insert new words or whole paragraphs anywhere in their writing, and the system will read back (again orally, helping the just-beginning reader) the whole writing sequence at any time the child wants. When the child is satisfied, and all desired revisions are complete, the unit will print out a final copy in several possible modes. One mode is identical to typing, another simulates hand-lettering (printed or cursive options, large or small print).
>
> Because of its extremely low cost, *Mother-Scribe* does not work with the lightning speed of some more expensive systems, but it seems that the unit is so finely tuned to children and their needs, that the speed factor becomes

unimportant. *Mother-Scribe* is extremely portable, needs no electric power source or batteries, and seems to just carry itself. It can use any grade, size and color of paper, saving you the need to visit your computer store for refills. In fact, it saves you needing to visit your computer store at all. A pad of paper, a pencil or pen, or at most a conventional typewriter, add one mother (fathers and older siblings and friends can work equally well) and one child, and the unit is off and running. Happy word processing!

Duck Journal

Pam Parriot wrote in Living Education, *5/83 ($15/yr.; PO Box 1051, Ojai CA 93023):*

In the past year and a half, Mia (8) has kept an on-going journal of her observations of her pet ducks. Beginning with four baby ducklings, she has chronicled their eating, sleeping, and swimming habits, their growth, the innate differences between species (she had two mallards and two Muscovites) as well as the differences in behavior between the sexes. Then, of course, there was the exciting, long-awaited day when they took their first flight and also the gradual emergence of the mating instinct (and the surprise to find what we thought was the male Muscovy turned out to be a female, and vice versa), not to mention the amusing and often distressing courtship routines.

We both delighted in discovering the first secret nesting spots. But the most incredible moment of all was watching the little baby ducklings break out of their shells and into a new world. I was every bit as excited as Mia was. Being a "city-slicker" myself, this was a first for both of us.

I first suggested the idea of writing about her ducks and she thought that would be fun. In the beginning, she started out actually writing it out herself, but this very quickly became a drudgery, and she began to lose interest in her journal.

Then I suggested that she dictate what she wanted to say, and I would write it all down for her. Well, after that she just took off and did pages at a time, where before it was all she could do to get down a couple of sentences. This way, we could concentrate more on the creative writing aspect (arranging her thoughts and putting things in a logical order that others reading it could understand, and bringing out pertinent and interesting facts). I felt that the technical aspect of having her do her own handwriting could be taken care of later, because I realized from observing her that insisting on her perfecting the technique of handwriting would kill the interest and enthusiasm of the whole project.

I took a lot of photographs of the ducks growing up, which she pasted into her book and wrote captions for. Then she decided she wanted to take some of her own pictures, so I got a little Instamatic camera for her to experiment with. She also did quite a few drawings in the book, including "technical drawings" of a duck's knee, the grooved "teeth" on the edge of their bills, and even, with unabashed innocence, a detailed sketch of the male duck's "private parts" which I didn't even know existed. She also pasted in several different kinds of feathers (down, body contour feathers, and flight feathers), and even picked off a few scales from their feet and taped them in.

The most fun that comes from reading through her two completed volumes is the refreshingly spontaneous perceptions of the world and its creatures as only a child can describe them. For instance, in one book Mia is describing how Strawberry, the male duck, mates with the females. She says, "Sometimes when the other ducks aren't looking, Strawberry runs up and jumps on top of them, but when he does it in the water, he tries to keep their heads down under the water so people won't notice, because he wants to keep it a secret."

Microscopes, Music & More

More from Nancy Wallace (NY):

We have a teeny patch of woods (and I mean teeny) in back of the garden and Bob and Vita (8) built a wonderful playhouse.... Ishmael (11) likes to read on the roof and Vita spends a great deal of time inside, making tempting treats for her tea parties.... The playhouse attracts lots of neighborhood children which is nice for Vita, mostly, but sometimes she feels her lack of privacy and would like to send them away but she doesn't know how. Fortunately, between school and summer camp, Vita doesn't get overdoses of children very often.

This spring we have become enthusiastic naturalists. Ithaca is famous for its wildflowers and we have been taking wildflower walks whenever we can. Vita has become an expert at identifying flowers and Ishmael sort of ambles along after her, storing up the more interesting names to use as characters for his plays.

Right around the house we have starlings, sparrows and cardinals nesting. Somehow it's wonderful to be able to sit around and watch two starling parents devotedly slaving to feed their babies. The cardinals, though, have been the most fun to watch. A few weeks ago it was nest building time. She surprised me by doing all the work and he spent his time just following her around.

Ishmael has been taking early morning walks, mostly, I think, because he loves the feeling of being alone, and yesterday he saw a deer, right on our street! Spring, we've discovered, is really the best time to do science. Just as I was beginning to feel guilty about not doing enough, the natural world showed me how silly I was being! One fun thing we've been doing is looking at marshy water under the microscope. Actually, we look at bits of algae or other water plants and we've been discovering all kinds of teensy creatures hovering in their midst—amoebas and paramecium and weird-looking insect larvae. The microscope we use is the one I had when I was a child and the magnification goes up to 300X. It's good for our purposes, but if I was going to buy one I might try to get one with greater magnification.... Vita can spend hours with the microscope and she loves to identify what we see with the help of a book we got from the library. Ishmael is a bit more absent-minded about the whole thing, although he does smile when he watches amoebas zipping around.

Music preoccupies him more and more and I am amazed at his creativity and his ability to concentrate for hours and hours at the piano, or while composing.... The problem now is that I think he works too hard, and yet he seems to enjoy himself, so I don't say anything. He's playing *big* pieces—Bach, Beethoven, Mendelssohn, Chopin.... Composing, though, is still his big passion.

Vita, meanwhile, is working hard at her music too. Sometimes, especially on the violin, she gets discouraged, since she is working on quite difficult music and the teacher has really been expecting Vita to play more perfectly than she really can.... But she loves what she's playing and she loves the violin, so it is up to me to moderate the teacher's expectations.... I think the problem is that the teacher is so impressed with Vita that she gets impatient for Vita to be even more impressive. On the other hand, this also means that she is encouraging Vita to use vibrato and she is getting her to experiment around in high positions, two things that Vita thinks are great fun. Vita still thinks of the piano as an instrument to relax on, which is good.

Vita has quit her ballet and art classes which has been nice for me since it's made my life less hectic, but I've wondered at her decision, since she loves dancing and art. I think her biggest problem was that the other kids in her classes weren't nearly as serious as she was (how could they be, after having spent the whole day in school?) and they goofed off so much that she was bothered and really irritated, since her teachers spent all their time trying to get the kids to pay attention. I am hoping to find an artist who will let Vita work in his/her studio, but I'm not sure what to do about dance.

One really nice thing that has happened this spring is that Ishmael has gotten really competent in math and Vita is learning how to spell. All I can attribute it to is some kind of physical maturity. Their brains must have just decided to grow some extra wrinkles, or something. Actually, in Ishmael's case, I think neglect helped a great deal. He didn't do any math while he was writing his play and since he really "wrote himself out" in the process, numbers became more interesting to him than words—and he was relaxed enough to discover that they could be fun. Vita, on the other hand, just got sick of being the worst speller in the family and decided to do something about it.

Vita has been spending hours at my desk reading the proofs of my book [*Better Than School*, Larson Publications, Sept. 1983] and she is very enthusiastic, which surprised me a little since I did touch on a lot of sensitive or at least personal subjects without consulting her. Anyway, she was inspired enough by the book to write (in secret) a whole account of the production of Ishmael's play, "I Love You More Than a Grapefruit Squirts." When she finally showed it to me I just loved it and as I was enthusing, she mentioned something about typing. I thought she meant that she wanted it typed, which seemed like a good idea and so, since I was busy (and since Bob was only working on a grant proposal that will affect our well-being for the next two years), I asked Bob if he would type it for me. When Vita heard me ask him, she threw a fit. . . . When we finally calmed her down, it turned out that what she had meant was that *she* wanted to type it, not one of us. So for the past two days she has been typing in her spare time.

She wrote a wonderful letter to Astrid Lindgren [author of *Pippi Longstocking*] asking her whether one of her books, *The Children Of Noisy Village*, was true. Ms. Lindgren sent her back a form letter, but it was really nicely done, so Vita was thrilled.

My father, who is a professor, told us that his best student, currently, dropped out of high school at the end of his junior year because he hated math and science. He spent his senior year reading (including 300 books on Israel) and apparently he did well enough on his S.A.T. and some other achievement tests that Stanford gladly let him in. Anyway, my father, who finally realized that you don't *have* to graduate from high school to get into college, suggested that we talk to the admissions people at Cornell in the next year or two to see what we would have to do to get Ishmael in at the earliest age possible. The idea seems attractive, in a way. I *know* that by the time he's 18, Ishmael will know so much about so many things that going to Cornell, and dealing with all the classes aimed at freshmen, would be ridiculous. . . . So the question is, should we try to get him ready to enter Cornell at, say, 14, or shouldn't we? If music wasn't an issue, I might be tempted. But as things stand, I don't think Ishmael would have the *time* to go to Cornell. Although he is tempted by the idea of studying history, literature, and languages, I don't think he could even imagine doing that at the expense of his music. . . . I get so mixed up when I think about his future. (He, of course, doesn't yet think much about it, he just composes, plays the piano, works on ear training, theory, etc., all day long, and at night he reads and writes—he's working on a play about gypsies). Anyway, I think we need to get an idea of what the best music conservatories expect of their incoming students.

Learning About Rocks Together

Susan Richman (PA) wrote us:

Jesse has launched into a great interest in rocks. We visited a wonderful cozy rock shop the other day, a home business run by a very old man; and Jesse has been busy now labeling his collection, testing rocks for hardness, listening to me read several rock-collecting children's books, doing much wondering and conjecturing. As usual, a whole new field is opening up to *me* too, and once again I'm finding that good informational books written for children are actually the proper place for *me* to begin investigations.

Earning Money For Computer

From a Florida parent:

When my son was nine, he got a TRS-80 home computer. For him to learn to use it, I had to read the manual and then teach him. Eventually, he gained the maturity to read the manual himself in the order he chose, and taught himself. Now with his new computer, a TI-99A, and being three years older, he has learned everything himself. When he needs help, he uses the phone and calls some adult members of his computer club.

My son is very busy with his computer lately. He just purchased "Extended Basic" from a friend who didn't use it, with money he makes working with his dad. This has increased his capabilities and he is very busy inventing a new game. He would work on it 24 hours a day if we let him. I still feel he should make his bed, eat breakfast, and do other small details of daily life. He does take a break occasionally to make more money so he can buy a "Speech Synthesizer."

About the job with his dad—they are starting a cement business, making birdbaths, flower pots, frogs, and other lawn ornaments. My son works as an apprentice, measuring the concrete and sand, running the cement mixer, oiling molds, setting things up, etc. He also has certain things he can make himself, which his father buys from him so we don't have to worry about the bookkeeping of having an employee. He enjoys it, he might be learning something, and he is earning money to support his computer habit. I'm sure that learning so much about computers now will give him an edge on getting a job in the future. If he could make money with the computer now, at home, he would be thrilled.

On Math

Bettelou Roberts wrote in the Western Pa. Homeschoolers Newsletter:

My husband gave Erin (5) his old calculator when he bought a new one. I showed her how she could push two different numbers and come up with a new and different number (addition). That was fun for a while, then I asked if I could play too, in a little different way. With the penny jar beside me, I had her push any number on the calculator while I laid out the same number of pennies. After pushing another number and laying out the same number of coins, she then pushed the equal button to see the new number. We then counted the pennies on the table and the look of wonder on her face stays with me yet. We then took turns counting pennies and pushing buttons, then she wanted to see if she could do both and checked herself. It was a wonderful new game for a while, and we both had fun discovering numbers again. I wasn't trying to teach her to add, my intention from the beginning was to show her that numbers can be fun. I don't want her to be frightened of them as I was. To me they were mysterious symbols that changed constantly and couldn't be depended upon to stay the same.

More from Susan Jaffer (pg. 1):

Joey (4) has a favorite question that goes like this: "How old will I be when Suzanne is 14?" Or, "How old will Daddy be when I'm 33?" With four people in the family besides Joey, this question has an almost infinite number of variations, and I suspect Joey has asked them all. I could see he wasn't learning much from my answers. (And besides, was getting *so* bored with the questions!) So I made a chart he could use to figure out the answers himself. Using a long piece of paper from a roll of leftover newsprint, drew a line 25" long and marked it off into 100 quarter-inch sections. Each section represented one year and were numbered from 1 to 100. Then I cut strips of paper to represent each member of the family. Since I am 35 years older than Joey, mine was 8¾" long (or 35 quarter-inches). I made his father's the same way, but since the girls are only 5 and 3 years older than Joey, for them I used a strip about 6" long and marked off the quarter-inch years with two arrows. To use the chart, Joey lines up the arrow on the left with his imagined age (say, 12) and reads off the age Suzanne will be (17) above the arrow on the right. Did I write all that clearly? It was easier to make and use than to write about.

From Jill Bastian (MI: see "The First Few Months," GWS 28):

Jan. 23: . . . Addition and subtraction math facts keep being shelved. But trying to find areas of rooms in the house and the size of my garden led to learning 2-digit by 2-digit multiplication during one long breakfast hour. We've also been working on borrowing to do subtraction when we make change in playing store.... Heather has learned that 0 plus or minus a number equals that number, that 1 plus or minus a number equals one more or less than that number, that 0 times any number equals 0, and that 1 times any number is that number. I have read no teacher's manuals on how to teach math. But for the multiplication problems, like 5 × 7, we talk about 5 7s or 7 5s, and she's counting by 1s, 2s, 's, 4s (almost mastered), 5s, and 10s. We learned that trick about 9's [GWS 18], too, from a friend's mom. I love math myself, and sometimes wonder if I should insist on her memorizing the facts. But then Heather starts figuring out complicated things in her head, and I get so excited, I forget all about the rote work.

June 3:.... It's amazing, but the homeschooling just keeps working. I can't even remember what it was like with Heather in public school. It seems so natural for her to be around here, learning as she goes along through each day. And she is learning! Every once in a while, I get on one of my "academic" kicks and require her to do certain paper and pencil activities. But, for example, when I orally quizzed her the other day on her addition and subtraction facts, including the teens, it was amazing how many of them she knew immediately, without having to stop and count. She's been learning them without workbook pages and hours of drill.

I know she can do many problems in her head—she does it all the time in everyday activities, like figuring change for items she's buying at a garage sale. She takes her spending money with her when we go. If she has enough money to buy something, she can buy it; if not, too bad. I'm trying to get her to see that the money only goes so far.... She has also learned the barter technique that adults often use at these sales.... She's getting more and more independent in these encounters; once she's comfortable in a situation and knows where I am, she's able to go off and do her looking and interacting all by herself.

Heather is fascinated with money and checks. Our local bank has told me that they do not allow checking accounts for persons under 18, I believe. So, I told Heather that when she learns how to do all of the procedures appropriate for having a checking account—writing in cursive, adding and subtracting amounts of money, filling out the deposit slips, writing numerals in words—I will go back to the bank and try to get them to make an exception in her case. For now, we have a "bank" set up at home. When she receives her weekly allowance (70 cents, because she's 7) she brings 45¢ to me (the banker) with a deposit slip (our old unused ones) all filled out. I stamp it with a date stamp that she bought with some previous allowance money; then I initial it and return it to her to use as a receipt. I put the money in a container. When she spends money, like at garage sales, we write checks afterward for the money she needed to take out for each transaction. The checks are made up (I plan to make a ditto and have copies run—we may even draw pictures on them to look like our real checks). I have showed Heather how to fill in the date, the person to whom the check is written or CASH, the amount of money in numerals and words, and explained about writing a neat legible signature in the same way each time. After she deposits her money or writes her checks, we complete the check register: she enters the deposits or withdrawals in the appropriate columns and calculates her balance on each transaction.... Our math lessons have never lasted so long or been so positively completed.

Now if she can just find a way to earn some more money.... I think she has plans for having a table at our garage sale next week and possibly selling garden produce or lemonade this summer.

Another neat activity that included using math was done with my dad. He visited recently, bringing some of his books and games that he had had when he was a boy or when I was a child. One such item that was a real hit was a pinball game. The object is to pull a spring-tensioned plunger and propel ten steel balls, one at a time, through a maze of slots and pins. If the balls land in the slots, you get the score listed. If they only hit the pins and fall to the bottom, you get nothing. To make the game more interesting, we made a gray ball worth double where it lands and the gold ball worth 3X. There's also a slot labeled *Double Score*. So as you play, you keep adding your scores onto your total, in your head. Heather quickly was getting scores of 1600, 2500, and even 4000. What a great way to learn larger numbers and how to say them (10 hundred is the same as one thousand, etc.).

German On Their Own

From Suzanne Alejandre (Ger.):

I enjoyed reading "Music in the Family" by Marion Pears in *GWS* 32. It's nice to read of other parents who pursue their own talents rather than trying to stimulate environments just for the benefit of their children. My mind is on this subject because I recently received a questionnaire from Jane Filstrup. She is writing a book tentatively titled "Bringing Up Baby Bilingual." Her twins are French/English bilingual—you printed her story in *GWS* 30. Anyway, her questionnaire implied that a parent would create an environment for the child to learn the other language. For example, one question asked, how strong was the motivation for the child to learn the other language? How hard or easy was it to provide a social context?

I answered her by trying to explain our approach to Niko and Lee's learning of German—we left them alone. Instead we have concentrated on learning German ourselves. Here is part of what I answered to Jane:

Learning a language is a very private experience. In fact, many learning experiences should be private. One of my major disagreements with a formal schooling experience is that these private learning experiences are tampered with. . . . I don't know if this is a direct quote from John Holt but it is an idea I decided on from reading *GWS*—the decisions should be left up to the individual when a skill or experience affects him or her only. For example, I would include such things as walking, speaking, reading, typing. . . . On the other hand, situations which affect more than the individual should have all who are affected involved. In our house that includes such things as noise level and fights!

Too many times, parents try to control what should be the child's (or in some cases, the adult's) experience. They want to know what the child knows in order to evaluate the child and make certain he/she knows "enough." . . . In my mind, it is often none of the parents' business. When a child or an adult is in control of his/her own learning, then it will meet his/her needs and that should be enough.

We still don't know how much German Niko or Lee know. They don't speak German with us. Our home language is American English. We only hear Niko and Lee speak German when we overhear them at the park or when they have their German-speaking friends over or when we are involved in conversations with them with Germans. We never quiz them or try to evaluate their performance. There are exceptions, though. We do compliment them, sometimes, as we would complement anyone who we admire. Also, we ask them for help sometimes! [See Suzanne's letter, "Kids Watch Parents Learn" in *GWS* 33.] . . . When the boys help us they are always discreet. They never shout out as I've heard many parents do who are trying to help their children.

For me, learning a language is a byproduct of developing a relationship with another person. That is why learning a language cannot (or rather, should not) be forced. A parent can set up all the social situations and motivations in the world, but unless the child wants to relate, then whether the language is English or Chinese, they won't speak it.

I realize that you are writing your book in part for readers who want to teach their children a second language yet live in the U.S. In my opinion, this should be approached from the idea that the parents want to learn or refresh or practice the second language. Thus the opportunity would be there and it would be up to the child whether he/she responded to it or not. Humans being as curious as they are, it would be rare to find a child who did not wish to try the other language.

[Suzanne continued in her letter to us:] . . .

Recently, we have been having rainy days, and Niko and Lee's friends have been coming to play here rather than meeting in the park. Kai (5) has been coming often. The three boys were playing in the same room where I was sewing and I overheard most of their conversation. One thing that struck me was that Niko, not once, spoke German to Lee! When he was talking just to Kai, he spoke German and when he was talking just to Lee, he spoke English. But what was most interesting was, when he was talking to both Kai and Lee, he used German and immediately translated into English! I learned a lot listening to him! Interesting, too, was his use of slang and his phrasing in both languages—he was not making direct translations, but rather, he said what was appropriate for each language.

After that experience, I realized why Lee probably doesn't ask Niko his translation questions (he always comes and asks Rich or me)—it's because Niko won't speak German with him. In my opinion, Niko can't speak German with Lee, it just doesn't come out. . . . Concerning this, the only other observation I have made has been with respect to married couples whose native languages are different. Of the couples I know, they all speak the language which they used when they initially met. This is despite the fact that they have moved to a country where another language is spoken and they both speak it.

Traveling Together

More from Jill Bastian (MI):

In April, Heather and I flew to Florida to help my father drive back to Michigan. Before we left on our trip, I wrote to about ten families listed in the *GWS* Directory who had children about Heather's age, and who lived near I-75 or I-69 where we would be traveling. I got five responses; we were able to visit four of the families.

Outside of Atlanta, we visited Connie Shaw and her children. The kids were shy for about 5 minutes; then they disappeared together. The main attraction was a treehouse in the back yard. There were books lining many walls of their home. We could only stay a short time; their oldest daughter really wanted Heather to stay longer. . . . We made our way to Berea, KY, in the rain and stayed at the Boone Tavern Hotel. We were waited on by the college students, had a great meal, and got to meet the Mehlers. They even came to their shop—he makes fine furniture—to show us the workroom and gallery at 9 o'clock at night. . . . We visited Bob Post and his daughter Safron in Pendleton, IN; in the afternoon, we were able to make connections with the Vanderburgs in Muncie—two more great experiences for Heather. Safron (8) is very able to take care of herself, and I trusted her to take Heather to the park, several blocks away and through town. We met them there after a detour to the library to see some shelves Bob had built. We had such a good time, and talked about many, many things. With the Vanderburgs, we shared how we had each decided to homeschool and what we were doing. Their children seem to be blooming because of the change, like Heather.

Heather was a delight to travel with. I had been apprehensive about this: I didn't want to have to play entertainment director for 1400 miles and 8 days. We took her back-pack full of activities, including many books. We started reading *The Secret Garden* (bought from you—I had never read it), a chapter at a time, several times a day. Even my dad got interested in the story; many times I read it aloud in the car as we were driving. We talked a lot; Heather had great fun eating out all the time; and we all managed to get along well together.

Music Class For Kids

From Carol Hughes in Miami:

Many people take it for granted that children of musical parents will also be good musicians. My husband and I are both professional musicians and our children are indeed showing signs of becoming adept on some kind of musical instruments. I started thinking why this is so. . . . While I was shopping with a friend for Christmas presents, for instance, she commented to me, "Do you realize that every toy you have bought makes a sound?"

When either of us gets up from playing the piano, both boys go over and start playing. We have offered our five-year-old, Evan, the chance for lessons from us but his reply is, "I already know how to play the piano." In fact, he has, on his own, found chords and played quite musical things. The boys have the opportunity to "jam" with us or dance around and around, whichever they are in the mood for. Evan will sit at the piano for forty-five minutes and play a third over and over and sing along with it. As a singer, I have a natural tendency to try and imitate almost any sound I hear. I encourage this in all children I meet.

As a result of these random observations, I started a "music class." It is for prenatal through five-year-olds. It begins with everyone playing along with whatever I am in the mood to play. So sometimes we have drums and harmonicas and ukuleles and sticks playing with a Bach invention or sometimes a blues tune by Eubie Blake. We trade instruments and take turns being the "soloist"—which means everyone has to play softly enough to hear one person the loudest. Each has a turn at being conductor and is the one who ends the piece.

We "write" music. That is, we make five lines on the blackboard with a free hand, and then I make a G clef, or F clef. Then everyone makes notes on the music and I try to play it on the piano. Sometimes they feel like drawing music monsters which makes for terrific giggles. One child who is four drew his first note and then promptly made a chord. There are things like this occurring constantly.

After playing and sometimes during listening (the children prefer playing to listening), I give them paper and crayons. The results are very interesting. One child drew long waving lines to represent sound waves.

The *most* important thing that is happening in this group is the feeling the children express of being persons who are making music. Most children's songs bore them and get little response. After Bach, Ella Fitzgerald, the *Grand Canyon Suite*, who wants to hear "Old McDonald"?

To the uninitiated, the sounds coming from the class are chaotic. To me, they are a never-ending source of joy.

Starting The Violin

A month or two ago I started to play the violin, not instead of the cello, which is still my #1 instrument, but in addition to it. I play no more than perhaps a half hour a day when I am in Boston, and not at all when on the road, when I take only my traveling cello with me.

For years I have thought vaguely that someday (when I had more time) I would take up the violin. Since I began listening to classical music, I have always liked the sound of the violin—the Beethoven Violin Concerto was my first favorite *classical* piece (My first favorite *symphonic* piece was Stravinsky's *Rite of Spring*). More recently, in the many years I have seen and heard the marvelous violins of the Boston Symphony Orchestra, I have been as much captivated by how their playing *looked* as by how it sounded. Music is a kind of athletics, and what these musicians were doing with their hands and arms looked so fluid, graceful, and sensuous that more and more I thought I would one day like to try it. Also, the further I advanced on the cello, the more I wondered what it would be like to play a stringed instrument in that very different position. In other words, playing the violin attracted me more and more, among other reasons, just as a problem in learning.

Another thought gave me an additional push. For some time I have felt that someday I would like to teach the cello, particularly to adult beginners, since unlike almost all teachers I understand many of the physical and psychological problems of beginning as an adult. More recently an even wilder thought crept into my mind, that if I could learn enough about the violin and viola at least to teach adult beginners, I could then organize my pupils into string quartets or perhaps even a string orchestra. This prompted all kinds of dreams of glory, all the more so when I found that some people are already doing this.

What gave me the final little push from fantasy into reality was seeing, in a catalog of a musical instrument company called Rhythm Band (from whom we get our recorder and the Pianica—see *GWS* 33), an ad for what they call a Practice Violin, which they sell to schools that want to introduce children to the violin but do not want or cannot afford to buy them real ones. The Practice Violin is a very cheap, very durable, very simplified, very unbeautiful imitation of a violin. Thinking that some parents might want to buy one for their children (or themselves), and that we might want to add it to our book and music list, and being in any case interested in all cheap musical instruments, I ordered one for the office. Soon it arrived, and though it looks odd, it works. The sound it makes is nowhere near as big or as beautiful as the sound of a real violin, but it is a musical and controllable sound. It is an instrument on which, without risking much money, one can at least learn a little about what violin playing is like.

Once it was in the office I could not keep my hands off it, and for a few minutes every day began to try to hold it under my chin like a real violinist. It was very awkward at first—more awkward than a real instrument would be, in fact, since this pseudo-violin is heavier and less well balanced than a real one. But I found that in a surprisingly short time I could indeed hold it for several minutes at a time with my chin and jaw. Soon I began to want to learn what a *real* violin and bow would feel and sound like. So I ordered from the SHAR catalogue (more on this later) the cheapest of their full-sized Suzuki violin outfits—violin, bow, and case.

When it arrived, I found to my dismay that because of the strange shape of its chin rest, it was much harder to hold than the Practice Violin. So one day I went to Boston Stringed Instruments (where my friend Vita Wallace, now a *real* violinist, got her first instrument), tried out a number of chin rests, and picked one that seemed fairly comfortable. Since then I have been playing a little every day I am in Boston. I have started to learn to play the songs in the *Suzuki Violin Book #1* (see our list), and so far have made it through about the first twelve of the songs, not elegantly, but reasonably accurately.

I am very surprised and pleased by the progress I have made in the ten to fifteen hours I have played. In that time I have made far more progress than I did in the same amount of time when I started the cello, though to some extent knowing how to play one stringed instrument makes it easier to learn to play another. I don't mean to imply that I sound good on the violin, for I don't; I sound like the beginner I am. But, at least until my still unaccustomed muscles get tired, I feel comfortable with the instrument; I can hold it securely with only my chin and jaw for quite a few minutes at a time; the basic position of my left arm and hand is essentially correct; my bow arm, though it wanders up and down the string and is still insecure when going from one string to another, is basically relaxed and smooth; after only a little practice my intonation becomes quite good; and though I don't make what anyone could call beautiful sounds (which would in any case be very difficult on such a cheap violin), I don't make the horrible scrapes and wails that so many beginners take years to escape. I am even making the beginnings of a very slow vibrato.

Even in this short time I have satisfied myself of two things: the violin, even for someone of my age, is not the impenetrable mystery that it is so often made out to be, and, as with my cello, if I could play it for the several hours a day I would like, I could in not too many years become, not a virtuoso, but a reasonably skillful player. I don't expect this to happen soon, because the cello is still my true love and will get most of what little playing time I can find. But even with limited playing time I intend and expect to get better on the violin and to have a lot of fun with it. Stand by for further reports.—JH

Saxophone Lesson With John Payne

Pat Farenga, our Managing Editor, has just started to play the saxophone, and he writes about his first lesson:

"Take this reed and shove it in your mouth."

I looked skeptically at the tall bearded man looking down at me—no mean feat since I'm six foot one. He urged me on, "Put it in your mouth and get it wet."

After I soaked the wood strip in my mouth I asked if I had to flip it over to get the other side wet. "Just putting it in your mouth will get it all wet. Here, look." He put his reed completely in his mouth and moved it around as if he was eating it. "Pretty soon you'll love the taste of wood," he mumbled, "You'll want it for spice in your food!"

He pulled the reed from his mouth and told me to come closer. Standing next to my husky mentor, I watched him carefully line-up the round end of the wet reed flush with the end of the mouthpiece. He then strapped the reed in place with a metal band and gave it to me to look at. Then he disassembled it and, smiling, handed it to me. "You try." he said.

John Payne's Music Center was first mentioned in *GWS* 28 and his patient, common-sense approach to teaching music generated my interest. However my wallet didn't generate enough money so I had to hold back on my desires to sing on the saxophone like Charlie Parker and content myself, as I have for fourteen years, playing jazz piano. But the piano was frustrating me. I had reached a threshold where I knew I needed a teacher to increase my technique, but I didn't want to spend money on lessons I only half wanted. Don't get me wrong—I still play and love the piano, but it no longer filled my musical needs. I thought about my situation and realized what an influence horn-players and especially the saxophone had on my piano-playing. My favorite pianists are Bud Powell, Horace Silver and Thelonious Monk, who play a lot of their solos like horn-players—one note snakelike be-bop blues solos. Though I began the piano with classical lessons, I soon became a hard-core jazz lover, and the sax always struck me as a jazz instrument. The saxophone, I decided, was where it was at for me. I spoke to John Holt about my feelings several times during the year, and he convinced me that money was really more of a procrastination than a major obstacle. Faced with this, and John's offer to rent me a sax if I paid for the lessons, I finally decided to take the risk.

John Payne instructed me to put the completed mouthpiece in my mouth and blow through it. Not a sound came out.

"Relax your mouth. Let the reed flutter against your lower lip and squawk like a duck. Like this." John sounded like a demented Donald Duck as he walked around his small studio creating some of the raunchiest noises heard in Boston. I tried to copy him, and emitted a weak-winded effluvial noise. "Yeah!" cried John. "Now do it with more breath, pushing your stomach in to push the air out of your lungs." He squawked on his mouthpiece again. I was a bit bewildered by his enthusiasm; after all, I had never blown into a mouthpiece before and I certainly wasn't making music yet. Warily, I blew into the mouthpiece again, tightening my mouth to seal the end of the mouthpiece off, and directing my breath into the piece. Squawk! "Do it again," said John, "And the next time you take a breath do it with your diaphragm; push your stomach out when you inhale, push in when you exhale." Following his advice I squawked again . . . and again . . . and again! "You're smokin', man!"

John picked up the neck of one of the saxophones in his studio and handed it to me. (When I first inquired about lessons, Pam, the Music Center's administrator, told me I wouldn't need a sax for my first lesson.) John pulled the neck off of his saxophone and placed his mouthpiece on the cork end; I did the same. Then we placed the completed neck into the body of the sax. John told me to be careful of making sure the slender tube that runs from one of the keys on the body to a bar on the neck is evenly placed under the bar. If it's moved too far to the left or to the right, the connection will be lost and the key won't work.

He made me put down the assembled sax and placed a fabric necklace with a hook at the end of it around my neck. Then he picked up my sax and placed it on my chest; I held it while he threaded the hook through an eyelet on the sax. When he let go, my neck felt a twinge of discomfort—the tenor saxophone weighed a lot more than I thought. John moved away from me and told me to adjust the neck-brace to make the mouthpiece reach my mouth comfortably. After I adjusted it, he placed my thumbs on their holds and told me to blow into the sax.

"What keys do I use?" I asked. "None. Just blow into it without hitting any of the keys."

I blew into it and produced nothing. I blew again and got a slight squawk. I blew again and nothing. Then when I blew once more I sounded a mid-range note and, yes, it sounded like a saxophone! All right! Then the sound trailed off into an inarticulate, sickly growl. John smiled at me and assured me, "You're smokin'!"

At first I wondered about the sincerity of such explosions of support, but I later realized that John's spontaneous reassurances that I was doing something right, no matter how small, would really give me heart later on. Working every day and pursuing familiar pastimes gave me a certain amount of confidence in my daily life that I was reluctant to abandon, and as I progressed down the unknown corridors of saxophony it was good to know, right from the beginning, that I had an open, friendly, and enthusiastic guide. John Payne's insistent confidence in me and his conviction that *anyone* can learn to play the saxophone at any age, without 10 hours of practice a day or "special talent," formed an early brace to combat my own doubts and reservations about my abilities. I thought it would take months just to get a sound out of the horn!

John walked behind me and put my fingers on their appropriate keys. "Have you ever taken typing? This is like home-position on a typewriter; no matter what you play, you will always return to this position. Get the feel of it. Hold your sax while you watch TV or listen to the radio, learn to make this an automatic grip. Now, let's hear you play a 'B.' What you have to do is push your left index finger down on the key and blow, from your diaphragm."

I took a deep breath, pushing my stomach out with my air intake pushed down the "B" key, and blew with all my force. There was a noticeable lack of sound for all my effort. I looked at John sheepishly and he told me to try again, this time putting a little more reed into my mouth. After a few more efforts I still had no sound.

"This can happen when someone tries to start on the tenor. Most folks start on the alto since it takes less breath, and then move on to the tenor. Let's put you on the alto and see if you get a sound."

I sadly removed the tenor sax from my neck—no Sonny Rollins? No Dexter Gordon? I'll have to settle for the alto sound, I thought, but I *really* want to play the tenor—it's is so much more expressive to my ears. I strapped the alto on and after two attempts I was sounding a "B"; an uncertain tone, but undeniably a "B" of some sort. John was sensitive to my enthusiasm for the tenor and he immediately suggested that since I got the "B" out of the alto, I should go back to the tenor and try to get the "B" on it using the exact same breath and lip contour. "Your lips should form a seal around the mouthpiece so all the air fills the chamber and none escapes around it."

I strapped the tenor on, placed my mouth around the reed, collected my breath and blew. No sound. "Put even more reed in your mouth," John said. "Give it a shot." I nearly swallowed the mouthpiece. I put at least 2/3 of it in my mouth, wrapped my lips around it and blew . . . and I produced a "B"! I felt like I just conquered Mt. Everest.

"That's it! Great! Now keep on making that 'B' while I get ready." I squeaked and squawked considerably, but every now and then a "B" emerged from the chaos. John pulled out a sheet with a carbon copy backing and wrote my name and the date at the top. He then made a note that I should place plenty of mouthpiece in my mouth. Then he opened an old beginner's sax book, *Tune-A-Day Book One*, and asked me if I could read music. I said yes, and we immediately skipped the first three pages of the book and went on to lesson one. "Producing a consistent sound and tone is the main goal of these early lessons, so don't worry if your fingers can't respond quickly enough or you can't follow the music. We'll work on that later. Most people don't even get a real note out of the thing for a few days, so you're already ahead of the game, especially since you already can read music."

John picked up his tenor and together we played Lesson One: four exercises with just the note "B." We played in four bar exercises, first combinations of half notes and half rests, then all half notes; then quarter notes and quarter rests. John pointed to the very first song in the book, eight bars of a theme from Beethoven's Seventh Symphony. I was a bit put off by the choice of tune; Beethoven's name never springs to my mind when I think of the sax, but before I could voice my grievance, John was telling me about the music. The upper stave was my part, the lower the teacher's. Mine was a cinch—good old "B" all the way through, in quarter and half notes. I felt some confidence and security return as I looked the music over in just those brief seconds—I can at least play this, no matter what it is, and I'll be making music on the sax! ... Eight bars later my obbligato squeaked to a halt just behind John's melody. I felt a childish flush of excitement. I say childish only because the feeling was so exhilarating, so new, that I was reminded of the thrills music gave me when I first discovered I could make it as a youngster, or of the excitement of getting an intriguing toy at Christmas. It's a feeling of discovery that only intermittently comes to me now as a "grown up." I had accomplished something I never thought I would find the time to do.

"I'm going to show you two more notes and then you'll be set for practice this week. When you hold down the keys under your index and middle fingers, at the same time, you get an 'A.'" He gave me time to sound an "A" before he spoke again, "And when you hold all three down, index, middle and fourth, you get a 'G.'" He demonstrated my new three notes for me on his sax, then let me do it several times. He drew a finger chart on my sheet to remind me of the left fingers' placement (my right hand did nothing so far except hold the sax). John asked me where I lived, then told me where the nearest and best place to rent a sax would be. "Go to Rayburn's and ask for Emilio. Tell him John Payne sent you and he'll take care of you. He'll show you how to put the reed on the mouthpiece, how to put the sax together, and whatever you need to know that you may forget from today. You should also buy the *Tune-A-Day* book while you're there; there's a fingering chart for all the notes on the saxophone in it and I want you to try and get up to lesson 4 for next week. But you can go further if you want. Tell Emilio you want a beginner's fairly closed, *not* metal, mouthpiece. Also a couple 1½ reeds." He wrote all this down for me as he spoke.

"Any special brand of reed?" "Try them all and see what works best for you. Do you know about the Music Center's Student Saxophone Choir?"

"I've heard about them."

"We play at the Oxford Ale House every Monday night. You should come down and hear us some night, we start at 9:30 and go to 10:30. If you like it we'll get you in the choir in nine months, maybe sooner. Who knows?"

"That sounds like fun." I couldn't believe it—not only would I learn the sax, but I'd be given the chance to play in a big band! Visions of Basie danced in my head.

"Here's my home phone number. Don't hesitate to call me if you get hung up on anything. If you can't read my fingering chart, if you forget how to hold it, anything; just give me a ring and I'm sure we can straighten it out over the phone." John smiled and we shook hands.

Outside the Music Center I felt a curious glow of adventure fill me as I waited for the subway. I'd never so much as blown into a saxophone and I learned how to put one together, hold it, and hit three notes. Not bad, I thought, not for someone who could never seem to make the time to learn a completely new set of skills like playing a wind instrument. But action erases doubt: I had gone from nothing to "B" to Beethoven in a half hour—what a blast!

Letter From Oklahoma

From Esther Rosen, 4635 NW, Lawton OK 73505:

I found out about *GWS* early in 1981 when we were living in Michigan. Our oldest son was in kindergarten and we were getting ready to pull him out. He'd quit drawing, singing, smiling, laughing, had skin rashes, stomach aches, and was generally a most unhappy little fellow. Some days it would be an hour or two before he would (could?) talk when he came home. We'd usually end up cuddling in a chair.

A friend loaned me all her copies of *GWS*. We found Clonlara mentioned so I got in touch with Pat Montgomery. We enrolled Joshua in their HBEP for his first grade year. That first day felt *so good* when the bus passed our drive (we were 18 miles from school). Then at 3:30 came the call—where was Joshua—had he moved? From there it went straight downhill—unannounced visits from the truant officer, once with the local superintendent and once to deliver a paper we had specifically asked to have mailed (he gave us a choice himself). The superintendent just didn't approve of what we were doing (he was losing too much money) and ended up going to the DA and saying we wouldn't send our son to school. Period. He forgot to mention Clonlara, the curriculum we turned in, the two certified teachers registered with the district as working with us, etc. So we were arrested.

What a horrible, scary time! Our 6-year-old was afraid to go to bed and was not sleeping well. I finally got him to talk and tell me why—he was afraid "they" were going to kidnap him and make him go to school. It's strange how something can be so frightening—I felt like I needed to stay inside with the drapes drawn just in case we had more unexpected visitors.

The whole thing was thrown out of court but cost us more than we could handle at a time when we were really struggling financially, having had several lay-offs.... Finally we ended up here in Oklahoma and things were fine. There are other homeschoolers and so far the schools aren't bothering us.

Massachusetts Success

From Gail and Jim McClymonds:

Thank you very much for your suggestions that helped us to write a letter to the Waltham [Mass.] School Committee requesting permission to teach our 6-year-old daughter, Charlene, at home next year. Writing that letter was a valuable experience for us because it congealed our thoughts on child rearing and it made us document how our home life was conducive to learning. Extra copies of the letter were also given to friends and relatives to explain what we were doing.

The reactions of the school officials to our request have been very favorable. We were prepared to face opposition, but we have had none. The Deputy School Superintendent who handled our request was especially supportive. He asked us for the names of some school districts in Massachusetts that have home schools to get some idea of how to proceed. (Thank you, *GWS*!) He then scheduled our request for the next school committee meeting.

Jim attended the school committee meeting and he explained our reasons for wanting to teach Charlene ourselves. Their greatest concern was how our progress could be monitored and documented. The Deputy School Superintendent recommended that our request should be approved and that a first-grade teacher and the principal of our elementary school would work with us closely and make periodic reports to the school committee. The motion passed unanimously, making us the first homeschoolers in Waltham. The meeting was open to the public and articles appeared in two local papers, one of them on the front page. Channel 7 also wanted to interview us, but we declined because we did not want the children exposed to that kind of public scrutiny.

We met with the Deputy School Superintendent and the principal a few days later. The principal was skeptical, but he pledged his full support and cooperation. He will make all the resources of the school open to us. He wants us to follow the first grade curriculum and use their text books, but this seems unnecessary to us, considering how well Charlene has progressed without text books. We decided not to press the issue, and hope that the success of our home school will convince him to give us more freedom later on.

The McClymonds sent us a copy of their letter to the school superintendent, which reads in full:

We are parents that live in Waltham and have three children: Charlene 6, Keith 3½, and Lydia 1. Dr. McClymonds is a scientist at Raytheon's Research Division in Lexington and has a PhD. in electrical engineering from Cornell University.

Mrs. McClymonds is a full-time homemaker and has a BA in fine arts from Ithaca College. Our oldest child, Charlene, will be the age for first grade in the fall, and our intention is to educate her ourselves in our home as an alternative to public or private schooling.

Our understanding of our legal right to have a home school and the procedure to be followed by school officials in approving a home school is based on the memorandum from the Massachusetts Department of Education concerning home education dated January 4, 1980 [available from Holt Associates, $1]. We have enclosed a copy of this memorandum for your convenience. The Massachusetts compulsory attendance statute C.L.c.76, s.1 provides for alternatives to public school or private school instruction by stating that ". . . such attendance shall not be required of a child . . . who is being otherwise instructed in a manner approved in advance by the superintendent or the school committee." The Massachusetts Supreme Judicial court ruled in *Commonwealth vs. Roberts*, 159 Mass. 372, 374 (1893) that the "otherwise instructed" statutory exemption allows home education by the parents "provided it is given in good faith and is sufficient in extent." Your office informed us by telephone that the first step in obtaining approval for our home school is to write you and the School Committee and explain our reasons for wanting to have a home school. We will gladly give our reasons below.

We believe that learning is best accomplished when a person is internally motivated and wants to learn. A home school has an ideal teacher-to-student ratio, so the feelings, interests, and attitudes of the child, which have such important roles in motivating the learning process, are known quite well by the parents. At home, the child is in a calm, positive atmosphere and learning is not inhibited by fear of failure, ridicule, humiliation, overstimulation and tension from competition. We do not wish to imply that we think that public school teachers are not dedicated, caring, and competent. But it cannot be denied that individual, loving, knowledgeable attention can be more abundant in a home school than in a classroom with 20 or more students and one teacher. In a classroom, the ability of each child to learn is directly related to his ability to conform his interests to a predetermined plan of learning. In a home school, the sequencing of subjects and the choosing of extra topics of interest is done by the ones who know him best, and learning is more rapid and intensive. We are convinced that homeschooling is the best educational situation for a child whose parents are able and willing to make the investment of their lives to make it work. What we want to do in our home school is what public school teachers would do if they had the opportunity to teach only two or three children. Also, the teaching of the parents' spiritual and moral beliefs can be integrated with learning most naturally if the child is taught at home by his parents.

It is a common belief that socialization is best accomplished when a child goes to school. We do not deny that learning to interact with children is important—we affirm this completely and it is an important goal for our home school—but we do not believe that children learn best to "get along" with others by having them interact in large groups when they are very young. Our observations of young children in large groups convince us that overstimulation, argumentativeness, and unkindness increase proportionately with the size of the group. We do not want our children to learn this kind of behavior. Rather, we have taught our children the Biblical basis for good character. In the home, where a child interacts with his siblings or with a few friends, good character is not overwhelmed by peer pressure. As a child matures and he has the ability to stand up for what is right, interaction in larger groups becomes feasible. Is this philosophy of socialization realistic? Yes, many parents who have written about their home schools state that their children have grown to be mature, independent thinkers and they are the leaders among their friends.

Our daily routine with the children has been very effective in teaching many skills to Charlene, although the education process has been much less formal than in public schools. Mrs. McClymonds makes a weekly trip to the library with the children, to acquaint them with the library and check out books, and she reads these books to Charlene and Keith for about 30 minutes per day before nap time. Charlene usually follows along when someone reads to her, and she has learned to read quite well in this way. Charlene has another reading time without Keith for about 20 minutes per day while Keith begins his nap. Mrs. McClymonds and Charlene have read the entire Laura Ingalls Wilder series, a few books from the Narnia series by C. S. Lewis, and from the Eddie series by Carolyn Haywood, and they are now reading *A Walk Across America* by Peter Jenkins. Before bedtime, Dr. McClymonds reads a Bible story to Charlene and Keith, and they discuss it together, and sometimes they will read a short library book, too. Charlene reads by herself often for entertainment, sometimes for as long as 30 minutes. She can choose from library books, our own children's books and her Bible. Sometimes Keith will have Charlene read a book to him while they are waiting for breakfast. Charlene often writes little "love notes" to Mama or Papa, and when Mrs. McClymonds writes letters to relatives and friends, Charlene adds a page of her own. Charlene was given a "Little Professor" calculator toy about a year ago and she mastered simple addition, subtraction, and multiplication in a short time. We have not encouraged her to learn more difficult arithmetic because she has no need for it at this time in her life.

Our plans for our home school are not very different from our present daily routine. Charlene is proud of her ability to read and write and she loves to use her new skills. We are pleased with her curiosity and we would like to see her develop more independence in learning by using the library to find books on topics of interest. We will also take "field trips" to support and stimulate the interests of the children. Our aim is to see the children develop their abilities to seek and learn independently, both through reading and firsthand observation of the world around them.

We plan to keep a portfolio or scrapbook for Charlene that will contain a list of the books she has read, samples of her writing and artwork and whatever else seems appropriate to document her progress. This portfolio would be made available occasionally to a public school official if this is the desire of the school committee.

We hope this letter adequately explains our reasons for wanting to have a home school for Charlene and what our home school is like. We hope for a favorable decision from you, allowing us to teach Charlene at home. We will be glad to answer any questions you may have in another letter or in person. We would also appreciate any suggestions you might have to help us in running our home school.

We know that our request to have a home school is the first one of its kind in Waltham, although there are many other home schools in the state. We can provide you with the names of other school districts that allow home schools if this would assist you. You may want to determine if it is possible for Charlene to be officially enrolled in the Waltham public schools as a child in a special program, so that you do not lose state aid.

Thank you for taking the time to consider our request.

Mennonites Win

A reader sent us this ruling from a case last fall in Minnesota:

> *In County Court, Criminal Division*
> *State of Minnesota v. Noah Hege and Ella Hege*
>
> *Findings Of Fact*
>
> 1. Noah and Ella Hege reside with their minor daughter, Eunice Hege, within the boundaries of school district 362, Koochiching County, Minnesota.
>
> 4. During the school year 1980 and 1981 and following, Eunice did not attend public school but was taught at her home by her mother, Ella Hege.
>
> 5. Ella Hege is not a certified teacher for the State of Minnesota and does not have the required degrees or education to

become a Minnesota certified grade school teacher.

6. Eunice Hege is enrolled as a student by correspondence in the Christian Light Education School out of Harrisonburg, Virginia. . . . It is an individualized curriculum and is basically self-instructional. It consists of courses in (1) Bible, (2) language art, (3) mathematics, (4) science, (5) social studies.

7. Eunice is doing passing work and is progressing at an acceptable rate as prescribed by her school.

8. Eunice Hege has completed the California Achievement Test after one year in the Christian Light School and scored average or above in all academic categories for her respective age and grade.

9. Ella, Noah and Eunice Hege are sincere Christian believers of the Mennonite faith.

10. It is their sincere and unshakable belief that a public education does not meet the needs of a student of their religious persuasion and is in fact an intrusion upon their privacy and their free exercise of their religion.

11. The Christian Light Education will successfully prepare Eunice Hege to become a productive, self-reliant, and self-sufficient member of the Mennonite community.

12. The State of Minnesota has failed to demonstrate a compelling interest or overriding public policy which would be superior to the rights of the defendants under the First and Fourteenth Amendments of the United States Constitution.

Memorandum

All the defendants in these cases are of the Mennonite faith. They are all good solid citizens and valuable members of this community. All of them appeared *pro se* [DR: literally, "for themselves"—without a lawyer]. Their entire defense was one of a religious nature. They wished to educate their children in their own way as they see fit so that their children will become self-reliant, self-sufficient, productive members of the Mennonite community and thus also of our State and Nation. One of the important parts of their faith is not to adopt worldly ways but to keep as best they can the religious and social customs and habits of their predecessors in faith. They consider it to be an intrusion and a violation of their right of privacy and their freedom to practice their religion, if forced to send their children to public school. They fear that a public education will alienate their children from their religious and social heritage and thus weaken and eventually put an end to their sect. It is their belief that the quality of education at their Christian schools is more suitable for children of their persuasion. They demonstrated to the court that all of their students have scored well on the California Achievement tests, indicating that their children are in fact being educated. Balanced against these facts, the State of Minnesota requires in Statutes 120.10 and following, that the curriculum and teachers must meet certain minimum standards to qualify as a school. Clearly, the Mennonite schools and teachers fail to qualify. That, however, does not mean they fail to educate. The State of Minnesota has an extremely important and vital interest in educating its young people. That interest, though important, in absence of an overriding public policy or compelling public interest on behalf of the State, is not superior to the First and Fourteenth Amendments of the Constitution.

That is the case here. The State has failed to show an overriding public policy or compelling interest that would be superior to the defendants' First and Fourteenth Amendment rights and thus the court found that although Minnesota Statutes 120.10 and following is constitutional on its face, it is not constitutional when applied to the defendants.

As an additional aside, the court might add that it has yet to see any of the children in question in juvenile court nor have any of the defendants, to the best of the court's recollection, appeared in any division of the County Court other than for the immediate cases.

Those comments sum up the type of people we are dealing with here. They are not criminals or child neglectors. They are sincere in their religious assertions and beliefs and their religion pervades their entire social fabric. We should be proud to have them as neighbors and citizens. We should trust them to educate and care for their children in their own way. We should grant to them their right to be free from government harassment and we should defend the exercise of their constitutional freedoms as though they were our own, because, in fact, they are.

These defendants have inherited the freedoms sought by our pilgrim fathers when they struggled ashore over 300 years ago. These defendants are exercising rights wrung from the kings of Britain by the blood of our patriots and defended down through the years by the bodies and lives of our citizenry and preserved and enlarged by our government for the general benefit of all. The State has not shown this court why those rights should be abridged.

—Peter N. Hemstad, Judge

September 15, 1982

"Definition Of School" Case

[DR:] Here is the Wisconsin Supreme court ruling described in GWS 33. Wisconsin readers should expect, as a consequence, the Wisconsin legislature to draft a definition of "private schools," and we hope they give their representatives their ideas and opinions.

From the opinion, written by Justice Shirley S. Abrahamson:

Wisconsin v. Laurence Popanz

No. 81-1493-CR

Filed April 26, 1983

Appeal from a judgment of the Circuit Court for Iowa County, James P. Fiedler, Circuit Judge. *Judgment reversed. Remanded.*

The circuit court adjudged Laurence C. Popanz guilty on two counts of violating Wisconsin's compulsory school attendance law. For the reasons we set forth we conclude that the phrase "private school as used in sec. 118.15(1)(a) is impermissibly vague.

In August of 1980, the defendant, Laurence C. Popanz, wrote to inform the district school administrator that he was a member of the Agency for the Church of the Free Thinker, Inc., a Wisconsin Corporation organized under ch. 181 of the Wisconsin Statutes, [and] that the Church administers "the Free Thinker School, a Private School located in Avoca, Wisconsin," . . . All three students were the defendant's daughters. . . . The defendant requested the children's school records along with recommendations regarding curriculum and asked the district school administrator to inform the school attendance officer about the matter "so that we can be informed of anything we must do to be in compliance with the law."

The defendant's letter initiated a series of communications between the defendant and the district school administrator relating to listing nonpublic schools in a Wisconsin Department of Public Instruction [DPI] publication entitled *Wisconsin Nonpublic School Directory*. The district school administrator testified that before he would recognize the defendant's school as a "private school" for purposes of the compulsory school attendance law, he would require that the defendant's school be listed in the directory, even though there is no such requirement in the statute or administrative regulations. The administrator testified that the listing requirement was a matter of his own "professional" standards.

The Chief of Information Services for the DPI, who is in charge of compiling the directory, testified that each district school administrator compiles the list of nonpublic schools in his or her district. In response to questioning seeking to ascertain whether the witness determined that the private schools adhered to any type of prescribed guidelines, he answered as follows:

"I do not. I collect the information and handle data. We do have a nonpublic school liaison person, Dr. Mildred Anderson, who counsels nonpublic schools, but I do not get involved in that and I'm sure there really are no official guidelines for nonpublic schools in the statutes."

The [district school] administrator testified that he personally needed to evaluate the schools to ensure that they comported with certain standards of which someone at the Department of Public Instruction had advised him orally, when the district administrator had consulted that person about another claimed private school. The standards the administrator claimed to use, or the questions he would ask, were as follows: Does the curriculum of the school provide sequential advancement of students? What are the facilities available? What are the educational backgrounds of the teachers? Are the instructional materials adequate? Is the time schedule consistent with that followed by the public schools? The administrator never asked these questions about the defendant's school because he never visited the school.

The defendant apparently took the position that he had made it clear to the administrator that . . . if the administrator required a visit to the school, the administrator should so advise the defendant. . . . The circuit court concluded that the administrator of the school district had advised the defendant that when his school was ready for evaluation, the defendant should contact the administrator and that the administrator and a representative of the DPI would then visit the school. . . . Because the defendant failed to request an evaluation, the administrator and the two school principals involved . . . requested the district attorney for Iowa County to institute proceedings against the defendant.

Even though the circuit court concluded that for the purposes of the compulsory school attendance law "the Wisconsin Statutes are singularly silent on the question of what constitutes a private school," it did not consider the constitutionality of the statute. The circuit court found the defendant guilty because he failed to establish that he had caused his daughters to attend a private school. He was sentenced to two consecutive 90-day terms.

The defendant maintains on appeal that sec. 118.15(1)(a) is void for vagueness. The state reminds us that there is a strong presumption favoring the constitutionality of a legislative enactment and that the court will construe the statute to preserve it if it is at all possible to do so.

There is no simple litmus-paper test to determine whether a criminal statute is void for vagueness. . . . Due process requires that the law set forth fair notice of the conduct prohibited or required and proper standards for enforcement of the law and adjudication. Before a court can invalidate a statute on the grounds of vagueness, it must conclude that "some ambiguity or uncertainty in the gross outlines of the duty imposed or conduct prohibited" appears in the statutes, "such that one bent on obedience may not discern when the region of proscribed conduct is neared, or such that the trier of fact in ascertaining guilt or innocence is relegated to creating and applying its own standards of culpability rather than applying standards prescribed in the statute or rule." *State v. Courtney*, 74 Wis.2d.

A criminal statute must be sufficiently definite to give a person of ordinary intelligence who seeks to avoid its penalties fair notice of conduct required or prohibited. "Vague laws may trap the innocent by not providing fair warning." *Grayned v. City of Rockford*, 408 US 104.

A criminal statute must also provide standards for those who enforce the laws. . . . The danger posed by a vague law is that officials charged with enforcing the law may apply it arbitrarily or the law may be so unclear that a trial court cannot properly instruct the jury as to the applicable law. "A vague law impermissibly delegates basic policy matters to policemen, judges, and juries for resolution on an ad hoc and subjective basis, with the attendant dangers of arbitrary and discriminatory application." *Grayned v. City of Rockford*.

Like this defendant, we have searched the statutes, administrative rules and regulations and official DPI writings for a definition of "private school" or criteria which an entity must meet to be classified as a "private school." . . . We have found neither a definition nor prescribed criteria. Nor does the phrase "private school" have a well-settled meaning in common parlance or in decisions of this court which could be used. . . . We therefore decline to adopt the definition of "private school" proposed by the court of appeals by the State Superintendent of Public Instruction in an *amicus* brief.

In *State v. White*, 109 Wis.2d 64, Ct. Ap. 1982, the court of appeals, combining a dictionary definition of "school" with language from various statutes that use the term "private school," interpreted the phrase "private school" as "an institution that meets prescribed curriculum and organizational requirements and that has any academic grade comparable to one included in the standard public school grade division." The court of appeals' decision . . . is hereby overruled.

The State Superintendent of Public Instruction, reading the statutes, court decisions, and dictionary definition of school together, proposed in an *amicus* brief that the phrase "private school" be defined as follows:

"[A] private school is a facility offering the various grade levels available in the public schools, and commonly understood by the public to be a 'school.' The commonly understood definition of 'school' is 'an institution for the instruction of children.' (*The American Heritage Dictionary*)."

"Thus, a private school is an educational institution. It is established for the primary purpose of providing instruction in the applicable grade levels, and its existence is continuing or perpetual rather than limited in duration to only the educational careers of specific persons now receiving instruction. In other words, particular students may come and go but the bona fide private school continues to hold its doors open to new students who will take the place of those who graduate or otherwise leave the school. . . ."

We are not convinced that these definitions are the only ones a citizen, an administrator, or a court using dictionary definitions, court decisions and the statutes could deduce. In any event the legislature or its delegated agent should define the phrase "private school"; citizens or the courts should not have to guess at its meaning.

Ad Commission

In *GWS* 30 we announced that we were going to start carrying advertising, as an additional way of bringing in the money we need to keep this office and *GWS* going, since subscriptions and book sales still fall a good deal short of meeting our expenses. We also suggested some ways in which readers might help us get ads. In *GWS* 31, to encourage readers to do this, we said that for every display ad recruited for us and sent in together with a check in payment, we would pay a commission of 10% of the cost of the ad. There has been some response to this offer, but so far much less than we hoped for and need. So, to encourage people still further, we are going to raise that ad commission to *20%*. It won't buy you a house or a car, but it could help pay some of your bills.

If my lecture income had remained what it was five or six years ago, or if we had (as we hope to have) two or three thousand more subscribers, or if our book business had kept on doubling as it did a year ago, we would not have such urgent need of new sources of income. But these things have not yet happened, so we will be grateful for any advertising you can get for us.

Other ways in which you can help keep *GWS* alive, well, and growing, include: (l) Getting us more new subscribers; (2) Buying more books and materials from us, or getting others to do so; (3) Finding fee-paying lectures for me; (4) Sending us a contribution in addition to your subscription. For whatever you can do, thanks very much.—JH

Late News Flash—J.H. Offers Workshop

Something I have wanted to do for some time, and have in fact been doing informally now and then, I am now going to start to do regularly. On the *third* Thursday of each month (our Open House is on the *second* Thurs.), starting Sept. 15, 5:30 p.m. on, I will have here in the office what we might call a Workshop for Bowed Stringed Instruments, both cello and violin (and viola if someone wants to bring one). People who want to find out what it feels like to make sounds on these instruments, or beginners who would like a little advice and help, can have a chance to do that at these very informal gatherings. I can provide one, maybe two real cellos, and my portable Travielo (which some of you may have seen in the office), and also a real violin and a playable pseudo-violin.

Since these workshops (at least at first) will require my presence, you should call the office in advance (617-437-1550) to make sure I will be there. If my travel schedule conflicts, we will suggest an alternate date, probably a week later.

Also, these will be *active* workshops; if you come, *you have to play*. If you want to learn a little about how to play the instruments "the right way," we can work on that. But if you just want to experiment with them, make some sounds, and have a good time, that's fine too, and a very good way to begin. This isn't school; I won't try to "teach" you anything unless you ask me to. But you have to do *something*; you can't just sit and watch.

I think we can have a lot of fun with this. If you own an instrument or can borrow one for the evening, it will help if you bring it. As always, children *who want to come* are welcome, but we don't (yet) have any small-sized instruments for them, so children much under eight might not have too much fun. I'm looking forward to seeing some of you there.—JH

New Books Available Here

How To Beat The S.A.T. (And All Standardized Multiple-choice Tests) by Michael Donner $3.55 + post). This book will probably be for many people one of the most *useful* of all the books on our list. It is not at all like, but a complement to, such books as *How To Take The S.A.T.* (*GWS* 20). For this book has nothing to do with the *knowledge* supposedly being tested. What it does have to do with is the ways in which the test-makers make up their right and wrong answers and decide where (among the five possible choices) to put the "correct" ones. It is, in short, a book about how you can substantially raise your test scores *without knowing the subject matter being tested.*

This will seem a strong, not to say fantastic claim, but Donner backs it up with experience and figures drawn from his analyses of real tests. Early in the book he writes:

> A simple experiment will prove that the methods presented in this book can definitely improve one's performance, and by a really substantial amount: Anyone who is able and willing to take (or has already taken) a sample test before reading this book and then a different version of the same test after reading this book will not fail to be impressed. . . . Indeed to my great satisfaction, when I took a series of six SAT-Math tests (enough to be statistically definitive), while applying only *five* of the principles in this book (Rules 2, 3, 5, 6, and 7) and *without even looking at the questions* but only at the answer choices, my average score per test was 140 points higher than random guessing would have produced, and higher than one-quarter of what all test-takers (test takers who benefited by looking at the questions) actually do score.

Let me emphasize once again, this is not a book about how to raise your score by knowing more of the right answers, but how to raise your score *without* knowing the answers. How can this be possible? When Donner looked at the answer sheets of a number of real tests, he found that.

The test maker *does* put appreciably fewer correct answers in columns A, C, or E than the laws of chance would have them contain. Moreover, he puts two or more successive correct answers in any one given column much less frequently than statistical probability.

From this observation comes Donner's Rule I—other things being equal, in choosing your answer avoid columns (or choices) "A," "C," and "E," and don't put two successive answers in the same column.

We described more of Donner's theories in *GWS* 25. Some are simple, others more complicated, but they all follow the same logic: test-makers use *systems* in making up their possible answers and placing the "correct" ones, and the better we understand those systems, the better we will do on all questions where we don't know the right answer and have to make some kind of a guess.

This is an extremely important book for parents of children who will be taking some kind of standardized test, and for many of these children themselves. I would guess that many children of ten or over, who were fairly good readers and had some interest in science and math, would find the book very interesting, for it is after all about how to solve puzzles and win at games, and children like to know about both.

I would also think that wherever parents were having or feared having difficulties with schools, particularly if they themselves did not go to college or perhaps even finish high school, they might do well, armed with the knowledge in this book, to take the S.A.T. tests themselves, and keep studying and taking them until they could get high scores. I'm not sure how Michael Donner was able to get the tests he needed to make this study (it seems most unlikely that the Educational Testing Service would have helped him), but if he could find a way to take Math S.A.T.'s and check his own answers six times, we ought to be able to. We will try, with any help you can give us, to find out how people can take (and if possible correct) these tests, as often as they want, with the least possible trouble and expense.

If these parents' test scores are, as they soon surely will be, much higher than the very low scores (combined Verbal plus Math scores of around 800, according to *U. S. News and World Report*) once obtained by most teachers, the schools will find it hard to claim convincingly that the parents are not competent to teach their children. As more and more homeschoolers and their children learn to beat these tests, either the schools will have to admit that we are better at teaching and learning, or they will have to claim, and so admit, as I have long insisted, that these tests don't really measure anything important, in which case they have no valid grounds for using them or insisting that we do. Either way, we win. When we beat these tests, we impress the schools (or the legislatures and courts); when we have beaten them often and badly enough, we will force the schools to give them up and find more realistic and useful ways of evaluating learning, which of course they ought long ago to have done anyway. A big first step in this direction will be for as many people as possible to read this most helpful book.

My Childhood, by Carl Nielsen ($5.40 + post). One of the unexpected delights of my last trip to Denmark was finding that this autobiographical fragment of the greatest Danish composer (and one of my favorites of all composers), which for a long time I had known about and hoped someday to read, was still in print and in an English translation—published by the company that first published and still publishes most of Nielsen's music. Like Emily Carr's *The Book Of Small* (*GWS* 19), this book, written during the last year or two of Nielsen's life, is a very vivid recollection of childhood from the point of view of old age, and is the only book I know of in which a great composer tells how he first began to hear, love, and make music.

Though of course we can never know what thoughts and feelings people may hide from the world, from all we know of Nielsen (who died in 1931) it does seem as if, among the great composers, he was an exceptionally cheerful, serene, strong, and happy person, and much of these qualities show through (as in his music) in this delightful memoir of his childhood and growing up. He was not a deliberately comic writer, trying to make us laugh in every sentence, but he could not help but notice, enjoy, and remember the comic side of everything that happened to him and around him, so this is in many places a very funny book. Beyond that, in his old age Nielsen remembered, and reminds us, how endlessly mysterious and fascinating to children is the adult world around them, even those parts that might strike us as most humdrum. It is the great gift and genius of children to find possibilities of magic and excitement in almost everything they do. On summer weekdays, since his family was very poor, Carl and his brothers had to work all day in a nearby brickyard, trimming bricks to even shape and size with a trowel, but even this seemingly monotonous work they managed to make into an exciting kind of sport.

As in Camara Laye's *The African Child* (*GWS* 29), like this the story of a poor village boy growing up, a spirit of happiness breathes from this book. Some of this must have had to do with the rural Denmark of his time, in which poverty, however severe (and it often was), rarely became what Illich has called "modern poverty," full of squalor, helplessness, envy, and shame. Some must have had to do with Nielsen's parents, who in their own strength, skillfulness, energy, and courage were themselves remarkable people. Much must have had to do with Carl's own temperament, which was probably sunny from the moment of his birth. And perhaps some of it had to do with the great music that was a central part of their lives—Carl's father was, among many other things, a musician and apparently a quite skillful one.

This presence of great music in the lives of poor people is a point that needs to be stressed. The ten in Nielsen's family lived in two small rooms and a kitchen in half of a cottage that he describes, without rancor, as "a mere hovel." Yet in this tiny house were several musical instruments; when Nielsen was six and in bed with the measles, his mother took from the wall a three-quarter sized violin and showed him how to play it. Music, much of it what we would call "classical," was everywhere in this rural area. The British writer, J. B. Priestley, who grew up in Bradford, a woolen-mill town in Yorkshire, once wrote that many of the very poor working-class families he knew had pianos and regularly played at least some of the music of Bach and other great masters. We can only wonder, when and how did the idea take hold that music, above all the greatest music, was the exclusive property of a small upper-middle class—and more to the point, how can we get rid of this idea.

Of his own life as a great musician, Nielsen writes:

> Why should I go forward along the road for which my brothers and others had equally good qualifications, some of

them perhaps better and greater? Will there come a time, I wonder, when human talents will have a chance to develop freely and fully, not haphazardly and crudely, but with fine observation, understanding, and tender care from the first groping start? I think so. . . . In my childhood days opportunities were few.

There is a sad irony in these words; the chances of a child as poor as Nielsen getting a musical education and experience as rich as his seem to me much smaller now than then. I can only hope that this may soon change, and that great music may once again become the common property of all people. Meanwhile, we have this lovely book to show us how for one person it came to be so.—JH

Editors—John Holt & Donna Richoux
Managing Editor—Patrick Farenga
Subscriptions & Books—Mark Pierce
Office Assistant—Mary Van Doren

Growing Without Schooling 35

October 1983

The center pages of this issue contain the complete catalog of "John Holt's Book and Music Store." If you would like some of our items for holiday gifts, we should receive your order no later than Nov. 30—please order early and avoid disappointment.

Our friend Nancy Wallace's book *Better Than School* has just been published and we'll be selling it here ($13.50 + post). John writes about it at length in this issue.

Another *GWS* reader and contributor, Maire Mullarney of Ireland, has a book out on her homeschooling experiences, *Anything School Can Do, You Can Do Better* (Published by Arlen House, Dublin, and Scribners, New York.) Maire wrote, "The book is top of paperback best-sellers for two weeks, and is out only three. All the reactions are positive, between people who remember their own schooldays or who are upset about their children's experiences. Many women have said that it improves their sense of their own value." Readers can order directly from Maire for $4 (Address: The Mill House, Whitechurch Rd, Rathfarnham, Dublin 14).

John and the Van Daams of Rhode Island got a last-minute invitation to appear on the NBC *Today* show Sept. 8, which some of you may have seen. Besides the events we mentioned in the last issue, John also spoke at a homeschooling meeting organized by Patty Arnold in Chagrin Falls, OH, Sept. 24, and at Edinboro College in Pennsylvania Sept. 29. He has recently been on radio shows from Buffalo and Austin, and on the Black National Radio show *Nighttalk*. The Canadian network CBC-TV featured him on a show about computers and education, and *Fortune* magazine interviewed him for their education issue. He was the cover story for the August issue of *Front Range*, a Boulder, CO publication! And we were pleased to see, among all the other clippings about home education we receive here, an article called "The ABC's of Homeschooling" from the Feb. '83 issue of *Black Family Magazine* (332 N. Michigan Av, Chicago IL 60601).

It was delightful to have the company and assistance of Robin Smith Schneider (PA) for two weeks in August; she worked as a volunteer in our office during her visit to Boston. A great help.— Donna Richoux

John Holt's Coming Schedule

November 3–4, 1983: Open Connections, Philadelphia PA. Thursday PM general public meeting, Friday PM homeschoolers meeting. Contact Peter Bergson, 215-527-1504 or 527-4982.

Nov. 10: Holt Associates Open House.

Nov. 17: John Holt's String Workshop (call 437-1550 to confirm).

Nov. 28 (tentative): State U. at Lexington, KY. Contact Libby Morley, 606-273-7816.

Nov. 30: Terre Haute, Indiana homeschoolers. Contact Mary Ann Simbol, 812-232-6311 x7350 or 317-653-8608.

Dec. 2: DePauw U., Greencastle IN. 9–11 a.m. Contact Myra Rosenhaus, 317-658-4864.

Dec. 3: Meeting with Central Indiana Home Educators. Contact Sherry Hamstra, 5724 Diana Dr, Indianapolis IN 46278.

Dec. 4 (tentative): Chicago homeschoolers. Contact Deb Martin, 312-968-6447.

Dec. 5 (tentative): Michigan Home Educators, Kalamazoo MI. Contact Len Locatis, 616-375-6196 or 657-6927.

Dec. 8: Holt Associates Open House.

Dec. 15: John Holt's String Workshop (call 437-1550 to confirm).

Playing versus Helping

From Toots Weier (WI):

I was rearranging some wall posters in the basement the other day. I intended to rehang them and use new tape to make them stay up. Well, Winter (almost 2) was right there wanting to be a part of the happenings (quite understandable!). "I do it! I do it!" It didn't dawn on me to actually have him *help*. Instead I cut off a piece of tape and handed it to him, figuring he'd play with it and I would continue hanging the posters. Play with it, he did. I had just hung a map of the U.S. and Winter thought it great fun to put the tape on the map and peel it off again. Only thing was, as he peeled the tape off, part of Georgia went with it.

He was about to do it again (on a different state) and I got all freaked out and was about to start jumping up and down when I realized he didn't want to play with a piece of tape so much as he wanted to help me. Or maybe he thought he *was* helping.... I gathered my senses, handed Winter a new piece of tape and gently directed him to the corner of the poster I was hanging. Very carefully he placed the tape on the corner at an angle and pressed it down. Oh, it was just a little bunchy, but it was so sweet! If only you could have seen the smile he flashed! And so we continued, me hanging posters, Winter taping them and flashing *such* a smile! The next day as we were passing through the basement he pointed to the posters and said, "Nice! Nice!" Very happy and proud!

Homeschooler At Harvard

On 8/30/83, the Boston Globe *ran a front-page story about Grant Colfax, a California boy who has been taught at home for the past eleven years, and who, accepted for admission by both Yale and Harvard, will enter Harvard this fall. An Associated Press story about him has appeared in newspapers in other parts of the country.*

A few highlights from the Globe *story:*

> The 18-year-old from Booneville, Calif., a rural town 100 miles north of San Francisco, was educated at home throughout his youth by his parents and his goats. "My mom and dad taught me English and math.... I learned about stuff like embryo transfer from the goats. Also economics. I breed baby goats and sell them for $500 apiece."

> Colfax says he has not missed much by not being able to mix with youngsters his age. "I joined a foreign film buffs group and I meet a lot of people selling my goats," he said. "Besides, this is a town of 750 people. I think my graduating class would have had 12 people in it. I guess I didn't miss much."

Mrs. Colfax said they ... bought a 50-acre ranch in Booneville 11 years ago. "Right away we decided that we had this raw piece of land, very remote and very wild, and just building the place up would be an education for our kids," she said. Besides Grant, they have three younger sons, all of whom are also being schooled at home.

Robert Cashion, the Harvard admissions officer who interviewed Grant, told the Associated Press that "the young man struck me as someone who really enjoyed the learning process. It was refreshing to see."

Schooling was worked in between building a house, planting the garden, laying telephone and electricity lines, and constructing a water system. "If we had a big project to do, and the weather was nice, then we put aside our studying," the youth said. "Later we found out that building a tool shed would help us understand the planes and angles in geometry."

[JH:] We're not running this story to show that all homeschoolers can get into Harvard (or Yale, etc.), or that they *should* go to Harvard, or that if they don't get into Harvard it means the parents did something wrong. The only point we want to make is that it is possible, given good test scores—Grant scored in the mid to high 600s in each section of the S.A.T.s—for young people to get into Harvard, Yale, and presumably other prestigious colleges, even though they may never have seen the inside of a school. In other words, there is no *policy* in these universities against admitting homeschoolers.

In fact, the news story suggests rather the opposite. The AP story quotes Robert Cashion, the admissions officer, as saying not just, "It was refreshing to see," but also, "It was really a remarkable thing." What was? That Grant Colfax enjoys the learning process. An interesting remark for a Harvard admissions officer to make. Of course, he might have meant that he did not expect anyone to enjoy learning who had not spent a lot of time in school. But I suspect that he meant the opposite, that Grant Colfax is in fact much more interested in learning than most kids who, like me many years ago, and probably most university students today, are mainly or only interested in grades.

At any rate, we have our answer to the question that so many parents ask: "If I teach my children at home, will they later on be able to get into good colleges?" The answer is Yes.

We just received this interesting note from Jeanne Finan (VA):

The nice thing about Grant Colfax going to Harvard is that suddenly it has made teaching my children at home acceptable to friends and family. After he was on *NBC Evening News,* my phone rang constantly—"Did you see the news tonight?" Suddenly we are not weird, crazy, or irresponsible any more. It is A.O.K. People can accept it. I find that a little strange but also I find it understandable. It gives others a long-range view—that a homeschooled child can actually get accepted to college—and Harvard at that (which is what impressed friends the most). Grant Colfax has indirectly done a public relations job that has benefitted many homeschoolers. I hope that all the publicity has not interrupted his life too much.

Court News

From the Montana Homeschoolers Association Newsletter, *7/83 (PO Box 1008, Belgrade MT 59714; $8/yr):*

Good News! Ware and Sharon Sutton from Broadview, MT do not have to spend their time in court any longer, because as of the end of June, their case has been dropped. . . . After a long and trying year I'm sure the Suttons could use a letter of encouragement from their fellow homeschoolers. Address your letters to Ward & Sharon Sutton, Broadview MT 59015.

From the N.M. Defensor-Chieftain, *7/18/83:*

Determined to continue to teach their three children at home, Don and Paula Edgington have appealed to the United States Supreme Court to review a recent decision made by the New Mexico Court of Appeals. The Edgingtons are appealing a decision made by the appelate court which reversed a decision made Sept. 3, 1982, by District Judge Edmund Kase III [*GWS* 32].

Neil Mertz, attorney for the Edgingtons . . . said that his application to the New Mexico Supreme Court was turned down on May 17.

Don Edgington said, "I think we have no choice but to file an application with the United States Supreme Court. Statistically, our chances are small that they will accept our case, but we think there's a good chance they will."

Mertz said that since the state appealed to the New Mexico Court of Appeals, he has been assisted by Winston Roberts-Hohl, a Santa Fe attorney.

From Family Report, *7/83 (36211 SE Sunset View, Washougal WA 98671; $15/yr):*

South Carolina: Attorney Orin G. Briggs of Columbia informs us of a great victory in the Scott and Susan Page case [*GWS* 34]. He writes, "As a result of this decision the Page family, and any other family in South Carolina that meets certain set standards, can teach their children at home. . . ." Dr. Raymond Moore testified as an expert witness on behalf of the Pages.

From Mrs. Robert Nicholson, 22601 Buena Vista Rd, Rockbridge OH 43149:

School officials did throw us in court, found us guilty of neglect, and ordered our children back to public school. We then had an appeal hearing April 1983 and are still waiting for their decision.

We did hit one good stroke of luck. Our court-appointed attorney kept going round and round, telling me they were right, we couldn't do anything about it. Then I wrote to the American Civil Liberties Union of Ohio. Both Bruce A. Campbell of Columbus and Helen Baker of Illinois ["Friendly Lawyers," *GWS* 33] wrote a beautiful brief for our appeal. They also contacted our lawyer—paid his way—he wrote a good brief and argued at our appeal. They got it so our attorney now knows what he is doing.

From Lynne Leffel, PO Box 094, Thompson OH 44086:

A short note on the Leffel case here. We dropped the appeal and decided to try again this year. We do not feel that we failed all the way around. We got the Superintendent to recognize that we mean business and that he has got to recognize the legitimacy of home education. During our trial the Superintendent came up with a guideline to follow in asking for permission to homeschool (a chronological procedure and a statement of what a curriculum should contain, i.e., minimum standards). We are following his steps and building the best facts to take up just in case we go to court again.

In brief:

Facing Court Action: Jennifer Scoggin (TX) and 4 other Clarendon families; attorney, Dave Haigler; Gilbert & Theresa Silveira, and Ross & Gloria Johnson, Monticello FL; attorney, Joseph Dallangera, Trenton

Charges Dismissed: George & Martha Zamber, San Antonio TX

Awaiting Appeal Decision: Tim & Jeanne Newstrom, Bemidji MN.—DR

News From Canada

Wendy Priesnitz sent us another change of address for the Canadian Alliance Of Homeschoolers and her magazine Child's Play: *195 Markville Rd, Unionville, Ont. L3R 4V8. She says, "We don't plan another move for a while!"*

A letter from Irene Todd in Manitoba:

Just a note to give you the new address of the *Manitoba Association For Schooling At Home* (MASH): 776 Victor St, Winnipeg, Man., R3E 1Y6.

We have a fairly loose organization, meeting about every two months, usually in the format of: meeting (an update on progress made by people who now have children of legal school age); potluck supper; and lots of time to chat, share ideas, play with children, etc. We seem to gain about two families every meeting, as word about us spreads across the province, with a total of about 20 families at the moment.

As for legalities of homeschooling in Manitoba—as it now stands, parents have to apply to the Department of Education for permission to homeschool over the age of seven years. One person is appointed to deal with these requests (among other things, I assume) and so far we have had no response from the Dept. of Ed. to these requests from families involved in MASH. We know of only one person in the province who has received permission and are hoping to meet with her shortly to see how she did it. Will fill you in when we get more information.

And from Bonnie Bitting (NB):

We should let you know that we, the Mann family, and the Gallant family have *finally* just received permission from the Minister of Ed. for the Province of New Brunswick to teach our children at home this year. We have been keeping Blossom at home for the past two years (the Manns have kept their son home the same, and the Gallants have been homeschooling 6 years now!) . . . It's been a real rigmarole with the local school board since last January over this, but now it's finally settled, at least until we have to be monitored again sometime this year. It looks like going directly to the Provincial authorities originally would have eliminated a lot of hassle by the local school board who apparently never had as much power as they thought they did. The Provincial authorities just required a brief visit by their "homeschool visitor" who seemed to be in too much of a hurry to get overly concerned about anything, as she was visiting all three families in one day, which necessitated her travelling about 180 miles from her home.

All three families had previously been called before the local superintendent, and then the school board, where on one night we overwhelmed them with each of our carefully written and quite thorough briefs concerning how and why we were homeschooling. Afterwards, they still didn't know what to do with us and considered testing at one point, but as we all refused, they gave us over to the Provincial. It all served to really convince us all of how well we were doing and made us aware of just how much we really do cover without realizing.

From A California Supt.

[DR:] The courteous tone of this letter from a California school superintendent to a would-be homeschooler suggests that some of last winter's confusion and furor about homeschooling (GWS 32) has died down:

August 8, 1983
Dear Mrs. P----,

There are areas of legal debate about home schools, and I am not qualified to discuss them. However, I will tell you of our current practices in this district which should provide adequate guidelines for your group.

1) People wishing to conduct schools in their homes complete the proper reporting form and submit it to the Office of the County Superintendent of Schools. This district receives a copy of the form but takes no action. We do not contest the establishment of home schools.

2) For elementary school grades (K–8) there is no such thing as accreditation or credit for courses. A home school may use any instructional method including correspondence courses. If a child from a home school later enters public school, the grade placement of the student would be determined by taking into account the recommendation by the home school and the results of any tests deemed necessary. The placement decision rests with the public school officials.

3) We are taking time to look into the advisability of having an independent study program agreement with a group such as yours. We will let you know as soon as our study is completed.

Sincerely,

William H. Newman, Superintendent, San Luis Coastal Unified School District, San Luis Obispo CA 93401

Local News

Arkansas: Robert and Ann Green of the *Christian Home Education Association* (PO Box 226, Mabelvale AR 72103) say that the news clipping from the *Arkansas Democrat* that we reprinted in *GWS* 34 was full of misinformation. The Greens quoted a 1979 letter from the State Attorney General's office to one of their state representatives, who had asked for an opinion on the mandatory school attendance law as it applies to private or parochial schools. The Attorney General's office stated, "The General Assembly has never enacted any legislation governing these schools; therefore, there is no specific level of education required of the teachers on the staff. There are no standards that a facility must meet to qualify as a private or parochial school since no standards exist. No agency has the responsibility for determining if an institution is a private or parochial school."

Australia: Lauris Jephcott writes in the 8/83 *Other Ways* (54 Park St, Hawthorn 3122), "My own view is that it is important to let authorities and others know of what we want in education, and why we are doing it. To this end we have made a few small beginnings—we have contacted the Minister of Education and all Victorian Regional Directors, sending copies of our booklets and *Other Ways*, and asking for comments and up-to-date information. So far a number of these officers have replied, have expressed interest in the group, and have passed on relevant information which will be used in updating the booklets. This will, I hope, lead further to the formulation of clear guidelines for home educating families and Education Department officers when applications for exemptions are being made.... Last week there came a request from the educational magazine which goes to all Victorian Department schools and teachers for information on home learners."

California: Suzanne Byrns writes, "Independent Study is alive and thriving in North San Juan. . . . In the mid-1970s, after existing in many one-room schools, the district decided that one sprawling campus would be built to house all 120 students. . . . In the fall of 1977, school construction was completed. Little more than five months later, a fire totally destroyed the new campus. . . . Parents went to work assisting in their children's learning by teaching at home under the direction of individual teachers. . . . A formal Independent Study program was established in 1979 . . . . The ease with which home instruction was implemented encouraged everyone involved." North San Juan has long been on our "Friendly School Districts" list; its mailing address is 18847 Oak Tree Rd, Nevada City CA 95959.

Lawrence Williams of *Oak Meadow School* (PO Box 1051, Ojai CA 93023) wrote in *Living Education*, 8/83, about the results of the Hackett case ("Homeschoolers in Court," *GWS* 34): "The outcome of all this for Oak Meadow and the Palisades Learning Center seems very favorable. Although the judge did not make a definitive ruling about the right of private schools to operate Independent Study Programs, she did make it clear that the burden of proof falls upon *the local school district* to prove that private schools do *not* have the right to operate such programs, for such limitations are not implicit in the California laws. . . . Accordingly, we will continue to operate the Palisades Learning Center for the benefit of families living in the Los Angeles area. "We are currently establishing a network of teachers throughout California who will act as Class Teachers for the Oak Meadow families in their area. These are *paid positions*. . . . Those who are interested should write or call the Oak Meadow School office."

Connecticut: Laura Pritchard (82 Woodland St, Meriden CT 06450; 634-0714) writes, "Please feel free to refer anyone interested in the Ct. homeschooling movement to me. I have a detailed list of CT homeschoolers (over 40) from throughout the state. We plan to hold statewide meetings every four months with field trips in between."

Florida: Ann Mordes wrote in the summer *FLASH.* newsletter (Rt 3 Box 215, Marianna FL 32446): "It's amazing just how many phone calls I have been receiving lately. Both from reporters and folks all over Florida. I was interviewed last week by Florida Wire Services, a TV outfit. . . . After 3½ hours of taping, I received about one minute of actual speaking time on TV!"

Indiana: Shery Hamstra (5724 Diana Dr, Indianapolis IN 46278) tells us that the *Central Indiana Home Educators Association* sponsored a statewide meeting Sept. 9–11, with guest speaker Pat Montgomery of Clonlara School, Ann Arbor, Michigan.

Iowa: The membership of homeschooling group O!KIDS has doubled to 50 families in the past two months, according to Barb Tetzlaff (202 SE 8th St, Ankeny IA 50021). Their newsletter costs $2 for 4 issues, and they will send a copy of the Iowa education laws for 35¢.

Kentucky: A reader told us that when she registered her home as a private school, the state sent her extensive forms inquiring about curriculum, philosophy, objectives, etc., and she didn't know if she was required to fill these out. I asked Ruth McCutchen of the *Kentucky Homeschoolers* (Rt 3 Box 11, Columbia KY 42728; newsletter $3/yr) if she knew anything about this, and she replied, "Several people phoned to ask me about them. Those forms and others are sent out every year. Our cooperation is always 'sincerely solicited' as they want the info for their data bank. *But* it *isn't required* so most of us just throw them away. . . . We don't want to be in anybody's computer more than necessary."

Maryland: Mr. and Mrs. David Hjembo (628 Londontown Rd, Edgewater MD 21037) write, "We in Maryland who are interested in homeschooling feel the need for better laws in this area. . . . We, along with Rev. and Mrs. Marcus Briggs, are planning to introduce to the state legislature your 'Preliminary Draft of Proposed Homeschooling Legislation.'" [Reprint available here, 10¢ +

SASE].

Massachusetts: Karen Kimball (163 Hingham St, Rockland MA 02370; 878-8093) says the *South Shore Homeschoolers Association* is meeting on the last Monday of each month. She writes, "We began a couple of years ago with Rockland homeschoolers and the group has expanded as people from other South Shore towns have contacted us.... We are putting notices of our meetings in area papers. We welcome anyone—they don't have to live on the South Shore."

Minnesota: According to the *Minnesota Homeschool Association Newsletter* (9825 Aquila Rd, Bloomington MN 55438; $5/10 iss.), 32 families came to their "First Annual Pot Luck Picnic" held at Glen and Sharon Hillestad's home Aug. 7. Main speaker was Joe Nathan of St. Paul, author of a book *Free To Teach*.

Missouri: We've mentioned the *Greenwood Forest Association* in *GWS* 24, #28, and #33—a rural community that welcomes homeschoolers. We should clarify that although all the land of the original development has been sold, some lots are available for resale, so anyone interested should write the association at Star Rt Box 70, Mountain View MO 65548.

New Jersey: From the *New Jersey Family Schools Assoc.* newsletter, 9/83: "FSA Fall Camping Trip—Rather than organize our own trip, we are again joining the fall camping trip of the *Eastern Cooperative Recreation School*. We did this with our spring camping trip and it worked out so well that we will continue doing so unless someone objects.... The program includes cooperative games, singing, folk dancing, dramatic games, walks, and swimming.... A rare, intergenerational group including nursing infants through octogenarians." Ann Bodine has been recommending the Eastern Cooperative Recreation School for some time—its mailing address is 324 Level Rd, Collegeville PA 19426.

New York: From an article on homeschooling in the Syracuse *Herald American,* 7/10/83: "There are no genuine statistics on the number of schools operated by parents in Central New York homes, but interviews with more than two dozen school board attorneys, district superintendents, university professors, and families uncovered evidence of at least 40 current cases in Onondaga and surrounding counties.... Douglas and Janeen Weeks said they received good cooperation from the Syracuse City School District while teaching their three children at home. Once, a junior high school principal called to offer any textbooks the family might need and another time the family borrowed some chemicals from the school for a science experiment on volcanoes...."

North Dakota: Cheryl Stover (2508 N 8th St #3, Fargo ND 58102) writes, "This year we moved to N.D., which makes no provision for homeschooling. So we have our work cut out for us. Last week we had an organizational meeting in Fargo for potential homeschoolers—eleven families were represented. We were pleased to see so much interest, especially since we did *very little* advertisin...."

Oklahoma: The new contact person for the Lawton chapter of the *Oklahoma Homeschool Association* is Linda Ashton, 907 Cheryl Circle, Lawton OK 73505; 405-248-2120.

Oregon: Toni Blum-Cates writes, "I've often wondered why there isn't much stuff in *GWS* from Oregon. I'm learning now that historically Oregon law has made it easier to homeschool. There are lots of folks out here doing it who never even heard of *GWS*. I hope to make more and more connections as Leah gets to school age."

Pennsylvania: Susan Richman wrote in *Western Pa. Homeschoolers*, Spring '83: "One district did not want to officially approve a family as homeschooling, although the superintendent was very supportive, but *did* suggest that the family enroll their son in a non-public school that was formed for independent study in their district! The district's lawyer felt more comfortable with this type of arrangement, and the family has been given no trouble...."

Utah: Ken Huffman, chairman of the board for the *Utah Home Education Association*, notified us that as of July 16, the president of UHEA is Don Taft (11666 S 675 E, Draper UT 84020; 571-5896).

Virginia: James O'Toole (Box 256, King

George VA 22485; 703-775-4867) phoned to say that the state's Joint Subcommittee on Home Education [*GWS* 32] has scheduled a public hearing on proposed legislation. The meeting will be at 10 AM, Nov. 21, at Senate Room B, General Assembly Building, Richmond. James asks that readers who are interested in attending the meeting contact him.

Wisconsin: From an Associated Press article in the *Wisconsin State Journal*, 8/22/83: "More parents than usual are trying to keep their children out of the classroom this year in the wake of a Wisconsin Supreme Court Decision that created a legal loophole [*GWS* 33 & #34].... Carl Carmichael, executive assistant to the state superintendent of public instruction, said he has received about a dozen letters from parents who say they'll educate their children at home this year.... Because the court found that state law does not adequately define what a school is, anyone can claim that home is a school and sidestep attendance laws, Carmichael said.... To close the loophole, the DPI is working with the legislators to come up with a definition of 'school.' He said the DPI does not anticipate a wave of truancy this fall, but he urged quick action on the definition in Madison..." —DR

Thoughts After Six Years

From Sue of Seattle:

This is written to you folks, of course, but also to the people who are curious about home (un-) schooling older kids.... We are beginning our seventh year of homeschooling. I have to tell you, in the beginning we had few doubts and lots of support for keeping the kids home. For starters we were legal—until Peter turned eight, compulsory age in Washington State. We enjoyed a lot of interest and support among our friends. I was still active in La Leche League, a real breeding ground of sympathy. Alternative lifestyles were "in," we were *doing* it. I developed convincing answers for those who asked the basic questions: "What about the social life?" "Don't you want them to go to college?" "You mean you *like* having them home all day?"

I think Peter was about 4th or 5th grade (we say things like that, "4th grade," "after school," etc.—it's a survival trick) when I realized the children of our "supporters" never got any older. Well, of course they did, but then they went to school ("Oh, sure," the reasoning goes, "I think schools in *general* are bad, but this is a good district and his teacher is just a *darling*") or the parents got interested in aerobic dancing or calligraphy, and new families with younger children took over. Homeschooling workshops I've been to were attended primarily by parents of preschoolers. Ditto for homeschooling sessions at LLL conferences, ditto for many of the contributors to *GWS*.

The questions from other people became less friendly and I no longer had the answers: "How will they measure up in junior high?" "Yeah, and what *about* the social life? What *about* college?" "What will you do when you get caught?" The doubts all along had been other people's doubts, but now I was reaching a point where there were no reassurances any more, and the other people's doubts were getting larger and more threatening.

"What about a *pro*gram? They have to be in a definite program. How do you expect them to keep up with their grade level?"

"They better buckle down and learn that cursive. Twelve years old and he can't even sign his name."

"You really should try to get legal. Is that what you want to teach them—dishonesty?"

"Tell me, dear, how long is this nonsense going to continue?" "Do you want them to be left out of *every*thing?"

"You're not stimulating them enough. In school they would be *chal*lenged. How do you expect them to know what's out in the world?"

God knows there are days when I don't know if the way we are going is better, days when I feel like we aren't doing anything, that I've abandoned them to raise themselves. They aren't especially creative. They don't do things like make total ecosystems in apple crates in the backyard that get monitored with instruments made from garden hose and mason jars. They don't publish their own newspapers or put on plays. Sometimes, many times, they're just plain bored. And I wonder: is it possible that school stimulates creativity in a way that just plain old *life* cannot?

I've never really done anything with them. But every time I think of something to teach them they already know it. Where do they learn all that stuff?

"Around."

The causes of the American Revolution? Come on. The structure of the atom? Long division?

A shrug. "Books, I guess."

"What do they do all day?" people ask me. Why is it that I don't know? *Why is it that I don't care*? We don't keep journals or go on field trips or categorize the day's activities into subject areas. I can't stand the dead smell of all those fake thought up things.

I see my children and I see the neighbor children and I see such a difference between them. But maybe the difference is simply that they are mine. And now, even to me the list of what I want for them is sounding more and more esoteric: for them I want excellence, a love of learning, an excitement with life.

"They will not be disciplined. . . . They will not have good study habits. . . . They will not know what they need to kno. . . ." (What do they need to know?)

"They will miss out on the social life of high school. . . . They will not learn how to play football. . . . They will miss riding the bus. . . ."

But there's no turning back now. I am in free-fall, just before it's time to open the chute. What if it won't open? *What if it isn't there*?

What I have always wanted for my children is freedom. But there is more. I want them to be able to survive in the natural world, and I want them to be able to survive in the man-made one. I want them to know where their contributions can best be made. I want them to have the skills for acquiring knowledge and the skills for assimilating it, the courage to change, because each new piece of knowledge requires a reorganizing within oneself. I want them to know how to read and how to type, how to use the library, how to write and speak articulately, how to solve problems. I want them to know how to get along on their own: how to manage their finances, hold on to a job, make or buy and mend their clothes. I want them to have good health habits, know first aid, CPR, how to cook, how to get from place to place. I want them to know how to "use their heads." I want them to have the skills and experience to feel comfortable in any setting, to feel comfortable with themselves. I want them to know themselves, to hunger and strive for excellence. I want them to have strong characters and clear values, to have self-confidence and a vigor that thrives. I want them to have endurance, self-discipline, ability to discern value, hope, and the capacity for joy.

"How do you know they're getting everything they'll need?" we're often asked. "How do you know they're keeping up?" This is a hard one to answer, because the concern springs from the fallacy that there exists some certain body of knowledge that children "must have," some collection of facts and theorems that make up the official curriculum, that over the years the certified teachers must manage somehow to pour into their empty brains. And this is simply not so.

It is neither the task nor the goal of true education to acquire a *particular* body of knowledge, but rather to sharpen the skills of acquisition and focus awareness on the capabilities of the brain. I wonder if maybe those people in charge of education don't really understand, themselves, the functioning of the brain's subconscious levels. It is not necessary to bring up and acknowledge all brain activity at a *conscious* level. And maybe here is where structured school programs run into trouble so much of the time, by messing around trying to get people to organize in the conscious part of their brains what is already (and *naturally*) working so well unconsciously. . . . Even alternative schools and homeschooling programs are guilty of this, with their daily journals that pigeonhole by subject the day's activities and discussions. What greater richness can be had and preserved by letting the memories stay all jumbled as they are where they can long be enjoyed, and allowing to be done at the subconscious levels of the brain the job of sorting and assimilating.

We want them to learn to "use their heads," by which we mean solve problems with resourcefulness. One day at the small print shop where I work one of our best customers brought in a booklet to be printed and bound: twenty-four pages plus cover with photographs on each page, 200 copies. Our normal turnaround for such a job would have been about a week, certainly several days. This was an emergency: they needed to put the finished booklets on a plane in less than two hours.

We accepted the job. Mission impossible.

The first several minutes were spent discussing how best to tackle the project. Every idea was aired, even the impractical, since often it is the suggestion of something crazy that triggers the unexpected ideal solution. When the plan was formulated we all set to work, working efficiently but carefully, each of us drawing on our store of accumulated knowledge in a kind of serendipity of useful information that is experienced, I'm sure, by others who work in high-pressure jobs. We finished the booklets, to the customer's great relief and satisfaction, in one hour and twenty-five minutes.

The experience was exhilarating and satisfying. By confronting the challenge each of us learned something new about his craft. We pleased an influential customer. We were well paid. It was a *real* challenge. It was a *personal* challenge in every dimension. Our confidence, as individuals and as a company, was built up by having the chance to test our limits. By focusing on our resources, i.e., our nerve and our wits, directly at the problem, we learned something new and valuable about ourselves.

Children need these kinds of challenges. The challenges must be their own, and they must be *real*. When the challenge is set up, a fake, not much of value can be gained. It doesn't count, it isn't real. Something's wrong when I'm congratulated for meeting a phony challenge. I've been conned. Or else it's you who have been conned, you the teacher for thinking something was important when it was not.

Aha! *Here* is the true crime in education, not the lies we tell Grandma and the neighbors about where the kids go to school, not our hiding from the truant officer, but this insidious weakening of moral fiber, this pretending that something (grades, test-scores, completing assignments, one set of facts, one list of books, one way of doing things) is important when it is not, this clouding of our sense of what is indeed real.

People, children, learn by having the opportunity to *do*. But something precious is lost when there is a teacher there directing things, evaluating. It is a matter of focus. In a situation such as at the print shop, the focus was on the problem itself; there was only that one measure of success. But in a classroom, in the challenge of a task set before the student(s) by the teacher, there is a double image, a competitiveness; and even in a one-to-one situation there is a desire to please.

When Peter was eleven he made a bet with an older friend (she was twenty) that he could go from Easter until the 4th of July without eating any sugar. No one else was involved on either side—this was strictly between the two of them. We continued to eat as much sugar as ever, sometimes even affectionately trying to tempt him to give in. He was scrupulously honest. It was as though he did not even *feel* any temptation to cheat. It was his own personal challenge, a matter of honor, a matter of achievement, and he did it.

This is how people grow—we want to know ourselves, know our limits, test them, and stretch them.

Why is it that we fear boredom and lack of structure so? Why do we get so nervous when there are no visible signs of "progress," when "he just bats around the house; I can't get him interested in anything"?

The truth, I think, is that we all need a lot of wild empty space. We reach plateaus when things are all of a sudden outgrown, and then we need to stop awhile, survey the lay of the land. We *need* those periods of boredom, damn it, *kids* need them, and they need to be allowed to work through them on their own. If I or someone else is always standing there, ready to shove something new and stimulating at them as soon as they slow down, where will there ever be the chance to stand apart and hold a finger to the wind? To contemplate the inner workings of themselves? School, even "homeschool," is no better than television—read this, listen to that, watch this clever thing over here, do what you're told and win gold stars/good grades/prestige/money from Mom and Dad. Whatsamatter, sonny, doesn't this interest you? Not to worry, just turn the dial, I'll offer you two dozen more tantalizing electives, no trouble for you, just walk through that door, read this book (this *particular* book), I'll entertain you with a lecture/video/Shakespeare to a rock beat, you can do it and still be a stranger to your soul.

I can't stop believing it is the nature of the species to seek excellence for its own sake.

I worry about a lot of things. I worry about depth. Is there depth in their lives? Do they feel the things I felt on my way to being me? I *don't* worry about cursive, but Grandma does. In my world, when people want to make something legible, they type. I can see how typing can be a useful skill. Even more important, for me, is some sort of personal scrawl, some quick personal shorthand (I don't always have a typewriter handy). But *cursive*? The last thing I wrote in cursive was a book report in 9th grade, twenty years ago.

We see through frames. For Grandma, writing in cursive is a symbol of being educated. That is what she has made her frame out of. To her the kids are illiterate. But her frame is a fallacy. Still, she can't let go of it. (By the way, they *do* know cursive. But they don't use it very often so it looks pretty raw.)

Or, perhaps it is just her need for visible proof. Okay, so look at them. They're happy, healthy. They read voraciously, have interests, hobbies, skills, ideas of things they want to try, glimpses of worlds that intrigue them. They get along with people of all ages, are popular with the kids in the neighborhood, even older teenagers (surprise), wear designer jeans and Nike shoes and say things like "awesome" and "grody" and listen to "Men at Work." They read (did I mention that? The G.E.D. exam is based almost entirely on reading) and can split and stack the firewood and calculate the cordage and figure the gas mileage on the cars and budget their earnings from part-time jobs and run out of money before the end of the month like everybody else.

They're fine. And I wonder: *what am I worried about?*

And yet—

And yet it *is* a leap of faith. You have to believe in certain basic things and then just trust. Believe in freedom first of all, and the self-motivating powers and the urgency of the soul to grow. And the power within the child to become one with the earth and his fellow beings—and maybe that's where all education leads, ultimately, to a binding back together of all people in a spirit of life, and a seeking to understand the universe.

More Long-Time Homeschoolers

From Maria Holt (ME), who has been homeschooling since 1973:

The most important thing I want to impress upon people about our family school is this: *we never taught anything*. My husband refused to allow it. The closest I came to "teaching" our four sons was during the evening reading-aloud session. We've waded, mulled, or stormed through the Old Testament, *War And Peace*, and *Moby Dick*, among many, many other classics. It was never required to come and listen, and one of our sons gave it up, preferring to read to himself. We provided for and supported the boys—never taught them. Their studies grew out of their own interests. They used all the local libraries and we sent for books from the state library. At one time, they spent months just fixing up an old fishing boat. We never really knew *what* they were learning! My husband says we won't know the success or failure of our homeschooling for a very long time, if *ever*. We always said they'd "graduate" from the home school when the direction of their lives was outward from home. And that is what happened. They have all managed the flight out without serious bruises. They all know how to work hard. They all get along well with all kinds and ages of people. What I treasure most is this: I see them liking learning. . . . They all have acquired interests and skills that do and will provide enjoyable learning for them now and throughout their entire lives, no matter what they do to earn a living. I think this is becoming more and more important in modern society.

Our children always knew we'd support them if they chose to re-enter public school. When two of them decided to go to college they made "getting into formal higher education" part of their curriculum and did it entirely on their own. They studied the college entrance requirements, brushed up in areas where they felt they were weak, and then did *very well* in school. *This* on a background of *no* formal teaching or schooling since second or third grade. The youngest, who "graduated" this past June, worked during his last two years at home at a local restaurant to earn money for flying lessons. (He had taught himself to read through a stamp collection and magazines about flying. He is a good historian. His specialty is the American Civil War, which, for him, developed from the stamp collection.) Now, at 18, he has been hired as a flight instructor at a respected flying school at Bradley Field in Hartford, Connecticut.

Here, I want to reminisce: Once, long ago when this particular son of ours was still a little boy, two officials of the state education department came to visit us quite unexpectedly. One of them pointed his finger at him and said he thought he was missing the boat by not going to dances and playing sports, and further, "Don't you think you'll grow up having the opinions of your parents and nobody else if you don't go to public school?" Our son looked a little surprised and said quietly, "No, I think that is a misconception. I have my own thoughts." I think that impressed our visitors as one of them said to me as they took their leave of us, "You have unusual children." I returned, "That is where you make your worst mistake." And I meant it. Our children are "average." There is not a genius among them.

All of our sons have registered to vote and are interested in government and current events. And, too, the youngest (longest in homeschool) is a member of our County Democratic Committee. I *am* a proud parent and not ashamed to say that our children have developed into valued members of their community.

Since we were not allowed to "homeschool" without getting an approved school status and my having to qualify for teacher certification (no one needed me to, except the state) we officially opened our doors to other parents and children in 1974. They had always been open on an unofficial basis as I documented in my "Genesis." We didn't particularly want to do this on an official basis at first, but we found people coming to us, often in desperation and exhaustion and distress. Their children simply were not growing and learning in the public schools.

Our school, with the help of the King Farm of Woolwich across the Kennebec River, became a haven for many children and parents. . . . All the families cooperated and we found we didn't need very much money. We have voluminous records of the success of the venture.

So, it is true, I did "teaching" at last. But hardly the kind that is offered up in public schools and not a *bit* of it did I attribute to my teacher certification studies. My life experiences and the rearing of five children gave me most of what I needed. And then, we were *all* teachers and *all* students! I did my share of self-motivated learning. Sometimes I thought we should have called ourselves "The I-Don't-Know-Let's-Find Out-School."

The children who were with us and have since moved away and re-entered public school are all doing well, according to their parents as well as by their own words. A few say they don't like public school much but can do the work and are making friends. (This is in direct contrast to their earlier public school problems and distress, sometimes related to home difficulties and sometimes not.) One child has decided to get out of public school and do home learning again. His younger brother decided to "stay in." (That's literally true as he lives in a little house without electricity and with an outhouse and by the beautiful sea where he hardly ever came indoors if he could help it! A real child of nature who seemed to blend right in with the wild creatures of the woods all around him. I think it must be hard for him to sit still so much of the day, but he is used to making decisions and living by them. He is only eight, but was allowed freely to come to this momentous decision and was able to do it with confidence. This is one of the great benefits of homeschooling.).

Custody Battle

From Gail Garuti-Frazer (MA):

Bianca (12) and Tanya (11) and I are starting our third year of homeschooling this fall. We have been through what many divorced homeschoolers must fear. I want to finally share what has happened while I look forward to our first free year together.

In early spring of 1981, I sent Bianca and Tanya's father a copy of your interview in *Mother Earth News* [#64, avail. here, $3] and a note that I was thinking of homeschooling. . . . He made it clear the subject was closed and he wanted to hear no more.

I have been on my own since 1975 when the girls were only 3 and 4, with sole custody. I simply went ahead as I had planned and didn't bother him again.

That fall, when he realized we were homeschooling, I can only say he freaked. He found that as long as I had sole custody there was nothing he could do. (It is interesting to add here that he did not know I had sole custody.) In Feb. '82, I received a Notice of Complaint for Modification, and found that he was suing for joint legal and physical custody. This began a year-long nightmare for the girls and me.

Let me explain for supporters of joint custody that not only have I raised the girls alone for eight years but that their father and I are diametrically opposed on everything. Examples: I serve juice, he serves Coke; I raise the girls as devout Catholics, he ridicules the church; they watch educational TV at home and Dukes of Hazzard at his house; there are no books in his house while at home we have walls and walls of books and all read often (I could go on forever).

When their father remarried in 1981, the girls began staying overnight regularly on Fridays because his wife started picking them up. When we started to homeschool he said he wanted them both Friday and Saturday nights so he could "counteract my influence." I didn't argue, hoping he would leave us alone otherwise. It is very hard for the girls to travel in and out of these "dimension warps" every week.

After being served with the Complaint for Modification, our days became a whirl of lawyer meetings, court dates, searches for documents, asking people for letters of recommendation, and finally an investigation by a court-appointed lawyer.

At a closed chambers hearing the judge stated that there would be no way he would grant joint custody to people who weren't even on speaking terms. This should have been a comfort to me but I interpreted it as a total win/lose situation. The stress seemed unbearable and I plummeted into depression with only enough drive to continue collecting letters of support and evidence on homeschooling. (At one point my lawyer said since I anticipated everything and had materials before he asked, why did I need him?) During the day I could only watch as the girls and I plodded through textbooks. I was terrified of going off on day trips, afraid *he* would accuse me of not following the schedule. We became as bound as our books.

The court-appointed lawyer finally submitted reports to the lawyers and the judge. A week before our final trial date, my lawyer called me in and read the report to me. Not only was it recommended that I retain sole custody, but the children, their home, their upbringing, their activities, and most importantly their homeschooling were addressed in such glowing adjectives there could be no doubt the judge would find in my favor. My lawyer also told me that the girls' father was dropping the suit.

It all ended with him losing some of what he had before, the girls and I losing a year of peace of mind, and my lawyer gaining $650.

So you see why this third year will be our first real year of homeschooling freedom. Best wishes to single parents and couples with their homeschooling efforts. Don't give up because someone else wants you to, ever.

Taking Teens Out

Borgny Parker (CT) writes:

From the beginning, our principal was cooperative and supportive. He helped by informing the school board and we were given permission in October, and Abigail did not have to attend school in the interim.

We chose to work through Clonlara School (MI) and we started off thinking that we would be following the public school day at home. That did not work well at all. Both David and I saw the need to keep our distance because we were putting Abi under the same pressures she was seeking to avoid. What evolved was our own blend of non-schooling, I guess. We saw Abigail take off in different directions by herself. She was very interested in American colonial history. She was constantly reading and very motivated to investigate. She read *Pride And Prejudice* several times and during this past year began to type her own copy of the book. This she is still doing. Of course, in the process she has learned to type quite well. [See DR's letter, "Learning to Type," *GWS* 12.]

The biggest change last year I think was Abigail's ability to take on something and continue with it until it is done, not just short-term projects or reports but other things as well. She has managed the raising and breeding of rabbits for a year, caring for and feeding them each day, logging their births, breeding times, keeping track of each litter from three different does. The number of rabbits is growing—the population now is 18 and expanding. This is so valuable, the ability to carry through on things. It is something that will help her in many other areas.

Another bonus of homeschooling is that Abigail and I have gotten to be real friends and much of the widening rift between us has gone. She is certainly her own person but that helps us to enjoy one another. It has been an important and wonderful year.

Now we are beginning high school at home through the University of Nebraska. Abi is looking forward to it. We will have a more demanding or structured program with an outside supervisor; but she is ready for that and, I might add, eager. But we want to preserve the same feeling about learning no matter what program.

From Marilyn Munsey (MA):

Thought I'd let you know about Mike's first year of homeschooling. He has been studying through courses of the American School, and has been able to learn on his own, at his own pace. It has turned out to be a good experience for him. He had finished the ninth grade by March's end, and then was able to make a dent on tenth grade work. I would heartily endorse the American School [850 E 58th, Chicago IL 60637] to anyone with a child in grades 9 through 12. It is run in a competent, professional way, and best of all the textbooks are brand new—no graffiti written on torn pages!

During the school year, I sent quarterly reports from the American School regarding Mike's progress to the attendance officer in Newton. And at this point in time it seems that the end-of-year testing will not be carried out. As requested, I called the attendance officer in June and was told that he would get back to me. I have heard nothing more. In fact, this past year has been so non-threatening that I now wonder why I was so afraid of those "school people" in the first place. We have been lucky to have had things work out. . . . I still remember your kind help to me while we were going through the turmoil—it meant a lot to me at the time.

On Teen Social Life

From a Tennessee mother:

Years ago I reasoned that I had "taught," nurtured, loved, encouraged my babies to take steps at their own paces, let them decide when they were ready to accomplish things they saw a need to accomplish—and that needn't stop arbitrarily at age 5 or 6 or 7. I have continued that role and they have continued to enjoy being themselves, pursuing their interests, and learning to be warm, affectionate human beings. They have never been in school and have had but very limited encounters with their peers (children of friends, library activities, etc.).

We enjoy one another, not only love but like each other. We have no "lessons," none of mine played the piano when they were 18 months or read when they were 3; none of them had read Dickens at 8 or showed any other feats of genius. They haven't knocked the top out of any standardized test (they haven't been given one, for that matter), but if there were tests for what I think education is all about (self-esteem, sensitivity to others' feelings, morality, etc.) I have no doubt they would score at the top. They have learned responsibility by having it. They have never been required to even wean or sleep alone unless they were ready to initiate such a move. We are all pleased so far with the results.

Oh yes, about "socialization," this summer has provided new sources for branching out. I have five children, ages "almost 15, 12, 10, 7, and 2. Since we keep our home education low key (our reply when asked "What school?" is "They have a tutor"), we are limited during the school year as to activities outside the home. My oldest decided she would like to do volunteer work at a nursing home so we found one nearby that would take her at age 14. She works two days a week from 10 a.m. until 3 p.m.. The residents adore her and the feeling is mutual. The nurses have only praise for how well she has fit right in and all think she must be 18. She talks to residents, takes them for walks, holds hands, feeds them. The residents look forward to her coming. Most of all, Lauren loves to hear their stories of the old days. (We also like to talk about the criticism I heard that if my children don't learn to get up to go to school every day, they'll *never* be disciplined to get up and go to a job when they are older! Balderdash, as Ashley Montagu says. Lauren voluntarily goes to bed before any of the rest of us so she can get up, get ready, then get me up to take her.)

My two older ones had a chance to be in a play which was given at a convention in another city this summer. They had never done anything like it before, but took to it easily and thoroughly enjoyed it. The club that put on the play is comprised of all ages of people, Jennifer and Lauren being the youngest. The play was a howling success before the banquet crowd of 900 people. I think they may have a flair for this kind of thing, but I can see that their strong sense of security and knowing themselves really well has helped a great deal.

Lauren auditioned and got a part on the spot (unusual, I was told) in one of the local children's theater productions. She has been with groups of her peers on a regular basis for weeks now. My husband said he had to laugh about his "poor unsocialized daughter" as he left her at rehearsal recently and watched her joking, moving so easily amongst them—not at all the picture of a socially retarded youngster hanging on the fringes, standing alone, apart from the crowd. Sure, Lauren still doesn't like the image of the typical or preppy teen and doesn't want to be lumped in that group, but she finds that she can relate, interact and find ways to communicate with the ones she works with. "It was actually less of a problem than I had anticipated," she told me.

Jennifer (12) enrolled in a stagecraft class at the same children's theater. She was singled out by the adults in charge to be stage manager for one of the plays because she seemed so mature and responsible. They had thought she was 14 or 15. She, too, works with the children very well and has had a summer of new experiences.

In the book *One Straw Revolution*, Mr. Fukuoka found that his trees that had been pruned and sprayed for insects for years, when left to grow naturally were weak and succumbed easily to insects and disease. . . . The ones that were never pruned and sprayed took longer to produce but were hardier and more productive overall. Men in charge of groves wanted more control of the tree's productivity and did not want to wait for results, thus the interference. Sound familiar?

Sylvia Young in Utah writes:

We have 10 children with the oldest in high school and the youngest at 8 months. . . . A question that was asked in *GWS* 33 was, does a homeschooled child around 11 to 13 become restless and want more socially. I would answer, "Yes." . . . They seem to want to extend out more to peers. . . . I have gone to the extra expense of art and dance classes and planned many field trips to make the home school seem worth staying in. About this time I notice all sorts of new avenues and talents blossoming, new hobbies surfacing and wanting to be tried—a lease of life that is exciting. But I don't seem to be able to keep the momentum going to keep them from saying, "I'm bored." They think going to school will solve that bored feeling.

My 15-year-old decided she wanted to go back to school and we compromised with a few classes. She took her driver's ed, band, and a religious class. She was on campus quite a bit, staying in the library during classes. At times she was made to feel that she was not learning anything so she had better go to all her classes and really learn. But she is definitely not going to give up her freedom.

Also last year we worked out a trade with a young mother with a college degree in math and computer science to exchange lessons for babysitting. It worked out great. My daughter (who had left school with a poor grade in math and a teacher who ridiculed her openly) jumped in with great vigor in algebra, geometry, and a college computer course.... Her teacher kept telling me that she just could not keep her from devouring everything she could in math.... I am torn on the subject of computers. Thank goodness for a neighbor with one, for exposure.

Let me mention here how well the Boy Scout program has offered a very excellent way to get an education. If you have ever read any of the merit badge pamphlets, you will see that they are small and efficient summaries of every interest or subject a boy would want to be exposed to. Plus, as an extra bonus, if needed, he receives a badge in a court of honor in recognition for his efforts in fulfilling the requirements.... You really get in and learn about botany, biology, photosynthesis, etc., all in the Environmental pamphlet.... The summaries are geared to junior high level, I think. But I have enjoyed learning from them as an adult.

And from Pennsylvania:

The past three years, we homeschooled through our local school district, but last July when we went in for our summer meeting with our local school officials, they turned us down, since both of our boys are now in high school, and my certificate legally only allows me to teach from kindergarten to sixth grade.

We were disappointed and wondered what we could do so late in the season, so we looked into schools with homeschooling programs. We found one fairly close to us, went to see them, and the boys were enrolled.

Part of our security coverage was to use a correspondence school for curriculum and grading, but after using the curriculum for only three weeks, we found ourselves so tied down to trying to pass tests, and trying to get everything super neat so we wouldn't have to do things over, and trying to get everything labeled correctly so it would be counted in the first place, that we felt that we would all be crazy if we didn't change. We had spent quite a bit of money on the curriculum and their tutoring, so we hated to give up so quickly. We stuck it out for nine weeks, called the school where our boys were enrolled and asked if we could quit with the correspondence school and work on what I had originally planned for the year. It was approved, and we were very relieved. It had been just like school!

We did use the correspondence school's books, since we paid for them, then we went on and covered everything I had planned, and the boys also were able to work on projects and read books they found along the way that interested them. I know that some people truly enjoy using correspondence schools, but it was not for us.... It was unbelievable how much we covered on our own.

Since our older son is interested in starting a computer business in the near future, we have been able to give him computer courses and electronics courses for credits toward graduation. We can hand pick what we specifically need for each boy, and we always have them help decide what courses they want to take within the state requirements for graduation.

The boys wanted me to write to you about "Asks About Teens," *GWS* 33. You see, each year in the summer they want to look into schools (with small enrollments) because they consider each year whether they want to return to school. They do not enjoy many large group activities, mostly small group ones, *but* they do miss having the opportunity to sort through a bunch of kids their own age and find some good friends with the same interests. We do not have many children in our neighborhood the same ages as they are, in fact, there is only one.

I'm not sure that teenagers who are restless would benefit any more or less from homeschooling than from public or private schooling. To us, it seems more of an emotional circumstance than a schooling problem. The boys are sometimes restless and say they want to be around children their own age, but mostly, when we talk about it more deeply, they want to be around those with the same interests as they have. You see, in elementary grades everyone was just basically interested in being together and playing, now they are changing into adults who have definite ideas about things and about what they want out of life.

The turmoil is a difficult one. . . . Sports activities and clubs serve to pass time and to let the kids be with others of their ages, but they do not necessarily fulfill their desire to have "one good friend my own age who enjoys many of the same things I do, and with whom I could get together as often as I wanted."

The boys have decided each year to continue homeschooling. We have it too good here at home. They are free to choose their courses, work at their own pace, and spend many hours working on projects and research they want to do for themselves. Their play or leisure time is basically up to them too, for as they need to eat or rest or change to another subject, they are free to take the time to do so whenever needed. No school can really beat that.

They wonder sometimes if they will space-warp through their teenage years, so we are giving much attention to socialization this year, and praying that the Lord will open up circumstances to meet these deep inner needs for our boys. I think many children in their early teen years do make a trade-off—about homeschooling it's "Well, I don't get to be with a lot of kids, but I get to be really free academically," and about going back to school, the trade-off is, "Well, I don't get to be free academically, but I get to be with lots of kids." It really depends on the child's priorities. . . . I feel children should be left to decide what the priorities are and aim at them, and with the option that if they find it wasn't what they wanted, they can change again, without recrimination.

Success Stories

From Telia Nunn (CA):

A few months ago I listened to John and Joseph Chilton Pearce speak in Vista, CA. That day had more impact on me than any day in years and I thank you both. I had taught both public and private Montessori school. Despite being a public school teacher, I thought I had escaped buying into the public school philosophy because I worked with gifted kids in the arts and created a very experiential program with artists from the community, or taught continuation school. That night I saw how I doubted that kids could learn *enough* without school. Worse yet, I began to see how my children felt that way. I began to see the reason behind a lot of the things I felt weren't right about my children's education.

My husband, a continuation high school principal, also heard you that night. Over the last months, we have overcome doubts and fears as we have learned, read *GWS* and *Teach Your Own*, and done some hard looking. We had several talks with our friend of 15 years, John Boston (CA)—I think you know him. We have decided to homeschool our children, two of whom have learned to be straight A students (who also have headaches and are often angry during the school year), and I never felt happier or looked forward with such joyous anticipation to how much *I* will learn and experience—and of course to the release into naturalness of learning for the girls. It is all one, this connection in a family, of learning, happiness, freedom, peace—we're in it together, and always have been. Leaving school is like taking down the last barrier to our connection with each other.

[From a later letter:] Two weeks ago, I told my daughters' principal I would be keeping the girls home from school and what led to my decision. In no way did I categorically put down public schools. I said rather that I could work with my children in a way that the schools might like to but cannot because of numbers and the prohibitive nature of institutions. I talked about wanting more experiential kinds of learning with the children setting the subject matter and pace. I then eased into the adverse effects of much of the social interaction and competition both social and academic.

Well—lo and behold—the principal agreed with me completely about my observations and said he would support my endeavors in any way he could. His support was not just official, but warm and genuine. . . . The district agreed to lend me any non-consumable materials I needed. The principal said my children could partake of school activities if they wanted as long as fulltime students weren't bumped from the class and the teacher was agreeable. The principal also asked me to loan him *Teach Your Own*. He's most interested.

All of the above was facilitated by the fact that I have a teaching credential. . . . So I will work towards making this a positive foundation for others who follow. Last Sunday our local *Times Advocate* newspaper did a huge spread on education including a piece on homeschooling with photos of John Boston. It stated there are 200 homeschooling families in San Diego County. . . . Anyone from the area who wanted to register with my "private school" for homeschooling purposes is welcome.

Loretta Heuer (MA) writes:

In June we met with the Superintendent and were pleasantly surprised to find him accepting, cooperative, and well-versed in the legalities of homeschooling even though we're the first family in Holliston to exercise the option for home education.

Like the McClymonds (*GWS* 34), we sent our copy of the "Mass. Memo" [avail. here, $1] along with our introductory letter. However, unlike them, we were not especially eager to discuss *why* we were choosing homeschooling. This approach was based on the section of the Mass. Memo which states that the parents' reasons for seeking the alternative may not be part of the approval process. Granted, we have deeply rooted reasons for wanting to keep Tad out of the schooled mainstream. But it was wiser, we felt, to concentrate on curriculum, materials, etc.—the issues which the school department had the legal right to consider. Meanwhile, we hoped that from our manner of approaching them and in our dealings with them we would be viewed as friendly, competent, and caring people.

This year Tad will be first grade age. However, since he is still technically eligible for kindergarten and since kindergarten is not mandated in Mass., we were not required to seek formal approval. That will come next year, but we plan to document this coming "school year" in a way that will ease the school's concerns about the level of supervision needed in the future. We intend to continue the system we used last year: a log book, a portfolio, and periodic anecdotal reports of Tad's progress. (This year we'll be using the town's reporting system which includes plenty of space for teacher comments. I *like* writing anecdotal reports; it's a joy to observe the process and to recall particular incidents that highlight the larger picture.)

We looked over the K–3 curricula but what we actually presented was a list of broad objectives and anticipated projects. . . . I think we were as concrete as they needed us to be while maintaining the flexibility we require.

We'll be able to utilize the school for any performances, courses, library work, etc., that may fit into our program.

This summer, in fact, Tad took a series of workshops given by the town. His choices were pottery, computers, and woodworking. We found it interesting that he selected areas where he'd be using equipment we don't have here at home. He had a good time learning and sampling. His only complaint was that the nastiness, name-calling, etc., displayed by some of the kids spoiled the climate and his chance of learning more. Quite frankly, I have never seen him so shocked and angry!

On reading. Tad devised an interesting method of self-instruction last fall when he was just beginning to read. During the weekly drives to my obstetrician's office, he would sit in the back seat of the car reading silently but spelling out the words he didn't know. He knew when he needed help, how to get just the amount of help he needed and how to avoid any well-intentioned reading lesson from me!

Interesting, too, that he taught himself to read silently whereas all the reading systems that I'm familiar with consider oral reading the first step.

From a South Carolina parent:

On June 9, we met with our superintendent and his assistant. The superintendent said that philosophically, he could see nothing wrong with what we wanted to do. He said he'd like to monitor us by testing the girls when the schoolchildren took the required tests. This was to check on the girls' progress and to help in working with any future situations that come up. The assistant wanted more details on our curriculum and mentioned visiting us each semester.

The superintendent said he wanted to help. His main concern was that the girls were educated. . . . Naturally, we were very pleased and extremely thankful over the outcome of this meeting! We feel blessed to have a cooperative superintendent.

And from Andrea Blackly (MA):

Sarah is five this year but is not going to kindergarten. I decided that in such a small town it would be best not to try to hide anything; I think that would only antagonize the people who think they are in charge. When we received an application for kindergarten registration, we wrote back to the principal innocently asking for the appropriate form, saying that Sarah was attending homeschool. We didn't ask, we just told them. The principal called the next day to set up an appointment.

We went ready to defend ourselves, but she was very supportive. She said she would probably keep her children out of school if she had any. She said a few somewhat derogatory things about her school which we neither agreed nor disagreed with, having decided ahead of time that we wouldn't say anything against the school. She offered us the support of her K–3 staff and any materials and equipment we want.

We don't have to do anything really for this year, because Sarah doesn't have to be in school until she is six. Next March we are supposed to submit our proposal to the school committee. One member of the school committee is a friend of mine and is for us all the way. Another is likely to be on our side, although I haven't discussed it with her directly. The third will be newly elected next spring. The people running for and getting elected to the school committee lately seem to be mothers who are dissatisfied with the schools and want to change them, as opposed to the businessmen who have run things in the past and are more interested in budgets than in children. I know the superintendent doesn't like the idea, but hopefully by next year we will have enough support to get around her.

I feel as if what we do this year is pretty important. I'd like to show them that we are serious. The principal wanted Sarah to go for screening. I agreed, thinking we might even find out something. We didn't! Sarah tested on about a third grade level, higher in vocabulary. Her strengths and weaknesses were just what we already knew. At least they have tested her and don't have to question our evaluation of her.

We are using Calvert because Sarah likes the structure, and we all like the materials. I find it very difficult to document our everyday activities as educational, only because standing back to evaluate what we are doing destroys the spontaneity of our days. Calvert is sort of an easy way to fulfill our requirements with as little paperwork as possible. We are very flexible with it, allowing Sarah to choose when and what she wants to do.

One of the problems we are experiencing is apparently universal. Abigail, who is three, wants to do all the same things Sarah does. I let her do what she can, and offer alternatives when she gets frustrated.

Sarah has just started reading books. They have a summer reading program at the library and she wanted to be part of it. The librarian was reluctant because she isn't in school yet, but Sarah insisted so they let her. She took out the first book on her list, brought it home, and sounded it out that afternoon. She read it several more times that day, to anyone who would listen, and also to herself. Now Abigail wants to read too!

Unschooler Sells Article

Homeschooler Heather Kapplow ("First Boston Family," GWS 27") had the following article published in East West Journal, *9/83. Heather says, "This is not quite up to date. I wrote it two years ago, a little after we had just starting homeschooling at the age of 9." We reprint the article with the permission of the* East West Journal:

> *My Home Is My School*—For the past century people have thought school is a building with lots of desks and a playground but now we are starting to change our minds.
>
> Many families across America are taking their children out of school and teaching them at home. Our family is one of them. I am ten years old and my sister Grace (who is seven) and I learn at home. We have done so for a few years.
>
> For about three months I worked in a museum. I helped with lots of things the other workers didn't have time to do. I like listening to Broadway musical records and singing while my father plays the piano. I study Spanish with my friends from Venezuela. I like being able to understand Spanish.
>
> Since I am at home I have more time to do what I like to do most, reading. I like to read mysteries such as Nancy Drew, the Hardy Boys, Encyclopedia Brown, and the Dana Girls mystery series. I also read *Romeo and Juliet, Hamlet, Cyrano de Bergerac,* and *The Miracle Worker*. I've thought of trying to write book reviews!
>
> In my house I am the lunch cook. I make all kinds of things like tofu salads, grilled cheese sandwiches, and noodles. I learn other things in the kitchen too. I use the stove, cut vegetables to make soup, and prepare the evening salad.
>
> I have my own method of doing math. I can do addition, subtraction, multiplication, and division. I work in workbooks as well as just everyday math. I solve the problems in my head and write the answers down on papers to save forever.
>
> Sometimes I teach myself how to do gymnastics on our trapeze bar. I hang upside down for a long time. I can stand on my hands and do back flips. Once my friend and I took apart an electric can opener and made it into an electric whirling stage. Sometimes I think up comic strips and then draw them and fill in the words. Whenever my father makes up music, I make up the lyrics.
>
> As a homeschooler I sometimes miss crowded schoolrooms and lots of other children. I just joined a Camp Fire group. Now I'll have a group of girls my own age to be with. I know I'm going to like it.
>
> I enjoy being a homeschooler very much and I will probably stay one for a long time.

A New Jersey Family

From the newsletter of the N.J. Family Schools Association:

> *Meet A Member—The Skidmore Family Of Gillette*. Carol Skidmore is a La Leche League leader in the Bernardsville group. She is also the business manager of a small Berkeley Heights centered food co-op. Her hobbies include sewing, gardening and needlework. Carol teaches cooperative games for the New Providence Recreation Department, finding that an enjoyable way to earn extra money. Often the Skidmore children come along to their mother's classes. Otherwise they visit their

grandparents who live in New Providence. Richard Skidmore is a mechanic at Bell Labs in Murray Hill. They have three children—Justin, 9, Sarah, 7½, and Natalie, 3.

Together the Skidmores have learned much about plumbing, electricity, and carpentry while finishing their basement and installing a new bathroom and, more recently, while completing a two room addition to their house. Carol has recently made slip covers for their sofa just by getting a book and following the instructions. What Richard and Carol have learned by doing this work themselves is an example of how the Skidmores hope their children will learn while being homeschooled.

Already the children are showing unusual autonomy and perseverance in some types of work. For example, Justin is a much-appreciated worker at the food co-op and helps out with counting, packaging, and other jobs more capably and responsibly than most children his age would. Justin also mows his own lawn all summer long as well as a neighbor's lawn. This past Halloween both Justin and Sarah sewed their own costumes from scratch, learning about pinning patterns, cutting precisely, and using the sewing machine with caution.

Carol writes, "We have homeschooled in many different ways these past two years. Sometimes we do a lot of academic type things and are quite structured. We use the Miquon Math course [*GWS* 14, 19] as well as Holt, Rinehart, and Winston Math. The children enjoy pattern blocks very much and have learned some computer programming in both the Logo and BASIC languages. At times we use standard reading, spelling, and languages. We visit the library at least twice a month and check out books on a variety of topics. I studied French for two years in high school and am enjoying relearning French along with my two older children, using "The Learnables" from the International Linguistics Corporation [*GWS* 31]. We do a 20-minute lesson each evening and the children find the lessons funny and enjoyable. We are now entering the third book of the course. Some day we intend to start Spanish or German using the same course.

"Occasionally we take a break from textbooks and concentrate on practical and equally important learnings such as sewing, cooking, and gardening. Most of the time we try to incorporate both ways. Just having three children around all the time can be challenging, so things are never the same.

"One thing that is usually a constant is that the children read every day. Sarah taught herself to read around her 6th birthday. I was just beginning to wonder how to start teaching her when I realized she was doing it on her own! I hope Natalie will follow the same way, but I am giving her a little bit of a start by writing her favorite words on cards for her. She recognized 25 or 30 words by her third birthday. Justin had been taught to read in school and always hated it. We now find that although reading is not his favorite activity, his dislike of it is gone."

In addition to the Skidmores' activities at home, Justin is a Cub Scout and member of the YMCA floor hockey league. Sarah is a Brownie and studies ballet. Sarah also plays the piano on her own, sometimes making rather pretty music with each hand playing a separate part. Sarah has resisted having her mother teach her piano, so Carol has been content to listen to the music that is all Sarah's own. Sarah does hear the first Suzuki tape occasionally and sometimes learns one of those songs with a friend of her own age. Both Sarah and Justin take swimming lessons at the YMCA from time to time.

The Skidmores participate regularly in *Family Schools Association* activity days. When asked what they like best about homeschooling, Sarah and Justin usually answer, "The activity days'" Carol sums up their experiences with homeschooling by saying, "Homeschooling is one of the best decisions we've made in recent years."

A Day At Home

From Janet Sarkett (AZ):

This is an account of a typical day of homeschool. Donavan (13) was, as always, the first one up. He enjoys the time to himself in the morning to exercise, cook breakfast, and complete his chores of feeding and watering the dogs, cats, and duck. Nathaniel (2) and I woke next. While I made a few phone calls, Nathaniel busied himself around the house doing this and that. He created a few telephones out of toys and other household objects—one for him and one for me. We arranged to go to the "bank" (a wooden wine keg in the living room). He got his bank book and checks from his "bill drawer" and also the stamp pad and stamps of shapes. . . . I merely acted as company.

By this time, Jeremiah (5) and Dad were getting up. Nathaniel bounded in, insisting that Dad read a book he had chosen, *Beowulf* in old English! After a few chapters, joking of Grendel, the guys moved out to the living room—a whole new scene of action. Nearly the entire floor area is built with block structures, some still under construction. There's a fire station, phone company, hospital, and I don't know what else. While breakfast was cooking, Jeremiah practiced "Twinkle, Twinkle, Little Star" on his small-sized piano. He played by ear, correcting himself as he went along. Nathaniel blew a kazoo and twanged a guitar. (We hope to buy him a small violin soon.)

Yoga exercises designed especially for children are a must at our house; the children are much more alert and calm throughout the day. After this, we all headed outside. I began to water the garden and hang clothes. A dying beetle was discovered. We discussed the life style of a bug. They patiently observed its death. Shortly thereafter, the cat brought a dead baby rabbit. I talked of how these creatures are sometimes gifts to us. Both boys were saddened and said they do not want these kinds of gifts. I wound up chasing the cat over fences and across yards with shovel in hand, hoping to bury the animal. Breathless, I declared that Nature can't be interfered with.

When we finally got to "work," the trucks (wagons) full of tools came out of the garage for the day. Nathaniel swung (I was still trying to hang clothes), then played with the hose in mud, watering the trees and the duck.

Dad came out with the power saw to make a small fence. Jeremiah and Dad sawed wood, then put up the fence, Jeremiah using his own wire cutters. Nathaniel gathered all the scraps, got his wood glue, and made two "canoes," using up all the scraps.

Jeremiah and Nathaniel went to their "saw mill." Jeremiah learned to climb a tree. They hooked up a hose in the branches for the water to run down, making a flood beneath the tree. Jeremiah, up in the tree, tightened all the branches with a pipe wrench to stop the leaks.

Jeremiah is learning to use the camera. He asked to take a picture of me writing this. I took one of him climbing his first tree. We had yogurt for lunch. Nathaniel counted them, tasted each one, and learned "blueberry," "raspberry," and "strawberry." Then back to work at the sawmill. We got a *Ranger Rick* magazine in the mail, browsed through it quickly, and filed it for nap time.

We took a break for watermelon. Nathaniel carefully picked out and counted each seed (1, 2, 3, 6, 7, 10, 14, 15). Jeremiah helped himself to herb tea in a small container just his size to minimize spills. Back again to work at the old saw mill. Now they're drilling with their own hand drills. Lots of holes in the ground. It's breezy and beautiful in the small crabapple tree.

Soon will be lots of stories and nap time. Then my time for whatever . . . cooking, cleaning, quilting, my mail-order herb business, reading books on child education, or Shakespearean plays. Now tell me, who has time for *teaching*?

My children have lots of toys, treasures (junk), and tools. They are responsible for them and do a fair job of cleaning-up and putting away.

I'm restraining myself from that adult compulsion to push information upon our children. My husband used to say that he felt as if he were student teaching and I the supervising teacher whenever he played with the kids. That's horrifying! I don't want to be referred to or thought of as a "teacher"—and I'm working on doing away with that title.

Sometimes, the kids want "formal" school. So we sit down at their table, and get out the box of school materials, mostly things that I've prepared for teaching reading, math, etc. A lesson will usually end with me sitting on the floor making sandpaper letters or gluing bright colors of felt on counters while they are far off into their own things, totally absorbed.

Today, Jeremiah awakened from his nap, asking for school. I asked what he wanted to do. He said, "Draw machines." We looked in the dictionary and read and studied diagrams of simple machines. He didn't want those—he wanted big working machines. He brought over his crane and copied it and recopied it, using an eraser and ruler, until it was perfect, with lots of details.

Growing Up Independent

Sue Karr (VA) writes:

My husband, I, Will (7), and Anna (4) live on 40 acres atop a mountain mainly because we love the wilderness. When we decided to homeschool, I was a little concerned about contact with other kids. After almost two years, I'm no longer concerned. We've found that when the kids spend a lot of time with other kids or running around to lots of places, they become disjointed. When we mostly stay home and center ourselves in our work, we become focused on who we really are and peace reigns supreme. We suspect that as they get older and pursue specific interests in more depth, they'll naturally make their own contacts with others. When I first started reading *GWS*, I suspected a little exaggeration in some of the descriptions of the kids' personalities and activities. At the risk of sounding gushy, I'm in awe of what my kids are becoming. Their relationship to us and each other has become truly beautiful. They create marvelous constructions with found objects *daily*, and any activity going on—from cooking, housework, gardening to the 140-year-old cabin we're reconstructing—they're involved. There are also days and days they're immersed together in intricate fantasies and dramas. We don't feel the need to entertain them or cart them around to activities to amuse them. They just naturally involve themselves with our work or create their own activities with incredible independence.

At Home With A Tutor

Beverly Garrett (MI) writes:

It's been exactly two years since I saw Ray Moore on a TV talk show . . . and that very day, I got the letter of notification off to the school authorities and got my children out. . . . Love keeping them home. Joanne, 17 this week, finished at 16 all subjects required by the state of Michigan—and she went to the National Institute of Florists. She graduated top of her class.

My Barbie is 12 in May. The only problem we have is finding work for her to do until she's 16. Her teacher has her into Shakespeare and she tests out at 12th grade in the literature classes (reading, composition, spelling, grammar). Math is coming along well, but more at 8th grade level. In just two years, she's grown from a frightened, defensive little third-grader into a young "teenybopper" who looks *down* at her mother and her teacher (since she's taller than we are!). . . . Oh yes, there *is* social life, music lessons, roller skating, foreign travel, art class, sewing class, church and weddings, lessons in signing for the deaf (my son can do the entire alphabet after watching Lindi on *Sesame Street*), reading Braille, going to the library, swimming lessons, doing *Annie* with the kids on the block, going to see Broadway plays, doing her own laundry, baking bread and Hungarian kaloch and cookies, playing the Lowry organ, piano, and autoharp, guitar lessons, gardening and floral arranging, making dolls (which can sell for $75) and doll clothes, shopping (all kinds), helping care for their wonderful grandfather and reading to him

(Barbie was his constant companion for three months and, for a child of 12, was an inspiration to all of us). She fills in the rest of her time helping my brother and his wife with their six-year-old and baby twins.... Barbie has been caring for them since they were brought home, and with her aunt's training, has become a qualified governess. She is also a "teacher"! Her brother has learned his shapes, colors, numbers, upper and lower case alphabet and the entire musical score of the play *Annie*, with Barbie's help. Oh, and we do have parties, so she has a great circle of friends. Many of them are pen pals, friends who have moved and still keep in touch.

Barbie's teacher, Sharrie, who works with Ronald Harrison's organization (*Educational Tutoring Northwest*, 22050 Meridian, Novi MI 48050; 348-8230), is a beautiful young woman, as well as a mother. She's like a big sister to Barbie. They do many things together—go shopping, play tennis, swim, even bake and make candies. We have grown to love her and her family. They use the telephone constantly. Plus Sharrie comes over for visits and so do we.... It's beautiful because we can make instant adjustments in schedules when necessary.

The teacher comes for 90 minutes twice a week. At the rate we're going, Barbie will graduate at 13, so I plan to reduce the tutoring to one lesson a week (I pay $18 per hour). This group is very well organized.... The director has spoken to our local authorities for us when they questioned our curriculum and the certification of the teachers.... So, it was well worth the expense, especially since these teachers are aware of what we're doing and think it's good.

Useful Legal Advice

[JH:] To a family who later won their case in court—the judge dismissed the charges against them—I sent some advice that might be useful to other families facing a hostile superintendent:

I think it might be a good idea to get down on paper as soon as you can a statement, as detailed as you can find time to make it, about what you have been doing and intend to do in the education of your children, why you are doing it that way, and how you have monitored and plan to keep monitoring the results. I would send copies of this to the Superintendent, all members of the school board, the State Superintendent (whatever his title maybe) and perhaps some of his assistants, including whoever is in charge of private schools (if there is such a position) and whoever is in charge of curriculum. A case might be made for sending a copy to the county attorney and perhaps also the state district attorney, perhaps the governor himself. These should not be blind copies, by which I mean that your statement should list at the end all persons who will receive a copy of it. This will make many of those who receive it think, "All those other people got this document, and they are probably reading it, and will expect me to read it, so I guess I'll have to." Many of them may feel that they ought to discuss it with some of the others. In other words, we want all these other officials to see this pet lawsuit of your Superintendent's as a great big pain in the neck.

It will probably also be useful, if you can't persuade the board and/or the state to drop the suit, to be able to show in court that all these educational officials *did* in fact know about your plan, your credentials, and the outstanding results you had achieved with your children. The question that will be raised in the mind of the judge will be, "Knowing all this, why did the state bring this suit?" All over the country the courts are terribly overburdened. Judges are everywhere frantically trying to find ways to reduce the enormous number of cases in which they are engulfed. Other things being anywhere equal they are likely to be very strongly prejudiced in favor of people who try to stay out of court, and against people who try to get in. And, as Justice Douglas once pointed out, judges' prejudices have a strong connection with judges' rulings. Most judges tend to look for legal reasons for ruling the way they would like to rule. In this case you can give the judge plenty of good reasons for being on your side.

Einstein Quotes

In the October '83 issue of the very interesting magazine *Science 83* ($15/yr., PO Box 10790, Des Moines IA 50340) I found these two quotes from Albert Einstein:

> The most beautiful experience we can have is the mysterious. It is the fundamental emotion that stands at the cradle of true art and true science. Whoever does not know it is as good as dead, and his eyes are dimmed.

> Direct observation of facts has always had for me a kind of magical attraction.

These quotes seem to me important, and in some circumstances perhaps very useful to homeschoolers—well worth quoting, for example, in a homeschool proposal—because they support so strongly what I have been saying about why children, above all when young, are so astonishingly good at learning. The tap root, the foundation stone, of all learning is observation, and children, at least when happy and healthy, are better observers than we are. They look at the world more intently and see it more sharply than we do precisely because it—all of it—seems both mysterious and magical to them, as it did to Einstein, and probably does to all really great scientists. One of the reasons why the compelled, controlled, competitive learning practiced in almost all schools (and too many homes) destroys so much of the learning power of children is precisely that it destroys so much of their sense that the world is magical and mysterious, and instead makes it look humdrum if not downright dangerous.—JH

PhD With "L.D."

Kathryn Finn (MA) writes:

My husband John Michael has all the symptoms of a learning disability *except* for trouble with reading. By this I mean that he mixes up words and letters when he writes and frequently writes them backwards. His handwriting can only be read by one or two of us who know him very well and he tends to stammer when he gets talking. *However*, he not only reads well but is highly educated. He has his PhD. in Nuclear Physics and is on the research staff at M.I.T. . . .

His mind is usually way ahead of his writing and talking (he doesn't stammer in a prepared talk). The main thing is that he has become quite successful in a highly demanding field anyway and it's not a problem for him. No one considers him to be handicapped. All he gets are a few jokes about absent-mindedness.

He feels that children would almost always find their minds ahead of their fingers and sees no reason why they should have to get the first draft perfect. No one demands this of adults and why should our standards be higher for children? So perhaps he can reassure some parents.

"Special Ed." Definitions

From Kathy Mingl (IL):

I thought you might like to see the letter Sue Radosti [*GWS* 32, "Surviving Ed. School" and "Improving Ed. Course") wrote to me about the definition of "hyperactivity." That was a bit of a shock, seeing that word written in connection with J.P., because it suddenly occurred to me that that's *exactly* how school authorities would see him!.

———

[From Sue's letter:] We attended a highly-recommended lecture on campus this week by a psychiatrist who spoke on "childhood stress." I'm not sure why I didn't walk out on him; I guess my cureless optimism kept me hoping he'd eventually say *something* that didn't make my blood boil! His presentation really captured the current trend among educators, at least on this campus. He talked for 30 minutes or more about "biological depression," listing all the symptoms and recommending—what else?—controlling it with drugs. *But* when he was asked to discuss the role of chemical imbalances in depression, he admitted that we really don't know much about the physical causes! He lumped "school phobia" (*GWS* 23) in with biological depression, saying that when a kid has great parents and a wonderful teacher but is developing a poor self-concept, sleeps in class, and gets headaches and stomach aches every day before school, we have to look to physical causes and cures. Since he had admitted to limited knowledge of physical causes, I don't know why he was suddenly so sure about the cause and effect sequence. It made me sick to sit there among some 200 future teachers who were blithely copying down all the symptoms of this latest childhood defect.

The story is much the same for hyperactivity: *there is no definition*, only symptoms, because they aren't really sure it exists at all! In my ed. classes, we're likely to be told once or twice that no one's sure of the causes, that no real evidence exists that there is such a thing as hyperactivity, but then we quickly rush on to the ubiquitous list of symptoms, since that's what we'll be tested over. In short, a whole army of future teachers are being trained to be pseudo-psychiatrists in the classroom, always on the lookout for the kid with the learning defect or behavioral disorder.... It's really a dangerous perspective, because it discredits the child's perceptions and creative functioning, labeling his actions as symptoms of a "problem" when they may very well be the healthiest response the kid can muster in a situation that's intolerable or threatening to him.

Here are the symptoms for hyperactivity we were given in class:

Overactivity:
An abundance of energy.
Needing less sleep than the average child.
Inability to sit still in class or at meals.
Talking a great deal.
Talking out of turn in class.
Being unusually loud.
Wearing out clothes and shoes faster than other children.
Inability to keep from touching other children's things and interfering with their activities.
Disrupting classes by clowning, etc.

Distractibility:
Refers to a tendency to:
Not get work done on schedule.
Daydream.
Be easily distracted by outside stimuli.
Be unable to attend to stories and maybe even TV.
Leaving projects unfinished in midstream.
Tune out teachers & parents when giving directions.
Unable to play with a card game, Monopoly, etc.

Impulsiveness:
Running into the street without looking.
Jumping into deep water without knowing how to swim.
Inability to save money for wanted objects.
Inability to keep secrets.
Talking sassy to teachers to show off for peers.
Doing dangerous things on the spur of the moment.

Excitability:
Being easily upset or unhappy.
Having a low frustration tolerance.
Not being able to take "no" for an answer.
Not being able to accept a delay.
Fighting over little things.
Crying more than the average child.

[DR: Later, Sue wrote us:]

I had been dreading the required "Intro to Special Ed." course ever since I first enrolled in the elementary ed. program, and now that I've finally taken it, I'm only grateful that it was during the shorter summer term so that it could be disposed of that much more quickly! I was pleasantly surprised during the first couple of weeks when we studied physical disabilities, because the instructor seemed very broad-minded and aware of the labeling issues, etc., and I learned a lot about things like spina bifida, cerebral palsy, and visual/auditory impairments. But eventually we got around to "behavior disorders," and I was appalled by the subtle shift in attitude. Suddenly, instead of adapting the environment to suit the needs of the child, the idea seemed to be to adapt the child to the environment (meaning the school environment, of course), using behavior modification or any other available technique to produce more "appropriate" behavior.

The definition we were given of a "learning disability" is as follows: "A cognitive impairment that is apparent only in the classroom and cannot be attributed to mental retardation (70 IQ or less), cultural deprivation, or a visual/auditory acuity disability." I don't know whether to cry or laugh over the obvious irony. I'm afraid it's not a laughing matter for the kids who don't fit the classroom mold.

The Mind Is Not A Muscle

The Sept. 6 issue of the *Christian Science Monitor* printed an article "Helping Your Child In Math," the kind of article you often see in newspapers. Like almost all such articles I have seen, it was full of misinformation, bad suggestions, and wrong ideas. Of all these, the worst was perhaps this:

> Does your child understand that mathematics is a skill like playing the piano or shooting free throws, and must be practiced regularly?

Wrong! 100% wrong. To think that after all these years, all these learned studies in the psychology of learning, and particularly of the mathematical learning of children, a major newspaper should print this nonsense. This false and outmoded idea is the root cause of the boring useless repetitive drudgery which makes up 95% of almost all school mathematics and which teaches almost all children to hate and fear math for all of their lives.

The mind is not a muscle. It does not have to be re-taught every day what it knows and understands. I *know* how to do multi-place multiplication, have known how for 50+ years. I do not need to do multiplication problems every day to be sure I don't forget it. *Muscles* do indeed have to be trained, and re-trained; even Heifetz did scales and exercises every day so that his fingers would hit the right notes. There is a famous old story of the musician (it has been attributed to many) who said, "If I miss a day's practice, I know the difference; if I miss two day's practice, the conductor knows the difference; if I miss three day's practice, the audience knows the difference." All true enough. But we do not have to do scales every day to remind ourselves what a scale *is*. Once we know that, we know it virtually forever.

If most people forget, as they do, most of what they are told and taught in school math classes, it is because they didn't want to learn this stuff in the first place, saw no need for it, no possible use for it, no connections between it and anything else. But more "drill" and drudgery will only make that situation worse, not better. If the schools insist on repeating this stupid mistake, as I guess they will, there's not much we can do about that. But we don't have to make that same mistake in our homes.—JH

Real-Life Learning

Toots Weier (WI) wrote:

> In our Office Practice class [at high school]. . . . I was introduced to a beast of a machine called a "marchant," used mainly for mathematics. I thought I never met any piece of office equipment as confusing and baffling as that marchant. Try as I did, I could make no sense of it. . . . I continually fought with that senseless machine, applying the teacher's knowledge and terms and methods and still that thing wouldn't behave. I gained nothing from the time wasted on struggling with it and almost crying at the confusion. A friend of mine had the same experience. I didn't give up because we were constantly being tested on it and someday we would probably have to use it in a real office, we were told.
>
> After graduating from high school, I landed a job at Mirra. I appeared for work as scheduled the first day. . . . There, by my desk, sat one of those giant machines . . . just gloating at me. My heart sank. What was I to do?
>
> There were three men and five other women in my office—all of whom were very friendly and helpful. . . . I confided almost tearfully to the

woman teaching me that I didn't know how to use that thing! She reassured me that it was easy. We sat down together at it for about a half hour. She explained a little, showed me a little, I used it and asked questions. And that was it! That's all there was to it—and it *was* easy. No fancy terms or methods were applied, because, after all, it was a simple, basic machine. And easy to use! Easy to learn! I told my friend of this and she couldn't believe me. It didn't seem possible.

[JH: Note that the "Real World" the schools worry so much about is in fact generally much more friendly and helpful than school.]

Figuring Out Magnets

From Heather Hynd ["A Good Question," GWS 27]:

Jason (now closing fast with his 8th birthday) is very interested in engines and things that move. A few months ago we saw a man playing with a remote control car. We all had a lot of fun watching that little car buzzing around all by itself. (Everyone who saw it started smiling!)

For ages, Jason thought of ways to make something move *without him touching it*. One day he got out his Legos and some magnets. He made a little vehicle from the Legos, strapped a magnet to it and with another magnet tried to pull it along. He was never fast enough to keep the magnets apart, but he kept at it. Finally, when he was beginning to tire of this, he discovered that, although magnets are attracted to each other, if he turned one over, they wouldn't stick, in fact, they seemed to have an invisible "bubble" that kept them apart. He quickly remade his car and with the "bubble" to keep the magnets apart, he happily "pushed" his little vehicle along! A far cry from the radio-controlled vehicle we first saw, but it worked enough for him. In the meantime he had spent hours working things out for himself and had learned a lot about magnets and their magical properties.

Watching Baby Learn

From an article by Nancy Plent (NJ) in the Unschoolers Network:

Eric was a baby we had given up hopes of having. I watched him appreciatively as we played together at baby things, and I tried to see the world through his eyes. I was impressed with the intensity of this small person and his passionate devotion to looking at every inch of his world. It was obvious that he was a solemn and serious scientist at work, unlocking the mysteries of salt shakers, specks of dust, and fingers that waggled when he willed them to. Plunk him down in any spot, and he made a serious study of his surroundings. Rule One became something like: let him play at whatever he chooses for as long as possible without interruption. Let him decide what's important to do.

When Eric began walking, we made some minor changes in the house so that he could move through his day feeling as competent as possible. His own door handle was installed on the back screen door, just two feet up from the bottom. An extra stair railing placed low helped him conquer the stairway early (and made us less likely to hover anxiously behind him) and the refrigerator juice shelf was placed down low. These things were easy and obvious.

When it came to "school subjects" it got a little harder to chart a course. Anything we might want to "teach" him would interrupt his own learning, the way ours had been interrupted. We were determined that he would have enough space to pursue his own directions. Afraid of doing the wrong thing, we made no effort to teach school things while we puzzled over the right way to go about it. He didn't bother to wait for us, but it took a while to notice that. We still thought we were going to have to teach him.

At the first stages of speech, his chubby finger was always aimed at something with a demanding "*uh?*" He was only satisfied when he received the name of the thing he pointed to. "*Uh?*" got him the names of the alphabet letters on his father's truck, the names of toys and household objects, and his neighborhood playmates' names.

One day in the car, I was busy trying to keep him poked back into his car seat with one hand, watch the road, and answer all of the excited "*uh?*" that filled the air. His head looked like it was on a swivel on these trips, and his eyes got especially big when a truck came toward us. On a hunch I decided to categorize trucks instead of just droning, "Yeah, big truck" when he pointed.

For several days, we went into tank truck, tractor-trailer, mail jeep, cement truck, dump truck, giving each one a specific name until I ran out of categories. A satisfied grunt and silence followed each name. And then the names started coming from him. He had learned the differences in a matter of days, and was clearly pleased and excited by it.

Giddy with "my" success, I figured we had formulated Rule Two; daily repetition promotes learning. It's the foundation of all public schooling, after all. And it's wrong. I tried the same technique with the flowers in our back yard. Every day carefully named each one, pointing and insisting with my tone of voice that he look where I pointed. No response, no repeating of the names. No remembering. No interest. Only when the interest came first was the learning as quick and thorough as it had been with the trucks. In a nutshell, I had the secret to learning. Pursue only what attracts. And truthfully, though I could tell dozens of the more subtle variations of that statement as the years have passed, that's what it all comes down to.

A Gift Giver

From Toni Blum-Cates (OR):

Leah (3½) regularly gives away her things to friends, strangers, newborn babies. She likes to wrap them up and make them into presents, or else gives them to someone immediately upon her noticing they are enjoying the thing. I have to bite my tongue to keep from saying, "But that's your favorite doll," or truck, or whatever. Of course! They are her favorites and so why wouldn't she want to share it all? Life *is* ever abundant, isn't it? Only Leah doesn't need affirmations to remind herself.

Saying "Thank You"

Only a few days before our little friend Anna Van Doren turned two, I had given her something in the office—I don't remember what it was, or whether she had asked for it. Anyway, when I gave it to her, she said, "Thank you." It was a real Thank You, a lovely little present in words, full of pleasure, affection, and gratitude. I said in reply, "Why, you're very welcome, lambkin," or something like that.

As far as I can remember, this was the first time she had ever said "Thank you" to me in response to my giving her something. The reason I mention it here is that this little person has never been *told* to say Thank You, either by her parents or any of us in the office. So why did she say it to me, if no one has told her to? How did she learn it? Because we adults always say Thank You to her when she gives us something or does something we ask her to, and because she hears us saying it to each other. By keen observation she has picked it up that when nice people (the only kind she knows) do something for each other, it is a little gift of love, and the one receiving the gift gives a little gift back. Since she wants to do what we do, she did the same thing. In time, it will become as natural as breathing.

How different from another kind of scene, which I have witnessed more times than I care to remember. A child is given something, perhaps something she or he asked for, perhaps a surprise present. As the child gazes on this gift, lost in pleasure, excitement, and curiosity, an adult voice says, often in a scolding or angry tone, "What do you say?" The child is snatched out of his world of awe and pleasure, is suddenly made to feel guilty and ashamed, hears what he understands very well is a threat—if he doesn't say "Thank you" something bad will happen to him. So, all pleasure gone, possibly even hating the present that has put him in this painful situation, he says grudgingly and sullenly, "Thank you."

Most of the parents who do this probably think and hope that they are teaching their children to feel gratitude and to show courtesy. But it is far more likely that what they are really teaching their children is only to be obsequious and servile to people more powerful than they are, and rude and overbearing to those less powerful. Some of the rudest and cruelest people I have ever seen or known are rich old people who never depart an inch from the rules of "good manners," but find ways within these rules to express in every word and gesture their contempt for everyone not their "social equals."

If I give some little gift to a child, and the parents start this what-do-you-say routine, if I know them well enough I may say, "Hey, wait a minute, give him a second to look at it." Or, if I can't say that, sometimes I can make the situation a little less painful for the child by telling him, after he has given me the required Thank You, that I thought about him before getting the gift, and that I really hope he likes it. Perhaps I may talk about what I have done with such a thing myself, or may suggest ways in which he might use it—anything to get his mind off the humiliating social event he has just been through, and back on the pleasures and possibilities of the gift itself.—JH

Competent Children

From Cindi Bigelow (PA):

Aeb (2½) is very intrigued with numbers, and is extremely mechanically minded. At Christmas time, he embarrassed his 13-year-old brother, Shawn, by teaching him how to work the new TV set. But, we do adjust. Just the other day, I heard Shawn angrily insisting that Aeb put down some toy and show Shawn how something or other worked. Not that Shawn isn't just as mechanically minded, it was just easier to get advice from someone who had experience with that particular object.

Shawn, for instance, just a few weeks ago repaired a non-functioning record player for my Sunday School class. I wouldn't have thought much of it if so many people didn't constantly remind me how incapable and untrustworthy children are! The postman still refuses to hand the mail to our 4½-year-old daughter when she is outside playing, and Gramma still drives or walks our 10½-year-old and *almost 14-year-old* the five blocks from her house, crossing streets so quiet, one could almost lay out good china in them to dry. . . . Besides which, years ago, they were both crossing one of the busiest streets in New Orleans to get to and from school every day.

Don't get me wrong—after many years of careful conditioning, I don't quite trust my children either. But we are all learning together, and we learn to trust them more and more each day; in exchange for which, they are learning to trust their parents more and more each day. Aeb is a big help in that respect, as he really calls me to task on my shortcomings. About a month ago, having had an extraordinarily long day which was only half over, I was tired and really snapping out crazy orders like "Sit still, be quiet," while helping his sister get her shoes on to go for a walk. Aeb got very annoyed with me and said, "Mommy, don't spank me'" To which I replied, still tired, "I won't spank you if you'll just sit still." "Mommy, you spank me with words!" Boy, did that ever stop me cold in my tracks; he was absolutely right, that was just what I had been doing, and when we went out the back door for our walk, they had a much more patient mother going with them.

Death In The Home

Ruth McCutchen (KY) wrote:

Early last year my dad was found to have inoperable cancer of the esophagus, stomach, and liver. He patiently endured two courses of debilitating radiation therapy and then refused any further medical "help." He chose to remain at home where my mother lovingly cared for him and where we grown children and not-so-grown homeschooled grandchildren could help and support them. He was able to move around his beloved home until about a week before he died. He was *not* drugged into a stupor and was aware of his family up to the last day when he slipped into a coma of sorts. There were some life-long friends who visited on his final day and my children (13, 11, and 8) and I arrived from our home 100 miles away, during that day. My brother and sister were also close at hand. On Sept. 7, he died in his feather bed, covered with a quilt he'd used on a many a cold winter night, surrounded by his family who sang and prayed him into his eternal rest.

My girls, who were a part of his life, his illness, and his death, have now experienced how rich and loving life can be at the far end of the continuum; and indeed, we're *all* the richer for having made his death a family experience.

Two weeks after his death, my mother fell and sustained a bad ankle fracture. For four weeks she was in a full-length cast, then knee-length for four weeks, then cast off but no weight-bearing for four weeks. She, too, was at home during this ordeal except for the initial trip to the hospital to get the leg set. My daughter Alison (13) spent one week during the first month with Mother, and was said to have been as valuable as an adult, cooking, keeping house, helping Mother get up with the walker.

Of course both of these experiences would have been watered down considerably if my children attended school. As it is, we were able to take many 2–3 day trips to Louisville to be with them.

For these reasons, I have been more than ordinarily thankful for the educational option we have chosen, that of home-based education. Truly these experiences have been "homeschooling" at its best.

Reading via Songs

Janey Smith (MO) wrote:

I received my book order August 9.... *Best Loved Songs Of The American People* is a wonderful collection, with interesting text, and reasonably easy accompaniment.

A thought—our Sarah, 6½, is an excellent reader. One of the many avenues she's pursued for teaching herself is singing. She loves to sing and this past year has loved finding songs she knows and following the words in songbooks. She also enjoyed singing in church choir and learning new songs and reading with music.

This is sort of another version of kids who "read" books they've actually memorized from hearing over and over.... Might be useful to someone else—kids learn lots of songs before they begin to read.

Standardized Tests At Home

From Tahca Ska (WI):

GWS 33 asked about using standardized tests at home. When threatened with court, we administered the California Standard Achievement test for two reasons. One, we felt the testing of the kids might be ordered by the court and we wanted to know of any weakness which we could address—did we need a little math cramming, or science perhaps? Two, we wanted the kids to be a bit more familiar with the tests themselves as the entire thing is quite alien to them.

We therefore stuck to the format and mode of presentation in the test manual with but one exception. As in the article in #33, we found the answer sheet could be confusing. We therefore allowed the children to make an answer sheet on lined paper. After the testing, we all looked at the standard answer sheets and agreed they were something bordering on stupid (one boy used the term "ugly"). I'm pleased to be able to write that both of my boys tested way above grade level.

[DR:] Wendy Priesnitz listed several Canadian sources for standardized tests in Issue #2 of *Child's Play*, and we sent for the catalogs. The first we received was an impressive 120-page booklet from *Guidance Centre*, Faculty of Education, University of Toronto, 252 Bloor St W, Toronto, Ont. Canada M5S 2Y3. Through it you can get "specimen sets" (usually a manual, sample tests, answer sheet, scoring information) for dozens of brands of tests, including the Stanford Achievement Tests. You must order on a school letterhead stationery.

Payment should be in Canadian funds.

Surely there must be more such sources of test materials in the U.S. besides the one in Kansas that we mentioned in *GWS* 33 and #26. Could someone please look into this and tell us what you find out?

Readers On Letter-Writing

From David Kent (TX):

Re your invitation in *GWS* 33 (p. 21) for reports of effective letters, I enclose a copy of a letter Carol and I sent to the National Geographic Society in 1979:

Thank you very much for your helpful letter of the 13th and the lecture brochure. . . . I see from the brochure that tickets are not available to children under eight, which may imply that children are not welcome at the lectures. I have two children, ages four and two, and wonder whether there is a way they could attend the lecture with me. The case pro: They have come with my husband and myself to performances at Trinity Theater in Georgetown, and not uttered a peep; the elder came with us to the Smithsonian-sponsored lecture by Margaret Mead at St. John's Church, and there received her compliment on his good behavior. Miss Mead's comment to the audience was, "This is a lecture about family and the community! Why is this the only family here to listen to it?" We take the precaution of sitting near the door in the event of the unlikely calamity, but to this date they have behaved as the children of a Society member ought to behave. The case con: The lectures are a series intended for adults. The policy of tickets to persons over seven must be administered consistently to avoid discontented members. Children are more likely to make an untoward noise than adults.

I have tried to place myself in your position, and have concluded that it would not do to have children at the late evening performances or lecture-screenings. However, I wonder whether there would be a suitable place at the 5 p.m. showings. I would appreciate hearing from you any suggestion you could give as to how we can attend the lectures as a family. I hope it will be possible to do, but will understand if it is not.

Thank you for your time; I look forward to hearing from you.

[David's note to us resumes:] We received a very friendly reply from Ms. Hess inviting us to bring the children to the lectures (and remarking incidentally that it was older children whom their parents sent alone to the programs who caused the only noise problem).

I entirely agree with your suggestion; I write this sort of letter constantly. . . . In 1979 the Arlington County library installed one of these offensive X-ray book-scanning devices at its exit door. I objected rather strongly by letter to this monument to distrust with its acknowledged radiation hazard; and the Director instituted a system of passes around it. Same story here at the University of Texas.

From Tahca Ska (WI):

Donna asks about letters that young folks have written. In our study of the Micronesian Trust Territories, we discussed Belau and the attempt by her citizens to maintain their constitutional ban on nuclear weapons within the Republic. My son felt strongly that the Belauan Constitution was every bit as important to them as the U.S. Constitution is to us. He sent a letter to Senator Proxmire who forwarded it to the Dept. of State. My son was pleased, indeed amazed when he received a personal letter from the State Dept. as well as a ream of material on their position. It is to my boy's credit that, in the face of this overwhelming informational assault, he remained convinced of the validity of his original point. He also was left with the feeling that—just perhaps—a single person's letter could have an impact.

And from Susan Jaffer (PA):

Whenever a book particularly moves me, or makes me laugh, or teaches me something exciting, or fills a need, I try to make it a point to write to the author. . . . The response, on the whole, has thrilled and astonished me. I have received long, warm, personal letters from many of my heroes. Some of these, and some others, have grown into continuing correspondences.

Once I wrote a second letter to an author, this time requesting information about another book of hers I was looking for, and she replied by sending me a copy of the book, which contained a truly beautiful inscription. But the most dramatic reward was realized very recently. A successful food writer I had been corresponding with (my first letter praised a cookbook I was having a great deal of fun with) had to turn down a publisher's request to create original tofu recipes for an upcoming cookbook. She recommended me for the job, and I did it! This left me richer by $736 and the real satisfaction of seeing my recipes in a book produced by one of my favorite publishers.

I asked my children today if they'd like to write to their favorite authors, and my 7-year-old jumped at the idea. She immediately sat down and wrote a charming letter to the author of her beloved *Wonders of Nature*, and included a poem she had written. She is planning to write some more letters tomorrow. I'm looking forward to my children's growing collection of letters from *their* authors!

Pen Pals Through Hobby

From Harold Ingraham (NY):

My daughter writes to many other people her own age (14). The correspondence according to her is very gratifying and supportive. She finds that the most interesting and constant pen pals are those she writes to in connection with her hobby—horses. The special interest seems to be the real catalyst for an exchange.... Michelle has 15 active pen pals through *Equus* magazine. She even corresponds with adults about horses. She is getting a good education by this exchange, not only in writing skills and personal manners but in the care and raising of horses.

Valuable Resource Person

From Maj. Lyman Barry, 9297 Shaw Town Line Rd, Nunda NY 14517:

In many years of teaching, I've found your criticisms of schools are all too true. Fortunately most of the time, I had sympathetic principals and now and then could step outside the bounds of strict curriculums and have fun with the students, especially in biology ... and in a course of plane geometry where I made the school buy me a set of surveyor's instruments and took the boys and girls outdoors to make maps of school grounds and streams and find out what real triangles were and that they were not just three-sided figures on paper!

I think I could interest younger children, say 6 or older, in nature studies (trees, plants, ecology, geology, microscope technique); history, especially the Revolution and Civil War; carpentry and building, printing (have a press); radio (have short wave and CB sets and marine transmitter); boating and canoeing (have a pond and life jackets). Also have stacks of French and German language records and during the war served as Intelligence Officer in England, France, Germany, Austria.... If any homeschoolers wanted to spend an afternoon or day (bring their own food), we could cover a variety of subjects. No charge, but my limit would be one day a week by prearrangement.... Would not want to act as tutor but just an "enrichment" program to arouse interest in some of many fields I enjoy myself. Might add that our house is a small "museum" especially rich in historical material, books, kodachromes (7,000!), guns back to flintlocks and powder horns, and camping and hiking material of every sort.

Family Needs Crew Member

From Rhuby Nolan, c/o Bieber, 2926 Franklin, San Francisco CA 94123:

Your suggestion in *Teach Your Own* of a live-in student has me so excited.... My husband Don, our 18 month-old son Dominic, and I live on our 36-foot sailboat. We hope to have another baby next year.... We are currently planning a long cruise (maybe a year) starting in Florida, cruising through the Caribbean Islands, through Panama, then to Seattle either via Hawaii or up the California coast. We could use a crew member, as

Dominic requires a *lot* of attention and love while we are at sea. So we could offer both experience with a child (or maybe two) and sailing experience, plus one of the best possible geography lessons! We would have to ask of this student a commitment to stay with us for the entire trip (after a two-to four-week trial) or until a replacement could be found. We also must warn of long hours (on-call 24 hours a day while at sea), cramped quarters, and our very simple lifestyle (no refrigerator, shower, hot water, or TV).

If these threats don't scare off any potential crew, perhaps Dominic will (that was said lovingly). Seriously, he's extremely aware, alert, and active, and does need a lot of attention, if only to keep him from throwing all our possessions (or himself) over the side. We call it the float test. Will a screwdriver float? A teddy bear? How about a bowl of soup? Maybe the laundry hanging to dry. . . . Oh, well, he'll eventually either outgrow this stage or run out of things to throw. [DR: John suggested they tie down, or tie floats to, everything that needed to be on deck.]

Dominic and I have lots of fun together watching birds (he knows the names of a half dozen of the most common water birds here in Florida), and going ashore to play more active games, ride his tricycle, go to the store or library, and do all the usual things that loving families share.

We are hoping to leave for the islands December of this year, and realize that might be short notice. . . . If we don't happen to find a crew member for this trip, we are planning trips in the (far-distant) future to Asia, Europe, Alaska, and who knows where.

House-Building School

From Bob Sonnenberg, 1001 Marshall Dr, Erie PA 16505:

I'm here in Bath, Maine, taking the 3-week course here at the *Shelter Institute* (38 Center Street, zip 04530). I read about the Shelter Institute in your book *Instead Of Education*.

This has been the *most* productive experience I've *ever* had in a school. I think that building houses, as taught here, is an excellent way to really learn many of the subjects taught in schools. Physics, mathematics, chemistry, geology, meteorology, political science, psychology, and even history are involved in the building process. The people at this school provide a great way to learn aspects of all those subjects and probably some I haven't mentioned.

Anyone of almost any age would gain from this course. If the readers of your newsletter don't know about it they should. . . . I'm now looking for work in either home building or some education-related (?) area.

[JH: Interesting to note that when the Shelter Institute first began, I think less than 10 years ago, it was the only such homebuilding school in the country. By now, according to several magazine stories I've read, there are close to forty of them. This is one kind of school I heartily approve of.]

On Buying Computers

A company that until now has made only video games, Coleco, has recently announced a new computer, called the Adam (because they think of it as the first of a long line? or because it is going to eat the Apple?), which will provide not just the computer but also a screen, a memory storage device (smaller and slower than a disk drive), and a fairly slow but adequate printer, all for about $600. Atari has also announced a similar machine, and rumor has it that within the next year or so IBM will put something similar on the market. This is a huge cut in price, all the more so when we consider that even the latest model machines are soon sold at well under list price in some of the big New York computer/camera stores (47th St. Camera, and others) that we have already written about, and whose ads can be regularly found in the second half of the main news section of the Sunday *New York Times*.

So, if these machines work well and are reasonably reliable (and it would be a good idea to wait long enough to find out), we may have on hand a $500 word processor which, if not quite as powerful as some of the bigger ones, would be perfectly adequate for everything that children, and perhaps many adults, might want to use it for. If these or some other companies produce Logo software for these machines, then we will have, at a quite reasonable price, the sort of computer for children that Seymour Papert wrote about in *Mindstorms* (*GWS* 24).

My guess would be that in another two or three years such computers may be available for $300 or less. It is not many years since Timex brought out a computer for $300 which they are now trying desperately to unload for $100. In advertisements in computer magazines, newspapers, and publications like the Boston magazine *WANT ADvertiser* (similar ones must exist in most big cities), in which individual people list things they are trying to sell, we can see a lot of computer equipment selling at as low as half its original list price. So don't be in a hurry to buy. It is clear that the computer manufacturers enormously overestimated the market for home computers, and for some time to come the market is going to be flooded with new and second-hand machines that private owners or the companies themselves are trying to sell. It should soon be possible to own a word processor—a very useful machine—for not much more than you would now pay for a correcting electric typewriter.

Still another reason for being cautious in buying is that many companies now making computer hardware and software are likely to be out of business within a few years. Even such giants in the industry as Timex and Atari have been taking very heavy losses. Several companies making small business computers, such as Fortune (which a computer expert friend of mine recommended for our office), Victor, and others, are in serious trouble. There is going to be a huge shakeout in this business in the next few years, and anyone thinking of investing much money in a computer might do well to wait till we can see who will be the survivors.

I suspect that in five years we at *GWS* will probably be using equipment that will make it possible for us to print *GWS* in real type rather than, as now, typewriter script. But right now nothing on the market tempts me to give up our "obsolete" Olivettis, which do well and easily the things we want them to do.—JH

Bank St. & Other Software

From Carol Krajcar (CA):

I am enjoying the back issues of *GWS* so much that I have to ration myself to only read one each day, or else I would have tried to read them all at once.

GWS 31 had several good articles about children and computers. There is getting to be more and more available software for children and preschoolers. Among my favorite software products for young children are products by *The Learning Company*, *Spinnaker Software*, and the *Xerox* Stickybear materials.

A most intriguing product that we recently purchased is a word processor for the Apple called the *Bank St. Writer* by *Broderbund Software* (1938 4th St, San Rafael CA 94901). It is very easy to use and has been successfully used by children. It does not have all the bells and whistles that a more expensive word processor would have, but it works well for writing letters, stories, and reports. I am writing this letter using the Bank Street Writer. Its list price is $69.95, but you can often find it discounted as much as 25%. I first read about the Bank Street Writer in the July issue of *Parent's Magazine*, and then read a review of it in two different computer magazines. I bought it for myself to use, and am very happy with it. It will run on an Apple II with 48K or an Apple IIe with one disk drive.

The August '83 issue of *Popular Computing* has several good articles on computers in education, and a 14-page article on different Logo products available for several types of microcomputers.

―――――――

Andrea Blackly (MA) writes:

As you can see, we have a computer. It's an Apple IIe. We have only had it for two months so we are just beginning to get used to it. We haven't done any systematic learning about it, we just use it and figure it out as we go along. Right now I am using the "Bank Street Writer" word processing program. I think it was designed for children, and is sold as a home word processor. It's very simple to use. You don't have to learn much of anything to get started because all the commands are listed on the screen.

Abigail (3) uses "KinderComp" by Spinnaker. It has a simple drawing program which she mastered in no time, and she does some very elaborate pictures. When she first started using it she would push a key and see if anything happened. When something did happen, she got very excited and said, "That was what I wanted it to do!" Now she is able to anticipate what will happen and is beginning to plan her drawings.

Sarah (5) uses "Delta Drawing" also by Spinnaker. She has figured it out on her own, and draws some neat complex pictures. She is also learning how the computer "thinks" and can usually figure out how the computer is going to interpret a given command. Sarah and I are learning Logo; learning a language to communicate with the computer will make it possible for us to do a lot more. "Delta Drawing" has limitations, particularly since it cannot save anything from one session to the next. It makes it hard to pick up where you left off. Sarah finds that frustrating at times; at other times, I think it is probably nice to know that whatever she does will be erased when the computer is turned off. It makes it non-threatening.

Both girls have dictated stories to me to type on the word processor. We go back to them some other time to edit them. They are learning to rewrite even before they can write! Right now they are working on a story for a contest in *Highlights*. Sarah sent in a picture to *Highlights* a while ago and they sent back a very nice letter thanking her for her work, and explaining the selection process, and why not everything submitted can be published. She was thrilled with the acknowledgement and felt very grown up.

From Ann Bodine (NJ):

Bank St. Writer is worth mentioning in *GWS*. It's the only word processor simple enough for young children.... My 8-year-old writes "The Bonyhard News" several times a week on the Bank St. Writer. He *never* wrote a newspaper before he learned to use Bank St. Writer (learning to use it took him about an hour).

For learning to touch type, the only program I've found which is entertaining enough to hold the interest of most young children is *Mastertype*.

And lastly, from Freda Davies:

Here are the main points of a review by John Anderson in *Creative Computing*, June '83, of the word processing program *Bank St. Writer* for Apple and Atari:

Simple, accessible, forthright, and consistent.

Although designed for ease of use by children, it is quite capable of producing professional results with any short document—for 10 or 12 page reports, it does just fine.

Up to 2300 words can be stored in single text file; files can be linked, so that larger documents can be stored.

Top of the screen always displays choices available to the user—can be selected by moving the highlighted bar to the desired choice.

A five-lesson tutorial included on the flip side of the disk is interactive, well-constructed—the quiz portion a little too demanding of exact compliance.

The manual is utterly unflawed.

Computer Vandalism—1

Something that I have felt sure would someday happen in the world of computers, has already started to happen. We might call it "computer vandalism."

Computer crime, using computers to steal or defraud, is of course nothing new. A few years ago Thomas Whiteside wrote a two or three part article for *The New Yorker* about people, usually employees of large corporations, who found ways to manipulate the company computers so as to enable them to embezzle large sums of money, often many millions of dollars. The article cited many such crimes, most or all of which took place in spite of elaborate and supposedly foolproof defenses. As is often true in cases of embezzlement, the companies generally did not prosecute the thieving employees; in many cases, they hired them as security officers, on the theory that if they were smart enough to crack the computer's security systems, they might be smart enough to figure out ways to prevent anyone else from doing it. Whiteside's informants were, however, generally skeptical about the possibility of designing secure yet usable systems. If a computer has a "door," through which good guys can get information, then sooner or later some bad guys will figure out how to get through the door.

This kind of computer crime—insiders manipulating a system for personal gain—I knew about. What I thought and feared would happen someday, as more and more computer data banks became accessible by phone, is that some people, just for the challenge and excitement of it, would break into some of these data systems and somehow mess them up. Like vandals spray painting on the walls, they would do harm for the sheer pleasure of showing to themselves and everyone else that they could.

This possibility of profitless (though not purposeless) invasion and at least partial destruction of data banks was one of the many reasons I doubted that we would ever see one of the many wonders that the computer prophets promise us, the day when anyone with a home computer can read any book in any library in the world. If anyone who wanted to could plug into the computer files of, say, the Library of Congress and read any book there (by the way, a very expensive way to read a book), what would prevent someone else from getting into those same files and destroying some of the books? It seemed only a matter of time before such things began to happen.

Well, they have begun to happen. The Aug. 22, 1983 issue of *Time* magazine reported:

A group of youths . . . used their home computers to penetrate a dozen computers in the U.S. and Canada. Included were Security Pacific National Bank in Los Angeles and the nuclear weapons laboratory in Los Alamos, N. Mex., both of which insisted that no real harm had been done. . . . The youngsters' prank was feasible because most of the penetrated computers had been linked by GTE Telnet Inc., which provides access to computer systems in 325 U.S. cities and 50 nations. Ron Zeitz, Telnet's public affairs director, said that gifted amateurs do occasionally get into unclassified data banks, but that classified military data are virtually impossible to intercept.

We can only ask ourselves, suppose some "real harm" had been done in the bank or the nuclear weapons laboratory, would those people have admitted it? And given his position, is it likely that the public affairs director of Telnet would have said anything other than what he did? And is a computer in a nuclear weapons laboratory really "unclassified"?

At any rate, the story was not over. In their issues of Aug. 29, 1983, both *Time* and *Newsweek* had full page stories about what has come to be called "the 414 Gang," 414 being the telephone area code for Milwaukee, where most of them live. One or more of them had broken into a computer of the Sloan-Kettering Cancer Center in New York, had erased some material in the computer's memory, and had put in a program that automatically sent to the 414s the code names of everyone who legitimately used the computer. The hospital called the police and the F.B.I., who tapped the phone lines coming into the machine. Nevertheless, they apparently were not able to track down the intruders until someone in Milwaukee sent them a tip, which finally put them on the right track.

Some excerpts from the *Time* story:

> Federal authorities were investigating seven members of the group . . . for illegally penetrating *dozens* of computer systems.

> How to safeguard information stored inside computers? The potential for fraud is awesome. The American banking system alone moves more than $400

billion between computers every day. Corporate data banks hold consumer records and business plans worth untold billions. Military computers contain secrets that, if stolen, could threaten U.S. security. Many of these machines are hooked into the telephone system, which enables them to communicate with other computers and with users in remote locations. But as the 414s have demonstrated, anyone with one of the popular new microcomputers has the potential, however remote, to unlock the secrets contained in machines operated by banks, hospitals, corporation and even military installations.

As networks of computers connected by phone lines grow, [putting computers under lock and key] becomes irrelevant. More elaborate precautions like passwords, dedicated telephone lines and voice analyzers offer some degree of security. Encryption, which scrambles messages, is perhaps the best way to protect data sent over the wires. It is expensive (up to $5000 per terminal) and difficult to use. Nonetheless, for those willing to pay the price, the technology for protection exists.

"For those willing to pay the price." Key words. For those willing, *and able*, to pay the price, the "computer revolution" may indeed hold out some tempting goodies. But let us not suppose that they will be available to everyone who can afford a $100 or even a $1000 computer.

The *Newsweek* story was much the same as *Time*'s. But there were some interesting additions:

> "There's an epidemic of malicious system hacking going on across the country," says consultant Donn B. Parker of SRI International in Menlo Park, Calif. "Every high school and university that teaches computer technology has this problem—either as a victim or as the source of students who do it."

> "We thought we had a very secure system," says Sloan-Kettering's Mohan [director of their computer service].

It is only a question of time, warns Adam Osborne, chairman of Osborne Computer Corp., before the financial community faces a catastrophic computer crime—a Three Mile Island-like financial disaster. "If this is what kids can do on a lark," says Osborne, "can you imagine what people are doing who are serious about this?"

What, if anything, does this have to do with you and me, aside from the obvious possibility that a bank might be wiped out in which we had savings, or that some financial or legal records, important or valuable to us, might be destroyed? The dangers may go a good deal further and deeper than that. Speaking of computers, I said in *GWS* 33 that for the convenience of computers and their users we might very soon be willing to make, and feel compelled to make, very unwelcome changes in our laws, customs, and ideas of right and wrong. What might some of these be? One place to look for answers might be *Newsweek*, which in its Sept. 5, 1983 issue had a cover story on computer vandalism, or "hacking," a word that originally meant any kind of serious exploration of computers, but that is coming to mean something more destructive and dangerous.

> The National Communications Security Committee—comprised of ranking officials from the Pentagon, CIA, Federal Emergency Management Agency and other agencies—is currently investigating computer security at the Treasury Department. Although federal officials were quick to point out that groups like the 414s had not breached secure computers, they were plainly trying to stop the epidemic of computer tampering. "It's time to put the fear of God into people," said Donald Latham, the Pentagon's deputy undersecretary of command control communications and intelligence.

What does Mr. Latham have in mind? The story does not say. It certainly looks as if the government, which already has a good deal more power over our personal lives than it used to, or ought to, is about to demand and get a great deal more. I'll have more to say about all this in *GWS* 36. —JH

Useful Music Publication

One of the most unusual, interesting, and useful publications I know is the *Journal of the Violin Society of America* (23 Culver Hill, Southampton NY 11968—membership $35/yr., which includes subscription to the journal). The membership of the society is made up largely of highly skilled professional musicians and highly skilled makers and repairers of bowed stringed instruments (including viola, cello, and bass), though they welcome unskilled but interested amateurs like myself. The journal, a fairly hefty quarterly, contains articles about the history, construction, and repair of the great instruments and bows; about the making and makers of fine modern instruments; about exhibitions and contests of these instruments; and about techniques of teaching and playing. I tend to think that any serious player of these instruments, whether professional, advanced student, or dedicated amateur, as well as anyone interested in their construction and repair, would do very well to join the society and read the journal.

Admittedly, the price is a bit high, but any serious string player will spend much more than this on lessons, strings, repairs, music, etc., and the $35 a year seems to me a very worthwhile investment. Perhaps a group of students or players, an adult class, or a Suzuki or similar group, could share the costs. For the journal, as well as being a close look into the inside of a strange, intense, and fascinating world, is full of useful information. Among other myths it will help dispel are (1) that the quality of the great old instruments is due to "lost secrets" and (2) that no one knows how to make instruments anywhere near as good as the old ones.

Worth noting that there is everywhere in the country a great shortage of skilled instrument-makers and repairers, and those that exist are swamped with work. People, young or not so young (one friend of mine went into this work in middle age) who like working with tools and wood and who are looking for a way in which they could earn a decent living while doing worthy and interesting work (which can also be done at home) might consider very seriously learning to repair stringed instruments and doing this as their full-time work. —JH

Starting A Town Orchestra

Kathryn Alexander (TX) writes:

By the way—we *did* start a community orchestra in Paris (Texas). First concert was Dec. 9th to standing room only audience in the junior college auditorium. I set it up for 10 rehearsals and then a concert. Some of the people went from barely reading music into a very *musical* concert. All ages and professions. It's the most enjoyable musical experience I've had since I was a 9-year-old cellist in *my* first orchestra. I'm conducting, coaching, nurturing, and challenging us to *make music* and have a wonderful time. Loved having the community respond as they did. It's the first orchestra in town in 50 years or more. About 12—15 strings, mostly my students, and about 15 wind/brass/percussion.

[JH: This is something I want to do myself someday.]

Violin Report

During my extensive travels this summer I was away from the violin for a month and a half or so, but when I more or less came to roost here in Boston in mid-August I began to play more regularly, perhaps ten or twenty minutes a day on most days. On Sept. 6 I began to keep a log of my exact playing time. From then until noon today, Sept. 13, I have played one hour and fifty-five minutes, which is much less than a serious student would spend on it, or than I would spend on it if I had as much time as I wanted, or indeed than I spend on the cello, which is still my main instrument. By now I have spent a total of something like thirty hours on the violin, and I am greatly surprised and encouraged by what I have been able to do in that time. I keep saying that we human beings are by nature learning creatures, but it is very exciting to discover once again that it is so. I am working on the tunes in the first Suzuki violin book (see our list). Of the 17 little pieces in the book I have played 14. To be sure, I played the last two very tentatively and clumsily, with many mistakes—in a more complicated piece, where I have several things to think about at once, the fingers of my left hand tend to "forget" which string they are on. But the first ten or so tunes I can play with quite a bit of confidence and security and a not too bad tone. Holding the violin under my jaw, and at first very awkward position of the left arm, are feeling more and more natural and comfortable. I can play for longer stretches without getting tired; this morning, after a layoff of several days, I played for twenty minutes. All this is very exciting and satisfying. What is even more satisfying is that, as I hoped would happen, I have already learned enough about the problems of getting started to be able to help other people get started. The other day I gave Mary Van Doren (who, like her husband Mark, has been a skillful trombone player) a first brief lesson, which we both enjoyed, and in which she learned a great deal. We're both looking forward to playing more, and playing more together.—JH

Concerns About Suzuki

From Judy Wenz (NE):

I enjoyed reading your comments about music and the Suzuki method in *GWS* 32.... I myself have some mixed feelings about the Suzuki method. Our children have had three teachers and we've gone to a Suzuki summer camp, and I see certain patterns the teachers have—in this area, anyway. One seems to be that the Suzuki teachers believe that a child who hasn't started lessons by age 4 is lost to the world of music. Another is that children should not be allowed to quit taking violin once they've started. This attitude amazes me. I wouldn't encourage a wavering child to quit, but, on the other hand, I wouldn't force an insistent child to continue. I've heard four or five teachers say that they forced their children to continue and then around age 11 (all seem to say the same age) the children suddenly come to love violin and thank the parents for making them stay with it. Music teachers in general seem so determined that their own children know music well. Why is that? What scientist forces his child to study science every day, or artist forces his child to "create" on a regular basis?

On the positive side, we do like the well-laid-out program Suzuki lessons have. Joshua, age 9, has been taking violin for five years and still loves it. I let him do a lot of "fiddling around" during practice time. He enjoys seeing what the violin can do.

Mail-Order Music Supplies

A very valuable resource for all who play or are thinking of playing bowed stringed instruments (violin, viola, cello, and bass) is the *Shar Products Co.* (PO Box 1411, Ann Arbor MI 48106), a mail order discount house that sells, at very low prices, practically everything related to these instruments. The table of contents of their catalog suggests the range of things covered: Bags for violin, viola, cello, and bass; Books; Bow Accessories; Bows; Bridges; Cases for Bows and Instruments; Children's Music Series; Chinrests; Endpins for cellos; Instruments; Lamps; Metronomes; Mutes; Pegs; Stands; Strings; Tools, Violinmakers; Tuning Forks; and many others. They also print a catalog of the enormous selection of music for stringed instruments that they sell, again at prices that you would be very unlikely to beat or match in most music stores. Even if you are close to a good local music store, Shar probably has a much wider range of music and equipment, and at lower prices. If you are not close to a good music store, and many people are not, these folks can be a life saver.

One of the nice things about the company is that it was started and is to a large degree run by members of one family, named something like Avsharian. One of their catalogs, which I can't lay my hands on at the moment, shows them all together, at least three generations of them, and all holding the stringed instruments which they apparently play together. If I lived near Ann Arbor I would love to meet them and hear them play.

The company is a joy to deal with—very quick service, everything well packed, etc. Call toll free from outside of Mich. 1-800-521-0791, from inside Mich. 1-800-482-1086. Local phone is (313) 665-7711.

One thing I bought from them is a very inexpensive violin, bow, and case, that they call their "Twinkle Violin Outfit." It comes in all sizes from full-size (4/4) to 1/16, suitable for very small children. I found the chinrest an awkward shape, and bought another at a local music store. Otherwise it seems a very decent little violin; no Strad, to be sure, but well worth its modest price. When I (a raw beginner) played it for Nancy Wallace, she was surprised by the quality of the tone.

Some other things that I bought from them and that I strongly recommend to players on any instruments are (1) a studio music stand; (2) Stand-Outs—extenders which fit on the sides of the stand and increase its width to 36", so that you can put both your individual part and the full score on the stand at once, which is often very handy; (3) A lamp that clips onto the top of the stand, solving the otherwise often difficult problem of finding a good light to play under. The folding portable stands that most people use are good for traveling, but for serious work the studio stand is much better and well worth the additional money.

I strongly recommend this company and their catalogs to all string players, whether skillful or beginners.—JH

[DR: By the way, several people have asked for the address of *Rhythm Band*, the company that sells the "practice violin" John described in *GWS* 34. It is PO Box 126, Fort Worth TX 76101. Prices on the practice violins range from $29.95 for the 1/4-size to $32.95 for the full-size.)

Portable Record Player

About a year ago Audio-Technica, which makes stereo cartridges, headphones, and other equipment, announced a product which I had been hoping for many years that someone would make— a portable record player. It was called Mister Disc and cost $200. When the mail order company JS & A offered it for $160, I bought one, thinking that it might be useful for some homeschooling families or their children. When it arrived, it seemed not only ingeniously designed but very well made, and when I played some records on it, using the ultralight headphones which came with it, it sounded quite good. I then tried it with my Sony MDR-80 headphones, which are as good as any I have heard anywhere, and found to my astonishment that with these it sounded just as good as my regular record player and amplifier, which even at discount prices would cost $400 or so to duplicate. Since then I have played it often, both off its batteries and off 120 volt AC, and every time I am delighted by the splendid quality of its sound.

The latest catalog from the mail order house Stereo Discounters Electronic World (6730 Santa Barbara Court, Baltimore MD 21227 Tel. 1-800-638-3920) lists the Mister Disc for $99. At this price it is an absolutely unbeatable bargain. At the same time the catalog from another good mail order house, Sound Reproduction Inc., 7 Industrial Road, Fairfield NJ 07006, lists the Sony MDR-80T headphones at $59, which is about half their official list price, and another great bargain. Putting the two together, you can get for $160 really high quality reproduction of recorded music, which you would otherwise have to spend more than twice as much to match.

A few other words about the Mister Disc. It is about 12" × 5" × 4". It has two headphone jacks, so that two people can listen over phones at the same time, and also output jacks, so that with what they call "patch cords" (available at any electronics shop) you can play it through an amplifier and speakers. The tone arm is so well balanced that it can be played in any position; indeed, there is a strap with which you can hang Mister Discover a hook, if you wish (to keep it away from small fingers, perhaps?). Even when played this way it sounds just as good as when horizontal. A wonderful machine for music lovers.—JH

Homeschooling Book Available Here

Better Than School, by Nancy Wallace ($13.50 + post). Nancy Wallace's book is out, and it's wonderful, even better than I remember it in manuscript, and I loved it then. It is the best book we have had about how homeschooling has worked and what it has been like in one family. Some might argue that the Wallace's are not "typical," but then, no homeschooling families are "typical."

The book is useful, among many other reasons, because the Wallaces were able, thanks to enormous tact, patience, stubbornness, and skill, to win the approval of a school board which was at first unanimously and angrily opposed. Their story is a textbook case of how to deal with such difficult school boards—who I think and hope are becoming more rare.

I would like to underscore here some things I said in my introduction to the book. It is clear from Nancy's own quite modest description of her children, Ishmael and Vita, that they are, musically and in other ways, very talented. In the introduction I said I thought they were even more talented than Nancy suggested, and I now think they are even more talented than I did when I wrote the introduction. There I said that the children were not on their way to Carnegie Hall, meaning that they would probably not become top-rank performing musicians. Four months later, I have changed my mind. It is possible that Ishmael may not choose the in some ways narrow career of a concert pianist, for his musical interests are wide, and he may well become even more interested in composing. But remembering the last time I heard him play, I would have to guess that if he wants to be a big-time concert pianist, he probably can. And Vita, who plays both piano and violin, seems to me to play as well as Ishmael did at her age. In addition to their musical talents, both of them love to write and write well, and Vita also loves to act and is very good at that. So there is no telling where they may go.

To this many school people would reply, as I have heard many times, that homeschooling parents like the Wallaces, taking their talented children out of the schools, leave them to struggle along with the less talented—they don't say "dregs," but "dregs" is probably what some of them are thinking. The answer, as I said in the introduction to the book, is that it is as sure as anything can be that neither Ishmael nor Vita would have been stars in school. Not only would they have done very badly in most school subjects, but they would almost certainly have had all kinds of damaging psychological labels stuck on them—Learning Disabled, Psychologically Disturbed, and the whole disgusting package. The school would have seen them not as assets only as problems, and would probably have convinced them that they were nothing but problems.

Only recently I heard sad news about a child whom I last saw, and loved, when she was just four years old. She was very much like Vita, energetic, enthusiastic, irrepressible, friendly, talkative, and full of ideas, opinions, and questions about everything. I worried a little, as I worry about every bright and energetic young child I meet, about what might happen to her when she got to school. There was reason enough to worry. When she got to school, she did not like it, and fiercely resisted its demand that she not move or speak except with its rare permission. Now, at age seven, mostly because of her resistance to school, she has been officially labeled as "schizophrenic." What is worse, she has learned to believe this of herself; in casual conversation, she will say that she is crazy. This dreadful thing could very easily have happened to one or both of the Wallace children, had they been forced to go to school.

Even in music the Wallace children showed no early signs of unusual talent. Ishmael did not have the perfect pitch he has now (Paul Hindemith always insisted that perfect pitch was teachable, or learnable), or any particular dexterity in his hands and fingers, and Vita's first violin teacher, though a fine musician, in no way found her a promising pupil. It took time for their talents to appear and to grow, and homeschooling gave them the time.

A very important point, which I wish I had thought to put into the introduction to the book, is this—Nancy Wallace did not begin to learn piano because she thought that this might "get the children interested" in music. She did it because she wanted to do it, for her own sake. Having started to learn piano, she asked Ishmael if he would like to do it with her. He said yes, but I haven't the slightest doubt that if he had said No, she would have gone on taking piano lessons herself, in which case he might have become interested later. Or he might not. OK either way. The point is, as I have long said to all homeschooling parents, that you can best help your children by making your own life as interesting as you can, and as you find things you like to do, make them available to your children as well. If you want to paint, paint—and then (if they want to) let them paint too. If you want to write, write—and let them write. Some years ago I said to two friends of mine, both writers, that if they bought (which they could easily afford) a typewriter for their child, he would have a chance to feel that *he too* was a writer. I don't think they have yet done so; as far as I know, their working and professional lives, so important to them, remain closed to him. This seems to me an unnecessary mistake. Nancy and Bob Wallace are both writers, and their children know about and often discuss with them their books and writing. I have said, our task is, as far as we can, to give children *access* to the world; but no part of that world is more interesting to them than our own lives and work.

The book shows both homeschooling families and schools themselves the way out of a seeming dilemma, which people may express as a question or as a statement. The question is often put to me, sometimes in anger, sometimes in pain, by teachers, who say, "Well, if learning is not the product of teaching, and if children can learn without being taught, what are we teachers for, what is it that we are supposed to do?" (To this Jim Herndon replied, "Pay attention, and give protection," an answer that can hardly be improved.) The statement comes out more like this: "Some people believe in giving their children guidance and structure"—by which is meant telling them what to do and making sure that they do it—"and other people, like John Holt, believe in just letting them learn on their own." *But these are not the only choices.* Ishmael and Vita Wallace are not told every day, "Now you must learn this, now you must learn that." But neither are they learning "on their own." They are not alone in the world. They live in very close contact and friendship with their parents, and other adults as well. What these adults do.

But that's why Nancy Wallace wrote this most interesting and valuable book, to tell you what those adults do. So read, enjoy, and find out.—JH

Other Books Available Here

The Young Person's Guide to Playing the Piano, by Sidney Harrison ($5.35 + post). This is not a book about how to play the piano in the sense of the Stewart and Suzuki piano books we sell here. Nor is it a collection of pieces and exercises—though here and there Harrison includes a few exercises of his own, mostly as an example of the kinds of problem-solving exercises that players might and should invent for themselves (as I often do on the cello). It is mostly aimed at young pianists who play seriously and with some skill. But I must add that I, who don't play the piano at all, find the book fascinating, full of insights about studying, playing, and performing, that would be helpful with any instrument. Beyond that, this book makes me more eager and determined than ever (someday) to learn the piano.

These few quotes (I could easily have picked dozens) will, I hope, give some of the flavor of this useful and delightful book:

> Of course you must know how to persuade and command the piano, but the first thing is to fall in love with it. Then it will persuade and command you, and you will never feel that spending time with your best friend is mere work or duty. For my part I fell in love with the piano at the age of four and have never fallen out of love.
>
> I seldom practiced with diligence. If I played something over and over again it was for one of two reasons. Either I was enjoying a second helping of something I enjoyed, *or I was searching for some knack that would make hours of practice unnecessary....* If I found the knack I was looking for I played the page again and again in sheer triumph. How clever of me! I had discovered how to play without practicing. Or had I really discovered how to practice?

Playing by ear is immensely important. So is improvising. We shall come to both later, but let us start with reading. I often think that the best way to learn this would be to find a tune by ear and then write it on paper.

If you practice a fast passage slowly ... pretend that it is slow music to be played with a proper respect for every sound. This is often a good approach to speed and power, but it will not work in every case. Every child knows that there is no slow way to hop or jump. An athlete jumping over hurdles ... cannot go through the motions slowly. There are some actions that can only be tried—and tried again and again—at speed.

This last was very reassuring to me. I am so fed up with hearing musicians say that the way to play faster—my biggest single problem on the cello—is to play everything very slowly. That's only part of the truth. Sure, you play it slowly to learn to do it right, but sooner or later you have to try to play it as fast as you can.

A final quote. Speaking now of the life of a concert pianist (but this would be good advice for many professional players of any instrument), Harrison says:

Amongst all the difficulties you must never let your piano become a nagging wife or a mere business asset. Your piano is your sweetheart and I hope you stay in love forever.

Anno's Counting Book, by Mitsumasa Anno (Hardback; $9.95 + post.) Some homeschooling friends in California showed me this lovely book, about the only one of these counting books that I have ever liked. In the first picture, for Zero, we see a gently rolling landscape, treeless and bare, covered with snow, with a little river running through it and a strip of empty blue sky behind. In the picture for 1, we have one each of sun, cloud, evergreen tree covered with snow, deciduous tree with bare branches, adult, child, bird, house, animal, and snowman. In the picture for 2, a month has gone by, the snow is beginning to melt, and we see two each of buildings, trucks, rabbits, children, roads, and trees as before. In #3 it is spring, and there are three of many different flowers, as well as boats in the river, butterflies, and objects in a field that I can't recognize. With each number we move a month further into the year, seeing new creatures or objects for the first time. There is a church in all the scenes from 2 on, and I just noticed, *this very second*, that in the picture for 5, the church clock points to five o'clock. (True for all numbers? See for yourself.) Instead of lining animals or objects up in a stiff little row, as in most counting books, here they are spread around the page, as naturally as if in a real village, so that children reading the book have to look for and find the objects on the page before they count them. Please, parents, don't spoil the surprise with leading questions like, "Now how many trees can we see on this page?" Let the child notice with surprise and pleasure, as I just did, that on the page for each number there is the matching number of people or animals or trees or whatever.

On one page there is a "mistake." But is it a mistake? Or did the painter put it there on purpose, to give us all something to notice and exclaim about?

All these pictures are painted with the greatest delicacy in subtle and beautiful watercolors, following the changing seasons until at the end we are in the middle of winter again. On every page so many things happen that we can easily make up not just one but many stories about all we see. In other words, this is not just a counting book but a story book as well. I can't imagine that any children will not enjoy it.

Los Tres Osos ($2.35 + post). The story of the Three Bears, told in Spanish by Hannah Hutchinson and charmingly illustrated with cartoons by Ed Nofziger. This is the first of a series of familiar children's stories told in Spanish that we plan to add to our list (in time we would like to find similar books in other languages). Except for a Spanish English glossary, there are only Spanish words in the book; what we know of the story, plus the illustrations, tell us what those words mean—which is, after all, how little children learn first to hear and speak and later to read their own language. For thirty years I have thought that an adult learning a foreign language could make a good start by reading children's books in that language, and indeed I did a little of that in 1953 when I was teaching myself Italian. So I am delighted to be able to add this book, and soon its companions, to our list. It is already, along with *Walk When The Moon Is Full*, one of the favorites of Anna Van Doren, age 2, who has often asked me to read it aloud to her. I do my best to explain that this story is in Spanish, but what she makes of it all I can't imagine. Still, if she keeps asking us to read it, she must be getting some pleasure or intuition of meaning from it, as I think many children, even very little children, will.

The Penguin Complete Father Brown, by G. K. Chesterton ($8 + post; contains *The Innocence Of Father Brown, The Wisdom Of —, The Incredulity Of —, The Secret Of —, and The Scandal Of —*).

I first saw one of the Father Brown stories when I was about ten, in an anthology of detective stories that my parents had lying about the house. The story was "The Oracle Of The Dog," which begins with Father Brown saying that he likes a dog as long as it isn't spelled backward. Who could resist reading ahead to find out what in the world he meant by that? When, a few years later, I found whole books of Father Brown stories, I plunged in like a glutton at a feast, and have been feasting on them ever since.

The titles alone are lure enough. "The Queer Feet," "The Invisible Man," "The Wrong Shape," "The Hammer Of God," "The God Of The Gongs," "The Arrow Of Heaven," "The Curse Of The Golden Cross," "The Blast Of The Book." Most of the crimes Father Brown is called on or happens to solve are murders; others are robberies, always of some rare and beautiful object, never anything as dull as money (though many of the murders are done for money). Most of the murders seemed to involve the supernatural—people disappearing from or being killed in sealed rooms, baffled bystanders saying, "But how could anyone possibly have. . . . But it's impossible that . . ." etc., etc. Just the kind of thing that imaginative and romantic children like. At the end, Father Brown makes sense of everything, which is fascinating and satisfying to children, because they so greatly need to make what sense they can of the puzzling world around them, and also, because solving a mystery is like finding a buried treasure.

Another thing I loved in the books was Chesterton's rich use of paradox, which I found later is in all his writing. A typical and famous sample: "Christianity has not been tried and found wanting; it has been found difficult and not tried." In these stories things are never what they seem, and usually quite the opposite. Children of about ten or eleven, just beginning to discover and enjoy wit, double meanings, puns, irony, will love this. Here, in one of the few really comic stories in the collection, "The Absence Of Mr. Glass," is Father Brown talking to Dr. Hood, a great criminologist (obviously a take-off on Sherlock Holmes) about the apparent but inexplicable disappearance of Mr. Glass, a supposed murder victim, who by elaborate Holmesian deduction Dr. Hood has described in minute detail:

> [Dr. Hood says] "In the absence of Mr. Glass—"
>
> "That's it, that's it," said the little priest, nodding quite eagerly, "That's the first idea to get fixed, the absence of Mr. Glass. He is so extremely absent. I suppose," he added reflectively, "that there was never anyone so absent as Mr. Glass."
>
> "Do you mean he is absent from the town?" demanded the doctor.
>
> "I mean he is absent from everywhere," answered Father Brown, "he is absent from the Nature of Things, so to speak."
>
> "Do you seriously mean," said the specialist with a smile, "that there is no such person?"
>
> The priest made a sign of assent. "It does seem a pity," he said.

How could any child philosopher—and they are all philosophers—resist that?

But I must emphasize that Chesterton did not write these stories for children, and might well have been surprised, though surely pleased, that children liked them. As I only learned when grown up, he wrote these stories for adults, and with a very serious purpose, to defend the Catholic Church, of which he was a member, and which was then very unpopular in England, against the charge of being impractical, unscientific, and full of preposterous superstitions. In every one of these stories it is Father Brown, and often he alone, who is the sensible, realistic, practical person, while all the supposed hardheaded rationalists around him are snatching at the wildest explanations of everything. "The Blast Of The Book," another one of the few comic stories, and a very funny one, ends with Father Brown explaining patiently why he looked in a book that was supposed to make everyone disappear who looked in it: "You see, I am not superstitious." Another story, "The Chief Mourner Of Marne," made clear to me for the first time the meaning and importance of something many non-Catholics find repugnant, the confessional. And "The Mistake Of The Machine," written seventy years ago, makes an argument against lie detectors (and in a way against all psychological testing, measuring, and meddling) that has not been improved on to this day, namely, that the machine, which supposedly cannot make a mistake, is always run by a human being, who can.

The final pleasure of this book is that through it we get to know Chesterton, an unusual, delightful, and admirable man and a true conservative, not at all like the people who today pin that badge on themselves. Were he alive now, he would certainly be a strong and witty defender of the right of people to teach their own children, a right which in his own lifetime he could hardly have imagined might someday be in question. To our great loss, the man is gone, but fortunately he has left to all of us, adults and children, these exciting, amusing, and instructive stories.

Stalky & Co., by Rudyard Kipling ($3.35 + post). My Uncle Tom read me this book aloud when I was visiting him at the age of about eleven. I loved it then and have ever since. It is one of the greatest of a kind of tale that humans everywhere have always loved to tell, about the powerless outwitting the powerful, and is probably the greatest of all tales about children outwitting adults. The children in this case are three boys, roommates in a 19th Century British military boarding school, where boys were trained for entry into the British equivalent of our West Point. Their enemies were their teachers, or most of them, harsh, sarcastic, embittered men, with whom they were in a state of constant war, and also some of the older boys in the school, who as in all traditional British boarding schools held absolute power over the younger students. The leader of the three was Stalky, surely one of the great heroes of literature. The second was McTurk, son of an Irish landowner. The third was the bespectacled, unathletic Beetle—Kipling himself, whose own boyhood was a misery, and who perhaps in this book got a kind of revenge on his earlier tormentors, winning in fiction all the battles which in bitter fact he had always lost. In story after story, in imaginative and hilarious ways, these three overcome the vastly stronger forces of authority arrayed against them.

When I read this book as a boy, the British Empire and its triumphs (or misdeeds) were nothing to me. When I came back to the book a few years ago, I thought I might be put off by an unspoken assumption that that Empire was the crowning achievement of human history. To my surprise, I enjoyed the book as much as ever, and realized something about it that I could never have realized as a boy, that it was a profoundly revolutionary book, a warning hidden in a comedy. Through the person of his hero, Stalky, Kipling was saying to his fellow Britons, if you want to keep your Empire you will have to change your ways. You cannot forever rule these hundreds of millions by force; if your rule is to endure, it must be by knowledge, love, and trust.

Thus, one reason why Stalky and friends could always escape their pursuers was that, alone among all the hundreds of people at the school, they had troubled to get to know the local people and their dialect, which most "educated" English people would have heard as little more than a language of ignorant savages, impossible to understand and not worth understanding. Because the boys knew, liked, and respected the local folk, in time of trouble these were automatically on their side, ready to give them without question whatever help they needed. Stalky himself learned the lesson, and years later, in India with the British Army, put it to good use. The Empire did not learn the lesson, and is gone.

But don't let all this talk mislead you. This is above all a comedy, mostly a broad slapstick comedy, which when I was a kid made me laugh myself almost sick. As comedy it will be read and enjoyed by most kids who read it, as I hope many will.

The Lady or the Tiger, and Other Logic Puzzles, by Raymond Smuliyan ($12.55 + post). About these and similar puzzles the author observes in his preface:

So many people I have met claim to hate math, and yet are enormously intrigued by any logic or math problem I give them, provided I present it in the form of a puzzle. I would not be at all surprised if good puzzle books prove to be one of the best cures for so-called "math anxiety." . . . In general, my own puzzle books tend to be different from others in that I am primarily concerned with puzzles that bear a deep and significant relation to important results in logic and mathematics.

The title of the book comes from the second chapter, which is a set of variations on the old story about the prisoner who must choose between two rooms, one of which contains a lady (whom he can presumably marry) and a tiger (which will presumably eat him). In the first of these puzzles, the king explains to the prisoner that the two rooms contain one lady each, or one tiger each, or a lady in one and a tiger in the other. On the door of the first room is a sign: "In This Room There Is A Lady, And In The Other Room There Is A Tiger;" on the second door, a sign saying, "In One Of These Rooms There Is A Lady, And In One Of These Rooms There Is A Tiger." The king tells the prisoner that one of these signs is true and the other false. Assuming the prisoner does not want to be eaten, which room does he choose?

There are in all twelve of these lady-tiger puzzles, each one a little more complicated and difficult than the one before. The next set of puzzles concern insane asylums. In these there are only doctors and patients, all truthful, but some of each totally sane and others totally insane. The sane ones are 100% accurate in their beliefs, the insane 100% inaccurate. A visiting inspector has been sent to determine whether there are any insane doctors or sane patients in each asylum. In the first puzzle, Inspector Craig speaks to two people, Jones and Smith. Jones tells him that Smith is a doctor. Later, Smith tells him that Jones is a patient. What does this tell Craig about these two men?

In the next set of puzzles things get a bit more complicated, since they take place in Transylvania, whose population is made up of vampires, who always lie, and humans, who always tell the truth. But, as in the hospital, half of the humans, and of the vampires, are sane, completely accurate in their beliefs, and half are insane, completely inaccurate. There are twelve of these puzzles, again, each a bit more complicated and difficult than the one before. In all of these sections, you will find the first puzzles easy enough. The last ones are far from easy. None of them require any knowledge of math; they could be solved by someone who had never heard of math. But as you solve these puzzles you will be learning, or figuring out for yourself, some ideas about mathematics that are a lot closer to the true work of modern mathematicians than any math you will learn in school.

At the end of each chapter are solutions to the puzzles, but you will be losing all of the fun of the book if you just spend a little time on each puzzle and then read the solution. This is a book to read slowly, as you might drink a rare and fine wine, a little sip at a time, savoring each sip. There's no rush! No one is going to give you a test, or a score! Don't read the solution to a puzzle until you think you have solved it, or until you have spent a long time working on it and feel so baffled that you can't stand it. So far, as I write this, I have only done a few of the lady-tiger and insane asylum puzzles. I don't know if I ever will do all the puzzles in the book. But over the years I expect to have a lot of fun trying. And if I make it to the end I will know quite a lot about Gödel's Incompleteness Theorem, one of the most important ideas and discoveries of modern mathematics, that up till now had never made any sense to me at all.

By the way, there's no reason why a group of people, say a family, couldn't work on these puzzles together; they might even be a lot more fun that way, sharing and testing ideas, as, when we were young, my sister and I used to sit next to my Grandmother on late Sunday afternoons and help her do the big Sunday crossword puzzle. And you might even try making up some puzzles of your own.

A Field Guide to the Dinosaurs, by David Lambert ($8 + post). This is the ultimate dinosaur book, the dinosaur book to end all dinosaur books. Everything you always wanted to know about dinosaurs but were afraid to ask—because you thought no one would know. Now you can know.

I can't improve on what the back cover says about the contents of this book:

> How and when did [the dinosaurs] evolve from lower reptiles? How did they differ from other animals? Were some . . . warm-blooded? What did they eat? What ate them? Did any dinosaurs care for their young? . . . Over 300 kinds of dinosaur. . . . Illustrations show where they lived, their family trees, what they looked like, and their size in comparison to a man. . . . What plants and animals shared the dinosaurs' habitat? How did the earth's lands, climates, and living things change during [those times]? What mysterious forces of nature killed off the dinosaurs? How were dinosaur remains preserved in rock? Who were the great dinosaur discoverers? How do scientists date the fossil remains? How do they rebuild fossil skeletons?

All this is indeed in the book. You will also learn as you read that arguments are still raging as to whether dinosaurs were cold-blooded or warm-blooded, or whether the big flesh-eating dinosaurs actually chased and killed their prey or merely fed on carrion? (I do not *wish* to believe that *Tyrannosaurus* only fed on carrion!) And you will also realize that much of our "knowledge" of dinosaurs is in fact ingenious guessing from very little evidence. Maybe 100 years from now a book like this will be written in which the pictures will look very different. Meanwhile, if you want to learn all that we *think* we know about these great and fascinating creatures, this is the place to find out.

The Word Processing Book, by Peter A. McWilliams ($8.95 + post). Our finding this book illustrates nicely what we have been saying about how (in the real world) people find out things. A young friend of ours, who works in a clothing store a few blocks away, but who also writes (he just went to Poland for a week to research a book), and works with computers, told me about this book, and kindly lent me his copy. I have only read a small part of the many millions of words written about computers, but this does seem to me one of the very best explaining books I have ever seen—clear, logical, well-placed, reassuring but uncondescending, and very funny.

It is so good that I will even forgive the author his subtitle: "A Short Course In Computer Literacy." On page 98 is some of the usual hype on this subject: ". . . a personal computer will give a student a skill that is valuable today, invaluable in five years and necessary in ten: computer literacy . . . [buying a computer] is the greatest investment parents can make in their child's future. . . ." Not true, for reasons I have already written about and will say still more about in a later *GWS*. The argument for buying children a computer is about the same as the argument for buying them violins; they may be able to have quite a lot of fun with it. But if by chance they don't, no great loss; they can get along fine without it, and don't let anyone tell you otherwise. If, sometime in the future, they want or need to learn to run one, they can learn it then, just as they can learn to fly a plane or ride a horse, if they want to do that.

Also on the front page: "If you write anything

from a letter a day to a book a month, reading this could change your life." More nonsense. If you write no more than a letter a day, or even five letters, you don't need a word processor, and until they are much cheaper (which may be very soon), it would be a waste of money to buy one. On the other hand, if you write many letters a day which need to look perfect, or if you are a student at a school that requires you to do much writing, or if you write or edit much for publication, then a word processor is indeed a very useful tool to have. This book will tell you all you need to know about what they are, how (in general) they work, and how to look for, buy, and use them.

One very useful feature of this book is that McWilliams reviews a number of the leading computers and printers on the market. Since these may change fairly rapidly—just the other day the Osborne Company, which made the first transportable computer and was generally felt to be one of the industry's leaders, went bankrupt—McWilliams offers to send an update on his book to any who ask (just send a self-addressed envelope with *two* 20¢ stamps).

A few notes. McWilliams strongly recommends *against* getting Apple, Atari, or Radio Shack computers if your main use for them will be word processing, for a number of reasons—awkward keyboards, bad video display, etc. Perhaps he will have changed his opinions in his latest Update #4. I would certainly check before buying any of these.

A machine he recommends is one of which I have heard and read other good things, the Kaypro II, another "portable" (26 lbs.) computer. These have been advertised at substantial discounts in the main news section of the Sunday *New York Times*. But all bets may be off when IBM puts out its low cost computer, the "Peanut." You might do well to wait for it.

Another piece of warning advice, from a different McWilliams' book:

> When you're considering spending $5,000 on any product, you expect from the salesperson a certain attention, kindness, politeness, expertise, or at least civility. In the world of buying a computer, you can either gently let go of that expectation now, or you can have it brutally taken from you later.

Even if you have no immediate thought of buying a computer, this book may still be worth reading, just as a clear and entertaining explanation of a subject that is and will remain very much in the news.—JH

Editors—John Holt & Donna Richoux
Managing Editor—Pat Farenga
Subscriptions & Books—Mark Pierce
Office Assistant—Mary Van Doren

Growing Without Schooling 36

December 1983

The Jan./Feb. issue of *Mother Earth News*, which should be out about the time you receive this *GWS*, will carry an article by me about how to homeschool. It will also recommend and quote from Nancy Wallace's new book *Better Than School (*see *GWS* 35). I will also write an article for *The Progressive* about what I call the metaphors of education; not sure when this will appear. And I am talking to the editors of *Phi Delta Kappan* about doing another article for them, about some simple and inexpensive ways to make the schools a little bit better.

On Sat. Nov. 19, I spoke to a statewide meeting of school boards in Nevada, saying why I thought it would be in their best interests to allow and support homeschooling, without imposing too restrictive conditions. The audience was polite though not enthusiastic. Later the President of the State Board of Education said to them that there was no longer any question of the state forbidding homeschooling, it was definitely legal, and the only question to discuss was under what conditions it would be allowed. For the time being the state seems ready to tell people that they can teach their kids at home as long as they do exactly what the schools do, a condition which most homeschoolers (and I) would find too restrictive and not acceptable. But it is encouraging that they are at least no longer thinking about trying to forbid homeschooling altogether.

On returning from my Nevada trip, I and our friends the Maher family taped a too-brief TV show with Steve Allen, musician, comedian, and one of the big stars of TV a decade or so ago. He did not learn until he reached the studio that he was going to be the interviewer for our show, so had no time to prepare; but even on this very short notice he asked good questions and was fun to work with.

While speaking in Philadelphia, I met my hosts' seven-year-old daughter, Amanda Bergson-Shilcock, who entirely on her own started and runs "A's Bakery." It is all her show; she makes and puts up posters, collects orders, buys the raw materials, bakes blueberry muffins and three different kinds of (delicious) cookies, fills the orders, collects the money, everything. I hope in a coming issue of *GWS* to tell, or to have her tell, her story at greater length.

We are happy to say that in recent weeks we have had the largest volume of book orders in our short history. Thanks for using us. As we've said before, one small but really helpful thing you can do is show or send our book list to as many people as possible.

I am leaving immediately for a 10-day trip to the Midwest, which (thanks to some organizing by *GWS* readers) includes talks at Eastern Illinois U., DePauw (IN) U., Indianapolis, Chicago, Northbrook IL, Kalamazoo MI, Ann Arbor, and Oakland U. (Rochester MI). I will be back in time for the Dec. 8 Open House, and a Dec. 12 meeting with Providence, RI homeschoolers.—John Holt

John's Coming Schedule

Jan. 12, 1984: Holt Associates Open House.
Jan. 28: Providence Learning Connection, Providence RI. Contact Joyce McFarlan, 401-274-9330. (Feb. 4 snow date).
Feb. 9: Holt Assoc. Open House.
Mar. 5: Project Excel, Suffolk U., Boston. Contact Glen Lewandowski, 723-4700 ext. 280.
Mar. 30: Eastern Washington University, Cheney WA. Contact Darleen Weller, 509-456-4401.
Mar. 31–Apr. 1: Seattle homeschoolers. Contact Deb Stewart, 206-435-5015.
Apr. 2 – 3: Home Schooling Fair, Spokane WA. Contact Nola Evans, 509-236-0267.
Apr. 16: University of Kentucky. Contact Libby Morley, 606-273-7816.

Grant Colfax Doing Well

From the San Francisco Examiner, *11/6/83:*

Scholar Who Never Went To School Likes Harvard—And Is Doing Well—
It's a long way from the coastal mountains of Mendocino County to

Harvard Yard, but except for a touch of homesickness and normal freshman jitters about grades, Grant Colfax is making the adjustment just fine.

"Things have calmed down pretty much," said the 18-year-old who drew international media attention after he was admitted to Harvard even though he had never attended school.

Colfax and his three younger brothers received all of their education from their parents at their mountaintop home near Boonville (CA).

Colfax said the media blitz surrounding his first two weeks at Harvard was "embarrassing." He went from never having watched television to appearing on *The Johnny Carson Show* ("which convinced me I don't want to be in show biz"), *Good Morning America* and more than a dozen other radio and TV shows.

When he arrived in Cambridge, he was besieged by reporters from as far away as Australia and Germany. CBS wanted a TV crew to follow him during his first day of classes. He refused, explaining, "I figured I had enough to worry about."

"The change (from studying at home) hasn't been that bad," Colfax said. "There is a lot of work. . . . The work isn't that hard, it's just the quantity of it. It requires a lot of organization. I have to learn to calm down at times. I have to learn I can't learn every detail like I could at home."

That lesson came swiftly. "After my first chemistry test I came out almost in tears because I had done so poorly," he said. "I felt so bad I called home and told them I might not make it." His intuition was correct. He got only 54% of the answers right. But on the Harvard curve, that was good enough for an A; 39% was worth a B on the test.

His midterm grades in his pre-med course of studies were an A in math, an A in Spanish and an A-minus in chemistry.

Colfax was one of only nine students selected for a freshman honors seminar on psychological issues in medicine. "There were 90 applications," said Dr. David Funder, a psychology professor who conducts the seminar. "I wanted to find people able to work independently, who didn't need to be spoon-fed, who were well-prepared."

Colfax more than met those qualifications, Funder said. "He's very energized and well-organized," the professor said, describing him as a "pretty remarkable young man."

His lack of formal schooling and the social interchange associated with it haven't hampered him, Colfax said. "I'm pretty outgoing."

"The main thing I miss is the quiet," Colfax said. "It's never quiet here. It makes you very tense. I have to get away from it a lot."

Notes from Donna

Looking back on our sixth full year of publication, I must say it was an eventful one for the staff. Two left (Peggy and Tim), one got engaged, then married (Pat), one had a baby (Mary Van Doren). Mark Pierce got pneumonia in September and was out for a week; in his absence we hired Mary Gray, who had been volunteering for us, and now both she and Mark are working on the book orders and subscriptions. Mary often brings her lively 5-year-old son Christopher to the office.

Time for a big end-of-the-year "Thank you!" to everyone who has worked as a volunteer for us. Special credit goes to: Mary Maher, for proofreading *GWS* and typing letters; Marilyn Pelrine, for mailing renewal postcards every two months; Kit Finn, for proofreading the big Directory in this issue. Other local volunteers who have helped this year in the office or at home include Mary Silva, Mary Steele, Mary Pelrine,

Pam Mitchell, Terry Burch, Mario Pagnoni, Ann Gilbert, Danny Desai, Fran Castelluccio, Sue Mojica, Jan Wrotnowski, and their families. Typists outside the Boston area included June and Allen Conley, Bob Post, Nanda Hills, Zeke Cameron, Cheryl Richardson, Kate Gilday, Jeanne Finan, Mary Friedl, Gary Floam, Diane Kephart. Thanks also to the families, such as the Prices (Susan, Matt, and Faith) of Florida who helped while they were visiting Boston.

A Win in Georgia

There have been two important rulings concerning homeschoolers in recent weeks, one win and one loss. First, the win. As reported in the Atlanta Constitution, *10/26/83:*

> The Georgia Supreme Court overturned the state's compulsory school attendance law Tuesday, calling it an "impermissibly vague" statute that fails to define a private school.
>
> In a 4–3 decision, the court issued the ruling in response to an appeal by Terry and Vickie Roemhild of Stephens County, who were arrested two years ago when, for religious reasons, they insisted on teaching their children at home instead of enrolling them in school.
>
> Under the compulsory attendance law, students aged 7 to 16 must attend public or private school. Although the law is clear in its definition of public school, it only vaguely defines a private school. As a result, many homeschoolers have complied with the law by registering their homes as private schools.
>
> "Although we agree that the word 'school' clearly puts one on notice that an organized education must be provided to the child, there are many questions concerning the scope, nature, and place of the education which are left unanswered by the state. . . ." said the ruling, written by Supreme Court Justice Richard Bell.
>
> Rusty Sewell, executive counsel for the governor, said Tuesday's decision means that the law is now in limbo. "Probably what it means is that you couldn't prosecute under that law if someone is teaching their children at home," Sewell said.

[DR:] The Justices' legal reasoning concerning "vagueness" drew heavily on the Wisconsin Supreme Court case *Wisconsin v. Popanz,* from which we quoted at length in *GWS* 34.

Connie Shaw of *Georgians for Freedom in Education* writes, "The overturning of the compulsory attendance law has created a mixed chorus of government and non-government reaction. A new law will most likely be voted on in this next legislative session which begins Monday, January 9, 1984. Our time is short. . . . If we are to influence our Georgia legislators in forming that new law to include home education, then we must combine forces with all home educators." The organization urges all Georgia readers to contact their legislators.

A Loss in Minnesota

The second ruling comes from Minnesota. On Aug. 31, a District Court upheld the conviction of homeschooler Jeanne Newstrom of Bemidji. Some quotes from that ruling, written by Judge Saetre:

> The main thrust of Mrs. Newstrom's defense relates to Subd. 2 of M.S. 120.10 and that her "qualifications are essentially equivalent to the minimum standards for public school teachers of the same grades or subjects. . . ."
>
> The qualifications for minimum standards for public teacher are . . . a bachelor's degree which must include a completed course in elementary school teaching and licensed as an elementary teacher by the State Board of Teaching.
>
> Mrs. Newstrom has the equivalent of one year of college in general courses, none of which include any courses in education. Mrs. Newstrom acknowledges

her lack of formal training and qualifications but claims that nonetheless she is qualified to teach her own children and offered evidence to compare the results of her daughter's education with the performance of children in public schools. The trial court sustained objections to this evidence on the ground that it was irrelevant to the issue of whether the defendant was qualified as a teacher. We agree with the trial court's ruling. The comparison would at best be mere conjecture insofar as Mrs. Newstrom's qualifications to teach are concerned. The trial court construed the word "qualifications" to mean educational qualifications acquired by formal education as well as informal training and correctly ruled that [whether] Mrs. Newstrom was in fact a good teacher or not was irrelevant.

Appellant simply does not realized or appreciate that every parent does not have complete freedom in selecting and determining the manner in which her children are to be educated.

[DR:] However, the Minnesota State Supreme Court has agreed to review the Newstroms' case, and attorney John E. Mack is hopeful that the *Popanz* (WI) and *Roemhild* (GA) decisions will be influential. Mr. Mack asked John Holt (among others) to file an *amicus curiae* brief on behalf on the Newstroms, and John agreed. He plans to write more about the weaknesses in this ruling in *GWS* 37.

Other Court News

Ann Mordes (FL) wrote in the FLASH newsletter:

We are happy to inform all of you that the case in Monticello (Jefferson County) against parents who were operating a "623" incorporated school was dropped due to "lack of evidence." The attorney was informed the day before the hearing was to have taken place.... [DR: The families involved were Gilbert and Theresa Silveira, and Ross and Gloria Johnson.] I'd like to compliment them in their choice of an attorney, Joseph P. Dallanegra, Jr. Mr. Dallanegra prepared a most thorough and truthful law brief. It was enough to educate not only the State Attorney, but also the Department of Education.

A news story reprinted in the Iowa newsletter, O!KIDS:

> *Parents Acquitted On Truancy Law Charges*—A Muscatine couple who withdrew their children from school to set up a home study program have been acquitted of charges that they violated Iowa's truancy laws.
>
> Ronnie and Nancy Shuler were accused by Muscatine school officials of failing to provide their three children with an educational program taught by a state-certified teacher and equivalent to public schooling.
>
> But in a ruling filed Tuesday, Muscatine County District Associate Judge James A. Weaver said he was not convinced beyond a reasonable doubt that the Shulers' home study program fell short of meeting those legal requirements.

[DR:] *In* GWS *34 we mentioned briefly that the Kirschenman family of Moorhead, MN had won their court case, but that was all we knew. Since then, the Kirschenmans have subscribed to* GWS, *and Shirley Kirschenman (MN) writes:*

I am enclosing a newspaper account of the results of our evidentiary hearing last spring. We *won*! Our handicapped child was neglected and worse—abused—in the local public school. It was just awful what was going on in that classroom.... He has improved 100% since getting him out of there. I have enjoyed teaching him.

At the time we had charges brought against us we did not know of your group or of others, but some of the homeschoolers elsewhere in Minnesota saw the account in their papers and got in touch with us. I must say they were a big help in helping us win the case. Dr. Moore gave us a lot of help and I also had information from John Holt which I gave to the judge as an exhibit.

From the local newspaper article Shirley sent:

> Becker County Judge Sigwel Wood has ruled that a Moorhead couple does not have to send their 11-year-old mentally and physically handicapped son to Moorhead public schools.
>
> The Kirschenmans have been teaching Stefan at home since they removed him from public school in May 1980.
>
> The judge also held that the compulsory attendance law did not apply in this case. Wood said the laws concerning education of handicapped children provide that parents may send a handicapped child to a school of their choice.
>
> "In this case, Stefan is attending a school ... insofar as he is being educated at home in all of the common branches as required for mentally handicapped child, and further ... Mr. and Mrs. Kirschenman do have qualifications which are essentially equivalent to the minimum standards for public school teachers of the same grades or subjects," Wood wrote.
>
> Mrs. Kirschenman has a nursing degree, worked as an Army pediatric nurse and also taught nursing at a California college. Mr. Kirschenman is a North Dakota State University engineering professor.
>
> Assistant Clay County Attorney Cathy Mills said the county will probably not appeal the case. Mills said Wood's finding that the Kirschenmans are qualified to teach Stefan precludes any appeal.

Other news in brief:

Awaiting trial: Jimmy Wilson, Vanceboro TN; attorney, Hugh D. Cox—The Millers, Maryland Line MD.

Awaiting ruling: The Wilkie family, Alpena MI.

Case appealed by state: Sheridan Road Baptist School, near Saginaw MI *GWS* 31 & 33).

Good News: Wa, Ky, Ms, Fl

From the Seattle Post-Intelligencer, *10/7/83:*

> Some parents could legally teach their children at home for the first time in state history if an experimental home-study program is approved today. The state Board of Education is expected to act on the proposal.... [DR: they *did* approve it.]
>
> Parents from the Stillaguamish Learning Exchange [see "Helpful Schools"], a two-year-old education cooperative headquartered near Arlington, said they would like to take part in the experiment. They said they would expect to be evaluated like any private school.
>
> About 150 Stillaguamish students are taught at home by their parents who are assisted and supervised by certificated instructors. The program was approved by the state board in 1982, but when the board learned this summer the program was a home-study project, it withheld approval.
>
> Under the state's attendance law, children from the ages of 8 through 14 not enrolled in either a private or public state "approved" school are considered truants.
>
> The home-study proposal from the state Superintendent of Public Instruction would establish two one-year experimental programs administered through a public school and a private school.
>
> The parents would tutor their own children under the supervision of a certificated teacher, who would be hired by the school.
>
> Teachers would train parents to be tutors and monitor no more than 20 children.

Each parent and student would meet with the teacher for at least one hour per week and keep daily progress records. The state superintendent's office would audit the program annually.

From Barb Soper (KY):

I had been told that the process of becoming a home school might take some time and trouble, so I immediately sent for your back issues (to glean all pertinent information) and called Mr. Pat West, Jr., the Superintendent of Non-Public Schools in Frankfort. Within a few days, I was shocked to receive all of the necessary information and an application form! ... I immediately called the local health department and the district fire marshal's office to request that they inspect our designated school area. Although I had been told that the officials who would be certifying (or, Lord forbid, not certifying) our school were very hard to please and downright rude, I was thoroughly impressed with the courteous, helpful and supportive response from both offices. ... By the end of July, I had received a 100% rating from the health department and the approval *and commendation* for cooperation from the Fire Marshal!

By the second week in August, our school had become approved by the State Department of Education, and my only other obligation was to notify the County Superintendent of Schools of the children's names and addresses by October 1, which I did.

Our school was sent data bank forms (which are sent out to all Kentucky schools) inquiring about our curriculum, schedule, philosophy, materials, etc., which I had been told by another homeschool family to expect [see *GWS* 35]. They had told me that I only needed to write N/A across the forms and return them or even throw them away! As I read through the forms, however, I realized that it might be helpful to the State Board of Education if I took the time to reply and to write down the philosophy behind our family's decision to learn at home. ... As I counted the number of books in our home and listed all of the wonderful things we have been learning together, I became more and more aware of how really fine our program is and of just how committed we all are to our homeschool. I felt very proud of my children as I reviewed the many accomplishments they have made already. For example, the 7-year-old has taught himself to read with confidence; the children save their own money to help support their new Mexican foster brother, with whom they correspond and for whom they have decided to learn Spanish; the children help teach art classes at a local nursing home and have "adopted" a wonderful gentleman to be their "grandfather"; we have taught ourselves the rudiments of Cuisenaire rods, and are learning Latin; the children are carefully raising gerbils and keeping records of the successive generations, eating habits, and all pertinent information that they can gather to go into a book they hope to publish . . . and on and on!

My proudest moment came when I received a phone call from Mr. West only a few days after I had returned the data forms. *He was kind enough to call me personally to commend our family on the fine program we had developed and to offer encouragement, praise, and any help we might need in the future.* I nearly wept with gratitude for his kindness and understanding, and I realized that the many negative responses to our decision to try homeschooling must have been hurting me more than I had realized.

[DR:] *Becky Howard (AR) sent us a copy of the new 10-page Mississippi compulsory education law, and marked the sections related to homeschooling. Looks like the Mississippi legislature went out of its way to protect the rights of homeschoolers. (Does anyone know why? Someone must have put a lot of effort into getting these favorable passages included in the bill.) The relevant parts:*

> Section 21 ... (2) The following terms as used in this section are defined as follows:
>
> (e) "School" means any public school in this state or any nonpublic school in this state which is in session each school year for at least 155 school days, except that

the "nonpublic" school term shall be the number of days that each school shall require for promotion from grade to grade.

(i) "Nonpublic school" for the purposes of this section shall mean an institution for the teaching of children, consisting of a physical plant, whether owned or leased, including a home, instructional staff members and students, and which is in session each school year. This definition shall include, but not be limited to, private, church, parochial and home instruction programs.

(3) A parent, guardian, or custodian of a compulsory-school-age child in this state shall cause such child to enroll in and attend a public school or legitimate nonpublic school for the period of time that such child is of compulsory school age, except under the following circumstances:

(c) When a compulsory-school age child is being educated in a legitimate home instruction program.... The parent, guardian or custodian of a compulsory-school-age child attending any nonpublic school... shall complete a "certificate of enrollment" in order to facilitate the administration of this section.

The form of the certificate of enrollment shall be prepared by the State Board of Education and shall be designed to obtain the following information only:

(i) The name, address, and date of birth of the compulsory-school age child;

(ii) The name and address of the parent, guardian, or custodian.

(iii) A simple description of the type of education the compulsory-school-age child is receiving and, if such child is enrolled in a nonpublic school, the name and address of such school; and

(iv) The signature of the parent.

For the purposes of this subsection, a legitimate nonpublic school or legitimate home instruction program shall be those not operated or instituted for the purpose of avoiding or circumventing the compulsory attendance law.

(9) Notwithstanding any provision or implication herein to the contrary, it is not the intention of this Section to impair the primary right and the obligation of the parent... to choose the proper education and training for such child, and nothing in this section shall ever be construed to grant, by implication or otherwise, to the State of Mississippi, any of its officers, agencies or subdivisions any right or authority to control, manage, supervise or make any suggestion as to the control, management or supervision of any private or parochial school or institution for the education or training of children, of any kind whatsoever that is not a public school according to the laws of this state; and this Section shall never be construed so as to grant, by implication or otherwise, any right or authority to any state agency or other entity to control, manage, supervise, provide for or affect the operation, management, program, curriculum, admissions policy or discipline of any such school or home instruction program.

A homeschooler in Florida wrote to Ann Mordes of FLASH:

The day after I talked to you, Mr. Jones (Health and Rehabilitative Services intake counselor) called and said that I had to have a certified teacher in order to be operating legally. I, of course, told him that he was misinformed, which he very heatedly denied. I asked him where I could see that requirement in writing, and he said Chapter 39. I asked him what it said exactly and he replied that all children must attend school between the ages of 6 and 16. I asked him where it said that any private school had to employ or have on its staff a state-certified teacher, to which he replied that he did not know right off but that he would find out. We ended our conversation with his assurance that he would let me know where to find a statute supporting his statements. I had also during the course of the conversation mentioned the H.R.S. manual's definition of "truancy" which he said was not accurate. I asked him to please look it up to make sure. He said he would. He also said that we were *definitely* going to (you guessed it) *court*! I was chagrined. Immediately upon my hanging up the phone, I started to worry and wonder what I was going to do.

Not fifteen minutes later the phone rang. It was Mr. Jones who told me, very nicely, that I was right about everything that I had said! The definition of truancy, that there was no requirement for any private school to have on its staff a state-certified teacher, and very few other requirements. He went on to say that as far as he could ascertain I was operating within the law (I had mentioned that I was open to the public and that we are supported in part by tuition and/or gifts) and that as far as he was concerned the case was closed and his report to the State (?) would say just that. He asked for a copy of my attendance records and said that was all he needed.

A few minutes later I received another call, this time from the school social worker, who apologized for all the trouble and frustration I had been put through. She said that it had been equally frustrating for them as they have received no help or legally-supported information from either the school board or the Dept. of Education. She asked me to send her copies of the papers I have and said that she would be very grateful. She also said that she hoped the role of the school board would be a more supportive one in the future. She also assured me that if she learns of anything I need to be doing to be in compliance with the law she will let me know.

I am taking your advice to get everything in writing. . . . Thank you also for putting me in touch with Mr. Dallanegra (attorney). We are arranging for him to conduct a seminar in this area soon. He gave me some advice also and even dictated the affidavit he advised me to send H.R.S. instead of the attendance records that they requested.

[DR: See also "Success in Florida," *GWS* 28, page 4.]

Informal School In Calif.

Karen Olin Johnston (CA) wrote:

The *San Fernando Valley Homeschoolers*, of which we are members, has really been growing! At recent meetings we've had as many as 13 mothers and 23 children. . . . Over the summer we met a few times rather informally, at parks and at the beach. As the school year approached, some of the older children expressed the desire to go to school, to be with kids their age. We decided to organize something among our own children to fill that need. So at present we are having these things happening:

Once a month we meet at a park, all ages welcome; and also families just considering homeschooling are welcome. While the children play and get to know one another, us mothers give each other moral support, share resources and news info, discuss *GWS*, swap stories, etc.

Once a week, part of the group (mostly 7–12 years old) meet at alternate houses for a more formal "school day." Everyone involved agreed that they were much more eager to sit down to do math or writing if there was someone to do it with. The first week, one mother led singing and beginning music notation lesson with the whole group; then one group worked with Cuisenaire rods while another group solved math problems with some Montessori materials. After lunch the whole group played a game to open them up to creative writing, and on the side there were one-on-one experiences going on with a home computer, the piano, and puzzles. Two babies and two four-year-olds just merged right in alongside the older children.

We're also planning "field trips" once a week. . . . Last week we visited a park which was the estate of a silent-movie star. It had farm animals, old western-style home, nature trail, etc. . . .

One thing we've all noticed is how well these kids play together. There is virtually no whining, tattling, or fighting. . . . One time you'll see a 10-year-old playing with a 22-month-old, and the next time you see her she'll be involved in a game with an 8-and a 12-year-old.

Our only level of organization is a telephone tree, which operates in a complete circle, so that anyone can instigate communication with the group. Also, as one family had already set up their home as a private school with an affidavit last year, many of the older children are "enrolled" in it this year, as some sort of protection.

Other Local News

Addresses for all homeschooling organizations are listed in the back of this issue.

Arizona: From an article headlined "Home-instruction program earns good marks in first year" in the *Arizona Republic, 10/2/83:*

> Richard L. Harris, school superintendent in Maricopa County, said he is pleased with the achievement test scores of the approximately 150 children in the county who were instructed at home last year. Of that number, 14 failed to show adequate progress on the California Achievement Test, Harris said. After testing by a psychologist, four of the 14 were denied homeschooling exemptions. "I was surprised there were as few as 14 who seemed to be having problems," Harris said . . . "I think the parents who are teaching at home are courageous. They're challenging us (the public schools) to do a better job. . . ."

The article also said the state had administered 314 proficiency tests to parents wishing to teach their own children, and 214 of those passed. It was unknown how many who failed retook the test later and passed.

Families for Home Education published the longest directory we've seen yet in a local newsletter—99 families in the greater Phoenix area.

California: A campaign to place the "school voucher" initiative on the '84 ballot has been started. For information, contact *Parents Choose Quality Education*, 1537 Hood Rd, Suite D, Sacramento CA 95825; 916-921-0575 or 444-8725.

Evella Troutt of the *L.A. County Christian Home Educators Association* writes, "We are affiliated with a statewide network called *Christian Home Educators Association* which is directed by Karen Woodfin and Susan Beatty. We are not locked in with any particular Christian church—most of our members would fit into the historical evangelical framework. Our main efforts have been directed at establishing local support groups, and providing basic guidance and information to prospective homeschooling families. We would be happy to work with any families you wish to refer to us. We do have a county newsletter which is directed toward local news of support groups and field trips. . . ."

Janet McCormick, the California State Department of Education Liaison to Non-Public Schools, expects over 5,000 private schools to register with the state in 1983–1984, says Pam Pacula in *Home Centered Learning*, 10/83.

Georgia: About 400 people attended a homeschooling conference featuring Dr. Raymond Moore on Oct. 24–25, according to Connie Shaw of *Georgians for Freedom in Education*.

Hawaii: From Barbara Hussey (HI): "We are a growing group of families here interested in homeschooling. . . . For now (and this is from a district superintendent of schools), there is no state policy on policing homeschoolers. It is allowed as long as basic requirements are followed: (1) Registration with the Department of Education; (2) 4-year college degree (which we don't have, but which we feel we can overcome as we have many years in college); (3) Submission of a basic program outline to the district superintendent."

Idaho: Elizabeth Good writes, "It appears that the State School Board here in Idaho is gearing up for a legislative offensive against homeschoolers in the next session of our legislature. The attorney general was asked by the State Board of Education to render an opinion on the state's compulsory education law as it relates to private and home schools. . . . One legislator is drafting a bill based in part on the Arizona law which includes the yearly testing of homeschooled children. Many of the homeschoolers are in favor of his bill because it 'makes us legal.' Others of us have a totally different philosophy of 'testing' and could not in good conscience support such a bill...."

Indiana: The Summer Bulletin of the *Home Education Resource Center* listed what it called "an excellent booklet for IN homeschoolers," entitled *Indiana Law and Home Education*, available from: *Education Data*, 6401 Velmar, Ft. Wayne IN 46815, SASE suggested.

Iowa: Barb Tetzlaff reports in the *O!KIDS* newsletter that the state has appointed a committee to study homeschooling and non-approved Christian schools. A neighbor of the Tetzlaffs, Dr. Gordon Shipp, President of Faith Baptist Bible College, is on the committee, and they loaned him materials on home education, including *GWS*. Some quotes from the paper he submitted Sept. 16: "I could not detect one *single* force that prompted home education. I did find a dedicated group of people that were making real sacrifices to educate their children. They were fine people within their communities. They were not hermits, nor were they withdrawn. Many of the parents were not highly educated themselves in formal processes. They were good communicators and expressive.... Let us allow them their freedom...."

Maryland: Manfred Smith sent back issues of the *Maryland Home Education Association* newsletter and wrote, "I have just discovered that you are *not* on our current mailing list! I'm very sorry! You probably have been wondering what is happening here in Maryland.... When I read in *GWS* 35 that the Hjembo family was introducing legislation on homeschooling, I became very concerned. Our law is fine the way it is (at this time).... We have sympathetic people in the State Dept. of Ed. Introducing a law would set forces in motion (teachers are *very strong* in MD) that our few numbers would be hard pressed to stop. I've talked with the Hjembos—their legislator was interested, but is not willing to do anything right now...."

Massachusetts: Mario Pagnoni (MA) and Elaine Rapp (NH) have given two seminars on homeschooling in Haverill, MA and Manchester, NH. Mario is giving a slideshow and demonstration on "Home Computers and Home Schooling" Feb. 12, 9–noon, at Northern Essex Community College, Haverhill.

Michigan: The *Michigan Association of Home Educators* has started a newsletter, $10/4 issues. Some quotes from its first issue: "15 months after starting this organization, we have the names of over 800 homeschooling or interested families.... [At] the Conference in Lansing May 21 ... the final headcount was 940 people. Of those that turned in the questionnaire, 50% were currently educating their children at home. The response given most often by families who weren't educating their children at home was that their children were too young."

Pat Montgomery of *Clonlara School* sent us a clipping from the Detroit Free Press about a State Representative, Timothy Walberg of Tipton, who is teaching his children at home. Walberg is on the state House Education Committee. Pat says, "An associate of Walberg met him in the House chambers when this news broke and told them that he was very upset because Walberg was doing homeschooling when, in fact, this other fellow wanted to be the first Representative doing it!"

Missouri: Saralee Rhoads of *Families for Home Education* wrote, "The *MO/Kansas Home Educators* group disbanded a couple years ago, and general consensus was that the state would leave us alone if we kept a low profile. Well, they didn't. Last year a bill came up which would have made all home educators in our state guilty of a misdemeanor until proven innocent! As a result, our group was formed, and has been growing ever since. In July we had 200 members, and now there are 300+ on the mailing list. We have conducted a study on the nature of homeschooling in our state, and are preparing for further legislative battles...."

Nebraska: Gary and Marilyn Miller (NE) formed a support group of homeschoolers in August. Marilyn writes, "We have grown to 70 families on our mailing list, many of whom have withdrawn children from the school system and are facing litigation...."

New York: Harold Ingraham of *Calumet School* writes, "A network of sorts among New York State unschoolers now exists. I say 'of sorts' because I abhor the idea of centralization. Therefore, I merely set out to instigate a contact system of like-minded persons.... Anyone who writes or calls me asking for area contacts will be given the name of their area's contact leader. A self-addressed stamped envelope will do the trick. I have also suggested that the area leader run a small notice in the local newspape...."

Ohio: Ruth Kirchhausen (OH) wrote, "Lynne Leffel asked me to let you know that they did get permission to teach Matthew and Jessica at home. The Geauga County superintendent signed the agreement.... Also another family in the county got a permit by claiming a religious exemption, neither of the parents having college degrees. So it seems the Leffels' court experience last year (although they were found guilty of truancy) has proven to the superintendent the seriousness of these homeschooling parents and he has grudgingly accepted their presence this yea...."

Ontario: Anna Myers is coordinator for a new organization, *Ontario Home Schoolers*; newsletter, $10/year.

Quebec: Another Canadian group, the *Quebec Homeschooling Advisory*, has started a newsletter ($2/year). They sent us a copy of proposed education legislation in the Quebec National Assembly; we don't know how different it is from the current law, but it does mention as an alternative to school attendance, "receiving instruction at home equivalent, in the opinion of the school board, to that provided at school."

Texas: The newsletter of the *Texas Coalition for Home Education* reports, "Governor Mark White has appointed Ross Perot to head a special education commission to study the Texas education system.... His preliminary recommendations include the following: (1) that children should start school at age 4, (2) that school hours sould be lengthened, and (3) that children should go to school year-round.... Please write Ross Perot today and express your views (Address: EDS, 7171 Forest Lane, Dallas TX 75230)."

Washington: In *GWS* 32, we reported that Washington homeschoolers were fighting and supporting several education bills in the state legislature. The outcome, as reported in the *Unschoolers' Project*: "Truancy H.B. 282 died in the House Rules Committee.... H.B. 492, a bill that would have extended the compulsory school age, died in the Education Committee.... S.B. 4095, a parental rights' bill that Debra (Stewart) did not think had a chance to get out of committee, went farther than in the last two years.... It was caught in a time crunch.... Next year we have been promised an 'Interim Study Committee' to examine the present law for constitutionality...."

A new homeschooling group in the Spokane area, the *Family Learning Exchange*, has started a lengthy monthly newsletter ($18/year).—DR

Thoughts on "Day After"

I watched "The Day After" with my friend, neighbor, and editor, Merloyd Lawrence, and a small group of her friends. I found the film very well done and often very moving. Early in the film I noticed a surprising reaction in myself. The suspense, as we waited for what we knew would happen, that the bombs would go off, became so unbearable that I began thinking in the back of my mind, "Hurry up, set it off, I can't stand the waiting." Later it occurred to me with real fear that many people may have begun or may soon begin to feel that way in real life—since it's coming sooner or later, let's get it over with.

After the film was over we all agreed, as has been pointed out in many news stories, that the film enormously underestimated the damage that would have been done by a nuclear attack of that size. The bomb over Kansas City would probably have started a very large firestorm, and at that time of year there would have been enough vegetation in the fields so that the storm would probably have burned its way all the way to and through Lawrence. Most of the injured would have been in very much worse shape than the ones we saw, many of them with massive burns, and many of them blinded like the little boy, since the reflex which makes us look toward a bright light is a very hard one to repress. Radiation sickness in its more advanced stages causes acute diarrhea and vomiting, which was not shown and was only once even hinted at. The problems of raising food would have been far more severe than what was suggested; not only were those farmers' tractors electrically burned out, but they had no fuel, no seed, and none of the chemical fertilizers and pesticides without which our large scale agriculture cannot grow crops at all.

And as my brother-in-law put it, "Whose cellar was that horse in?" Where *did* that healthy horse come from?

A day or two later I talked on the phone with my sister in New Mexico. She told me that a number of young people in her town who saw the show had an interesting reaction, one I would not have expected. The special effects in the show, particularly the pictures of the injured and dying, were so much *less* bloody and horrible than the special effects these young people are used to seeing in the crime and horror films they regularly watch that they were bored and disappointed. "Is that all?" they asked. "Is that what all this fuss was about? Big deal!"

Many of you will have already learned from articles in the press about the danger that Carl Sagan in the panel spoke of after the film. There seems to be very strong evidence that even a small (small?) nuclear attack or exchange, involving as little (little?) as 100 megatons, would throw so much fine dust and smoke into the upper atmosphere that for several years the temperatures at the earth's surface would be greatly lowered, probably to well below freezing. Scientists from many countries, including Russia, who have seen the figures and the arguments seem to agree that this is so. I would add something that I have not yet seen in print, that even a much less drastic reduction in average year-round temperature, perhaps as little as twenty degrees, would be enough to reduce our agricultural output by eighty or ninety percent.

This very high probability of what Sagan called "the nuclear winter" seems to me to contain a very strong possibility of hope. For it is simply not true, as Schultz and Kissinger said after the panel, that preventing nuclear war has been the #1 aim of our government, or any government. The superpowers have from the beginning always thought of nuclear war as a possible option, an acceptable if costly and dangerous way to get something they could not get any other way. Both sides dream—fortunately, it has so far been only a dream—of a day when they could, if they chose, drop nuclear weapons on their enemy without having to worry about any being dropped on them in return. In the jargon of the times, this is called a "credible first strike possibility." This is what all this talk about so-called Star Wars weapons—anti-missile lasers, etc.—is about. If we could just find a way to destroy all enemy missiles in the air, dream the military leaders, then we could drop ours without any danger of retaliation.

The "nuclear winter," if this is accepted as being true or highly probable, should put an end to such foolish dreams, and might well give us the reason and impetus the big powers need to do what so far they have never done, despite their talk, which is to get serious about winding down and rolling back the nuclear arms race. For if it is the case that your own nuclear weapons will kill you, *no matter where they go off,* then even the most hard-nosed general or fanatic hawk (on either side) will soon have to agree that talk about "superiority" or "first-strike capability" or even "equality" makes no sense. A weapon that will kill the person who shoots it, no matter where he aims it, is not a weapon. If 100 megatons, *exploded anywhere*, will be enough to wipe out most life in the Northern Hemisphere, then even the feeblest wits should be able to figure out that stockpiles of 10–20 thousand megatons make no sense.

So out of all this gloomy talk may come a message of real hope. Let us do what we can to make it so.—JH

Famous Unschooler

Simone T., age 13, wrote in the 10/83 Hostex Exchange:

> Agatha Christie was eight years younger than her sister and brother, Marjorie and Louis. When it was time for them to go to school, their mother, Clarissa Margaret Beochmer Miller, firmly

believed in education. Marjorie was sent to a boarding school, and Louis was sent to public school. When it was Agatha's turn to go, her mother's views had changed. She now believed that education destroyed a child's brain and was ruinous to eyesight. Her mother tutored her at home, but she was sent out for certain special classes—art, singing, Swedish exercise, and cookery—just like I am.

Agatha Christie started writing very young. She used to tell stories to her mother every night. One night her mother told her to write the story down instead. Agatha next tried poems; then she wrote a long novel. She said some of the early writing wasn't too bad, but the whole thing was pretty poor. She later had much encouragement from Eden Phillpotts, a near neighbor, who was also a writer.

Her first whodunit, *The Mysterious Affair at Styles*, was an attempt to outwit her sister. Marjorie had challenged Agatha to write a mystery that she couldn't figure out after reading the first chapter. Agatha succeeded in stumping her sister.

Two "Special Ed" Kids Free

From Larraine Falk (IL):

I have been educating my son, J.D. (9½), at home for 1½ years. Many times during those years I have wanted to write and thank you for your inspiration.... If it wasn't for you, *GWS*, and *Teach Your Own*, we would not have found out about homeschooling, or had the courage to do it.

J.D. always loved learning, he is very curious and creative, and was reading by age 4. By 2nd grade, he read on a 7th grade level. However, while he was in school, I saw his creativity drop. He no longer did art projects at home. He refused to do any work in school unless it interested him. If pressured to do the work, he erupted into tantrums which the teachers were not able to handle and he was sent home. I was truly perplexed by the whole thing as I knew him to love learning.

In the middle of the first grade, we put him in a private school, thinking that the public school was the problem. Things improved but not greatly. We started meeting with the principal who was also a clinical psychologist. We followed eagerly all of the suggestions of the principal. Most of the time I intuitively felt they were bad suggestions. However, this person was an expert in child development and I was only a concerned first-time parent. Therefore, she must be right. At any rate, her suggestions did not help much.

In the beginning of second grade, the private school would not take him, so we put him back in public school, this time in the behavior disorder class, which was the only way they would take him. Things became much worse. He was being sent home from school several times a week for tantrums. All of the progress he had made in the private school disappeared. At this point we were desperate. We hated parenthood, our only child, ourselves. It was sheer hell. *The "experts" even told us we were bad parents and J. D. would probably end up institutionalized.*

One day I was watching J.D. in swim class in the bleachers. The woman next to me started talking to me out of the blue, and told me about her son's problems in school, and how she was planning to take him out of school and teach him at home. I had never heard of homeschooling. The idea hit me like a thunderbolt and I knew that it was the answer. I bought *Teach Your Own* on the woman's suggestion and attended a homeschoolers' meeting in the area. Within a month we had taken J.D. out of school.

Two weeks after homeschooling began, many friends commented to me how relaxed J.D. seemed, how mature he had become, how loving and giving he was, how open and friendly he had become, etc., etc. This was after only *two weeks*! After a few months of homeschooling, our home life became very loving, warm, and wonderful. My husband and I even started to talk about having another child.... We had definitely not wanted any more children while J.D. was in school! Parenting was too awful. But it became rewarding, fulfilling, and enjoyable.

So much so, that we now have an adorable baby girl, Alisa, 3½ months old.

Alisa's arrival has been perfect for J.D.'s emotional growth. He adores her and cares for her. J.D. can't wait for her to wake up in the morning and be with her all day. Kids sure miss a lot of loving relationships with their siblings when they go to school all day long.

It took about a year for the school wounds to heal, for J.D. to become creative and fully interested in learning again. It has taken me about 1½ years to be able to write about it or really talk about it.

J.D. gets along with other kids so well now. Socialization in school was a very negative experience. School children seem to love being mean to the sensitive, intelligent ones. J. D. has no trouble making friends now.

From Mary Ann Daniels, 7 Birchwood Trailer Pk, Fishkill NY 12524:

You have ended three of the most horrible years of our lives. Our daughter is now a homeschooler.

Since she entered the door at kindergarten, she rebelled against paperwork. She went steadily downhill and me with her. She's been in three different schools and hasn't hit a teacher yet who could handle her. Last year we learned she was "hyperactive." She was thrown on Ritalin by a neurologist. It didn't help much, and when it was wearing off she had unexplained crying spells. I went to the library to learn more about "hyperactivity" and found Dr. Ben Feingold's book, *Why Your Child Is Hyperactive.* I placed Judy on his all-natural diet, and we couldn't believe the change that took place. Her behavior changed, her health changed—but her attitude about school didn't.

I began reading your books and they helped me understand her better. In fact, your books made me reflect back on my own school years. I began to realize that Judy was a lot like me—very selective in what she wanted to learn.

We had a lot of pressure put on us by her second-grade teacher to have her tested. . . . Our guilt feelings made us go along with it. The psychologist told me she thought Judy had an auditory language processing problem. I had been told this when she was in kindergarten, but we felt all along her problem was motivation. . . . I will never forget the day I had to be at the meeting to label her. I had all I could do not to cry, as I felt I was doing her an injustice. She is about as learning disabled as I am!

Around this time I was in a bookstore and *Teach Your Own* caught my eye. I bought it and can honestly say it was the best investment I ever made. I began building a case for Judy to be taught at home. I had kept everything on her (report cards, psychological reports, and my own log). At the close of school I sent an eight-page letter with fifteen enclosures to the State Department of Education requesting permission to homeschool her. I had enrolled her with the Calvert School and listed all the texts to be used for her third grade curriculum along with a week's lesson plan. The State wrote and told me under the N.Y.S. Education Law I could teach her at home. I just had to present my program to the local superintendent for approval. I brought all the material I had prepared for the State to the superintendent. Two days later I received permission to teach Judy at home.

You can never know the relief I feel. I know my daughter can learn, and a lot better than she was learning in school. Three years of agony are over. Judy is no longer "learning disabled." I started working with her four weeks ago and I have noticed a change already. She was convinced she was stupid, but now she sees she is learning.

Ray Moore Offers Curriculum

Dr. Raymond Moore, author of *Better Late Than Early, School Can Wait, Home-Spun Schools,* and *Home-Grown Kids,* is now offering a correspondence course for grades 1–8 through the *Hewitt-Moore Child Development Center.* According to the brochure, the intention is "to provide a program that (1) contains carefully selected Christ-centered materials from a variety of publishing houses; (2) is not too structured; (3) avoids myths and nonsense stories; (4) plans for no formal schooling before about 8 or 10; (5) lists costs clearly and specifies what services are offered (personal counsel, tests, legal advice, etc.). . . . Cost is $250 tuition plus $100–$200 in books. Address for more information: PO Box 9, Washougal WA 98671.—DR

Teen Works At Science Museum

From a reader in New England:

I was interested in what te mother of teenagers ("Asks About Teens," *GWS* 33) had to say and ask. We have been having a similar situation with our "all but" 13-year-old daughter—a restlessness, a desire to have a friend her age. We, also, don't get together with other homeschoolers (there are none that we know of in this area) and we just don't know any families whom we see regularly with kids around that age. I know these things would help. We live in the country, fairly isolated and simply.

So far we have found one thing that has helped. Since spring, our daughter has been volunteering at a science museum two days a week. To say that she loves it is an understatement! She's been doing a great deal of work in the museum's "mount room," cataloging their collections and learning names (in scientific as well as laymen's terms) of many birds and mammals in the process. (She quizzes us on the scientific names and we have great times trying to guess what animal it is!) She's become quite the birder. Occasionally she gets to go on a field trip with the museum's naturalist. And we all got to go (at special staff rates) on a whale watch sponsored by the museum. (For anyone who hasn't done that, *please* do, if at all possible—*definitely*, an experience of a lifetime! Hopefully we can repeat it again and again. . . .)

The naturalist, by the way, has been very impressed by both of our children's obvious love of and knowledge of nature. He said that he'd be more than happy to take them out into the field any time. All the museum staff thinks that it's wonderful that our daughter has the chance to be doing this and have been very supportive, giving her a range of things to do to broaden her experiences there. Occasionally she will take over for the receptionist, and the accountant wants to teach her some of that. She can use the cash register and she helps get out mailings at times. Everyone has found what a good worker she is and the demand has become high! Her major focus is and will be, at her request, the natural history work.

None of this has meant much interaction with people her age, though there was a teen-age girl there over the summer which was nice for both of them. This particular girl goes to school but has had a hard time making friends there because she is considered "different." She plays the cello, for one thing, and was so glad to find another kid who thought that was great! She and our daughter went camping and hiking together and had a great summer. It's been hard for them to get together since school started as they live far from each other.

High school is becoming the issue—to go or not to go next year. We have found a very small alternative high school within reach (though not an easy reach) which we are looking into. School isn't wanted, but a chance to meet some kids is. Our daughter wants somewhere to go sometimes where there are kids but does not want to give up the museum. This alternative school will take kids part-time, offers internships, independent study, all sorts of things. They work around the student instead of the other way around and think that homeschooling is great. . . . May be just the thing.

Our 9-year-old son seems to have no complaints and spends his time reading or playing with and observing nature. He says that he's going to be a scholar, builder of ships—both the water and space type—a homesteader, and a naturalist. Sounds like a busy and interesting life ahead!

John, I wanted to comment on "Spaceship School," *GWS* 34. You could have been writing about my niece. . . . She will not do anything unless there is a chance of seeing or meeting "cute boys." Hardly anything is done for itself—what can be enjoyed by simply doing it or what can be learned from it. How sad. When our daughter told her about the museum work, her question was, "Are there any cute boys?" Since the only males at the museum are men rather than boys, her response was, "Oh, I wouldn't like it then." I realize that it's a natural time to begin taking an interest in the opposite sex, but it is not *un*natural to have other interests also!

I, too, would like to see more about teens in *GWS*. . . . We know of only one other homeschooling family with a teen-ager and they live in a different part of the state.

How She Met Dates

Joyce Kinmont wrote in the October Tender Tutor:

> Andrea, our social butterfly, has thoroughly enjoyed her three hours a day at the high school, but I hope there will be a better place for the rest of my children to go. The question, of course, is: Can a girl have a social life without going to the high school? And what *that* really means is: How will she meet any *boys*?
>
> When Andrea turned 17 this summer we made a list of all the boys she had gone out with in the year she had been dating. There were eleven. Six of them were already out of school. Of those six, two were in our church ward, two she met in plays they were in at the community theater, one she met at a clogging class, and one has been a good friend since she was twelve. Another boy was from a different high school, and she met him at the theater. She did meet four of the eleven boys at the high school, but she also met these same boys at church dances.
>
> So, if she had never attended the high school, her dating life would have been basically the same!

J.P. And Calvert

From Kathy Mingl (IL):

> J.P. has started 1st grade (Calvert) . . . . I didn't send for the course just because it was "time for him to start school," as nearly everyone said— though I didn't argue. I *asked* him if he wanted me to get it for him, and he said he did. This boy has *plans*, you see—he intends to build helicopters and walkie-talkies from kits, design robots and spaceships, and find out where to prospect for gold, etc., etc. . . . He has come to his own decision that he wants to learn how to read and solve number problems (actually, he does know the mechanics of reading, he just has gaps in his theory, and lacks zip). He's willing to accept schoolwork as a help in practicing his skills, but only in the areas where he needs it—if the games and puzzles are too easy, he loses interest (he says, "The tricky ones are neater").
>
> For $225, Calvert sent him two boxes of books, instructions, and supplies—paper, crayons, pencils, etc. J.P. freaked out over the riches—*all his*! He made me drag the desk we'd saved for him out of the garage and put it in his room right away, and he was stashing all his stuff in it even before he let me finish screwing the legs and handles on—he just climbed over me.
>
> I was a bit intimidated by it all, myself, so at first I tried doing it "by the book," until I could figure out what the heck I was doing. Well, that didn't work—for some reason, I felt like a *teacher*. J.P. got antsy, and I got irritable. Doing a little bit of each subject just long enough for the kid to get interested, and then switching to something else, makes him feel like the whole business is *your* idea, not his. Asking "know-it-all" questions all the time gets sadly in the way of scientific rapport.
>
> Most of all, I can't imagine what kind of kid this course is addressed to. It's true that they tell you to "accept the child as he is," and modify the program "in the light of his interests and abilities." The directions say to find out what areas the child has trouble with and make up more lessons for him to practice—but what they do *not* tell you is what to do with their dratted program when the kid swallows their little morsel of learning whole, not to mention the spoon and half your arm, and then brightly looks up for more. . . . It seems to me that *anyone* who had reached the ripe old age of 5½ would be beyond the speed of this 1st grade stuff, and yet, I have it on the authority of J.P.'s godmother, an elementary schoolteacher, that these are the standard texts the public schools use, and the workbooks are much more colorful and interesting—she got quite excited about them, as a

matter of fact. J.P. does need work in the areas they cover, not so much for information as to clarify what he knows in his own head, but he has a naturally wide range of interests, and a good ability to duplicate what he sees and hears, so his "curriculum" has to be considerably padded out.

For instance, the other day we were supposed to "review the sound for the letter b" by means of my printing the words *bed* and *bat* on a sheet of paper, telling the "pupil" what the words are, and asking him if they begin with the same letter, and also the same sound! Well, what we *did* do was skip that part entirely. I think I'm going to have J.P. just do the test pages until we get to something with a little meat on it. We zipped through the workbook exercise; I was supposed to *tell* him what the pictures were, and ask him if they started with the same sound as "bug," but really, it's not *safe* to insult J.P.'s intelligence like that—I told him what they wanted and let him figure it out for himself. Then we hit the next lesson, comparing rhyming words, but instead of the incredibly tedious process the directions called for, we made up stories, with J.P. writing down all the words he could think of that ended with the same sound, and both of us trying to fill in the action: "*Dad* was *sad* when his boy was *bad*. Mom was *mad* and said 'You *cad*! Is this a new *fad*?' So she spanked her *lad* with a paper *pad*, and when she stopped, he said, '*Gad*, am I *glad*!'" Pat and his adventure with the ubiquitous rat was another classic.

The next day, J.P. did several lessons in his arithmetic workbook, which involved learning to draw the numbers 0–9. Of course, he knows those already, but he had never considered them in the light of legibility, which is rather a different problem from merely recognizing them. He was quite interested, but he naturally objected a bit to doing it exactly the way the *book* said to. I didn't insist, but I told him just to try it the way they suggested and see what worked best, because the main thing was to be able to tell what they were supposed to be, and beyond that, you can get as fancy as you want. (I had showed him my *Encyclopedia of Phototype Styles* which has *5000* letter and number designs.) He wrote 0–9 all the way through several times, galloped on through 19, noticed that $10 + 10 = 20$, and then got all excited about a dot-to-dot puzzle in his workbook. He dragged all his dot-to-dot coloring books out and did puzzles for the rest of the day, some of them with numbers up to 60! (I think those are very good, by the way, especially the ones that include letter-dot puzzles as well, because he practices things like "What comes after K?," not just saying all of them straight through, like the alphabet song. *I* get mixed up on those, too.)

With science, J.P. is so busy with his own lines of investigation that he goes for long stretches without any interest in the book. Then one day he did five plant experiments (sprouting seeds in dark and light, rooting cuttings, collecting different kinds of seeds, etc.) in one morning. Letting him figure the pictures out for himself and staying out of it as much as possible seems to work best. The next lesson mentioned "reptiles" on the first page, and we never got beyond that—we looked the word up in the dictionary, went through his *Reptiles and Amphibians* book, looked up where boa constrictors come from on the globe, got off into geography, magnetic poles, geo- vs. helio-centrism, Galileo, official persecution, and the theory of continental drift.

By the way, another area where J.P. and Calvert part company is this "correct study posture" business. When J.P. works, he stands, kneels, or sprawls. When he is especially happy about what he's doing, he bounces, hops, dances, or "flies" (flings himself at things). When he's tired of doing something, he falls down in a heap. When he's excited (because they thought they could fool him, but they sure couldn't! He's too smart for them!), he spins like a whirlwind. He *does* sit sometimes, but it's mostly in my lap, and if he's still it's because he's parked somewhere, like on the floor when I'm trying to make supper. J.P. can't be creative without getting his whole body into it—there's so much energy it just has to spill over. ("Dear, dear—hyperactive," right?)

All of this may sound like tepid approval of Calvert, but really, they have a very nice, consumer-oriented product. The fact that they've been in business for over 75 years lends a certain comforting respectability to the situation— something to fall back on when you have to defend yourself from people who can't see the *real* issues. Of course, their "Advisory Teaching Service" is another $130, and they don't give you any certificates or other impressive pieces of paper to flash at relatives or officials without that. I can't imagine J.P. and any "advisory teacher" seeing eye-to-eye, any more than he and a public school teacher would, so we dispensed with that.

I know this is old stuff to you, but it's become very real to Tony and me right now that slowing J.P. down into a narrow, public-school kindergarten pattern would be about as useful to him as chopping a baby bird's wings off in order to teach him to walk. J.P. is still very little—his attention is flighty, and his self-discipline almost non-existent. His social development is healthy, but rudimentary; his grasp of ethical principles is remarkable, but elusive in application. If he does go to school eventually, I want him to have all those things down first, including being able to hold his own when he knows he's right, even in a difference of opinion with an adult.

Life At Home

From Virginia Schewe (IL):

Our home school (Hookdale Christian Academy, Inc.) is sailing along with ever-increasing success. After the initial rebellion against anything that even remotely resembled public school structure, the youngsters have made and settled nicely into their own tailor-made schedules.

Since we are a farm family, quite a number of our science projects are closely tied to agriculture. The latest project is a fish farm—complete with 10-gallon aquarium for the showy stuff and a 5-gallon nursery tank.... The long winter days don't look so long any more with the fish to care for.

Both boys did a man's work in the fields this past farming season, and *they feel good about themselves!* We put them on the payroll and they did a swell job.... Mark (14) learned how to operate the combine and he also drilled (planted) over 100 acres of wheat this fall. Bill (13) did most of the disking and field cultivating just ahead of the planter, plus hauling the harvested grain. Marsha (9) was the radio dispatcher—we use 2-way radios to keep track of everyone since most of us are strung out over a 5-mile-long area during farming season. She has "patch-through" mastered. And all this in addition to the regular reading, writing, and 'rithmetic.

Quite by accident this summer, I opened the doors to genealogy and suddenly history became very interesting to the youngsters. After we discovered that a great-grandpa had been in the Army during the Civil War, did a little research in the service records, traced his path, and read about the battles he had taken part in, the Civil War wasn't just some old dumb scrap any more.

From Robyn Midouhas (NJ):

We are keeping our 6-year-old son Stephen home this year. Last year he attended a private Christian school which we felt was too structured. We are using an informal curriculum (Dr. Raymond Moore's) with him and he is spending time in my husband's architectural office each week.

Our public school system has been very supportive—not that they totally agree, but they will leave it up to us. We didn't even have to show a curriculum!

Since we've started homeschooling, we look at everything in life as a learning experience.... We bought a set of World Book encyclopedias and are constantly using them as a reference.

Billie Jean Bryant (GA) wrote:

Channel 11 in Atlanta is doing a 30-minute feature on homeschooling. We are to be filmed and I plan to have the children simply doing what they usually do: some studying and reading; constructing sound equipment; doing needlework; playing guitar and flute; cooking; caring for goats, snakes, and dogs; studying birds; assisting the handicapped to ride horses; learning gardening from neighbors; canning; dancing; skating; fishing.... Do you think

More On Saxophone Lessons

Pat Farenga's continued adventures with the sax (GWS 34):

The store was neatly arrayed with displays of various musical instruments.... Noticing the 8x10 glossy photos of famous contemporary horn players that hung below the shiny new saxophones, I felt a bit intimidated. They were all inscribed to this effect, "To Emilio, Thanks for your help. Best, Sonny Rollins." What am I doing here? I thought.

"Can I help you?" asked the man with curly white-hair who stood behind the counter.

"John Payne sent me here. He told me to ask for Emilio."

"I'm Emilio. What can I do for you?"

"I just had my first sax lesson yesterday and I'd like to rent a tenor sax."

"I don't think we have any in stock. Let me check." Emilio returned empty-handed. "I don't have any used tenors. I can let you have an alto; it's cheaper."

"I just started and I really want to play tenor."

"Are you a full-time student in town?"

"No. I work as a dorm director at the Boston Conservatory."

Emilio was very unimpressed. I quickly added, "And I work part-time at Holt Associates. It's a small company on Boylston Street."

Emilio looked at me cannily, then he said, "I trust you. I'll tell you what. I have a new Yamaha tenor I can rent you."

"That's great! Just show me how to take care of it."

"I'll show you everything you need to get started," Emilio said as he left me. The sax he gave me was still wrapped in its original packing. Emilio told me how to assemble and maintain it, then turned the sax over to my charge.

Later that day I went back to my dormitory and unpacked the sax. I examined it closely, trying to see how its labyrinth of holes, connections, and levers work. I then strapped the sax around my neck and prepared to hit one of the three notes I learned the day before. It was astounding! I spent at least ten minutes blowing into the thing and all I got out of it was a blue face. I removed the mouthpiece from the sax and tried to make some of the obnoxious sounds we made during yesterday's lesson. After some experimenting with different mouth positions I finally found the one that produced the proper noise. Then I tried to make the noise again. I was walking around my room, carefully squeaking and squawking when I heard a loud knock on my door, followed by a dorm resident's concerned and baffled voice, "Are you all right, Pat?" I knew then it was going to be a weird experience learning something new.

One thing neither John Payne nor anyone else ever warned me about the saxophone is that it numbs your mouth into granite. When a player's "chops" were described as good or bad, I thought they referred to their improvisational originality, not to their facial muscles. As I rubbed my numb jowls and massaged the back of my jaw bone below the ear, I realized what "chops" are: the limits of one's blowing abilities.

I worked on the first four lessons in my *Tune-A-Day* book, and by the next week's lesson I was able to play "The Little A and B March," "Merrily We Roll Along," and other timeless favorites of the sax repertoire.

My second lesson included information about slurring and tonguing notes, both aspects of playing that I'm still working on. John told me to read and do the material *but to go on before mastering it.* "Don't get hung up on this stuff. If it doesn't come, skip it for now. The important thing is to keep you getting a consistent sound from the instrument." During that lesson John showed me how all the notes I learned in the previous lessons could be put together to form the scale of D major. "Once you learn a few more scales we'll have you improvising, and even in the choir," John would tell me. John always reminds me where my practice and lessons will lead me and what I can do with the knowledge I'm picking up every week. Everything—improvising, playing in the Choir, playing in a small ensemble, learning my favorite songs off records—all of these are made to be within my reach. That's something that gets neglected a lot when you're learning something new; seeing how you can benefit from it in the long run.

It is especially nice knowing that no one but me decides how fast I will be travelling towards these goals. If I stop for a breather while I do something else, my lessons slow down accordingly; if I whiz through my assignments, John will load me up with more than enough to keep me busy. My proficiency on the sax is still in the very green beginner's stage, but that's not important to me now. Now that I've started and gotten sounds out of it I feel ready to dig in for the long haul. I haven't any desire to become a card-carrying musician, but I do want to be able to get together with a group of likeminded folks and play "Satin Doll" with some skill and creativity.

What was very helpful in getting me to enjoy practicing was learning a Blues Scale in my second lesson. John Payne told me to just "mess around with it" at the same time I was doing Lessons 4–10 in the *Tune-A-Day* book. The Blues scale sounds so good on the sax; and since the blues is the basis of Jazz and Rock and Roll, you realize you can do exciting things with this readily identifiable sound.

[To be continued.]

A Single Parent's Year

From Lynne Norris (IN):

Jan. 11: This is a very hard letter to write. I feel very much a failure.

The reason being that I've had to put my son, Daniel, into school. It is every bit as awful as we expected. But finally life on working welfare in New York City became absolutely untenable. I moved back to my old home town in Indiana in hopes that financially things would improve. They haven't. Being a single parent the financial burden falls on me. I have very little earning power as it is, and none of my cottage industry skills can support us anymore. I have no one who can watch Daniel while I work, he is too small to leave alone eight hours a day, and cannot afford to pay anyone to look in on him. We live in a fairly isolated area. When I say he would be *alone* if left as a latchkey child, he would really be alone. The only babysitter I can afford is the school system. We feel awful. Especially since the first words out of the new principal's mouth were that children who misbehaved would be paddled.

I wasn't "done in" by the school system. I was done in by Reaganomics. I can't even renew my subscription. I don't have as much money off of welfare as I did when I was on.... Out here I couldn't even look for work with a small child in tow. I guess my advice to other single parents is to stay in the largest metropolitan area. Situations can be much more flexible that way.

John wrote back:

1) Cheer up! The game isn't over yet.

2) You're not a failure.

3) We'll keep sending you *GWS*, at least for this year. Maybe you can get us some other subscriptions, or perhaps an ad for the magazine.

4) Don't worry quite so much about the school. The school game is not hard to play, once you know it's a game. It's a dumb, boring, stupid, often cruel place, and it's a shame children should have to waste so much time there, but any smart kid, and I'm sure your Daniel is smart, can figure out how to do most of the things s/he has to do, and how to stay out of such kinds of trouble as s/he could get into. Think of school as a game which you and he have to play together for a while, perhaps no more than a year or two. Perhaps much less.

5) I don't know whether Daniel is too young to be a latchkey kid. Why not let him be the judge of that? Say to him, "Here are the choices: play the school game, or be at home alone during the school day. Which do you want to try?"

6) I looked on the map, and see you're not far from Louisville, where we have some homeschoolers. I know some of them, and they are very nice folks.... Why not make contact with them? It would probably encourage you to meet some of them and go to some of their meetings, etc. Get them to put you on whatever mailing list they have. If for any reason life at school gets very bad,

you might be able to send Daniel to spend a few days, or a week, or more if you both like, as a kind of vacation from school. Someone over there might be able to find you a job, or help you find one, or take care of Daniel during the day, or whatever.

Don't despair! There's lots of time left to run, and plenty of friends out there, and some of them not too far away. Write again soon, tell us how things are going. Good luck to you both.

[Lynne wrote in May:] I was able to locate only one family in Louisville. We did get together one evening socially, but the mother is somewhat ambiguous about what she wants for her son. Also her children are younger than Daniel.... They are, however, knowledgeable and friendly people.

After I put my son into school in January, I met with the new Superintendent of the New Albany-Floyd County Schools, Dr. Tracy Dust. He willingly spent two hours with me, discussing my past experience in teaching, gifted education advocacy, curriculum ideas, homeschooling, and what mutual exchanges we might have. Dr. Dust said that if I decide to homeschool again that he would like to work with me rather than against me. He is familiar with the concept and practice of homeschooling from other school districts he has served.

Daniel has found that school is as boring as we thought it would be.... I must admit there was some curiosity on both our parts as to whether he could "make it," when many had accused us of living in a fantasy world. Daniel adapted to school within two weeks. The kids like him, despite his inability to understand the hostility between boys and girls. I have explained this to him, but he still doesn't like it. Though his first reading test came out a year below grade level, I did not pay much attention to it.... He had never had a standardized test before. The general attitude was "We told you so." After two weeks the teacher was keeling over how well he could read, how well-behaved, how intelligent, etc., Daniel was.... He finished the year in the top quarter of the class. We refused to get caught up in the notion of rushing to beat schedules, feeling guilty or "bad" for talking in the lunchroom (they are not allowed to talk at lunch time), or just plain bad scholarship that came out of the school in the form of textbooks, announcements, and misinformation. The children who attend the school are, for the most part, what might be termed "culturally disadvantaged."... These children's lives revolve around their family, the shopping mall, and television.

Since Daniel had to do 14 book reports in the half year, as opposed to the other children having all year to do the 14, he quit reading for recreation. He finished the reports about four weeks ago. Last night he picked up his first book for fun. He did win a two-county writing contest. He won for a prose piece on the baby bird we raised last summer. The piece was written in December, before he went to school.

We have been continuing an art class held at a local art supply store. The teacher is one the school system laid off. She is quite good and Daniel loves going. He also takes dancing lessons and is an excellent swimmer. This summer we will also do an art project and a natural history project for the county's Mini-4H exhibit. Again, this is stuff the school does not do. What this school experiment has demonstrated is that we were right, Daniel and I. We also learned that sometimes we have to compromise and adjust, but that we can survive once we know the game, as John said.

As to this fall, it seems unlikely that Daniel will go to school. I have been very lucky in picking up a class to teach at the local university in Freshman Composition.... Daniel can wait in the student lounge while I teach.... Also, I may do some teaching for another university.... If I have just two classes to teach we'll do OK.

Nov. 11: My negotiations with Dr. Dust continued throughout the summer. I brought him my homeschooling records, stressed my growing knowledge of community resources, and my interest in current trends regarding all types of schooling. I introduced him to Daniel.... Though Dr. Dust and I have points of philosophical disagreement, he has been very generous with his time, and we have developed a mutual respect for one another's position.

The upshot is that we have permission to homeschool. I do send in informal end-of-month reports, though these are not requested. I want to demonstrate my cooperation so if anything unpleasant should occur, my cooperation, good planning, and record-keeping would be evident.

Daniel and I spent the summer gardening; working on the 4-H exhibits; visiting museums, an industrial site and a health care facility; attending on-going programs at the public library; and digging one day at an archeological site.

I've had a little better luck at job hunting.... The state vocational college hired me to teach English, and a third college asked me to direct a play for them in the spring. In each instance Daniel can go with me, sit in the student study area, and do his work. Anybody who has tried "adjuncting" knows how little it pays. Teaching, preparation, and grading time brings the wage to $4 an hour without any benefits. But it does allow us to homeschool, and that's something no other jobs around here could do.

This fall Daniel is still taking art class, but has traded dancing for a children's bowling league. He has fallen in love with anything that flies, prompting unsupervised building of plane models, massive library research (he found out who the Wright brothers were a week before I was going to have him look them up), and the keeping of a journal which includes names of planes, names of models he wants, sketches and ideas for things that fly. There is a lot of hot-air ballooning around here, so we try to see that as much as we can. Neither a school nor I could have gotten Daniel to do as much writing and record-keeping as his own interest in flying has done. (Incidentally, we have found that any kind of oil or acrylic paints do fine on plastic models, thereby saving buying any expensive model paint.)

I have done two impromptu lectures on homeschooling in my classes, since my day students noticed that I had a 9-year-old in tow. Only a few thought it odd, but I suspect that is because what the locals call a "laid-back attitude" is actually mental inertia.... About half had not been inside a public library for years, so I took them on a field trip. None knew how to use the card catalog.... They had no idea that the library contained technical books, best-sellers, records, pictures, or children's books (some are parents). These students must have a high school diploma or a G.E.D. to enroll in the school. This is beyond sad. This is tragic.

So, though our finances remain at rock bottom and we have huge waves of homesickness for New York City, the home of our hearts, we are able to get on with the important work at hand: learning, living, and caring in the way that is best for us.... As soon as my November checks are in I will pay for this year's renewal to *GWS* and I graciously thank you for the past year's freebie.

Responses To "On Guilt"

From Susan Jaffer (PA):

I'd like to comment on John's response to the mother who felt guilty (*GWS* 33); it was excellent. La Leche League receives many letters on the subject of guilt, and their replies usually center around the statement that they present ideals. I always suspected that many of the mothers weren't guilty at all, but resentful. They were uncomfortable with the idea of natural childbirth, they didn't bond with their newborns, and they didn't want to breastfeed at least not the League way. So there was LLL telling the world about all these things that are best for babies, and that naturally generates a lot of hostility and defensive behavior in those mothers who aren't giving their babies the "best."

This is not to say I've always been the perfect breastfeeder or unschooler; in fact, I managed to totally foul up my first nursing experience. Sure, LLL's newsletter occasionally reminds me of those mistakes, but that doesn't dilute the fact that it helped me enormously when I successfully nursed my second and third babies.

As for *GWS*, some of its ideas have been entirely new to me; some I don't even agree with (yet?). But many of these ideas have inspired me to make some changes. I have to confess that for years I inadvertently discouraged my children from exploring new areas of capability because of my aversion to mess-making (I have a terrible time with my own messes and can never keep up with them) and lack of patience. *GWS* is teaching (did I say "teaching"?) me to change my ways. I've also learned that while being a good talker has certain advantages, it is also a good idea to refrain from reacting verbally to one's children once in a while. (A nice way of saying I'm learning to keep my mouth shut.) And on the positive side, *GWS* has enabled me to see that in many ways I have provided a wonderful home school for my kids. We are all ravenous readers, enthusiastic artists, and ever-curious explorers of nature.

One of the things I like best about your newsletter is that it reflects your open attitude. That is, you share letters from people who are doing homeschooling in a multitude of ways—or not doing it at all. All of their opinions count, they are all treated with respect—and no one is ever made to feel guilty.

Toots Weier (WI) wrote:

The article John wrote ("On Guilt," *GWS* 33) about his friend criticizing *GWS* for writing so much about "Superkids" was very interesting. I had wondered myself why so much was written about the above average homeschooled children, those who are not only very intelligent but also have a great variety of interests. I found John's reply to be very important.

Forest (8) has *never* had a vast assortment of interests. Before he could read, he drew picture after picture, every day. I marvelled at them all, each one unique and so very special. I believed he had a genuine talent in art, but knew of nobody who could encourage him to pursue it in a way that he would benefit and expand his talent.

Now that he can read, he reads a great part of the day away. It's been months since he's drawn a picture. I believe that through his reading he will also be exploring and may find new interests through that.

For a short while he was very interested in violin. I had taken him to a Suzuki class so that we could sit and watch. He thought it looked like fun, and was sure he wanted to start lessons. Well, as it was, we couldn't start right then, and now that we can, he's lost interest. I was really looking forward to hearing music in our home. . . . I'm thinking that possibly sitting in on a class again will spark his interest.

I don't think the lack of interest in our children points to them as being lazy or careless. It's more a matter of what they are exposed to and what's available. In town, 20 miles from here, the children's theater was holding auditions for a Christmas play. I asked Forest if he was interested in trying out and he said *no*. It would have meant a lot of chasing around, but I was willing to do it if he had been interested.

I did check out 4-H while they had a booth set up at the county fair. Since then I got a call from a very friendly woman who gave me all the information on 4-H. I passed it on to Forest and he is rather excited, especially since they encourage the participation of parents. The only drawback is that 8 years is the youngest age that can join which leaves Horizon Blue (5) out. He is disappointed, but that will be a very special time for either Steve or myself to have with him while Forest is at the meeting with one of us.

Disapproving Relatives

[DR:] A number of recent letters have mentioned the same issue. Some excerpts:

Our only problem now is the fact that my folks are adamantly against this decision. My father was a school superintendent.

My husband's mother is opposed to homeschooling. She doesn't feel that an "untrained" person knows enough. But she taught all her five children music and most of them can play beautifully.

The most difficult thing is when people you love openly disapprove of what you're doing. My parents were visiting for two weeks this summer and were constantly on my case about sending my son to school. They truly love him and are worried about him and no amount of talking convinces them that this is best for him. They are sure he'll grow up to be a social misfit. The fact that he reads and writes far beyond his years is actually a point *against* him. "He'll be *too* smart to have any friends." I can't win!

He does have lots of friends of all ages but they really believe he *needs* to be with a group of 30 kids his own age! When I recount some of the cruel treatment he suffered in school, they say he has to learn to "take it" or he won't survive in the outside world.

Nothing I say helps. They think this is just another of my rebellious streaks.... I'd be interested to hear how other homeschoolers cope with beloved grandparents who greatly oppose homeschooling.

Most of our relatives will be totally against this (as if it is any of their business), as they are about our lifestyle and macrobiotic vegetarian diet. They're already asking if our son can count numbers, blah, blah, blah.

When we make our decision about how we plan to handle the letter to the superintendent, I would like to give a copy to those asking. I would like to tell them not to discuss this subject in front our children, as I don't want them being hassled, like "Don't you want to go to school?" and "You'll have to learn to eat other foods," etc....

A recent visit from my parents included a rather unsatisfactory discussion on homeschooling. They have been silently disapproving since I first hinted at the possibility we might keep our children home, about three years ago. We had all conveniently avoided any further discussion on the subject until their last visit. I was very patient, but became inwardly very frustrated with them. I tried giving them factual information, stating the legality of homeschooling in this state, why we wanted to, etc. My parents are difficult to begin with, but the whole conversation left me feeling like I'd wasted my breath. I offered them the opportunity to read material I have, and gave them two of John's reprints. They think it is illegal, we'll wind up in court, they could never have taught me, and what's wrong with sending your child on the school bus with his lunch pail and having him come home again with all his papers to show you?

I finally decided *they are defensive because they consider my doing things different as an accusation that what they did with me was wrong.* I guess they are that insecure about having raised four kids that they can't look beyond that to see that they raised four very good human beings who are all doing well. I've made special attempts to praise them as parents and grandparents.

J.P. Meets Homeschoolers

More from Kathy Mingl (IL):

About the same time that J.P.'s schoolwork came, Tony turned the wood-working business over to me and took a job as an electronics employment counselor.... J.P. is naturally saddened that his daddy has to be away from us all day, but in a way, his schoolwork helps with that, because now he has something just as important and impressive to do during the day that he can surprise Tony with when he gets home. (And of course, J.P. is entirely in favor of making money.)

Still, it's a loss, and he feels a bit isolated with his friends off at school, so we called up a homeschooler in Arlington Heights, and got in touch with the House group in that area. We went to one of their open-house meetings at Susan Oldberg's house in Northbrook, so that J.P. could see *other* kids who go to school at home. Boy, did he see other kids! They had a guy who'd raised a wolf give a talk and show movies, and the place was *swarming*. J.P. was a bit overwhelmed at first, and spent a lot of time in my lap, but then he found a cat, a friend, and a geodesic jungle-gym sort of thing, and when it was time to go home, I thought I was going to have to lasso him. They go on field trips, too—J.P. would like that, I'm sure.

I was feeling a bit flattened at the time, myself, because now that J.P. is actually "school-age," some of the people who were supportive of our ideas are deserting the ranks. One of our favorite relatives has become unexpectedly critical of us (though she couldn't come out in the open and tell *us*), and I was inclined to feel rather puzzled and hurt. I talked to some of the homeschoolers at that open-house about it, though, and one of them, Kathy Catino, who gave J.P. and me a ride there, nailed it down pretty good, I thought. She said that people who *know* they should be doing something like homeschooling but are terrified of going against the norm feel *threatened* when they hear about it, and that makes you almost an enemy. It's not that they don't agree with you, it's that they do, and it scares them to death. Tony and I were very struck by the logic of that, and it made us feel a little better.

As it turns out, I've talked to this relative since, and though can't say the situation is resolved, she did tell me that her youngest boy had *begged* her to let him stay home from school this year, and she had refused because she didn't feel she could handle it. So there you are.

Just started reading *GWS* 35.... I would like to comment on Sue of Seattle's "Thoughts After Six Years": obviously she and her family don't like things like keeping journals and going on "field trips," but speaking in mild defense of such things, if you *enjoy* something, it isn't "fakey." As she says, it's thinking up activities you *don't* care about, for someone else's approval or admiration, that's fake.

Why Did They Stop?

We need to hear, and are very eager to hear, from families whose children were for a while homeschooled but have for one reason or another now gone back to school. Some of the things we would like to know are:

1) Was it mostly the children or the parents who made this decision about going back to school?

2) If it was the children, was it mostly because they were tired of homeschooling and just wanted a change; or because there was some particular study or sport or activity that they wanted to do at school; or because they mostly wanted to check out the social scene and meet a larger number of other children; or if something else, what?

3) If it was mostly the parents' decision, what were their reasons? Lack of time, pressure of other commitments, resistance from the children, or what?

4) Did the children go back to school with the understanding that if they didn't want to stay, they did not have to, and could always go back to homeschooling? Or did they go with the understanding that, like most children, they were going to have to stay in school whether they liked it or not? Or was there perhaps an understanding that they would have to stay, like it or not, through some definite time period, after which the question of going or not going could be opened again?

5) What have been some of the experiences and reactions of the children going back to school? If they had gone to school before they homeschooled, do they like school more, or less, this second time than they did the first time? Do they like being at school more, or less, than they expected to? If there are some good things about the experience and some bad, what are some of these? Do they feel they are treated in any special way, perhaps unkindly, perhaps kindly, by the school because of their previous homeschooling; in other words, is the school punishing them for having been homeschoolers, or does it seem to be going out of its way a little to make them feel at home and welcome, or are they just treated pretty much like the other kids?

6) Do they have any trouble with the schoolwork, and if so, with what aspects of it?

We tend to feel here that a family which has been teaching its children at home does not stop being a homeschooling family just because the children want to try school for a while, as long as the parents continue to offer the children the choice of homeschooling if they want it. Only if that choice is withdrawn and the children are told that they have to go to school whether they like it or not, would we feel that the family had given up homeschooling. If some of you have truly given up homeschooling, we would like to know some of the reasons why, if you care to tell us. We will not (or will do our best not to) try to argue you out of your decision, but if we can learn something about why homeschooling did not seem to work for you, we may be able to solve some of these problems for families that are still doing it. For anything you may be able to tell us, we will be very grateful.—JH

Fan Mail

We enjoy your newsletter immensely. I always get two copies, make notations of interest in one and send to family and friends I know are skeptical or interested in homeschooling. On the other I make notations of legal matters or points of interest that I feel may help us if we ever need to go to court or to aid in enacting legislation for homeschoolers. This goes into my education file along with clippings of articles which support our feelings of what's happening in the schools today (low literacy, violence, etc.).—*Barbara Hussey (HI)*.

You know, many times I've felt like writing "letters to the editor" in newspapers or magazines, but I never went through with it. I suppose one reason was laziness. Another, fear of sounding uneducated and illogical. But most of all I didn't believe it would accomplish anything. Since my ideas usually differ from society's norms anyway I felt I would probably do my cause more harm than good (home birth, homeschooling, nutrition, and an Edgar Cayce view of life and death) by appearing overly emotional on the issue with few facts, said in an incorrect letter form with possible grammatical, spelling, and punctuation errors. With *GWS*, on the other hand, I feel the majority of readers are more accepting and willing to see beyond incorrect structure to hear my ideas, to listen to the "me" hiding behind the words. I'm willing to give part of myself to what feels like a supportive family.

I had written a short letter when I subscribed to *GWS*, describing the basics of our unschooling situation. A couple of months ago, I received a postcard from Donna asking how things were going for our son. She made me feel that someone out there really does care. Also I was so grateful that she had carefully worded it, so if our postal clerk read it she wouldn't know what Donna was really referring to!—*Maggie Meyer, Ohio*

I love it when *GWS* gets here. First I have a quick look for letters from friends or people I know through my work with *Nurturing* magazine, then I try to read it. That's the hard part—I'll be halfway down a letter and a title will catch my eye, so I start on another, then back to the first. I think I should take up speed reading, I cannot get enough in my head at once. I have to explore its every page, find the words that express exactly what I feel, suffer with the families who are having a hard time, be happy for those who have won the battle and can now teach and learn fully with nothing hanging over them. Like a lover returning after time apart, I must search each part to see that there are no changes, make sure the feelings come through the same, and find out that we are still going along the same path. There comes a time, after I have checked each page, read parts of letters, seen who is new in the directory, that I do settle down to read. When a friend wanted to borrow my back issues I was most reluctant to lend them even though I know she will treat them as I do. It was just the thought of them not being here in case I needed to turn to one of them.—*Karen Dixon (Ontario)*.

Family In The Country

From Karen Schadel (NY):

Aug. 16: We recently moved to a small (16 beautiful acres) home in the country.... Our elevation is over 1400 feet so we have the valley and countryside just before our eyes.... We hope to build a small addition this fall which will enable the children to observe, participate, and learn from the experience.

We heat solely with wood.... my kids have always loved to participate in stacking, storing, and bringing it in. We have periodically suffered from either a water shortage or a total water loss.... However, we're learning so much about water—supply, purity, maintenance, conservation, pressure, flow rate, plumbing, and much more—all with the children silently watching what is taking place and later discussing it with us with wonderful comprehension.

When we discovered there were bats on our property, probably residing in our barn or an old tree stump, I was a bit taken aback. We rushed to the library and scrounged for books and information on bats.... My honest intention was to learn how to rid ourselves of them. How could I possibly live with bats??!! My 7-year-old was enthralled and retained nearly every bit of material we pored through, and my 5-year-old was equally enticed by them. Only Mom couldn't handle the thought of a bat in my hair (a hard myth to shake) or a rabid bat who might bite an unsuspecting child (actually, not a likely event, I later learned). The more we read, the more we all (especially me) learned about bats. With the arrival of the black flies which were followed by a horde of mosquitoes, I came to welcome and truly appreciate the role of the little brown bats who were living with us and eating all those bugs.... Now we will often, one or all of us, go to the window or venture outdoors to watch the bats appear as nightfall arrives.

Oct. 17: Things are hectic now. The excavation is done for the addition and we watched the masons erect the foundation today. The children are observing so much and will start more active participation with the carpentry work, as their father will be involved with this, and all the finishing work, which will take us years to complete. But it gives us something to look forward to, to plan for and to work together on as family projects. Meaningful work, as John says, is really the best teacher, and helps to build a good self-image and feeling of worth. The children are at their best when doing adult jobs or projects that have significance—I rarely see the same look on their faces when they are playing with toys or just spending idle time.

For example, recently we began digging potatoes from our garden—the same ones the children carefully helped us plant in the spring. They spent a lot of time digging each hole and marvelling over the number of potatoes in each hill and the size of each potato. We carried them down from our garden located well behind the house.... What they did was *very* important to them and they did a *very* good job. And the best part was when we cooked and ate their potatoes—did they ever taste good!

The boys now have two miniature lops (rabbits) that were purchased for them by a friend.... We visited two rabbitries in our area before they could decide. The first farm had 450 rabbits and they didn't like any of them! So on to the next farm, where they bought an aguti doe and a broken (spotted) buck. We did the necessary reading to educate ourselves in the basic needs and care of rabbits before our trip to the rabbit farms, so we were prepared to purchase them and eager to have these pets: the children's first responsibility to an animal totally dependent on them for its existence.

While at the second rabbit farm (something I recorded in my journal as a field trip), we were given a grand tour by the owner. She questioned why my oldest wasn't in school. I felt the situation a safe one in which to say he was being taught at home. For some reason this had a very positive effect on her (she was the mother of five, her youngest just beginning kindergarten) and she proceeded to share an incredible amount of knowledge with us—especially Joshua. She directed much of what she said or showed to him and used his name when talking with him. She demonstrated how to hold a rabbit properly to prevent being clawed. She explained how to clip their nails if necessary. She showed us the way their teeth should be lined up, what a malocclusion was, and how to determine if a rabbit was ill by feeling its nose and observing its dietary intake and elimination patterns.... She explained how to prepare a nesting box and when to place the expectant mother in it. We were allowed to see and touch kits (baby rabbits) that were only *one* day old. She told us that a rabbit kindles (gives birth) in about 30 days following conception and that the newborn kits are hairless, blind, and deaf. We observed the tiny kits all pink and new as they jumped about in the nesting box, looking very much like popcorn in a kettle as they searched for their mother to nurse. We were told how important it is to wash your hands after handling the rabbits to decrease the possibility of spreading disease. She demonstrated how a wire cage is torched with a propane flame in order to sanitize it before allowing a new rabbit to reside there, and also to remove molting rabbit fur that adheres to the wire. We left the rabbit farm with our two miniature lops in the back of the car and much new knowledge, facts, and information stored away in our heads. Joshua retained every bit of what he saw and was told that day.... This was the best start they could have had.

Oct 2: Since we moved to the country, we can no longer enjoy the convenience of setting our garbage at the curb and watching it be hauled away to who-knows-where. Instead we must make weekly trips to our local dump about four miles away—but we enjoy these trips more than I ever imagined. The boys began going with their father and I quickly saw that they were hauling home nearly as much as they were hauling away.

Seth (5) spotted a fishing pole exactly sized for him and after we brought it home, untangled the line, and purchased a hook and sinker, it was in perfect working condition. Joshua (7) discovered an old discarded record player way beyond repair, but still of interest to him, so it was also brought home along with a chair with only three legs. He has explored, dissected, and investigated the insides of the record player and further disassembled the chair. What he's learned, I'm not sure, but he has occupied himself and enjoyed the time spent with his "treasures."... Among my husband's finds have been a wooden style toilet tank with brass fixtures, a dresser (incredibly warped but still sporting some very nice antique hardware), screening, metal, wood scraps, and sheetrock.

Since I didn't want to miss out on all the fun, I hopped into the truck one Saturday morning with the whole crew, which by this time included 2-year-old Sadrah, and ventured to the dump to see what treasures I would uncover. I was astonished to find a large wooden bowl (with a small crack), an orange straw hat (perfect for dress-up), two small metal enamel bowls, a paper party tablecloth (unopened), and a full-sized wool blanket (beige and lavender striped with a few burdocks stuck to it). All of these items were clean and in good to excellent condition.

A big discussion followed involving waste, recycling, donations, charity, value, and more. Granted, we didn't really *need* any of what we found, but we're making use of almost all of it. The dresser was returned to the dump less its hardware and I expect the record player will find its way back sometime when Joshua has finished with it. But the blanket is on Seth's bed, the hat is in the toy basket, the wooden bowl has become a decorative addition by our front steps next to my plants, the metal bowls were temporarily used as food dishes for our rabbits and are now part of our sandbox equipment, and so on. The dump is not a very lovely spot to visit, but I didn't see any rats, either.... We anticipate each trip in wonderment of what new treasures we'll uncover.

The Changing World Economy

The *Boston Globe* of 9/26/83 published a story about industrial workers around the world that, though few paid it much attention, seemed to me as important as any news story I have seen in years. They showed a table of "Total hourly compensation for production workers in manufacturing. These figures include fringe benefits, bonuses, medical coverage and employer social welfare contributions."

The figures:

United States—$11.79
Canada—$10.77
Sweden—$10.33
France—$8.15
Italy—$7.39
United Kingdom—$6.67
Japan—$5.82
Israel—$4.67
Venezuela—$3.98
Brazil—$2.43
Mexico—$1.97
Singapore—$1.77
Taiwan—$1.57
Hong Kong—$1.55
South Korea—$1.22
India (1979)—*$0.37*
Sri Lanka (1981)—*$.21*

We can easily see why Atari recently moved most of its production facilities from California to Hong Kong, and why a factory worker in Hong Kong was quoted in this same *Globe* story as saying that she knew it was only a matter of time before her job disappeared into Sri Lanka.

One of the countries missing from these tables is the most significant of all—China. I would guess that China's average hourly industrial wage was somewhat above India's 37 cents, but probably well below South Korea's $1.22 and probably well below $1.00. With India's more than 600 million people and China's more than a billion, there is in the world a virtually inexhaustible supply of industrial workers ready to work for less than, probably much less than $1 per hour.

The economic future of the rich industrial nations of the West, and probably even of Japan itself (which has already lost most of its shipbuilding industry to South Korea), is written in these figures. For about two decades these nations were able to employ, at high wages, just about everyone who wanted to do industrial work. For the first time in history, factory workers could think of owning cars, a home, sending children to college, joining the true middle class. That day is gone, probably forever. The industrial, money economies of these nations have already dropped out many of their workers, and in the next decade or two are sure to drop out a great many more.

"High-tech" will not save us. Atari, like many companies, as we know, is already doing its manufacturing in Hong Kong. Anything a company can train a $10 an hour worker to do today, it can train a $1 an hour worker to do tomorrow—and will. *Homesteader's News, Mother Earth News*, and others tell us about people who have chosen to learn how to live outside the money economy. Millions of others won't get the choice; they are going to have to learn the same thing, whether they like it or not.

Those with a taste for irony may perhaps enjoy the thought that what a century or so of Socialism and Communism have not been able to do—reduce the gap between the poor and the rich peoples of the world—may be done in a decade or two, is in fact being done right now, by profit-seeking multinational corporations.

What is the point of all of this for homeschoolers? Just this: that this country as a whole is going to have to begin to give some serious thought to some things that already interest many homeschoolers but have so far not been of the slightest interest to schools—economy, efficiency, thrift. "Use it up, wear it out, make it do, do without." "A penny saved is a penny earned." Things like that. No child can be said any more to go into the world and the future even moderately prepared who has not learned, perhaps among many other things, how to live healthily, productively, and happily on very little money, how to do for herself or himself a great many things that most of us now only think of paying others to do. (Incidentally, there was a plumbing disaster in my apartment not long ago, and out of necessity—to keep my apartment from being flooded out—I played some part in helping to get it fixed.)—JH

Children in The Workplace

From Marta Clark in Kentucky:

You asked about unschooling and working parents. Since Joy Thomas and I started a business two months ago, I can tell you how we have worked things out. I have two children (4 and 1) and she has two (4 and 2). Rather than split them up among the various preschools and daycare centers, we hired one babysitter to watch all of them in her home. The important features of this arrangement were (1) the brothers and sisters and friends were all kept together instead of being split up by age; (2) we could work with the babysitter about food (no sweets), TV watching, and discipline; (3) the care was consistent instead of being given by whoever was working that day; (4) the woman became emotionally involved with the children and they with her, which is impossible in the usual daycare school with its changing students and teachers.

The only drawback to this wonderful setup—it is too expensive to continue because our new business needs the money we have been paying the sitter. But, since things have settled down so that we both don't need to work all the time, we are going to take turns working at the business (an exercise studio/health club) and being at our homes with all four children. We are also fixing up the office at work for the children so they can be with us there for a couple of hours every day. Our husbands will also be seeing more of their children than they were before we started the business!

The two four-year-olds *love* the exercise studio—they think it's lots of fun to work out, meet new people, and go out to eat. The two-year-old is also fairly well-behaved there. The one-year-old prevents me from getting anything done at work so I have stopped trying—I get too frustrated and angry with him. The problems with keeping the children at work are that they quarrel with each other enough to distract us and our customers, and they can't last the hours that we work—late lunch, etc. So the combination of paying a babysitter, their fathers keeping them at home, one of us taking all the children, and bringing them one at a time to work is working very well for us.

Tree Planter Update

In "Tree Planters," way back in *GWS* 7, we told about a 15-year-old in Los Angeles who started planting trees in Southern California and organized others to do so. The "Tree People" are going stronger than ever, and we think *GWS* families in the L.A. area might want to work with them. According to their newsletter, the *Seedling News* (12601 Mulholland Dr, Beverly Hills CA 90210; 213-769-2663), the organization set a goal of planting 1,000,000 trees before the 1984 Olympics. They have gotten support from the government, nurseries, celebrities, and thousands of volunteer tree-planters. Sounds like a good way for young people, especially, to do some work they can see is worth doing.—DR

Success Stories

Elaine Gale (MA) wrote:

Two weeks ago I went before a public session of a school board meeting to request homeschooling for my daughter, Leah. I was not able to appear before this time because the Superintendent checked my curriculum with the department heads, met with me twice, and tested my daughter with the Detroit Learning Abilities Test, the Spache Reading Test, and a math test devised and administered by a local principal. The superintendent made a recommendation for us to the school board. He said that my curriculum (*Weimar College Child Development Program*, Box A, Weimar CA 95736) was better than the public school except our math book only went up to the 6s in multiplication (I also got Elmer Brooks' *Math-It Kit* from Weimar—excellent!). He told them that Leah was tested and scored several grade levels above hers (3rd).

I had given her the Iowa Basic Skills Test before I received her materials from Weimar. She scored well above average in everything but spelling. You see, Leah turned 8 October '82 but *I did not start any formal schooling until six months ago.*

Oh, I also gave a hand-out to all the members of the school board with information about "socialization," peer pressure, etc., and the concept of waiting until age 8–10 to start formal schooling. I answered several questions from the school committee, received a compliment, and got unanimous approval!

From Nan and David Erbaugh (OH):

We have two sons, Zachary (6) and Noah (1½). We held Zachary out of kindergarten last year with no hassles—our school system even recommends delaying the start of children with summer birthdays, especially boys. This summer we spoke to the superintendent about approving us for homeschooling. We pointed out that we knew we didn't *have* to do anything to get approval until Zachary turned 7. He was quite nice and said he wanted us to do what was most comfortable for us. All he needed was a letter from us stating our objections to public schools, why we felt qualified to teach, and what our plan of education would be.

He approved our plans within a week.

The reason we did all of this now is that we knew he was amenable to homeschooling, and our school district has a history of not keeping superintendents for more than 2 or 3 years. This superintendent is now in his third year.

A side note—the fact that I was a French and English teacher in junior high and high school and my husband has a psychology degree seemed to make the superintendent feel good about our teaching.

[DR: See also "Notifying Superintendent Early," GWS 34.]

From another Ohio parent:

We were turned in to the school—we hadn't registered our son at all.... We were therefore forced to visit the superintendent sooner than we had planned on (in fact I was considering not going at all, hoping we were invisible to the so-called authorities, while my husband felt it would be better to go before they found out about us).

We typed up a 4-page single-spaced paper on our views with an emphasis on the religious side. We have many other reasons, including almost all the ones mentioned in *Teach Your Own*.... I basically wrote the paper myself with my husband adding cohesion, editing out irrelevant or possibly misleading sections, and putting it all together.

When we walked into the superintendent's office we were pleasantly greeted by his secretary. Maybe it was our imagination, but it seemed to us like every office worker, the janitor, and even the principal popped out all over to get a look at us. The superintendent himself was polite yet distant. We handed him our paper and asked him to read it right then and there so he'd know how we felt. He was hesitant.... Finally he read it and we watched him raise his eyebrows here and there.

He told us he had never heard that he had this legal power to allow homeschooling and he'd have his lawyer check into it. He told us he'd get back with us soon and let us know what he intends to do. That was back in October '82 and still no word from him. Our lawyer said to leave well enough alone and not to call to ask what he intends to do. So we are assuming that the superintendent is letting us keep our son home.

From Katharine Houk (NY):

July 20: I am enclosing a copy of the letter my husband and I sent to the superintendent and school board members of our local school. It has been almost a month since it was sent and we have heard nothing. My husband is an attorney at the N.Y. State Education Department and he thinks that to stress *cooperation* with the school district is vitally important—which is why our letter does so.

Tahra (13) is tremendously excited about learning at home (is this the "honeymoon period" I've heard tell of?) and she has already plunged into reading and writing projects on her own this summer. I am nagged by the feeling that we are waiting for something because we haven't yet heard from the school.

Our letter is not revolutionary in any sense and borrows from other *GWS* letters.

Sept. 30: Shortly after I wrote you, we heard from the superintendent. He called my husband at work (at the State Ed. Dept.) and we set up a time to meet with him and the high school principal. They gave us the enclosed information sheet (#1). My husband said, "If we're going to do all this then we might as well send Tahra to school." We talked for a couple of hours with them; it was a friendly meeting. They commended us for what we wanted to attempt and recognized our sincerity. By the end of the meeting they had relaxed on all the requirements but the monthly reports and the attendance record.

Tahra is very happy at home and I love having her around. Our workplace is leisurely. I worried about the monthly report, though. Then two days ago I got a call from the high school principal. He said he wanted to meet to tell us what the school district expects for the monthly reports.

I went into his office this morning fearing the worst—testing, timesheets, multi-page reports, etc. Instead he handed us Sheet #2 [DR: a yes/no checklist as to whether objectives are being met and records are being kept] and said that is all we have to submit each month!

We still can't believe how easy they are making it for us. . . . We are first in our district to homeschool at the high school level. . . . The local paper has already called me for an interview on homeschooling; I told them to call back at the end of the year when I've had more experience (and the relationship with the school has stabilized).

[DR:] A number of readers have told us of sending a letter to their superintendent and waiting in uneasy suspense for weeks, months, or occasionally even years for an answer. It is a good idea to put at the end of such a letter (and in fact, any official business-type letter) a short statement of *exactly what action you would like the other party to take, and by what date you expect it.* Precisely what this will be will depend on the laws in your state, the circumstances in your district, etc. For example, it might be sending written approval, phoning to schedule a meeting, or arranging for you to appear before the school board.

Or, you can use the good "negative" option mentioned in the early issues of *GWS*: "If we do *not* hear from you by—we will assume we have your full approval." In either case, you are spurring the official to make *some* sort of decision instead of allowing your letter to become buried in an in-basket.

Research On Late Starters

From Raymond and Dorothy Moore's (WA) newsletter Family Report:

In the August 30 issue of *USA Today* was a bit of interesting news citing a seven-year study of 70 children in Cincinnati showing that 81% of boys who waited a year to start school had above-average grades compared to only 47% of those who started early. 100% of the girls who waited had above-average grades while only 60% of the younger girls did.

California Ruling: School Negligence

In a long and very thoroughly researched legal brief prepared by Nick Davenny of Kalamazoo, Mich. for the defense of his own homeschooling program [*GWS* 30], I found something I have been wanting to find for some time—the citations (legal references) for a quotation from a very important California ruling that I described in *GWS* 1. In this case a San Francisco family, whose son (though never designated as needing any special help and in any event never having received any) was graduated from high school with no better than fifth grade reading skills, sued the schools for negligence. They charged the schools had failed to take the necessary steps to insure that the boy received an adequate education. The San Francisco Unified School District, in defending themselves, offered a very interesting argument. They said, in effect, that they could not be declared negligent for having failed to do the right thing by this child, *because no one knew what the right thing was.* The Superior Court dismissed the parents' suit and the Appeals Court upheld the dismissal, saying:

> Unlike the activity of the highway or the marketplace, classroom methodology affords no readily acceptable standards or care, or cause, or injury. The science of pedagogy itself is fraught with different and conflicting theories of how or what a child should be taught, and any layman might—and commonly does—have his own emphatic views on the subject.

Peter W. v. San Francisco Unified School District, 60 Cal. App. 3d 826, 131 Cal. Rptr. 854, at 860-861 (1976).

In two or three similar cases in other parts of the country, the courts have in like manner refused to award damages against the schools, almost certainly for these two practical policy reasons: first, if the schools have to pay damages for every child they fail to educate, they will soon be broke, and secondly, because if the courts awarded such damages to one family their courtrooms would soon be full of hundreds of other families seeking similar damages. But even though, for reasons of public policy, the courts have denied these families the redress to which justice surely entitled them, they have in doing so given homeschoolers the legal argument quoted above, which we may in many cases be able to put to very good use. For it should be obvious to all but the most hopelessly biased judges that the schools cannot defend themselves against charges of negligence by saying that no one really knows how children should be educated, and then in the next breath turn around and say that they are the only people who know and that everyone must do it exactly their way.

I think it might be very useful for some of our California friends with a taste for legal research to look into this case further, and find out if possible in greater detail what the schools said in their own defense and what the courts said in supporting them. For any more such information, we will be very grateful.—JH

Her First School

By Annie Horrocks in Home Centered Learning, *8/83 (34 Katrina Ln, San Anselmo CA 94960; $5/yr):*

> A long time ago—20 years, in fact—our oldest daughter in first grade mentioned that she hadn't learned anything before she started school. I asked her where she'd learned to dress and feed herself. Where did she learn her numbers, colors, and letters? Who had read many books to her before she began school about insects, weather, animals, families, and more? Where had she come to know about our God and His works? How was it that she knew that baby people and baby animals must be treated gently and with love?
>
> A startled look came across our child's face and she realized that her first school had been home. Being a homeschooler is not new, it's just that some of us are choosing to carry it beyond society's norm of 5 to 6 years. In all truth, we are homeschoolers all our lives.

Boy with Rings

One Sunday morning a month or two ago, as I was walking up Boylston Street to the office, a little boy gave me still another glimpse of the workings of the mind of a very young child. He was out with his mother, who told me that he was about fourteen months old. He was walking around the metal tables and chairs of the outdoor section of a restaurant, which for him were something like a maze. Every now and then he would try to climb one of the chairs. His nice mother kept close enough to be able to ward off danger, but far enough away so that he felt, not watched or hovered over, but free to roam and explore.

As I watched him with pleasure I noted that he carried, usually in his left hand, a couple of brightly colored plastic rings, big enough for him to use as bracelets. Every so often he would stick his right hand through the rings, so that for a while he was wearing both of them on his right arm. So he continued to explore and I to watch. Then I began to see a curious thing. Now and then it would happen that the two rings were lying, loose and separate, on the ground or on a chair. The little boy would pick up one of them, stick his right arm through it, and push it up his arm about to the elbow. Then he would spy the other ring, and the thought would clearly come into his mind that he wanted it on his arm beside the one already there. But at this point, to my great astonishment, he showed that he could not remember *how* that ring on his arm had got there, for instead of putting his right hand through the second ring, he would instead put the second ring right beside the one he already had on his arm, and pat it, as if to make it stick and stay there, and he was always surprised and mildly vexed that it would not stick, but kept falling off.

After trying a few times he would give up, and continue walking around, between, and under the chairs and tables. Then the rings would again summon his attention. If he happened to have them both in his left hand, he could get them both on his right arm, as before. But if he had only one ring in his left hand and the other somewhere else, he would go through that same procedure, first putting one ring on his right arm, then finding the second ring and trying to stick it on next to the first.

During the twenty minutes or so I watched him,

he tried to solve that problem three or four times, without success. I am sure that sometime during the next few months he did solve the problem, and wish I could have been around to see him do it. As it was, it was fascinating to watch this tiny baffled scientist at work on the problem, and useful to be reminded what an enormous number of similar problems (which to us have long since ceased to look like problems) little children have to grapple with, puzzle over, and finally solve.—JH

Testing Young Children

From Nancy Dumke (CO):

You might find this interesting. Claire was exposed to her first formal testing situation at the tender age of 3! It happened at her medical check-up and it's apparently routine for doctors to administer this developmental test. . . . The doctor's questions and Claire's responses instantly reinforced all my objections to schools and tests. For example: Dr. Ned (whom she knows and likes and feels fairly comfortable with) handed Claire a bottle with a raisin inside and said, "Can you take this raisin out of the bottle?" "Yes," said Claire, and she proceeded to stick her finger through the narrow opening to *take* the raisin out. It was extremely frustrating. "She's so literal," I said to the doctor. Well, she finally got the raisin out, and ate it, but she hadn't done it the correct way, so Dr. Ned tried again. "This time," he said, "can you take the raisin out without using your finger?" Well, of course she tried using her thumb! "Can you take the raisin out without using your finger *or* your thumb?" he asked. "Sure," said Claire, and turned the bottle upside down, dropped the raisin into her other hand, and popped it into her mouth.

Then came question and answer time. "What do you do when you're cold, Claire?" asked Dr. Ned. I could just feel her mind racing from situation to situation, trying to fit the question into a frame of reference. She said nothing. He repeated the question, but she just looked at him, so he went on to the next. "What do you do when you're tired?" "I go to sleep." "What do you do when you're hungry?" "I eat some food." "What do you do when you're cold?" This time she was ready: "If I'm at the pool," she said, "I wrap up in a towel." (Later at home she kept answering the question: "If I'm cold in bed, I pull up the covers." "If I'm cold in winter, I put on my ski jacket.")

I can remember so clearly taking tests in school and wracking my brain trying to decide which of several possible answers was the "right" one. Or thinking that the answer was so obvious and easy that it couldn't be right, it must be a trick question. Later, Claire and I talked about what a hard time the doctor had asking the question. . . . I wanted to be sure she understood that the problem was his, not hers. Claire thought the whole thing was very interesting and fun, but it's easy to see how a child with less self-confidence could be upset by such a test.

From Lynne Thunderstorm (BC):

When I read Ann Miles' letter in GWS 34 concerning the "Which does not belong?" game she played with her 4-year-old, we decided to try it with 3½-year-old Raven. The results we got were hilarious and only confirmed my belief that looking for "correct" answers is completely irrelevant!

"Which does not belong: a guitar, a horse, a harmonica, an autoharp?"

"The guitar."

"Oh, but that's something to make music with and a horse isn't."

"No, silly, I *like* horses." So, she eliminated the one she didn't *like*.

"Which does not belong: onions, apples, rocking chairs, garlic?"

She laughed. "Onions and garlic do *not*!"

Certainly, when I named the categories, she answered "correctly." But when I merely listed items, she easily made choices that were right for her, and was able to tell us why she eliminated the thing.

In The Mail

Thanks for "Liking School Is Not Enough" and "Spaceship School," *GWS* 34. Those articles, and our growing convictions, helped us to decide we would *not* put Maia in kindergarten next year even though she wants to go. Since we've made that decision and let her know firmly that we are a "homeschooling family," she seems to have accepted it. We'll see how it goes when her friends leave for kindergarten next year, though.—*Denise Hodges (WI).*

In response to "Blaming The Unconventional," *GWS* 33: Yes, homeschooling can be blamed for everything, but we must be careful not to present the opinion that homeschooling is the answer to everything. I had a friend who didn't want to share her problem concerning her daughter because she thought I would think that she wouldn't have that problem if she would just homeschool! —*Terri Walker (MN).*

I first found that my desire to teach could not be satisfied in traditional schools. My experience in public schools was a nightmare, even though I was considered a "good" teacher by students and professionals.... My second grand realization was that my desire to teach was no more than a desire to have children. I have never felt the need to work outside the home, to teach or to work with kids (my previous goals) since the day Becca was born.... Believe me, as the daughter of a very feminist, liberal-thinking mother, it was quite a shock to realize that I don't have to "work" to be a worthwhile contributing member of society.—*Patti Pitcher (MI).*

There are five families in the area with a total of 10 children who are homeschooling. This winter we were able to obtain the old armory gymnasium every Monday afternoon free of charge. The kids would roller-skate, play basketball, volleyball, badminton, kickball, etc. Even the preschoolers were included.—*Gary & Diann Foster (KY).*

We always seem to have a yard full of kids. I suppose they feel free to come around. We have teenagers to toddlers open the gate and join the activity or create their own. Perhaps they are intrigued by the noise, laughter, and fun. I've no argument for who comes in, and have never had to ask anyone to leave, even though there are arguments and occasional fights. What can you expect when there are two or twenty kids together?—*An Iowa Reader.*

I have a day care business at home, and recently put an ad in the paper, to be different, which started out, "Homeschooling family will care for your baby/child...." I'd never seen one like it, and I got a very nice 8-year-old boy who's never been to public schools. Both his parents are now working days and needed care where they hadn't before. They are still teaching him and he plays here with my 5-year-old girl, Forest, and reads to her.—*Linda Rieken (AZ).*

Young Writers Still Needed

Pat Stone of Mother Earth News *tells us that he needs more articles by young people for the "Mother's Children" feature. He writes:*

It's incorrect to say I'm running out of material ... but I do occasionally go through too-lean times. That's not good, 'cause I'd like to keep this feature alive. There's not that many paying markets I know about for young writers.

The basic purpose of "Mother's Children" is to share how-to projects initiated and carried out by younger children and teenagers. The author should be *both* the person who did the project *and* the one who writes the article. I'm open to a wide range of possibilities.... We've run everything from "How I Changed the New York State Income Tax Laws for Minors" to "How to Make Food Jewelry Out of Bread Dough" ... from "I Ran our Farm's Giant Combine Just like the Men Do" to "Make a Ball out of a Pig Bladder" ... and including more ordinary topics like making herb vinegars or beef jerky. I also like to see money-making ideas: it's nice when we can give other young people ways for earning their own money.

I respond to all queries and do everything I can to help the author work the article up (including sending a page of writing guidelines).

Our payment for the column runs from $100 to

$200 (that includes paying for photos), which is the same we would pay an adult writer for the same work. The better the writing and pictures—a frequent problem is bad pix—and the more exciting the topic, the higher the payment.

Homeschoolers tend to be a pretty self-directed group, so I've gotten a lot of good articles from your readers. Hope to get more!

[DR: Pat recommends that all young authors send in a query—that is, a letter telling about the story they'd like to do—before writing a full article. Address, 105 Stoney Mountain Rd, Hendersonville NC 28791.]

On Reading

Joyce Kinmont (UT) wrote in the Tender Tutor*:*

> I made a little book for Becky (3) that she dearly loves. I went through some old pictures, then bought a little photo album to put them in. Under each picture I wrote a short sentence. The first page has the title, "When Becky Was a Baby." The pages are:
>
> Picture of Becky at the stove—"Becky liked to cook."
>
> Picture of her in a wig—"Becky had too much hair."
>
> Holding stuffed animals—"Becky had three dogs."
>
> With a ski cap pulled down over her face—"Where did Becky go?"
>
> And so on. We are now taking pictures of Milli to make her a book. . . . Since she is older there will be more writing with them.

From Lyn Cargill in Australia:

Skye (2½) is learning to read. I tried the Glenn Doman approach when she was about 20 months but although she loved the cards, she preferred to "write" on them and cut them up. I wasn't keen enough to bother teaching her, so I let her destroy them all. Recently I made some new cards (names of friends) and put them aside, ready for when she showed an interest. She's been asking what words say and demanding to know the exact name of everything.

While looking for something, she found the cards and asked me to read them. She loves them and asks me to read them several times a day. Sometimes she reads them correctly, sometimes she makes mistakes which I ignore—but she makes me find the card and tells me what it really is. Her favorite game is for Mum to look perplexed and say, "Um, um, um" and she then "helps" me.

As long as she's interested I'll make her cards. Then we'll move on to home-made books. She already has a few. I always take heaps of photos on holidays or special occasions and make a book out of them. It helps her remember the occasion.

[A later note:] After a month or so break, Skye found her cards again. Remembered them all. Still prefers people's names to anything else.

Science with J.P.

From Kathy Mingl (IL):

We've been launching butterflies from our bedroom window this summer—we've always let the milkweed plants grow for the monarchs, and this year we brought in some eggs and raised the caterpillars in wide-mouth gallon jars, on top of the refrigerator. As they turned to chrysalises (*lovely* things—they look like gold-and-jade ornaments), we transferred them to a bouquet of sticks in a glass vase above the radio, where we can watch them ripen. As soon as they begin to get dark and the wing patterns show through, we put them in the bedroom window to "hatch."

We missed the first one—I woke up to find a note from my dad: "Pupa monarched—rescued him from cat and released outside—healthy little tyke." The next three that were ready, Tony, J.P. and I stayed up all night to watch, and though J.P. only managed to keep himself awake until 1:00, he held the first one to emerge (a female) on his finger while she dried her wings, and fed her sugar water from a toothpick. When we let them go the next morning, the two males were just anxious to take off, but J.P.'s little female seemed to remember him and stayed behind, tasting his finger with her tongue when he took her up on it. He fed her again, and then held her out the window until she finally decided to leave. It's quite a feeling to see them go sailing off over the house—you almost feel as if you had something to do with it. Something awfully allegorical there, don't you think?

We had another blessed event right on the kitchen table, while J.P. was eating lunch. This time the whole family got to watch—my mother was home, so we ran to get her as soon as J.P. yelled that things were happening. J.P. explained the entire process to her, and showed her how to tell that this one was a *boy* butterfly. My mother was fascinated—do you know, she's *never* seen a butterfly hatch before? My father maintained that *his* butterfly (the one he'd rescued and taken outside), had been the biggest.

Altogether, I think we've raised 20 monarchs, and though one time we had five fluttering on the screen at the same time, for the most part the hatchings have been staggered enough that we weren't overwhelmed. I think it was a good number, because the little things have a sly genius for waiting till your back is turned before they do something interesting (we *still* don't know where the "zipper" is!).

Some of the interests J.P. has been pursuing on his own lately are experiments with fire and chemistry, under my supervision (I tell him to say he's lighting candles, *not* lighting matches—gives a much less alarming picture), soldering, electronics and computers with Tony, geology (he's fascinated by volcanoes, and has started a rock collection; his eternal passion is prospecting for gold all over the back yard), and cooking. He's been learning to tell time and spell his name and address, and he has a long-standing interest in the working of bodies, and in hand-taming wild birds. J.P. is a very busy boy.

Something really fascinating has come up with J.P.'s fire experiments lately. He's been going through boxes of kitchen matches, mostly just lighting them and blowing them out, and using up all the candles in the house, but he's begun to venture into new scientific territory. I restrict his investigations to the kitchen table, with an adult in the vicinity, but other than that, I don't bother him too much. When he first wanted to try it, he was a little scared, so I showed him all the ways I could think of to put fires *out*—water, baking soda, pot-lids, fire extinguishers, etc.—and I even showed him how to call the fire department. Little by little he started trying different things on his own, and his interest led us down some remarkable byways of discussion—chemistry, history, mythology, fire-fighting and prevention, survival skills, and Murphy's Law (it's *easy* to start a fire when you *don't need* one). The other day, J.P. showed me something I didn't know—you can ignite a match by holding it *above* a flame, without even touching it. Really, if you're willing to learn yourself, raising a child can be a fascinating scientific exchange.

Learning Russian At Home

Barb Tetzlaff (IA) wrote in the O!KIDS *newsletter #2:*

> Our 8-year-old recently demonstrated an interest in learning the Russian language. He is very concerned with the Russian threat, nuclear freeze, etc. He decided that if he could find out how the Russians speak, live, and think he might better understand the dilemma.
>
> We were happy that he was showing an interest in any language at all because when he was in public school, he vehemently protested being force-fed Spanish (and consequently retained nothing!). We were not totally optimistic, however, thinking about how difficult (and potentially disappointing) it might prove to be for Josh. I had only a high school Spanish background and my husband had studied Latin in ninth grade. But we have always believed that when an interest is indicated it should be nurtured.
>
> We checked out a Russian language record from the library and forged ahead. Repeating phrases from the book that went along with the record turned out to

be rather dull. So I decided to try and make picture cards so that Josh could associate what he was saying with a picture. I plunged through stacks of old magazines searching for pictures that were interesting or humorous. Josh was curious as I worked along but he did not want to help create the cards (which I think would have been the ideal way to go about it).

When I'd finished, I had 38 colorful pictures glued to sturdy paper (8½ x 11). I went through the cards with Josh using the pronunciations we had learned from our record. Josh was even able to guess at the meanings by using the pictures. He then went over to his father and excitedly showed him the cards. He said he would now teach his father the phrases and sentences, and proceeded to do so while using my *exact* inflections, mannerisms, jokes, etc.!

It has been months since we began and we still can remember almost all of the 38 phrases. All we need to do to jog our memory is to bring the picture to mind and the phrase comes forth as well.

[Barb later wrote us:] One hot Saturday in July . . . I casually mentioned that I felt I needed to sit down and rest. . . . Jason replied in Russian, "Ya hachi s'iest" (I want to sit down). We had not even looked at our Russian language picture cards for several months and yet he knew just which phrase would be appropriate. . . . He remembers almost all of the phrases because it was his interest we nurtured. We didn't have to push and prod. We had *fun* learning together!

In Defense Of TV

Wendy Wartes (WA) wrote to John:

In the past there has been mention by readers, as well as yourself, of the lack of merit in television viewing. I would like to describe my use of TV and why I disagree.

First of all, my husband and I control the use of TV, not the children. Though my children are still young, I don't anticipate a problem later as this has been firmly established. The TV is only turned on for a specific program and is turned off immediately afterwards.

We rarely watch any commercial TV. Occasionally a special or a movie such as *Stanley and Livingston* or *Tom Sawyer* is seen by the whole family. I speak out critically of commercials, asking the children what it is the ads want us to do or buy. I have had my five-year-old try to sell me make-believe products and pointed out how he used nice words to make it sell. He has been told that advertisers are people who write words for actors to speak to do the same thing. He can readily see that the product would not sell if they said it tasted terrible or cost too much.

On Sunday, I sit down with my TV schedule and the monthly public TV magazine, *Dial* (I subscribe to this) and mark those programs of merit. Then we don't turn TV on except for those shows. Last month we watched public TV shows on Arctic wolves and Australian animals. How else could we have seen the actual birth of an embryonic kangaroo and its journey up the mother's stomach and final attachment to a nipple in her pouch to continue development?

Because I know what topics are coming up, through the *Dial* magazine, I check out books on the same topic at the library. Then if an interest is sparked, we don't have to wait to learn more. Just as a field trip can lead to other topics, so can TV if used wisely. . . . Many quality programs such as *National Geographic* and *Nova* are repeated once during the day and twice during the evening. Thus, we have the chance for reviewing it if our reading fanned an interest, with several days in between.

I've never been fortunate enough to travel and though I hope my children will have the first-hand opportunity to view other countries, I truly feel TV can fill a gap. In many cases the photographer can take the viewer to places no tourist can go. The show *Four Castles* is a good case in point. On a real trip to Wales, few of us would ever view these castles in such detail. . . . Coming soon is a 3-part series on the geology of the American West, a special on trains, a National Geographic update on

Hillary and Everest, Tanzanian wildlife, and the whooping crane.

I liken TV to a guest in my house. If I had company and the person spoke vulgarities, threw garbage around, and undermined my children's morals, I certainly would never invite them back. If, though, the company showed us spectacular photos of a recent trip and then helped explain the history of that country, they'd be invited back many times.

Computer News

In *GWS* 35 I wrote about Coleco's coming small computer, the "Adam." It was first announced for summer, then promised for October, then for Christmas. As of Nov. 15, it is still not in the local stores, though very much in the ads. Dealers, afraid of losing their Christmas business, are saying that Adam will appear any day, that supplies will be limited at first, and that sales will be made on a first-come first-served basis. In other words, if you hope to give someone an Adam for Christmas you must pay for it now; if it doesn't arrive in time for Christmas that is your tough luck, and (your money now safely in the store's bank) you'll just have to wait patiently until it does.

By now IBM has shown its small computer, called "PCjr" (Personal Computer junior). About it Peter Mitchell, electronics engineer and chief computer expert of the *Boston Phoenix*, writes:

Now that it has been unveiled, the machine itself comes as an anticlimax. If it were not graced by those three magic initials [IBM], its prospects for success would be rather dim. Objectively, it is an overpriced, disappointing assemblage of rather ordinary hardware.

In both word processing and video games, the two most popular uses for home computers, the IBM is notably weak. . . . The $670 that buys only the IBM keyboard would get you a complete Atari Writer system or the entire Coleco Adam system. E. F. Schumacher, author of *Small Is Beautiful* (see our list), would get some ironic amusement from this. Only a company as big as IBM would dare offer a product this bad, and with every reason to believe that it will be a commercial success.

The *Phoenix* also predicts that in 1984 we will see a number of truly portable computers, that is, capable of battery operation and weighing ten pounds or less (as opposed to the 25 lb. "transportable"), with a full Liquid Crystal Display screen, substantial memory, word processing capability, etc. If the price is low enough, such a machine might be useful to us in this office.

Meanwhile the Osborne Corporation, who made the first of the transportable computers, and in spite of having last year over $100 million in sales, has just gone bankrupt. Accountants who had been called in to review the company's books gave Adam Osborne, the founder and president, the unwelcome news that during a time when he had thought the company was earning money it had in fact lost $8 million, and barring a miracle would soon have to close.

This confirms vividly what I said in an earlier *GWS* about information not being a substitute for intelligence and judgment. Certainly, if access to computer experts and computer information could save a business, it should have saved this one. But information based on mistaken views of reality is worse than none, and as Osborne found out, the more of it you have, the worse off you are.

The press accounts of the end of this company said that when Osborne first learned of his unexpected losses and hence the imminent probable failure of his company, before he told anyone else this news, he sold $1.5 million of his personal stock to another one of the company's directors. Later, when the company decided to close, it told a large number of its employees that it was sending them on indefinite furlough (since if it fired them outright it would have to give them the severance pay to which they were entitled) and gave them *two hours* to clear their things out of the office. I wondered, "Why two hours? What was the big rush?" These two reports may throw some useful light on the notion that the people who make computers are primarily moved by some deep concern for the well-being of the human race.

Texas Instruments, one of the giants of the field, has decided after huge losses to drop out of the home computer market altogether. Apple's profits were down 78% from the previous year, and it may soon be in worse trouble. It made a huge engineering and capital investment in a fairly expensive home computer called the Lisa, in which you give the machine instructions by using a little table-top gadget called a "mouse" to move a cursor on the screen, thus making it unnecessary to memorize or carry out complicated instructions. An ingenious idea, which Apple hoped would keep them at the head of the pack for some time. But it has already been technologically outdated by a new machine from Hewlett-Packard in which you give the machine the same kind of instructions just by touching the screen with your finger. What this will do to the huge sales Apple anticipated for Lisa remains to be seen.

So the dance goes on. The *Phoenix* reports that for a given capability, the price of a new computer is halved every two years. Also, second-hand machines generally sell for about half their original price. The Commodore VIC can now be had, new, for $50, and a second-hand VIC is considered to be without commercial value; if you have one and don't want it, give it away, it's not worth the trouble it would take you to sell it. As always, the moral is, unless you have a real business need for a computer, don't be in a hurry to buy, and if you buy, buy cheap.—JH

Computers: For

From Mario Pagnoni (MA):

A year ago we decided to test the homeschooling waters. Here in Massachusetts the legal waterway had already been bridged and my 13 years of teaching also worked in our favor. We expected, and got, no trouble from school authorities.

We were fascinated by the potential of the home computer and intrigued with the prospects of utilizing it as an educational tool. And for me, homeschooling was an opportunity to combine three loves: my children, education, and writing (I'd attempt a book on home education—possibly with a slant toward computers).

At the outset we knew nothing about computers. And personally, I am a basket case around machines. I can't even figure out how to run the digital watch my kids gave me last Father's Day. Our 10-year-old son James is the only one who can program it. When I try to set it, the bloody thing ends up playing Yankee Doodle during meetings. "I, ah, don't know how to work it," I try to explain. "You see my, ah, son. . . ."

Nevertheless, we researched personal computers as best we could and finally opted for Apple. There was more software for the Apple than any other computer. We found programs for word processing, database management, and an incredible array of games and educational packages. Most importantly, there were two Apple users' clubs within a 30-minute drive of our home. While support is sometimes rare from computer dealers, it is readily available at a friendly users' club. Before I knew it I was not only a club member, but co-editor of its newsletter, and author of a regular column called "Computers for Absolute Beginners." The column was my way of insuring that there would be at least one piece in the publication that I could understand.

But was all this computer stuff the antithesis of homeschooling? Were we to turn our children over to the computer? I mean, homeschooling is people oriented. It can be tremendously rewarding and bring a family closer together. Everything we heard about computers indicated that they would come between people. But the more we worked with the machine the more we realized that it neither brought us together nor tore us apart. It was just a tool—a powerful tool. It was part of our educational program, but it could never *be* the educational program.

Our biggest computer problem was software. There was so much available and so little that was good. By sharing ideas at the computer club we learned how to sift through the trash and select worthwhile programs. Much of the available software only provides drill and practice. At first I thought, "Who needs a $2000 microcomputer to teach multiplication tables—flash cards do the job nicely for 79 cents." But drill is only one use for a micro. And that mechanized drill instructor frees teacher time for more creative endeavors. All those years of teaching made me progressive enough to know that drill is not the ultimate in education. But, on the other hand, I'm still conservative enough to know that there's a place for it. The better drill programs feature sound effects and graphics and can be entertaining enough to take the drudgery out of practice. Kids also appreciate the fact that feedback is immediate—no need to wait for teacher to correct and return papers. Being non-judgmental is another plus for the micro—you can't disappoint the computer.

One evening a friend of mine interrupted his son who was pounding feverishly at the computer keyboard. The youngster was working late into the night on an entertaining program called "Musical Math Teacher." Drilling the user on basic math facts, the program rewards correct answers with a brief musical interlude, and keeps a running percentage score. "What are you doing working so late?" asked the parent. "Well, I got one problem wrong earlier," answered the fifth-grader, "and since then I've worked my score up to 99% correct and I'm not going to bed until I get all the way back to 100%."

We favor programs that have an editor mode. They're the kind that allow you to enter your own data into the program. One such program, a vocabulary builder called "Word Attack," let us enter our own word lists into its video game mode. With nifty sound effects and graphics (two sure hits with kids), our boys enjoyed learning their lessons. Still, I can't help but remember that computer instructor who warned that, "Learning is best done *not* at a video game pace."

We find simulation-type programs like "Lemonade Stand" and "The Oregon Trail" particularly valuable. They simulate real life situations. "The Oregon Trail," a pioneer adventure, requires that you manage your food, avoid hostile Indians and natural disasters, and make it across country. "Lemonade Stand" challenges your business skills. You check the daily weather report, input the number of advertising signs you'll purchase, and indicate how much lemonade you'll produce and its price per glass. I've given up playing this one with my kids. Have you any idea how embarrassing it is to file bankruptcy for a lemonade stand?

Another favorite program called "Snooper Troops" transforms students into detectives. Their case is a mystery that requires map-making and note-taking to unravel. Our boys work together on the program, sometimes brain-storming clues, sometimes arguing over which suspect to interrogate next. There's always lots of interaction going on—between the boys, and between the boys and the machine. It's a far cry from people's image of isolated, sullen children silently droning away at the keyboard.

Perhaps the most valuable educational use for a microcomputer is word processing. . . . When children become familiar with "electronic cut and paste" (moving passages around the body of their text) they begin to analyze the very fabric of writing. They marvel at the effects of rearranging the words in a sentence. Moreover, they become acutely aware of the logical progression of thoughts expressed in writing. Their writing gradually becomes clear and uncluttered.

Computerists are often surprised to hear that our children work with the "Apple Writer II" (a sophisticated word processing package). They expect that they would utilize a simpler WP program like "Bank Street Writer" [*GWS* 35], designed to be simple enough for children. After several brief sessions of watching me "manipulate text" with Apple Writer, they had it mastered. Of course, it took me six weeks to figure out the manual, but that's another story.

One of the most rewarding activities for our children has been pen pal letters. [DR: See James Pagnoni's letter in *GWS* 33.] Right in the middle of his love affair with the WP I was surprised to find James *handwriting* a letter. "Why aren't you using the computer?" I asked. "Oh, no special reason," he fibbed. "James," I persisted, "you've used word processing for all your writing the last few weeks—you even tried to stuff your Jedi Fan Club membership card into the printer."

"Well . . . you know my new friend—the one who's kind of poor? Well . . . I just figured that he might feel bad. I mean, seeing that computer printout might remind him . . . of all the stuff other people have that he doesn't."

Our home school has been a tremendous success. We are convinced that no school in the country, public or private, could have done for us what we did for ourselves this past year. . . . And all of this from people who a year ago didn't know software from Tupperware.

And Against

Lynne Thunderstorm (BC) wrote:

We live in an isolated valley with wild mountains on all sides. We live with a sense of the seasons and the earth in all that we do, and try to let this awareness grow in our children. We don't keep up with all the latest happenings, so that when we went out last winter to visit our family in New York State, we were surprised by the computer phenomenon. It seemed that everybody had or was saving up for computers, everybody was buying the latest games, and everyone knew how to play.

Since then, the so-called need for computer literacy has been jumping out at me from everything I read, from *MS.* to *GWS*—or so I thought. Thank goodness John wrote what he did in *GWS* 33. I think we need something large scale, though, more along the lines of Jerry Mander's *Arguments For The Elimination Of Television.*

The whole thing seems spooky to me, and I was only exposed to computer buffs for five weeks. I saw my father and his friends sitting in front of a noisy box for hours and hours each day. In fact, from the time he came home from work until bedtime, his sounds of frustration or success could be heard mingled with the bashes and buzzes of the machine. He wanted to share his new interest with me—for hours and hours. I couldn't even pretend enthusiasm after the first hilarious encounter with Pac Man, but these games were enough to hold him enthralled for hours every day, for months on end. The image of my dad, whom I will not be able to visit very many times, sitting alone in the family room playing his games, saddens me.

A cousin I hadn't seen for 15 years visited while I was there. He and his two daughters, on vacation from school (he "teaches"), didn't feel like taking a walk, talking, bike riding, doing yoga with me, or anything. It was either lie in front of the TV, or sit in front of the screen with levers in their hands. Or, lie on the couch with stereo earphones on. Just like my father.

Younger kids had pocket games that went everywhere with them. People praised the new inventions for increasing eye-hand coordination, as if ancient basket weavers hadn't done that. They called it creative, marvellous, entertaining.

All I saw was how the latest toy or learning device, call it what you will, tended to remove people one step more from their connection with each other and with the earth. People spoke of developing a relationship with their machines, of spending time with their computers to get to know them better. That sounds scary. It is one more step away from developing relationships with living, breathing organisms. And when you think that the content of many of these manufactured games—all that I saw—was shooting, bopping, killing, and that the dialogue was often, "There, I got you, you little ——," or "Oh, no, I'm gonna crash," the absurdity of talking about relating looms larger.

Vicarious living. I understand that computers are useful. Like their technological counterparts, snowmobiles and penicillin, they have a place in the world, and certainly in the economy. But when masses of people fall for the latest gadgets and clothing styles, there is always a trade-off, and someone always gets rich.

I picture some little child sitting in a soundproof booth punching buttons all alone, maybe with earphones, and the child is "learning" something. Something that maybe other children used to learn with someone's knee pressed against hers, and a warm human voice exchanging information. Blip, blip, blip.

Nava had an uneasy feeling when he read the *National Geographic* article on computers. He told me that it seemed as if people felt the computer were going to solve a lot of problems in the world, to make the world a better place to live in, to help kids learn more, give people more jobs, on and on. That's a lot of faith to have in something, and that something seems to take the control of people's lives one step farther away from them.

Nava tried to write what made him uneasy. "Having repaired and worked with heavy machinery in factories and mills, having developed a homestead, built a few houses, learned to grow nearly all our own food, I can see that the computer is one more step removed from basic production, from the human interrelating and work that makes the world go around. The computer is a manipulating tool, useful, but not the thing that makes the food or the goods we need. It can juggle information, but it can't replace real human skills, real work of people making things happen. What's scary is when people think it can."

Such a hard one to talk about! The nightmarish image of a man alone in a room with a machine for company, when the rest of the family, the far distant family, would have loved his company; or two kids hunched over a machine, madly pushing buttons, like their lives depended on it—these are the things I think of when I think of computers. My mother writes that the computer is revolutionizing her office, scaring her, increasing her workload, and my cousins write that computers are teaching them better than teachers can.

You are right to ask what we will have gained in twenty years.

Computer Vandalism—2

In *GWS* 35, I quoted from articles in *Time* and *Newsweek* on "computer vandalism," the invasion and sometimes destruction of computer databanks simply for the sake of excitement, and I began to discuss the implications of this. Here is more from the *Newsweek* story:

> the ["414 Gang" in Milwaukee] stumbled across an electronic bulletin board in New York called OSUNY. The board was a treasure trove: messages posted by other users gave codes and phone numbers to get free access to MCI and Sprint long-distance telephone services, *ways to escape having unauthorized phone calls traced* [emphasis added] and a panoply of network telephone numbers and directions for accessing major computer systems around the country.

> Hackers like the 414s were essentially exploiting weaknesses in systems that were designed to be easy to use and relatively open ... Telenet, Tymnet and other networks are designed so that thousands of legitimate users can gain access to the computers quickly.

> Only half of the states now have laws against computer crime, and legal experts argue that cases like the Milwaukee 414s break-ins are going to have to be covered by new legislation. "We can't have horse-and-buggy laws in a Buck Rogers era," said Arthur R. Miller, Professor of Law at Harvard Law School. ... Moreover, there is no federal law specifically prohibiting unauthorized access to computers.

> *The vast majority* [emphasis added] of white collar crime cases in one way or another involve computers.

> The Computer Security Act of 1983 ... would mandate a fine of up to $50,000 or a five-year jail sentence for robbing or abusing federal or private computers used in interstate commerce.

From a front page story in the Sept. 5, 1983, *New York Times*, we get this additional information:

> The number of young people roaming without authorization through some of the nation's most sophisticated computer systems runs into the hundreds and possibly thousands, according to computer crime experts. Further, they say, the number is growing hand-in-hand with the boom in personal computers.

> Many computer enthusiasts scoff at the Milwaukee group. "They are the least of what's going on in this world," said a 19-year-old university student in Chicago who calls himself Mr. Xerox. "They are the ones who get caught, which means they really don't know what they're doing."

Those who are most knowledgeable in the computer world say the preponderance of unauthorized penetrations into commercial, academic, and government computers are never discovered. "Most computers don't have the mechanisms in place to know that they've had an intruder," said Robert P. Campbell, president of Advance Information Management Inc. in Woodbridge, Va., "and most don't have the ability to go back and reconstruct what happened."

The manipulation of telephone systems to communicate endlessly over long-distance lines for free is fairly common, the crime experts say. . . . The "pirates" regularly use long-distance lines for transmitting stolen computer programs to electronic acquaintances across the country, and such a transmission often takes more than half an hour. They either bypass telephone billing mechanisms or use a code that results in the bill's being sent to a subscriber to one of the long-distance telephone systems. There is a bimonthly newsletter published in New York that contains detailed information on how to break into computers and manipulate telephones.

Once again, what does this have to do with all of us who only want to own computers for innocent reasons, like playing games, or doing some word processing, or reading a few books from a distant library? It may have a great deal to do with us, and with such foundations of our legal system as the assumption of innocence and the burden of proof. Consider: suppose the government accuses us of having, say, robbed a bank. We could of course defend ourselves against the charge by proving that we were somewhere else. But we do not *have* to do even that much. The burden of proof is not on us to show that we were not at the bank, but on the government to show beyond reasonable doubt that we *were*, and this means among other requirements that it must produce witnesses who will swear they saw us there. Now suppose instead that some years in the future the government accuses us of having tampered with someone's computer. What must it show, in order to convict us? What *can* it show, what is there for it to show, other than that certain illegal calls were traced to our telephone number? How could we possibly defend ourselves against such a charge? Suppose some malicious hackers had figured out what it will probably be very easy for them to figure out, as indeed they may well have already—a way to make a call from one number while making it look as if it came from another? How then could we show our innocence? "But Your Honor, it's all a mistake!"

History has shown very plainly that when the government, and other holders of wealth and power, feel themselves in danger, they will take steps to reduce this danger, and if these happen to do away with certain constitutional rights of citizens, so much the worse for them. We may be absolutely certain that Congress and the Legislatures, and above all the present Supreme Court, will give the government whatever legislation and powers it thinks it may need to prosecute computer vandals, and before we jump up and down and sing happy songs about the wonderful computer revolution, we might think a little about what some of these laws and these powers might turn out to be.—JH

Superlearning

I'd like to ask if any of our readers have had any first-hand experience with an instructional method called *Superlearning* (450 7th Ave., Suite 500, New York NY 10123), which involves the use of tapes, and if so, what their experience has been. Some of what I have read about the results of the method sounds promising; on the other hand, there is a high-pressure quality to their catalog that I don't much like. But there might be a valuable resource for homeschoolers there, and if so, I'd like to take advantage of it.—JH

Education "Stores"

I recently visited *Sentinel Teacher Supply* and found it to be a homeschoolers' paradise! Games, stickers, workbooks, etc. Also a Christian Education room. The salespeople were welcoming.

... Great source of materials! Catalog available: 2200 W Alameda Av, Denver CO 80223.—*Janis Martinez, Colorado Homeschooling Network Newsletter.*

The *Tennessee Book Company*, 410 Harding Industrial Drive, PO Box 110110, Nashville TN 37211, sells textbooks to the schools. Prices are wholesale whether you buy one or 100. There's a reading room where you can compare the books of 65 different publishers. Fill out your order, call yourself a school, pay, and you have your books, no questions asked. Prices are cheaper than buying direct from the publisher, and no shipping charge.—*A Tennessee Reader.*

[DR:] If you would like to find such a place in your area where you can examine textbooks and other educational materials first-hand, check the Yellow Pages under "School Supplies" and "Book Dealers."

Stencils From X-Rays

From Leslie Westrum (IN):

If anyone is interested in stenciling, I've found a financial shortcut. Cardboard stencils don't hold up well, and the mylar store-bought kind cost a fortune. But you can make your own designs with an exacto-knife or razor blade and old X-rays. Just go to your local hospital and ask for used X-rays— they usually just throw them away. This plastic is sturdier than the commercial stencil stuff. I used it to stencil hearts on my kitchen wall and it worked *great*! ... The standard size is 10" x 12"—a good size to work with. It cuts easily if your blade is sharp. Aside from stenciling—the X-rays themselves are great for teaching your kids about anatomy.... You sure can't beat the price!

Piano And Recorder

Susan Richman (PA) wrote:

Little Molly (3 months old) has been a real spur to Jesse's piano playing—she calms down almost instantly when he plays for her, a wonderfully appreciative audience! He plays on and off throughout the day now. He discovered *on his own* that he could use *all* his fingers, not just his index finger, and even both hands—he said that doing Chisanbop gave him the idea! He really notices how his little songs sound smoother when he uses all fingers. He's still enjoying experiments with chords. He once corrected me when I was telling a friend about how he was *learning* to play piano. "I'm not *learning* to play piano, I'm *playing* piano," he said adamantly. He loves playing his little repertoire of memorized songs to anyone who will listen.

Jacob also takes his time at the piano, pretending to play Jesse's songs from *Mrs. Stewart*, often turning to the proper page and singing the numbers or words.

Glad to see you're offering the Aulos recorder now (*GWS* 33). I've found that as a mother with young ones, the recorder can't be beat—can't be *broken* by two-year-olds, either. I usually try to bring mine along on hikes in the woods. I find I'm much more patient in letting Jesse and Jacob play as long as they like, building "rock islands" in our creek or digging in sand, if I have my recorder with me so I can be playing, too. Easy to carry with a baby—I don't know too many mothers who could easily manage, say, a cello *and* a babe on hip. We all had a wonderful walk out in the woods the other day boys playing in the stream, Molly looking up at the waving-to-her tree branches, kicking and smiling, and me having a long time for recorder playing. Very nice to be able to take a musical instrument outside. I always feel in tune with all the shepherds of the world!

I have discovered a nice recorder book, *The Recorder Guide* by Johanna Klubach and Arthur Nikta. It's a teaching guide, and mostly is full of very simple but delightful duets from the folk heritage of the world. Easy sight-reading, and the book is also full of charming old etchings and drawings of people playing recorder.

A Mysterious Gift

One of our readers, learning that I had taken up the violin, called me one day from New Jersey to say that she had an old violin in the house that she wanted to give me. (Down, boy! This is not a Strad-in-the-attic story.) I suggested that she try to sell it, but she said she would rather have me have it. I said that was very nice of her, and we arranged to meet when I was in N.J. giving a lecture. Came the evening, and just as I was about to begin, a lady came in with a violin, thrust it into my hands, and walked right out again. I had expected and hoped to have time to thank her, and learn a bit about the instrument and its history in her family, but there was no time. I don't even know her name.

Later, in my motel, I opened the case and looked at, and tried, the violin. It looked very nice, with a beautifully grained back and sides (ribs), and though the strings were old and the bow poor, it made a mellow sound. It is at my friend Horst Kloss's shop right now, getting the back glued up, a new bridge cut, new strings put in, and so on. I am eager to start playing it. Meanwhile, it is important that my unknown benefactor get in touch with me, so that I can tell her something about the instrument.—JH

New Tape Available Here

Wallace Family Concert #2 (1983) ($8 for 90 min. cassette). Our first Wallace Family Concert tape was made in June 1982, when Vita was just 7 and Ishmael not quite 11. They planned and gave the concert mostly in order to make a recording to send to relatives and friends, and I added it to our list so that others could hear a family learning and making classical music together. Also, I thought there would probably be more concerts and recordings in the future, and that some might later find it interesting to have a record of where, musically speaking, the family had come from.

There have been other concerts since. In one, in November 1982, I was a guest artist; in one part of the concert, Ishmael and I played a sonata for cello and piano. At that concert we had a very small audience—one other homeschooling family. This year the Wallaces decided to put on a somewhat larger and more formal concert, with invitations (prepared by Vita) sent out to a number of guests, and program notes for all the music, written by Ishmael. On the big day—I had just driven up after some lectures in the Philadelphia area—every chair in the house was pressed into service for the 20 or so adults and children who arrived. This is a tape of the entire occasion, complete with applause and shouts of "Encore"! If you listen to this tape over headphones, which I like to do when listening alone, you will feel you are there.

The first music you will hear is the first movement of a piano quartet which Ishmael has written for the family. (By now he has mostly completed the other movements, but only the first movement had been rehearsed for this concert.) In this we hear the first recorded appearance on cello of Bob Wallace, who has been playing for only about a year and a half. In following selections we hear Vita on the piano, then Ishmael on the piano playing the *Children's* suite by Debussy, and also two fascinating compositions of his own, then Vita on violin accompanied by Ishmael, then Ishmael on piano again. As in a professional concert, the performers do not announce their pieces, so we will provide a copy of the program, along with the program notes.

This is for me not only a souvenir in sound of a very happy gathering of family and friends of all ages, but also a record of the continuing musical growth of this music-loving family. If you already know their earlier tape, you will find it very hard to believe how much both the children have improved. Ishmael no longer sounds like a "child" pianist, but like a mature artist that I would be glad to hear on any occasion, and Vita in her turn has progressed amazingly on both piano and violin.

All in all, a wonderful proof, in music, that it is not true that children will never do anything difficult or worthwhile unless they are made to. For this is music played only for love.—JH

New Books Available Here

Black Foremothers, by Dorothy Sterling ($6.25 + post). This is the story of a too-little known part of our history, the lives of three black women who were among the pioneers in the long and hard effort, not ended yet, to free black people, first from slavery, then from legal and political discrimination. It is hard to believe, and indeed many young people may still not know, that more than eighty years after our country was founded, not only was it legal in many parts of the country to own slaves, but in all parts of the country it was a crime to help slaves escape from slavery.

All of these stories remind us what long, hard, patient, often discouraging effort it takes to do away with long-established customs and wrongs. The most exciting of these stories is the first, the Life of Ellen Craft. Born in 1826, she was the only one of these women to grow up a slave. When she was 22, she and her new husband, William, afraid they might be separated from each other, or from their children if they should have any, decided to try to escape to the North and freedom. Their plan was a daring one. Since she was light skinned, she planned to disguise herself as an invalid Southern gentleman, and her husband as her servant.

Most of the details that made her disguise plausible were devised by Ellen. Realizing with a sudden pang that she would be asked to sign hotel registers, she made up a bandage and sling for her right arm to explain her inability to write. A poultice—a bulky, wet bandage, tied from chin to head, toothache style, would conceal her beardlessness. Then, looking in a mirror, she saw that her eyes might register fear, anger, dismay, and she sent William downtown for a final purchase—a pair of green spectacles. The story of their escape is almost unbearably exciting—it might someday make a wonderful film, though it may be some time before such a film is made.

If the other two women in this book did not face quite the same degree of danger as Ellen Craft, they still had to overcome every kind of difficulty. Ida Wells at age 16, lost both parents to yellow fever, and had to come home to take care of five young children. To keep the family from being broken up, she went to work as a schoolteacher so that she could support them. Later she became the first black woman journalist, and for most of her life remained one of the most tireless, eloquent, and effective speakers against racial injustice.

This book is a useful supplement and corrective to the very incomplete American history that has always been and is now taught in our schools, even the "best" schools. It is also an exciting and well told story, from which, in these difficult times, we may all gain much needed strength and courage.

Mrs. Frisby and the Rats of NIMH, by Robert O'Brien ($1.75 + post). This is one of my very favorite animal adventure stories. Mrs. Frisby is a widowed field mouse, facing a terrible dilemma. Spring is coming, and she and her children must move from their winter home in the field of a farmer, whose spring plowing will destroy their dwelling, to their summer home in nearby woods. But her youngest child is very ill, and to make such a long journey this early in the year will certainly kill him. She seeks advice and help, and is told to try to make contact with some mysterious rats in her neighborhood. These, we learn, are the rats of NIMH. What does NIMH stand for? National Institute of Mental Health. What did that have to do with these rats? The scientists of NIMH did an experiment on the rats to see if they could increase their intelligence. Did they succeed? They did, beyond their wildest dreams. And from this beginning follows this exciting story.

Once begun, it is very hard to put down. It is a wonderful bedtime-read-aloud story, since the author, like all great story-tellers, ends almost every chapter with a new piece of important information, a new danger, or a new way of overcoming danger, so that readers can hardly wait to see what happens next. Also, the book raises a question for its child-philosopher readers that has always been and is now a matter of passionate concern to many adults: What is intelligence? How can we recognize it, or test it, or measure it? How would really intelligent creatures, under the control of more powerful creatures, behave? (This story, like any schoolroom, provides one good answer—they would conceal most of their intelligence.) What would truly intelligent creatures have as their aim in life? To this question the book gives a very good and I think true answer—for these super intelligent rats do indeed have an ambition, a goal, for which they are ready to risk their lives. What it is, I will let readers find out.

I have read that a full-length film, an animated cartoon, was made from this book, and that it is one of the best of such films ever made. If it turns up near you, it might be worth seeing—and if you see it, please give us a report. Meanwhile, don't miss this wonderful book.

The Chinese Word for Horse, And Other Stories, by John Lewis & Peter Rigby ($5.35 + post). This unique, surprising, and beautiful book is both about the three stories it tells and about the Chinese written language it uses to tell them. The illustrations which help tell the stories are themselves made up of Chinese written characters (each of which stands for a whole word), or slightly modified versions of these. Thus the true Chinese word for horse, with only a few changes, becomes an easily recognized but still very Chinese looking picture of a horse; the Chinese word for tree, in the same way, becomes a very beautiful picture of a forest. The true Chinese characters are always painted with a brush in a very vivid Chinese red; all the other illustrations, also painted with a brush, are in black. The boldness of these shapes and colors make this a strikingly beautiful book. Some children may be inspired by it to want to make Chinese or pseudo-Chinese characters of their own.

One of the fascinating and beautiful things we learn from this book is the way Chinese combines words for things to make words for other things, or even abstract ideas. Thus the Chinese word for "shed" is the word for "cart" with a little roof drawn over it. To the word for "tree" Chinese adds three shapes representing the open mouths of birds, to get the word for "birdsong." The Chinese word for "thrift" is a picture of a storehouse, with two sheaves of grain hanging under the roof. And the Chinese word for "thief" is the picture for "man," with a sheaf of grain on each side, as if under each arm. This is a very powerful reminder that a thief not only steals another's work but his food, in short, that he does him a serious injury.

It may well be true that the Chinese are constantly reminded by their written language what it is they are really talking about; the shapes of the symbols remind them of the realness of the thing.

To be sure, such pictographic languages have serious disadvantages. It takes a very long time for the Chinese to learn enough symbols to use their written language well—time that a simpler system (which the Chinese are right now trying to develop) might have freed to use in other ways. But the concrete nature of this written language may to some extent protect them from the over-abstraction of thought which is one of the great curses and dangers of our Western life.

In any case, this is a fascinating book to look at and read, as well as an interesting glimpse into a very different way of thinking and writing.

A High Wind in Jamaica, by Richard Hughes ($2.25 + post). This book, set in the 19th century, about a group of children who, while on their way to England from their island home in the Caribbean, are captured by pirates, is not only an exciting adventure story but also one of the first, and one of the greatest, fictional psychological portraits of children, above all of its ten-year-old heroine Emily. Few books I have read have captured or intuited so vividly and convincingly what it might feel like to be a child, above all in these special circumstances. Hughes' understanding of children seems to me amazingly accurate, with perhaps one exception, the question of their ability to become attached to people, places, things—he says they don't, I say they often do.

The book, like another favorite of mine, *Jeremy*, which I will add to our list if it ever comes back into print, was not written for children but for adults—it is an adult novel, about children. But the story is so exciting, the children so real, and the descriptions of life in the tropics and at sea so lifelike, that I think any children of ten or over, and perhaps even some younger; would love the book, which I myself have read many times, always with the greatest pleasure.—JH

Rubber Stamp Kit Available Here

STA-TITE Printing Kit ($11, no extra postage charge). What we have here is in effect the world's smallest and least expensive printing press. It was designed to be used, not by children, but by adults in offices. But I think it may be something that many children will much enjoy using, and that may make easier and more exciting their first exploration of the world of reading and writing.

As Glenda Bissex, in her wonderful book *Gnys at Wrk* (*GWS* 24, 25) has pointed out (along with many others), many and perhaps even most children, if they had a chance, would rather approach the world of reading through the world of writing rather than the other way round. What makes this very natural approach hard and unpleasant for most children is the sheer physical difficulty of making letters at all, let alone letters they would feel proud to look at and to show others.

I have felt for some time that if children had an easy way to make letters, they might, like Paul Bissex, be much more interested in writing as a way of expressing their thoughts. Hence my long-standing interest in typewriters for children—I still feel strongly that anyone who can afford the needed $100 or so would be very wise to buy some kind of electric typewriter for their children. (Manual typewriters are too hard for small fingers.) And I also agree strongly with what Seymour Papert said in *Mindstorms* (*GWS* 24) and Mario Pagnoni has said in a more recent letter to us, that many or most children would find word processors a great incentive to writing.

At the same time I have been looking for something much cheaper and simpler, a set of letter stamps that even young children could use. Until recently, those I had seen seemed much too expensive for most parents, on the order of $1 per letter. Then one day, looking through one of the many office supply catalogs that come in our mail, I saw an ad for these rubber stamps, which looked as though they might be just what we were looking for.

This is a kit, designed to enable offices to make their own custom designed rubber stamps. In the kit are a number of rubber letters and numerals, plus the basic stamp into which you can insert whatever letters and numbers you need to make your own personal message. This particular set has four or five each of the letters, both capitals (about ¼" high) and lower case, and two or three of each of the numerals, which should be enough to write most of the messages that could fit on the stamp— 4-5 lines of print with about 20 characters per line. I should think children might have quite a bit of fun with this. I can imagine using the stamp to send some short message to a child, who would then use it to send a message in return. Or children might use it to send the same message or letter to a number of people—perhaps a Christmas card or other greeting. Readers will no doubt invent their own ways of using these pads—please let us know what you and your children do with them.

A word of advice and one of caution. The kit supplies tweezers for inserting and removing letters, but I find them a little awkward to use and think most children would find them impossible. Fingers can do the job better. As for caution, the stamp pad provided is a regular office stamp pad using *non-washable* ink, so take needed precautions. I have not yet found a stamp pad with washable ink; if you know of any, please let us know. It is possible to buy un-inked pads. We tried using water colors with one of these, but the letters were much too faint to be interesting. Perhaps washable colors for felt-tipped pens would work better. So far we have not had time to try such an experiment. If any of you try it, or find some other good colors to use in un-inked pads, please let us know. For the time being, I would probably not trust a two-year-old with these pads, but think that four-year-olds could be trusted to use them properly—on paper only. With these minimal controls, I think many of you and your children may find this a very interesting and helpful tool.— JH

Editors—John Holt & Donna Richoux
Managing Editor—Pat Farenga
Subscriptions & Books—Mark Pierce & Mary Gray
Office Assistant—Mary Van Doren

Growing Without Schooling 37

January 1984

On Dec. 20 Dr. Raymond Moore, and Nancy, Bob, Ishmael, and Vita Wallace were on the *Donahue* show, which we saw two weeks later here in Boston. I thought the homeschoolers, and homeschooling, did very well. I wish that the Wallace's and Ray Moore had been given time to talk in a little more depth; they mostly had to slip a word in edgewise where they could, and Bob Wallace was hardly ever able even to finish a sentence. I also wish that Ishmael and Vita had been given a little more time to show some of their musical skill, which in itself would have been a strong argument for homeschooling. But even so, the homeschool team made many important points.

What struck me most about the show was how much the audience seemed to be on the homeschool side. I did not keep an accurate count, but it seemed to me that about three-quarters or more of what was said during the program either strongly supported homeschooling or was sympathetic to it. Several families in the studio audience, including one black family, spoke enthusiastically about teaching their own children at home, and one 16-year-old homeschooled boy said that he was taking a number of college courses. Hard to ask for much better than that. It was very different indeed in 1978 when Bob and Linda Sessions and their children were with me on the show. As I recall, we had only one strong supporter in the audience, and many angry opponents. So perhaps public opinion has swung a little our way. Let us hope so; we are likely to face some tough legislative battles in a number of states this year and in coming years, and we will need all the public support we can get.

The most exciting news is that our homeschooling friend Mario Pagnoni has signed a contract with Larson Publications, publishers of Nancy Wallace's *Better Than School*, to publish his first book, now entitled *The Complete Guide To Homeschooling*. Publication date should be sometime next fall. As we get more definite news about title, price, and availability, we will let you know. Meanwhile, congratulations to Mario! And may this book be the first of many!

Within the next week or two, as I write this, I expect to sign a contract with Addison Wesley for a new book, of which a working title is *The Three R's At Home* (or perhaps *"The Basics" At Home*). This will be, for the most part, about the many ways in which children, usually outside of any designed learning environment and with little or no formal instruction, figure out for themselves a great deal of essential knowledge about language, reading, numbers, and the like. It will also be about ways in which adults, parents or teachers, can make it easier for them to do this. This will be my first book with Addison Wesley, though I will be continuing to work with my friend, neighbor, and editor Merloyd Lawrence. The book should be finished this year and in print sometime next year.

Good news from one of our youngest authors. *Mother Earth News* has accepted a story which Vita Wallace (8) wrote about the concert which she and her family gave early in November (we have a tape of this in our catalog). She still has to take some photographs to go with it, so I would guess that the story will appear perhaps sometime next summer.

As I said in *GWS* 36, the current (Jan./Feb.'84) issue of *Mother Earth News* has an article by me called, "So You Want to Home School," a good summary of the different legal ways to homeschool and the steps to take to carry them out. Also printed with the article is an excellent short review of Nancy Wallace's *Better Than School*, with some very good excerpts. As always, there are a number of other very interesting articles in this issue of *Mother Earth News*, including an interview with Dr. Andrew Saul called, "You Can Be Your Own Doctor," at the end of which is an exceedingly useful list of basic medical reference books (usually not easy to find), with information about how to get them. This interview, and these books, would be a good supplement to *Confessions of a Medical Heretic*, which we sell here.—John Holt

John Holt's Coming Schedule

Mar. 5, 1984: Project Excel, Suffolk U., Boston. Contact Glen Lewandowski, 723-4700 ext. 280.

Mar. 8: Holt Associates Open House (second Thurs. each month).

Mar. 15: John Holt Music Workshop (3rd Thurs. each month—call 437-1550 to confirm).

Mar. 30: Eastern Washington University, Cheney WA. Contact Darleen Weller, 509-456-4401.

Mar. 31–Apr. 1: Seattle homeschoolers. Contact Deb Stewart, 206-435-5015.

Apr. 2–3: Home Schooling Fair, Spokane WA. Contact Nola Evans, 509-326-0267.

Apr. 4: Montana Homeschooling Association. Contact Debbie Kersten, Box 144, Manhattan MT 59741.

Apr. 8 (Tentative): East Stroudsburg U., E. Stroudsburg PA. 2 p.m. Contact Ann Cameron, 1743 Pokono Av, Stroudsburg PA 18360.

Apr. 16: University of Kentucky. Contact Libby Morley, 606-273-7816.

Anyone who wants to coordinate other meetings or lectures around these times, contact Pat Farenga.

Another Home-Schooler At College

James Salisbury (ID) sent us this clipping from the Provo, Utah Herald, *about one of his former* John Learning Center *students:*

> Amy Louise Hovenden ... starts school at Brigham Young University in January. ... Amy [14] is the youngest freshman ever to be accepted to the university.
>
> She feels no major qualms about starting college at an age younger than most. "I feel excited and a little nervous," she said. "But I don't see any problems with it. The other students are just people, too."
>
> Amy will take general education courses at first, but plans to major in music, with emphasis on piano performance and teaching.
>
> "My mother wanted to keep me at home for a few more years, but my father said what I was studying was the same material as the 100 and 200 level courses he took at BYU," she said. "So we decided I would give college a try."
>
> Amy had to undergo nearly three months of intense scrutiny by college entrance boards to determine her social readiness as well as her scholastic ability. "She was thoroughly checked for emotional stability, and was found to be very 'balanced.' That of course made us all feel better about it," Mrs. Hovenden said. "The examiners certainly did their homework, but were very gracious and helpful."
>
> Amy scored a 29 on the ACT college entrance test [JH: out of a possible 36—about the same as Grant Colfax's scores], and was awarded a dean's scholarship, which pays one-half of tuition costs.
>
> The oldest of nine children, *she and her brothers and sisters have been schooled by their parents at "Sterling Academy" home school.*
>
> Amy has already almost completed seven course credits of college home study classes.
>
> Amy will continue to live at home in Orem, with her parents driving her to school. "Our family is very close and we enjoy having her here," her father said.

Lawyer With No Law School

A UPI story from San Francisco, reprinted in the Davis (CA) Enterprise, *1/17/84:*

> A grandmother whose last formal education was at Willits High School 32 years ago has taken and passed the difficult California State Bar examination without the benefit of a diploma from a law school.
>
> Myrna Oglesby, 48, a mother of five and

a long-time Ukiah legal secretary, prepared for the exam by "reading the law"—a method all but abandoned in the 20th century.

A total of 3,906 law-school graduates learned last month that they had flunked the examination. The number was 51% of those who took it. To qualify to take the exam without being a law school graduate, one must:

Pass a Bar Association college equivalency test.

Work in the office of an attorney or judge willing to devote at least five hours a week to one-on-one educational supervision.

And study a minimum of 18 hours per week outside the office for 48 weeks of each year with the tutor filing a report every six months with the State Bar on the content.

Oglesby's mentor was lawyer Jared Carter who taught her for five years before she felt ready to tackle the bar exam.

She said in a recent interview that key advantages to reading for the law were "saving classroom time by doing it my way instead of listening to some lectures that, perhaps, wouldn't have been beneficial" and "the fact that I had my own personal tutor—which you don't get in large law school."

Carter said, "I think it's absolutely remarkable that she accomplished this."

Notes From Donna

New Reprints: We are offering two more reprints here for 10¢ each. The first has two articles recently written by John for *USA Today*, "Same 'cure' won't help schools" and "Home schooling lets a child's mind grow." The other new reprint (on the suggestion of a reader) is "Homeschooler at Harvard," the articles from *GWS* 35 and #36 on Grant Colfax.

We are running the list of all our reprints in the back of this issue, since it has changed so much in the last year and it was not quite correct in our Fall catalog. If you order one or two reprints without buying other material from us, please send a self-addressed stamped envelope as well.

Learning Disability Resource: From Thomas Armstrong (*Latebloomers*, PO Box 2647, Berkeley CA 94702): "I finally got my book proposal for *The Learning Disability Lie* finished after a year of research and writing, and it is now in the hands of my agent. . . . I feel really excited about the work as it is a comprehensive indictment of the whole learning disability mess (including research indicating that the tests don't test for L.D., that the programs don't cure L.D., etc., etc.) and at the same time provides positive alternatives. . . . I'm sending along a resource sheet which represents sources I have culled from my research that question the learning disability paradigm. On the other side are learning resources that parents can use. . . . I would be glad to send a copy of this resource sheet to any of your readers who send me a SAS. . . ."

Michigan Legal Brief: In *GWS* 30 we told about homeschooling parent Nick Dennany who wrote a 300+ page legal brief that a judge praised as being unusually thorough and precise. We have learned that Mr. Dennany is selling copies of his brief for "not too much"—contact him at 728 Mabel, Kalamazoo MI 49007; 616-382-2887.

Indexing Needed: We sure could use an index for the issues of GWS starting with #31. Is someone willing to take this on? You could use the categories in Rachael Solem's index of #1–30 as a starting point.—Donna Richoux

Mixed News From Kansas

From the Wichita (KS) Eagle-Beacon, *12/23/83:*

> The Wichita public school district will not interfere with parents who educate their children at home . . . as long as the parents have registered as a non-accredited private school, said Ted Shackelford, coordinator of student concerns and services.

Shackelford said he has learned of six Wichita families that may be homeschooling. He said officials will "absolutely not" make any decisions about the quality of education provided by parents who teach their children in their homes.

Shackelford said he didn't know which agency should assess home schools. The state Department of Education has no authority over non-accredited private schools, beyond requiring that they register with the department.

If parents are teaching their children at home without reporting to the Department of Education, Shackelford said, the school district will report them to the Kansas Department of Social and Rehabilitation Services for investigation of possible child neglect.

Dave Kester, an attorney for the state Department of Education, said the school district's policy complies with state law. "If they register as a private school, then the presumption is that they're a private school and they're within the law," Kester said. "I can be real sympathetic with the position of the Wichita Board of Education on this. . . . You can almost get into a thicket when you try to determine whether it's a private school and whether the teachers are competent or not."

But Verne Stephens, education programs specialist with the state education department, said registering with the state doesn't guarantee that a child is receiving the education required by law.

Kester said he thinks homeschooling violates state law, but he said the law is "confused and ambiguous."

The law doesn't mention home schools. Children between the ages of 7 and 16 are required to attend an accredited or non-accredited school. . . . The law requires that teachers in non-accredited schools be "competent" and the school be in session for the same period of time as accredited schools. But the law doesn't define competence.

Last year, 122 non-accredited private schools registered with the department. The Kansas Supreme Court ruled on Dec. 2 that a Johnson County couple had violated mandatory attendance laws when they established a home school for their two school-age children. Bonnie and Tom Sawyer of Spring Hill had registered their school with the state. But the court decided Bonnie Sawyer was not a "competent" teacher.

Court News

From the Santa Fe New Mexican, *12/18/83:*

On Dec. 7 a Carlsbad judge ruled that four families who took their children out of school to teach them at home through the auspices of the Santa Fe Community School were within their legal rights. Similar suits have been won by others teaching children at home under the SFCS program. "To my knowledge, we were the first in the country," says Ed Nagle of his school's home study program, which was started in 1975 and now has 200 students from 47 states enrolled.

The enrollment fee is $100 a year. . . . About 500 students have enrolled in the program since its inception, he says. "All of them have gone on to the grade level we have recommended if they transfer to another school," says Nagel. Three went on to college after graduating from Santa Fe Community School.

[DR:] U.S. District Judge Conrad Cyr in Maine issued a ruling on Dec. 20 in the case of *Bangor Baptist Church, et al v. Maine* that limits the state's power over private schools. A group of Christian schools had been unwilling to seek approval to operate, and with the assistance of William Ball, a lawyer well versed in matters of religious and educational freedom, had filed suit against the state. The judge agreed that although the state had the power to approve private schools, it did not have the power to close down non-approved ones, and he pointed out that the state already had established procedures of prosecuting parents for truancy. He also implied the parents could get legal exemption for their children's attendance at the non-approved schools through the "equivalent instruction" clause of the Maine statutes.

There appear to have been two very similar decisions against North Carolina homeschoolers, one in the Fourth U.S. Circuit Court of Appeals, the other in the North Carolina Court of Appeals.

We learned about the first from the Fall '83 NCACS Newsletter:

> In the case of *Duro v. District Attorney* (82-1806), Peter Duro, a fundamentalist Christian, claimed public and nonpublic schools would corrupt his five school-age children. The appeals court said last July 14 that North Carolina has "an interest in compulsory education which is of sufficient magnitude to override Duro's religious interest" under the First Amendment of the Constitution.
>
> Duro's wife teaches their children at home, but she doesn't have a teaching certificate and hasn't been trained as a teacher. Duro failed to demonstrate that home instruction will prepare his children to be self-sufficient participants in our modern society or enable them to participate intelligently in our political system, which, as the U.S. Supreme Court stated, is a compelling interest of the state.

[DR:] A reader sent this A.P. news story, dated 12/7/83, concerning the other N.C. loss. Because the language is so similar, I suspect the federal case influenced this decision:

> *Home School Ruling Overturned*
>
> The North Carolina Court of Appeals . . . on Tuesday reversed a lower court decision allowing a Harnett County couple to teach their children at home because of their religious beliefs.
>
> "The state . . . has a compelling interest in providing access to education for all in order to prepare future citizens to participate effectively and intelligently in our political system and to prepare individuals to be self-reliant and self-sufficient," said the decision, written by Judge Sidney S. Eagles Jr. "The state has no means by which to ensure that children who are at home are receiving an education. . . ."
>
> Larry Delconte [*GWS* 25] and his wife had set up one room in their home with desks, a blackboard, textbooks and other teaching materials for their two school-age children. . . . Delconte, a college-educated machinist, and his wife belong to a nondenominational fundamentalist group.

Other news in brief:

Charges Dismissed: The Lloyds, 65 Glendale Park, Rochester NY 14613---Julie and Alan Sutherland, Gainesville FL; enrolled in Mordes Academy, Rt 3 Box 215, Marianna FL 32446; attorney, Joseph Dallanegra.

Won Appeal At District Court: Mr. & Mrs. Don Budke, St. Joseph's Academy, Rt 2, Underwood MN 56586. (State is appealing to Minn. Supreme Court.)

Appealing A Loss: Jerry & Camilla Wilke, Alpena MI.

Facing Court Action: Lola Lochridge, Cadillac MI---Bill Martin, Bronson MI---Pete Olson, PO Box 1357, Windsor CO 80550.

Legislative News

A number of state legislatures or Departments of Education are attempting to change laws and regulations concerning homeschooling. Many of these same battles went on a year ago, during the 1983 legislative sessions. Here is our most recent news. I should hardly need add that we hope that all of our readers in these states will make their opinions known by writing or phoning their legislators, the committee chairmen, the governor, etc. (The organizations mentioned can give you more information):

Georgia: As we reported in *GWS* 36, the Georgia Supreme Court struck down the compulsory attendance laws because there was no definition of "private school." Connie Shaw of *Georgians For Freedom In Education* (404-923-9932) says, "There is a widespread consensus among school officials, legislators, and the governor's office that a law for attendance must be passed during this session of the General Assembly. Truancy officers are reporting cases of children not attending school because the attendance law is no longer in effect."

Connie says that the first bill proposed by the chairman of the Senate Education Committee, John Foster, did not allow for home study and House leaders told him it would never pass. Foster quickly added some provisions allowing for home study, but that included many provisions homeschoolers do not like, such as requiring them to pay for testing every year, and withdrawing permission if the children test below average.

Louisiana: The newsletter of the *Northwest Chapter of Citizens for Home Education* (4453 Finley Dr, Shreveport LA 71105; 865-4939; $2/yr.) reports: "Governor-elect Edwin Edwards has publicly stated that he intends to lead the fight to repeal the Home Study law. He also has indicated that he intends to push for further regulation of private church schools." Representative Woody Jenkins held a statewide meeting Jan.10 to help formulate strategy to preserve the current law.

Maryland: The 12/83 newsletter of the *Maryland Home Education Association* (301-730-0073) printed a list of what appear to be proposed state regulations for Maryland homeschoolers. They include a requirement that teachers in home study programs be certified for each subject taught, or have a college degree, or get a waiver from the local superintendent of schools. The State Board was scheduled to hold a hearing on these regulations Jan. 25.

New Hampshire: Barb Parshley (NH) sent us a memo dated 7/19/83 entitled "Amendments to State Board of Education's Home Education Regulations," written by Charles Marston. Many of the amendments appear to be minor clarifications, but one substantive change is to specify that parents must complete an application at least 60 days prior to keeping their children out of school. Barb says several homeschooling families have been meeting regularly to work out proposals to share with the state on approving and evaluating home education programs. The next meeting is at the Concord Library, March 20, 10 a.m.

Tennessee: From a letter by Gail Neal and Ed Falkowski (615-732-4827): "You may or may not know of the Rochelle bill which has been in the works for about a year now. . . . Homeschoolers object strenuously to this bill because it puts the burden of proving that a quality education is being provided onto the parents. . . . Representative Bobby Wood has just introduced a bill (no number yet—introduced 1/10/84) which is *very* favorable for homeschoolers, so favorable that I doubt it will make it through the committee as it stands). . . . It lists about eight alternatives for parents, any *one* of which would satisfy the compulsory school law."

The letter continues, "There is an organization forming now called *Home Education Association of Tennessee (HEAT)* which will be a way of getting up-to-date information on lobbying efforts, etc. . . . There are several hundred members, most of whom were present at a conference done by Dr. Raymond Moore and two Tennessee lawyers. . . . Since my only exposure to the homeschooling movement had been through *GWS* and John Holt's books, I was amazed to learn that many of the people at the conference had not heard of either of them. . . . Yet this is encouraging to me because the more broad-based support for homeschooling is, the better chance of favorable legislation. . . . If you want more information on HEAT, write to Larry Crain, Attorney, First American Center, 12th Floor, Nashville TN 37238. . . ."

Virginia: Connie Schwartz sent us information on the new group *Home Educators Association of Virginia*, PO Box 15266, Richmond VA 23227; 804266-6652. She reported that the legislature is working on a bill that would allow for homeschooling if a parent has a college degree or uses an approved correspondence school, and if the children are tested regularly.

Washington: Helen and Mark Hegener, who are starting a magazine called *Home Education* (PO Box 218, Tonasket WA 98855; 509-486-2449; $20/12 iss.) sent us a copy of Senate Bill 3033 which would allow for homeschooling, require standardized tests each year, and permit homeschoolers to enroll part-time in public schools and use their services.

Wisconsin: Given the State Supreme Court's ruling in *Popanz* [*GWS* 33, 34] about the "vagueness" in the compulsory school law, it was no surprise to learn that the Wisconsin legislature is trying to pass a definition of private school. It was a disappointment, however, to learn that it was anti-homeschool ("Instruction at the institution does not occur on premises used primarily as a private residence. . . ." "The majority of pupils at the institution are neither related to nor under the guardianship of any instructor at the institution"). Susan Brooks of the *Wisconsin Regional Coalition of Alternative Community Schools* (715-237-2402) says this was an old bill that has failed for years, but it has been given new momentum by the court decision. It is now called Assembly Bill 887 and Sue expected it to be scheduled for a public hearing after Jan.18. She also says that Governor Earl wants the bill passed before elections.—DR

Other Local News

Addresses of homeschooling organizations can be found in *GWS* 36, or send $1 for our "Home Schooling Resource List."

Connecticut: Laura Pritchard of the *Connecticut Homeschoolers Association* writes, "Our new commissioner of education, Dr. Trozzi, recently was on a TV discussion outlining the direction of education. He supports an entrance age of 4 years, longer school year, and all-day kindergartens, among other points . . . . Perhaps these new proposals will scare people into action . . . ." Laura also says the group has organized a "Lending Library" and a "Skills Pool."

Hawaii: Dr. Raymond Moore (Hewitt Research Foundation, PO Box 9, Washougal WA 98671) wrote us, "A major victory in Hawaii. Ensign Mark Snively was turned down by Supt. of Education Donnis Thompson. Then he gave her our Columbia U. *Record* monograph. She reversed and approved his home school . . . ."

Indiana: From Sharon Griffith, 306 S Rangeline Rd, Anderson IN 46012: "The group in Madison-Delaware County is growing and doing very well. The mailing list is close to 100 . . . . We have twice-monthly field trips which the children really enjoy. One activity I am really pleased with is our monthly visit to a local nursing home. Four families take the children for a home school 'show-and-tell' time and some singing. The children are proving to be very sociable and communicate across generations. . . ."

And Darlene Sartore (see IN Directory) says, "We will begin hosting a monthly support meeting for home educators on the first Saturday of each month starting Feb. 4, 1984. Write or call for directions (812-779-3616). We are midway between Evansville and Vincennes in southern Indiana. . . ."

Kansas: Bonnie Sawyer is helping to put on an all-day seminar with Dr. Ray Moore on April 9. For info, call 913-686-2310 or write her at 19985 Renner Rd, Spring Hill KS 66083.

New York: In the last two weeks, reporters from three major media in New York City have called us about doing stories on homeschooling. We have never had many NYC families in our Directory, and some who are there have unlisted phone numbers. If you are presently homeschooling in New York City and would not mind being interviewed, it would be most helpful if you would drop me a note with your phone number so I could pass it on to reporters.

Homeschooling parent Richard Fahey of the *Homesteading School* (Oxford NY 13816) is offering a "Home Education Workshop" June 17–20. Send him 2 stamps for more info.—DR

Phone Instead Of Address

[DR:] Some time back, we suggested that readers who would like to make contact with other homeschoolers but who did not want to write letters, list their telephone number in the Directory instead of a mailing address. About this, one reader writes, "I chose to list my phone number because I find it far easier to cope with the children and talk than to write, but if people fear being deluged with calls, they needn't worry—I've only gotten 10 or so in more than a year. Most have been from families just moving to the area who want to connect fast and I really enjoy helping them.... The rest have been desirous of interviews with homeschoolers and I've found the phone a comfortably distant way to deal with them, whether I've chosen to say yes or no."

A Grown Unschooler

From Roberta Archer in El Paso:

I just discovered *Teach Your Own*, much to my delight. My parents were both missionaries in Mexico, Cuba, and the Dominican Republic. I spent many of these years without "schooling" as such. Part of that time we had the Calvert course, but again I was allowed to teach myself and to go at my own pace. Other times were spent in the jungles of Mexico with my father, doing everything from teaching children my age Bible stories and English, to riding horseback (the villagers would come to the all-day church service and I would have my pick of the horses tethered there meanwhile).

Back home in Mexico City, I had my own small "restaurant business" in a corner of our large yard. I would make tortillas from the "masa" and turn them into all kinds of Mexican "antojitos" (appetizers) and sell them to the Bible school students that Mother and Dad were teaching, during their morning and afternoon breaks. I remember that each morning I would invest the same amount and that I always doubled my money. I would put the 100% profit away and then go back to the corner store and the "tortilleria" and buy ingredients for the next morning with the original investment amount. On Saturdays I would go with our housekeeper to the big market and buy little baby chicks, raise them, sell the eggs to the "student kitchen," and again I had more profit.

These are just a few of the (what I consider) rich experiences I had. I would not exchange any of them for a "normal school life"!

I returned with my brother to the USA when I was about 15. My former experiences helped me to cope with a country, experiences, and people that I was no longer familiar with. Also to be able to know what to do when I found myself stranded in a small town in Pennsylvania with the date fast approaching when I had to be in Knoxville, Tenn. I coped, didn't panic, and made it there in time to start high school, a regimented, religious boarding school on the demerit system. However, I don't have negative memories concerning this, and finished all high school courses in 1½ years and two summers. I found I was ahead of others in my classes and had far more experience in many areas than they.

I finished college and am now working as a Federally Certified Court interpreter. I also had no difficulties with this (other than seeing firsthand how we treat other human beings).

Kids In The Workplace

From Margaret Sadoway (MA):

Our 4-year-old son Solon has been in and out of our small natural foods store ever since we bought it when he was 11 months old. At first we had fond (naive) images of him spending most of his time there, quietly playing with his toys. Ha! At 12 months he dumped a bucket of whole corn into one of black-eyed peas; at 13 months he regularly chose to practice crawling through broken glass and garbage in the parking lot; at 14 months he delighted and exasperated parents and customers alike by frequently insisting on running the $150 juicer unassisted; at 15 months he was enrolled in a nursery school two days a week while we thought things over.

We were strongly committed to the idea of having him at the store for several reasons. First, we feel strongly (like John, I think) that a very alienating factor in children's lives today is their nearly total exclusion from all adult work. Next, we really couldn't afford much childcare and if one of us could have Solon at the store, then the other could have a few hours a week for drawing and writing, activities we were not willing to mix with a toddler. Finally, we had become interested in home learning long before Solon was born and knew the store was a treasure trove of educational possibilities.

It has been, too. By 2½, Solon had learned to use a knife to open cartons and to price the contents (and everything else in sight) by himself. At 2¾ he startled us by what he'd put together about other commercial supply lines: spotting a tank truck on the road ahead of us, he said, "Dat oil truck's going to gas place (station), fill it all up so cars can come and get more gas." At 3 he started approaching customers with his own nutritional advice ("You know, you have to brush your teeth after all that honey"). By 3½ he'd learned to read price tags from left to right, punch in the corresponding number on our fancy cash register, hit a department key, then sub-total and total. Just when I was sure he was learning to tell coins apart, he lost all interest in the cash register for several months. When he just as suddenly returned to it, he'd somehow learned to differentiate the six departments on his own and knew all the coins, so began making change when told "Give her two quarters, a nickel, three pennies and a five-dollar bill."

Customers fainted, of course, and I hear some readers groaning that this is yet another "super-kid" story.... Maybe they will feel better if I add that at 4½ Solon refuses even to try to dress himself, is in nighttime diapers, has not quite given up the nursing relationship, is in awe of 4-year-olds who can spend a night away from their mothers, and certainly doesn't play the violin. Could there be a connection, in his case? Has lack of pressure about weaning, dressing, and sleeping freed his energies for other learning? No child can "progress" on all fronts simultaneously.

We encourage other children to use the cash register, with interesting results. 4-year-olds are likely to bang away with little respect for the machine, to Solon's amazement. It seems that children who are allowed to touch nearly everything from an early age rarely damage them or even misuse them. 6-year-olds can work it alone within ten minutes while 12-year-olds sometimes take a little longer. One 7-year-old liked running it so much that she checked customers out alone for several hours in a row. We bit our tongues (a little proud of ourselves!) and intervened only when we noticed what Solon calls "hurry customers." In between sales, she repeatedly counted *all* the cash in the drawer, $200–400, and added it up on the calculator, even though she knew one key on the register would give her the answer directly. At the end of the day, the money came out right! But the next day a sad thing happened. Her father came to visit, watched her nervously, then began a steady patter, all in a kind voice, "Are you sure that's right? How much change should you give? I'll show you a faster way. "Within a few minutes she made more mistakes than all the previous day and let us take over until her father left.

Don't let me give the impression that having children at the store is ideal or even easy. Most worthwhile things in life call for a struggle. For two years, until he was about 3½, we rarely had Solon at the store for more than half an hour at a time and then only when two adults were present. Usually, we each spent half the day with Solon and half at the store, a nearly ideal situation for all three of us except that our only free time was those few hours a week that Solon was at nursery school. Suddenly even that ended, as he announced that "Every time I start a puzzle, they tell me it's time for lunch," and that he was never going back. Once we made sure he was serious, we were actually glad to be forced into the no-school situation that we'd really intended all along.

So we reshuffled our schedules, realizing Solon was ready to spend much larger chunks of time at the store, 3, 5, even 10 hours. We made room for his record player, fleet of vehicles, and other necessities, and all began learning. He's learned that helping customers comes before stories, that flinging shopping baskets at innocent people who took one without realizing they are his race cars is not what we consider good communication, and that swearing vigorously at customers gets a different reaction from Mom than trying out profanity at home.

I've learned that seemingly urgent work can be postponed or finished more quickly, that letting him add up long columns of figures on our calculator is actually faster and more fun than trying to dissuade him, and how to deal with the few customers who are actually rude or indifferent to Solon (how dare they!).

I think that waiting until our late thirties to have a child gave us an insight that much younger parents might not have. On days when I can't get anything done due to Solon's interruptions, I force myself to remember all those books I never wrote, all those projects I never finished in the 15 long years *before* he was born.

And from Kathy Epling (CA):

Since I work with my child at the local bookstore we are very public. It is interesting that most (though not all) people respond with interest and positive energy when Garth (6) informs them he's homeschooled. It's usually in the context of his ringing up their sale at the cash register—they comment, "Gee, you'll do real well at math in school," and he says, "Well, I'm homeschooled," whereupon they turn to me in disbelief (so few people listen to children or take them seriously) and I confirm it. Then *usually* a good discussion results.

Working In A Pet Shop

From Scott Maher (MA), age 13:

In September I went down to the Wakefield Pet shop and asked the owner Steve, whom I already had known, if there would be any way I could come down and help. I told him how I was a homeschooler and that I could come down in the mornings. Steve said we could try it out for a while and see what we think.

I went down on a Monday at 10:30 and first he showed me around and showed me how things are done.... I started off feeding the birds and cleaning their cages. Next I swept the floor and fed the fish. Then I fed and watered the small animals, lizards, rabbits, guinea pigs, and cats. Some days I clean filters in the fish tanks and test the pH of the water; other days I clean the cages and clean the glass. I have helped unload shipments and put stock away.

I have been working there almost four months now. I have waited on customers, given them advice, taken inventory, and I even take care of the shop if Steve has to leave. Soon I will be learning how to use the cash register.

There are two other boys my age who come down and help after school is out. The way we get paid is: $2 in trade for every hour we work, or $1 in money.

I think the best part of it is learning about all of the different animals, fish and birds and learning how to take care of them. I have been put in charge of lizards and small animals. It is a lot of fun to help our customers.

And In An Orchard

In GWS *22, we asked readers to tell us about the relationship between their children and their work. Lucy Lilly (AZ) wrote:*

In the very rural area in which we live, there are not many employment opportunities, especially if one wants to spend any time with family. So instead of having only one income source, we've had to develop many part-time jobs. One of our favorites is seasonal orchard work. We've just finished apple harvest and are looking forward to pruning. Chuck and I and our children (7, 5, and 3) as well as another couple who are teaching us the work and their son, make up a crew of workers. The children enjoy getting together each day in the orchard to play, as none of them have neighbors to play with at home.

We work with virtually no interruptions from the children in contrast to when I'm working at home with their father away at a job and the children are constantly under my feet. When both parents are working at home they play pretty well independently but it seems that when there is a crew of people busy around them, then they stay busy, too.... Of course, we interact more closely with them during breaks in the work.

One day a week I volunteer my time to the local library as the story-time reader.... Daniel (7) attends and is my helper. As we are fairly new to the area, this work has given me the opportunity to meet many children and their parents. I've even met one woman who has become interested in homeschooling.

On Her Own At 10

From Arkansas:

July 4: My daughter (10) has been unschooling since April, but we've done nothing in the way of academics. (This is fine with me, so far.) My concerns are her sometimes boredom and "the authorities" finding out when the school year starts.

She has been staying home with my 2-year-old (and sometimes, her stepfather) while I go to carpentry school. While at home, she reads lots of library books. Her choices are novels only—lots of mysteries, girls growing up, etc. She also bakes and cooks and goes for walks.

Now during the summer, she is doing well while I am gone as she has playmates besides her 2-year-old sister. But come late August I am at a loss as to what is best for her.

My current husband and I are no longer together. So it looks like I will be gone on a full-time job most of the time. I know I can't keep Angela on as a permanent babysitter—she gets burned out. There's too much constant responsibility, and the 2-year-old treats her like she's the mom.

Nov. 23: I'm managing to work only part-time, but even so, Angela is basically on her own most of the time.

She reads, reads, and reads. Mostly library books, mostly fiction. (We don't have a TV.) She found a small fractions workbook and multiplication workbook at a bookstore. We do them gradually and sometimes not at all. Now she says she'd like to do weekly spelling words. OK.

As far as the school officials (my biggest concern), so far I just haven't let them know of her existence and hope to keep it that way. All records she had of schooling were in a different state.

GWS 35 had some very encouraging letters for me, especially from Sue in Seattle. It made me think of my own situation.

At Home In Israel

Haim Chertok wrote in the Jerusalem Post Magazine, *5/7/82:*

> "You can't do it! Maybe it's okay in America, but here you can't do it!"

This we heard, not from one Israeli friend but from virtually everyone we consulted.... Ignoring this prudential din, my wife and I and our 12-year-old son Ted decided two years ago to withdraw Ted from the 7th grade class of his Dimona junior high school (religious) in order to take charge of his education ourselves.

Ted's dropping out was more practical than ideological, a decision fuelled as much by despair as by hope. Fortunately, the incredulity of most Israelis was overmatched by the supportive and growing American and British community in Yeroham where we have lived for nearly five years now. Without their active help, we could never have succeeded.

We would not have embarked on this path had we not concluded that keeping Ted within the Israeli school system was positively harmful. He was learning not to value but to waste his time, to equate the numbers on his tests and report card with getting an education. In the absence of any serious hopes of amelioration, and chary about sending our 12-year-old to board at some school or yeshiva 40 or 100 km away, we felt we had no real alternative.

How did we proceed? We saw home learning as an opportunity for Ted to learn *how* to learn, to learn to take responsibility for his own education. At the start of each week, he would schedule his hours of classes, study, and outside activities. He was responsible to himself to fulfill the schedule which he (with our assistance at the start) created. And one of his first and most important learning projects was to keep a daily journal (in English). This became not only an instrument of self-reflection but a self-check on his studies and a means to use and polish his English, which we all felt was important for him. (Now Ted is back in school but he still maintains his journal.)

Then I surveyed our friends and acquaintances to see which of them had the time and inclination to teach with regularity something he/she was enthusiastic about. The result was, I think, a curriculum which would be the envy of most school kids his age. Twice a week, Ted studied Gemara with our neighbor Moshe. Both were cheered by the arrangement, and Ted now gets top grades in his religious subjects. With another neighbor, Leah, Ted (for a semester) reviewed Hebrew grammar, read some stories, and wrote short essays in Hebrew. And for the entire year and a half Ted studied mathematics once a week with Dina, a high school math teacher. In return, I (and later Ted himself) tutored their younger son in English.

Ted developed a friendship also with an American student, an environmental major.... Many mornings they'd be off at 4 a.m. to the Yeroham Lake for a morning's bird watching, and for a hike to watch the sunrise (and for a geology lesson) at the Yeroham crater. Ted became proficient at recognizing and collecting desert plants, which later he and John studied under a microscope. Ted and I worked together on literature, my field. After some thought, we decided to focus on Greek literature because it seemed sufficiently self-contained to be cohesive, is important, and fun, and usually neglected in Israeli schools. Over the next 18 months, Ted and I read through background words like Edith Hamilton's *The Greek Way* and *Mythology*, Kitto's *The Greeks*, and Finley's *The World Of Odysseus*. His "texts" were the *Iliad* and the *Odyssey*, the plays of Sophocles and Aristophanes (he didn't like Aeschylus), and the Platonic dialogues. After completing a work, Ted wrote a paper (in English), often comparing some aspect of it to a Biblical theme or character. The result is that Ted now has a fine background in Greek thought and literature, enjoys reading, and is able to write an acceptable essay in English.

Interspersed among the Greeks we read other works like *Catcher In The Rye*, *A Separate Peace*, some of the Bagrut stories, and novels by Mark Twain, Golding, and Saroyan. All in all, I'm satisfied that Ted absorbed a love of books and learning.

Was Ted cut off from his friends? Hardly! A member of Bnei Akiva, he took part in all their activities.

I suspect that the school authorities were aware of our "dereliction." They did not interfere.

It would be misleading to suggest that everything went smoothly, that Ted never felt isolated, never wasted an hour, and that there was no clash between the parental and teacher roles. But from very early on it was clear that we were embarked on an exciting experiment for us all.... Now that he is 14 and lives away from home, we both miss our learning sessions immensely.

[Haim wrote an update in 1983:]

Ted re-entered the school system in the ninth grade.... Both he and I were convinced that our experiment was a success, but there were several reasons for re-entry, not the least of which was the need to prepare for the battery of Bagrut (matriculation) exams which all Israeli high school students must pass in order to proceed (after the army) to university.... It also seemed reasonable for an older Ted to test himself and what he'd learned within a traditional school environment. What we both knew, however, was that if he found learning with classmates at yeshiva genuinely distasteful or seriously counter-productive, that we would contrive means to continue outside of the system in spite of the rigidity of Bagrut requirements.

With the beginning of tenth grade, the yeshiva began to respond positively to the situation. . . . In December, Ted announced that he was offered the option to skip the rest of the 10th grade and to jump (after Hanukah vacation) into 11th grade.

It certainly wasn't easy this last spring. Suddenly, Ted was in eleventh grade facing four Bagrut exams that very June with a new class to integrate into. . . . Ted's grades on his report card for the second trimester went down, and there were times during the spring when it was plain that he wondered whether he had chosen the right course. But by the end of June, Ted had been accepted by his classmates, done nicely in all his courses, and passed all his Bagrut exams.

It's plain to me that hours of our learning together two to three years ago have borne fruit. He takes pleasure in learning and in creating. That he now pursues his learning within a traditional system is not, I feel, a sign of regress, for he has learned how to make that environment adapt to meet *his* needs for growth and learning.

Down's Syndrome Unschooler

Janet Bennett (NJ), who wrote at length in GWS 11 *about the homeschooling of her daughter who has Down's syndrome, wrote the following article for the* New York Times *which was published 12/11/83:*

> She does forward rolls and one-handed cartwheels, and she spins on the uneven parallel bars. She does leg presses, bench presses and curls on the universal machine.
>
> She does a jazz dance routine that threatens to get the place raided, and she swims, bicycles, and goes ice-skating.
>
> She types and does needlepoint; she volunteers in the local hospital's Gift Shop, waiting on customers, and she has an acting and singing class every Friday.
>
> In her spare time, she has Down's syndrome.
>
> She is my 21-year-old daughter, Kathryn. She has never been in special-education classes; in fact, for the last five years, she has not gone to school at all.
>
> Oh, she has had schooling, all right, but not the usual kind. She went to private nursery school and kindergarten with children who were not handicapped. Then we found a public-school system that was running an open-school experiment, and Kathryn went there for four years in a class of 90 children. Finally, for two years she was in a class of eight girls in a private Catholic school.
>
> Kathryn did well in those places. She learned to read—and well—but she learned more than academic things; she learned how to be a child and not how to be a Down's syndrome person.
>
> Her models were not perfect, and they were all different, but she didn't have a collection of handicapped behavior and speech to copy. Neither did she learn to mirror the self-reinforcing patterns of other children with Down's syndrome.
>
> No, Kathryn did not "keep up" with the classes she was in. The emphasis on individualizing in these schools meant that each child was offered what seemed to be appropriate at the time.
>
> Those early years were certainly better than I had ever imagined they would be when I was told in 1962 to institutionalize Kathryn, not to tell our other children where she was or to ever visit her and that she would probably lie on a pillow all her life.

But better years were to come.

In 1977, when Kathryn was 15, I took her out of school. I had a feeling that there was a better way than school.

After having three older children make their way valiantly through the conventional system, I was sick of the whole school business anyway—the schedules that ran our lives, the permission slips and book covers, the conferences and the milk money.

And I was nagged by a sense that even an individualized approach, if done in the context of a school and its structures, just could not be individualized enough.

For the last five years, Kathryn and I have been free. We sleep late in the morning, go for walks at midday, schedule doctor appointments and go grocery shopping when no one else is around. And Kathryn has learned all the things I have mentioned—and more.

I teach her some things. Right now, we are learning geography, especially about China, where her older sister, a journalist, is spending a couple of years. And we have spent a lot of time taking pictures—of seasons, of weather and of our town and neighborhood—as jumping-off points for exercises in writing stories.

A good friend gives classes in cooking and mathematics (paying restaurant bills, how to tip, and balancing Kathryn's checkbook). They also practice relaying telephone messages, making collect calls and learning the etiquette of answering machines.

We go to the shore in May and November as freely as in August. We go out to lunch most Mondays, and go to conventions with my husband with nary a permission slip.

How we have done this and what we do day by day is not really the point, though. What is really important is what I have found out about what Kathryn is capable of—how much she knows, how her mind works, how she learns—things I could not have known as well if she had stayed in school. I would certainly never have known them if she had been in special education from the beginning.

I talk with her and watch her as I did when she was in school, as I did with the other children. But in those days, the school ultimately called all the shots and defined the context and the plan.

The work and planning I do with Kathryn now do not take all that much time, sometimes only 15 minutes a day. But now I can see the whole thing: the beginning, middle and end of the process of learning.

I see Kathryn as herself, not as one point along a scale of other points.

At home, I watched as Kathryn learned the keyboard of our electric typewriter in one week. I watched as she made a rank order out of a long list of possible courses, not once blinking an eye as I explained what a rank order was. I watched as she—all 4 feet 10 inches of her—maneuvered our Plymouth Valiant through a course laid out with rocks in a parking lot.

The whole thing has been the best of all possible worlds for Kathryn and me.

I always knew that Kathryn had great potential, that she could shoot for the moon. But she surprised even me by what she has accomplished, by what she is really like, now that I see her without the filter of a school system.

[Janet added in a note to us:] For parents of Down's syndrome kids, there's a good newsletter, mainly medical information but very clearly written ... $5 year from 10404 Leslie Ct, Silver Springs MD 20902 address it to *Down's Syndrome*.

The Making Of A Homeschooler

From a Texas parent:

I sent my oldest child to public school. I had taught her how to read and recognize her colors, how to tie her shoes, the alphabet, and how to write her name. She was spot-reading words in various books. After her first week in school, she came home with work-papers on colors. I noticed she had missed some. When I asked her about it, she just shrugged her shoulders and hung her head. As time went on, she regressed. I knew, and she knew, that she could do the work, but she evidently was too bored.

In the first grade, they told me she was failing reading. I asked for the book she was reading from so I could tutor her. She read fine for me. I asked her about it, and she told me the teacher tried to hurry her and told her she couldn't read. . . . A couple of days later I noticed Rebecca's attitude changing about herself. It's pretty sick to see a 7-year-old child sit and cry and tell me how stupid she is because she can't read the way the teacher expects her to.

My second child was belittled by the other children because she couldn't write a letter of the alphabet correctly. I took her out of school, after I found out the teacher yelled at her to do her work instead of explaining it to her. I got away with it by telling them I'd start her again next year. I heard a teacher tell her students that she didn't care if they didn't learn anything, that she'd get paid whether they learned or not!

It is my belief that when talking to or teaching a child, that when you see they don't understand, that you would (without even thinking about it) try it from a different angle. Doing this is what I term common sense. Seeing teachers not backing up to hit the subject from a different angle so all students can understand, and instead leaving them behind to wander for the rest of the school year, is absurd.

We called Austin to see if homeschooling was legal in Texas. They told us no. [DR: However, many Texas readers have told us they have called their home a private school with little trouble.] We were also told by the gentleman we were talking to, he didn't blame us for not wanting to send our kids to public school. He said, "I don't even send my own kids to public school." To me that's pretty poor when the State Board of Education doesn't even stand behind public schools!

I took the children out of school the last two months of the school year. We moved to a small town and I didn't enroll them. I taught them until 3:30 or 4 p.m. so the neighbors wouldn't be suspicious. My husband marveled at how much they had learned in two months. I thought I wasn't doing so well, until he told me that I had taught them in two months what they should learn in a year of schooling.

My kindergartner is reading a certain book I have, also my 4-year-old is reading. They are doing addition and subtraction and writing sentences. My 7-year-old who was told she could not read is reading from a 3rd grade reader. She writes stories, counts to 800 and could go to 1000 but gets bored. They all love books and cry to go to the library. My 1½-year-old colors and counts to 3 and loves books. She thinks she can do whatever her sisters do! Right now they are learning to swim.

In the short time I have taught them I have felt their closeness to me. They no longer say, "I'm stupid, I can't do it." They decide what they will learn for the day. They know they have to read and write and do math. They pick out things like learning about planets, the moon, stars, animals, flowers. They enjoy themselves.

I hope I haven't bored you with this letter. But I just had to tell you these things. Maybe they will help others see the light.

On Learning Disabilities

[JH:] A friend of mine, a Professor of Education at whose university I spoke not long ago, sent on to me a letter that one of his students had written him about my talk. In my reply to him I said in part:

The trouble with the phrase "learning disability" is that it does not make clear whether it refers to *an observed phenomenon*, say, the fact that Billy has trouble reading words or writes them backwards, or *an inferred cause of that phenomenon*, say, that Billy does this because of something in the physical structure of his brain. In other words, it does not make the basic distinction which we know in medicine as the difference between symptoms—what the doctor can see, feel, etc.—and diagnosis what the doctor thinks is the cause of the symptoms. This distinction is so crucial that I don't see how we can talk usefully about the learning problems of children unless we make it.

My experience both as a teacher and a learner, and since at age 60 I have just begun to play the violin I am encountering many learning difficulties, is that stress, anxiety, fear of failure or disapproval, are enormously productive of these difficulties, so much so that I would say that something like 90% of the art of teaching lies in being able first to recognize stress in learners and then in being able to reduce it.

Stress Affects IQ Test

From Learning, *9/83:*

> Recent findings about stress and IQ scores should cause educators and psychologists to pause the next time they're tempted to base their decisions about a kid's future on the results of the Wechsler Intelligence Scale for Children.
>
> Bernard Brown and Lilian Rosenbaum, researchers from Georgetown University, found that when children they studied were under emotional or physical stress, they scored an average of 13 percentage points lower than youngsters who were functioning virtually worry-free.
>
> The researchers found that as the number of stress factors with which a child must deal increased, IQ scores decreased. Stress appeared to worsen a child's verbal ability and his proficiency in distinguishing shapes, causing 12 percent declines in scores on vocabulary and visual discrimination subtests.
>
> Even more dramatic was the finding that when children under high stress are held back a grade *or placed in a special education-class,* their IQ scores declined 15.5 percent, suggesting that these common school procedures are not having the intended positive effect on kids.

Single copies of "Stress Effects on I.Q." by Bernard Brown and Lilian Rosenbaum are available free from the Georgetown Family Center, Georgetown U. Medical Center, 4380 MacArthur Blvd NW, Washington DC 20007.

[JH:] Some brief observations about this article.

1) It supports my claim that what schools call "learning disabilities" may in most cases simply be reactions to stress.

2) Parents can quote this study to show that if their children are learning in the more relaxed and comfortable environment of the home, they will be likely to learn more than if they were at school.

3) Parents who are required by state law or their own agreement with the local schools to submit their children to periodic achievement tests can cite this study to show that if their children are tested in the unfamiliar and therefore more stressful environment of the school, their test scores are likely to be substantially lowered, and therefore, that these tests may well be invalid unless given a home.

4) Since, in the name of "raising standards," "ending social promotion," etc., the schools are about to start making large numbers of children repeat grades unless they have achieved certain levels, we can expect that even more schoolchildren will have severe learning problems.

"Test" For Emotional Maturity

[DR:] People have asked us, "If a homeschooled child returns to public school and has no correspondence school records, how does the school decide what grade he/she belongs in?" As far as we know, children are placed with their age group, and the most that can happen is that the schools will test the child to determine if s/he belongs in the higher or lower of the two possible grades. One parent has written us about a sad

experience concerning this:

We have recently moved here to Illinois from Missouri. . . . In Mo., like so many of the people that I knew, we didn't keep records. . . . We did not have the funds for correspondence schools for four kids.

Why did I allow my children to go back to public school after having them at home for three years? . . . They were hoping that the public schools would be better here in Illinois.

My older son was scheduled for testing that, I was told at the time, was to see if he was qualified to handle tenth grade curriculum . . . The testing went without notification. I had indeed given consent, but with the stipulation I would be aware of the date as I wanted to be there. I was notified afterwards, and only then when I was asked if I could come to the school for a hearing on the results.

The testing turned out to be for emotional capabilities. . . . Here we are talking about a sixteen-year-old boy/young man who is very well-liked, who my neighbors consider to be the most trustworthy kid they have ever met. . . . I have had neighbors tell me in my front yard it was so nice to have a kid in the neighborhood that used manners. He has people requesting his services for babysitting. He uses power tools to make beautiful toys for these kids. But the school has deemed him immature.

My son was tested on his family relationship and relationship toward his peers. . . . One question was how he felt about his family and he answered he loved his family and enjoyed being with us a great deal. Another question was on music—he liked some rock and roll, but also liked symphony because it relaxed him. . . . The last question really angered him. If a friend was being jumped by 4 or 5 guys would he help or get help. He answered he'd help his friend, because he may not be close enough to find help. These were judged immature.

So he was put into the 9th grade. I have some of his work books from Scott-Foresman Grade 10—he did beautiful work—but this was not acceptable.

He is going to quit now. . . . I have also been given the go-ahead to take my older daughter out. . . . My two younger ones won't go back next year either. . . . The school counselors and the school have accepted my choice of a private home school (Clonlara School in Ann Arbor, Michigan).

From Home To School—And Back

From Bonnie Miesel (MI):

May 30: My oldest daughter is turning 8—the age we promised to give her "the choice." She's decided to try a formal classroom for a semester. Her reasons are to meet more friends and to see what school is like. I've begun interviewing principals in the area, asking questions which bring out their philosophy of education. What I am looking for is one who sees living as learning or at least believes learning is possible outside the classroom.

In evaluating our homeschooling with Jennifer up to this point, I find it to have been successful. We really do not spend much time daily on workbooks and yet she is near the end of third grade math, music, far ahead in reading, etc. She has several areas of interest in people: for Multiple Sclerosis she has read over 100 books to raise money; she reads books on blindness (Helen Keller, Louis Braille) and knows the sign language alphabet for the deaf; she enjoys visiting older people and making "cheer-up" cards for them.

A friend of mine who taught herself to play the recorder in college and played in classical groups has been teaching Jennifer and me to play. We've come to the point where we are picking up other songbooks and familiar songs to play for fun. Duets really sound nice (their beauty is our reward for practicing). In the process Jennifer has learned notes, timing, etc.

Her "Physical Education" class is an acrobatics class at a dance school. Afternoons she plays baseball (kids range from 4 to 12) and shoots basketball, etc. Roller-skating, bowling, and swimming are also favorites.

I guess what I consider "success" is her interest in people and her well-rounded activities. She is becoming capable and dependable in doing household jobs too: baking, washing, cleaning her room, etc. When we went to the Michigan State Conference of Home Educators, she asked to stay in the lobby with some other girls during the long afternoon session. I hesitated, saying, "But you don't know them." She came right back with, "Mom, I know how to make friends with them." And she did.

Our four-year-old is learning almost solo. She loves dot-to-dot so her counting is perfect up to 40. She's always discovering exciting things like, "Mommy! Five take away three makes two!" She draws quite realistically. She also spends hours and hours playing house with our two-year-old. Baking is one of her favorite experiments—using recipes "from my head." Usually they are edible.

We still have problems at times with cooperation and getting along [*GWS* 26]. I'm going to watch and see if this problem becomes better or worse when the oldest is gone from 8 a.m. to 3 p.m..

Dec. 11: To fill you in on our 8-year-old trying a public classroom beginning in September.... Academically, her spelling was poor because I had not insisted on her memorizing lists of words but had expected that her extensive reading and her letter writing would eventually build up her spelling vocabulary. Her first two tests were disasters until she got the hang of memorizing. Now she gets every word right.

On math she's OK, but spends so much time doing the same things over and over. The teacher noted that she asks for a lot of personal help when they begin anything new (probably because she's used to it). She hates science and social studies because mostly she spends lots of time copying sentences from the text. But overall she has her work done on time (no nagging from me) and is unhappy if her grades are not A or B.

I should have explained that she is one year ahead of her age group. She was tested by the school psychologist for placement. Consequently many of the school staff are very positive and enthusiastic about what homeschooling did for her. They asked many questions about our methods, and suggested I write a little book on Jennifer's homeschooling to be "published" in the school. (I am planning to do just that. However, I'm finding it impossible to lift a "typical" day or week from our journal. There's too much variety....)

If this sounds like a successful adjustment-to-school story, it is *not*. Most morning there's a stomach-ache—I can't remember those complaints before.... She was crying in her pillow one night about being "no good in music and hating it anyway." The teacher had moved her off the bells when she had missed the rhythm.... I reminded her that music is more than bells, that she had already been playing recorder for a year at home, etc.

She's also finding that in a group of 25 kids she does *not* find 25 new friends (contrary to the comments often made about having so many more friends when you go to school). In homeschool, *most of the kids she knew and had contact with were friends*. Now out of 25 in school, she finds one or two, and sometimes those change from one week to another.

So at the end of the first semester she is wanting to come back home. At the same time, the 9-year-old daughter of a single mother will begin homeschooling with us. Her mother approached the school saying she wants to try a full-time tutoring environment for her daughter who increasingly neglects her schoolwork although she has always tested very high. We are all excited about the ideas we want to work on, projects, reading, field trips, etc.

Our five-year-old tells people she is going to *real school* at home and Jennifer is going to *pretend school*. People try to tell her she has it turned around but she sticks to her labels. We had been talking about how we do real things in home school and that in public school they pretend they are doing things but they are only reading about them or acting like they are buying things using play money, etc.

On Teacher Quality

Mario Pagnoni (MA) wrote:

A study published by the Educational Testing

Service in 1951 rated students' scores on draft deferment exams. Of the 97,800 college freshmen tested, those who scored highest were students of engineering, with 68% passing; then came the physical sciences, 64%; biological sciences, 59%; social sciences, 57%; the humanities 52%; general arts, 48%; business, 42%; agriculture, 37%; and then, at the very bottom, education with only 27% passing.

In a Pennsylvania study the median IQ score for 26,000 randomly selected high school seniors was higher than the median for college Education students. The high schoolers did better than the university students *in the very subjects the education majors were preparing to teach.* (*What's Happened To Teacher?* by Myron Brenton, 1970.) [See "What's Wrong with Teachers?" *GWS* 32.]

Teacher Effectiveness

At a weekend conference of the Nevada Association of School Boards last November, while waiting for my own turn to address the meeting, I heard a most interesting talk by a man who in his home state of Missouri is apparently one of the leading advocates of and experts on merit pay for teachers. He is Dr. Charles McKenna, Superintendent of Schools, Ladue Board of Education, 9703 Conway Rd., St. Louis MO 63124. At one point in his talk he said that schools have traditionally given extra pay to teachers on the basis of (1) professional training (2) experience in teaching.

He then astonished the meeting, or at least me, by saying that all the research done on teacher effectiveness (which he did not define) showed *that it had no connection whatever with either training or experience.* I was not surprised to learn that this was so, since years ago I had learned this through my own experience. But I was surprised to hear a professional educator say it, and to hear that it was backed up by respectable research. By the way, Dr. McKenna did not say what, if anything, teacher effectiveness *was* connected to, and since no one there asked, I did not think it was my place to. Since then I have written him to ask what more he could tell me about this research, or how I might learn more about it. So far I have not had a reply; if and when I do, I will let readers know. But even the little information given here might be useful for homeschoolers to quote to educators, legislators, judges, media people, or skeptical friends and neighbors, who claim that paid teachers can teach children better than parents because they have more training and experience.

Perhaps some of the "Professors and Allies" on our list might be able to tell us more about this research on teacher effectiveness, or might be willing to write to Dr. McKenna to see what he can tell them. Anything you know or can find out on this matter, we would be very glad to hear about.— JH

The Schools' Failures

From an editorial in US News and World Report, *2/24/83:*

> As many as 26 million Americans are "functionally illiterate," and 46 million more operate "at a marginal level or below."
>
> Chairman Paul Simon listened as Education Secretary Terrel Bell gave that information to the House Subcommittee on Postsecondary Education. At about the same time, a hearing sponsored jointly with the House Subcommittee on Elementary, Secondary, and Vocational Education, under Carl Perkins, elicited the following from the National Science Foundation:
>
> In 1981, nationwide, half the teachers newly employed for high school science and mathematics *were not certified to teach those subjects.*

[JH:] An article entitled "See Dick and Jane Learn to Love Reading" in the same issue said in part:

> Surveys indicate that more children are choosing not to read, viewing it as a meaningless exercise no longer needed in an electronic world.

Reading tests given throughout the 1970s by the National Assessment of Educational Progress found that fewer than 30% of 17-year-olds tested could analyze a text in order to support a theme or conclusion. The study also found that the further children progressed in school, the less they liked reading. While 80% of 9-year-olds reported enjoying reading very much, only 50% of 13-year-olds rated their reading enjoyment that high.

Since the mid-70s, *several schools* have adopted a program known as "Sustained silent reading." Under that system, each student and employee, from the principal to the janitor, is expected to drop whatever he or she is doing and read for *about 15 minutes.*

[JH:] We will keep our eyes open here for articles like these in newspapers and magazines, and we'll be grateful if our readers will pass along to us any such stories they find. Some of these we will print in *GWS*, so that readers in all parts of the country may pass the information on to their state legislators, above all to those who seem to feel that only in schools can children learn anything.

As in talking to the courts about the shortcomings and failures of schools (such as "Graduates Lack Skills," *GWS* 31), we must be careful how we use this information. We must make clear to legislators that we are not asking them either to condemn or change the schools. Trying to make schools better by passing various kinds of laws "mandating" that they become better not only doesn't make them better but usually makes them worse, since the effect of such laws is always and necessarily to *reduce* the independence, authority, and freedom of teachers. These are the *only* things that can or will make schools better, and the lack of them will continue to keep or drive the most able, creative, and responsible teachers out of the schools. All we are asking the legislatures to say, perhaps in some version of the proposed legislation printed in *GWS* 30, is that that minority of the public who are deeply dissatisfied with the schools' philosophy, methods, and performance, and which believes that it can provide a substantially better education for its own children, should have the right to do so.

Teacher Examinations

The Washington Post *of 1/8/84 published an article by Alison Muscatine, "If I Can Pass It, This Test Is A Joke," about the National Teacher's Exam. It said, in part:*

> I have never taken an education course in my life . . . but recently I joined 70,000 aspiring teachers and took the National Teachers' Exam.
>
> The NTE, developed by the Educational Testing Service in Princeton, has been used since 1950. It is the teaching profession's only standardized measure of a prospective teacher's academic achievement and "professional knowledge"—the educational jargon for teaching techniques and philosophy.
>
> I went into the NTE with no advance preparation and was more than a little nervous about my "test-taking abilities," not to mention my moronic knowledge of elementary math.
>
> Only a few questions required some factual knowledge. . . . I found the math section surprisingly easy. And except for failing to identify some types of rock formations or geographic characteristics of Africa, I also survived the science part.
>
> After a lunch break we returned for the test on "professional knowledge." . . . This came down to a series of questions about how to treat Johnny's parents when they complain that he has too much homework. With no training in education, I found answers to the "process and context" questions by relying on simple reason and logic.
>
> By the end of the day, I felt as if I had taken a high school equivalency test—the kind that leads to a high school diploma for dropouts—not a test

designed to evaluate America's future teachers.

When I got my results six weeks later, they came as no real surprise. On "professional knowledge," I scored right in the middle of all those taking the test. In communications [the language section] I was in the top 1 percent, and in general knowledge, in the top 9 percent.

Do we need a test that really is not much of a test at all of the knowledge, abilities, and personal qualities that the nation clearly needs in its teachers?

[JH:] The Jan. 9, 1984 issue of *Newsweek* published an article about teachers in Houston, Texas taking a test, also developed by the Educational Testing Service, called the PPST Pre-Professional Skills Test, designed to screen college students training to become teachers. *Newsweek*'s reporter, Barbara Burgower, a former teacher, writes in part:

When the PPST was first given to 3,200 teachers last March, cheating was so widespread that one-fourth of the scores were invalidated. The results were unimpressive. With 174 points out of 190 needed to pass, 44% of the teachers failed reading and 46% failed math; 26% failed to gain the 172 points needed to pass the writing section. To help teachers prepare for the test, district officials set up a series of cram courses at Houston Community College. Perhaps inevitably, some of the teachers who took the preparation classes began acting a lot like their own students, passing notes, talking among themselves and serving up wisecracks to the instructors. . . . The six-week math class I attended . . . provided a review of high-school geometry and algebra and an update on metrics. One of the questions on the sample test we took at the beginning of the course asked: A liter is the same as (A) 1000 milliliters, (B) 1000 centimeters, (C) 10 milliliters, (D) 100 centimeters, (E) 100 milliliters. The correct answer is (A). *Half the teachers in my class failed a similar test given at the end of the course* [JH emphasis].

The results in other courses were equally depressing. Reading instructor Larry Marky told me that about a quarter of the teachers in those classes scored below the sixth grade level at the beginning of the course and improved to perhaps the ninth-grade level by the end of the four-week review. . . . One instructor told me that only 4 of the 19 teachers in her class passed the writing course.

Just weeks after taking the test, I would be hard pressed to compute the area of a trapezoid again. . . . "There are 21-year-old college graduates who could outperform me on this test because they've just had this stuff," says Norma Pittman (a 19-year veteran special education teacher), "but I know a whole lot more than they do." What Houston needs is a way of finding out just how much more the Norma Pittmans know about the actual subjects they teach.

[JH:] What Houston really needs is a way of finding out how much students know about the subjects they are taught. It seems astonishing that no one has yet figured out that if tests are not a very good way of testing the knowledge of teachers, they can't be a very good way of testing the knowledge of children. The article says that the Superintendent of Schools "freely doubts his ability to pass the math portion." Norma Pittman says that the college students test better "because they've just had this stuff." Can't they put two and two together?

While lecturing at a mid-Western university I met a professor of Mathematics who told me, among other things, that he had given a sixth grade math test to 40 Elementary Education students in his classes, and that *only one had passed*. The student who had brought me to the university then said that in her department the same test had been given to 36 students, of whom three had passed.

Many people, hearing stories like this, will think angrily, "Why didn't they teach these students that math when they were in school? Why didn't they make sure they learned it?" I'm sure they did. I haven't the slightest doubt that if we fished around in the school transcripts of these would-be teachers, we could find some kind of test scores showing that at some point in their lives they "knew" sixth grade math. The problem is that since, like the great majority of the general public, they were never interested in any of that math and never had any use for it, they have forgotten most of it.

I am really very grateful to teacher Norma Pittman of Houston, for giving us, in her indignation and anger, just the right words to describe the whole elaborate curriculum of the schools: This Stuff. College graduates, she says, can get better test scores "because they've just had this stuff, but I know a whole lot more than they do." I'm sure she does. Since she no longer knows most of This Stuff, what then should she teach? *What she knows*—whatever that is. Here in her classrooms are a group of young people, desperately eager (whether they admit it or not) to learn something more about the world, how it works, why it works the way it does, how to get along in it, how to find something worth doing in it. Here is this woman who one way or another knows more about these things than they do. Why not let her help them as best she can in their search to find answers to these questions, instead of vainly doing what years before people did to her—trying to fill their heads full of This Stuff? If she teaches them what she knows, and when they ask her (as they will) things she doesn't know, if she tries, like good homeschooling parents, to find the answers, she and her students will all grow smarter in the process— the opposite of what happens now.

Let me say again what I first said in *How Children Fail*, twenty years ago. *Nobody knows This Stuff.* Few of the students who get A's in their exams in our elite schools and colleges could even pass those same exams if they were given them without warning a year later. Very few professors at our leading universities could pass even freshman exams in any area outside their own field. Very few practicing doctors could pass most of the exams they had to take in medical school. And so on.

But for the time being it looks as if for some time to come we are going to go on with this silly game, spending $150+ billion a year trying to push into students' heads various versions of This Stuff. It also looks as if more and more states and school districts, like Houston, are going to be testing teachers to see what little fragments of This Stuff they still remember. If so, homeschooling parents may be able to use this to their advantage, by taking those same tests themselves. Under Arizona law a number of parents have already done this, and like the reporters quoted above, have told us that the tests are relatively easy. It seems very likely that most homeschooling parents, if they do take these tests, will score substantially higher than most teachers in their state or area. If so, it will be hard for the schools even to claim, far less prove, that these parents are less qualified to teach their children than "professional teachers."

It might be worthwhile to find out whether your state or local district gives or plans to give some kind of competency tests to its teachers, and if so, how you might go about taking that same test. If you do this, please let us know anything you find out, either about the procedures to follow, the nature of the tests themselves, the scores you get if you take such tests, and the response of the educational authorities if you tell them these scores.

Inner City Private Schools

[JH:] This powerful answer to the claim that only the public schools can help poor kids appeared in the *Education Voucher Institute News*, 2/83:

> A recent study of inner city private schools, conducted and published by the Catholic League for Religious and Civil Rights, offers new insights into who attends these schools and why parents select and support them. Working with a team of distinguished educators, the League conducted an in-depth study of fifty-four schools in eight cities, all of which were found to be Title I schools with at least a 70% minority enrollment. Data collected by the League was generated through questionnaires administered to parents, teachers, and

principals during the 1978–79 academic year.

The study revealed that the educational levels of inner city school parents were only slightly higher than the national average. No evidence was present to indicate that these schools draw students from better educated families at the expense of public schools.

Critics of private schools often point to them as being elitist in nature. This charge is usually based on the assumption that admission and exclusion policies are used selectively to insure a model student population. Examination of school records, however, revealed only a modest tendency toward admission selectivity and virtually no selective exclusions or school expulsions. Records also indicated that these schools open their doors to public school transfers, even when they may not involve the most desirable or ideal students.

While the schools studied were Catholic, nearly one-third of all students of these schools were Protestant. Among blacks attending, this percentage was even higher, with 53% reporting themselves as Protestant. . . . Fully two-thirds of all parents responding to the survey were found to have been educated in public schools.

Most inner city parents chose private schools because of positive attitudes they held about education offered in the schools of their choice, rather than as a negative reaction to the public schools in their areas. Three out of every four parents who responded to the survey gave pro-private school reasons for selection while only one-fifth held negative attitudes about public schools. Private schools were chosen primarily for the educational quality they offered, with the presence of moral and religious instruction being a secondary consideration.

Tuition costs at schools surveyed ranged from $200 to $800 per year with the median charge being $399.50. A total of 72% of parents surveyed reported incomes of $14,999 or less, yet 55% of all responding families reported having more than one child attending these schools. This financial commitment on the part of poor parents to bear the burden of private school tuition is probably the most eloquent testimony about the willingness and ability of parents to exercise choice to improve educational opportunity for their children.

Teaching Outside Of School

[JH:] A good friend of mine is Susannah Sheffer (now at Swarthmore College, Swarthmore PA 19081), who first read some of my books while in fifth grade and has been corresponding with me about them, and about many other things, ever since. Recently she wrote:

> I think I told you that I was doing work in a nearby school, doing philosophy with kids. Do you remember saying that you'd rather not see kids at all than see them in school? I knew it, I've known it for years. I thought, well, if I can make philosophy a voluntary thing as it was in the program in which I worked last year, it'll be all right. One part of me suspected the impossibility, but I tried to convince myself that the good outweighed the bad.
>
> Well, John, you can say you told me so, but I suppose that I needed to see for myself. The second session that I had there was discouraging, angering, and saddening. The kids told me that they wanted me to stay and to come back. But we could not successfully battle the school's great enemy, noise. I told them I didn't care if they were noisy, it was fine with me, but there were people with greater authority who minded and they wouldn't let me come back if they didn't like what went on. The kids, however, and I see this completely, were so thoroughly in a prison mentality that they

could not break out of it. I asked them if they were only quiet when there was someone around whom they were afraid of, and they said yes.

I was not at that point told to leave. I chose to anyway, convinced in a kind of rock-bottom way that school was a horrible place to see and to *be* children. Still, I remember how much kids who visited the Museum of Philosophy enjoyed the experiments they did there, and it is still very important to me to get philosophy into the world of "regular people." I'm putting my mind to thoughts of other ways to do this.

A friend and I are running a creative writing workshop for kids ages 9–12, completely independent of any school, just neighborhood interested kids, held in a nice lodge on this campus. . . . We ran an ad in the local paper and put up a couple of posters in our small college town. The ad said simply, "Do you know a child who is between the ages of nine and twelve and loves creative writing? We provide a unique workshop at no cost."

We had no idea what would happen, but before long we were getting phone calls, and were able to begin with six kids on the date we intended. We'd met with each kid beforehand to get an idea of what kind of writing they wanted to do, and to make sure that they really wanted to spend two hours on Saturday afternoons writing, and it wasn't that their parents were making them do this. We needn't have feared; each of the kids who telephoned us passed our mild requirement for admission at the first meeting—each thought it would be fun to spend those hours writing.

We met on campus for seven sessions. We received no academic credit for the workshop; among other reasons, we wanted to be there as voluntarily as the kids. We had few rules except that no one ever had to read aloud during the Saturday sessions and that no one had to do an assignment over the week. We gave out lists of the correct spelling of words they'd misspelled but told them they didn't have to look at them unless they felt like thinking about spelling. We had very little in the way of philosophy except that as serious writers ourselves we felt that people learn to write better by writing, that we'd do better if we wrote about what we knew and what was important in our lives, and if we knew that we never *had* to show our writing to anyone else, and we never made the kids do something we would have minded doing ourselves.

[JH: This writing workshop seems like something that some homeschoolers might like to do in their own community.]

Life At Home

From Darlene Graham (TX)—see "Success Stories," GWS 26:

We're in our third year of running Pine Ridge Academy and at long last I am feeling really comfortable and confident with it all. I guess sometimes it takes that long, so, anyone listening, don't feel discouraged if your school program doesn't work like magic from day one. We have found that the longer our children were in public school, the harder it was for them to re-develop their own natural curiosity and creativity.

Grant is 17 now and works as a carpenter while preparing to take his G.E.D. test. Suddenly he sees a world full of realistic goals to be accomplished. The local school has enrolled him in Driver Education, to begin in January. They didn't ask questions and were very helpful.

Graham, 14, has taken a breather from his violin lessons, much to my disappointment, at first. It took me a while to realize that even if he never touches it again, he has learned some valuable lessons in self-discipline *and* self-confidence. He does quite a lot of auto repair with my husband, and is becoming very skilled and responsible. At his age, he loves anything to do with cars, and never complains about unloading livestock feed since it involves driving to the barn, backing up, etc., and maybe going once or twice up and down the driveway for good measure.

Crystall (11) is back to her flute practice, and so far, no headaches. Last year she was "teething"—no kidding—and we felt that was contributing to the terrible headaches she got from playing flute.

A few years ago, *all four* of our children were teething at the same time, and was that ever a year of it! Their ages ranged from 2 to 13. Dr. Spock didn't prepare me for that! (Or for much of anything else, for that matter.)

Ginger is nearly 6 and it's exciting to watch her learn. We are pleased with the Alpha-Omega books and she seems delighted. We don't mess around with anything that resembles busywork, and she progresses rapidly.

The other day Grant sorted through some of his old notebooks and found he couldn't even read his handwriting from a few years ago! The children's handwriting has improved tremendously now that they have less of it to do, and more time to do it.

From Barb Tetzlaff (IA):

I got an idea for "*What if*" cards from an old Language Arts and Skills book.... Although the book says it develops verbal expression and reasoning and analytical skills, we found it to be just a fun game and a neat way to learn more about each other. All you need to do is print on one side of a card the enticing words "*What if . . . .*" and on the other side any hypothetical thought you fancy, such as "*What if*—people used fish instead of money?" I made ten cards and Josh insisted we do them all right away, he had so much fun! Then he couldn't wait to talk them over with his father. He also asked some good friends of ours the questions. I never saw that kind of excitement and joy from Josh in public school.

One week Josh played all week by setting up a tiny toy city complete with an airport, restaurant, store, football field, roads, homes, zoo . . . anything he thought you'd find in a real city. His city grew to fill three tables and he was very proud of it and anxious to point out interesting facets of it, like the water tower he created for it.

For several years now Josh has labored at organizing and pricing his collections of stamps, baseball cards, and comic books. He spends hours at categorization. When he is tired, he sets it all aside for a while. It finally literally paid off for him when an acquaintance who collects cards purchased 3,000 of Josh's cards for $75! Quite a first sale for an eight-year-old.

One day Josh found me making my own Valentine postcards to send to friends. He promptly joined in on the fun and made some to send out to his friends. Now, if instead I'd said, "Josh, here are the materials, work on this and have fun," I know he'd have done nothing or done such a sloppy, begrudging job that it would have been better having him not do it at all.

When we were first married, Wayne and I had made cassettes of humorous newscasts from scripts we'd written. Josh was intrigued and after hearing ours, went off to his room to make his own. His current interest in baseball led him to taping himself as a sportscaster. To this day, I can remember his quavering rendition of the voice of the elderly Babe Ruth moaning about how Hank Aaron beat him out for the most-home-runs title. Josh made five tapes altogether.

Josh and a favorite uncle of his worked together on soldering wires into the figure of a man (bespectacled with a head of wiry hair), checking a light-beam burglar alarm, and fixing an electrical motor. It's a special relationship because they work on grown-up projects that we have no talent for ourselves.

A mother in Ohio writes:

Lately our son has been on a kick of designing computers (on paper) that are his idea of what they should be—not anywhere near a real computer. Or he takes strings, rubber bands, pieces of wire, bones, and toilet paper tubes and makes "heaters." Some of them have "generators" attached. But if I try to get him to read (a library fiction or nonfiction or a phonetic reader) he balks and fidgets and can't read some of the easiest material.... He may be beyond his age level in other subjects (he does love math), but we don't think the superintendent would be too impressed with that if he can't read.

He enjoys talking to us about his interests and I'm getting exhausted from hearing over and over and over and over and over and over and over again about his machine he's going to build when he's 21 that will go to anywhere in outer space, even to the sun. "Can anything break my machine? What will happen if it crashes into an asteroid? What is the strongest metal I can put on it?" and on and on. He watches very little TV, hardly anything commercial, and his favorite shows are *Cosmos, Nova, Life On Earth, 3-2-1 Contact,* and *You Asked For It.*

[DR: This parent wrote a few months later that her son was now reading better, though still a little below grade level.]

Mary Friedl (IL; GWS 26) writes:

Everything's going fine here. Kids are doing great. Since September, Adam (3) has learned to recognize numbers 1–10, say numbers 1–12, add and subtract. He's learned to recognize all the letters, a few words, and can also write a few words.

Nathan (6) has gone through K–3 in mathematics. He can add, subtract, multiply, and divide. He does 100- and 250-piece puzzles, can find almost *anything* on the globe or a map. He's reading the Wizard of Oz series. The three of us are taking an exercise class on TV together. Nathan really throws himself into it.

We've organized *many* neighborhood parties. We're working on an egg hunt now for Easter. Kids do planning, decorating, invitations and most of the work. Sometimes they even get the invitees to help in preparation.

We go on many field trips, both on weekends and during the week. Sometimes, as last week, we make a field trip twice, because we enjoy it so much or because we didn't get to see everything. We often study about what we'll see before we go and what we saw after the trip.

Nature science and reading are our favorite topics. Science is not even on the curriculum in our kindergarten–1st grade in public school. If Nathan were in school they'd be "teaching him to read phonetically." What a joke; he's been reading—well—for over four years!.

Esther Rosen, whose family is moving to Germany, writes:

The boys have already figured what their allowances will be in marks. The landlord speaks no English so we're even more motivated to learn German. The 8-year-old (who spent most of kindergarten in public school) is very afraid of making mistakes and will only listen to the tapes and repeat phrases alone. . . . The 5-year-old jumps right in.

It's fascinating to see how Adrian (5) has taught himself about numbers. Two months ago, he could just count to 10. We got a new encyclopedia and he started copying the numbers from the spines (1–24) and counting objects ("What comes after 10? What comes after 11?"). Suddenly I realized he was typing numbers one day and counting by 100s. The next day he was counting by 10s starting at 5 (I wonder why 5?) and was all the way up to 95. Nobody's done anything but answer questions when he asks. Adrian still doesn't know the names of all the numbers (he said today there were 5 books in the top row he doesn't know the name of) but he's doing problems like 50 + 50 + 50 + 50 = 200.

Joshua (8) is starting to read. It's so hard not to interfere and "teach" him, especially when I know we'll be seeing my family where most of the other grandchildren were reading quite early. A few weeks ago, Joshua suddenly realized that he could spell. It was such a revelation! He wrote "gas mask," "castle," "can," and "help" on the blackboard. He was so proud. But he's still totally uninterested in any help from me that's not his idea.

I remember reading quite a while ago something John wrote about the confusion over right and left [*GWS* 3]. I have a young friend who has always been confused. One day while we were talking about it, I discovered that to him right and left meant "write hand" and left hand. He's left handed and never could understand why his "right" hand wasn't his "writing" hand.

PS—Forgive the messy letter. The baby always "helps" by sitting on my letters, taking my pens, etc.

And from Susanna Sutton (NM):

We have been homeschooling for about two years and on the whole are quite pleased with it. There are days (which come to almost everyone, I suppose) though, that I would like to wash my hands of the whole thing. That is when being able to read the newsletter is such a boost. There are times I worry unnecessarily, when complaining and bickering are the order of the day and it all seems chaotic, but sometimes great ideas come from floundering around with an "I don't know what to do" attitude, ideas that carryover for several days.

I try to let my three children direct their activities and come to their own conclusions. It's hard to not pressure Harry (6) to do reading and spelling drills, but I do leave him alone and he is learning to read in his own way, very slowly and rather secretly. Also my oldest, Timothea (10) is a voracious reader but only wants to read stories. Sometimes I try to interest her in history or science but she knows what she wants to read. She had the most public schooling and often has the hardest time filling her days with productive, interesting, and fun things to do.

Paulie (8) went to kindergarten for several months, hated it, dropped out and then finished the last couple of months. She went to first grade, hated it, dropped out midway and has never turned back. She used to be (both girls were) cross, tired, a screaming meemie when she went to school, and now she is a happy child who can sing when she feels like it, make earth dams with her brother any time the urge comes, or just "do nothing" happily and contentedly.

We recently moved from the Zuni reservation where John, my husband, taught woodshop at the high school, to Albuquerque.... Living in a city is so different from our quiet, routine existence in the country. So many opportunities to do things—to me it is a bit overwhelming. To the children, though, it is all grist for their mill. They have plenty of time to do the things closest to their hearts and still play with their friends and help me out.

I don't miss the time I would have alone, not when such positive development is going on. After all, children are only around for 10 or 15 years and then they are wanting to be away and do things on their own.

A Different Curriculum

Joyce Kinmont (UT) wrote in the September Tender Tutor:

> This summer I took a hard look at what we have accomplished in our eight years of homeschooling. I made a list of the things we had done: we memorized times tables (every single year!); we worked at reading with daily phonics lessons and read from a number of readers, for the most part trite; we wrote in everyone's journal every day, which was great, but tedious. I began to wonder what would have happened if I had waited until the children were older, say junior high age, to begin these things. Would they have learned them faster and easier, thus saving a great deal of time? I think they would have. Or would they have gone ahead without me and learned these things anyway? I think they would have done that too.
>
> Now, I'm not saying that there was anything wrong with those academic activities.... But when I looked at the list of things we have *not* had time for, I began to question my priorities. The things we never seemed to get around to included art, music, sewing, service projects in our ward, birthday parties, making personal birthday cards for our family, recognizing new babies in our ward, visiting the elderly. In short, I had devoted my energies to things that could have waited, while the things that give emotional and spiritual development didn't get done. If I could do it all I would, but since I can't, this year's curriculum will be based on the high priority activities.
>
> Our first time will be order. As part of

our school this year we will learn to keep our house neat. We will eliminate tons of clutter and organize that which is left.

Our curriculum will center on art and music. We are buying a Casio keyboard this year instead of a lot of books, and we will sing together every day. (There is reading and math in music.) We will put together a little birthday program that we can take to the members of our ward.

Then I will spend more time reading *to* my children. I'm not nearly so interested in having them do a lot of reading themselves (since there is little they can read that is really important) as I am in filling their heads with uplifting thoughts and lofty ideals from good literature. Then we will work on art, painting pictures for pleasure and to give away. And we will learn to sew.

Our children did want math books, and we let them choose their own inexpensive ones to do if and when they choose.... Last year I supplied art materials for use in their free time; this year math materials are for use in their free time.

One reason I have the faith to adopt this philosophy is that I have already seen it work with Andi and Ritchie. Ritchie had such a fear of anything labeled "math" that we never did work on fractions. Yet when he needed them for his drafting class last year, I helped two evenings and that was all he needed. Andrea has never had a formal English class; I have just answered questions when she had them. But she signed up for a Senior English class at the high school this year, and after two days she can see that she will have no trouble fitting in.

What this means is that I am now ready to stand up and say, "My children may be *below* grade level in some subjects. We intend it that way. We are educating from a different priority list, in a different order. But by the end of their schooling they will have mastered these areas, together with a lot more for which they would not otherwise have had the time."

A Mother's Notebooks

This anonymous story was reprinted in Arizona Families for Home Education, *12/83:*

I have a Korean friend, a very gifted woman who is able to write, edit, organize, lead Bible classes and speak in public. In addition, she's a gracious hostess, a skilled gardener and flower arranger, and a wise counselor. "Is there anything you can't do?" I asked her one day. "You're so confident about tackling so many different ventures. What's your secret?"

My friend smiled. Then she said, "It's no secret. My mother found a way to give each of her six children a feeling of confidence. She kept a careful notebook on each one of us. Every month she took our pictures individually. And in the notebook, alongside our photo, she wrote all the things she observed in each of us that she wished to commend or affirm. I remember how my brothers and sisters and I could hardly wait until the end of each month to read what Mother had written. It gave us assurance and self-respect and encouraged us to build on our good points."

What a wonderful way to record the growth of a child—the development of both his physical self and his human resources.

Mother Learns The Most

From Mary Maher (MA):

I was remembering days spent with my beloved grandmother. I loved to sew, and had learned practically everything I needed to know from her about sewing. She could make clothes without patterns, and I had learned to do this by watching her and sewing alongside her. She never said, "Now do this," or "You can't do it that way." She just let me sit next to her, and I was always free to use materials, needles, sewing machine, whatever I needed. I made an entire wardrobe for my dolls—I still have the clothes today, and they are quite sophisticated for a 12-year-old child to have created without patterns.

So, years later when I had a chance to take sewing lessons in high school, I signed up right away. That year, sewing became a chore. We couldn't do *anything* until the teacher had checked our work, and very often I would find myself ripping out all that I had done. When I finished making the dress and skirt in that class, I threw them away. I didn't go near a sewing machine for seven years.

But the happy memories of sewing with my grandmother won out in the end, and I have since gone back to sewing, and find it still gives me a great deal of pleasure and satisfaction. . . . I never remember my grandmother making a big deal of what I had made—she'd usually just smile at me. That was enough. That smile said better than words ever could, that she loved me and liked sharing her time with me.

Maybe I'm the one who has benefited the most from homeschooling and reading *GWS*. I'm beginning to look at the ways in which I learn things, and I've found out that I'm a very scared learner. Did I do it right? Will I remember how to do it again? What if someone saw me doing it wrong? All these nagging doubts! I never want this for my children. I hope they will always jump into things and never worry about whether or not they're getting it right.

I joined a camera club recently. At first, I thought about all the reasons I *shouldn't* join—there were too many professionals in this club, and I knew nothing about photography, and on and on. But I did join and it's been great. Sure, these people are professionals, but they are very eager to help others learn. They let me be in charge of getting the slides ready for competitions, and this had made me feel very useful. Each month one member runs a workshop on some aspect of photography that s/he can do especially well, such as black-and-white print photography, drawing with light, night photography, etc. I even felt confident enough to enter three of my slides in a recent competition. Mandy (8) comes along to these meetings with me. She never says much, but I know she's taking it all in.

Mandy has found something she loves to do, and is quite good at—ice skating. She takes lessons, and is so pleased at all the tricks—as she calls them—that she has learned to do. She had spent all last winter practicing on her own without lessons, but she was getting frustrated. She longed to be able to spin around, go backwards, jump, etc., and asked if she could take lessons this year. We found a skating club in Stoneham. The teachers are wonderful—there's no shame in doing it wrong or in falling down a lot. When a goal you have been working toward is reasonably well accomplished, you get a badge, and can move ahead to a more challenging class.

Mandy has skated since she was 2. One day she wanted to skate with the big kids, so I found her Scott's old skates and explained that the ice was *very* slippery and she'd need to hold my hand until she got the feel of it. As soon as she got out on the ice, she told me to let go of her hand. Her words were (I'll never forget them) "Me do it self!" And she did. Whenever she fell she'd just laugh and get right up. That day was the beginning of her love for skating.

She learned to ride her bike the same way. Get on, falloff, get on again. She wouldn't allow any interference or help. When she had finally learned how, she came in and announced (with a twinkle in her eye) that she still couldn't ride that bike, and needed our help. Of course, when we went out to "help" she was already riding it, and laughing about the trick she had played on us.

Queries

[DR:] Sometimes readers ask us questions that we don't know how to answer and that have not yet been discussed in *GWS*. We are printing two of them, and we invite readers to respond. We will publish the most interesting answers, and will forward all responses to the askers.

First, "How do you feel about the Chisanbop method of finger calculation? I recently borrowed a copy of their home study book.... My feelings are mixed.... I'd like some feedback from others who have used the method. My son is 5½. He likes to come up with sums in his head.... He is just beginning to do some written addition and subtraction problems...."—J.B.

And, "How do you handle homeschoolers fighting with each other? I have two boys at home and the learning part works great, but their bickering and quarreling drives me crazy. It makes me wonder sometimes if I can stand to have them around, even though I can see plainly it's so much better for them to be home...."—A.C.

On Discipline

At just about every meeting of homeschoolers at which I have spoken, we spend quite a bit of time discussing the question, or problem, of discipline. So I thought I would say a few words about it here.

A good place to begin is by looking at the problem of discipline in the schools. A large majority of the general public says, year after year, that they consider discipline to be the number one problem of the schools. But, as I said in a recent letter to Bob Cole at *Phi Delta Kappan*, it is never clear, from the way the question is put to them, just what they mean by that. Do they mean that they think the discipline is bad in the schools their own children go to, or the schools in their own community? Or are they thinking of other communities, notably large cities? I suspect that a large number of these people are not thinking so much about the schools in their own communities as of big city schools, full of poor kids (probably minority kids), raising all kinds of Cain.

To the extent that people are unhappy about the discipline in the schools in their own community, it is still not clear what it is they don't like. Do they think there ought to be more "You must do this" rules, or more "You mustn't do this" rules, or both, and if so, of what kinds? Or do they think that the rules are OK but that they are not enforced, that the students are too often allowed to ignore them? Or do they think that, even though the rules are enforced, the punishments for breaking them are not severe enough, and if so, what kinds of punishments would they prefer? More corporal punishment? More and longer suspensions from school? As far as I can tell, people in the school business have not made much effort to find answers to these important questions.

It seems very likely that a large majority of homeschoolers and of the general public assume that the main reason schools have such problems with discipline is that they don't care about it. Nothing could be further from the truth. The schools are, always have been, obsessed with discipline. In 1965 I reviewed for *Book Week* a book called *Learning To Teach In Urban Schools* (the review appears, under the title "Blackboard Bungle," in my book *The Underachieving School*). The book was the story, told in their own words, of four young teachers' five years of teaching in urban slum schools. At one point one of them says, typically, "In order to establish discipline in a class *so that eventually you will be able to teach* [JH emphasis], you have to set up routines and everlastingly enforce them." About this and similar remarks, the editor wrote, "Every beginning teacher worries about discipline. There is but one thought in the minds of most neophyte teachers: 'Will the children obey me?'"

About this I wrote:

These quotes can only begin to suggest these teachers' panicky obsession with order, control, obedience, discipline. Their model of education and the classroom is an assembly line in a factory. Down the line come the children, a row of empty jugs; beside the line, each in his place, stand the teachers, pouring into these jugs out of containers marked English, math, etc., prescribed quantities of knowledge. The pouring is easy—anyone can do that; anyone can do the things they tell you to do in the teachers' manuals. The real problem, the teacher's real job, is to get children to sit still on the conveyor belt while he does the pouring. This is why these teachers, like almost all teachers, think that learning is a by-product of order, that if you can just create the order, the learning must follow.

A few years later James Herndon's very funny, very important, and in the end very sad book, *The Way It Spozed To Be*, appeared. (It is now out of print, but we are selling used copies for $3, and I hope someday we can get it back in print.) It was a realistic, comic, horrifying picture of a school trying, and hopelessly failing, to put into practice this mistaken notion that learning follows order. In his own classroom Herndon discovered what I wrote in "Blackboard Bungle": "Any order we get [in urban schools] is going to have to be a by-product of real learning, learning that satisfies the curiosity of the children, that helps them to make some sense of their lives and the world they live in." For discovering and applying this, he was fired, despite the fact that at the end of the year, when everywhere else the coercive order of the school had broken down completely, his own classes were working and his students learning.

Describing what a large team of researchers had found in visits to schools all over the country, Charles Silberman wrote, in *Crisis In The Classroom*, "Adults . . . fail to appreciate what grim, joyless places most American schools are, how oppressive and petty are the rules by which they are governed, what an appalling lack of civility obtains on the part of teachers and principals. . . ." And this was when the schools were supposedly "permissive." They are surely much more rigid, oppressive, and punitive now.

A few years ago Adah Maurer, in her anti-corporal punishment magazine *The Last Resort*, reported that on the basis of a survey sent to school districts all over the country, she estimated (in my opinion very conservatively) that official corporal punishment, formal beatings with paddles in the principal's office, recorded in some kind of log, take place about 1.25 *million* times a year. There is probably several times that much unofficial and unrecorded violence against children by school staff. According to research I have seen (it may have been in *The Last Resort*), no schools anywhere in the world, except perhaps in the British Commonwealth, treat children as harshly as ours.

No, the reason our schools have so much trouble with discipline is not that they don't believe in it, but that they don't understand it. The thing they don't understand about it is exactly what is very well understood by any reasonably experienced and competent Army sergeant—that rules, threats, punishment, fear are not the most important but the least important part of discipline, the small tip of a very large iceberg. Of course, any functioning human organization, military or non-military, whether it be a family, a business, an orchestra, an athletic team, a hospital, or a school, has to have some rules, and some way of seeing that these are obeyed, and some kind of penalties for those who do not obey them. But the relation of these things to discipline is the relation of the crutch or the aspirin bottle to health. The crutch and aspirin bottle do not create health; we use them only when health has broken down. In the same way, rules and punishments do not create discipline, but are used only when it has temporarily broken down.

What *creates* discipline, as any competent sergeant, or anyone who has ever been part of any highly effective, high-morale human organization, is something altogether different, indeed almost the exact opposite. The mix includes love of and pride in one's work; a belief in the reasons for which the work is done, what might be called the mission of the organization; affection and concern for one's fellow members or workers; respect for one's leaders, which does not mean fear of them, but a belief in their competency, fairness, and dedication; and a conviction that one's own contribution to the work or the organization is noticed and valued, that one does not just see oneself but is seen by all others as a valuable member of the team. There may be other ingredients, but these are essential. Simply to name them is to see how little of them exists in most schools, where the work is dull, meaningless, useless; where the most important mission of the school is keeping kids out of the adults' hair; where many students will do anything, including cheat, to get ahead; where many of the teachers are contemptuous, unfair, and often visibly incompetent; where one earns success (if at all) by faking knowledge and hiding one's strongest feelings and convictions.

Then there is the all-important matter of courtesy. In the mid-60s I taught for two summers at the Urban School, a small, private, evening high school, most of whose students were inner city kids. The mother of one of these students told us this story. One day, half-teasing, she was challenging her son to explain to her what he liked so much about the school. For a while he could not find reasons that would stand up to her questioning. Finally he blurted out, "Listen, Mom, I've been going to school for eleven years now, and this is the first time anyone has ever said, 'Please' to me!" Many teachers would defend their "appalling incivility" by saying that if they were courteous to their students, it would undermine their authority. On the contrary, it would strengthen it. But since, in their own lives as students and as teachers they have probably never experienced much courtesy, there is little reason for them to understand how it works.

At college, when I was in the Naval Officer Reserve Training Corps, one of the enlisted men attached to the unit one day interrupted the regular class work to tell us something very important. "You men are going to be commanding enlisted men pretty soon, and if you want them to work well for you, and give their best, here is one thing you've got to remember. *Never use sarcasm!*" Surprised by his vehemence, we asked him why that was so important. What he said I have never forgotten. If you tell someone under your authority, someone who may not be very clever with words, to do a job, and you don't like the way he has done it, and say, "I don't think you did a good job on that, there's this or that or the other wrong with it," he can deal with that. If your criticism seems justified, he can accept it and learn from it; if not, he can try to explain or defend himself. But if you say, in a tone of heavy sarcasm, "That was some great job you did the other day," he has no way of responding. He can't explain or defend himself because, literally speaking, he hasn't been criticized, though in fact he knows he has.

The schools have never learned this. Even at the university level, sarcasm is one of the most used weapons in the teacher's arsenal. Over the years I have asked a number of education students whether they had ever been warned against using sarcasm with or on their pupils. No one ever said yes. Teachers use sarcasm on children to make them feel bad about themselves, thinking this will make them easier to control. They do not understand that it will make most of them much harder to control.

Seeing that in the past hundred years the schools (like most of the general public) have not been able to learn these simple truths about discipline, and seeing no slightest sign that they are about to learn them now, I must conclude that the discipline problems of the schools are not likely to get better and may well get worse. But we don't need to make all their mistakes in teaching our own children. In the next *GWS* I will relate what I have said here about discipline to the question of living with children in the home.—JH

School Memories

Toots Weier (WI) wrote:

I am in the middle of reading *Teach Your Own*, and would like to share some thoughts with you.... At the beginning of the book I was moved to tears reading about the cruelty children have suffered in schools (not just by teachers, by peers as well). I have heard horror stories of physical and verbal abuse of children in schools. Beatings, locked in closets and boxes, humiliation, teasing, just to name a few. I am not ignorant to what takes place in this world, but being reminded of it made me cry.

It was also knowing that I was a part of it in my years at school. At different times, ages, and classes, I was the one to tease and "pick on" another classmate—or—*be* the one *being* teased and picked on. I couldn't be more ashamed now of my behavior then—if only I had known the suffering I was causing. That took place mostly from grade school through 9th grade.

Then I entered high school and things were a bit different.... For a while, anyway. I was somewhat meeker and quieter. After all, here I was in senior high school, and only a sophomore! There were juniors and seniors *above* me! I guess I felt threatened in a way.... I didn't even take the classes I really wanted to (such as art) because it might have meant getting in with juniors and seniors who would laugh at me or think I was dumb. As it turned out, I *did* end up in classes (mandatory ones, like science) with those older kids I wanted to avoid. My guesses weren't wrong, I was scorned by them for just *being* a sophomore—nothing else mattered.

Well, I finally became a senior, and I was anything but "cool." Maybe to my peers I was, because I smoked in forbidden places, skipped classes, etc. But my behavior was totally destructive to any class I was in. *Learning* wasn't my thing, I wasn't interested. Especially in science, psychology, history, civics, etc.,—the classes we had to take. I cheated my way through those classes with a "D" or "D-." I didn't learn *anything* from them.

It's a wonder I wasn't kicked out of school altogether. (Possibly because I *did* know my limits.) I knew which classes I could goof off in and get away with it. But as for those teachers whose authority was never questioned—I knew better than to give them *any* grief. I attended their classes and kept my eyes open and cheated and passed by the skin of my teeth. . . . The classes whose teachers were less serious, or more patient, or whatever, were no more of a learning experience for me. It was more fun to have other classmates laughing at me than to pay attention to what was being taught! And I loved making the teachers angry, I just enjoyed it! When they would get so mad they couldn't stand me, I would get sent to the vice-principal's office. There I would sit in his waiting room—the only girl among 3–6 boys and I thought that was funny! So did the other kids passing by, they would wave and laugh or say something, so it was great fun to sit there. The more I could get away with or even *not* get away with, the better.

I don't believe I am stupid if I was to be measured common-sense-wise. But in terms of *knowing* things (i.e., about the world, countries, states, government) I *am* stupid. At times I feel a bit fearful about being a homeschooling parent. If ever I was to be tested—if ever someone should look back to high school records of me—what then? *Peer pressure.* I knew it well. I was pressured into lightening my long dark brown hair—I didn't *want* to. . . . But if I didn't, that meant I was "so old-fashioned" and I didn't like the sound of that, so I bleached my hair, using peroxide. Again, and again, until it turned a funny red.

Peer pressure. Isn't that the reason I started wearing make-up? "You'd look so nice with a little blush, a little eyeliner, a little mascara, a little . . . until I ended up looking like "The Painted Lady" as the boys on the school bus called me.

I didn't *want* to pluck my eyebrows. That was the dumbest thing I ever heard of—I thought it was kind of sick to hurt yourself like that. But, I was hassled almost every day about my eyebrows so I finally gave in and started plucking. It never made any sense to me, it hurt besides, but I gave in to the satisfaction of the others.

Making School Compulsory

The New York Times *of 9/12/83 has an interesting story by Reginald Stuart about Mississippi education. He writes, in part:*

> Sweeping changes in the public school system were approved last year by voters and legislators. . . . One new measure is the state's first compulsory attendance law with a penalty for parents who fail to comply. Until the 1960s the state had a mandatory attendance law, but it contained much weaker provisions. That law was dropped when lawsuits to desegregate the public schools burgeoned and whites began leaving to attend private schools.
>
> State officials estimate that about 10 percent of the school-age children in Mississippi were not enrolled in school before the changes were enacted.
>
> The new attendance law specified for the first time that attendance officers are to police compliance. The law applies to pupils 6 to 8 years old this year, and one year will be added to the upper limit annually until the age of 14 is reached.

[JH:] Since I have long felt that making school

attendance compulsory was one of the worst mistakes the schools ever made, I find it enormously interesting that in the absence of this compulsion 90% of the children in Mississippi, a poor state with presumably less interest in education than many, should have gone to school anyway. I doubt whether the *true* attendance figures of any state in the union are much higher than that, and in all our big cities even the official figures do not come close to it. It will be interesting to find out whether these Mississippi attendance figures are raised or lowered by the new compulsory laws.

It is worth noting, too, what the story does not point out: that the legislature was only willing to pass the laws on condition that there would be absolutely no regulation of private schools [*GWS* 36].

The "peg" of the story, as newspaper people say, is a child in Jackson named Wanda Jean Tarver who at age 11, along with her 13-year-old sister, is going to school for the first time. The story gives no other information about her social and economic background, but only says that the mother of the girls could not explain why she had not enrolled her children earlier. Wanda Jean says that she likes school: "They give you good food, air conditioning, and you have lots of friends." She also says that she is eager to learn to read, and later, to go to college.

It will be interesting to see how long it takes Wanda Jean to learn to read (or pass reading tests) as well as the average of her age-mates. Even if it takes her six years, her learning rate will be twice that of the schools; if four years, 2 ½ times the official rate; if three years, three times the official rate, and so on. The experience of these late starting children may give us some very important (and to the schools perhaps unwelcome) information about the benefits or drawbacks of late entry. I have written to Mr. Stuart, suggesting that it might be interesting from time to time to check up on the progress of these late starters, and asking him to let me know whatever he finds out. But *GWS* readers in Mississippi may find it easier to check up on this from close at hand.

One other point. The story says that Wanda Jean cannot read. I wonder about this. Does it mean that she cannot pass reading tests, or answer school-type questions about initial consonants, etc.? Or does it mean that there are literally *no* words that Wanda Jean can read, that she has no knowledge of reading whatever? I find that very hard to believe. I think of the story Herb Kohl told, years ago, about the ten-year-old Hispanic boy whom the New York City schools had said could not read but whom Herb found to have a sight-reading vocabulary of over 200 words. If someone offered Wanda Jean a dollar, or even a quarter, for every written word she could correctly identify, how many would she get? And if it should turn out that in fact she really cannot read *anything*, how did that happen? Were there no written words in the environment where she grew up? Was she never curious about what some of them said? Did she never ask? If she never asked her mother or anyone else for any help in reading and her mother never offered her any, I suspect it was because both of them thought that reading was something you could only learn in school, by being taught by an official "teacher." We have all seen the bumper sticker, "If You Can Read, Thank A Teacher." The obvious corollary is, no teacher, no reading. Some more fortunate people know better, but many poor people may well believe it. If only Wanda Jean and her mother had known how easy reading is for children to learn, with a little help, and how easy it is for parents to give that help, the story might have been different.

At any rate, it would be very interesting to learn more of the progress of Wanda Jean and the many Mississippi children like her.

Two Useful Schools

From James Salisbury (ID):

I was trained to be a professional conductor but taught piano lessons while attending Brigham Young University. After a couple of years as professional musician (but still keeping 20 to 40 piano students) I soon realized that I was more successful and happier while working with children and since it is next to impossible to make a living only by teaching music to small children, I returned to university life to get another degree in education.

I had been teaching music according to the inspired wisdom of Shinichi Suzuki (whose method is often referred to in *GWS* pages) and was extremely taken back by the dictatorial methods the university was teaching future teachers! I was very nearly kicked out of the program because I could not make myself consent to the forced methods of public school methodology. I was, in fact, booted out of my first attempt at student teaching and they finally found a principal and a supervisor who understood that I was not crazy but could justify a more freedom-based approach. . . . but I still had to compromise my convictions considerably before they passed my practice teaching.

I accepted a position in a private school "for the gifted and talented." . . . But still they had a forced curriculum, threats of punishment and little of the true freedom of the mind that they advertised.

So with some friends and a few dedicated parents I helped to start yet another "alternative school" which attracted many families. With John's kind permission we named it the *John Holt Learning Center*. Freedom-searching teachers were and are in abundance looking for jobs and our students are the happiest bunch of people anywhere. We also have many homeschool families listed on a correspondence basis.

Many parents come to us and say, "Johnny is the happiest he has been in his entire life and he is finally loving to learn to read, study, and explore—but things are so informal around here, I think we could almost accomplish as much at home!" I was *delighted* to hear this, for the parents are invariably harder to "teach" than the students.

The John Holt Learning Center is still going strong as a correspondence school because the learning happens in the home, the library, the planetarium, the shopping mall, the theater, the concert hall, the farm, the factory. We firmly tell all prospective families that they can certainly learn as much without us (bad for the school's income, but why lie?). Many families enjoy "belonging to a school." They can tell inquiring local school people that their children are enrolled in a parochial school, which makes them exempt from the stewardship of superintendents and politicians in most states. We are "accredited" (now that's an interesting story) and our high school diploma satisfies the laws of the State of Utah and is accepted at Universities nationwide.

I have moved to Twin Falls, Idaho, to help in the Southern Idaho Suzuki program. . . . I am still the ex-officio headmaster of the John Holt Learning Center, and handle much of the correspondence work myself even though the address of the JHLC is still in Utah (PO Box 520794, Salt Lake City UT 84152) and most of the secretarial work is being handled by its parents and supporters in Utah.

[JH:] David Snow, who in recent years founded the *Platte River Free School* (4344 Bryant St., Denver CO 80211), sent us a copy of the prospectus of the school. Some of it we'd like to quote here, since it is an excellent statement of what the school believes and how it works. The school itself, like the *John Holt Learning Center*, would be a very good model for any who might want to start such a school elsewhere. Indeed, if legislatures were to pass unfavorable laws, we might have to start such schools in many places in order to make homeschooling possible there.

The prospectus, *An Introduction to the Platte River Free School*, says in part:

> The Platte River Free School is a day school dedicated to non-structured, free learning. We are founded in the libertarian educational theory of John Holt, Carl Rogers, Francisco Ferrer, Paul Goodman, A. S. Neill and others. The environment of the school provides space for kids to do what they choose without direction, restriction, or guidance from teachers or experts. Some students seek assistance or guidance—which is provided upon request—but the philosophy of the school encourages free, independent thought and action that does not require external authority or reinforcement. We trust that children can and will choose to be self-directed and work through situations without adult involvement.
>
> All families are encouraged to select homeschooling as their learning option

before they come to the Free School. We believe that home-based lifestyles are the healthiest alternatives in a somewhat disjointed world. We believe that homeschooling should be the first priority before families select to come to the Free School. We do provide a day school for children who are unable to homeschool, or for children who choose to participate in the activities of the school as an augmentation to homeschooling.

Community-based learning is the mainstay of the "official" school activities. We conduct three to four field trips each week. These are also "process" activities; we do not seek "closure" or relating such field trips to a specific academic activity. The issue of such trips is the trips themselves, not "What we learn from going to the museum," or "How does the trip to the zoo relate to what we read about animals?" The trip is its own end, and each child can deduce this independently. Ideas for trips and arrangements are conducted by students; teachers often assist if requested.

The school supports and assists homeschoolers by providing resource help, consultation, field trips and activities, transcript development, and other needs.

We serve students ranging in age from 5 to 18 years old. We do not police kids; they are permitted and encouraged to use their time wisely and independently. We trust that they know how to make such choices. We do not operate on time schedules; we open at 8:30 a.m. and most kids leave between 2 and 2:30 p.m. But students can arrive and leave anywhere within that framework. We believe that all children are "gifted" and are all encouraged to "be as gifted as they may choose," as Earl Kelley so nicely put it. We trust kids and know that they will trust other kids and adults in such an environment.

Please visit us and see the process in operation.

A Cambridge Family's Curriculum

[DR:] Here is the curriculum written by Dorothy and Michael Bridges (MA) for their son Joshua (10), who in December became the first homeschooler approved by the city of Cambridge. Note that, like the curriculum by Lynn Kapplow in GWS *27, it is written largely in the present tense, which allows the family to avoid making too many promises about what Josh will learn, while still painting a vivid picture of a rich learning environment:*

Joshua finds much pleasure in reading and reading is one of our favorite activities that we as a family love to share. Every morning after breakfast, Joshua reads aloud to us from a book which the three of us have previously chosen together. The amount of time spent reading is usually at least thirty minutes in the morning and thirty minutes in the evening. Choosing a book which all three of us will enjoy involves Joshua in a process of sharing reviews or giving reports or relating recommendations by friends. Sources from which Joshua draws are our *Growing Without Schooling* newsletter: published by John Holt, the Central Square branch library, the Cambridge Main Library and their suggested reading lists for fifth and sixth graders. We frequently browse through book stores in Harvard Square, and have quite a selection of classics in our own library at home. Accompanying this proposal is a list of books Joshua plans on reading this year. Some of these books will be read aloud with the family while others will be read by Joshua privately. This is probably an incomplete list of what will actually be read this year as newfound interests will supplement the list throughout the year.

Joshua is currently reading aloud to us from Will James' autobiography, *Lone Cowboy*. One reason we enjoy reading aloud as a family is because it affords us a focus and stimulation for further topics of discussion. Josh doesn't simply read from the book but shares with us his thoughts and feelings and relevant experiences as we do with him. While we read at these times, we take notes of things we want to remember, augment our vocabulary list, and make use of our grammar book as necessary. For instance, the dialect in *Lone Cowboy* is often difficult for even Michael and me to decipher (Texan slang from the late 1800s), so we found it helpful to teach Josh to dissect sentences into subject and predicate to figure out some rather perplexing sentences. Meeting the challenge has greatly increased and strengthened Josh's confidence and in three days, he went from having to repeat certain sentences several times in order to gain their meaning, to a point where he was comfortable dramatizing the dialogue.

We don't teach grammar as a separate subject but integrate it into all of our sessions which involve reading, writing, and discussing, referring to the *Perrin-Smith Handbook of Current English* whenever the need arises. In doing so, we are striving to increase Josh's language arts skills in an active and conscious way. One of Josh's current projects, which we have titled "The Philosophy of Education," is a good example of how he is gaining in the areas of language arts. He is writing letters to various public, private, and alternative schools in the Boston area, asking to be invited to investigate how their educational philosophies differ by coming and observing, asking questions, and interviewing teachers and students. Here he is learning letter composition, proper typewritten letter form, sentence structure, punctuation, spelling, communicative and inter-personal skills.

We are encouraging Josh to write daily in a private journal. He also enjoys writing stories which he shares. We will be using a workbook called *Continual Surprise* by Donald Murray and Burton Albert Jr. from the Reader's Digest Educational Division for stimulating creative writing skills.

Josh also plans to write to some of his favorite authors, first on the list being Judy Blume.

History—We are beginning our leap into recorded world history by reading some of the shorter and simpler Platonic dialogues, starting with *Crito* and *Ion* and hopefully parts of the *Apology* and then working to develop the setting in which Plato and Socrates lived; i.e., ancient Greek history and culture, its geography and mythology. We plan on paralleling our historic jaunt with a philosophic jaunt, introducing simplified versions of the basic thoughts of the important philosophers, starting with Plato, Aristotle, Bacon, and Spinoza and examining the corresponding historical and cultural settings which produced them. We are also developing our perspective on the geography of the world, starting in ancient Athens and reaching out from there to conquer ever new territories. We are using *A Child's History of the World* by V. M. Hillyer, *The Story of Philosophy* by Will Durant, *The World Book Encyclopedia*, and a Jowett translation of the dialogues, predigesting and editing out some of the more difficult material.

Typing—*Typing For Everyone* by Nathan Levine, Arco Publishing, and working on our computer.

Computer—Commodore VIC-20. Using Turtlegraphics to learn programming, and also Basic Part One.

Art—*Drawing On The Right Side Of The Brain*, A Course Enhancing Creativity and Artistic Confidence by Betty Edwards, and two-hour, monthly meetings with an artist friend who teaches at the Museum of Fine Arts, Judy Friebert.

Math—We do basic math drill work while we're jogging and Josh is riding his bike or jogging with us around Fresh Pond, so he's learning to perform some more and less complex math operations in his head using algorithmic techniques and the distributive properties of numbers. We are using the Random House Mathematics Program at least thirty minutes a day or an hour every other day to introduce math concepts in concordance with drill work. It covers sets, properties of numbers, different number systems, estimating, number theory, fractions, measurement, geometry, decimals, ratio and percent, statistics, rational numbers, probability, equations and inequalities, functions and graphs, constructions and logic. We also bring ideas to Joshua from *Mathematician's Delight* by W. W. Sawyer.

Physical Education—Josh loves basketball and softball. This past summer he learned to sail at Boston's Community Boating. He earned his solo card and plans to practice for a helmsman's card when the sailing season reopens in the spring. He enjoys swimming, essentially teaching himself and passing the necessary swimming test to qualify for sailing lessons. He enjoys ice skating in winter. At an easy jog, he is able to run the full two and a half miles around Fresh Pond. He is learning tennis, does daily push-ups and chin-ups (on a chinning bar at home) and some Tai Chi exercises which are good for his asthmatic condition. We are planning to renew his membership at the Arlington Boy's Club to take advantage of the gym and swimming pool throughout the winter. Josh recently purchased a new dirt bike which he rides daily.

Music—Josh loves music. He makes up his own songs and dances and has learned some songs his dad has written, especially the one written for him when he was born. He has recently been experimenting with friends' instruments, his sister's guitar, Khalik's violin and Kathy's congos and his mother's flute. We will continue to encourage his investigations and should he one day proclaim a particular interest, we will help him follow through on it.

Business—Josh wrote a little book when he was six and we built him a stand on a stroller and the next thing we knew he was selling copies at MIT. At seven, he was in business for himself and receiving letters from his admiring readership. This year, he learned about capital investment with his own peanut business, needing to invest sometimes as much as $48.00 in peanuts so he'd have peanuts available when business was available. He also learned about supply and demand and the price fluctuation that goes along with it.

Science—Our ten volume set, *The Book of Popular Science*, and the *World Book Encyclopedia* can easily satisfy our ambitions in the sciences for this year. Basically, we want him to know what all the sciences are and to have a basic understanding of what each science entails—and where some sciences intersect. We belong to the Science Museum and Josh is starting classes there every other Saturday with Mr. Pauli, a dynamic and irresistible teaching personality. We also use the library at the Science Museum and go there just to read sometimes. We'll spend from one to two weeks on each science the first time around, and each succeeding time around, go deeper into each field.

Joshua has stated that he would have no objections to testing at the end of the year.

List of Questions

Su Rannells (CA) writes:

At our urging, this year our school district established complete home school (Independent Study) as one of the alternatives that parents in our community could choose. Kate's father and I traded a partial school situation (2 days a week in a one room school) for a complete home learning program.

In John's talk in Sacramento, he spoke of keeping a record, a "portfolio" of your child's learning experiences. I have always found this difficult to do but lately it struck me that keeping a list of Kate's *questions* might be the best "portfolio" of all. Her questions are the measures for me that her mind is actively exploring uncharted waters and they let me in on the many places her mind travels, and they also determine what books we get from the library. The questions fascinate and astonish me for all they represent. A recent sample from the last couple of days:

1. How did the first tree get on earth?
2. What are tires made of? How do they make tires black?
3. Can birds poop when they fly?
4. How come this is called Dutchman's Britches? (A wildflower)
5. What makes 200?
6. What does "confidence" mean?

Einstein On Education

Our old friend Manas *(Box 32112, El Sereno Station, L.A. 90032, $10/yr), from which we have drawn many good quotes, just quoted these useful and beautiful words by Einstein from* Einstein And The Poet *(Branden Press, Brookline Village MA 02147; $10):*

The basis of true thinking is intuition;

this is what makes me abhor our present-day school system. It splits each science into several categories; yet truth is only attained by a totality of experience. I was never attracted by specialization. I always wanted to know nature, creation itself. The mystery of life attracted me. My religion is to use my thinking faculties, as much as I can, to know what seems unknowable. Have you ever stopped to consider that reading books, or gathering facts, has never led to any scientific discovery? Intuition is the prime factor in our achievements.

The world consists of real objects, and there are consistent laws underlying them. If we want to honor God, then let us use our reason and intellect to grasp these laws, which form the basis of a perfect mechanism. The concepts of space and time are many centuries old, but that didn't hinder me from questioning them.

From Writing To Reading

[JH:] A friend sent me a story from the *New York Times* (8/24/82) about a man I knew and liked many years ago. The story underlines in many ways what I said in the review of Glenda Bissex's book *Gnys At Wrk* (*GWS* 24, 25). From the *Times* story:

> Seven years ago, John Henry Martin, a lifelong educator, came out of retirement and began "with one child at a time," as he says, to test the theory that children ought to learn to read by first being taught to write. Since then, he and Evelyn Martin, his wife, have applied that theory to more than 900 youngsters, aged 5 and 6.

> Working under the auspices of their own J.H.M. Corporation in Stuart, Fla., they have confounded old-line reading experts and attracted the attention of school people looking for a better mousetrap. [JH: A reading program called "The Writing Road To Reading," by Romola Spaulding, has been in print for at least twenty years.] Last week [IBM] began a major test of Dr. Martin's "writing to read" program, in which 10,000 kindergarten and first grade pupils in at least seven states will participate.

> Dr. Martin came to view the traditional way of teaching children to read first, then to write, as the "curse of teaching." The idea of "writing to read" led him back to "the very, very old approach." Up to World War I, he points out, every child started with a slate and piece of chalk, and reading and writing were never taught separately. But somewhere between 1910 and 1920, the slate—"a symbol of rural poverty" was taken away, and the process of reading became purely visual.

> "But I discovered that human hands were entry points into a child's brain," he adds. [JH: Something that Maria Montessori said over a century ago.] "Children begin intuitively to write. If you have a sound symbol connection, the child can put sounds on paper." That is the basis of writing to read.

> He believes that when reading comes first, the English language, with all its irrationalities, makes children feel that they themselves are irrational or stupid. Yet all normal 5-year-olds already possess a vocabulary of 2,000 to 4,000 words and are able to express complex ideas orally. When we teach children to write, we build on that knowledge, Dr. Martin says. "As they learn to write, they learn to read—the two processes are interdependent."

> "Children's minds are extraordinarily logical," he says. "We try to exploit their logic." How? The children at first write by learning those symbols, or letters, that represent the sounds they make when they speak. They quickly understand that there is a difference between "sound spelling" and "book spelling," and, says Dr. Martin, as the two spellings are used in parallel, the transition comes naturally. But they are spared the initial difficulty that confronts them, when reading comes first, of facing the irrationality of the

differences between, say, "through" and "threw," or "bear" and "bare."

How does the computer help? If you believe in the importance of tutoring individual children but can't have 10 million teachers for 10 million children . . . the computer becomes an individual tutor. The one provided by IBM is capable of acting as typewriter, primer, tape recorder and television screen. It produces color, sound and even chant. For example, the computer may show the picture of a cat, say the word, ask the child to repeat it, and then spell the word "cat."... After this, there may be a rhythmic tune, and the computer asks the child to clap hands while chanting the words along with the computer.

"How do you think," asks Dr. Martin, "man transmitted sacred literature for millennia, without writing it down?" The answer, he believes, is "by rhythmic chant. In order to get the child's total physical involvement, the computer chants."

With or without the computer, the writing-to-read system relies initially on the child's phonetic spelling—making natural speech visible, letting the sounds from the mouth be coded on paper or screen, without attention to the inconsistencies of English spelling. A typical story, written by a first grader after four to six months under Dr. Martin's program, came out as follows:

"One day I took a trip to outer spas. On the way I saw a Marshon so I landed on Mars to see the Marshon and I made friends with him. He told me all about spas and we had lots of fun together." To Dr. Martin, this—along with test results—is proof that, despite the initial "sound spelling," the children become better spellers than those taught with the traditional reading-first approach. They also scored high on standardized reading tests.

When the project is subjected to its large-scale tests beginning next month, it will be examined in big city schools and in a mountain county in North Carolina. . . . Since it flies in the face of so much traditional theory and practice, it will undoubtedly be scrutinized by friends and critics alike, and debated by reading and writing experts.

―――――

[JH:] It is amusing, though frustrating, to watch schools rediscovering the wheel over and over again. In the late '50s Prof. Omar K. Moore set up an arrangement—much more cumbersome than today's computers make available —which made it possible for children, when they hit keys on a typewriter, not only to see the letters but to hear the sounds made by those letters. By simply making such equipment accessible to children, and with a minimum of anything that could be called "teaching," he was able to help three- and four-year-old children to teach themselves to read. This brought down on his head the wrath of all the early childhood experts, who said that learning to read was bad for children this age. Despite impressive results, Moore was never able to get more than a handful of schools to try this method with children of any age. After a while he gave up and went on to something else—I haven't heard from or of him in years. Maybe Dr. Martin and the IBM folks will have a little more luck. I hope so. We'll see.

What can we homeschoolers get from all this? Well, I think if we give children *access* to things which will make writing easy for them—typewriters, magnetic letters for the refrigerator door, rubber letter stamps, stencils—most of them will do a lot of writing and from it will learn much about reading.

[DR: We contacted Dr. Martin's corporation, which promised to send current info on the program.]

A Day Full Of Learning

Clare Cole writes in Other Ways, *the journal of the home and alternative school movement in Australia:*

The thing which encourages me the most is the striking difference between *how* my children learn in comparison to their schooled peers.

A few weeks ago Megan, Holly, and I were visiting friends after dinner. Their nine-year-old daughter, who attends state school, was starting to do her homework, which she had remembered just before bedtime. She expressed real anxiety and concern that she would get into trouble if she didn't do it. Her mum and dad reassured her and said that they would help her get it done in the morning. She agreed, but said she wanted to try and remember her spelling words and asked her dad to help. They spent 15–20 minutes going over her list and she really tried hard but was frustrated and angry with herself for "being so dumb"! She had a standard list of 10 words appropriate for her age and reading level—none of them terribly difficult, but *all* of them totally *irrelevant* to anything she was involved or interested in at that point in time.

The following journal entry shows how, after a busy and social day, Megan (9) spontaneously organizes her own spelling lessons and Holly (5) chooses activities which, with just a little help from mum, are constantly extending her use of language.

July 7, 1983: Rose had a day off and came to Family Home School this morning, and together with James, Robbie, Megan and Holly, they played happily for hours, mainly dressing up and acting out complicated and imaginative games of their own creation. They played on the see-saw (from Hawthorn toy library), read stories, looked at books and drew pictures, etc. Megan and Holly went off with Rosie at about 3:30 to visit and play for a few hours, came home just before dinner and were off again roller skating with their dad from 7:30 to 9:30.

When they arrived home Megan decided to make herself a "crossword book." She got a bundle of old magazines, picked out all the crosswords she thought were not too easy, but not too hard, then set about cutting them out and gluing them into an exercise book. Holly asked her for an exercise book and sat doing a beautiful front page saying "Holly's writing book" with a great deal of concentration and a sense of ease and relaxation. She then said to me, "What will I write?" but before I could respond she said, "I know, I think I'll write the alphabet first!" and proceeded to do just that. She wrote some letters in upper case and some in lower case. All were in the right sequence with only J, N, S written backwards. I played a guessing game with her, asking how many could she see written backwards.

She read through her letters one by one saying each sound, and picked out the three letters which were the wrong way. I asked her if she wanted to do a whole line of each of the three (principle being practice makes perfect) and she enthusiastically agreed and took her book and pen with her to bed. When I went in to read her bedtime story she showed me what she had done. Not only had she done a line of each (the right way round), but she had done a complete upper case alphabet and a complete lower case alphabet on the next page. I commented on how great it was, and she said she did all "little letters" and all "big letters" because it looked better.

Asking Questions, Keeping Quiet

From Teaching And The Art Of Questioning *by J. T. Dillon, published by the Phi Delta Kappa Educational Foundation, 1983:*

The intent of most why questions is not to seek any answer at all. Even given amiable intent, a why-question functions to express such things as objections, disapproval, and criticism; the response is to defend, withdraw, or attack. From long experience children have learned that there is, in fact, no meaningful answer to a why-question.

"Tommy, why are you doing the dishes?"

"Lynn, why didn't you do the dishes?"

"Chris, why are you sitting there reading a book instead of doing the dishes?"

Tommy, Lynn, and Chris know that it is foolish to give *their reasons* (as if it were their reasons that were being called for). When we react to a student's contributions or behavior by means of a why-question, we risk communicating that what he is saying or doing is wrong or stupid.

Just such a case happened to me recently in a doctor's office. The doctor had told me the treatment for my condition and he began to write his notes. I asked him a question about the treatment because I was confused and I wanted to get it right. He looked up and said in a high pitch, "Why are you asking these questions?" I thought, I could tell this guy my reasons—ignorance, confusion, need, anxiety—but he doesn't want my reasons, he wants to scold me; so I waited, and he did. "You're not listening to me. I told you, blank-blank-blank." He repeated precisely the phrase that had confused me to begin with, and he left the room. I went to the nurse and got the right instructions. Because of the status differential, it is socially more permissible to ask a question of a nurse than a doctor; and, as is well known, nurses respond more readily. Doctor-patient conversations are similar to teacher-student ones. The doctor asks the questions—simple, response-constraining ones—at a fast pace. The patient responds briefly; the patient asks very few questions; the doctor typically replies with a counter question.

Certainly, there are times when a sincere why-question occurs to a teacher, but the teacher must be sure that the student *receives* it as a sincere why-question. A teacher might consider using one of the alternatives to questions, because they convey better than a why-question that the teacher is genuinely interested in learning the student's reasons for saying or thinking something.

In elementary grades, teachers have been found to reply with a counter question to two of every three pupil questions. A counter question has the force of rejecting student initiative, of refusing to the student the right to ask a question, of withholding cooperation in the exchange, and of wresting control of the interchange away from the student and back to the teacher. Now the student must answer the teacher's question. A counter question says: "I'm the one who asks the questions around here. You answer them."

Deliberate silence is the most intriguing alternative to questions and one of the most effective. It is the simplest yet the hardest to practice. And it is the most difficult for everyone in the class to get used to.

Say nothing at all. When a student pauses, falters, or has ostensibly finished speaking, maintain a deliberate, attentive, and appreciative silence lasting 3–5 seconds. Chances are that the speaker will resume or another student will enter in.

Deliberate silence is difficult for teachers because they feel impelled to speak out of a sense of responsibility, if not anxiety, for maintaining and directing classroom discourse. For many teachers a period of silence seems to be awkward, perhaps wasteful.

To use this technique.... the teacher must learn how long three seconds actually last and then rehearse that duration between two sentences spoken aloud.... In class it might help to nod or murmur while waiting for the student to resume.... For years everyone has been conditioned to hearing the teacher start to speak within less than a second after the student's last syllable.

To speak up at the first second's pause or on the first flawed phrase is merely to grab the floor and dismiss the speaker; it is no less an interruption than when someone is speaking—indeed, someone *is* speaking.

Surprised By Reading

The other day Mary Wolk and daughters Rebecca (7) and Deborah (5), visiting Boston from Los Angeles, came into the office to ask some questions, and give us some much needed help. While Rebecca worked steadily, Deborah, between short bursts of work, played our new ½-sized violin, talked to all of us, and amused herself in other ways. Since I had not been reading to her or talking about reading, I was surprised when she said to me solemnly, "I don't know how to read." Since she seemed to feel a little badly about this, I said, "That's OK, one of these days you'll figure it out." Whether reassured or not, she dropped the subject.

The next evening, at the Open House, her mother told me this story. At 11 o'clock or so Wednesday night Deborah woke up and came into her mother's room, saying that she could not sleep. Mary (who was reading some back issues of *GWS*) said, "This is my time to myself, and I'm reading, so you'll have to be very quiet. Why don't you get a book of your own and read to yourself." Deborah said, "But I don't know how to read." Mary said that she could just look at the book and see if there were some words she knew, and if so, perhaps put a little line underneath them. So Deborah settled herself with a book, *Danny And The Dinosaur*, and her mother went back to her own reading. Soon she was astonished to hear a soft voice reading aloud, slowly, the words of the story. Since Deborah had never heard that book read aloud, she had to be reading it herself. After a while she realized this, and said with great excitement, "Mommy, I know how to read, I can read this book." Needless to say, much joy all round.

So much of children's learning goes on in their subconscious that it is futile and foolish to try to keep track of what they are learning by constantly asking them questions about it. Obviously Deborah did not figure out reading between 2 and 11 p.m. that Wednesday. Most of what she needed to know in order to read, she already knew when she told me, meaning to be truthful, that she could not. But she did not know she knew it. Indeed, Mary said that only a day or two before Deborah, seeing her older sister reading, had said irritably, with an envy that was not put on, "Why does she have to read so much?"

If Mary, or anyone, had put pressure on this child by quizzing her about her reading, she would have replied, perfectly truthfully, by saying, "I don't know." What is worse, that unforced, unhurried, unworried process by which her subconscious mind was working out the patterns of reading, might well have come to a stop. It would have been very easy by such quizzing not only to confirm this child in her belief that she did not know how to read, but to convince her that she was too dumb to learn.

This is the great and fatal flaw in Piaget. Even in the early sixties, when his work was just beginning to come into educational fashion, I knew, simply from what I had seen of young children in schools, and even younger ones out of schools, that he was just plain wrong in much of what he said about children's thinking, what they could and couldn't do. How had such an intelligent and observant man made such serious mistakes? There seemed to me then three serious flaws in his method, which was basically to study children's thinking by asking them questions about it. (These flaws, by the way, are inherent in all psychological research of this kind, whether done with children or adults.) The first was that they didn't understand the real meaning of his questions; the second, that he didn't understand the real meaning of their answers. The third, perhaps even more important, was that the children were often not even trying to tell him what they really thought, but, like all people being questioned by some higher authority, were trying to guess and give him the answer they thought he wanted.

I described these three flaws in his method in, among other things, *The Underachieving School*. But now I see that there is an even more serious flaw in his and everyone else's efforts to learn, by asking them questions, what children know. It is that much of the time, like Deborah, *they don't know what they know*, certainly not well enough to be able to talk about it. When Deborah assured me that she could not read, she probably had a reading vocabulary of at least several hundred words. But if I had asked her to name all the words she knew, she might have been able to name at most a few dozen, might well have insisted that she did not know any at all. We should keep making this point to schools, educators, and legislators: testing children's learning not only usually fails to reveal it, but may often even destroy it.

Well, if asking them questions won't tell us what children know, how then do we find out? By paying attention to what they *do*, above all when they are doing what they have chosen to do, and don't think that we're watching. To find out how well they read, *notice what they read*. It is as simple as that.

Today, learning psychologists are beginning to try to find out what children know by giving them ways to put their knowledge into action. In the next *GWS* I will describe how their results are confirming what I have said for many years about Piaget's work, and how we can use these facts in dealing with schools.—JH

Free Books—School Discards

From Kathy Bare (OK):

We heard we could get free books from Oklahoma public schools. We found a room full of elementary schoolbooks, ours for the taking, at the Lincoln School in Tulsa. They had two more rooms which contained thousands of junior high and high school books. These books are discarded books the teachers no longer plan to use; but most of the elementary ones have *never* been used. Some of them are published within the last couple of years and were the same type of books (which had been "updated" in the catalogues) we were planning to order.

[JH: We have run stories like this from other parts of the country. Small wonder the schools are short of money.]

8-Year-Old's Magazine

From Ellen Duncan, RD 2 Box 413, Halifax PA 17032:

We have been homeschooling since October '82, and never dreamed we could have so much fun!

I am sending you a copy of each of the first four issues of my 8-year-old daughter's magazine *The Jibber Jabber*. . . . I have found *The Jibber Jabber* has done much to relax Laura's attitude toward written composition. The two years she spent in public school so restricted her that she became afraid to write anything. I admit the first issue of her magazine created a bit of anxiety and a few tears. The use of an interview feature really helped. In this way she could organize her thoughts as questions. With the interviewee supplying the information, the pressure of knowing what to say was removed and with it went much of the anxiety. So far, Laura has interviewed only people she knows. There are many interesting people in our area who are patient and willing to pause long enough for a young interviewer to take notes.

Every aspect of *The Jibber Jabber* experience has been beneficial—from doing the layout to rushing for a deadline! Personal notes of acknowledgement to contributors are now dashed off instead of agonized over because there simply isn't time to worry.

Fortunately, the expense of copying isn't overwhelming, thanks to a local firm which allows us the use of its copier if we buy the paper. Laura is seeking contributors of all ages and she felt perhaps other homeschoolers would enjoy seeing their creations in print. She stresses that *The Jibber Jabber* is for fun and that everything is printed as it comes to her (with the exception of spelling bloopers). . . . Children who don't yet write can dictate their contributions to Mom or Dad, as her 3-year-old sister Ann has done. . . . Contributions can be of any nature—puzzles, stories, interviews, jokes, drawings, poetry, etc.

Laura sees that every contributor receives a copy of *The Jibber Jabber* containing his/her work.

On Reading And Writing

From Kathy Mingl (IL):

J.P. woke me up the other night complaining of bad dreams. I told him to remember it and tell it to me in the morning, and I'd help him write it down. He made a book of it, complete with illustrations, and hasn't woken up crying since. Apparently turning it around into an exciting adventure story, like a "scary movie," put him enough in control of the whole thing that now *he* pursues the dream to find out what happens, instead of *it* chasing *him*. It wasn't hard for me to be impressed and "bug-eyed" when he told me the scary parts, because I can remember how I was at his age. I just wish someone had thought of turning *mine* into stories—I might be a famous science fiction writer by now!

From Jane Gaffney in Australia:

I started showing books to Liesl (now 16 months old) when she was 4 months old. I would choose ones with big bright pictures and set her between my legs on the floor to look at them and talk about them. She really does love books. She often just sits by herself and looks through them, sometimes chattering away to herself about what she sees. Several times a day she'll come up to me with a book in her hand which she wants me to look at with her. If she's miserable about something, I just have to suggest looking at a book and her face lights up instantly. However, she *will not* let me read the words. Whenever I try she screws up her face and tries to close the book up. The only reading I can get away with is some nursery rhymes if they're sing-songy or if I can do some flamboyant actions along with them. I guess at this stage she just doesn't want to be bogged down by a lot of mumbo jumbo she doesn't understand. She likes to look at the pictures and recognize things she knows and talk about those things with me. She likes to tell her own story.

Which isn't to say she's not at all interested in print—she is. She likes to look at our books which are often *all* print and she loves to get hold of some official looking piece of paper—a brochure or magazine—and pretend she's reading it. I've noticed she always holds her books up the right way (and ours too where there's no pictures to give away which way is up) so she must be taking it in. . . . Also, she never tears books, except for pop-up books, whose characters have been known to lose their arms and legs. I must admit, I can hardly wait until she wants to be read some of the wonderful stories I've got waiting for her.

From a California parent:

My 6-year-old taught himself to read at age 5 with no more than a knowledge of consonant sounds and a lot of questions on his part "What's that word say?" He is an excellent reader now, reading long books regularly. Vocabulary and difficult sentence structure are no obstacle to him. He enthusiastically reads the difficult English of *The Boy's King Arthur* or the King James Bible with no difficulty at all, provided the story interests him. If the ideas are on his level of comprehension and interest, he can read anything with excellent understanding.

Now this is my interesting observation: he was playing a word game where you match cards together and come up with simple three-letter words. It was supposed to teach phonics. I was amazed to find that he could not recognize simple words like *did* and *tip*. I'm sure this was because they were just words out of context in a list. He knows how to read sentences and paragraphs—*not* words. I noticed that when he first began to read that he seemed to recognize whole phrases, not individual words.

A Helpful Librarian

[JH:] Sherry Early (8104 Parkdale Dr, Austin TX 78758) has made a very generous offer that I think might be most helpful to many homeschoolers, not least of all because it will help them (and us) answer questions like, "Well, what are you going to do if your kid wants to learn chemistry?" She writes:

I am employed as a school librarian here in Austin, and I believe I have a skill that I can use to help homeschoolers. I would like to do annotated subject bibliographies for parents or for children who are looking for books and materials on a specific subject. For example, when my husband was young he was interested in making fireworks. He read everything about fireworks that was available in his small hometown library, but he still needed more information. A librarian could have directed him to *Books In Print* or other bibliographical sources, but even those wouldn't have told him which books to buy on his limited budget. In Austin, I have access to the reference collection and review sources of the University of Texas libraries in addition to a fine public library system and my own school libraries. Our school system receives review copies of recently published books, and I am able to examine these. I could produce a typewritten two to five page annotated bibliography on any subject from fantasy fiction to electronics. I could answer questions such as:

1) Where can I find books in Spanish for my children who are learning a second language and what are some good books in Spanish that are available in the U.S.?

2) Our family just bought a home computer, and we're trying to decide what educational software to buy for it. Do you have any suggestions?

3) Our family is planning to visit Japan next summer. What are some books we could read together that would give us some idea of Japanese life and culture?

4) I am nine years old, and my favorite books are the Narnia Chronicles by C. W. Lewis. What other books can I read about magic and about other worlds?

I could give other examples, but I think you get the idea. I would like for people to write me giving me as much information as possible about what it is they need, and then I will respond within a reasonable amount of time with a bibliography and a letter answering their questions. I think for now I'll just do the bibliographies and let people pay me whatever it is worth to them or whatever they can afford. If the postage and time involved get out of hand, I may have to charge a set amount since school librarians aren't wealthy people.

Foreign Books and Info

From the brochure of the Information Center On Children's Cultures, *a service of UNICEF (331 E 8th St, New York NY 10016; 212-686-5522):*

The Library of the *Information Center On Children's Cultures* is a collection of:

educational and cultural materials in English about children of other lands (chiefly materials that have been designed for use by children) and

primary source material, usually in the languages of the country, created for, about and by children from many lands with emphasis on children of the developing countries.

Materials in all media are included: books, periodicals, pamphlets, films, filmstrips, tape and disc recordings, pictures and photographs, children's art, games, musical instruments, and others.

What does the center do most of the time? It answers questions close to 5,000 each year, by mail, by phone, and in person.

Whom do the questions come from? Mostly from: individual teachers, individual children, church group leaders, Scout leaders, scholars, librarians, newspaper and magazine editors, children's book editors, writers and illustrators, university students, parents.

What are some of the typical questions answered by the center?

Where can I get a Pen Pal?

What can you tell me about the children in the country of ___?

Where can I get pictures of children from ___?

Where can I get children's books in the ___ language?

Where can I find the description of children's folklore (games, songs, play, etc.) in the country of ___?

How are the questions answered? They are usually answered by sending mimeographed sheets or photocopied materials and reading lists containing the actual information, or by referring the inquirer to another place where the actual information can be obtained.

Please send a self-addressed, stamped envelope when requesting information by mail.

[DR:] Here's an example of the kind of help the *Information Center* provides. When the Marschners (LA) wanted to know where to find good children's books in Spanish, the Center's librarian sent them exhaustive information on publishers and on libraries with large Spanish language collections. She suggested the family use the Interlibrary Loan service of their public library, which is what they did.

Another resource for foreign language study: Jane Filstrup, who wrote *"Bilingual Family"* in *GWS* 30, says, "We are members of the *French Institute* (22 E 60th St, NY NY 10022; 355-6100), which lends French books by mail at small charge to people anywhere in the US. Very helpful librarian, Mr. F. Gitner. Membership in the library only is something on the order of $20 per year. . . ." Do readers know of any other such organizations?

Using Math

Linda Butler (UT) wrote:

I'd like to share with you an experience I recently had with math. Your "Thoughts on Counting" [*GWS* 1] came to mind and I realized that I, too, looked at numbers as these magical elves, who acted totally on their own, or under orders from some higher power, but were never to be understood, let alone manipulated, by me.

I was trying to figure out whether a certain magazine was still a good value or not. To determine the number of pages of actual reading material I subtracted the number of pages of ads from the total number of pages. I also counted the articles. I had two formulas: (1) Total pages minus pages of ads equals number of pages of articles and features; and (2) Number of pages of articles and features divided by number of articles equals average length per article.

What I was doing was comparing an early issue to a recent one. I felt that the articles were getting shorter and more superficial, and I did find this to be true. The early issue averaged 4.4 pages per article while the recent one averaged only 1.8 pages.

Feeling successful thus far I continued. It was fun to use these numbers to solve problems—I was getting those elves to work for me!

Then I decided to figure out what percentage of each magazine was ads and how much I was paying per page of reading material. I even had my calculator at hand. But I suddenly couldn't figure which number to divide into which. My mind began to freeze up. I thought later about your fifth graders in *How Children Fail*, and how they'd panic, especially if they felt they had to perform for a teacher. I would have fallen apart—even as a supposedly mature adult. And I wasn't under any pressure but that of my own making. I started punching in numbers and getting wrong answers. I asked my husband for help.

Now both of us have college degrees—I have a BA in Humanities, Steve has a BS in Psychology and a Master's in Social Work. Neither of us is good at all in math, but managed to get around the University requirement—I did so by learning two foreign languages. My math education generally ceased around grade 7. I somehow managed to get through high school algebra and geometry but have since forgotten every bit of it. This is unfortunate, because I'm now getting interested in learning math and using it, and also I feel that I need to know and understand math so I don't destroy it for my children (or my children for it), as I hope to teach them at home when they reach school age.

Back to my situation. My husband had no idea of how to find percent but he helped me estimate the approximate percentage. This helped a lot because I'd had the right answer all along but couldn't recognize it. (I forgot about moving the decimal point.)

To figure out the cost per page I set up a story problem, and, talking aloud to myself, plugged in the numbers and got the right answers (I did make a few mistakes, too, but I knew that 24¢ per page was a bit high!)

At any rate, here I was, a 28-year-old college graduate, mother of two, feeling quite fulfilled and, yes, excited too, that I had solved a sixth grade math problem.

I have no idea how I'll teach my kids math. My 2½-year-old loves to count and yes, we do count objects just as you suggest. I figure that the only thing a young child rattling off a chain of numbers is good for is impressing people.

Please, lead me to some sources that will help me to learn math and help me to teach my children.

P.S. As I read this I want to comment on my speaking out loud to myself as I solved the cost per page problem. By speaking to myself I could concentrate even harder on the problem at hand. It helped keep my mind centered on what I was trying to do. I notice Jessica (2½) speaking aloud to herself quite often, especially when she's deeply involved in her work (play). It seems to help shut out other people and distractions. Have others observed this, too?

[JH: see next *GWS* for my reply.]

Letters On Computers

From Don Porter (NY):

I read with interest the computer items in *GWS* 31.... My son (11), a homeschooler, benefits enormously from using our Atari 400. Both he and his sister (10) have learned math facts using a simple drill program that I wrote. They like to use the computer, whether for skill practice or game playing. Many children may not react so positively, but John and Judy have gained skill and confidence using the computer in a mode that is not really very stimulating.

I see I have started right off confronting the dread "computer drill-and-practice is deadening" cliché. That may be true for many kids. For John and Judy it has been a great boon. They are quite proud of their accomplishments. Incidentally, John is now expanding his vocabulary very handily through another drill program—it presents words and asks for definitions.

Through commercially available educational software, John has also gained other valuable skills: suffixes, prefixes, punctuation, fractions, etc. It is annoying that much of what is available is not very good, either pedagogically or in its use of the computer. What is surprising is that it works—at least for John.

The *People's Computer Company* sponsors local groups who want to start up "Computer Towns," places where people of all ages have access to computers, with instruction, assistance, mutual aid, etc. They have a newsletter —address, 1263 El Camino Real, Menlo Park, CA 94025.

Another group that started up from folks seized with the excitement of kids using computers is *Young People's Logo Association*, 1208 Hillsdale Dr, Richardson TX 75081. Their newsletter *Turtle News* keeps kids and adults informed and excited about Logo. Membership is $9 for those 18 and younger, and $25 for others. They have information about setting up "Turtle Learning Center" chapters—sort of a backyard version of "Computer Town." They also offer advice on the best hardware and software for Logo—a question raised in *GWS* 31.

―――――――

And from Judy Gelner (CO):

Our son Kendall (14) is the one who primarily uses the computer. He had access to a computer for two years (5th and 6th grade) in school. When we got our computer, he barely knew any BASIC. Apparently what he really learned at school was how to load a pre-packaged program. It seems to me to be less of a tool if that's all you can do with it. Since homeschooling this year, he has learned quite a bit.

Last spring, in preparation for our school, we started looking around for a computer.... After some thought, we decided the best thing to do would be to choose the absolutely cheapest computer around, use it, and then someday when that mythical ship came in, we would be able to spend our money more wisely when purchasing a bigger system. We bought a Sinclair—now a Timex-1000. The price is now $30–$60 in our area, and the 16K RAM, which we recommend, is an additional $40. You will also need a small black-and-white TV plus a cassette tape recorder, preferably with a counter. We haven't found anything any other computer can do that ours doesn't have the capability for, except color and high resolution graphics.

We have found that its disadvantages are either not substantial or even became an advantage for beginners. The first disadvantage is the membrane keyboard. Kids who are not used to typing don't object as much as anyone who is used to typing. Like most things, once you get used to the feel of the keyboard, you can type in programs fairly rapidly. Many of its functions like PRINT are one-key entries, so that cuts down on the typing.

Another disadvantage is that programs load on a cassette tape recorder which is much slower than the floppy discs that computers such as Apple use. However, programs on tapes cannot be coded or "locked" to prevent copying, so a beginner can more easily study what someone else has done to achieve an effect and even change something if he so chooses.

A third disadvantage is that there is not much commercial software (programming) available at stores you can walk into.... I think that may change.... Meanwhile, a subscription to *Sync*, a magazine which deals only with the Timex 1000, is full of programs and peripherals you can order by mail, as well as giving you printed programs in the magazine to try on your own. As you type them in, you learn quite a bit about programming.

[From a later letter:] We no longer hope for a bigger system such as Apple, just the new $160–$200 model 2068 that is coming out. It has color and high resolution graphics. We were looking at some promotional literature for teachers which suggested Timex 1000 for grade school, an intermediate model for junior high, and the 2068 for 11th grade and up. Kendall could hardly believe it. After one year of work he is definitely ready for the 2068.

Nature Walks With A "Teacher"

More from Mary Maher (MA):

In *GWS* 33, you ran an ad for a natural science course to be held in Cambridge. I contacted Jeanie Tibbils, and learned that *I* would have to accompany my kids on this course, since it would be held out of doors and in all weather. I knew I didn't want to take this course, but I'd take it "for the children's sake." Every week for 10 weeks, from 9:30 –11:30, we would meet Jeanie at Fresh Pond. At first, I was worrying, would Jeanie ask me questions I couldn't answer? Would she quiz me? Make me write essays? How dreadful!

None of these things happened. In fact, the children and I had a most wonderful 10 weeks. Jeanie was great—not a "teacher," but a guide and a friend.

Each week brought new experiences as we walked through the woods, and gradually learned the names of plants, fungus, ducks, trees, wild flowers, etc. The children became very adept at climbing huge willow trees and jumping over creeks. We observed things up close with hand lenses and field glasses. A favorite activity was sitting by the pond very quietly with our notebooks, and writing down everything we observed. We learned what plants we could eat (and did so), and which ones we could use for making tea. The kids brought home birds' and bees' nests, and things to look at under our microscope. We delighted in finding the tunnels under the grass where the voles can run and not be seen by predators.... We discovered that Mandy (8) is the most observant of us all. In her very quiet way, she would discover and point out things that the rest of us had missed.

In contrast to our joyful experiences together,

we often saw a school group who visited the area as part of their class time. These kids were made to stand still and listen to the teacher *teaching* them about the environment. They were clearly not enjoying themselves, and were not experiencing any of the joys that we were so free to partake of.... They couldn't run, or get their feet wet in the pond, or climb trees, or search in hidden places, or talk.... I *really* saw for the first time how artificial school learning really is. These children weren't in a classroom, but they might just as well have been, for they showed no interest at all in their surroundings.

Mandy was fascinated by this group, and would wander away from us so as to get a better look at this (to her) very strange gathering. One day, she saw the teacher slap a child, then the child began to cry. Mandy was horrified.... She made it very clear that she would *never* go to school "where people treat you mean." I assured her that she would never have to.

For anyone living in the Boston area, I would highly recommend Jeanie's class.... Just as I was finishing this letter, Scott (13) gave me a story he wrote about the class. It gives a better idea of what we did:

[Scott wrote:] On our 9th trip, Amanda and I ran through dried goldenrod stalks, playing tag. There was a field full of it, and it was about 5½ feet tall. To run through it, we had to keep our arms in front of us, so we could brush it to the side as we ran.

Later on, we found a small rabbit about the same size as the one we found before, hiding in some tall grass near the goldenrod. He stood real still, hoping that I wouldn't see him, but I did. Then I called my sister over and she saw it too. We started to get closer to it and it started running. It zigzagged around and went into a briar patch and stood still. By the time we got near it, it was in the patch too deep for us to get a good look.

We continued walking down the road, and got to some good climbing trees. I climbed up near the top of a willow tree and my sister got only a little way up. Amanda wanted to climb an ash tree, so I followed her over to it, and I got to the top and she swung around on the lower branches. After a while, we got down and went over to a place where a man had cut down grape vines growing on a small ash tree.

We made wreaths out of the vines.... First, we took a thick piece of vine and wrapped it in a circle and twisted it around itself. Then we took another piece of vine a little smaller this time, and twisted that in and out of the other vine. We continued doing this until we had a thick, round wreath.

After doing that, we walked over to an area that had Japanese Knotweed (American Bamboo). It has seed pods out this time of year. The seeds are in individual cases, and are the same color as the seed cases on a money tree plant. They are about a quarter of an inch wide and each have a little black seed inside. We clipped some of this and stuck it in our wreaths. Then we went to pick the bittersweet, which is little orange berries with yellow caps around them. Once the caps fall off an orange shell opens up; there is a bright red berry inside. We put little pieces of bittersweet on the wreath and we were finished. We brought the wreaths home and my mother hung hers on the front porch, and I gave mine to my aunt, and my sister gave hers to my grandparents.

[DR:] Jean Tibbils is continuing to offer her science course; for information, call her at 617-876-8829.

Playing In A Museum

From Aletha Solter (CA):

My son (6½) goes to an open alternative class (K–3) which is a part of the local public school here in Goleta. The class was started because I and some other parents requested such an alternative, submitted a written proposal to the school board, and managed to find 20 other families who were also interested. Several of the families would be homeschoolers if it weren't for the class (myself included).

I recently took four children from the open alternative class to the Natural History Museum.... In the bird room there were hawks and eagles suspended from the ceiling with wings outstretched ready to attack. I said to the children: "How do you think it would feel to be a mouse and to look up and see hungry birds like that swooping down towards you?" No sooner had I said that, than the children were instantly transformed into mice scurrying around looking for shelter. They soon disappeared from sight under the large display cases in the center of the room, peeking out from time to time to see if their predators were still there. This went on for a while; then they asked me to be a bird and try to catch them. There I was, flying around searching for mice to eat. Any visible arm or leg from under the display cases was likely to be attacked, to their great delight. (Luckily, nobody else entered the room while this "lesson" in predator/prey relationships was taking place!)

At the blue whale skeleton, the four children were, of course, immediately swallowed by the whale. There they were, huddled together inside the belly of the largest animal ever to have lived, with a look of awe and excitement on their faces.

I couldn't help but be struck by the contrast when we saw other groups of children in the museum being led around by their teacher, and listening politely and obediently to long lectures and explanations. These children looked so bored, and they were so passive compared to the four from our class.... Perhaps the greatest mistake we adults make with children is to separate play from learning, and to impose on them the ridiculous notion that they cannot have fun while learning.

Real Science Education

From "Why Kids Fail To Learn Science and What To Do About It," by Michael Rossman (Reprinted with special permission of Learning: The Magazine for Creative Teaching, *September 1983. Copyright 1983 by Pitman Learning Inc., 19 Davis Dr. Belmont CA 94002):*

> Breast-beating over science education has begun. The statistics emerge as a national disgrace: Russia graduates four times as many engineers as the United States, and clever Japan graduates twice as many. Comparisons of how many study how much science in secondary school show us falling far behind. Science education seems to be a national disaster area, a prime target for massive remedial programs vital to the "reindustrialization" of America.

> Myself, I taught science part-time for a decade in an alternative school.... What I teach is somewhat idiosyncratic, since I don't follow a standardized curriculum, but go from one thing to another from year to year as my interests and the children's move. I do come back often to favorite and basic ground: how the body works, the transmutations of energy, life through the microscope. But there's always time to take advantage of the moment—just why did Mount St. Helens erupt?

> During children's early years, before science is separated from other aspects of their lives, I try to teach that it is natural to us, that it's natural to see with scientific eyes almost everything in the world.

> I do it mainly by becoming like a child myself.... As we fondle snake and fossil and the morning's surprise mushroom, notice someone's bruise or wonder why the tape on the solar housing peeled this time, what I teach remains always the same. I teach that each place we cast our attention is worthy of attention, each pebble and leaf and odd trick of light is a door to wonder.... an intricate story open to whoever wants to see and know. I teach that it's natural to *really pay attention* to what we encounter and behold— sometimes simply by observing, sometimes by prying with the mind, always with marvel at how everything connects.

> It's an easy curriculum even without microscopes, since everything's grist for the mill. The true subject is not the world, but how to be a person in it. And how else could a person be, than to notice what's what and wonder why?

Children find this process natural, until they're taught that *noticing what* and *wondering why* and *finding out* are special activities reserved for a special sort of people. Most have a natural appetite for the ways of learning that we later call "science."

This appetite grows if it's fed and fades if it's starved. Children engaged with people who *notice* and *wonder* and *find out* tend to learn to do likewise. This learning begins at home, as early language does—but usually it goes on much less than it might, because most parents have themselves lacked encouragement to develop their own capacities of noticing, wondering, and finding out.

Our educational system treats science as if it were something *out there* to be learned, "objective," beyond the self. Well, the world may be so, but science itself is not. Science is a human attitude and posture, a way of knowing. What passes for "science education" concentrates on teaching students about *what* and *how* other people have seen and known. Only incidentally does it teach learners how to see and know by themselves.... Indeed, ordinary "science education" may inhibit the development of natural scientific capacities.

Museum Run By Kids

From a brochure on The Museum Of The Hudson Highlands *in Cornwall-on-Hudson, NY:*

Most of us think of a museum as a place where people go to look at things, but— how did those things get there? Who decided what should be shown? Who collected and organized them into groupings? Who designed the displays and cases they are shown in?

At the Museum of the Hudson Highlands, the answer is: school-age youngsters.

This unusual project was started by local teenagers, is maintained by them, and today involves both grade school and high school students.

The Museum.... specializes in exhibits of live animals, fish, reptiles, and birds. It features wildlife native to the region.

School children are natural born collectors. All they need is some adult encouragement, a place to house their findings, some art and construction materials, and you have a fine starting-point for a museum.

The Museum was organized as a summer project. The town donated one room in Town Hall and appointed a Director. The Museum membership and collections grew into a year-round project occupying ten rooms in Town Hall. A donation from a local resident built the present 2-wing building located on 40 acres of woodland. The site now includes three nature trails laid out and maintained by Workshop youngsters. The Museum now employs four full-time professional staff members, who share the "doing" with the youngsters.

At 3 p.m., the Museum bus picks up youngsters at school. Attendance is purely voluntary but there are usually plenty of hands available because the Museum functions as a social meeting ground as well as a fascinating workshop.

Some youngsters may work on a special museum display, e.g., a bulletin board on animal bounties or a diagram-history of the bony structure of reptiles. They will plan it, create artwork for it, build and decorate display cases, hand letter display signs. Others will work with the animals—feed them, clean the cages, help in raising the worms, mealy bugs and live mice that are used as food. Others may act as tour guides for visiting public.... On Sundays, again youngsters are present to keep things going.

Workshop members, under the direction of one particularly gifted teenage writer, are preparing a brochure which will describe each animal in the collection and give interesting facts about it. All research and writing is being done by the teenagers themselves. When finished, the Brochure will be on sale at the Museum Sales Desk.

Hudson Highlands Museum hopes to add an additional wing in the near future. On their own, the youngsters suggested they undertake a house-to-house canvass to raise the initial funds needed for this project.

Museum Workshop members are often called upon by local residents to rescue, or remove to safer quarters, wild animals that have wandered into yards, gardens, etc. They are also asked to identify poisonous shrubs and berries. This consulting service is a tribute to the youngsters' acquired knowledge of wildlife habits and habitats.

Hudson Highlands is an example of joint funding.... The Town of Cornwall owns and operates the Museum, pays the director's salary, pays most of the curator's salary, and provides a film projector. The Cornwall Board of Education funds most of the Summer Junior Workshop. The New York State Council on the Arts pays for two assistants and the materials used in museum exhibits. Individual donations pay for part of the curator's salary and for part of the Summer Junior Workshop; foundation gifts paid for the present building and provide the Museum bus and trailer. Other sources of income are a donation box, an annual membership drive, and the Sales Desk in the Museum.

[DR:] The brochure was prepared by the *National Commission On Resources For Youth* (605 Commonwealth, Boston 02215; 617-353-3309), an organization with a wealth of information on projects that have involved young people in their communities—working with food banks, hospitals, libraries, consumer complaints, tutoring, etc. We hope to publish more of their reports in *GWS*. Meanwhile, any of you who are concerned with the question of how to involve young people in serious work might send for NCRY's list of publications.

Science Resources

We were sent a sample copy of *Zoobooks* and thought that some of our readers might find them attractive and not too expensive. The booklet we received, *Elephants*, has 18 pages full of colorful paintings and photos, and lots of interesting facts: "The ears of an African elephant weigh about 110 pounds *each*"; "An elephant can actually pick up a single blade of grass with its trunk"; "Elephants are wonderful swimmers." There is a fascinating composite picture of 14 elephant ancestors (woolly mammoths, etc.). The amount of information in the text is probably no more than in a good encyclopedia article, but the number of illustrations is what makes it appealing.

Other booklets in the series are *Endangered Animals, Birds of Prey, Big Cats, Baby Animals, Wild Horses, Giraffes, Whales, Bears, Snakes*, and *The Apes*. They are published by *Wildlife Education* (930 W Washington St, San Diego CA 92103) as a subscription series—you normally receive one every 5–6 weeks, though we learned you can ask for a whole set of 10 at once. For a limited time they are making a special offer of 10 booklets for $9.95 (normal rate is $14).

A catalog *GWS* readers might find useful and enjoyable is the *Sir-Plus* catalog of *JerryCo* (601 Linden Pl, Evanston IL 60202; 312-475-8440; quarterly, 50¢ per issue). It describes itself as carrying "industrial and military surplus all aimed at teachers, tinkerers, labs, small manufacturers, model shops, collectors of the bizarre, astronomers, artists, do-it-yourselfers, small retailers, gadgeteers, flea marketeers, the curious, or anyone seeking hard-to-find items...."

Examples of some interesting items from their 1/84 issue: hyper flex wire (used by sculptors—

"very pliable and totally forgiving"), $2 for 32 feet; a small solar motor, $1.75; Ivory tower puzzle, $1; 573 foot roll of plain paper, $3.75; lenses that make things appear bigger, smaller, or upside down, $1 each; and much more, including magnets, boxes, bottles, electronic parts, and photographic equipment. The catalog is delightful to browse through, as it is full of puns and humorous descriptions, with lots of fanciful suggestions on how to use the more peculiar gizmos.—DR

From Pat Williams (KY):

A resource for science study for kids and adults is the *Biological Materials Catalogue* of the *Carolina Biological Supply Company* (Burlington NC 27215). It is available free to science teachers and those in the life sciences profession. If you are homeschooling your children, you can probably honestly say you are a science teacher (among many other things). It is a beautiful catalog of almost 1000 pages full of everything you would need to do science teaching on all levels. It contains living and 24 preserved animals, skeletons, microscope slides, computers and educational computer programs in science, games and puzzles, books (over 60 pages), filmstrips, models (eyes, hearts, teeth, flowers), charts, mineral samples, fossil samples, apparatus of all kinds, chemicals, and much more. Most of the items are not inexpensive, but there are some affordable items, and almost everything is something you can't buy at local stores. Where else is a child interested in biology going to find a fetal pig to dissect ($8.55), a human pumping heart model kit ($10), or a set of fossil shark teeth ($13.95)? Even if you never buy anything, a lot could be learned from the pictures of the items in the catalog. My husband and I enjoyed looking at it for hours.

[DR: The *Arizona Families for Home Education* newsletter listed the addresses of Carolina Biological Supply and several other similar companies: *Connecticut Valley Biological Supply*, Valley Rd, Southampton MA 01073; *Sargent-Welch Scientific Company*, 7300 N. Linden Av, Skokie IL 60076; E.G. Steinhilber, Box 888, Oshkosh WI 54901; and *Ward's Natural Science Establishment*, PO Box 1712, Rochester NY 14603.]

Trying Out Embroidery

From Karen Schadel (NY)—see "Family in the Country," GWS 36:

Recently while in the fabric section of a department store, Joshua noticed some embroidery floss as it was lined up and displayed with its beautiful assortment of colors. He inquired as to what you did with this colored thread. This simple question led me to purchase each of the children an embroidery hoop, embroidery needles, a yard of muslin and an assortment of floss.

Immediately when we arrived home the sewing began. I quickly demonstrated what to do as I was anxious to begin a knitting project of my own. Seth (5) needed quite a bit of threading and re-threading—I soon learned to double strand his floss and knot it for him. He experimented with some abstract lines and created triangles on his fabric along with making frequent color changes. He was definitely pleased with his ability to make the thread do as he wanted it to.

Joshua (7) caught on quickly and was able to thread and knot his own floss as well as sew with a single strand. His first creation was a group of hearts that encircled a purple J. He is currently working on a very pretty original design. He started with a stitched line border in purple, his favorite color. Then he made stem and leaf lines and intends to place different colored flowers on the stems with yellow centers. Next he stitched a shining sun in the upper left area. Truly, this isn't that original, but what intrigues me is how he is doing all this free-hand and with good control and planning.

Joshua decided he would show Sadrah (2) how to use her hoop, as she was asleep when I gave my demonstration. She was pestering him so much whenever he tried to work on his that this must have seemed like a solution for peace to him. He cut the muslin, clamped and tightened the hoop, adjusted the fabric, cut a length of floss, threaded and knotted a needle, and sat down on the floor to sew with Sadrah. He let her do it all with a little verbal coaching to encourage her in pushing the needle and pulling it through. When they brought it to show me I was really amazed. It was basically a design with different lengths and colors of floss that overlapped and went in all directions, but Sadrah was tickled by her sewing and begged to do more. I never considered giving Joshua a needle and thread when he was just 2, although he did begin to sew by doing buttons on scrap material when he was about 4. Yet, here was Sadrah pushing and pulling on a needle and not once stabbing herself. Actually neither did Joshua or Seth, except when they first started and laid their hoops on their thighs. They quickly discovered they needed to hold it up off their laps when pushing the needle down through the hoop. Joshua and Sadrah laugh as Sadrah pretends to poke herself and squeals, "Ouchie, ouch!"

J.P.'S Crayon Flowers

More from Kathy Mingl (IL):

I showed J.P. something I liked to do when I was little—melting crayons. You printed something once in GWS about how disappointing the effects you get with crayons are—sort of pale and "skippy." The results are much different if you heat them in a candle flame first—it's like painting with melted wax, and the colors are very rich and beautiful.

J.P. took it a step further, though. I was working in the other room, and he brought me a present he'd made for me—a perfect, tiny cup-like flower, out of crayon-wax. He had dropped a bit in his water cup, just to see what would happen. We played with it all afternoon, and we found that if you let the melted wax drip from a little higher, you get petal-like effects, and if you drop it just above the water, it looks like a single lily-of-the valley blossom. Sometimes you can even get one with a tiny stem underneath. You do have to be careful just to drop it, though, and not let it splash, or the "petals" will break up into individual specks of wax. We're collecting all the best specimens to make an arrangement.

Pat Plays the Blues

The continuing adventures of Pat Farenga learning to play saxophone:

My third lesson was when things really began to turn on for me. After a brief discussion of last week's lessons and a quick spot check on playing 8 bars of Schumann's "Evening Song," John Payne put an album on his turntable. "Did you practice the Blues Scale? Good, 'cause that's all you have to play on this cut." John immediately started to play the blues on his sax over a slow rhythm track coming from his speakers. Piano, bass and drum are supplied and the rest is up to you. After a chorus it was my turn, and I tentatively played the blues scale up and down in time to the music. I kept losing the octave key D and G (it really is a cinch to play now, but then it was murder!) and John egged me on to keep going and take a second chorus. This time I just played the root notes, alternating the rhythm a bit. I played a total of three different notes over 12 bars of music but that was enough; I was totally hooked—I was playing in a band! I forgot to take a breath and didn't hit the next note right; I went down in a blaze of very flat B-flats. John picked up and played a few choruses, always staying within the range of the G-blues scale. Very simply and quite expertly John created a model solo for me to refer to for ideas—and he used only the nine notes he taught me the whole time! He told me to try and copy some of his licks off the tape he made of us playing, and to buy the *Nothing But The Blues* play-along record by Jamey Aebersold.

The afternoon that I went home with the Blues album and played along with it in my room was a gas. I never played with or accompanied anyone in my first seven years of piano lessons, and here I was playing in a quartet after three saxophone lessons. John Payne kept telling me you don't need to know a lot to make music and he's right. I didn't know how to properly use 70% of the saxophone then, and right now I still don't know what a number of the keys are for, but I've been playing and creating real music almost since I started my lessons with him.

Next week's lesson came and we played the

first cut from the album I was supposed to learn, "Slow Blues in F." I soloed first and played a very safe and slow solo, adhering devoutly to the KISS principle I learned from my piano lessons: Keep It Simple Stupid. But John picked up on what I was doing and practically played the same notes I did, only he made an interesting solo out of it. When he was done I felt the ball was now in my court. OK, watch me hit that high G—oops.

"Keep going. Don't stop." encouraged John.

I finished a chorus and listened to John. This sequence repeated itself until the song finished. John pointed out some things I could do to make my solos more interesting, like holding notes over the points where the chords changed and using rests for the punctuation of rhythm and melody instead of gasping for air. He wrote out four more blues scales for me and noted the songs I could play them with on the album. At no point was I taught any of the melodies for them that are in the book. We were just improvising freely every time we played. I would go home and listen to the tape of us playing and though my sound was akin to a moose-call, it heartened me to think I was capable of creating music without endless scale drills and boring rote exercises.

These would be given to me eventually, but even these are turned into a game by John. He calls it his "hammer and tongs" method. Rather than practicing written out scales and a bunch of scales disguised as songs under the title "Exercise in G" or "Waltz in E," he has you make twelve flash cards, one for each key. Then you're to shuffle the cards and play the arpeggio and scale for the card you turn up. He has you time yourself playing the shuffled scales, always trying to beat your previous time. Then he applies this work at the same time to particular songs on the play-along albums that require you to improvise with those scales.

We choose the songs together too. I like jazz, but other students like rock and others, standard pop songs; we all learn what we like when we want to and John never looks down his nose at you for wanting to play Bruce Springsteen over Duke Ellington. "I love all types of music," he once told me, "I can listen to John Coltrane and then turn on some sixties bubble-gum tune, like something by the Archies, and I can get pleasure and learn something from them both."

In my fourth lesson I completed the *Tune-A-Day* book, learned five blues scales and could use them on seven cuts from the album, and was given my first steps towards becoming a member in the Student Saxophone Choir. John gave me the tenor parts to "Keep On Doin' It," a jazz-rock song, and "South," a big band tune from the twenties by Bennie Moten. I went home and blew away on these tunes like a man possessed: I was determined to learn them. But when I had my lesson my mouth was so tired I kept letting air escape from the sides. The muscles just wouldn't work! John added this note on my assignment sheet: "Don't wear out your chops!"

[Next *GWS*: Pat plays in public!]

Self-Taught Musicians

[JH:] In my files I found an old newspaper article about Gunther Schuller, written shortly after he became head of the New England Conservatory of Music, a position he held with great distinction (all the while continuing to compose and conduct) for a number of years. What caught my eye in the story were these words:

> The life of Gunther Schuller is an incredible story of how the musical Establishment can (or at least could) be brought to its knees by a boy who is driven by a desire to make music and to make it as he hears it. At the age of 12, he began to participate actively in music, joining the St. Thomas Choir School as a boy soprano and also taking up the study of composition, flute, and later the French horn.
>
> He started composing at the age of 14 and developed so rapidly in his study of the French horn [JH: an extremely difficult instrument] that in 1942, at the incredibly young age of 16 he accepted a professional position with the Ballet Theatre Orchestra. At 17 he became Principal French horn with the Cincinnati Symphony and the following year

performed his own Horn Concerto with the orchestra directed by Sir Eugene Goossens. By the time he was 19, he had accepted a position in the Metropolitan Orchestra, a post which he held until he resigned in 1959 (by that time he was Principal horn) to devote more time to creative work. The very fact that he educated himself outside of any educational institution has helped him to understand what kind of training is really necessary for a musician. In his speech at the [New England Conservatory] Centennial Dinner, he addressed himself to this point:

"Forgive me for becoming autobiographical for a moment, but I do it only to make a point. I stand before you as one of the original dropouts. I do not have any degrees, and I do not have even a high school diploma. Now I'm not advocating this necessarily as a road to higher education, and I am aware of the fact that times have changed tremendously in the twenty-four years since I left high school. But I have the feeling I would not have been a very good music student in, for example, the rigid programs which allow for almost no electives, which some of our schools demand."

[JH:] For some time now, we have offered on our list two recordings of the Tapiola Children's Choir from Finland. When their conductor, Erkki Pohjola, started the choir in 1963 at the Tapiola Secondary School, it was just an ordinary school choir. By ten years later it was acknowledged to be perhaps the finest children's chorus in the world, and one of the finest of any kind.

What I only learned later (from a record jacket) is that although Mr. Pohjola is an accomplished violist and a member of a leading Finnish string quartet (the other members being his sister and his two brothers), he is entirely self-taught as a choral conductor and indeed never sang in a chorus.

Two more stories about self-taught musicians. First, from *Newsweek*, 9/20/82:

Renting New York's Avery Fisher Hall to conduct a symphony orchestra before 2700 VIP's is the kind of derring-do nobody did until Gilbert Kaplan raised his baton last week. Barely able to read music 15 months ago, the millionaire publisher led 119 instrumentalists and a chorus of 200 through Mahler's dauntingly difficult *Resurrection Symphony*. Kaplan, 41, directed the 90-minute, 209 page opus without a score. The concert was an act of pure passion. Kaplan is an ardent amateur musician who plays the piano by ear, once built a harpsichord for fun and has been haunted by "a crazy relationship" with the Mahler symphony since first hearing it 18 years ago.

The notion of actually performing the *Resurrection* began to gnaw at Kaplan in 1979. He sounded out professional musicians. They told him, as one maestro said, that the idea was "preposterous.". . . . Finally, the publisher found a young conductor willing to help; Charles Bornstein, now musical director of the Newfoundland Symphony, spent the summer of 1981 working with Kaplan nine hours a day. By the end of August, Kaplan had mastered rudimentary conducting technique and memorized the first movement. By late September, he'd weathered an audition with the American Symphony Orchestra. . . . "Our initial reaction," confesses a cellist, "was, 'Oh my God, what are we getting into?'"

Sometimes Kaplan wondered too. . . . He practiced doggedly each day. . . . flew to Amsterdam and Tokyo to analyze symphony performances; he collared every accessible conductor. . . . toiled over Mahler's treacherous changes of tempo. By the end of 12 full rehearsals with the orchestra, Kaplan's growing expertise had won over his instrumentalists.

What the black-tie audience applauded last week—with a five minute standing ovation—was more complex. . . . Kaplan conducted with a control and ardor that awed even some professionals.

To Kaplan, risk is what the $125,000 extravaganza was about. "There are so many people who don't try things because they are afraid of failure," he explained. "I simply *had* to do this." Acting out his own "hare-brained scheme," he hopes, may encourage others "to pursue what really matters to them and take risks."

(Part of Kaplan's dream was a realistic fallback position; had his memory gone blank in mid-performance, he planned to turn and announce, "Ladies and gentlemen, dinner is served.")

[From *Inc.* magazine, 11/83:]

Wrote critic Leighton Kerner in *The Village Voice*, ".... It turned out to be one of the five or six most profoundly realized Mahler Seconds I have heard in a quarter-century.".... Indeed, the response was so favorable among listeners and musicians alike that the ASO invited Kaplan to conduct the work again last April at Carnegie Hall. Since then, he has received firm offers to do the same in London and Tokyo next year.

[JH:] Lastly, from an editorial in *The Christian Science Monitor* (I wish I knew more about this):

We have always liked stories of secret millionaires who, when refused lodging in a hotel, walk out and buy the establishment lock, stock, and barrel. We were therefore particularly amused at reading the story of Jim Graham, an 18-year-old English lad.

Although he apparently has had little or no formal musical training, Jim has been strongly drawn to music. His first hope and ambition was to be a member of the local school choir. Alas, this ambition came to naught. When Jim stood up to sing it was found that he persistently flatted his notes, and so was gently bounced from the choir.

Not to be robbed of a musical career, Jim went to the local public library, drew out books on music, and taught himself to write music. The result? He has now amazed English music critics and experts by writing a full orchestral symphony. Furthermore, the symphony has been chosen by Britain's Royal College of Music for a premier performance in the very town where he failed to make the choir.

Violin Update

Since my last violin report in *GWS* 35 I have been playing more or less regularly, about 15–30 min. per day, while I am in Boston, though during a couple of weeks when I was traveling and fighting a bad cold, I played very little. On the whole, I keep improving slowly. Holding the violin and placing the left hand continue to become easier, the muscles are stronger, and being more confident I can relax more while playing, using only those muscles that need to be used. A couple of times I have been able to practice for almost an hour, and ready for more at the end. I have been doing quite a bit of work on the Minuet 2 in the first Suzuki book, which is a good deal more complicated than any of the pieces before it, and with a little practice I can play it through without many stops or mistakes. Elegant it isn't, but it is recognizably the tune, and the sound isn't too bad.

When I play, much of my work consists of standing in front of a mirror or reflecting window and training my right arm to draw a straight bow across the strings. For some reason this is somewhat harder to do with the low G string than with the higher A and E strings. Since my arm can't "tell" by itself when I am making a straight bow, I have to rely on what I can see in the mirror to give the needed feedback. But the arm seems to be learning. Even when off it is never very far off. Other than keeping the bow stroke straight, I try to make my right arm and hand in motion *v* as much as possible like what I see when I look at the wonderful violinists of the Boston Symphony. At the same time, I try to keep the sound as musical and even as possible. It seems to work. While on my travels, I met a young college student, a very talented player, who may well decide to become a professional musician. He felt that the position of my arms, hands, etc. were very good, and that I was off to a sound start.

On the basis of my brief acquaintance with the violin so far, and very much to the contrary of what I had expected, my impression is that a violin is not a harder instrument for an adult to begin than the cello. True, the playing position is at first a bit awkward, whereas that of the cello is somewhat more natural. But, at least for someone with a small and not very strong or flexible left hand, like mine, it has been a long hard struggle, by no means over yet, to train into that hand the kind of strength, flexibility, and quickness that cello playing demands. The violin, so far at least, seems less demanding, though of course I begin with a hand already somewhat trained by the cello, so the comparison may not be wholly fair. In any case, the violin is not an impenetrable mystery or a fierce enemy, but a very "user-friendly" instrument.

Visiting the Wallaces the other day, I played a little bit on Nancy's viola, and loved its sound. The lowest string on the violin, the G, makes a kind of croaky sound—the instrument is not big enough to vibrate very naturally at that frequency. But the low C string of the viola is wonderfully rich and resonant, a little like the voice of Tallulah Bankhead, for those old enough to remember her. The viola has two great advantages for adults: in the first place, in chamber and orchestra music, its parts tend to be simpler; in the second place, violists are everywhere scarce, so that even when not very good you can be sure in most places of finding a musical welcome. Switching from one "chin-fiddle" to another is not very hard; most musicians who play either of them at all well can usually play passably well on the other. So you can start with whichever you like best, and later switch if you choose to. I intend someday to be able to play them both. Right now, the cello comes first and the violin second; the viola will just have to wait.

(1/12/84) Since I wrote the above, three adults and two children (12 and 7), none of whom had ever played a violin before, have all taken a shot at playing my cheap violin. Watching and hearing them experiment with it made two things clear. The first is that, next to the piano itself, there is probably no "classical" instrument on which it is so easy for a complete beginner to pick out a tune. You don't have to "know how" to play a given note. If you draw the bow across a string and press that same string down with a finger of the other (left) hand, you will get a note. If it's too low, slide that finger toward you; if too high, slide it away from you, until you get the note you want. As in singing, you can find any note you want by trial and error. Even on as simple an instrument as the recorder you cannot do this; you have to know what holes to cover with your fingers, and what holes to leave open, in order to get the note you want. For this reason the bowed stringed instruments (violin, viola, cello) are great for experimenting, fooling around, trying to play simple tunes. All five of my friends did this. Younger children (and others as well) may be more interested in just seeing how many sounds, or simply how much sound, they can get from the instrument.

The other thing I learned is that, contrary to what the experts say, it is not hard to get a quite pleasant sound out of the violin. Indeed, for many years I have believed and said that the cello was perhaps a better instrument for beginners because you could make a fairly nice sound on it right away, whereas with the violin you had to play for years before you could learn *not* to make unpleasant sounds. Not so. You may not be able to play a tune on the violin, let alone a difficult tune, when you first pick it up. But you *can* make a very nice sound. The trick, which my friends all learned very quickly by themselves, without my saying anything, is not to push too hard on the string.

To sum up, though learning to play the violin well may take years of intense concentration and effort, learning to have fun with it, to make interesting and agreeable sounds and even a little simple music, takes almost no time at all. So, if you're at all tempted, do give it a try.—JH

Children & Stringed Instruments

From Kathryn Alexander (TX); see "Starting a Town Orchestra," GWS 35:

A comment about how my children are involved in string playing. I'm not doing anything too formal. However, as I was practicing for a lecture demonstration, Jennifer (4) was playing her 1/8 size violin like a cello. As I reached climactic points in my playing (Kodaly Unaccompanied) and was concentrating very intently, I became aware of a great deal of activity off to my left, where my daughter was madly playing tremolo to match the emotional intensity of the passage. As my musical involvement became more lyric, so did hers. I'm sure that is the way to get young children involved in the true substance of music.

Julie, my almost-18-month-old, is a very interesting musical person. Before she was born, when I would play cello, or bass, or accompany a student on the banjo, she would always move over to where the instrument was resting on my stomach. After she was born, she was always in the studio when I was teaching, and gradually, about the time she began walking, would come over to my cello and demand to play it. I hold her on my right leg and let her put her foot in the curve of the cello. She holds the bow and plays quite vigorously back and forth across the lower strings. She has a look of absolute rapture as she does this. She and Jennifer take turns when I play at home.

Julie is also very conscious of what she is imitating. When Jennifer plays her violin, Julie insists on holding it as a violin, even though I keep trying to set her up as a cellist, since it's easier to balance it for her. Julie also gets a marvelous full tone, pizzicato, plucking the cello, since she does it with such joy, rather than being intimidated by the experience.

Violins for Sale Here

Violins ($100—includes fine tuners, bow, chin-rest, case, rosin; price includes postage). We have found someone who can supply us with new violins (made in Italy) at a lower price than we have been able to find anywhere else, and we are offering them for sale here. I bought one of the 1/4-sized violins and have been using it here in the office, and it seems a very decent, sweet-toned instrument. If you can find a used violin, *in good condition,* for less than this, it may be a good bargain. But if it is not in good condition it may not be a bargain at all: if it has been badly repaired in the past, its tone may suffer, and in any case to get it well repaired may cost you almost as much as a new violin. On the whole, I would advise against buying a used violin unless you can find in your area someone with experience in teaching violin to children, or a good instrument repairer. If they say OK, OK. Otherwise, I think one of these new violins is your best bet.

Violins come in different sizes, to fit different sized children. The sizes we offer are 4/4 (full size), 3/4, 1/2, 1/4, 1/8, and 1/16 (all same price). Someone with experience in teaching children can tell you what size violin would be best for your child. If there is no such person near you, then we can advise you. We will need to know how old the child is and how tall, and it would be useful to know how fast the child is growing; if she or he is growing fast, and is, so to speak, on the borderline between two violin sizes, it will make sense to get the larger size, rather than have the child quickly outgrow the smaller instrument. On the other hand, if there is a younger child coming along to use the smaller instrument, you could start the older child with that and get a larger instrument when needed.

Just to give you a rough idea, two children we know, one 4'2" tall, the other a bit shorter, are about to start using 1/2-sized violins, which will be a bit large for them at first but which they should grow into in a few months. A child much under 4 feet would probably do better with a 1/4-sized violin. Get local advice if you can; if not, ask us.

We are also offering a specially made *shoulder pad* for $7.50. It fits between the shoulder and the bottom of the violin, has a plush-padded rest and rubber-protected "feet" where it touches the violin, and has two elastic loops to hold it in place instead of the usual one loop. It comes in 4/4, 3/4, 1/2, and 1/4 sizes.

You will need something with which to tune

the violin. There are several possibilities: (1) an A 440 tuning fork, easy to get at any music store; (2) a pitch-pipe—I would suggest getting a chromatic pitch-pipe rather than one of the little ones that only make four notes; (3) if you already have some kind of electronic keyboard instrument, it will probably have an accurate A; (4) some electronic metronomes, such as the Seiko we sell here (see *GWS* 33), sound a 440 cycle A; (5) if you have in your house a piano which you keep well-tuned, you can tune from that; indeed, whenever the violin plays along with the piano, it will have to use the piano A.

There are other things to know about tuning, using, and caring for a violin, but rather than print them here, we will make up an information sheet which we will send to violin buyers. If you have other questions, don't hesitate to write. Let me say once again that the violin is a very good beginner's instrument and that I have heard a number of people with no musical experience whatever get very pleasant sounds from it.—JH

New Book Available Here

Powers Of Ten—On The Relative Size of Things in the Universe, by Philip and Phylis Morrison ($27 + post). This is the most interesting, imaginative, far-reaching, mind-stretching, beautiful book on science that I have ever seen. It was inspired by a book I first saw many years ago, and would long since have added to our list, had it not (like so many good books) gone out of print. That book was *Cosmic View: The Universe In Forty Jumps*, written by a Dutch teacher named Kees Boeke. (If you ever run across it, in library or bookstore, borrow or buy it.)

Boeke's book was based on a most ingenious idea. He began with a picture of a Dutch girl, sitting in a big chair and holding in her lap a white cat, girl and chair filling up most of the picture. He then asked himself, "What would we see if we moved ten times further away?" This gave him his second picture of the girl, now much smaller, in the middle of a field. Around her he drew a little square, which represented the boundaries of the first picture, thus reminding us of what we had been able to see there.

In the third picture we see a part of the city in which she lives, with the entire field of the second picture in the middle of it, and the girl just a dot in the middle. In the next picture we see most of the city, and the girl and cat are much too small to be seen at all.

And so, page by page, we keep jumping back from the girl, and the surface of the earth, getting ten times further away with each jump. As we move away, jump by jump, we see the whole earth, later the inner planets, and then the entire solar system. Soon the planets disappear and we see only the sun, then later the galaxy of which our sun is a part. Twenty-five of those jumps bring us to the very edge of the visible universe, seeing everything human beings now have the power to see. If, as we may well do in the next century (if we don't destroy ourselves), we build large telescopes on the moon or in space, we will be able to make some more jumps, but I would guess probably not more than perhaps two or three.

Then Kees Boeke went back to the girl and this time showed us what we would see if each time we came ten times *closer*. Two jumps show us a close-up of her skin; a few more take us into the world of the smallest living creatures, such as cells; a few more take us out of the world of living matter (and of photography itself) and into the imagined world of molecules, atoms, electrons; and in 15 jumps we are in the center of the atomic nucleus, as far as our instruments and imaginations will take us. Perhaps in another generation or two we will be able to take another jump or two inward, but probably not more than that.

Thus 40 of these jumps have taken us from the smallest things we can "see" to the largest. It is a magnificent idea, and I always regret not having bought more copies of *Cosmic View* while it was still in print.

Now, fortunately, the idea has been brought back to life. The architect Charles Eames, best known for the bucket-shaped plastic chair he designed, and his wife Ray Eames, with the help of Philip and Phylis Morrison, the authors of this book, made a film called *Powers of Ten*, based on Kees Boeke's *Cosmic View*. From the photos taken for the film (which I would love to see), and with much additional material, the Morrisons have made this astonishing and beautiful book.

In many ways it is a great extension of and improvement on the original. For one thing, where Boeke gave us black and white drawings, *Powers of Ten* gives us photographs, the first of these of a young man asleep after a picnic, in a park in Chicago on the edge of Lake Michigan. These are in color where color is visible—and it is worth noting that nine jumps outward and six jumps inward from our original picture take us into a world where, in effect, there is no color, or none that we can see, which I guess is the same thing. For another, there is a great deal more text, introducing many ideas about size and scale that are not in the original book. And, along with the main illustrations, the Morrisons have given us many additional ones, which show us more about the large or small worlds shown in the main picture than that picture alone can tell us.

This book, more than almost any I can remember, gives us a glimpse of the unity, the excitement and adventure, what we could almost call the romance of the physical sciences. Hearing every day the many ways in which an often corrupted and distorted science has filled our world more and more full of dangerous and destructive materials and devices, I had begun myself, like many people, to think of science as a mysterious and sinister kind of magic, and to forget that at its best, properly understood and carried on in a responsible and ethical spirit, it can still be one of the most exciting and beautiful things that human beings do.

The powers-that-be keep saying they are worried because so few young people seem to be going into science, which will make us drop behind the Russians, Japanese, etc. This kind of talk only makes the problem worse—one of the reasons so many young people *don't* want to go into science is that it seems to them only in the business of making more and more destructive weapons, or keeping up with or getting ahead of somebody else. But if many more young people could see this book (preferably outside of school), quite a few of them might once again see science, above all the physical sciences, as a fascinating and worthy work they might someday want to do.

As fascinating as the illustrations may be, the accompanying text was not written for children, and would probably be beyond the powers of most children of ten. Children of twelve, already interested in science and good at reading, could probably read it by themselves and get a great deal out of it, though they might have questions about certain words or ideas. But many children quite a bit younger than that would probably enjoy very much having the book read to them by anyone who had a fair idea of what it was about. Most children I have known have always been very interested in the ideas of size, very large and very small things, motion through space—all of them central and easily graspable themes of this book.

The book is expensive, to be sure, but it is worth every penny of it. I know of nothing like it anywhere else. It is beautifully designed, laid out, and printed, a delight to the eye as well as the mind. If a conventional publisher, rather than the magazine *Scientific American*, were publishing it, it would probably cost much more. At this price, it is a bargain; no five less expensive books about science that you might buy would come close to conveying so much information in such a striking and unified way. It is a kind of guided tour, not just of the whole universe, but also of the structure and history of science itself.

Any of you who own computers, or plan to, will pay this much or more for many of your programs, and few if any programs could compare with it.

For some, however, as much as they might want it, it may still be too expensive. In that case, you might combine with other homeschooling parents to buy and own it jointly; or you might persuade your local library to buy it, perhaps showing them this review; or, if you are on good terms with your local schools, you might persuade their library, or their science department, to buy it; or a nearby college or university library might be persuaded to get it. But one way or another, all homeschooling families owe it to themselves to see this unique book.—JH

Other Books And Materials Here

Whitey's First Roundup ($1.75 + post) and *Whitey Takes A Trip* ($1.75 + post), by Glen Rounds. These delightful books are the first two of a series about a boy of perhaps 10 or 11 who for several years has lived with his Uncle Torval on a western cattle ranch, where as far as his strength and skill allow, he does the work of a regular ranch hand. The books are short, only about 90 pages, in fairly large print. But they are in no way little kids' books; though simply told, they are serious in tone, an accurate picture of the life of a boy living and working with grown men in the real world of dry country ranching. I would think they would be ideal for boys of 8 to 12 who are not very good readers but for reasons of pride are no longer willing to read books written for younger children.

In the first book Whitey goes with his uncle and many cowhands on a big, old-style round-up. The first day he does camp chores for the cook; the next day he rides out with the hands to round up cattle that have strayed through the countryside. At first this seems exciting, but ".... before the morning was more than half over Whitey had decided that the roundup was like most ranch business—more work than excitement." Still, most children who read this would give anything to be there with him.

In the second book Whitey rides off alone to take a team of horses over to a neighboring ranch, a day and a half's ride away. In this short trip he fixes a wheel of his wagon, has his horses get away during the night, finds them next day, finds a man who has been thrown from a buggy, sets his broken leg, and gets him into town—all these tasks taking skill, intelligence, patience, and courage. Whitey seems to me the kind of person that most kids would like to identify with—responsible, resourceful, competent, a solver of problems—a boy who does real and useful work, instead of just another suburban kid getting into trouble with his teachers or younger brothers or whatever.

These little books preach no sermons, but they say a lot about what it means to be a good human being. When Whitey finds the man who was thrown from his buggy, lying helpless and in pain in a ditch with a broken leg, with a very real chance of dying of thirst before anyone can find him, the man says to him, "Howdy, son. I'm pleased to see you, believe me." That's all. But many children who read those simple words may draw courage from them long after they think they have forgotten them.

Caperucita Roja ($2.35 + post). Little Red Riding Hood, told in Spanish by Hannah Hutchinson and illustrated with amusing cartoons by Ed Nofziger. The second in our series of children's stories told in Spanish (the first was *Los Tres Osos*—The Three Bears—reviewed in *GWS* 35). As in the first book, the story is told entirely in Spanish, but those who know the story, and even some who don't, will be able to figure out for themselves most of the Spanish words, and for any they can't, there is a vocabulary in front. By the way, the story has been pasteurized a little—the wolf doesn't eat either the grandmother or Little Red Riding Hood, and the hunter doesn't kill the wolf. It's a good exciting story anyway. We'll have more of these in the future.

The Broken Ear ($4.50 + post); *Flight 714* ($4.50 + post); *Cigars of the Pharoahs* ($4.50 + post); *The Castafiore Emerald* ($4.50 + post). Four more exciting books about Tintin, the famous boy journalist-detective, still in his brown knickers and white socks. As always, complicated and mysterious plots (they would make wonderful movies), plenty of suspense, action, and adventure, plenty of slapstick humor, pictures so well-drawn and interesting that in themselves they provide food for much thought, and more actual reading matter than you would find in many children's books. Everyone's favorite.

All-Of-A-Kind Family, by Sydney Taylor ($2 + post). This charming book, from which comes the illustration on the front page of our catalog, is about a family of five girls, 12, 10, 8, 6, and 4, and at the end of the book, a baby brother, growing up in New York City's lower East side around the turn of the century. The girls are called the all-of-a-kind family because their clothes all look very much alike, being the cheapest and longest wearing that their mother can buy or make. The picture we get of these lively and happy children and their loving parents and many relatives would make this book fun to read no matter where the story was set, but I particularly like it for three reasons. In the first place, the story takes place in a city, and reminds us that, like country life, city life can have its own satisfactions and pleasures. In the second place, the family, and all the people in the story, are poor, living in what we would call a slum; yet many of these poor and very hard-working people had much dignity, joy, and genuine culture in their lives. In the third place, the family is Jewish; not only did the book tell me many things I did not know about Jewish religion and customs, but it shows how interesting, exciting, and reassuring it is for children to grow up in a culture so full of meaningful ritual and tradition, and to do things that people have done for thousands of years before them. A lovely story; I look forward eagerly to reading the next books in the series.

Alphabet Art—Thirteen ABCs From Around The World, by Leonard Fisher ($9.85 + post). This book is itself a work of art, a set of drawings of thirteen alphabets in use today—Arabic, Cherokee, Chinese (a modern phonetic version), Cyrillic, Eskimo, Gaelic, German, Greek, Hebrew, Japanese (phonetic version), Sanskrit, Thai, and Tibetan. The letters of each of these alphabets are beautifully calligraphed in a handsome soft rust color with a touch of purple in it. With the letters Mr. Fisher has given us a short history of each of the alphabets, and also an illustration, in the same colored ink relieved with white, showing some aspect of the culture using the alphabet. All of this is beautifully laid out and printed, a lovely example of the bookmaker's craft.

Children of many ages, and adults too, will find many reasons for being fascinated with this book. Children just learning their own alphabet may be amazed to find out that there are many languages whose letters are completely different from ours. Some may want to trace or copy those letters; some may want to invent letters of their own. Slightly older children may also be fascinated with the history of these alphabets, may want to know if there are still other alphabets in the world (there are many), and how can they find out more about them. Both younger and older children may be struck, as I am, by the vigor and beauty of the shapes that human beings have invented to represent the sounds of their speech.

I can't think of any particularly useful reason to own this book—you certainly won't get quizzed about it on any test. But I am sure that it will bring much wonder and pleasure to most of those who read it.

Pentel Water Colors (box of 12 tubes) ($2.25, no extra postage charge). I've been wanting to add some water colors to our catalog for some time, and this is a very nice small set for beginners. Tubes (which are what working artists use) are much better than those flat cakes in metal boxes. Squeeze out a little paint as you need it, save the rest for next time. (My guess is that for very little children, adults had better do the squeezing—I can't think of anything more fun than to squeeze all the paint out in one big squoosh.) You will have to be a little careful about not losing the tops of the tubes, but if you do, you can probably seal the tubes just as well with some transparent or masking tape. The tubes fit neatly into a little molded plastic box, so they won't rattle around—at least, not if they're *in* the box. The tube of white paint is about half again as big as the others. We assume you can find paintbrushes; if you have trouble, let us know. Kids who get serious about painting will want bigger tubes than these, and perhaps more colors. But this is a good set to start with.

Individual Chalk Board ($1.80 + post). All the children I know like to write on what I still tend to call the "blackboard"—even though it's now usually green. Here's an easy way to do it at home. These chalkboards are 13 x 9 ½ inches, made of the same material as chalkboards in school, composition board covered with some kind of green material. Ideal for scribbling, drawing pictures, making big letters, leaving messages, doing scratch work for math, etc. Clean them off with a damp rag or paper towel. For most purposes, much better than even the cheapest scratch paper. We don't supply chalk, but if you have trouble finding any, let us know. These chalkboards are so useful and such fun to play with that you may want to order several. Wonderful, inexpensive and welcome presents for other people's children.

Think Good Thoughts About A Pussycat, by George Booth ($3.60 + post). A collection of cartoons, mostly from *The New Yorker*. I have just read through the book, for perhaps the tenth time, and as always I laughed my way all through it. I don't know who makes me laugh the most, his cave men, totally disorganized auto mechanics, grumpy old men, fierce dogs, or even fiercer old ladies. Choose your own favorites.

The Great Composers Calendar For 1984 ($5.35 + post). For each month, a portrait in color of a famous composer, often with very interesting biographical information. On each date, a little nugget of musical information. On each month, a riddle in the form of a short poem. The answer to each riddle provides a letter, and the twelve letters put together make the answer to the Grand Puzzle (which I have just this minute solved). For music lovers, a splendid calendar, one that will be worth keeping even when 1984 is over.

Suzuki Violin School, Book 2 ($4.30 + post); *Suzuki Cello School, Book 1* ($5.15 + post); *Suzuki Cello School, Record 1* ($11.65 + post). The first Suzuki cello book has most but not all of the tunes in the first Suzuki violin book (also available here, $4.75 + postage). They are, however, written in different keys to make fingering easier, so don't assume that your Suzuki violinist and Suzuki cellist will be able to play these songs in unison.

On the cello record, the player is Ronald Leonard, Principal Cellist of the Los Angeles Philharmonic, so you and your children will hear cello playing at its best. The record is in split-stereo, with the cello on one channel and the accompanying piano on the other. If your stereo amplifier has a balance control, as most do, you can use it to hear cello alone, or piano alone, or both together. Very small, Walkman-type machines will usually not have this control.

The cello book has some nice pictures of children playing the cello. Some of the photos show the children's instruments with little pieces of tape on the fingerboard in what is called "first position," to "show" the children where to put their fingers. This is standard Suzuki practice, and if your children study with a Suzuki group they will have to do it. But as I have said before, it makes no sense to me whatever, and seems to me to violate the essential principal of Suzuki, which is that the *ear* (not the eye) guides the hand. It's not worth arguing with the Suzuki people about, but I would get the markers off as soon as you can; if they helped good players to play better, you would see good players using them.

Swami And Friends, by R. K. Narayan ($3.65 + post). This book is the first of a series of novels about life in the small Indian town of Malgudi, written in the 1930s by the man whom many feel is the finest Indian writer in English. It is about a year in the life of a boy, Swaminathan, whose age is never given but who I would guess was about nine or ten, and is one of the most perceptive, touching, and funniest books about children ever written. It is in some ways very like *Tom Sawyer*, but with important exceptions. Like Tom, Swami lives mostly in a world of dreams, wild threats and boasts, grandiose schemes, and like Tom, he sees the outside world, of parents, home, and above all school, mostly as a nuisance that interferes with his fantasy life and keeps causing him trouble. The difference between Tom and Swami, though, is that, though occasionally set back by the real world, Tom usually manages to get the best of it, and to find ways to turn some of his grand projects into reality. Not Swami. If Tom is sooner or later always a winner, poor Swami is always a loser. He never comes out on top. But he never stops struggling, either, and this tale of his struggles is side-splitting.

If anything, Narayan sees even more deeply into the inner life of young boys than Twain. Here is Swami, watching a fight between two friends:

> The fighters, rolling and rolling, were everywhere in the field. The headmaster and the peon easily picked them apart, much to the astonishment of Swaminathan, who had thought till then that the strength that Somu or Mani possessed was not possessed by anyone else in the world.

There are a hundred bits I would like to quote: Swami and his baby brother; Swami, under the watchful eye of his father, cleaning the dust off the school books that he was supposed to be reading during summer vacation; Swami getting ready to study for exams by making an elaborate list of needed supplies; Swami trying by magic to turn copper coins into gold ones so that he can buy a hoop (actually a bicycle wheel without a tire); Swami taking joyous part in a riot outside the school; Swami and friends making elaborate plans for a cricket match (this episode reminds me of the famous joke that if you want to find true Englishmen, go to New Delhi). But I will limit myself to two. Here are boys in school, the day after the riot, trying to account for why they were not in school on that day:

> The fifth said that his grandmother died suddenly just as he was starting for the school. The headmaster asked him if he could bring a letter from his father. No. He had no father. Then, who was his guardian. His grandmother. But the grandmother was dead, was she not? No. It was another grandmother. The headmaster asked how many grandmothers a person could have. No answer. Could he bring a letter from his neighbors? No, he could not. None of his neighbors could read or write, because he lived in one of the more illiterate parts of Ellaman Street. Then the headmaster offered to send a teacher to this illiterate locality to ascertain from the boy's neighbors if the death of the grandmother was a fact. A pause, some perspiration and then the answer that the neighbors could not possibly know anything about it, since the grandmother died in the village.

I have been laughing all the way through this as I typed it. And here is poor Swami being tutored in arithmetic by his father:

> Father held the arithmetic book open and dictated: "Rama has ten mangoes with which he wants to earn fifteen annas. Krishna wants only four mangoes. How much will Krishna have to pay?"
>
> Swaminathan gazed and gazed at this sum, and every time he read it, it seemed to acquire a new meaning. He had the feeling of having stepped into a fearful maze. His mouth began to water at the thought of mangoes. He wondered what made Rama fix fifteen annas for ten mangoes. What kind of a man was Rama? [Some time later] "Have you done the sum?" Father asked, looking over the newspaper he was reading.
>
> "Father, will you tell me if the mangoes were ripe?"
>
> Father regarded him for a while and smothering a smile remarked, "Do the sum first. I will tell you whether the fruits were ripe, afterwards."
>
> Swaminathan felt utterly helpless. If only Father would tell him whether Rama was trying to sell ripe fruits or unripe ones! Of what avail would it be to tell him afterwards? He felt strongly that the answer to this question contained the key to the whole problem. It would be scandalous to expect fifteen annas for ten unripe mangoes. But even if he did, it wouldn't be unlike Rama, whom Swaminathan was steadily beginning to hate and invest with the darkest qualities.

And so on, for an agonized half-hour. What a wonderful glimpse into the baffled mind of someone, probably typical of many people, who keeps trying to breathe a little life into the abstract corpse-world of mathematics.

Narayan's style is so simple that it seems hardly a style at all. With Mark Twain, you are aware of the virtuoso writer at work, choosing his words, constructing and polishing his elaborate sentences. When a joke is coming, Twain lets you know—and it is none the less funny for all that. Not so Narayan, of whose presence as writer and storyteller we are hardly aware. He simply shows us this absurd and utterly true-to-life little boy, in his desperate and comic struggle with an unyielding world; the story itself, not his way of telling it, is what makes us laugh. And laugh I am sure you will.—JH

Editors—John Holt & Donna Richoux
Managing Editor—Pat Farenga
Subscriptions & Books—Mary Gray & Steve Rupprecht
Office Assistant—Mary Van Doren

Growing Without Schooling 38

March 1984

In recent weeks, Virginia and Georgia have passed education laws that are largely favorable for homeschooling. You'll find the exact wording of these laws, plus John Holt's thoughts on them, later in this issue.

We were sorry to learn that Peter Perchemlides, the Amherst, MA homeschooler, died in January after a long illness. He was 47. The court case that he initiated in 1978 resulted in statewide standards for considering homeschooling requests, and dozens of Mass. families have benefited from them. We have also seen the influence of the *Perchemlides* decision in homeschooling policies of other states.

A related piece of news—John saw in the *Boston Globe* that John Greaney, the judge who wrote the *Perchemlides* decision, is the newly-appointed chief justice of the state Appellate Division. Good to know, if a Mass. court case were ever to get that far!

In early February, Virginia homeschoolers arranged to fly John to Richmond to testify on behalf of the homeschooling bill. Since then, John has done radio interviews in Rochester, Saskatoon, and Seattle, and is about to leave for a week's trip to Washington State and Montana. A writer for *Time* magazine interviewed him recently and said a homeschooling story should appear soon.

An article by John called "Why Teachers Fail" appears in the April '84 issue of *Progressive*. We'll have reprints available here for 10¢ (SASE required if you are not ordering other materials from us).

The January issue of *The Iconoclast*, published by Roy Masters' *Foundation For Human Understanding*, reprinted an excerpt from John's book *The Underachieving School*, and it also has a classified ad from Pamela Hackett (213-936-9666) and Cathy Levesque saying, "We are starting a Letter-Writing Association to simultaneously direct our letters to Public Officials to let them know we want Home Education in California."

Cher Bateman (NV) says she wrote to David Colfax, the father of Grant ("Homeschooler at Harvard," *GWS* 35). In his reply, he said, "We are just finishing a book on homeschooling."

The latest issue of *Homesteaders News* announces their 7th Annual *Homesteaders Good Life Get-Together*, at Naples, NY, July 19–21. John has done homeschooling workshops at two of these; he says he enjoyed the Get-Togethers very much and would be at this one if he were not going to be lecturing on the West Coast. So Norm Lee invited me instead, and it looks as if I can be there. The Get-together offers more than 30 workshops in self-reliant living, as well as dancing, music, camping, etc. For more information, write to PO Box 517-1, Naples NY 14512.

Readers who are Catholic might want to send for the "Charter of the Rights of the Family," presented by the Holy See on Oct. 22, 1983. Copies are available from the Catholic League for Religious and Civil Rights, 1100 W Wells St, Milwaukee WI 53233. It has some very strong and supportive language for homeschooling, such as "Parents have the right to educate their children in conformity with their moral and religious convictions. . . . The rights of parents are violated when a compulsory system of education is imposed by the state from which all religious formation is excluded. The primary right of parents to educate their children must be upheld in all forms of collaboration between parents, teachers, and school authorities. . . ."

In *GWS* 31, we printed Rena Caudle's request that readers send cards and stickers to her son Jeremy (1417 Fir St, Everett WA 98201), who had a brain tumor. She writes that Jeremy has filled two scrapbooks with letters, cards, photos, stamps, and drawings, and that he treasures it. The latest body scan showed no tumors at present, "so we can relax again for another few months."

There was an error in last issue's story about Amy Hovenden, the 14-year-old homeschooler who entered Brigham Young University. She was formerly one of James Salisbury's piano students, not a student of his *John Holt Learning Center*.

We have missed the help of Mary Gray in our book and subscription department for a number of weeks now—she came down with mononucleosis. If all goes well, she'll be back in April. Meanwhile, I sent a plea for help to local subscribers, and have gotten eight or nine new volunteers, which is exciting.—Donna Richoux

John Holt's Coming Schedule

Apr. 15, 1984: Kentucky Home Schoolers Association. Contact Libby Morley, 606-273-7816.

Apr. 16: U. of Kentucky. Contact Gail Duckworth, 606-257-3294.

Apr. 18: Conference on Homeschooling, U.S. Dept. of Education, Washington D.C. Contact Dr. Charles J. O'Malley, 202-472-9610.

Apr. 19: John Holt's Music Workshop (3rd Thurs. each month—call 437-1550 to confirm).

Apr. 26–28: Nova Scotia Reading Association, Mt. St. Vincent Univ., Halifax. Contact Jane Baskwill, 902-584-3692.

May 6: E. Stroudsburg U., E. Stroudsburg PA. 2 p.m.. Contact Ann Cameron, 717-421-5022.

May 10: Holt Associates Open House (2nd Thurs. of each month).

June 22 (tentative): Southeastern Regional Conference of Alternative Educators, Arthur Morgan School, Burnsville NC 28714. Contact Kate Brown, 704-675-4262.

July 18 (tentative): College of Ed., Washington State U., Pullman WA. Contact Denis Conners, 509-335-5023.

Anyone who wants to coordinate other meetings or lectures around these times, contact Patrick Farenga.

11-Year-Old Columnist

The Washington Post, *11/22/83:*

> Rawson Stoval (11) likes video games. He likes them so much that when he was nine he picked, shelled, halved, and sold close to $200 worth of pecans from his parents' back yard in Abilene, Texas, to pay for his first Atari video computer system.
>
> But after a few months, the system lost its thrill. Stovall decided he wanted to design his own games, and began his column, "The Vid Kid," to raise enough money for an advanced home computer. The column, which reviews new games and offers technical advice, is syndicated and now runs in 11 papers.

The Stovall family bought an Atari 800 in February, but Rawson hasn't had time to design any games yet; he's too busy testing new games for his column, and working on his book, which Doubleday will release next spring.

Long-Time Homeschooler

From Erika Du Bois (NS):

Yes, we educated our five children almost entirely at home, and it has been a tremendous success. This does not mean that all of them have gone into university, though some have and another is heading that way now after some years of self-support in the big wide world. I think it's a great mistake to use university entrance as the sole measure of educational success.

Yesterday I phoned my lawyer and made an appointment to come in and study the Nova Scotia Education Act with a view to getting the very few home-teaching parents here together into a supportive structure for others. We're heading for a period of change and (I think) further degradation of our public schools here, and I think we'll really have something to contribute to our community, and that we should stop hiding ourselves in the woods! The reason I can do this is that my youngest decided to try out 9th grade in the local school, and my 19-year-old is doing a year of work here on the farm along with setting up a small custom shingle cutting business.

The difficult years for me seem to be the high school ones and I wonder if that is because the usual general curriculum does not suit a homeschooler who has been able to develop some very serious, in-depth interests, and therefore glossing over the top is no longer appropriate or meaningful—people have to do real things.

My third is about to approach the University of Arizona for entrance—I'll let you know. He has none of the usual pieces of paper at all.

An excellent correspondence program comes from: *Parents Union School*, Murray House, Vandon St, London S.W.1, England. [DR: This is the old address of the *World Wide Educational Service*, which moved recently to Strode House, 44/50 Osnaburgh St, London NW1 3NN.] I used this service and thought the materials were great, but that was some years ago. Their philosophy of education, their principles make sense!

Carmelita Hinton once said to me: *If I were going back into teaching again, I would never teach six-year-olds to read.* Her idea, as elaborated later, was that 6-year-olds should be doing, making, touching and living, forming real relationships, gathering *raw material*, and not living life through a book....

Here's my last word to parents: No matter how much better you *think* you could or should be doing, or how much of a hash you make (*really*) from time to time, it's much better than school. This is what I know for sure from Alex's few months in Grade 9 where no one gives much of a damn and 1½ hours of work take a 7-hour day to accomplish—plus homework. He is pleasing his teachers and getting good marks, whatever that signifies. His background was simple in the extreme: lots of stories (*reading aloud*), history for fun and interest, some basic math over the worst cold snaps of two winters, about eight months of schoolroom-type working in all. An old letter reminded me that he did not read until age 10½, though he'd gone over a few "Tom & Betty" books in disgust at 5 years or so. At about the same age (10½), writing was easy, too.

We are extremely disappointed with the public school curriculum and inefficiency—all that time for nothing—and are wondering again about alternatives. He wants time to study for his ham radio operator's license, and it's hard to do that along with the fatigues of the school day.

Famous Unschoolers

The Marschners (TX) sent this quote from A Treasury of the Great Children's Book Illustrators:

Beatrix Potter's own schoolroom was confined to the nursery where she worked alone with a governess, a course of education she did not find unfavorable in retrospect. "Thank goodness, my education was neglected," she wrote many years later. "I was never sent to school.... The reason I am glad I did not go to school—it would have rubbed off some of the originality (if I had not died of shyness or been killed with over-pressure). I fancy I could have been taught anything if I had been caught young; but it was in the days when parents kept governesses, and only boys went to school in most families."

These solitary hours were consumed by three interests: her writing, her art, and a study of the flora and fauna surrounding her. When she was thirteen years old, she began to make almost daily entries into a journal.

The Marschners also sent these reminiscences about General George Patton by his daughter:

His aunt Nannie Wilson, gentle as the dove and stubborn as the mule, decided out of hand that Georgie, whom she worshipped, was too delicate to go to school, so she kept him home and read aloud to him. For this reason he didn't learn to read or write until he was 12 years old.... Aunt Nannie was a tremendous influence on George's life. She pressed the study of the Bible on him, as a library of history and religion. He knew a great deal of it by heart, and one of his favorite quotes was, "As a man thinketh, so is he." Aunt Nannie read aloud all of the *Iliad*, the *Odyssey*, Pliny, Plutarch's Lives, all the books on Napoleon, and Xenophon, and the March of the Ten Thousand, all about Alexander the Great, Shakespeare, Ben Jonson, Marlowe, Piers Plowman, Pilgrim's Progress—all the books we all should read and never have time to..... All his life he could come up with a quotation for anything and everything. History was his playmate and his mentor and probably the greatest influence in his life..... His sister, my Aunt Anita, told us that one time he wanted to play Achilles, dragging the body of Hector around the walls of Troy behind his pony Peachblossom, and the only way she avoided being Hector was by finding a huge dead rat to take her place. He brought himself up in the company of heroes, and he wanted to be among them. . . . .

From London Times' *wire service:*

> Hephzibah Menuhin Hauser, pianist sister of violinist Yehudi Menuhin and, like her brother, internationally acclaimed while she was still a child, died here Thursday. . . . .
>
> She devoted herself mainly to chamber music and played hundreds of sonata recitals around the world with her more famous brother.
>
> Their first recordings in 1932, when she was 12 and Yehudi 16, won the national Prix du Disque in France.
>
> Like Yehudi, she had scant early formal schooling. Her brother once recalled she spent only five days at one San Francisco school, where she left after being classed as educationally backward.
>
> Her parents took her home and taught her to read and write within a year. She was never sent to school again.

From a speech by Georgia State Senator John Foster, 2/6/84:

> A review of educational history opened my eyes to the large number of our past and present leaders who were taught at home. Some of the names are: Thomas Jefferson. . . . Abraham Lincoln. . . . Thomas Alva Edison. . . . Albert Einstein. . . . General Douglas MacArthur. . . . all of the Roosevelts. [A name] from the present that surprised me [is] Supreme Court Justice Sandra Day O'Connor.

[DR:] this last one surprised us, too. Could someone look this up and send us more information? When Justice O'Connor joined the bench a few years ago, there must have been biographical articles about her in the newsmagazines.

News From Alabama

From Lee Gonet of Alabama Citizens for Home Education, *Rt 3 Box 360D, Montgomery AL 36110 (phone 205-265-1221):*

> We have always wanted to teach our children at home, even before they were born! We recently moved to Alabama, where I found out immediately that the law was very unfavorable. . . . I was discouraged, but set about forming a group for support and info swapping.
>
> Then one of our members received a newspaper clipping from her mother in Huntsville about a homeschooling family being taken to court (Sharon & Ed Pangelinan, 1012 Bedford Dr. SW, Decatur AL). So I called Sharon to offer our support and let her know that there were others in the state.
>
> It turns out many people have called the Pangelinans for the same reasons. As far as Sharon and I can figure there is a group of about 30 families in Huntsville, 25 in Birmingham, ours in Montgomery, and groups starting in Florence, Lake Guntersville, and West Blocton. . . . Sharon is going to send me a list of everyone who has contacted her and I in turn will send out information and a questionnaire, and start a statewide newsletter. Sharon also gave me the name of a sympathetic journalist at the Montgomery newspaper who would like to do a story, and so we should have even more people contacting us.
>
> How are people homeschooling in this state? For the most part, they are *hiding*. A few have become "satellite schools," but many are simply afraid to take their children out of school. One family in our group was about to be arrested and so moved out of the county to avoid going to jail, and Sharon has been told her children could be taken away from her. Sharon and Ed considered moving or becoming a satellite school, but felt someone had to challenge our state laws, and through their courageous efforts, many homeschoolers are coming out of hiding.

Laws Proposed—Texas, Kansas

The Dallas Morning News, *3/2/84:*

> A subcommittee of H. Ross Perot's education panel recommended Thursday that parents be allowed to educate their children at home through the 6th grade under the supervision of local schools.
>
> The subcommittee chairman, state Sen. Carl Parker, said he and the other panel members don't believe in educating children at home. But Parker said the practice should be legitimized because many parents now teach their children at home in violation of state law.
>
> A number of such parents appeared before the Perot committee during a recent meeting in Dallas.... "It's going on now, and we should regulate it," Parker said. "They (the parents) are afraid to let the kids go out and play during break because the truant officer might catch them."
>
> Under the homeschooling proposal, parents wanting to teach their children at home would be required to register them at the public school they normally would attend so they could take standardized achievement tests.
>
> The parent or guardian designated as the instructor also would have to pass the Texas Assessment of Basic Skills test given to all 9th grade students.
>
> Home-taught students would be required to attend regular classes if they scored below average on achievement tests. The parent or guardian instructor also would have to keep attendance records and file a study plan with the school district. The state would reimburse the schools for their cost in complying with the proposed law.

[DR:] Jean Kasten (KS) sent this clipping from the *Wichita Eagle-Beacon*, 2/19/84, and said that Marti and Mark Ahlman (11 Anderson Ct, Newton KS 67114) are forming a committee to work on legislation. From the story:

> Children being taught at home by their parents would be required to pass competency tests under a bill pending in the Kansas Legislature.
>
> Sen. Paul Hess, R-Wichita, has introduced legislation to require children taught at home to pass standardized examinations in math and reading. The measure would, for the first time, award clear-cut legal status to the practice of teaching children at home.
>
> More than 100 families across Kansas have rejected public and established schools, and teach their children at home.
>
> Under Hess's bill, parents who teach their children at home would be legally required to register as non-accredited private schools. Their children would have to demonstrate "the attainment of minimum competency objectives in basic skills" by passing the same Kansas minimum competency test now administered to all public school students five times during their school years — in grades 2, 4, 6, 8, and 11..... Those who failed would be required to transfer to a public or an established private school. The State Board of Education would decide how the test would be given and what the passing grades would be.
>
> Harold Blackburn, Kansas commissioner of education, said the state board wants the Legislature to postpone consideration of the bill for a year. "The ramifications of home study are quite substantial," Blackburn said. "I can't see that there would be an opportunity to gather all the information needed for the board to make a policy decision (this session)."
>
> Donna Penaire.... who is president of the *Teaching Parents Association*, a group of about 80 local families who teach their children at home.... said she wouldn't object to the testing, because she plans to test her son anyway. But she said she thought the bill would create a

double standard. Public school students aren't penalized if they perform poorly on the test, she said, "but they'll kick them out of home school if they fail the test."

Sally Buxton, a registered Wichita parent who teaches her children at home, said she does not object to tests as long as the children are not expected to meet standards different from those applied to public and private school students.

"Uproar" In Missouri

From the Kansas City, Mo. Star, *1/22/84:*

Trouble surfaced in eastern Missouri last fall. Social workers investigating reports of children not attending school in St. Charles County cracked down, demanding to see home school curriculums, referring cases to juvenile courts.

Homeschoolers felt they were being harassed. In response to their complaints, Sen. Fred Dyer, a St. Charles Republican, arranged a meeting in December with officials of the Division of Family Services, the Department of Education, and local juvenile courts.

What resulted was official acknowledgment that the state had not handled home school cases consistently.

"Quite frankly I wasn't aware until we got into the situation that we did not have refined guidelines," said Joseph O'Hara, director of the Division of Family Services.

Statewide guidelines were drawn up and distributed this month: All social workers who find parents educating their children at home must turn that information over immediately to the juvenile court, which will then decide if the home school program is adequate.

Although the guidelines simply put into force a regulatory process implicit in the statutes, homeschoolers are in an uproar because, with some isolated exceptions, they have been allowed to exist without oversight until now.

A sympathetic legislator, Rep. William McKenna, a Democrat from Jefferson County, is sponsoring a bill that would remove home schools entirely from the purview of Family Services by removing the crime of "educational neglect" from child abuse and neglect statutes.

But critics on the other side say the Family Services guidelines aren't tough enough. They provide homeschoolers with an easy escape clause: Any parent who can prove he is operating an incorporated day school will be left alone.

All it takes to become an incorporated day school is a few pages of paperwork and a $10 filing fee, state officials said. There are no other requirements.

Juvenile courts are equally ill prepared to determine the merits of home schools. Present Missouri law is vague about what constitutes an acceptable alternate education. . . . .Judge Parrish [who serves on the Missouri Children's Services Commission], like many others in the legal and educational arena, would like to see more regulation of home schools. Among their suggestions: minimum course standards; periodic competency testing of the students; a college education for the parent-teacher; and prior approval of curriculum by local school superintendents.

But these criteria are not required of private schools, homeschoolers say. Why should they be singled out?

Although homeschoolers see their freedom threatened by the biases of individual juvenile court judges, Missouri still clearly is a haven for homeschoolers compared with most other states.

One bill about to be introduced by a Missouri legislator would. . . . require parents to notify the superintendent of the local school district that they plan to educate their children at home. In return, the public schools would provide school library access, textbooks, and testing and counseling services to parents requesting them for their children.

The bill, sponsored by Rep. Sandra Reeves, a Kansas City Democrat, also would place the burden upon the parents to prove, if challenged, that their school provides "regular, daily instruction designed to prepare the child to become a competent, knowledgeable citizen of the community and state." Mrs. Reeves doesn't think much of the measure's chances this session.

Legislative and State News

Connecticut: Laura Pritchard of the *Connecticut Homeschoolers Association* writes, "In my last letter, I mentioned numerous items being considered by our Commissioner Tirozzi. Several of those have been put in bill form: Bill 5485—compulsory school entrance age lowered to 5. Bill 5487—increasing the kindergarten school day to a full four hours. Bill 5217—statewide mastery testing at the 6th and 8th grade level.... A study is in progress considering lowering school entrance age down to 4. "We have attended board of education meetings, as well as public hearings (there have been 3 to date, with several more planned....) We developed a flyer and had 4,000 copies printed. These were circulated to all the homeschoolers, as well as concerned parents from other walks of life. We have tried to stress the importance of writing letters and spreading the word. We have found that there has been very little media coverage and many people were not aware of this proposal.

"The Education Committee must finish its business by the third week in March.... We have developed a network of homeschoolers willing to spread news throughout their district...."

Illinois: Mary Friedl (IL) sent us copies of several papers on homeschooling that have circulated among Regional Superintendents in Illinois, including a memo by Paul Studnucki, Asst. Supt. of the Livingston County Schools, and a draft entitled "Suggested Procedures for Determining Program Equivalency and Compliance with Compulsory Attendance Requirements Through Parent-Taught Home Instruction."

This draft says, "Parents are expected to substantiate that the child's reasonable academic and social needs are being appropriately considered and addressed." In particular, the parents must establish they will teach the same branches of learning taught in the public school, that the length of instruction time will be basically equivalent, that they are competent instructors, and finally, that the child will be given standardized achievement tests every year, either with the public school students or independently. The draft says, "In addition to the foregoing options, certain situations may require an evaluation of progress that is less formal than standardized testing, such as an oral examination, review of projects, etc."

We have never heard that standardized testing is required by law in Illinois, and we advise readers in that state to voice their opinions on this draft before it becomes final. There is no name or address anywhere on the draft so we're not sure where your letters will do the most good, but you could try the State Department of Education, the Illinois Association of Regional Superintendents of Schools, and your own Regional Superintendent. If you cannot get a copy of this draft elsewhere, send me a SASE.

Kentucky: Margaret Wheeler reported in Issue #2 of the *Kentucky Home Schoolers Exchange* that Senate Bill 22 would require that achievement tests be given to all private school students in grades 3, 5, 7 and 10. She says a second piece of legislation, not yet formulated, would enable the state to take "remedial actions" if private school students failed to show achievement as determined by the State Board of Ed.

She writes, "Leading the opposition is Senate Minority Leader Gene Huff. (If you feel so inclined, call him a message of support on the toll-free hotline, 1-800-372-2985).... There have been *no reported problems* with the education afforded by our private, parochial, and church schools, so why should the state interfere? Even Senator Gibson, the bill's sponsor, said, 'I agree that you do a better job in your schools.'. . . . The public school liaison with private schools in Jefferson Co. was opposed to this bill. He testified that 'parents working together to provide an education for their children unencumbered by state regulations, can do wonders. . . . If it ain't broke, stop tryin' to fix it!'"

Margaret says there is another toll-free number, 1-800-372-2993, to inquire as to the status of a bill.

Maine: Last fall, Maria Holt (ME) wrote, "Carolyn Sturtevant, who is charge of curriculum for Maine's Dept. of Education and Cultural Services, suggested a bill for the legislature that would put the responsibility for home education squarely on the shoulders of the parents. We will be working on this, though the necessity seems strange to me. . . ."

Maryland: From the *Maryland Home Education Association* newsletter, 2/84: "A capacity-plus crowd of homeschooling supporters showed up at the second annual State Board hearings on Jan. 25, 1984. . . . No less than 72 homeschoolers testified in opposition to the proposed by-law. Unlike last year's hearing, the tone this time was more serious—and militant. . . . The board of education decided to make some kind of decision in the near future."

Minnesota: From the newsletter of the *Minnesota Home Schoolers Network*: "During the middle of March there will be a meeting at the state capital. Legislators want to meet with homeschool families in order to find out what we want for an education bill. This meeting is being set up by Bill Parker. The Parker family was forced to move from Alexandria because they were educating their daughter at home. . . . If you cannot make the meeting, write to: Don Anderson, 144 State Office Blvd, St. Paul MN 55155 or call him at 296-6455. It would be a good idea for homeschool families to write to their own representatives. . . . Also drop a note to Ruth Randall, Commissioner of Education. She has been holding meetings all over the state in order to get input from people regarding education. . . ."

Nevada: Cher Bateman (NV) writes the Department of Education has written Draft 5 of the Proposed Regulations. They are calling for (1) a NV certified teacher, or (2) a NV cert. teacher acting in a consulting capacity a certain number of hours per week, or (3) enrollment in a correspondence school. They are not specifying a NV approved correspondence school. The consultory teacher provision would be waived after two years of a successful program. I believe other children in the family would be automatically exempt from these provisions after having the first child pass the tests for two years. . . ."

New Hampshire: Barb Parshley tells us that nearly all of the proposed changes to the NH Home Education Regulations have passed, except the one we thought was most controversial. Instead of requiring that children must stay in school until the family's application is approved, a procedure that takes 60 days or more, the regulations now say the local superintendent may allow the child to be at home until a decision is made.

New York: Katharine Houk (NY) writes, "I'm enclosing a copy of the guidelines for home instruction that the NY State Ed. Dept. came out with in January, in case you haven't seen them. My husband [who works there] says they've been getting an increasing number of calls about homeschooling in his office." The guidelines say that NY permits parents to instruct their children at home if they get prior approval from the public school superintendent. (Note: "prior approval" is *not* in the actual NY statute.) Parents are told to provide lists of subjects to be taught and the curriculum materials to be used, a daily schedule and calendar for the year, a description of their qualifications, attendance reporting procedures, and a plan for evaluation. Standardized testing is strongly recommended but not required. A "Question/Answer" page says that local school officials may, at their discretion, accept credits earned through a home instruction program towards a diploma, and, if they wish, allow the child to use the library and other school facilities.

Washington: Apparently there was quite a battle in Washington State to get favorable homeschooling legislation passed. According to Wendy Wartes of *Teaching Parents Association* (206-483-6642), after a homeschooling bill was killed last year, the chairman of the Education Committee agreed to appoint an interim committee to study the problems and write another bill. The result was this year's Senate Bill 4364 (not 3033 as I said in *GWS* 37), which would allow homeschooling but under considerable regulation. Some homeschoolers began calling for its defeat and offered another bill, House Bill 1337, which would allow homeschooling with practically no regulation. As a result, S.B. 4364 was modified to say that parents who were high school graduates or had a G.E.D. would be considered "qualified to teach," and that home education may be less structured than that provided in a classroom. But many homeschoolers still actively opposed the bill, and time ran out before it could come to a vote. H.B. 1337 also died in committee.

Wendy says, "I really think the Legislature wants to pass a homeschooling bill but is in a quandary of how to do it. If we continue to fight ourselves I get the feeling they will say to heck with it. At least that's what the sponsor of 4364 is feeling. He doesn't even wish to discuss homeschooling now.... And he is Chairman of the Senate Ed. Committee." Wendy is on the interim committee to prepare a new bill, and hopes to pull together a broader base of support before next January's session (which will be longer—120 days, instead of 60 days).

Wisconsin: As we go to press, the Wisconsin legislature is struggling to pass an education bill before the session ends April 6. The version passed by the Assembly says that the state superintendent shall approve a private home-based educational program if it provides (1) at least 875 hours of instruction each school year, and (2) a "sequentially progressive curriculum of fundamental instruction in the subject areas of reading, language arts, mathematics, social studies, science, and health." The bill specifically says a private school cannot be a private home-based educational program. However, Susan Brooks (715-237-2402) says there have been a flurry of amendments proposed. Check the back page of this issue for any last minute news.—DR

Duro Case: North Carolina

[DR:] We learned from U.S. News and World Report, *2/6/84, that on Jan. 23 the U.S. Supreme Court refused to hear the case of* Duro v. District Attorney, 2nd Judicial District home *of North Carolina. I called and then visited the law library of the U. S. Court of Appeals in Boston to get a copy of the lower court ruling, which was decided 7/14/83 and published in the* Federal Reporter, 2nd Series, *Vol. 712, p. 96-100.*

In that decision, as we reported in GWS *37, the U.S. Court of Appeals (4th Circuit) ruled against homeschoolers Peter and Carol Duro, reversing an earlier U.S. District Court ruling (GWS 29). Here are some excerpts from the decision, written by Judge K. K. Hall:*

> Duro and his wife are Pentecostalists. This religion does not require that children be taught at home; in fact, the majority of children whose parents are members of the Pentecostal Church, which the Duros attend, are enrolled in a public school. Notwithstanding this, Duro refuses to enroll his children in a public school or the only available nonpublic school....
>
> According to Duro, exposing his children to others who do not share his religious beliefs would corrupt them ... However ... he admits that when they reach 18 years of age, he expects them to "go out and work ... in the world."
>
> Although Mrs. Duro has assumed the responsibility for teaching the children, she does not possess a teaching certificate and has never been trained as a teacher. She implements a "self-teaching" program, the Alpha Omega Christian Curriculum.The district court relied heavily upon *Wisconsin v. Yoder*, 406 U.S. 205, 92 S. Ct. 1526, 32 L.Ed.2d 15 (1972), in holding that North Carolina's compulsory school attendance law was unconstitutional, as it applied to

Duro. In *Yoder*, the Court held that there are two issues which must be considered in cases such as this: (1) whether a sincere religious belief exists, and (2) whether the state's interest in compulsory education is of sufficient magnitude to override the interest claimed by the parents under the Free Exercise Clause of the First Amendment. The Court recognized that generally a state has a compelling interest in compulsory education, in order to "prepare citizens to participate effectively and intelligently in our political system" and to "prepare individuals to be self-reliant and self-sufficient participants in society...."

The district court found that Duro, like the parents in *Yoder*, expressed a sincere religious belief that school enrollment would corrupt his children. We find, however, that the district court, in reaching its conclusion, incorrectly interpreted and applied *Yoder*, because it arose in an entirely different factual context from the present case. Nevertheless, in balancing Duro's religious belief against North Carolina's interest in compulsory education, keeping in mind both the children's future well-being and their state constitutional right to an education, we find the balance in this case tips in favor of the state. The Duros, unlike their Amish counterparts [in *Yoder*], are not members of a community which has existed for three centuries and has a long history of being a successful, self-sufficient, segment of American society. Furthermore, in *Yoder*, the Amish children attended public school through the 8th grade and then obtained informal vocational training to enable them to assimilate into the self-contained Amish community. However, in the present case, Duro refuses to enroll his children in any public or nonpublic school for any length of time, but still expects them to be fully integrated and live normally in the modern world upon reaching the age of 18.

Duro has not demonstrated that home instruction will prepare his children to be self-sufficient participants in our modern society or enable them to participate intelligently in our political system, which, as the Supreme Court stated, is a compelling interest of the state.

Despite Duro's sincere religious belief, we hold that the welfare of the children is paramount and that their future well-being mandates attendance at a public or nonpublic school.

Other Court News

[DR:] We learned from Ray Moore's *Family Report*, 2/84 that the U.S. Supreme Court also refused to hear the appeal of Don and Paula Edgington of New Mexico (*GWS* 32, 35). Meanwhile, the Edgingtons have formed a New Mexico corporation and moved the "place of instruction" outside their home.

From the Quebec Homeschooling Advisory Newsletter, *9/83:*

> In our May issue, we reported on a case where the father was found guilty of keeping his 8-year-old son away from school.... A lawyer was able to track down the judgment, available for $5 from *Jurisprudence Express*, 276 St Jacques, Suite 310, Montreal, H2Y 1N3. Ask for Jugement #83-42, Tribunal de la Jeunesse, Beauharnois (Valleyfield) 760-42-000003-82, 1982/11/30.
>
> It would appear the Tribunal was not satisfied that "enseignement efficace" [efficient instruction] was provided by antiquated textbooks, and that Phys. Ed., science, art, or catechism were taught at all. It would appear that "efficace" was measured in terms of what the present day Quebec curriculum contains; "elements de culture et de sociabilite" were likewise lacking. The qualifications of the tutor were also questioned [she hadn't gone past Grade 8 herself].

From the Ann Arbor News, *1/15/84:*

Branch County Juvenile Judge Edward DeVito granted approval of [a] homeschooling plan Friday after William Martin's eighth appearance in his court in Coldwater. The plan allows the girl, Mollie Martin, to be taught using materials supplied by the Clonlara School in Ann Arbor and ends a string of hearings that at one point landed her father in jail for contempt of court.

DeVito purged the contempt of court finding after Martin changed both the curriculum he was using and the teacher who was overseeing Mollie's education. Testifying on [his] behalf Friday were Pat Montgomery, who operates the Clonlara School, and Sherrie Ankner, a certified teacher.

From a recent Boston Herald, *about the Papia family of Sharon, MA:*

> The Papias pulled their 10-year-old daughter out of school over a year ago when she was entering fourth grade and received School Department approval for their planned curriculum.
>
> But, the Papias said, when they decided to keep their 12-year-old daughter home this year, the School Department filed charges against them in Stoughton District Court.
>
> "We were not being supplied information necessary to show that the parents were teaching their plan or how well the children were doing," Sharon School Supt. John Maloney said.
>
> The case was continued for a year without a finding while the School Department and the Papias attempt to come to an agreement.

Other court news in brief:

Case dismissed, but state is appealing: Mark & Karen Buckner, 917 E. Flora, Tampa FL 33604—Fred & Leonora Senczyszyn, 7506 Sanibel Circle N, Temple Terrace FL 33617

State Supreme Court accepts case: Mr. & Mrs. Don Budke, Rt 2, Underwood MN 56586---Jeanne & Timothy Newstrom, Bovey MN (*GWS* 36)

Appealing to Circuit Court: Steve & Debbie Cooper, 1621 Five Springs Rd, Tiftonia TN.

Organizational News

Addresses of all groups can be found in *GWS* 36, or on our "Home Schooling Resource List" ($1).

Arizona: Barbara Lawson (AZ) wrote, "Shirley Gardner, Sherri Pitman, and I did the taping with Rita Davenport for her TV show *Open House*, and it went very well. I was very, very impressed with both Shirley and Sherri.... Both of them were extremely articulate, and said some beautiful, perfect things about homeschooling that I would like to have said.... I have also sent a copy of *Teach Your Own* to Rita personally...."

Australia: The *Alternative Education Resource Group* (54 Park St, Hawthorn 3122) is planning Australia's first ever national conference of home educators, for three days in September or October this year. They say if any *GWS* readers can get to Melbourne for the conference, they can stay with home educating families.

California: Connie Pfeil (CA) says, "We have formed a support group here in the San Francisco suburbs. We had 10 mothers and a bunch of kids (all moving too fast to count) here in Concord for a potluck on Jan. 7. The moral support is wonderful, as is the diversity of our views and methods. The common bond is our concern for our kids and our ability to search for options...."

An article in the *Sacramento Union*, 1/15/84, says that in 1982–83 there were 1,338 private schools in the state with an enrollment of 10 or less, up from 958 the year before.

Jane Williams of the *California Home Education Clearinghouse* writes, "There are several small homeschooling groups in the Sacramento, Placer Co., El Dorado Co. areas.... There is no formal communication network.... I am attempting a new method of disseminating information.... a *Master Calendar Of Homeschooling Events*. Any group or family in this area who is planning a field trip, meeting, etc., which they would like to have open to other homeschooling families, may call me at 916-791-4467, and have the event placed on the Master Calendar. . . . Any homeschooling families or group leaders who wish to know what events are taking place in any given week or month can call me and I will give them the information. . . ."

Florida: Ann Mordes of FLASH says, "I have (along with Barbara Plunket) recently decided to do away with the FLASH newsletter in favor of Joseph Dallanegra's newsletter (PO Box 759, Trenton FL 32693; 904-463-7188), which is better done and more factual. He is, after all, teaching his kids at home. . . ." Ann also reports that the *Florida Federation Of Women For Responsible Legislation* (6520 SW 134th Dr, Miami FL 33156) is planning to lobby for a change in the school attendance statute.

Illinois: The group HOUSE has reorganized, it is now composed of independent local chapters, with a statewide address being maintained only to answer general inquiries about homeschooling. Apparently the group was becoming too big and diverse for any small number of workers to manage.

Iowa: From *O!KIDS* Issue #4: "Due to increased printing costs, the *O!KIDS* newsletter will cost $3 per year. . . . Our legal pages have been updated and now include the Sessions' ruling. Please send SASE and 20¢ to receive. . . . Current membership: 90 families!" The newsletter printed a story about an Iowa school board approving a homeschooling junior high student, and listed three certified teachers willing to help homeschoolers.

Manitoba: David McConkey sent us the first two issues of the Manitoba Assoc. For Schooling At Home (MASH) newsletter. Subscriptions are $5 per year; send to MASH, 776 Victor St, Winnipeg R3E 1Y6. The group is holding get-togethers the third Saturday of May, July, Sept., and November.

Massachusetts: Gail Gray (MA) writes, "Last year we had a few get-togethers for people in the Pioneer Valley wishing to talk to each other about homeschooling. . . . Now they have started up again and seem helpful. . . . Interested persons could call me at 413-253-7447 or Martha Krawczyk at 549-6379."

Minnesota: From Sharon Hillestad of the *Minnesota Home School Network*: "Faye Getchell and I have made four radio appearances last month and were in one of the newspapers. Each time we hear from one or two new families. More radio programs are scheduled. . . . The *Minnesota Christian Home Education Association* held an all-day seminar in January. 276 people paid $12 apiece to attend. . . ."

Montana: The Jan. '84 issue of the *Montana Homeschoolers Association* newsletter lists "support group contacts" in Miles City, Glendive, Bynum, Fairfield, Whitehall, Dillon, Shepherd, Billings, Missoula, and Kalispell. The group is forming a statewide "Hotline" for legislative news.

Nebraska: The *Nebraska Christian Home School Association* is publishing a monthly magazine, *Home School Journal* (Box 1245, Columbus NE 68601). Subscriptions are $12 per year.

New Mexico: Kay Goodsell reports the formation of *New Mexico Home Educators.* "We have two addresses that can be contacted: 3833 Madrid NE, Albuquerque NM 87111, or PO Box 13383, Albuquerque NM 87192."

North Carolina: From Kim Golden, 691 Sportsman Dr, Concord NC 28025: "We thought you would like to know about our newly-formed organization, *North Carolinians for Home Education.* As you know, homeschooling is next to impossible in our state. We intend to have a bill introduced to the 1985 legislature that will specifically allow home education as satisfying our state's constitutional mandate to provide our children with a 'means of education.' We are at present six to eight families, all but one with preschool age children. . . . We have an advantage now, since we aren't facing criminal charges, legal expenses, etc., and want to work to keep it that way. . . . We are printing up about 1000 brochures with a Q/A approach to the superiority of home instruction, a list of the articles in the N.C. constitution which we feel provide legal sanction for home education, and addresses to write for info.

. . ."

Ohio: Elizabeth Burns (419-289-8013) announced there will be a statewide homeschooling picnic July 28 at Mohican State Park.

Ontario: Sue Pound (Ont.) writes, "We operate a homeschooling private school with four other families. We meet once a month or so to exchange ideas and get the kids together. Our relationship with the Ministry of Education has been very good and we have encountered few problems legally. There is more paperwork for us than there would be if we worked with the local school board, but we enjoy more freedom in designing our own curriculum. . . ."

Pennsylvania: Peter Bergson of *Open Connections School* (312 Bryn Mawr Av, Bryn Mawr PA 19010; 215-527-1504 or 527-4982) says a support group for eastern Pa. is forming, called P.E.N.C.I.L. (Pennsylvania East Network of Children Learning Independently). He says, "Children are involved in the content of the newsletter and will help to get it out to subscribers. . . ."

Rhode Island: Peter Van Daam (401-274-8897) is publishing a monthly newsletter, *Rhode Islanders for Constitutional Education*. He says over 70 people have been attending a monthly meeting.

Wyoming: The *Montana Homeschoolers Association* bulletin lists two "support group contacts" in northern Wyoming. Contact Steve and Michelle Dolan, Box 2878, Cody WY 82414 (307-527-7052) or Dave and Susan Hoffert, Clark HCR, Powell 82435 (645-2403).

Advice From PA Official

Susan Richman wrote in Issue #7 of Western PA Homeschoolers*:*

> Katie White and I were asked to talk about homeschooling on the KDKA Roy Fox Show in late August. Roy had Mr. Billman from the Dept. of Ed. in Harrisburg on the line also, who stressed that Pennsylvanians were lucky to have three ways to meet the compulsory education requirements—public, or private schooling, or home/tutorial teaching. Several families told me that they'd been seriously considering homeschooling, and hearing the radio show gave them the boost needed to really get going making it a reality.
>
> KDKA-TV also ran a spot about a homeschooling family, the Tribous, on *Evening Magazine* in the early fall. . . . Interestingly enough, the family was chosen for the feature when the mother called the station to try to arrange for a visit for their daughter to see how a TV studio operated. The station inquired about what school the child attended, saying that they usually only took school groups for tours. Upon finding out that the child was taught at home by her parents, KDKA turned the tables and said that *they* had been wanting to do a piece on homeschooling, and could *Evening Magazine* visit *them*!
>
> We're now seeing several districts that are cooperating with more than one family, and a number of families are now in their second and third years of official homeschooling with district approval. Many have mentioned to me that securing continuing approval has been a very easy matter, often completed through a simple written request.
>
> Negotiating during the summer months, if you are taking a child out of school, seems to bring the happiest results. School people often seem to feel *very* threatened and very possessive of your child if you try to remove him or her mid-term.
>
> During this past fall I've had several opportunities to talk by phone with Douglas Boelhouwer (717-783-5146), the man in the Pa. Dept. of Ed. who handles inquiries about homeschooling. I had heard from a homeschooling family that Mr. Boelhouwer's office was sending out a packet of information to superintendents who requested guidance in dealing with parents. This packet includes copies of agreements made

between other Pa. districts and families. I had hoped that Mr. B. might send *me* copies of those agreements, too. (He does refer families to our network, and he *subscribes* to *GWS*.) Mr. B. felt that the contract/agreements held too much personal "in-house" information, but he did tell me what guidelines he offers parents in dealing with their districts.

First, Mr. B. felt it was imperative for families to have a well-written, cogent *rationale* for their homeschooling choice—a statement of their philosophy of education and *why* they wanted to teach their child at home.

Second, parents need to describe their educational program, that is, what they plan to do in each subject area mentioned in the Pa. School Code. I think, here, it is vital for parents to let school people know you *have* direction, goals, plans, or they may think you simply *have* no idea on what to do. They think you will need their books and curriculum.

Third, parents must describe their qualifications as teachers of their children. Here Mr. B. made it *very* clear that he knew that it was not required for parents to be certified teachers or even college graduates, "but if a parent has an 8th grade or a 12th grade education, they have to show in some way that they *are* qualified." I imagine he was thinking of parents documenting their life experience/self-taught learning, any relevant work experiences (volunteer included, of course), and any written references. I think, too, that it can be a real help for families to think of asking certified teacher friends to be listed as "educational consultants." There are a number of certified teachers in our directory (my husband and I are two) who would be happy to be resource people. Indeed, our network and *GWS* could be listed as resources.

Fourth, Boelhouwer felt parents had to then guarantee that there would be a minimum of 180 days of instruction (I think most of us can practically guarantee that there will be 365 days of "instruction"!). Here Boelhouwer and I digressed a bit to discuss a situation where a family had been asked to follow the school calendar and to hold home instruction during the regular hours of the school day. The family made it very clear that they would take advantage of the flexibility of the home situation, and *not* stick to a rigid time schedule. Boelhouwer agreed that this was of course fine, although he did quibble a bit about what constitutes "instruction." At one point he said, "Why, some people would say that if a kid skips to school while whistling, that he's had physical education *and* a music class, and that is just *not so!*" If some grown-up *tells* a child to skip or *tells* a child to whistle, I guess that's an entirely different matter.

Fifth, Boelhouwer then recommended parents include a written statement on how they plan to deal with the child's socialization. Although he recognized that this of course was not legally required in any way, he felt that it would be wise to be ready with answers to this question. He thought parents might want to tackle this from the standpoint of how they were preparing the child for leadership, how they were positively building the child's self-image and self-concept.

Last, Mr. Boelhouwer felt it was imperative for parents to agree to participate in standardized testing. Apparently there is a new state plan for mandatory achievement testing at the 3rd, 5th, and 8th grade levels (I'm a bit fuzzy about this, seems to be part of Gov. Thornburgh's "Plan for Excellence in Pa. Education"). Mr. B. said that these test scores should be used to evaluate the student's progress in homeschooling, but then qualified this by saying that there generally would be improvement from year to year on these tests *just by virtue of daily life and normal growing and incidental learning*. I have also heard, from a mother who talked to

Boelhouwer, that he was very supportive of her insisting that her child be tested individually rather than in a regular classroom with a group of strange agemates.

Further, Mr. Boelhouwer and I discussed a recent situation where a family was being asked to submit weekly lesson plans, allow unlimited home-monitoring visits, take the National Teacher's Exam, and use the district's curriculum and books. Mr. Boelhouwer's reaction was a bit surprising—he was first astounded ("What! They want to keep closer tabs on that child than any other in the district!"), then he said, *laughing*, "Well, the family should agree to it all, just say, 'Sure, we'll do it!" I was a bit taken aback, when he continued, laughing, "The district will *never do it*; it's a scare tactic. They'll *never* want to spend so much time with this one family.... Once the family agrees to it all, they'll probably back right down!" Interesting perspective, I thought.

Official Suggests Transfer

We received this letter from Lynn P. Hartzler, who is in charge of Alternative Education and Independent Study in the Calif. State Dept. of Education:

Superintendent Honig has requested that I respond to the letter in which you enclosed a portion of a letter from a California correspondent who expressed strong disappointment with the response of the Santee School District to a request for cooperation in setting up an Independent Study agreement in lieu of operating a private school. We deeply regret the type of attitude apparently expressed by the district spokesperson referred to and note that other districts have exercised their option to serve the type of parents who wrote to you. Districts have the option and this department encourages them to respond affirmatively but the law does not mandate the program.

Since roughly half of the public school districts in California do offer independent study to some extent (including many in San Diego County), parents may be able to turn from a non-cooperative school district to one that will work with them through *an inter-district transfer*. This is a legal means for shifting the responsibility for educating the student from the district in which the family resides to another which is in a better position to offer the specialized service desired.

As you may have noticed, there is substantial interest in homeschooling in many parts of California and in the press in general. I was recently contacted, for example, by a writer for *Newsweek* magazine who was gathering information for a special story on the subject. My mail and record of phone calls indicate that homeschooling is probably the primary growth area within alternative education.

Thank you for printing in GWS stories of school districts that are cooperating with homeschooling families. We hope that you will have more of these stories in the future and that this option will eventually become so commonplace as to no longer "make news." We know of several developments under the direction of county superintendents of schools in northern California which appear to be quite newsworthy and about which the educators and families involved seem to be very enthusiastic. If you would like to know more about these, please let me know and I will put you in touch with the people who can describe what is happening. There is also an interesting model fairly well developed in the Ramona School District (near San Diego), not far from where your disgruntled correspondent lives.

School Story

A story from Joyce Kinmont (UT): When a little boy returned from his first day at school, he said, "I'm really worried about that teacher. Do you know what she did? She held up four crayons, and *she* asked *us* what colors they were!"

A Feisty Goat Farmer

From a syndicated column by Nicholas Von Hoffman, 2/19/84, about Christine Solem of Albemarle County, Virginia:

The authorities stopped Solem from selling her raw, unpasteurized goat milk to 15 customers. She went to court and, miracle of miracles, found a judge with some horse sense, who remarked that, "I am unprepared and certainly unwilling to say that the customer is to be protected from himself when he knows what he is getting and is asking for it."

Naturally the Commonwealth of Virginia's apparatchiks appealed to the State Supreme Court where horse sense is not in great supply and therefore won over Solem, who complied by getting out of the goat-milk business and getting into the goat rental business. You could rent a goat from her; she would take care of it and give you the milk. Now they have put her out of rent-a-goat, but undaunted, she wrote the authorities a letter saying: "I am sure you will be pleased to know that I have temporarily gone out of the milk business and gone into the manure business. Since there are no legal problems with selling goat manure, business should move briskly ahead. In addition, if we have any extra goat's milk, each person who buys one 8-gallon bag of composted goat manure for $3 will receive, absolutely free, one gallon of raw, unpasteurized goat's milk."

Start A Non-Profit Corp.?

Running *GWS*, helping homeschoolers, has proved to be far more interesting but also far more demanding than we guessed at the beginning. As you readers know, we have had to spend much time talking to people who were having difficulties with school authorities, as well as gathering and putting out information about school policies, legislation, and court decisions. There are not many economies of scale available; when our readership doubles, so does most of our work.

We are hoping and trying to reach the point where a combination of *GWS* subscriptions and book sales will meet all our expenses, but we are a long way from it yet, even with my own income from lecture fees and book and magazine royalties added in. This last year, our expenses were about $20,000 greater than our income. Now in some ways this was not a typical year; because my editor was changing publishing houses, which took some time, it was a year in which I did not have any book in the works, and so, no advance royalties. I will have some this year and next year, and, I hope, in following years, so these deficits should not be as high.

On the other hand, my lecture income has been declining steadily for years now and may well to continue to decline. I am not a big enough celebrity to be attractive to the college students, who support a large part of the lecture business, and I have become too radical to be acceptable at most educational meetings and conferences. This could change, particularly as more and more educators come to realize that homeschooling is here to stay and that the best thing for them to do will be to learn how to live with it. But there is no reason to expect this to happen in the near future.

We had hoped to help meet these deficits by taking ads in *GWS*, but our campaigns for advertising have been very slow to get off the ground. I think we can and will do better here, but it may take a long time. We simply do not have enough subscribers and readers to be tempting to most advertisers.

We have a few ideas about ways in which we can expand our book and music business, and also perhaps find new subscribers for *GWS*. But these will take time to put into effect, and still more time to show whatever results they produce. Meanwhile, it is only prudent to look for other sources of income. For this reason I am considering the possibility of starting a non-profit, tax-exempt corporation, called perhaps *Friends Of Homeschooling* (other suggested names welcome), to support many parts of our work.

I looked into this idea a few years ago, but let it drop, first, because I thought and hoped we might not need it, and secondly, because homeschooling was so controversial that there seemed little chance of getting enough tax-deductible contributions to make the effort worthwhile. This, however, may no longer be true. Homeschooling has been enough in the news and has become respectable enough so that we just might be able to find a few small foundations that would be willing to make some small gifts to it, or perhaps underwrite certain projects that we have never had the money to do, like publishing some of our own books about homeschooling law, or math, or computers, or music, or science, or bringing back into print some good books that are no longer available.

It also seems possible, if gifts to *Friends Of Homeschooling* were tax-deductible, that our present and former readers might be willing to make some small contributions. Enough of these could make a big difference. If five hundred people would each year give $5 apiece, and five hundred more $10 apiece, and another 100 $25 apiece, and 50 $100 apiece, it would move the wolf quite a few paces back from the door. So I would like to ask you a question, to which I hope you will give the most accurate guess you can. Suppose we started *Friends Of Homeschooling* and suppose contributions to it were tax-deductible. Roughly how much do you think you might contribute per year? This would of course be in addition to whatever you might spend on *GWS* subscriptions and/or books, music, etc., from our catalog.

Please let me emphasize again that what I am asking for right now is a guess, not a promise or a pledge. I do beg you to make this guess as realistic and accurate as you can, so that we can better judge whether it makes sense to go ahead with this project. If we do go ahead, it will probably take us six months or more to draw up articles of incorporation, write by-laws, select or find officers and a board (the smallest possible) of trustees, all required by law, and then to get the desired tax-deductible status. Naturally, with all the other things we do, we don't want to take this much time and effort unless we have good reason to believe it will bring in enough money to make it worthwhile. May we please hear from you about this within the next month? For whatever you can tell us, thanks very much.—JH

Going Back To School

In "Why Did They Stop?" in GWS *36, John asked families whose children were for a while homeschooled but have gone back to school to tell about their experiences. Here are some of the replies. First, from Diane Gilman (WA):*

Our 12-year-old *chose* to go back to school this year—after 2½ years of homeschooling. He is at the top of his classes and was amazed at how little the kids knew when he first started back. . . . He's there by his choice and if he wants to stop, that's fine, too. . . . He is, in fact, enjoying school. . . . Early on in the year he wanted to participate in an extended learning theater production. The competition was high as to who would be chosen so they selected on the basis of a standardized test. Ian hadn't been tested since he'd been out of school 2½ years, but he wanted to be in the play so took the two tests the next day. . . . He scored 99 on the English and 96 on the math. What does that say about our public schools if kids out of school can do that well?

So far his return is positive for all of us, whereas school before made us all miserable, so we feel the timing of his choice is right.

[From a later letter:] Ian told us last night that he has decided to finish this year at the public school, but then go back to homeschool. He is enjoying this year, but he is also missing being master of his own time. . . . He has his home school time planned as far as what he wants to do next year. I was overjoyed at his decision and maturity.

From Sally Ford in Oregon:

Our oldest son went to kindergarten. Then we kept him at home for first grade. We sent him back to second grade because we got so much criticism from relatives for keeping him home, especially since he couldn't read very well. We had no support group (other than your newsletter) and I think that contributed to our sending him back. . . . He understood he was to go to school in second grade, but after that he could be homeschooled.

He loved going to school, and is now in 3rd grade. He felt he was treated pretty much like the other kids. The only bad part of going back to school, he says, was the other kids who knew him wondered (and I guess kept asking) why he didn't go to first grade. He decided to go to 3rd grade because he likes recess, has fun being around other kids. Also we have a 3-year-old and a 9-month-old and he says I'm too busy taking care of them to give him much attention!

When he started second grade, I'd say it took him till Christmas to catch up to the average second grader. Now in the 3rd grade, he's doing better than average in all areas but reading (he says he still hates to read). We have four children and will always keep homeschooling as an option for them. I can almost see my first grader already not wanting to finish the year.

We all decided that maybe part-time school would be the best. The 3rd grader says he'd like to stay home Mondays because Sunday night he dreads the thought of going to school, but once he's there, it's OK. The first grader already stays home on Thursdays, his dad's day off.

From a Florida parent:

My three children wanted to go back to school for companionship of other children in the classroom. They wanted to be involved in the high school activities. This was the only reason. We partially agree that this is important so we allowed them to do so.

They were allowed to come back home if they wanted to. It was understood that they *would* come back home if they did not keep their grades up to a standard set by us.

They did not have any problems with schoolwork when returning to school. My daughter is maintaining a B average in 11th grade.

And from New York:

When I decided to do homeschooling with Rick, I felt he should stay home at least through first grade and possibly through fourth grade. The decision to go to first grade, after a year of homeschooling, was his, not mine. One homeschooling friend of mine advised against letting him go, saying, "He doesn't know what he's getting into." I figured he'd know what it was like once he got there—and I never considered the decision to go to school to be irreversible.

The desire to be with other kids his age was the biggest factor in Rick's decision to go to school. My efforts to work out non-school socializing didn't work out well at all. I'm not saying it *couldn't* work out, but for us it *didn't*. By the end of the first week of school, Rick had a friend come over to play. It was a great day for him.

Academically, Rick has been doing quite well—it's obvious I did as good a job of preparing him as the kindergarten teacher could have—actually better, I'm sure.

I still definitely consider myself to be a homeschooling parent in my approach to my kid and particularly in my sense that I'm the one responsible for my kid's education. I have encouraged other parents to homeschool, and may very well do it again sometime.

For the first month, Rick loved school, but by mid-December the routine and some inappropriate assignments began to get him down. At this point we are on a sort of middle course—Rick goes to school when he feels up for it, usually 3 or 4 days a week. I'm not ready to pull him out completely yet, but I'm sure not ready to enforce their rules on my kid. . . . The school is not aware of my current policy—I send absence notes about headaches, colds, stomach aches—there's enough of that this time of year anyway.

One thing I want to make clear—I *never* accept "I don't want to go to school today" from a sleepy child snuggled into a warm bed on a cold morning. I used to hear that from my daughter when she was in 4th grade and my response was, "Get dressed, have breakfast, and *then* we'll decide." For her that was always enough to get her going *and* going to school. But when Rick is dressed and fed and still doesn't want to go, I let him stay home.

Learning Stories

Anna Myers (Ont.) writes:

To give you an example of Drew's approach to learning, I'll tell you about our ski experience. We got a call from friends saying that skiing was free for the day at the local ski club. Beginner lessons were free, too. At first both kids wanted to go and then I noticed Drew (10) got quieter and quieter. Then he said he'd be embarrassed if he didn't know how to ski. I said there were lessons for beginners so he could learn really quickly. That did it—no way would he go to lessons unless he *already knew* how to do it. So-o-o-o, we stayed home and Drew dug the old skis out of the shed and skied down the slope in front of our house until he felt competent enough to take lessons! It's like cleaning your house before the cleaning lady comes so she won't see it dirty.

From Car Oliver (LA):

For some time I had been contemplating how I would help our six-year-old daughter, Autumn, to learn to ride a two-wheeler bicycle. One Sunday afternoon recently Autumn popped the question to me, "Mom, when are you going to teach me to ride a big bike?" So we got out there, in the road, and began lesson #1, right? Wrong! All I remember is how little we accomplished.

But one morning I drove to a nearby store and when I returned only about a half hour later, our bunch came running over to the car with big oversized grins on their faces. . . . I was really stumped, thinking to myself, "I've only been gone 30 minutes. What world-changing event could have occurred in this short amount of time?" . . . Joshua had succeeded at teaching not only his sister, but his younger brother simultaneously, how to ride a two-wheeler bike!

All he did was to have one get on while he held on to the bike firmly, and he then just gave it a gentle 2–3 step push and released. (All of this took place on a slightly downhill grassy padded section of yard.) At this angle the bike will glide a good ways giving the child a chance to feel the balance and get some pedaling in. Autumn, at 6, got the knack of pedaling and was able to keep things going a ways through the grass while dodging trees. Caleb (4) just takes a run and keels over when the hill gives up its velocity. Using a very low training bike presents just a short spill to the padded ground below, so the child is not frightened and is eager to try again, seeing if he can further his run the next time.

From Allen Myers (NH):

I have been resisting my own pushes and those of others to teach Eben (5) how to ice skate. My approach has been to let him get used to being on skates at his own pace; to pull him around so he could get used to the feeling of motion, balance, turning, etc. I admit to occasional intense frustration at progress beyond this "free ride" and occasional bouts of shuffling. But one day Eben wanted to catch up with a friend, and shuffling along the sidewalls wasn't getting him there. So he pushed off and began skating across the ice! A look of incredible excitement and exuberance crossed his face as he suddenly realized what he was doing, and shouted, "I'm skating, Daddy! I'm skating!!" Enough said.

Carolyn Civitarese (PA) wrote:

We gave Sunshine a United States puzzle when she was somewhere around 2½ years old. The pieces were made of a thin cardboard and she needed help handling them at first. As she would take out each piece I would name the state and perhaps tell a short story (such as "Maine—that's where Grandmom lives"). Before she was able to manipulate all the pieces in place, she was able to name them. At three, she can name a state just from its shape found pictured almost anywhere.

I don't want you to think I'm bragging. This learning happened because she was interested and both her parents took the time to answer, "What's this one called?" hundreds of times. Neither of us expected her to learn the names of the states. She just did.

From Tennessee:

My son (6) does not like to learn from his mistakes, because he can't stand to *make* mistakes. He prefers to hang back and study something for a long time without trying it then he just *does* it. With his toilet learning, for example, he refused adamantly to try, insisting (in near-terror sometimes) on continuing to wear a diaper. So I tried not to pressure him and just waited . . . and waited . . . and waited. Finally, one day he requested to wear underwear, and that was it. Without a backward glance he was out of diapers, and he's never even had an accident (as a long-time bed wetter myself, I continue to be amazed at that).

Now that he is not in school, I feel pressured for him to be at least at the same level as his age-mates. . . . Well, I've learned by now about the way he learns, and I see him hanging about the periphery of reading, and I know that he probably *can* read a little; but I also know that he's not going to do it until he's good and ready. So, again, I wait.

Just last night he drew a picture and added cartoon "balloons" in which he printed "Yo, He-Man" and "Ha ha ha ha ha!" I thought he must have copied the words from something (he has enjoyed copying captions from comic books), but he had written it completely on his own. I down-played my reaction because that's the way we have to be with him. Too much praise or enthusiasm somehow puts too much pressure on him, and he backs away from anything that elicits that kind of response. So I just sort of accepted his accomplishment, and he went on. . . . When he does actually sit down and read, I'll try to be just as matter-of-fact about it.

I hate to think what would happen to him in a school. . . . He would probably be labeled "learning disabled" or worse.

―――――

And from Sue Radosti (IL):

Some of my most valuable lessons last summer were taught to me by a 9-year-old girl. She was enrolled in a summer art program on campus, and my Art Methods class worked as teacher's aides for the program. We were one-on-one, so Lindsey had my undivided attention. I think we were both pretty uncomfortable with the arrangement at first; she obviously didn't need much help, and I felt awkward watching her every move and feeling obligated to comment on her work. I finally got bored and decided to do some drawing and painting of my own—and Lindsey was delighted! She paid very little attention to me whenever I tried to directly teach her anything, but if I sat down with a sheet of paper and crayons, we always had a lively exchange of ideas, often creating a joint project. Lindsey never seemed overly concerned about the finished product, and any effort (usually by the supervising teacher) to make her concentrate on accuracy never failed to squelch her joy in the act of creating.

On Piaget and Learning

In *GWS* 37, in the article "Surprised By Reading" (p. 19), I showed that often to a large degree children are not aware *that* they are learning, or *what* they are learning, and do not know what they know. This underscores other things that I have said about children's learning in my books, notably *How Children Learn*, and in many articles in *GWS*. Children do not move from ignorance about a given thing to knowledge of it in one sudden step, like going to a light, which has been off, and turning it on. For children do not *acquire* knowledge, but *make* it, as scientists do, by observing, wondering, theorizing, and then testing and revising these theories. To go from the point of making a new theory to the point of being sure that it is true often takes them a long time. Most of the time they are not aware of these processes, this scientific method, that they are continually using; they do not know that they are observing, theorizing, and testing and revising theories, and would be surprised and baffled if you told them so. At any particular moment in their growth their minds are full of theories about various aspects of the world around them, including language, which they are constantly testing, but not for the life of them could they tell you what these theories are. As I said in *GWS* 37, we cannot help these unconscious processes by meddling with them. Even when we are trying our best to be helpful, by assisting or improving these processes, we can only do harm.

In "Surprised by Reading" I also said that because Piaget, brilliant and original thinker though he was, did not understand this about children, both the method he used to try to learn about children's thinking and the conclusions he drew from it were fatally wrong. I added that psychologists were increasingly finding in experiments with children that this was so, and that I would in this issue report on some of the results of their experiments. The article I intended to quote from was one by Maya Pines that appeared a few months ago in the magazine *Psychology Today*. I thought I knew where I had put it, but when I went to put my hands on it, it was not there, and I can't find it. So the quotes will have to wait until I can get another copy of the article. (Perhaps a reader can send me a copy.)

What I can say about these experiments, just from what I remember of this and other articles, is, first, that when they give children a way of showing what they know in *actions* instead of words, the results of Piaget's earlier experiments are reversed, and the children show that they are indeed capable of doing many things that he said they could not do. Children as young as two have now been shown able to do exactly the kind of formal, logical reasoning that he declared was impossible. My other recollection of the article is that it supports something I have said about children for a long time, most recently in the chapter on "Fantasy" in the revised *How Children Learn*, that if we want children to do formal reasoning with different kinds of abstract quantities and shapes, whether these be Cuisenaire rods or Montessori materials or lumps of clay or whatever, we must give them time to do what I can only call "de-abstract" these objects, in other words, to use fantasy and play to put some real life and meaning into them. Thus, to invent an example, if we give a child a small set of wooden colored blocks to play with, and give her time to invent a game in which these become, say, a Mommy, Daddy, and three children, we can not then fool that child into saying there are more or fewer blocks just by changing their arrangement in space. Shuffle those blocks around however we will, the child will still recognize that here is the Mommy block, here the Daddy block, and so on until all the block family is accounted for.

I think here of Schumacher's lovely story about the old shepherd's advice to the young shepherd. "Don't count the sheep," he said, "or else they won't thrive." By this he meant that if you counted the sheep you would turn each real, live, unique animal into an abstraction or a symbol of a sheep, everyone like every other, sheep = sheep = sheep, and so would begin to lose sight of them as individual sheep, and fail to notice whether they were remaining healthy, energetic, their best sheep selves.

What we easily forget, in our passionate 20th century love affair with abstract thinking, is that to make an abstraction out of some part of reality we must take some meaning *out* of it. This makes it so much easier for us to think about whatever it is, manipulate it, measure it, put it into numbers, put it into a computer, that we tend more often than not to think that our abstraction is larger and more real than the reality of which it is only a small part, and to ignore the reality we threw away in order to make our abstraction. We think, as I have said many times, that whatever we can't count, doesn't count. The schools count the children, or countable things they try to get the children to do, and so like the bad shepherd they come to think that these numbers are more real than the children themselves. Soon they forget to look at the children, forget even *how* to look at children. Naturally they fail to notice whether they thrive, forget or never learn how to tell whether they are thriving or not, and so in turn, fail to learn what kinds of things help or prevent their thriving. The uniqueness of my own *How Children Fail* lay only in this, that I looked at the real children, saw after a while that they were not thriving, and so could begin to think about *what I was doing* that was preventing them from thriving, and what I might and ought to do instead.

Children resist this continual abstracting (remember poor Swami in #37 and his problem of the mangoes), because their chief business in life is finding and making meaning, putting meaning *into* a world, which must at first seem wholly meaningless to them. It is not a weakness on their part but a strength, that they are more passionately interested in reality and meaning than we are, and struggle to preserve it, find it, invent it, wherever and however they can.

One of the children who has most recently shown to me, once again, that little children can and do make use of formal reasoning in their life and growth is Bridget Finn (4), who often comes to the office with her two sisters when their mother Kit comes in to help us. I first noticed a couple of months ago that Bridgie was saying things like "Him moved the boxes" and "Her took the crayons." This surprised me. I have often heard little children say "Me want this," etc., though not all do—one of my now grown-up niece's first utterances was "I some," meaning "I want some, give me some." But I had never heard a child say "Her do this" or "Him do that." What we have to realize about this is that it is *not* imitation. Bridgie has never heard *anyone* use "her" and "him" as the subjects of verbs. This is her own application of her own mini-theory of the English language. In this she is using both inductive and deductive reasoning. From other people's use of the words "her" and "him" she arrived at the correct generalization that these were what we (but not she) call "pronouns," words that can stand in the place of a noun or a proper name. From there she deduced her particular and in my experience unique rule that she could use these same pronouns as the subjects of verbs. And even as I write about this it occurs to me that she has already stopped doing it—I can't remember her saying that the last few times she has been in the office. So she has already tested her theory about English against her observations of other people's use of it, and seeing that her theory doesn't fit, has changed it. If this is not formal reasoning, nothing is.

Another interesting incident that further confirms this article is that Deborah Wolk, the little girl of "Surprised By Reading," came back to the office a few weeks later for a final visit before she and her family returned to the West Coast. During our short time together she said something—I can't quote her exact words—that told me that, even though she could remember a time when she *did* read, she still was not sure that she *could* read, that is, do it any time she wanted. She still does not truly *own* this new piece of knowledge. I now know just how she feels. I am in the process of having that same experience myself, of slowly acquiring not just a new piece but a new kind of knowledge, which I have not had long enough to feel that I truly have it. What this is all about I will describe in the next article.—JH

Learning Perfect Pitch

A few weeks ago I decided that I was going to try to do something I have often thought of doing— learn the exact note A to which musicians traditionally tune. The pitch of A is of course a matter of convention, or agreement. Most musicians around the world have agreed to put it at 440 Hz, which means the sound we get from something vibrating 440 times a second. (The Hz is an abbreviation for Hertz, the name of the scientist who did a lot of the pioneer work in the physics of sound.)

Most musicians or musically inclined people have, as I do, what is called good "relative pitch," which in a nutshell means that we can sing in tune, can remember and reproduce the musical intervals between one note and another. But very few people, even musicians, have what is called "perfect pitch," that is, the ability to name, by letter (A, C, E flat, or whatever) any note that they hear. Musicians argue about whether this is a useful skill or talent to have. I have always felt rather in awe of people who, like my older friend Izler Solomon the conductor and my younger friend Ishmael Wallace the composer and pianist, have absolute pitch. It seemed to me something of a mystery.

But remembering that playing the cello once seemed equally a mystery, and that the great composer and teacher Paul Hindemith always maintained, and on the basis of some experience, that people could learn perfect pitch, I decided, as I say, that I would learn the A. The way to do it is, of course, every so often to tap an A-440 tuning fork or to blow through an A pitch-pipe or hit an A on the piano, sing the note, and then some time later sing the note again, then sound the fork or pipe or piano, and see how close you came. And so on until you learn it.

I have been at this now for perhaps three weeks. When I started I might hit the A one time in three or four. After a week or so I was hitting it about one out of two. By now I am hitting it eighty or ninety percent of the time. If I am off, I am almost never off more than a semitone, and I almost always know which way I am off—that is, if I think, "This may be a little low," it is low and not high. When I sing the A after not thinking about it for a while, what usually happens is that I guess a note, sing it, think, "That sounds and feels (in my throat) a little low," and sing it higher. This second guess is the one I test against the tuning fork, and it usually turns out to be right.

But it still feels to me as reading feels to Deborah Wolk, a mystery and a miracle, not something I can count on. I am always surprised when I get it right. I would certainly not bet money on it. If I did, even though now I am getting it eight or nine times out of ten, I would probably demand 10-1 odds. And I am sure that under any kind of stress my success rate would be much lower.

If and when I come to feel secure in the A, I will see if I can learn some other notes. From time to time I will make further reports on this experiment.—JH

Earns Degree, Fixes Engines

From the Florida reader who said in GWS 34 she was slowly working toward a teaching certificate:

I learned I can get a Bachelor of Independent Studies degree from the University of South Florida (Tampa FL 33620) which is equal to any bachelor degree. This involves a reading list in certain areas of knowledge, interaction with a faculty member by mail or phone, and attending a two week seminar in the summer for each area of study. It sounds like something I can handle with my family responsibilities.

Meanwhile, my son (12) and I are taking a small engines repair class two nights a week, through adult education. This is the same class taught to the junior high kids, but in the evening. We bring our own engines to repair. It is attended mainly by retired gentlemen, but this time my 72-year-old mother-in-law and my son and I added a little variety to the class. We really learned a lot in spite of all the help we got from these very nice old men who couldn't believe we were capable. So far we have repaired three lawn mowers and a go-cart. This includes grinding valves and installing new piston rings and gaskets.

On Discipline—2

People who push this or that way of raising and disciplining children always say that their methods "work." The question is, what do they mean by "work"? No doubt disciplining children in certain ways will in time produce certain kinds of adults, but before we decide what these ways should be, we have to know what kind of adults we want.

Many writers about discipline seem to want adults who will do anything and everything that anyone in a position of authority tells them to do. That idea needs a very careful second look. There were many people like that in Germany not so long ago, and they made a government and a society that was one of the worst, probably *the* worst, that the world has ever known. In its twelve years of life Nazi Germany killed something close to thirty million people, and if it had won its war in Russia it would have killed a great many more; it had serious and well worked out plans to exterminate, not just Jews but also what it called "the Slavic race," which might well have meant a hundred or two hundred million people.

Most of the great crimes and cruelties of history were done by people who were just carrying out orders. As was shown in the book *Obedience To Authority* (in our catalog), there are many people right now, in this and other supposedly free countries, who, simply in the course of what they believe to be a scientific experiment, are willing to inflict terrible pain and even death on someone they believe to be an innocent participant in the same experiment, merely because a scientific authority figure tells them to do so.

I am afraid of such people, afraid of what they might do to others, afraid of what they might (if ordered) do to me. We already have far too many of this kind of people around, and I don't want to make more. What I do want is to help children grow up to be self-disciplined, responsible, civilized human beings. This is the farthest thing in the world from, indeed the very opposite of, the kind of cowed and resentful savages we have so many of, always sneaking looks over their shoulders to see who is watching, always trying to find something they can get away with, always looking for another chance to say, "You can't make me! You can't stop me!"

I always hated it, and still do, when children, in my classrooms or elsewhere, acted or act that way. When I meet new children, I always want to get as quickly as possible to the point where they are open and aboveboard with me, so that instead of playing Cops and Robbers type games with each other we can get on with the serious work of finding sensible and decent ways of living and working together.

Such matters are rarely if ever talked about in any of the many books I have seen about discipline. The writers of these books talk as if from the point of view of adults there were only two kinds of child behavior, obedient or rebellious. But, as a teacher friend very helpfully pointed out to me years ago, there are not two kinds of behavior but three: dependent, counter-dependent, and independent. The dependent child says, "Tell me what to do, and I'll do it but I won't do anything at all until you tell me." The counter-dependent child says, "Tell me what to do, and I'll refuse to do it." The independent child says, "You don't have to tell me what to do, I have plenty of things to do, and most of the time you don't need to tell me what not to do either, because I'm smart enough to watch you and other people I like and trust, and try to act as you do."

The schools, and most parents, and most writers of books about discipline, do not understand that dependence and counter-dependence are just two varieties of what is essentially the same kind of behavior, while independence is a very different kind of behavior altogether. Instead, they act as if independence was only a slightly milder form of, or a first step toward, counter-dependence or rebelliousness, as if independence in children was dangerous while dependence was safe. But not so. The cowed savage, the resentful slave is always likely to turn on you if he gets a chance. I have long lost count of the number of times I have heard about some really dreadful criminal—torturer, mass murderer—who during his growing up was always a model of good behavior. It is only civilized, responsible, principled human beings who can be trusted not to do bad, destructive, cruel things, *even* when no one is looking, *even* when everyone else is doing them, *even* when someone tells them to do them. That's the kind of adults I would like children to grow up to be.

In *GWS* 19 I reviewed what was then and is still my favorite of all historical novels, Thornton Wilder's *The Ides Of March*, an imaginative reconstruction, in the form of letters written by or to various prominent Romans, chiefly Caesar, of the last days of the Roman republic. In one of these letters Caesar says:

> I am surrounded by and hate those reformers who can only establish an order by laws, which repress the subject and drain him of his joy and aggression. Cato and Brutus envision a state of industrious mice. . . . Happy would I be if it could be said of me that like Cytheria I could train the unbroken horse without robbing him of the fire in his eye and the delight in his speed.

Here I think of our dear little office friend Anna, now almost three, who like many other small visitors here has plenty of fire in her eye and is full of delight in her equivalent of the horse's speed—energy, curiosity, enthusiasm. And I think of something I first saw when I was in my twenties, only just beginning to realize that I liked and was interested in children. I was visiting, as I did often, a friend who was involved in my work, and who had told me more than once that he believed in strict parental discipline. We sat down in the living room and began to talk. None of his four children were around. After some time one of them slipped quietly into the room, said a brief hello to me, busied herself for a while with something at the far end of the room, and after a while slipped out again as quietly as she had come in. Her father and I went on talking and joking. A few minutes later the first child reappeared, then later a second, then a third, and eventually all four, this time staying in the room and listening to our conversation. But on some of my other visits, the first child would disappear and we would not see any of the others until dinner. After a while I realized what was happening; the first child was coming in on a scouting mission to see whether Daddy was safe to be with, something I had learned to do myself as a young child. And I was sad, because my friend really did like his children and did not understand the game, and the reason for the game, his children were playing, did not understand that to some extent he had made himself, for them, into a source of danger.

Many years later, after I had become a teacher, and had come to know many young children and the many signs and signals by which they show their thoughts and feelings, I saw another and more extreme, but very common example of the results of this kind of discipline. The father in this case was a rancher, who having been told a little about my ideas said almost angrily that he didn't believe in any of that permissive nonsense. His children (girls of four and six) were being raised under strict discipline, including spanking. It didn't take long to see that the children had already become specialists in fooling and seducing Daddy, and almost never dealt with him in any other way. Sometimes they did this with simpering smiles and cute little tricks, child movie star style; almost always they pretended to be much younger than they were; and whenever they felt in danger, they acted babyish, pretended to be scared, or to cry. Around us visitors, when Daddy wasn't around, they acted like normal children of their age, curious, mostly serious, shy but friendly. Since Daddy hardly ever saw any other children and so could not know what children were like when they were on the level, he was easily fooled. Again, it was sad to see; for the sake of a discipline which, because his children were so good at fooling him, he often did not achieve, he had mostly lost the possibility of having them as his friends, and of being a friend to them, and so, of being a true civilizing influence on them, which he could well have been, since he was on the whole a very admirable man from whom they could have learned a great deal.

In the next issue, I will continue this discussion of discipline, and also answer a question that many readers may be asking: where did I learn, and where have I put into practice, my own ideas about discipline.—JH

A "Grandteacher"

From Jacque Williamson (WV):

Besides having two pen pals his age, Nathan (6) has a "grandteacher." She is a retired teacher (the professor who introduced me to John Holt's books when I was in graduate school!). She encouraged our plans to homeschool and helped us design our plan for first grade. She sends Nathan letters, puzzles she makes up, clippings, and tall tales of ridiculously funny stories which they both enjoy exchanging. She enjoys hearing from him and really lavishes attention on him through the mail. It encourages Nathan to write and dictate letters, to try to read her rebus stories, to figure out her puzzles. For her, it allows her to keep up her interest in young children, despite living in a retirement home, to find pictures of interest to him, and to use things she used as a teacher. It is mutually beneficial. It seems there must be other retired people who would also enjoy having a homeschool friend.

"Help" And Real Help

From Jane Gaffney in Australia see "A Continuum Baby," GWS 34:

Liesl (16 months) is hardly at all interested in playing with toys. She might spend half an hour a day playing with toys. She is much more interested in doing what I am doing or using grown-up things. She has recently started "helping" me with washing up and hanging out clothes. I wash up at the suds sink while she stands on a chair in front of the rinsing sink with a towel tied around her. Her job is supposedly to put the rinsed things into the drying rack but she tends to get distracted by all those interesting pouring devices, and thinks it's just as much fun to take things out of the drying rack and put them back into the washing water. As you can imagine, it sometimes becomes a rather wet and prolonged business, but she enjoys herself so much it's worth it and the washing up does eventually get done.

Hanging clothes out is less of an ordeal. In fact, she really is a help. She picks up each item out of the basket and hands it up to me to hang out. I can see real joy in her face at being truly useful. I hope that by encouraging her in this way (or at least not actively discouraging her by making her feel she's a useless nuisance which is what often happens to babies), she will continue to enjoy doing such things and not be spending a lot of energy later on trying *not* to help as a lot of children seem to do.

New Law Passed—Virginia

In its session early this year, the Virginia Legislature passed a homeschooling law that is not only a generally good and workable bill, but is in some important respects perhaps the most significant of all such bills yet passed, and one that might very well serve as a model for many other states. Entitled House Bill No. 535, it begins by saying that a parent must send any child between the ages of 5 and 17 to school, or have the child tutored, or provide home instruction, as described below:

Instruction in the home of a child or children by the parent, guardian or other person having control or charge of such child or children, shall not be classified or defined as a private, denominational or parochial school.

22.1-254.1 Declaration of policy: requirements for home instruction of children.

A. When the requirements of this section have been satisfied, instruction of children by their parents in their home is an acceptable alternative form of education under the policy of the Commonwealth of Virginia. Any parent of any child who will have reached the fifth birthday on or before September 30 of any school year and who has not passed the seventeenth birthday may elect to provide home instruction in lieu of school attendance if he (1) holds a baccalaureate degree in any subject from an accredited institution of higher education; or (2) is a teacher of qualifications prescribed by the Board of Education; or (3) has enrolled the child or children in a correspondence course approved by the Board of Education; or (4) provides a program of study or curriculum which, in the judgement of the division superintendent, includes the standards of learning objectives adopted by the Board of Education for language arts and mathematics and provides evidence that the parent is able to provide an adequate education for the child.

B. Any parent who elects to provide home instruction in lieu of school attendance shall annually notify the division superintendent in August of his intention to so instruct the child and provide a description of the curriculum to be followed for the coming year and evidence of having met one of the criteria for providing home instruction as required by paragraph A of this section. The division superintendent shall notify the Superintendent of Public Instruction of the persons approved to provide home instruction.

C. The parent who elects to provide home instruction shall provide the division superintendent by August 1 following the school year in which the child has received home instruction with either (1) evidence that the child has attained a composite score above the fortieth percentile on a battery of achievement tests which have been approved by the Board of Education for use in the public schools or (2) an evaluation or assessment which, in the judgment of the division superintendent, indicates that the child is achieving an adequate level of educational growth and progress.

In the event that evidence of progress as required in this paragraph is not provided by the parent, home instruction shall cease and the parent shall make other arrangements for the education of the child which comply with 22.1-254 of the Code of Virginia.

D. For purposes of this section, "parent" means the biological parent or adoptive parent, guardian, or other person having control or charge of a child.

Nothing in this section shall prohibit a pupil and his parents from obtaining an excuse from school attendance by reason of bona fide religious training or belief pursuant to S. 22.1-257 of this Code.

E. Any party aggrieved by a decision of the division superintendent may appeal his decision within thirty days to an independent hearing officer. . . . The costs of the hearing shall be borne by The Party Appealing.

And Georgia

The other state to pass new homeschooling legislation recently is Georgia. Senate Bill 504 struck much of the compulsory education law, and provided requirements for both private schools and home study programs. The new law reads:

20-2-690 . . . The term "private school" means an institution meeting the following criteria or requirements:

1) The primary purpose of the institution is to provide education or, if the primary purpose of the institution is religious in nature, the institution shall provide the basic academic educational program specified in paragraph (4) of this subsection;

2) The institution is privately controlled and operates on a continuing basis;

3) The institution provides instruction each 12 months for the equivalent of 180 school days of education with each school day consisting of at least four and one-half school hours;

4) The institution provides a basic academic educational program, which includes, but is not limited to, reading, language arts, mathematics, social studies, and science;

5) Within 30 days after the beginning of each school year, it shall be the duty of the administrator of each private school to provide to the superintendent of schools of each local public school district which has residents enrolled in the private school a list of the name, age, and residence of each resident so enrolled. At the end of each school month, it shall be the duty of the administrator of each private school to notify the superintendent of each local public school district of the name, age, and residence of each student residing in the public school district who enrolls or terminates enrollment at the private school during the immediately preceding school month. Enrollment records and reports shall not be used for any purpose except providing necessary enrollment information, except with the permission of the parent or guardian of a child or pursuant to the subpoena of a court of competent jurisdiction; and

6) Any building used by the institution for private school purposes meets all health and safety standards established under state law and local ordinances.

Parents or guardians may teach their children at home in a *home study program* which meets the following requirements:

1) The parent, parents, or guardian must submit within 30 days after the establishment of a home study program and by September 1 annually thereafter a declaration of intent to utilize a home study program to the superintendent of schools of the local school district in which the home study program is located;

2) The declaration shall include a list of the names and ages of the students who are enrolled in the home study program, the address where the home study program is located, and a statement of

the 12-month period that is to be considered the school year for that home study program. Enrollment records and reports shall not be used for any purpose except providing necessary enrollment information, except with the permission of the parent or guardian of a child or pursuant to the subpoena of a court of competent jurisdiction.

3) Parents or guardians may teach only their own children in the home study program provided the teaching parent or guardian possesses at least a high school diploma or the equivalent GED certificate, but the parents or guardians may employ a tutor who holds at least a baccalaureate college degree to teach such children;

4) The home study program shall provide a basic academic educational program, which includes, but is not limited to, reading, language arts, mathematics, social studies, and science;

5) The home study program must provide instruction each 12 months to home study students equivalent to 180 school days of education with each school day consisting of at least four and one-half school hours unless the child is physically unable to comply with the above rule;

6) Attendance records for the home study program shall be kept and shall be submitted at the end of each month to the superintendent of schools of the local school district in which the home study program is located. Attendance records and reports shall not be used for any purpose except providing necessary attendance information, except with the permission of the parent or guardian of a child or pursuant to the subpoena of a court of competent jurisdiction;

7) Students in home study programs shall be subject to an appropriate nationally standardized testing program administered in consultation with a person trained in the administration and interpretation of norm reference tests to evaluate their educational progress at least every three years beginning at the end of the third grade and records of such tests and scores shall be retained but shall not be required to be submitted to public educational authorities; and

8) The home study program instructor shall write an annual progress assessment report which shall include the instructor's individualized assessment of the student's academic progress in each of the subject areas specified in paragraph (4) of this subsection, and such progress reports shall be retained by the parent, parents, or guardian of children in the home study program for a period of at least three years.

Any person who operates a home study program without complying with the requirements shall be guilty of a misdemeanor and upon conviction shall be punished by a fine not to exceed $100.

[JH:] The newsletter of *Georgians for Freedom in Education*, 3/1/84, says:

> Georgians for Freedom in Education worked very closely with all who were involved in getting SB 504 written and passed. . . . We do not foresee the Department of Education challenging or threatening any family who wants to teach their children at home under this present administration, unless the parents decide not to comply with the new law. Therefore, we encourage every family to honor this law if at all possible.
>
> For those parents who for one reason or another do not want to be recognized as a home study program, we encourage them to enroll as satellites of private schools.
>
> Senator John Foster proved himself again and again a friend to those who are earnestly desiring to teach their children at home. A very strong opponent in the 1983 GA Assembly, this year he reversed his decision against home educators and became a very strong ally.

[JH:] There is so much other useful information and advice in this newsletter, relating to the passage of this bill and the steps to be taken in following it up, that people involved in or planning legislative campaigns in other states might be wise to order a copy of it, either from G.F.F.E. (PO Box 69, Palmetto GA 30268) or from us. In either case, please send S.A.S.E. and a dollar or two to cover costs.

Comments On the New Laws

We could say of the Virginia and Georgia homeschooling laws that they have closed a loophole but opened a door. In more rural terms, they have made the fence much harder to crawl under, but have then put in a gate. I consider this a big step forward, though some homeschoolers will disagree. They liked crawling under the fence because you didn't have to talk to anyone; with a gate, there's going to be someone standing there whom you have to talk to. But, as we have said here before, the states were bound to fix those fences anyway; the unregulated private school option was always a temporary one at best.

In Virginia the loophole had in fact been plugged and the fence made crawl-proof even before the bill was passed, since the state Supreme Court had already ruled that a family teaching their own children at home could not be considered a private school. There was in fact no legal way for Virginians to teach their own children, and the state was getting ready to take to court a large number of families who had been using the private school option. So the law has turned what could have been an extremely unfavorable situation into a very favorable one.

Though it is somewhat more restrictive than the Georgia and some other state laws, notably Louisiana (which will soon be up for review), the Virginia law seems to me in some ways to be a more important precedent. For one thing, the state educational authorities seem perfectly ready to live with it. While the bill was in the house, the State Board of Education passed by a vote of six to two a resolution supporting it. After the bill passed, Theo Giesy, a pioneer and leader of the homeschooling movement in Virginia, talked to a number of the district superintendents who will now have the authority to approve or disapprove many homeschooling programs. She said that all she talked to seemed satisfied with the bill and intended to interpret it liberally. Time will tell how liberal they really are; for the moment, it does seem as if this bill makes Virginia one of the best homeschooling states. And it does not look as if every year we are going to have to go back to the legislature and fight to save the bill's life. Whereas in states such as Louisiana homeschoolers may have won glorious legislative victories, but only in a war that is still going on, in Virginia it looks as if the war between educators and homeschoolers is over.

As a model for other state legislatures to copy, the Virginia law seems to me more persuasive and acceptable. I doubt that there are more than two or three states, if that many, that are likely in any near future to pass a homeschooling law as liberal as Georgia's, whereas a dozen or more might well pass a law more like Virginia's. One thing that helped get such an unrestrictive law passed in Georgia may have been that the state superintendent, who opposed the bill, has some powerful enemies in the legislature, for whom his opposing a bill is a good reason to be for it. This is not likely to be true in most state legislatures, where in general state superintendents tend to be very influential.

At the Virginia hearings I was struck by the great friendliness, respect, and support shown by the legislators to the homeschoolers. They did all they could to make us, adults and children, feel welcome and at home. They were clearly impressed by the excellence of our testimony and the happiness and maturity of our children, and were eager to write a law under which we could legally continue to educate these children.

Two short observations about the Virginia law. Though it says that a single family in their home cannot be a private school, it still does not say what a private school is, so parents who do not wish to or are not able to use the other provisions of the law to teach their own children may be able, by joining with others like themselves, to make what the courts will consider a private school. As for the clause excusing children from school attendance "by reason of bona fide religious training or belief," the courts are likely in interpreting this to apply a strict *Yoder* test, i.e., are you a member of an established sect which *as a matter of doctrine* forbids your sending your children to school. It is not likely that this clause will be very helpful to most families.

It would be unrealistic and unwise to suppose that legislators are by nature hostile to homeschoolers and that only by intimidating them can we get good homeschooling laws. We are a long way from being able to intimidate legislators. In every state in the union public school employees outnumber homeschoolers by at least ten or twenty to one. When large numbers of homeschoolers descend on a state capital to protest a bad law or ask for a good one, it is very unlikely that legislators think, "I'd better vote their way or they'll have me out of office." What they probably do think is something more like, "If these folks are determined and organized enough to put on this kind of demonstration, we can trust them to do a good job of educating their own children." The legislators are not intimidated by our demonstration so much as persuaded. And even if we had every reason to believe of a particular legislator that only intimidation would bring him our way, it would still be good tactics to talk to him as if we were trying to persuade.

In my testimony to the Virginia legislators I said some things that in one form or another we might be wise to say to all legislators considering home education legislation.

> I would like to thank you . . . for all the hard work that you have done on this legislation. It is not easy in this matter to reconcile the legitimate but conflicting Constitutional claims of parents and the state, and I congratulate you on the skill with which you have addressed this difficult task.

In conclusion I would like to say that in guiding homeschooling, the state will best serve its interests and those of its children by guiding with a very light rein. Time has shown that the overwhelming majority of homeschoolers, whatever may be their educational background, are conscientious and capable and do an excellent job of teaching their own children. Time has also shown that in doing so they use a very wide variety of curricula, timetables, methods, materials, and means of evaluation, according to the needs and learning styles of their children. The state would be wise, in whatever ways it can, to protect and encourage this pedagogical diversity, not least of all because from it may well come many ideas that can prove very helpful to the schools themselves, which for many years to come most children will continue to attend.

A final general comment. My strong feeling is that in the next few years most legislatures will want to legitimize homeschooling, that is, to provide explicitly legal ways for parents to do it. At the same time they are almost certain to demand some kind of state supervision and control; even the sponsor of the very liberal Georgia law, in his speech to his colleagues proposing and defending his bill, said over and over again that he was *not* proposing totally unregulated homeschooling. In insisting that the states do have a Constitutional interest in the education of children, the legislatures are strongly supported by both state and federal courts, most recently in *Duro*, about which we write elsewhere in this issue and which I will discuss at greater length in coming issues. No use to ask them for a blank check; they will not give us one.

It will, I think, be a tactical mistake for homeschoolers, as some have done, to oppose all legislation which does not seem to them ideal, that is, which allows homeschooling with virtually no restriction. Unless the conditions are outrageously restrictive, i.e., requiring all homeschoolers to have teachers' certificates, or requiring them to adhere strictly to the curricula and timetables of the public schools, we would be wiser to give at least qualified support to any homeschooling laws the legislatures produce, even while expressing whatever reservations we may have. It is puzzling, distressing, and in the end irritating for legislators who have worked hard on a bill to hear homeschoolers testifying both for and against it; it makes them begin to wonder, perhaps, how intelligent we really are. In Virginia this conflicting testimony did no harm; in Washington, it not only resulted in neither of two bills being passed, either one of which would have been better than the present situation, but caused an influential sponsor of one of the bills to say, for the moment at least, that he was not interested in sponsoring any future bills. And it is possible, human nature being what it is, that a legislature which is continually blocked in its efforts to make homeschooling legal may decide that the next best thing is to make it illegal. If legislatures are trying, as I believe more and more of them will try, to help us, we would be wise to meet them half way.—JH

Not A Good Way

[DR:] On Dec. 8, 1983, the Maine Supreme Court unanimously denied the appeal of Patrick and Dianne McDonough, who had refused to seek approval for homeschooling their children, and who acted as their own lawyers in court. We hope other homeschoolers can learn from their experience. From the ruling written by Justice McKusick:

> At the hearing before the District Court, the State presented undisputed evidence tending to prove the following facts. On August 25, 1982, Leonard Ney, the superintendent of School Administrative District No. 64, was informed by the principal of the elementary school in Bradford, that there were some children of school age living in the Bradford area who were not yet enrolled for the upcoming school year. The principal directed him to the McDonough home. When the superintendent visited there on August 27, he was greeted in the front yard by Mrs. McDonough. Superintendent Ney observed four children looking out the windows of the house and was informed by Mrs. McDonough that three of her four children were of school age. . . . She told Ney that she and her husband had decided not to enroll the children in school. In reply, Superintendent Ney explained to Mrs. McDonough that "home education plans" were permitted but that a formal procedure for approval was required.
>
> A meeting was arranged between Superintendent Ney and Mr. McDonough at Ney's office in early September. At that meeting Ney told Mr. McDonough that he must either enroll his children in school or submit a home instruction plan to the board of directors of the school district. After being duly notified, Mr. and Mrs. McDonough attended a school board meeting held on September 27, 1982. There Mr. McDonough, asserting a constitutional right to educate his children at home, told the board that he had not submitted a home instruction plan and that he had not obtained any permission from the superintendent or the school board to keep the children at home. . . . By unanimous vote the school board found the McDonough children to be truant.
>
> At oral argument, defendants conceded that they do not base their claim of a right to educate their children at home on the Free Exercise Clause of the United States Constitution (First Amendment). Instead, defendants rely on a variety of other provisions in the state and federal constitutions, including the remainder of the First Amendment and Amendments 4, 5, 8, 9, 10, 13, and 14 to the U.S. Constitution, as well as sections 1, 2, 3, 5, 6, 6-A, and 24 of Article I of the Maine Constitution. Defendants' brief indicates that their claim of a right to educate their children at home is based fundamentally on the guarantee in the 14th Amendment to the U.S. Constitution that no state shall deprive

any person of liberty without due process of law.

The statute that the McDonoughs challenge neither compels every student to attend a public school nor prohibits home education. It provides in part:

"A child shall be excused from attending a public day school if he obtains equivalent instruction in a private school *or in any other manner arranged* for by the school committee or the board of directors and if the equivalent instruction is approved by the commissioner. 20 MRSA S 911(3) (A)."

This provision acknowledges the right of parents to educate their children at home. It defends against abuse of that right by requiring that parents obtain the approval of school officials for home educational programs. If approval is denied by the local school committee or board of directors, the statute further provides that an aggrieved parent may appeal to the Commissioner of Educational and Cultural Services. . . . If their appeal in turn is denied by the commissioner, parents have judicial review available to them in the Superior Court.Despite repeated invitations by the superintendent of their school district, the McDonoughs consistently refused to submit a proposal for home instruction of their children. As a result, school authorities never had an opportunity to consider the McDonoughs' claim of a right to educate their children at home.We find that the requirement in section 911 that parents seek the approval of school authorities for home educational plans is fully justified by the state's "high responsibility for education of its citizens." (*Wisconsin v. Yoder*, 406 US 213) For the state to allow home education without imposing some standards as to quality and duration would be, in many cases, to allow parents to deprive their children of any education whatsoever. Not all parents who would hold their children out of school under such an unlimited exception to the compulsory education statute would have the sincere desire, which is no doubt present in the instant case, to provide their children with adequate instruction. Furthermore, many parents, even though they have a sincere desire to educate their children at home, lack the necessary training and facilities to do so. Defendants in fact make no argument that the requirement of prior approval of home instruction plans violates the state or federal constitution. In any event, we do not find anything unreasonable in that requirement.

In short, where the state has provided a reasonable procedure whereby defendants may vindicate their asserted right to educate their children at home, they may not ignore that procedure and then appeal to this court claiming that their right has been denied. Defendants are not barred by this decision from submitting a home instruction proposal to their local school board at any time in the future. If their proposal is denied, they may pursue the avenues of appeal we have outlined above. However, until they obtain approval for a home educational program or qualify for some other statutory exception, they are required by law to keep their children enrolled in public school.

[Footnote #5:] Defendants do argue before this court that their constitutional privilege against self-incrimination was violated by the requirement that they apply for and obtain prior approval for a home instruction plan. This argument has no merit. Under the express terms of both the federal and state constitutions, the privilege against self-incrimination applies only to criminal cases. . . . Furthermore, the record in this civil violation proceeding is devoid of any showing on the part of defendants as to how information required in an application for approval of a home instruction proposal would tend to convict them in a criminal prosecution.

"Writing To Read" Is Working

In "From Writing to Reading," GWS 37, we wrote about a program to help children to read by having them first write on computers, that has recently been started by Dr. John Henry Martin, working with the IBM Corporation. Since then, Dr. Martin's company (JHM Corp., 511 S Federal Hwy, Stuart FL 33494; 305-286-3055) sent us a more up-to-date report on this work: an article by Bernard Asbell in the New York Times Magazine, *2/26/84, entitled "Writers' Workshop at Age 5," and sub headed "A new system is teaching children how to write letters before they read. And, with the aid of computers, it is resulting in a startling increase in youthful literacy." It says, in part:*

> On the morning I watched her, Christal [a 6-year-old black child] wasn't writing with a pencil, although she can. She was composing on a Selectric typewriter. Furthermore, in kindergarten she's learned to build letters into words by working on a computer. She learned so well that Christal knows how to write down anything she can say. I'll repeat: She knows how to write anything she can say. And so do most of her 75 or so classmates (their teachers estimate that, at most, nine or 10 might need a little prompting). Specially selected verbal prodigies? Not at all. They have just graduated from the three regular kindergarten rooms of an ordinary public school of an ordinary Southern hosiery-milling town, Burlington, N.C., where the average I.Q. of schoolchildren— tested from the third grade on—happens to match the national average just about on the nose. What is happening with these North Carolina children is also happening in every other school in Burlington; in kindergartens of Raleigh, the state capital, and in the rustic village of Brevard . . . as well as in several Florida schools. It is happening in big-city public schools in Houston, Washington and Boston. . . . 105 schools in 17 school systems. Unlike many educational demonstrations . . . which often are proclaimed successes based on testing only a few hundred or even a few dozen children, this one involves 10,000 5- and 6-year-olds, white and black, Hispanic and Asian and Indian, of every income level. The two-year demonstration will be completed this June.

> "It wasn't easy for us to agree to participate." [Says Floretta D. McKenzie, Washington's superintendent of schools]. "When you say you're going to let a machine instruct, and that it will succeed where some of us have not, that's hard for us educators to accept."

> The project is the brainchild of Dr. John Henry Martin, former school superintendent of Mt. Vernon, NY, and a lifelong student of how children begin learning to read and write. He calls his method "Writing to Read". . . . What is new about Dr. Martin's method is not the computer, not the typewriter, not even the earlier than usual start at the age of 5. It is a system of teaching a child how to convert the sounds he already speaks into "sounds" he can write, or as Dr. Martin puts it, "having children understand that they can talk with their fingers on paper." The system aims at allowing the child to write at the upper levels of his ability to think and talk. Having mastered the encoding of written language, logically the child should also be able to read at the upper levels of his individual ability to recognize and understand words. Writing to Read is the first effort at programming this old idea in meticulous detail, offering it to a broad range of children, and carefully testing its results.

> A full-scale evaluation by the Education Testing Service of Princeton, NJ, will be issued after the current school year. But last June, many of the participating school districts released their own one-year measurements, based chiefly on giving kindergartners and some first-graders a standard first-grade California Achievement Test. With striking consistency, both geographically and

demographically, the children as a group scored higher in reading skills than 89 percent of their peers. The typical child comes to kindergarten with a working vocabulary of 2,000 to 4,000 words. Rather than help him expand that remarkable linguistic achievement, which the child has brought off with *no formal instruction*, the school usually issues him a standard first-grade reading book that narrows his mind to about 400 words, and a spelling book that runs to even fewer words.

Christal Graves's teacher, Betty Coley, after 20 years in conventional kindergartens and early grades, still blinks in near disbelief at what she sees in her own room: "The other day, a first-grader wrote a story that had Switzerland in it. After she wrote it, she asked me if she spelled it right. She had 'Switserlin.' No, I didn't correct her. I just told her to be on the lookout for the way books spell it. She'll see and remember it. . . ."

Education professionals, on first hearing of Writing to Read, almost always recoil at the thought of permitting children to spell incorrectly without immediate correction. Usually—but not always—they withdraw their objections upon hearing that within two years, tests show these children to be better spellers than most.

The practice of starting children to read at 6, like much educational practice, appears to be observed mainly because it is observed. "If you ask teachers to tell you why," said Dr. Martin, "you get statistical generalizations that are shallowly based on faulty research." He cited some studies from the 1930s, indicating that children below the age of 6½ didn't learn as well as those over that age. "They didn't—by the reading methods used, which we now reject."

IBM bought the sales rights to Writing to Read in 1982. Dr. Martin's toughest condition—which IBM accepted—was that they must underwrite, to the tune of $2 million, the current two-year national demonstration and the Educational Testing Service evaluation. . . . These commitments pale before the potential profits to IBM from computers and software if Writing to Read is widely adopted by schools. . . . IBM estimates that a school can install Writing to Read at a cost of about $60 per year per kindergarten child. . . . By present standards of per-pupil cost [$1500 to over $4000] that added cost is scarcely an obstacle. [Says Dr. James E. Surratt, Burlington's superintendent of schools] "This is the first time in a long time that I've seen schools give a child something that was the most important thing in his life. You know, I hate to admit that."

[JH:] When I last saw Dr. Martin, probably at least fifteen years ago, and after he had resigned as superintendent of schools in Mt. Vernon, he said to me that he had decided that schools could not be changed in any significant way from the inside, and was going to see if he could find a way to change them from the outside. It looks as if he just might have found it.

There is nothing really new about anything in his program—with one exception, of which more in a minute. As I said in in *GWS* 37, just about everything Martin is doing with typewriters was done in the '50s in much the same way, by Dr. O. K. Moore, who even called his typewriters "Talking Typewriters." The idea of having children write freely, using their own invented but surprisingly phonic spellings for words has been pursued, researched, and reported for years, by (among many others) Carol Chomsky and Charles Read. In my own *The Underachieving School* I describe once letting first graders write freely, spelling for them on the board any words they wanted spelled. They worked for forty minutes and would have gone on if not interrupted by lunch hour. A number of other teachers have described similar work. Years later, Glenda Bissex, in the wonderful book *Gnys At Wrk* (*GWS* 24, 25) described how her son figured out for himself how to write, and along with it, how to read, by actually writing things (at home) that he wanted to write.

What Martin is doing, people have been doing for years, always with spectacularly good results. For just as many years, all but a handful of schools and teachers have turned their backs on these successes. The comments of teachers in this *Times* article suggest how fiercely most educators would ordinarily resist this program. It is indeed hard for educators to accept that children can easily learn in a few months, with a machine, what most teachers find hard to teach them in years. Educators do indeed "recoil," usually with indignation and anger, from the idea of letting children make mistakes, in spelling or anything else, without immediately correcting them, often harshly. Ordinarily there would be little chance of such a radical program being adopted on any wide scale in the schools. Even computers, fashionable as they are, would not have been enough to make it happen—neither in this country nor in France has Seymour Papert been able to get more than a few schools to make a sustained and imaginative use of Logo (see *Mindstorms, GWS* 24).

The great social invention of Dr. Martin's that may succeed in getting this program into the schools on a wide scale lies in the three magic letters: IBM. The fact that this huge, rich, smart, resourceful, and generally much admired corporation has been persuaded to take an interest in this program is the one thing that gives it a real chance of succeeding. IBM will not give up easily the enormous profits they stand to get from it. If even after a successful demonstration the schools drag their feet in accepting it, IBM will surely take their case to the public and to the legislatures.

Meanwhile I think we might do well, in whatever ways we can, to call this program to the attention of our schools, our media, and our politicians. As it turns out, Boston is taking part in the demonstration project, so it's very possible that if the results are as good as they seem almost certain to be, our schools will adopt the method on a large scale. I intend to do whatever I can to make sure that they do. I have already written our superintendent to congratulate him on taking part in the demonstration and to urge him to put the program into all our schools as soon as possible. In bringing this matter to the attention of schools and in arousing public support for it, homeschoolers can show by our acts first, that we are very much interested in the learning and growth of all children, and secondly, that homeschoolers are not an enemy but an ally of the schools and should be seen and treated that way.

Letters On Reading

Karen Schadel (NY) sent us a copy of a long, enthusiastic letter she wrote to Nancy Wallace after reading Nancy's book Better Than School *(avail. here, $13.50 + post). She said, in part:*

I noticed a similarity between Vita and Joshua regarding their reading. Joshua also refuses to sound out new words and seems to read by memory or context. I've completely given up trying to introduce or continue with phonetics. He simply resists so much; it takes all the enjoyment out of our reading times.

He has just started to really read again, and this time he's reading to Sadrah from picture books we have at home. In between I watched him and saw that he could read most anything he wanted to from a catalogue, food labels, road signs, store signs, or selected words from magazines and books, so I wasn't too worried. I realized he just needed time to come around. He isn't reading big books yet although he recently expressed the desire to be able to read a big "chapter" book because I had to stop too often during a very suspenseful story and he could hardly wait for me to read again.

[DR: Karen later wrote to us:] In *Better Than School*, Nancy Wallace mentioned the "Little Bear" books by Else Holmelund Minarik. I made a mental note regarding them and at our next library visit, we found two of them. I showed one to Joshua (7) and stated it was a book I thought he could read. He wasn't too interested, but I felt he was ready for just a little push since he had been expressing the desire to read a "big book." So right there we opened the book and I said, "Just read the first sentence." He did! Then I encouraged him on to the next sentence and we progressed to the next page, and pretty soon we were both laughing at how cute and funny the Little Bear character was.

After three pages I was distracted to attend to my daughter. When I looked to find Joshua, he had settled into a beanbag chair next to the fireplace and was actually reading. I asked him to tell me about what was happening and he proceeded to detail the story to me. He held the book open and read as we walked from the library to the car and drove 20 minutes to our house. And what surprised me the most was his ability to read silently. It seems I remember first learning to read aloud and then acquiring the ability to read silently. I also remember other children in school who were scolded for reading aloud when they weren't supposed to and also for moving their lips while reading.

This all led me to believe that Joshua was more than ready to read, but is the type who waits until he can do something really well before he does it— such was his pattern with talking and walking. For quite some time now, I believe he has been reading to himself—not books, but words from the world around him. Had I not investigated the "Little Bear" books, he might have gone on indefinitely reading our picture books to his sister, but not filling his need for a book of his own to read to himself that told a story.

As Joshua is my first child, I realize I am guilty of sometimes presenting him with the opportunity to experience something he might not otherwise come up with or try on his own. Yet I can generally read his signals and I know when to back off. If he had responded negatively that day in the library, I would have dropped the issue.

Peeka Schevens wrote in the Colorado Homeschooling Network Newsletter, *2/84:*

> Magnus (6) has been hounding me to teach him to read. This morning I told him that at 9:30 we were to start working on reading. He cleared his little table and got a pad, pencil, and his index cards. I left the breakfast dishes and brought a couple of books with very simple vocabulary. I asked Magnus if he wanted to learn the words from the books so he could read them, but he made up a simple poem this morning: "One, two, Jordan and you," (Jordan is his younger brother) and said he wanted to learn to read that.
>
> I told him how to spell the words and he wrote them in a list on a blank page. Then he decided to illustrate with a picture of Jordan and me fishing because the J reminded him of a fish hook. When that was done he copied each word onto an index card. With the list in front of him for reference, he shuffled the cards and read each one.
>
> Then he suggested that I write some words and I suggested I write the same words so we could match pairs. At that point we played a modified version of "Go Fish" with five pairs of words.
>
> I really like the fact that he started hounding me to help him. Having an appetite for knowledge is much more beneficial than being over-fed. And, by the way, before we started and as soon as we were finished, Magnus kept encouraging and teaching Jordan (4) that he could read, too.

From Susan Price (FL):

I think you go overboard in telling people not to teach their children. Most of us were not taught to read by our parents and so we don't have the model in our minds that we have about so many other things that we teach our children without hardly even thinking about them—like how to tie your shoes, how to work a zipper, how to cook, how to hold your silverware right, etc., etc., etc. As a result, people have to make a more conscious effort to teach their kids to read. Yes, it's possible for kids to learn to read completely on their own, but it's a lot easier for them if they get some (non-pressured) help.

What Ann did [DR: Susan visited Ann Bodine in N.J. last year] with her children was to write words on index cards, one word per card. You could ask the child what words he wants to learn.

Ann says be sure to put in "poop!" A person who wrote an article in *Mothering* suggested doing one new word a day. I saw Ann going through her words with David. If he didn't know the word, she made up a sentence with the word being the last word in it and letting him see if he could fill in the last word. Ann said that after Jonathan had learned only 300 words, he had gotten a good enough intuitive grasp of phonics that he could read any new word he came to. She said that Karina wasn't able to pick up phonics so easily, so she spent a couple of hours teaching her phonics and that was all she needed.

For people who want to try out teaching phonics to their kids, I have a suggestion on how to do it easily. . . . I just wrote a list of rhyming words, like rat, mat, cat, sat, etc., and then read through them several times myself as I pointed to them, then had Faith read along with me several times until she wanted to read through them herself. She liked doing this, so we did a lot of lists this way. The more we did it, the more she got so she needed me reading them fewer times before she went ahead herself.

Another thing to do with a beginning reader is to show him a word on a page, like *the*, and see if he can find the rest of the *the*'s on that page. And go through the rest of the book finding them. Faith used to like to do this. . . . She would circle the words lightly with a pencil.

While *The Cat in the Hat* and *The Cat in the Hat Comes Back* are okay, kids don't like books that are barely-disguised phonics lessons, in my experience—they want books with a good story line. . . . What my kids love are the Berenstein Bear books (the hardcover ones in rhyme). And *Go, Dog, Go!* is great.

With Matt, we are doing comics. I have stopped having him do a certain number of pages a day (or a certain number of frames of the comic). What we do generally, now, is that he reads the short "balloons" and I read the long ones. I go by his guidance on which ones I should read. I'll wait a second to see if he's going to read one and go ahead if he doesn't. . . . I will often say the first word or two to start him off.

Matt just read a comic book on his own—out loud—while we were waiting for Faith to get her shoes on before we went to the store. . . . It was the same comic he's read the last few days—about Donald and the boys trying to catch frogs. Comics are really fantastic. Donald's three nephews are always so resourceful and smarter than he is—and always getting into all sorts of adult adventures. One of the guys in the comic Matt read was Colonel O'Corn—I didn't get that for a while. You ought to sell comics!

[JH: What I say about teaching is, don't teach them unless asked. Doing things for their own sake where children can see them, is not the same as doing things you otherwise would not do *so that* the children can see you doing them. I admit the line between is not always clear, but I can usually tell the difference between natural talk to children and "teaching" talk.]

And from Illinois:

I have enrolled my children in Clonlara. . . . My 13-year-old son is very involved with Dungeons and Dragons, creating his own mazes, monsters, and characters. As he has never read a book (or anything else) by his own choice, I'm encouraged that he reads everything he can get his hands on concerning D&D. He is also beginning to raise finches, and we just had the excitement of seeing the first three eggs. (I took him to the library to get a book about finches, and he has been interested in my reading it to him.) When he was little, he read "Cat-in-the-Hat" type books to me, and I read a great deal to him. In school he read as much of the schoolbooks as he felt he had to, but he has never completed a book because he wanted to, or even a book that he was required to write a book report on. He used to buy books at school and check them out from the library, but he has never read more than a few pages in them.

He just finds no pleasure in reading, and it grieves me. I have always had this pleasure, and perhaps even have read too much. We have a library in the house, 56 shelves of books, with about 10 shelves devoted solely to children's books. I have always read to the children, and they both still enjoy this. My 8-year-old reads for his own enjoyment several hours a day, but I have so far been unable to interest his big brother in a book enough that he will want to finish it. I have started books and given them to him, and they remain unfinished.

My plan for this year is to not make him read anything unless he chooses to. So far, he is reading the Dungeons and Dragons handbooks, and reads the Adventure computer games (for TI99/4A), and he did read two chapters of a book about gorillas after a trip to the zoo, but that has been it.

The Drawbacks Of Reading

From Penny Barker (OH)—see "Five Years At Home," GWS *27:*

A subject I have been going over in my mind for about six months now is this reading question. I agree with you that reading is a useful skill, but it is only that. It seems that we have made a very much larger ado over this skill than is necessary or even desirable.

In the last year all five of my children have become regular ornithologists. They have spotted and identified 36 different birds around our home. They have observed all kinds of nests and eggs and can identify many birds from their songs and calls as well as make the calls on their Audubon bird caller. The children's ages are 5, 6, 9, 10, and 15, and the way they discuss their recent sightings and discoveries you would think they were all the same age. Britt, the 15-year-old, as the reader, does help with the identification details the Peterson Field Guide offers when the others bring the book to her, after they have located the photo of the bird in the Guide.... The reading in the Field Guide is a *very small part* of the actual bird watching and the four younger children do not feel any loss of status or inferiority because they cannot yet read the Field Guide.

After having been a Montessori teacher for eight years, and having seen parents push reading to the exclusion of all other skills, I have really down-played the reading with my own children in the six years I've been unschooling. Partly because of this, Britt does not see herself as superior to her younger siblings in regard to the bird watching. Their observations and input she sees as every bit as worthy as hers.

Now this is the observation she came up with the other day in regard to an 11-year-old visitor. (We have children spend time with us here on the farmstead during the summer who are prep schooled, public schooled, private schooled.) She was amazed that this visitor was much, much more interested in looking at the bird in the Field Guide than watching the actual bird, and also much more interested in writing a "report" on the bird from the information in the Field Guide and then showing the report to me for approval. This was an intelligent girl supposedly extremely interested in birds. Britt was amazed at her lack of interest in the *actual* bird and her focus on the written word instead. I have observed this many times over the past seven summers.

When a mother or father has told me how very much their child likes to read, how far above grade level he or she reads and then that child spends a week with us here at the farm where reading is done only in the evenings, that child has a very difficult time coming to grips with the actual *doing* of things. It's as if they would rather *read* about it than *do* it. In contrast, children who come here who have difficulty with reading and writing by school standards often excel in the actual work and life of the farmstead. They go home having experienced so much and seem really fulfilled.

My own children take in the world around them so whole-heartedly every single day. They read for pleasure only in the evenings and then usually only in the winter when cold weather keeps them close to the stove. Britt will go to the vet books and other reference books any time she needs them, and Maggie (10) will struggle through her *Shepherd's Guidebook* if she has a problem with her flock of sheep.

I also notice that the non-readers in the family have memorized much more of the bird information than Britt who writes her information down and then feels she can forget it since it is recorded. The non-readers always have the information at hand because they have memorized it. Interesting, isn't it? (I've been referring mainly to the bird example but the same things apply to all of the other interests they have.)

I will never keep any of them from reading when they want to, of course, but I really think parents can make reading *too* important just by being *too* thrilled when their child recognizes a letter for the first time. I've been rather thrilled that my 9-and 10-year-olds have taken a late interest in this abstraction. They take in so much sensorially. No matter how many times the Great Blue Heron flies over the house, they will watch and watch until he is completely out of sight. This is in contrast to the "gifted" readers who will give a quick glance and a disinterested "Yeah" when the great bird is pointed out to them in flight. Very sad. I am not an anti-intellectual (I read to all five of mine every night from 1 to 2 hours from all kinds of literature) but I'm just wondering if reading a little later might not be *better* than reading so early.

In his reply, John wrote:

Your point about reading reminded me of something I read years ago in an essay by the great British essayist William Hazlitt. He wrote an article about reading, which could be turned, almost word for word, into what a lot of people (including me) are saying about TV.

Briefly, Hazlitt's point was yours, that people will substitute reading about things for looking at things. I love reading and read a great deal (I hate to think how much), but I never allow myself to forget that someone, somewhere, has to see or do something directly before it can be written about. I still learn a lot more by looking and listening and thinking about what I see and hear, than I do by reading.

I read a lot when I was a kid, but I think I read in the way and for the same reasons that a lot of people watch TV, because the imagined world of books was more interesting and less threatening than the real world I lived in.

Real Experience vs. TV

From Donna Jordan (CA):

One line in Wendy Wartes' letter ("In Defense of TV," *GWS* 36) struck me.... She writes, "I have never been fortunate enough to travel and though I hope my children will have the first-hand opportunity to view other countries, I truly feel TV can fill the gap." I haven't travelled much either, partly no money, partly because it's not something I do very easily and yet, when I watch TV, I don't have the feeling that I'm experiencing what it's like to be somewhere else. I mostly feel like I'm sitting, ignoring the people around me, and wasting my time. Even the few programs I've watched that seemed interesting at the time have escaped my memory. Although I do remember some frightening images, I don't remember any information.

Every year when I was a child we went to Ida and Danny's house to look at their slides from the latest trip. They didn't have any children but they did have a little theater in their house. We saw slides of Ida in India, Ida in Africa, Ida next to the Eiffel Tower, etc. The slides weren't very interesting, but Ida was quite interesting. She was very modern with puffy blonde hair and kind of loud. I remember how her house looked, I heard stereo sound there for the first time, I got locked in the bathroom there once, I looked out at the lake through the huge picture window, and watched the cocker spaniels race up and down in their pen. I don't remember thinking it would be fun to go to France but it was fun to be at someone else's house. The experience of Ida and her house is what was real for me.

I would say that an hour walk near your house would yield more of real interest than a TV show about wolves in the Arctic. Do you know the people around you? Do you know all the plants and animals? Do you know what's under the ground? The wires overhead? Which way the wind blows? Can you draw a picture of your house? What color is the house two doors down? How do the plants and animals change with the seasons? Does someone nearby need your help with something? How fast can you walk? How slow? It seems that we're always trying to take in more and more of the world yet we know very little about our own surroundings. Children especially love and deserve a detailed look at what's nearby.

And . . . how about pretending to be a wolf? Write and read stories and poems about wolves, make wolf masks, draw wolves, sculpt a wolf (how about life size out of chicken wire and papier-mâché?), write wolfy music, listen to *Peter and the Wolf* and then go ahead and be a wolf for a while. Once you have a TV image of a wolf it's just about impossible to be a wolf yourself; the TV has made it too clear that you aren't a wolf. It seems to take the soul out of the wolf and leave you the "real" image of fur, claws, and teeth.

I think what it boils down to, is why do we learn what we learn? Why bother? . . . To be continually somewhat interested in something kind of interesting seems to me to be of little value; what is exciting is to be deeply involved in something. I think we not only love our children for who they are but because they force us to be deeply involved, which is exciting albeit sometimes very difficult. It is the depth of our feeling for life which makes us "world travellers," not the mere fact that we've paid for a plane ticket.

Even the "educational" TV leaves us sitting, staring. Drawing, dancing, reading, singing, sculpting, writing, playing about anything is far more fascinating than staring about it. Whatever you may lose in accuracy you'll make up for in passion. And who knows? You may end up in the Arctic, the beloved friend of the wolves.

Home Eye Test

From California:

I've found that when my 7-year-old's eyes are tested at the doctor's office they say he needs glasses. We even have a prescription for him. But when I test him at home with a little home test chart (from *Northern California Society to Prevent Blindness*, PO Box 18042, San Francisco CA 94118; 415-387-0934), he has *better* than adequate vision. He can read a whole extra line past the "OK" line. I think this has something to do with the fluorescent lights at the doctor's office and the anxiety of testing itself. He also has no trouble seeing anything he wants to.

Making Photo Book

Margaret Sadoway (MA) who, with her son Solon, was in the office with us for two weeks in February, giving us much valuable help, showed me a wonderful book she had made for him. About this she writes:

After returning from six weeks in Greece, I hit upon a particularly successful record of our trip for Solon (4). I filled an inexpensive 24-page mini-album (3½" × 5") with color snapshots, then wrote captions on self-sticking labels cut to various sizes, depending on how much of the photograph I could afford to cover. All that remained was to stick the labels on the plastic over each photo, leaving the pictures themselves unmarred. Now, 1½ years later, Solon still loves the book (bless him, after the hours it took me to make!), probably partly because it's all told from his point of view, or more fairly, from my impressions of his point of view. It begins, "Hi! I'm Solon. I have a passport, a ticket, and a new backpack. . . . After we took off, Mom said the white things under our plane were clouds. At first I didn't believe her. It seems pretty silly to have clouds *under* you. . . ."

He also enjoys a large map of our neighborhood that we made by taping together several large sheets of paper, then drawing buildings and streets on it. The streets are wide enough for his small vehicles. . . . He provides the busiest fire department for miles around.

Entered Writing Contest

From Sharon Hillestad (MN), who told in GWS *33 about her daughter's decision to enter a writing contest for novels by teenagers:*

Holly did finish the book in time to enter the Avon Flare contest for teenage writers. It was quite an experience to make that deadline. She had to miss a day and a half of school to finish this homeschool project. We sent it "express" to get it there on the last acceptable date. She didn't win but got a nice letter with the return of the manuscript. There were 540 entries. I think the company will run the contest again.

Entering this contest has given Holly a direction for her life. She wants to be a writer. She is rewriting her book now—works on it after she does her homework from school. At school she gets very little opportunity to write. In fact the students have the choice of writing book reports or drawing pictures about the story. She did so many worksheets for English—lots of crossword puzzles and comma worksheets—but no writing, except book reports.

Writing Contest Info

[DR:] *Someone sent us information on a writing contest for children, but unfortunately, its deadline was too soon for there to be any point in announcing it in* GWS. *I asked Sherry Early (TX), the "Helpful Librarian" of* GWS 37, *if she could find out anything about such contests so that we could let our readers know in time. After a few weeks of research, she wrote back:*

First of all, I didn't really find what you asked for—a list of writing contests for young people. If any publication has such a list, I was unable to find it. *The Writer*, a magazine for aspiring writers of all ages, does the next best thing. *The Writer* has a monthly column entitled "Prize Offers" which lists "selected literary prizes for unpublished manuscripts." ... It is a monthly publication; the subscription rate is $15 per year. The address is 8 Arlington St, Boston MA 02116.

I found announcements of contests in the following periodicals:

Creative Child and Adult Quarterly, National Association for Creative Children and Adults, 8080 Springvalley Dr., Cincinnati OH 45236. *Quill and Scroll*, School of Journalism, U. of Iowa, Iowa City IA 52242. This magazine is directed toward high school journalism students. *Writer's Digest*, 9933 Alliance Rd, Cincinnati OH 45242. This is the "other" magazine for aspiring writers. It had a lot of ads in the classified section for poetry contests especially, but many of them required an entry fee. I wasn't sure how reputable the contests were, but homeschooling families interested in this sort of thing might want to take a look at the magazine.

English Journal, National Council of teachers of English, 1111 Kenyon Rd, Urbana IL 61801.

Instructor and *School Library Journal* have also carried announcements in the past. ...

Some of these periodicals, *SLJ*, *Instructor*, *Writer's Digest*, and *The Writer*, should be available in most public libraries of any size. Interested homeschoolers would just need to check every month or so and see what they could find.

Also, for those who think they are ready to submit their work to a magazine or book publisher and try to make a sale, the book *Writer's Market* gives names and addresses of hundreds of publishers, big and small, and tells what kinds of work they are looking for. I would recommend that anyone who is interested in getting into print look at the current year's *Writer's Market* first of all.

———

[DR:] *Here are the specific announcements that Sherry sent. In each case, you should write to the address given for complete entry rules. First, about the* Young Playwrights Festival, *from* Creative Child & Adult:

Playwrights up to 18 years of age are invited to send scripts for production to: *The Foundation of the Dramatists Guild*, 234 W 44th St, New York NY 10036. The deadline for entries is July 1. A star-studded selection committee chose the seven plays for 1983 [including] Stephen Sondheim, Jules Feiffer. ... In the previous two years, more than 700 plays were received and 45 states were represented, student authors eight to eighteen. Award-winning directors were in charge of the productions. The plays were jointly produced by The Foundation of the Dramatists Guild and the Circle Repertory Company, 99 7th Av S, NYC 10014.

———

[DR:] The *Creative Child & Adult* also sponsors its own "Creative Career Interviews" contest. Apparently, the child interviews someone with a "creative career" (in the arts), using a standard questionnaire, and submits it to NACCA with a $5 entrance fee. The rules say, "Awards of U.S. Government Bonds, books, art materials and NACCA publications will be given when the judges feel works are merited. Entries may be forwarded at any time." For complete rules and the entry form, write to NACCA, 8080 Springvalley Dr, Cincinnati OH 45236.

From an ad in the *English Journal*, 2/84: "*Third Annual North American Essay Contest*. . . . This year prizes will be awarded in *two separate age categories*—those entries 19 and under, and those 20 through 29. Cash awards for both categories will be: *First prize*—$500; *Second prize*—$250; *Multiple third prizes*—$50. Entries must be postmarked before *July 15, 1984*. . . ." For essay topics and complete rules, write to *The Humanist Essay Contest*, PO Box 146, Amherst NY 14226-0146.

We'd like to hear about it if any homeschoolers enter these contests. And, if you learn of similar opportunities, please pass them on.

Magazines Seek Children's Work

[DR:] *Sherry Early also said there are two magazines that are made up of children's work,* Chart Your Course! *and* Stone Soup. *Neither one pays for material, but that might not matter to some children. Both are colorful, professional magazines.*

First, the guidelines for submitting work sent by Stone Soup *(subscriptions, $16/year):*

Stone Soup is a literary magazine by children up to age 13. Stories, poems, and pictures are accepted for publication. Send all work to P.O. Box 83, Santa Cruz CA 95063.

Fiction and Poetry Guidelines—There is no need to type or copy over manuscripts before sending them to *Stone Soup*. If you would like the work returned, enclose a self-addressed stamped envelope.

We will consider for publication any story or poem written by a child, regardless of the child's writing skills (spelling, grammar, handwriting), as long as the work is not based on an obvious formula or cliché.

We have no length limitations. In fact, we like receiving long stories.

Art Guidelines: Pictures may be any size, any color, and any number of colors. We can reproduce paintings as easily as pen drawings.

Reporting Time: Within six weeks of a submission, we will notify you of our intentions. We usually publish work three months to a year after notification of acceptance.

Payment: we pay contributors in complimentary copies.

And from Chart Your Course! *(subscriptions, $17.50/yr.):*

1) All work must be original. A statement, signed and dated by the child's legal guardian or teacher attesting to the originality of each item, must accompany all work.

2) We are looking for the very best material (cartoons, reviews, songs, articles, puzzles, photographs, comic strips, interviews, stories, art work, poems, activities, games, editorials, plays, etc.) we can find by gifted, creative, and talented children for all children to enjoy.

3) Each child may submit as many pieces of work as desired. Each piece must be labeled with the name, birthdate, grade, school, and home address of the child.

4) All work must be accompanied by a self-addressed stamped envelope. The stamps must be sufficient to cover postage and the envelope must be large enough for all of the work.

5) Activities requiring solutions must be accompanied by the correct answers.

6) Drawn items must be done in black ink. Clear, well-focused photographs or color transparencies of the full color art are acceptable.

7) Only glossy finished photographs and 35mm transparencies are acceptable. It is difficult to reproduce other types.

8) Those submitting accepted material will receive a copy of the *Chart Your Course!* issue in which their work appears.

9) Mail all material to P.O. Box 6448, Mobile AL 36660.

Typewriter Is Effective

The New York Times Magazine *article on Dr. John Henry Martin's* Writing To Read *program (see elsewhere this issue) quoted him as saying:*

Of all the fads and fancies that have captivated education in recent years, scarcely any has been validated as much as the use of the typewriter as an improver of children's learning. There have been more than 600 studies, the best of them by Ben Wood of Columbia (University) in the 1930s, involving 15,000 children. He showed that if children from first grade through eighth grade simply had free access to a typewriter, *with no formal instruction on it*, they did better than children who didn't—in all subjects, from arithmetic and science to reading and composition. The typewriter is 110 years old, but it's never caught on in the schools.

[JH:] This backs up what I have been saying about children for 25 years or so now, that they love typewriters, use them every chance they can get, learn a lot from them, and that we ought to make sure they have access to them, or better yet, have typewriters of their own.

It also shows, sadly enough, that schools and educators don't even pay any attention to their own research. More than 600 studies! How could they possibly have ignored, and continue to ignore, such a weight of evidence. Dr. Martin's quote may well be worth adding to homeschooling proposals, particularly in districts that you feel may not be very cooperative.

Well, we homeschoolers can do better. If you don't have a typewriter in your home that your children can use whenever they want (we have two in the office for just that purpose), then please get one.

Electronic Bargains

A recent ad of *47th Street Computer* (36 E 19 St, NY NY 10003; 800-221-7774), in the second news section of the Sunday *New York Times* (in which they regularly advertise), has some remarkable bargains and a very interesting offer. Among the bargains are a $70 manual portable typewriter from Olympia (a very good German brand); an Olivetti correcting electronic portable for $250; the Texas Instruments TI99/4A computer for $70 (original price $300); a complete Commodore word processor, with printer and software, for $900; a Kaypro II computer (about whom everyone says good things), plus word processing software and letter quality printer, for $2000; and so on.

The unusual offer reads as follows: "If you live out of town and want to purchase any *Kaypro*, or the *Epson QX-10* computer system . . . we will pay your roundtrip airfare from Baltimore, Boston, Buffalo, Pittsburgh (and other named cities). Call for details." For some, this might be worth looking into.

Consumer Reports did a recent report on small home computers (under $1000). Each machine had its advantages, but overall they preferred the Atari 600XL and its companion equipment. (The Atari 800XL, with larger memory, costs $100 more and is probably worth the difference.) Ads in a recent Sunday *New York Times* for *47th St. Computer* and also *Executive Photo & Supply Corp.* (120 W 31 St, NYC, tel. 800-223-7323) offer this equipment at well below list price; a "package" including the 600XL computer, a letter-quality printer, a recorder for storing text, and a word-processing program, costs $575 or so. For about $250 more, you can get the Atari disk drive. Executive Photo also offers for $759 a package including the Commodore Vic-64 with disk drive and printer. Neither of these packages includes a monitor; for this you can use a TV set.

In *GWS* 33, we wrote about a very small portable electric typewriter, the *Brother EP-20*, which I felt might be ideal for children (all who have seen mine have been fascinated with it). Since then *Brother* has produced two newer versions of the same machine. The EP-22 has a 2K (about 400 words) text memory, within which you can edit text—this is about as much as any young child is likely to write—and a "buffer," which I presume means that at the end of a line you can keep typing while the typing head is returning to begin printing the next line (on the original EP-20 you must wait until the typing head has returned, which breaks up your rhythm). With the slightly larger but still very compact EP-44 you get a 4K memory and, what some may find very important, a much higher quality of type, very close to letter quality. Executive Photo sells the original EP-20 for $140 and the EP-22 for $177. Both seem to me a good buy, either for children, or for people who would use the machine mostly to type their own letters or rough drafts, though I think the EP-22 is probably well worth the extra $37. *47th St. Computer* sells the EP-44 for $289; the difference is well worth it for students, writers, etc., who have to submit their writings to teachers or editors, many of whom will not accept the less legible dot-matrix printing of the smaller machines.

In *GWS* 35 (p. 27) I wrote about a wonderful portable stereo record player called *Mister Disc*, then available for $99. The latest catalog from *Markline* (Box C-5, Belmont MA 02178), offers it for $89. As I said before, it is an absolutely unbeatable bargain. The sound quality is excellent, equal to systems costing three or four times as much.

The machine runs on three C batteries. For another $12.95, you can get from Markline an adapter that will enable you to run it off your regular AC house current. If you use many batteries and have a battery recharger (a good investment), no need to get the adapter. If not, the adapter is probably worthwhile.

Two people can listen to Mister Disc over headphones at the same time. A very small and quite good set of phones comes with it, but in *GWS* 35 I recommended that you get Sony MDR-80T headphones, which are as good as any on the market, and which were then available for $59. Now *Illinois Audio* (12 E Delaware Pl, Chicago IL 60611) sells the same phones for $47, another great bargain, and worth getting no matter what kind of equipment you may have. With phones, you can listen without disturbing others; what's more important, you get a much better quality of sound than you can get over loudspeakers, unless you can spend thousands of dollars on equipment.

My hunch is that Mister Disc has not been a great commercial success (I never see it advertised), and that the company may be dumping its stock and taking it off the market, so if you have a use for this machine or think you may have later, say when children get older, I would suggest getting it now; nothing this good at such a low price is likely to come along for some time.—JH

Using Cuisenaire Rods

Susan Richman wrote in Western Pa. Homeschoolers *#7:*

> As many parents are not familiar with Cuisenaire rods and their many possible uses, I thought I'd share here how our boys have used them over several years.
>
> First, a bit of description—the rods are wooden (now available in plastic—a bit cheaper, but not as pleasing aesthetically) blocks in 10 graduating sizes from a one centimeter cube to a 10 centimeter rod. You can build a "stairway" of rods from smallest to longest. Each length is always the same color—red rods are always 2 cm long, blues are always 9 cm, etc. A small set of the rods costs about $7 in most catalogs. There are no markings or numerals on the rods.
>
> Jesse certainly spent a very long time building and playing freely with rods. All the time, though, he was learning about

these lengths and their relationships. As a 2½-year-old he'd figured out that all reds, say, were always the same size. He worked with great concentration on paving rod "roads" of different widths, fitting in rods exactly. The rods became barns, trains, families. He discovered stairway patterns, and for a good while made lots of variations on these—what would happen if a yellow rod was added to each step, could stairways go up and down, could stairways be built on top of stairways? We talked a lot about which rods were longer, which shorter, which ones when put together, equaled others. Our language gradually came closer to that of mathematics. We talked of "black minus purple equals light green" or "3 light greens equals 1 blue."

Although it's hard now to remember just when we began relating the rods to number ideas, I know we just very naturally began talking in Cuisenaire terms throughout the day. Lengths of objects became "Oh, that's about as long as a purple," or "I think my fingers are about a black long" (this usually followed by testing out with actual rods). Once when Jesse was asked to pick up 10 things from the kitchen floor, and had found 5, we laughed about how he needed to find an "orange" worth of things, and had already found a "yellow," another "yellow" to go. A dozen was referred to as an orange plus a red, or 2 dark greens or 4 light greens, or 3 purples. Lots of talk of halves and quarters while measuring whole wheat flour for baking led us to look into these relationships in the rods—could Jesse find half an orange, half a purple, half a blue? This was quite intriguing to Jesse, as he found that some rods didn't have even halves, and we began discussing ideas of odd and even numbers. Jesse made stairways of all odd rods and all even rods. We've examined thirds, quarters, fifths, sixths. We've used rods on a simple balance scale, having fun with balancing different combinations of rods.

Somehow I think it was important that we didn't let the rods become just props for other play. Although Jesse and Jacob both fantasized richly *with* the rods, we didn't mix Cuisenaire rods in with Lincoln logs, say, or use them as people for Tonka trucks, or stir them in with sand for pretend witch's brew. They were always a bit special, used only in certain places, carefully picked up, kept in certain containers. We found it helpful to either use them on rectangular trays or on an old second-hand coffee table with a raised edge (it's now called our "Cuisenaire table"). This kept the rods in one place, not falling scattered about, and also gave the boys a firm edge to line rods up against. We literally never put them away anymore, but always have them out ready for a moment's use.

Once Jesse figured out how to show 100 with rods (10 oranges). Then he wanted to try to show one thousand. This took lots of work, as our set only has about 17 orange rods. He worked very systematically and diligently—the "200" square was made of all yellow rods, the "300" square was made from 10 blacks and 10 light greens, etc. These larger numbers have taken on quite a reality for Jesse. It reminds me of an experience I had as a 6-year-old. I was lying in bed one night, counting as high as I could. I reached 100. Unsure what came next, I began saying "200 . . . 300 . . . 400 . . . 500." I stopped quickly, almost heady with the thought of how high I'd gone, but sensing that perhaps something might be wrong. I had no way to test out my counting ideas, no model of how these bigger numbers really worked. Jesse has rods to give him a very concrete way of imagining them.

Jesse seemed to really need, as well as enjoy, the concreteness of the rods. Written numerals meant little to him before almost age 6, even though we came upon numerals frequently on clocks, calendars, store advertisements, in books and games. The wiggles on paper just didn't carry meanings for him like the rods that he could tangibly feel and compare. With rods, addition combinations, say, are real, rather than "math facts" to be memorized and drilled. I was amazed that the very first time Jesse saw written-down addition problems this fall he had absolutely no difficulty. I'd made a simple addition "concentration" game—1 + 5 could be matched to 3 + 3 or 2 + 4, or 5 + 1, or 6 + 0, etc. Jesse thought it was great fun, and suggested other combinations I hadn't thought of. "Why couldn't you put 1 + 1 + 1 for 3?" He lined up the cards in order, like he's done with rods, made a new game of adding up the *columns* of numbers, got out his rods to help him check his answers.

[DR: A free catalog is available from the *Cuisenaire Co. Of America*, 12 Church St, New Rochelle NY 10805.)

Math and Common Sense

[JH:] I wrote in reply to Linda Butler's letter on using math (see *GWS* 37, page 21):

Thanks so much for your wonderful letter. In a very concrete way (usually the best way) it raises, and helps to answer, some very large and important questions about math, of which the most important of all is the question that millions of tormented schoolchildren must have asked themselves over the years: "What is math *for*, anyway?"

The answer, as I eventually figured out for myself, long after I was out of school, was that people invented math partly for the reason they invented music, that it was fascinating and beautiful, and partly for the practical reason that it helped them solve problems that they wanted or needed to solve and could not solve, or solve as easily, any other way. One of the earliest of these may have been, "How can I be sure that all the sheep I went out with in the morning are with me when I bring them home at night?" Another might have been, "How can I tell how big my field is if every spring the floods of the Nile wipe out all the boundary marks?" And so on.

You are right, it certainly is exciting to figure out how to solve a problem that you really want to solve. When I talk to meetings of teachers about children and learning, it often happens that someone says, usually in an angry tone of voice, "Learning can't all be fun!" (What they usually mean by this is, "Learning can't *ever* be fun, or it isn't really learning.") They are so wrong about this. Figuring things out, solving problems, is about as much fun as anything we human beings know how to do. For pleasure and excitement, hardly anything beats it, and few things come even close.

Your letter also illustrates a good point or two about what is called "heuristics," which means the strategies of solving problems, in other words, what you do when you're not sure what to do. In the matter of figuring out percentages, when you are not sure which number to divide into which, what you and your husband did was a smart thing—estimate the right answer, then do the problem both ways, and see which way gives an answer close to your estimate. Another similar method would be this. Assuming that you know that 50% of something means half of it, make up a very simple problem, of which you know that 50% will be the right answer. Thus: "There are six people in a room, and three of them are women. What percentage of the people in the room are women?" You have a 3 and a 6 there, and are not sure which to divide into which. If you divide the 3 into the 6, you get the answer 2, and no matter what you do with the decimal point, you can't make that turn into a 50. So you divide the 6 into the 3, and get .5 for an answer. Well, 5 is not 50, but you can make it 50 by moving the decimal two places to the right. So it looks as if, to find what percentage a small thing is of a big thing, you divide the big thing into the small thing, and then multiply your answer by 100 (or move the decimal point two places to the right, which is the same thing as multiplying by 100).

Or you could say to yourself, "1 is 50% of 2," which would suggest that you had to divide the 2 into the 1, rather than the other way round.

Or you might say to yourself, "Since 50% is the same as ½, then 50% must mean the same as 50/100 or fifty one-hundredths."

In other words, start with what you know, and use a little guesswork, or common sense, or whatever you want to call it, to figure out what you don't know.

When I was in school, scientists and engineers used slide rules to do quick calculations. I knew that slide rules existed, but had never used one. One day I found myself in a spot where, in a short time, I had to do a lot of problems involving calculation. I knew the only way I could get them done was by using a slide rule, so obviously I had to figure out how to use it. So I made up some very simple problems, like $2 \times 3 = 6$, and then pushed and pulled things around on the slide rule until I got the right answer. Then I checked that with a couple of other simple problems, and when the method worked with them, I knew I could use the slide rule on the harder problems. So when you're not sure which of two or three methods to use, try all of them on a simple problem and see which one gives you the answer that you know is right.

About counting, I feel as strongly as ever that it is a waste of time and probably not a good thing to *teach* children to count aloud. But every so often I hear our little office companion, Anna Van Doren, now 2½, count off a string of numbers up to 8 or 10. No one has "taught" her to do it. How did she learn it? What does she think she's doing when she does it? I don't know, and probably she doesn't know. Maybe she has heard people counting aloud to themselves when they were counting out money, or something. As long as she isn't being taught or made to count, but just does it for her own reasons, it's probably OK.

You ask about ways to help you and your children learn math. By the time you have read all the back issues of *GWS*, you will have plenty of ideas to work with, as well as the names of a number of books, most of them on our catalog, that will also be helpful. If, in reading those books, or anywhere else, you run into a problem with math that you can't work out, write us about it and we'll try to help.

Finally, I entirely agree that talking out loud while you're trying to solve a tough problem is very helpful. I hear children do it all the time, and I sometimes do it myself. With the tone of your voice you can emphasize relationships and connections that, sitting there on the paper, may not be so clear. Thus, you could say with heavy emphasis, as if explaining something to someone else, "Now, *if* such and such is so, and *since* this other thing is also so, *then* this other thing *has* to be so. Isn't that right?" Pretending that you are explaining something to someone else helps you understand it better, and pretending that you are asking a question of someone else does the same thing. Also, if you have made a mistake, you are more likely to notice it if you say it out loud—it will sound "funny."

One of the many things that makes learning in school, and in particular figuring out math problems, much harder for many children is that they aren't permitted to think out loud in this way. [DR: See also "Talking to Yourself," *GWS* 30.]

Thanks again for your letter, and if and when you have other Math adventures, let us know.

Foreign Language Resources

From Frank Hubeny (ME):

Donna mentioned in *GWS* 37 the *French Institute* which loans French books and wondered if there were any other such organizations. I think the best, and cheapest, source for foreign language materials is a state university library. In Maine, for instance, a library card costs a one-time fee of $3, and the quantity of foreign titles at the U. of Maine at Orono takes up most of one floor of the library. There are even French tapes in the learning materials center of the library. Couple a good library with a shortwave receiver and you have just about everything really necessary to learn the more commonly studied foreign languages.

A shortwave receiver is a radio which picks up more than local AM and FM. It is not a transmitter so you do not need a license nor any special expertise to operate it. Just turn it on. For some good information on these radios, see *The Next Whole Earth Catalog* under "Communications radio." They cost $100–$300 which is somewhat less than the price of a good language program on cassettes.

About using a state university library without actually going there. This can be done, of course, by using interlibrary loan and it is the way I used it up to four years ago, when for some reason, I felt that I needed some information right away and drove to Orono to get it. That incident forced me to overcome my shyness and sense of intimidation and I haven't used interlibrary loan since. Unless you need a specific book or article, relying on interlibrary loan actually restricts you. By going to a large library, you can see directly what sort of literature is available, opening horizons a local public library cannot even touch.

In a year or so, I plan to begin learning German to read some mathematics I'm interested in. . . . At the university library I would then find out (1) where the German-language books are so I could browse through those stacks periodically; (2) what German-language periodicals were available; (3) whether there was a German-language newspaper in the reading room; (4) what German-language recordings were in the listening room or the learning materials collection; and (5) what reference books on or about German were available. The last item is made easy by first knowing about Sheehy, *A Guide to Reference Books*. . . . Another general reference source is Schwann's *Record and Tape Guide* for recordings of German plays and poems.

Possibly one disadvantage of relying on a university library is that the material is usually "adult." . . . But I would hazard the rule of thumb that anyone with the motivation to pursue a self-taught language program is old enough for any material available in a university library.

[DR:] This leads to another question, prompted also by a letter from Barbara Stoutner (ID), who is looking for stories recorded by native speakers of other languages, with written translations or transcriptions, if possible. Cassettes of children's books in *English* are now easily available in American stores—usually a picture book and tape come packaged together. Do any of our readers (particularly those of you who live outside the U.S.) know if such children's book/tape combinations are available in other languages? I bet the Japanese, for example, have such things for their children. If so, please tell us whatever you can about who sells such materials and how we can get them.

Good Gardening Info

[JH:] The current issue (#41) of *Homesteader's News* (PO Box 517-1, Naples NY 14512; $1.75) has, among much other useful information about self-reliant life, the best and clearest articles about raised-bed gardening that I have yet seen. If you are gardening or thinking about it, you would do well to read it—even if you think you know quite a lot about raised-bed gardening. At the end of the article Norm Lee writes, based on what he and Sherry have actually done, beginning with poor soil and spending almost no money (because they *have* almost no money):

Anyone with a few square feet of garden space, no matter how poor the soil, can raise more than $2.00 worth of food a year on each of these square feet if they prepare raised beds as we've shown here. Conventional gardeners are advised to reduce their garden area to a fraction of their former space when converting to the deep-compost method, unless they plan to feed the neighbors or start a roadside stand!

A Cello Adventure

While on my December lecture tour in the mid-West, I arranged to spend a few hours with David Chickering, who plays cello in the Chicago Symphony (one of the world's greatest orchestras), and who ran an ad in *GWS* 36 and 37, offering to live with a rural homeschooling family and share his love of music.

When I got off the train in Union Station on Sunday morning, he met me, cello in hand. He said, "Let's go over to Orchestra Hall (where the Chicago Symphony plays) and see what's going on." When we arrived, no one was using the stage, so he said, "Let's go out and make a little music." In no time at all there I was, sitting at the front edge of the stage of one of the world's most famous concert halls, playing my cello to 2500 empty seats and imagining them full. After a while he tried my traveling cello, which he found surprisingly good, and let me play his cello, a beautiful Guarneri, one of the great old Italian instruments, ten times better than the best cello I have ever played. What a difference such an instrument can make! I could have played it forever. He was very encouraging, said I got quite a nice sound out of it. For a while we took turns, one of us playing while the other went through the empty hall, listening to the sound from various locations. Then we played a few duets.

Then off for lunch and much interesting conversation. He is an intelligent, friendly, and delightful young man as well as an expert and versatile musician, and any family with whom he lives for a while will gain not only much knowledge of music but much pleasure from his company. I envy you the experience. (David can be reached at 1220 Jarvis St, Chicago IL 60626.)—JH

Pat Plays In Public

The continuing adventures of Pat Farenga learning to play sax (see GWS 34, 36, 37):

After two months of lessons, John Payne felt I was ready to become a member of the Student Sax Choir, which performs every Monday night in Harvard Square. I was horrified, "I barely know anything!" I protested. He told me that if I wanted to wait I could, but he felt I could do it and benefit from it. He assured me I wouldn't have to play everything and that I could do one of two things when I encountered sections that were too tough for me to play, "You can just not play, or you can keep the sax in your mouth and look like you're playing. With thirty other saxes going no one's going to notice you're not making a sound, but you'll look cool!" We laughed and I decided, "What can I lose?" So I practiced some more choir tunes John gave me at the lesson and decided to check out the choir that Monday night.

The Oxford Ale House isn't the most glamorous night spot in town, but when I walked in it for the first time as a sax choir member it became a special place to me. I entered and heard the cacophony of 30 or so saxophones warming-up. What a wild noise! I introduced myself to Duncan Martin, the choir's arranger and conductor, and he placed me in the tenor section. Then he tuned everybody to his liking, and began rehearsal. During the 90 minutes that followed we ran over trouble spots in songs the choir had been performing for a while, learned a new tune Duncan had just arranged for us, and chattered quietly to one another every so often. The loose, informal atmosphere and Duncan's focused, clear and humorous tutoring make rehearsals a pleasure. Not only does he teach us group dynamics as a band, but he'll take the time to explain the best way to finger a certain note, how to make the octave key "D" sound in tune, and so on. Duncan's animation and energy are amazing for a teacher who must go over the same thing day after day with his students. He's the only person I can think of who could make something as dry as "music theory" come to life.

During our break after rehearsal and before we play, I got to know some choir members, and was pleased to discover what a remarkable collection of people and talents comprise the choir. There are all sorts of ages and occupations represented among the thirty plus saxophone players. There are a number of grade school students, some teenagers, a lot of men and women in the 20–30-year-old age group, and a few folks in their forties and early fifties. They are lawyers, nurses, students, factory workers, tree surgeons, and so on; all playing at different levels of saxophone competency. You don't have to be a student at the Center to join the Choir. All you have to do is pay your $10 a month dues (for materials and Duncan's time) and show up for rehearsals.

After the break, John Payne, backed by piano, bass, and drum players (all of whom are teachers at the Music Center) plays a song before he brings the choir out to join him. I've heard John play before in concert and know he and his band are all fine musicians, but sometimes I'll hear them do things at the Ale House that make me wish I had a tape recorder. The snap, crackle, and pop of their rhythm and sound immediately lets you know you are listening to professionals. On their best nights you can almost see the energy they exude as they create their solos and interact as a band. They are good models for the aspiring soloists in the choir.

The music stands were set up and I readied my sax as Duncan counted down the rhythm for the first choir tune, "Tom Cat," a funky jazz number. I could only play a few measures of the melody before I had to stop and wait for some notes I knew. The whole sound and excitement of the choir I felt during rehearsal was now highly charged as the rhythm section moved us through the tune. (Having "real musicians" back you up can often hide some of the choirs' "clams" as well as add to the excitement.) During those parts when I played I felt an exhilaration from the total sound my sax is helping to create. It's a total blast interjecting the tenor's two-cents in the holes created by the altos' syncopations. What really is fun though, is hearing how John Payne weaves his solos in and out of our background licks. Recently there have been "guest soloists" from the choir who get up and play the lead while John Payne will step down into whatever section needs an extra horn the most (he teaches and plays soprano, alto, tenor, baritone, flute and clarinet).

Duncan's conducting is very explicit. He combines clear cuing with a good sense of humor as he tries to decrease our nervousness before an audience and make us have fun while we're performing. When we get too deep into an arrangement or worry about how we're sounding he'll hold up signs that say, "SMILE," or "I LOVE YOU" or "GET HIP."

The choir's songbook is an imaginative mix of current songs (Al Jarreau's "Roof Garden"), old favorites ("In The Mood"), standards ("Nobody Knows The Trouble I've Seen") and jazz tunes ("Let's Jump With Symphony Sid"). It's to Duncan's credit that these clever and challenging arrangements can hold such a diverse group's interest over the years.

The last of our 5 songs on my first evening was Stevie Wonder's "Sir Duke," an up-tempo number with a lot of notes; I think I played four of them that night. When it was over I spoke to John Holt, who was there with his tape recorder, and when I listen back to the tape of our conversation I am surprised by the amount of enthusiasm and happiness I had that night. It really was, and still is, a peak moment playing in a band before a paying crowd. (All right, the admission charge is only a dollar, but that counts, right?)

From the atrocious sounds of my first lesson, to the somewhat less atrocious sounds of my current lessons after seven months, it has helped me keep to my practicing knowing that at least once a week I'll be playing for a live audience. (I say "at least" because we have sometimes gotten other gigs as well, such as playing for a United Way fundraiser.)

Other music schools could learn a lot from Payne's example. Their emphasis on competition and grades probably keeps a lot of their students from truly excelling in what they want to do with their individual talents. . . . And the musicians aren't having nearly as much fun making their music as we do.

New Books Available Here

Making Things: The Handbook of Creative Discovery, by Ann Wiseman $7.95 + post). We decided to offer this book after several readers recommended it enthusiastically. It gives directions for over 100 craft projects for children, gathered from the author's experience of working with thousands of children in elementary schools and in programs such as the Boston Children's Museum. Many of the projects can be done with materials and tools that are around the house—scissors, paper, crayons, glue, yarn, pencils, coat hangers, cardboard, cans. Others require materials that can be scavenged—pieces of cloth, wood, leather, screening, glass—or inexpensively bought—ink, dye, paints, plaster of paris, paraffin, dowels.

A few of the projects that caught my eye: weaving a belt on a loom made of plastic drinking straws; making paper; sewing clothes without patterns. The complexity of the procedures range from very simple (cutting and bending paper to make a stand-up village) to fairly demanding (carving a willow whistle). I recognize some of the projects from the craft books of my childhood, like potato block printing, and hand puppets from socks or paper bags, but many others are new to me, such as ironing a crayon drawing on cloth to make it permanent; making "stained glass" out of crayons, paper, and oil; or the cardboard and string "racing turtles" (Ms. Wiseman says, "My mother introduced this game to us as children and I've never seen it played anywhere. Yet it is so simple and such fun, especially when grownups join in.") There's a section on the unusual soap bubble devices that the Boston Children's Museum developed—with a loop of string on sticks and some practice, you are supposed to be able to make a huge bubble. And there's a xylophone made out of electrician's pipe (75¢ for 10 feet); John heard one of these once and says the sound was wonderful. Oh, and you can make a pendulum that traces designs in sand—I've seen one of those in a museum, too. Many of the items would be suitable for children to make as birthday or Christmas gifts for friends and relatives, such as jewelry, macramé, toys, and candles.

There are plenty of drawings, and the written directions vary from extremely brief to quite detailed. I imagine that children browsing through this book would find some projects they could do entirely on their own; for others they would need some guidance from an adult; and there are still others that would be a challenge to the ingenuity of both a parent and child, working together. One of the nicest things about this book is its encouragement of the reader to be flexible, creative, to adapt the instructions to a variety of materials. As the author says in the introduction, the answer to "Is this right?" is "Right by whose standards? What is right? The right that makes things work, please, or improve. Give permission to experiment—that is right."—DR

The Stars: A New Way To See Them, by H. A. Rey ($8.95 + post). I have been on the lookout for a good book about that part of astronomy which is about the position and movement of stars and planets in the sky, and not about how big or hot they are or what they are made of or how they were made. As often happens, one of our readers showed us this book, which is much the best we have seen. Published in 1952, it has been in print ever since, and deserves to be. It is full of interesting information, understandable explanations of things we may never have understood, and many excellent illustrations that really do help make them clear. It begins with these welcoming words:

> This book is meant for people who want to know just enough about the stars to be able to go out at night and find the major constellations, for the mere pleasure of it. Of course you can enjoy the stars without knowing them. But if you know them at least a little, the pleasure is infinitely greater. It is fun to watch them announce the seasons, to see them rise at the expected times and places and follow their paths year in, year out, more reliable than anything else.
>
> Besides, if you know the stars you are not easily lost. They tell you the time and direction on land, on sea, and in the air, and this can be valuable on many occasions.
>
> And should you venture into outer space, anywhere in the solar system, where no earthly landmarks exist, the constellations would be your only guideposts, and familiar ones, too.
>
> This book . . . shows the constellations in a new, graphic way, as shapes which suggest what the names imply: it shows the group of stars known as the Great Bear, in the *shape* of a bear . . . and so on.

What a nice, patient, friendly voice behind these words. Rey is a wonderful teacher, doesn't rush us along too fast, makes sure we know what he means by the words he uses—small things, but important. In the book he shows us, first, diagrams of the major constellations; then later, pictures of what the whole sky will look like, at least in those latitudes in the Northern Hemisphere (25–55 degrees North) within which the U. S., southern Canada, and most of Europe are located, at different times of the year; still later, much more information about the motion of the earth and moon, and the apparent motion of the stars.

One interesting thing he tells us that I never knew. The earth's axis now points toward the star we call Polaris, the Pole Star, but it did not always and will not always do so; because of the wobble of the earth's axis, it will slowly move away from Polaris, and in 12,000 years will point very close to the bright star Vega. From there it will take 25,000 years before it comes back to Polaris again. However, we will not see this happen; during our lifetimes, and the lifetimes of our children, grandchildren, and many generations to come, we can count on Polaris to keep showing us due North.

A most delightful and informative book.

Myths And Legends Of The Indians Of The Southwest: Navajo, Pima, Apache, by Bertha Dutton and Caroline Olin ($2.95 + post). A fascinating story of where these Indians came from, how they lived and worked, the stories they invented and told to explain the world's and their own existence, and how they invented and still make sand paintings, a unique and beautiful art form. As the book says:

> Sand paintings (sometimes called dry paintings—for not all materials used are sand) are made by trickling dry pulverized pigments between thumb and forefinger. These are chiefly red, yellow, and white sands from natural sandstone, black charcoal, colored cornmeals, crushed flower petals, and plant pollens. They are placed on a smooth layer of desert sand . . . [or] buckskin or cloth. . . . A painting may be a few centimeters in size or as large as several meters across. . . . After a painting is used ceremonially, it is destroyed immediately.

It is hard to believe sand painting even when you see it. The cover of this book shows a sand painting, done from memory, since Navajo religion forbids photographing or copying sand paintings. Those straight lines are done absolutely freehand; there are no guiding ruled lines, no sketches. The painter simply begins, and works steadily, changing nothing, until the painting is finished.

All this and much other information in this interesting book.

Great Women Composers ($3.50 + post). Another in our series of books about composers, with pictures of each one and a short biographical sketch on the facing page. Some of these women composers I have known about for some time, like Fanny Mendelssohn (sister of Felix); Clara Schumann (wife of Robert); Lili Boulanger, an enormously gifted Frenchwoman who died very young and whose older sister Nadia became the most famous teacher of composers of this century; Dame Ethel Smythe, whose picture is on the cover; and Boston's own Amy Beach, who having while very young composed some excellent works gave it up almost completely when she married. There are others I had never heard of and am glad to know about. And I know one that they don't mention and that I'll bet very few people know about, an American woman named Pauline Hall who lived most of her life in Norway, where she wrote a fascinating impressionist piece called "Black Birds." By now many women are composing, so perhaps we will soon have enough for another book. Meanwhile, this is a must for young musicians and music lovers.

Should I Teach My Kids At Home? A workbook for parents by Kate Kerman ($4.50 + post). The author of *Who Does What When*, a very popular item in our catalog, has written another very useful booklet for people who are teaching or thinking about teaching their own children.

Her own introduction sums up the book very well:

> I am not writing this pamphlet as a series of answers to the questions and doubts you have in your mind about teaching your kids at home. I want it rather to be a series of questions for *you* to answer in the hopes that your answers will help you decide if and how homeschooling might work for you. I have been teaching my kids at home since Ada, age 11, was born. . . . I like homeschooling, and am happy with the results I see in my kids,

but I don't think it is the right answer for every family. In talking and corresponding with many people on the subject, I have seen the need for some help on deciding whether or not to teach kids at home. ... Although I am clearly biased in favor of homeschooling for my own family, I hope I have written this in such a way as to let you find out for yourself whether homeschooling, public school, or a private school would best fit your family's needs.

The subjects to be discussed are divided into four main groups: family, child, you, outside factors. Under each of these, Kate Kerman asks a number of questions on the right hand page, such as "How much time do you spend together as a family now?" and "What is your child interested in most particularly right now? Is there time to pursue this interest in school?" On the facing page, she discusses some of the ways in which she and her family deal with these questions. The questions are pointed and practical, and Kate deals with them in a very sensible and non-dogmatic way. One could quote the book forever, but two quotes seem to me particularly important, the first of them something that could and should be said in one way or another in every family's homeschooling proposal:

> Having watched kids learning at home, I have gradually reached the conclusion that a deep interest in practically any subject is likely to lead the child to most of the subject areas taught in school. ... It would be difficult for a child to be interested in any subject deeply for a long time without learning something about language and numbers and writing words ...

> I have come to the conclusion that when you try something a bit different, many people look on it as a direct criticism of the way they did it, or are doing it. Then people who are not completely comfortable with the choices they made may choose to defend themselves by attacking you.

This book should make many new friends for homeschooling, persuade many people to undertake it, and help many of those who do undertake it, to do it better.

Using A Law Library ($5 + post), published by HALT, a legal reform organization (201 Mass. Ave. NE, Suite 319, Wash. D.C. 20002). This is a short, clear, well organized, and absolutely invaluable guide to research into the law, including statutes, regulations, and court decisions. If you want to find out what the law has to say about homeschooling or anything else, this book will tell you how to find out.

In addition, it tells you what kinds of law libraries there are, where to find them (an appendix lists by states 450 law libraries open to the public), what are your rights of use, and if you have to ask for permission, of whom you must ask it.

It also contains a very good short explanation of the American legal and judicial systems—what kinds of laws there are, which ones take precedence over others (the U. S. Constitution is of course at the top), which courts decide about which laws, how the courts themselves are organized, and so on. One vital point: "The U.S. Constitution is the bedrock in American law, and the U.S. Supreme Court is the final arbitrator of what that law is." In other words, as Justice Holmes put it many years ago, "The Constitution is what the judges say it is." What counts is not what we think or hope the Constitution means as we read it, but what judges have said (or might say) about the meaning of those words.

I cannot exaggerate the importance and usefulness of this book. Anyone wanting to do legal research on any subject, and particularly homeschoolers who may face court action, should not be without it.

MATHPLOTS 2: Building Blocks for Mathematics: being at home with math, by Kate Kerman ($3 + post). Another of Kate Kerman's booklets, written out of her experience with her own and other homeschooled children. This one is so full of interesting and practical ideas and just plain common sense (nothing rarer!) that it is hard to choose what best to quote. It begins:

> I am hoping by putting out this pamphlet and others in the *MATHPLOTS* series that we can help parents confront and reduce their fear of mathematics or of teaching and learning mathematics with their children, whether their children are learning at home or in a school.
>
> I think that people are natural learners—that children come into the world with a zest and drive for figuring out how things work, and how they fit into the big picture.... I don't think that people learn any given subject in an outline, one-step-following-another fashion. I think learning comes in spurts and stops, in times of intense expansion, and in times of reflection and consolidation.... Children and adults only learn in a dramatic fashion when they want to, when they know they have a reason (pleasure often being a very strong reason) to find out about something.
>
> I am not offering an orderly progression through the subject of mathematics [JH: there *is* no such orderly progression]. I hope to offer some insights into how much mathematics a typical preschool child is engaged in, and to give you as a parent-teacher a framework to use when you are observing your child learn, and when you are learning about mathematics yourself.
>
> I am coming to see mathematics in terms of *the information it can store up for you.*
>
> Most of the major mathematical areas can be and are part of even very small children's lives: geometry, set theory, measure and money, logic, probability and statistics, perhaps even the beginning understandings of algebra, trigonometry, topology and calculus. I am hoping this series of pamphlets will give parent-teachers some understanding of these subject areas—enough to reduce their hesitation about mathematics and to foster in their children an ability to cope with if not enjoy the mathematical aspects of their lives.
>
> Little kids ... love to find out about the world. It is very important to them to figure out how things work, how they fit into the scheme of things. They are experimenters, and will patiently try the same experiment tens, hundreds or thousands of times to make sure that results are consistent. ... Babies don't learn at someone else's bidding. ... Little children ask a lot of questions, and learn a lot from your answers, but they aren't generally looking for much information at a time. They signal to you quickly if you are telling them more than they want to know. Pay attention to those signals if you can.

From this point Kate Kerman goes on to discuss the major mathematical areas listed above, and many ingenious ways in which these areas can be made more enticing and understandable for children, and for the parents too—for I suspect this book will be at least as helpful to many of them as for their kids.

Bumpee Gardening Catalog, by Ken Lawless ($4.95 + post). I showed Mary Van Doren this book, a take-off on seed catalogs, that Nancy Wallace had just sent me, and she all but fell out of her chair laughing at it. So we decided to add it to our catalog. Last year Mary and Mark Van Doren and Mark's father Jim joined forces to buy a house near Boston. No sooner had they spotted the tiny front yard than they began to plan a garden. The other day Mary came into the office loaded down with seed catalogs, and started to mail "a few" orders for seeds. To my unpracticed eyes it looked as if they had enough to seed the entire King Ranch, with plenty of seeds left over, but maybe all gardens start out that way. Many of you, living in the country, know seed catalogs well and have probably just been looking through a few of your own, so you should get quite a few laughs from this full-color satire. (It was written and photographed, by the way, by a homeschooling family in Northern New York State.)

Hard to say what in this book made me laugh the most, but one of my special favorites is certainly the Attack Zucchini. The photo shows an intruder, knocked unconscious and pinned to the ground by a zucchini as big as he is, which has fallen or maybe even leaped upon him. On the cover is a photo of someone holding a tomato about four feet in diameter. Inside is a preposterous ad for "Toy-Bilt" tillers. But I won't give away any more surprises, except perhaps to say, be sure to read *all* the book, including such official looking things as order forms, guarantees, early order discounts, etc. Not a word of it is serious. An ideal gift for all gardeners.

Confessions of a Medical Heretic, by Robert S. Mendelsohn, M.D. ($3.65 + post). Dr. Mendelsohn, whose bulletin *The People's Doctor* (Box 982, Evanston IL 60204) some of you may know, is an experienced and distinguished physician, who in this book gives us some extremely important advice about doctors, hospitals, and drugs. In two words—Watch Out!

The back jacket of the book sums it up:

> Twenty-five years as a practicing physician have convinced Dr. Mendelsohn that (1) Annual physical examinations are a health risk. (2) Hospitals are dangerous places for the sick. (3) Most operations do little good and many do harm. (4) Medical testing laboratories are scandalously inaccurate. (5) Many drugs cause more problems than they cure. (6) The X-ray machine is the most pervasive and most dangerous tool in the doctor's office.

Dr. Mendelsohn begins with these words:

> I do not believe in Modern Medicine. I am a medical heretic. My aim in this book is to persuade you to become a heretic, too.
>
> I haven't always been a medical heretic. I once believed in Modern Medicine.
>
> In medical school, I failed to look deeply into a study that was going on around me, of the effects of the hormone DES— because I believed. Who could have suspected that twenty years later we would discover that DES causes vaginal cancer and genital abnormalities in children born to women receiving the drug during pregnancy?
>
> I confess that I failed to be suspicious of oxygen therapy for premature infants, even though the best equipped and most advanced premature nurseries had an incidence of partial or total blindness of around *ninety percent* of all low birth weight infants. . . .
>
> A year or two later it was proved that the cause [of blindness] was the high concentration of oxygen administered to the premies.
>
> I believe that despite all the super technology . . . the greatest danger to your health is the doctor who practices Modern Medicine.
>
> I believe that Modern Medicine's treatments for disease are seldom effective, and that they're often more dangerous than the diseases they're designed to treat.
>
> I believe the dangers are compounded by the widespread use of dangerous procedures for non-diseases.
>
> I believe that more than ninety percent of Modern Medicine could disappear from the face of the earth—doctors, hospitals, drugs, and equipment—and the effect on our health would be immediate and beneficial.

Strong words! Yet he backs them up. He gives so many examples of outrageously careless and dangerous medical practice that it would be tempting to quote them—but there are too many. One way of summarizing many of them would be to say that many doctors either do not know the risks of the drugs or procedures they recommend, or if they know, won't tell you. Nor will they tell you, unless you press them hard, what is the track record, what are the chances of success, of these same procedures.

A few years ago, at the T.C. Anderson Cancer

Clinic in Houston, one of the leading orthodox cancer hospitals in the country, and a true temple of Modern Medicine, I heard doctors say that they considered a treatment successful—in this case they were talking about chemotherapy—if it produced a *ten percent* increase in the number of patients who were alive five years after the initial diagnosis. Yet this treatment is enormously expensive—one child they were talking about had had over $250,000 worth of treatment—and produces not only great suffering but very destructive side effects, including, as I remember, the almost total destruction of the body's immune system, so that there is a very real question of how many of these statistical "survivors" will survive another year or two. But these same doctors can and did in my hearing denounce as "quackery" methods of treatment involving such low-cost therapies as diet, vitamins, etc., that have demonstrated much higher increases in success rates than ten percent.

The most dangerous thing you can possibly do, if you cannot avoid being a doctor's patient, is to be what most doctors would call a Good Patient, one who asks no questions, and believes and does everything that the doctor tells him. Though some of you may disagree with some of Dr. Mendelsohn's opinions on what we could properly consider non-medical subjects, I hope his book will persuade many of you not to be Good Patients, or better yet, patients at all, but instead, as you already do in the matter of education, to take a vigorous, determined, skeptical, and informed responsibility for your own and your children's health.

And if I were a young person with a leaning toward medicine, I think I would like to ask Dr. Mendelsohn, "What should I learn, where can I go, what can I do to become and remain a good doctor?"

Never Too Late, by John Holt ($4.50 + post). This book, which might be called the life story (so far) of a late starter in music, is now back in print in our own 8½ × 11" Pinchpenny Press edition. (A year or so ago the publishers, without giving me any opportunity to buy them, destroyed the remaining 1500 copies they had in stock—a fairly common occurrence in publishing, I am told by people who know about such things.) Dozens of people have written and said that reading *Never Too Late* inspired and encouraged them to do what they had long wanted but never quite had the courage to do—begin the serious study of music. My oldest such correspondent was a man who, having never played any musical instruments, took up the cello in his mid-70s and a few years later, like myself, was playing in an amateur orchestra, and also like myself, struggling hard to catch maybe half the notes they were playing, and finding this one of the most exciting things he had done in his life. Just last night, as I write, a young woman came up to me after the Boston Symphony concert, asked if I was John Holt, and hearing that I was, then said that because of this book she had just started to play the violin and was studying in a class otherwise entirely made up of children and having a wonderful time.

You should particularly read this book if you have learned or been taught to think that you are "tone-deaf" and therefore incapable of singing or playing a musical instrument. It is not so. The condition of, as the old saying goes, "not being able to carry a tune in a bucket," is easily cured, and this book will show you how, with the help of any friend who can carry a tune, you can cure it.

Of all the books I have written, this was perhaps the most fun to write, dealing as it does with what has always been one of the chief pleasures of my life. I hope you enjoy the reading as much as I enjoyed the writing.—JH

Other Material Available Here

Aulos Alto And Sopranino Recorders (alto $15, sopranino $9 + post). In *GWS* 33 we offered for sale the Aulos soprano recorder, an ideal beginning and family instrument, and so many people have bought them that we are now adding the alto and sopranino to our list. As you probably know or can guess, the alto recorder is larger than the soprano, and plays in a lower register, and the sopranino is smaller than the soprano and plays higher. The alto has a lovely soft, mellow voice and is ideal for playing duets with the soprano. Many of these duets have been published, and experienced recorder players can probably tell you what they are and how to get them. By the way, if you find some music you like, please tell us, for we would like to add some of this music to our list.

The great advantage of the sopranino, for families, is that since it is smaller than the soprano, and the holes are therefore closer together, young children can more easily cover those holes with their fingers, while the soprano may be a little too big for them to play comfortably. And it too makes a good companion for the soprano and alto. All you then need is a tenor recorder, the biggest of them all, and you can play recorder quartets, of which there is a big literature. Perhaps in time, if there seems enough interest, we will add the tenor recorder to our list. Meanwhile, I hope you enjoy these.

Pat Farenga Plays In Public! ($8 for 90 min. cassette). *GWS* readers will have read, most recently in this issue, that our friend and Managing Editor, Pat Farenga (already a jazz pianist) began last April to play the tenor saxophone, studying under a most remarkable musician and teacher named John Payne, who believes as I do that anyone of any age who wants to can quite quickly learn to play a musical instrument well enough to get much pleasure from doing it. As you also know, Payne runs a music school, and has organized his students, many of whom, like Pat, have been playing for only a year or less, into a Sax Choir which regularly performs in public.

After Pat had had only five lessons (he was an enthusiastic student and had had considerable previous musical experience), John felt that Pat was ready for his first appearance with the Choir, then playing weekly at the Oxford Ale House in Cambridge. I went to hear him, and I made a very good tape of the occasion. First we hear a small group of John's more advanced students, then John himself on flute with his own professional jazz quartet, then the 30-person Sax Choir itself—a very exciting record of amateur music making in its best sense.

Later in the year Pat joined one of the small ensembles into which Payne organizes his students, and on March 4 of this year made his public debut with his group, which also included (on guitar) Steve Rupprecht, also on our staff, who joined us at *GWS* when Mark Pierce left. I made a good tape of this session, which we also hear on this cassette. The group is amazingly good, partly because an experienced and excellent drummer played with them, which makes a big difference, but partly because Pat, Steve, and friends all played with such spirit and imagination. They don't sound like students! And they do sound as if they were having a wonderful time—which they were.

All in all, an exciting record in sound of the first year of an adult beginner's musical exploration and adventure.

Fine Point Color Pens (in plastic holders) (set of 12, $6; set of 24, $12). Color, porous tip pens have been on the market for years. Artists and art teachers have called them the best of all media for the unskilled, and they're probably right; I know I've had a lot of fun with them, just making fancy colored doodles—though I guess in skillful hands they can do a lot more than that. I've had in mind that we might one day add some of them to our list, and not long ago, at the home of some unschoolers, I saw a set that I specially liked; the points stay firm and don't get mushy, the colors are vivid, the caps fit smoothly and snugly at either end, and the pens themselves, which have a nice shape, are the same color as the ink, so that in the words of the old saying, what you see is what you get. Best of all, they come in a little plastic wallet-like kind of holder, which folds over to make something about the size of a book. Makes it a little easier for children (or adults) to keep all the pens in a set in the same place. Of course, not even the Japanese have quite managed to design a pen that, left on the floor by its last user, will of its own accord return to its proper place in the holder; it still takes human hands to do that. But once in their holder the pens will stay there until next called for. The 12 color set includes red, pink, orange, yellow, two shades of greens, two blues, purple, brown, gray, and black; the 24 color set has a greater variety of hues in all the colors. These handsome sets will invite much use. Wonderful for presents.

The Faces Of Greece: A Permanent Calendar, designed by Margaret and Jack Sadoway ($3.50 + post). How can a calendar be permanent? Easy, show the Sadoways (other letters from Margaret in *GWS* 37 and this issue). After all, a month has to begin with a certain day of the week, and there are only seven ways it can do this. All 31-day months which begin with the same day of the week have the same calendar, no matter what the year. So to take care of all possible 31-day months, you need only seven 31-day calendars, one beginning with Sunday, one beginning with Monday, and so on. Seven more calendars for the 30-day months will take care of all of them, and seven more 29-day calendars take care of all the Februarys (on non-leap years, just forget the 29 at the end).

What you then have to know, for the month you are interested in, is which day of the week it begins with. A table on the back page of this calendar tells you that; look up the year, and then the month, and a number tells you which page of the calendar to use. Want to find what day of the week you were born on? What day of the week Christmas will be on ten years from now? This calendar will tell you. Many children with a mathematical or scientific bent will love this.

What has all this to do with Greece? On each page of the calendar is a beautiful black-and-white photograph (taken by Margaret) of one or more of the people of Greece. A few of these are children, some are young or middle-aged, many are old, and all show a wonderful directness and vitality. These photographs, beautifully reproduced and printed (in Greece), are in themselves a work of art, and well worth the price of the calendar.

Since the calendar is quite small (5½" wide × 11" high), and since in any case to write in it would spoil it as a permanent calendar, it is not an engagement calendar, only a reminder of days and dates. Many (children and others) will enjoy it for what they can find out in it, others for its beautiful photographs and elegant design—a calendar that you do not need to and will not want to throw away. It has a spiral binding at the top with a loop, so that you can hang it. Another ideal small gift.—JH

Editors—John Holt & Donna Richoux
Managing Editor—Pat Farenga
Subscriptions & Books—Mary Gray & Steve Rupprecht
Office Assistant—Mary Van Doren

Growing Without Schooling 39

May 1984

As we could only expect in a big and diverse country like ours, the homeschooling picture is mixed. Most families are having it easy, some hard. On the whole, though, we seem to be winning much more than we are losing in our struggle for respectability and legitimacy. Legislatures seem more and more of a mind to make homeschooling explicitly legal, but with some restrictions. If we can avoid wasting our time trying to get rid of all restrictions, we should be able to use our energy and our growing political savvy to insure that such restrictions as there are are minimal, reasonable, and easy to live with. At the same time I would say that the number of school people who feel that they can and should stamp out homeschooling altogether continues to decline, while the number who are ready to live with it, and even to give it strong support, continues slowly to rise. In short, I feel that the odds are continually improving that families who want to teach their own children *and who go about this the right way* are going to be able to do so with little or no trouble. What the right way is, we have of course discussed at length, and will continue to discuss in *GWS*. In a nutshell, we should try not to attack, startle, or terrify the schools, and to show them instead that we are smart, serious, reasonable, courteous, resourceful, and determined.

The response to our article about starting a tax-exempt corporation called Friends of Homeschooling (*GWS* 38, p 7.) has been encouraging. May we ask that you look or look again at that article and tell us your thoughts. We plan fairly soon to write about it to all former subscribers; perhaps a number of them, who feel that they no longer need *GWS*, will want to help us keep it going for others who do need it.

The article I wrote for *The Progressive*, which they, rather to my regret, entitled "How Teachers Fail," was reprinted in the May 14 issue of *Newsday*, a very large newspaper that serves Long Island. They gave it the much better title, "Educational Metaphors That Crush Kids."

In Ithaca not long ago I saw three performances of Ishmael Wallace's new musical play—his third, all produced (wonderfully!) at the First Street Playhouse. Except for Vita Wallace and one other child, the cast was made up of adults, most of them experienced singers and actors (it was Bob Wallace's first appearance on stage), and all of them excellent. The play was very funny; some of the Saturday night audience were laughing so hard I thought they might have to be carried out, or given oxygen, or something.

Nancy Wallace's wonderful homeschooling book, *Better Than School*, sold over 1000 copies in its first three months, which is very good for a book by a new author, published by a small company. This will be a word-of-mouth book, so if you have read and liked it, please tell others about it (or buy it for them). By the way, the publishers have no immediate plan to put it into paperback.

Speaking of books, we just had an order, from a public school in California, for one each of every book on our list! A splendid example for everyone.

Dr. Raymond Moore (Hewitt Research Center, PO Box 9, Washougal WA) has started to publish some curriculum materials in reading and math, and would like to have homeschoolers act as distributors for his material. People interested should get in touch with him.

We have had several foreign visitors in recent months. From Sweden came my old friend Ake Bystrom, who arranged my tour to his country in early 1982. From England came John Farrow, Co-Director of Kilworthy (in Devon), a community of teen-agers and adults; and later, my friend the physicist David Deutsch, who wrote us (*GWS* 29) about apprenticeship as a way of learning advanced physics, and with him his two young friends Ben and Rudge Brown—John Holt

John Holt's Coming Schedule

July 12, 1984: Holt Associates Open House (2nd Thurs. of each month).

July 19: A.A. Cleveland Conference, College of Ed., Washington State U., Pullman WA. Contact

Denis Conners, 509-335-5023.

Sept. 8 (tentative): Connecticut Homeschoolers Association. Contact Laura Pritchard, 203-634-0714.

Sept. 28: Sunrise Session, D'Youville College, Buffalo NY 14201. 8 a.m. Contact Robert DiSibio, 716-881-3200, ext. 6112.

Anyone who wants to coordinate other meetings or lectures around these times, contact Patrick Farenga.

"Young Children" Supplement

We are pleased to announce a new publication available from our office, *Young Children: Natural Learners.* This is the first-ever GWS supplement, made up of letters from GWS readers and articles by John Holt. This is *not* a collection of old material reprinted from GWS, but all-new stories which we simply have not had room to print.

The entire supplement relates to children from birth to age 6—living with them, watching them learn, coping with their demands, teaching them (or trying to!), the important role of play, deciding whether to send them to preschool or school, and more. One article by John Holt describes how a six-year-old intertwines work and play in our office. Although many of the letter-writers do not expect to send their children to school, this GWS supplement is *not* specifically about homeschooling, and could be read and enjoyed by many parents and others who are not interested in homeschooling as such. So this could be the perfect gift for your friends and relatives, as a way of introducing them to our beliefs about the way children learn, and to give them many great ideas on what they can do with their children.

For now, the price of this supplement is $1, including postage. As soon as I send this issue of GWS to the printer, I will be putting together the supplement, which will be 8 pages in the same 3-column format as GWS. So it will be available by the time you read this. We may print supplements on this or other topics in the future, depending on the abundance of material, our time constraints, and the success of this one.

So, for all of you who have told us you just can't get enough of GWS—here's your chance to get a little more! You won't find this kind of encouragement and support anywhere else.— Donna Richoux

News from Clonlara

Pat Montgomery sent us the April issue of Home Educator, *the newsletter for her* Home Based Education Program *(Clonlara School, 1289 Jewett St, Ann Arbor MI 48104). Some interesting excerpts:*

> The number enrolled in 1978: 3 students; the number in 1983: 632 students.
>
> In the current school year, 37 homeschool families were contacted by local school officials. Two were threatened with a court suit by those officials. Each of the 37 consulted with HBEP and let us handle the contacts. None of the families had to consult a lawyer; none was taken to court.
>
> Out of a total of seven high-school-aged students who completed the HBEP program in 1983, each went on to college or university (two to business college, three to community colleges, and two to universities).
>
> Clonlara School-Based Education Program does provide standardized tests, the California Achievement Test, for homeschool students. . . . We administer the test in either of the following ways: (1) the entire packet, including the administrator's manual, is sent to the family, the teacher then administers the test after becoming familiar with the manual and with our own written explanation of procedures; or (2) . . . a teacher from an alternative school near to the family's home administers the CAT to the homeschoolers. The entire packet is then returned to HBEP. . . . An explanation of the scores and each interpretation is then sent to the homeschool. The cost is $20 per family (it does not matter how many children a family has enrolled in their homeschool).

In January, the "rear portable" classroom here on campus was rearranged to accommodate homeschoolers from the area. Actually some families come from as far as 60 miles away to attend the sessions here.... All of the resources of the campus school are available to the homeschoolers.

Last January, also, Jackie Beecher (MI) and I met to develop an idea about instituting satellite schools in as many areas of the state and country as we possibly can.... Jackie's was the first satellite.... She opened a room in her Emmett, MI home to area homeschoolers on certain days of the week and acted as tutor for several students; her books and materials were made available to them. Janine Timo of Pinckney, MI followed suit in February.... Valerie Carrier [in Lansing] was next.... If you are interested in being a *Clonlara Satellite School*, contact Pat, preferably by mail, for details.

Notes From Donna

Dr. Mendelsohn an Ally: Toots Weier (WI) writes, "I see that Dr. Robert Mendelsohn's book *Confessions of a Medical Heretic* is available through *GWS*. Wonderful! ... We attended a seminar with Dr. Mendelsohn as the guest speaker. ... A woman in the audience questioned him about his obviously strong opposition to routine immunizations of children and how to deal with entering the children in school without being immunized.... His answer: 'If you are smart enough not to immunize, you are smart enough to teach your children at home.'"

Want to be an Alaska School Superintendent? A reader writes, "I am on the school board of a rural school district and hope that after elections in October there will be a majority of board members who will favor exchanging our present superintendent for a new one.... Could I look to you for some advice and suggestions about sources for recruiting a school administrator who would be sympathetic to 'Holtian' educational philosophy?" If you are interested and think you qualify, I can put you in touch with this reader.

Justice O'Connor not a homeschooler: As I suspected, the quote in the last issue about Sandra Day O'Connor was an error—she went to several private and public schools in Texas. However, one article I found implied she did not start school till age 8, though this was not clear.

Canadian Homeschooling Book: Wendy Priesnitz (195 Markville Rd, Unionville, Ont. L3R 4V8) says in her newsletter *Child's Play* that she is writing a book on homeschooling in Canada. If you'd like to help, send for the questionnaire she has prepared (it is not necessary to identify yourself on it).

Another young writer makes a sale: Toni Lenhardt (OR) says that *Mother Earth News* sent a check and a contract to her daughter Brooke (5) for an article she dictated on "Brooke's Books." Brooke makes and sells blank books with a variety of decorated covers. When the homeschooling newsletter *Family Centered Learning* ran a notice offering her books for $1 each, Brooke got quite a few orders, according to Toni. "She tells me what she wants to write to each customer and I type it up."

A Big Thank-you to everyone who helped with our latest booklist mailing, especially to Kit Finn, who coordinated the entire project. Other local volunteers were Loretta Heuer, Mary Silva, Pam Mitchell, Ann Gilbert, Rosemary Larking, Mary Maher, Jim Sterling, Jeanne Gaouette, John Woodman, Mary Pelrine, and their families. Typists across the country were Eldon Evans, Marie Hartwell, Pamela Lewin, Linda Rieken, Bonnie Speir, Carol Hughes, and Susan Rhodes.—DR

Ally in Utah

From Leslie Westrum (IN):

I wrote to Professor Arnoldsen (Brigham Young University) who is on the *GWS* "Professor and Allies" list [*GWS* 36], and he's really terrific! He sent me some good material, things that he and others had written on freedom, learning, how schools do and don't work, etc.... He said that following the children's lead—letting them show us what they are ready to learn—is the best way to teach. . . . He's a delightful man, totally in support of homeschooling.

New Wisconsin Law

On May 9, the Governor of Wisconsin signed Assembly Bill 887, which read, in part:

> 115.30 (3) On or before each October 15, each administrator of a public or private school system or a home-based private educational program shall submit, on forms provided by the department, a statement of the enrollment on the 3rd Friday of September in the elementary and high school grades under his or her jurisdiction to the department which shall prepare such report as will enable the public and private schools and home-based private educational programs to make projections regarding school buildings, teacher supply and funds required. The administrator of each private school system and home-based private educational program shall indicate in his or her report whether the system or program meets all of the criteria under section 118. 165 (1).
>
> Instruction in a home-based private educational program that meets all of the criteria under S. 118.165 (1) may be substituted for attendance at a public or private school.
>
> *118.165 Private schools.* (1) An institution is a private school if its educational program meets all of the following criteria:
>
> (a) The primary purpose of the program is to provide private or religious-based education.
>
> (b) The program is privately controlled.
>
> (c) The program provides at least 875 hours of instruction each school year.
>
> (d) The program provides a sequentially progressive curriculum of fundamental instruction in reading, language arts, mathematics, social studies, science and health. This subsection does not require the program to include in its curriculum any concept, topic or practice in conflict with the program's religious doctrines or to exclude from its curriculum any concept, topic, or practice consistent with the program's religious doctrines.
>
> (e) The program is not operated or instituted for the purpose of avoiding or circumventing the compulsory school attendance requirement under S. 118. 15(1) (a).
>
> (2) An institution may request the state superintendent to approve the institution's educational program as a private school. The state superintendent shall base his or her approval solely on the criteria under sub. (1).

[DR:] The original form of the bill would have closed the loophole of homeschoolers calling their homes "private schools." This would force them instead to get approval for home instruction through the Department of Public Instruction, which has a long history of being erratic and harassing families.

Homeschoolers did not find out about that bill until late in 1983, and immediately started alerting as many others as they could. At a public hearing on Jan. 25, over 2,000 people showed up, the overwhelming majority opposing the bill. The next few months were full of visiting representatives, writing letters, phoning, arranging media coverage, etc. Sue Brooks wrote in the newsletter of the *Wisconsin Regional Coalition of Alternative Community Schools,* "Several of us 'volunteer lobbyists' were in the Capitol [in February] talking with reps and *waiting* to find out when AB887 would be on the floor for a vote. As soon as we found out, we all called our contacts back home—*the next day the phones were ringing off the hooks!* Secretaries and aides were comparing notes in the hall: 'How many did you get this morning?' . . . At that moment it became crystal clear to me that the press is important, lobbying is important—*but*, if you want to make an impression in Madison, make *sure* that informed constituents are contacting their representatives! It was a *great* thing to see and hear!"

As the bill went through various committees, votes, etc., it changed form. Homeschooler Janet Kassel prepared what turned out to be important testimony, documenting many instances in which the Department of Public Education had acted irresponsibly (failing to answer homeschooling requests, turning them down for no apparent reason, demanding applications of unreasonable length, making derogatory comments on personal character, etc.). Sue Brooks says it was also important to reassure representatives that there were already laws on the books concerning children who didn't go to any kind of school (truancy investigations, consultations, reports), so there was no need to deal with that in this bill.

Legislative & State News

Alaska: Jack Lash sent us a copy of a bill passed by the 1984 Legislature that says, among other things, that nothing requires religious or other private schools to be licensed by the state. It also has an interesting "kicker" about test scores that reads, "The composite test results of a religious or other private school operated in compliance with AS 14.45.100-140 are not public information unless each public school (1) is also required to administer a nationally standardized test . . . and (2) the composite test results for each public school are public information."

The office of the state's Centralized Correspondence Study (Dept. of Ed., Pouch GA, Juneau AK 99811; 907-465-2835) sent us information on their home-study program which is available free to Alaska residents. It says, "The 1983 enrollment of 1,154 was an all-time high. . . . Enrollment has increased nearly 30% the last four years. . . . In May the CCS K–8 program was declared one of the nation's exemplary education programs by the U.S. Dept. of Education. . . ."

Arizona: According to the *Families for Home Education* newsletter, "Dr. Moore came here to speak to the Senate Education Committee concerning Bill 1125. The part of the bill that we were interested in was the section trying to change the mandatory beginning school age in Arizona from 8 years to 6 years. Since 90% of the children are already attending at that age there seems to be no reason to change the age. It would have made an inconvenience for many homeschoolers, requiring them to take the test earlier than they had planned. Anyhow, Dr. Moore made a very good presentation plus some excellent remarks from Sherri Pitman and this section of the bill was unanimously dropped."

California: A new brochure on Independent Study, the program that public school districts can use to approve homeschooling, is available from the Office of Alternative Education and Independent Study, Calif. State Dept. of Education, 721 Capitol Mall, Sacramento CA 95814.

Connecticut: Laura Pritchard tells us that the legislative proposal for a 5-year mandatory school entrance age has been dropped for the present, as has the all-day kindergarten. She sent a newspaper article that quoted one legislator as saying, "I've never had as much mail on any issue in my 10 years here as I have had on this one." (See *GWS* 38).

Illinois: Mary Friedl told us that the draft on "Suggested Procedures for Determining Program Equivalency" of homeschooling (*GWS* 38) has been dropped. Instead, the committee of Regional Superintendents working on this issue have proposed a one-page form for homeschooling parents to fill out, called a "Statement of Assurance." Homeschoolers have seen a draft of this form and are trying to make some changes in it.

Kentucky: Libbie Morley writes, "It seems that a strong effort will be made in the next few legislative sessions to extend the annual testing requirement to private schools. The bill this winter was easily squashed in hearing, largely through the efforts of the church school lobby (*GWS* 38). . . . Another reason for its defeat this year was funding as the state would not be able to require the private schools to pay for these tests."

Louisiana: The legislature is in the midst of considering changes to the laws regarding private schools and homeschoolers. June Conley told us on the phone that it appears some sort of compromise will have to be worked out—the state wants homeschooling to be legitimate, but also wants some sort of control over it.

Maine: The *Maine Home Education* newsletter published a long anti-homeschooling statement by the president of the Northeast Regional Elementary Principal's Association, and urged all homeschoolers in the state to send their responses to the Dept. of Education and Cultural Services.

Minnesota: From the *Minnesota Homeschool Network Newsletter*: "On March 28, a couple of dozen homeschoolers met with Independent Republican legislators on the education committee. . . . It was the consensus of the legislators that we ought not to push for a homeschool law right now until the Minnesota Supreme Court ruled on the two homeschool court cases now pending. Their concern was that powerful special interest groups in education (I think they are referring to teachers unions and school board associations) would turn a homeschool bill into a law that would restrict home schools greatly. As one of the legislators commented, 'The only people not represented to our education committee are parents and students. You're the first I've seen.' It was suggested that we gather a committee of homeschoolers to work with the legislators about the specifics of a homeschool bill. The legislators were very cordial, and the homeschool families present felt good about the communication that took place. . . ."

Nebraska: The legislature passed a bill saying that schools that do not wish to comply with the usual requirements (which includes certified teachers) may instead submit evidence annually to show that (1) they meet minimum health and safety standards; (2) they keep attendance records; (3) they provide instruction in basic areas; (4) the teachers have passed a nationally recognized teacher competency exam, or provide some other evidence of competency.

New Hampshire: The *New Hampshire Homeschooling Association* would like people to get a copy of the new homeschooling regulations from Charles Marston, State Dept. of Education, 101 Pleasant St, Concord NH 03301, review them, and send their comments directly to Charles Marston and to Elaine Rapp of NHHEA.

Texas: Martha Bigley writes, "From listening to the debates before yesterday's election, I found that the Texas State Board of Education is *not* against home education. I heard two of them say that they would support home education, that it is a choice parents should be allowed to make. . . . In June (maybe) the Governor will call for a special session of the Texas legislature to consider education and road improvement. . . . One of the main recommendations is that children should start school at age 4, and that kindergarten should be all day classes. . . ."

Martha also sent us a copy of a letter that Carl A. Parker, Chairman of the Senate Education Committee, wrote to her, in which he said: "The Legislative Action Subcommittee had recommended to the full Select Committee on Public Education that home schools be exempted from compulsory attendance laws for grades K–6 if the student maintains certain achievement levels through testing at the local school district. . . . I was subsequently convinced through conversations with homeschooling advocates that the issue cannot be so simply dealt with. It appears that many homeschooling advocates are divided in what they want to happen with homeschooling in this state. Therefore . . . I moved to remove the recommendation from the report pending further study. . . ."

Washington: In order to write a bill that will have as much support as possible, the homeschooling organizations are sending out a survey, developed by Jon Wartes of the *Teaching Parents Association*. It looks to be very thorough and well-written; results will be available some time after August 1.—DR

Court News

The Washington Post, *4/28/84:*

> A judge in Anne Arundel County Circuit Court today dismissed for lack of evidence a case against a Maryland couple charged with violating the state's compulsory school attendance law by educating their children at home.

Following two days of intricate testimony on what constitutes education, Judge James Cawood said the state failed to provide evidence that Kathleen Miller of Laurel isn't providing "regular, thorough instruction" to her children, Terry Jr., 12, and Deborah, 8. The jury, therefore, had no facts to deliberate, the judge said.

The case, brought by the state against Kathleen and Terry Miller who withdrew their children from public school two years ago, was widely regarded as a test of the state's compulsory attendance law.

In announcing his decision to the jury, Cawood said, "We're not trying the value of education here. I will stand behind that any time I can. And we're not debating whether public schools are better than home learning."

Instead, he said, it was a matter of the state "shooting itself in the foot" because it did not collect evidence prior to the trial to prove that the Millers were violating the law. The law requires all children from the ages of 6 to 16 to attend public school "unless the child is otherwise receiving regular, thorough instruction during the school year in the studies usually taught in the public schools to children of the same age."

Anne Arundel Schools Superintendent Edward J. Anderson has interpreted the law to mean that children must attend either public or private schools and, unlike some neighboring county superintendents, has refused to allow home education.

Cawood said school officials' assumption that the only comparable education was in a school was wrong under current law and that the real issue was determining whether the programs were similar. "The state cannot approve home education programs and turn around and say you can't use them," he said.

Mrs. Miller has used programs from the Calvert School of Baltimore and the Home Education Institute of Takoma Park to educate her children.

Dennis Younger, curriculum director for the county board of education, today testified that the Calvert program used by Mrs. Miller in the 1982–83 school year was not comparable to county curriculum because it allowed fewer hours of study and did not provide for physical education, art, and some other subjects.

However, A. Dale Swecker, a state accreditation specialist who monitors home study programs in the state, said the Calvert program provides "appropriate" instruction for elementary-age children.

Mrs. Miller testified that she supplemented the Calvert program in those areas. The state had no evidence to the contrary.

Other expert witnesses called by the Miller's attorney said tests of the Miller children indicated they were receiving regular instruction and were working above grade level in most subject areas. Marilyn Nicholas, an assistant professor of education at Towson State University, said she found Mrs. Miller, who has a high school education, to be a "warm and loving teacher . . . responsive to the children's needs."

The Chicago Tribune, 4/17/84:

A Riverside woman's campaign to educate her five children at home got a boost Monday when prosecutors agreed to postpone her trial on educational neglect charges while she works out an acceptable curriculum with local school officials.

[Marietta Rubien] had taught her children at home for more than year before a Cook County Juvenile Court judge last December ordered them returned to a formal school.

Rubien could have lost wardship of her children if educational neglect was proven in a trial.

Teresa Magnazini, an assistant state's attorney, said the main issue no longer is whether Rubien should keep her children. Rather, she said, it is whether the suburban mother can create a homeschool program that will be acceptable to the two local school districts.

From the April newsletter of Christian Home Schools *(8731 NE Everett St, Portland OR 97220):*

In Mariposa, a small town in northern central California, the school board tried to get one of our member families to enroll their child in public school through threatened court action.

There is a private Christian school in the area which decided to try an independent study program with the family. This was accomplished and now the school district is trying to decide what they can do further, under the law, to force the child into the public school.

The legislature in California has passed legislation authorizing and encouraging this type of alternative within the public school. Therefore, if the public school can set up independent study, then the private school must have that right also. The school attendance supervisor is quite perplexed by the turn of events and is asking to see the curriculum.

[DR: See the Hackett case, *GWS* 34 & #35.]

The St. Louis Post-Dispatch, *3/27/84:*

Two conservative Christian families who teach their children at home have filed a suit contending that state officials and school districts have conspired to deprive them of their religious rights.

The class-action suit was filed Monday in U.S. District Court in St. Louis. Defendants in the suit include Arthur L. Mallory, state commissioner of education, and Joseph J. O'Hara, director of the Division of Family Services.

The plaintiffs—including David and Deenie Ellis and their daughter, Elisha, 8, of Augusta in St. Charles County—are asking the court to declare unconstitutional Missouri laws used to justify the intervention of child abuse investigators into homeschool operations.

Others joining in the suit were Charles A. and Marcia Bowles of Warrenton, and *Families for Home Education*, a Kansas City-based association of Missouri parents who operate home schools.

The Ellises and the Bowles are among at least 24 families in counties surrounding St. Louis claiming to be victims of harassment from officials. The parents contend that their reputations have been damaged by their being "stigmatized" as "incapable of caring for their children."

[DR:] *From a letter by the president of the Nebraska State Education Association, published in the March newsletter of the* Nebraska Christian Homeschool Association:

On January 27, 1984, the Nebraska Supreme Court in *State Ex. Rel. Douglas v. Morrow* upheld the constitutionality of the teacher certification requirements set forth in state regulation. The Morrows were operating a home school for their children and neither of them held a Nebraska Teaching Certificate. The court found that, notwithstanding their religious views, the Morrows had not complied with state law. The court held that the requirement of the State that all teachers hold a valid teaching certificate does not interfere with or violate Morrow's religious beliefs or other constitutional rights. . . .

[DR: However, see also "Legislative News," this issue.]

The Birmingham, Alabama Post-Herald, *4/6/84:*

Two Decatur residents who refused to send their children back to Decatur schools after Christmas vacation were ordered to spend 90 days in the Morgan County jail yesterday for violating the state's compulsory education laws.

Edmund and Sharon Pangelinan [*GWS* 38]—who want to educate their children at home—can reduce the sentence to 10 days in jail and a two year supervised probation if their 9-year-old and 7-year-old daughter are brought back from Connecticut and sent to school.

The Pangelinans instead appealed the decision to Morgan County Circuit Court and vowed to continue their fight. . . . "Our defense may have appeared weak, but we felt we were going to lose on this level and we will present more of our case in circuit court," [Mrs. Pangelinan] said, "We'll take this thing to the Supreme Court if we have to. . . ."

Deputy Morgan County District Attorney Paul Mathews argued during a four-hour trial that the couple had never tried to meet state regulations for the home teaching they advocate. "We had intended to take our plan to the school board but found out it was held a night early and once the warrants were issued we just decided we would not," [Mrs. Pangelinan] said.

Dr. Byron Nelson, superintendent of Decatur city schools . . . said the state requires that home teaching plans guarantee instruction a minimum three hours daily between the hours of 8 a.m. and 4 p.m. for at least 120 days a year in a plan the local school system must approve. . . . "Personally I've not had the first home teaching plan submitted to me in 13½ years as a superintendent," he said.

Other court news in brief:

County drops case: Maginess & Erin Dowling, West Palm Beach FL; after they agreed to enroll two other children in their home school.

Facing court action: The Golson family, Columbia MD—Stephen Beckett, Cambridge ME

Released from jail Feb. 23: Six fathers in Louisville, Nebraska; after they agreed not to send their children to a particular Christian school.—DR

Homeschooler Graduates Early

The Maine Home Education *newsletter reprinted this article from the Lewiston (ME) Daily Sun, 3/13/84:*

High school graduation has come early for Tom Kane of Wilton Road, Farmington. The 14-year-old Kane . . . has received word that he has passed the final examinations at the John Holt Learning Center, a school for the gifted and talented.

In making the announcement, Headmaster James Salisbury stated, "I am pleased to congratulate you for graduation with the highest honors (summa cum laude, valedictorian). Your course work and graduation test was unquestionably one of the finest submissions we have had in our five year history, indeed a beautiful bit of research and thoughtful writing. . . . We recommend you warmly to university work."

The school is named for John Holt of Boston. . . . U.S. Secretary of Education Terrel H. Bell is one of the directors.

Kane's major subjects were astrophysics, literature, and creative writing.

Kane said he has not completed his plans for the future. Currently under consideration is the University of Maine, Farmington, where he has already taken some courses for credit. Another possibility is Bates, he said. Dean Mary Kendall has indicated Kane would be accepted for study at the Lewiston College. The youth remains active at Sandy River School, where he has been a student since 1978.

Some of Tom Kane's plans for the immediate future include traveling in Europe during late spring and early summer with the John Holt Learning Center, visiting museums, attending theaters in London and the Passion Play. Kane is also thinking of attending an international astronomy camp in West Germany this summer, then attending Spitz Space Systems graduate credit course in observatory and planetarium education in Philadelphia in August.

The newsletter also printed this note from Jean Kane (MI):

You asked why we chose the John Holt Learning Center.

(1) We wanted an accepted, accredited high school diploma to clear ourselves with the public school.

(2) Of course Tom could have gotten that at other schools (Calvert, American, etc.) but we liked the "academic excellence" of this school's requirements and courses in: 4 years of English literature and creative writing; algebra, geometry (plane and solid) and trig; sciences including physics; proficiency in foreign languages; history. . . . An old fashioned college-oriented private school flavor.

(3) We thought this bettered the "old fashioned" school, though, because all the emphasis is on personal initiative and endeavor—creative approach—self-motivation. More of home study, which we like.

(4) The school did more than just put us on our own. (We were already there.) Through their guidance and direction, we—the whole family but especially Tom—discover new ideas, books, courses of study which we had never thought of and find fascinating.

[DR: For more about the John Holt Learning Center, see GWS 37 p. 15, or write them at PO Box 520794, Salt Lake City UT 84152.]

Long-Time Homeschoolers

Susan McKnight in Texas wrote:

Mary Schwalm in Dallas has been homeschooling for some 20+ years. I had the privilege of hearing her give an informal talk to the Ft. Worth homeschoolers recently about her experiences with her now 20-year-old twins and her youngest son, aged 13 or 14, who is still being schooled at home. Many of her experiences were similar to those of other *GWS* families; for example, her boys read later than she thought they would—ages 9 or 10; they watched a tree in their yard every day for a year and noted its seasonal changes. What is important to me about her experiences is that her homeschooling methods are so *pure* and *untouched* by the flood of curriculum and resources I find myself bombarded with.

One comment she made about children beginning to read still sticks in my mind. "It's what children bring with them (in their minds) to their reading that's important. Children who have been read to and with, and children who have engaged in thousands of meaningful activities and had the chance to question and discuss with other adults, have a more enriched reading experience."

From Kandy Light of Ohio:

We have been doing homeschool for eight years now! Five of our six children (17 to 2) are school age.

They are turning out to be well adjusted, not socially deprived, and (I thank God) not your "average" kid. They are able to speak intelligently, and not about the latest TV show or rock group. Some may think we've sheltered them but I did not want them to know about the perversions of society until they were older. All of that comes soon enough.

We have been asked to speak to a few

homeschooling parents or those interested, twice now. The last time, 70 people showed up in someone's living room. There is quite an interest in homeschool, much more than when we started eight years ago. There were several public school teachers at the last meeting who were either doing homeschool with their own kids or interested in doing so.

I could write a book on our experiences over the years. In New York we were confronted by the school authorities and finally, heartily approved as a private school. Here in Ohio we are "laying low"—or trying to—but everyone knows about us, it seems. People I've never seen before are constantly coming up to ask me about homeschool. I suppose it's a matter of time before we are "inspected" again.

N.J. Open Houses

[JH:] To what Nancy Plent said about the New Jersey Unschoolers "Open House" in *GWS* 32, I would like to add some excerpts from an article she wrote in the *Unschoolers Network*:

> A year ago, we decided to chuck all of the things we were doing up to then in favor of a monthly Open House. No meetings, no workshops, no changing locations, no plans; just come on over and visit. Post cards went out to the entire local mailing list, saying this was the last card they would get. (Whew! Hadn't realized what a pain it was to send those cards each time!) Everybody was invited to come over on the first Tuesday of each month.
>
> At first, we got a movie from the local library each month, but that, too, proved to be too much structure and we settled for getting one now and then. In the summer, we sat outside and the kids splashed in the pool. Sometimes out-of-state families passed through NJ and spent the afternoon with us. New mothers came and said they were glad to know we were around for when they would be homeschooling. I don't think any of us knew exactly what we wanted to do with this day, but doing nothing spectacular proved to be just right.
>
> One of the good things that has happened was that people who came here often met other people they could get together with on other days, too. Three families who met here are taking their children to a local gym class together, and no, we aren't going to make that a "group trip" . . . it's much more relaxed this way.
>
> To people just starting groups, I'd say try not to get sidetracked by having too much purpose and schedule. It's easy to get high on ideas, and tempting to try and carry them all out. The burn-out phase comes on very suddenly when a group tries to translate too many ideals into reality. I really feel that alternative people would experience much less of a sense of isolation if they could focus more on getting to know each other as people, as less on causes and meetings and activities.

Organization News

Addresses of all homeschooling groups are either in the back of this issue or in *GWS* 36. Or, send $1 for our Homeschooling Resource List.

Arizona: Liz Prohaska of *Sunset Hill School* writes, "A group which includes 15 families and 33 children are getting together once a month. The adults talk and the kids play. We usually meet in a park. . . . Four of us with children of similar ages get together 2–3 times a week. A few of the children in the group take a pottery class together once a week at a pottery studio in town. The teacher has been surprised at how self-directed the kids are. . . . We are gradually building up enrollment in our school of independent study students. We just enrolled 4 children from California, our first out-of-state students. . . ."

California: Suzanne Bischof of North Hollywood writes: "A local church has formed a satellite support group for homeschool parents. Monthly meetings have grown from a dozen or so in private homes to over a hundred interested parents and children meeting at a church. Field trips have been organized...."

Beth DeRoos (CA) arranged a homeschooling seminar at Stanford University May 28. She told us in April that more than 400 had signed up, at $15 apiece.

Colorado: Nancy Dumke of the *Colorado Homeschooling Network* has revised and expanded their Legal Packet, which is available for $6.25 (write to Judy Gelner, 7490 W Apache, Sedalia CO 80135).

Florida: Ann Mordes says, "We will again begin to put out the FLASH newsletter, but this will be on an irregular basis."

Indiana: According to two newspaper stories, one homeschooling Indiana parent is a judge (Kenneth Johnson, Marion County Superior Court 2), and one is a school board member (Richard Merrion, Danville School District)!

Iowa: Issue #5 of *O!KIDS* ($3/yr., 202 SE 8th St, Ankeny IA 50021) lists support group meetings in: north, south, and west Des Moines, Story City, Rolfe, Waterloo, Ida Grove, Sioux City, Ames, Marshalltown, and Ankeny.

Montana: Patty Barnett of Missoula wrote in the *Montana Homeschoolers* newsletter, "We decided to hold a small homeschool workshop ... given by parents who were actually teaching, which would be free.... Printing 300 posters cost about $20. We sent one to every church in town, and in surrounding areas, along with a cover letter asking them to please display them on their bulletin boards. Then volunteers hit the town with the rest of them. Public service spots were put on several radio stations and we had a piece in the "Community Briefs" section of the newspaper.... Including people already belonging to the group, there were about 50 people attending!...."

Missouri: Cynthia Fels of the *Holistic Educational Activities Directory*, RR 1 Box 45, Defiance MO 63341, says her group is starting a home study program with a large group of parents in southwest Missouri.

Oregon: From Toni Lenhardt (OR): "There is now a Portland network/group of homeschoolers who met to hear Lawrence Williams of *Oak Meadow School* (connected with homeschooling)— he was inspiring...."

Quebec: Helen Fox (Que.) writes, "For people who dream of moving to a nice little bit of countryside where they can leave their doors unlocked.... Quebec is a fascinating province, full of educational opportunities for homeschooling families. There is a wonderful ethnic mix in Montreal, cultural festivals and activities abound, great restaurants are everywhere, public transportation is clean and safe, and people walk the streets at midnight just for fun. The opportunity for young children to become fluently bilingual by simple, daily contact with French playmates is unequalled.... It is still possible to buy land not too far from the city to garden, write, watch the kids climb trees, and feel at peace.

"There are about 30 homeschooling families in the Montreal area.... Individual school boards may react very differently to requests. The arrangement may be as simple as drawing up plans on paper to provide a certain number of hours of instruction in specific subjects.... Prospective immigrants would be wise to contact Jocelyn Maskerman at 4650 Acadia, Lachine, Que. H8T lN5, Tel. 514-637-5790. She edits the *Quebec Homeschooling Advisory Newsletter*...."

VA—Ed Wilhelm (Rt 1 Box 127-C4, Bent Mtn VA 24059) sent us the "Human Resources Directory" he helped put together, which lists skills that about 75 people in the area are willing to share or want to learn. Anyone in the general area (west of Roanoke) would do well to contact Ed about this.—DR

GWS Videotapes?

A number of people have suggested over the years that we might make available videotapes of some of my talks about homeschooling (perhaps other people's as well). We have not done it for several reasons: (1) we thought that too few of our readers had videotape machines to make it worthwhile; (2) we didn't know who would win the competition between the incompatible Betamax and VHS formats (it looks as if VHS has); (3) we thought that some new technology might make both formats obsolete (which right now looks unlikely).

To help us look into this a bit further, would you please tell us if you have or are about to get a videotape machine, and what kind. Thanks very much.—JH

Success Stories

From Jan Evergreen (WV):

We are all enjoying homeschooling this year. The kids spend three days a week with a friend of ours who either works with them here on the farm or takes them on trips to places they want to go. A few other children are involved also—we have arranged to be a legal private school called Harmony Hill School. The main requirement is that the kids keep diaries. We have on file the few simple state requirements. So far we have not had any problems.

The local school is aware of our status and we have taught a basket class there. The children were fascinated to see how well our kids could make baskets. Ours were amazed to see so many kids in one room. They were comfortable talking about their learning and private school, and seemed to make friends quickly. They were attracted to the social aspects of school.

So I understand that I need to renew my efforts in getting them out to dance classes, music lessons, and playtime with friends. As they get older they are more comfortable spending a night away, which helps in driving on these mountain roads.

Diana Bissell (OH) writes:

I am teaching my children at home. The local school superintendent has given me permission to do this. I am happy he didn't cause any grief over the subject, but I am not very happy about all the meetings [weekly], lesson plans, minutes-spent-per-subject, and grade reports I have to complete. I still feel the public school system has the control over the children. All the meetings, etc., take a lot of time and this time could be spent with my children. Plus, how can you write every minute and every detail you have given for instruction?

Both my children are more relaxed and happier now.... They are no longer afraid to question something they don't understand or want to know more about. Both children are getting along better with each other and with the people around them. When they have their chosen friends to the house they enjoy the time much more. They are finally learning and accepting that emotional and intellectual growth doesn't have to be painful.

Our daughter hasn't had any problem with allergies and asthma since she has been in our school. Our son hasn't had strep throat, ear infections, or pneumonia since attending our school. Plus, the children no longer have a nervous stomach.

From Nancy McGrath (NY):

We recently went for our yearly visit to our principal and a meeting with the psychologist. It was a positive experience though we have been informed we must change school districts (we have changed residences). The principal said he enjoyed sharing in the homeschooling experience with us and he felt good about what we were doing and he had no doubt it was good for our son to be offered such an opportunity.... After two years, relatives have begun to stop shaking their heads and see there is a possibility of learning without schooling.

From Marti Holmes (MI):

Although we had been homeschooling for four years without the slightest hint of trouble from the courts or the school system, it was still a bit of a relief when my son turned 16 last December. Now he is officially past the age of mandatory school attendance, and it's good to have all that behind us.

When a new center was formed for the "gifted and talented," Dale enrolled for their art class. Our local school has graciously provided bus transportation to and from the Center each day.... Although I often rage privately at the carry-over of "schoolism," Dale has dealt well with the demands and is tolerant of their (sometimes) authoritarian style. The Center accepted Dale as a homeschooler without comment, although all the rest of the students spend the other half of the school day at a regular school.... Dale has enjoyed the exposure to the other young artists, the teaching staff, and their marvelous materials and equipment.... The Center brings in performing artists, community leaders, and all sorts of interesting folks.... We feel truly fortunate.

Dale wrote to a local college last fall, asking if they would enroll a person without any high school credits or credentials. A very positive response was received, congratulating him on "planning ahead" and inviting him in for a conference. The director of admissions said, "Your academic credibility is a real hurdle, but one that we should be able to work through...."

So the future holds good possibilities, at least. . . . Homeschooling has not closed any doors that I can see, and has provided rich, full years of living (rather than "preparing for life").

From Jacque Williamson (WV):

This year we have made the break and are totally homeschooling (last year we did part time in the schools for kindergarten). I took John's suggestion and typed a 10-page letter to our board in which I listed our qualifications, our resources at home (wow, it's impressive to count all the books and all the indoor and outdoor learning resources!) and how our children have been learning. I listed all the required subjects, then told what our children had been doing and how we noticed they learn best. I did very little of "here's what we will do" but did list textbooks and workbooks we would have at our disposal as that means a lot here. I carefully did not say, "We will be using these books for instruction" nor did I give any schedule but assured them we would spend more than the required time on the subjects as the learning (life!) goes on constantly here, with no regard to holidays and clocks.

The lack of schedule was the only thing that bothered them but I think I adequately explained that schooling two children at home cannot be done the same way as in schools (at least at our house). I wanted them to understand that if and when anyone pays a visit, they know that they may or may not find our boys academically engaged in the school sense of the word.

Handing them several copies of our proposal was definitely putting our best foot forward and having copies of the law and both *GWS* and *Alternatives in Education* (our W.V. newsletter) let them know we knew what was legal. We had no trouble with approval and the assistant superintendent even asked for a copy of *Alternatives* (I had no extra *GWS* to give!) and later spoke very appreciatively of it, as it helped him know how to handle us.

Comparing To School Kids

From a New Jersey reader:

Quite often I go through these crises when I'm afraid my son is not keeping up with kids his age who attend school—especially in math. After all, to be quite honest, the most I can get him to do in math is about 30 minutes every other day.

Feeling insecure one day, I called a neighbor who is a year older than Noah and a good student. I asked her if she would bring her math book with her on our weekly swimming trip at the Y. After looking through her math book I was relieved to see he was actually ahead in multiplication, division, and fractions.

I hadn't seen anything on measurements so I asked her what about things like gallons, quarts, and pints. She said that she had that, in second grade. So I said, "How many quarts in a gallon?" She didn't know. "How many pints in a quart?" Still didn't know. She said she got an A on it in second grade but had forgotten it. Again I felt relief. He was no worse off than her and she was a grade ahead of him.

I asked another 5th grade friend the same questions. She said the same thing. She had it in second grade, passed all her tests, but couldn't remember any of it.

Another similar incident was when my mother was showing me a spelling test my niece got an A on. I was impressed by the words she could spell. She is the same age as my son and I doubted he could correctly spell half of them. I asked her to spell some for me. She couldn't, and was surprised that I expected her to. After all, she had taken that test several weeks before.

Changes Ideas about School

From Susan Peterson (MD):

I'm afraid that until I read your books, I thought of free schools as places where hippie types lounged around and smoked dope or where bratty kids ran wild. This was the picture painted by my parents who were both elementary school teachers in public schools. I feel that they were (they are now retired) hard working and devoted to their jobs, but they definitely believed that you couldn't teach unless the kids would sit still, be quiet, and listen to you. I had imbibed their attitude. What I resented in my children's schools was not the compulsion but that they used all that compulsion and bribery and then for what? Crawling at a snail's pace through stupid workbooks and watered down, condescending textbooks.

Your books broke in upon us as a startling surprise. Certainly if anyone had summarized their conclusions to me I would have rejected them out of hand. Had they been filled with airy speculations I would also have rejected them. I suppose that what makes them so compelling is that you show how your ideas gradually developed from attempts to teach certain things to real children. Also your descriptions of how real learning works fit my own experience in learning since I left school.

For instance, in trying to understand birth, I read all the popular books on the subject and many obstetrical textbooks, including quite a few old ones in 20 year jumps in order to see the development of certain attitudes and practices. Later I sat in on the obstetrics class given in the local nursing school and discovered that I knew everything that they were teaching—a large part of it, I strongly disagreed with.... This study culminated in three beautiful, "medically unattended" home births. Another example is that when I became a Christian and then a Catholic, I taught myself a great deal of theology and church history using my college library.... I am also a gardener and I see this study as extending over many, many years to come as I try new vegetables and new techniques, and also learn about fruit trees, berry bushes, grape vines, perennial flowers.... One success in this field is that I have learned to grow all kinds of oriental vegetables—bok choy, mizuna, shungiku—which are beautiful and which we love to eat.

My husband has also taught himself many things. While working in a restaurant he studied cooking at home, reading Escoffier and many other books and practicing, and as a result was able to become the chef of a French restaurant. He is now on the faculty of a Culinary Arts Institute and he commented that his students were paying $8,000 a year to learn what he learned while being *paid* $8,000 a year and more! While working as a chef for these past ten years, he has continued to study philosophy, poetry, psychology, taught himself some Swedish, learned a little Indian sign language.

But that children could proceed in this way! When I was in second grade I had learned to read quite well—tested about 5th grade level—and I said to my parents, "Now that I can read, I don't need to go to school any more, because if I want to learn anything I can just read about it in a book." I was so confident in this belief, its logic was so irrefutable, that I expected my parents to say, "Yes, you're right. You don't have to go to school any more." Instead, they laughed indulgently and often quoted this remark to me as one of those cute things children say.

Before my oldest son went to kindergarten I "taught" him to read—that is, while I was cooking or changing a baby's diapers, he would come to me, crayon and paper in hand, and say, "How do you spell bus? How do you spell cat? How do you spell black?" I told him, and he would go and write them over and over. He had a special interest in writing and the alphabet itself, while being able to read was a kind of sideline. At about 4½, he said that he was tired of those letters, he knew them all, weren't there any other letters. So I gave him my Greek textbook from college and he set about copying the Greek alphabet and learning the names of the letters.

Then he went off to kindergarten—so eagerly, school was where he was going to learn so much more than he had been learning at home. And they made him "learn" the names and the sounds of the letters which he had known since he was two.

Besides that they colored in pictures, learned the names of the colors, and counted to 20 (he could count to 500). When I complained, the reaction was, "Here's another mother who thinks her kid's a genius." His own estimate of what he could do dropped so far that he stopped learning the Greek letters, stopped learning arithmetic, stopped learning everything, it seemed. Also he couldn't draw any more pictures for a long time. It didn't occur to me that I could have taken him out. ... Now (at 9) he is a master of doing the absolute minimum to get by. Strangely enough he has terrible handwriting and hates to put anything on paper.

[From a later letter:] This has been our first year of homeschooling. We are legal, as a "church school." Not too many super extra-special wonderful things have happened—but a lot of bad things at least have been avoided. I believe we are rescuing Winnie (our second child) from psychological devastation. The others at least spend only one or two hours a day on formalized schoolwork instead of six. They—and I—can get enough sleep. I used to spend two hours a day driving to and from school—I prefer to spend it teaching, even if it isn't always peaceful. My one hesitation is that my oldest son and I rub each other the wrong way and we are thrown together a lot this way.

Husband Changes Mind

Mha Atma Kaur Khalsa (CA) wrote:

My husband at first was opposed to homeschooling, thinking it was just a fad with me and not really understanding what it was all about. He is very busy with his work. I would choose chapters out of your books, Nancy Wallace's book, and stories out of *GWS*, and set them on the table with his meals and ask him to read them. When we would go out to dinner or for a walk, just the two of us, I would tell him about the benefits of homeschool and the disadvantages of school as I was discovering and learning on my own from my reading. He began to favor my ideas as he began to understand what it was all about. He agreed to let me take our younger son, Siri Atma (6) out of school, but felt I should not take Sat Sarbat (10, the one with "L.D.") out since he did not feel I could help him very much.

I was only up to about Issue #23 in *GWS* at that time, and had not run across any success stories with children similar to Sat Sarbat, so I wrote to *GWS* for help—asking for someone to correspond with or reference to articles in *GWS*. Donna Richoux sent me two names of moms who had homeschooled kids with "L.D." One of the morns answered my letter and got a friend of hers to write me too. Their letters really helped. I found more L.D. articles in *GWS* and my husband about two weeks ago said he was glad I was into homeschooling and that I could keep Sat Sarbat home next year.

I am glad I went slow and steady with my husband, though I must admit at times I thought I would go crazy with desperation in being alone in my beliefs about homeschooling (the first local people I wrote to out of *GWS* did not respond). ... I now have his solid support and I did not make him angry or resentful towards me by being pushy.

Parents' Work Arrangements

From Wendy Priesnitz (Ont.):

On the subject of working parents and homeschooling: we have found the perfect solution, for the short term at least. We have had a family business in the past, but found that it took up a huge amount of our time and energy, even though it allowed us to work at home and travel around the country a bit with the girls. But right now, both Rolf and I are working at the home of some friends, also homeschoolers. Rolf is putting in their plumbing and heating systems (it is a huge house, so it is a big job) and I am working with them on their home business. The girls go with us when they want, and have a great time playing with their friend. The two families have great lunchtime discussions, we work flexible hours, and everyone benefits. I think that with more networking done among homeschooling families, others could work out situations such as this, at least on a temporary basis.

From Peggy Buchanan (OR), who wrote about learning to be a midwife in GWS *24:*

As a single parent for the last two years, I have found homeschooling to fit in well to our family scene. I am fortunate to work out of my home, so my children are welcome. They learned early on when they were expected to be quite "respectful of privacy" and when I was available to them. They enjoy going on appointments with me and we get a lot of mileage out of our car rides to and fro. . . . I find that my children are welcome in many aspects that are untraditional, but work well. I hope you continue to encourage single parents in their homeschooling efforts.

From Patti Murphy (MA):

Shawn (7) has been a tremendous help around the house. In addition to mothering four children, I am also a weaver. I just recently got a production loom at home and that enables me to put in between 20–30 hours a week weaving. The first month was hard but now that we have all worked out a bit of a schedule it works out all right. I work while the baby sleeps and do cooking and cleaning when she's awake. The only thing I don't like about it is I feel I should spend more time teaching Shawn. But we need the money and it's an ideal job as I am able to be home all the time.

It's probably a blessing that I don't have that extra bit of time to instruct him. I was talking with another home-schooler about my guilt feelings for putting so much responsibility on Shawn as far as household chores and she jokingly told me—he will probably really go for the school work just to get a break! He doesn't seem to mind any housework except dishes so I do those. If he learns nothing else he knows how to run a house and take care of young children.

Kids Earning Money

Helen Kepler (AZ) wrote:

Solomon and Persephone have been selling bunches of mistletoe at the shopping mall. My sister-in-law, who works at one of the stores in the mall, assured us the security guards would throw them out since no soliciting is allowed there. However, Solomon tells me he believes one of the guards bought some from him. I don't know if it's because they are children that they have been allowed to stay and sell, or if it's a case of Christmas spirit, or if it could be they are such an attraction for the mall. They both have hand puppets this year which they operate through holes cut in the bottom of their mistletoe boxes. The little kids in the mall are all thrilled to see the bear and cat come to life passing out the mistletoe. Solomon and Persephone are quite proud of their profits.

From Penny Barker (OH):

Britt (15) wrote a letter to our local newspaper asking if she could sell them a few word puzzles she'd written. They responded by asking her to submit a *weekly* puzzle column with her photo and are paying her $5 for each puzzle. I've enclosed one of her puzzles. She submits it ready for printing and has earned $30 so far. . . . [DR: The puzzle is the "Word Search" kind—15 rows and columns of apparently nonsensical letters in which twenty or so words are concealed.]

Maggie (10) has the go-ahead from Pat Stone to write an article on her sheep for *Mother Earth News*. ["Young Writers Still Needed," *GWS* 36.] Britt finally decided to spend some of the money she got from *her* article in *Mother Earth News*. She is purchasing a 12 record set of Chopin piano pieces for herself.

Work: A Part of Life

More from Penny Barker (OH):

In reading your review of *The African Child* (*GWS* 29), I couldn't help but see the many similarities between the culture described in the small African village and the Amish community here in Ohio. The Amish thrive on work and it is an integral part of their life. Everyday chores and upkeep are done by everyone in the family from the 5-year-olds on up. Larger jobs such as barn building, oat thrashing, spring cleaning, cooking for weddings, are done by larger numbers of people in their church community. . . . Whenever any Amish couple or family move to a new farm, they become members of that particular church district and contribute their labor to the events in that area. Corn husking and quilting are two other work events that they do together as small- to medium-sized groups. Children grow up attending these "work parties" as well as attending to their many work duties at home. Work is never considered bad but rather as a part of life or a friendly social time. My Amish neighbor did say to me the other day that it was noticed that between the ages of 7 and 14 (8th grade is the last grade required by law for Amish children), the children were distracted by school and were not able to be as attentive, thorough, or responsible about their work at home. Still, she said, once they were home again they usually focused in on home duties. Before school attendance was made compulsory for the Amish, the children learned everything they needed to be a very responsible member of their community from being at home and participating in all of the things going on at their farms and in their communities.

One of the sad things I have discovered from talking with various Amish mothers is that where not too many years ago the children from an early age were revered as real contributors on the farm, now many Amish mothers are looking forward to those hours that the young ones are away so they can get their work done. I can just see how the schools are changing this community, which has all the elements of J. H. Van Den Berg's "healthy community."

Last week we had eleven 7-to 13-year-old visitors here for five days and what seemed to be most absent in their lives was physical work basic to their upkeep as human beings. We did everything—washed dishes many times a day, made bread, churned butter, made dog biscuits (my 5-year-old did this spontaneously with a group of 7-year-olds who were amazed that you didn't *have* to *buy* dog biscuits and more amazed that I would let a 5-year-old do this task *completely* unaided by an adult), pitched hay, planted fruit trees, started vegetables inside, built birdhouses, spread manure on pastures, repaired the hogs' nest, gathered eggs, swept up after ourselves many times (amazing to see how many children do not know how to hold a broom or carry a bucket, but wonderful to see them finally learn how). Most of them absolutely thrive in doing this labor that seems to have been denied them. They are also amazed to learn they can work with many different aged people and learn from each other, My 7-year-old was taking a 13-year-old girl with him to feed the new calf. . . . The calf has to be bottle-fed and a special formula of milk replacer mixed up to go into the bottle. Ben was getting everything out to prepare the formula, when the 13-year-old visitor came into the kitchen and asked me how to mix it up and I very truthfully told her that Ben knew how but I had no idea. She was amazed to think that she was going to learn something from this very small boy. The thing is that he learned how to mix up the formula from his 9-year-old brother who learned it from his 10-year-old sister the year before who learned it from her 15-year-old sister two years ago and she learned from the directions on the back of the milk replacer bag, and neither Richard nor I have ever had occasion to mix it up, so we really don't know how to do it!

One father of a 7-year-old boy said to me as he left his son here last week, "I hope there will be other children here his age." . . . I tried to let him know his child would be with other people, not just "peers." As it turned out, when he was with our other three 7-year-old visitors, he acted like a robot or machine of some sort or was generally silly, seeming to seek some sort of peer approval. As Richard and I and my children related to him in a straight way about things that really mattered to what we were doing, he seemed to bring himself to a different level.

In sitting around the breakfast, lunch, and supper table with these eleven children, I noted a high degree of linguistic skills—not particularly pertinent topics but a lot of complex words and sentences. Then when we would go to our chores and projects I was stunned (as I always am) by the very low degree of bodily-kinesthetic skills they possess.

I also notice a strong absence of listening skills. I find many children are very interested in what they have to say, but not real good at listening to what others have to say. . . . I notice that my own children who will talk *a lot* to each other and us, will grow very quiet and attentive when we have adult visitors and will spend the whole visit just listening. . . . I really think they have this pertinent attitude to life that allows them to listen when they think something is worth listening to and talking when it seems their words will *really* contribute to the subject at hand. They do not have a need to talk simply to be noticed.

Draw Kids into Your World

Sue Radosti (IN) wrote:

The Continuum Concept has really changed my feelings about becoming a mother. . . . I've known people who focused their lives so totally on their children that they didn't have anything else to talk about, no other interests or concerns, and I was beginning to get the impression that it's not possible to lead an active life without neglecting your children! *The Continuum Concept* (and obviously, all of *GWS*) has helped me to see that it's not only possible but healthy to integrate parenting with the rest of life, by drawing the children into the parents' world rather than creating an isolated, limited, contrived world for the children (which places just as many restrictions on the parents!).

As a *GWS* friend of mine once explained to me, when she is actively pursuing her own interests, her children can come along and pick quality learning from her like fruit from a tree (I love that analogy!), and her role as a parent cannot be distinguished from her identity as an active, learning human being. There is a unity and fluidity in that sort of family relationship that surpasses all of my effort to describe it with the usual labels.

Behaving In Public

From Toots Weier (WI):

I would like to comment on the letter by David Kent (*GWS* 35). His concern was directed to the fact that tickets were not available to children under 8 years of age to attend lectures sponsored by the National Geographic Society. His protest, I felt, was totally and understandably legitimate. I commend him for speaking up for children's rights. . . . It seems that often children are seen as nuisances, noisemakers, restless and whining beings who are not in control of their behavior. . . . Of course, not all children are well-behaved. . . . But given a chance, they can prove their worth!

Recently, The Friends of Animals sponsored a film at the local museum by a wildlife sanctuary. It stated that families were welcome and so I took our three children, my brother and two sisters to view it. Weren't we surprised, first of all at the small attendance of people—a few adults and only one other child. Secondly, we had no idea that we had just sat in the front row of what was to be the Friends of Animals' *Annual Meeting* and the film was to follow!

The point I want to make is that our children, ages 8, 5, and 2, were completely silent and still through the entire meeting (which even I thought to be *very* boring as it included electing officers, etc.). . . . After the meeting, there was a small lunch for everyone in attendance. It was at that time that many of the adults went up to my children and praised them for being so well behaved. (Talk about a proud mother!).

Children Help Save Wildlife

From Karen Johnston (CA —"Wildlife Volunteer at 9," GWS 34):

Donna's article, "The Power of Letter-Writing," in *GWS* 33 interested me. . . . Part of the activities of the *Elsa Clubs* is the involvement of young people in current conservation efforts. So many kids want to actually *help* animals in trouble, in addition to just *learning* about them (which is, of course, the first step to finding solutions).

In the Elsa Clubs we have had several letter-writing and petition campaigns designed for children. These have been campaigns to help species as diverse as the tule elk, harp seal, and California condor. The most impressive results were obtained when we successfully halted an effort by sports-hunters to have the leopard removed from the endangered species list so that they could bring back leopard trophies from Africa. A massive letter-writing and petition campaign was launched, which included the involvement of thousands and thousands of children from across the country. We feel that their input contributed to the leopard's continued protection.

[DR: Club membership costs $7.50. Address, PO Box 4572, N Hollywood CA 91607.]

Living in Jamaica

Rachael Solem ("Kids on a Boat," GWS 23; "On the Road," #28) wrote last winter from Jamaica, where her family rented a house:

Fisher and John-Eli (4) take long walks and meet all sort of people—mountain men making charcoal, fishermen catching shrimp, builders, boat-makers. John is especially fond of walking with a stick, and is getting good at finding his way along fairly small paths up in the hills around us.

Briana (7) is a good enough reader now to read to him and our trips to the library are an important part of our week. The kids have an allotment of three books between them and have learned how to find an assortment appropriate to both of them for two weeks. . . . I am also writing several stories for them for Christmas. I have found my painting skills to be good enough to consider illustrating the books, and another mother wants me to make some for her kids, too. At first I tried to keep the words within what I know to be Briana's reading vocabulary, but then I scattered a few new ones in here and there as I had to—and why not? How else will she expand her knowledge? She reads more from sight and context than phonics anyway. In my usual guiding manner I have been "helping" her sound words out, unless I catch myself and just read the word for her. . . . There is often so much else going on in a child's life—so much living to be done in between what we think of as lessons that those skills we consider necessary and are so anxious for kids to acquire are, for the kids, just another thing to do—perhaps a bit more of a hassle as they perceive our anxiety and must deal with *that* on top of the lesson.

Briana and John-Eli have been in school and want to return for the next term in three weeks. We chose this because of the need for them to see other kids and for this purpose the schooling has been good. Briana understands "Jamaica-talk" and had several parts in the Christmas play and can visit some other children now. John-Eli is happy just about anywhere, and certainly so near his sister. Academically, the school is not very demanding and the atmosphere is hardly conducive to any kind of study. It is dark and noisy. When I begin to wonder if Briana is acquiring all the necessary information, all I need do is ask, in conversation, some pertinent questions which challenge her powers of observation and memory. Just now we were talking of reptiles and I asked how big she thought a lizard was, one that we saw from the car on a tree, ten feet from us, some days ago. It was the biggest we've seen here. Her estimation was the same as mine, and what more could I ask?

The kids have become prolific artists in the absence of TV and old friends. They are sharpening their skills of socializing, observation, drawing, swimming, and talking. Talks go on and on. Everything is open for discussion. Briana's questions range from "the biggest number in the whole world" and our number system, to the whole life of Jesus, especially how he died and why he is so special, to the way poetry is written, to why money is different and dollars of different value. I picked up a book of poetry which is daily read. We are still making friends with the chameleons. . . . They are fast and I am not, but the kids have lots of other pets which are held for observation for a time and then let go: caterpillars, hermit crabs, lightning bugs, beetles, and grasshoppers have graced our veranda in jars or Frisbees, mostly on John-E's hands. He talks to them in the most soothing voice I have ever heard.

We play cards—concentration (John-E is very good, as Briana is, of course) and 21. . . . Every time I try to learn one of the Jamaican card games, whoever is teaching changes the rules, and I often lose, quite baffled. The Jamaican kids especially are flexible with playing-etiquette. "Irie," they say, all's well. We live with an old woman who keeps herself fit and active with long walks to her garden, keeping laying hens, hand washing, cooking over a wood fire, and generally living the typical Jamaican life. This was new to us, of course, and the slaughter of a goat and a chicken, the gathering of eggs, shelling of quarts and quarts of "peas" (kidney beans), were all novel and fun, and are now part of a simple routine. Briana has brought to my attention the growth stages of a coconut, and daily collects and opens almonds from the tree by the beach.

As much as I imagined my raising of children to happen in a very controlled and rooted way, this seems to not be the way our life is. It hasn't been for some years, actually. Fisher is a traveller now, and there is much to be learned from travel and living abroad, so here is where the lessons begin. Both kids seem to be good at getting knowledge and using it from every source they find. They are getting less afraid of looking, too.

Mexico Adventure

From Anna Quinn-Smith (OR):

Mexico in May '83 was a big adventure. We dealt with Mexico City hype, new currency, exploring where *we* wanted to. Kris and I truly enjoyed the sights and "light-sound" show at Teotihuacan outside Mexico City. She ran to the top of the Pyramid of the Sun! Visited a friend in San Miguel de Allende, and made many new friends at Cinco de Mayo festivities and on early morning walks over cobbled streets. Language presented no real barrier, there were other ways to communicate with our fellow species! Kris had her 12th birthday there and celebrated with an early morning private swim at a local hot springs resort— three pools, each warmer than the last, surrounded by stone parapets and full of banana trees, flowers, birds—wonderful! We felt we could live on Mexican-siesta schedules forever. Visited a friend from Idaho who plays in the symphony orchestra in Mexico City; and on our last full day there, Kris had appendicitis and was operated on! So—no Disneyland side trip, but five days in a Spanish-speaking hospital—with no ice or air conditioning or stomachable food to recuperate by. Only our doctor spoke some English, and that wasn't much! Such an experience! I camped out in her hospital room and interceded where I could. She learned quickly how to ask for an outside telephone line, a variety of juices, and other basic necessities— Dónde está el baño por favor? Pronto!

Elitist Snobs?

Nancy Wallace (NY) wrote to a local paper that had published a review of her book Better Than School *(avail. here, $14.95):*

Ms. Halpern says that because they are taught at home, Vita and Ishmael are missing out on the opportunity to be aware of "differing lifestyles and cultures," and since she implies that they may not be able to "move toward an understanding and acceptance of diversities that are neither better nor inferior," . . . it sets up the (perhaps unconscious) implication that we are, in effect, elitist snobs.

Actually, it seems to me that, despite the good intentions and the strongly-held liberal values of many teachers (and administrators) like Ann Halpern, it is the schools, not homeschoolers, who end up teaching their students that some people are better than others. They do this by focusing on certain skills (mainly those having to do with literacy and mathematics) and rewarding children's excellence in these skills to the practical exclusion of everything else, except perhaps sports. When, as is so often the case, minority and poor children are prominent among those who do poorly in school, they are judged (and judge themselves) accordingly.

When I first went to kindergarten in California, I quickly learned that the Mexican-American children—sons and daughters of migrant workers— didn't know their letters and often didn't even know their colors, whereas many of the children of the professors in town already knew how to read. Not only were we aware of this, but it soon became obvious that the Mexican-American kids were never going to "catch up." School taught us that writing and spelling correctly were more important than picking apricots and putting them in bushel baskets without bruising them, and that math was more important that being able to look after your younger brothers and sisters all day long while your parents were working in the fields. My children, on the other hand, do not judge other children, or themselves, in the way that school taught me to. Instead, they look upon each person they meet as a potentially worthy human being.

As for Ms. Halpern's fear that Vita and Ishmael won't have opportunities to meet different kinds of people, just the opposite is true. They come with us to political meetings and to lectures at the colleges, they have opportunities to travel and to see how other people live and work, and in any case, between the First Street Playhouse, the Community School of Music and Art, and all of the afternoon classes that they go to, they have plenty of opportunities to befriend people of all kinds.

OK To Be Ordinary

From Deirdre Purdy (WV):

Thoughts on superkids and guilt [*GWS* 33, 36]: (1) When I have written *GWS*, I always find, as I describe the children, how good they sound on paper. Of course, I emphasize the positive—not to brag or hide the truth, but because that is the point of the letter. We are more likely to be writing with the good news about homeschool; less likely to be describing our child with many interests and ideas but little follow-through, or so busy talking he can't listen, or—an ordinary kid.

(2) And, John, don't you have a bias toward to the positive also? So your newsletter encourages discussion of the positive rather than the negative aspects of child raising and educating, and emphasizes solutions over problems. And who, as editor, could fail to print the stories of the homeschooled child who runs her own bakery, writes a symphony, goes to Harvard?

Of course it's a mistaken attitude to feel lessened by others' accomplishments, but who has never been guilty of it? . . . But I want to make my big plea for this: it's OK to be ordinary, living your days out well and happily without newsworthy accomplishments, just everyday going forward, living and learning.

Jed, at 9, is the main local D&D dungeon master for which he prepared himself by diligently studying many arcane and abstruse texts. Hannah taught herself cursive and is an excellent housekeeper. But how many other projects are strewn behind them, unfinished (and picked up by me?) How many hours spent reading Nancy Drew, the Hardy boys, Adventure comics? And how many hours spent fighting with each other, spacing around, helping us and "helping" us? Sometimes a project has their complete concentration, but that might as often be a 2-day Monopoly binge as anything that could be shown, a finished "product."

And in all of this they are very like me. When I was in school I was whipped to a frenzy of producing papers, book reports, posters, projects, and, especially, good grades, as well as holding offices and joining clubs. Eighty percent was for show. Let them be unproductive. I rejoice that they can entertain themselves, all day, every day. And I have every expectation that as they mature their application and ability to carry through their schemes will mature also. But now, they are children. I urge other parents not to berate themselves or their children because they and their children are only ordinary. Let us freely admire those who produce while allowing to ourselves and others that it is also all right not to.

[JH:] About being "positively oriented"—I admit it. Today, when the headlines daily shriek new dangers and disasters, there seems no point in using scarce space in *GWS* to tell people that things are tough all over, and specifically, that children are passionate, temperamental, changeable, impulsive, proud, and strong-willed, and that as a result of these qualities (which I do *not* consider vices) are often unreasonable and difficult. We all know this, and I have been saying it for years.

Nor have I ever been in the business of saying that children who have certain clearly visible and impressive accomplishments are "better" than others. If readers cannot avoid making such comparisons and pecking-orders, that is their mistake and their problem, and we accept no responsibility for it. As we have said before, we have a very practical reason for printing all the good news we can find about the doings of children. We homeschoolers have to contend with two extremely popular ideas: (1) Children can do nothing good, since they are no good. (2) Children may occasionally do something good, but only if some adult makes them. In every way we can, we will continue to show that these ideas are wrong.

So please keep on helping us do this, by sending us all the good news you can find about your own or other kids, and we will print all we can find room for. We are in a way a big family, so let's all rejoice together in the accomplishments of our children. Of course, if you have real problems, tell us about those too, so that together we may find remedies. But it is in no way a problem that your child does not happen to have done something or other that some other child has done, whether that be writing a song or playing the tuba or getting into Harvard.

Kids' Hour

From Marcia Kolb (VA):

After Aaron's birth, my life was so taken up with a new baby again, I wanted to devise a special way to make sure that my girls would not be neglected. We started "Kids' Hour." Sometime in the early afternoon they have a whole hour of my undivided attention. The time is spent doing something of *their* own choosing. Some days we read for an hour, sometimes we play games or draw or paint or have a craft time or a nature walk or whatever.... We've sometimes had so much fun that the hour extends to 1½ or 2 hours. Aaron is usually nursing or sleeping in my arms, or in the baby carrier. With the concentrated time in the afternoon, they are usually much happier the rest of the day and don't feel neglected or left out because of the baby. It's a priority time and I don't take any phone calls during this period. I notice during spells where we've gotten away from "Kids' Hour" that their behavior is more difficult to deal with and we have more bad days.

Thoughts on Fighting

In "Queries," GWS 37, we invited responses to a reader's question, "How do you handle homeschoolers fighting with each other? It makes me wonder sometimes if I can stand to have them around." Here are excerpts from some of the answers:

I have found with my own four children that fighting is generally a result of *a little too much* family togetherness. As much as I love my husband and children, I find I love them so much more after a little private time to recharge my batteries, and I believe children have this same need. So one of the best solutions is to separate potential squabblers regularly *before* they get tired and cross with each other. An hour or so of "You in this room and you in that room" generally produces eager companions. With more than two children, it pays to periodically have them change the configuration in which they pair or group up in their activities.

Sometimes a situation arises where one child has caused injury to a sibling, whether by accident, carelessness, or (it happens!) just plain orneriness. My standard remedy, rather than dish out punishment, is to assign the child who caused the injury (or *appeared* to cause it—these things are seldom one-sided) to be personal nurse to the injured child. It's amazing how quickly anger dissipates and compassion takes over, not to mention the opportunity to learn a few emergency first-aid techniques.... Generally recovery is remarkably swift!—*Darlene Graham* (TX).

―――――――

My children, too, are always fighting. I thought that this was something we would be saved from by having home births, prolonged nursing, family bed, and homeschooling. But I've discovered that love and closeness can breed discontent also. Our entire family of four is together 24 hours a day. Sometimes I feel like I'm in the middle of a battleground. If one child approaches another who is involved in something, I know that in a minute there will be a tussle ending in crying.

A lot of the problem is boredom. I don't always feel like entertaining them or having a part in their projects. Sometimes I feel guilty . . . but what we're striving for is kids who can create and do on their own, not wait around for entertainment and directions.

Almost accidentally I have found some answers to this problem. Two months ago, we made a long distance move. . . . My husband and I were exhausted and stopped being able to wake up at 7 a.m. with the kids. So, for the first time in our life, we closed the door and told them to keep quiet and let Mommy and Daddy sleep. Two hours (of quiet!) later I awoke feeling apprehensive, only to find that they had somehow managed to make themselves breakfast. Jeremiah (8) had read a couple of books to Serena (5) and together they were happily playing a board game. Having no audience there was no reason for competition, and so they pulled together instead of against each other.

The kids still hang around me all day, not wanting to go outside unless I come, too. But as soon as I push them out alone and they set off on a hike together, to explore the woods or whatever (unknown dangers!), I notice that they each reach for the other's hand. . . . Put them in some sort of situation where they have to depend on each other (instead of you) and they'll learn slowly but surely how much they mean to each other.—*Pam Gingold* (CA).

I think it helps to give them language they can use. "Please let me use your rocket eraser." "I'd like to play by myself now. We can play that game later." It *really* helps to listen for things you like to hear and tell them. "I liked hearing you boys getting along with each other." "I hope you'll say that more often."—*M. Wilkie*.

When the children started fighting, I would force them to confront each other by sitting in chairs opposite each other about three feet apart. They had to be silent, just looking at each other. I would set the timer for five or ten minutes. If they fooled around I would reset the timer. At first I had to physically enforce this and it took them 30 minutes to finally sit still and confront for 5 minutes. Soon they wised up and would just sit down and get it over with. I haven't found it necessary to have them do this for the last two years. They bicker so seldom.

Another thing is that television watching often makes people quarrelsome. . . . Hans was absolutely addicted. But we still wanted access to the TV for our video and for selected shows. Finally my husband cut the end of the cord off, and added a female plug end. On a short cord he put two male plugs. I just pop the little cord into my purse and I've got control even when I'm not home.—*Sharon Hillestad* (MN).

I have found that the less running around I do, less time in the car, more streamlined meals, grocery shopping twice a month, less clutter in the house, the calmer I am *and* the calmer the children are. Fighting seems to escalate when we are tired, hurried, and/or unorganized.—*Joanie Gillispie* (CA).

On Discipline—3

In Parts 1 and 2 of this extended article (see *GWS* 37 and #38), I made the point, first, that the reason schools have such generally bad discipline is not that they don't want it but that they don't understand it, and secondly, that systems of discipline which rest mainly on rules, threats, and punishments may produce for a while the appearance of success, but in the longer run are likely to do harm. At the end of Part Two of the article I raised the question, where did I learn, and where have I put into practice, my own ideas about discipline.

The first part of the answer to that question is, from teaching. At one time or another I have taught, in schools, all ages of children from first grade through twelfth. My first four years of teaching were in a small coeducational boarding school in the Colorado Mountains, in which students and faculty did all the manual work of the school. As a teacher of English, French, and Math, I dealt with students in classes; being in charge of a boys' dormitory, I was a kind of substitute parent, responsible for getting kids up in the morning and to bed at night, keeping the dorm more or less clean, and maintaining some kind of order; as a coach of soccer and baseball, I was in charge there; and I directed groups of students in many of the different kinds of work we often had to do on campus. Since the school was new, small, and broke, we had to take what students we could get, and some of these were very disturbed and difficult indeed.

Later in Boston I taught for two summers at a small evening private school, most of whose students were from the inner city, on the whole very unsuccessful in their regular public schools. Since they were at our school by choice, they were not violent; but they were certainly not docile, a long way from anyone's idea of ideal students. Many of them told us years later, by the way, that they gained enormously from their few weeks' experience in our little school.

Also, one of the elementary schools at which I taught was near the bottom of the local private school pecking order, and so could not be choosy about students. Some of these were smart and delightful kids, but many were very difficult children, who had been kicked out of other schools, private and in one case even public, and had been diagnosed as disabled, disturbed, retarded, etc. So I have had to deal with a number of children of many ages whom other adults, often including professional specialists, had found almost impossible to manage. Not only did I manage them, but in all but one or two cases I helped to civilize them, helped them to understand and master some of their problems, and to begin to live more constructively and happily. By other people's standards, and by my own, my methods of discipline worked, even on children on whom the conventional methods had been tried, and failed, for many years.

Though I have never had children of my own, over the years I have spent a great deal of time with other people's young children, often in circumstances in which I had some responsibility for their behavior. For the past few years, here in the *GWS* office, there has hardly been a day when we have not had with us at least one small child, either of someone working here or of visitors. Our policy has been and is to let children have the run of the office and to do pretty much what they like, as long as they don't impede our work too much or damage or destroy things. If and when this happens, I don't hesitate to say "No," not least of all because I don't think it would be fair for me always to have the fun of being with the children, but to give parents the less pleasant job of saying "No" to them. As a result, we who work here full-time and the many parents of young children who come to the office have a good working understanding of what children are and are not allowed to do. Also, aside from protecting our personal and office property, I take an interest in the children; if I hear a little voice begin to wail, I very often look to see what has gone wrong and if there is some way I can help, which often there is. So if I have not had and probably never will have (which I regret) the experience of being a full-time parent, there are probably not many people who have had as much experience in dealing with a variety of children of all ages.

One way to say some of what I want try to say about discipline is to tell again a story about something that happened when I was teaching fifth grade. I taught most subjects in the curriculum, but for some classes the children had to go to other rooms. One of these was French, which the children detested, and with good reason—the woman who taught the class obviously did not like children and did not like having to teach them French. One day, when the time came for the class to go to French, one girl, a very intelligent, proud, spirited child, with much fire in her eye, stayed at her desk, reading a book. I said to her that it was time to go to French. She read on. I said it again. No response. I said that I didn't blame her for not liking French, but that the rules of the school required her to go to French and required me to make sure she went, and that if I had to I *would* make her go, even if I had to take her there myself. Still no response. I said,

"Well, I'm sorry if that's the way it has to be," and started toward her desk. Without even looking up, she went on reading, until I was about three feet away. Then she jumped up, slammed the book shut, and in a furious voice said, "All right, I'm going, I'm going! But it's just *brute force* that's making me go, just *brute force!*" I said, "You're absolutely right, it's nothing but brute force." And off she went, without another word. Neither of us ever mentioned the incident again, and from then on, she went to French without delay or protest.

Not only did she not give me any trouble about French; she did not give me any trouble about anything. In fact, she was one of the three leaders in a class which, without such leaders, would have been almost impossible to teach. Yet her parents, who "believed in discipline," considered her a problem. So did her former teachers at this school. So, I learned many years later, did most of the teachers who taught her later. (One of the other two leaders in this class was also a child whom everyone, parents and teachers, had previously found hard to handle.)

Some may say here, perhaps with some exasperation, "But isn't what you did exactly what all the books on discipline tell us to do, tell the child what to do and then, if she doesn't do it, give her some punishment?" The answer is No. What I did was *not* what all the books tell you to do but something quite different. I told her what the rules of the school required her to do, and I made it clear that I was ready to make her do it. But I did not *punish* her. Indeed I did not in any way try to make her feel that she had committed any kind of "crime" for which punishment was deserved. I did not defend, by pretending to believe in it, the rule which I was enforcing, and I did not ask her to believe or pretend to believe in it. I did not insult her intelligence by claiming that her being made to go to this French class was in any way a good thing. The school taught or rather went through the motions of teaching French for reasons of snob appeal only —it was what all the fancy private schools in the area did, so in order to get students this school felt it had to do it too. I knew then as now that this kind of teaching, even if well done, is a waste of time and money; the children quickly forget what little they learn, and in any case, any half smart child would learn more French in a few weeks in France, or Quebec, than they would learn in years of this teaching. Beyond that, the French teacher in this school taught French very badly; I could have done much better myself.

I would have been happy to say all this to the child if she had ever asked me, which she never did. She was bright enough to understand and probably even to accept the school's reason for putting French in the catalog, namely, that without it many parents, including probably her own, would not have sent their children to the school. Perhaps she already understood this without my needing to say it. Meanwhile, as I say, I did not insult her by pretending to speak from a position of moral authority which I knew I did not have. In this matter I was simply acting as an agent and instrument of what she quite rightly called "brute force," which is to say, an aspect of reality. Being like most children a realist, she was ready to accept this brute force. *What she was not ready to accept was this brute force pretending to be something else*—an expression of reason, or truth, or justice. And this is what a great many children, including I am sure many who become very severe discipline problems, can't stand.

Reason. Truth. Justice. These are the things that, whether they know it or not, and even before they know the names of such things, children expect, want, and need to find in their encounters with the adults who run their lives. They want to see us behaving sensibly, honestly, fairly. These ideas do not get much space or attention in any of the articles or books on discipline that I have ever seen. Some will say that it is OK, maybe even a good thing, to explain to children your reasons for giving them orders—but, they hasten to add, only after they have obeyed them, which is of course too late for any serious discussion about whether the orders ought to have been given in the first place. About honesty, about admitting our real motives for giving children the orders we give them, they say very little, and about fairness they say nothing at all. Oh, they do say that you must be consistent in your demands and that what you demand of one child you must demand of the others, which is true enough as far as it goes. But they never for a second consider the possibility that for us to have the power to make these demands of children is in itself not fair. We can perhaps explain and excuse it in terms of brute force reality, the ignorance and helplessness of children, but we cannot call it justice. Children feel and resent this very strongly. I remember that I was no older than nine or ten when I realized with amazement and anger, and being a realist then accepted, that my parents as a matter of course spoke to me in a way they would not speak to anyone else in the world, not even their hired servants. The rules of minimal courtesy which held force everywhere in the adult world obviously did not apply to me. To the adults, I was something less than a full human being.

Everything I have said about discipline so far I can sum up in these words—our ways of disciplining children are not likely to be effective, in the long run or even the short, unless and except as we think of children and treat them as full human beings.

Since I still have more to say on this subject, I will continue in a later issue.—JH

Overcoming Shyness

Deirdre Cox wrote in the Illinois newsletter, The HOUSE Door:

> I know that most people who know me will be truly shocked—but I was very shy until my early twenties (I didn't date until I was 20 years old). I don't know, or care, what may have been the causes of my shyness. What I do care about is how I overcame it. Since socialization is the #1 question regarding home education, I imagine that a home educator who has a shy child is probably acutely aware of this "problem."
>
> One thing my parents did for me was to send me to drama class. I would highly recommend this to anyone else out there! The skills I learned in dealing with an audience of 100–200, I was able to use in dealing with people one-to-one.... It also makes a nice addition to your child's English studies. If drama lessons aren't readily available (check out your local park district—many have free or cheap classes for children 8 or older), I would also suggest lessons dealing with the development of the body. Classes such as self-defense, gymnastics or tumbling help to increase the child's sense of being able to do *something*.... I have a gut feeling that things relating to body development are more critical to improving self-esteem than are, say, music lessons.
>
> What I consider to be the most important "cure" for shyness is getting out of yourself and helping others. Once I started getting involved in volunteer work, I found I didn't have time to be shy—there were meetings to attend, too many things to do. Admittedly, volunteer work for younger children is more difficult to find. Look around for literacy programs that an older child might tutor at. Little Brothers of the Poor in Chicago have several volunteer programs that children can do. One that I find nice, for even my five-year-old, is the telephone volunteer whereby your child (with your supervision) calls an elderly person once a week to make sure everything is OK, and just to chat. The elderly love talking to a young child (usually) and the child is learning valuable lessons about taking care of others.
>
> Finally, don't push—if you maintain a non-competitive environment with some social contact, eventually the child will outgrow the shyness—even if it isn't until adulthood!

More on Duro Case

In *GWS* 38 we quoted some excerpts from the ruling of the U.S. Court of Appeals (4th Circuit) in the case of *Duro v. District Attorney, 2nd Judicial District of North Carolina.* Since there is considerable misunderstanding about the meaning of this case, let me try to make more clear what the court did and did not say.

The court did *not* say that homeschooling, however done, under whatever circumstances and by whatever means, was illegal. It is of the greatest importance that we correct this mistaken interpretation of the court's ruling, since it seems to be gaining wide circulation. It appeared in an article on the legal status of homeschooling which was published in a leading education journal, and which said, incorrectly, that the court's ruling had given to the legislatures of at least those states within the fourth district, and perhaps all states, the right to declare all homeschooling flatly illegal. Not long after, at a meeting of educators at the Department of Education in Washington to which I was invited (with two others) to speak about homeschooling, one of the other speakers, a staunch and well-informed defender of homeschoolers in his own state, made the same remark (which I quickly corrected). Today I see that the latest issue of *Tender Tutor*, Joyce Kinmont's homeschooling newsletter (2770 South 1000 West, Perry UT 84302), says "in North Carolina the Court of Appeals ruled that a couple could not educate their children at home," the implication being that no families could do so. But this is not what the court said.

What the court said in *Duro* was that a family could not say that because of their religious belief they had a right to teach their children *and to say nothing to the state about it*. At issue was not a family's right to teach their own children under certain prescribed conditions, but their right to teach them without any conditions whatever. The Duro family had claimed, misinterpreting the U.S. Supreme Court's decision in *Wisconsin v. Yoder* in a way that many others have misinterpreted it, that because of that decision all they had to do to avoid sending their children to school was merely to say that their religious beliefs forbade their doing so. The Circuit Court went on to point out, as we have done in *GWS*, what the Supreme Court *did* say, which is that to gain such religious exemption from school attendance you must belong to an established church which as a matter of doctrine forbids that attendance (or as in the case of the Amish, forbids it beyond a certain age). In other words, the court said once again, "You can't get out of sending your children to school *merely* by saying that it offends your personal religious beliefs."

It is important to understand that if the court had ruled in favor of the Duro family, it would quite simply have abolished compulsory schooling. No doubt the Duros, and many others, including many readers of *GWS*, think this would be a fine idea. But the fact is that the courts are not going to do this, not least of all because if they did, an angry electorate would immediately cause to be passed a constitutional amendment making compulsory schooling explicitly constitutional. We must not fool ourselves about this. Compulsory schooling is one of the most popular of all political ideas. The overwhelming majority of Americans, parents or not, do not want to have children under their feet all day, and demand some kind of tax-supported institution where they can (in more ways than one) shut them up. That is above all else what schools are for. A court decision to do away with compulsory schooling would be about as unpopular, and about as quickly reversed, as a decision to do away with the armed forces.

In its ruling in *Duro* the court said:

> In *Yoder*, the [Supreme] Court held that there are two issues which must be considered in cases such as this. . . . 2) whether the state's interest in compulsory education is of sufficient magnitude to override *the interest claimed by the parents under the Free Exercise Clause of the First Amendment* (JH emphasis).

But this latter interest was precisely the Duros' claim that the First Amendment gave them, because of their religious beliefs, the right to teach their children *without telling the state anything about it.*

Later the court said:

> Duro has not demonstrated that home instruction will prepare his children to be self-sufficient participants in our modern society or enable them to participate intelligently in our political system, which, as the Supreme Court stated, *is a compelling interest of the state.* (JH

emphasis).

But the reason that Duro did not demonstrate that home instruction satisfied that compelling interest was that *he did not try* to demonstrate it, claiming that under the First Amendment he did not have to. Once again, it is only this claim that the court disallowed. The court did not say that homeschooling, no matter how done, could never satisfy the compelling interest of the state, but only that Duro did not demonstrate that *he* could satisfy it. This may seem like a fine distinction, but the law is made up of fine distinctions, and this one is of crucial importance. For it is not at all hard for homeschoolers to demonstrate, as many have already done, that homeschooling is at least as likely and probably much more likely to satisfy the compelling interest of the state than the great majority of public schools.

Properly understood, then, *Duro* can and should be more of a help than a hindrance to homeschoolers. It should discourage us from rushing into the courts (which in any case we should stay out of as long as we can) with weak and losing cases, claiming non-existent First Amendment rights, and instead greatly increase the chances that, if and when we are forced into court, we will go in with arguments so strong that they are almost certain to win.—JH

On Children and Language

[JH:] Bob Wallace (NY) sent me a copy of a *New York Times* article, "The Seven Wonders of the World, Updated," by Lewis Thomas, chancellor of the Sloan-Kettering Cancer Center in New York City, and author of a number of deservedly popular books of essays, one of which, *The Lives Of A Cell*, is in our catalog. The entire article is so fascinating that I am glad it appears in his new book.

I quote this selection about children because I think it could be a very useful part of any parents' statement about their reasons for wanting to teach their own children at home. In the first place, what Dr. Thomas says about children is true, important, and like all his writing, beautifully put. In the second place, he is a doctor, not just a PhD. but a real medical doctor, and his words are likely to carry considerable weight with professional educators, who envy "real" doctors their wealth and prestige, and their apparent monopoly over what most people see as vast stores of mysterious and secret knowledge. So if you like this quote, by all means use it in any plan you write up for the schools.

I particularly like his idea about children inventing language. It is not as far-fetched as it might seem. It is well known, among people who study children's language, that many children, above all identical twins, have while quite young invented wholly original and often quite complicated languages for use among themselves.

Thomas writes:

> The sixth Wonder of the modern world is a human child, any child. I used to wonder about childhood and the evolution of our species. It seemed to me unparsimonious to keep expending all that energy on such a long period of vulnerability and defenselessness, with nothing to show for it, in biological terms, beyond the feckless, irresponsible pleasure of childhood. After all, I used to think, it is one-sixth of a whole human life span!
>
> Why didn't our evolution take care of that, allowing us to jump more quickly from our juvenile to our adult (and, as I had thought) productive stage of life? I had forgotten about language, the single human trait that marks us out as specifically human, the property that enables our survival as the most compulsively, biologically, obsessively social of all creatures on earth, more interdependent and interconnected even than the famous social insects. I had forgotten that, and forgotten that children do that in childhood. Language is what childhood is for.
>
> What I hadn't known, until recently, is that children not only learn language— any old language you like—they can make language, any new language they

like.

Sometime between 1880 and 1910, Hawaiian Creole appeared as the common language of the sugar plantation workers in Hawaii—a genuine, complex speech with its own syntactical sentence structure and tight grammatical rules, containing words borrowed from the other tongues spoken by the first settlers: English, Japanese, Korean, Spanish, and Hawaiian.

Professor Bickerton has analyzed this new Creole and discovered that it closely resembles, in the details of its grammar, other Creole tongues in other colonial settings elsewhere in the world. It is fundamentally different from all the languages spoken in the homes of the different ethnic groups. It is a new language. When it appeared, it could not be understood or spoken by the adult generation who arrived in 1880, nor could the American overseers comprehend it.

Bickerton's great discovery is that this brand-new language, never heard or spoken before, must have been made by the first generation of children—syntax, grammatical rules, sentence structure, metaphors and all. There it is: children make language. Not only are children biologically equipped to learn speech, if necessary they can manufacture it out of their collective heads, and in perfection at that.

It puts childhood in a new light, I think. No wonder we need a long childhood; pity it can't be longer. When languages shift and change, as all languages always have done, maybe it is the children who do the changing. If it were not for the generations of children, maybe we would all still be speaking Hittite, or original Indo-European. And when human speech first appeared, probably sometime within the last 100,000 years or so, no time at all as evolution goes, turning our species from whatever it was down from the trees, inspecting its thumbs, trying to make friends, into our kind of creature, heads filled with metaphors, memories, awareness, fear of death and all, maybe it was the children who started it off.

Maybe language required for its beginning nothing more than a critical mass of children, raised together, going at each other in close quarters for a long time. Maybe, when it first started up in some newly stabilized agricultural or hunting-gathering community, the parents and elders around the communal fire wondered, wordlessly, what those incessant sounds being made by the children were, and wondered why the children seemed so enchanted.

Learning Stories

From Suzanne Alejandre (Ger.):

One of those perfectly-timed family learning experiences happened last night. We were having dinner by candlelight and for some reason Niko asked Rich about when he was a navigator. Perhaps his questions were spurred by the airplane sticker book he had been working on in the day—but, whatever the case, there ensued a 1½ hour discussion on airplanes, navigation, a pilot's job, airplanes landing on short runways, etc. After each topic, Rich seemed willing to stop the discussion but Niko and Lee very eagerly continued it. Rich still has some of his navigation charts (from 1972–81 he was a navigator on the C-141, which is an Air Force cargo plane) and he got one out to show the boys. Again, he was only offering the information that the boys asked for, rather than taking the chance to deliver a lecture. While all of this was going on, I tried to keep quiet since Niko and Lee seemed intent on hearing all the answers from the "expert." I did, however, ask some questions of my own.

It struck me as being a rare experience for children to have such discussions with their father. . . . I can remember asking my father something, then later being sorry since he wouldn't ever answer the question I had posed but would lecture on the topic I had asked about. He never would be talking with me, but instead, he would talk *at* me. I never felt any communication. But, last night, communication was buzzing through the air! Niko is almost 7 now and Lee is almost 5 so their attention spans and comprehension have really lengthened—that was quite evident last night.

Rich and I talked about it later that night and his comment was that it was so nice to have someone actually interested in what he knew about.

Lois Sunflower (PA) writes:

Cliff and I are swimming instructors from way back. So, of course, when we had children, our friends and relatives wanted to know when we would start teaching our kids to swim. With our first son, Beorn, who is now 6, we went through the regular baby swimming skills which are basically for getting the child used to the water. He didn't like this experience much, but we persevered, continuing to introduce new skills over the next couple of years. By the time he was 4, he hated the water, and we hated what we had done. So we finally left him alone. . . . We decided that just playing would be our new approach with our children in the water.

Phoebe, now 4, loved water play from Day 1. Burleigh, now 3, did not think much of it, but luckily for him, we let him sit on the side for as long as he wanted. All of a sudden at age 2, he jumped in the water one day and now he cries only when it's time to get out, when Mom and Dad have reached the prune stage.

And Beorn? Well, after watching his sister and brother for a while, he got himself back in the water. Within two weeks, he was swimming underwater and diving in. By the end of the summer, he was making progress in all four competitive swimming strokes. (His only introduction to these was watching his mom and dad swim in Masters Swimming Meets).

By the way, the U.S. Masters Swim Program is a nice example of many adults learning something new. It's a competitive swim program for people age 20–80 and up. Some of the swimmers have competed in the past, even on a world class level, but the majority of the participants are new at competitive swimming. The atmosphere is great as everyone involved appreciates your individual effort and improvement, no matter what your skill level. . . . If someone is interested in Masters, they should contact their local YM-YWCA or Aquatic Club.

Cliff and I have given up trying to force-teach any swimming skills. We sure are happy, not to mention that the pressure is off poor Beorn. It's nice that kids are so forgiving. Now sometimes he'll ask us to help him with his swimming and once in a while he gives me a pointer or two on my breast stroke. It's so easy! Why do we try to make teaching our own so hard?

A New Jersey reader wrote:

Recently we put together The Visible Woman and Man. They are put out by Revell. They are models of the human body with a skeleton, vital organs, and see-through skin. The woman has parts to simulate pregnancy.

It's recommended for 10-year-olds to adult. With help, a younger child could do it. The 2, 3 and 4-year-olds I babysit enjoyed watching it be put together. They especially loved the baby in the womb, the skeleton, and the skull with the moveable jaw.

My son (9) was excited about putting them together. He showed them to everyone who came to visit. One day he was showing them to a teacher friend. She wanted to know, could he tell her the names of the organs? I was surprised when he solemnly said, "No." . . . I reminded him that he was the one who put most of the organs in the body. He said, "Oh, you mean like the heart, lungs, and liver?" I said yes and he looked quite relieved.

If I hadn't been there to turn it around, that incident could have put a damper on his enthusiasm, and he might not have gone on, later that day, to cutting out a 4-foot paper model of skeleton, including a moveable jaw, elbow, and knee bones.

Rick Sprout (NY) writes:

When I was a kid, there was a next-door

neighbor named Mr. Davis. I don't know exactly how old I was, 7 or 8, but he was probably 60–65. He was the closest to my ideal of a naturalist in the best sense of the word. His knowledge of birds, wildflowers, gardening, and stars was, I now realize, remarkable. As I was a friendly and curious little boy, Mr. Davis made the perfect partner. We spent almost the entire summer either down by the river, in our backyards, or with his extensive library. I learned how to make compost, suet sticks, and identify a host of birds, flowers, and constellations.

When fall returned and school started again, our visits were cut shorter and shorter. You can't imagine my horror at discovering that my interest in birds, flowers, and nature in general was considered "sissy" or unmanly in some way, not only by other male students, but by teachers as well. Being rather quick to catch on that enjoying birds was "odd," unless, I suppose you shot them, I began to spend more time away from Mr. Davis *and* from my schoolmates who had branded me early on for being different.

After finishing *Teach Your Own*, one of the first things we did was to get rid of our TV. While you don't mention it, the elimination of TV had been brewing in the back of our minds for a long time. We started doing things again. As it was close to Christmas, I decided to make suet sticks for gifts. . . . My mother, upon receiving the suet stick, recalled my long ago friendship with Mr. Davis. It was the perfect explanation about our desire to keep Jonah out of school. My parents had said in the past, "But you've *got* to have some type of schooling," but now we're at least talking.

Pamela Pacula (CA) wrote in Home Centered Learning #6:

I was discussing homeschooling with a physician (orthopedic surgeon) recently, who wondered how parents had the time and ability to teach their children. . . . Before I could elaborate, he remembered how he had been such an early riser as a young boy, that his parents bought him a set of encyclopedias, hoping he would have something to do during the early morning hours when the rest of the house was asleep. He recalled how he had read them from A to Z, many times over, until he had them practically memorized. He realized how much he had learned on his own without being taught.

Teresa Tittley (Que.) writes:

In *GWS* 35, Toots Weier related her frustrating high school experience with a certain office machine and then the ease with which she learned to use it once she was on the job. I had a similar experience in my own life. When I was in 10th grade, I took Home Ec. and it was a disaster. Oh, I passed the course well enough, but I didn't enjoy it at all. The main reason Mom wanted me to take it was to learn how to sew. She is an excellent seamstress and she knew this was a skill both useful and enjoyable. But I couldn't get the knack of it, though I really did try. I got out of that course with the "knowledge" that I'd never, ever be able to sew.

Later, I took a summer sewing class offered by a sewing machine company at a local shopping mall. It was worse than at school, and I gave up.

Quite a few years later, my dad offered to buy me a sewing machine. I guess my parents never gave up hope! Anyway, to my great surprise, I found that suddenly I was very interested in learning to use my new machine. I went through the instruction booklet, bought some patterns, and within a couple of months I was making all of the children's clothes and most of my own. I became so adept that my friends began to come to me with difficult patterns to get my help, or to have me do their buttonholes and other finishing details. Sewing is now one of my most rewarding pastimes!

We are homeschooling our three children and I hope I can remember this lesson. I like to encourage them to try many different things, but I won't get upset if they don't seem to catch on to things I may think are important for them to know. I realize that they can learn just about anything they really need or want to, and it's never too late to begin.

How The Brain Works

Here are excerpts from an article by Leslie A. Hart, "Programs, Patterns, and Downshifting in

Learning to Read" (Reading Teacher, Oct. '83). A full reprint is available from Hart at 129 Pelham Rd, 6-C, New Rochelle NY 10805; 914-632-9029. Like much of what we print in GWS, *there is valuable ammunition here for parents to quote when explaining to officials why they prefer homeschooling:*

> The new insights into the human brain arise from many disciplines.... I have sought to synthesize from the remarkable achievements in these fields a modern, brain-based, comprehensive theory of human learning. Mine, called Proster Theory, appears to have been the first to be published and has won some attention and acceptance.... My emphasis has been on theory that can be immediately applied to schooling.
>
> It should be pointed out that brain-based theory and rapidly growing cognitive psychology do not embellish common practices and beliefs; rather, they often conflict head-on. Consider, for example, a statement by Wittrock (1978, p.101), a leader in relating new findings to education: "The brain does not usually learn in the sense of accepting or recording information from teachers." That view, I have found, usually leaves teachers gasping. Wittrock amplifies (1981, p. 261): "Within a cognitive approach one does not teach in the everyday sense of the word. Instead one designs and conducts the educational activities that facilitate the learners' active construction of verbal and imaginal mental processes."
>
> "Active" here means that these processes are under the control of individual learners, not that of the teacher. The same idea is expressed by Good and Brophy (1980, p. 104), who have moved toward the cognitive brain view: "Learning is a dynamic and active process. We are not passive containers into which knowledge is poured; we are active information processors who decode information coming in and recode it in our own terms in the process of learning it." "In our own terms" again means in individual, different, internal ways.
>
> *Programs.* "Program" simply means a fairly fixed sequence of steps to achieve some goal. Brain researchers are in firm agreement that in general we operate by programs (Young, 1978). For example, to get dressed you may consciously select a shirt or blouse, which you then put on "automatically." You may have trouble later saying which arm you put in first, or in what order you buttoned it up—the program has been so well established that you simply run it off without thinking.
>
> Looking at words as programs can be instructive. A program is needed to utter a word. We have long known from Lenneberg (1967) and others that speech requires tremendously complex sequences of hundreds of neuromuscular events, in exact order; we can observe the process of acquiring and refining such programs as we see two-year-olds learning to talk. Later a program is needed to read a word, and still others to print it, write it in cursive style, type it, or write it in capitals. These programs may be in some cases expanded to word groups or phrases, as is easily seen in typing. The brain has no problem storing these programs, as they are built, using its more than 30 billion neurons.
>
> *Patterns.* Pattern-detecting, the process of extracting meaningful patterns from confusion, is now recognized by investigators of the brain as one of its most essential functions.
>
> The pattern-detecting ability of even small children is revealed in such remarks as "I wented to see the sheeps and I falled down." Plainly the child is not imitating adult speech, but has detected subtle rules for past tense and plurals, and is loath to adopt exceptions. At 5, a youngster has no problem separating *chair* from *stool, sofa, bench,* and other seats, yet cannot explain the features that make a chair a chair.

(Offhand, few adults can, either!) But this ability depends on having seen a variety of furniture, chairs and non-chairs, and having had input and feedback on what they were called.

Pattern-detecting and recognizing capacity, however, is natural. It does not have to be taught, and we can even doubt that it can be directly taught. Evolution has designed the brain for this use.

Programs and patterns link up in the brain to permit us to act. . . . The letter M, for instance, is a pattern, which is why we can recognize it in a thousand variations of form, color, size, or material. We recognize a song by tune and rhythm whether sung or played on instruments even badly.

In almost any real situation, the pattern does not stand isolated and naked. Rather, we have to extract it from confusion, ignoring what is irrelevant and what communication theorists call noise, like static in a radio or extraneous elements of interference on the television. Strange as it may sound, presenting the pattern naked to a learner may hinder, not help, because it shortcuts the normal extraction process that the brain has been built to do.

With these concepts, well accepted in brain and cognitive circles, we can see more clearly how a child learns to understand the language heard in the home—which is mostly at adult level, often fragmentary, random, unplanned, uncontrolled, and about the polar opposite of the logical, graded progression good teaching is supposed to demand. But gradually, from this total confusion, the infant begins to sort out sound patterns and relate them to things and actions and even ideas—not by simple association, but in a complex way based on probability. The patterns may be only vaguely comprehended at the outset, but they are gradually perceived with more and more precision. To use a familiar example, *daddy* may be thought at first to mean any man, and only later a certain person, and only much later a relationship—a friend also has a daddy.

Considering the difficulty of the task, children's common success in gaining command of language under these circumstances must be viewed as amazing. Yet observation (and now a large body of research) shows that we can expect children to learn if they are given sufficient input (that is, they hear enough varied talk) and if they are able to get enough feedback on the results of their communication efforts from people or circumstances. Motivation is not a problem; by virtue of being human, children are intensely interested in mastering language, which increases their control of their world. We need only observe preschool children to see this.

Approaching reading from this direction, we can hardly miss the close parallel between extracting and recognizing patterns from sound sequences and from visible symbol sequences. Equally, building a program to utter a word parallels building a program to write a word. Reading and writing, then, can be seen as extensions of the language interests and operations which the children have been pursuing with enthusiasm and success, using the built-in powers of the brain.

But suddenly this child may be thrust into an initial reading class where all this is turned upside down. Abruptly, the child who was guiding his own learning actively is now told to be passive and suffer being aggressively taught. The boy or girl who was learning so well in an individual way, at individual pace, from individual input, must conform to a group method. Reading and writing may be presented not as extensions of early language learning, but as new subjects to be learned by logic, stated rules, and analysis of parts—approaches very far away from the program-building and pattern-detection that has worked so well.

The brain, we now know, does not work by logical progression along a single channel, as most electronic computers; it uses multiple channels—usually a great many—and comes up not with a precise answer but with an approximation or probability (Brazier, 1962). We must concede that children learn to use language in the home and associated activities, with very little gross failure if they get normal input and feedback. Nor can we close our eyes to the fact that this learning occurs, without instruction in the school sense, from input that is in general unplanned, fortuitous, random, ungraded, and in no way logically presented.

On the other hand, we can hardly deny the large amount of weak learning and gross failure that stems from conventional, logical, graded instruction.

Quite the worst feature of this instruction, I submit, is the use of logically selected and graded vocabularies, on the utterly unfounded assumption that short, regular words are easier to deal with than longer ones. Considering pattern detection, we see that 300 basal words present little range of pattern variation, and so are harder to separate. This may bring a letter-by-letter approach, even more crippling and impractical, as Smith (1978) and others have shown. Meanwhile, the great bulk of the child's real language experiences is being excluded, rigorously.

To illustrate, a preschool child is likely to know words such as *kitchen, toothbrush, supermarket, hamburger, refrigerator, television, electronic, spaghetti, bathroom, commercial, hospital, explosion* . . . words of this complexity (the list could be many times longer) will in most cases not enter "official" vocabularies for years. Reading instruction typically cuts the child off from his or her normal language and real world.

Still more serious a consequence is that the limited, graded vocabulary, as many observers have remarked, makes basal readers barren, stilted, and dull. In simplest terms, they are not worth reading. From a program-pattern viewpoint, they are disastrous because the text does not often contain the normal patterns of spelling, speech, or meaning conveyance. There is no way students can extract patterns that are not there.

[DR: Hart lists 15 references at the end of his article, including Kenneth Goodman's article "Reading: The Key is in the Children's Language," The Reading Teacher, 3/82; Understanding Reading by Frank Smith (Holt, Rinehart, and Winston, 1978); and Hart's own book How The Brain Works (Basic Books, 1975) which is available from him for $15.95.]

Going Back To School—2

More responses to "Why Did They Stop?" (GWS 36 & 38). First, from Joan Johnson (MI):

We homeschooled for two years in Kentucky with exciting results, then moved to Michigan last September. . . . We put the children in school here because we were swamped with closing our lawn & garden business, new job, new state, new house that needs finishing and new baby beginning to crawl, etc.—and the children wanted to go and meet friends.

They thought they would stick out like sore thumbs in public school and be laughed at and looked down on for being homeschooled. Deep down, I think they believed the taunts of Kentucky friends that they hadn't learned anything. The lawn & garden business had not left Milt and me much time with any of the older four. . . . But the children had bloomed. Amy and Becky had begun propagating plants, Amy got fish (well researched), Tim got a gerbil and built a mini-bike, getting to know bike repairmen and wheeling and dealing. He also did landscaping, drove the truck, learned some of the business. They all did that. . . . But they were just "having fun," not "learning."

Anyhow, all are now A students. Becky has

been filling out work sheets daily until I finally got her tested—she's "gifted" as is Tim (the others haven't been tested) and the school principal is working out a special program for her. Tim is enjoying the social scene and sliding through classes with almost no homework. I don't know what he's learning. Amy isn't learning much and is counseling girls in her class. She did a puppet show with a group of girls on her own strength and much push—*no* support from her teacher. She suffers a lot from the cliquishness of the girls. She is becoming a fantastic writer after school on her own and reads constantly. They all say the classes are boring but they must remain in school for the social access.

Our home has been quite a battleground since the children began school. They are all so tense and ready to fight at the drop of a hat. I can see the difference now that we are four days into vacation and they are more relaxed.

From Gretchen Denniston in PA:

After considering several options, we finally went with using Calvert for Laurel's first year.... I felt quite up to going for another year at home, but Laurel felt differently. We left it up in the air for the summer. I wasn't sure I wanted to leave that big a decision up to her. But as time went by it was obvious that going to school was what she really wanted to do. I debated with myself about how strongly to tell her that if school didn't "work out" that I would have to take her out.... The bussing worked out differently this year and takes up just under an hour in addition to the 6½ hour school day. So things looked good.

Laurel enjoyed 2nd grade from the start and has no desire to homeschool, which makes me sad because I really enjoyed it. She does have some on-going problems, especially with staying on task. I find that I have to stay with her and keep urging her on with homework assignments, as I had to do last year when we were at home. She is easily distracted and loved to talk with the others in class. The teacher has been most flexible and creative and has tried a variety of ways to help Laurel. (There are 17 in Laurel's class). I've been able to satisfy some of my desires to see that Laurel does well by being a classroom volunteer. I help the teacher one morning a week. We don't know what the future holds—depends what we find where we live next. My experience has given me the confidence to know that I *can* teach the kids myself—at least in the early years.

And from Texas:

We enrolled the boys in a private school last fall. Why? One reason is that we wanted to buy a house (which we have done), and my wife needed to work so that we could have the income to qualify. Mind you, we're no better off, as the tuition eats up her income; but it enabled us to qualify for the loan. The other reason is that my wife was not happy; our older boy had become a real handful, as he is very aggressive in the pursuit of knowledge. He thought he was bored and unchallenged by our informal curriculum, yet he would become very upset every time he encountered something that he did not understand immediately. My wife was just not satisfied with her handling of the situation, and became discouraged; but oh, how a year back in school can make one appreciate what a good thing one had!

This school is a well-regarded private school, and it really is excellent *academically*. Socially, it stinks. John, everything you ever wrote about the negative social aspects of schools certainly applies to this one. If anything, it is worse than the public schools.

The headmaster is a very interesting and open-minded fellow. He was intrigued by the thought of admitting homeschooled children.... Without any preparation, our older boy tested out at the very top percentile of the seventh grade, and our younger was well above the average for second grade. So, they were each placed a grade ahead of the usual. Guess what? They are both honor students. Despite my general dislike of testing and grading, I am proud of both of them ... it also speaks well of our homeschooling methods and qualifications (although neither of us has a college degree).

Most people were surprised that the boys were not terribly introverted—especially the younger, who had never been in school before. What do they think —that we raised them in a vacuum? That school is the only place where children see each other? ... Both of them have done very well in resisting peer pressure, especially the older one. This was one of my biggest worries, considering his age and his lack of resistance when he was in public school. I'm a true believer that homeschooling has helped solidify all the moral and ethical values we have ever instilled in them.

We will definitely be homeschooling again in the fall. It will be more structured; both the boys are happier when they have specific goals to reach and specific things to accomplish. We intend to obtain or establish an appropriate high school level curriculum for our older son. He's ready, willing, and certainly able. My wife will do the majority of the teaching next year, but the by fall of 1985, I hope to be in a position to do it myself.

Quitting Ed. School

Sue Radosti (IN—"Surviving Ed. School," GWS 32) sent us a copy of a letter she wrote to Kathy Mingl (IL):

In your very first letter to me, you told me that your dad had quit his teacher ed. program just one credit before graduation, and I remember thinking, "Surely one more credit couldn't have made much difference." But I sure know better now. I started my student teaching last week, and after only three days, I knew that there was no way I could go through with it. (Actually, after three days I was so distraught that I didn't know up from down, but as I pulled myself back together, I figured out that the tension headaches and uncontrollable tears were just futile efforts to fight off the decision I'd really made in the very first day.) It was one thing to watch other people dominate and stifle children, or to *be* dominated and stifled, but actually playing the role of prison warden myself was more than I could handle. Every time I found myself scolding a kid for talking or pressuring another to finish an assignment on time or frowning at another's truly funny attempts to ease the boredom of the routine (and the list could go on forever), I would suddenly wonder how I could possibly justify my actions to John Holt, to you, to my husband, or—ultimately—to myself. I could never ignore the fact that I was practicing the exact opposite of everything I preach, at the expense of 23 7-year-olds, and I was so embarrassed/ashamed/repulsed by that, I couldn't live with it, even for "eight short weeks"—or three days, for that matter!

My mom, with sincere good intentions, tried to encourage me with the argument that I could eventually help so many more kids than I would be hurting in these eight weeks, and since there wasn't anything I could do to stop them from being hurt anyway.... There's a certain amount of pragmatic appeal in that line of thinking, but somehow it seems very similar to telling a conscientious objector that he can have an office job if he'll just serve at the front for eight weeks, and isn't killing a *few* people (who are going to be killed by *someone* anyway) a lot better than killing a lot? Some comfort.

I was very moved by your last paragraph in "J.P. and Calvert" [*GWS* 36]. I have finally seen for myself one of the kids that the school authorities are wanting to label "hyperactive," and my heart bled for the kid. He was very young, seeming younger than his 6 or 7 years, and he had *no* interest in the repetitive busywork required of him. Watching him in his reading group, I was astounded by how little he *needed* to pay attention to keep up with what was going on. He would be playing with his pencil or bugging the kid next to him or looking around the room, and the teacher would ask him a question in order to embarrass him into paying more attention, and as soon as he knew what she was asking, he had the answer. Whenever he would sit in his seat long enough to really work at something, he didn't have any problems in doing the assigned tasks—but he much preferred to be up and around the room, talking to other kids, playing games, and just generally socializing. The teacher told me the very first day that she was convinced he had a medical problem that actually prevented him from sitting still, and she had convinced his parents to take him to a doctor for diagnosis and (hopefully) drug treatment. He made a shambles of any instructional time, and I found myself feeling just as aggravated with him and expecting him to be "good" like the other kids in the class.

But then one afternoon we had a substitute teacher in the room for a couple of hours, and she had the whole class in the palm of her hand while she related a very suspenseful account of her experience in a Texas hurricane. The room was so quiet you could have heard a pin drop, and I looked over at Ryan to see what he was (or wasn't!) doing. For the first time, he looked completely relaxed; the tension was gone from his jaw, and his face and entire body looked soft and loose as he sat there in a trance, sucking his thumb absentmindedly, engrossed in the story. I thought, "My God, he's just a very little boy!" ... When we went into another room to watch a film, he stopped and looked at me wistfully as I sat on the floor with a couple of little girls trying to crowd onto my lap. He sat nearby, bugging the heck out of anyone within reach of him, but gradually sidling closer and closer to us, until he sneaked under my arm and cuddled up with us for a moment or two. ... I wondered if a few more hugs and a lot fewer worksheets might contribute more to that child's development! (The teacher, when I proposed working independently with Ryan and the other two "problem" boys, responded that so much individual attention would only reinforce their behavior and that they needed to learn to function in the whole group, not on their own. Sigh.)

I went over to the campus and had my credits transferred into a liberal arts degree program, and I can still graduate in May. ... While I relaxed and let my brain unscramble itself this week, I finally got around to reading (devouring!) Jim Herndon's books from the library. Wow! I don't think anything could have made me feel better about my decision. When I read in *How To Survive In Your Native Land* about the father who cried over the schools having convinced him that his kindergarten son was "bad," I felt such a jolt of recognition, thinking immediately of "hyperactive" Ryan.

Grads Lack Basic Skills

From the front page story in the national newspaper USA Today *of 5/24/84, under the headline "Bosses say H.S. grads lack basic skills":*

> Too many high school graduates are unemployable because they lack basic skills needed to hold a job, a panel of employers said Wednesday.
>
> The panel represented employers from major corporations, independent businesses and the federal government. It said many youths with diplomas can't read, write, compute, express themselves or understand instructions well enough to be employed.
>
> The report noted its findings confirm "much of the general criticism that has been made of American education."
>
> The committee—appointed by the National Academy of Sciences—also said:
>
> Computer literacy is overrated and a "lousy trade-off" as a substitute for basic skills.
>
> Panel chairman Richard Heckert, chief operating officer of the Du Pont Co., says the computer soon will be a simple tool that "even a clod like me" can operate.
>
> Heckert likens the computer revolution to the automobile revolution that "didn't produce a country full of sophisticated auto mechanics. It produced a country full of people who can stick a key in a slot."

[JH:] Please note again that it is at least ten years since the schools all over the country announced to newspaper headlines and magazine cover stories that they were going to get tough and go "Back to the Basics." These are the results.

What should we homeschoolers do with stories like this? It's probably not helpful to add to the chorus of complaints about schools—*unless we are attacked*, whether in the media, legislatures, or courts. Any time some educational official (or anyone else) says publicly that only the schools can prepare children for adult life, etc., and that home schools cannot hope to match the good job the schools are doing with their trained and professional teachers, etc., will be a good time to offer this statement (and others like it) in rebuttal.

It might be a particularly good idea to bring this statement to the attention of legislators who are or may be considering homeschooling legislation, particularly if these have already expressed any hostility to homeschooling or a belief that education must be left solely to professional educators.

It would probably be wise *not* to use statements like this in homeschooling proposals, except perhaps in those cases where school officials have already been markedly skeptical or hostile.

Response to "Sue of Seattle"

From Nancy Wallace (NY):

I found *GWS* 35 stimulating, perhaps because there were so many long-term homeschoolers who wrote about their older kids. I particularly liked the letter from "Sue of Seattle" since she described so graphically the questioning that we all do from time to time about the way we raise our children.

A strange thing happened to Vita and me the other day at her violin lesson. Vita (8) was playing a piece in second position and she and her teacher counted all the notes in the piece that would cause the open strings to vibrate sympathetically if she played them in tune. Vita counted 19 notes. Then the teacher asked her how many notes there were in the piece altogether and Vita set out to count them one by one. To save time, the teacher suggested that she multiply the number of notes in each measure (4) by the number of measures (8). After an excruciating silence, while Vita, I knew, was trying to figure out what 8×4 was, the teacher finally told her. The teacher was nice about it, but I also think she must have thought our home-school was a bit lax. And since she's read my book [*Better Than School*], where I describe how Vita loves math, she must have been confused, since like most people, she equates math with *math facts*. Anyway, I think Vita and I initially felt a little badly about the whole thing, and I don't think Vita will ever again forget what 8×4 is.

But unlike Sue, who doesn't keep a journal, I *do*, and all I have to do is flip through the pages to remember that with her multiplication chart in hand, Vita can multiply 2 and 3 digit numbers, divide equally large numbers, and find common denominators. And I can see, too, that until last year (6th grade), Ishmael didn't know his multiplication tables either. Now he does, by the way, and it just happened, without anyone being aware of the process. The point of all this is that journals *do* help—they can remind me of how Vita and Ishmael spend their days, and they can remind me of all the wonderful things they do. I really think that we have to stay as much in touch with our kids as possible, so that little incidents like the one I described don't throw us.

The other reason for staying in touch with our kids is that it's fun. I think I understand what Sue means when she says that she doesn't know and doesn't care what her kids do all day long. . . . But what I do care about is that Vita and Ishmael like to talk to me, that they like to tell me what they are doing and all about the things that interest them. I just love it when Ishmael comes up to me while I'm doing the dishes and says, "You know, I think I've just worked out a plan for a cello sonata. The first section will start with a slow cello solo, followed by the piano. . . ." Or when Vita tells me the plot of a book she's reading when I go up to kiss her good night. . . . I never grill the kids about their projects with the idea of evaluating them. Instead, we talk, and care about each other's occupations, because we're friends.

I often feel very self-conscious about all the time we spend on music. . . . In fact, when I'm explaining to homeschoolers or new acquaintances that I just *can't* be bothered in the morning, I usually tell them that it's "our time for school." I let them assume that "school" means math and writing, even though perhaps it is dishonest, because almost no one takes music seriously enough to understand that we really *do* need peace and quiet in the morning to work on the piano and violin.

The rest of what we do is far less formal. . . .

We don't get out the math books on a regular basis any more because we simply don't have time. But every so often, perhaps as much as three times a month, Vita will come up to me and say, "Mommy, I don't have anything to do," and then, before I can even open my mouth, she'll say, "Don't tell me! I know what you're going to say. You're going to tell me to do some math!" We both laugh, and then more often than not, she actually gets out her math books. In this haphazard way she accomplishes a lot, mostly, I think, because she doesn't do any drill work. She busies herself learning procedures, not memorizing math facts.

So often I get so excited about what we are doing only to be reminded that many people simply don't approve, no matter how terrific the kids seem. ... When I heard, for example, that one of my relatives "disagreed" with my book I could feel the bitterness welling up inside me and I could feel, again, all the misery we faced when Ishmael was in school. How could he disagree with the book? How could he disagree with the fact that Vita and Ishmael are happy, thriving, and incredibly productive? How could he disagree with the fact that Ishmael almost died in school?

Math & Real Life

Frances Kelly in Montana wrote in response to "Using Math," GWS *37:*

Myles (4) had a desire to use the phone so I told him he had to learn to recognize the numbers on it first. This he has done and now uses the phone quite readily. We have a pocket calculator sitting around which the boys play with freely. Also a digital clock and they are both making an effort to learn to tell time.

When I pay the bills they both help (sometimes I get nothing accomplished). I read numbers off that I'm adding and subtracting, and Myles makes an effort to write them down. I also do my math out loud sometimes, asking what's such-and-such minus such-and-such. So the kids feel they're involved in the process.

What I'm suggesting is explore with your children. There is no need to swamp yourself with books on math. When a question comes up that you have no answer for, then is the time to search for it. And your children will most likely be able to help you find it.

From Karen Olin Johnston (CA):

Currently we are doing many repairs to our house. ... I had thought that Fawn (10) and Melanie (4) would have to be on their own in regards to education, because I would be busy working. ... But the renovations themselves have provided so much to learn about. Both girls have become adept at removing hinges and knobs from cupboard doors, and choosing the right screwdrivers. Also, helping to paint using brushes and rollers. Math has tied in with the work, too. We put a suspended ceiling in the playroom we built. Fawn helped me measure, then draw out a scale map, including choosing which ceiling tiles would be left empty for light fixtures. When we went to the building supply store, Fawn was able to help choose which tiles, and also knew how many of each tile, bracket, etc., was needed by referring to our map. We had another long math lesson when it came time to measure the entire house and map out all the areas for which we were purchasing new carpet. Sure, it took longer to include my daughter in all these figurings, but what she learned about measurement—perimeter, square footage and yardage, translating inches to feet-and-inches, creating scale drawings—and relating all this to real life, was invaluable.

Robin Vant wrote in the New Zealand homeschooling newsletter Prunes *(120 Eskdale Rd, Auckland 10):*

> *And Now, Loo Math*—A recent notable math exercise revolved around the toilet. The question was, "How much water does your toilet use in a week?" This required, first, the collection and second, the analysis of the relevant data.
>
> Obviously, we have to know how many times the toilet was flushed. So a chart appeared on the wall of the toilet, inscribed "Please make a tally mark each

time you flush the loo." . . . Some doubts about the accuracy of some of the data collected tally groups with six strokes were seen, and some days recorded suspiciously high totals. Nevertheless, reasonably reliable data for seven days was assembled, ranging from a low of 14 to a high of 22. Now what? No hesitation—"find the average" add up all the day totals and divide by 7—result 17½ (what is "half a flush?"—couldn't get them to suggest any meaning for this).

The other necessary information is, "How much water does the cistern hold?" Father initially says 10 liters, then isn't so sure. How to check? Father had done it once before, on a quiet Sunday when everybody else was out, by reading the water meter, then flushing the toilet 10 times, and then reading the meter again.

This didn't seem to appeal, so a more direct attack was made. Flush the cistern with the float held up to stop the cistern refilling, then pour in a liter at a time until it is full again. Surely a recipe for disaster—two children standing on the toilet seat, one holding up the float and the other pouring in water out of a measuring jug—but they were reasonably happy with their answer—"It holds 8 liters."

I don't think they ever finished the final calculation (about a thousand liters a week, if you are interested), but there is a fine bar graph on the kitchen wall summarizing the daily flush tallies.

And from Nona Perez (CA):

Recently my mother took an adult math refresher class. Her first homework assignment was to list all the ways in which she used math every day. The first few on her list were easy: figuring her paycheck, measurements in recipes, and how far a tank of gas would take her. Beyond that, she drew a blank. This surprised me, and we went through it together. She soon became amazed at how much math she used without knowing it *was* math, such as, how many bales of hay will feed the horses for a season; how far can she hike and still get home before dark; how much food to buy for a family dinner; how much paint to buy for a poster; etc., etc. Evidently, the word "math" made her put up a mental block.

My five-year-old, Carlos, walked into the kitchen recently, asking for a cookie. He walked over, grabbed a cookie, and walked away saying there were 16 cookies. He did *not* have time to count them one by one, but there were four stacks of four, and he knew, before I did, just how many cookies there were. We count everything, and add, subtract, and multiply. . . . I have a tendency not to tell them they're "multiplying" or whatever, until they know the function.

On Finger-Math

In response to "Queries," *GWS* 37: a few years ago I found a book on Chisanbop in the library and thought it was very interesting. In the two weeks I had it, I learned to do quite a number of the calculations, but the kids balked at my attempts to get them interested in it.

Now Ginger, age 6, has begun doing computations in her head, and after reading J.B.'s question, I began to analyze whether or not I ought to begin teaching her some form of "fingermath." However, something about the delighted expression on her face when she comes to me with her latest numerical discovery tells me that working with these figures in her head without any mechanical aids like paper and pencil, fingers, and even Cuisenaire rods, is a very important part of her development. My conclusion is to let her continue this particular stage of learning, which she seems to find very exciting, and not introduce something that she might find artificial and distracting.—*Darlene Graham* (TX).

On Chisanbop: I know nothing about that particular method but assume it is similar to Edwin M. Lieberthal's *The Complete Book of Fingermath*. I started teaching Hans fingermath when he was five. He learned to count to 99 using his ten fingers. Later I showed him how to add small numbers and just recently he learned how to subtract using his fingers. He is now 8½. I think it is great. First of all, Hans has problems thinking in the abstract. Arithmetic problems written down with all the little boxes just confused him. There would be months when we did nothing with fingermath, yet he did not lose the knowledge from lesson to lesson.

Hans can now easily do the Miquon Math Lab workbooks. The little boxes no longer confuse him. He does math drills on our computer and because he can subtract 57 from 92 using his fingers he can beat the timer. . . . He often adds things in his head in order to shortcut the fingers. He really feels comfortable with numbers—plus, being able to do something no one else can do is fun.

My experience in teaching this to older children has been dismal. They are not willing to drill. Little children love it. . . . Teaching fingermath is like teaching a game.—*Sharon Hillestad* (MN).

Letters On Computers

From an Arizona reader:

About the impact computers have made on our homeschool. . . . We have two: Atari 800 and Apple II. . . . It started with the usual: kids programming in BASIC, kids playing games, and all that sort of thing. The younger children spent quite a bit of time just copying out of books, and making lists of what they copied.

One of the most attractive early things they did was to use the Video Easel to draw the most fantastic designs. They learned how to design complex "blinkers" (replicating patterns)—the latest one had 20 stages! They also learned all the features used in the prepared designs that come in the cartridge, so they could draw the same kind of thing, but they also figured out some brand-new stuff that no one else seems to know. The youngest children to use the cartridge had just turned two. The Music Composer was used in some most interesting ways. I typed in about 50 hymns, and the children sometimes get the hymnal and sing along with the computer. Several of the children learned to read music well enough to type in hymns, too, just from the act of typing them in. Martha (10) learned how to read music quite well in only three days! Later, several of the children began to make up their own tunes occasionally.

Martha has been making files of drawings, using graphics characters, which we will be using in programs to teach foreign language. She also wrote programs that ask various riddles, and if you get the answer wrong, the computer heaves an insult at you! . . . Our 16-year-old, who was a positive flop in organized school, taught himself assembly language programming, and is working on some program or other almost constantly. He programs well enough to earn money at it.

But the really surprising thing that happened was when we gained access to a national network of computers. One of the interesting features on this system is a program called "CB Simulator" which enables users to talk to each other, much in the same style as real CB radio, with handles, etc. Through this medium, the three oldest children learned to type very quickly and accurately, and their spelling improved immensely. They met several people with whom they now exchange letters. The first of those is a young woman, married but with no children, who seems to spend most of her spare time writing to my children (and lately, myself), and sending them all kinds of interesting things. My children have written the most fabulous letters and stories for her! Another person we met later actually came to visit us, and when he returned home, he sent us a lovely large volume all about Pittsburgh. Our oldest child read that, and is now an expert on Pittsburgh. Other people have sent us things like a fabulous book on the Voyager missions, complete with spectacular photographs of Jupiter and Saturn. . . . The children's social skills have developed considerably, and they talk easily with people of all ages. I bet you never guessed that computers could lead to such uncommon social opportunities!

And from Cyndi Bigelow (PA):

We finally got a computer for the kids. I sold

enough dolls at Christmas to buy them a little inexpensive one (Aquarius by Mattel—it has quite a few add-ons to build it up as the children become more adept).

Shawn (14) and Jamin (11) spend most of their time programming the computer. They have found a way to use BASIC language and program in Logo functions. Unfortunately, I don't get to use it very often, so I'm not sure how they are doing it. When we first got the computer, we had a marvelous math lesson. The boys were programming spirals, but couldn't figure how to change the shape.... Mommy to the rescue. I got out the math book and showed them why their computer program had "cos" and "sin" in it, and how to understand it. Noses went into the math book for some quick study, and then back to the computer.

Last week, everyone was making their own computers out of cardboard boxes, and then they would take turns being inside each other's box, feeding out information, and rattling off strange sounding terms—*s n error, ok, m o error, ok, error in line 020, run.*

Phys. Ed. At Home

More from Karen Johnston (CA):

One aspect of homeschooling that some people may not stop to think about is physical exercise. My daughter Fawn is not the type to be real active. She went from being a very slim person to a rather chubby person during the first year of our homeschooling.... It was our pediatrician (who is very supportive of our homeschooling) who suggested that this could be because of less physical activity—after all, we didn't have any group games or sports or planned "recess" at home! Once we made this a conscious part of our education, Fawn's extra weight began to disappear.

I've found that any one type of activity is attractive for a month or two, then Fawn finds an alternative way to keep in shape. Her methods have ranged from joining me in my twice-weekly aerobics class at the park (kids are very welcome), to watching and exercising with "Mousercise" (a show on the Disney cable TV station), to taking dogs for a jog around the block every morning. She also takes classes at the parks—sometimes it's been ballet, sometimes gymnastics, and currently ice skating. Thank goodness for our terrific parks program with really affordable classes.

Pen Pal Results

[DR:] Wondering whether our list of "Children Wanting Pen Pals" *was doing any good, I wrote to the families in the first listing (*GWS *33) and asked what kind of results they had. Here are their answers:*

No, Jeb received not one letter. He did write to two from another homeschool newsletter but had no response. He is in the process of writing to two more that were listed in *GWS* 37 with I hope better results.... I enjoyed foreign as well as American pen pals as a child. I think Jeb got discouraged since he is not much inclined toward reading or writing but I am encouraging him to do it since I believe it will increase his interest in both.—*Cher Bateman* (NV).

———

I have 7 pen pals. They live all over the United States—2 in California, 1 in Wisconsin, 1 in Maine, 1 in Ohio, 1 in Georgia, and 1 in Kentucky. It is fun getting letters and writing them too.—*Laila Gatts.*

As Laila said, she received 7 replies to her request for pen pals and she is still writing to all but one of them. It seemed rather overwhelming at first—trying to keep up with all the letters—so we made 7 maps of the U.S. and marked the names, addresses, and locations of all the pen pals and sent one to each girl—so they can all write to each other. Laila has received pictures of almost all the girls (all *are* girls) and she has sent her picture to all. It's fun—they exchange cards, stickers, thoughts, etc. And the by-products of this fun are real writing (organizing thoughts and punctuation), real spelling—real communication.—*Carol Gatts* (MN).

———

Since Eric owes 4 different pen pals letters, I decided I'd respond to your postcard.... He's received letters from four kids who saw his name on the list and he wrote to two that he saw on the list, so he's got 6 pen pals so far. (He calls them "friend pals.") Two of the letters came long after *GWS* 33 had listed him. In fact, one came just last week. There are a couple more he wants to write to on the latest list.

One family that lives very near us saw his name and called us on the phone. That has worked out beautifully. They are most helpful and their 12-year-old and Eric enjoy each other's company. In fact their 16-year-old is now my one and only babysitter.... Another Ohio family wrote Eric and we have gone over there once and found them great people, too. They have five kids and live on 100 acres.... I wrote to the mother of one of Eric's pen pals in West Virginia and she answered me back the other day.—*Maggie Meyer*.

Since my name was printed in the *GWS*, five people have written to me and all of us continue to write back and forth. I haven't written to any other children in the column as these five keep me busy enough. Thanks for the service.—*Thomas Wyton*.

Our three older boys (9, 7, 5) received a lot of responses, averaging about 4 to 5 each. It is still ongoing. They tend to like writing to special pals. I usually write all or part of the letter but they dictate what they want to say. They draw pictures, send stickers, maps, etc. The boys are indescribable in their excitement when they receive a letter. The real bond is that they are homeschoolers, *plus* they have similar interests. We love it! —*Margaret Partlow* (IL).

"Cluster" Technique

Daphne Denny in California wrote:

I found a book in our local library that I am thoroughly enjoying: *Writing The Natural Way* by Dr. Gabriele Lusser Rico, published in 1983 by J.P. Tarcher.... On the cover it says, "Using Right Brain Techniques to Release Your Expressive Powers." The author is an English professor and this book is apparently what her writing courses are all about.

I have always wanted to be a professional writer, and I've felt certain deep down inside that I could do it, but still the words never came out and sounded as powerful on paper as they did in my head. Getting the first sentences down was agony, and then getting everything to sound coherent and unified was impossible. But I've been very pleased with the writings I've come up with as a result of the exercises.... The imagery has been rich and deep and it pours out with ease. I no longer sound like I'm writing for my ninth grade English teacher.

I haven't introduced the technique to my children. My 13-year-old daughter enjoys writing stories and her ideas seem to flow out so naturally that she doesn't need it. Maybe it's mostly for those of us who have been too schooled.

PS—Something my daughter has been doing lately to give her stories more pizzazz. Instead of simply writing them down, she now tells them into our tape recorder, and then plays them back a sentence at a time and writes them down. It has helped her to put a lot more realistic dialogue in. She doesn't get so bogged down with the tedious job of writing the story while the ideas are still fresh in her mind that she loses interest. The transcribing from the tape recorder can take as long as she wants it to.

[DR:] We happened to have a copy of *Writing the Natural Way* in the office, and after browsing through it, I thought *GWS* readers might like to know the author's basic idea. Dr. Rico recommends a technique she calls "clustering," which you do for one to two minutes, to loosen up the mind—a way to get ideas flowing and to avoid the paralyzing fear of having to put one word after another in a sentence.

To "cluster," you start with a key word or phrase—in the examples, she suggests "time," "afraid," "family," "help," "web," "body"—write it on the paper, and circle it. Then as other words or phrases come to mind, you write them down, circle them, and connect them with arrows. When one train of thought is exhausted, you go back to the central word and start again. One cluster she shows looks like this (key word, "bend"):

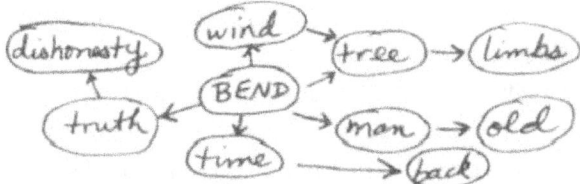

Dr. Rico says, "You will know when to stop clustering through a sudden, strong urge to write, usually after one or two minutes, when you feel a shift that says 'Aha! I think I know what I want to say.' If it doesn't happen suddenly, this awareness of a direction will creep up on you more gradually, as though someone were slowly unveiling a sculpture."

If even writing a cluster seems difficult, she suggests drawing the arrows and empty circles anyway; then as you relax, "you will find yourself filling in those inviting empty circles with the associations that are inevitably triggered by the nucleus word."

It looks like a simple enough idea. If any other GWS readers try this, do let us know your reactions.

Reading Resource

From Mha Atma Kaur Khalsa (CA):

I am rather excited about the "I Can Read Books" by *Harper & Row* (Dept. 128, 10 E 53rd St, NY NY 10022). They sell the "Little Bear" books [see "Letters on Reading," *GWS* 38] and many others just as charming.... They sell to schools— and easily sold to me—at a 35% discount with a very low shipping fee when you order 10 books or more. So their $3 paperbacks cost $2.

Book Raves

My sons (7½ and 6) loved *Swallows and Amazons* [DR: $3.95 + postage; all books in this article are available here] which I read to them about six months ago. Orion is now reading it on his own and also favorite parts to his brother. They have been camping out in our yard the past few nights and they refer to John and me as "natives." They are up with the sun and birds and ready to adventure.—*Barbara Plunket* (FL).

I just this evening finished reading Randall Jarrell's *The Animal Family* [$2.25] and we are *all* in love with it! We completed it in just two evenings of reading aloud.... I think it took, well, maybe all of three sentences before both boys were utterly immersed and hooked.... We talked about the story all through the day, Jesse drawing and labeling pictures of all the family.... We especially enjoyed all the language discussions— learning new language, making "mistakes" in language, having no base for understanding a foreign idea.I bought, read, and *loved* Nancy Wallace's book *Better Than School* [$14.95]. Wrote to her about it. Jesse and Jacob have just finished varnishing their *own* raft for our pond, after being inspired by my reading to them about Ishmael's. I'll be recommending her book heartily. . . . Especially loved the look into the children's play—it reminded me of the complex adventures my boys spin together with *their* blocks and "little people."—*Susan Richman* (PA).

I very much appreciate your book sales service. ... It's like Christmas when the box comes and we always enjoy the books we get! I personally felt especially helped and inspired by *The Continuum Concept* [$2.50] and *Better Than School*. I've actually read *Better Than School* over a couple of times. Nancy Wallace's book has been tremendously helpful to me! One of my goals is to read most of the books about children that you recommend. I am currently reading *Gnys at Wrk* [$17.50] and I love it! I figure if I've spent my whole life absorbing ideas about children which I now feel are partially and sometimes wholly inaccurate, harmful, and wrong, I can use all the good and correct input that I can get to retrain myself. Glenda Bissex's book helps me to try hard to not stomp on my son's style of learning by correcting him.—*Mha Atma Kaur Khalsa* (CA).

I've started on the exercises in *Drawing On The Right Side Of The Brain* [$9.95] and it is delightful. I was unprepared for this—didn't really believe I could draw.... I was an art major in high school, and in all that time I was never taught to draw. One of my teachers said drawing is something you either can or can't do, period. . . . After all these years I'm finally learning to *see*, and it has changed the way I look at everything!— *Leslie Westrum* (IN).

We recently read *Helen Keller* [$1.95] and *Martin Luther King* [$1.95]. After I finished reading them aloud to Heather, chapter by chapter, then she was eager to read them again—with her reading aloud to me. . . . We were so impressed with these biographies. . . . Heather just loves them; she likes to read about real people in storybook form, especially easy ones that she can read herself once I have read it the first time. . . . We'll peruse the latest book list and send in another order; you have us hooked.—*Jill Bastian* (MI).

Aerial Photos

From David Kramer in Calif.:

I went down to the city hall to get an aerial photo of my neighborhood. They have a set of 2 x 3-foot negatives for the city, and for the nominal fee of one dollar they ran Sheet 21 through a blueprint machine to make a copy for me. And what a fascinating thing it is! Even though it covers one and half square miles and the method of reproduction does not give the best resolution (a Photostat would be better but much more expensive), I can see the white lines on the streets along with the arrows for the right and left-turn lanes. With a magnifying glass, I can discern telephone poles by their shadows and tell if a tiny car is a sedan or a station wagon. Of course, I picked out the mobile home where I live. I had a little trouble with a dark, perfect square surrounded by trees. Couldn't be a baseball diamond since there was no pitcher's mound and no infield or outfield. It turned out to be a lawn-bowl green in a local park.

I can't imagine any kid not being intrigued by an aerial photo of his/her neighborhood. A blueprint like mine, however, will eventually fade. If kept rolled up away from light when not in use, it should last for over a year, and the cost is so slight that there shouldn't be any fuss over marking it up or coloring in areas, etc.

There are other kinds of aerial photos called stereo photos which you view with a simple set of lenses like the old stereopticon. Everything is 3-D! The geology department at your local university can tell you where to get these, and a book on field geology will have information on how they are used. I don't know how expensive they are, however. Sets of stereo photos are professional tools.

I once had an aerial photo hanging on a wall of my office. . . . Everyone came in and looked at it, of course, but I really was surprised by the number of people who could *not* find the building they were working in on the photo! And it was a big building, too—part of a complex. I didn't realize that a lot of folks have trouble in orienting themselves to maps and the like.

Watching Court Trials

From Susannah Sheffer ("Teaching Outside of School," GWS 37):

I recently discovered a new kind of resource that I don't think I've ever seen mentioned in *GWS*. It sounds odd, but it's free, accessible, interesting, and fun—it's sitting in on trials. A friend and I were in a nearby town, by no means a large one, and decided to try it, vaguely remembering that this was something any citizen could do (except in special cases). Sure enough, we wandered in with no questions asked, and I've never listened so willingly or interestedly. Sometime later I tried it again in New York, and the next day I found I'd been watching a trial which made the headlines. I don't know why this is so interesting, but it carries the weight of something so *real*, not TV, not even book drama, but real human lives, and the judicial process in action, and seeing how all sorts of procedural things are done. And since it *is* free and accessible, as I said, it struck me as a good thing.

Art Tips

I am curious about the impression people may

get about the *Pentel Water Colors* described in *GWS* 37 [available here, $2.75 for a set of 12 colors]. I am a watercolorist and people are usually surprised to see my dried colors in my palette. Watercolor artists do not put out fresh paint each time. It is expensive and unnecessary. We just wet them and paint.

Another handy art-saver tip is to drill holes in a 2×4 wood scrap and shove the plastic tips of markers in. We haven't wasted marking pens because they dried out or lost a top for two months now.... The children always put them away and the cap is of course the holder.—*Janet Roelle* (MI).

About rubber stamps (*GWS* 36) ... The children use ink-pads with supervision but like to use washable magic markers to vary colors—coloring the stamp individually.—*Katharine Houk* (NY).

It would be very easy to cut block letters from weather stripping and stick them to small empty thread spools or one-inch sections of dowel. This way you could make an inexpensive printing kit for kids who don't have the coordination needed with a kit like STA-TITE (*GWS* 36) ... I just remembered a way to make a stamp pad like we did in kindergarten. Fold a couple of paper towels several times each way till you've got a stamp-pad sized rectangle. Wet the toweling (it might be a good idea to put it on a saucer, cottage cheese carton lid, or something like that). Then put a spoonful of tempera paint on the wet towel and rub it in with the back of the spoon. I haven't tried this with small stamps, but it works OK with large ones.—*Leslie Westrum* (IN).

Child Weavers In Egypt

[DR:] *Two readers sent us information on a remarkable experiment in children's art, the weaving studio at Harraniya, Egypt. David Kramer (CA) sent an article from* Aramco World, *Sept. '82, with many photographs of the richly-colored, intricate tapestries made by the people of the village. From the article:*

Ali Selim took nearly a year to weave his masterpiece—a tapestry three meters long, depicting one full day in the life of an Egyptian village. Its completion, however, represented the culmination of an unusual experiment begun 38 years before by Ramses Wissa Wassif, then a young Cairo architect, his wife Sophie, and her father, Habib Gorgi—another man with a theory on the source of artistic gifts.

This experiment was based on a belief of the Austrian expressionist painter, Oskar Kokoschka, that all children are born geniuses, but lose their genius because of life's faulty teaching. "It begins with the parents and goes on with teachers and if they don't get him, the other children will," Kokoschka said.

Like Kokoschka, Ramses Wissa Wassif and his family came to believe that very young children the world over are capable of making wondrously beautiful things, if only given the chance. And like Gorgi—who thought ancient Egypt's skill in sculpture still survived in today's children (see *Aramco World*, Jan. '82)—Ramses Wassif decided to put his theory to the test by getting to children before their God-given talents evaporated.

Unlike Kokoschka, Ramses believed that education need not necessarily stifle creativity; indeed, it could be used to liberate it. "I had the conviction," he said, "that every human being was born an artist, but that his gifts could be brought out only if artistic creation was encouraged by the practice of a craft from early childhood."

In 1952, Ramses, Habib, and Sophie bought a small piece of land beside a canal outside the village of Harraniya ... In a setting of vegetable gardens and fields of corn, they built a small studio, domed, vaulted and whitewashed in the traditional manner, to which they invited the children of Harraniya to come and play. They then picked 18 children—the eldest 10, the youngest 8—none of whom had ever had a lesson, or touched a loom, and provided each of them with a small upright loom and supplies of locally grown wool.

At first, the only images to appear on the looms were irregular lines of color—a line of red, a line of yellow or perhaps black. One girl made two "legs" and said it was a bird. Another made four and said it was a cow. They could not, at first, make forms. Then, suddenly, the miracle happened: the children began to create—actually create—what must be called works of art. Madame Sophie Wassif says that "one child made a complete tree with a bird alongside . . . the bird as big as the tree. This was the beginning."

Because Wassif regarded adult criticism as a paralyzing intrusion on the child's imagination, no criticism was allowed. In the closely guarded environment of the studio, each child was free to work at whatever came into his or her mind—and they were thus able to develop confidence in their work, and to depend solely on their own imaginations.

In a little more than a year, a profusion of images began to emerge from the children's looms: geese and ducks seen every morning on the nearby irrigation canal, Ahmad's water buffalo coming to drink and Sharira's chickens. But there were also fantasies: pink sheep, purple horses, and birds that fly without opening their wings—all woven with an imaginative power and vision that only children possess.

From the beginning, Wassif forbade the children to make preliminary drawings. The child had to visualize his picture and keep it in mind until the weaving was finished. As each tapestry progressed, the completed portion was rolled up so that the child was compelled to retain the initial purity of his conception until it was finished. Then, when the tapestry was completed and unrolled, the children exclaimed: "How did this happen?" "Did I do this?" A sense of triumph began to possess the children.

A section of the garden surrounding the studio was used to grow dye plants . . . and over wood fires and steaming pots set up in the garden, the children were introduced to the magic of dyeing their own wools, according to the colors they needed for their next tapestry.

The children who began Wassif's experiment nearly 30 years ago, no longer think and weave the way they did then. They have matured into sophisticated artists, capable of subtle color and fine shading. . . . There have been a number of important exhibitions of Harraniya tapestries in Cairo, Paris, Zurich, Rome, London, and Stockholm. . . . Many now grace the walls of galleries and collectors around the world.

Though Ramses Wissa Wassif died in 1974, his wife Sophie still carries on, offering encouragement when it is needed. "Only yesterday one of the new boys was sitting on the grass. He had all his colors spread out in front of him and he called out: 'What will be my next piece?' I said: 'Oh, what beautiful colors you have there laid on the grass. Put these colors onto the loom.' And so he began."

[DR:] Barbara Stoutner (ID) also sent an article on the Wissa Wassif studio, from The Friend *magazine (50 E North Temple, S.L.C. UT 84150), and a chapter from a book by Wassif, written 15 years or so after the experiment began. Some excerpts from this book:*

I should make it clear from the outset, that these children were not selected for any particular trait or exceptional characteristic. . . . I had to restrict the numbers according to my means.

I chose that means of expression, weaving, which seemed to me to have certain essential advantages, though the mastery of the technique requires a long period of fruition. On the other hand, from the very beginning a child can find something in it. . . . The weaving loom itself is very simple: it is the loom with the high warp, has been used since prehistoric times.

The wools are dyed in natural colors—indigo, cochineal, madder and wood-waxen or yellows—colors that have proved their worth since the days of antiquity, colors that harmonize well. . . . I am sometimes compelled to restrict the scale of colors.

It goes without saying that I do nothing that might restrict freedom of the children's expression. I make no criticism for I do not want to substitute argument for emotion and criticism gives rise to doubts and often starts a person on false trails. These young artists have never seen any recognized "works of art" and their inspiration springs entirely from within themselves and from their environment, and their contact with nature.

Work goes on throughout the week without surveillance or constraint. Though the children are the entire masters of their own time, they are all, nevertheless, very assiduous. We pay them only one visit a week to distribute the colored wools and to maintain contact.

The first contact was made by organizing games—then we agreed to meet again during the following weeks. I was admirably backed up by my wife, who knew how to maintain regular contact with these children and their families on a social footing. We met every week so as to get to know one another better, and it was not until several months later that we proposed to the children the idea of weaving on small looms.

But it may be asked, what good is there in seeking to revive a form of work that is outmoded? . . . The decor of our lives has become neat and elegant, but without soul. . . . A return to that individual form of expression which is the essence of craft art is alone capable of filling the emptiness from which our epoch is suffering ever more and more. . . . Normal education—too early and for far too long a period—prohibits a child from expressing itself freely.

Cheap Instruments

Since *GWS* 37, when I first wrote about the violins we are selling, I have learned, for one thing, that they are *not* made in Italy, but in China. It takes a lot of hand work to make a violin (or viola, or cello), even the most inexpensive ones, and if the workers are paid Western-style wages, the instruments will be too expensive for most homeschoolers to afford. One of our readers seemed somewhat distressed by the idea of buying a violin made in China. As I see it, if our public servant, the President, can go to China (and enjoy himself there), we the citizens have every right to buy Chinese violins.

The other thing I have learned is that these very inexpensive instruments have an astonishingly good sound. I compared one of our full-sized violins (now $110) to a 19th century European violin worth over $2000, and while the latter had a richer tone on the C string (the lowest string), on the other three strings there was little difference between them. No doubt the better instrument is more responsive, as violinists would say, "speaks more easily," and would be better for playing difficult music. For the kind of music we beginners will be playing, the difference doesn't make any difference, and the very inexpensive violin will be just as good.

On my travels I compared one of our 1/4-sized violins with another that had probably cost at least twice as much. For tone, ours seemed clearly the better of the two. These not very elegant looking violins are plenty good enough for beginners, and a child or adult would have to make much progress before it would make sense to buy a significantly better, and therefore much more expensive instrument. In fact, the first piece of equipment you should upgrade would be the bow.

The biggest surprise of all came when, on my

travels, I played for the first time a very inexpensive, mass-produced plywood cello, the kind that I, like most cellists, have always dismissed as the lowest of the low. To my astonishment, I found that the instrument, though it weighed a ton, had a pleasant warm voice throughout its range, did not have any terrible wolf notes, and was quite easy to play—much easier to play and nicer to hear than many more expensive cellos that I have played and even owned. In coming months I hope to try one of the inexpensive Chinese cellos; if it is anywhere near as good as the one I played, we will probably start selling them too.—JH

Teaching Yourself with Suzuki

A Montana reader writes:

I own a violin and have never played a musical instrument, have no access to an instructor (live out in the sticks). Is it possible to teach oneself with Suzuki books and records? If not, is there any other method by which a person could teach oneself? I have three children at home whom I would like to teach music, but I must learn with them.

I am learning math with my children. I have never been good at math, always being sure I could not do it, counting on my fingers and yet now I find the answers were always there in my head but I would never allow myself to trust them, for fear of being wrong, I suppose. I am now allowing myself to give the answers although I still check on my fingers at times to see if I'm right. I am just now building up my confidence at age 26. I want my children not to lose that confidence.

A thought on dyslexia: I find my children, as they grow and develop, first crawl backwards before forward. In the walker they learn to roll backwards before forward. Why not in writing?

[JH:] In reply I wrote:

Yes indeed, it is possible to teach yourself and your children the violin (and/or other bowed stringed instruments) with the aid of Suzuki books and materials, and other materials which you may learn about from us or from others, or perhaps find or invent for yourselves. There is so much courage and common sense in your letter that I have no doubt at all that you can do a very good job of it.

You do not need the proverbial weekly lessons in order to learn a musical instrument. Nathan Milstein, one of the great violinists of this century, said in an interview a few years ago that the importance of music teachers was greatly exaggerated, and that most of what he learned about playing the violin he figured out for himself and by watching and hearing good players. I am largely self-taught on the cello, and though I am no expert and not likely ever to be, I have been told by experts that my basic technique is sound. About a year ago, at age 60, I began to play the violin. I have never had a lesson, and though I am rarely able to play more than fifteen minutes a day, if at all, I have again been told by good players that my fundamental technique is good. What I have done, quite simply, is watch good cellists and violinists, listen to them in person and on recordings, and then, playing in front of mirrors or reflecting windows, and often recording my own playing and then listening to it, to try to make myself look and sound the way the good players do. Basically, that's the method I recommend to you.

I see by the map that you are not far from Missoula, and though I don't know the music scene there, I suspect that perhaps in the university, perhaps in a local orchestra, there will be some skilled violinists whom you can watch, listen to, and learn from. If there is a music department in the university, they are sure to have many student and faculty recitals and concerts. If there is not a good orchestra in Missoula, I know there is in Spokane, Wash., and it might be fun and a good idea for you and perhaps your children, depending on their age and their ability to sit quietly through a concert (not all can, and if they can't, don't take them), to go there to hear a concert or two, above all if there is a violin soloist playing. You might also be able, in Missoula and/or Spokane, to arrange to attend some rehearsals—as much as I love concerts, I enjoy rehearsals even more, and learn more from them.

If you don't have a record player, I would recommend the Mister Disc we wrote about in

GWS 35 and 38. I would also strongly suggest that you buy a small tape recorder, so that you and your children can now and then record your own playing and compare it with recordings of the songs you are learning to play. It will be much better for *you* to learn to hear the difference between expert playing and your own than to have teachers point it out to you. What you need to do is put the sight and sound of good playing in your own eyes and ears, so that as you play you can constantly correct and improve yourself. Indeed I would say without hesitation that no one can become a skilled musician who does not learn to do this.

Of the inexpensive Walkman-type cassette recorders, perhaps the best are made by Aiwa. The Sony Professional Walkman, which costs about twice as much, is a very high quality machine, well worth the price if you can afford it. You might see what is available in Missoula, so that if your machine needs to be fixed someone can take care of that. Of course, you don't really have to have a *stereo* recorder; mono recorders are much cheaper, and at least at the start will do as well, though stereo recordings are more lifelike and exciting, and worth having in the long run.

If you do not have, or have ready access to, a piano, organ, or harpsichord, I would suggest that you get a very inexpensive keyboard instrument, perhaps the Pianica in our catalog (reviewed in GWS 33), perhaps one of those little Casio electronic pianos (the cheapest cost about $50). You will find it useful, and not at all hard, to learn how to look at simple written music and pick out the notes on your keyboard. This will enable you to learn tunes for which you may have the written music but not a recording, and also, to write down some tunes you may think up yourselves. A little knowledge of the keyboard is very useful, no matter what instrument you play.

When you go to rehearsals or concerts, sit near the violinists, watch them carefully, from different angles, see what they do with their arms and hands. Then, when you get home, try to make yourself look the same in a mirror. You might get to know a few violinists, students or otherwise; if so, without signing up for anything as formal as regular lessons, you could ask them now and then to show you a few things, or to check your own technique and make some corrections. And as you are doing all of this, be sure that you and your children are having fun with the violin. Experiment, improvise, fool around! Think of yourselves not just as imitators of good musicians, which you will try to be, but also as explorers and scientists, which is the spirit in which I approach music.

We will say more in *GWS* about all this, and I even hope someday to write a book about it. For the time being, full speed ahead! Do let us know from time to time about your musical adventures. The things you learn may be very inspiring, helpful, and encouraging to many other people who would like to do what you are doing. Good luck to you all.

Getting a Synthesizer

From Luella Porter (IN):

We have acquired a tool that other *GWS* musicians might find useful—a synthesizer. In my efforts to become a pianist as an adult, I found it desirable to practice in the evening when the family was in bed, but I didn't want to disturb them (or the neighbors). So I began thinking about getting something I could play silently and hear the music through headphones. After considering organs and electric pianos, I came to decide on a synthesizer.

We chose a Juno 6 by Roland. It has over 5 octaves, and with an octave transpose up and down (on a switch), it is only two notes short of a piano keyboard. It also transposes to any key instantly. I like the sound of an organ, and it does everything an organ does, plus the synthesizer sounds. I think the instrument duplications are better than those I've heard on organs. Practicing the classics is much more exciting. I set it for harpsichord when I play music written for harpsichord, strings when playing music for strings. Meredith (3½) has duplicated wind, sounds from Star Wars, and animal sounds. She likes to tell stories that she makes up while doing the sound effects on the synthesizer.

It takes up little space—I use our desk top. This would be great for those who live in apartments or who move frequently. Ours only weighs 30 pounds, and road cases are available. I used to dread missing practice time when we went away for a weekend, but now my keyboard can come with me. Prices range from $300 on up for new instruments, and there is an active used market around here.

For composers, Roland now makes the Juno 60, which can be connected with certain computers that print musical notation as you play! It also has preprogrammed patches (settings), so you punch in a 2-digit number to instantly get a certain sound. This seems to be the trend that they are going toward.

Synthesizers are complex like computers, so take your time in deciding what you need. I found music stores to be very good about letting me spend hours working with them and learning their capabilities. I found price variations of 50% on the same model from store to store, so it pays to shop around.

I still have much to learn about electronic music, but I'd be happy to try to answer any questions.

Letters on Music

Jesse is ready for *Mrs. Stewart's Book I*—he's now added two chords to most songs, has memorized a good dozen and a half songs, knows about minor chords and how to form them. Today our piano tuner came, and Jesse found it especially neat to see the *pattern* the piano hammers made when he played major and then minor chords. Jesse was also inspired by hearing that John was timing himself on violin (*GWS* 37)—immediately suggested that we time *his* playing. He enters on his own calendar his time for each day. Today he played *80 minutes*! How different his attitude is from my attitude toward flute practice as a child—in 5th grade the school group-lesson teacher talked to us sternly about the need for practicing more and then handed us all fill-in "practice Record Sheets," to be *signed* by our parents each day. We all clearly took this as a type of punishment, and although I was usually a very honest child, I soon found myself doing things like filling in "0" minutes, having my mother sign it, and then sneaking in a "3" before that zero.—*Susan Richman* (PA).

A note about our piano playing. I've discovered that the best way to interest Siri Atma in playing is for me to play. Often, but not always, he'll come over and excitedly ask for his turn. He is quite sensitive about being corrected and I aim to be very respectful of this when I help him. He tends to like to quit or get silly when he's doing something that is hard for him—last time we played I was delighted to be able to help him past such a point by singing the tune—it seemed like he just naturally got the right notes with my lead to follow. He does not like me to play any notes to show him how. I have mentioned getting lessons, but presently plan to wait until he is more enthusiastic. We are using the Stewart Preschool books. We listen to the Suzuki record, but haven't attempted to do much with it yet.—*Mha Atma Kaur Khalsa* (CA).

Michael bought me a recorder while we were in the city—an alto. He plays a tenor himself, and the holes are too far apart for my fingers. If he hadn't pointed out the problem to me I'd have gone on thinking I was just "not musical." Now, with a recorder that fits my hands, I'm suddenly not so "unmusical" any more. What a nice feeling! I've got a long ways to go before I'm ready to play at Madison Square Garden—but I can play notes that sound clear now instead of the slurs and beeps you get when your fingers won't quite reach.—*Leslie Westrum* (IN).

[JH:] In my travels, or through letters, I meet more and more families in which the children (and often the parents) are busily and skillfully making music. Off the top of my head I think of a number I have seen or heard from recently: the Vogts in Lexington, Ky.; the Van Daams in Providence R.I.; the Kahns in Portland, Me.; the Cameron-Shicks in Stroudsburg, Pa.; the Wallaces in Ithaca, N.Y.; the Barkers in Millersburg, Ohio; the Schallenbergs in Oceanside, Ca.; the Salisburys in Twin Falls, Idaho. Please let us know about music in your family.

Using Language Tapes

From Penny Barker (OH):

All five of the children have been using the International Linguistics tapes [see "Want Ads"] for about two months and every night after I've blown out the lamp I hear them speaking German to one another. Each of them has learned enough to contribute to this nightly ritual. We are on our second series of tapes. It is very much like the Suzuki mother-tongue approach and we're quite pleased.

New Books Available Here

Read By Ear—An All-In-One Recorder Book, by Richard S. Perry ($3.95 + post). This is an excellent beginner's instruction book for all the recorders—sopranino, soprano, and alto (which we sell), and tenor (which we do not yet sell, but may). The cover-page subtitle is "With a Suzuki approach, as presented at Suzuki institutes in the USA and Canada." The Suzuki approach that Perry has followed is the very sensible one of having people learn the beginnings of music notation *not* by being shown various musical symbols and then being told what they "mean," but by beginning with rhythmic phrases and tunes that his readers will know already and then showing what these look like in written music. This is perhaps most important with respect to rhythm. Most readers can probably grasp more or less easily the idea that lines and spaces in written music stand for different white notes on the piano; but talk about half-notes, quarter-notes, eighth-notes, dots doubling the value of the note, etc., just confuse and terrify them, all the more so since so few of them were ever good at fractions. This book avoids or jumps right over all this unnecessary mystery and terror.

The book contains fingerings for all the recorders. There are also a number of well-known songs, some to be played in unison, others as duets, trios, or even quartets. A fine text, which should quickly make the beginner ready to explore the big world of recorder music.

Oxford Picture Dictionary of American English, English-Spanish edition ($4.50 + post). In my review of the original (English only) *Oxford Picture Dictionary*, in *GWS* 17, I wrote: " . . . parents have put signs on well-known objects around the house—door, chair, table, etc.—so that children can look at each of these written words and know what they mean. The Richard Scarry books [also] give children a large number of written words, with pictures to make clear what the words mean. This Oxford Picture Dictionary . . . does the same thing. It includes over 2000 common English words, with pictures illustrating them. The words and pictures are grouped in familiar scenes: Clothes; In The City; At The Supermarket; the Kitchen; the Bedroom; etc. There's no plot or story line, just pictures and names of things. . . ."

This new edition is the same book, only for every picture the word is written in both English (in black) and Spanish (in blue). At the end of the book are two lists, one of all the English words, one of the Spanish. Nothing fancy, but a great deal of information here. And it occurs to me that it would not be hard for resourceful parents and/or children to invent their own stories using these scenes.

Are All The Giants Dead? by Mary Norton ($2.50 + post). This fascinating book is by the author of the books about the Borrowers, but it is very different from them, or from any other children's book I know. An ordinary, present-day boy, who likes science fiction and space travel, is taken every so often on a visit to the land of fairy tales. But Time has invaded that magic land. The famous characters are there—Beauty and the Beast, Cinderella, Sleeping Beauty, the Wicked Witch, and the two Jacks, Jack of the Beanstalk and Jack the Giant Killer. But they are all old, past their prime, their beauty and powers gone (or so they feel). In this world the boy, James, meets a young Princess, who suddenly faces a terrible danger. Though he has been warned not to interfere in the lives of Fairy Land people, he tries to help her. Their efforts take them to the world where the giants once lived, but no more, since now they are all dead. Or are they?

What a wonderful writer Mary Norton is. I found myself thinking once again how much better the best children's books are than almost any of the books now written for adults. The urgent requirements of writing for children bring out the best in writers. It certainly does with Mary Norton, who aside from being an original and spellbinding storyteller has (like Ursula Le Guin, and like many English writers) a great love of and feel for nature.

And, as is often true of the best children's books, the surprising and moving ending of this one has a gentle but much-needed message for all of us.

Drive It 'Till It Drops, by Joe Troise ($4.95 + post). Since most homeschoolers don't have much money but do have to own a car, we're listing this book because it's the best one I've seen about how to own and run a car with the least possible trouble and expense. The author is an experienced mechanic and writes out of long experience and a healthy supply of skepticism and common sense. He is also a very good writer, unpretentious, clear, friendly, and funny without straining at it. Some of his conclusions may surprise you, as they did me. Among other things, he says, and convincingly, that just from the point of view of saving money you would do better to buy (or keep) an old car, even a gas hog, than buy a brand new one, however "economical." The title of the book refers to one way (but not the only way) of owning and keeping a car, probably the cheapest of all if you don't use it for long trips.

If I owned a car, I would want Joe Troise nearby to fix it. Not owning one, I'd like to know him anyway; I'll bet he has interesting and sensible things to say about many things beside cars. Meanwhile, I think that many of you will find this a very useful as well as amusing book.

Lifetimes, text by Bryan Mellonie, illustrations by Robert Ingpen ($6.95 + post). This book (first published in Australia), which I see as something to be read aloud to young children if and when they ask questions about death or the time seems otherwise appropriate, is subtitled "The beautiful way to explain death to children." Well, it is not quite that; no one, including the world's leading biologists, knows more than a tiny bit about the processes with which and because of which living creatures die. What this book does show, and in a beautiful way, is that all living creatures do in fact die, that each one has its proper lifespan, and that its death is a part of as well as the end of its life. I think this is a thing that young children can understand, and that it is good for them to know. Along with the text, which is simple, poetic, and elegiac in tone—a gifted and sensitive composer might be able to set quite beautiful music to it—are some of the most beautiful watercolor paintings I have seen. Some remind me of some of the work of Andrew Wyeth; others, of some of the paintings in *Gnomes* (in our catalog). All of them catch in a most vivid way the liveness of life and the silence, stillness, and sureness of death. They remind us what we can too easily forget, that life is a wonderful gift, and that we should be happy and grateful to have as much of it as we have. A treasure of a book.

Wally's Stories, by Vivian Gussin Paley ($12.95 + post). This is one of the most charming, captivating, adorable books about little children that I have ever read. It is a report, by a very sensitive and affectionate teacher, of a large number of conversations and arguments that the children in her kindergarten class had during a school year. I don't believe I have ever read a book about a group of children this age that brought them so vividly and delightfully to life. I was sad when the book ended, because I had come to feel I knew these children, and now I had to say goodbye to them. I wished there had been, could be, a sequel, many sequels. The children talk about tooth fairies (about which they are experts), other fairies, witches, magicians, robbers, God—all of them different kinds of supernatural beings, but very carefully distinguished from each other in their powers. They talked about babies, fish, beans, Santa Claus, presents, Christmas, pulleys, numbers, monsters, and many other things. All this talk is utterly delightful, and Mrs. Paley is extraordinarily skillful in the way she gets the talk going and then lets it run. Unlike so many adults, she can really listen to children and think about what they mean.

And here arises my one reservation about the book, which has been strong enough so that I have at times thought of taking it off our list. Not only do I think that Mrs. Paley quite often seriously misinterprets the talk of the children, but I think that she enormously *over*estimates the degree to which we *can* learn, from children's talk about the world, what their real picture of it is. My guess would be that she is a strong believer in Piaget, and quite a few of her conversations sound to me like efforts to use her class to prove that Piaget was right. At the very end of the book she writes: "Our contract reads more like this: if you will keep trying to explain yourselves I will keep showing you how to think about the problems you need to solve." I greatly fear that many readers of this book will take this as a description of what a "good" teacher should do in a classroom (or parent at home), and it reminds me uncomfortably of a lot of what Bill Hull and I spent our time doing when we taught fifth grade together—trying to find out what wrong ideas were in the children's minds, so that we could then think of ways to put them right. I now feel this was a mistake, and that our efforts to understand children's confusions may often only have led them into deeper confusion. Children, even at 10, certainly at 5, are not very aware of the processes by which they gradually construct an increasingly accurate and reliable mental model of the world, and any attempts by us to force these processes into awareness so that we can then adjust or correct them are likely to do various kinds of harm, one of which may be to prod the children into verbal "explanations" of this or that which have little or nothing to do with what their model of reality really is.

The fact is that children do not generally talk "to explain themselves," and indeed ordinarily have no interest at all in doing so, least of all to adults. The very idea of "understanding" oneself or others is meaningless to a child, except in the immediate and practical sense of understanding what someone else *wants*. What actually happened in Mrs. Paley's classroom, much of the time, was that she would ask a question, and the children would then talk. Mrs. Paley then assumed, as many people would, that the children were talking *so that* she could get an answer to her question. Most probably, what the children understood about all this was that Mrs. Paley's question was clearly a signal that they should start talking about something, which they were always happy to do—how few little children, after all, are given any chance at all to talk at school, far less about something interesting and with someone who really likes them and does not criticize or judge what they say. But this does not mean that they understood that there was a particular confusion in Mrs. Paley's mind and were talking so as to clear it up.

I suspect that in future issues of *GWS* I may have more to say about children's talk and what we may or may not be able to learn from it. For the time being I will only say that Mrs. Paley's classroom must have been one in a thousand (10,000?) and that it would have been a great joy to spend some time in it with her and these passionate, imaginative, argumentative, but in the end very affectionate and compassionate little people. For most of us, reading this book is the closest we can come to that, and I hope you will enjoy doing it as much as I have.—JH

Other Materials Available Here

Platero, An Elegy for Two Young Guitarists and Narrator, ($11.50 + post). Music composed and narrated by Ray Sealey, played by Karen Chapman (14) and Andrea Hayman (12); text from the book *Platero And I*, written in 1905–12 by the great Spanish poet and Nobel Prize winner Juan Ramon Jimenez. This is a unique and very beautiful record. The music and the playing are lovely, the story and the descriptive and poetic language will appeal to all from the youngest children to adults, and Sealey's narration is perfect, expressive without overpowering the delicate music, full of feeling without being sentimental.

In the record jacket notes, Sealey says that some years ago friends gave him *Platero And I*, which he had never heard of (nor had I until I bought this record). He writes, "In later years . . .

teaching guitar to young people, I contemplated writing some duets for two young students who often practiced together. What had always disturbed me was that much music composed for young hands was oriented to the technical and not the spiritual level of young people. . . . I was busily conjuring up some highly descriptive and evocative music to make things a little more interesting for my young players when . . . *Platero And I* sprang into mind. . . . Writing a movement for each of their weekly lessons, a structure gradually evolved and *Platero*, as it is called here, eventually took on a life of its own. . . ."

The story, which is about a little Spanish boy and his pet burro, is still in print and I expect we will soon add it, too, to our catalog. Meanwhile, I cannot imagine anyone not loving this story and this music.

Pitch-Pipes: Chromatic ($9.40 + post); for violin ($5.00 + post); for Spanish guitar ($5.50 + post). These are the simplest and cheapest devices you can get for tuning instruments. They all work the same; a small metal reed (thin strip of metal), like the kind used in harmonicas, vibrates when you blow past it, to give you the desired note. The chromatic pipe, circular in shape, gives you all 12 notes of the chromatic scale (all the white and black keys of the piano), from C to the next higher C. Very useful for teaching yourself sight singing, or for figuring out the sound of a tune of which you have the written music. The violin pipe gives you the notes for the four strings of the violin, G-D-A-E (reading from low string to high), the guitar pipe the notes E-G-A-B-D-E. The chromatic pipe comes in a square plastic box. The violin and guitar pipes are small and might be easily mislaid; I would suggest tying them with a string to the instrument case, or perhaps even getting more than one of each. Essential tools for musicians.

Hearing Protectors ($22; price includes postage). These are the gadgets that you see people wearing who work outside at airports. I first bought a pair when I was interested in free schools. Most of these were in cramped spaces, and when the children were free, as we thought they should be, to talk as loud as they wanted, the noise was often painful. It occurred to me that being able to cut down some of the noise might make being in such schools more pleasant for teachers and children. But for various reasons I never pursued this.

About four summers ago something set off a loud steady noise in my right ear. Loving music as I do, the possibility that I might lose a lot of my hearing was frightening. I decided that before going to doctors I would try wearing the hearing protectors, thinking that if I could protect my ear from further loud noise it might cure itself, which it did. By this time I had come to enjoy the increased quiet, and had grown used to the constant pressure of the protectors around my ears. I had also read that among a primitive tribe of people in Africa who live in an almost noiseless environment, old people, unlike old people almost everywhere else, had suffered virtually no loss of hearing. I decided that except when it was unnecessary or clearly inappropriate, I would wear the protectors all the time, which I have done since. I wear them on city streets, in subways or planes, in the office while typing, whenever there is more noise around me than I want to hear. They have made my life much more pleasant, I have had no more hearing problems, and I think my hearing is somewhat better than when I started wearing them. They are some of the most useful tools I have ever owned.

These protectors do not give absolute silence. They reduce the noise level about 30 decibels, which means that you can hear almost everything you would hear without them, even conversation, but much less. Above all, they cut down on the kinds of noises that are most penetrating and painful, like sirens, pile drivers, screeching wheels on the subway.

What has this to do with *GWS* readers, most of whom don't live in the city? Just this—of all the painful noises I know, by far the most painful, even unbearable, is the loud crying or screaming of babies or young children. You will still hear them through these protectors, but so much less that instead of being driven half-frantic by the noise you will be more able to think about how to stop it, or at least to endure it. But they would also be useful for taking naps in a noisy house, or for otherwise cutting down on unwanted sound—barking dogs, loud music, chain saws, etc. As I say, they have improved my life and might well improve yours. Beyond that, children of all ages find them fascinating.—JH

Editors—John Holt & Donna Richoux
Managing Editor—Pat Farenga
Subscriptions & Books—Steve Rupprecht & Jim Hayes
Office Assistant—Mary Van Doren

Growing Without Schooling 40

July 1984

Just came back from a trip to Phoenix, where I taped a short interview with the Rita Davenport show and later spoke to a meeting of homeschoolers; to San Diego, where I spoke to a number of meetings of homeschoolers in what is obviously a very active area; and then on to Washington state, where (with many others) I spoke at the Cleveland Conference at Washington State University in Pullman, and then later at some very well attended and enthusiastic public meetings in Wenatchee, in the heart of the fruit country. The Cleveland Conference, held annually, ordinarily brings together school administrators and architects to discuss school curriculums and buildings. This year the sponsors of the conference decided to discuss instead the question of the law as it relates to independent schools, mostly religious, and homeschooling. Whether for this reason or some other, only about half the usual number attended, but these seemed to find the conference lively and stimulating.

Returned home to hear the very welcome news that our dear friend and colleague Donna is going to be married this November, probably in the Boston suburb of Concord, to Franklin Ross, who, among other things, works at the Museum of Comparative Zoology at Harvard.

Another old friend and staff member, Jim Hayes, has left to work full time at the Westin Hotel. His place is being taken by Ross Campbell, who arrived here recently from the West Coast to work as a volunteer, and now becomes one of the regular crew. Mary Gray, meanwhile, is recovering somewhat from mononucleosis, so it may not be too long before she is with us again.

The response to our recent story about possibly starting a tax-exempt corporation called Friends of Homeschooling has been so encouraging (about $6000 in donation estimates) that we have decided to go ahead. Barring unforeseen and extremely unlikely legal difficulties (there are thousands of tax-exempt corporations of a similar nature), we should have the new corporation formed by the end of the year, though it will of course take some time after that to get our tax-deductible status from the Internal Revenue Service.

More good news about homeschoolers and college admission. Theo Giesy, one of our pioneer homeschoolers in Virginia, wrote me that her son Darrin, who has not been to school in the many years I have known him, has been admitted to Antioch College, one of our most selective colleges, for this coming fall.

Brief note on late starts in reading. Heard from one homeschool friend that her youngest child, age 11 last winter, has only in the last year or less taken an interest in reading and is now reading well, and in fact wrote me a very interesting and well-spelled letter. And on my travels I met a 10½-year-old boy who only began reading four months or so ago and is now reading far beyond his grade level. Will try to get a little more complete story about these by no means atypical children. Children learn very quickly when they have chosen to do so for their own reasons. How much trouble and pain would be saved if more schools could only learn this.

—John Holt

John Holt's Coming Schedule

Sept. 8, 1984: Connecticut Homeschoolers Association. Contact Laura Pritchard, 203-634-0714.

Sept. 13: Holt Associates Open House (second Thursday of each month, 6-8 p.m.).

Sept. 28: Sunrise Session, D'Youville College, Buffalo NY 14201. 8 AM. Contact Robert DiSibio, 716-881-3200, ext. 6112.

Oct. 13: Missouri homeschoolers. U. of Mo., Rolla. Contact Albert Hobart, 314-674-3296.

Anyone who wants to coordinate other meetings or lectures around these times, contact Patrick Farenga.

GWS T-Shirt Contest

Ever want to create an award-winning design? Now you can indulge in your most creative talents—enter your design for our first-ever *GWS T-Shirt Contest*. Mary and Richard Zimman, the owners of the company *Horseshirts!*, have offered to sponsor the contest. The rules are:

1) The winner will be awarded $25.

2) Entries must be no larger than 8" wide and 10" high, drawn in black ink on white paper, and be camera-ready original artwork.

3) All entries must have name and address of the entrant on the back.

4) Multiple entries are acceptable.

5) Judging will be by *GWS* in conjunction with Horseshirts! Inc.

6) The winning design will be imprinted on T-shirts as a fundraising and publicity activity for *GWS*.

7) Entries should be postmarked no later than Oct. 31, 1984.

Once a winner is chosen, the winning design will be printed on Hanes 50/50 T-shirts in 8 sizes (4 youth and 4 adult). The postpaid prices will be $4.75 for youth and $5.25 for adult sizes. *GWS* will receive one dollar for every T-shirt sold, so create a design that'll sell a million! We look forward to your creations and encourage all ages to enter. Good Luck!—Pat Farenga

Report On *GWS* Supplement

Delighted to see that *Young Children: Natural Learners* is moving briskly—over 100 sold so far, with new orders steadily coming in. I'm especially pleased that many people are buying copies for their friends and relatives.

For those of you who did not see the announcement in *GWS* 39, *Young Children: Natural Learners* is the first-ever "*GWS* Supplement," made of letters and articles we have not had room for in the regular magazine, and all pertaining to children from birth to age 6. It turned out to be *12* pages, not 8, in the *GWS* format with a few illustrations.

In the introduction, I wrote, after a few words on our history: "Through *GWS*, a sizable network has formed of people concerned about the true nature of learning. To our delight, many of our readers have written us about the way they and their children actually do learn, and it has been our great pleasure to print these perceptive, warm, and often witty letters in *GWS*. Through these shared experiences, like the ones you will find in these pages, a new picture is emerging of what the role of the parents may be in producing children who are happy, creative, and independent—parents who trust their children's innate ability to learn, who provide only as much help as the child asks for, and who allow the child to become involved in *their* lives and work instead of narrowing their world down to the traditional limits of childhood. We hope you will find these letters and articles stimulating and encouraging."

Several of the stories relate to family businesses—an employer in New Hampshire who *requires* workers to bring preschool-age children; starting family-style health food store; a 3-year-old who answers the phone for her parents' construction firm. Some of the other titles: "When a Toddler Interferes," "Twos Aren't Terrible," "Having Faith in Special Kids," "Learning to Ice Skate," and "Thoughts on Preschool."

As I expected, because the printing and postage costs are higher than we estimated, we have had to raise the price already to $2, including postage (make checks payable to Holt Associates). But to encourage the multiple orders to continue, the price will be $1.50 each for 2 or more shipped at one time to one address.

We'd love to hear feedback on this booklet. The first response we got was from Joyce Spurgin in Oklahoma: "I received *Young Children: Natural Learners* today. . . . It is just what I needed. When will you have another issue? . . . If it was a regular periodical, I would subscribe!" —Donna Richoux

Notes From Donna

Looks like the next four months are going to be very, very busy, what with the wedding, moving house, and the projects at work—the fall booklist mailing, updating the Directory, the Mass. kindergarten law (see "Legislative News")—not to mention *GWS* itself every two months. I'm getting rather nervous about how it will all get done. But I suppose, with lots of help, I'll make it through!

Franklin Ross and I met several years ago contra-dancing (we plan to have a caller and musicians at our wedding!). He's very different from me in some ways—I was good in school and am a habitual reader, whereas Frank learned almost everything in his field from direct experience; he spent about 10 years travelling around North America, collecting and studying reptiles and amphibians for museums. I find him to be strong and capable and thoughtful, and I'm sure we'll be happy.

Ross needs a home: When Ross Campbell came from California to help in our office, he was planning to live with a friend. But that fell through, and right now he's staying for a month with the Matilsky family (*GWS* readers), and is looking for other such places, fairly close to our office, where he could trade some household and childcare work for room and board. Ross is also a fine violinist (trained by Suzuki methods) and would be happy to share his music with families. Please call the office (437-1550) if interested—we'd like to keep him in the area as long as possible!

Cheap handout: Tired of loaning out your back issues of *GWS* and never getting them back? We have about 30 copies of *GWS* 37 that were goofed up in printing—each consists of two sets of pages 9–24 instead of 1–32. You could take them apart and have two partial samples for people to get an idea of what *GWS* is about. All we ask is that you pay the postage—50¢ each (specify "Printer's Goof.") If we run out, we'll return your check *if* it was made out separately; otherwise, we'll issue a credit slip.

Safety concern: Michael Kern of Washington wrote in response to Sharon Hillestad's idea (*GWS* 39) about modifying the TV plug to control her family's TV watching: "This would create two serious electrical hazards. Male plugs should always receive current, rather than deliver it, because the conductors are exposed, and would present full house current if touched. Very possibly a lethal shock. I'm sure the idea was to always plug into the TV cord, then the wall—but if your concentration slips, or a guest doesn't know the system—ZAP. The other hazard involves polarized plugs. Most TVs are designed so the +/- polarity is always the same. This is to reduce the shock and fire hazard from the TV itself. One would have to carefully maintain that polarity in any modification to the cord. . . ."

Good news from California: From the Summer '84 *CoEvolution Quarterly*, reprinted in *Georgians for Freedom in Education*: "Last year at San Juan Ridge Union Elementary School in northern California, a whopping 15% of the students were enrolled in Independent Study." The San Juan district is on our "Friendly School District" list (*GWS* 36).—DR

Selling Used Materials

[DR:] Several of you have asked if we could print your offers to buy or sell—or even give away—books, magazines, and so on. We have simply been too short on room to do this and have suggested you try the local newsletters. Now comes this good idea from Jeff and Kim Golden of North Carolinians For Home Education (PO Box 752, Concord NC 28025; 704-782-3930):

Trading Post—Many of you have curriculum materials which your children are no longer using, yet are still useable, while others can't or don't wish to pay retail price for materials they will use for only a year. This can apply to teaching aids, student or teacher texts, audio materials, reference books, or even hobby, craft, or science equipment which is no longer used. If you have, or are looking for any of these things, send us a full description of the item: title, publisher, grade level, subject, condition, etc.—any information that would help identify what you're offering or seeking. Please be sure to include your name, address or phone number—some way for interested persons to reach you. We ask that you enclose $1 to help cover the printing/mailing costs for the *Trading Post*.

[DR:] Kim says they'd be happy to run listings from outside of North Carolina, since most actual sales will be done by mail anyway. We will print the address of the *Trading Post* in *GWS* from time to time, the way we do for the *Network for Educational Travel*, (which is at 1853 East Shore Dr, Ithaca NY 14850).

By the way, when the question of selling used Calvert materials arose in an early issue of *GWS*, someone said the school makes customers sign an agreement not to sell or give away its books. However, a reader recently sent us a copy of Calvert's Enrollment Agreement, and it turns out that only the *Lesson Manual* is restricted in this way.

News From North Carolina

More from the newsletter of North Carolinians For Home Education.

> We strongly recommend that you enroll your children in one of the several regional schools currently being formed for parents who wish to teach their own children.... The schools have an opening day when all the students meet at a central location, and meet about once a month thereafter. Otherwise, the students are taught in the finest of classrooms, by the best of teachers: in their own homes, by their own parents.
>
> For more information, call: John McKinley, 704-683-4471, Asheville area; Terry Manahan, 704-233-4568, Charlotte area; Claudia Eldridge, 919-885-0743, HP/Greensboro; Debbie Leverette, 919-544-2809, Raleigh area; Susan Oates, 919-291-4137, Wilson/Rocky Mt.
>
> Or you can form your own nonpublic school, as long as you have one student from outside your family (his/her parent can teach that student in own home).

Court News

Two important points to remember about the *Duro* decision [*GWS* 38, 39]: (1) The state's "compelling interest" in the education of its citizens was upheld: we *are* accountable to the state for the education of our children. (2) It was not the validity of home education which was in question in this case: Duro did not even try to prove that his children were being properly educated, claiming, rather, that the state had no right to compel their education, in view of his First Amendment religious liberties. This ruling was in no way a comment on the acceptability or legality of home education, but a ruling on the right of the State to ensure that its citizens are being prepared to take their places as responsible members of a democratic society.

The Delcontes [*GWS* 25, 37] were charged with violating compulsory attendance laws in educating their children at home.... The issue here, however, is not that the state claims that the children are not being educated, or even that their education is inadequate, but that, based on a December 1983 opinion by the Attorney General, Rufus Edmisten, a home school does not qualify as a school.... In deciding this case, the judges must decide if the Attorney General's opinion is legally valid or not. The case is currently before the North Carolina Supreme Court.... Decision is expected to be issued in September.

The Catos [*GWS* 26].... received a favorable ruling from District Judge Warren, and have continued teaching Lori at home.

The Gottfrieds of Randolph County.... had charges dropped the week of their court appearance because they received private school status by forming a private school with another family.

The McKinleys and Millers, both of Buncombe County ... both had their cases dismissed at pre-trial hearings.... Both have since either gotten private school status, or enrolled their children in a private school.

And From Missouri

New law: Carol Myers-Brown (MO) tells us

that the legislature passed a bill which would stop the Family Services division from investigating reports of homeschooling, and instead, transfer that responsibility to the local district attorney and the school district. The law will be in effect for only one year, so Carol says homeschoolers are organizing, establishing phone trees and raising money in order to get favorable legislation passed in 1985. She says she now knows of about 1,000 interested families in the state, and is sure there are many more.

Preliminary injunction: Earlier this year, the suit initiated by *Families For Home Education* and families in Warren and St. Charles County succeeded in getting a preliminary injunction to stop the harassment by Family Services.

Ozarks peaceful: Albert Hobart (MO) writes, "Fortunately, harassment by social workers hasn't been a statewide phenomenon, and homeschoolers in our part of Missouri have had relatively few legal difficulties. In fact, homeschooling in the Ozarks seems to be doing better than ever. Recently, for example, the *Rolla Daily News* included two favorable articles featuring several local homeschooling families. . . . Since then we've had a couple of homeschooling get-togethers to give interested parents a chance to meet experienced homeschooling families. . . . We plan to get together about every two months, and everyone is welcome to contribute to our newsletter. For more information, phone Carol Ratliff (314-341-3216) or me (314-674-3296). . . ."

State convention: Albert also told us he enjoyed the Missouri homeschoolers convention sponsored by *Families For Home Education* in June. A state legislator and two lawyers were on one panel discussion.

Helpful school: Carol Brown also wrote, "We're a school for homeschoolers. We live in an old stagecoach stop. . . . We meet once a week (more or less) so our children can have a day together. Last year a child came whose father was the principal of a public school. . . . Our latest interest is creative play and dramatics. . . . Our community has a nearby theater which has been out of commission since piano-playing silent movies.

It's open now!" For more information, contact the *Little Piney School*, Rt 1 Box 20, Newburg MO 65550; 314-762-2036.—DR

Other Legislative/State News

Illinois: Mary Friedl (IL) wrote, "That last draft I sent you called a Statement of Assurance was passed (not approved) by the Illinois State Board of Education. Some regional superintendents plan on using it for the '84–85 school year. They say it'll be voluntary and will only be used for statistical purposes (but that's not what some regional superintendents have said). The State Board made it clear that this was a first step toward regulation."

Sally B. Pancrazio, Manager of Research and Statistics for the State Board of Education, put together a summary of comments made by four homeschoolers (Karen Demmin, Mary Friedl, J. Lynn Currie, and Deborah Saalfeld) on the new form. Their concerns included the fact that the Statement of Assurance asked for information that private schools did not have to submit; that the question about "the highest level of education attained by the instructor" could be used against the parents; and that the form had to be notarized.

Becky Currie reported in the Springfield HOUSE newsletter, "Representative John Birkinbine in Cook Co. District 57 is in favor of homeschooling. His own child(ren?) attend Christian Liberty Academy's day school. His address is 1336 Shermer Rd, Northbrook IL 60062; phone 312-564-3490. He may be of help to us in initiating some positive homeschooling legislation."

And Dee Cox wrote in the *Chicago HOUSE Door* #2: "On March 27, Dorothy Werner and I attended a lecture given by Dr. Donald Gill (head of the Illinois State Board of Education) and Dr. Richard Wagner. . . . Dr. Gill stated that one of his goals was to change state mandates from 'You shall take such and such subjects' to 'You shall prove competency in such subjects.' I asked Dr. Gill if these new mandates would affect private schools, he stated, 'Why, no, I can't mandate private schools.' I have written him a letter to elaborate on this issue, and to see if it directly applies to home schools. . . ."

Kansas: Daniel Glynn sent a copy of Senate Bill 712, which would allow homeschooling if (1) the parents notify the State Board of Education before Sept. 15; and (2) the child "demonstrates the attainment of minimum competency objectives" based on reading and math examinations administered by the state each spring.

Daniel says, "I honestly haven't heard how it currently stands, but I don't see much advantage to the bill as written. Legally speaking, I would rather be considered a private school under the current law than be considered as homeschooling under the proposed bill. . . . The only requirements for a Kansas private, nonaccredited school are (1) a "competent" instructor (not construed to mean degreed or certified), and (2) in session substantially the same amount of time as the public schools (which is easy to prove). Kansas cases are usually lost on the competency question, which is often a matter of presentation or flaws in representation, as the lawyer in the Sawyer case admitted at a meeting I attended. (By the way, when that loss was publicized, I made sure to write a letter to the superintendent here explaining the ruling and stating that it had no bearing on our situation whatsoever; he told me he appreciated the letter.). . . ."

Louisiana: From the newsletter of *Citizens For Home Education, Northwest LA. Chapter*: "During this last legislative session, three bills were introduced concerning homeschooling. First—Repeal of Home Study. The sponsor of this bill, Rep. Alphonse Jackson, withdrew this bill before it got to committee. Second—Screening and Testing of Home-study Children upon re-entry into the public school system—this passed with little or no objection from homeschoolers. The third and most opposed bill required mandatory testing of home study children. The bill was amended to the following that passed both houses and is now the "new" home study law. Most homeschoolers view this new law as a victory even though there are now more restrictions; the opposition feels that an adequate compromise has been made and will probably be less likely to severely attack our right to homeschool for a while (we hope!)"

The substance of the third bill, now R.S. 17-236. 1: A parent shall apply to the state Board of Elementary and Secondary Education for approval within 30 days of starting to homeschool. The initial application shall be approved if the parent certifies that the home study program will offer a sustained curriculum of quality at least equal to that offered by the public schools. For a renewal application to be approved, any of these conditions must be met: (1) the parent submits a packet of materials such as a complete outline of subjects taught during the previous year, lists of books, copies of the student's work, copies of tests, progress reports by third parties, etc., for the Board's approval; (2) the child passes a competency-based education examination which will be offered by the local school board and the State; (3) the child scores at or above grade level on an approved standardized test such as the California Achievement Test; or (4) a certified teacher submits a statement saying the teacher has examined the program and finds it at least equal to that offered by public schools (the Board may review this evaluation).

Maine: In the beginning of June, Maine homeschoolers learned of a 24-page draft of homeschooling guidelines, written by the State Dept. of Education with no input from homeschoolers. 150–250 people, including Dr. Raymond Moore, showed up at a hearing June 13, protesting the lack of input as well as some of the proposed restrictions, and got considerable TV and newspaper coverage. As a result, four homeschoolers were asked to be on an advisory committee, along with four school superintendents and three Department officials, to work on the guidelines.

Maryland: The State Board passed the homeschooling regulations it had proposed last January. These require a family to submit a written schedule and "specific instructional objectives" in order to show that the program provides "regular, thorough and comparable instruction of those subjects usually taught in public schools to children of the same age." A correspondence course is acceptable if specifically approved by the local superintendent. A homeschooling parent must have a Maryland teaching certificate, be a college graduate, or get a waiver from the local superintendent. The superintendent is also responsible for monitoring progress and determining placement upon readmission to school.

Massachusetts: Part of a big education reform package (House Bill 5704—Section 20, Paragraph 2B(d), and Section 28) would lower the compulsory school attendance age to 5 and require districts to offer 4-year-old programs. We at Holt Associates expect to do a mailing to the 1000–1500 Massachusetts names in our files, asking people to write or phone their legislators. The bill is due to be voted on soon after the summer recess ends Sept. 27. To find out the bill's current status, call the State House at 617-722-2700.

Nevada: Marian Sorenson writes, "The new Nevada regulations are enclosed. They are not the best, but after months of work, it seemed the best compromise we could get. Most of us feel that we can live with them. . . . Most families know a certified teacher who is willing at no cost or a nominal fee to meet the consultation requirement. . . . There may be some who are concerned enough to fight for a more relaxed set of regulations, and if so, I'll help them. Selfishly, though, because we can accomplish our goals under this set, I'll do just that and not make waves. . . ."

The new regulations allow four alternatives for homeschoolers: (1) a certified teacher as tutor; (2) a parent with an appropriate teaching certificate; (3) "consultation" with a certified teacher, for at least 25 hours during the year, on planning, teaching, and learning problems; or (4) an approved correspondence program. A child must be tested *before* being excused from school attendance. For the board to renew the "grant of excuse," it must see evidence of "reasonable educational progress," such as test scores. Students in grades 1, 2, 4, 5, 7, and 8 must be given the same standardized tests as public school students. The requirement for a consultant *must be waived* after one year when it has been demonstrated that the child has made reasonable educational progress. The waiver will apply if other children in the family are excused at a later date from school attendance.

Ohio: An article from the *Yellow Springs (OH) News*, 2/1/84, said: "The State of Ohio, as part of its educational reform program, has extended its guidelines for approval of educational options—but gives local school districts the authority to set their own standards. . . . In essence, the state offers its approval to optional programs as long as the students participating in them demonstrate—by their performance on tests—that they are being adequately educated. These options include home-based instruction, mentor education, independent study, tutoring, educational travel, and correspondence courses. . . . The new state guidelines call for students in home-based programs to be supervised and evaluated by certified teachers—but the actual day-to-day instruction may be done by non-certified persons. . . . These homeschooled students could be enrolled in public schools, and receive public school credit for the courses they complete. . . ."

We have not succeeded in getting a copy of these state guidelines. Can anyone help?

Virginia: Jim O'Toole and Theo Giesy both sent copies of a memo written by the State Dept. of Education and sent to all Division Superintendents, summarizing the new homeschooling law which took effect July 1, and including a copy of the one-page form to be filled out by homeschooling families. One of the ways to homeschool legally is to use a correspondence course approved by the board of education; Jim sent lists of courses the Board was considering in June, and said it postponed any decision until it heard from the Attorney General on what exactly "approval" would mean.

Washington: A reader whose husband is on a school board sent the April bulletin of the *Washington State School Directors' Association*, which included this paragraph: "Home schools—Resolution of this issue will be determined in 1984. All indicators point to solutions which favor the homeschoolers unless public school educators get pro-active to prevent the zealots from riding roughshod. Homeschool advocates want testing programs, materials, equipment, instruction, medical care, accountability and everybody's blessing. . . . all provided by the local public schools. Some assertive legislation, introduced by the supporters of public education, can dampen this issue."—DR

Court News

The Arkansas Democrat, *5/22/84:*

> The Arkansas Supreme Court on Monday affirmed a Pulaski County Circuit Court decision against Wayne Burrow [*GWS* 34 & 35], who was charged with refusing to send a minor to school.
>
> Burrow was found guilty in Pulaski County Municipal Court and then convicted in circuit court and fined $1,000.
>
> Burrow said he was educating his daughter at home using curriculum supplied by a correspondence school.
>
> On appeal, he argued that the law was vague and it violated the free exercise clause in the constitution. He also argued that the trial court erred in finding that a state statute gives the state the power to approve private schools.
>
> The Supreme Court said that compulsory school attendance laws have been struck down in other states, but refused to consider that question in this case. The court said Burrow did not have the standing to raise the issue.
>
> "We think someone of average intelligence would readily recognize that appellant's educational methods do not constitute a school within the common understanding of the word," the court said. The court said Burrow's daughter was the only student and that there were no certified teachers.
>
> In a dissenting opinion, Justice Darrell Hickman said the court avoided the issue, passed over decisions from other states, and "has put its power to ill use simply to punish non-conformity."
>
> Hickman said there is no law defining a private school in Arkansas.
>
> "In my judgment Burrow loses because he refuses to conform, thereby threatening the power of the political establishment, and not because he committed a crime," Hickman said. "The state has the power to punish this man, but it doesn't have the right."

From Helen Baker (440 Addison Av, Elmhurst IL 60126), who is on our "Friendly Lawyers" list:

> Last year I did an amicus brief for the ACLU of Ohio for an Ohio couple who wanted to educate their children at home and who had been harassed under the "neglect" statute. On appeal, the court agreed with my various arguments (the statute can't be used where there is no neglect, the school had a duty to provide the parents with information on how they could conform to state standards, the parents' due process rights were violated, etc.) and told the superintendent to provide the parents with the sought-after information. In the meantime, the two children had returned to public school. The case was argued in April, 1983, but the court didn't hand down its opinion until Nov. 1 (incredible) and the superintendent dawdled in complying until March '84 and probably would still be dawdling except that the parents' attorney finally decided to push. I am still working with the parents (what do most attorneys know about the nitty-gritty of homeschooling?)

[DR:] In January, Pamela Lewin of Ohio sent us clippings about Dan and Deborah Johnson of Jamestown, OH, who were being prosecuted for truancy. Pamela now gives this update: "I called and spoke with Deborah this morning. She said that they had enrolled their child in the *Dayton Christian Schools* program and they are homeschooling as a satellite school. She said that all charges were dropped when they did this and they have had no problems since then. . . ."

From the Providence, RI Journal-Bulletin, *6/25/84:*

Lorraine King had kept her daughter, Danielle, out of the Central Falls school system, because she felt she could do a better job educating her at home. But she did not file an alternate educational program with the School Committee. She was tried by a jury last year, found guilty and was fined $700. The law invoked against Mrs. King was unclear, according to Department of Education lawyer Forrest Avila. Should her penalty have been a flat $20? Or should it have been the $700 that Judge John Najarian imposed—$20 for each of the 35 days of truancy that the school district listed on its complaint?

At the time Mrs. King's case went to trial, the statute did not say. It does now. A series of changes, adopted at the request of Family Court judges, were signed into law recently by Governor Garrahy. The changes went into effect immediately.

The new statute increases the fine to $50 and directs judges to levy it "for each day or part of a day that the child fails to attend school.". . . . If parents keep a child out of school for more than 30 days in a school year, they can be charged with a misdemeanor, fined $500 and sentenced to six months in jail. . . . The new law also allows school districts to pursue a civil case against parents, instead of a criminal one. The new law, Najarian said, should not scare parents. State law still allows parents to formally teach their children at home, as long as the local school committee agrees to the parents' education program.

Lorraine King's case was up for review one day last week. . . . She had enrolled Danielle in a correspondence course, and Najarian had suspended her fine. They reviewed tests Danielle took at the end of the year. She scored at or above grade level in every major subject.

Najarian continued the case until December, to make sure that Mrs. King keeps her daughter in the correspondence course next year.

From Diane Elder (TX):

In August of '83, an agreement was reached by the Bexar County District Attorney, and Jean Witteman and me, both representatives of the San Antonio Homeschoolers Association. The DA, Sam Milsap, agreed that he would no longer prosecute homeschoolers. We had been working with him for nine months, and his decision came after his staff had thoroughly researched our claim that homeschooling does not violate any Texas statutes. . . . Milsap forwarded his research to the state Attorney General for a ruling, which Milsap was sure would be favorable. The Attorney General said he cannot make a ruling while homeschooling litigation in Galveston is pending.

And from Don Miller (TX):

I talked with our friends in Houston who lost in J.P. court and appealed to County court. Egon Tausch ["Friendly Lawyers," *GWS* 36] of San Antonio was their lawyer. He filed a pre-trial motion, which was granted, that eliminated the testimony of the state's only witness, the assistant superintendent of the school district involved. This person, while acting as a truant officer, failed to advise the defendant of her rights in regard to legal action. Mr. Tausch also filed a motion regarding the question of the constitutionality of the compulsory attendance law. The motion was not ruled on, but it would have been if they had gone to trial. The prosecution offered a compromise which was accepted. The defendant pleaded nolo to one charge and the other 24 were dropped. The fine was $25. The judge said that if they went to trial, he would likely grant the motion regarding constitutionality and rule in the defendant's favor. Because of the expenses involved, the defendant chose to bargain. The child has continued in homeschooling.

Other court news in brief:

Charges dropped: The Golsons, Howard County, MD; atty. Dale Reid

Appealing in U.S. District Court: Mark Fresh, Ashtabula OH

Appealing a loss: Robin and Connie Starnes, Sanford FL

Organizational News

If your state or local group has a newsletter, we would appreciate very much being on your mailing list, so that we can share your news, ideas, and concerns with others.

Addresses of these groups can be found in *GWS* 36 or our *Home Schooling Resource List*, $1.

Arizona: Mesa members of *Families For Home Education* arranged to take the annual achievement tests together. Shirley Gardner wrote, "A great time was had by all! We had videos and nutritious snacks available for the children during their breaks and for the mothers who stayed and visited with each other.... Everyone came away feeling we need to get together like this more often! We feel that the children probably did well on their tests because of the relaxing atmosphere that surrounded them...."

California: Oak Meadow School has expanded its homeschooling program through Grade 12.

Miriam Mangione (NV) says that *Christian Home Educators* recently held an exciting convention in downtown Los Angeles with over 1100 participants. And Beth DeRoos (CA) says that over 500 parents attended the May 28th all-day seminar at Stanford University—and over 100 had to be turned away at the door! "While those attending came from every area of California, the two areas with the largest number of homeschoolers were Marin County and Santa Clara County."

There is a group of homeschoolers in the San Diego area that meets once a week. Contact Cathy Camp, 9174 Rosedale Dr, Spring Valley CA 92077.

Colorado: Raymond and Dorothy Moore will run a seminar Sept. 17 in Littleton. For information, call 789-4309.

Georgia: Interesting items from the July newsletter of *Georgians For Freedom In Education*:

1. "A letter has been written from our organization to chairmen of the departments of education of leading colleges and universities in the area. We are asking them if they would join with us in sharing expenses to bring John Holt to Atlanta in October or November.

2. "Copies are available of an ad put together for our organization. The ad is to identify parents in your area who are teaching their children and who would be interested in sharing learning experiences, organizing field trips, and maybe forming a support group.

3. "Copies are available of Georgia's curriculum outline for grades K–12. The outline is 30 pages long. Send $4.50 (to GFFIE, 4818 Joy Ln, Lilburn GA 30247)...."

Idaho: The *Family Education Association Idaho* (PO Box 171, Buhl ID 83316) is publishing a bi-monthly newsletter for $6/yr.

Maine: On July 25, the *Maine Home Education Association* had a day-long picnic in combination with the Maine Summer Institute, which was sponsoring a series of talks by Ivan Illich and John Ohliger (*Basic Choices*).

Massachusetts: Boston area homeschoolers have been meeting to go bowling, play softball and soccer, and go on field trips. If interested in joining them, call Jeanne Gaouette in Newburyport (465-3768) or Wendy Baruch in Cambridge (497-9170).

Manitoba: From the MASH newsletter #3: "About 20 children (4–12) and 10 parents attended the February tour of the Museum of Man and Nature, and the April tour of the Legislative Building.... At the March Get-Together we watched the tape of the recent *Donahue* program which featured the homeschooling Wallace family and Raymond Moore. The program was very good. ..."

Michigan: 90 people attended the "First Annual Conference" of Clonlara School, which is also sponsoring a "huge get-together" August 24–26 in Mason, MI. Featured speakers will be State Senator Alan Cropsey, State Rep. Tim Walberg, and Dr. Pat

Montgomery.

Montana: Linda McFarlane writes, "We are trying to make the *Flathead Valley Homeschooling Association* a non-profit group. . . . Our music classes have been so popular and successful, starting at 2 years old. We have all experienced our children singing and making up songs every day."

Nevada: *Las Vegas Home Education* is publishing a monthly newsletter ($3.50/6 months; Peggy Hamlen, 6244 Fargo Av, Las Vegas NV 89107; 8705688) and hopes to run a state convention in October.

New York: Karen Schadel wrote, "In February, I arranged for a pot luck dinner in the Syracuse area for those who are homeschooling (very few) or who are interested. . . . The format was just to come, bring a dish, and socialize *one* with another. We did go around the room just prior to eating and quickly identified ourselves and our families (husbands and children were highly encouraged to attend). I indicated that I did not feel in a position to organize anything further. . . . I suggested people get phone numbers and addresses on their own. . . . About 50–60 people attended, including children. We rented a large room with kitchen facilities at a neighborhood community center, asking each family to give $1 toward the cost. As far as I know nothing further has resulted from the evening, but I found it enjoyable. . . ."

North Carolina: Over 40 families attended the second statewide meeting of *North Carolinians For Home Education*, which has published an elegant brochure on questions about homeschooling.

Oklahoma: Lynn Zimms sent a copy of the *Oklahoma City Homeschooling Newsletter*. To get on their mailing list, contact Patty Morwood, 14212 Piedmont Rd, Piedmont OK 73078; 405-373-1098.

Texas: Diane Elder wrote, "Apparently the homeschooling group in San Antonio is no longer meeting. The group, unfortunately, divided over religious/secular issues. There was a lot of back-stabbing, name calling, and all the rest of that kind of thing. Makes me sad!"

Utah: Laurie Huffman told us on the phone that the homeschooling situation in Utah is "blissful" with the exception of one district. The *Utah Home Education Association* has 400–500 active "Associated Families," and its annual convention is in August.

Washington: In the last issue we said that the *Teaching Parents Association* in Washington State sent out a survey to help in preparing legislation. Wendy Wartes (16109 NE 169 Pl, Woodinville WA 98072) says "If anyone outside WA would like a copy of the survey for possible use in their state, they could send $1 for a copy. We have tried to list major choices so it should be applicable to other states." She will also send a copy of the survey results for $2.—DR

Results Of Homeschooling

From an article by Dr. Raymond Moore in Moody *magazine, 3/84:*

> When five western New York state couples who taught their children at home were challenged for truancy, each couple agreed to let the local school superintendent give their children the Stanford Achievement Test, one of the nation's more demanding measures. Although the national average on this test is 50 [percentile], all seven youngsters scored between 90 and 99 [percentile].

In Wallace, Nebraska, high school graduate Vickie Rice [*GWS* 13] helped her daughter, who was failing sixth grade, by teaching her at home. Vickie taught Leslie Sue only an hour or two daily; during the rest of each day, the two worked as a team in their small family hotel. Nine months later, Leslie Sue's academic standing had risen almost three grade levels.

Famous Unschooler

From Home Based News *(MI), 5/84:*

> Did you know Frank Lloyd Wright was homeschooled? He owed his success to his mother. She was an immigrant from Wales and a schoolteacher. His father was a traveling preacher and a musician.

As the family moved all over the country, Frank's mother took charge of his education.

He never graduated from high school. When he moved to Chicago, he rose quickly in the architectural profession. At age 26, he was operating his own business.

There are several good children's biographies about Frank Lloyd Wright. Check at your local library.

Homeschooler Graduates Early

A UPI story from Hillsdale, MI:

M. Coleman Miller graduates from Hillsdale College in May with straight A's and degrees in mathematics and physics.

M. Coleman Miller is 15.

Julian Stanley, director of [Johns Hopkins University's] mathematically precocious youth program, calls Miller "one of the most remarkable college graduates I've ever known. He is also very versatile.... He's good at three fields (mathematics, physics, and computers). And he's also very athletic."

Stanley has worked with about 300 gifted students in the past three years. He said Miller is one of the most sought-after graduate students in the nation.

Miller was taught at home until he was 10, enrolled in college at 11 and also managed to become adept at karate and basketball.

Although he does not have a high school diploma, Hillsdale College admitted him at 11 because of remarkably high Scholastic Aptitude Test scores.

Miller attributed part of his educational success to schooling at home from his parents Lincoln and JoAnne Miller—both teachers. "My parents educated me. Mostly my father in mathematics and science and my mother in English. I spent half-days at home and half-days at school during grade school." Miller said his parents sent him to school half-days for social contact.

He entered the fifth grade at 10 and simultaneously took science and mathematics courses in high school.

Working & Learning In Zambia

From Laura Hills (Box 23, Kafue, Zambia) who is a missionary:

David, our youngest child, had one year in a nursery school, one year in first grade, and about five months of 4th grade in U.S. schools. He attended a Zambian school for three years, from the second half of Grade 2 to the first half of Grade 5. In this school he was the only white pupil and the only one who heard English spoken in the home. School, however, was taught in English, with Tonga (the vernacular) taught as one class only. Hence you can see the academic standards which were possible to maintain were not very high.... I tried to do some supplemental work with him from Calvert School.... This, however, went very slowly as anyone knows who has attempted extra school after their child has completed a full day of public school. We did some things and skipped some things (we did not subscribe to the Advisory Teaching Service).

When we returned to Zambia in 1977 after Dave had spent several months in Grade 4 in Michigan, we went to live on a houseboat—became nomads in a sense—and since that time, Dave has not been in any public school. We struggled with Calvert through the beginning of 7th grade. In May 1980, we were called home because of a very serious health problem for one of our older daughters. At this time I first read the Plowboy interview with you, John, in *Mother Earth News*. This intrigued me and I got and read one or two of your books from the library and ordered a subscription to *GWS*.

What I read really supported my observations of the way children learn, made both with my own children (including trying to teach Dave) and watching the way the Zambian children learn. Not the ones in school only, but those many who were unable to go to school—mostly because there are not enough schools in Zambia for all children. They learn by mimicking adults, they learn by using real tools, by doing real things. Girls by the age of 2 or 3 have their own tiny tin can of water which they carry back from the well or river on their head along with their mothers who have their own six gallon tin full of water on their own head. Girls of this age have their own corn cob or rag, etc., tied on their backs like a baby—but girls of 5 or 6 have their baby brother or sister strapped on their backs part of the time. This is not forced child labor—this is what children *want* to do. And the examples could go on and on. Zambian children learn the survival skills they will need as adults in a normal, natural way because they want to and because they see adults doing them. They will not learn how to read by themselves because the printed word is not readily available nor used by most adults (in the rural areas, anyway).

We were in the states for 17 months in 1980 and '81. *GWS* gave us the courage to not insist Dave go to school during this time—he did not want to attend. When we returned to Zambia he also did not want to go to boarding school for secondary school. Boarding school was the only possible way, since we moved up and down the river, too far from any day school. This surprised me as we had had a lot of friction over the Calvert courses, with "When are we going to get them done?" When Mom was ready, he was not—and he saw that Mom had a lot of excuses (even if good ones) when he might have been more willing. Neither one of us really had it as a top priority, I guess.

So we sent for the American School course which he chose himself out of several possibilities. We had not finished Grade 7, only barely started it. But because he was considerably older than most 7th graders he felt a bit touchy about being "behind." So we skipped the rest of Grade 7 and all of Grade 8 and decided to try Grade 9 to see if it would be too difficult. It was not and thanks to *GWS* I no longer pressured him. It was his course, anyway—he had bought the whole four-year course with money he had earned working on his uncle's blueberry farm the summer of '81. So he felt responsible and did it whenever he wanted to (which was oftener than when I had pushed him, incidentally). I do not think that to date he has gotten any less than 90% on any exam they have sent back. He is in the third year now.

Meantime he was learning in many other ways. His dad always made it a point of teaching him the various things he was involved in. David learned carpentry while helping to build our first houseboat (a glorified Huckleberry Finn raft, floated on 49 oil drums). He learned mechanics while repairing our various outboard engines and pickup trucks. Lately he has been learning diesel mechanics as we now have a diesel houseboat and diesel pickup. He learned to drive a speedboat when he was 11, being careful, among other things, to watch out for hippos that like to stay submerged until you are upon them. Then he could take his mother up the river to the houseboat while his dad drove the vehicle around by road. I never did learn to drive the speedboat and in the rainy season the road was often impassable, so I did not want to drive then. He learned to survey and helped his father mark farms for the farmers and later plots for the fishermen. After that at a crucial stage of digging a canal, when his father had to be away for three days, he was able to use what he had learned to keep a huge excavator working on the level. This meant being there from 6 a.m. to 4 p.m. or so when the excavator operator quit for the day. A long day and a big responsibility for a boy only 12 years old! But he loved it because he was using a skill he had learned and doing an adult job. He learned metal work, fiberglassing, and more carpentry when he helped build our present houseboat onto a 24-foot trimaran hull, two and a half years ago. Six months ago he began helping a nearby Seventh Day Adventist mission build a similar superstructure onto the same kind of hull for a medical launch.

He learned a lot of things while helping to build the other boat: how to live and work with a team other than his parents, how to weld, and many other things. They were very happy to have his help and especially the knowledge he had picked up in making the first boat for us. So he had the added bonus of being able to feel useful to someone else. He now is teaching the mission driver how to operate the boat and how to navigate the very intricate maze of waterways which make up the Kafue Flats. This he learned by being our driver for the first twelve trips. Yes, he still is probably a bit "behind" academically, since he is now 17 and is still in Grade 11. But he speaks three Zambian languages fluently so that Zambians who do not see him while speaking are convinced he is a Zambian, and he understands three other Zambian languages. (His parents are not yet fluent in the first one.) He still finds many other things which seem to be more of a priority than academic studies—like repairing a waffle iron today for another family. Or repairing a shoe for his Zambian friend with his "speedy stitcher" (I forgot to mention his leatherworking abilities), a shoe which if it had been owned by most people in the US would have long ago been thrown out. His friend was extremely happy to have it made "like new" again. And tomorrow Dave leaves with the health boat for another two-week trip giving further training to their driver. In between stops he will translate for them, so he won't have much time for school then either. But we are no longer concerned about those "academic studies" and neither is he. They *will* be done—later on when there is time.

Four On Their Own

From an Oregon reader:

"On Her Own at 10" in GWS 37 moved me to write.... I am also a single mother (of four teenagers). My children have been out of school for six years now.

When I first took them out of school in '78 there was pure chaos in our home. They did nothing but fight, only taking breaks to eat and use the toilet, for about six months. I didn't try to do anything with them because I knew they had a big adjustment to make.

When I first took them out of school, their father and I were still together, so I wasn't working. I took the gang on plenty of field trips to distract them from their boredom which led to fighting.

When separation became imminent between their father and me, I began to take in sewing and other children to care for. The children were helpful with both endeavors. We worked together on various money-making schemes which were fun, educational and profitable.

The important thing, I felt, was that we stayed together. Their father had abandoned them, so I could not.

As time went on the children got involved in various projects, all of which were beneficial in several ways. The single most beneficial project was their stamp collection. That went up and down in importance for them over the years until they sold out at a profit last year.

My children also read a lot. They take 10–15 books out of the library at a time, and read most of them cover to cover. I take them to community meetings with me so they can learn how our local government works, and I also take them to patriot meetings. When I had to get a full-time job a little over a year ago, I made sure that it was all right for at least one of the children to come to work with me some of the time. Sometimes all four of them have come with me. The deal is that they must not be disruptive and must be helpful.

Together the children and I have worked out numerous problems that had existed between us for years. We have established a good solid working relationship. My priority has always been the children first, and as a result things have always worked out one way or another.

Pressure's Off In Nebraska

From Ronaele Berry (NE), whose five children are ages 13 to 3:

We are *so* isolated—at least now the legal pressures have been removed (trial dropped at the last minute so we'd have a chance to comply with the new Nebraska law [GWS 39]) so the isolation isn't quite as threatening. Still—we receive a certain amount of "hate" comments from neighbors and others who are sorry we are "getting away with it." They worry about the "poor abused little children"—"How will they ever get an education?" "Whatever will happen to them?". . . . We almost always hear the comments second-hand so can give no rebuttal.

This spring in preparing for our trial we decided to have the children tested, as our district attorney had said she would view willingness for testing and appropriate results as reasons for withdrawing charges. So we talked to Pat Montgomery at Clonlara where the girls had been enrolled earlier and she sent CAT for the three girls plus a "Teachers Competency" for myself. We had made arrangements with a local teacher to administer/monitor the tests. All the children thought the tests were easy. (Pat had sent some pre-tests for practice so they were comfortable with the style). They all tested grade level and above on all tests. Incidentally, *my* test was easy, too. It was interesting to feel my brain settle into the old "test-taking gear" and really plow right through it. The math problems brought to mind whole pages of math I could see as though the books were open before me. I missed four on the entire test.

I am hoping my score from this test will be accepted by the State Department. Otherwise I will have to take the National Teachers Exam. A county superintendent told me no parent would be able to pass this test with 50% or above so he recommended trying all the other options first (i.e., sending letters of recommendation, high school transcript, etc.) Anyone know if the Nat'l Teachers Exam really is this difficult?

I enjoy *living* with my kids and do not like the idea of having to insert "force-feeding" to prepare for tests (which we did before the tests this spring because we could not have withstood the repercussions of low test scores—children removed from us, we could go to jail, etc.). We *know* our children are bright and intelligent but our everyday living had not really prepared them for test type learning.

I have spent *very* little time sitting down with a child for "lessons." They all have *Yearbooks* (1505 Wellington Dr, Bedford VA 24523) which they really like but they work at them very sporadically—when they are in the mood.

Susan Peterson says in *GWS* 39, "Now (at 9) he is a master of doing the absolute minimum to get by. . . ." This is *exactly* the attitude displayed by my three older kids when asked to do *anything* they do not wish to do. Especially true if ever I try to get them to write in a journal or do schoolwork of any kind. It has taken me almost two years to learn that it never pays for me to brightly, subtly, or any other way push schoolwork or make suggestions or hints about something being educational. They are not sullen or nasty about it—they just give it the absolute minimum of attention and effort and drop it.

"Not too many super extra-special wonderful things have happened"—Does my ol' heart good to hear that from another homeschooling mother. I sometimes get depressed reading about all the super things some children do/are doing. It would give *me* so much pleasure to say my children are excelling in their music, their writing, or that they have grand business ventures, high ambition, high motivation, etc. I do have to fight my own anxiety and need for my children to excel. But the truth is without pressure from school and teachers they have not pursued any of their interests they seemed to have while in school. . . . I do sometimes feel that I need to pressure them but I am so uncomfortable with doing that that I don't.

If I were to say that my children excelled at anything it would be at verbal *communication* and *perception* and *sensitivity* about other people (no tests to measure this!). . . . We discuss moral issues, political issues, social mores, ethics. *Everything* comes up for discussion. They may be more qualified (informed) to vote in local, state, and national issues than many registered voters! This is one of the government's concerns about education—that the future citizens would be wise and capable voters—again—no tests show this ability and intelligence!

"OK To Be Ordinary" (*GWS* 39) was just what I needed to read! So I've got ordinary kids, capable of running a house, entertaining themselves all day, communicating with people of all ages, discussing theories, ideals, realities. [DR: But this is *not* "ordinary"—very few kids can do all that.] Why then do I retain this almost physical longing for them to play the piano more, draw more, create more, write more???

One thing I have done for a while, without making any big deal of it, has been to limit library visits. I allow other things to crowd them out. It seemed to me that all other plans and projects went wanting until the library books were read. I would see nothing but bodies draped around, behind, over, under furniture as girls read and read and read. We would discuss what they read—I get lots of verbal book reports!—but their energy seemed to fizzle out through the books. They've been without new books to read for almost two months. Of course, they re-read books from our own home library but they can be more easily distracted from them so they've all been doing more sewing, cooking, playing, badminton, baseball, skating, bike-riding, working (for neighbors for money).

School Once A Week

Deirdre Purdy (WV) wrote in Alternatives in Education *(Rt 3 Box 305, Chloe WV 25235; $3/yr):*

> Last school year, Jed, now 9, and Hannah, now 6, went to "Talented and Gifted" at the local elementary school one afternoon a week. This is a special education program available at all the public schools in the state.... My husband and I knew and particularly liked the teacher so felt it would be a good program, some excitement for the children, and would allow them to familiarize themselves with the school. They enjoyed T&G; however, three of the four regular participants were homeschoolers, and the class had no contact with the rest of the school as it was held in a separate trailer.
>
> This year we wanted them to continue with T&G, and they wanted to go, but we thought it would be good for them to go to their assigned school class in the morning and have regular school activities for the day, except to spend the few hours in T&G. Our thinking was that school is the main experience of children in this society, and it would be good for them to know what it was about, get to know the ropes, maybe meet children their age, and give us a day off.
>
> Jed and Hannah's initial reaction was extremely negative. The first Monday morning we woke them at 6:30 they began to fuss, whine, fight with us and each other, couldn't eat, didn't have anything to wear, and made us all miserable. The first Mondays they attended were all like this before school, although they always came home saying they had had a good day. Neither of them liked getting to school early.
>
> I started driving them Monday mornings so they could arrive just as class started rather than having to wait in the cafeteria, and they both appreciated that. Also they kept having good days and would come home full of tales of everything their teachers had said, how someone got in trouble and had to stand in the corner, a question they answered right.... the usual school stories. However, the whining and complaining kept up, beginning Sunday afternoon, about how tomorrow was Monday, their day of torture, and we were so mean making them go to school. They are both very adept at argument and brought out all the reasons why home school was superior, how they hadn't learned anything, and now they had learned their way around at school as we had wanted, so they didn't need to go any longer.
>
> Finally, about Thanksgiving, I said, "Okay, we certainly won't make you go to school. It's up to you. Go or don't go. Just stop complaining about it all the time. You know you always say you had a great day when you get home." Since then they've been going every Monday. Occasionally they forget and complain out of habit, but we remind them that it's up to them. (However, I think that if we hadn't encouraged them to go until they were somewhat familiar, when we left it

up to them they would have quit right off. I think.)

On Thanksgiving, though, when we were saying what we were thankful for, they both said they were thankful they only had to go to school one day a week. If they've learned anything of importance at school, that's it: what school's like. They are comfortable at the school building, know and are known by children their age, feel more a part of the general community. They are accepted now, no longer new kids, and many of their classmates envy them their freedom. Wally and I really enjoy our day of freedom also, though by 4 p.m. we are anxious to see them again.

As for scholastic matters, it has not seemed to make the slightest bit of difference.... Jed did realize that he was behind his grade level in arithmetic. (He's always refused to do any arithmetic problems, have any explained or shown to him, and if we try, has been known to throw himself over backward so he lands on his head. Still, through some sort of osmosis, he's learned a lot of math, fractions, percentages, plus arithmetic operations, but never by seeing a problem written down.) Since starting school, he asked me (!) to give him some arithmetic problems and applied himself for about a half-hour once a week for 5 or 6 weeks. At the end of that time he took the CTBS test and scored above the 90th percentile in arithmetic. Also he likes his language arts teacher so much he's learning cursive for her. These are the only academic plusses I can think of (I'm not even sure script handwriting is a plus. I'd rather see him learn to use a keyboard), but we didn't send them for academics.The academic minuses are more obvious. Hannah comes home with sheaves of paper, so much I worry about the waste. They are purple ditto sheets, copied from coloring books, or workbook pages of "reading" and arithmetic. I say "reading," in quotes, for it's a picture of a can or a boy or a ball or a nail, and the student has to pick out the right word. This, despite the fact that Hannah has been reading for more than a year. Arithmetic is the same, adding 2+3 and 3+2, though she's ahead of her brother in adding 3-figure numbers together in her head. So there's the mental waste, too. Hannah can be a dramatic and interesting artist, but her crayon pictures done at school are not even recognizable as her (or anyone's) creations—they're not creations, just scribble on the colors to get done.

Then there's the social silliness. Even in the elementary grades, the talk is all of boy and girlfriends, who do you love, and who's in love with you. My kids think this is silly, thank goodness. But it's easier for a fourth grade boy and second grade girl to pass off than it will be later. A friend, a girl, who goes to fourth grade once a week and to Talented and Gifted, has a harder time because the girls wear makeup, talk only about their boyfriends, and look down on anyone who doesn't wear designer jeans. And that means her.

Learning In Groups

From Anna Myers of the Ontario Homeschoolers Association*:*

Our homeschoolers' trips have been excellent! We've been through a cookie factory, to the theater, on nature walks through conservation areas, and to a Shakespeare play (Macbeth) at which two of the six-year-olds were enthralled! We have a hands-on program at Pioneer Village, and a cruise around Toronto harbour coming up in the future.

At the Macbeth play one of the actors travelled home to Toronto with us on the train. He followed our group in, so he could ask us how we liked the performance, and he had a captive audience for himself the whole trip home. He told us how the ghost Banquo came up and down through the floor, what the "blood" was made of, how the swords "broke," and how they made the smoke. We found out how they made the weird sisters have ugly eyes. ... They told him about homeschooling too—so he learned something that day!.

From Susan Macauley in England:

Several families home educating their children have set up a local support scheme. . . . We include children from a small working-class school, and children from the local "public" [private] schools. Adults can and do participate, too.

It consists of optional afternoon and evening activities and learning groups. Some are free, given/led by parents or friends. Some groups pay a specialist teacher (speech and drama, Shakespeare plays, music and band, craft, French conversation). The volunteer groups include an indoor swimming pool outing weekly (we now have a couple of local handicapped children coming, too), a weekly nature walk, woodwork, knitting, and arts and crafts. It is going very well. . . . It was inspired by *Instead Of Education*.

Success Stories

From Kathleen Hatley in Oklahoma:

We are a family of homeschoolers—Mom, Dad, and four sons ages 11, 7, 5, and 2. My husband and I have been interested in alternatives to formal schooling since the 1970s, when we participated in the development of an accredited University Without Walls program. Homeschooling for our children seemed a natural outgrowth of our own educational process.

We are fortunate to be living here in Oklahoma, a state which seems, at this point, to be quite sympathetic to the homeschooler. A spokesman for a large religious university here recently estimated that homeschoolers save the state $1,000,000 a year—and there is no pending legislation to regulate home schools, thanks in part, I'm sure, to the many non-regulated religious schools. We live on ten acres of rural land and run our own business, so the children have numerous opportunities for gardening, carpentry, nature study, and learning basic survival skills, as well as experiencing the family business. We pursue an experiential approach to math, utilizing many of the commercially available materials such as Cuisenaire rods, Geo-boards, pattern blocks, etc., as well as many home-made materials and games. We have also been using *The Learning Science Program*, developed by a Piaget-influenced professor here in Oklahoma, a hands-on approach to science which helps to develop scientific thinking skills. It is geared towards educators who are not science specialists, so much of it is quite useful to the parent-educator. We supplement that with work with magnets, compass, electronics boards, microscope, mechanical gadgets of all sorts, etc.

I am quite sold on the idea of letting a child's interests direct his/her learning. Last year, our 7-year-old taught himself to read fluently in a couple of months (we tossed out the basal reader in two weeks) and proceeded to spend his days devouring the World Book encyclopedia and full-length novels. He also developed an incredible interest in geography and drew over 200 accurate maps, most from memory, of every spot on the globe. These included details such as cities, rivers, mountain ranges, etc. I could relate many other instances of self-directed learning.

I meet a fair number of people who are interested in homeschooling, but their main concern seems to be the "socialization" process. I do believe in the usefulness of academic peer experiences—learning and doing together—beyond what the normal sports and play time can offer. We are very involved in a program in a nearby university town which helps to fill this gap for us—an educational enrichment cooperative. Our co-op offers workshops and classes in areas as diverse as entomology, creative dramatics, dance, the physics of music, gems and minerals, foreign languages, electron microscope, laser beams and holographs, meteorology, environmental studies, sign language, computer programming, and much much more! It is run completely by parents (mostly public schoolers) and has generated a lot of community support. . . . A lot of work is involved in getting something like this started, but it really is a good opportunity to share skills and ideas with other families (and spread the word about homeschooling in the process).

From Valerie Vaughan (MA), who wrote "Single Mother's Arrangements" *in* GWS *32:*

I have received approval from the Superintendent to teach Gabriel (6) at home '84–'85, and the support of the local elementary school principal. Boy, did I work hard, but everyone in authority was more than cooperative. I was lucky to have open-minded school authorities who appreciated my creative and assertive approach, as well as my commitment to do the job. In fact, they thanked *me* for being so cooperative!

About my present work/child care arrangements. I managed to eliminate all the driving Gabe and I were doing—it got to be too much—and for about a year we traded with parents of other kids (mostly younger kids who weren't in school or whose parents, like me, worked odd hours not 9 to 5). We have now moved a little more into the country and are living on the top floor of a farmhouse, where kids and animals abound in the neighborhood. Gabe still has a wide age range of friends (2 to 9) which I think is *fine* and really preferable to the narrow range that school and society forces on most kids.... We are still trading childcare with neighbors and friends and I still work part time, including Saturdays, when childcare is easier.... Of course in the fall, we will have to rearrange everything. Fortunately, I am leaving single parenthood soon (getting married to my employer!), so I can rearrange my work and still have financial support.

I have permission to teach Gabe pretty much the way I want to, so we start our "25 hours a week program" in September, and it includes more music and arts than is usually found in school. If anybody out there wants a copy of all the written materials I exchanged with the school authorities, I'd be glad to send it for $2.

One thing I have done is scour the local used book shops for old school books. We don't use them the way they were intended, but they make good resources, *especially* the ones from the 1920s and '30s.

I have been especially inspired by Rudolf Steiner's writings and Waldorf school materials.... This philosophy of education has much to tell us about the imagination of children, and especially an understanding of how we learn.... The Waldorf/Steiner Education Catalog is available from *St George Book Service,* PO Box 225, Spring Valley NY 10977.

Harriet Whinkey wrote in Alternatives in Education *(WV):*

Our daughter, M'Linda, is a homeschooler, using the Pensacola Christian Correspondence School curriculum.... (In September) Mr. Ronald Blankenship, Superintendent of Schools for Calhoun County, informed me that we had two options: put our daughter in public school, or take her out of state to complete the school year. Otherwise, Dane and I were looking at certain and immediate prosecution. He said that there was no nice way to put it: that we were subject to fine and/or imprisonment.

I got out *Mother Earth News,* No. 64, and at the end of their interview with John Holt found an address for Holt Associates in Boston and put through a call. Talked with Mr. Holt himself. I explained our situation to him, and he said, "Oh no, you have several other alternatives." Hallelujah! So he put me in touch with Deirdre Purdy, and she put me in touch with others. As a result of their input, I filed a request the same day with Mr. Roy Truby, State Superintendent of Schools, to operate a private school under Exemption K. At the same time I wrote Mr. Blankenship of our decision, sending him a copy of our letter to Mr. Truby. On October 20, we received Mr. Truby's letter of recognition.

I have realized my need for contact, interaction, with other homeschooling families. We had been doing our own thing, quietly, not wanting to cause the public school system any problems. But I can see now that we should have been in touch with other homeschoolers all along. I need that support, and I will be most happy to share whatever experiences we have had with others. And lastly, I feel a need to actively work for more wide-spread recognition of the legality of homeschooling. Why should we be made to feel like criminals? I'm not going to *hide* any longer!

And from Daniel Glynn (KS):

We've just completed our first year of schooling our kids at home. Actually, "unschooling" is more descriptive of what we're doing, but under current Kansas law we have to consider ourselves as operating a private, non-accredited school called "The Everyday School."

Our homeschooling experience has been very good, and we're completely satisfied with what we're doing. The year zipped by and the kids didn't miss school a bit (what's to miss?). They have their friends and are doing very well "socially," which is of course what everyone was concerned about when we told them what we were going to do. Our 6-year-old recently participated in his first public presentation ever, a piano recital; he had to face an unfamiliar grand piano in the center of the college auditorium stage in front of over a hundred parents and children. He handled it smoothly and confidently.

The other concern of people (of course) is how our son will learn to read without ever going to school. We weren't concerned, and he has started reading without a lot of effort. The girls, 11 and 9, had attended school through 4th and 2nd grades. They both read a lot and write letters and do all kinds of projects. In other words, all three are flourishing "normally" and healthily without school. And, as all unschoolers know, our home and family life routine has been greatly simplified by getting out from under the 24 hours-a-day control exerted by the school system.

The people and school officials here are very cooperative in that they accept what we're doing. . . . I'm sure that my background and position in education helps a great deal in getting that acceptance (community college instructor of English—former high school teacher), although I know myself that degrees and certificates have no necessary connection to education.

What I did was to write a lengthy letter to the district superintendent stating our plans to homeschool, reviewing the law for him, assuring him that our decision was thoroughly researched and thought out, and asking for his passive cooperation (not for his approval or permission, neither of which is necessary). In addition, I enclosed copies of laws, attorney general opinions, and letters written by the attorney for the State Dept. of Education which, if read closely, advocate a "hands-off" policy toward sincere private, non-accredited schools. As part of my research I met with that attorney and discussed what we had in mind, and although he cannot encourage homeschooling (which by definition is not yet legal) he did suggest that we'd have no problem establishing the private, non-accredited school.

I sent the material to the superintendent in April, while our girls were still in school and well before we wanted to start official homeschooling the following August. I made it clear that one chief purpose of my letter was to *inform* him completely about our plans so he wouldn't be surprised by small-town gossip about the Glynn kids not going to school. In other words, he was the *first* to know, not the last, as happens to some superintendents.

I did not state our specific philosophy or reasons for homeschooling, which by necessity would challenge his own position. . . . The key, I think, in avoiding legal trouble is to present yourself as sincere, reasonable, thoughtful, thorough, confident, caring, and so on. Perception is everything; that is, how the homeschooling parents are *perceived by* the school figures and community people makes a great difference. And to create that perception in their minds takes some work and thought.

From A Quebec Homeschooler

Soma Morse, age 14, writes:

I've read a few issues of your newsletter and thought I'd send along a letter with my pen pal listing. I guess you could say that most of my life I have been a homeschooler. I went to kindergarten, which was a good experience for me, but then came Grade One. An awfully quick change from a "Let's have fun and learn at the same time" theme to *sit up straight, keep your mouth shut and do your work* theme. I think that's when many children lose their yearning to learn. I was then taken out of school because of transportation problems and my parents got permission to teach me at home (apparently so the town wouldn't have to fix our road so the bus could come in). So Grade 2 was homeschooling. We then moved somewhere else where I went to most of Grade 3 at an excellent school. We then moved *back* to where we were previously living and I was taught at home with books from the school, which were returned at the end of the year at the same time I took tests for the school. The school was getting about $2000 a year of which my parents did not get any.

I was taught at home like this until Grade 7, when I went to the local high school. It took me most of a year to get used to it and make friends. I passed Grade 7 with an 81% average. What had happened was that the road was fixed a bit and the bus brought in.... But unfortunately, I had to get up at 6 a.m., get ready, walk 8/10 of a mile (which under Quebec laws is legal; your walk has to be more than a mile before they will bring the bus in), then have an awful backroad 1-hour-and-40-minute bus ride.... This early-to-rise, late-to-bed with homework and whatnot made me tired but I kept on.

Then my mare Penny had a foal (Aravis). All summer holidays we got to know Aravis, then after I went back to school that fall, the foal changed gradually into a mean stubborn animal because I was not there to give her my attention and training. Around this time, the late nights and early mornings—not to mention an awful bus ride with a rude bus driver who occasionally smoked and drove too fast— got to me, so I told my vice-principal that unless they brought the bus in my drive I would not go.... The bussing boss said no, so I haven't gone since February.... It seems almost that the people who run the school did not take me seriously as they sent me a form for enrolling next year and letters saying "Soma is a responsible student, well-liked by her teachers and peers," etc., also letters saying "We think you are making a mistake." At the school there is a very high level of children who have lost their desire to learn and many kids who want to quit but their parents would kick them out of the house if they did so. I really enjoyed school while there but I couldn't handle the back and forth thing, I would be tired and grouchy. So at the point where I was thinking about refusing to go to school, I realized, "Animals or school? You can have one but not both."

So now I am *happily* training Aravis, and Penny has another on the way. Now Aravis is worth at least $400. I think I am a much happier person now that I'm not going to school. The only thing I miss is my friends and the social part of it.

California Teacher Test

In "Teacher Examinations," *GWS 37, John wrote: "It seems very likely that most homeschooling parents, if they do take these tests, will score substantially higher than most teachers in their state or area. If so, it will be hard for the schools even to claim, far less to prove, that these parents are less qualified to teach their children than 'professional teachers.'" He asked readers to let us know anything they find out about such tests in their state. A response from Sue Laurente (CA):*

I don't believe that California has or plans to give tests to teachers who already have their credentials. However, every candidate for a credential and anyone who wants to be a substitute teacher must take the CBEST (California Basic Educational Skills Test). It has three sections: reading comprehension, math, and writing. The reading section consists of paragraphs with questions about each one. The math section is pretty comprehensive and is the part that causes the most people trouble. A thorough review before the test is advisable. Those two sections are typical computer-graded multiple-choice. In the writing section, there are two topics to write about—usually one where you describe an important event or person in your life and the other where you must express an opinion and support it.

It isn't an easy test but it isn't overly hard either. If you fail one or two sections out of the three, you can take just those over again. It costs $32 and is given several times a year. Information about the CBEST can be obtained from any college or university offering teacher education courses or by writing CBEST Program, Box 1904, Berkeley CA 94701. Hope this information is of use to someone.

Teaching Is No Mystery

[JH:] The following quotes are from a letter I wrote to a magazine in reply to an article saying that teaching should be more "professional." They may be of use to readers who meet that argument:

> Teaching is not, ought not to be, and cannot be made to be a mystery, in [the article writer's] words, "a body of knowledge which its members alone possess." It is a timeless and universal human activity, something we all do throughout our lives in all our relations with other humans. This is not to say that some people don't do it better than others, or that people cannot learn—almost entirely from experience—to do it better. In this respect it is perhaps akin to cooking. There is indeed a considerable body of knowledge about cooking, but it was not created in and cannot be confined in *schools of cooking*. By study and practice you can learn to be an expert cook, and you don't have to go to a school to do it—indeed many expert chefs are self-taught. The same is true and will always be true of teaching.
>
> The most important thing any teacher has to learn, not to be learned in any school of education I ever heard of, can be expressed in seven words: *Learning is not the product of teaching.* Learning is the product of the activity of learners, who, beginning at birth, create knowledge from experience in exactly the way scientists do, by observing, wondering, theorizing, and testing and refining their theories, which is how children learn to crawl, walk, talk, and so on. Only when we understand that this is true can we begin to understand in what ways outsiders, whether parents, paid teachers, or whatever, can best support this learner-initiated and learner-controlled activity.

Certificates & Teacher Quality

In GWS 30, John pointed out that many prestigious private schools do not necessarily hire teachers with state certificates, and that this fact could help those homeschoolers who were challenging a teaching credential requirement in their state. On this subject, Eleanor Siegl (WA), director of the Little School near Seattle, wrote:

Washington State does, indeed, have a law requiring that all teachers in both public and private schools be certified by the state. Passed in 1910, the law as it pertains to private schools was rather lenient, since the state was reluctant to take on the Catholic Church which for a long time provided the only private schools. In recent times, however, the office of the State Superintendent of Public Instruction has included the certification of teachers in its "compliance" requirements for state recognition of a private school.

Some of the Pacific Northwest Association member schools have taken exception to the certification requirement, feeling that experts in specific subject areas who may be PhDs or people with practical experience could well be better qualified to teach than certified teachers, many of whom are admittedly limited in their scope.... Consequently, PNAIS formed a committee to try to break down the narrowness of interpretation of "What is a qualified teacher?" I'm enclosing a copy of Dan Ayrault's paper. It received polite attention and little response but efforts are continuing.

———

[DR:] *Some excerpts from the paper by Dan Ayrault:*

> *Statement To Commission On Schools Of The Northwest Association Of Schools And Colleges*

On behalf of the Pacific Northwest Association of Independent Schools (PNAIS)

December 5, 1982

Over the years we have frequently been asked at these meetings why independent schools do not have all faculty certified. In addition to the matter of state laws, isn't it obviously desirable for teachers to have formal pedagogical training before they begin teaching?

We must be candid to say that our schools have simply not observed over the years a strong correlation between effectiveness of student learning, or even the quality of instruction on the one hand, and the possession of a teaching certificate on the other. This is different from saying that a correlation does not exist, because the numbers we deal with are small. Nor does it suggest that we mean to be contemptuous of state laws regarding certification. We simply find that some of our strongest teachers are certified while some are not, and some of our average or unsatisfactory teachers are certified while some are not. Generally we consider the certificate to be a neutral to somewhat positive element within our perception of a candidate's qualifications, but we definitely place it in a subsidiary category, well below such factors as integrity, maturity, a genuine interest in young people, enthusiasm, energy, curiosity, intelligence, strong academic scholarship, commitment to high standards, an alert sensitivity to other people young and old, and that elusive quality of personality that permits some adults to establish potent and influential relationships with young people.

These elements . . . are so compellingly important. . . . that we are reluctant to limit our capacity to secure the strongest possible combination of such qualities. The pool of human beings who possess these qualities in abundance is limited; we believe a pressing responsibility to students and to their parents is to draw into teaching those people who in our honest, professional judgment offer the greatest potential. Indeed, because no one is required to attend our schools, we will not long have students unless we perform this function thoroughly and well. We are aware of no data to give us assurance that restricting our teacher search to credentialed candidates only would improve the quality of instruction in our schools. In fact, when we look around our schools our own experience declares otherwise.

It would be foolish not to acknowledge that the strong people we seek to attract into teaching do arrive with some ideas about the principles behind effective or ineffective instruction. They do not start from scratch. The Stanford School in Redmond, which specializes in work with students who have problems which hinder optimal learning. . . . finds most graduates of teacher certification programs trained to be good "classroom managers." The Stanford School believes that the concept of classroom management, the attitudes which lie behind this, will actually hinder the kind of instruction they believe most effective with their students. The number of teachers they hire is small enough so that the only practical approach is to train their own teachers. (It is interesting to note that various school districts currently contract with the Stanford School to provide schooling for some of their students. This indicates a belief that learning for these special students is more effectively accomplished in the Stanford School's setting, despite the fact that not all Stanford teachers are certified. . . .)

The example above suggests that another possible route to "credentialing" would be to determine if the results of a given school are effective. (It is only indirectly to that end that the credential of an individual teacher is relevant.) Such an assessment may not always be clear, but where the results do appear to be demonstrably good, through test data or incremental progress measures, for example, or through the kind of on-site periodic evaluations conducted by the NW Association or the PNAIS, then, if requested, certification might be waived as moot.

Advantages Of Homeschooling

Sharon Griffith (IN) spoke about homeschooling to a college education class and also a meeting of interested people, and sent us a copy of her outline, notes, and other written material. Two of her lists that readers may find useful for their own writing and discussions:

Advantages Of Homeschooling

1. Freedom to pursue curiosity and interests (prevents "burnout"—turnoff to learning).
2. Time to treat all questions seriously and find answers (low student-teacher ratio is key).
3. More opportunity for personal verbal interactions.
4. Formal education can be introduced at the "right" time (readiness is extremely variable).
5. Prevention of sex discrimination (especially for boys at school entrance age, and because of favoritism of teachers for girls).
6. Freedom to pursue learning at own rate and ability to capitalize on individual differences (students are not *pushed* or *held back*).
7. Harmony of values—security.
8. Provides incentive and encouragement to discover life work (by experience with real world).
9. Time for fantasy and private times.
10. Atmosphere of confidence and trust.
11. Provides access to *real* world. Encourages *doing*. Learning has real purpose.
12. Protects from overstimulation. School takes up too much time and energy (which is not effectively used there). Free time not spent recovering from the overstimulation of school.
13. Produces happier, more inquisitive human beings and happier families (is *"family* saving").
14. Provides best atmosphere (conditions) for acquiring a good sense of self-worth, competence, independence, sensitivity, sense of humor—to deal with the realities of life.
15. Provides opportunity for self-evaluation on basis of progress, potential and mastery.

Our Goals

a. To promote good health practices: good nutrition, ample rest, exercise (in order to encourage physical readiness to learn with a clear alert mind).

b. To provide a pleasant learning environment: proper light, fresh air, comfortable temperature, comfortable furnishings, reasonable order, emotional stability.

c. To maintain consistent, loving discipline.

d. To foster motivation—by providing a wide variety of opportunities for study, within and without a basic framework of fundamental areas and encourage learning by doing.

e. To evaluate readiness for various tasks according to knowledge of changing physical, social, mental and moral development of the child.

f. To learn *with* them and enjoy their discoveries and achievements.

g. To provide a schooling experience uniquely compatible with our spiritual values and philosophy of education.

h. To provide the time for our children to develop their "consuming" or special interests—without necessitating a harried lifestyle.

i. To meet the need for active learning from real life situations and to provide a place where learning is not separate from the rest of life.

j. To provide for "mastery learning" (measuring own progress and achieving a competence level), thus eliminating grade competition, and providing a solid base for future learning.

All of the above should encourage the child to love sincerely (God and man), adopt a healthful life style, work responsibly, communicate clearly, enjoy beauty, reason perceptively, conduct personal business prudently, and relate intelligently to the environment.

The Role Of The State

[JH:] This excerpt from my testimony in February before a joint hearing of the Education Committees of the Virginia legislatures makes some points that I think we would be wise to make, in one form or another, in all legislative hearings:

> I would like to thank you, first of all for making it possible for me to testify at these hearings, but more importantly, for all the hard work that you have done on this legislation. It is not easy in this matter to reconcile the legitimate but conflicting Constitutional claims of parents and the state, and I congratulate the delegates for the skill with which they have addressed this difficult task.
>
> The argument is sometimes made that regarding the education of children the state has no rights, and that parents who wish to teach their own children for reasons of religious conviction can do what they like. I respect those who make this argument, but I disagree with it. In the first place, the United States Supreme Court has ruled many times that the states do in fact have a constitutional interest in the education of children. In the second place, even if this were not the law, I would say that it ought to be. Homeschooling seems to me an excellent idea, with an excellent track record; but even the best ideas have possibilities of mis-use and abuse, and children have the right as citizens to be protected against these. As we reject the claim, which some school authorities have frequently and publicly made, that children are the property of the state, to do with what it likes, so we must reject equally the claim that they are the property of their parents, to do with what they like. Children, by virtue of being American citizens, have important rights of their own, including the right of access to useful information, and these rights the state is morally bound to protect.
>
> Let me say again that the delegates have done a commendable job at the difficult task of reconciling these conflicting rights and duties of parents and state.
>
> In conclusion I would like to say in guiding homeschooling, the Commonwealth will best serve its interests and those of its children by guiding with a very light rein. Time has shown that the overwhelming majority of homeschoolers, whatever may be their educational background, are conscientious and capable and do an excellent job of teaching their own children. Time has also shown that in doing so they use a very wide variety of curricula, timetables, methods, materials, and means of evaluation, according to the needs and learning styles of their children. The Commonwealth would be wise, in whatever ways it can, to protect and encourage this pedagogical diversity, not least of all because from it may well come many ideas that can prove very helpful to the schools themselves, which for many years to come most children will continue to attend.

Main Source Of Income?

A letter from Cincinnati:

I am single and have no children and desire to use my teaching certificate to help homeschoolers. I would also like to make this my main source of income. Please send me any information about the successes and failures of teachers who are trying to do this. Is it economically feasible?

Donna wrote in reply:

Glad to hear you want to help homeschoolers. As of yet, we have never heard of anyone whose main source of income was helping homeschoolers. But there's always a first time. In the five years I've been here, we've gotten several letters like yours and I have sent the people ideas and asked them to let me know if they have any success. I can't remember hearing from any of those people again.

Some of your options. To start (or join) an alternative school, and help homeschoolers on the side. This is what a number of people have done, like Ed Nagel, Pat Montgomery, Liz Prohaska and so on—see our "Helpful Private Schools" list in *GWS* 36. Pat Montgomery, who also heads the *National Coalition For Alternative Community Schools* (1289 Jewett St, Ann Arbor MI 48104) would probably be the best person to consult about this.

Or, there are home-bound teachers employed by school districts. There are even some private tutoring agencies, though we never hear much from these, either—I've asked them how they work. I believe there are some on our "Certified Teachers" list (*GWS* 36).

Or, if you are willing to live in the country, with a homesteading type family, teaching/take care of children in exchange for room and board, there have been a number of people who have offered such situations. You'd have to be flexible—willing to go where the work is. There was even someone who wanted a helper on their ocean-going sailboat (*GWS* 35).

You could try asking some of the people listed in our "Certified Teachers" column if they have earned any money by being on there. A few of them may have.... We'd be interested in hearing about this if they did.

Beyond that, I'm not sure. To make money, you have to offer some sort of service that someone is willing to pay for, and the whole idea of homeschooling is that parents can do it *themselves*, without paying anybody. Talk with homeschoolers in your area, and see if you can put your finger on some sort of need that they would be willing to pay for—someone to take the kids off their hands for a day, or someone to provide educational materials, or some kind of legal security.

Good luck. You may have to come to the same wrenching decision that thousands of others of us former teachers have done, namely, that the direction of your life may have to be in something not involving teaching, formally, at all. What John always advises people who want to work with children is, find some kind of *real work* to do, something that needs doing in the world, and after you get into that, find a way to involve children in it, too.

Do let us know how things go.

Montessori: Philosophy Vs. Practice

From a Virginia reader:

I am deeply interested in Maria Montessori's philosophy, which I don't feel is very much at odds with Mr. Holt's. I am reading all her books right now and visited the most recent Montessori Education Center here. I expected to be completely captivated by the school and feel that my children would be very deprived if they didn't go.... I was relieved to find my children would not be missing a thing by staying home with me until they were five.

They allowed me to observe the classes in progress and I got the immediate impression that many of these children were unhappy. I had children come up to me (at least 10) asking whose mommy I was, etc. I was in another classroom where six children were clinging to the teacher as she walked around the room. I was appalled by the attitude of the teacher and especially the teacher's assistant. The teacher continually singled out one or two children for chastisement for rudeness, etc., in a loud voice. Incidentally, this particular school is one of the most expensive private schools in the area.

From another VA parent:

I found a Montessori school which at least seemed a little better than most preschools. At least no one talks *at* the kids all morning! For sure my son was intimidated the first year—so many *neat* things in the classroom, but you have to know *just* how or else! He also lost much of his incredible fantasy play capacity. He was in from October till April when I could stand it no longer. I took him out.

My older two have had two years of traditional school and one or two of Montessori. They despise it. They still score very highly (for what it's worth) on achievement tests, but who *cares*? They hate it.

And from Penny Barker (OH), a former Montessori teacher:

I think the Montessori philosophy, with its respect for the child, awakening of the senses, correction of error in the material, and the orderly environment, is a very good basis for child rearing. I have my doubts about the timing of the sensitive periods, the need for the specific Montessori materials, and the preschool environment. I have found from experience that there is a much greater range to the sensitive periods in all given areas than 3–6 years. I feel the materials are beautiful, but they take the child's focus of attention from the natural world around him and place it on these *objects*. Most all of the subject areas can be given to the child without *any* of the materials.

As far as preschool, I feel that what Dr. Montessori did in Italy with the slum children (bringing them away from their immediate families) may have been good in that particular situation of working mothers, unsanitary living conditions, great poverty. But somehow in America, bringing all these little ones away from mothers, fathers, siblings, and full environment into a classroom setting where there is only a *limited* amount the children can do with the available materials is unnecessary and stifling.... Sending them to school at 3 begins the early dependence on the peer group as well as taking them out of a world where life is really going on and putting them in a building where only a very small part of life is going on and it is not *real* but "set up" for them, thus beginning their first step in alienation from reality. For many children, once they are in a setting with a great number of peers they never again feel comfortable without it—they long for it when not in it and have a feeling of missing out—they may even feel off-balance or out of sorts when not with a group.

I know of a 4-year-old whose mother is an artist and pianist and whose father is a poet and stone worker; she has a baby sister and they live in a beautiful rural valley with woods and stream nearby. This little girl cries when taken away from the presence of other children and so the mother will spend 50 minutes driving away from the beautiful valley, away from the pastures, woods, and streams, into a town where her daughter can spend her afternoon in a building with other children. At home the mother will be painting, playing Bach, working in the garden, tending the baby; Father will be writing, pruning trees, and gathering stone. But the little girl will be with a teacher (who would probably rather be somewhere else) coloring in papers the teacher hands out. I really don't think it would be much better for her to be building a tower of graded cubes (in a Montessori school). Her home environment seems so much richer.

On Kids And Work

From Karen Schadel (NY):

We went strawberry picking at a local farm. I had been told it would be best not to bring the children, but I knew Joshua (7) and Seth (6) would want to be included—Sadrah, too, but the sight of a 2½-year-old might make them too nervous. Thinking it would be best to take them separately, I first took Joshua with me and on my next picking Seth went along. No one said anything further about the presence of children, and I was especially careful to explain where walking was permitted and how to remove only the ripened berries from the plants. They both were dedicated and serious pickers who attended to the business of berry-gathering right alongside me on an equal level. They knew of the owner's request to leave them at home when I came picking and maybe this inspired them to do an especially good job to show that children can be as responsible and careful as most adults are.

We found a similar thing to be true when it came time to start garden preparations. They were all ready and at my elbow as I started the indoor plants and began planning where everything would go in the garden. They seemed so interested that I decided they should have their own garden space. They were given seeds and helped with picking stone and other garden work to ready the soil for planting. I explained that I would answer any questions they might have, show them how something was planted if they wanted, and make suggestions only, but would not nag them to weed, water, or anything that would take away from the pleasure I wanted them to have in growing their own gardens. They loved the idea and were very careful to follow planting directions and plan what to plant where, and how much space to save for later plantings, etc. They have been exceptionally attentive to their gardens—even Sadrah, who decided she must be in on the act. Just the other day they proudly picked their first bowl of peas and posed for a photograph. They are now anxiously awaiting their squash and cucumber blossoms and plan to grow a cucumber in a bottle and carve their names on small pumpkins and watch them grow.

All three of them dug and dug and dug with their father as he prepared a deep trench to start an asparagus bed. Again they worked right beside him, doing the same heavy work and keeping right up with him. They are always at their best in these situations—more agreeable, less argumentative, more open and communicative and seem freer and happier than at other times.

Mimi Wagner, whose family is in the Middle East, wrote in Western PA Homeschoolers #8:

> Since funds are a bit tight this year, Jon, Damon and I started working at the American school store 1½ hours a day. It's kind of like a home-business having the kids there. Jon (7) has become very good at making change (real life math) in the local currency, Bahraini Dinar. I never taught him how or what the different bills and coins represented. I only answered his questions. After we'd worked there for about six weeks he just started handling customers, with confidence no less. He knows the entire inventory of the store and is very quick to answer questions of prices, sizes, colors. He's quite proud of himself (and he should be) especially when now and again one of his peers comes to buy something and is amazed to find that Jon *really works* there, and is not just doing what I tell him to.
>
> Damon (3) is in charge of giving out the indicated "granola snack," usually asked for by color, of which we carry 15 different kinds. As in Jon's case, I never taught Damon what the colors were, or the flavors for that matter. One day after we'd been working there for about three weeks, he just decided that that was his job and no one else had better try and take it from him! He has proven himself worthy of the position. I might add that he did not know the names of colors before we started the job and was a bit shy with strangers. Not so anymore! Damon has also designated himself the official "ice-cream-spoon-giver-outer." Both Jon and Damon also have decided that they *do not* need or want my help with restocking these items. Damon likes sorting the money in the cash box as well (coins: small, medium, and large; bills: red, purple, blue, green, pink). It's been a good experience for us all.

Fun, Not Extraordinary

Margaret Davis (WA) wrote:

Several of the stories in *GWS* made me feel at times that maybe I should expect more from our boys. Our guys do not make computer programs (we don't have a computer), they do not make music (we have a piano, pump organ, guitar, banjo just because I like them) or write plays (I can't get them to write more than a thank-you to grandparents), no scientific experiments or signs of budding genius. But they can tell you how our farm is run much better than I can at times. They can list off weeds, crops, what was damaged by what (insect, weather, chemicals), what should be done and when and why. They care for their livestock—small flock of chickens and rabbits. They are fun to be around.

Our curriculum is very relaxed and for us it works best. We do the regular school book work in the morning—math, English, printing, whichever school book grabs their interest at that time. If none does, I grab them and say "Do it," so we aren't real lax. Then at noon they escape outside, from then on our day is very free. We all read something. The old *Book of Knowledge* of Dad's is great for interesting talks. We branch off from the moon to history to poetry. . . . I have learned to let them find out on their own. If we stick with one particular subject it seems like it doesn't stay stuck for very long.

I guess what I'm trying to say is for others not to feel they have to be outstanding. Like we tell our kids, they are outstanding in their field—it's corny, especially if they are in the wheat field at the time. It has taken two years for our older boy Justin to be fun to be around again. A friend says she thinks he's something else. He is funny. Our youngest, Ethan, only went to kindergarten so does not have a lot of hang-ups to get rid of, and it's fun to watch and be part of his learning. What they know, they know because it is important for them and our living. Have we finally become real homeschoolers? I think so. It's a wonderful feeling to be friends with your kids.

Mom Keeps Busy

Madalene Murphy (PA) wrote in the Western PA Homeschoolers:

> A discovery it took me almost two years of homeschooling to make: whenever the kids are working at something that requires my presence to answer an occasional question or simply to provide moral support, I have to have something to keep *my* hands busy so I stay out of their work except when they need or want me. Sometimes this can be accomplished while I am doing kitchen work, if the project lends itself to the kitchen floor or table. But I must be doing something that tolerates frequent interruptions or I will end up getting more frustrated instead of less. I started doing some quilting this year and have found that it fits the requirements of the situation perfectly. So I'm getting a lot of practice at something I enjoy doing and at the same time can sit benignly while Christian ponders the spelling of a word in a letter he's writing or Emily tries to figure out the sales tax on something she wants to buy or Clare tries for the fifteenth time to build a house by standing the orange Cuisenaire rods on end, and I never—well, at least a lot less than I used to—offer any of those "helpful hints" that would usually only interrupt their train of thought.

Being Flexible With Calvert

From Luella Porter (IN):

I've read comments in *GWS* about how Calvert is too regimented and petty, but I disagree. Any program has to be adjusted to the child's needs and interests in order to work well. The Calvert "teacher's manual" says the same thing. From the kindergarten manual:

> These subjects are to be approached experimentally and tentatively. As you will see when you encounter them in the daily lessons, they are to be used in accordance with the response of each individual child.

I wonder if people are afraid to change the program around to suit the child. Maybe our own school training makes us feel we must accept it as is or reject it altogether.

On days when we do Calvert, we do about a week's worth, so I plan the group of lessons so we can do them in blocks of each subject. Since nobody wants to stop something that is fun, we plunge way ahead in some lessons. We skip the parts Meredith (3) already knows (most of it) so we move *fast* through the course. Yet having the program gives us plenty of new ideas and things to do.

And I do mean *us*. I am having a great time doing this with her, making up poems, pasting, painting, coloring, collecting spiders (I always wanted to do that), and much more. From a selfish point of view, homeschooling has given me the excuse to relearn Spanish, play the piano, and never feel guilty for not being out there holding an office job. Life is good and getting better every day.

The point is, Calvert is what you make it, and its general acceptance by schools makes its use worthwhile to us. Besides, we like it.

Violence Against Children

[JH:] Many of you have written us about the cruelty and violence in schools, of children against children and of children and adults against each other. Why is there so much of it? A column by

Anne Taylor Fleming in the Sept. 5 *Boston Herald* points to at least one of the answers. She writes:

> Recently roaming the California coast for a week in a car.... my husband and I were struck by some of the behavior and habits of our fellow travelers. First off, there seems to be not a man or woman motorist anymore without a bumper sticker declaring his or her love for this or that, for a certain religion or radio station or baseball team or bar, even. "I Love Jesus," "I Love LA," "I Love Cats"—the freeways are now full of such protestations.
>
> (But) wherever we went, on whatever beach we walked, there were beer cans and bottle tops and potato chip bags left willy-nilly, a veritable carpet of trash.
>
> Even harder to imagine, and the most troubling thing we saw on our random journey, is how tough so many parents are on their children. I'm not talking about child abuse in the strict sense, rather about something more subtle but no less damaging. We were unhappy witnesses to countless scenes in which an angry parent harshly rebuked or yanked a young child barely more than a baby—from his or her seat for no more than accidentally tipping over a glass of milk.
>
> So much anger, so much of it directed at the young. The adults did sometimes verbally bristle at each other, but the brunt of their angers fell on the children.
>
> We were moving mostly through small seaside towns, rural-suburban places where most of the mothers were plump and young.... Their equally young husbands, prematurely beer bellied, many of them, seemed so obviously wistful. Young couples feeling locked in, looking as if they feel locked in, their children the most obvious reminder of just how locked in.
>
> We were vacationing, as I said, in small towns, in modest motels, among people obviously of limited resources, and the level of just general rage on the streets was palpable. And more often than not the children were the unwitting targets of the rage, as I suppose in a way were the beaches themselves. But it was the children, so many of their faces in a kind of pre-cringe, who provided such an odd juxtaposition to all those bumper stickers proclaiming all that love.

[JH]: In the '50s and '60s, supposedly for most people a more hopeful and happy time than today, I drove alone many times from the East coast to Colorado and New Mexico, going either to the school in Colorado where I taught for four years, or to New Mexico or Colorado to visit my sister and her family. It was summertime, and the highway restaurants where I stopped for gas and a bite to eat were full of the kinds of young families Anne Fleming writes about, on their way to and from national parks or visits with grandparents or whatever—anyway, on vacation, supposedly having a good time. I was appalled to see how harsh, angry, and violent many of them were with their children, shouting at them, threatening them, giving them peremptory orders (they would not have talked to their dog in such a tone of voice), pulling them this way and that and even striking them, for the most trivial of offenses or in many cases no offense at all that I could see. Even allowing for the fact that long automobile trips with children can be wearing, and may not show families at their best, the amount of anger and violence that I saw was surprising and distressing. It put into my mind the thought, which many years of further observation have only strongly confirmed, that large numbers of Americans do not like children, including, or perhaps especially, their own.

And it was then, driving in the beautiful mountain country of Colorado and New Mexico, that I first noticed motorists throwing trash and garbage, often great bags of it, out their car windows as they drove along, and realized that this kind of needless defacing of the landscape was not an act of carelessness but of anger and aggression, someone saying to an Invisible but always present Other, "There, you -----, take that!" If you can't hit your real enemies, next best thing is to hit whoever's handiest, and for that purpose children are ideal. The 9/5/83 issue of *Time* has a long cover story about violence within the family, of husbands against wives (and, occasionally, the reverse), and both of them against children. This tragic and horrifying problem is growing worse, as it always does in bad times, when people worry themselves sick about their jobs, their bills, their future.

At any rate, this habitual verbal and/or physical violence by adults against children is surely one of the root causes of violence by children in school, and one for which the schools themselves bear no responsibility at all. Children who have been cruelly treated tend to treat others cruelly, for three reasons; they have learned the habit, they want revenge, and they have so little sense of their own worth that they can only make themselves feel a little better, briefly, by making others feel even worse. To this cause of violence and cruelty we must add two others which are the responsibility of the schools, and which tend to make what could be (as Dennison, Herndon, and many others have shown) a manageable problem into an unmanageable one. The first is that they set the children against each other in an endless competition for a very (and deliberately) limited supply of adult approval and rewards. There are only enough carrots for a few; the rest get the stick, of punishment, humiliation, failure. The result, as an all adult societies of extreme scarcity, is that many children, even those not normally cruel, in their great need to be one of the few winners, their fear of being a loser, and the envy, resentment, and anger they feel for the obvious or even potential winners, behave badly. The second is that far too many adults in schools dislike, distrust, and above all fear children, and treat them with what Charles Silberman called "appalling incivility," and even outright violence. What was even before school a vicious cycle of fear and cruelty begins to wind down ever more steeply.

What this means for homeschoolers is that the social life of schools, already in most places bad or intolerable, is almost certain to get even worse, so that it becomes even more important for us to keep our children out of it and to find or make for them some healthier and more natural alternative.

Maple Syrup Adventure

From Karen Schadel (NY):

This spring we decided rather suddenly and unpreparedly that we were going to make our own maple syrup. The entire process, from the time the idea came to us until we were finished, was one of the neatest times we've had. It was a real family project with all of us joining together to make it happen.

We began by noticing that others had already hung their sap buckets, and wondered if we could do it, too. We stopped and gathered some information and ideas by just simply chatting with people who were doing it on a small-scale/backyard basis. Next, a trip to the library gave us bulletin information printed by the Cooperative Extension from the vertical files, and several books including *The Maple Sugar Book* by Helen and Scott Nearing, a book in the juvenile section titled *Maple Sugar For Windy Foot*, and a photo/descriptive one called *Sugaring Time*. The blending of the real with the fictitious was perfect and we were really getting ready!

Through a series of phone calls, one to our local Co-operative Extension division, we learned of a nearby sugar house and a not-so-nearby supplier of sugaring items. A "field trip" to the sugar house gave us an idea of how it is done on a large scale and some pointers, but basically left us feeling like it might be too much for us to handle. But we were too far into the idea to turn back.

The weather turned cold and the first early sap run was over. On a blizzard-type day we got into the car and searched through the blowing snow to find the sugaring supplier. We wanted to be ready for the next run! We purchased what we needed and also looked around at the big evaporators and elaborate supplies used by syrup/sugar makers who do this as a business.

It seemed like the more reading we did and knowledge we acquired, the more confusing it became. It had seemed fairly simple at first, but was appearing more and more like a very skilled process that we weren't knowledgeable enough to do on our own. Then I realized the description *sounded* complicated, such as the directions for tying your shoes would if written down and you'd never done it before yourself or seen it done. So we decided to keep going and not give up, but just do one step at a time.

We borrowed a brace and purchased a standard bit for drilling the holes, but next came the tree identification. Without the characteristic maple leaf, many of them appeared the same to us, and with time running short (we just didn't want to miss the next run as the suspense was building in all of us as to whether we could really do this) we didn't want to spend time studying books to help us identify the maples by bark and shape, so we sought the help of a neighbor who pointed out our sugar maples to us.

We decided we'd carry the sap down to the house and keep the sugaring nearby so it could be watched more carefully. The wood supply became a lot of the scraps and old lumber that had cluttered our property when we bought it. Initially we cursed all of it for its untidy appearance, and had said it must all go! But now we look at each piece of wood and item of "junk" in a new light and wonder what we can use it for. With these decisions made we tapped our first tree and applauded ourselves—except no sap came to the end of our plastic spile—too cold yet!

My husband had come up with our collection system which consisted of plastic spiles connected to about a yard of plastic tubing that was inserted to the cap of a plastic cider/milk jug that had had a hole drilled into it with the brace and bit, thus creating a closed system. We also punctured tiny air vents in the handles with the point of a nail and in this way practically eliminated the concern about bugs, debris, etc.

The tapping (25 spouts) was completed on a warm sunny day, with everyone getting a chance to use the brace and bit, and the sap was running again. The kids all put their mouths right on the tap and drank the sweetness of the trees as it ran right into their tummies! Sadrah (2½) said it tasted better than breastmilk! We were all in awe of how it works and looked back for history-type information. . . . We learned the Indians were essentially responsible for its discovery.

The building of our outdoor evaporator was no simple job either, but my husband's knowledge and experience in woodstoves proved quite valuable. We constructed the firebox with cinder blocks and had a chimney with stove pipe to draw away the smoke that might otherwise flavor the syrup while it was cooking. . . . The kids helped carry buckets of sap, or cared for Sadrah while Ed and I marched up and down the hill in either snow or slippery mud (I was interested in losing weight so I welcomed the hikes, but later discovered we were eating too many pancakes and waffles for me to drop any pounds!). Joshua and Seth helped cut wood using either a bow saw or an axe and were content to spend large amounts of time "just chopping." They each had their own maple tree, now, too, and would proudly go to it at least twice daily to see how it was producing and which taps gave out more sap according to the side of the tree it was on. We began calculating how much syrup we could hope for, as one source said each tap could give as much as a quart of finished syrup—let's see. . . . 25 taps, 4 quarts in a gallon—roughly 6 gallons! It seemed too good to be true. But it takes 40 gallons of sap to produce just one gallon of syrup. We finally decided that 2 gallons would be a satisfactory and strived-for amount.

We finally had enough to start cooking. We'd read so much about what a delicate and exact process this was that we felt insecure again, although we felt ourselves already to be "experienced" in identifying trees and tapping and collecting maple sap—how quickly we learn! So, we did each step awkwardly. . . . We had to test our boiling point of water which according to our elevation (or maybe just the thermometer we used) was 5 degrees lower than the 212 degrees usually known as the boiling point. We discussed all this and related it to the fact the sap becomes syrup when it reaches 7 degrees above the boiling point of water. Then we made our first *small* quart of backyard syrup! Although it didn't taste like commercially produced syrup, it was still sweet, amber-colored, and tasty, and it flavored our whole-wheat waffles and pancakes with a wonderful maple taste that we all loved!

We had bought a maple candy form so we went right into maple candy production. The kids loved it and the special shapes were a real treat. Maple candy, we learned, can be cooked too far past the syrup point, resulting in a scorched, cement-like ending. One batch was ruined and we grieved over it since so much effort had been necessary to reach that point and it seemed wasted. But we continued with the syrup production—collecting, cooking, eating, and gaining more confidence and experience with each batch. In the end we believe our total to be around 5 gallons of syrup, but we ate too much to have an accurate amount. But we do have jars of golden syrup on our pantry shelves, awaiting the winter months.

When I look back at all we did, realize the many areas the children were exposed to—the "field trips," library visits, communications with experienced individuals (social skills), ratios, weights and measurements, fractions, temperatures, recycling and so much more. And I also remember thinking that had they been in school they might have missed a large amount of this *as had I when I grew up. My family made maple syrup every spring,* but due to my school attendance was a passive observer and knew almost nothing more than that buckets hung on trees collecting sap and you cooked it and ate it.

Family Backpacking Trip

Penny Barker (OH) wrote:

Our three-week backpacking trip in the Chisos Mountains of Texas was a wonderful experience for us all.... Waking very early in the mornings and with no timepiece, we learned to tell the time by the exact position of the Big Dipper and Orion. We packed in our own food but did eat the pads and fruit from the prickly pear cactus and the pinon nuts from the pine trees. Our five-year-old, Jonah, became especially adept at getting the fruit of the prickly pear with knife and pliers without getting the painful cactus hairs in his fingers.... The children became very aware of the absence of water and what makes a desert a desert. They all rejoiced when we found a mountain spring dripping water. By counting and filling a container they learned how to figure the flow rate of the water as well as a good deal about patience.

Everyone was able to carry part of our gear. Jonah (5) and Ben (7) were able to carry 7–10 lb. packs, Dan (9) and Maggie (10) carried 15–18 lb. packs; Britt (15) carried about 25 lbs. and Richard and I were able to carry 35 to 50 lb. packs. Everyone realized how important their part of the load-carrying was to the entire group since items were divided up into groupings of use and the only individual items each carried was his washrag, toothbrush, and sleeping bag.

Group Nature Walks

Jean Tibbils (219 Harvard St, Cambridge MA 02139) wrote:

Mary Maher (MA) said that you wanted to know what the response was to her article in *GWS* 37 about the homeschooling natural science class. We've had a new class going since April 3; it meets once a week. There are 17 children and adults in the class, and the kids are ages 3½, 6, 7, 8, 9, 9, 10, 11, 12, 13 and 14.

The kids get along well and *really* appreciate the social aspects of the group, as do the parents. I thought that such a large group might scare off the wildlife, and it does, but this is compensated for by the extra eyes and ears for finding wildlife in the first place. Most of the people keep some form of journal. I think the favorite activities so far (other than tree-climbing and picnicking) have been rescuing goldfish trapped in trenches that are slowly drying out and looking at tiny pond animals through a $2.50 field microscope. The goldfish are huge—one was 9" long. The group is large and only those individuals who stick right by me "get" everything, but I think this works out fine.

I'd like to continue this next year, but don't know how to publicize it. It costs each person less per hour than group art or music lessons, and everyone seems to *love* it.

Free Nature Posters

From Linda Butler (UT):

We picked up several great posters from a local office of the Forest Service. They're large and have pictures of fish, insects, flowers, animals. They were all free, and the kids (3, 1½) love them. Right now we just point out red bugs, blue bugs, ants, etc., but as they get older they can learn their names if they so desire. If you don't live near an office, perhaps you could write to one in your state. They gave the kids a few Smokey the Bear trinkets and stickers which the kids liked, too.

Science That Needs Doing

These paragraphs from an article by Harvard biology professor Edward O. Wilson in Nature Conservancy News, *11/83, suggest the vast amount of true scientific research that still needs doing—and that homeschoolers might do:*

> Think of scooping up a handful of soil and leaf litter and placing it on a white cloth—as a field biologist would do—for closer examination. This unprepossessing lump contains more order and richness of structure, and particularly of history, than the entire surface of all the other (lifeless) planets. It is a miniature wilderness that would take almost forever to explore, should we choose to make the organisms in it the objects of serious biological study.
>
> Most biologists estimate that there are between three and ten million species of plants, animals, and microorganisms on Earth. But there are additional sound reasons, based on new data from tropical forests, to place the figure at closer to 30 million. In fact, the exact number cannot even be guessed because, incredibly, most species have yet to be discovered. Among those already classified, no more than a dozen have been studied in as much detail as the fruit fly, the horse, or maize. And experts are quick to point out that the biology of even these paradigms remains poorly explored.
>
> The accelerating destruction of natural habitats and the extinction of species is eliminating important opportunities for future biological research. We are rapidly narrowing not only potential scientific knowledge but also the commensurate benefits these species might have for the human race.
>
> To take a practical example, Norman Myers has estimated that societies around the world use about 7,000 kinds of plants for food and have come to depend—to a frightening degree—on about 15 highly domesticated forms. Yet at least 75,000 species exist that are edible, and even the relatively modest amount of research on plant diversity conducted thus far has revealed many among these that are potentially superior to the crop plants in prevalent use.

[DR:] This last subject, in particular, is one that *GWS* readers can explore now. For a year or so I've been using Peterson's *Field Guide To Edible Wild Plants* to gather berries, nuts, leaves, roots, and even flowers to eat, and it's been fun and satisfying. There are a number of regional field guides available to help you identify and prepare wild foods, which are not only to be found in woods and swamps, but also in cities and suburbs—probably even in your own lawn.

"Computers In Ed." Conference

From Sheryl Schuff (IN):

We attended a conference sponsored by the National Institute of Education (the research arm of the U.S. Dept. of Education) concerning the use of computers for education in the home. Stephen was invited by Tom Ascik (who learned of us through *GWS*) to participate in a panel discussion of parents explaining how they used computers with their children. All four of the panelists were involved in homeschooling to some degree. Mario Pagnoni (MA) was one of the panelists.... Although many of the attendees were parents, few were there in that capacity. Most were "educators," "administrators," "policy-makers," and computer software publishers and vendors.

The vendors publicly confirmed our thoughts that they write and sell software to make money. Their primary concern is not to produce a quality product; rather, one that will sell to the home market. They have packaging and promotion down pat and are thoroughly insulting to parents as they maintain that we don't know what type of software we need and don't have the ability to evaluate what's available. Although they agreed that there was a need for more creative software and for software specifically designed for certain audiences, e.g., functional illiterates and the physically and/or emotionally handicapped, they were unanimous in their decisions not to commit their own money to these developments because they were certain not to show enough profit.

The "educators" confirmed our worst fears of the school systems. They informed us that children are naturally inquisitive, creative, eager to learn, *until they enter school*. Then they must be "socialized," "edu-tained," grouped, labeled, and measured. There is neither the time nor the facilities to handle individual learners' needs, styles, or abilities. In the computer software area, they must use products that can be plugged in, turned on, and used by each child in his (for example) 10-minute session at the computer each week. Software that is open-ended, creative, learner-directed is not appropriate for school use, they say. It can, however, be used in a home setting where children have more time to pursue their interests without regard to the constraints that are necessary (in their opinion) in school. Unintentionally, I'm sure, they built a very strong case for homeschooling.

They also showed a great desire to control the educational computing that takes place in the home. At least one "progressive" school district is using its volume purchasing power to offer certain computers at attractive discounts to parents, but, in effect, limiting their choices of "acceptable" machines. And several parents reported incidents of schools' refusal to accept homework that had been prepared using a word processing program. Their excuse the computer had *done* the work, not the child. Unbelievable.

The pervasive tone of the conference was that "computer literacy" (however the school chooses to define it) is mandated and that the use of computers for educational purposes will solve all the current problems of the school systems. We don't agree with either of these ideas. As Stephen explained in his prepared remarks at the conference, we view the computer as just another material which we have made available to our children. It is available when and *if* they choose to use it. . . . We have tried to convey the attitude that its use is no more or less important than their books, building blocks, paints, etc. Even though we both are computer professionals (we run a consulting business), we do not think that computer programming ability is a necessary or even important skill for our children to master.

TV: For And Against

Joyce Kinmont, in her excellent magazine Tender Tutor *(2770 S 1000 W, Perry UT 84302; $9/yr) makes an interesting point about television:*

> Television, some say, robs the imagination. Television to most people means soap operas, *MASH*, and Home Box Office. There *is* very little of any real value on TV, but what is good is really good, and it enhances, complements, or stimulates the imagination.
>
> For instance, when Ritchie watched a program on monorail trains, he came away with his own idea for designing a railroad system. When the children and I read a book about a Mississippi steamboat pilot, nothing in our imaginations painted so vivid a picture as a television program about Mark Twain that we saw shortly thereafter. How can one possibly "imagine" the damages of a flood, the appearance of the Statue of Liberty, or the beauty of the Rose Parade from the written word.

From Brenda Jinkins (TN):

Although we have homeschooled for four years, the last eight months without a TV have been the best. Our old color set just faded way, and we were all watching very little upon its last gasp. Then it just naturally followed, after recuperating from surprisingly bad withdrawal symptoms, for us to do without a TV indefinitely. The emphasis on things rather than people, the repetitive negative news, and the universal themes on nearly all network programming of both emotional and philosophical cowardice come clear to us now with only occasional glimpses of the Great Time-Eater and Escape Machine.

Kids & Money

From "What Nobody Else Will Tell Your Child About Money," McCall's *magazine, 3/84:*

> *Savings*:.... As soon as a child starts to save and more than quarters are at stake, a savings account should be opened. But don't open the account *for* your child; take advantage of youthful enthusiasm and involve your child in the procedure. Just obtain a Social Security number for him or her—application forms are available at many banks and thrifts—and go in together to open the account. Tell your child what banking is all about. Explain that banks pay interest on money for the privilege of using that money, just as people who borrow money pay interest.
>
> Be sure to make it clear that banks circulate money, rather than keeping it locked up. Otherwise your child may be horrified at withdrawing a five-dollar bill instead of the five ones that were deposited. (You should, of course, permit withdrawals. If you don't, your child may become turned off to the whole idea of saving.)
>
> Once a child can sign his name, he should be eligible to open a savings account. But banks set their own rules, and some—especially larger commercial banks—may turn young children away. Others impose sizable service charges on small accounts, charges that negate the interest. Look for an institution—very likely a savings and loan or a credit union—that welcomes children and has minimal fees. At the Hi-Plains Teachers Credit Union in Plainville, Kansas, for instance, children are encouraged to come in and make their own deposits; dividends are entered in passbooks in red so the child can clearly see the interest that has been earned. There's an annual raffle, too, with a ticket issued for each five dollars saved by depositors age 16 and under. And small children are helped to count and wrap coins for their own accounts.
>
> Wherever your child saves, keep the account active, if only to record periodic interest, so that there's no risk of the money being turned over to the state. Note: Children should make out new signature cards every few years to reflect their changing handwriting.
>
> *Checking*: ... One father I know opens a checking account for his children as they reach age 12. He deposits money to cover the cost of school lunches, recreation and visits to the orthodontist. The children write the checks and—just as important—balance the checkbooks. Some parents try this approach with make-believe checks, issued in lieu of spending money. The real thing, if you can arrange it, is even better.
>
> Here, too, credit unions are in the lead. At the Educational Employees Credit Union in Fort Worth, Texas, the Buckaroos is a savings group for 7-to-13-year-olds. Members up to age 11 get a tour of the credit union and some basic money-management lessons. 12- and 13-year-olds who deposit at least $25 get a free checking account, together with an hour-long training course on how to write checks and balance a checkbook.
>
> Children of junior-high-school age can take over some of your bill-paying chores, by writing checks—for your signature—for telephone or electric bills.

The dollars-and-cents figures, in fact, will make them realize more than you could by lecturing that such services cost real money.

Investing: . . . . Why not buy one or more shares of common stock for your child, in a company he's heard of, such as Toys "R" Us? 12-to-15-year-olds might be even more interested in computer stocks.

Owning just one share entitles the child to the quarterly and annual reports, and most children love to get mail in their own name. You can also show them how to follow the stock's progress in the daily stock-market tables. And dividends can be reinvested so that statements will reflect regular additions to the account.

David Polen, president of [an] investment-advisory firm. . . . suggests that a mutual fund is preferable to individual stocks as a learning experience. "One stock could turn out to be a superstock," he notes, "or it could collapse. . . ." A mutual fund, on the other hand, represents investment in a variety of stocks and, therefore, a solid foundation of investment experience.

Whether you choose individual stocks or mutual funds, however, you'll find that a minor is not legally allowed to buy securities. You can make the purchase for your child under the Uniform Gift to Minors Act in your state. It's an easy procedure, set up by any stockbroker. . . . Just remember that, even though you are the custodian, your child is the legal owner of the account and is entitled to the money when he or she reaches legal age.

Credit: A credit union in Topeka, Kansas, has offered bicycle loans, at 8 percent, to children under 17. With a maximum loan of $200—co-signed by parents, to be repaid in one year—the Kansas Credit Union hopes to teach young people about money management while building customers for the future. . . . The youngest recipient so far is 3½.

Typewriters At Home. From Peggy Carkeet (CA):

I received *GWS* 38 recently and read "'Writing to Read' is Working" and "Typewriter is Effective" and was inspired to uncover the 1920(?) Underwood that I inherited this year from my 98-year-old grandpa. I showed it to Brent (4½), briefly explained how to load the paper, thumb space and loosen the paper. I then got out *One Fish, Two Fish* by Dr. Seuss and said, "You might enjoy practicing with this."

Brent normally is asleep by 8 or 9 p.m.. He sat for three *solid* hours last night typing out page after page from the book, then illustrating each sentence. In the morning he didn't want any breakfast, but went right to work again in his underwear from 7 a.m. until 11 a.m. when I interfered and suggested he eat and take a break. *And* he is picking up words: a, fish, red, dad.

I've tried using large flash cards to teach him to read and he gets thoroughly bored after about 10 minutes—quite a difference from 3–4 *hours*. I've always heard how *short* a child's attention span is.

From Jennifer Gemmell in Tulsa:

Following John Holt's suggestion, we bought Trahern (4) a typewriter for his birthday which we casually left on the table in his room. Eventually he began asking the names of letters as he pecked at the keys and composed sentences to send to his grandmother in Australia. Soon after that, Trahern began making books which he illustrated with scenes from Star Wars, having me write the captions which he composed. Then he decided he could write the captions himself. At first he had me write the letters on another piece of paper so he could copy them, but now I only have to spell for him as he has learned the entire alphabet. All this in the space of a few weeks and without any initiative or effort on my part.

Janet Roelle (MI) wrote:

I have been pleasantly surprised about using the typewriter with Jason (6). He had many ear infections as an infant and didn't talk between 15 months to three years, and was not understandable when he did talk. He has seen many specialists. If he were in school he would have been in the "Learning Disabled" class and have more problems (I have been encouraged by the letters in *GWS* about L.D., deafness, and Down's Syndrome). . . . J, K, A were the same to him, as were P, B, C, E, D, G, T, V, Z. After speaking with a doctor in Speech Pathology at the University of Michigan, who labels his problem as a Phonological Rule Disorder, I felt I could do what an expensive therapist could do. Also, I could do it in comfortable surroundings without the "something is wrong with you" connotation. Of course, I was told, "He may not cooperate for you as well as a therapist since you are his mother." Many people say this is a problem with homeschooling. Anyway, Jason *works* great and is proud that he can "hear" the sounds now. He still has to conquer the belief he has that something is wrong with him and he can't learn to read.

Back to the typewriter. He wants to type letters to mail for freebies, so I tell him letter by letter. He has to hear me correctly, then distinguish the letter on the keyboard. This is not a speech drill to him and he is often surprised that certain words begin with the letter they do. Contrary to the speech therapist, I felt he also needed visual cues. On the typewriter he can write several words without me spelling them. He is phonetically reading approximately 100 words. When he reads these words he says the "s" which he usually omits. He also works at "l" and "r" which are still not natural to him (developmentally, these two letters may not be correctly pronounced by any child until about 7).

Since I removed Jason from the Pre-Primary Hearing Impaired program, he has changed from an L.D. self-conscious, low-self-esteem, quiet, non-verbal child to doing 1st-grade Miquon math, reading simple words, and comfortably playing with any other boys and girls.

And At School

From a North Carolina reader:

I couldn't resist writing to you about the "Writing to Read" program using IBM computers and typewriters in kindergarten. My son was involved in the program last year and it turned out to be far from what you described in *GWS* 37 and 38. First of all, his teacher did not like the program and told everyone so. It was very regimented. There was very little freedom to write. There were 10 computer books that the children went through and had to memorize how to spell the words before they were passed to the next level. The children were very competitive to get through these books as quickly as possible. My son was very nervous the night before a test and was one of the last in the class to finish Book 10. He spent several sleepless nights afraid he could not learn to spell "uniform." His best friend was one of the top in the class as far as finishing the books went, but his mother also noticed the competitiveness and worrying.

The children did not like the typewriters after the first month. The teacher made a large chart of words for them to type. They did not know what words they were typing. They were copying! They could type their own words but few did. While helping out one day, I had to keep reminding the children to type. They would quit and just sit there. . . . We have a typewriter at home and my son likes to type at home.

The "Writing to Read" program is famous for the phonetic stories the children write. My son never wrote a story. He did write a few sentences the last two weeks of school. Some children did write stories, but certainly not all students. My son felt very dumb in this program. He has now finished first grade using a basal reading program and scored in the 75th percentile on achievement tests, so he *isn't* dumb. Next year, I understand the school system will use another reading program called "Success." This will be his third year in school and the third reading program.

Using the "Writing to Read" program took a lot of time. They worked two hours a day with the program in a lab. They did not have time for traditional kindergarten activities and my son missed out on a lot of fun things.

I think this is a prime example of a good program that doesn't work in the public schools. It would be good for homeschoolers since you would remove the competitiveness and just let them type when they wanted.

Jesse Becomes A Writer

Susan Richman (PA) wrote in the Western Pa. Homeschoolers #8:

Over the past half year, Jesse (6) has become a writer. Those of you who've received our *W. PA Children's Magazine* have read some of his stories and poems—these were all dictated, as at the time they were composed Jesse's knowledge of encoding written language was very sparse, and forming letters was slow, exacting work. For him to have written out his own pieces then would have been akin to us, as adults, having to carve our words in marble, with dull chisels at that—a pretty arduous task. Jesse dabbled some with our electric typewriter, enjoying pretending to be typing fast, enjoying typing small parts of letters he'd dictated to his "Mother/Scribe." He was completely dependent, though, on copying my written out correct spellings of words he needed. Early on he wanted his spellings to be *right*. I'd read in *GWS* about children happily "sound spelling" when they began to write on their own, and wondered if Jesse would ever take off in this way. I thought for a good while that his temperament was just averse to the idea. That has now all changed.

A bit of chronology may help put his growing in perspective. . . . In September '83, we began a few small routines that proved helpful and eventually led up to sound-spelling. Jesse and I decided that he would write out the whole alphabet each month, upper and lower case, for display in our living room. He understood that we'd be keeping these handwriting samples in our portfolio of work that we show to our school district periodically. September's alphabet was a tortuous affair. Jesse hadn't written much over the summer, and his letters were wobbly, awkward, uncomfortable for him to form. He was also severely critical of his work, would cut out any "wrong" letters and tape on a new piece of paper—the whole alphabet was a twisting segmented crumple. He kept at the job, though—the task had become self-chosen.

Then sometime that month Jesse was hanging about the kitchen table while I was cooking supper. I laid down a sheet of blank paper and suggested that he write something, anything at all, just write. He began, and by the time the stew was ready to serve he'd proudly written out several lines of wobbly print. He wrote only disconnected words, "safe" words that he was sure he knew how to spell (Mommy, Daddy, etc.).

From that night on, he wrote almost daily, and I felt progress was happening. He was growing physically more comfortable with pencil and paper, he was writing out lots *more* each day, he seemed pleased with what he was doing. Oddly, he decided that he would just keep *re*writing what he'd written the day before, maybe adding a new line, even slowly beginning to put his separate words into little sentences ("cat sat Daddy" became "the cat sat on top of Daddy"). There was some movement going on, but I could see that Jesse was grinding deeper into his rut of only using correct spellings, and so limiting terribly what he might say. He would occasionally snap, when I urged him to perhaps write something *new* as it was getting a bit boring for him to just read the same thing over and over every day, "But I'm trying to learn all these words *first* before go on to any others!" Writing was becoming mechanical for him—he was seeing it as an exercise in penmanship and correct spelling. He still did it willingly and with interest, proud of his growing ease, but I was becoming distressed that he was not seeing writing as a communication tool any more. I knew, too, that his plan to learn each word perfectly before going on to others was a doomed one—too limiting, too slow. Think how stunted our *oral* vocabularies would be if we had tried that tactic at age 2!

Our break-through came when my husband and I both read a book by George Riemer, *How They Murdered The Second "R"* (W.W. Norton, 1969). Among other things, the book strongly advocates using some way of simplifying the sound/spelling correspondences in English for beginning writers, feeling our unreliable language is "a hell of a trick to play on a little kid." The book is full of wonderful examples of genuine writing done by 6–7-year-old children who felt unencumbered by the onus of spelling correctly. These children wrote whatever they could *say*, their written vocabularies were not limited by what select batch of short-vowel words they had just been doled out in reading or spelling class. The book in many ways supports the ideas in Glenda Bissex's wonderful book *Gyns at Wrk* (Genius at Work), available from John Holt's Book Store, which describes the author's son's development in writing and reading through his invented spellings. Jesse, unlike Bissex's son Paul, didn't come up with the idea of inventive spellings on his own—he had apparently never thought of it. To Jesse, spellings were "givens," something you copied and eventually just knew. They came from the outside-in, not the inside-out.

Jesse finally understood and took to heart the idea of "sound-spelling" when Howard had Jesse's favorite puppet, Monkey, begin to "sound-spell" messages and questions to Jesse.... Jesse began writing little statements and replies to Monkey, sound-spelling "because Monkey would find it easier to read." The playful situation made it possible for Jesse to not worry about correctness. Howard also wrote out a vowel chart for Jesse (he knew sounds of most consonants fairly well), using basically the "Unifon" simplified spelling system (where all long vowels are written ae, ee, ie, oe, ue, each sound getting only *one* spelling pattern). I also was reading Jesse parts of *How They Murdered The Second "R"* aloud, and that also seemed to give him confidence in this new approach. He could readily tell which writings from the book were done by the inventive spellers and which were done by the "Dick and Jane" group—the latter were stilted and chopped, not at all the natural voices of children. Within a month Jesse was writing whole little stories. He was also using written language for real purposes—little notes to Howard ("Doet feel BADLee DADDY love Jesse I wil not teez yoo Tunite"), signs on block buildings or drawings ("Dun Bie Jesse"). In the beginning writing was incredibly hard work. Jesse would at times burst into frustrated tears when I couldn't make out what he'd written, or sometimes he'd be unable to remember what word it was he was writing as he was so buried in dissecting the smaller sounds within the word. I, too, had a lot of *patience* to learn. I had to learn not to question or correct his spellings, but just try to do the best I could to understand his *meanings*. A quote from *The Second "R"* helped me out here:

"Parents are so permissive about a baby's beginning speech that they hear *mama* and *dada* when he's merely clearing his throat. They'd never insist that their baby pronounce their first and last names fully and clearly or even mo-ther or fa-ther. But they see no parallel importance in a child's first writings and they pick and nag at his spellings."

Just as usually a sensitive parent is the best person to understand a toddler's beginning spoken language, so too we're the ones most likely to be able to decipher the first rough written words. We know the context of our children's thoughts so well that we're more likely to be able to predict their meanings.

Jesse needed me to be near, physically, while he wrote during his early spurt. He would need to ask me for sounds he didn't know (I was surprised how often *sh, th, ch, ou*—"harder" sounds we hadn't worked on much before—came up). He needed me to reread his writing aloud for him, as at that point he couldn't always read back what he'd written. . . . I was pleased he would *try* any word at all, long words with several syllables, anything. All words were his.

My mother wondered over Christmas, while delightedly reading Jesse's little note that began "Hie Grammo," when Jesse might ever learn to spell correctly. . . . As Bissex noted with her son, there is clearly no danger of Jesse developing "bad habits," as his spellings are thought out new each time he meets a word; he is not merely repeating marks on paper that he made once before. Also, Jesse is very aware that he is moving towards *"real"* spelling, and knows that certain situations (addresses on envelopes, for instance) are inappropriate places for invented spellings. We've read children's books on the history of our language, and this has helped him understand the somewhat snarled, though rich, roots of English, and so why we have so many odd spellings.

He usually pronounces *th* as something close to *z*, and so in his early writings he'd happily write *zn* for "then." He's now aware of this difference; indeed at times he's *over*-compensated, once correcting his *wuz* ("was") to *wuth*. He also did what John Holt mentioned in an old *GWS*—spontaneously wrote *chraen* for "train," and indeed this is closer to what most of us *do* say!

Jesse is no longer terribly touchy about his writing. His handwriting has even improved greatly, and more lower-case letters are proudly sprinkled through his capitals. He needs no reminding about spaces between words, he's gaining rudimentary knowledge of what sentences are and how we punctuate them (he *loves* exclamation points!), and can take low-key questions about sounds he may have left out of a word, in mature stride. He writes almost daily, and no longer needs me nearby when he writes, even seems to be savoring now the *privacy* of the writing act. We discuss writing a lot, everything from "writer's block" to needs for editing and proofreading for *adults'* writing (he sees *my* rough drafts!) to how writers come up with ideas or how writers borrow and change others' ideas, to why most young kids in schools don't write much (Jesse was astounded to discover our 9-year-old neighbor clearly felt *copying* an encyclopedia article was "writing"). And Jesse has gone from writing *"cat sat daddy"* to "Win cats ar siting dan thae git a rool lok" (when cats are sitting down they get a royal look). Why, my wooden-sword-loving son even now loves the old saying, "The pen is mightier than the sword."

A Writing Club

Daniel Fitzgerald (CO) sent this clipping from a local paper:

> A group of enterprising youngsters in south Greeley have spent their summer days producing newspapers, comics, books, plays, and poems.
>
> The group—a semi-secret club that calls itself *Comics*—meets regularly in the bedroom of Shawn Oster: "We have TV trays set up for everybody to work. Some of us draw cartoons and some write. We have panels between us so nobody can take the other guy's ideas or stories."
>
> In addition to 10-year-old Shawn, the members of *Comics* include his sister Shana Oster, 13, Justine Fitzgerald, 11, and her sister, Sara, 8. . . . Shawn and Justine are the leaders of *Comics*, but all members have important tasks:
>
> There are two family newspapers, published on an irregular basis. Dubbed *Family Edition*, the newspapers contain stories, poems, sports, illustrations, comic strips, puzzles and want ads. "We sell them for five cents," Sara said. "If nobody buys them, we'll give them away. If people start buying the papers,

we might raise the price to 6 or 7 cents." The front stories involve family happenings, such as the unfortunate death of Harry the cat. Editorials hit on topics of cleaning one's room or family responsibilities. The want ads include such notes as "Lost: mom's black thread. Reward—2 cents" and "Jobs: Cleaning the kitchen and bedroom. Pay is voluntary."

Justine is writing her own adventure novel, which currently is untitled. However, it does have 17 chapters, all typewritten. Justine said she learned to type when she was 8 years old. The story involves "two kids who go into a cave and find a strange world." She is illustrating the story herself. "That's what I'd like to do when I grow up. Write adventure stories and illustrate them myself."

In a small, brown briefcase, Shawn carries a number of cartoons he has drawn. The characters have strange names: Buzler, Big Cheeks, Lard, Ta, Star Sight and Psycho Jackson ("brother of Michael Jackson"). Completely businesslike, Shawn took his briefcase to *The Tribune* in an effort to sell "or even give away free" his comic strip. Although he was turned down, he's still optimistic about his future: "I'd like to be a professional cartoonist someday, and draw a cartoon strip like *Garfield*."

Shana wrote a 10-page play titled "The Princesses," and is currently working on other stories. "I like to write about kings and queens and princesses the best," she said. "The play is about a boy in search of three princesses and the adventures he has trying to find them." The members of *Comics* still ride their bicycles and run through the lawn sprinklers in the summer, but they also devote much of their time to the writing projects. "We try to work on them every day," Shawn said.

[DR:] *Dan also wrote to us:*

Justine and Sara have been homeschooling all this past year and the experience has only gotten better instead of worse. Now that it is summer, kids from all around the neighborhood come calling for the girls. Justine has formed a club that has four members. Then, they were asked to join the *Comics* club. And, they were both asked to join still another club run by another group of kids I don't even know yet but who are in their summer recreation group at the campus. They have been in 4-H and have played on the volleyball team, plus they are in the middle of their softball season.... They both can now hit, catch, know and interpret the rules, throw, etc. Their days are filled with activity and they seem quite happy.

In one month I must return to work after being on a two-year educational leave. We will all be in Osan, Korea, where I'll be teaching elementary school.... I don't know what the future of our homeschooling endeavor will be. But, I know that this past year has been one of great adventure, much real learning, and a sense of rich fulfillment.

Overcoming School Effects

From Vermont:

We have pulled our 7-year-old son out of school.... He reached the point where he would sit and blankly stare at a piece of work placed before him, all the while softly repeating over and over, almost as if he was in a hypnotic state, "*I am dumb.*" The first time I witnessed this, I was stunned, completely speechless. It was not so much that it was a shock (which, of course, it was) but the expression of utter hopelessness that was on his face—and what was really the crux of the matter was, he *knew* the material. He proved it to himself this Friday when he breezed through the same page of work here at home. The only difference is that he knows we will not find fault with every little thing that might be wrong.

The teacher had been hammering on such asinine things like, his letter O's are round, not oval in shape; some of his letters do not always touch the line; etc., etc. The first time I gave him some vocabulary words to write, he took over 22 minutes to write 9 or 10 words. It was write two letters, erase; write one letter, erase; he was a nervous wreck by the time he got it done and had it (what he considered) acceptable. We explained to him that in our "homeschool," we didn't want erasing every 10 seconds; that we didn't care what the letters looked like as long as we could read his work and it was spelled correctly. He is slowly beginning to realize that we mean it and will not become angry with him or make a federal case out of every little mistake—so what if his letter "t" in the word "cat" is leaning slightly or his number 10 has the 1 smaller than the zero?

After a week and half at home, being constantly assured that there is nothing wrong with him and that he is far from stupid, he is beginning to lose the whipped-dog expression on his face and actually smile and laugh again. He is slowly becoming the bright, inquisitive little boy he was back in September.

More Info On Writing Contests

From the brochure of the Young Playwrights Festival *(GWS 38):*

> Have you ever dreamed of becoming a writer? The Foundation of The Dramatists Guild invites you to participate in the annual playwriting festival open to young people aged 18 and under. The selected plays will receive fully professional productions in New York City. The authors will be given one year's membership in The Dramatists Guild, America's organization for professional playwrights, and an opportunity to attend and contribute to the rehearsal process; they will also receive a royalty. Entries must be submitted no later than July 1. Receipt of plays will be acknowledged. Participants will receive written evaluations of their work, but scripts will not be returned.
>
> *Some points to remember:*
>
> In plays, the story is told through speech and action rather than just description.
>
> Avoid using a narrator, if possible.
>
> Stage directions are useful, but don't overdo them.
>
> Avoid too many characters—we suggest that you try to limit the number of actors required to no more than nine or ten. This will facilitate casting.
>
> In the theater, unlike film or television, you cannot switch easily from one elaborate setting to another. Keep in mind that whatever you write has to be acted out on a stage in front of an audience.
>
> Have a look at a printed play-script to see the way you put things on the page.
>
> *Here's what to do:*
>
> The choice of subject, style, form and length is up to you. Collaborations and group written plays are eligible.
>
> Scripts must be entirely written by one or more people who are under the age of 19.
>
> Scripts must be typed and securely bound.
>
> Submit a copy of your play and keep the original at home.
>
> Plays submitted to previous Young Playwrights Festivals are not eligible.
>
> Film scripts, screenplays and musicals are not eligible, nor are adaptations of other authors' work.
>
> On the title page of your play, please list your name, date of birth, address and telephone number. You may be asked at some point to submit proof of age.
>
> Send a copy of your typed manuscript by July 1 to Young Playwrights Festival, The Foundation of The Dramatists Guild, 234 W 44 St, New York NY 10036.
>
> Eleven plays by writers aged 12 to 18 will be presented. . . . [A quote from

Jason Brown, 12, a 1984 winner]: "I decided to write about something I knew about, reality. So I just wrote about my parents' divorce. The hardest part in writing it was editing. My mom helped me a little by telling me to write each sentence like I was sending a telegram to London and each word cost a dollar."

The Young Playwrights Festival is made possible in part by a grant from Exxon Corporation. Support has also been provided by a number of corporations, foundations, and individuals.

[DR: Edith Oliver reviewed this year's festival in the May 21 *New Yorker*; she particularly liked one play *Fixed Up* by 16-year-old Patricia Durkin, and said it was "so funny and rings so true that it can be considered a finished piece of work and sent on its way."]

A letter from Avon Publishers:

Thank you for your inquiry about the 1985 Avon/Flare Young Adult Novel Competition. Here are the submission requirements and prize information:

You are eligible to submit a manuscript if you will be no younger than 13 and no older than 18 years of age as of December 31, 1984.

Each manuscript should be approximately 125 to 200 pages, or about 30,000 to 50,000 words (based on 250 words per page). All manuscripts must be typed, double-spaced, on a single side of the page only. Be sure to keep a copy.

With your manuscript, please enclose a letter that includes your name, address, telephone number, age, and a short description of your novel. Also enclose the following:

1. A self-addressed, stamped postcard so that we can let you know we have received your submission.

2. A self-addressed, stamped envelope for return of manuscript.

3. A self-addressed, stamped postcard for us to notify you of the winner (optional).

If you win this competition, your novel will be published by Avon/Flare for an advance of $5,000 against royalties. A parent or guardian's signature (consent) will be required on your publishing contract.

We will accept completed manuscripts from *January 1 through August 31, 1985*, at the following address: Avon/Flare Novel Competition, Avon Books, 1790 Broadway, Room 1204, New York NY 10019. If you have any further questions, please write or call us (212-399-1384).

[DR:] More writing contests for young people [*GWS* 38], these from a book called *How To Enter And Win Fiction Writing Contests* by Alan Gadney (Facts on File Publications, NY NY):

Youth Magazine Creative Arts Awards, 132 W 31st St, New York NY 10001. Open to U.S. youth age 13–19. Categories: Short Story, Poetry, Play. Winners published in *Youth Magazine* (1505 Race St, Rm 1203, Philadelphia PA 19102; 215-568-3950). Deadline May.

Scholastic Writing Awards, 50 W 44th St, NY NY 10036. Open to US & Canadian students (public or nonpublic school) under 20, Grades 7–12. Categories: Short Story, Poetry, Script-Play. Cash and scholarship awards $10–500, also typewriters, Papermate products. Deadline February.

Seventeen's Annual Fiction Contest, 850 Third Av, NY NY 10022; 212-759-8100. U.S. Ages 13–20. Awards $50–$500. Deadline June.

More Magazines By Children

I've found another magazine that would be helpful in giving our homeschoolers a chance at being published [*GWS* 38, "Magazines Seek Children's Work"]. It's called *Young People Today*. The magazine is written, edited and published by young people under 20 years of age, who are also responsible for layout, illustrations and photography. In the copy I got they said, "Other young people, to the age of 20, are encouraged to use this communicable vehicle for free expression, be it through creative writing, creative art, research, an opinion, the sharing of an experience, humor, or any other form desired." They stated that "contributors have been remunerated for their works, when published." Their address is PO Box 19438, Los Angeles CA 90010-9990; phone 213-487-4154.—*John Boston* (CA).

A magazine by and for children—writing of all kinds and line drawings—*McGuffey Writer*, 400 McGuffey Hall, Miami University, Oxford OH 45056. $5/year subscription (3 issues), 12 pages per issue. Through 8th grade.—*Lynne Norris* (IN).

Learning To Love Books

Judy Cornell (FL) wrote to John:

Until about age 32, I hated reading books. I can recall loving to go to the library in elementary school and checking out books with pretty pictures on the smooth, cellophane covers. I would come home eagerly anticipating an exciting experience and become discouraged after reading and not finding it interesting. Being a slow, word-for-word reader, if the book moved slowly with much description, I became bored.

What changed my whole outlook (and my life) was an article you wrote about a conversation with your sister for *Redbook Magazine* in 1967 ["How Teachers Make Children Hate Reading," reprinted in *The Underachieving School*]. I realized then that I believed there was something wrong with me if I couldn't finish a book and not that the book didn't interest me. Consequently, this guilt feeling kept me from trying another until I finished the first which I never did.

When I realized this after reading your article, I decided to start a reading program. I would ask my friends about their favorite books and why they liked them. Then, if it seemed like something I'd enjoy, I'd begin it and as you suggested, if I didn't care about the characters after thirty pages or so, I'd forget it and not feel guilty.

I'll never forget my first attempt: *The Exorcist*. I couldn't put it down and since then I've become an avid reader. I must limit my reading only because there are not enough hours in the day.... My life changed so much that I went on to get a degree in English Education.

History Through Fiction

A California reader wrote:

This month our evening reading is *Lorna Doone*—a very enjoyable and humorous old classic—and I'm filling in on the side with the history of the Stuarts and their descendants.... I became interested in history (and it turned into a lifelong passion) through reading historical novels as a teenager and am convinced now that a good way of teaching children is to read a rousing good story of a historical period, and fill in the dates and other data on the side. While reading *A Tale of Two Cities*, I also read selections from Carlyle's *French Revolution* and a biography of Louis and Marie Antoinette, and the children were fascinated.

Sculpture Catalog

From Albert Hobart (MO):

Have you ever told your readers about *Sculpture House*? It sells by mail the most complete array of sculpture tools and materials I've seen anywhere. (I used to be a sculptor, so I've always had an interest in this sort of thing.) For example, the catalog lists a wide variety of high quality wood carving chisels and mallets, stone carving sets, clay modeling tools, scrapers, knives, handmade files, waxes, plasters and casting stones, armatures, molding making aids, potters supplies, sculpture stands, and even kilns.

Homeschoolers, especially, might appreciate the many varieties of modeling clays. One type my son (14) enjoys is "Boneware," a water-based clay which hardens into permanent form without firing. There are two colors, gray and terra cotta. The 25 lb. package we ordered three years ago cost $16, and we still have some left. A little goes a long way.

There's no charge for the Sculpture House catalog which is easy to read and includes numerous illustrations. Here's the address: 38 E 30th St, NY NY 10016; 212-679-7474.

Textbook Catalogs

Way back in *GWS* 15, I said there didn't seem to be any easy way of buying textbooks through the mail—you had to write to individual publishers, of which there are dozens. Finally we have heard of some companies that sell a wide selection of texts, new and used, from many publishers.

First is *Wilcox & Follett Book Co.*, 1000 W Washington Blvd, Chicago IL 60607; toll-free no. 1-800-621-4272 (in Illinois 1-800-621-1474). The 144-page free catalog lists hundreds of books, classified by subject, most $5 or less, and almost all under $10. Only problem I see is that you only have the titles to judge by.

Second is *Adams Book Co.*, 537 Sackett St, Brooklyn NY 11217; 1-800-221-0909. Be prepared to give the name of your school. At press time we are still waiting for the catalog, which Nancy Fletcher of Florida says has "a broad selection of new and used and also has paperbacks and workbooks."

By the way, neither Nancy Fletcher nor Deborah Schwabach, who in *GWS* 16 and 17 offered low-cost used texts to *GWS* readers, is providing that service any longer. Deborah said she sold (or in some cases gave away) around 1500–2000 books through that *GWS* story!

The *Home Centered Learning* newsletter (CA) lists a third catalog: "*Textbooks For Christian Schools*—A comprehensive catalog for those interested in Christian-based curriculum. *Bob Jones University Press*, Greenville SC 29614."—DR

On Suzuki Instruction

James Salisbury (PO Box 2261, Twin Falls ID 83303) wrote:

Isn't it funny how so many music teachers who call themselves "Suzuki Teachers" have never read the writings of Shinichi Suzuki? ... I appreciate the frequent references to Suzuki methodology in *GWS*, but it is unfortunate that self-proclaimed proponents of Suzuki philosophy so badly misrepresent it. John told me once that the same thing has happened to the teachings of Maria Montessori; practices in "Montessori Schools" seldom comply with her inspired respect for the mind of the child.

Dr. Suzuki not only revolutionized music instruction but has labored diligently to reform education to comply with the natural ability of the child to learn all things from math to foreign languages, in the same way that the child learns his mother tongue. These principles are simple and need only to be reawakened in all of us. ... not studied like a complicated methodology to be taken as a college course! The best Suzuki teachers are fine *self*-disciplined, genuinely loving musicians who have mastered their instrument, and loving, teachable parents who simply provide a home where beautiful, simple music is as common to the home environment as is the native language; casual but constant, always encouraging and never, never, never, *never* forced!

"*To force the curriculum is to produce the dropout.*" This is the heart of the Shinichi Suzuki philosophy and there is no axiom of education, or life, that is more true. Nor did it begin with Dr. Suzuki. Show me a virtuoso musician prodigy and you will see someone from a musical home where the instrument was loved and accessible, but not forced as everyone believes.

Yes, for over 12 years I, too, have tried to live up to the title of Suzuki teacher. Naturally I think it would be nice if my three children would become fine musicians. But I would just as soon they became fine, honest plumbers, sailors, doctors, scientists, beekeepers. In the meantime, my children happen to love to play the violin, the piano, the recorder, and can't wait to get their hands on my flute, my clarinet, or my trumpet. I don't give them lessons until they beg for them. They may not practice unless they have "been good." They like their music precisely because it is not forced.

They want to play the piano because they see a couple of dozen other eager children come over for lessons for which their parents have paid dearly, and because they see how much I love to play the piano. They also see how much I love to play the violin and the clarinet. (I'm terrible at the violin and the clarinet but they sense how much I yearn to do it.) So they beg me daily to let them get out the little 10th sized instrument and "practice" (this is not a dreaded word at our house). We put the instrument away *before* they lose interest and they look forward to the next session.

When a parent brings their child to begin lessons, the hardest task is to carefully nurture the parent to be loving, to joyfully play the beautiful recorded music in the home, and *not* to force the curriculum. I do not teach the child in the common sense. I show him, I love him, I encourage him. He listens inadvertently, then curiously. His mother (usually) and I show him how to sit (when he is ready), how and where to put his fingers (when he is ready), and without exception, he teaches himself. Suzuki teachers, like public school teachers, are deluding themselves if they think teaching, in itself, is a "professional" technical undertaking.

Glenn Doman says, "The man to whom information comes in dreary tasks along with threats of punishment is unlikely to be a student in after years, while those to whom it comes in natural forms, at the proper times, are likely to continue through life that self-instruction begun in youth."

One more misconception about the Suzuki method needs to be corrected. A person does *not* need to be under five to be a good Suzuki student! When Masaru Ibuka, friend of Suzuki and President of Sony International, said "Kindergarten Is Too Late" (the title of his excellent book), he only meant, as John Holt almost identically said in *The Underachieving School*, that every child, before his first day of school, "is smarter, more curious, less afraid of what he doesn't know, better at finding and figuring things out, more confident, resourceful, persistent, and independent, than he will ever again be for the rest of his life.". . . . But Ibuka does not argue with John's insistence that, if you really want to learn something, it's really "Never Too Late.". . . The hunger for knowledge may be clouded over by so many years of formal schooling, but is seldom totally damaged.

Changing Music Teachers

From a Maine reader:

Dec. 2: I have been wanting to write to you for help with the Suzuki program that my son (4) and I are now in. We are encouraged to force our kids to practice, stickers are given out for certain numbers of hours of practice per week, and for performing in certain ways during class.

I do not force or pressure my son to practice and I've made it clear to him that if he wants to earn stickers it's totally up to him—I don't care one way or another. I continue to pursue my own violin and piano study with great pleasure and he loves going to violin, watching the other children play and dreaming of his own future in the group. My fear is that the competition and the "do-it-for-a-gold-star" fever will infect him and rob him of his own initiative and motivation in studying *anything*. Do you have any ideas about this? I badly need reassurance and support. I feel quite alone in my beliefs and attitude toward practice and discipline.

[DR:] We sent a copy of this letter to James Salisbury, who sent the parent many of the same thoughts as appear in his article in this issue. The reader then wrote us:

Feb. 8—Eight million thanks for forwarding my desperate little note to James Salisbury. The supportive letter he sent me was tremendous. I was beginning to think that John Holt and I were the only people in the world who believe that children can direct their own learning in music as in other areas. And to be honest, I thought maybe he and I were *wrong*. Music is so important to me that I don't want to be wrong about it—don't want to ruin it for my son.

Now there's a third person! Three of us can't be totally off our rockers.

I wrote back to James with some more specific questions about how to handle the stars and general lack of faith in the program we are in. I am considering looking for another teacher.

June 25: We have left the Suzuki program we were in. Shortly after the supportive letter from

James, I decided this would be our last year even if my son wanted to stay in the program (although he showed signs of being unhappy while there), *I* was too unhappy to stay. A few weeks after I made that decision, my son said he'd had it, and we dropped out abruptly but with great relief. . . . The poor kid really believed, and I think still somewhat believes, and worse yet *I* somewhat believed, that a person has to put up with that sort of denigration and disrespect to learn to play an instrument. He declared that although he wanted to *play* the violin, he'd had it with *studying* the violin. Fine, I said.

I found another teacher and decided to make very clear what my values were *before* my son got involved. I said I was interested in studying violin for myself, whether or not my son ever takes an interest again. I said that I did not want to proceed with any lessons for my son until *he* asked for them (got this tip from James). And I asked her about practicing. She said that she thought rewards were necessary, but that she respected however parents wanted to handle it, that she understood every family and every child had a different balance to their interests and that she felt it was important to respect that. And finally she said that enjoyment was the most important thing.

It sounded to both of us like we would get along, so I am studying with her and loving it. My son so far has not wanted to go with me—he gets out his violin every so often and polishes it and plays around with it, but I think his other teaching experience makes him leery of accompanying me. I am hoping to be able to play with my new teacher's group playing class in the fall. I think I'll be the only adult! This is very exciting to me.

That's where we are with music. At first I was quite angry that my son had developed negative feelings about studying an instrument through poor teaching, but now I see it as a valuable learning experience with our own son, about children being in charge of their own education, and will be most hesitant to compromise our philosophy in the future.

Thrilled With Violin

We got our violin [from Holt Associates] and we're thrilled with it. The tone is beautiful. We've only had it five days but between the four of us we've already produced one of the following: a pretty-close scale, a pretty good phrase from a favorite tune, and an excellent squeaking door. We think there's even violin on Michael Jackson's *Thriller* album. Onward and upward!—*Mary Stone (OR).*

Music Lessons On Tape

From the Black Sheer Review, *a magazine on Northeast folk music:*

> There is an enormous wealth of traditional music in this country, and short of having a professional teacher come right into your living room for a private lesson, Happy Traum's *Homespun Tapes* just might be the best way for the budding musician to learn the real thing. The tapes are clear, informal and fun. The teaching programs range from the basics on each instrument to some very ornate pieces, and each tape is accompanied by an instruction book written either in tablature or standard musical notation. Tapes for beginners are explicit in telling the novice player exactly where the fingers go, how to hold the instrument, and what kind of tone production to aim for. "When selecting teachers, I talk to them first," [Traum] says. "Some musicians may be excellent performers, but may not be able to express themselves. I have to choose people who can talk and can analyze their playing. It's not always easy for musicians to do that because a lot of them play spontaneously. . . . I sit with the instructors, ask them questions, and organize their material for them so it comes out being very lucid."

> Today, Homespun offers about 275 individual lessons taught by over thirty artists. . . . The latest brainstorm at Homespun Tapes is Homespun Video Tapes.

[DR:] We got Homespun Tapes' free catalog,

which is available from Box 694, Woodstock NY 12498. It lists lessons for: guitar (many styles), electric guitar, acoustic bass, electric bass, banjo, fiddle, mandolin, hammer dulcimer, Appalachian dulcimer, harmonica, piano, autoharp, mouth harp, pennywhistle, and ear training. Some of the more famous teachers are Merle Watson, Mike Seeger, John Sebastian, and Jean Ritchie. A single cassette lesson with supplemental printed material costs $12.95; a series of three, $32.50; of six, $65 (reel-to-reel tapes available).

Homeschooling Book Here

Anything School Can Do, You Can Do Better, by Maire Mullarney ($5.95 + post). Here is another delightful book on homeschooling, from Ireland, by a *GWS* reader who taught all of her own children at home until they were eight or nine (and later wished that she had taught them at home a lot longer). I hope it will not be long till I meet Maire Mullarney; she comes across very strongly out of the pages of her own book, a sensitive, affectionate, smart, no-nonsense person. One of the things I like most about her is that she had so much fun with her children and had such a wonderful sense of the kind of things that children found fun.

To give a little of the flavor of Maire, her children, and the book, some quotes—but I wish I had room for many more:

> I am puzzled when I hear a mother say, "Teach them at home? I would never have the patience!" What do they think happens at school?

> As soon as Barbara could stand with her hands held, I found myself giving her little jumps. Soon we were counting the jumps up to ten. Years went by and new toddlers were clamoring for jumps, as were the others, up to nine or ten. This game must have helped the younger ones to internalize the meaning of number. It certainly helped them to get splendid bounce, going well up over my head to just miss the kitchen ceiling.

> When Barbara was about a year old, I gave her some powder paint in a saucer, mixed with water to make a thick cream, and a long-handled paint brush. An enamel table top turned on its side [JH: what a great idea!] made a good surface to spread colour on, and made it easier to show her how to use the brush. Putting paint on an upright surface does not lend itself to leaning heavily on the brush. . . . This worked so well that no baby went past a year without meeting a paint brush.

> It should be evident from the first part of the book that I found staying home with interested children much more fun than either of the "jobs" I had beforehand. . . . It was the learning together that gave zest to the days.

> After some eighteen quiet years of child-watching I had come to realize that school was a time-wasting and inefficient attempt to enable one generation to share knowledge with the next. When the elders felt the need to subdue the young by beating and humiliating them, that went beyond mere inefficiency. It had not dawned on me that sharing knowledge was only a minor purpose of the system.

> My share of the activity did not take any extra time. I moved the baby around with me. . . . Gardening, sewing, cooking, and reading fit in with paying some attention to a baby. We would lie on a rug together, indoors or out; baby on tummy, mirror to reach for; on her back, kicking at a sheet of coloured paper held by parent; or parent on back, arms straight up, holding flying baby. . . . Time spent in shared activity showed itself to be an investment. Babies who have had a solid chunk of full parental attention feel confident enough to potter around and explore for the rest of the day, making contact from time to time.

> If I were able to return to the beginning I would see that every child had a chance to learn to play an instrument, just as every child had a chance to learn to read.

Looking back I see [Alasdar] out in the garden, rocking quietly on a very small rocking horse, then bringing over a bucket of tasty stones to feed it.

[Thomas] did not bother to read until he was five, when he brought me a model he had made of a bird on a nest. I admired it, then wrote on a card, *nest, bird, wing, twig*. As soon as he realized there were books about birds he very quickly learned to read.

[JH:] In a later chapter Maire Mullarney tells us what the children, now grown up, the oldest 36, did in and with their lives. They are a very varied and interesting crew. For several school was visibly harmful, and might have been much more so had Maire not moved quickly to prevent further harm. But even when she was able to find for the younger children smaller schools, which did not beat children (then common in Ireland, now I believe forbidden), and which had some interesting teachers, they learned very little that had anything to do with their later lives. Only one of the eleven is interested in what we might think of as a school-like activity (mathematics).

The book is so full of delights that, other than to mention them, I won't say much about my disagreements with it. MM is a strong believer in Montessori materials and methods. I think she gives them far too much credit and herself far too little. Given the kind of mother (and also loving father) they had, I think the children would have grown up interesting and smart even if she had never heard of Montessori. MM seems to feel, perhaps less strongly than at one time, that little people aren't going to learn things unless kindly and loving big people somehow teach them. Early in the book she describes how she taught shapes (circle, square, etc.) to her babies when they were less than a year old. Because she was so ingenious, and so gentle and loving, I'm sure it was fun for the baby, and it probably did little harm or none at all. But as I have said before in *GWS*—*no one ever taught me shapes*! The idea that, unless taught, people might somehow grow up in the modern world not knowing what a circle or a square is seems to me bizarre.

MM is also a strong believer in formal instruction in reading, and by a strict use of what I call single-letter-phonics. As I have often said, neither seems to me necessary, far less efficient. As she did it, it worked, almost all her children learned to read well and early. In a house like theirs, full of words, ideas, books, and with parents who loved reading, I think the children would have learned to read anyway. I must note that from her descriptions of them, it does not seem that the written word plays a very important part in their lives.

However, I would not want to let such disagreements get between anyone and this book, our introduction to a very smart, loving, sensitive woman and her children. The book, by the way, has gained much attention in Ireland, and sparked considerable interest in homeschooling, so if any homeschoolers are tempted, as I surely am, to visit Ireland, meeting Maire Mullarney is another good reason.

Book On Legalities Here

Home Education And Constitutional Liberties, by John Whitehead and Wendell Bird ($5.95 + post). This short, thoroughly researched, well organized, and clearly written book seems to me, with a few exceptions, to be one of the most valuable legal resources, tools, or weapons for homeschoolers to have appeared in some time. With the exceptions noted, no book or article I have seen so well sums up and argues the historical and legal case for homeschooling. Virtually all homeschoolers would be wise to own it or have a copy within easy reach, above all homeschoolers who face or fear they might face hostile action by school authorities and/or the courts. And, at least in states where the right to homeschooling is not clearly and strongly established, homeschoolers might also be wise to send this book to their state representatives, the governor (no need for everyone to send one), and perhaps leading state educational officials.

The heart of the book, and of the legal argument for homeschooling, the constitutional ground on which we stand, is summed up as:

> In fact, any question of First [JH: or any other] Amendment freedoms.... is viewed by courts within a three-step process. First, there must be a First [JH: or other] Amendment Right that conflicts with a governmental program or requirement. Second, the state must have burdened [i.e., made difficult or impossible] the exercise of that right. And third, there must not be any compelling state interest that justifies the burden; or if there is, the state must have satisfied that interest by the least burdensome means possible.

Any statutory prohibition against home education should be presumed unconstitutional, as several court decisions have held or assumed. If a statute can be construed to preserve its constitutionality, it should be so construed. This means, for example, that a statute that mentions only public or private education should be interpreted to include home education within the definition of "private education." If not, the law would be unconstitutional. [JH: the book notes that the courts have split about 50-50 on this last argument.]

Any burdensome regulation of home education is also unconstitutional (just as burdensome regulation of religious schools is unconstitutional).The book is in effect a condensed and simplified legal brief. But for parents facing prosecution in court Whitehead and Bird are prepared to offer in support something even more powerful than this book. A footnote on page 10 of the book says:

> On behalf of the Rutherford Institute, the authors have prepared an exhaustive legal brief, with thorough appendix, that provides a technical legal defense of home education. The brief was filed in the Georgia Supreme Court, the Minnesota Supreme Court, the North Carolina Supreme Court, the Arkansas Court of Appeals, and other courts. The Rutherford Institute will file this brief in similar cases. For more information, write The Rutherford Institute, Box 510, Manassas VA 22110.

Note that the homeschoolers won in Georgia; the Minnesota case is as I write still pending; and the North Carolina family lost. The long brief, while powerful, is not infallible.

What are my reservations about *Home Education And Constitutional Liberties*? First, in the chapter "Freedom Of Religion," it overstates what the courts have actually said about the right of parents to homeschool for religious reasons, and later defends this position by calling "erroneous" some of what the Supreme Court said in *Yoder* and just about all the Appeals Court said in *Duro* (an exceedingly important case). From reading this book one might get the impression that in *Yoder* the Court gave very broad support to homeschooling for religious reasons, whereas in fact the support given, as we have more than once said in *GWS*, was very narrow.

In a late chapter, the book speaks of "erroneous" court cases. It seems an odd and unhelpful use of the word. One might as well speak of "erroneous" legislation. One can always say of a given court ruling that it was unfair or unjust or badly reasoned or self-contradictory, or that wiser and better judges would have ruled differently. None of this makes any difference. A ruling is a ruling, and unless and until overturned by a later ruling, it is the law. The authors say that in *Duro* the U.S. Court of Appeals made nine fundamental constitutional errors. Perhaps so. But the fact that the Supreme Court refused to hear the appeal clearly indicates that they did not consider them to *be* errors. The fact is, as we have pointed out in *GWS*, the courts in *Yoder* and *Duro* have explicitly refused to give religious homeschoolers the blank check that Whitehead and Bird think they should have, and that readers of this book might be led to believe they do have. We cannot say to the state, "I am teaching my children for religious reasons, and therefore, what I do is none of your business."

In the chapter "The Least Burdensome Means," Whitehead and Bird say, quite rightly, "Allowance for home education constitutes the least burdensome means for assuring any state interest in education." This is an excellent argument and should be quoted verbatim. But then they go on to say, "Standardized testing, because of grade inflation, is now considered by many as the most meaningful measure of educational achievement." This is a most dubious assertion, and for many years considerable numbers of educators, myself among them, have for many different reasons strongly disputed it. To require that all home education programs be judged and justified by standardized test scores strikes me as an extremely burdensome requirement, supported by almost no evidence, and one that would be highly objectionable to me and to many homeschoolers. In a given situation, it may be tactically wise for homeschoolers to submit to it, as I have now and then advised them to do, but we ought never to accept it as generally necessary or proper.

In the last chapter of the book, "Practical Suggestions for Home Education," which contains some useful advice, the authors make some proposals with which I strongly disagree and which I urge readers to ignore:

> for the best legal protection, a home instruction program should operate as closely as possible to a "traditional" school within the home. This means that those involved in home instruction programs should, at least.... (1) Annually have their children take standardized achievement tests.... administered by someone other than the parents.... (2) Keep detailed records of actual days and hours of study (3) Prepare a lesson plan which chronicles textbooks and the pages covered for each subject assignment given on each day of instruction.... (4) Administer and maintain regular tests for each subject. These tests should be administered as frequently as those in the public schools and other private schools. (5) Provide a structured environment for instruction; that is, the children should have desks.

If you believe, as on the basis of long experience I emphatically do, that it is the standard assumptions and daily practices of conventional schools that block and prevent children's learning and soon destroy their love of independent investigation and thought, then the above advice can only seem like saying; "It's OK to give your children the same old school poison, as long as they drink it out of a different bottle." What difference does the bottle make, or the building? I recall, as I often do, the young Canadian homeschooler saying to her anxious and over-teaching mother, "Mom, if I'm going to have to do all this school junk, I'd rather do it in school." She was right—wherever it happens, school junk is school junk, forced learning is faked learning. The whole point of homeschooling, at least for many parents, is to be able to do something radically and wholly different from what is done in schools, to allow children to continue to be the kind of independent, self-motivated, voracious explorers and learners we all were when we were very young, before others began trying to coerce, control, and measure our learning.

Some readers will disagree with me about this, or perhaps my other reservations about this book. If so, they are of course free to ignore them. But if you agree with some or all of these reservations, but decide anyway, as I recommend, to send this book to a state representative or other official, I also recommend that along with the book you send these reservations, perhaps in the form of a copy of this review, or even better in your own words. Otherwise, you may give a wrong impression of what you believe and want.

In any case, there are many ways to use this thoughtful and timely book, and I hope that many thousands of homeschoolers will make use of it.

—JH

Other Books Available Here

A House Is A House For Me, by Mary Ann Hoberman, illus. by Betty Fraser ($3.95 + post). This unique and lovely book is a long rhyming poem, first about living creatures and the various places they live in, and then later about inanimate objects and the other kinds of objects that *they* can be found in. She begins:

A hill is a house for an ant, an ant.

A hive is a house for a bee.

A hole is a house for a mole or a mouse.

And a house is a house for me!

And here we see a picture of a small boy reading in a tree house built of scrap lumber. The poem goes on, one of the most ingenious and delightful pieces of light verse I have ever read. Each time we come to the title line, the picture shows a child or children in one of the kinds of shelters they like to find or make for themselves— in a couple of cardboard boxes, under a big umbrella, under a table with a sheet draped over it, a hollowed out pile of snow, a sheet draped over a line to make a tent. The illustrations, in color, are done in minute and realistic detail, but also with much fantasy and wit—I particularly love the picture of a duchess sitting up in bed with her knitting and banjo, surrounded by plans of castles and thinking hard about what kind she wants to build for herself. The children themselves are adorable; we feel their intentness and busyness. Finally in the last verse, the truth we cannot be reminded of too often:

A flower's at home in a garden.

A donkey's at home in a stall.

Each creature that's known has a house
of its own

And the earth is a house for us all.

Many Moons, by James Thurber ($3.95 + post). James Thurber, *New Yorker* colleague and friend of E.B. White, and one of the great American humorous writers of the '30s through '50s, wrote, as far as I know, only two books for children, but they are so good that I wish he had written many more. This one, which Mary Van Doren showed me, is charming, perfect for children up to eight or nine, though children quite a bit older might well enjoy it for its quiet Thurberish irony and wit. I can think of no limit to the number of times I would be ready to read it aloud.

The story is simple. A King's little daughter (the book says age ten, but she seems more like six or seven) falls ill, and says she will only get well if she can have the moon. The loving worried father tells his wise men to get the moon for her, but they say no, it can't be done, it's too big, too far away. The King is in despair till his Jester gives him wise advice: since it is the child who wants the moon, why not ask her how big she thinks it is? What she says, and what happens, makes this lovely story.

The delicate water-color illustrations go beautifully with the text. One of the most endearing things about them is that in all pictures of the little Princess, whatever she is doing, whether sleeping or playing and jumping rope in the garden, she has a tiny little crown, not much bigger than a grown-up's thumb, perched right on top of her head. Nothing shows or hints what keeps it on; it's supposed to be there and stay there, so it does. A pure delight.

As I Was Crossing Boston Common, by Norma Farber, pictures by Arnold Lobel ($3.95 + post). Mary Van Doren, who has put us onto many good books, showed us this lovely little picture book for younger children. The teller of the story is a box-shelled tortoise (the kind kids get for pets). We see it at the very lower left hand corner of the first picture. The text for the first four pages reads:

> As I was crossing Boston Common
> Not very fast, not very slow
> I met a man with a creature in tow.
> Its collar was labeled *Angwantibo*.
> I thought it rather uncommon.
>
> As I was crossing Boston Common—
> Not very fast, not very slow—
> Angwantibo passed with a *Boobok* in tow...

And so, through the book, each new page introduces a new animal or two, each being towed by the one before. The drawings, in pen and ink with a light overwash of muted colors, are detailed and accurate, but have a whimsical quality—the animals seem almost as surprised by this strange procession as we are. And the poem continues its almost musical chant till the end of the procession and its little surprise.

This book is, in short, what our ancestors used to call a Bestiary, a book of animals, usually exotic, sometimes imaginary, sometimes, as in this case, real (though mostly unknown to me). But it is also something else, and not until the very end of the animal procession did I realize, with astonishment, what it was. My excuse for this mental lapse is that I was fascinated by the animals and lulled by the poem—as you will be. This will be a favorite read-aloud book.

Cars And How They Go, by Joanna Cole, illus. by Gail Gibbons ($9.95 + post). The dust jacket says that this book is for ages 7–11; my guess is that any kids of that age who liked machines enough to want to read the book in the first place would be able to understand all or nearly all of it. The dust jacket also says that the author "is known for her ability to explain complex ideas in simple terms." I emphatically agree; this is one of the finest pieces of explaining I have ever seen. She has the great and rare gift of knowing where to begin an explanation, of knowing what must be put in and what can be left out, and of not telling you too much, or too much all at once. The light-hearted illustrations (in color) are a perfect match for the text.

Any child (or adult) who reads through this book will know a great deal more about cars than I knew when at age twenty I first went into the Navy, where for the first time I saw what the insides of engines and other machines looked like. In fact, this book, slim as it is, will probably tell you more about cars than is known by most people driving them today. So if you feel a little uncertain about what's down there underneath all the shiny paint, you can always sneak this book out of your child's room for a quick look.

Conceptual Physics, by Paul Hewitt ($23.95 + post). I've been looking off and on for some time for a good general introductory physics text, and this one seems excellent. The problem for all people who write such texts is, since there are many different branches of physics, in what order should one present them. Hewitt has wisely begun with the study of motion; not only is motion a very common event, something we see, experience, and think about every day, but since it was one of the first aspects of visible reality that human beings did think about, in discussing it Hewitt is able to tell us a little about the history of physics, how certain discoveries led to new questions and so to new discoveries.

This is a college text, but don't be put off by that. Years ago, when Jud Jerome and his then 11-year-old son Topher were looking for a text from which to learn algebra together, they found that college texts were the only ones they could tolerate; the others over-simplified or talked down to the reader. Hewitt writes clearly and explains well; outside of scientific terms, which any student of physics must get to know anyway, there are not many words that an interested twelve-year-old would not know or could not soon figure out. The many black-and-white drawings are helpful.

A word about the title. Why "Conceptual"? Because most physics texts are full of illustrative problems which require a great deal of calculation. Since Hewitt was writing this book mostly for college students who wanted or needed to know something about physics but who were not and did not plan to be scientists, he wisely framed his end-of-chapter questions to get the students to think about the ideas and principles in the text; if and when calculation is involved, it is very simple, do-it-in-your-head kind of stuff.

I was sorry to see him waste a couple of pages on dumb talk about space colonies. But I forgive him, first, because there is very little of the air of gee-whiz science-worship in the book, and second, because of a nice little photo of sheets hung out to dry on a clothesline, with the dead-pan caption, "Solar powered clothes dryer." On the important question of the prudent and responsible use of scientific knowledge, his heart is in the right place. All in all, a very good, clear, comprehensive introduction to a fascinating, important, and for many people, forbidding subject.

A Sampler Of Lifestyles—Womanhood and Youth in Colonial Lyme [Conn.], by Mary Sterling

Bakke ($6.95 + post). Here is another fine example of a kind of history book I wish we had more of, books about the everyday lives of "ordinary" people. In the acknowledgements the author writes: "From old diaries, documents, newspapers, State Archives records, genealogies, and oral traditions the picture of both daily life and special occasions brings to life women and young people in the time prior to 1800." It makes me wonder in passing where future historians will look to find such records of us. Few people keep diaries any more, and the paper and ink with which modern high-speed presses print our newspapers and books guarantee that, barring some miracle-method of preservation, they will crumble to dust within a few generations.

At any rate, we have this record of earlier times, and it tells us many interesting and some surprising things about women in pre-1800 New England. They were a very long way from being the kind of sheltered, submissive, powerless, fragile creatures we sometimes imagine.

Concerning the lives of the young, which were busy and active and full of time for vigorous play, the author writes:

> Not all of girls' work was done skillfully and expeditiously, in spite of supervision by elders.... Diary confessions to scorching preserves and flirting with father's apprentices seem normal; and a reader perceives that such kindly, gentle, loving instructive oversight gave individuals a sense of being needed and that what they did was important. They had a secure niche in the family's life.

On the legal and economic rights of women:

> Though the statute legalizing a woman's administration of the estate of her deceased husband came in 1784 by Connecticut as a state, actual practice had given her this power in the colonial period at least a hundred years before that.... Not only were widows functioning as executors of their husbands' estates in the 17th Century, but were making bequests executed as legal.... Aside from this, in the 17th Century women had more legal prerogatives than in the 19th. Because husbands were often away, women were accustomed to the management of a farm, or shop, or trade.... We get a picture of colonial women quite different from the stereotype of a property-less and legally helpless drudge in a patriarchal society. Functioning with all the necessary legal guarantees, one hundred sixty women in New London County, alone, are listed as heads of households in the first Census of the United States, 1790.

> Literary and romantic notions of the helpless female, dimly subject to male domination, and a legal nonentity prove to be just that—notions—when the stories of real women who helped make this country become known.

In short, the industrialization of America did not raise but lowered the general position of women in society, by turning more and more of their necessary and skilled work into industrial jobs, by organizing these jobs (needlessly) into a hierarchy of higher and lower, and by assigning a much greater proportion of these lower jobs to women. From this most interesting book we get a picture of how different it once was and, perhaps, a vision of how different it might be again.

Worms Eat My Garbage by Mary Appelhof ($5.95 + post). This book tells how the author uses the kind of fast-breeding worm usually called red wigglers or manure worms, which she keeps in a moderate-sized (4–6 sq. ft.) box in her kitchen, to eat up her organic garbage (as opposed to trash) and to convert it into the most fertile and productive of all growing mediums. It's the best book I have seen, first, about the worms themselves, what kind of critters they are, how they live, mate, breed, and secondly, about how to raise them on a small scale.

There is much to be said for having some of these worms in or near the house. In the first place, they convert a nuisance into a valuable asset. In the second place, they are (perhaps along with ants) the most trouble-free of all pets or domestic livestock.

Put them in a container with enough food, make sure their bedding, which can be shredded paper, little bits of cardboard, etc., is moist enough—they like things pretty wet—and you can forget about them for weeks on end. The children I have seen who have seen them, after a few ritual cries of "Gross!" and "Yucky!", find them fascinating. They lend themselves very well to all kinds of small-scale but genuine science projects, calling for observation, measurement, and so on: how fast do they multiply, what sort of things do they like to eat, how long does it take their eggs to hatch, how long does it take newly hatched worms (not much thicker than threads) to mature, and so on.

Those of you who have read some of the earlier issues of *GWS* will know that I have been raising them in a small enclosed patio outside my basement apartment. They are still there, more of them than ever. What they like to eat almost as much as anything is plain old brown corrugated cardboard, as in cardboard boxes. They gobble it up, and, as I have said, turn it into the richest imaginable soil. Seems almost too good to be true. People who want to garden, have bad soil, and cannot easily find organic materials to make compost, may find this the easiest way to enrich their soil.

I would amend Mrs. Appelhof's wise words about worms in a couple of small respects. It is not always true that they can't stand plastic. I am raising some of them, and seeing them breed and thrive, in two plastic yogurt containers, and also in a plastic shopping bag. I would add that they much prefer cardboard to leaves; leaves have to be well rotted before worms will eat them, whereas they will tear into cardboard just as soon as it gets moist enough for them to eat it. There are in short many ways to keep and feed these almost miraculously useful little creatures. Reading this clear and informative book is a good way to start.

Cancer And Vitamin C, by Ewan Cameron and Linus Pauling ($5.95 + post). This may well be one of the two or three most important books, perhaps the most important, ever written about medicine for the general public. Since I have known for at least five years about Linus Pauling's work with vitamin C, and for at least a couple of years belonged to his Institute of Science and Medicine and read its quarterly bulletins, I regret that it has taken me so long to read this book and to add it to our list. Since about 400,000 people die of cancer every year (about a fifth of deaths from all causes), and since it is estimated that about a third of all Americans will get cancer sometime in their lives, this is clearly a subject that prudent people, above all if they already have cancer or know someone who has it, ought to know something about. I don't know a better place to start than this book, from which we can gain much information, understanding, and hope.

The preface states the central message of the book:

> Some years ago we developed the idea that regular high intakes of vitamin C (ascorbic acid, or its several biologically active salts known as ascorbates) play some part both in the prevention of cancer and in the treatment of established cancer. Evidence steadily accumulates to support this view. [JH: The book was published in 1979; since then, the evidence has continued to grow stronger.]

> During the last twenty years about ten billion dollars has been spent on cancer research, in the effort to get some control of the disease.... Despite this great expenditure and the corresponding great effort, not much has been achieved.

For most kinds of cancer, those involving solid tumors in adults, which lead to 95 percent of the cancer deaths, there has been essentially no change in overall incidence and mortality during recent years.

In short, for most kinds of cancer, including the most dangerous kinds, the orthodox treatments you would probably be given by most doctors or hospitals are generally very expensive, often crippling and extremely painful, and usually ineffective. Cameron and Pauling here present powerful evidence that supplementing or replacing these treatments with large doses of vitamin C has been and would be beneficial for large numbers of patients.

In spirit as well as content this is a scientific book, not a fervent plea or dramatic exposé—though certainly, given his experience, Pauling could have been forgiven for writing one. Perhaps because he still hopes to win over the medical establishment, he does not say what I have no hesitation in saying, that by almost wholly ignoring vitamin C as a cancer treatment and denying it (by denying funds for the necessary large scale research) a chance to prove itself, the cancer establishment is at least morally responsible for the painful and premature or unnecessary deaths of millions of human beings. I hope this may change, but as of 1984 this research into the use of vitamin C is still being done almost entirely by Pauling's own Institute of Science and Medicine (440 Page Mill Rd., Palo Alto CA 94306), struggling to keep alive on what it can raise from private sources. It seems almost unthinkable that this vital work, probably the most important work being done in the entire field of medicine, might end with Dr. Pauling's death, or simply the drying up of private funds, but it is possible, and only steady support by concerned persons for his institute will prevent it.

I'll say in passing that if I were a young person interested in biology and medicine I could hardly think of a more satisfying and important place in which to work, since there one would do the kind of scientific research of which one could feel really proud.

Though *Cancer And Vitamin C* is a scientific book, it is not at all obscure or difficult to read; indeed it is one of the most interesting, understandable, and even exciting books on a scientific topic that I have read. If it does nothing else for us, it should at least take some of the mystery and terror out of what has become a kind of Black Plague of our time.—JH

Other Items Available Here

Cellos (Price below includes fine tuners, bow, case, rosin, and postage). In *GWS* 37 I described the inexpensive violins, made in China, that we are making available to our readers. Since our supplier, Kathryn Alexander, also supplies violas and cellos, I asked her to send me a tape of herself playing one of the cellos, which she has done. On it she plays, for comparison's sake the same piece on the cello she uses professionally. As with the violins, the sound of the cello is surprisingly good; I have heard quite a few instruments that cost a lot more and sounded worse. So we are adding them to our catalog. They come in six sizes: 1/10 or 1/8, $379.50; 1/4 or 1/2, $399.50; 3/4 or 4/4 (full-size) $429.50. If you have near you cello teachers who teach children, they can advise you what size to order. If not, tell us the child's age and height, and perhaps the height of the parents (since this will give a clue as to how fast the child is likely to grow) and we will advise you.

By the way, Kathryn Alexander does sell European-made instruments (which cost roughly three times as much as the Chinese), so if any of you want to spend the extra money for what will be a much better-looking and somewhat better-sounding and easier-playing instrument, let us know. But as I said in *GWS* 39, I think the Chinese instruments are not only adequate but very good for novice players.

Kolstein's Violin And Cello Rosin ($6.95 + post). The rosin that is supplied with the inexpensive violins we sell, though it works, is not very good, and one of the best small investments you can make toward making your playing easier and better sounding is to get a good rosin, of which Kolstein's is the best I know. I first learned about it at the Center for Chamber Music at Apple Hill, N.H. I had been using a very well known rosin, the kind recommended by most music stores, but my cello was resisting me and I was having to put a lot of pressure on the strings in order to make them "speak." One of the Apple Hill professionals asked me if I had ever tried Kolstein's rosin, and when I said I hadn't, urged me to try some of his. I was astonished what a difference it made. I needed less of it on the bow hairs, it stayed on longer, and it gripped the string better. It didn't turn my ugly duckling cello into a swan, but it made it noticeably easier to play, and I have been using it ever since. It is in fact a very good buy, since you don't have to use much of it at a time, and you don't have to use it often. I strongly recommend it.

Smith And Hawken's Catalog Of Garden Tools ($1.00 *including* post). When Paul Hawken, who started Erewhon, the enormously successful natural foods company, finally sold it for a large sum, he enjoyed his retirement for a while but soon became restless and looked about for something to do, specifically, for an interesting, useful, and he hoped profitable business to run. He decided to sell garden tools, the finest that he could find, and the company which he helped start soon began importing from England a line of what experts seemed to feel were the best designed, best made, and most durable garden tools in the world. This is their catalog, all in color. We carry it for the same reasons we carry the Garrett Wade tool catalog: some people may want to buy some of the tools in it, but it any case it is a very handsome book, fun to look at, and from which you may learn some useful things about gardening. You may even find that a tool you needed but couldn't find or didn't know existed, does in fact exist. But even if you don't garden at all, it is a pleasure to look at color photographs of beautiful and useful objects made with thought, care, and love.

Mother Earth News Issue #85 ($3 + post). This is the issue that contains my article, "So You Want To Homeschool," plus some good excerpts from Nancy Wallace's *Better Than School*. The article is the best short piece I have seen in print, not about why you should teach your own children, but about *how* to do it once you have decided. Early in this issue of *GWS* we say that homeschooling will probably become easier for most parents, provided they go about it the right way. This article shows what "the right way" is. It would be a very useful piece to show to parents who are thinking about homeschooling, and it might be a very good piece for would-be homeschoolers to show to school officials, who will be calmed and reassured by its reasonable and conciliatory tone, and by the fact that it appears in a magazine of *Mother Earth News'* size and reputation.

And of course, the 192-page magazine is packed full of good ideas on energy, cooking, gardening, building houses, using tools, medical self-care, and more. Of special interest are Norm and Sherrie Lee's (*Homesteaders News*) "Four-Season Gardening Plan," the design for TMEN's successful composting toilet, and a ten-page section on how to knit and crochet.—JH

Editors—John Holt & Donna Richoux
Managing Editor—Patrick Farenga
Subscriptions & Books—Steve Rupprecht & Ross Campbell
Office Assistant—Mary Van Doren

About John Holt

John Holt (1923–1985) is the author of *How Children Learn* and *How Children Fail*, which together have sold over 2 million copies, and eight other books about children and learning. His work has been translated into more than 14 languages. For years a leading figure in school reform, John Holt became increasingly interested in how children learn outside of school. The magazine he founded to support such efforts, *Growing Without Schooling*, reflects his practical philosophy of how children and adults learn throughout their lives.

To learn more about homeschooling, unschooling, and the work and life of John Holt, visit www.johnholtgws.com.

www.ingramcontent.com/pod-product-compliance
Lightning Source LLC
Chambersburg PA
CBHW082221090526
44585CB00020BA/2128